College Board AP Topic Outline
Macroeconomics

Krugman's Economics for AP*

College Board AP Topic Outline
Microeconomics

Krugman's Economics for AP*

I. **Basic Economic Concepts** (8–14%)

A. Scarcity, choice, and opportunity cost

B. Production possibilities curve

C. Comparative advantage, absolute advantage, specialization, and trade

D. Economic systems

E. Property rights and the role of incentives

F. Marginal analysis

Section 1: Basic Economic Concepts

Module 1   The Study of Economics

Module 3   The Production Possibilities Curve Model

Module 4   Comparative Advantage and Trade

Module 1   The Study of Economics

Module 1   The Study of Economics

Module 1   The Study of Economics

II. **The Nature and Function of Product Markets** (55–70%)

A. Supply and demand

1. Market equilibrium

2. Determinants of supply and demand

3. Price and quantity controls

Section 2: Supply and Demand

Module 5   Supply and Demand: Introduction and Demand

Module 6   Supply and Demand: Supply and Equilibrium

Module 7   Supply and Demand: Changes in Supply and Demand

Module 8   Supply and Demand: Price Controls

Module 9   Supply and Demand: Quantity Controls

4. Elasticity

Section 9: Behind the Demand Curve: Theory of Consumer Choice

Module 46   Income and Substitution Effects and Elasticity

Module 47   Interpreting Price Elasticity of demand

Module 48   Other Elasticities

Module 49   Consumer and Producer Surplus

5. Consumer surplus, producer surplus, and market efficiency

6. Tax incidence and deadweight loss

B. Theory of consumer choice

Module 50   Efficiency and deadweight Loss

Module 51   Utility Maximization

C. Production and costs

1. Production functions

2. Marginal product and diminishing returns

3. Short-run costs

4. Long-run costs and economies of scale

5. Cost minimizing input combination

Section 10: Behind the Supply Curve: Profit, Production, and Costs

Module 54   The Production Function

Module 54   The Production Function

Module 55   Firm Costs

Module 56   Long Run Costs and Economies of Scale

Module 72   Cost Minimizing Input Combinations

D. Firm behavior and market structure

1. Profit

Module 57   Introduction to Market Structures

Module 52   Defining Profit

Module 53   Profit Maximization

2. Perfect competition

Section 11: Market Structures: Perfect Competition and Monopoly

Module 58   Introduction to Perfect Competition

Module 59   Graphing Perfect Competition

Module 60   Long-Run Outcomes in Perfect Competition

3. Monopoly

Module 61   Introduction to Monopoly

Module 62   Monopoly and Public policy

Module 63   Price Discrimination

College Board AP Topic Outline
Microeconomics

Krugman's Economics for AP*

KRUGMAN'S
ECONOMICS for AP*

KRUGMAN'S ECONOMICS for AP*

Margaret Ray and David Anderson

University of Mary Washington   Centre College

Adapted from *Economics,* Second Edition
by Paul Krugman and Robin Wells

*AP is a trademark registered and/or owned by the College Board,
which was not involved in the production of, and does not endorse, this product.

WORTH PUBLISHERS/BFW

Further credits appear on page xxxvii, which is an extension of this copyright page.

Director, BFW High School: Craig Bleyer
Executive Editor: Ann Heath
Development Editor: Rebecca Kohn
Senior Consultant: Andreas Bentz
Assistant Editor: Dora Figueiredo
Media Editor: Marie McHale
Executive Marketing Manager: Cindi Weiss
Marketing Manager: Janie Pierce-Bratcher
Art Director: Babs Reingold
Cover Designer: Lissi Sigillo
Interior Designer: TSI Graphics
Photo Editor: Cecilia Varas
Photo Researcher: Dena Digilio Betz
Associate Managing Editor: Tracey Kuehn
Project Editor: Kerry O'Shaughnessy
Production Manager: Barbara Seixas
Composition: TSI Graphics
Printing and Binding: RR Donnelley

Library of Congress Control Number: 2010940245

ISBN-13: 978-1-4292-1827-6
ISBN-10: 1-4292-1827-4

Printed in the United States of America

Third printing

Worth Publishers
41 Madison Avenue
New York, NY 10010
www.bfwpub.com/highschool

To beginning students everywhere,
which we all were at one time.

About the Authors

Margaret Ray is Professor of Economics at the University of Mary Washington, where she specializes in teaching introductory economics. She received her BS in Economics from Oklahoma State University and her PhD in Economics from the University of Tennessee. Her research is primarily in the areas of economic education and equine industry economics. In 2003 she taught AP Economics at Collegiate School in Virginia. Ray received the National Council on Economic Education's Excellence in Teaching Economics award in 1991. She has been involved in the AP Economics program since 1992, serving as a reader and question leader, writing test items, overseeing the AP course audit, writing College Board "*Special Focus*" articles, and contributing activities to the National Council on Economic Education's *AP Economics* resource. She has been a College Board Endorsed Consultant for economics since 2001 and she conducts several professional development workshops and institutes each year. She currently serves on the Steering Committee for the College Board's AP National Conference.

David Anderson is the Paul G. Blazer Professor of Economics at Centre College. He received his BA in Economics from the University of Michigan and his MA and PhD in Economics from Duke University. Anderson is a leading authority on AP Economics and speaks regularly at the International AP Economics Teacher Conference, the National AP Conference, and regional AP Economics workshops. He has authored dozens of scholarly articles and ten books, including *Cracking the AP Economics Exam, Favorite Ways to Learn Economics, Environmental Economics and Natural Resource Management, Contemporary Economics for Managers, Treading Lightly*, and *Economics by Example*. His research is primarily on economic education, environmental economics, law and economics, and labor economics. Anderson teaches courses in each of these fields and loves teaching introductory economics. He lives in Danville, Kentucky with his wife and two children.

Supplements Team

Eric Dodge
Teachers Resource Binder, Test Bank

Eric is Professor of Economics and Business Administration at Hanover College in Indiana. He received his BA from the University of Puget Sound and his MA and PhD from the University of Oregon. Eric has been involved with AP Economics for more than ten years and has served as reader, table leader, and question leader.

Paul Krugman, recipient of the 2008 Nobel Memorial Prize in Economics, is Professor of Economics at Princeton University, where he regularly teaches the principles course. He received his BA from Yale and his PhD from MIT. Prior to his current position, he taught at Yale, Stanford, and MIT. He also spent a year on the staff of the Council of Economic Advisers in 1982–1983. His research is mainly in the area of international trade, where he is one of the founders of the "new trade theory," which focuses on increasing returns and imperfect competition. He also works in international finance, with a concentration in currency crises. In 1991, Krugman received the American Economic Association's John Bates Clark medal. In addition to his teaching and academic research, Krugman writes extensively for nontechnical audiences. Krugman is a regular op-ed columnist for the *New York Times*. His latest trade book, *The Conscience of a Liberal,* is a best-selling study of the political economy of economic inequality and its relationship with political polarization from the Gilded Age to the present. His earlier books, *Peddling Prosperity* and *The Age of Diminished Expectations,* have become modern classics.

Robin Wells was a Lecturer and Researcher in Economics at Princeton University. She received her BA from the University of Chicago and her PhD from the University of California at Berkeley; she then did postdoctoral work at MIT. She has taught at the University of Michigan, the University of Southampton (United Kingdom), Stanford, and MIT. The subject of her teaching and research is the theory of organizations and incentives.

David Mayer
Strive for a 5, Lecture PowerPoint Presentations

Dave teaches at Churchill High School in San Antonio, Texas. He received a BA in Economics from Texas A&M University and earned his MA at University of Texas, San Antonio. He has been teaching the AP Economics course since 2004, and began working as an AP Economics reader and then table leader in 2006. Dave is a College Board Endorsed Consultant for economics and he conducts several professional development workshops and institutes each year. He is the author of *The Everything Economics Book* published by Adams Media in 2010. David lives in San Antonio with his wife Courtney and children Caty and Colin.

Brief Contents

Contents

Contents

Contents

Contents

Contents

Contents

Preface

"If you want to be listened to, you should put in time listening." —Marge Piercy

FROM MARGARET AND DAVE

We understand the unique challenges of teaching and learning AP Economics. This book is the culmination of our combined 35 years of work with AP Economics students and teachers. We have seen the challenges first hand, and we have listened to the concerns and solutions of the many remarkable teachers with whom it has been our privilege to work. The creation of this book draws from our experience in every facet of AP-level education, from teaching high school classes to leading AP Economics professional development programs. We have designed this book and its ancillary resources to be the most effective possible resources to help teachers and students succeed in AP Economics.

It is clear that the foundation of any effective AP Economics course is a high quality, college level textbook. The impetus for this project was the recognition that, while any college level introductory textbook can be adapted for use in an AP Economics course, no existing textbook is sufficient for the task. The existing textbooks cover large amounts of material that is *not* included on the AP Course Outline and omit important topics that are on the Outline. Teachers using existing textbooks must navigate around unnecessary chapters, cover chapters with some relevant topics but lots of superfluous information, and search for supplementary materials to cover topics not addressed in the text. These problems hinder the effectiveness of standard textbooks and make extra work for both teachers and students. While some other college level books have been printed as "AP Editions," the changes in those editions are little more than new labels and covers. This book is different. It is made specifically to satisfy the goals of the AP Economics teacher and student.

Intent on promoting the efficiency and effectiveness of AP Economics courses, we started with the best available college-level introduction to economics–Krugman and Wells' *Economics*, second edition. The first edition of the Krugman and Wells textbook was a resounding success, quickly becoming one of the best-selling college economics textbooks. AP Economics teachers embraced the textbook for its clear explanations and storytelling approach. The second edition of *Economics* became even more popular and successful. We knew that it would be the best foundation for an AP adaptation. Our goal was to retain the features of *Economics* that make it a winner, while crafting it to closely follow the AP syllabus and speak to a high school audience. We hope the result will serve as the best possible textbook for teaching and learning AP Economics.

The Organization of This Book and How to Use It

The organization of this book is inspired by our goal of adapting the parent book to best support AP Economics teachers and students. The sequence of sections and modules conforms to both the AP Topic Outline and a traditional sequence of material that has been found to be pedagogically effective. The sections and modules are grouped into building blocks in which conceptual material learned at one stage is built upon and then integrated into the conceptual material covered in the next stage. All material included in the AP Economics Course Description is included here, and all material included here is related to AP course requirements. Following is a walkthrough of the sections in the book:

Note: The material covered in sections 1 and 2 is found on both the AP Macroeconomics and the AP Microeconomics Topic Outlines

Section 1: Basic Economic Concepts

The first section initiates students into the study of economics, including scarcity, choice and opportunity cost. Module 1 provides students with definitions of basic terms in economics. Module 2 provides an overview of the study of macroeconomics, including economic growth, unemployment, inflation, and the business cycle. Modules 3 and 4 present the production possibilities curve model and use it to explain comparative and absolute advantage, specialization and exchange.

Section 2: Supply and Demand

Section 2 begins with an opening story that uses the market for coffee beans to illustrate supply and demand, market equilibrium, and surplus and shortage. Modules 5, 6, and 7 introduce the important parts of the supply and demand model; demand, supply, and equilibrium. Module 8 and 9 teach students how to use the model to analyze price and quantity in markets.

Macroeconomics

Sections 3–8 cover the material found exclusively on the AP Macroeconomics Topic Outline.

Section 3: Measurement of Economic Performance

In Section 3, we provide an overview of the topics in macroeconomics that provides the foundation for models that are covered in later sections. Modules 10 and 11 introduce the circular flow model and gross domestic product.

Modules 12 and 13 teach students how to define, measure, and categorize the types of unemployment. The definition and measurement of inflation, price indices (real versus nominal values), and the costs of inflation are presented in Modules 14 and 15.

Section 4: National Income and Price Determination

Section 4 introduces national income and price determination and presents the aggregate supply and demand model, which is the foundation for the material presented in later sections. Modules 16, 17, 18, and 19 introduce individual parts for the model; income and expenditures, aggregate demand, aggregate supply, and equilibrium in the model. Macreoconomics equilibrium and economics fluctuations (including fiscal policy and the multiplier) are presented in Modules 20 and 21.

Section 5: Financial Sector

In Section 5, money, banks, and the Federal Reserve are added to our model of the macroeconomy. Modules 22, 23, and 24 present basic concepts and their definitions; saving, investment, financial assets, money, the money supply, and the time value of money. Module 25 introduces banking and the creation of money in the economy. Central banks and the Federal Reserve System are included in Modules 26 and 27. Finally, the money market and monetary policy, including the loanable funds market, are presented in Modules 28 and 29.

Section 6: Inflation, Unemployment and Stabilization Policies

Section 6 continues with coverage of monetary and fiscal policies. Module 30 focuses on fiscal policy and the implications of government deficits and debt. Module 31 focuses on monetary policy and its effect on the interest rate. Modules 32 and 33 look in detail at the types of inflation, disinflation, and deflation, while Module 34 introduces both the short-run and long-run Phillips curve. Finally, Modules 35 and 36 present some history of macroeconomic thought as it leads to the modern macroeconomic consensus, emphasizing the role of expectations in macroeconomic policy.

Section 7: Economic Growth and Productivity

Economic growth and the role of productivity are the focus in Section 7. Module 37 defines and discusses long-run economic growth and Module 38 emphasizes the role of productivity in generating economic growth. Module 39 looks at how differences in human and physical capital,

research and development, and technology lead to differences in long-run economic growth and how growth policy can be used to facilitate economic growth in the long run. Finally, Module 40 reviews and highlights how economic growth plays a role in the macroeconomic models developed in earlier sections.

Section 8: Open Economy: International Trade and Finance

Section 8 adds the international sector to the macroeconomic models presented in previous sections. Module 41 introduces balance of payments accounts. Modules 42 and 43 develop the foreign exchange market and exchange rate policy. Module 44 links the foreign exchange market to financial markets and the markets for goods and services through a discussion of exchange rates and macroeconomic policy.

Module 45 Module 45 shows students how the models they have studied throughout the course can be applied to answer real-world questions, like the type they will see on the AP exam.

Microeconomics

Section 9 begins coverage of the material exclusive to the AP Microeconomics Topic Outline. The first section of the AP Microeconomics Topic Outline, "Nature and Function of Product Markets," is quite large, representing 55–75% of the course material. We break this material into five sections: 2, 9, 10, 11, and 12.

Section 9: Behind the Demand Curve: Consumer Choice

This section looks more closely at topics related to the demand curve. Module 46 explains how the income and substitution effects relate to a downward sloping demand curve and presents the concept of elasticity. Module 47 is devoted to developing price elasticity while Module 48 explains three additional elasticity measures important in economics. Consumer and producer surplus are presented in Modules 49 and 50 and are used to explain deadweight loss. Finally, Module 51 presents consumer theory and utility maximization.

Section 10: Behind the Supply Curve: Profit, Production, and Costs

Section 10 shifts to a more detailed discussion of the supply curve. This section introduces the production and cost concepts used throughout the following sections. The section begins with a discussion of profit and profit maximization in Modules 52 and 53. Module 54 develops the production function. Modules 55 and 56 introduce cost concepts, both short-run and long-run. The last module provides an introduction to the market structures covered in Sections 11 and 12.

Section 11: Market Structures: Perfect Competition and Monopoly

Section 11 presents the perfect competition and monopoly market structures. Modules 58-60 present perfect competition. Modules 58 and 59 develop the perfect competition model and graphs. Module 60 presents the long-run outcomes under perfect competition. Modules 61–63 present the monopoly market structure. Module 61 develops the basic monopoly model. Module 62 presents public policies toward monopoly and Module 63 explains the practice of price discrimination.

Section 12: Market Structures: Imperfect Competition

This section introduces the imperfectly competitive market structures: oligopoly and monopolistic competition. Module 64 introduces oligopoly and Module 66 discusses oligopoly market structures in the real world. Game theory as it relates to oligopoly is given special attention in Module 65. Module 67 explains monopolistic competition. Module 68 covers product differentiation under monopolistic competition with special focus on the role of advertising.

Section 13: Factor Markets

This section begins with Module 69, an introduction to factor markets and factor demand. Modules 70 and 71 present the markets for land, capital, and labor. Module 72 explains how to find the cost-minimizing combination of inputs. The last module in the section discusses the marginal productivity theory of income distribution and various sources of wage differentials.

Section 14: Market Failure and the Role of Government

This section focuses on the conditions under which markets fail and explains public and private approaches to market failure. Modules 74 and 75 discuss externalities and the public policies and private remedies available to address them. Module 76 covers public goods. Module 77 presents the use of antitrust law and government regulation to promote competition. Module 78 explains theories of income distribution and income inequality.

The appendix to Section 14 provides enrichment modules. While not currently part of the material on the AP Topic Outline, these modules contain extensions of the material presented in AP courses. They provide enrichment materials for advanced students or for coverage after the AP exam. This material may also be considered for inclusion on the AP Topic Outline in the future. Module 79 presents the economics of information, including adverse selection and moral hazard. Module 80 discusses indifference curves and consumer choice, an extension of the material in Module 51.

The AP Edition: What's Different?

Perhaps the most important feature of the AP adaptation of *Economics* is what has been left unchanged. We retain Paul Krugman's fresh voice and lively writing style, which AP students find easy to understand. We also adhere to the general approach of the parent book:

> "To achieve deeper levels of understanding of the real world through economics, students must learn to appreciate the kinds of trade-offs and ambiguities that economists and policy makers face when applying their models to real-world problems. We believe this approach will make students more insightful and more effective participants in our common economic, social, and political lives."

Finally, we have been careful to maintain the international focus and global coverage of issues from *Economics*, 2e.

However, we have made significant changes in the original book to meet the specific needs of AP Economics teachers and students. Here are the major adaptations:

Close Adherence to the AP Topic Outline and Terminology

We have carefully followed the AP Topic Outlines for Macroeconomics and Microeconomics and included all of the material required for the course. The book covers the course material using the same terminology students will see on the AP Economics Exam. When there is more than one term that can be used in a particular situation, we have introduced students to each of the terms they might see on the exam and made it clear that the terms are synonymous. Because it closely conforms to the required course material and introduces AP exam terminology, this book helps students learn the material and terminology they will see on their AP Economics Exam.

AP Course-friendly Organization

This book is arranged by sections that correspond to the AP Topic Outline provided by the College Board. Each section is divided into 4–7 modules. Each module breaks the course material into a pedagogically appropriate unit that is designed to be presented in one class period, with additional class periods for activities, demonstrations, and reinforcement, as needed. This organization takes teachers and students through the required AP course material in a sequence and at a pace designed for optimal success for students in AP economics classes.

Relevant Examples

The Krugman and Wells textbook was lauded for its use of relevant and interesting examples to teach economic principles. We have retained this approach and many of the examples from the parent book. However, we have modified, added, or replaced examples to speak specifically to a high school audience.

Practice for the AP Exam

Each module in the book ends with AP review material including sample multiple-choice and free-response questions related to the content in the module. The multiple-choice questions are written in the style of the AP exam with five distracters. Two sample free-response questions are included for each module, the first of which includes a sample grading rubric. Providing the rubric helps students to prepare for the format of the AP exam and to better understand how their responses will be graded (which will help them to provide better responses on the exam). In addition, Module 45 *"Putting it All Together"* is devoted to showing students how to use the economic principles they have learned in macroeconomics to answer comprehensive questions like the long question typically found on the AP Economics Exams.

Supplements

The teacher and student supplements have been designed by experts in AP economics to facilitate teaching and learning. The instructor's resources are comprehensive enough to guide new AP teachers through their first years of teaching AP economics but also provide unique ideas and suggestions that will help experienced teachers enhance their courses. The student's resources help students through both the course and preparation for the AP exam. All supplement materials are developed to adhere to the AP course outline, goals, and testing format.

Economics by Example

David Anderson's *Economics by Example* has become a leading supplemental resource for AP economics courses. Each book is bundled with a copy of the Anderson book, and suggestions for how to use it in an AP economics course are integrated throughout the text and the instructor materials.

Advantages of This Book

This book has all of the advantages found in the parent book as well as many new advantages unique to the AP adaptation:

➤ **Created by a Team with Insight**. The team of authors for this project has a wealth of experience with AP economics. This book is the result of extensive collaboration within the team as well as incredible support from highly qualified AP content reviewers and accuracy checkers at all points along the way.

➤ **Created Specifically to Meet the Needs of AP Economics Teachers and Students.** From the Table of Contents through the supplements, this project is specifically designed to meet the needs of AP teachers and students. The outline of the book follows the AP topic outline, the terminology in the book conforms to accepted terminology used in AP materials and on the AP exam, and supplements provide everything new or experienced teachers and students need to be sucessful in an AP economics course.

➤ **Chapters build intuition through realistic examples.** In every chapter, real-world examples, stories, applications, and case studies teach the core concepts and motivate student learning. The best way to introduce concepts and reinforce them is through real-world examples; students simply relate more easily to them.

➤ **Pedagogical features reinforce learning.** The book includes a genuinely helpful set of features that are illustrated and described later in the Preface.

➤ **Modules are accessible and entertaining.** A fluid and friendly writing style makes concepts accessible. Whenever possible, the book uses examples that are familiar to students: choosing which college to attend, paying a high price for a cup of coffee, or deciding where to eat at the food court at the local shopping mall.

➤ **Although easy to understand, the book also prepares students for the AP exam and further coursework.** Too often, instructors find that selecting a textbook means choosing between two unappealing alternatives: a textbook that is "easy to teach" but leaves major gaps in students' understanding, or a textbook that is "hard to teach" but adequately prepares students for the AP exam and future coursework. This is an easy-to-understand textbook that offers the best of both worlds.

Tools for Learning...Getting the Most from This Book

Each section and its modules are structured around a common set of features designed to help students learn while keeping them engaged.

The **section outline** lists the modules that comprise the section and suggests a relevant chapter in Dave Anderson's book, *Economics by Example,* which is packaged with this text.

Opening Story Each section opens with a compelling story that often extends through the modules. The opening stories are designed to illustrate important concepts, to build intuition with realistic examples, and then to encourage students to read on and learn more.

---

section 4

Module 16 Income and Expenditure

Module 17 Aggregate Demand: Introduction and Determinants

Module 18 Aggregate Supply: Introduction and Determinants

Module 19 Equilibrium in the Aggregate Demand–Aggregate Supply Model

Module 20 Economic Policy and the Aggregate Demand–Aggregate Supply Model

Module 21 Fiscal Policy and the Multiplier

Economics by Example:
"How Much Debt Is Too Much?"

National Income and Price Determination

FROM BOOM TO BUST

Ft. Myers, Florida, was a boom town in 2003, 2004, and most of 2005. Jobs were plentiful: by 2005 the unemployment rate was less than 3%. The shopping malls were humming, and new stores were opening everywhere.

But then the boom went bust. Jobs became scarce, and by 2009 the unemployment rate had reached 14%. Stores had few customers, and many were closing. One new business was flourishing, however. Marc Joseph, a real estate agent, began offering "foreclosure tours": visits to homes that had been seized by banks after the owners were unable to make mortgage payments.

What happened? Ft. Myers boomed from 2003 to 2005 because of a surge in home construction, fueled in part by speculators who bought houses not to live in, but because they believed they could resell those houses at much higher prices. Home construction gave jobs to construction workers, electricians, real estate agents, and others. And these workers, in turn, spent money locally, creating jobs for sales workers, waiters, gardeners, pool cleaners, and more. These workers also spent money locally, creating further expansion, and so on.

The boom turned into a bust when home construction came to a virtual halt. It turned out that speculation had been feeding on itself: people were buying houses as investments, then selling them to other people who were also buying houses as investments, and the prices had risen to levels far beyond what people who actually wanted to live in houses were willing to pay.

The abrupt collapse of the housing market pulled the local economy down with it, as the process that had created the earlier boom operated in reverse.

The boom and bust in Ft. Myers illustrates, on a small scale, the way booms and busts often happen for the economy as a whole. The business cycle is often driven by ups or downs in investment spending—either residential investment spending (that is, spending on home construction) or nonresidential investment spending (such as spending on construction of office buildings, factories, and shopping malls). Changes in investment spending, in turn, indirectly lead to changes in consumer spending, which magnify—or *multiply*—the effect of the investment spending changes on the economy as a whole.

In this section we'll study how this process works on a grand scale. As a first step, we introduce *multiplier* analysis and show how it helps us understand the business cycle. In Module 17 we explain *aggregate demand* and its two most important components, consumer spending and investment spending. Module 18 introduces *aggregate supply,* the other half of the model used to analyze economic fluctuations. We will then be ready to explore how aggregate supply and aggregate demand determine the levels of prices and real output in an economy. Finally, we will use the aggregate demand-aggregate supply model to visualize the state of the economy and examine the effects of economic policy.

Courtesy of the Dallas Morning News

157

What you will learn in this **Module:**

- How scarcity and choice are central to the study of economics

- The importance of opportunity cost in individual choice and decision making

- The difference between positive economics and normative economics

- When economists agree and why they sometimes disagree

- What makes macroeconomics different from microeconomics

Economics is the study of scarcity and choice.

Individual choice is decisions by individuals about what to do, which necessarily involve decisions about what not to do.

An **economy** is a system for coordinating a society's productive and consumptive activities.

In a **market economy,** the decisions of individual producers and consumers largely determine what, how, and for whom to produce, with little government involvement in the decisions.

Module 1
The Study of Economics

Individual Choice: The Core of Economics

Economics is the study of scarcity and choice. Every economic issue involves, at its most basic level, **individual choice**—decisions by individuals about what to do and what *not* to do. In fact, you might say that it isn't economics if it isn't about choice.

Step into a big store such as Walmart or Target. There are thousands of different products available, and it is extremely unlikely that you—or anyone else—could afford to buy everything you might want to have. And anyway, there's only so much space in your room. Given the limitations on your budget and your living space, you must choose which products to buy and which to leave on the shelf.

The fact that those products are on the shelf in the first place involves choice—the store manager chose to put them there, and the manufacturers of the products chose to produce them. The **economy** is a system that coordinates choices about production with choices about consumption, and distributes goods and services to the people who want them. The United States has a **market economy,** in which production and consumption are the result of decentralized decisions by many firms and individuals. There is no central authority telling people what to produce or where to ship it. Each individual producer makes what he or she thinks will be most profitable, and each consumer buys what he or she chooses.

All economic activities involve individual choice. Let's take a closer look at what this means for the study of economics.

Resources Are Scarce

You can't always get what you want. Almost everyone would like to have a beautiful house in a great location (and help with the housecleaning), two or three luxury cars, _____ vacations in fancy hotels. Even in a rich country like the United States, _____ must make choices—whether to go to _____ to make do with a small backyard or _____ and is cheaper.

fyi

The Great Tortilla Crisis

"Thousands in Mexico City protest rising food prices." So read a recent headline in the *New York Times*. Specifically, the demonstrators were protesting a sharp rise in the price of tortillas, a staple food of Mexico's poor, which had gone from 25 cents a pound to between 35 and 45 cents a pound in just a few months.

Why were tortilla prices soaring? It was a classic example of what happens to equilibrium prices when supply falls. Tortillas are made from corn; much of Mexico's corn is imported from the United States, with the price of corn in both countries basically set in the U.S. corn market. And U.S. corn prices were rising rapidly thanks to surging demand in a new market: the market for ethanol.

Ethanol's big break came with the Energy Policy Act of 2005, which mandated the use of a large quantity of "renewable" fuels starting in 2006, and rising steadily thereafter. In practice, that meant increased use of ethanol. Ethanol producers rushed to build new production facilities and quickly began buying lots of corn. The result was a rightward shift of the demand curve for corn, leading to a sharp rise in the price of corn. And since corn is an input in the production of tortillas, a sharp rise in the price of corn led to a fall in the supply of tortillas and higher prices for tortilla consumers.

The increase in the price of corn was good news in Iowa, where farmers began planting

A cook prepares tortillas made with four different types of corn in a restaurant in Mexico City.

more corn than ever before. But it was bad news for Mexican consumers, who found themselves paying more for their tortillas.

Engaging examples provide a context for important concepts

section 2

Module 5 Supply and Demand: Introduction and Demand

Module 6 Supply and Demand: Supply and Equilibrium

Module 7 Supply and Demand: Changes in Supply and Demand

Module 8 Supply and Demand: Price Controls (Ceilings and Floors)

Module 9 Supply and Demand: Quantity Controls

Economics by Example:
"The Coffee Market's Hot; Why Are Bean Prices Not?"

Supply and Demand

For those who need a cappuccino, mocha latte, or Frappuccino to get through the day, coffee drinking can become an expensive habit. And on October 6, 2006, the habit got a little more expensive. On that day, Starbucks raised its drink prices for the first time in six years. The average price of coffee beverages at the world's leading chain of coffeehouses rose about 11 cents per cup.

Starbucks had kept its prices unchanged for six years. So what compelled them to finally raise their prices in the fall of 2006? Mainly the fact that the cost of a major ingredient—coffee beans—had gone up significantly. In fact, coffee bean prices doubled between 2002 and 2006.

Who decided to raise the prices of coffee beans? Nobody: prices went up because of events outside anyone's control. Specifically, the main cause of rising bean prices was a significant decrease in the supply of coffee beans from the world's two leading coffee exporters: Brazil and

Vietnam. In Brazil, the decrease in supply was a delayed reaction to low prices earlier in the decade, which led coffee growers to cut back on planting. In Vietnam, the problem was weather: a prolonged drought sharply reduced coffee harvests.

And a lower supply of coffee beans from Vietnam or Brazil inevitably translates into a higher price of coffee on Main Street. It's just a matter of supply and demand.

What do we mean by that? Many people use "supply and demand" as a sort of catchphrase to mean "the laws of the marketplace at work." To economists, however, the concept of supply and demand has a precise meaning: it is a *model* of how a market behaves.

In this section, we lay out the pieces that make up the *supply and demand model,* put them together, and show how this model can be used to understand how many—but not all—markets behave.

Section 2 uses the supply of coffee beans and the price of coffee at the local Starbucks to teach the supply and demand model.

Jed Jacobsohn/Getty Images

47

Clearly labeled graphs help to explain complex ideas

figure 5.3

A Movement Along the Demand Curve Versus a Shift of the Demand Curve

The rise in the quantity demanded when going from point *A* to point *B* reflects a movement along the demand curve: it is the result of a fall in the price of the good. The rise in the quantity demanded when going from point *A* to point *C* reflects a change in demand: this shift to the right [reflects a rise] in the quantity demanded at

> Figure 5.3 shows the difference between *movement* along the demand curve and a *shift* in demand, providing a clear presentation of a difficult topic.

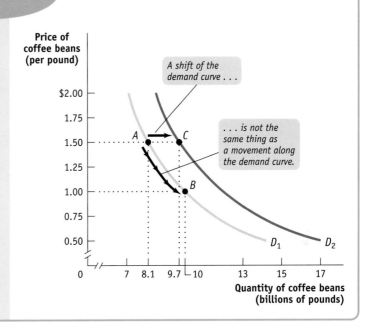

figure 6.3

Movement Along the [Demand] Curve Versus [the] Supply Curve

[The rise in the] quantity supplied when [going from point] *A* to point *B* reflects a [movement alon]g the supply curve: it is the result of a rise in the price of the good. The increase in quantity supplied when going from point *A* to point *C* reflects a change in supply: this shift to the right is the result of an increase in the quantity supplied at any given price.

> Figure 6.3 in the following module illustrates the same concept for the supply curve

> Color is used consistently to distinguish between demand (blue) and supply (red) curves.

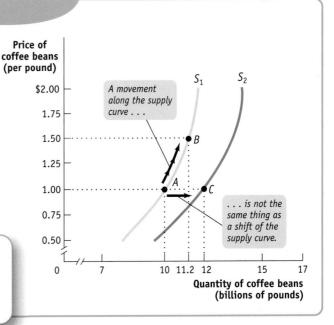

Each module concludes with a unique AP Review

Module 1 APReview

Solutions appear at the back of the book.

Check Your Understanding

1. What are the four categories of resources? Give an example of a resource from each category.

2. What type of resource is each of the following?
   a. time spent flipping hamburgers at a restaurant
   b. a bulldozer
   c. a river

3. You make $45,000 per year at your current job with Whiz Kids Consultants. You are considering a job offer from Brainiacs, Inc., which would pay you $50,000 per year. Which of the following are elements of the opportunity cost of accepting the new job at Brainiacs, Inc.? Answer yes or no, and explain your answer.

   a. the increased time spent commuting to your new job
   b. the $45,000 salary from your old job
   c. the more spacious office at your new job

4. Identify each of the following statements as positive or normative, and explain your answer.
   a. Society should take measures to prevent people from engaging in dangerous personal behavior.
   b. People who engage in dangerous personal behavior impose higher costs on society through higher medical costs.

> **Check Your Understanding** review questions allow students to immediately test their understanding of a module. By checking their answers with those found in the back of the book, students will know when they need to reread the module before moving on.

Tackle the Test: Multiple-Choice Questions

1. Which of the following is an example of a resource?
   I. petroleum
   II. a factory
   III. a cheeseburger dinner
   a. I only
   b. II only
   c. III only
   d. I and II only
   e. I, II, and III

2. Which of the following situations represent(s) resource scarcity?
   I. Rapidly growing economies experience increasing levels of water pollution.
   II. There is a finite amount of petroleum in the physical environment.
   III. Cassette tapes are no longer being produced.
   a. I only
   b. II only
   c. III only
   d. I and II only
   e. I, II, and III

3. Suppose that you prefer reading a book you already own to watching TV and that you prefer watching TV to listening to music. If these are your only three choices, what is the opportunity cost of reading?

   a. watching TV and listening to music
   b. watching TV
   c. listening to music
   d. sleeping
   e. the price of the book

4. Which of the following statements is/are normative?
   I. The price of gasoline is rising.
   II. The price of gasoline is too high.
   III. Gas prices are expected to fall in the near future.
   a. I only
   b. II only
   c. III only
   d. I and III only
   e. I, II, and III

5. Which of the following questions is studied in microeconomics?
   a. Should I go to college or get a job after I graduate?
   b. What government policies should be adopted to promote employment in the economy?
   c. How many people are employed in the economy this year?
   d. Has the overall level of prices in the economy increased or decreased this year?
   e. What determines the overall salary levels paid to workers in a given year?

> The **Tackle the Test** feature presents five AP-style multiple-choice questions, with solutions, to help students become comfortable with the types of questions they will see in the multiple choice section of the AP exam.

Tackle the Test: Free-Response Questions

1. Define resources, and list the four categories of resources. What characteristic of resources results in the need to make choices?

   Answer (6 points)

   1 point: Resources are anything that can be used to produce something else.

   1 point each: The four categories of the economy's resources are land, labor, capital, and entrepreneurship.

   1 point: The characteristic that results in the need to make choices is scarcity.

2. In what type of economic analysis do questions have a "right" or "wrong" answer? In what type of economic analysis do questions not necessarily have a "right" answer? On what type of economic analysis do economists tend to disagree most frequently? Why might economists disagree? Explain.

> In addition, two **AP-style free-response questions** are provided. A sample grading rubric is given for the first FRQ to teach students how these question are graded on the AP exam and to help them learn how to write thoughtful answers.

Each Section ends with a comprehensive review and problem set

Section 4 Review

Summary

1. The **consumption function** shows how an individual household's consumer spending is determined by its current disposable income. The **aggregate consumption function** shows the relationship for the entire

9. Changes in commodity prices, nominal wages, and productivity lead to changes in producers' profits and shift the short-run aggregate supply curve.

10. In the long run, all prices, including nominal wages, are ... its **potential out-** ... potential out- ... e in response to ... put will fall. If po- ... e output, nominal

Key Terms

Marginal propensity to consume (*MPC*), p. 159
Marginal propensity to save (*MPS*), p. 159
Autonomous change in aggregate spending, p. 160
Multiplier, p. 160

Interest rate effect of a change in the aggregate price level, p. 174
Fiscal policy, p. 176
Monetary policy, p. 177
Aggregate supply curve, p. 179
Nominal ... p. 180

Demand shock, p. 191
Supply shock, p. 192
Stagflation, ...
Long-run ma...
Recessionary ...
...

End-of-Section Review and Problems In addition to the opportunities for review at the end of every module, each section ends with a brief but complete Summary of the key concepts, a list of key terms, and a comprehensive set of end-of-chapter problems.

Problems

1. A fall in the value of the dollar against other currencies makes U.S. final goods and services cheaper to foreigners even though the U.S. aggregate price level stays the same. As a result, foreigners demand more American aggregate output. Your study part-

ner says that this represents a movement down the aggregate demand curve because foreigners are demanding more in response to a lower price. You, however, insist that this represents a rightward shift of the aggregate demand curve. Who is right? Explain.

Putting it All Together The final module in the macro part of the book, Module 45, shows students how to use what they have learned to answer comprehensive, "real-world" questions about the macroeconomy, like the type they will see in the free-response section of the AP exam.

Appendix 14 provides enrichment modules for greater insight into microeconomics.

section 14

Module 79: The Economics of Information
Economics by Example: "How Gullible Are We?"
Module 80: Indifference Curves and Consumer Choice
Economics by Example: "Why Is Cash the Ultimate Gift?"

Module 45
Putting It All Together

Having completed our study of the basic macroeconomic models, we can use them to analyze scenarios and evaluate policy recommendations. In this module we develop a step-by-step approach to macroeconomic analysis. You can adapt this approach to problems involving any macroeconomic model, including models of aggregate demand and supply, production possibilities, money markets, and the ... to combine mastery of the ... to analyze a new scenario

Appendix

...alysis

...ut the macroeconomy take ...ion, most macroeconomic

...ow where to start.

...or a policy response to the

...e initial, short-run effects.

...un effects run their course, ...will move toward its long-

For example, you might be asked to consider the following scenario and answer the associated questions.

Assume the U.S. economy is currently operating at an aggregate output level above potential output. Draw a correctly labeled graph showing aggregate demand, short-run aggregate supply, long-run aggregate supply, equilibrium output, and the aggregate price level. Now assume that the Federal Reserve conducts contractionary monetary policy. Identify the open-market operation the Fed would conduct,

Supplements and Media

We are pleased to offer an enhanced and completely revised supplements and media package to accompany this textbook. The package has been crafted by experienced AP teachers to help instructors teach their AP Economics course and to give students the tools to develop their skills in economics and succeed on the AP Economics Exam.

For Instructors

Teachers Resource Binder The TRB, written by Eric Dodge, is a comprehensive resource for AP Economics teachers that provides suggestions for organizing an AP Economics course, including a sample syllabus, teaching strategies, suggested resources, and AP tips that will prove helpful for new and experienced AP teachers alike. In addition, the following components are provided for each module:

- Student learning objectives
- Key economic concepts
- Common student difficulties
- Class presentation ideas
- Pacing guides to suggest how much class time to spend on the module
- Sample lectures
- In-class demonstrations and activities
- Solutions to AP Review problems from the textbook

Instructor's Resource CD-ROM The CD-ROM contains all text figures (in JPEG and PPT formats), PowerPoint lecture slides, and detailed solutions to all of CYU, Tackle the Test, and end-of-section problems. Using the Instructor's Resource CD-ROM, the teacher can easily build classroom presentations or enhance online courses.

Printed Test Bank The Test Bank, written by Eric Dodge, provides a wide range of AP-style multiple choice and short answer questions appropriate for assessing student comprehension, interpretation, analysis, and synthesis skills. With close to 3000 questions, the Test Bank offers multiple-choice questions designed for comprehensive coverage of the AP course concepts. Questions have been checked for correlation with the text content and notation, overall usability, and accuracy.

The questions are organized by Section, keyed to the pertinent module(s), and categorized by degree of difficulty. The Test Bank includes questions designed to represent the various question formats used on the AP exam. It contains questions based on the graphs that appear in the book. These questions ask students to use the graphical models developed in the textbook and to interpret the information presented in the graph. Selected questions are paired with scenarios to reinforce comprehension.

ExamView® Software The Printed Test Bank is available in computerized format with ExamView. ExamView Test Generator guides teachers through the process of creating online or paper tests and quizzes quickly and easily. Users may select from our extensive bank of more than 3000 test questions or use the step-by-step tutorial to write their own questions. Tests may be printed in many different types of formats to provide maximum flexibility or may be administered on line using the ExamView Player. Questions may be sorted according to various information fields and scrambled to create different versions of tests.

Lecture PowerPoint Presentation Created by David Mayer and Margaret Ray, the enhanced PowerPoint presentation slides are designed to assist teachers with lecture preparation and presentations. The slides contain graphs, data tables, and bulleted lists of key concepts suitable for lecture presentation. Key figures from the text are replicated and animated to demonstrate how they build. *Notes to the Instructor* are included to provide added tips, class exercises, examples, and explanations to enhance classroom presentations. The PowerPoint presentations may also be customized by adding personalized data, questions, and lecture notes. The files may be accessed on the instructor's side of the Web site or on the Instructor's Resource CD-ROM.

For Students

Strive for a 5 Prepared by Margaret Ray and David Mayer, this guide serves as a study guide for students as they complete the course and as an AP test preparation resource. It reinforces the topics and key concepts covered in the text and on the AP exam.

The study guide component of *Strive for a 5* begins with an overview of the sections to provide a big picture context and to review how the textbook content correlates to the AP exam weighting and then shifts to a module by module review. The coverage for each module is organized as follows:

Before You Read the Module

- Summary: an opening paragraph that provides a brief overview of the chapter.
- Learning Objectives: a numbered list outlining and describing the most important concepts in the module.
- A review and discussion of key models and/or graphs introduced in the module.

While You Read the Module

- ➤ Key Terms: a list of boldface key terms —including room for definitions and note-taking.
- ➤ What to watch for: A list of questions that prompt students to look for key information as they read, with space left for answers and note taking.

After You Read the Module

- ➤ Review questions: fill-in-the blank questions that review important material in the module.
- ➤ Featured graph: a graphing exercise that helps students understand and draw the important graphs in the module.
- ➤ Practice questions: study questions, and sample free response questions to help review the material in the module.

Answer Key

- ➤ Solutions: detailed solutions to the Questions, and Exercises in the Study Guide.

The AP preparation section of *Strive for a 5* is a comprehensive test review resource. It begins with a diagnostic pre-test and instructions to help students determine where to focus their test preparation efforts. Test preparation tips, suggestions for setting a test preparation schedule, and advice on how to study effectively and efficiently in preparation for the AP exam are also featured. Finally, sample practice tests that simulate the AP exam with solutions and sample grading rubrics are provided. Information about purchasing the *Strive for a 5* guide may be found on the Web site.

Krugman's Economics for AP*, eBook The eBook fully integrates the text with the student media including animated graphs. The eBook also offers a range of customization features including bookmarking, highlighting, note-taking, plus a convenient glossary.

Book Companion Web Site for Students and Instructors

www.bfwpub.com/highschool/Krugman_AP_Econ
The companion Web site offers valuable tools for both instructors—including access to the contents of the Instructors Resource CD and suggestions for additional resources—and for students—additional opportunities for self-testing and review. For additional information on the supplements package and other offerings check out the Web site.

Acknowledgments

Our deep appreciation and heartfelt thanks to the following individuals who wrote and/or helped to develop and critique various components in the supplements package:

Melanie Fox, Austin College, Sherman, TX, who wrote the *Online Tests and Quizzes and Cumulative AP Tests for Macroeconomics*

Amy Shrout, Holy Cross College at Notre Dame, Indiana who wrote the *Online Tests and Quizzes and Cumulative AP Tests for Microeconomics*

Mike Fullington, Port Charlotte High School, Port Charlotte, FL.

Robert Graham, Hanover College, Hanover, IN

Brian Held, Loyola High School, Los Angeles, CA

Woodrow W. Hughes, Jr., Converse College, Spartansburg, SC

Holly Jones, The Pennington School, Pennington, NJ

Robert Zywicki, Montgomery High School, Skillman, NJ

We are also want to offer our gratitude to the following experienced AP-teacher reviewers who helped us to shape this text.

Patricia Brazill, *Irondequoit High School, Rochester, NY*

Matthew Bohnenkamp, *Marian Catholic High School, Chicago Heights, IL*

Ralph Colson, *Stephen F. Austin High School, Austin, TX*

Anthony O. Gyapong, *Penn State University, Abington, PA*

Martin Inde, *Willis High School, Willis, TX*

Mary Kohelis, *Brooke High School, Follansbee, WV*

David Mayer, *Winston Churchill High School, San Antonio, TX*

Francis C. McMann, *George Washington High, Cedar Rapids, IA*

Dianna Miller, *Florida Virtual School, FL*

Diana Reichenbach, *Miami Palmetto Senior High School, Miami, FL*

James Spellicy, *Lowell High School, San Francisco, CA*

Kevin Starnes, *Garden Grove HS, Lake Forest, CA*

Shaun Waldron, *Niles West High School, Skokie, IL*

Marsha Williams, *The Bronx High School of Science, Bronx, NY*

Sandra Wright, *Adlai Stevenson High School, Lincolnshire, IL*

We are indebted to the following reviewers, class testers, survey participants, and other contributors whose input helped guide the second edition of Krugman and Wells' *Economics*.

Carlos Aguilar, *El Paso Community College;* Terence Alexander, *Iowa State University;* Morris Altman, *University of Saskatchewan;* Farhad Ameen, *State University of New York, Westchester Community College;* Christopher P. Ball,

Quinnipiac University; Sue Bartlett, *University of South Florida;* Scott Beaulier, *Mercer University;* David Bernotas, *University of Georgia;* Marc Bilodeau, *Indiana University and Purdue University, Indianapolis;* Kelly Blanchard, *Purdue University;* Anne Bresnock, *California State Polytechnic University;* Douglas M. Brown, *Georgetown University;* Joseph Calhoun, *Florida State University;* Douglas Campbell, *University of Memphis;* Kevin Carlson, *University of Massachusetts,* Boston; Andrew J. Cassey, *Washington State University;* Shirley Cassing, *University of Pittsburgh;* Sewin Chan, *New York University;* Mitchell M. Charkiewicz, *Central Connecticut State University;* Joni S. Charles, *Texas State University, San Marcos;* Adhip Chaudhuri, *Georgetown University;* Eric P. Chiang, *Florida Atlantic University;* Hayley H. Chouinard, *Washington State University;* Kenny Christianson, *Binghamton University;* Lisa Citron, *Cascadia Community College;* Steven L. Cobb, *University of North Texas;* Barbara Z. Connolly, *Westchester Community College;* Stephen Conroy, *University of San Diego;* Thomas E. Cooper, *Georgetown University;* Cesar Corredor, *Texas A&M University and University of Texas,* Tyler; Jim F. Couch, *University of Northern Alabama;* Daniel Daly, *Regis University;* H. Evren Damar, *Pacific Lutheran University;* Antony Davies, *Duquesne University;* Greg Delemeester, *Marietta College;* Patrick Dolenc, *Keene State College;* Christine Doyle-Burke, *Framingham State College;* Ding Du, *South Dakota State University;* Jerry Dunn, *Southwestern Oklahoma State University;* Robert R. Dunn, *Washington and Jefferson College;* Ann Eike, *University of Kentucky;* Tisha L. N. Emerson, *Baylor University;* Hadi Salehi Esfahani, *University of Illinois;* William Feipel, *Illinois Central College;* Rudy Fichtenbaum, *Wright State University;* David W. Findlay, *Colby College;* Mary Flannery, *University of California, Santa Cruz;* Robert Francis, *Shoreline Community College;* Shelby Frost, *Georgia State University;* Frank Gallant, *George Fox University;* Robert Gazzale, *Williams College;* Robert Godby, *University of Wyoming;* Michael Goode, *Central Piedmont Community College;* Douglas E. Goodman, *University of Puget Sound;* Marvin Gordon, *University of Illinois at Chicago;* Kathryn Graddy, *Brandeis University;* Alan Day Haight, *State University of New York, Cortland;* Mehdi Haririan, *Bloomsburg University;* Clyde A. Haulman, *College of William and Mary;* Richard R. Hawkins, *University of West Florida;* Mickey A. Hepner, *University of Central Oklahoma;* Michael Hilmer, *San Diego State University;* Tia Hilmer, *San Diego State University;* Jane Himarios, *University of Texas, Arlington;* Jim Holcomb, *University of Texas, El Paso;* Don Holley, *Boise State University;* Alexander Holmes, *University of Oklahoma;* Julie Holzner, *Los Angeles City College;* Robert N. Horn, *James Madison University;* Steven Husted, *University of Pittsburgh;* John O. Ifediora, *University of Wisconsin, Platteville;* Hiro Ito, *Portland State University;* Mike Javanmard, *RioHondo Community College;* Robert T. Jerome, *James Madison University;* Shirley Johnson-Lans, *Vassar College;* David Kalist, *Shippensburg University;* Lillian Kamal, *Northwestern University;* Roger T. Kaufman, *Smith College;* Herb Kessel, *St. Michael's College;*

Rehim Kiliç, *Georgia Institute of Technology;* Grace Kim, *University of Michigan, Dearborn;* Michael Kimmitt, *University of Hawaii, Manoa;* Robert Kling, *Colorado State University;* Sherrie Kossoudji, *University of Michigan;* Charles Kroncke, *College of Mount Saint Joseph;* Reuben Kyle, *Middle Tennessee State University (retired);* Katherine Lande-Schmeiser, *University of Minnesota, Twin Cities;* David Lehr, *Longwood College;* Mary Jane Lenon, *Providence College;* Mary H. Lesser, *Iona College;* Solina Lindahl, *California Polytechnic Institute, San Luis Obispo;* Haiyong Liu, *East Carolina University;* Jane S. Lopus, *California State University, East Bay;* María José Luengo-Prado, *Northeastern University;* Rotua Lumbantobing, *North Carolina State University;* Ed Lyell, *Adams State College;* John Marangos, *Colorado State University;* Ralph D. May, *Southwestern Oklahoma State University;* Wayne McCaffery, *University of Wisconsin, Madison;* Larry McRae, *Appalachian State University;* Mary Ruth J. McRae, *Appalachian State University;* Ellen E. Meade, *American University;* Meghan Millea, *Mississippi State University;* Norman C. Miller, *Miami University (of Ohio);* Khan A. Mohabbat, *Northern Illinois University;* Myra L. Moore, *University of Georgia;* Jay Morris, *Champlain College in Burlington;* Akira Motomura, *Stonehill College;* Kevin J. Murphy, *Oakland University;* Robert Murphy, *Boston College;* Ranganath Murthy, *Bucknell University;* Anthony Myatt, *University of New Brunswick, Canada;* Randy A. Nelson, *Colby College;* Charles Newton, *Houston Community College;* Daniel X. Nguyen, *Purdue University;* Dmitri Nizovtsev, *Washburn University;* Thomas A. Odegaard, *Baylor University;* Constantin Oglobin, *Georgia Southern University;* Charles C. Okeke, *College of Southern Nevada;* Terry Olson, *Truman State University;* Una Okonkwo Osili, *Indiana University and Purdue University, Indianapolis;* Maxwell Oteng, *University of California, Davis;* P. Marcelo Oviedo, *Iowa State University;* Jeff Owen, *Gustavus Adolphus College;* James Palmieri, *Simpson College;* Walter G. Park, *American University;* Elliott Parker, *University of Nevada, Reno;* Michael Perelman, *California State University, Chico;* Nathan Perry, *Utah State University;* Dean Peterson, *Seattle University;* Ken Peterson, *Furman University;* Paul Pieper, *University of Illinois at Chicago;* Dennis L. Placone, *Clemson University;* Michael Polcen, *Northern Virginia Community College;* Raymond A. Polchow, *Zane State College;* Linnea Polgreen, *University of Iowa;* Eileen Rabach, *Santa Monica College;* Matthew Rafferty, *Quinnipiac University;* Jaishankar Raman, *Valparaiso University;* Margaret Ray, *Mary Washington College;* Helen Roberts, *University of Illinois at Chicago;* Jeffrey Rubin, *Rutgers University, New Brunswick;* Rose M. Rubin, *University of Memphis;* Lynda Rush, *California State Polytechnic University, Pomona;* Michael Ryan, *Western Michigan University;* Sara Saderion, *Houston Community College;* Djavad Salehi-Isfahani, *Virginia Tech;* Elizabeth Sawyer Kelly, *University of Wisconsin;* Jesse A. Schwartz, *Kennesaw State University;* Chad Settle, *University of Tulsa;* Steve Shapiro, *University of North Florida;* Robert L. Shoffner III, *Central Piedmont Community College;* Joseph Sicilian,

University of Kansas; Judy Smrha, *Baker University;* John Solow, *University of Iowa;* John Somers, *Portland Community College;* Stephen Stageberg, *University of Mary Washington;* Monty Stanford, *DeVry University;* Rebecca Stein, *University of Pennsylvania;* William K. Tabb, *Queens College, City University of New York (retired);* Sarinda Taengnoi, *University of Wisconsin, Oshkosh;* Henry Terrell, *University of Maryland;* Rebecca Achée Thornton, *University of Houston;* Michael Toma, *Armstrong Atlantic State University;* Brian Trinque, *University of Texas, Austin;* Boone A. Turchi, *University of North Carolina, Chapel Hill;* Nora Underwood, *University of Central Florida;* J. S. Uppal, *State University of New York, Albany;* John Vahaly, *University of Louisville;* Jose J. Vazquez-Cognet, *University of Illinois, Urbana-Champaign;* Daniel Vazzana, *Georgetown College;* Roger H. von Haefen, *North Carolina State University;* Andreas Waldkirch, *Colby College;* Christopher Waller, *University of Notre Dame;* Gregory Wassall, *Northeastern University;* Robert Whaples, *Wake Forest University;* Thomas White, *Assumption College;* Jennifer P. Wissink, *Cornell University;* Mark Witte, *Northwestern University;* Kristen M. Wolfe, *St. Johns River Community College;* Larry Wolfenbarger, *Macon State College;* Louise B. Wolitz, *University of Texas, Austin;* Gavin Wright, *Stanford University;* Bill Yang, *Georgia Southern University;* Jason Zimmerman, *South Dakota State University.*

We must also thank the many people at Worth Publishers for their contributions and the talented team of consultants and contributors they assembled to work with us. Executive Editor Ann Heath was a mastermind behind the scenes, juggling documents, encouraging excellence, and gracefully putting out fires. Dora Figueiredo, assistant editor extraordinaire, assisted with manuscript preparation and helped to coordinate the impressive collection of print supplements that accompany our book.

As in Krugman and Wells' *Economics,* 2e, Andreas Bentz did yeoman's work, granting us the ability to focus on larger issues because we could trust him to focus on the details. Andreas helped to ensure consistency and accuracy as we developed the manuscript. We count ourselves fortunate to have Andreas help us with this adaptation. Development editor Rebecca Kohn's sharp eye and commonsense appraisals were critical in helping us to make good decisions about how to rework the material from Krugman and Well's *Econcomics,* 2e to meet the organizational needs of this book. Executive Development Editor Sharon Balbos played an important role in ensuring that all of our new figures were consistent with the established styles. Many thanks go to Eric P. Chiang, Florida Atlantic University, for his invaluable contributions in accuracy checking the end-of-module CYU and Tackle the Test questions and the end-of-section problems and solutions. Eric also brought us James Watson, who assisted us with extremely quick and thorough data research for updating the content and for accuracy checking second pages. We also thank Dan Heath for his close review of second pages.

We have had an incredible production and design team on this book, people whose hard work, creativity, dedication, and patience continue to amaze us. Thank you all: Tracey Kuehn and Kerry O'Shaughnessy for producing this book; Kevin Kall, Lissi Sigillo, and TSI Graphics for their beautiful interior design and the absolutely spectacular cover; Barbara Seixas, who worked her magic once again on the manufacturing end and despite the vagaries of the project schedule; Cecilia Varas and Dena Dibiglio Betz for photo research; Stacey Alexander, Laura McGinn, and Jenny Chiu for coordinating the production on all supplemental materials. Thanks to our marketing managers, Cindi Weiss, Nicole Sheppard, and Janie Pierce-Bratcher for their tireless advocacy of this book, and to Marie McHale for her work on the media.

It is a thrill to behold a book that one has written; but it's a particularly special thrill to behold a book so beautifully published.

Margaret Ray   *David Anderson*

Cover photo credits

First row: Making American toys: *Feng Li/Getty Images;* Euro Disneyland: *Picture Partners/Alamy;* Currency exchange house, México: *Keith Dannemiller/Alamy;* Bridge: *PhotoDisc;* **Second row:** Trading floor: *Image Source;* Girl with purple scarf: *PhotoDisc;* Tokyo: *Tom Bonaventure/ Photographer's Choice RF /Getty Images;* Double-decker bus: *Flat Earth Images;* **Third row:** Flags: *PhotoDisc;* Tomatoes: *Royalty-Free/Corbis;* Jean shopping: *Getty Images/Somos;* Windmills: *Photodisc/Getty Images;* **Fourth row:** Engineers: *PhotoDisc;* House building: *Photodisc;* Tugboat: *Flat Earth Images;* Cows: *Stockbyte;* **Fifth row:** Job search: *Freefall Images/Alamy;* Coffee: *Getty Images;* Red Prius: *iStockphoto;* Oil wells: *iStockphoto.*

"The TLC Taxi Medallion" is a registered trademark of the City of New York. All rights reserved.

p. vi: Photo of David Anderson by Donna Anderson.

Chapter-opener photo credits

p. 2, Getty Images/Somos RF; p. 10, American Stock/Getty Images; p. 16, 20th Century Fox/Dreamworks/The Kobal Collection; p. 23, Dreamworks/The Kobal Collection/Cooper, Andrew; p. 48, Getty Images; p. 59, Philippe Colombi/PhotoDisc/Getty Images; p. 71, © Steve Raymer/Corbis; p. 77, iStockphoto; p. 88, iStockphoto; p. 102, Spencer Platt/Getty Images; p. 112, © Peter Menzel/menzelphoto.com; p. 118, Spencer Platt/Getty Images; p. 126, AP Photo/Marcio Jose Sanchez; p. 134, AP Photo/Paul Sakuma; p. 142, Getty Images/Glowimages; p. 158, Maria Teijeiro/Digital Vision/Getty Images; p. 172, Getty Images/Blend Images; p. 179, Digital Vision; p. 190, © Kurt Brady/Alamy; p. 199, © Jeff Greenberg/Alamy; p. 209, AP Photo/Rich Pedroncelli; p. 222, © Michael Belardo/Alamy; p. 231, iStockphoto; p. 237, Photo by Oli Scarff/Getty Images; p. 243, Tim Boyle/Getty Images; p. 253, © Corbis Premium RF/Alamy; p. 262, Reuters/Joe Pavel/Federal Reserve Board/Handout; p. 268, iStockphoto; p. 277, © Brad Schloss/Icon SMI/Corbis; p. 296, Timothy A. Clary/AFP/Getty Images; p. 307, Chip Somodevilla/Getty Images; p. 315, iStockphoto; p. 321, Desmond Kwande/AFP/Getty Images; p. 331, Tom Bonaventure/Photographer's Choice RF/Getty Images; p. 343, AP Photo; p. 355, AP Photo/Gerald Herbert; p. 368, Stockbyte/Getty Images; p. 376, AP Photo/Jacques Brinon; p. 387, FocusJapan/Alamy; p. 398, Jetta Productions/Getty Images; p. 410, © Picture Partners/Alamy; p. 421, Photo by Udo Weitz/Bloomberg via Getty Images; p. 431, Udo Weitz/Bloomberg via Getty Images; p. 437, PhotosIndia.com LLC/Alamy; p. 443, iStockphoto; p. 458, © Joe Belanger/Alamy; p. 466, iStockphoto; p. 475, iStockphoto; p. 482, Photoedit; p. 495, © Chloe Johnson/Alamy; p. 511, © DAJ/Imagestate; p. 530, iStockphoto; p. 536, Michael Melford/National Geographic/Getty Images; p. 542, Felipe Dupouy/Lifesize/Getty Images; p. 548, © Terrance Klassen/AgeFotostock; p. 559, © Modern Landscapes/Alamy; p. 567, © Chris A Crumley/Alamy; p. 584, © UpperCut Images/Alamy; p. 590, Brand New Images/Getty Images; p. 599, Getty Images; p. 608, Corbis; p. 617, Mario Tama/Getty Images; p. 624, Dena Digilio Betz; p. 638, Bloomberg via Getty Images; p. 644, Frances M. Roberts; p. 652, © Richard Levine/Alamy; p. 659, AP Photo/Kiichiro Sato; p. 668, Alamy; p. 680, Digital Vision; p. 690, iStockphoto; p. 695, © LOOK Die Bildagentur der Fotografen GmbH/Alamy; p. 706, © Barry Sweet/epa/Corbis; p. 711, Getty Images/Hola Images RF; p. 724, iStockphoto; p. 731, iStockphoto; p. 743, © imac/Alamy; p. 754, AP Photo/The Record, Mike McMahon; p. 761, iStockphoto; p. 782, iStockphoto; p. 787, iStockphoto.

KRUGMAN'S
ECONOMICS for AP*

section 1

Basic Economic Concepts

COMMON GROUND

The annual meeting of the American Economic Association draws thousands of economists, young and old, famous and obscure. There are booksellers, business meetings, and quite a few job interviews. But mainly the economists gather to talk and listen. During the busiest times, 60 or more presentations may be taking place simultaneously, on questions that range from the future of the stock market to who does the cooking in two-earner families.

What do these people have in common? An expert on the stock market probably knows very little about the economics of housework, and vice versa. Yet an economist who wanders into the wrong seminar and ends up listening to presentations on some unfamiliar topic is nonetheless likely to hear much that is familiar. The reason is that all economic analysis is based on a set of common principles that apply to many different issues.

Some of these principles involve *individual choice*—for economics is, first of all, about the choices that individuals make. Do you choose to work during the summer or take a backpacking trip? Do you buy a new CD or go to a movie? These decisions involve *making a choice* from among a limited number of alternatives—limited because no one can have everything that he or she wants. Every question in economics at its most basic level involves individuals making choices.

But to understand how an economy works, you need to understand more than how individ-

uals make choices. None of us lives like Robinson Crusoe, alone on an island—we must make decisions in an environment that is shaped by the decisions of others. Indeed, in our global economy even the simplest decisions you make—say, what to have for breakfast—are shaped by the decisions of thousands of other people, from the banana grower in Costa Rica who decided to grow the fruit you eat to the farmer in Iowa who provided the corn in your cornflakes. And because each of us depends on so many others—and they, in turn, depend on us—our choices interact. So although all economics at a basic level is about individual choice, in order to understand behavior within an economy we must also understand economic *interaction*—how my choices affect your choices, and vice versa.

Many important economic interactions can be understood by looking at the markets for individual goods—for example, the market for corn. But we must also understand economy-wide interactions in order to understand how they can lead to the ups and downs we see in the economy as a whole.

In this section we discuss the study of economics and the difference between microeconomics and macroeconomics. We also introduce the major topics within macroeconomics and the use of models to study the macroeconomy. Finally, we present the production possibilities curve model and use it to understand basic economic activity, including trade between two economies. Because the study of economics relies on graphical models, an appendix on the use of graphs follows the end of this section.

One must choose!

ADMIT ONE

?

1

- How scarcity and choice are central to the study of economics

- The importance of opportunity cost in individual choice and decision making

- The difference between positive economics and normative economics

- When economists agree and why they sometimes disagree

- What makes macroeconomics different from microeconomics

Economics is the study of scarcity and choice.

Individual choice is decisions by individuals about what to do, which necessarily involve decisions about what not to do.

An **economy** is a system for coordinating a society's productive and consumptive activities.

In a **market economy,** the decisions of individual producers and consumers largely determine what, how, and for whom to produce, with little government involvement in the decisions.

In a **command economy,** industry is publicly owned and a central authority makes production and consumption decisions.

Incentives are rewards or punishments that motivate particular choices.

Module 1
The Study of Economics

Individual Choice: The Core of Economics

Economics is the study of scarcity and choice. Every economic issue involves, at its most basic level, **individual choice**—decisions by individuals about what to do and what *not* to do. In fact, you might say that it isn't economics if it isn't about choice.

Step into a big store such as Walmart or Target. There are thousands of different products available, and it is extremely unlikely that you—or anyone else—could afford to buy everything you might want to have. And anyway, there's only so much space in your room. Given the limitations on your budget and your living space, you must choose which products to buy and which to leave on the shelf.

The fact that those products are on the shelf in the first place involves choice—the store manager chose to put them there, and the manufacturers of the products chose to produce them. The **economy** is a system that coordinates choices about production with choices about consumption, and distributes goods and services to the people who want them. The United States has a **market economy,** in which production and consumption are the result of decentralized decisions by many firms and individuals. There is no central authority telling people what to produce or where to ship it. Each individual producer makes what he or she thinks will be most profitable, and each consumer buys what he or she chooses.

An alternative to a market economy is a **command economy,** in which industry is publicly owned and there *is* a central authority making production and consumption decisions. Command economies have been tried, most notably in the Soviet Union between 1917 and 1991, but they didn't work very well. Producers in the Soviet Union routinely found themselves unable to produce because they did not have crucial raw materials, or they succeeded in producing but then found nobody wanted what the central authority had them produce. Consumers were often unable to find necessary items—command economies are famous for long lines at shops.

At the root of the problem with command economies is a lack of **incentives,** which are rewards or punishments that motivate particular choices. In market economies, producers are free to charge higher prices when there is a shortage of something, and to keep the resulting profits. High prices and profits provide incentives for producers to make more of the most-needed goods and services and eliminate shortages.

In fact, economists tend to be skeptical of any attempt to change people's behavior that doesn't change their incentives. For example, a plan that calls on manufacturers to reduce pollution voluntarily probably won't be effective; a plan that gives them a financial incentive to do so is more likely to succeed.

Property rights, which establish ownership and grant individuals the right to trade goods and services with each other, create many of the incentives in market economies. With the right to own property comes the incentive to produce things of value, either to keep, or to trade for mutual gain. And ownership creates an incentive to put resources to their best possible use. Property rights to a lake, for example, give the owners an incentive not to pollute that lake if its use for recreation, serenity, or sale has greater value.

In any economy, the decisions of what to do with the next ton of pollution, the next hour of free time, and the next dollar of spending money are *marginal decisions.* They involve trade-offs at the margin: comparing the costs and benefits of doing a little bit more of an activity versus a little bit less. The gain from doing something one more time is called the *marginal benefit.* The cost of doing something one more time is the *marginal cost.* If the marginal benefit of making another car, reading another page, or buying another latte exceeds the marginal cost, the activity should continue. Otherwise, it should not. The study of such decisions is known as **marginal analysis,** plays a central role in economics because the formula of doing things until the marginal benefit no longer exceeds the marginal cost is the key to deciding "how much" to do of any activity.

All economic activities involve individual choice. Let's take a closer look at what this means for the study of economics.

Resources Are Scarce

You can't always get what you want. Almost everyone would like to have a beautiful house in a great location (and help with the housecleaning), two or three luxury cars, and frequent vacations in fancy hotels. But even in a rich country like the United States, not many families can afford all of that. So they must make choices—whether to go to Disney World this year or buy a better car, whether to make do with a small backyard or accept a longer commute in order to live where land is cheaper.

Limited income isn't the only thing that keeps people from having everything they want. Time is also in limited supply: there are only 24 hours in a day. And because the time we have is limited, choosing to spend time on one activity also means choosing not to spend time on a different activity—spending time studying for an exam means forgoing a night at the movies. Indeed, many people feel so limited by the number of hours in the day that they are willing to trade money for time. For example, convenience stores usually charge higher prices than larger supermarkets. But they fulfill a valuable role by catering to customers who would rather pay more than spend the time traveling farther to a supermarket where they might also have to wait in longer lines.

Why do individuals have to make choices? The ultimate reason is that *resources are scarce.* A **resource** is anything that can be used to produce something else. The economy's resources, sometimes called *factors of production,* can be classified into four categories: **land** (including timber, water, minerals, and all other resources that come from nature), **labor** (the effort of workers), **capital** (machinery, buildings, tools, and all other manufactured goods used to make other goods and services), and **entrepreneurship** (risk taking, innovation, and the organization of resources for production). A resource is **scarce** when there is not enough of it available to satisfy the various ways a society wants to use it. For example, there are limited supplies of oil and coal, which currently provide most of the energy used to produce and deliver everything we buy. And in a growing world economy with a rapidly increasing human population, even clean air and water have become scarce resources.

Just as individuals must make choices, the scarcity of resources means that society as a whole must make choices. One way for a society to make choices is simply to allow

Property rights establish ownership and grant individuals the right to trade goods and services with each other.

Marginal analysis is the study of the costs and benefits of doing a little bit more of an activity versus a little bit less.

A **resource** is anything that can be used to produce something else.

Land refers to all resources that come from nature, such as minerals, timber and petroleum.

Labor is the effort of workers.

Capital refers to manufactured goods used to make other goods and services.

Entrepreneurship describes the efforts of entrepreneurs in organizing resources for production, taking risks to create new enterprises, and innovating to develop new products and production processes.

A **scarce** resource is not available in sufficient quantities to satisfy all the various ways a society wants to use it.

them to emerge as the result of many individual choices. For example, there are only so many hours in a week, and Americans must decide how to spend their time. How many hours will they spend going to supermarkets to get lower prices rather than saving time by shopping at convenience stores? The answer is the sum of individual decisions: each of the millions of individuals in the economy makes his or her own choice about where to shop, and society's choice is simply the sum of those individual decisions.

For various reasons, there are some decisions that a society decides are best not left to individual choice. For example, two of the authors live in an area that until recently was mainly farmland but is now being rapidly built up. Most local residents feel that the community would be a more pleasant place to live if some of the land were left undeveloped. But no individual has an incentive to keep his or her land as open space, rather than sell it to a developer. So a trend has emerged in many communities across the United States of local governments purchasing undeveloped land and preserving it as open space. Decisions about how to use scarce resources are often best left to individuals but sometimes should be made at a higher, community-wide, level.

Opportunity Cost: The Real Cost of Something Is What You Must Give Up to Get It

Suppose it is the last term before you graduate and you must decide which college to attend. You have narrowed your choices to a small liberal arts college near home or a large state university several hours away. If you decide to attend the local liberal arts college, what is the cost of that decision? Of course, you will have to pay for tuition, books, and housing, no matter which college you choose. Added to the cost of choosing the local college is the forgone opportunity to attend the large state university, your next best alternative. Economists call the value of what you must give up when you make a particular choice an **opportunity cost.**

Opportunity costs are crucial to individual choice because, in the end, all costs are opportunity costs. That's because with every choice, an alternative is forgone—money or time spent on one thing can't be spent on another. If you spend $15 on a pizza, you forgo the opportunity to spend that $15 on a steak. If you spend Saturday afternoon at the park, you can't spend Saturday afternoon doing homework. And if you attend one school, you can't attend another.

The park and school examples show that economists are concerned with more than just costs paid in dollars and cents. The forgone opportunity to do homework has no direct monetary cost, but it is an opportunity cost nonetheless. And if the local college and the state university have the same tuition and fees, the cost of choosing one school over the other has nothing to do with payments and everything to do with forgone opportunities.

Now suppose tuition and fees at the state university are $5,000 less than at the local college. In that case, what you give up to attend the local college is the ability to attend the state university *plus* the enjoyment you could have gained from spending $5,000 on other things. So the opportunity cost of a choice includes all the costs, whether or not they are monetary costs, of making that choice.

The choice to go to college *at all* provides an important final example of opportunity costs. High school graduates can either go to college or seek immediate employment. Even with a full scholarship that would make college "free" in terms of monetary costs, going to college would still be an expensive proposition because most young people, if they were not in college, would have a job. By going to college, students forgo the income they could have earned if they had gone straight to work instead. Therefore, the opportunity cost of attending college is the value of all necessary monetary payments for tuition and fees *plus* the forgone income from the best available job that could take the place of going to college.

For most people the value of a college degree far exceeds the value of alternative earnings, with notable exceptions. The opportunity cost of going to college is high for people who could earn a lot during what would otherwise be their college years. Basketball

LeBron James understood the concept of opportunity cost.

star LeBron James bypassed college because the opportunity cost would have included his $13 million contract with the Cleveland Cavaliers and even more from corporate sponsors Nike and Coca-Cola. Golfer Tiger Woods, Microsoft co-founder Bill Gates, and actor Matt Damon are among the high achievers who decided the opportunity cost of completing college was too much to swallow.

Microeconomics Versus Macroeconomics

We have presented economics as the study of choices and described how, at its most basic level, economics is about individual choice. The branch of economics concerned with how individuals make decisions and how these decisions interact is called **microeconomics.** Microeconomics focuses on choices made by individuals, households, or firms—the smaller parts that make up the economy as a whole.

Macroeconomics focuses on the bigger picture—the overall ups and downs of the economy. When you study macroeconomics, you learn how economists explain these fluctuations and how governments can use economic policy to minimize the damage they cause. Macroeconomics focuses on **economic aggregates**—economic measures such as the unemployment rate, the inflation rate, and gross domestic product—that summarize data across many different markets.

Table 1.1 lists some typical questions that involve economics. A microeconomic version of the question appears on the left, paired with a similar macroeconomic question on the right. By comparing the questions, you can begin to get a sense of the difference between microeconomics and macroeconomics.

Microeconomics is the study of how people make decisions and how those decisions interact.

Macroeconomics is concerned with the overall ups and downs in the economy.

Economic aggregates are economic measures that summarize data across many different markets.

table **1.1**

Microeconomic Versus Macroeconomic Questions

Microeconomic Questions	Macroeconomic Questions
Should I go to college or get a job after high school?	How many people are employed in the economy as a whole this year?
What determines the salary that Citibank offers to a new college graduate?	What determines the overall salary levels paid to workers in a given year?
What determines the cost to a high school of offering a new course?	What determines the overall level of prices in the economy as a whole?
What government policies should be adopted to make it easier for low-income students to attend college?	What government policies should be adopted to promote employment and growth in the economy as a whole?
What determines the number of iPhones exported to France?	What determines the overall trade in goods, services, and financial assets between the United States and the rest of the world?

As these questions illustrate, microeconomics focuses on how individuals and firms make decisions, and the consequences of those decisions. For example, a school will use microeconomics to determine how much it would cost to offer a new course, which includes the instructor's salary, the cost of class materials, and so on. By weighing the costs and benefits, the school can then decide whether or not to offer the course. Macroeconomics, in contrast, examines the *overall* behavior of the economy—how the actions of all of the individuals and firms in the economy interact to produce a particular economy-wide level of economic performance. For example, macroeconomics is concerned with the general level of prices in the economy and how high or low they are relative to prices last year, rather than with the price of a particular good or service.

Positive Versus Normative Economics

Economic analysis, as we will see throughout this book, draws on a set of basic economic principles. But how are these principles applied? That depends on the purpose of the analysis. Economic analysis that is used to answer questions about the way the world works, questions that have definite right and wrong answers, is known as **positive economics.** In contrast, economic analysis that involves saying how the world *should* work is known as **normative economics.**

Imagine that you are an economic adviser to the governor of your state and the governor is considering a change to the toll charged along the state turnpike. Below are three questions the governor might ask you.

1. How much revenue will the tolls yield next year?

2. How much would that revenue increase if the toll were raised from $1.00 to $1.50?

3. Should the toll be raised, bearing in mind that a toll increase would likely reduce traffic and air pollution near the road but impose some financial hardship on frequent commuters?

There is a big difference between the first two questions and the third one. The first two are questions about facts. Your forecast of next year's toll revenue without any increase will be proved right or wrong when the numbers actually come in. Your estimate of the impact of a change in the toll is a little harder to check—the increase in revenue depends on other factors besides the toll, and it may be hard to disentangle the causes of any change in revenue. Still, in principle there is only one right answer.

But the question of whether or not tolls should be raised may not have a "right" answer—two people who agree on the effects of a higher toll could still disagree about whether raising the toll is a good idea. For example, someone who lives near the turnpike but doesn't commute on it will care a lot about noise and air pollution but not so much about commuting costs. A regular commuter who doesn't live near the turnpike will have the opposite priorities.

Should the toll be raised?

This example highlights a key distinction between the two roles of economic analysis and presents another way to think about the distinction between positive and normative analysis: positive economics is about description, and normative economics is about prescription. Positive economics occupies most of the time and effort of the economics profession.

Looking back at the three questions the governor might ask, it is worth noting a subtle but important difference between questions 1 and 2. Question 1 asks for a simple prediction about next year's revenue—a forecast. Question 2 is a "what if" question, asking how revenue would change if the toll were to change. Economists are often called upon to answer both types of questions. Economic *models,* which provide simplified representations of reality such as graphs or equations, are especially useful for answering "what if" questions.

The answers to such questions often serve as a guide to policy, but they are still predictions, not prescriptions. That is, they tell you what will happen if a policy is changed, but they don't tell you whether or not that result is good. Suppose that your economic model tells you that the governor's proposed increase in highway tolls will raise property values in communities near the road but will tax or inconvenience people who currently use the turnpike to get to work. Does that information make this proposed toll increase a good idea or a bad one? It depends on whom you ask. As we've just seen, someone who is very concerned with the communities near the road will support the increase, but someone who is very concerned with the welfare of drivers will feel differently. That's a value judgment—it's not a question of positive economic analysis.

Still, economists often do engage in normative economics and give policy advice. How can they do this when there may be no "right" answer? One answer is that economists are also citizens, and we all have our opinions. But economic analysis can often be used to show that some policies are clearly better than others, regardless of individual opinions.

Suppose that policies A and B achieve the same goal, but policy A makes everyone better off than policy B—or at least makes some people better off without making other people worse off. Then A is clearly more efficient than B. That's not a value judgment: we're talking about how best to achieve a goal, not about the goal itself.

For example, two different policies have been used to help low-income families obtain housing: rent control, which limits the rents landlords are allowed to charge, and rent subsidies, which provide families with additional money with which to pay rent. Almost all economists agree that subsidies are the more efficient policy. (In a later module we'll see why this is so.) And so the great majority of economists, whatever their personal politics, favor subsidies over rent control.

When policies can be clearly ranked in this way, then economists generally agree. But it is no secret that economists sometimes disagree.

When and Why Economists Disagree

Economists have a reputation for arguing with each other. Where does this reputation come from?

One important answer is that media coverage tends to exaggerate the real differences in views among economists. If nearly all economists agree on an issue—for example, the proposition that rent controls lead to housing shortages—reporters and editors are likely to conclude that there is no story worth covering, and so the professional consensus tends to go unreported. But when there is some issue on which prominent economists take opposing sides—for example, whether cutting taxes right now would help the economy—that does make a good news story. So you hear much more about the areas of disagreement among economists than you do about the many areas of agreement.

It is also worth remembering that economics is, unavoidably, often tied up in politics. On a number of issues, powerful interest groups know what opinions they want to hear. Therefore, they have an incentive to find and promote economists who profess those opinions, which gives these economists a prominence and visibility out of proportion to their support among their colleagues.

Although the appearance of disagreement among economists exceeds the reality, it remains true that economists often *do* disagree about important things. For example, some highly respected economists argue vehemently that the U.S. government should replace the income tax with a *value-added tax* (a national sales tax, which is the main source of government revenue in many European countries). Other equally respected economists disagree. What are the sources of this difference of opinion?

One important source of differences is in values: as in any diverse group of individuals, reasonable people can differ. In comparison to an income tax, a value-added tax typically falls more heavily on people with low incomes. So an economist who values a society with more social and income equality will likely oppose a value-added tax. An economist with different values will be less likely to oppose it.

A second important source of differences arises from the way economists conduct economic analysis. Economists base their conclusions on models formed by making simplifying assumptions about reality. Two economists can legitimately disagree about which simplifications are appropriate—and therefore arrive at different conclusions.

Suppose that the U.S. government was considering a value-added tax. Economist A may rely on a simplification of reality that focuses on the administrative costs of tax systems—that is, the costs of monitoring compliance, processing tax forms, collecting the tax, and so on. This economist might then point to the well-known high costs of administering a value-added tax and argue against the change. But economist B may think that the right way to approach the question is to ignore the administrative

costs and focus on how the proposed law would change individual savings behavior. This economist might point to studies suggesting that value-added taxes promote higher consumer saving, a desirable result. Because the economists have made different simplifying assumptions, they arrive at different conclusions. And so the two economists may find themselves on different sides of the issue.

Most such disputes are eventually resolved by the accumulation of evidence that shows which of the various simplifying assumptions made by economists does a better job of fitting the facts. However, in economics, as in any science, it can take a long time before research settles important disputes—decades, in some cases. And since the economy is always changing in ways that make old approaches invalid or raise new policy questions, there are always new issues on which economists disagree. The policy maker must then decide which economist to believe.

Module 1 AP Review

Solutions appear at the back of the book.

Check Your Understanding

1. What are the four categories of resources? Give an example of a resource from each category.

2. What type of resource is each of the following?
   a. time spent flipping hamburgers at a restaurant
   b. a bulldozer
   c. a river

3. You make $45,000 per year at your current job with Whiz Kids Consultants. You are considering a job offer from Brainiacs, Inc., which would pay you $50,000 per year. Which of the following are elements of the opportunity cost of accepting the new job at Brainiacs, Inc.? Answer yes or no, and explain your answer.

   a. the increased time spent commuting to your new job
   b. the $45,000 salary from your old job
   c. the more spacious office at your new job

4. Identify each of the following statements as positive or normative, and explain your answer.
   a. Society should take measures to prevent people from engaging in dangerous personal behavior.
   b. People who engage in dangerous personal behavior impose higher costs on society through higher medical costs.

Tackle the Test: Multiple-Choice Questions

1. Which of the following is an example of a resource?
     I. petroleum
     II. a factory
     III. a cheeseburger dinner
   a. I only
   b. II only
   c. III only
   d. I and II only
   e. I, II, and III

2. Which of the following situations represent(s) resource scarcity?
     I. Rapidly growing economies experience increasing levels of water pollution.
     II. There is a finite amount of petroleum in the physical environment.
     III. Cassette tapes are no longer being produced.
   a. I only
   b. II only
   c. III only
   d. I and II only
   e. I, II, and III

3. Suppose that you prefer reading a book you already own to watching TV and that you prefer watching TV to listening to music. If these are your only three choices, what is the opportunity cost of reading?

   a. watching TV and listening to music
   b. watching TV
   c. listening to music
   d. sleeping
   e. the price of the book

4. Which of the following statements is/are normative?
     I. The price of gasoline is rising.
     II. The price of gasoline is too high.
     III. Gas prices are expected to fall in the near future.
   a. I only
   b. II only
   c. III only
   d. I and III only
   e. I, II, and III

5. Which of the following questions is studied in microeconomics?
   a. Should I go to college or get a job after I graduate?
   b. What government policies should be adopted to promote employment in the economy?
   c. How many people are employed in the economy this year?
   d. Has the overall level of prices in the economy increased or decreased this year?
   e. What determines the overall salary levels paid to workers in a given year?

Tackle the Test: Free-Response Questions

1. Define resources, and list the four categories of resources. What characteristic of resources results in the need to make choices?

   Answer (6 points)

   1 point: Resources are anything that can be used to produce something else.

   1 point each: The four categories of the economy's resources are land, labor, capital, and entrepreneurship.

   1 point: The characteristic that results in the need to make choices is scarcity.

2. In what type of economic analysis do questions have a "right" or "wrong" answer? In what type of economic analysis do questions not necessarily have a "right" answer? On what type of economic analysis do economists tend to disagree most frequently? Why might economists disagree? Explain.

- What a business cycle is and why policy makers seek to diminish the severity of business cycles

- How employment and unemployment are measured and how they change over the business cycle

- The definition of aggregate output and how it changes over the business cycle

- The meaning of inflation and deflation and why price stability is preferred

- How economic growth determines a country's standard of living

- Why models—simplified representations of reality—play a crucial role in economics

Module 2
Introduction to Macroeconomics

Today many people enjoy walking, biking, and horseback riding through New York's beautiful Central Park. But in 1932 there were many people living there in squalor. At that time, Central Park contained one of the many "Hoovervilles"—the shantytowns that had sprung up across America as a result of a catastrophic economic slump that had started in 1929. Millions of people were out of work and unable to feed, clothe, and house themselves and their families. Beginning in 1933, the U.S. economy would stage a partial recovery. But joblessness stayed high throughout the 1930s—a period that came to be known as the Great Depression.

Why "Hooverville"? These shantytowns were named after President Herbert Hoover, who had been elected president in 1928. When the Depression struck, people blamed the president: neither he nor his economic advisers seemed to understand what had happened or to know what to do. At that time, the field of macroeconomics was still in its infancy. It was only after the economy was plunged into catastrophe that economists began to closely examine how the macroeconomy works and to develop policies that might prevent such disasters in the future. To this day, the effort to understand economic slumps and find ways to prevent them is at the core of macroeconomics.

In this module we will begin to explore the key features of macroeconomic analysis. We will look at some of the field's major concerns, including business cycles, employment, aggregate output, price stability, and economic growth.

The **business cycle** is the short-run alternation between economic downturns, known as recessions, and economic upturns, known as expansions.

A **depression** is a very deep and prolonged downturn.

Recessions are periods of economic downturns when output and employment are falling.

Expansions, or recoveries, are periods of economic upturns when output and employment are rising.

The Business Cycle

The alternation between economic downturns and upturns in the macroeconomy is known as the **business cycle.** A **depression** is a very deep and prolonged downturn; fortunately, the United States hasn't had one since the Great Depression of the 1930s. Instead, we have experienced less prolonged economic downturns known as **recessions,** periods in which output and employment are falling. These are followed by economic upturns—periods in which output and employment are rising—known as **expansions** (sometimes called *recoveries*). According to the National Bureau of Economic Research

figure 2.1

The U.S. Unemployment Rate and the Timing of Business Cycles, 1989–2009

The unemployment rate, a measure of jobless-ness, rises sharply during recessions (indi-cated by shaded areas) and usually falls during expansions.

Source: Bureau of Labor Statistics.

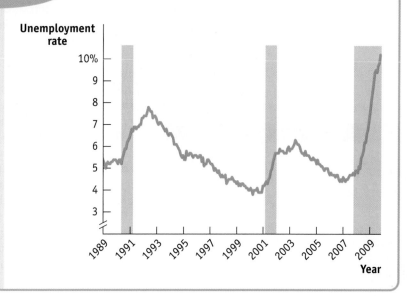

there have been 11 recessions in the United States since World War II. During that pe-riod the average recession has lasted 10 months, and the average expansion has lasted 57 months. The average length of a business cycle, from the beginning of a recession to the beginning of the next recession, has been 5 years and 7 months. The shortest business cycle was 18 months, and the longest was 10 years and 8 months. The most recent eco-nomic downturn started in December, 2007. Figure 2.1 shows the history of the U.S. un-employment rate since 1989 and the timing of business cycles. Recessions are indicated in the figure by the shaded areas.

The business cycle is an enduring feature of the economy. But even though ups and downs seem to be inevitable, most people believe that macroeconomic analysis has guided policies that help smooth out the business cycle and stabilize the economy.

What happens during a business cycle, and how can macroeconomic policies ad-dress the downturns? Let's look at three issues: employment and unemployment, ag-gregate output, and inflation and deflation.

fyi

Defining Recessions and Expansions

Some readers may be wondering exactly how recessions and expansions are defined. The an-swer is that there is no exact definition!

In many countries, economists adopt the rule that a recession is a period of at least two consecutive quarters (a quarter is three months), during which aggregate output falls. The two-consecutive-quarter requirement is designed to avoid classifying brief hiccups in the economy's performance, with no lasting significance, as recessions.

Sometimes, however, this definition seems too strict. For example, an economy that has three months of sharply declining output, then three months of slightly positive growth, then another three months of rapid decline, should surely be considered to have endured a nine-month recession.

In the United States, we try to avoid such misclassifications by assigning the task of determining when a recession begins and ends to an independent panel of experts at the National Bureau of Economic Research (NBER). This panel looks at a variety of economic indicators, with the main focus on employment and produc-tion, but ultimately, the panel makes a judg-ment call.

Sometimes this judgment is controversial. In fact, there is lingering controversy over the 2001 recession. According to the NBER, that recession began in March 2001 and ended in November 2001, when output began rising. Some critics argue, however, that the recession really began several months earlier, when industrial produc-tion began falling. Other critics argue that the re-cession didn't really end in 2001 because employment continued to fall and the job market remained weak for another year and a half.

Employment, Unemployment, and the Business Cycle

Although not as severe as a depression, a recession is clearly an undesirable event. Like a depression, a recession leads to joblessness, reduced production, reduced incomes, and lower living standards.

To understand how job loss relates to the adverse effects of recessions, we need to understand something about how the labor force is structured. **Employment** is the total number of people currently working for pay, and **unemployment** is the total number of people who are actively looking for work but aren't currently employed. A country's **labor force** is the sum of employment and unemployment.

Finding a job was difficult in 2009.

The **unemployment rate**—the percentage of the labor force that is unemployed—is usually a good indicator of what conditions are like in the job market: a high unemployment rate signals a poor job market in which jobs are hard to find; a low unemployment rate indicates a good job market in which jobs are relatively easy to find. In general, during recessions the unemployment rate is rising, and during expansions it is falling. Look again at Figure 2.1, which shows the unemployment rate from 1989 through 2009. The graph shows significant changes in the unemployment rate. Note that even in the most prosperous times there is some unemployment. A booming economy, like that of the late 1990s, can push the unemployment rate down to 4% or even lower. But a severe recession, like the one that began in 2007, can push the unemployment rate into double digits.

Aggregate Output and the Business Cycle

Rising unemployment is the most painful consequence of a recession, and falling unemployment the most urgently desired feature of an expansion. But the business cycle isn't just about jobs—it's also about **output:** the quantity of goods and services produced. During the business cycle, the economy's level of output and its unemployment rate move in opposite directions. At lower levels of output, fewer workers are needed, and the unemployment rate is relatively high. Growth in output requires the efforts of more workers, which lowers the unemployment rate. To measure the rise and fall of an economy's output, we look at **aggregate output**—the economy's total production of goods and services for a given time period, usually a year. Aggregate output normally falls during recessions and rises during expansions.

Inflation, Deflation, and Price Stability

In 1970 the average production worker in the United States was paid $3.40 an hour. By October 2009 the average hourly earnings for such a worker had risen to $18.74 an hour. Three cheers for economic progress!

But wait—American workers were paid much more in 2009, but they also faced a much higher cost of living. In 1970 a dozen eggs cost only about $0.58; by October 2009 that was up to $1.60. The price of a loaf of white bread went from about $0.20 to $1.39. And the price of a gallon of gasoline rose from just $0.33 to $2.61. If we compare the percentage increase in hourly earnings between 1970 and October 2009 with the increases in the prices of some standard items, we see that the average worker's paycheck goes just about as far today as it did in 1970. In other words, the increase in the cost of living wiped out many, if not all, of the wage gains of the typical worker from 1970 to 2009. What caused this situation?

Between 1970 and 2009 the economy experienced substantial **inflation,** a rise in the overall price level. The opposite of inflation is **deflation,** a fall in the overall price level. A change in the prices of a few goods changes the opportunity cost of purchasing those goods but does not constitute inflation or deflation. These terms are reserved for more general changes in the prices of goods and services throughout the economy.

Employment is the number of people currently employed in the economy.

Unemployment is the number of people who are actively looking for work but aren't currently employed.

The **labor force** is equal to the sum of employment and unemployment.

The **unemployment rate** is the percentage of the labor force that is unemployed.

Output is the quantity of goods and services produced.

Aggregate output is the economy's total production of goods and services for a given time period.

A rising overall price level is **inflation.**

A falling overall price level is **deflation.**

Both inflation and deflation can pose problems for the economy. Inflation discourages people from holding on to cash, because if the price level is rising, cash loses value. That is, if the price level rises, a dollar will buy less than it would before. As we will see later in our more detailed discussion of inflation, in periods of rapidly rising prices, people stop holding cash altogether and instead trade goods for goods.

Deflation can cause the opposite problem. That is, if the overall price level falls, a dollar will buy more than it would before. In this situation it can be more attractive for people with cash to hold on to it than to invest in new factories and other productive assets. This can deepen a recession.

In later modules we will look at other costs of inflation and deflation. For now we note that, in general, economists regard **price stability**—meaning that the overall price level is changing either not at all or only very slowly—as a desirable goal because it helps keep the economy stable.

The economy has **price stability** when the aggregate price level is changing only slowly.

Economic growth is an increase in the maximum amount of goods and services an economy can produce.

Economic Growth

In 1955 Americans were delighted with the nation's prosperity. The economy was expanding, consumer goods that had been rationed during World War II were available for everyone to buy, and most Americans believed, rightly, that they were better off than citizens of any other nation, past or present. Yet by today's standards Americans were quite poor in 1955. For example, in 1955 only 33% of American homes contained washing machines, and hardly anyone had air conditioning. If we turn the clock back to 1905, we find that life for most Americans was startlingly primitive by today's standards.

Why are the vast majority of Americans today able to afford conveniences that many lacked in 1955? The answer is **economic growth,** an increase in the maximum possible output of an economy. Unlike the short-term increases in aggregate output that occur as an economy recovers from a downturn in the business cycle, economic growth is an increase in productive capacity that permits a sustained rise in aggregate output over time. Figure 2.2 shows annual figures for U.S. real gross domestic product (GDP) per capita—the value of final goods and services produced in the U.S. per person—from 1900 to 2009. As a result of this economic growth, the U.S. economy's aggregate output per person was almost nine times as large in 2009 as it was in 1900.

figure 2.2

Growth, the Long View

Over the long run, growth in real GDP per capita has dwarfed the ups and downs of the business cycle. Except for the recession that began the Great Depression, recessions are almost invisible.

Source: Angus Maddison, "Statistics on World Population, GDP and Per Capita GDP, 1–2006 AD," http://www.ggdc.net/maddison; Bureau of Economic Analysis.

Economic growth is fundamental to a nation's prosperity. A sustained rise in output per person allows for higher wages and a rising standard of living. The need for economic growth is urgent in poorer, less developed countries, where a lack of basic necessities makes growth a central concern of economic policy.

As you will see when studying macroeconomics, the goal of economic growth can be in conflict with the goal of hastening recovery from an economic downturn. What is good for economic growth can be bad for short-run stabilization of the business cycle, and vice versa.

We have seen that macroeconomics is concerned with the long-run trends in aggregate output as well as the short-run ups and downs of the business cycle. Now that we have a general understanding of the important topics studied in macroeconomics, we are almost ready to apply economic principles to real economic issues. To do this requires one more step—an understanding of how economists use *models*.

The Use of Models in Economics

In 1901, one year after their first glider flights at Kitty Hawk, the Wright brothers built something else that would change the world—a wind tunnel. This was an apparatus that let them experiment with many different designs for wings and control surfaces. These experiments gave them knowledge that would make heavier-than-air flight possible. Needless to say, testing an airplane design in a wind tunnel is cheaper and safer than building a full-scale version and hoping it will fly. More generally, models play a crucial role in almost all scientific research—economics included.

A **model** is any simplified version of reality that is used to better understand real-life situations. But how do we create a simplified representation of an economic situation? One possibility—an economist's equivalent of a wind tunnel—is to find or create a real but simplified economy. For example, economists interested in the economic role of money have studied the system of exchange that developed in World War II prison camps, in which cigarettes became a universally accepted form of payment, even among prisoners who didn't smoke.

Another possibility is to simulate the workings of the economy on a computer. For example, when changes in tax law are proposed, government officials use *tax models*—large mathematical computer programs—to assess how the proposed changes would affect different groups of people.

Models are important because their simplicity allows economists to focus on the effects of only one change at a time. That is, they allow us to hold everything else constant and to study how one change affects the overall economic outcome. So when building economic models, an important assumption is the **other things equal assumption,** which means that all other relevant factors remain unchanged. Sometimes the Latin phrase *ceteris paribus,* which means "other things equal," is used.

But it isn't always possible to find or create a small-scale version of the whole economy, and a computer program is only as good as the data it uses. (Programmers have a saying: garbage in, garbage out.) For many purposes, the most effective form of economic modeling is the construction of "thought experiments": simplified, hypothetical versions of real-life situations. And as you will see throughout this book, economists' models are very often in the form of a graph. In the next module, we will look at the *production possibilities curve,* a model that helps economists think about the choices every economy faces.

Module 2 AP Review

Solutions appear at the back of the book.

Check Your Understanding

1. Why do we talk about business cycles for the economy as a whole, rather than just talking about the ups and downs of particular industries?

2. Describe who gets hurt in a recession and how they are hurt.

Tackle the Test: Multiple-Choice Questions

1. During the recession phase of a business cycle, which of the following is likely to increase?
   a. the unemployment rate
   b. the price level
   c. economic growth rates
   d. the labor force
   e. wages

2. The labor force is made up of everyone who is
   a. employed.
   b. old enough to work.
   c. actively seeking work.
   d. employed or unemployed.
   e. employed or capable of working.

3. A sustained increase in aggregate output over several decades represents
   a. an expansion.
   b. a recovery.
   c. a recession.
   d. a depression.
   e. economic growth.

4. Which of the following is the most likely result of inflation?
   a. falling employment
   b. a dollar will buy more than it did before
   c. people are discouraged from holding cash
   d. price stability
   e. low aggregate output per capita

5. The other things equal assumption allows economists to
   a. avoid making assumptions about reality.
   b. focus on the effects of only one change at a time.
   c. oversimplify.
   d. allow nothing to change in their model.
   e. reflect all aspects of the real world in their model.

Tackle the Test: Free-Response Questions

1. Define an expansion and economic growth, and explain the difference between the two concepts.

2. Define inflation, and explain why an increase in the price of donuts does not indicate that inflation has occurred.

Answer (3 points)

1 point: An expansion is the period of recovery after an economic downturn.

1 point: Economic growth is an increase in the productive capacity of the economy.

1 point: An expansion can occur regardless of any increase in the economy's long-term potential for production, and it only lasts until the next downturn, while economic growth increases the economy's ability to produce more goods and services over the long term.

- The importance of trade-offs in economic analysis

- What the production possibilities curve model tells us about efficiency, opportunity cost, and economic growth

- The two sources of economic growth—increases in the availability of resources and improvements in technology

Module 3
The Production Possibilities Curve Model

A good economic model can be a tremendous aid to understanding. In this module, we look at the *production possibilities curve*, a model that helps economists think about the *trade-offs* every economy faces. The production possibilities curve helps us understand three important aspects of the real economy: efficiency, opportunity cost, and economic growth.

Trade-offs: The Production Possibilities Curve

The 2000 hit movie *Cast Away,* starring Tom Hanks, was an update of the classic story of Robinson Crusoe, the hero of Daniel Defoe's eighteenth-century novel. Hanks played the role of a sole survivor of a plane crash who was stranded on a remote island. As in the original story of Robinson Crusoe, the Hanks character had limited resources: the natural resources of the island, a few items he managed to salvage from the plane, and, of course, his own time and effort. With only these resources, he had to make a life. In effect, he became a one-man economy.

One of the important principles of economics we introduced in Module 1 was that resources are scarce. As a result, any economy—whether it contains one person or millions of people—faces trade-offs. You make a **trade-off** when you give up something in order to have something else. For example, if a castaway devotes more resources to catching fish, he benefits by catching more fish, but he cannot use those same resources to gather coconuts, so the trade-off is that he has fewer coconuts.

To think about the trade-offs necessary in any economy, economists often use the **production possibilities curve** model. The idea behind this model is to improve our understanding of trade-offs by considering a simplified economy that produces only two goods. This simplification enables us to show the trade-offs graphically.

Figure 3.1 shows a hypothetical production possibilities curve for Tom, a castaway alone on an island, who must make a trade-off between fish production and coconut

You make a **trade-off** when you give up something in order to have something else.

The **production possibilities curve** illustrates the trade-offs facing an economy that produces only two goods. It shows the maximum quantity of one good that can be produced for each possible quantity of the other good produced.

figure 3.1

The Production Possibilities Curve

The production possibilities curve illustrates the trade-offs facing an economy that produces two goods. It shows the maximum quantity of one good that can be produced, given the quantity of the other good produced. Here, the maximum quantity of coconuts that Tom can gather depends on the quantity of fish he catches, and vice versa. His feasible production is shown by the area *inside* or *on* the curve. Production at point *C* is feasible but not efficient. Points *A* and *B* are feasible and efficient in production, but point *D* is not feasible.

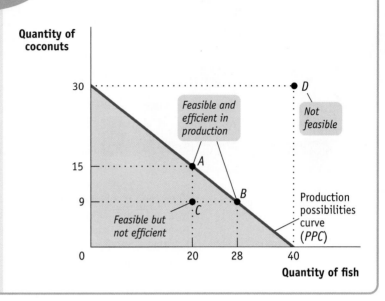

production. The curve shows the maximum quantity of fish Tom can catch during a week *given* the quantity of coconuts he gathers, and vice versa. That is, it answers questions of the form, "What is the maximum quantity of fish Tom can catch if he also gathers 9 (or 15, or 30) coconuts?"

There is a crucial distinction between points *inside* or *on* the production possibilities curve (the shaded area) and points *outside* the production possibilities curve. If a production point lies inside or on the curve—like point *C*, at which Tom catches 20 fish and gathers 9 coconuts—it is feasible. After all, the curve tells us that if Tom catches 20 fish, he could also gather a maximum of 15 coconuts, so he could certainly gather 9 coconuts. However, a production point that lies outside the curve—such as point *D*, which would have Tom catching 40 fish and gathering 30 coconuts—isn't feasible.

In Figure 3.1 the production possibilities curve intersects the horizontal axis at 40 fish. This means that if Tom devoted all his resources to catching fish, he would catch 40 fish per week but would have no resources left over to gather coconuts. The production possibilities curve intersects the vertical axis at 30 coconuts. This means that if Tom devoted all his resources to gathering coconuts, he could gather 30 coconuts per week but would have no resources left over to catch fish. Thus, if Tom wants 30 coconuts, the trade-off is that he can't have any fish.

The curve also shows less extreme trade-offs. For example, if Tom decides to catch 20 fish, he would be able to gather at most 15 coconuts; this production choice is illustrated by point *A*. If Tom decides to catch 28 fish, he could gather at most 9 coconuts, as shown by point *B*.

Thinking in terms of a production possibilities curve simplifies the complexities of reality. The real-world economy produces millions of different goods. Even a castaway on an island would produce more than two different items (for example, he would need clothing and housing as well as food). But in this model we imagine an economy that produces only two goods, because in a model with many goods, it would be much harder to study trade-offs, efficiency, and economic growth.

Efficiency

The production possibilities curve is useful for illustrating the general economic concept of efficiency. An economy is **efficient** if there are no missed opportunities—meaning that there is no way to make some people better off without making other people worse off. For example, suppose a course you are taking meets in a classroom that is

An economy is **efficient** if there is no way to make anyone better off without making at least one person worse off.

A crowded classroom reflects ineffi- ciency if switching to a larger classroom would make some students better off without making anyone worse off.

too small for the number of students—some may be forced to sit on the floor or stand—despite the fact that a larger classroom nearby is empty during the same period. Economists would say that this is an *inefficient* use of resources because there is a way to make some people better off without making anyone worse off—after all, the larger classroom is empty. The school is not using its resources efficiently. When an economy is using all of its resources efficiently, the only way one person can be made better off is by rearranging the use of resources in such a way that the change makes someone else worse off. So in our classroom example, if all larger classrooms were already fully occupied, we could say that the school was run in an efficient way; your classmates could be made better off only by making people in the larger classroom worse off—by moving them to the room that is too small.

Returning to our castaway example, as long as Tom produces a combination of coconuts and fish that is on the production possibilities curve, his production is efficient. At point *A,* the 15 coconuts he gathers are the maximum quantity he can get *given* that he has chosen to catch 20 fish; at point *B,* the 9 coconuts he gathers are the maximum he can get *given* his choice to catch 28 fish; and so on. If an economy is producing at a point on its production possibilities curve, we say that the economy is *efficient in production.*

But suppose that for some reason Tom was at point *C,* producing 20 fish and 9 coconuts. Then this one-person economy would definitely not be efficient in production, and would therefore be *inefficient:* it is missing the opportunity to produce more of both goods.

Another example of inefficiency in production occurs when people in an economy are involuntarily unemployed: they want to work but are unable to find jobs. When that happens, the economy is not efficient in production because it could produce more output if those people were employed. The production possibilities curve shows the amount that can *possibly* be produced if all resources are fully employed. In other words, changes in unemployment move the economy closer to, or further away from, the production possibilities curve (PPC). But the curve itself is determined by what would be possible if there were full employment in the economy. Greater unemployment is represented by points farther below the PPC—the economy is not reaching its possibilities if it is not using all of its resources. Lower unemployment is represented by points closer to the PPC—as unemployment decreases, the economy moves closer to reaching its possibilities.

Although the production possibilities curve helps clarify what it means for an economy to be efficient in production, it's important to understand that efficiency in production is only *part* of what's required for the economy as a whole to be efficient. Efficiency also requires that the economy allocate its resources so that consumers are as well off as possible. If an economy does this, we say that it is *efficient in allocation.* To see why efficiency in allocation is as important as efficiency in production, notice that points *A* and *B* in Figure 3.1 both represent situations in which the economy is efficient in production, because in each case it can't produce more of one good without producing less of the other. But these two situations may not be equally desirable. Suppose that Tom prefers point *B* to point *A*—that is, he would rather consume 28 fish and 9 coconuts than 20 fish and 15 coconuts. Then point *A* is inefficient from the point of view of the economy as a whole: it's possible to make Tom better off without making anyone else worse off. (Of course, in this castaway economy there isn't anyone else; Tom is all alone.)

This example shows that efficiency for the economy as a whole requires *both* efficiency in production and efficiency in allocation. To be efficient, an economy must produce as much of each good as it can, given the production of other goods, and it must also produce the mix of goods that people want to consume.

Opportunity Cost

The production possibilities curve is also useful as a reminder that the true cost of any good is not only its price, but also everything else in addition to money that must be given up in order to get that good—the *opportunity cost*. If, for example, Tom decides to go from point *A* to point *B,* he will produce 8 more fish but 6 fewer coconuts. So the opportunity cost of those 8 fish is the 6 coconuts not gathered. Since 8 extra fish have an opportunity cost of 6 coconuts, 1 fish has an opportunity cost of $^6/_8 = ^3/_4$ of a coconut.

Is the opportunity cost of an extra fish in terms of coconuts always the same, no matter how many fish Tom catches? In the example illustrated by Figure 3.1, the answer is yes. If Tom increases his catch from 28 to 40 fish, an increase of 12, the number of coconuts he gathers falls from 9 to zero. So his opportunity cost per additional fish is $^9/_{12} = ^3/_4$ of a coconut, the same as it was when his catch went from 20 fish to 28. However, the fact that in this example the opportunity cost of an additional fish in terms of coconuts is always the same is a result of an assumption we've made, an assumption that's reflected in the way Figure 3.1 is drawn. Specifically, whenever we assume that the opportunity cost of an additional unit of a good doesn't change regardless of the output mix, the production possibilities curve is a straight line.

Moreover, as you might have already guessed, the slope of a straight-line production possibilities curve is equal to the opportunity cost—specifically, the opportunity cost for the good measured on the horizontal axis in terms of the good measured on the vertical axis. In Figure 3.1, the production possibilities curve has a *constant slope* of $-^3/_4$, implying that Tom faces a *constant opportunity cost* per fish equal to $^3/_4$ of a coconut. (A review of how to calculate the slope of a straight line is found in the Section I Appendix.) This is the simplest case, but the production possibilities curve model can also be used to examine situations in which opportunity costs change as the mix of output changes.

Figure 3.2 illustrates a different assumption, a case in which Tom faces *increasing opportunity cost.* Here, the more fish he catches, the more coconuts he has to give up to catch an additional fish, and vice versa. For example, to go from producing zero fish to producing 20 fish, he has to give up 5 coconuts. That is, the opportunity cost of those 20 fish is 5 coconuts. But to increase his fish production from 20 to 40—that is, to produce an additional 20 fish—he must give up 25 more coconuts, a much higher opportunity cost. As you can see in Figure 3.2, when opportunity costs are increasing rather

---

figure 3.2

Increasing Opportunity Cost

The bowed-out shape of the production possibilities curve reflects increasing opportunity cost. In this example, to produce the first 20 fish, Tom must give up 5 coconuts. But to produce an additional 20 fish, he must give up 25 more coconuts.

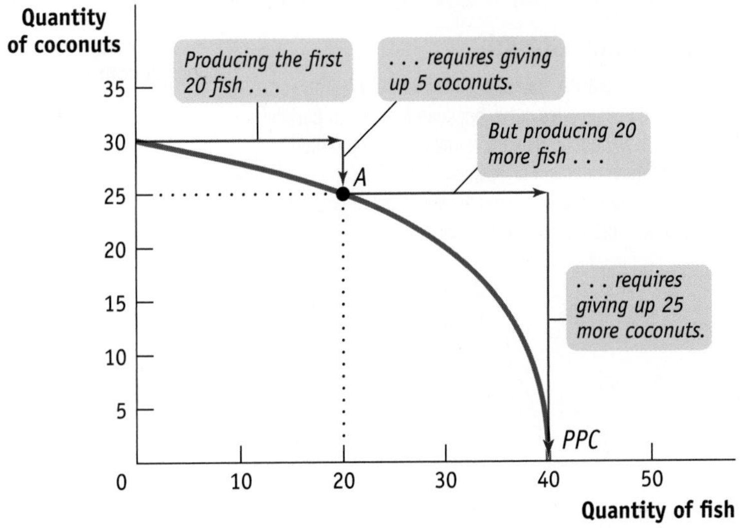

than constant, the production possibilities curve is a bowed-out curve rather than a straight line.

Although it's often useful to work with the simple assumption that the production possibilities curve is a straight line, economists believe that in reality, opportunity costs are typically increasing. When only a small amount of a good is produced, the opportunity cost of producing that good is relatively low because the economy needs to use only those resources that are especially well suited for its production. For example, if an economy grows only a small amount of corn, that corn can be grown in places where the soil and climate are perfect for growing corn but less suitable for growing anything else, such as wheat. So growing that corn involves giving up only a small amount of potential wheat output. Once the economy grows a lot of corn, however, land that is well suited for wheat but isn't so great for corn must be used to produce corn anyway. As a result, the additional corn production involves sacrificing considerably more wheat production. In other words, as more of a good is produced, its opportunity cost typically rises because well-suited inputs are used up and less adaptable inputs must be used instead.

Economic Growth

Finally, the production possibilities curve helps us understand what it means to talk about *economic growth*. We introduced the concept of economic growth in Module 2, saying that it allows *a sustained rise in aggregate output*. We learned that economic growth is one of the fundamental features of the economy. But are we really justified in saying that the economy has grown over time? After all, although the U.S. economy produces more of many things than it did a century ago, it produces less of other things—for example, horse-drawn carriages. In other words, production of many goods is actually down. So how can we say for sure that the economy as a whole has grown?

The answer, illustrated in Figure 3.3, is that economic growth means an *expansion of the economy's production possibilities:* the economy *can* produce more of everything. For example, if Tom's production is initially at point *A* (20 fish and 25 coconuts), economic growth means that he could move to point *E* (25 fish and 30 coconuts). Point *E* lies outside the original curve, so in the production possibilities curve model, growth is shown as an outward shift of the curve. Unless the PPC shifts outward, the points beyond the PPC are unattainable. Those points beyond a given PPC are beyond the economy's possibilities.

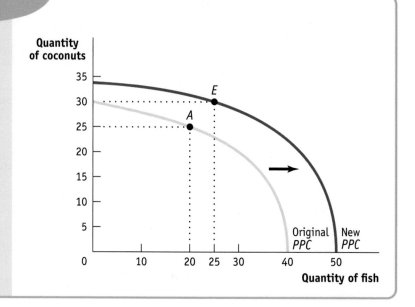

figure 3.3

Economic Growth

Economic growth results in an *outward shift* of the production possibilities curve because production possibilities are expanded. The economy can now produce more of everything. For example, if production is initially at point *A* (20 fish and 25 coconuts), it could move to point *E* (25 fish and 30 coconuts).

What can cause the production possibilities curve to shift outward? There are two general sources of economic growth. One is an increase in the resources used to produce goods and services: labor, land, capital, and entrepreneurship. To see how adding to an economy's resources leads to economic growth, suppose that Tom finds a fishing net washed ashore on the beach. The fishing net is a resource he can use to produce more fish in the course of a day spent fishing. We can't say how many more fish Tom will catch; that depends on how much time he decides to spend fishing now that he has the net. But because the net makes his fishing more productive, he can catch more fish without reducing the number of coconuts he gathers, or he can gather more coconuts without reducing his fish catch. So his production possibilities curve shifts outward.

The other source of economic growth is progress in **technology,** the technical means for the production of goods and services. Suppose Tom figures out a better way either to catch fish or to gather coconuts—say, by inventing a fishing hook or a wagon for transporting coconuts. Either invention would shift his production possibilities curve outward. However, the shift would not be a simple outward expansion of every point along the PPC. Technology specific to the production of only one good has no effect if all resources are devoted to the other good: a fishing hook will be of no use if Tom produces nothing but coconuts. So the point on the PPC that represents the number of coconuts that can be produced if there is no fishing will not change. In real-world economies, innovations in the techniques we use to produce goods and services have been a crucial force behind economic growth.

Again, economic growth means an increase in what the economy *can* produce. What the economy actually produces depends on the choices people make. After his production possibilities expand, Tom might not choose to produce both more fish and more coconuts; he might choose to increase production of only one good, or he might even choose to produce less of one good. For example, if he gets better at catching fish, he might decide to go on an all-fish diet and skip the coconuts, just as the introduction of motor vehicles led most people to give up horse-drawn carriages. But even if, for some reason, he chooses to produce either fewer coconuts or fewer fish than before, we would still say that his economy has grown, because he *could* have produced more of everything. If an economy's PPC shifts inward, the economy has become smaller. This could happen if the economy loses resources or technology (for example, if it experiences war or a natural disaster).

The production possibilities curve is a very simplified model of an economy, yet it teaches us important lessons about real-life economies. It gives us our first clear sense of what constitutes economic efficiency, it illustrates the concept of opportunity cost, and it makes clear what economic growth is all about.

Technology is the technical means for producing goods and services.

M o d u l e ③ A P R e v i e w

Solutions appear at the back of the book.

Check Your Understanding

1. True or false? Explain your answer.
   a. An increase in the amount of resources available to Tom for use in producing coconuts and fish does not change his production possibilities curve.
   b. A technological change that allows Tom to catch more fish relative to any amount of coconuts gathered results in a change in his production possibilities curve.
   c. Points inside a production possibilities curve are efficient and points outside a production possibilities curve are inefficient.

Tackle the Test: Multiple-Choice Questions

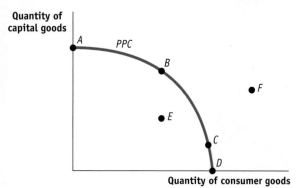

Quantity of capital goods

Quantity of consumer goods

Refer to the graph above to answer the following questions.

1. Which point(s) on the graph represent efficiency in production?
   a. *B* and *C*
   b. *A* and *D*
   c. *A, B, C,* and *D*
   d. *A, B, C, D,* and *E*
   e. *A, B, C, D, E,* and *F*

2. For this economy, an increase in the quantity of capital goods produced without a corresponding decrease in the quantity of consumer goods produced
   a. cannot happen because there is always an opportunity cost.
   b. is represented by a movement from point *E* to point *A*.
   c. is represented by a movement from point *C* to point *B*.
   d. is represented by a movement from point *E* to point *B*.
   e. is only possible with an increase in resources or technology.

3. An increase in unemployment could be represented by a movement from point
   a. *D* to point *C*.
   b. *B* to point *A*.
   c. *C* to point *F*.
   d. *B* to point *E*.
   e. *E* to point *B*.

4. Which of the following might allow this economy to move from point *B* to point *F*?
   a. more workers
   b. discovery of new resources
   c. building new factories
   d. technological advances
   e. all of the above

5. This production possibilities curve shows the trade-off between consumer goods and capital goods. Since capital goods are a resource, an increase in the production of capital goods today will increase the economy's production possibilities in the future. Therefore, all other things equal (*ceteris paribus*), producing at which point today will result in the largest outward shift of the PPC in the future?
   a. *A*
   b. *B*
   c. *C*
   d. *D*
   e. *E*

Tackle the Test: Free-Response Questions

1. Refer to the graph below. Assume that the country is producing at point *C*.

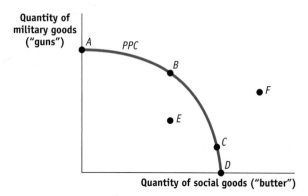

Quantity of military goods ("guns")

Quantity of social goods ("butter")

   a. Does this country's production possibilities curve exhibit increasing opportunity costs? Explain.
   b. If this country were to go to war, the most likely move would be from point *C* to which point? Explain.
   c. If the economy entered into a recession, the country would move from point *C* to which point? Explain.

Answer (6 points)

1 point: Yes

1 point: The PPC is concave (bowed outward), so with each additional unit of butter produced, the opportunity cost in terms of gun production (indicated by the slope of the line) increases. Likewise, as more guns are produced, the opportunity cost in terms of butter increases.

1 point: *B*

1 point: The country would choose an efficient point with more (but not all) military goods with which to fight the war. Point A would be an unlikely choice because at that point there is no production of any social goods, some of which are needed to maintain a minimal standard of living.

1 point: *E*

1 point: A recession, which causes unemployment, is represented by a point below the PPC.

2. Assume that an economy can choose between producing food and producing shelter at a constant opportunity cost. Draw a correctly labeled production possibilities curve for the economy. On your graph:
   a. Use the letter *E* to label one of the points that is efficient in production.
   b. Use the letter *U* to label one of the points at which there might be unemployment.
   c. Use the letter *I* to label one of the points that is not feasible.

Module 4
Comparative Advantage and Trade

What you will learn in this Module:

- How trade leads to gains for an individual or an economy

- The difference between absolute advantage and comparative advantage

- How comparative advantage leads to gains from trade in the global marketplace

Gains from Trade

A family could try to take care of all its own needs—growing its own food, sewing its own clothing, providing itself with entertainment, and writing its own economics textbooks. But trying to live that way would be very hard. The key to a much better standard of living for everyone is **trade,** in which people divide tasks among themselves and each person provides a good or service that other people want in return for different goods and services that he or she wants.

The reason we have an economy, but not many self-sufficient individuals, is that there are **gains from trade:** by dividing tasks and trading, two people (or 7 billion people) can each get more of what they want than they could get by being self-sufficient. Gains from trade arise, in particular, from this division of tasks, which economists call **specialization**—a situation in which different people each engage in a different task.

The advantages of specialization, and the resulting gains from trade, were the starting point for Adam Smith's 1776 book *The Wealth of Nations,* which many regard as the beginning of economics as a discipline. Smith's book begins with a description of an eighteenth-century pin factory where, rather than each of the 10 workers making a pin from start to finish, each worker specialized in one of the many steps in pin-making:

> One man draws out the wire, another straights it, a third cuts it, a fourth points it, a fifth grinds it at the top for receiving the head; to make the head requires two or three distinct operations; to put it on, is a particular business, to whiten the pins is another; it is even a trade by itself to put them into the paper; and the important business of making a pin is, in this manner, divided into about eighteen distinct operations. . . . Those ten persons, therefore, could make among them upwards of forty-eight thousand pins in a day. But if they had all wrought separately and independently, and without any of them having been educated to this particular business, they certainly could not each of them have made twenty, perhaps not one pin a day. . . .

The same principle applies when we look at how people divide tasks among themselves and trade in an economy. The economy, as a whole, can produce more when each person *specializes* in a task and *trades* with others.

In a market economy, individuals engage in **trade:** they provide goods and services to others and receive goods and services in return.

There are **gains from trade:** people can get more of what they want through trade than they could if they tried to be self-sufficient. This increase in output is due to **specialization:** each person specializes in the task that he or she is good at performing.

The benefits of specialization are the reason a person typically focuses on the production of only one type of good or service. It takes many years of study and experience to become a doctor; it also takes many years of study and experience to become a commercial airline pilot. Many doctors might have the potential to become excellent pilots, and vice versa, but it is very unlikely that anyone who decided to pursue both careers would be as good a pilot or as good a doctor as someone who specialized in only one of those professions. So it is to everyone's advantage when individuals specialize in their career choices.

Markets are what allow a doctor and a pilot to specialize in their respective fields. Because markets for commercial flights and for doctors' services exist, a doctor is assured that she can find a flight and a pilot is assured that he can find a doctor. As long as individuals know that they can find the goods and services that they want in the market, they are willing to forgo self-sufficiency and are willing to specialize.

Comparative Advantage and Gains from Trade

The production possibilities curve model is particularly useful for illustrating gains from trade—trade based on *comparative advantage*. Let's stick with Tom stranded on his island, but now let's suppose that a second castaway, who just happens to be named Hank, is washed ashore. Can they benefit from trading with each other?

It's obvious that there will be potential gains from trade if the two castaways do different things particularly well. For example, if Tom is a skilled fisherman and Hank is very good at climbing trees, clearly it makes sense for Tom to catch fish and Hank to gather coconuts—and for the two men to trade the products of their efforts.

But one of the most important insights in all of economics is that there are gains from trade even if one of the trading parties isn't especially good at anything. Suppose, for example, that Hank is less well suited to primitive life than Tom; he's not nearly as good at catching fish, and compared to Tom, even his coconut-gathering leaves something to be desired. Nonetheless, what we'll see is that both Tom and Hank can live better by trading with each other than either could alone.

For the purposes of this example, let's go back to the simple case of straight-line production possibilities curves. Tom's production possibilities are represented by the production possibilities curve in panel (a) of Figure 4.1, which is the same as the

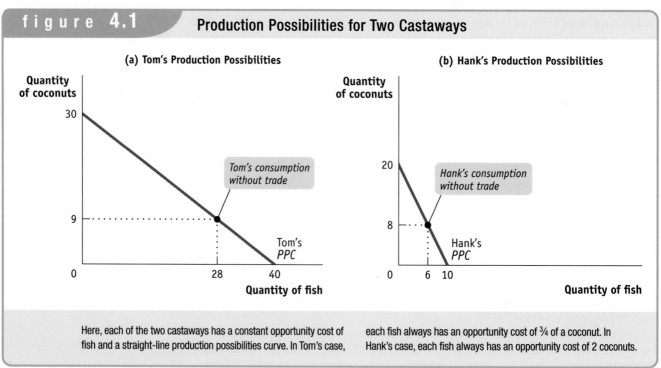

figure 4.1   Production Possibilities for Two Castaways

(a) Tom's Production Possibilities

Quantity of coconuts

30

Tom's consumption without trade

9

Tom's PPC

0   28   40

Quantity of fish

(b) Hank's Production Possibilities

Quantity of coconuts

20

Hank's consumption without trade

8

Hank's PPC

0   6   10

Quantity of fish

Here, each of the two castaways has a constant opportunity cost of fish and a straight-line production possibilities curve. In Tom's case, each fish always has an opportunity cost of ¾ of a coconut. In Hank's case, each fish always has an opportunity cost of 2 coconuts.

production possibilities curve in Figure 3.1 (page 17). According to this PPC, Tom could catch 40 fish, but only if he gathered no coconuts, and he could gather 30 coconuts, but only if he caught no fish. Recall that this means that the slope of his production possibilities curve is $-\frac{3}{4}$: his opportunity cost of 1 fish is $\frac{3}{4}$ of a coconut.

Panel (b) of Figure 4.1 shows Hank's production possibilities. Like Tom's, Hank's production possibilities curve is a straight line, implying a constant opportunity cost of fish in terms of coconuts. His production possibilities curve has a constant slope of -2. Hank is less productive all around: at most he can produce 10 fish or 20 coconuts. But he is particularly bad at fishing: whereas Tom sacrifices $\frac{3}{4}$ of a coconut per fish caught, for Hank the opportunity cost of a fish is 2 whole coconuts. Table 4.1 summarizes the two castaways' opportunity costs of fish and coconuts.

table 4.1

Tom's and Hank's Opportunity Costs of Fish and Coconuts

	Tom's Opportunity Cost	Hank's Opportunity Cost
One fish	3/4 coconut	2 coconuts
One coconut	4/3 fish	1/2 fish

Now, Tom and Hank could go their separate ways, each living on his own side of the island, catching his own fish and gathering his own coconuts. Let's suppose that they start out that way and make the consumption choices shown in Figure 4.1: in the absence of trade, Tom consumes 28 fish and 9 coconuts per week, while Hank consumes 6 fish and 8 coconuts.

But is this the best they can do? No, it isn't. Given that the two castaways have different opportunity costs, they can strike a deal that makes both of them better off.

Table 4.2 shows how such a deal works: Tom specializes in the production of fish, catching 40 per week, and gives 10 to Hank. Meanwhile, Hank specializes in the production of coconuts, gathering 20 per week, and gives 10 to Tom. The result is shown in Figure 4.2 on the next page. Tom now consumes more of both goods than before: instead of 28 fish and 9 coconuts, he consumes 30 fish and 10 coconuts. Hank also consumes more, going from 6 fish and 8 coconuts to 10 fish and 10 coconuts. As Table 4.2 also shows, both Tom and Hank experience gains from trade: Tom's consumption of fish increases by two, and his consumption of coconuts increases by one. Hank's consumption of fish increases by four, and his consumption of coconuts increases by two.

table 4.2

How the Castaways Gain from Trade

		Without Trade		With Trade		Gains from Trade
		Production	Consumption	Production	Consumption	
Tom	Fish	28	28	40	30	+2
	Coconuts	9	9	0	10	+1
Hank	Fish	6	6	0	10	+4
	Coconuts	8	8	20	10	+2

So both castaways are better off when they each specialize in what they are good at and trade with each other. It's a good idea for Tom to catch the fish for both of them, because his opportunity cost of a fish is only $\frac{3}{4}$ of a coconut not gathered versus 2 coconuts for Hank. Correspondingly, it's a good idea for Hank to gather coconuts for both of them.

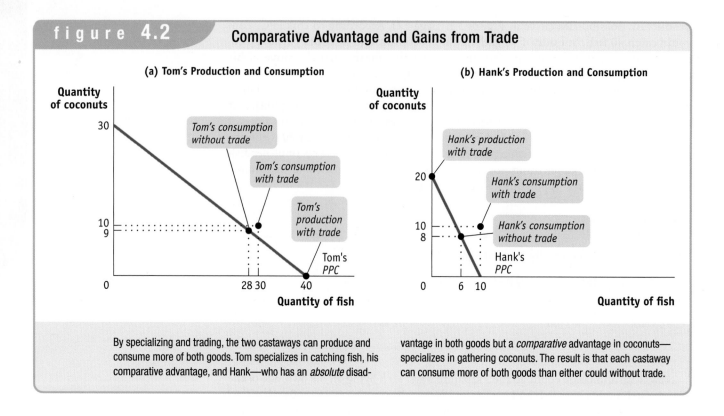

figure 4.2 — Comparative Advantage and Gains from Trade

(a) Tom's Production and Consumption

Quantity of coconuts

Tom's consumption without trade

Tom's consumption with trade

Tom's production with trade

Tom's PPC

Quantity of fish

(b) Hank's Production and Consumption

Quantity of coconuts

Hank's production with trade

Hank's consumption with trade

Hank's consumption without trade

Hank's PPC

Quantity of fish

By specializing and trading, the two castaways can produce and consume more of both goods. Tom specializes in catching fish, his comparative advantage, and Hank—who has an *absolute* disad-vantage in both goods but a *comparative* advantage in coconuts—specializes in gathering coconuts. The result is that each castaway can consume more of both goods than either could without trade.

An individual has a **comparative advantage** in producing a good or service if the opportunity cost of producing the good or service is lower for that individual than for other people.

Or we could describe the situation in a different way. Because Tom is so good at catching fish, his opportunity cost of gathering coconuts is high: ⅓ of a fish not caught for every coconut gathered. Because Hank is a pretty poor fisherman, his opportunity cost of gathering coconuts is much less, only ½ of a fish per coconut.

An individual has a **comparative advantage** in producing something if the opportunity cost of that production is lower for that individual than for other people. In other words, Hank has a comparative advantage over Tom in producing a particular good or service if Hank's opportunity cost of producing that good or service is lower than Tom's. In this case, Hank has a comparative advantage in gathering coconuts and Tom has a comparative advantage in catching fish.

One point of clarification needs to be made before we proceed further. You may have wondered why Tom and Hank traded 10 fish for 10 coconuts. Why not some other deal, like trading 15 coconuts for 5 fish? The answer to that question has two parts. First, there may indeed be deals other than 10 fish for 10 coconuts that Tom and Hank are willing to agree to. Second, there are some deals that we can, however, safely rule out—such as 15 coconuts for 5 fish. To understand why, reexamine Table 4.1 and consider Hank first. When Hank works on his own without trading with Tom, his opportunity cost of 1 fish is 2 coconuts. Therefore, it's clear that Hank will not accept any deal with Tom in which he must give up more than 2 coconuts per fish—otherwise, he's better off not trading at all. So we can rule out a deal that requires Hank to pay 3 coconuts per fish—such as trading 15 coconuts for 5 fish. But Hank will accept a trade in which he pays less than 2 coconuts per fish—such as paying 1 coconut for 1 fish. Likewise, Tom will reject a deal that requires him to give up more than ⅓ of a fish per coconut. For example, Tom would refuse a trade that required him to give up 10 fish for 6 coconuts. But he will accept a deal where he pays less than ⅓ of a fish per coconut—and 1 fish for 1 coconut works. You can check for yourself why a trade of 1 fish for 1½ coconuts would also be acceptable to both Tom and Hank. So the point to remember is that Tom and Hank will be willing to engage in a trade only if the "price" of the good each person is obtaining from the trade is less than his own opportunity cost of producing the good himself. Moreover, that's a general statement that is true whenever two parties trade voluntarily.

The story of Tom and Hank clearly simplifies reality. Yet it teaches us some very important lessons that also apply to the real economy.

First, the model provides a clear illustration of the gains from trade. By agreeing to specialize and provide goods to each other, Tom and Hank can produce more; therefore, both are better off than if each tried to be self-sufficient.

Second, the model demonstrates a very important point that is often overlooked in real-world arguments: as long as people have different opportunity costs, *everyone has a comparative advantage in something, and everyone has a comparative disadvantage in something.*

Notice that in our example Tom is actually better than Hank at producing both goods: Tom can catch more fish in a week, and he can also gather more coconuts. That is, Tom has an **absolute advantage** in both activities: he can produce more output with a given amount of input (in this case, his time) than Hank. You might therefore be tempted to think that Tom has nothing to gain from trading with less competent Hank.

But we've just seen that Tom can indeed benefit from a deal with Hank, because *comparative,* not *absolute,* advantage is the basis for mutual gain. It doesn't matter that it takes Hank more time to gather a coconut; what matters is that for him the opportunity cost of that coconut in terms of fish is lower. So Hank, despite his absolute disadvantage, even in coconuts, has a comparative advantage in coconut-gathering. Meanwhile Tom, who can use his time better by catching fish, has a comparative disadvantage in coconut-gathering.

If comparative advantage were relevant only to castaways, it might not be that interesting. However, the idea of comparative advantage applies to many activities in the

> An individual has an **absolute advantage** in producing a good or service if he or she can make more of it with a given amount of time and resources. Having an absolute advantage is not the same thing as having a comparative advantage.

fyi

Rich Nation, Poor Nation

Try taking off your clothes—at a suitable time and in a suitable place, of course—and take a look at the labels inside that say where the clothes were made. It's a very good bet that much, if not most, of your clothing was manufactured overseas, in a country that is much poorer than the United States is—say, in El Salvador, Sri Lanka, or Bangladesh.

Why are these countries so much poorer than the United States? The immediate reason is that their economies are much less *productive*—firms in these countries are just not able to produce as much from a given quantity of resources as comparable firms in the United States or other wealthy countries. Why countries differ so much in productivity is a deep question—indeed, one of the main questions that preoccupy economists. But in any case, the difference in productivity is a fact.

But if the economies of these countries are so much less productive than ours, how is it that they make so much of our clothing? Why don't we do it for ourselves?

The answer is "comparative advantage." Just about every industry in Bangladesh is much less productive than the corresponding industry in the United States. But the productivity difference between rich and poor countries varies across goods; there is a very great difference in the production of sophisticated goods such as aircraft but not as great a difference in the production of simpler goods such as clothing. So Bangladesh's position with regard to clothing production is like Hank's position with respect to coconut gathering: he's not as good at it as his fellow castaway is, but it's the thing he does comparatively well.

Although Bangladesh is at an absolute disadvantage compared with the United States in almost everything, it has a comparative advantage

Although less productive than American workers, Bangladeshi workers have a comparative advantage in clothing production.

in clothing production. This means that both the United States and Bangladesh are able to consume more because they specialize in producing different things, with Bangladesh supplying our clothing and the United States supplying Bangladesh with more sophisticated goods.

economy. Perhaps its most important application is in trade—not between individuals, but between countries. So let's look briefly at how the model of comparative advantage helps in understanding both the causes and the effects of international trade.

Comparative Advantage and International Trade

Look at the label on a manufactured good sold in the United States, and there's a good chance you will find that it was produced in some other country—in China or Japan or even in Canada. On the other hand, many U.S. industries sell a large portion of their output overseas. (This is particularly true for the agriculture, high technology, and entertainment industries.)

Should we celebrate this international exchange of goods and services, or should it cause us concern? Politicians and the public often question the desirability of international trade, arguing that the nation should produce goods for itself rather than buy them from foreigners. Industries around the world demand protection from foreign competition: Japanese farmers want to keep out American rice, and American steelworkers want to keep out European steel. These demands are often supported by public opinion.

Economists, however, have a very positive view of international trade. Why? Because they view it in terms of comparative advantage.

Figure 4.3 shows, with a simple example, how international trade can be interpreted in terms of comparative advantage. Although the example is hypothetical, it is based on an actual pattern of international trade: American exports of pork to Canada and Canadian exports of aircraft to the United States. Panels (a) and (b) illustrate hypothetical production possibilities curves for the United States and Canada, with pork measured on the horizontal axis and aircraft measured on the vertical axis. The U.S. production possibilities curve is flatter than the Canadian production possibilities curve, implying that producing one more ton of pork costs fewer aircraft in the

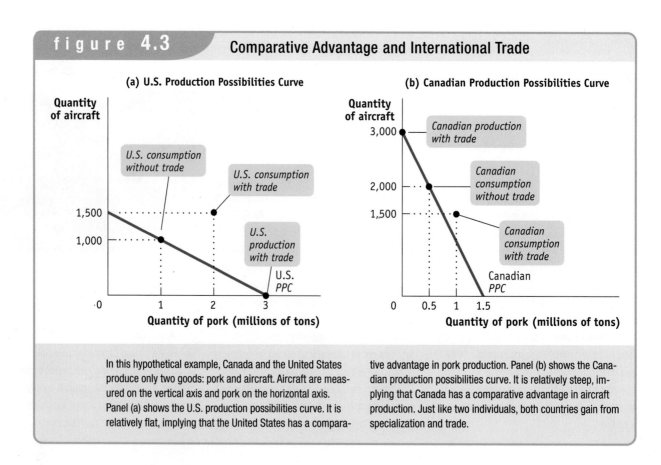

figure 4.3 **Comparative Advantage and International Trade**

In this hypothetical example, Canada and the United States produce only two goods: pork and aircraft. Aircraft are measured on the vertical axis and pork on the horizontal axis. Panel (a) shows the U.S. production possibilities curve. It is relatively flat, implying that the United States has a comparative advantage in pork production. Panel (b) shows the Canadian production possibilities curve. It is relatively steep, implying that Canada has a comparative advantage in aircraft production. Just like two individuals, both countries gain from specialization and trade.

United States than it does in Canada. This means that the United States has a comparative advantage in pork and Canada has a comparative advantage in aircraft.

Although the consumption points in Figure 4.3 are hypothetical, they illustrate a general principle: just like the example of Tom and Hank, the United States and Canada can both achieve mutual gains from trade. If the United States concentrates on producing pork and ships some of its output to Canada, while Canada concentrates on aircraft and ships some of its output to the United States, both countries can consume more than if they insisted on being self-sufficient.

Moreover, these mutual gains don't depend on each country's being better at producing one kind of good. Even if one country has, say, higher output per person-hour in both industries—that is, even if one country has an absolute advantage in both industries—there are still mutual gains from trade.

Module 4 AP Review

Solutions appear at the back of the book.

Check Your Understanding

1. In Italy, an automobile can be produced by 8 workers in one day and a washing machine by 3 workers in one day. In the United States, an automobile can be produced by 6 workers in one day, and a washing machine by 2 workers in one day.
   a. Which country has an absolute advantage in the production of automobiles? In washing machines?
   b. Which country has a comparative advantage in the production of washing machines? In automobiles?
   c. What type of specialization results in the greatest gains from trade between the two countries?

2. Refer to the story of Tom and Hank illustrated by Figure 4.1 in the text. Explain why Tom and Hank are willing to engage in a trade of 1 fish for 1½ coconuts.

Tackle the Test: Multiple-Choice Questions

Refer to the graph below to answer the following questions.

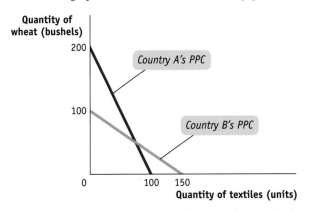

1. Use the graph to determine which country has an absolute advantage in producing each good.

Absolute advantage in wheat production	Absolute advantage in textile production
a. Country A	Country B
b. Country A	Country A
c. Country B	Country A
d. Country B	Country B
e. Country A	Neither Country

2. For country A, the opportunity cost of a bushel of wheat is
   a. ½ units of textiles
   b. ⅔ units of textiles
   c. 1⅓ units of textiles
   d. 1½ units of textiles
   e. 2 units of textiles

3. Use the graph to determine which country has a comparative advantage in producing each good.

Comparative advantage in wheat production	Comparative advantage in textile production
a. Country A	Country B
b. Country A	Country A
c. Country B	Country A
d. Country B	Country B
e. Country A	Neither Country

4. If the two countries specialize and trade, which of the choices below describes the countries' imports?

Import Wheat	Import Textiles
a. Country A	Country A
b. Country A	Country B
c. Country B	Country B
d. Country B	Country A
e. Neither Country	Country B

5. What is the highest price Country B is willing to pay to buy wheat from Country A?
   a. ½ units of textiles
   b. ⅔ units of textiles
   c. 1 unit of textiles
   d. 1½ units of textiles
   e. 2 units of textiles

Tackle the Test: Free-Response Questions

1. Refer to the graph below to answer the following questions.

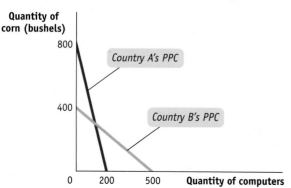

Quantity of corn (bushels)

800 — Country A's PPC

400 — Country B's PPC

0   200   500   **Quantity of computers**

   a. What is the opportunity cost of a bushel of corn in each country?
   b. Which country has an absolute advantage in computer production? Explain.
   c. Which country has a comparative advantage in corn production? Explain.
   d. If each country specializes, what good will Country B import? Explain.
   e. What is the minimum price Country A will accept to export corn to Country B? Explain.

2. Refer to the table below to answer the following questions. These two countries are producing textiles and wheat using equal amounts of resources.

| | Weekly output per worker | |
	Country A	Country B
Bushels of Wheat	15	10
Units of Textiles	60	60

   a. What is the opportunity cost of producing a bushel of wheat for each country?
   b. Which country has the absolute advantage in wheat production?
   c. Which country has the comparative advantage in textile production? Explain.

Answer (9 points)

1 point: Country A, ¼ computers; Country B, 1¼ computers

1 point: Country B

1 point: Because Country B can produce more computers than Country A (500 versus 200)

1 point: Country A

1 point: Because Country A can produce corn at a lower opportunity cost (¼ versus 1¼ computers)

1 point: Corn

1 point: Country B has a comparative advantage in the production of computers, so it will produce computers and import corn (Country A has a comparative advantage in corn production, so it will specialize in corn and import computers from Country B).

1 point: ¼ computers

1 point: Country A's opportunity cost of producing corn is ¼ computers, so that is the lowest price they will accept to sell corn to Country B.

Section Ⓘ Review

Summary

The Study of Economics

1. Everyone has to make choices about what to do and what *not* to do. **Individual choice** is the basis of **economics**—if it doesn't involve choice, it isn't economics. The **economy** is a system that coordinates choices about production and consumption. In a **market economy,** these choices are made by many firms and individuals. In a **command economy,** these choices are made by a central authority. **Incentives** are rewards or punishments that motivate particular choices, and can be lacking in a command economy where producers cannot set their own prices or keep their own profits. **Property rights** create incentives in market economies by establishing ownership and granting individuals the right to trade goods and services for mutual gain. In any economy, decisions are informed by **marginal analysis**—the study of the costs and benefits of doing something a little bit more or a little bit less.

2. The reason choices must be made is that **resources**—anything that can be used to produce something else—are **scarce.** The four categories of resources are **land, labor, capital** and **entrepreneurship.** Individuals are limited in their choices by money and time; economies are limited by their supplies of resources.

3. Because you must choose among limited alternatives, the true cost of anything is what you must give up to get it—all costs are **opportunity costs.**

4. Economists use economic models for both **positive economics,** which describes how the economy works, and for **normative economics,** which prescribes how the economy *should* work. Positive economics often involves making forecasts. Economics can determine correct answers for positive questions, but typically not for normative questions, which involve value judgments. Exceptions occur when policies designed to achieve a certain prescription can be clearly ranked in terms of efficiency.

5. There are two main reasons economists disagree. One, they may disagree about which simplifications to make in a model. Two, economists may disagree—like everyone else—about values.

6. **Microeconomics** is the branch of economics that studies how people make decisions and how those decisions interact. **Macroeconomics** is concerned with the overall ups and downs of the economy, and focuses on **economic aggregates** such as the unemployment rate and gross domestic product, that summarize data across many different markets.

Introduction to Macroeconomics

7. Economies experience ups and downs in economic activity. This pattern is called the **business cycle.**

8. With respect to the business cycle, economists are interested in the levels of **aggregate output, unemployment** and **inflation.**

9. Over longer periods of time, economists focus on **economic growth.**

10. Almost all economics is based on **models,** "thought experiments" or simplified versions of reality, many of which use analytical tools such as mathematics and graphs. An important assumption in economic models is the **other things equal (*ceteris paribus*) assumption,** which allows analysis of the effect of change in one factor by holding all other relevant factors unchanged.

The Production Possibilities Curve Model

11. One important economic model is the **production possibilities curve,** which illustrates the **trade-offs** facing an economy that produces only two goods. The production possibilities curve illustrates three elements: opportunity cost (showing how much less of one good must be produced if more of the other good is produced), **efficiency** (an economy is efficient in production if it produces on the production possibilities curve and efficient in allocation if it produces the mix of goods and services that people want to consume), and economic growth (an outward shift of the production possibilities curve).

12. There are two basic sources of growth in the production possibilities curve model: an increase in resources and improved **technology.**

13. There are **gains from trade:** by engaging in the **trade** of goods and services with one another, the members of an economy can all be made better off. Underlying gains from trade are the advantages of **specialization,** of having individuals specialize in the tasks they are comparatively good at.

Comparative Advantage and Trade

14. **Comparative advantage** explains the source of gains from trade between individuals and countries. Everyone has a comparative advantage in something—some good or service in which that person has a lower opportunity cost than everyone else. But it is often confused with **absolute advantage,** an ability to produce more of a particular good or service than anyone else. This confusion leads some to erroneously conclude that there are no gains from trade between people or countries.

Key Terms

Problems

1. Imagine a firm that manufactures textiles (pants and shirts). List the four categories of resources, and for each category, give an example of a specific resource that the firm might use to manufacture textiles.

2. Describe some of the opportunity costs of the following choices.

   a. Attend college instead of taking a job.

   b. Watch a movie instead of studying for an exam.

   c. Ride the bus instead of driving your car.

3. Use the concept of opportunity cost to explain the following situations.

   a. More people choose to get graduate degrees when the job market is poor.

   b. More people choose to do their own home repairs when the economy is slow and hourly wages are down.

   c. There are more parks in suburban areas than in urban areas.

   d. Convenience stores, which have higher prices than supermarkets, cater to busy people.

4. A representative of the U.S. clothing industry recently made this statement: "Workers in Asia often work in sweatshop conditions earning only pennies an hour. American workers are more productive and, as a result, earn higher wages. In order to preserve the dignity of the American workplace, the government should enact legislation banning imports of low-wage Asian clothing."

   a. Which parts of this quotation are positive statements? Which parts are normative statements?

   b. Is the policy that is being advocated consistent with the statement about the wages and productivities of American and Asian workers?

   c. Would such a policy make some Americans better off without making any other Americans worse off? That is, would this policy be efficient from the viewpoint of all Americans?

   d. Would low-wage Asian workers benefit from or be hurt by such a policy?

5. Are the following statements true or false? Explain your answers.

   a. "When people must pay higher taxes on their wage earnings, it reduces their incentive to work" is a positive statement.

   b. "We should lower taxes to encourage more work" is a positive statement.

   c. Economics cannot always be used to determine what society ought to do.

   d. "The system of public education in this country generates greater benefits to society than the cost of running the system" is a normative statement.

   e. All disagreements among economists are generated by the media.

6. Why do we consider a business-cycle expansion to be different from economic growth?

7. Evaluate this statement: "It is easier to build an economic model that accurately reflects events that have already occurred than to build an economic model to forecast future events." Do you think that this is true or not? Why? What does this imply about the difficulties of building good economic models?

8. Suppose Atlantis is a small, isolated island in the South Atlantic. The inhabitants grow potatoes and catch fish. The accompanying table shows the maximum annual output combinations of potatoes and fish that can be produced. Obviously, given their limited resources and available technology, as they use more of their resources for potato production, there are fewer resources available for catching fish.

Maximum annual output options	Quantity of potatoes (pounds)	Quantity of fish (pounds)
A	1,000	0
B	800	300
C	600	500
D	400	600
E	200	650
F	0	675

a. Draw a production possibilities curve with potatoes on the horizontal axis and fish on the vertical axis, and illustrate these options, showing points *A–F*.

b. Can Atlantis produce 500 pounds of fish and 800 pounds of potatoes? Explain. Where would this point lie relative to the production possibilities curve?

c. What is the opportunity cost of increasing the annual output of potatoes from 600 to 800 pounds?

d. What is the opportunity cost of increasing the annual output of potatoes from 200 to 400 pounds?

e. Explain why the answers to parts c and d are not the same. What does this imply about the slope of the production possibilities curve?

9. Two important industries on the island of Bermuda are fishing and tourism. According to data from the World Resources Institute and the Bermuda Department of Statistics, in the year 2000 the 307 registered fishermen in Bermuda caught 286 metric tons of marine fish. And the 3,409 people employed by hotels produced 538,000 hotel stays (measured by the number of visitor arrivals). Suppose that this production point is efficient in production. Assume also that the opportunity cost of one additional metric ton of fish is 2,000 hotel stays and that this opportunity cost is constant (the opportunity cost does not change).

a. If all 307 registered fishermen were to be employed by hotels (in addition to the 3,409 people already working in hotels), how many hotel stays could Bermuda produce?

b. If all 3,409 hotel employees were to become fishermen (in addition to the 307 fishermen already working in the fishing industry), how many metric tons of fish could Bermuda produce?

c. Draw a production possibilities curve for Bermuda, with fish on the horizontal axis and hotel stays on the vertical axis, and label Bermuda's actual production point for the year 2000.

10. In the ancient country of Roma, only two goods, spaghetti and meatballs, are produced. There are two tribes in Roma, the Tivoli and the Frivoli. By themselves, the Tivoli each month can produce either 30 pounds of spaghetti and no meatballs, or 50 pounds of meatballs and no spaghetti, or any combination in between. The Frivoli, by themselves, each month can produce 40 pounds of spaghetti and no meatballs, or 30 pounds of meatballs and no spaghetti, or any combination in between.

a. Assume that all production possibilities curves are straight lines. Draw one diagram showing the monthly production possibilities curve for the Tivoli and another showing the monthly production possibilities curve for the Frivoli.

b. Which tribe has the comparative advantage in spaghetti production? In meatball production?

In A.D. 100, the Frivoli discovered a new technique for making meatballs that doubled the quantity of meatballs they could produce each month.

c. Draw the new monthly production possibilities curve for the Frivoli.

d. After the innovation, which tribe had an absolute advantage in producing meatballs? In producing spaghetti? Which had the comparative advantage in meatball production? In spaghetti production?

11. According to data from the U.S. Department of Agriculture's National Agricultural Statistics Service, 124 million acres of land in the United States were used for wheat or corn farming in 2004. Of those 124 million acres, farmers used 50 million acres to grow 2.158 billion bushels of wheat, and 74 million acres of land to grow 11.807 billion bushels of corn. Suppose that U.S. wheat and corn farming is efficient in production. At that production point, the opportunity cost of producing one additional bushel of wheat is 1.7 fewer bushels of corn. However, farmers have increasing opportunity costs, so additional bushels of wheat have an opportunity cost greater than 1.7 bushels of corn. For each of the production points described below, decide whether that production point is (i) feasible and efficient in production, (ii) feasible but not efficient in production, (iii) not feasible, or (iv) uncertain as to whether or not it is feasible.

a. From their original production point, farmers use 40 million acres of land to produce 1.8 billion bushels of wheat, and they use 60 million acres of land to produce 9 billion bushels of corn. The remaining 24 million acres are left unused.

b. From their original production point, farmers transfer 40 million acres of land from corn to wheat production. They now produce 3.158 billion bushels of wheat and 10.107 billion bushels of corn.

c. From their original production point, farmers reduce their production of wheat to 2 billion bushels and increase their production of corn to 12.044 billion bushels. Along the production possibilities curve, the opportunity cost of going from 11.807 billion bushels of corn to 12.044 billion bushels of corn is 0.666 bushel of wheat per bushel of corn.

12. The Hatfield family lives on the east side of the Hatatoochie River, and the McCoy family lives on the west side. Each family's diet consists of fried chicken and corn-on-the-cob, and each is self-sufficient, raising their own chickens and growing their own corn. Explain the conditions under which each of the following statements would be true.

a. The two families are made better off when the Hatfields specialize in raising chickens, the McCoys specialize in growing corn, and the two families trade.

b. The two families are made better off when the McCoys specialize in raising chickens, the Hatfields specialize in growing corn, and the two families trade.

13. According to the U.S. Census Bureau, in July 2006 the United States exported aircraft worth $1 billion to China and imported aircraft worth only $19,000 from China. During the same month, however, the United States imported $83 million worth of men's trousers, slacks, and jeans from China but exported only $8,000 worth of trousers, slacks, and jeans to China. Using what you have learned about how trade is determined by comparative advantage, answer the following questions.

a. Which country has the comparative advantage in aircraft production? In production of trousers, slacks, and jeans?

b. Can you determine which country has the absolute advantage in aircraft production? In production of trousers, slacks, and jeans?

14. Peter Pundit, an economics reporter, states that the European Union (EU) is increasing its productivity very rapidly in all industries. He claims that this productivity advance is so rapid that output from the EU in these industries will soon exceed that of the United States and, as a result, the United States will no longer benefit from trade with the EU.

a. Do you think Peter Pundit is correct or not? If not, what do you think is the source of his mistake?

b. If the EU and the United States continue to trade, what do you think will characterize the goods that the EU exports to the United States and the goods that the United States exports to the EU?

What you will learn in this **Module:**

- The importance of graphs in studying economics
- The basic components of a graph
- How graphs illustrate the relationship between variables
- How to calculate the slope of a line or curve and what the slope value means
- How to calculate areas represented on graphs
- How to interpret numerical graphs

Section ①Appendix Graphs in Economics

Getting the Picture

Whether you're reading about economics in the *Wall Street Journal* or in your economics textbook, you will see many graphs. Visual presentations can make it much easier to understand verbal descriptions, numerical information, or ideas. In economics, graphs are the type of visual presentation used to facilitate understanding. To fully understand the ideas and information being discussed, you need to know how to interpret these visual aids. This module explains how graphs are constructed and interpreted and how they are used in economics.

Graphs, Variables, and Economic Models

One reason to attend college is that a bachelor's degree provides access to higher-paying jobs. Additional degrees, such as MBAs or law degrees, increase earnings even more. If you were to read an article about the relationship between educational attainment and income, you would probably see a graph showing the income levels for workers with different levels of education. This graph would depict the idea that, in general, having more education increases a person's income. This graph, like most graphs in economics, would depict the relationship between two economic variables. A **variable** is a quantity that can take on more than one value, such as the number of years of education a person has, the price of a can of soda, or a household's income.

As you learned in this Section, economic analysis relies heavily on *models,* simplified descriptions of real situations. Most economic models describe the relationship between two variables, simplified by holding constant other variables that may affect the relationship. For example, an economic model might describe the relationship between the price of a can of soda and the number of cans of soda that consumers will buy, assuming that everything else that affects consumers' purchases of soda stays constant. This type of model can be described mathematically or verbally, but illustrating the relationship in a graph makes it easier to understand. Next we show how graphs that depict economic models are constructed and interpreted.

How Graphs Work

Most graphs in economics are based on a grid built around two perpendicular lines that show the values of two variables, helping you visualize the relationship between them. So a first step in understanding the use of such graphs is to see how this system works.

Two-Variable Graphs

Figure A.1 shows a typical two-variable graph. It illustrates the data in the accompanying table on outside temperature and the number of sodas a typical vendor can expect to sell at a baseball stadium during one game. The first column shows the values of outside temperature (the first variable) and the second column shows the values of the number of sodas sold (the second variable). Five combinations or pairs of the two variables are shown, denoted by points A through E in the third column.

Now let's turn to graphing the data in this table. In any two-variable graph, one variable is called the *x*-variable and the other is called the *y*-variable. Here we have made

figure A.1 — Plotting Points on a Two-Variable Graph

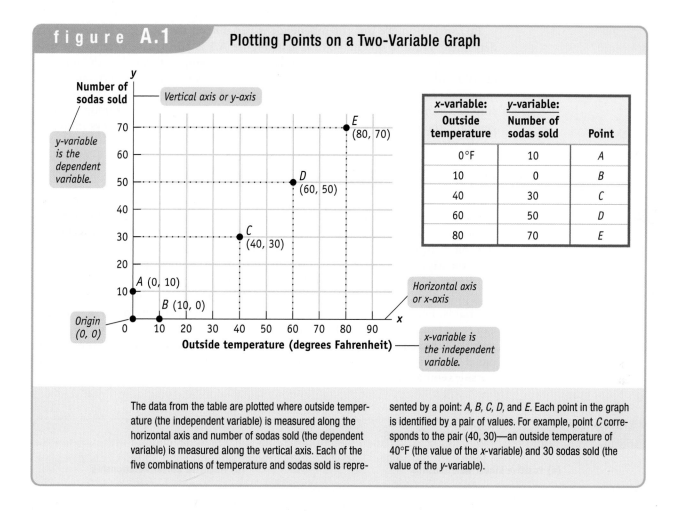

x-variable: Outside temperature	y-variable: Number of sodas sold	Point
0°F	10	A
10	0	B
40	30	C
60	50	D
80	70	E

The data from the table are plotted where outside temperature (the independent variable) is measured along the horizontal axis and number of sodas sold (the dependent variable) is measured along the vertical axis. Each of the five combinations of temperature and sodas sold is represented by a point: A, B, C, D, and E. Each point in the graph is identified by a pair of values. For example, point C corresponds to the pair (40, 30)—an outside temperature of 40°F (the value of the x-variable) and 30 sodas sold (the value of the y-variable).

outside temperature the *x*-variable and number of sodas sold the *y*-variable. The solid horizontal line in the graph is called the **horizontal axis** or **x-axis,** and values of the *x*-variable—outside temperature—are measured along it. Similarly, the solid vertical line in the graph is called the **vertical axis** or **y-axis,** and values of the *y*-variable—number of sodas sold—are measured along it. At the **origin,** the point where the two axes meet, each variable is equal to zero. As you move rightward from the origin along the *x*-axis, values of the *x*-variable are positive and increasing. As you move up from the origin along the *y*-axis, values of the *y*-variable are positive and increasing.

You can plot each of the five points *A* through *E* on this graph by using a pair of numbers—the values that the *x*-variable and the *y*-variable take on for a given point. In Figure A.1, at point *C*, the *x*-variable takes on the value 40 and the *y*-variable takes on the value 30. You plot point *C* by drawing a line straight up from 40 on the *x*-axis and a horizontal line across from 30 on the *y*-axis. We write point *C* as (40, 30). We write the origin as (0, 0).

Looking at point *A* and point *B* in Figure A.1, you can see that when one of the variables for a point has a value of zero, it will lie on one of the axes. If the value of the *x*-variable is zero, the point will lie on the vertical axis, like point *A*. If the value of the *y*-variable is zero, the point will lie on the horizontal axis, like point *B*.

Most graphs that depict relationships between two economic variables represent a **causal relationship,** a relationship in which the value taken by one variable directly influences or determines the value taken by the other variable. In a causal relationship, the determining variable is called the **independent variable;** the variable it determines is called the **dependent variable.** In our example of soda sales, the outside temperature is the independent variable. It directly influences the number of sodas that are sold, which is the dependent variable in this case.

By convention, we put the independent variable on the horizontal axis and the dependent variable on the vertical axis. Figure A.1 is constructed consistent with this convention: the independent variable (outside temperature) is on the horizontal axis and the dependent variable (number of sodas sold) is on the vertical axis. An important exception to this convention is in graphs showing the economic relationship between the price of a product and quantity of the product: although price is generally the independent variable that determines quantity, it is always measured on the vertical axis.

Curves on a Graph

Panel (a) of Figure A.2 contains some of the same information as Figure A.1, with a line drawn through the points B, C, D, and E. Such a line on a graph is called a **curve,** regardless of whether it is a straight line or a curved line. If the curve that shows the relationship between two variables is a straight line, or linear, the variables have a **linear relationship.** When the curve is not a straight line, or nonlinear, the variables have a **nonlinear relationship.**

A point on a curve indicates the value of the y-variable for a specific value of the x-variable. For example, point D indicates that at a temperature of 60°F, a vendor can expect to sell 50 sodas. The shape and orientation of a curve reveal the general nature of the relationship between the two variables. The upward tilt of the curve in panel (a) of Figure A.2 suggests that vendors can expect to sell more sodas at higher outside temperatures.

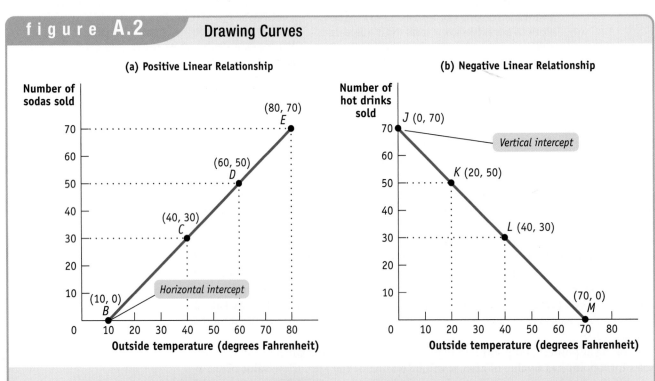

figure A.2 **Drawing Curves**

(a) Positive Linear Relationship

(b) Negative Linear Relationship

The curve in panel (a) illustrates the relationship between the two variables, outside temperature and number of sodas sold. The two variables have a positive linear relationship: positive because the curve has an upward tilt, and linear because it is a straight line. The curve implies that an increase in the x-variable (outside temperature) leads to an increase in the y-variable (number of sodas sold). The curve in panel (b) is also a straight line, but it tilts downward. The two variables here,

outside temperature and number of hot drinks sold, have a negative linear relationship: an increase in the x-variable (outside temperature) leads to a decrease in the y-variable (number of hot drinks sold). The curve in panel (a) has a horizontal intercept at point B, where it hits the horizontal axis. The curve in panel (b) has a vertical intercept at point J, where it hits the vertical axis, and a horizontal intercept at point M, where it hits the horizontal axis.

When variables are related in this way—that is, when an increase in one variable is associated with an increase in the other variable—the variables are said to have a **positive relationship.** It is illustrated by a curve that slopes upward from left to right. Because this curve is also linear, the relationship between outside temperature and number of sodas sold illustrated by the curve in panel (a) of Figure A.2 is a positive linear relationship.

When an increase in one variable is associated with a decrease in the other variable, the two variables are said to have a **negative relationship.** It is illustrated by a curve that slopes downward from left to right, like the curve in panel (b) of Figure A.2. Because this curve is also linear, the relationship it depicts is a negative linear relationship. Two variables that might have such a relationship are the outside temperature and the number of hot drinks a vendor can expect to sell at a baseball stadium.

Return for a moment to the curve in panel (a) of Figure A.2, and you can see that it hits the horizontal axis at point *B*. This point, known as the **horizontal intercept,** shows the value of the *x*-variable when the value of the *y*-variable is zero. In panel (b) of Figure A.2, the curve hits the vertical axis at point *J*. This point, called the **vertical intercept,** indicates the value of the *y*-variable when the value of the *x*-variable is zero.

A Key Concept: The Slope of a Curve

The **slope** of a curve is a measure of how steep it is; the slope indicates how sensitive the *y*-variable is to a change in the *x*-variable. In our example of outside temperature and the number of cans of soda a vendor can expect to sell, the slope of the curve would indicate how many more cans of soda the vendor could expect to sell with each 1° increase in temperature. Interpreted this way, the slope gives meaningful information. Even without numbers for *x* and *y,* it is possible to arrive at important conclusions about the relationship between the two variables by examining the slope of a curve at various points.

The Slope of a Linear Curve

Along a linear curve the slope, or steepness, is measured by dividing the "rise" between two points on the curve by the "run" between those same two points. The rise is the amount that *y* changes, and the run is the amount that *x* changes. Here is the formula:

$$\frac{\text{Change in } y}{\text{Change in } x} = \frac{\Delta y}{\Delta x} = \text{Slope}$$

In the formula, the symbol Δ (the Greek uppercase delta) stands for "change in." When a variable increases, the change in that variable is positive; when a variable decreases, the change in that variable is negative.

The slope of a curve is positive when the rise (the change in the *y*-variable) has the same sign as the run (the change in the *x*-variable). That's because when two numbers have the same sign, the ratio of those two numbers is positive. The curve in panel (a) of Figure A.2 has a positive slope: along the curve, both the *y*-variable and the *x*-variable increase. The slope of a curve is negative when the rise and the run have different signs. That's because when two numbers have different signs, the ratio of those two numbers is negative. The curve in panel (b) of Figure A.2 has a negative slope: along the curve, an increase in the *x*-variable is associated with a decrease in the *y*-variable.

Figure A.3 illustrates how to calculate the slope of a linear curve. Let's focus first on panel (a). From point *A* to point *B* the value of the *y*-variable changes from 25 to 20 and the value of the *x*-variable changes from 10 to 20. So the slope of the line between these two points is

$$\frac{\text{Change in } y}{\text{Change in } x} = \frac{\Delta y}{\Delta x} = \frac{-5}{10} = -\frac{1}{2} = -0.5$$

Because a straight line is equally steep at all points, the slope of a straight line is the same at all points. In other words, a straight line has a constant slope. You can check

(a) Negative Constant Slope

(b) Positive Constant Slope

Panels (a) and (b) show two linear curves. Between points A and B on the curve in panel (a), the change in y (the rise) is -5 and the change in x (the run) is 10. So the slope from A to B is $\frac{\Delta y}{\Delta x} = \frac{-5}{10} = -\frac{1}{2} = -0.5$, where the negative sign indicates that the curve is downward sloping. In panel (b), the curve has a slope from A to B of $\frac{\Delta y}{\Delta x} = \frac{10}{2} = 5$. The slope from C to D is $\frac{\Delta y}{\Delta x} = \frac{20}{4} = 5$. The slope is positive, indicating that the curve is upward sloping. Furthermore, the slope between A and B is the same as the slope between C and D, making this a linear curve. The slope of a linear curve is constant: it is the same regardless of where it is calculated along the curve.

this by calculating the slope of the linear curve between points A and B and between points C and D in panel (b) of Figure A.3.

$$\frac{\Delta y}{\Delta x} = \frac{10}{2} = 5$$

$$\frac{\Delta y}{\Delta x} = \frac{20}{4} = 5$$

Horizontal and Vertical Curves and Their Slopes

When a curve is horizontal, the value of y along that curve never changes—it is constant. Everywhere along the curve, the change in y is zero. Now, zero divided by any number is zero. So regardless of the value of the change in x, the slope of a horizontal curve is always zero.

If a curve is vertical, the value of x along the curve never changes—it is constant. Everywhere along the curve, the change in x is zero. This means that the slope of a vertical line is a ratio with zero in the denominator. A ratio with zero in the denominator is equal to infinity—that is, an infinitely large number. So the slope of a vertical line is equal to infinity.

A vertical or a horizontal curve has a special implication: it means that the x-variable and the y-variable are unrelated. Two variables are unrelated when a change in one variable (the independent variable) has no effect on the other variable (the dependent variable). To put it a slightly different way, two variables are unrelated when the dependent variable is constant regardless of the value of the independent variable. If, as is usual, the y-variable is the dependent variable, the curve is horizontal. If the dependent variable is the x-variable, the curve is vertical.

The Slope of a Nonlinear Curve

A **nonlinear curve** is one in which the slope changes as you move along it. Panels (a), (b), (c), and (d) of Figure A.4 show various nonlinear curves. Panels (a) and (b) show nonlinear curves whose slopes change as you follow the line's progression, but the slopes always remain positive. Although both curves tilt upward, the curve in panel (a) gets steeper as the line moves from left to right in contrast to the curve in panel (b),

figure A.4 Nonlinear Curves

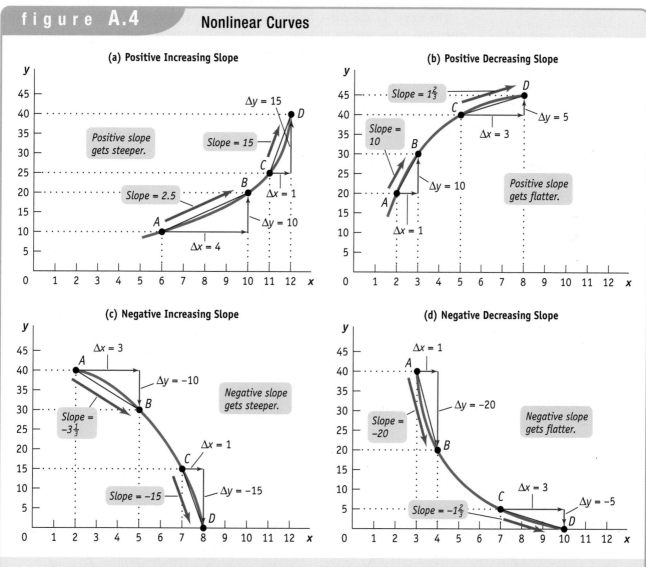

In panel (a) the slope of the curve from A to B is $\frac{\Delta y}{\Delta x} = \frac{10}{4} = 2.5$, and from C to D it is $\frac{\Delta y}{\Delta x} = \frac{15}{1} = 15$. The slope is positive and increasing; it gets steeper as it moves to the right. In panel (b) the slope of the curve from A to B is $\frac{\Delta y}{\Delta x} = \frac{10}{1} = 10$, and from C to D it is $\frac{\Delta y}{\Delta x} = \frac{5}{3} = 1\frac{2}{3}$. The slope is positive and decreasing; it gets flatter as it moves to the right. In panel (c) the slope from A to B is $\frac{\Delta y}{\Delta x} = \frac{-10}{3} = -3\frac{1}{3}$, and from C to D it is $\frac{\Delta y}{\Delta x} = \frac{-15}{1} = -15$. The slope is negative and increasing; it gets steeper as it moves to the right.

And in panel (d) the slope from A to B is $\frac{\Delta y}{\Delta x} = \frac{-20}{1} = -20$, and from C to D it is $\frac{\Delta y}{\Delta x} = \frac{-5}{3} = -1\frac{2}{3}$. The slope is negative and decreasing; it gets flatter as it moves to the right. The slope in each case has been calculated by using the *arc method*—that is, by drawing a straight line connecting two points along a curve. The average slope between those two points is equal to the slope of the straight line between those two points.

which gets flatter. A curve that is upward sloping and gets steeper, as in panel (a), is said to have *positive increasing* slope. A curve that is upward sloping but gets flatter, as in panel (b), is said to have *positive decreasing* slope.

When we calculate the slope along these nonlinear curves, we obtain different values for the slope at different points. How the slope changes along the curve determines the curve's shape. For example, in panel (a) of Figure A.4, the slope of the curve is a positive number that steadily increases as the line moves from left to right, whereas in panel (b), the slope is a positive number that steadily decreases.

The slopes of the curves in panels (c) and (d) are negative numbers. Economists often prefer to express a negative number as its **absolute value,** which is the value of the negative number without the minus sign. In general, we denote the absolute value of a number by two parallel bars around the number; for example, the absolute value of −4 is written as $|-4| = 4$. In panel (c), the absolute value of the slope steadily increases as the line moves from left to right. The curve therefore has *negative increasing* slope. And in panel (d), the absolute value of the slope of the curve steadily decreases along the curve. This curve therefore has *negative decreasing* slope.

Maximum and Minimum Points

The slope of a nonlinear curve can change from positive to negative or vice versa. When the slope of a curve changes from positive to negative, it creates what is called a *maximum* point of the curve. When the slope of a curve changes from negative to positive, it creates a *minimum* point.

Panel (a) of Figure A.5 illustrates a curve in which the slope changes from positive to negative as the line moves from left to right. When x is between 0 and 50, the slope of the curve is positive. At x equal to 50, the curve attains its highest point—the largest value of y along the curve. This point is called the **maximum** of the curve. When x exceeds 50, the slope becomes negative as the curve turns downward. Many important curves in economics, such as the curve that represents how the profit of a firm changes as it produces more output, are hill-shaped like this one.

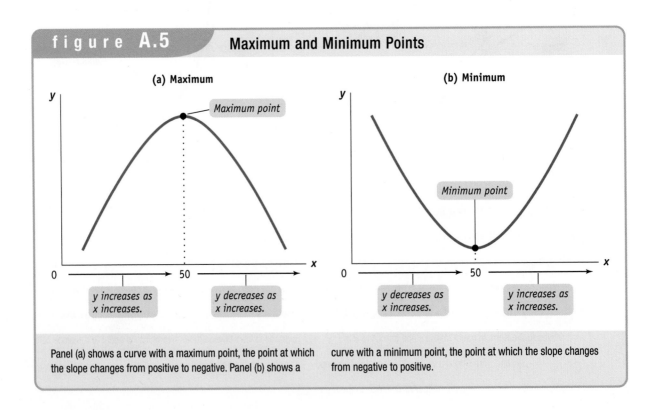

figure A.5   Maximum and Minimum Points

(a) Maximum

Maximum point

y increases as x increases.   *y decreases as x increases.*

(b) Minimum

Minimum point

y decreases as x increases.   *y increases as x increases.*

Panel (a) shows a curve with a maximum point, the point at which the slope changes from positive to negative. Panel (b) shows a curve with a minimum point, the point at which the slope changes from negative to positive.

In contrast, the curve shown in panel (b) of Figure A.5 is U-shaped: it has a slope that changes from negative to positive. At x equal to 50, the curve reaches its lowest point—the smallest value of y along the curve. This point is called the **minimum** of the curve. Various important curves in economics, such as the curve that represents how a firm's cost per unit changes as output increases, are U-shaped like this one.

Calculating the Area Below or Above a Curve

Sometimes it is useful to be able to measure the size of the area below or above a curve. To keep things simple, we'll only calculate the area below or above a linear curve.

How large is the shaded area below the linear curve in panel (a) of Figure A.6? First, note that this area has the shape of a right triangle. A right triangle is a triangle in which two adjacent sides form a 90° angle. We will refer to one of these sides as the *height* of the triangle and the other side as the *base* of the triangle. For our purposes, it doesn't matter which of these two sides we refer to as the base and which as the height. Calculating the area of a right triangle is straightforward: multiply the height of the triangle by the base of the triangle, and divide the result by 2. The height of the triangle in panel (a) of Figure A.6 is $10 - 4 = 6$. And the base of the triangle is $3 - 0 = 3$. So the area of that triangle is

$$\frac{6 \times 3}{2} = 9$$

How about the shaded area above the linear curve in panel (b) of Figure A.6? We can use the same formula to calculate the area of this right triangle. The height of the triangle is $8 - 2 = 6$. And the base of the triangle is $4 - 0 = 4$. So the area of that triangle is

$$\frac{6 \times 4}{2} = 12$$

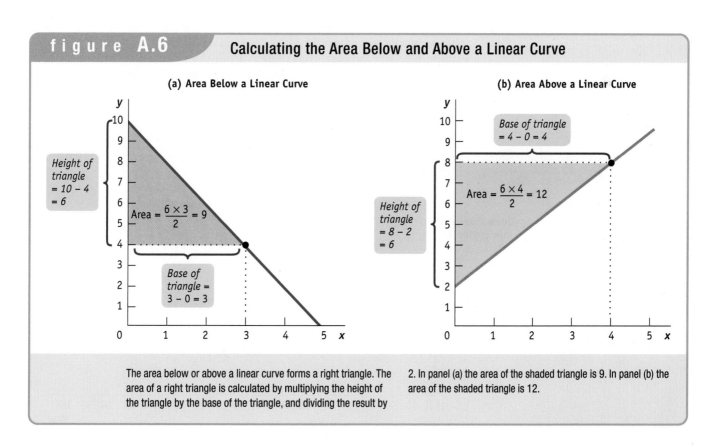

figure A.6 — Calculating the Area Below and Above a Linear Curve

(a) Area Below a Linear Curve

Height of triangle $= 10 - 4 = 6$

Area $= \dfrac{6 \times 3}{2} = 9$

Base of triangle $= 3 - 0 = 3$

(b) Area Above a Linear Curve

Base of triangle $= 4 - 0 = 4$

Area $= \dfrac{6 \times 4}{2} = 12$

Height of triangle $= 8 - 2 = 6$

The area below or above a linear curve forms a right triangle. The area of a right triangle is calculated by multiplying the height of the triangle by the base of the triangle, and dividing the result by

2. In panel (a) the area of the shaded triangle is 9. In panel (b) the area of the shaded triangle is 12.

Graphs That Depict Numerical Information

Graphs can also be used as a convenient way to summarize and display data without assuming some underlying causal relationship. Graphs that simply display numerical information are called *numerical graphs*. Here we will consider four types of numerical graphs: *time-series graphs, scatter diagrams, pie charts,* and *bar graphs*. These are widely used to display real empirical data about different economic variables, because they often help economists and policy makers identify patterns or trends in the economy.

Types of Numerical Graphs

You have probably seen graphs in newspapers that show what has happened over time to economic variables such as the unemployment rate or stock prices. A **time-series graph** has successive dates on the horizontal axis and the values of a variable that occurred on those dates on the vertical axis. For example, Figure A.7 shows the unemployment rate in the United States from 1989 to late 2006. A line connecting the points that correspond to the unemployment rate for each month during those years gives a clear idea of the overall trend in unemployment during that period. Note the two short diagonal lines toward the bottom of the *y*-axis in Figure A.7. This *truncation sign* indicates that a piece of the axis—here, unemployment rates below 4%—was cut to save space.

Figure A.8 is an example of a different kind of numerical graph. It represents information from a sample of 158 countries on average life expectancy and gross national product (GNP) per capita—a rough measure of a country's standard of living. Each point in the graph indicates an average resident's life expectancy and the log of GNP per capita for a given country. (Economists have found that the log of GNP rather than the simple level of GNP is more closely tied to average life expectancy.) The points lying in the upper right of the graph, which show combinations of high life expectancy and high log of GNP per capita, represent economically advanced countries such as the United States. Points lying in the bottom left of the graph, which show combinations of low life expectancy and low log of GNP per capita, represent economically less advanced countries such as Afghanistan and Sierra Leone. The pattern of points indicates that there is a positive relationship between life expectancy and log of GNP per capita: on the whole, people live longer in countries with a higher standard of living. This type of graph is called a **scatter diagram,** a diagram in which each point corresponds to an actual observation of the *x*-variable and

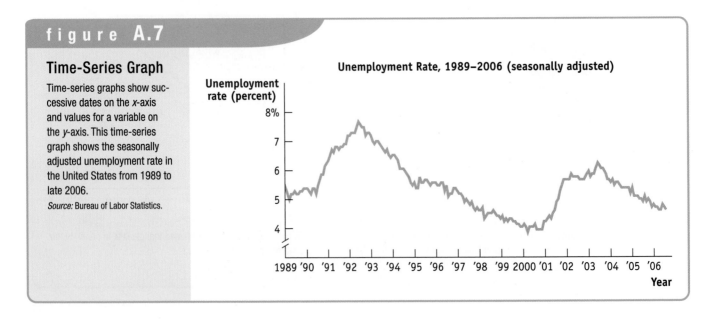

figure A.7

Time-Series Graph

Time-series graphs show successive dates on the *x*-axis and values for a variable on the *y*-axis. This time-series graph shows the seasonally adjusted unemployment rate in the United States from 1989 to late 2006.

Source: Bureau of Labor Statistics.

figure A.8

Scatter Diagram

In a scatter diagram, each point represents the corresponding values of the *x*- and *y*-variables for a given observation. Here, each point indicates the observed average life expectancy and the log of GNP per capita of a given country for a sample of 158 countries. The upward-sloping fitted line here is the best approximation of the general relationship between the two variables.

Source: Eduard Bos et al., *Health, Nutrition, and Population Indicators: A Statistical Handbook* (Washington, DC: World Bank, 1999).

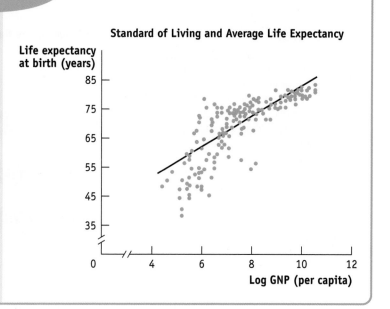

Standard of Living and Average Life Expectancy

the *y*-variable. In scatter diagrams, a curve is typically fitted to the scatter of points; that is, a curve is drawn that approximates as closely as possible the general relationship between the variables. As you can see, the fitted curve in Figure A.8 is upward-sloping, indicating the underlying positive relationship between the two variables. Scatter diagrams are often used to show how a general relationship can be inferred from a set of data.

A **pie chart** shows the share of a total amount that is accounted for by various components, usually expressed in percentages. For example, Figure A.9 is a pie chart that depicts the various sources of revenue for the U.S. government budget in 2005, expressed in percentages of the total revenue amount, $2,153.9 billion. As you can see, social insurance receipts (the revenues collected to fund Social Security, Medicare, and unemployment insurance) accounted for 37% of total government revenue, and individual income tax receipts accounted for 43%.

figure A.9

Pie Chart

A pie chart shows the percentages of a total amount that can be attributed to various components. This pie chart shows the percentages of total federal revenues received from each source.

Source: Office of Management and Budget.

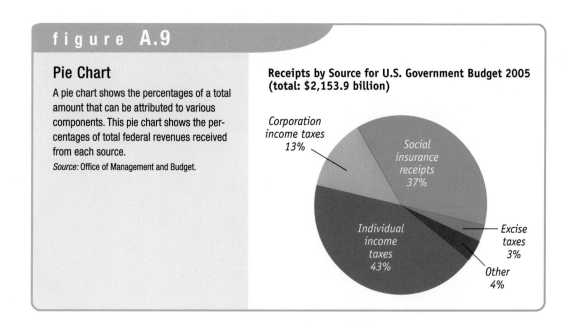

Receipts by Source for U.S. Government Budget 2005 (total: $2,153.9 billion)

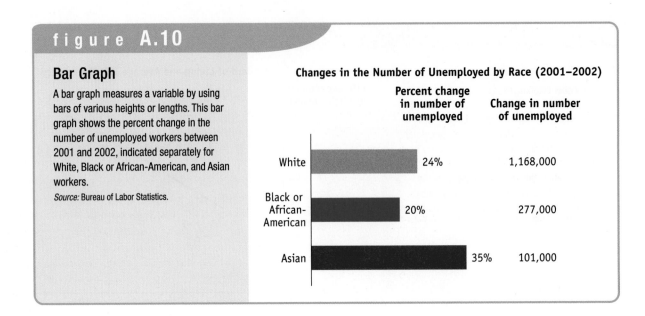

Bar Graph

A bar graph measures a variable by using bars of various heights or lengths. This bar graph shows the percent change in the number of unemployed workers between 2001 and 2002, indicated separately for White, Black or African-American, and Asian workers.

Source: Bureau of Labor Statistics.

Changes in the Number of Unemployed by Race (2001–2002)

	Percent change in number of unemployed	Change in number of unemployed
White	24%	1,168,000
Black or African-American	20%	277,000
Asian	35%	101,000

Bar graphs use bars of various heights or lengths to indicate values of a variable. In the bar graph in Figure A.10, the bars show the percent change in the number of unemployed workers in the United States from 2001 to 2002, indicated separately for White, Black or African-American, and Asian workers. Exact values of the variable that is being measured may be written at the end of the bar, as in this figure. For instance, the number of unemployed Asian workers in the United States increased by 35% between 2001 and 2002. But even without the precise values, comparing the heights or lengths of the bars can give useful insight into the relative magnitudes of the different values of the variable.

Solutions appear at the back of the book.

Check Your Understanding

1. Study the four accompanying diagrams. Consider the following statements and indicate which diagram matches each statement. For each statement, tell which variable would appear on the horizontal axis and which on the vertical. In each of these statements, is the slope positive, negative, zero, or infinity?

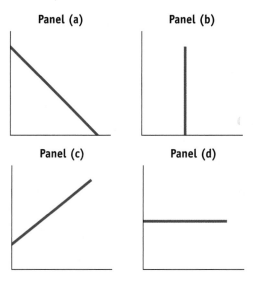

Panel (a)   **Panel (b)**

Panel (c)   **Panel (d)**

a. If the price of movies increases, fewer consumers go to see movies.

b. Workers with more experience typically have higher incomes than less experienced workers.

c. Regardless of the temperature outside, Americans consume the same number of hot dogs per day.

d. Consumers buy more frozen yogurt when the price of ice cream goes up.

e. Research finds no relationship between the number of diet books purchased and the number of pounds lost by the average dieter.

f. Regardless of its price, there is no change in the quantity of salt that Americans buy.

2. During the Reagan administration, economist Arthur Laffer argued in favor of lowering income tax rates in order to increase tax revenues. Like most economists, he believed that at tax rates above a certain level, tax revenue would fall (because high taxes would discourage some people from working) and that people would refuse to work at all if they received no income after paying taxes. This relationship between tax rates and tax revenue is graphically summarized in what is widely known as the Laffer curve. Plot the Laffer curve relationship, assuming that it has the shape of a nonlinear curve. The following questions will help you construct the graph.

a. Which is the independent variable? Which is the dependent variable? On which axis do you therefore measure the income tax rate? On which axis do you measure income tax revenue?

b. What would tax revenue be at a 0% income tax rate?

c. The maximum possible income tax rate is 100%. What would tax revenue be at a 100% income tax rate?

d. Estimates now show that the maximum point on the Laffer curve is (approximately) at a tax rate of 80%. For tax rates less than 80%, how would you describe the relationship between the tax rate and tax revenue, and how is this relationship reflected in the slope? For tax rates higher than 80%, how would you describe the relationship between the tax rate and tax revenue, and how is this relationship reflected in the slope?

Supply and Demand

For those who need a cappuccino, mocha latte, or Frappuccino to get through the day, coffee drinking can become an expensive habit. And on October 6, 2006, the habit got a little more expensive. On that day, Starbucks raised its drink prices for the first time in six years. The average price of coffee beverages at the world's leading chain of coffeehouses rose about 11 cents per cup.

Starbucks had kept its prices unchanged for six years. So what compelled them to finally raise their prices in the fall of 2006? Mainly the fact that the cost of a major ingredient—coffee beans—had gone up significantly. In fact, coffee bean prices doubled between 2002 and 2006.

Who decided to raise the prices of coffee beans? Nobody: prices went up because of events outside anyone's control. Specifically, the main cause of rising bean prices was a significant decrease in the supply of coffee beans from the world's two leading coffee exporters: Brazil and Vietnam. In Brazil, the decrease in supply was a delayed reaction to low prices earlier in the decade, which led coffee growers to cut back on planting. In Vietnam, the problem was weather: a prolonged drought sharply reduced coffee harvests.

And a lower supply of coffee beans from Vietnam or Brazil inevitably translates into a higher price of coffee on Main Street. It's just a matter of supply and demand.

What do we mean by that? Many people use "supply and demand" as a sort of catchphrase to mean "the laws of the marketplace at work." To economists, however, the concept of supply and demand has a precise meaning: it is a *model* of how a market behaves.

In this section, we lay out the pieces that make up the *supply and demand model,* put them together, and show how this model can be used to understand how many—but not all—markets behave.

Jed Jacobsohn/Getty Images

47

Module ⑤ Supply and Demand: Introduction and Demand

Supply and Demand: A Model of a Competitive Market

Coffee bean sellers and coffee bean buyers constitute a *market*—a group of producers and consumers who exchange a good or service for payment. In this section, we'll focus on a particular type of market known as a *competitive market*. Roughly, a **competitive market** is a market in which there are many buyers and sellers of the same good or service. More precisely, the key feature of a competitive market is that no individual's actions have a noticeable effect on the price at which the good or service is sold. It's important to understand, however, that this is not an accurate description of every market. For example, it's not an accurate description of the market for cola beverages. That's because in the market for cola beverages, Coca-Cola and Pepsi account for such a large proportion of total sales that they are able to influence the price at which cola beverages are bought and sold. But it *is* an accurate description of the market for coffee beans. The global marketplace for coffee beans is so huge that even a coffee retailer as large as Starbucks accounts for only a tiny fraction of transactions, making it unable to influence the price at which coffee beans are bought and sold.

It's a little hard to explain why competitive markets are different from other markets until we've seen how a competitive market works. For now, let's just say that it's easier to model competitive markets than other markets. When taking an exam, it's always a good strategy to begin by answering the easier questions. In this book, we're going to do the same thing. So we will start with competitive markets.

When a market is competitive, its behavior is well described by the **supply and demand model.** Because many markets *are* competitive, the supply and demand model is a very useful one indeed.

A **competitive market** is a market in which there are many buyers and sellers of the same good or service, none of whom can influence the price at which the good or service is sold.

The **supply and demand model** is a model of how a competitive market works.

There are five key elements in this model:

- The *demand curve*
- The *supply curve*
- The set of factors that cause the demand curve to shift and the set of factors that cause the supply curve to shift
- The *market equilibrium*, which includes the *equilibrium price* and *equilibrium quantity*
- The way the market equilibrium changes when the supply curve or demand curve shifts

To explain the supply and demand model, we will examine each of these elements in turn. In this module we begin with demand.

The Demand Curve

How many pounds of coffee beans do consumers around the world want to buy in a given year? You might at first think that we can answer this question by multiplying the number of cups of coffee drunk around the world each day by the weight of the coffee beans it takes to brew a cup, and then multiplying by 365. But that's not enough to answer the question because how many pounds of coffee beans consumers want to buy—and therefore how much coffee people want to drink—depends on the price of coffee beans. When the price of coffee rises, as it did in 2006, some people drink less, perhaps switching completely to other caffeinated beverages, such as tea or Coca-Cola. (Yes, there are people who drink Coke in the morning.) In general, the quantity of coffee beans, or of any good or service that people want to buy (taking "want" to mean they are willing and able to buy it), depends on the price. The higher the price, the less of the good or service people want to purchase; alternatively, the lower the price, the more they want to purchase.

So the answer to the question "How many pounds of coffee beans do consumers want to buy?" depends on the price of coffee beans. If you don't yet know what the price will be, you can start by making a table of how many pounds of coffee beans people would want to buy at a number of different prices. Such a table is known as a *demand schedule*. This, in turn, can be used to draw a *demand curve*, which is one of the key elements of the supply and demand model.

The Demand Schedule and the Demand Curve

A **demand schedule** is a table showing how much of a good or service consumers will want to buy at different prices. On the right side of Figure 5.1 on the next page, we show a hypothetical demand schedule for coffee beans. It's hypothetical in that it doesn't use actual data on the world demand for coffee beans and it assumes that all coffee beans are of equal quality (with our apologies to coffee connoisseurs).

According to the table, if coffee beans cost $1 a pound, consumers around the world will want to purchase 10 billion pounds of coffee beans over the course of a year. If the price is $1.25 a pound, they will want to buy only 8.9 billion pounds; if the price is only $0.75 a pound, they will want to buy 11.5 billion pounds; and so on. So the higher the price, the fewer pounds of coffee beans consumers will want to purchase. In other words, as the price rises, the **quantity demanded** of coffee beans—the actual amount consumers are willing to buy at some specific price—falls.

The graph in Figure 5.1 is a visual representation of the information in the table. The vertical axis shows the price of a pound of coffee beans and the horizontal axis shows the quantity of coffee beans. Each point on the graph corresponds to one of the entries in the table. The curve that connects these points is a **demand curve.** A demand curve is a graphical representation of the demand schedule, another way of showing the relationship between the quantity demanded and the price.

Note that the demand curve shown in Figure 5.1 slopes downward. This reflects the general proposition that a higher price reduces the quantity demanded. For example, some people who drink two cups of coffee a day when beans are $1 per pound will cut down to

A **demand schedule** shows how much of a good or service consumers will be willing and able to buy at different prices.

The **quantity demanded** is the actual amount of a good or service consumers are willing and able to buy at some specific price.

A **demand curve** is a graphical representation of the demand schedule. It shows the relationship between quantity demanded and price.

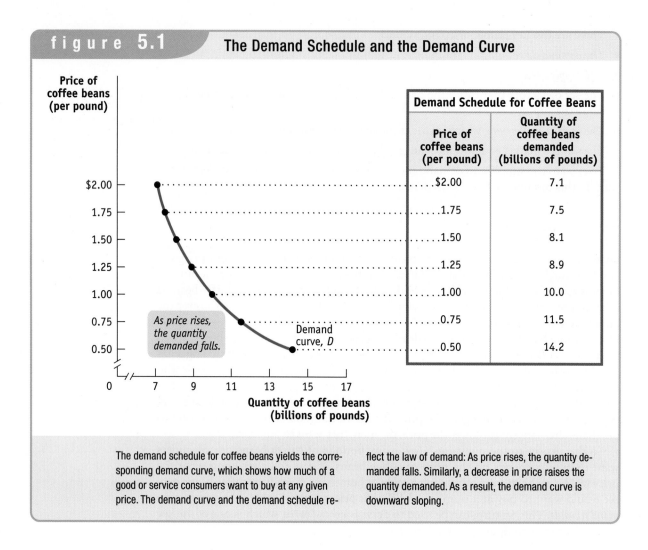

figure 5.1 The Demand Schedule and the Demand Curve

As price rises, the quantity demanded falls.

Demand curve, *D*

Demand Schedule for Coffee Beans	
Price of coffee beans (per pound)	Quantity of coffee beans demanded (billions of pounds)
$2.00	7.1
1.75	7.5
1.50	8.1
1.25	8.9
1.00	10.0
0.75	11.5
0.50	14.2

The demand schedule for coffee beans yields the corresponding demand curve, which shows how much of a good or service consumers want to buy at any given price. The demand curve and the demand schedule reflect the law of demand: As price rises, the quantity demanded falls. Similarly, a decrease in price raises the quantity demanded. As a result, the demand curve is downward sloping.

> The **law of demand** says that a higher price for a good or service, all other things being equal, leads people to demand a smaller quantity of that good or service.

one cup when beans are $2 per pound. Similarly, some who drink one cup when beans are $1 a pound will drink tea instead if the price doubles to $2 per pound and so on. In the real world, demand curves almost always slope downward. (The exceptions are so rare that for practical purposes we can ignore them.) Generally, the proposition that a higher price for a good, all other things being equal, leads people to demand a smaller quantity of that good is so reliable that economists are willing to call it a "law"—the **law of demand.**

Shifts of the Demand Curve

Even though coffee prices were a lot higher in 2006 than they had been in 2002, total world consumption of coffee was higher in 2006. How can we reconcile this fact with the law of demand, which says that a higher price reduces the quantity demanded, all other things being equal?

The answer lies in the crucial phrase *all other things being equal*. In this case, all other things weren't equal: the world had changed between 2002 and 2006, in ways that increased the quantity of coffee demanded at any given price. For one thing, the world's population, and therefore the number of potential coffee drinkers, increased. In addition, the growing popularity of different types of coffee beverages, like lattes and cappuccinos, led to an increase in the quantity demanded at any given price. Figure 5.2 illustrates this phenomenon using the demand schedule and demand curve for coffee beans. (As before, the numbers in Figure 5.2 are hypothetical.)

The table in Figure 5.2 shows two demand schedules. The first is a demand schedule for 2002, the same one shown in Figure 5.1. The second is a demand schedule for 2006.

figure 5.2   An Increase in Demand

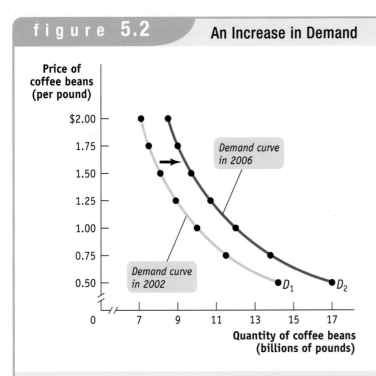

Demand Schedules for Coffee Beans		
Price of coffee beans (per pound)	**Quantity of coffee beans demanded (billions of pounds)**	
	in 2002	in 2006
$2.00	7.1	8.5
1.75	7.5	9.0
1.50	8.1	9.7
1.25	8.9	10.7
1.00	10.0	12.0
0.75	11.5	13.8
0.50	14.2	17.0

An increase in the population and other factors generate an increase in demand—a rise in the quantity demanded at any given price. This is represented by the two demand schedules—one showing demand in 2002, before the rise in population, the other showing demand in 2006, after the rise in population—and their corresponding demand curves. The increase in demand shifts the demand curve to the right.

It differs from the 2002 demand schedule due to factors such as a larger population and the greater popularity of lattes, factors that led to an increase in the quantity of coffee beans demanded at any given price. So at each price, the 2006 schedule shows a larger quantity demanded than the 2002 schedule. For example, the quantity of coffee beans consumers wanted to buy at a price of $1 per pound increased from 10 billion to 12 billion pounds per year, the quantity demanded at $1.25 per pound went from 8.9 billion to 10.7 billion pounds, and so on.

What is clear from this example is that the changes that occurred between 2002 and 2006 generated a *new* demand schedule, one in which the quantity demanded was greater at any given price than in the original demand schedule. The two curves in Figure 5.2 show the same information graphically. As you can see, the demand schedule for 2006 corresponds to a new demand curve, D_2, that is to the right of the demand curve for 2002, D_1. This **change in demand** shows the increase in the quantity demanded at any given price, represented by the shift in position of the original demand curve, D_1, to its new location at D_2.

It's crucial to make the distinction between such changes in demand and **movements along the demand curve,** changes in the quantity demanded of a good that result from a change in that good's price. Figure 5.3 on the next page illustrates the difference.

The movement from point A to point B is a movement along the demand curve: the quantity demanded rises due to a fall in price as you move down D_1. Here, a fall in the price of coffee beans from $1.50 to $1 per pound generates a rise in the quantity demanded from 8.1 billion to 10 billion pounds per year. But the quantity demanded can also rise when the price is unchanged if there is an *increase in demand*—a rightward shift of the demand curve. This is illustrated in Figure 5.3 by the shift of the demand curve from D_1 to D_2. Holding the price constant at $1.50 a pound, the quantity demanded rises from 8.1 billion pounds at point A on D_1 to 9.7 billion pounds at point C on D_2.

A **change in demand** is a shift of the demand curve, which changes the quantity demanded at any given price.

A **movement along the demand curve** is a change in the quantity demanded of a good that is the result of a change in that good's price.

figure 5.3

A Movement Along the Demand Curve Versus a Shift of the Demand Curve

The rise in the quantity demanded when going from point *A* to point *B* reflects a movement along the demand curve: it is the result of a fall in the price of the good. The rise in the quantity demanded when going from point *A* to point *C* reflects a change in demand: this shift to the right is the result of a rise in the quantity demanded at any given price.

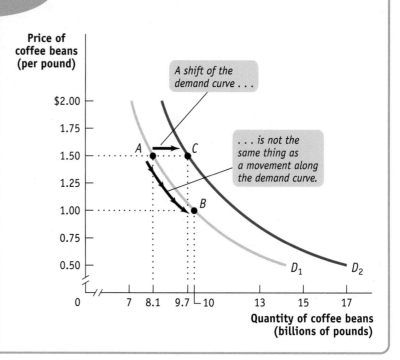

When economists talk about a "change in demand," saying "the demand for *X* increased" or "the demand for *Y* decreased," they mean that the demand curve for *X* or *Y* shifted—*not* that the quantity demanded rose or fell because of a change in the price.

Understanding Shifts of the Demand Curve

Figure 5.4 illustrates the two basic ways in which demand curves can shift. When economists talk about an "increase in demand," they mean a *rightward* shift of the demand curve: at any given price, consumers demand a larger quantity of the good or service than

figure 5.4

Shifts of the Demand Curve

Any event that increases demand shifts the demand curve to the right, reflecting a rise in the quantity demanded at any given price. Any event that decreases demand shifts the demand curve to the left, reflecting a fall in the quantity demanded at any given price.

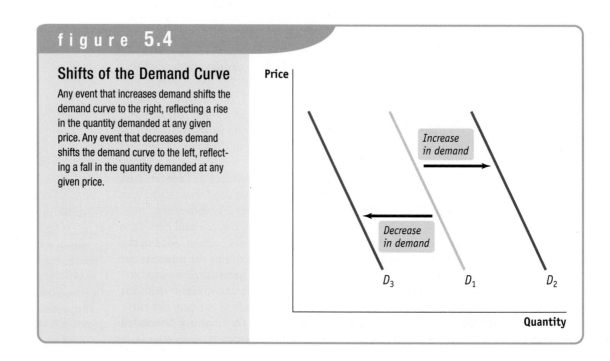

before. This is shown by the rightward shift of the original demand curve D_1 to D_2. And when economists talk about a "decrease in demand," they mean a *leftward* shift of the demand curve: at any given price, consumers demand a smaller quantity of the good or service than before. This is shown by the leftward shift of the original demand curve D_1 to D_3.

What caused the demand curve for coffee beans to shift? We have already mentioned two reasons: changes in population and a change in the popularity of coffee beverages. If you think about it, you can come up with other things that would be likely to shift the demand curve for coffee beans. For example, suppose that the price of tea rises. This will induce some people who previously drank tea to drink coffee instead, increasing the demand for coffee beans.

Economists believe that there are five principal factors that shift the demand curve for a good or service:

- Changes in the prices of related goods or services
- Changes in income
- Changes in tastes
- Changes in expectations
- Changes in the number of consumers

Although this is not an exhaustive list, it contains the five most important factors that can shift demand curves. So when we say that the quantity of a good or service demanded falls as its price rises, all other things being equal, we are in fact stating that the factors that shift demand are remaining unchanged. Let's now explore, in more detail, how those factors shift the demand curve.

Changes in the Prices of Related Goods or Services While there's nothing quite like a good cup of coffee to start your day, a cup or two of strong tea isn't a bad alternative. Tea is what economists call a *substitute* for coffee. A pair of goods are **substitutes** if a rise in the price of one good (coffee) makes consumers more willing to buy the other good (tea). Substitutes are usually goods that in some way serve a similar function: concerts and theater plays, muffins and doughnuts, train rides and air flights. A rise in the price of the alternative good induces some consumers to purchase the original good *instead* of it, shifting demand for the original good to the right.

But sometimes a fall in the price of one good makes consumers *more* willing to buy another good. Such pairs of goods are known as **complements.** Complements are usually goods that in some sense are consumed together: computers and software, cappuccinos and croissants, cars and gasoline. Because consumers like to consume a good and its complement together, a change in the price of one of the goods will affect the demand for its complement. In particular, when the price of one good rises, the demand for its complement decreases, shifting the demand curve for the complement to the left. So the October 2006 rise in Starbucks's cappuccino prices is likely to have precipitated a leftward shift of the demand curve for croissants, as people consumed fewer cappuccinos and croissants. Likewise, when the price of one good falls, the quantity demanded of its complement rises, shifting the demand curve for the complement to the right. This means that if, for some reason, the price of cappuccinos falls, we should see a rightward shift of the demand curve for croissants as people consume more cappuccinos *and* croissants.

Changes in Income When individuals have more income, they are normally more likely to purchase a good at any given price. For example, if a family's income rises, it is more likely to take that summer trip to Disney World—and therefore also more likely to buy plane tickets. So a rise in consumer incomes will cause the demand curves for most goods to shift to the right.

Why do we say "most goods," not "all goods"? Most goods are **normal goods**—the demand for them increases when consumer income rises. However, the demand for

Two goods are **substitutes** if a rise in the price of one of the goods leads to an increase in the demand for the other good.

Two goods are **complements** if a rise in the price of one of the goods leads to a decrease in the demand for the other good.

When a rise in income increases the demand for a good—the normal case—it is a **normal good.**

some products falls when income rises. Goods for which demand decreases when income rises are known as **inferior goods.** Usually an inferior good is one that is considered less desirable than more expensive alternatives—such as a bus ride versus a taxi ride. When they can afford to, people stop buying an inferior good and switch their consumption to the preferred, more expensive alternative. So when a good is inferior, a rise in income shifts the demand curve to the left. And, not surprisingly, a fall in income shifts the demand curve to the right.

One example of the distinction between normal and inferior goods that has drawn considerable attention in the business press is the difference between so-called casual-dining restaurants such as Applebee's and Olive Garden and fast-food chains such as McDonald's and KFC. When their incomes rise, Americans tend to eat out more at casual-dining restaurants. However, some of this increased dining out comes at the expense of fast-food venues—to some extent, people visit McDonald's less once they can afford to move upscale. So casual dining is a normal good, while fast-food appears to be an inferior good.

Changes in Tastes Why do people want what they want? Fortunately, we don't need to answer that question—we just need to acknowledge that people have certain preferences, or tastes, that determine what they choose to consume and that these tastes can change. Economists usually lump together changes in demand due to fads, beliefs, cultural shifts, and so on under the heading of changes in *tastes,* or *preferences.*

For example, once upon a time men wore hats. Up until around World War II, a respectable man wasn't fully dressed unless he wore a dignified hat along with his suit. But the returning GIs adopted a more informal style, perhaps due to the rigors of the war. And President Eisenhower, who had been supreme commander of Allied Forces before becoming president, often went hatless. After World War II, it was clear that the demand curve for hats had shifted leftward, reflecting a decrease in the demand for hats.

We've already mentioned one way in which changing tastes played a role in the increase in the demand for coffee beans from 2002 to 2006: the increase in the popularity of coffee beverages such as lattes and cappuccinos. In addition, there was another route by which changing tastes increased worldwide demand for coffee beans: the switch by consumers in traditionally tea-drinking countries to coffee. "In 1999," reported *Roast* magazine, "the ratio of Russian tea drinkers to coffee drinkers was five to one. In 2005, the ratio is roughly two to one."

Economists have little to say about the forces that influence consumers' tastes. (Marketers and advertisers, however, have plenty to say about them!) However, a *change* in tastes has a predictable impact on demand. When tastes change in favor of a good, more people want to buy it at any given price, so the demand curve shifts to the right. When tastes change against a good, fewer people want to buy it at any given price, so the demand curve shifts to the left.

Changes in Expectations When consumers have some choice about when to make a purchase, current demand for a good is often affected by expectations about its future price. For example, savvy shoppers often wait for seasonal sales—say, buying next year's holiday gifts during the post-holiday markdowns. In this case, expectations of a future drop in price lead to a decrease in demand today. Alternatively, expectations of a future rise in price are likely to cause an increase in demand today. For example, savvy shoppers, knowing that Starbucks was going to increase the price of its coffee

Photodisc

beans on October 6, 2006, would stock up on Starbucks coffee beans before that date.

Expected changes in future income can also lead to changes in demand: if you expect your income to rise in the future, you will typically borrow today and increase your demand for certain goods; and if you expect your income to fall in the future, you are likely to save today and reduce your demand for some goods.

Changes in the Number of Consumers As we've already noted, one of the reasons for rising coffee demand between 2002 and 2006 was a growing world population. Because of population growth, overall demand for coffee would have risen even if each individual coffee-drinker's demand for coffee had remained unchanged.

Let's introduce a new concept: the **individual demand curve**, which shows the relationship between quantity demanded and price for an individual consumer. For example, suppose that Darla is a consumer of coffee beans and that panel (a) of Figure 5.5 shows how many pounds of coffee beans she will buy per year at any given price per pound. Then D_{Darla} is Darla's individual demand curve.

An **individual demand curve** illustrates the relationship between quantity demanded and price for an individual consumer.

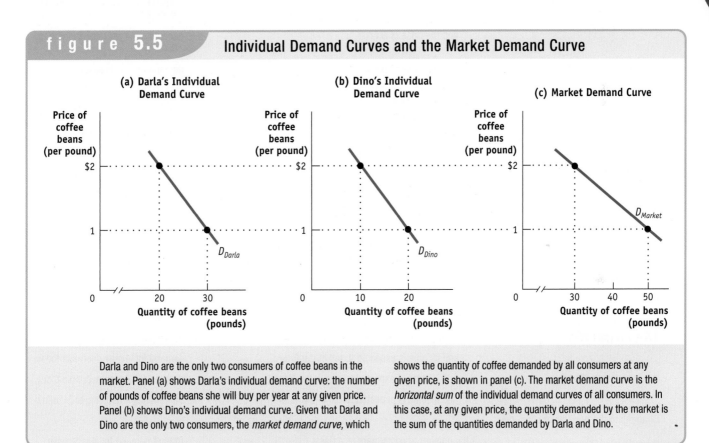

figure 5.5 **Individual Demand Curves and the Market Demand Curve**

Darla and Dino are the only two consumers of coffee beans in the market. Panel (a) shows Darla's individual demand curve: the number of pounds of coffee beans she will buy per year at any given price. Panel (b) shows Dino's individual demand curve. Given that Darla and Dino are the only two consumers, the *market demand curve,* which shows the quantity of coffee demanded by all consumers at any given price, is shown in panel (c). The market demand curve is the *horizontal sum* of the individual demand curves of all consumers. In this case, at any given price, the quantity demanded by the market is the sum of the quantities demanded by Darla and Dino.

The *market demand curve* shows how the combined quantity demanded by all consumers depends on the market price of that good. (Most of the time, when economists refer to the demand curve, they mean the market demand curve.) The market demand curve is the *horizontal sum* of the individual demand curves of all consumers in that market. To see what we mean by the term *horizontal sum,* assume for a moment that there are only two consumers of coffee, Darla and Dino. Dino's individual demand curve, $D_{Dino,}$ is shown in panel (b). Panel (c) shows the market demand curve. At any given price, the quantity demanded by the market is the sum of the quantities demanded by Darla and Dino. For example, at a price of $2 per pound, Darla demands

20 pounds of coffee beans per year and Dino demands 10 pounds per year. So the quantity demanded by the market is 30 pounds per year.

Clearly, the quantity demanded by the market at any given price is larger with Dino present than it would be if Darla were the only consumer. The quantity demanded at any given price would be even larger if we added a third consumer, then a fourth, and so on. So an increase in the number of consumers leads to an increase in demand.

For an overview of the factors that shift demand, see Table 5.1.

table **5.1**

Factors That Shift Demand

Changes in the prices of related goods or services		
If *A* and *B* are **substitutes** . . .	. . . and the price of *B* rises, . . .	. . . demand for *A* increases (shifts to the right).
	. . . and the price of *B* falls, . . .	. . . demand for *A* decreases (shifts to the left).
If A and B are **complements** . . .	. . . and the price of *B* rises, . . .	. . . demand for *A* decreases.
	. . . and the price of *B* falls, . . .	. . . demand for *A* increases.
Changes in income		
If *A* is a **normal good** . . .	. . . and income rises, . . .	. . . demand for *A* increases.
	. . . and income falls, . . .	. . . demand for *A* decreases.
If *A* is an **inferior good** . . .	. . . and income rises, . . .	. . . demand for *A* decreases.
	. . . and income falls, . . .	. . . demand for *A* increases.
Changes in tastes		
	If tastes change in favor of *A*, . . .	. . . demand for *A* increases.
	If tastes change against *A*, . . .	. . . demand for *A* decreases.
Changes in expectations		
	If the price of *A* is expected to rise in the future, . . .	. . . demand for *A* increases today.
	If the price of *A* is expected to fall in the future, . . .	. . . demand for *A* decreases today.
If A is a **normal good** . . .	. . . and income is expected to rise in the future, . . .	. . . demand for *A* may increase today.
	. . . and income is expected to fall in the future, . . .	. . . demand for *A* may decrease today.
If A is an **inferior good** . . .	. . . and income is expected to rise in the future, . . .	. . . demand for *A* may decrease today.
	. . . and income is expected to fall in the future, . . .	. . . demand for *A* may increase today.
Changes in the number of consumers		
	If the number of consumers of *A* rises, . . .	. . . market demand for *A* increases.
	If the number of consumers of *A* falls, . . .	. . . market demand for *A* decreases.

fyi

Beating the Traffic

All big cities have traffic problems, and many local authorities try to discourage driving in the crowded city center. If we think of an auto trip to the city center as a good that people consume, we can use the economics of demand to analyze anti-traffic policies.

One common strategy of local governments is to reduce the demand for auto trips by lowering the prices of substitutes. Many metropolitan areas subsidize bus and rail service, hoping to lure commuters out of their cars.

An alternative strategy is to raise the price of complements: several major U.S. cities impose high taxes on commercial parking garages, both to raise revenue and to discourage people from driving into the city. Short time limits on parking meters, combined with vigilant parking enforcement, is a related tactic.

However, few cities have been willing to adopt the politically controversial direct approach: reducing congestion by raising the price of driving. So it was a shock when, in 2003, London imposed a "congestion charge" on all cars entering the city center during business hours—currently £8 (about $13) for drivers who pay on the same day they travel.

Compliance is monitored with automatic cameras that photograph license plates. People can either pay the charge in advance or pay it by midnight of the day they have driven. If they pay on the day after they have driven, the charge increases to £10 (about $16). And if they don't pay and are caught, a fine of £120 (about $192) is imposed for each transgression. (A full description of the rules can be found at www.cclondon.com.)

Not surprisingly, the result of the new policy confirms the law of demand: three years after the charge was put in place, traffic in central London was about 10 percent lower than before the

London's bold policy to charge cars a fee to enter the city center proved effective in reducing traffic congestion.

charge. In February 2007, the British government doubled the area of London covered by the congestion charge, and it suggested that it might institute congestion charging across the country by 2015. Several American and European municipalities, having seen the success of London's congestion charge, have said that they are seriously considering adopting a congestion charge as well.

Module 5 AP Review

Solutions appear at the back of the book.

Check Your Understanding

1. Explain whether each of the following events represents (i) a *change in demand* (a *shift of* the demand curve) or (ii) a *movement along* the demand curve (a *change in the quantity demanded*).
   a. A store owner finds that customers are willing to pay more for umbrellas on rainy days.
   b. When XYZ Telecom, a long-distance telephone service provider, offered reduced rates on weekends, its volume of weekend calling increased sharply.
   c. People buy more long-stem roses the week of Valentine's Day, even though the prices are higher than at other times during the year.
   d. A sharp rise in the price of gasoline leads many commuters to join carpools in order to reduce their gasoline purchases.

Tackle the Test: Multiple-Choice Questions

1. Which of the following would increase demand for a normal good? A decrease in
   a. price.
   b. income.
   c. the price of a substitute.
   d. consumer taste for a good.
   e. the price of a complement.

2. A decrease in the price of butter would most likely decrease the demand for
   a. margarine.
   b. bagels.
   c. jelly.
   d. milk.
   e. syrup.

3. If an increase in income leads to a decrease in demand, the good is
   a. a complement.
   b. a substitute.
   c. inferior.
   d. abnormal.
   e. normal.

4. Which of the following will occur if consumers expect the price of a good to fall in the coming months?
   a. The quantity demanded will rise today.
   b. The quantity demanded will remain the same today.
   c. Demand will increase today.
   d. Demand will decrease today.
   e. No change will occur today.

5. Which of the following will increase the demand for disposable diapers?
   a. a new "baby boom"
   b. concern over the environmental effect of landfills
   c. a decrease in the price of cloth diapers
   d. a move toward earlier potty training of children
   e. a decrease in the price of disposable diapers

Tackle the Test: Free-Response Questions

1. Create a table with two hypothetical prices for a good and two corresponding quantities demanded. Choose the prices and quantities so that they illustrate the law of demand. Using your data, draw a correctly labeled graph showing the demand curve for the good. Using the same graph, illustrate an increase in demand for the good.

2. Draw a correctly labeled graph showing the demand for apples. On your graph, illustrate what happens to the demand for apples if a new report from the Surgeon General finds that an apple a day really *does* keep the doctor away.

Answer (6 points)

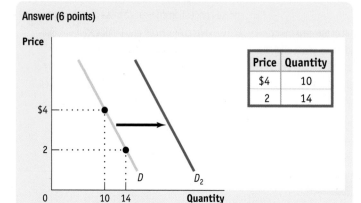

Price	Quantity
$4	10
2	14

1 point: Table with data labeled "Price" (or "P") and "Quantity" (or "Q")

1 point: Values in the table show a negative relationship between P and Q

1 point: Graph with "Price" on the vertical axis and "Quantity" on the horizontal axis

1 point: Negatively sloped curve labeled "Demand" or "D"

1 point: Demand curve correctly plots the data from the table

1 point: A second demand curve (with a label such as D_2) shown to the right of the original demand curve

Module 6
Supply and Demand: Supply and Equilibrium

What you will learn in this Module:

- What the supply curve is
- The difference between movements along the supply curve and changes in supply
- The factors that shift the supply curve
- How supply and demand curves determine a market's equilibrium price and equilibrium quantity
- In the case of a shortage or surplus, how price moves the market back to equilibrium

The Supply Curve

Some parts of the world are especially well suited to growing coffee beans, which is why, as the lyrics of an old song put it, "There's an awful lot of coffee in Brazil." But even in Brazil, some land is better suited to growing coffee than other land. Whether Brazilian farmers restrict their coffee-growing to only the most ideal locations or expand it to less suitable land depends on the price they expect to get for their beans. Moreover, there are many other areas in the world where coffee beans could be grown—such as Madagascar and Vietnam. Whether farmers there actually grow coffee depends, again, on the price.

So just as the quantity of coffee beans that consumers want to buy depends on the price they have to pay, the quantity that producers are willing to produce and sell—the **quantity supplied**—depends on the price they are offered.

The Supply Schedule and the Supply Curve

The table in Figure 6.1 on the next page shows how the quantity of coffee beans made available varies with the price—that is, it shows a hypothetical **supply schedule** for coffee beans.

A supply schedule works the same way as the demand schedule shown in Figure 5.1: in this case, the table shows the quantity of coffee beans farmers are willing to sell at different prices. At a price of $0.50 per pound, farmers are willing to sell only 8 billion pounds of coffee beans per year. At $0.75 per pound, they're willing to sell 9.1 billion pounds. At $1, they're willing to sell 10 billion pounds, and so on.

In the same way that a demand schedule can be represented graphically by a demand curve, a supply schedule can be represented by a **supply curve,** as shown in Figure 6.1. Each point on the curve represents an entry from the table.

Suppose that the price of coffee beans rises from $1 to $1.25; we can see that the quantity of coffee beans farmers are willing to sell rises from 10 billion to 10.7 billion pounds. This is the normal situation for a supply curve, reflecting the general proposition that a higher price leads to a higher quantity supplied. Some economists refer to

The **quantity supplied** is the actual amount of a good or service producers are willing to sell at some specific price.

A **supply schedule** shows how much of a good or service producers will supply at different prices.

A **supply curve** shows the relationship between quantity supplied and price.

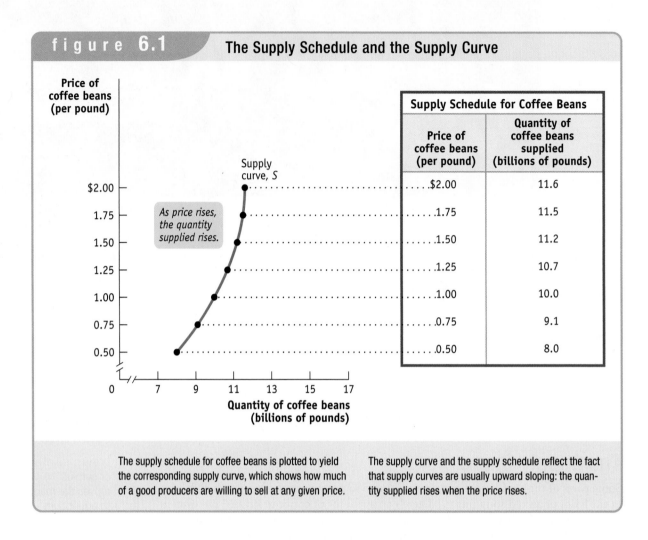

figure 6.1 The Supply Schedule and the Supply Curve

Price of coffee beans (per pound)

Supply curve, S

As price rises, the quantity supplied rises.

Supply Schedule for Coffee Beans	
Price of coffee beans (per pound)	Quantity of coffee beans supplied (billions of pounds)
$2.00	11.6
1.75	11.5
1.50	11.2
1.25	10.7
1.00	10.0
0.75	9.1
0.50	8.0

Quantity of coffee beans (billions of pounds)

The supply schedule for coffee beans is plotted to yield the corresponding supply curve, which shows how much of a good producers are willing to sell at any given price.

The supply curve and the supply schedule reflect the fact that supply curves are usually upward sloping: the quantity supplied rises when the price rises.

this relationship as the **law of supply.** Generally, the price and quantity supplied are positively related. So just as demand curves normally slope downward, supply curves normally slope upward: the higher the price being offered, the more of any good or service producers are willing to sell.

Shifts of the Supply Curve

Compared to earlier trends, coffee beans were unusually cheap in the early years of the twenty-first century. One reason was the emergence of new coffee bean–producing countries, which began competing with the traditional sources in Latin America. Vietnam, in particular, emerged as a big new source of coffee beans. Figure 6.2 illustrates this event in terms of the supply schedule and the supply curve for coffee beans.

The table in Figure 6.2 shows two supply schedules. The schedule before new producers such as Vietnam arrived on the scene is the same one as in Figure 6.1. The second schedule shows the supply of coffee beans *after* the entry of new producers. Just as a change in the demand schedule leads to a shift of the demand curve, a change in the supply schedule leads to a shift of the supply curve—a **change in supply.** This is shown in Figure 6.2 by the shift of the supply curve before the entry of the new producers, S_1, to its new position after the entry of the new producers, S_2. Notice that S_2 lies to the right of S_1, a reflection of the fact that the quantity supplied increases at any given price.

As in the analysis of demand, it's crucial to draw a distinction between such changes in supply and **movements along the supply curve**—changes in the quantity supplied that result from a change in price. We can see this difference in

The **law of supply** says that, other things being equal, the price and quantity supplied of a good are positively related.

A **change in supply** is a shift of the supply curve, which changes the quantity supplied at any given price.

A **movement along the supply curve** is a change in the quantity supplied of a good that is the result of a change in that good's price.

figure 6.2 — An Increase in Supply

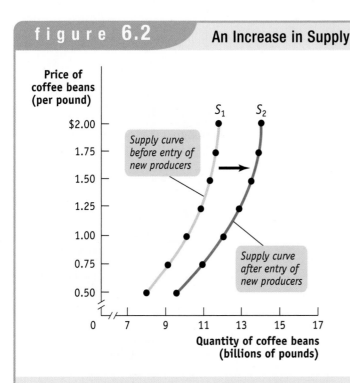

Supply Schedules for Coffee Beans		
Price of coffee beans (per pound)	Quantity of coffee beans supplied (billions of pounds)	
	Before entry	After entry
$2.00	11.6	13.9
1.75	11.5	13.8
1.50	11.2	13.4
1.25	10.7	12.8
1.00	10.0	12.0
0.75	9.1	10.9
0.50	8.0	9.6

The entry of Vietnam into the coffee bean business generated an increase in supply—a rise in the quantity supplied at any given price. This event is represented by the two supply schedules—one showing supply before Vietnam's entry, the other showing supply after Vietnam came in—and their corresponding supply curves. The increase in supply shifts the supply curve to the right.

Figure 6.3 on the next page. The movement from point *A* to point *B* is a movement along the supply curve: the quantity supplied rises along S_1 due to a rise in price. Here, a rise in price from $1 to $1.50 leads to a rise in the quantity supplied from 10 billion to 11.2 billion pounds of coffee beans. But the quantity supplied can also rise when the price is unchanged if there is an increase in supply—a rightward shift of the supply curve. This is shown by the rightward shift of the supply curve from S_1 to S_2. Holding price constant at $1, the quantity supplied rises from 10 billion pounds at point *A* on S_1 to 12 billion pounds at point *C* on S_2.

Understanding Shifts of the Supply Curve

Figure 6.4 on the next page illustrates the two basic ways in which supply curves can shift. When economists talk about an "increase in supply," they mean a *rightward* shift of the supply curve: at any given price, producers supply a larger quantity of the good than before. This is shown in Figure 6.4 by the rightward shift of the original supply curve S_1 to S_2. And when economists talk about a "decrease in supply," they mean a *leftward* shift of the supply curve: at any given price, producers supply a smaller quantity of the good than before. This is represented by the leftward shift of S_1 to S_3.

Economists believe that shifts of the supply curve for a good or service are mainly the result of five factors (though, as in the case of demand, there are other possible causes):

- Changes in input prices
- Changes in the prices of related goods or services
- Changes in technology
- Changes in expectations
- Changes in the number of producers

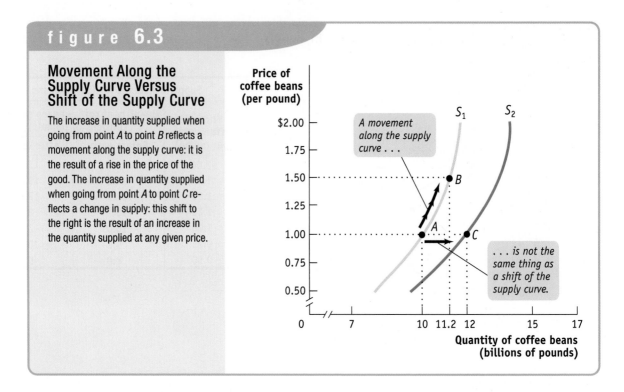

figure 6.3

Movement Along the Supply Curve Versus Shift of the Supply Curve

The increase in quantity supplied when going from point *A* to point *B* reflects a movement along the supply curve: it is the result of a rise in the price of the good. The increase in quantity supplied when going from point *A* to point *C* reflects a change in supply: this shift to the right is the result of an increase in the quantity supplied at any given price.

Changes in Input Prices To produce output, you need inputs. For example, to make vanilla ice cream, you need vanilla beans, cream, sugar, and so on. An **input** is anything used to produce a good or service. Inputs, like output, have prices. And an increase in the price of an input makes the production of the final good more costly for those who produce and sell it. So producers are less willing to supply the final good at any given price, and the supply curve shifts to the left. For example, newspaper publishers buy large quantities of newsprint (the paper on which newspapers are printed). When newsprint prices rose sharply in 1994–1995, the supply of newspapers fell: several newspapers went out of business and a number of new publishing ventures were canceled.

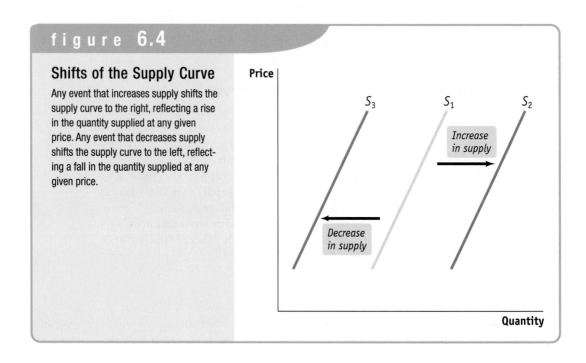

figure 6.4

Shifts of the Supply Curve

Any event that increases supply shifts the supply curve to the right, reflecting a rise in the quantity supplied at any given price. Any event that decreases supply shifts the supply curve to the left, reflecting a fall in the quantity supplied at any given price.

Similarly, a fall in the price of an input makes the production of the final good less costly for sellers. They are more willing to supply the good at any given price, and the supply curve shifts to the right.

Changes in the Prices of Related Goods or Services A single producer often produces a mix of goods rather than a single product. For example, an oil refinery produces gasoline from crude oil, but it also produces heating oil and other products from the same raw material. When a producer sells several products, the quantity of any one good it is willing to supply at any given price depends on the prices of its other co-produced goods. This effect can run in either direction. An oil refinery will supply less gasoline at any given price when the price of heating oil rises, shifting the supply curve for gasoline to the left. But it will supply more gasoline at any given price when the price of heating oil falls, shifting the supply curve for gasoline to the right. This means that gasoline and other co-produced oil products are *substitutes in production* for refiners. In contrast, due to the nature of the production process, other goods can be *complements in production*. For example, producers of crude oil—oil-well drillers—often find that oil wells also produce natural gas as a by-product of oil extraction. The higher the price at which drillers can sell natural gas, the more oil wells they will drill and the more oil they will supply at any given price for oil. As a result, natural gas is a complement in production for crude oil.

istockphoto

Changes in Technology When economists talk about "technology," they don't necessarily mean high technology—they mean all the methods people can use to turn inputs into useful goods and services. In that sense, the whole complex sequence of activities that turn corn from an Iowa farm into cornflakes on your breakfast table is technology. And when better technology becomes available, reducing the cost of production—that is, letting a producer spend less on inputs yet produce the same output—supply increases, and the supply curve shifts to the right. For example, an improved strain of corn that is more resistant to disease makes farmers willing to supply more corn at any given price.

Changes in Expectations Just as changes in expectations can shift the demand curve, they can also shift the supply curve. When suppliers have some choice about when they put their good up for sale, changes in the expected future price of the good can lead a supplier to supply less or more of the good today. For example, consider the fact that gasoline and other oil products are often stored for significant periods of time at oil refineries before being sold to consumers. In fact, storage is normally part of producers' business strategy. Knowing that the demand for gasoline peaks in the summer, oil refiners normally store some of their gasoline produced during the spring for summer sale. Similarly, knowing that the demand for heating oil peaks in the winter, they normally store some of their heating oil produced during the fall for winter sale. In each case, there's a decision to be made between selling the product now versus storing it for later sale. Which choice a producer makes depends on a comparison of the current price versus the expected future price, among other factors. This example illustrates how changes in expectations can alter supply: an increase in the anticipated future price of a good or service reduces supply today, a leftward shift of the supply curve. But a fall in the anticipated future price increases supply today, a rightward shift of the supply curve.

Changes in the Number of Producers Just as changes in the number of consumers affect the demand curve, changes in the number of producers affect the supply curve. Let's examine the **individual supply curve,** which shows the relationship between

An **individual supply curve** illustrates the relationship between quantity supplied and price for an individual producer.

A farmer in Brazil sorts coffee beans by tossing them into the air. With advances in technology, more beans can be sorted in less time, and the supply curve shifts to the right.

quantity supplied and price for an individual producer. For example, suppose that Mr. Figueroa is a Brazilian coffee farmer and that panel (a) of Figure 6.5 shows how many pounds of beans he will supply per year at any given price. Then $S_{Figueroa}$ is his individual supply curve.

The *market supply curve* shows how the combined total quantity supplied by all individual producers in the market depends on the market price of that good. Just as the market demand curve is the horizontal sum of the individual demand curves of all consumers, the market supply curve is the horizontal sum of the individual supply curves of all producers. Assume for a moment that there are only two producers of coffee beans, Mr. Figueroa and Mr. Bien Pho, a Vietnamese coffee farmer. Mr. Bien Pho's individual supply curve is shown in panel (b). Panel (c) shows the market supply curve. At any given price, the quantity supplied to the market is the sum of the quantities supplied by Mr. Figueroa and Mr. Bien Pho. For example, at a price of $2 per pound, Mr. Figueroa supplies 3,000 pounds of coffee beans per year and Mr. Bien Pho supplies 2,000 pounds per year, making the quantity supplied to the market 5,000 pounds.

Clearly, the quantity supplied to the market at any given price is larger with Mr. Bien Pho present than it would be if Mr. Figueroa were the only supplier. The quantity supplied at a given price would be even larger if we added a third producer, then a fourth, and so on. So an increase in the number of producers leads to an increase in supply and a rightward shift of the supply curve.

For an overview of the factors that shift supply, see Table 6.1.

figure 6.5   The Individual Supply Curve and the Market Supply Curve

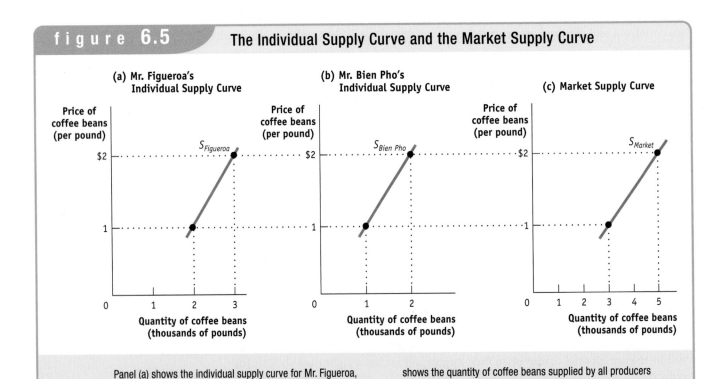

Panel (a) shows the individual supply curve for Mr. Figueroa, $S_{Figueroa}$, which indicates the quantity of coffee beans he will sell at any given price. Panel (b) shows the individual supply curve for Mr. Bien Pho, $S_{Bien\ Pho}$. The market supply curve, which shows the quantity of coffee beans supplied by all producers at any given price, is shown in panel (c). The market supply curve is the horizontal sum of the individual supply curves of all producers.

table **6.1**

Factors That Shift Supply

Changes in input prices		
	If the price of an input used to produce A rises, . . .	. . . supply of A decreases (shifts to the left).
	If the price of an input used to produce A falls, . . .	. . . supply of A increases (shifts to the right).
Changes in the prices of related goods or services		
If A and B are substitutes in production . . .	. . . and the price of B rises, . . .	. . . supply of A decreases.
	. . . and the price of B falls, . . .	. . . supply of A increases.
If A and B are complements in production . . .	. . . and the price of B rises, . . .	. . . supply of A increases.
	. . . and the price of B falls, . . .	. . . supply of A decreases.
Changes in technology		
	If the technology used to produce A improves, . . .	. . . supply of A increases.
Changes in expectations		
	If the price of A is expected to rise in the future, . . .	. . . supply of A decreases today.
	If the price of A is expected to fall in the future, . . .	. . . supply of A increases today.
Changes in the number of producers		
	If the number of producers of A rises, . . .	. . . market supply of A increases.
	If the number of producers of A falls, . . .	. . . market supply of A decreases.

Only Creatures Small and Pampered

During the 1970s, British television featured a popular show titled *All Creatures Great and Small.* It chronicled the real life of James Herriot, a country veterinarian who tended to cows, pigs, sheep, horses, and the occasional house pet, often under arduous conditions, in rural England during the 1930s. The show made it clear that in those days the local vet was a critical member of farming communities, saving valuable farm animals and helping farmers survive financially. And it was also clear that Mr. Herriot considered his life's work well spent.

But that was then and this is now. According to a 2007 article in the *New York Times,* the United States has experienced a severe decline in the number of farm veterinarians over the past two decades. The source of the problem is competition. As the number of household pets has increased and the incomes of pet owners have grown, the demand for pet veterinarians has increased sharply. As a result, vets are being drawn away from the business of caring for farm animals into the more lucrative business of caring for pets. As one vet stated, she began her career caring for farm animals but changed her mind after "doing a C-section on a cow and it's 50 bucks. Do a C-section on a Chihuahua and you get $300. It's the money. I hate to say that."

How can we translate this into supply and demand curves? Farm veterinary services and pet veterinary services are like gasoline and fuel oil: they're related goods that are substitutes in production. A veterinarian typically specializes in one type of practice or the other, and that decision often depends on the going price for the service. America's growing pet population, combined with the increased willingness of doting owners to spend on their companions' care, has driven up the price of pet veterinary services. As a result, fewer and fewer veterinarians have gone into farm animal practice. So the supply curve of farm veterinarians has shifted leftward—fewer farm veterinarians are offering their services at any given price.

In the end, farmers understand that it is all a matter of dollars and cents—that they get fewer veterinarians because they are unwilling to pay more. As one farmer, who had recently lost an expensive cow due to the unavailability of a veterinarian, stated, "The fact that there's nothing you can do, you accept it as a business expense now. You didn't used to. If you have livestock, sooner or later you're going to have deadstock." (Although we should note that this farmer *could* have chosen to pay more for a vet who would have then saved his cow.)

Supply, Demand, and Equilibrium

We have now covered the first three key elements in the supply and demand model: the demand curve, the supply curve, and the set of factors that shift each curve. The next step is to put these elements together to show how they can be used to predict the actual price at which the good is bought and sold, as well as the actual quantity transacted.

In competitive markets this interaction of supply and demand tends to move toward what economists call *equilibrium*. Imagine a busy afternoon at your local supermarket; there are long lines at the checkout counters. Then one of the previously closed registers opens. The first thing that happens is a rush to the newly opened register. But soon enough things settle down and shoppers have rearranged themselves so that the line at the newly opened register is about as long as all the others. This situation—all the checkout lines are now the same length, and none of the shoppers can be better off by doing something different—is what economists call **equilibrium.**

The concept of equilibrium helps us understand the price at which a good or service is bought and sold as well as the quantity transacted of the good or service. A competitive market is in equilibrium when the price has moved to a level at which the quantity of a good demanded equals the quantity of that good supplied. At that price, no individual seller could make herself better off by offering to sell either more or less of the good and no individual buyer could make himself better off by offering to buy more or less of the good. Recall the shoppers at the supermarket who cannot make themselves better off (cannot save time) by changing lines. Similarly, at the market equilibrium, the price has moved to a level that exactly matches the quantity demanded by consumers to the quantity supplied by sellers.

The price that matches the quantity supplied and the quantity demanded is the **equilibrium price;** the quantity bought and sold at that price is the **equilibrium quantity.** The equilibrium price is also known as the **market-clearing price:** it is the price that "clears the market" by ensuring that every buyer willing to pay that price finds a seller willing to sell at that price, and vice versa. So how do we find the equilibrium price and quantity?

Finding the Equilibrium Price and Quantity

The easiest way to determine the equilibrium price and quantity in a market is by putting the supply curve and the demand curve on the same diagram. Since the supply curve shows the quantity supplied at any given price and the demand curve shows the quantity demanded at any given price, the price at which the two curves cross is the equilibrium price: the price at which quantity supplied equals quantity demanded.

Figure 6.6 combines the demand curve from Figure 5.1 and the supply curve from Figure 6.1. They *intersect* at point *E,* which is the equilibrium of this market; that is, $1 is the equilibrium price and 10 billion pounds is the equilibrium quantity.

Let's confirm that point *E* fits our definition of equilibrium. At a price of $1 per pound, coffee bean producers are willing to sell 10 billion pounds a year and coffee bean consumers want to buy 10 billion pounds a year. So at the price of $1 a pound, the quantity of coffee beans supplied equals the quantity demanded. Notice that at any other price the market would not clear: some willing buyers would not be able to find a willing seller, or vice versa. More specifically, if the price were more than $1, the quantity supplied would exceed the quantity demanded; if the price were less than $1, the quantity demanded would exceed the quantity supplied.

The model of supply and demand, then, predicts that given the curves shown in Figure 6.6, 10 billion pounds of coffee beans would change hands at a price of $1 per pound. But how can we be sure that the market will arrive at the equilibrium price? We begin by answering three simple questions:

An economic situation is in **equilibrium** when no individual would be better off doing something different.

A competitive market is in equilibrium when price has moved to a level at which the quantity demanded of a good equals the quantity supplied of that good. The price at which this takes place is the **equilibrium price,** also referred to as the **market-clearing price.** The quantity of the good bought and sold at that price is the **equilibrium quantity.**

YEAH, I KNOW IT'S PRICEY, BUT I ONLY GOTTA SELL *ONE* GLASS AND I'M SET FOR LIFE.

Lemonade $1,000,000 a glass

© Dan Piraro, 1996 Dist. By Universal Press Syndicate

©DAN PIRARO 1996   DIST. BY UNIVERSAL PRESS SYND.

WWW.CREENSOURCE.COM/BIZARRO

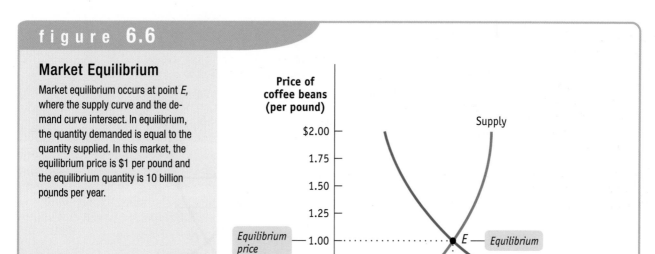

figure 6.6

Market Equilibrium

Market equilibrium occurs at point *E*, where the supply curve and the demand curve intersect. In equilibrium, the quantity demanded is equal to the quantity supplied. In this market, the equilibrium price is $1 per pound and the equilibrium quantity is 10 billion pounds per year.

1. Why do all sales and purchases in a market take place at the same price?
2. Why does the market price fall if it is above the equilibrium price?
3. Why does the market price rise if it is below the equilibrium price?

Why Do All Sales and Purchases in a Market Take Place at the Same Price?

There are some markets in which the same good can sell for many different prices, depending on who is selling or who is buying. For example, have you ever bought a souvenir in a "tourist trap" and then seen the same item on sale somewhere else (perhaps even in the shop next door) for a lower price? Because tourists don't know which shops offer the best deals and don't have time for comparison shopping, sellers in tourist areas can charge different prices for the same good.

But in any market where the buyers and sellers have both been around for some time, sales and purchases tend to converge at a generally uniform price, so that we can safely talk about *the* market price. It's easy to see why. Suppose a seller offered a potential buyer a price noticeably above what the buyer knew other people to be paying. The buyer would clearly be better off shopping elsewhere—unless the seller was prepared to offer a better deal. Conversely, a seller would not be willing to sell for significantly less than the amount he knew most buyers were paying; he would be better off waiting to get a more reasonable customer. So in any well-established, ongoing market, all sellers receive and all buyers pay approximately the same price. This is what we call the *market price*.

Why Does the Market Price Fall If It Is Above the Equilibrium Price?

Suppose the supply and demand curves are as shown in Figure 6.6 but the market price is above the equilibrium level of $1—say, $1.50. This situation is illustrated in Figure 6.7 on the next page. Why can't the price stay there?

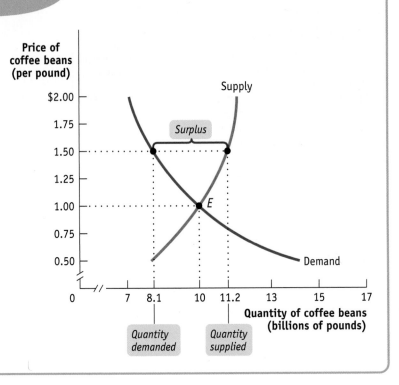

figure 6.7

Price Above Its Equilibrium Level Creates a Surplus

The market price of $1.50 is above the equilibrium price of $1. This creates a surplus: at a price of $1.50, producers would like to sell 11.2 billion pounds but consumers want to buy only 8.1 billion pounds, so there is a surplus of 3.1 billion pounds. This surplus will push the price down until it reaches the equilibrium price of $1.

There is a **surplus** of a good when the quantity supplied exceeds the quantity demanded. Surpluses occur when the price is above its equilibrium level.

There is a **shortage** of a good when the quantity demanded exceeds the quantity supplied. Shortages occur when the price is below its equilibrium level.

As the figure shows, at a price of $1.50 there would be more coffee beans available than consumers wanted to buy: 11.2 billion pounds, versus 8.1 billion pounds. The difference of 3.1 billion pounds is the **surplus**—also known as the *excess supply*—of coffee beans at $1.50.

This surplus means that some coffee producers are frustrated: at the current price, they cannot find consumers who want to buy their coffee beans. The surplus offers an incentive for those frustrated would-be sellers to offer a lower price in order to poach business from other producers and entice more consumers to buy. The result of this price cutting will be to push the prevailing price down until it reaches the equilibrium price. So the price of a good will fall whenever there is a surplus—that is, whenever the market price is above its equilibrium level.

Why Does the Market Price Rise If It Is Below the Equilibrium Price?

Now suppose the price is below its equilibrium level—say, at $0.75 per pound, as shown in Figure 6.8. In this case, the quantity demanded, 11.5 billion pounds, exceeds the quantity supplied, 9.1 billion pounds, implying that there are would-be buyers who cannot find coffee beans: there is a **shortage**—also known as an *excess demand*—of 2.4 billion pounds.

When there is a shortage, there are frustrated would-be buyers—people who want to purchase coffee beans but cannot find willing sellers at the current price. In this situation, either buyers will offer more than the prevailing price or sellers will realize that they can charge higher prices. Either way, the result is to drive up the prevailing price. This bidding up of prices happens whenever there are shortages—and there will be shortages whenever the price is below its equilibrium level. So the market price will always rise if it is below the equilibrium level.

figure 6.8

Price Below Its Equilibrium Level Creates a Shortage

The market price of $0.75 is below the equilibrium price of $1. This creates a shortage: consumers want to buy 11.5 billion pounds, but only 9.1 billion pounds are for sale, so there is a shortage of 2.4 billion pounds. This shortage will push the price up until it reaches the equilibrium price of $1.

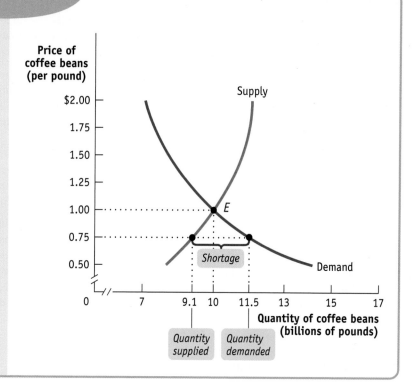

Using Equilibrium to Describe Markets

We have now seen that a market tends to have a single price, the equilibrium price. If the market price is above the equilibrium level, the ensuing surplus leads buyers and sellers to take actions that lower the price. And if the market price is below the equilibrium level, the ensuing shortage leads buyers and sellers to take actions that raise the price. So the market price always *moves toward* the equilibrium price, the price at which there is neither surplus nor shortage.

Module 6 AP Review

Solutions appear at the back of the book.

Check Your Understanding

1. Explain whether each of the following events represents (i) a *change in* supply or (ii) a *movement along* the supply curve.
   a. During a real estate boom that causes house prices to rise, more homeowners put their houses up for sale.
   b. Many strawberry farmers open temporary roadside stands during harvest season, even though prices are usually low at that time.
   c. Immediately after the school year begins, fewer young people are available to work. Fast-food chains must raise wages, which represent the price of labor, to attract workers.
   d. Many construction workers temporarily move to areas that have suffered hurricane damage, lured by higher wages.
   e. Since new technologies have made it possible to build larger cruise ships (which are cheaper to run per passenger), Caribbean cruise lines have offered more cabins, at lower prices, than before.

2. In the following three situations, the market is initially in equilibrium. After each event described below, does a surplus or shortage exist at the original equilibrium price? What will happen to the equilibrium price as a result?
   a. In 2010 there was a bumper crop of wine grapes.
   b. After a hurricane, Florida hoteliers often find that many people cancel their upcoming vacations, leaving them with empty hotel rooms.
   c. After a heavy snowfall, many people want to buy second-hand snowblowers at the local tool shop.

Tackle the Test: Multiple-Choice Questions

1. Which of the following will decrease the supply of good "X"?
   a. There is a technological advance that affects the production of *all* goods.
   b. The price of good "X" falls.
   c. The price of good "Y" (which consumers regard as a substitute for good "X") decreases.
   d. The wages of workers producing good "X" increase.
   e. The demand for good "X" decreases.

2. An increase in the demand for steak will lead to an increase in which of the following?
   a. the supply of steak
   b. the supply of hamburger (a substitute in production)
   c. the supply of chicken (a substitute in consumption)
   d. the supply of leather (a complement in production)
   e. the demand for leather

3. A technological advance in textbook production will lead to which of the following?
   a. a decrease in textbook supply
   b. an increase in textbook demand
   c. an increase in textbook supply
   d. a movement along the supply curve for textbooks
   e. an increase in textbook prices

4. Which of the following is true at equilibrium?
   a. The supply schedule is identical to the demand schedule at every price.
   b. The quantity demanded is the same as the quantity supplied.
   c. The quantity is zero.
   d. Every consumer who enjoys the good can consume it.
   e. Producers could not make any more of the product regardless of the price.

5. The market price of a good will tend to rise if
   a. demand decreases.
   b. supply increases.
   c. it is above the equilibrium price.
   d. it is below the equilibrium price.
   e. demand shifts to the left.

Tackle the Test: Free-Response Questions

1. Draw a correctly labeled graph showing the market for tomatoes in equilibrium. Label the equilibrium price "P_E" and the equilibrium quantity "Q_E." On your graph, draw a horizontal line indicating a price, labeled "P_C", that would lead to a shortage of tomatoes. Label the size of the shortage on your graph.

2. Draw a correctly labeled graph showing the market for oranges in equilibrium. Show on your graph how a hurricane that destroys large numbers of orange groves in Florida will affect supply and demand, if at all.

Answer (6 points)

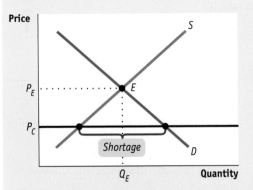

1 point: Graph with the vertical axis labeled "Price" or "P" and the horizontal axis labeled "Quantity" or "Q"

1 point: Downward sloping demand curve labeled "Demand" or "D"

1 point: Upward sloping supply curve labeled "Supply" or "S"

1 point: Equilibrium price "P_E" labeled on the vertical axis and quantity "Q_E" labeled on the horizontal axis at the intersection of the supply and demand curves

1 point: Price line at a price "P_C" below the equilibrium price

1 point: Correct indication of the shortage, which is the horizontal distance between the quantity demanded and the quantity supplied at the height of P_C

Module 7
Supply and Demand: Changes in Equilibrium

What you will learn in this **Module:**

- How equilibrium price and quantity are affected when there is a change in either supply or demand

- How equilibrium price and quantity are affected when there is a simultaneous change in both supply and demand

Changes in Supply and Demand

The emergence of Vietnam as a major coffee-producing country came as a surprise, but the subsequent fall in the price of coffee beans was no surprise at all. Suddenly, the quantity of coffee beans available at any given price rose—that is, there was an increase in supply. Predictably, the increase in supply lowered the equilibrium price.

The entry of Vietnamese producers into the coffee bean business was an example of an event that shifted the supply curve for a good without affecting the demand curve. There are many such events. There are also events that shift the demand curve without shifting the supply curve. For example, a medical report that chocolate is good for you increases the demand for chocolate but does not affect the supply. That is, events often shift either the supply curve or the demand curve, but not both; it is therefore useful to ask what happens in each case.

We have seen that when a curve shifts, the equilibrium price and quantity change. We will now concentrate on exactly how the shift of a curve alters the equilibrium price and quantity.

What Happens When the Demand Curve Shifts

Coffee and tea are substitutes: if the price of tea rises, the demand for coffee will increase, and if the price of tea falls, the demand for coffee will decrease. But how does the price of tea affect the *market equilibrium* for coffee?

Figure 7.1 on the next page shows the effect of a rise in the price of tea on the market for coffee. The rise in the price of tea increases the demand for coffee. Point E_1 shows the original equilibrium, with P_1 the equilibrium price and Q_1 the equilibrium quantity bought and sold.

An increase in demand is indicated by a *rightward* shift of the demand curve from D_1 to D_2. At the original market price, P_1, this market is no longer in equilibrium: a shortage occurs because the quantity demanded exceeds the quantity supplied. So the price of coffee rises and generates an increase in the quantity supplied, an upward

figure 7.1

Equilibrium and Shifts of the Demand Curve

The original equilibrium in the market for coffee is at E_1, at the intersection of the supply curve and the original demand curve, D_1. A rise in the price of tea, a substitute, shifts the demand curve rightward to D_2. A shortage exists at the original price, P_1, causing both the price and quantity supplied to rise, a movement along the supply curve. A new equilibrium is reached at E_2, with a higher equilibrium price, P_2, and a higher equilibrium quantity, Q_2. When demand for a good or service increases, the equilibrium price and the equilibrium quantity of the good or service both rise.

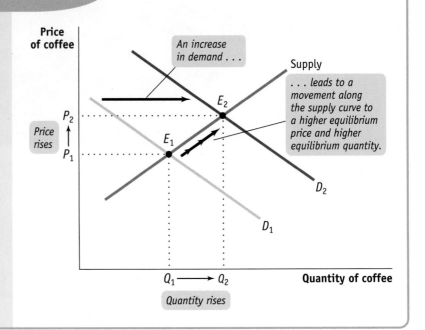

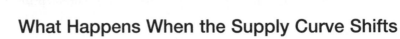

movement along the supply curve. A new equilibrium is established at point E_2, with a higher equilibrium price, P_2, and higher equilibrium quantity, Q_2. This sequence of events reflects a general principle: *When demand for a good or service increases, the equilibrium price and the equilibrium quantity of the good or service both rise.*

What would happen in the reverse case, a fall in the price of tea? A fall in the price of tea reduces the demand for coffee, shifting the demand curve to the *left*. At the original price, a surplus occurs as quantity supplied exceeds quantity demanded. The price falls and leads to a decrease in the quantity supplied, resulting in a lower equilibrium price and a lower equilibrium quantity. This illustrates another general principle: *When demand for a good or service decreases, the equilibrium price and the equilibrium quantity of the good or service both fall.*

To summarize how a market responds to a change in demand: *An increase in demand leads to a rise in both the equilibrium price and the equilibrium quantity. A decrease in demand leads to a fall in both the equilibrium price and the equilibrium quantity.*

What Happens When the Supply Curve Shifts

In the real world, it is a bit easier to predict changes in supply than changes in demand. Physical factors that affect supply, like the availability of inputs, are easier to get a handle on than the fickle tastes that affect demand. Still, with supply as with demand, what we can best predict are the *effects* of shifts of the supply curve.

As we mentioned earlier, a prolonged drought in Vietnam sharply reduced its production of coffee beans. Figure 7.2 shows how this shift affected the market equilibrium. The original equilibrium is at E_1, the point of intersection of the original supply curve, S_1, and the demand curve, with an equilibrium price, P_1, and equilibrium quantity, Q_1. As a result of the drought, supply falls and S_1 shifts *leftward* to S_2. At the original price, P_1, a shortage of coffee beans now exists and the market is no longer in equilibrium. The shortage causes a rise in price and a fall in quantity demanded, an upward movement along the demand curve. The new equilibrium is at E_2, with an equilibrium price, P_2, and an equilibrium quantity, Q_2. In the new equilibrium, E_2, the price

figure 7.2

Equilibrium and Shifts of the Supply Curve

The original equilibrium in the market for coffee beans is at E_1. A drought causes a fall in the supply of coffee beans and shifts the supply curve leftward from S_1 to S_2. A new equilibrium is established at E_2, with a higher equilibrium price, P_2, and a lower equilibrium quantity, Q_2.

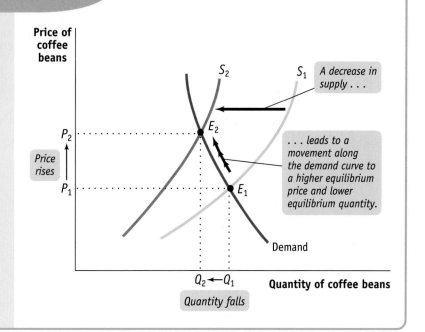

is higher and the equilibrium quantity is lower than before. This may be stated as a general principle: *When supply of a good or service decreases, the equilibrium price of the good or service rises and the equilibrium quantity of the good or service falls.*

What happens to the market when supply increases? An increase in supply leads to a *rightward* shift of the supply curve. At the original price, a surplus now exists; as a result, the equilibrium price falls and the quantity demanded rises. This describes what happened to the market for coffee beans when Vietnam entered the field. We can formulate a general principle: *When supply of a good or service increases, the equilibrium price of the good or service falls and the equilibrium quantity of the good or service rises.*

To summarize how a market responds to a change in supply: *An increase in supply leads to a fall in the equilibrium price and a rise in the equilibrium quantity. A decrease in supply leads to a rise in the equilibrium price and a fall in the equilibrium quantity.*

Simultaneous Shifts of Supply and Demand Curves

Finally, it sometimes happens that events shift *both* the demand and supply curves at the same time. This is not unusual; in real life, supply curves and demand curves for many goods and services typically shift quite often because the economic environment continually changes. Figure 7.3 on the next page illustrates two examples of simultaneous shifts. In both panels there is an increase in demand—that is, a rightward shift of the demand curve, from D_1 to D_2—say, for example, representing the increase in the demand for coffee due to changing tastes. Notice that the rightward shift in panel (a) is larger than the one in panel (b): we can suppose that panel (a) represents a year in which many more people than usual choose to drink double lattes and panel (b) represents a year with only a small increase in coffee demand. Both panels also show a decrease in supply—that is, a leftward shift of the supply curve from S_1 to S_2. Also notice that the leftward shift in panel (b) is large relative to the one in panel (a); we can suppose that panel (b) represents the effect of a particularly extreme drought in Vietnam and panel (a) represents the effect of a much less severe weather event.

In both cases, the equilibrium price rises from P_1 to P_2 as the equilibrium moves from E_1 to E_2. But what happens to the equilibrium quantity, the quantity of coffee bought and sold? In panel (a), the increase in demand is large relative to the decrease in supply,

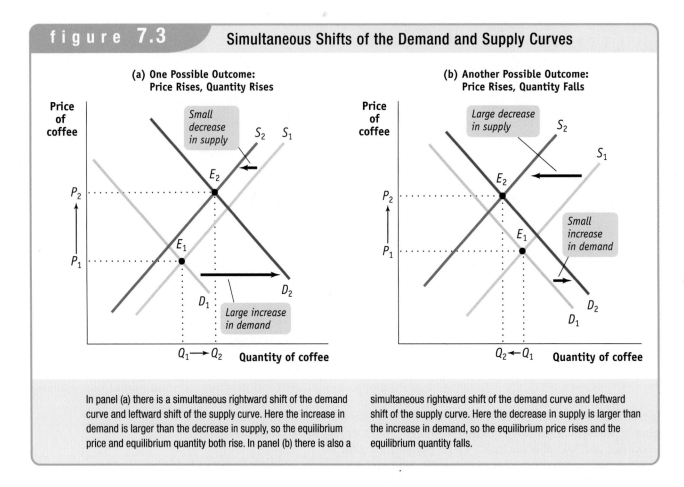

figure 7.3   Simultaneous Shifts of the Demand and Supply Curves

(a) One Possible Outcome:
Price Rises, Quantity Rises

(b) Another Possible Outcome:
Price Rises, Quantity Falls

In panel (a) there is a simultaneous rightward shift of the demand curve and leftward shift of the supply curve. Here the increase in demand is larger than the decrease in supply, so the equilibrium price and equilibrium quantity both rise. In panel (b) there is also a simultaneous rightward shift of the demand curve and leftward shift of the supply curve. Here the decrease in supply is larger than the increase in demand, so the equilibrium price rises and the equilibrium quantity falls.

and the equilibrium quantity rises as a result. In panel (b), the decrease in supply is large relative to the increase in demand, and the equilibrium quantity falls as a result. That is, when demand increases and supply decreases, the actual quantity bought and sold can go either way, depending on *how much* the demand and supply curves have shifted.

In general, when supply and demand shift in opposite directions, we can't predict what the ultimate effect will be on the quantity bought and sold. What we can say is that a curve that shifts a disproportionately greater distance than the other curve will have a disproportionately greater effect on the quantity bought and sold. That said, we can make the following prediction about the outcome when the supply and demand curves shift in opposite directions:

- When demand increases and supply decreases, the equilibrium price rises but the change in the equilibrium quantity is ambiguous.

- When demand decreases and supply increases, the equilibrium price falls but the change in the equilibrium quantity is ambiguous.

But suppose that the demand and supply curves shift in the same direction. This was the case in the global market for coffee beans, in which both supply and demand increased over the past decade. Can we safely make any predictions about the changes in price and quantity? In this situation, the change in quantity bought and sold can be predicted but the change in price is ambiguous. The two possible outcomes when the supply and demand curves shift in the same direction (which you should check for yourself) are as follows:

- When both demand and supply increase, the equilibrium quantity increases but the change in equilibrium price is ambiguous.

- When both demand and supply decrease, the equilibrium quantity decreases but the change in equilibrium price is ambiguous.

fyi

The Great Tortilla Crisis

"Thousands in Mexico City protest rising food prices." So read a recent headline in the *New York Times*. Specifically, the demonstrators were protesting a sharp rise in the price of tortillas, a staple food of Mexico's poor, which had gone from 25 cents a pound to between 35 and 45 cents a pound in just a few months.

Why were tortilla prices soaring? It was a classic example of what happens to equilibrium prices when supply falls. Tortillas are made from corn; much of Mexico's corn is imported from the United States, with the price of corn in both countries basically set in the U.S. corn market. And U.S. corn prices were rising rapidly thanks to surging demand in a new market: the market for ethanol.

Ethanol's big break came with the Energy Policy Act of 2005, which mandated the use of a large quantity of "renewable" fuels starting in 2006, and rising steadily thereafter. In practice, that meant increased use of ethanol. Ethanol producers rushed to build new production facilities and quickly began buying lots of corn. The result was a rightward shift of the demand curve for corn, leading to a sharp rise in the price of corn. And since corn is an input in the production of tortillas, a sharp rise in the price of corn led to a fall in the supply of tortillas and higher prices for tortilla consumers.

The increase in the price of corn was good news in Iowa, where farmers began planting

A cook prepares tortillas made with four different types of corn in a restaurant in Mexico City.

more corn than ever before. But it was bad news for Mexican consumers, who found themselves paying more for their tortillas.

Module 7 APReview

Solutions appear at the back of the book.

Check Your Understanding

1. For each of the following examples, explain how the indicated change affects supply or demand for the good in question and how the shift you describe affects equilibrium price and quantity.
   a. As the price of gasoline fell in the United States during the 1990s, more people bought large cars.
   b. As technological innovation has lowered the cost of recycling used paper, fresh paper made from recycled stock is used more frequently.
   c. When a local cable company offers cheaper pay-per-view films, local movie theaters have more unfilled seats.

2. Periodically, a computer chip maker like Intel introduces a new chip that is faster than the previous one. In response, demand for computers using the earlier chip decreases as customers put off purchases in anticipation of machines containing the new chip. Simultaneously, computer makers increase their production of computers containing the earlier chip in order to clear out their stocks of those chips.

   Draw two diagrams of the market for computers containing the earlier chip: (a) one in which the equilibrium quantity falls in response to these events and (b) one in which the equilibrium quantity rises. What happens to the equilibrium price in each diagram?

Tackle the Test: Multiple-Choice Questions

1. Which of the following describes what will happen in the market for tomatoes if a salmonella outbreak is attributed to tainted tomatoes?
   a. Supply will decrease and price will increase.
   b. Supply will decrease and price will decrease.
   c. Demand will decrease and price will increase.
   d. Demand will decrease and price will decrease.
   e. Supply and demand will both decrease.

2. Which of the following will lead to an increase in the equilibrium price of product "X"? A(n)
   a. increase in consumer incomes if product "X" is an inferior good
   b. increase in the price of machinery used to produce product "X"
   c. technological advance in the production of good "X"
   d. decrease in the price of good "Y" (a substitute for good "X")
   e. expectation by consumers that the price of good "X" is going to fall

3. The equilibrium price will rise, but equilibrium quantity may increase, decrease, or stay the same if
   a. demand increases and supply decreases.
   b. demand increases and supply increases.
   c. demand decreases and supply increases.
   d. demand decreases and supply decreases.
   e. demand increases and supply does not change.

4. An increase in the number of buyers and a technological advance will cause
   a. demand to increase and supply to increase.
   b. demand to increase and supply to decrease.
   c. demand to decrease and supply to increase.
   d. demand to decrease and supply to decrease.
   e. no change in demand and an increase in supply.

5. Which of the following is certainly true if demand and supply increase at the same time?
   a. The equilibrium price will increase.
   b. The equilibrium price will decrease.
   c. The equilibrium quantity will increase.
   d. The equilibrium quantity will decrease.
   e. The equilibrium quantity may increase, decrease, or stay the same.

Tackle the Test: Free-Response Questions

1. Draw a correctly labeled graph showing the SUV market in equilibrium. On your graph, show the effect on equilibrium price and quantity in the market for SUVs if the price of gasoline increases.

2. Draw a correctly labeled graph showing the market for cups of coffee in equilibrium. On your graph, show the effect of a decrease in the price of coffee beans on equilibrium price and equilibrium quantity in the market for cups of coffee.

Answer (5 points)

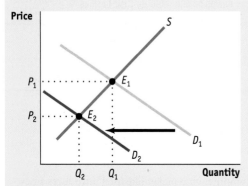

1 point: The vertical axis is labeled "Price" (or "P") and the horizontal axis is labeled "Quantity"' (or "Q").

1 point: The graph shows a downward sloping demand curve and an upward sloping supply curve (*with labels*).

1 point: Equilibrium price and quantity are found where supply and demand intersect and are labeled *on the appropriate axes*.

1 point: A new (*and labeled*) demand curve is shown to the left of the original demand curve.

1 point: The new equilibrium price and quantity are found at the intersection of the original supply curve and the new demand curve and are labeled *on the appropriate axes*.

Module 8
Supply and Demand: Price Controls (Ceilings and Floors)

What you will learn in this Module:

- The meaning of price controls, one way government intervenes in markets
- How price controls can create problems and make a market inefficient
- Why economists are often deeply skeptical of attempts to intervene in markets
- Who benefits and who loses from price controls, and why they are used despite their well-known problems

Why Governments Control Prices

You learned in Module 6 that a market moves to equilibrium—that is, the market price moves to the level at which the quantity supplied equals the quantity demanded. But this equilibrium price does not necessarily please either buyers or sellers.

After all, buyers would always like to pay less if they could, and sometimes they can make a strong moral or political case that they should pay lower prices. For example, what if the equilibrium between supply and demand for apartments in a major city leads to rental rates that an average working person can't afford? In that case, a government might well be under pressure to impose limits on the rents landlords can charge.

Sellers, however, would always like to get more money for what they sell, and sometimes they can make a strong moral or political case that they should receive higher prices. For example, consider the labor market: the price for an hour of a worker's time is the wage rate. What if the equilibrium between supply and demand for less skilled workers leads to wage rates that yield an income below the poverty level? In that case, a government might well be pressured to require employers to pay a rate no lower than some specified minimum wage.

In other words, there is often a strong political demand for governments to intervene in markets. And powerful interests can make a compelling case that a market intervention favoring them is "fair." When a government intervenes to regulate prices, we say that it imposes **price controls.** These controls typically take the form of either an upper limit, a **price ceiling,** or a lower limit, a **price floor.**

Unfortunately, it's not that easy to tell a market what to do. As we will now see, when a government tries to legislate prices—whether it legislates them *down* by imposing a price ceiling or *up* by imposing a price floor—there are certain predictable and unpleasant side effects.

Price controls are legal restrictions on how high or low a market price may go. They can take two forms: a **price ceiling,** a maximum price sellers are allowed to charge for a good or service, or a **price floor,** a minimum price buyers are required to pay for a good or service.

We make an important assumption in this module: the markets in question are efficient before price controls are imposed. Markets can sometimes be inefficient—for example, a market dominated by a monopolist, a single seller who has the power to influence the market price. When markets are inefficient, price controls don't necessarily cause problems and can potentially move the market closer to efficiency. In practice, however, price controls often *are* imposed on efficient markets—like the New York City apartment market. And so the analysis in this module applies to many important real-world situations.

Price Ceilings

Aside from rent control, there are not many price ceilings in the United States today. But at times they have been widespread. Price ceilings are typically imposed during crises—wars, harvest failures, natural disasters—because these events often lead to sudden price increases that hurt many people but produce big gains for a lucky few. The U.S. government imposed ceilings on many prices during World War II: the war sharply increased demand for raw materials, such as aluminum and steel, and price controls prevented those with access to these raw materials from earning huge profits. Price controls on oil were imposed in 1973, when an embargo by Arab oil-exporting countries seemed likely to generate huge profits for U.S. oil companies. Price controls were imposed on California's wholesale electricity market in 2001, when a shortage created big profits for a few power-generating companies but led to higher electricity bills for consumers.

Rent control in New York is, believe it or not, a legacy of World War II: it was imposed because wartime production created an economic boom, which increased demand for apartments at a time when the labor and raw materials that might have been used to build them were being used to win the war instead. Although most price controls were removed soon after the war ended, New York's rent limits were retained and gradually extended to buildings not previously covered, leading to some very strange situations.

You can rent a one-bedroom apartment in Manhattan on fairly short notice—if you are able and willing to pay several thousand dollars a month and live in a less-than-desirable area. Yet some people pay only a small fraction of this for comparable apartments, and others pay hardly more for bigger apartments in better locations.

Aside from producing great deals for some renters, however, what are the broader consequences of New York's rent-control system? To answer this question, we turn to the supply and demand model.

Modeling a Price Ceiling

To see what can go wrong when a government imposes a price ceiling on an efficient market, consider Figure 8.1, which shows a simplified model of the market for apartments in New York. For the sake of simplicity, we imagine that all apartments are exactly the same and so would rent for the same price in an unregulated market. The table in the figure shows the demand and supply schedules; the demand and supply curves are shown on the left. We show the quantity of apartments on the horizontal axis and the monthly rent per apartment on the vertical axis. You can see that in an unregulated market the equilibrium would be at point *E*: 2 million apartments would be rented for $1,000 each per month.

Now suppose that the government imposes a price ceiling, limiting rents to a price below the equilibrium price—say, no more than $800.

Figure 8.2 shows the effect of the price ceiling, represented by the line at $800. At the enforced rental rate of $800, landlords have less incentive to offer apartments, so they won't be willing to supply as many as they would at the equilibrium rate of $1,000. They will choose point *A* on the supply curve, offering only 1.8 million apartments for rent, 200,000 fewer than in the unregulated market. At the same time, more people will want to rent apartments at a price of $800 than at the equilibrium price of $1,000; as shown at point *B* on the demand curve, at a monthly rent of $800 the quantity of apartments

figure 8.1
The Market for Apartments in the Absence of Government Controls

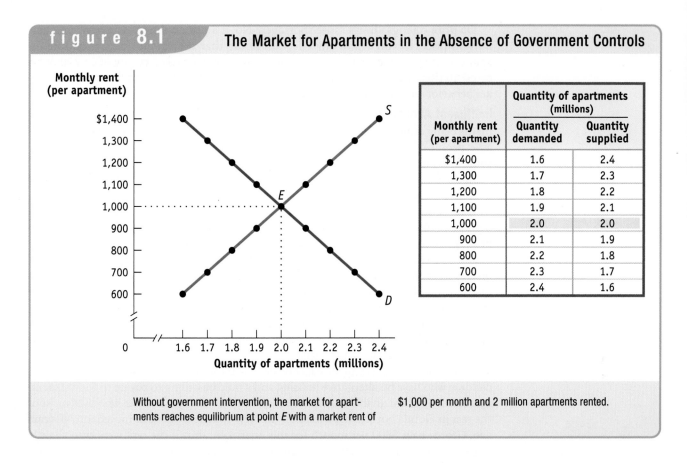

Monthly rent (per apartment)	Quantity of apartments (millions)	
	Quantity demanded	Quantity supplied
$1,400	1.6	2.4
1,300	1.7	2.3
1,200	1.8	2.2
1,100	1.9	2.1
1,000	2.0	2.0
900	2.1	1.9
800	2.2	1.8
700	2.3	1.7
600	2.4	1.6

Without government intervention, the market for apartments reaches equilibrium at point *E* with a market rent of $1,000 per month and 2 million apartments rented.

demanded rises to 2.2 million, 200,000 more than in the unregulated market and 400,000 more than are actually available at the price of $800. So there is now a persistent shortage of rental housing: at that price, 400,000 more people want to rent than are able to find apartments.

figure 8.2

The Effects of a Price Ceiling

The black horizontal line represents the government-imposed price ceiling on rents of $800 per month. This price ceiling reduces the quantity of apartments supplied to 1.8 million, point *A*, and increases the quantity demanded to 2.2 million, point *B*. This creates a persistent shortage of 400,000 units: 400,000 people who want apartments at the legal rent of $800 but cannot get them.

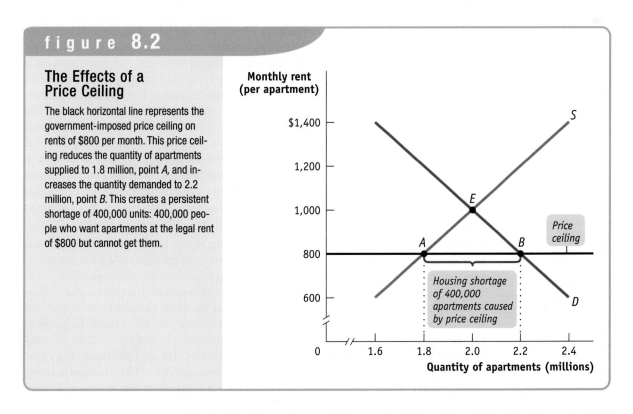

Do price ceilings always cause shortages? No. If a price ceiling is set above the equilibrium price, it won't have any effect. Suppose that the equilibrium rental rate on apartments is $1,000 per month and the city government sets a ceiling of $1,200. Who cares? In this case, the price ceiling won't be binding—it won't actually constrain market behavior—and it will have no effect.

Inefficient Allocation to Consumers Rent control doesn't just lead to too few apartments being available. It can also lead to misallocation of the apartments that are available: people who badly need a place to live may not be able to find an apartment, while some apartments may be occupied by people with much less urgent needs.

In the case shown in Figure 8.2, 2.2 million people would like to rent an apartment at $800 per month, but only 1.8 million apartments are available. Of those 2.2 million who are seeking an apartment, some want an apartment badly and are willing to pay a high price to get one. Others have a less urgent need and are only willing to pay a low price, perhaps because they have alternative housing. An efficient allocation of apartments would reflect these differences: people who really want an apartment will get one and people who aren't all that eager to find an apartment won't. In an inefficient distribution of apartments, the opposite will happen: some people who are not especially eager to find an apartment will get one and others who are very eager to find an apartment won't. Because people usually get apartments through luck or personal connections under rent control, it generally results in an **inefficient allocation to consumers** of the few apartments available.

To see the inefficiency involved, consider the plight of the Lees, a family with young children who have no alternative housing and would be willing to pay up to $1,500 for an apartment—but are unable to find one. Also consider George, a retiree who lives most of the year in Florida but still has a lease on the New York apartment he moved into 40 years ago. George pays $800 per month for this apartment, but if the rent were even slightly more—say, $850—he would give it up and stay with his children when he is in New York.

This allocation of apartments—George has one and the Lees do not—is a missed opportunity: there is a way to make the Lees and George both better off at no additional cost. The Lees would be happy to pay George, say, $1,200 a month to sublease his apartment, which he would happily accept since the apartment is worth no more than $849 a month to him. George would prefer the money he gets from the Lees to keeping his apartment; the Lees would prefer to have the apartment rather than the money. So both would be made better off by this transaction—and nobody else would be made worse off.

Generally, if people who really want apartments could sublease them from people who are less eager to live there, both those who gain apartments and those who trade their occupancy for money would be better off. However, subletting is illegal under rent control because it would occur at prices above the price ceiling. The fact that subletting is illegal doesn't mean it never happens. In fact, chasing down illegal subletting is a major business for New York private investigators. A 2007 report in the *New York Times* described how private investigators use hidden cameras and other tricks to prove that the legal tenants in rent-controlled apartments actually live in the suburbs, or even in other states, and have sublet their apartments at two or three times the controlled rent. This subletting is a kind of illegal activity, which we will discuss shortly. For now, just notice that the aggressive pursuit of illegal subletting surely discourages the practice, so there isn't enough subletting to eliminate the inefficient allocation of apartments.

Wasted Resources Another reason a price ceiling causes inefficiency is that it leads to **wasted resources:** people expend money, effort, and time to cope with the shortages caused by the price ceiling. Back in 1979, U.S. price controls on gasoline led to shortages that forced millions of Americans to spend hours each week waiting in lines at gas stations. The opportunity cost of the time spent in gas lines—the wages not earned, the leisure time not enjoyed—constituted wasted resources from the point of view of consumers and of the economy as a whole. Because of rent control, the Lees will spend all their spare time for several months searching for an apartment, time they would rather have spent working or engaged in family activities. That is, there is an opportunity cost to the Lees' prolonged search for an apartment—the leisure or income

Price ceilings often lead to inefficiency in the form of **inefficient allocation to consumers:** people who want the good badly and are willing to pay a high price don't get it, and those who care relatively little about the good and are only willing to pay a relatively low price do get it.

Price ceilings typically lead to inefficiency in the form of **wasted resources:** people expend money, effort, and time to cope with the shortages caused by the price ceiling.

they had to forgo. If the market for apartments worked freely, the Lees would quickly find an apartment at the equilibrium rent of $1,000, leaving them time to earn more or to enjoy themselves—an outcome that would make them better off without making anyone else worse off. Again, rent control creates missed opportunities.

Inefficiently Low Quality Yet another way a price ceiling causes inefficiency is by causing goods to be of inefficiently low quality. **Inefficiently low quality** means that sellers offer low-quality goods at a low price even though buyers would rather have higher quality and are willing to pay a higher price for it.

Signs advertising apartments to rent or sublet are common in New York City.

Again, consider rent control. Landlords have no incentive to provide better conditions because they cannot raise rents to cover their repair costs but are able to find tenants easily. In many cases, tenants would be willing to pay much more for improved conditions than it would cost for the landlord to provide them—for example, the upgrade of an antiquated electrical system that cannot safely run air conditioners or computers. But any additional payment for such improvements would be legally considered a rent increase, which is prohibited. Indeed, rent-controlled apartments are notoriously badly maintained, rarely painted, subject to frequent electrical and plumbing problems, sometimes even hazardous to inhabit. As one former manager of Manhattan buildings explained, "At unregulated apartments we'd do most things that the tenants requested. But on the rent-regulated units, we did absolutely only what the law required. . . . We had a perverse incentive to make those tenants unhappy. With regulated apartments, the ultimate objective is to get people out of the building [because rents can be raised for new tenants]."

This whole situation is a missed opportunity—some tenants would be happy to pay for better conditions, and landlords would be happy to provide them for payment. But such an exchange would occur only if the market were allowed to operate freely.

Black Markets And that leads us to a last aspect of price ceilings: the incentive they provide for illegal activities, specifically the emergence of **black markets.** We have already described one kind of black market activity—illegal subletting by tenants. But it does not stop there. Clearly, there is a temptation for a landlord to say to a potential tenant, "Look, you can have the place if you slip me an extra few hundred in cash each month"—and for the tenant to agree, if he or she is one of those people who would be willing to pay much more than the maximum legal rent.

What's wrong with black markets? In general, it's a bad thing if people break *any* law because it encourages disrespect for the law in general. Worse yet, in this case illegal activity worsens the position of those who try to be honest. If the Lees are scrupulous about upholding the rent-control law but other people—who may need an apartment less than the Lees—are willing to bribe landlords, the Lees may *never* find an apartment.

So Why Are There Price Ceilings?

We have seen three common results of price ceilings:

- a persistent shortage of the good
- inefficiency arising from this persistent shortage in the form of inefficiently low quantity, inefficient allocation of the good to consumers, resources wasted in searching for the good, and the inefficiently low quality of the good offered for sale
- the emergence of illegal, black market activity

Given these unpleasant consequences, why do governments still sometimes impose price ceilings? Why does rent control, in particular, persist in New York?

One answer is that although price ceilings may have adverse effects, they do benefit some people. In practice, New York's rent-control rules—which are more complex than our

Price ceilings often lead to inefficiency in that the goods being offered are of **inefficiently low quality:** sellers offer low quality goods at a low price even though buyers would prefer a higher quality at a higher price.

A **black market** is a market in which goods or services are bought and sold illegally—either because it is illegal to sell them at all or because the prices charged are legally prohibited by a price ceiling.

simple model—hurt most residents but give a small minority of renters much cheaper housing than they would get in an unregulated market. And those who benefit from the controls may be better organized and more vocal than those who are harmed by them.

Also, when price ceilings have been in effect for a long time, buyers may not have a realistic idea of what would happen without them. In our previous example, the rental rate in an unregulated market (Figure 8.1) would be only 25% higher than in the regulated market (Figure 8.2): $1,000 instead of $800. But how would renters know that? Indeed, they might have heard about black market transactions at much higher prices—the Lees or some other family paying George $1,200 or more—and would not realize that these black market prices are much higher than the price that would prevail in a fully unregulated market.

A last answer is that government officials often do not understand supply and demand analysis! It is a great mistake to suppose that economic policies in the real world are always sensible or well informed.

Price Floors

Sometimes governments intervene to push market prices up instead of down. *Price floors* have been widely legislated for agricultural products, such as wheat and milk, as a way to support the incomes of farmers. Historically, there were also price floors on such services as trucking and air travel, although these were phased out by the U.S. government in the 1970s. If you have ever worked in a fast-food restaurant, you are likely to have encountered a price floor: governments in the United States and many other countries maintain a lower limit on the hourly wage rate of a worker's labor—that is, a floor on the price of labor—called the **minimum wage.**

Just like price ceilings, price floors are intended to help some people but generate predictable and undesirable side effects. Figure 8.3 shows hypothetical supply and demand

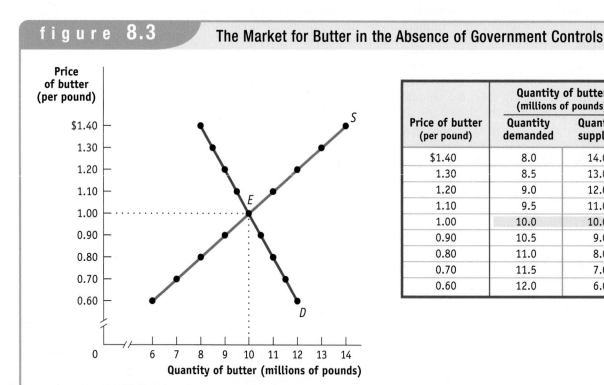

figure 8.3

The Market for Butter in the Absence of Government Controls

Price of butter (per pound)	Quantity of butter (millions of pounds)	
	Quantity demanded	Quantity supplied
$1.40	8.0	14.0
1.30	8.5	13.0
1.20	9.0	12.0
1.10	9.5	11.0
1.00	10.0	10.0
0.90	10.5	9.0
0.80	11.0	8.0
0.70	11.5	7.0
0.60	12.0	6.0

Without government intervention, the market for butter reaches equilibrium at a price of $1 per pound with 10 million pounds of butter bought and sold.

curves for butter. Left to itself, the market would move to equilibrium at point *E*, with 10 million pounds of butter bought and sold at a price of $1 per pound.

Now suppose that the government, in order to help dairy farmers, imposes a price floor on butter of $1.20 per pound. Its effects are shown in Figure 8.4, where the line at $1.20 represents the price floor. At a price of $1.20 per pound, producers would want to supply 12 million pounds (point *B* on the supply curve) but consumers would want to buy only 9 million pounds (point *A* on the demand curve). So the price floor leads to a persistent surplus of 3 million pounds of butter.

Does a price floor always lead to an unwanted surplus? No. Just as in the case of a price ceiling, the floor may not be binding—that is, it may be irrelevant. If the equilibrium price of butter is $1 per pound but the floor is set at only $0.80, the floor has no effect.

But suppose that a price floor *is* binding: what happens to the unwanted surplus? The answer depends on government policy. In the case of agricultural price floors, governments buy up unwanted surplus. As a result, the U.S. government has at times found itself warehousing thousands of tons of butter, cheese, and other farm products. (The European Commission, which administers price floors for a number of European countries, once found itself the owner of a so-called butter mountain, equal in weight to the entire population of Austria.) The government then has to find a way to dispose of these unwanted goods.

Some countries pay exporters to sell products at a loss overseas; this is standard procedure for the European Union. The United States gives surplus food away to schools, which use the products in school lunches. In some cases, governments have actually destroyed the surplus production. To avoid the problem of dealing with the unwanted surplus, the U.S. government typically pays farmers not to produce the products at all.

When the government is not prepared to purchase the unwanted surplus, a price floor means that would-be sellers cannot find buyers. This is what happens when there is a price floor on the wage rate paid for an hour of labor, the *minimum wage:* when the minimum wage is above the equilibrium wage rate, some people who are willing to work—that is, sell labor—cannot find buyers—that is, employers—willing to give them jobs.

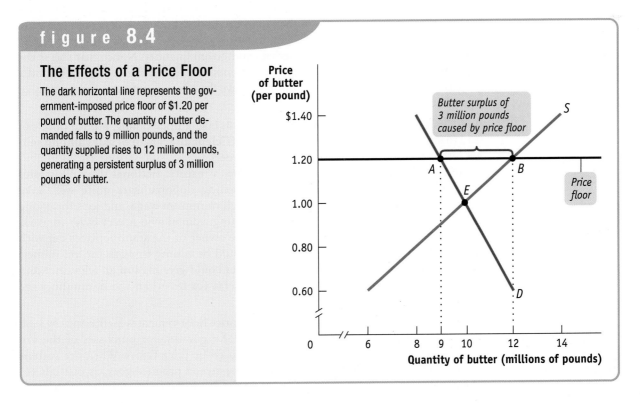

figure 8.4

The Effects of a Price Floor

The dark horizontal line represents the government-imposed price floor of $1.20 per pound of butter. The quantity of butter demanded falls to 9 million pounds, and the quantity supplied rises to 12 million pounds, generating a persistent surplus of 3 million pounds of butter.

Price Floors and School Lunches

When you were in grade school, did your school offer free or very cheap lunches? If so, you were probably a beneficiary of price floors.

Where did all the cheap food come from? During the 1930s, when the U.S. economy was going through the Great Depression, a prolonged economic slump, prices were low and farmers were suffering severely. In an effort to help rural Americans, the U.S. government imposed price floors on a number of agricultural products. The system of agricultural price floors—officially called price support programs—continues to this day. Among the products subject to price support are sugar and various dairy products; at times grains, beef, and pork have also had a minimum price.

The big problem with any attempt to impose a price floor is that it creates a surplus. To some extent the U.S. Department of Agriculture has tried to head off surpluses by taking steps to reduce supply; for example, by paying farmers *not* to grow crops. As a last resort, however, the U.S. government has been willing to buy up the surplus, taking the excess supply off the market.

But then what? The government has to find a way to get rid of the agricultural products it has bought. It can't just sell them: that would depress market prices, forcing the government to buy the stuff right back. So it has to give it away in ways that don't depress market prices. One of the ways it does this is by giving surplus food, free, to school lunch programs. These gifts are known as "bonus foods." Along with financial aid, bonus foods are what allow many school districts to provide free or very cheap lunches to their students. Is this a story with a happy ending?

Not really. Nutritionists, concerned about growing child obesity in the United States, place part of the blame on those bonus foods. Schools get whatever the government has too much of—and that has tended to include a lot of dairy products, beef, and corn, and not much in the way of fresh vegetables or fruit. As a result, school lunches that make extensive use of bonus foods tend to be very high in fat and calories. So this is a case in which there is such a thing as a free lunch— but this lunch may be bad for your health.

How a Price Floor Causes Inefficiency

The persistent surplus that results from a price floor creates missed opportunities— inefficiencies—that resemble those created by the shortage that results from a price ceiling.

Inefficiently Low Quantity Because a price floor raises the price of a good to consumers, it reduces the quantity of that good demanded; because sellers can't sell more units of a good than buyers are willing to buy, a price floor reduces the quantity of a good bought and sold below the market equilibrium quantity. Notice that this is the *same* effect as a price ceiling. You might be tempted to think that a price floor and a price ceiling have opposite effects, but both have the effect of reducing the quantity of a good bought and sold.

Inefficient Allocation of Sales Among Sellers Like a price ceiling, a price floor can lead to *inefficient allocation*—but in this case **inefficient allocation of sales among sellers** rather than inefficient allocation to consumers.

An episode from the Belgian movie *Rosetta,* a realistic fictional story, illustrates the problem of inefficient allocation of selling opportunities quite well. Like many European countries, Belgium has a high minimum wage, and jobs for young people are scarce. At one point Rosetta, a young woman who is very eager to work, loses her job at a fast-food stand because the owner of the stand replaces her with his son—a very reluctant worker. Rosetta would be willing to work for less money, and with the money he would save, the owner could give his son an allowance and let him do something else. But to hire Rosetta for less than the minimum wage would be illegal.

Wasted Resources Also like a price ceiling, a price floor generates inefficiency by *wasting resources*. The most graphic examples involve government purchases of the unwanted surpluses of agricultural products caused by price floors. When the surplus production is simply destroyed, and when the stored produce goes, as officials euphemistically put it, "out of condition" and must be thrown away, it is pure waste.

Price floors lead to **inefficient allocation of sales among sellers:** those who would be willing to sell the good at the lowest price are not always those who manage to sell it.

Price floors also lead to wasted time and effort. Consider the minimum wage. Would-be workers who spend many hours searching for jobs, or waiting in line in the hope of getting jobs, play the same role in the case of price floors as hapless families searching for apartments in the case of price ceilings.

Inefficiently High Quality Again like price ceilings, price floors lead to inefficiency in the quality of goods produced.

We've seen that when there is a price ceiling, suppliers produce goods that are of inefficiently low quality: buyers prefer higher-quality products and are willing to pay for them, but sellers refuse to improve the quality of their products because the price ceiling prevents their being compensated for doing so. This same logic applies to price floors, but in reverse: suppliers offer goods of **inefficiently high quality.**

Price floors often lead to inefficiency in that goods of **inefficiently high quality** are offered: sellers offer high-quality goods at a high price, even though buyers would prefer a lower quality at a lower price.

How can this be? Isn't high quality a good thing? Yes, but only if it is worth the cost. Suppose that suppliers spend a lot to make goods of very high quality but that this quality isn't worth much to consumers, who would rather receive the money spent on that quality in the form of a lower price. This represents a missed opportunity: suppliers and buyers could make a mutually beneficial deal in which buyers got goods of lower quality for a much lower price.

A good example of the inefficiency of excessive quality comes from the days when transatlantic airfares were set artificially high by international treaty. Forbidden to compete for customers by offering lower ticket prices, airlines instead offered expensive services, like lavish in-flight meals that went largely uneaten. At one point the regulators tried to restrict this practice by defining maximum service standards—for example, that snack service should consist of no more than a sandwich. One airline then introduced what it called a "Scandinavian Sandwich," a towering affair that forced the convening of another conference to define *sandwich*. All of this was wasteful, especially considering that what passengers really wanted was less food and lower airfares.

istockphoto

Since the deregulation of U.S. airlines in the 1970s, American passengers have experienced a large decrease in ticket prices accompanied by a decrease in the quality of in-flight service—smaller seats, lower-quality food, and so on. Everyone complains about the service—but thanks to lower fares, the number of people flying on U.S. carriers has grown several hundred percent since airline deregulation.

Illegal Activity Finally, like price ceilings, price floors provide incentives for illegal activity. For example, in countries where the minimum wage is far above the equilibrium wage rate, workers desperate for jobs sometimes agree to work off the books for employers who conceal their employment from the government—or bribe the government inspectors. This practice, known in Europe as "black labor," is especially common in southern European countries such as Italy and Spain.

So Why Are There Price Floors?

To sum up, a price floor creates various negative side effects:

- a persistent surplus of the good
- inefficiency arising from the persistent surplus in the form of inefficiently low quantity, inefficient allocation of sales among sellers, wasted resources, and an inefficiently high level of quality offered by suppliers
- the temptation to engage in illegal activity, particularly bribery and corruption of government officials

So why do governments impose price floors when they have so many negative side effects? The reasons are similar to those for imposing price ceilings. Government officials often disregard warnings about the consequences of price floors either because they believe that the relevant market is poorly described by the supply and demand model or, more often, because they do not understand the model. Above all, just as price ceilings are often imposed because they benefit some influential buyers of a good, price floors are often imposed because they benefit some influential sellers.

Solutions appear at the back of the book.

Check Your Understanding

1. On game days, homeowners near Middletown University's stadium used to rent parking spaces in their driveways to fans at a going rate of $11. A new town ordinance now sets a maximum parking fee of $7. Use the accompanying supply and demand diagram to explain how each of the following can result from the price ceiling.

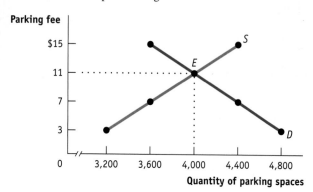

a. Some homeowners now think it's not worth the hassle to rent out spaces.

b. Some fans who used to carpool to the game now drive alone.

c. Some fans can't find parking and leave without seeing the game.

Explain how each of the following adverse effects arises from the price ceiling.

d. Some fans now arrive several hours early to find parking.

e. Friends of homeowners near the stadium regularly attend games, even if they aren't big fans. But some serious fans have given up because of the parking situation.

f. Some homeowners rent spaces for more than $7 but pretend that the buyers are nonpaying friends or family.

2. True or false? Explain your answer. A price ceiling below the equilibrium price in an otherwise efficient market does the following:

a. increases quantity supplied

b. makes some people who want to consume the good worse off

c. makes all producers worse off

3. The state legislature mandates a price floor for gasoline of P_F per gallon. Assess the following statements and illustrate your answer using the figure provided.

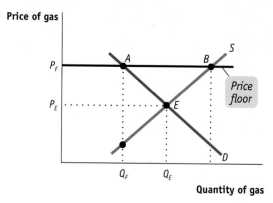

a. Proponents of the law claim it will increase the income of gas station owners. Opponents claim it will hurt gas station owners because they will lose customers.

b. Proponents claim consumers will be better off because gas stations will provide better service. Opponents claim consumers will be generally worse off because they prefer to buy gas at cheaper prices.

c. Proponents claim that they are helping gas station owners without hurting anyone else. Opponents claim that consumers are hurt and will end up doing things like buying gas in a nearby state or on the black market.

Tackle the Test: Multiple-Choice Questions

1. To be effective, a price ceiling must be set
   I. above the equilibrium price.
   II. in the housing market.
   III. to achieve the equilibrium market quantity.

   a. I
   b. II
   c. III
   d. I, II, and III
   e. None of the above

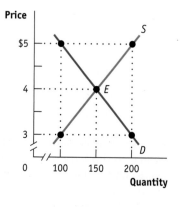

2. Refer to the graph provided. A price floor set at $5 will result in
   a. a shortage of 100 units.
   b. a surplus of 100 units.
   c. a shortage of 200 units.
   d. a surplus of 200 units.
   e. a surplus of 50 units.

3. Effective price ceilings are inefficient because they
   a. create shortages.
   b. lead to wasted resources.
   c. decrease quality.
   d. create black markets.
   e. do all of the above.

4. Refer to the graph provided. If the government establishes a minimum wage at $10, how many workers will benefit from the higher wage?

   a. 30
   b. 50
   c. 60
   d. 80
   e. 110

5. Refer to the graph for question 4. With a minimum wage of $10, how many workers are unemployed (would like to work, but are unable to find a job)?
   a. 30
   b. 50
   c. 60
   d. 80
   e. 110

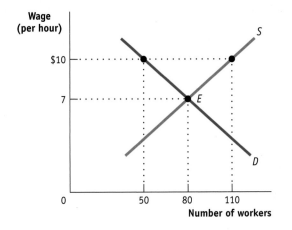

Tackle the Test: Free-Response Questions

1. Refer to the graph provided to answer the following questions.

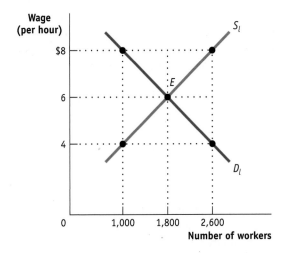

   a. What are the equilibrium wage and quantity of workers in this market?
   b. For it to be effective, where would the government have to set a minimum wage?
   c. If the government set a minimum wage at $8,

   i.   how many workers would supply their labor?
   ii. how many workers would be hired?
   iii. how many workers would want to work that did *not* want to work for the equilibrium wage?
   iv. how many previously employed workers would no longer have a job?

   Answer (6 points)

   1 point: wage = $6, quantity of labor = 1,800

   1 point: anywhere above $6

   1 point: 2,600 workers would supply their labor

   1 point: 1,000 workers would be hired

   1 point: 800 (the number of workers who would want to work for $8 but did not supply labor for $6)

   1 point: 800 (at equilibrium, 1,800 workers were hired, at a wage of $8, 1,000 workers would be hired. 1,800 − 1,000 = 800)

2. Draw a correctly labeled graph of a housing market in equilibrium. On your graph, illustrate an effective legal limit (ceiling) on rent. Identify the quantity of housing demanded, the quantity of housing supplied, and the size of the resulting surplus or shortage.

- The meaning of quantity controls, another way government intervenes in markets

- How quantity controls create problems and can make a market inefficient

- Who benefits and who loses from quantity controls, and why they are used despite their well-known problems

Module 9
Supply and Demand: Quantity Controls

Controlling Quantities

In the 1930s, New York City instituted a system of licensing for taxicabs: only taxis with a "medallion" were allowed to pick up passengers. Because this system was intended to ensure quality, medallion owners were supposed to maintain certain standards, including safety and cleanliness. A total of 11,787 medallions were issued, with taxi owners paying $10 for each medallion.

In 1995, there were still only 11,787 licensed taxicabs in New York, even though the city had meanwhile become the financial capital of the world, a place where hundreds of thousands of people in a hurry tried to hail a cab every day. (An additional 400 medallions were issued in 1995, and after several rounds of sales of additional medallions, today there are 13,257 medallions.)

The result of this restriction on the number of taxis was that a New York City taxi medallion became very valuable: if you wanted to operate a taxi in New York, you had to lease a medallion from someone else or buy one for a going price of several hundred thousand dollars.

It turns out that this story is not unique; other cities introduced similar medallion systems in the 1930s and, like New York, have issued few new medallions since. In San Francisco and Boston, as in New York, taxi medallions trade for six-figure prices.

A taxi medallion system is a form of **quantity control,** or **quota,** by which the government regulates the quantity of a good that can be bought and sold rather than regulating the price. Typically, the government limits quantity in a market by issuing **licenses;** only people with a license can legally supply the good. A taxi medallion is just such a license. The government of New York City limits the number of taxi rides that can be sold by limiting the number of taxis to only those who hold medallions. There are many other cases of quantity controls, ranging from limits on how much foreign currency (for instance, British pounds or Mexican pesos) people are allowed to buy to the quantity of clams New Jersey fishing boats are allowed to catch.

A **quantity control,** or **quota,** is an upper limit on the quantity of some good that can be bought or sold.

A **license** gives its owner the right to supply a good or service.

Some attempts to control quantities are undertaken for good economic reasons, some for bad ones. In many cases, as we will see, quantity controls introduced to address a temporary problem become politically hard to remove later because the beneficiaries don't want them abolished, even after the original reason for their existence is long gone. But whatever the reasons for such controls, they have certain predictable—and usually undesirable—economic consequences.

The **demand price** of a given quantity is the price at which consumers will demand that quantity.

The Anatomy of Quantity Controls

To understand why a New York taxi medallion is worth so much money, we consider a simplified version of the market for taxi rides, shown in Figure 9.1. Just as we assumed in the analysis of rent control that all apartments were the same, we now suppose that all taxi rides are the same—ignoring the real-world complication that some taxi rides are longer, and so more expensive, than others. The table in the figure shows supply and demand schedules. The equilibrium—indicated by point E in the figure and by the shaded entries in the table—is a fare of $5 per ride, with 10 million rides taken per year. (You'll see in a minute why we present the equilibrium this way.)

The New York medallion system limits the number of taxis, but each taxi driver can offer as many rides as he or she can manage. (Now you know why New York taxi drivers are so aggressive!) To simplify our analysis, however, we will assume that a medallion system limits the number of taxi rides that can legally be given to 8 million per year.

Until now, we have derived the demand curve by answering questions of the form: "How many taxi rides will passengers want to take if the price is $5 per ride?" But it is possible to reverse the question and ask instead: "At what price will consumers want to buy 10 million rides per year?" The price at which consumers want to buy a given quantity—in this case, 10 million rides at $5 per ride—is the **demand price** of that

---

figure 9.1   The Market for Taxi Rides in the Absence of Government Controls

Fare (per ride)	Quantity of rides (millions per year)	
	Quantity demanded	Quantity supplied
$7.00	6	14
6.50	7	13
6.00	8	12
5.50	9	11
5.00	10	10
4.50	11	9
4.00	12	8
3.50	13	7
3.00	14	6

Without government intervention, the market reaches equilibrium with 10 million rides taken per year at a fare of $5 per ride.

The **supply price** of a given quantity is the price at which producers will supply that quantity.

quantity. You can see from the demand schedule in Figure 9.1 that the demand price of 6 million rides is $7 per ride, the demand price of 7 million rides is $6.50 per ride, and so on.

Similarly, the supply curve represents the answer to questions of the form: "How many taxi rides would taxi drivers supply at a price of $5 each?" But we can also reverse this question to ask: "At what price will producers be willing to supply 10 million rides per year?" The price at which producers will supply a given quantity—in this case, 10 million rides at $5 per ride—is the **supply price** of that quantity. We can see from the supply schedule in Figure 9.1 that the supply price of 6 million rides is $3 per ride, the supply price of 7 million rides is $3.50 per ride, and so on.

Now we are ready to analyze a quota. We have assumed that the city government limits the quantity of taxi rides to 8 million per year. Medallions, each of which carries the right to provide a certain number of taxi rides per year, are made available to selected people in such a way that a total of 8 million rides will be provided. Medallion holders may then either drive their own taxis or rent their medallions to others for a fee.

Figure 9.2 shows the resulting market for taxi rides, with the black vertical line at 8 million rides per year representing the quota. Because the quantity of rides is limited to 8 million, consumers must be at point *A* on the demand curve, corresponding to the shaded entry in the demand schedule: the demand price of 8 million rides is $6 per ride. Meanwhile, taxi drivers must be at point *B* on the supply curve, corresponding to the shaded entry in the supply schedule: the supply price of 8 million rides is $4 per ride.

But how can the price received by taxi drivers be $4 when the price paid by taxi riders is $6? The answer is that in addition to the market in taxi rides, there is also a market in medallions. Medallion-holders may not always want to drive their taxis: they

figure 9.2   Effect of a Quota on the Market for Taxi Rides

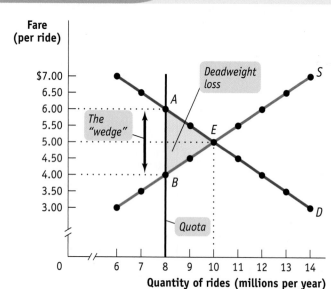

Fare (per ride)	Quantity of rides (millions per year)	
	Quantity demanded	Quantity supplied
$7.00	6	14
6.50	7	13
6.00	8	12
5.50	9	11
5.00	10	10
4.50	11	9
4.00	12	8
3.50	13	7
3.00	14	6

The table shows the demand price and the supply price corresponding to each quantity: the price at which that quantity would be demanded and supplied, respectively. The city government imposes a quota of 8 million rides by selling enough medallions for only 8 million rides, represented by the black vertical line. The price paid by consumers rises to $6 per ride, the demand price of 8 million rides, shown by point *A*. The sup-

ply price of 8 million rides is only $4 per ride, shown by point *B*. The difference between these two prices is the quota rent per ride, the earnings that accrue to the owner of a medallion. The quota rent drives a wedge between the demand price and the supply price. Because the quota discourages mutually beneficial transactions, it creates a deadweight loss equal to the shaded triangle.

may be ill or on vacation. Those who do not want to drive their own taxis will sell the right to use the medallion to someone else. So we need to consider two sets of transactions here, and so two prices: (1) the transactions in taxi rides and the price at which these will occur and (2) the transactions in medallions and the price at which these will occur. It turns out that since we are looking at two markets, the $4 and $6 prices will both be right.

To see how this all works, consider two imaginary New York taxi drivers, Sunil and Harriet. Sunil has a medallion but can't use it because he's recovering from a severely sprained wrist. So he's looking to rent his medallion out to someone else. Harriet doesn't have a medallion but would like to rent one. Furthermore, at any point in time there are many other people like Harriet who would like to rent a medallion. Suppose Sunil agrees to rent his medallion to Harriet. To make things simple, assume that any driver can give only one ride per day and that Sunil is renting his medallion to Harriet for one day. What rental price will they agree on?

To answer this question, we need to look at the transactions from the viewpoints of both drivers. Once she has the medallion, Harriet knows she can make $6 per day—the demand price of a ride under the quota. And she is willing to rent the medallion only if she makes at least $4 per day—the supply price of a ride under the quota. So Sunil cannot demand a rent of more than $2—the difference between $6 and $4. And if Harriet offered Sunil less than $2—say, $1.50—there would be other eager drivers willing to offer him more, up to $2. So, in order to get the medallion, Harriet must offer Sunil at least $2. Since the rent can be no more than $2 and no less than $2, it must be exactly $2.

It is no coincidence that $2 is exactly the difference between $6, the demand price of 8 million rides, and $4, the supply price of 8 million rides. In every case in which the supply of a good is legally restricted, there is a **wedge** between the demand price of the quantity transacted and the supply price of the quantity transacted. This wedge, illustrated by the double-headed arrow in Figure 9.2, has a special name: the **quota rent.** It is the earnings that accrue to the medallion holder from ownership of a valuable commodity, the medallion. In the case of Sunil and Harriet, the quota rent of $2 goes to Sunil because he owns the medallion, and the remaining $4 from the total fare of $6 goes to Harriet.

So Figure 9.2 also illustrates the quota rent in the market for New York taxi rides. The quota limits the quantity of rides to 8 million per year, a quantity at which the demand price of $6 exceeds the supply price of $4. The wedge between these two prices, $2, is the quota rent that results from the restrictions placed on the quantity of taxi rides in this market.

But wait a second. What if Sunil doesn't rent out his medallion? What if he uses it himself? Doesn't this mean that he gets a price of $6? No, not really. Even if Sunil doesn't rent out his medallion, he could have rented it out, which means that the medallion has an *opportunity cost* of $2: if Sunil decides to use his own medallion and drive his own taxi rather than renting his medallion to Harriet, the $2 represents his opportunity cost of not renting out his medallion. That is, the $2 quota rent is now the rental income he forgoes by driving his own taxi. In effect, Sunil is in two businesses—the taxi-driving business and the medallion-renting business. He makes $4 per ride from driving his taxi and $2 per ride from renting out his medallion. It doesn't make any difference that in this particular case he has rented his medallion to himself! So regardless of whether the medallion owner uses the medallion himself or herself, or rents it to others, it is a valuable asset. And this is represented in the going price for a New York City taxi medallion. Notice, by the way, that quotas—like price ceilings and price floors—don't always have a real effect. If the quota were set at 12 million rides—that is, above the equilibrium quantity in an unregulated market—it would have no effect because it would not be binding.

A quantity control, or quota, drives a **wedge** between the demand price and the supply price of a good; that is, the price paid by buyers ends up being higher than that received by sellers. The difference between the demand and supply price at the quota amount is the **quota rent,** the earnings that accrue to the license-holder from ownership of the right to sell the good. It is equal to the market price of the license when the licenses are traded.

PNI Ltd./Picture Quest

New York City: An empty cab is hard to find.

is the lost gains associated with transactions that do not occur due to market intervention.

The Costs of Quantity Controls

Like price controls, quantity controls can have some predictable and undesirable side effects. The first is the by-now-familiar problem of inefficiency due to missed opportunities: quantity controls prevent mutually beneficial transactions from occurring, transactions that would benefit both buyers and sellers. Looking back at Figure 9.2, you can see that starting at the quota of 8 million rides, New Yorkers would be willing to pay at least $5.50 per ride for an additional 1 million rides and that taxi drivers would be willing to provide those rides as long as they got at least $4.50 per ride. These are rides that would have taken place if there had been no quota. The same is true for the next 1 million rides: New Yorkers would be willing to pay at least $5 per ride when the quantity of rides is increased from 9 to 10 million, and taxi drivers would be willing to provide those rides as long as they got at least $5 per ride. Again, these rides would have occurred without the quota. Only when the market has reached the unregulated market equilibrium quantity of 10 million rides are there no "missed-opportunity rides"—the quota of 8 million rides has caused 2 million "missed-opportunity rides." A buyer would be willing to buy the good at a price that the seller would be willing to accept, but such a transaction does not occur because it is forbidden by the quota. Economists have a special term for the lost gains from missed opportunities such as these: **deadweight loss.** Generally, when the demand price exceeds the supply price, there is a deadweight loss. Figure 9.2 illustrates the deadweight loss with a shaded triangle between the demand and supply curves. This triangle represents the missed gains from taxi rides prevented by the quota, a loss that is experienced by both disappointed would-be riders and frustrated would-be drivers.

Because there are transactions that people would like to make but are not allowed to, quantity controls generate an incentive to evade them or even to break the law. New York's taxi industry again provides clear examples. Taxi regulation applies only to those drivers who are hailed by passengers on the street. A car service that makes prearranged pickups does not need a medallion. As a result, such hired cars provide much of the service that might otherwise be provided by taxis, as in other cities. In addition, there are substantial numbers of unlicensed cabs that simply defy the law by picking up passengers without a medallion. Because these cabs are illegal, their drivers are completely unregulated, and they generate a disproportionately large share of traffic accidents in New York City.

The Clams of New Jersey

Forget the refineries along the Jersey Turnpike; one industry that New Jersey *really* dominates is clam fishing. In 2005 the Garden State supplied 71% of the country's surf clams, whose tongues are used in fried-clam dinners, and 92% of the quahogs, which are used to make clam chowder.

In the 1980s, however, excessive fishing threatened to wipe out New Jersey's clam beds. To save the resource, the U.S. government introduced a clam quota, which sets an overall limit on the number of bushels of clams that may be caught and allocates licenses to owners of fishing boats based on their historical catches.

A fried clam feast is a favorite on the Jersey shore.

Notice, by the way, that this is an example of a quota that is probably justified by broader economic and environmental considerations—

unlike the New York taxicab quota, which has long since lost any economic rationale. Still, whatever its rationale, the New Jersey clam quota works the same way as any other quota.

Once the quota system was established, many boat owners stopped fishing for clams. They realized that rather than operate a boat part time, it was more profitable to sell or rent their licenses to someone else, who could then assemble enough licenses to operate a boat full time. Today, there are about 50 New Jersey boats fishing for clams; the license required to operate one is worth more than the boat itself.

In fact, in 2004 the hardships caused by the limited number of New York taxis led city leaders to authorize an increase in the number of licensed taxis. In a series of sales, the city sold more than 1,000 new medallions, to bring the total number up to the current 13,257 medallions—a move that certainly cheered New York riders. But those who already owned medallions were less happy with the increase; they understood that the nearly 1,000 new taxis would reduce or eliminate the shortage of taxis. As a result, taxi drivers anticipated a decline in their revenues as they would no longer always be assured of finding willing customers. And, in turn, the value of a medallion would fall. So to placate the medallion owners, city officials also raised taxi fares: by 25% in 2004, and again—by a smaller percentage—in 2006. Although taxis are now easier to find, a ride now costs more—and that price increase slightly diminished the newfound cheer of New York taxi riders.

Module 9 AP Review

Solutions appear at the back of the book.

Check Your Understanding

1. Suppose that the supply and demand for taxi rides is given by Figure 9.1 and a quota is set at 6 million rides. Replicate the graph from Figure 9.1, and identify each of the following on your graph:
   a. the price of a ride
   b. the quota rent
   c. the deadweight loss resulting from the quota

Suppose the quota on taxi rides is increased to 9 million.
   d. What happens to the quota rent and the deadweight loss?

2. Again replicate the graph from Figure 9.1. Suppose that the quota is 8 million rides and that demand decreases due to a decline in tourism. Show on your graph the smallest parallel leftward shift in demand that would result in the quota no longer having an effect on the market.

Tackle the Test: Multiple-Choice Questions

Refer to the graph provided for questions 1–3.

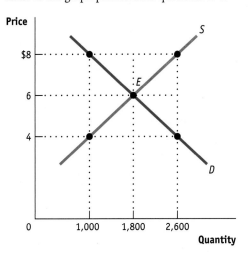

1. If the government established a quota of 1,000 in this market, the demand price would be
   a. less than $4.
   b. $4.
   c. $6.
   d. $8.
   e. more than $8.

2. If the government established a quota of 1,000 in this market, the supply price would be
   a. less than $4.
   b. $4.
   c. $6.
   d. $8.
   e. more than $8.

3. If the government established a quota of 1,000 in this market, the quota rent would be
   a. $2.
   b. $4.
   c. $6.
   d. $8.
   e. more than $8.

4. Quotas lead to which of the following?
   I. inefficiency due to missed opportunities
   II. incentives to evade or break the law
   III. a surplus in the market
   a. I
   b. II
   c. III
   d. I and II
   e. I, II, and III

5. Which of the following would decrease the effect of a quota on a market? A(n)
   a. decrease in demand
   b. increase in supply
   c. increase in demand
   d. price ceiling above the equilibrium price
   e. none of the above

Tackle the Test: Free-Response Questions

1. Draw a correctly labeled graph illustrating hypothetical supply and demand curves for the U.S. automobile market. Label the equilibrium price and quantity. Suppose the government institutes a quota to limit automobile production. Draw a vertical line labeled "$Q_{ineffective}$" to show the level of a quota that would have no effect on the market. Draw a vertical line labeled "$Q_{effective}$" to show the level of a quota that would have an effect on the market. Shade in and label the deadweight loss resulting from the effective quota.

2. Draw a correctly labeled graph of the market for taxicab rides. On the graph, draw and label a vertical line showing the level of an effective quota. Label the demand price, the supply price, and the quota rent.

Answer (5 points)

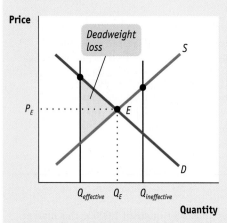

1 point: Correctly labeled supply and demand diagram (vertical axis labeled "Price" or "P," horizontal axis labeled "Quantity" or "Q," upward sloping supply curve with label, downward sloping demand curve with label)

1 point: Equilibrium at the intersection of supply and demand with the equilibrium price labeled on the vertical axis and the equilibrium quantity labeled on the horizontal axis

1 point: Vertical line to the right of equilibrium quantity labeled $Q_{ineffective}$

1 point: Vertical line to the left of equilibrium quantity labeled $Q_{effective}$

1 point: The triangle to the right of the effective quota line and to the left of supply and demand shaded in and labeled as the deadweight loss

---

Section ② Review

Summary

1. The **supply and demand model** illustrates how a **competitive market,** one with many buyers and sellers of the same product, works.

2. The **demand schedule** shows the **quantity demanded** at each price and is represented graphically by a **demand curve.** The **law of demand** says that demand

curves slope downward, meaning that as price decreases, the quantity demanded increases.

3. A **movement along the demand curve** occurs when the price changes and causes a change in the quantity demanded. When economists talk of **changes in demand,** they mean shifts of the demand curve—a change in the quantity demanded at any given price. An increase in demand causes a rightward shift of the demand curve. A decrease in demand causes a leftward shift.

4. There are five main factors that shift the demand curve:
   - A change in the prices of related goods, such as **substitutes** or **complements**
   - A change in income: when income rises, the demand for **normal goods** increases and the demand for **inferior goods** decreases
   - A change in tastes
   - A change in expectations
   - A change in the number of consumers

5. The **supply schedule** shows the **quantity supplied** at each price and is represented graphically by a **supply curve.** Supply curves usually slope upward.

6. A **movement along the supply curve** occurs when the price changes and causes a change in the quantity supplied. When economists talk of **changes in supply,** they mean shifts of the supply curve—a change in the quantity supplied at any given price. An increase in supply causes a rightward shift of the supply curve. A decrease in supply causes a leftward shift.

7. There are five main factors that shift the supply curve:
   - A change in **input** prices
   - A change in the prices of related goods and services
   - A change in technology
   - A change in expectations
   - A change in the number of producers

8. The supply and demand model is based on the principle that the price in a market moves to its **equilibrium price,** or **market-clearing price,** the price at which the quantity demanded is equal to the quantity supplied. This quantity is the **equilibrium quantity.** When the price is above its market-clearing level, there is a **surplus** that pushes the price down. When the price is below its market-clearing level, there is a **shortage** that pushes the price up.

9. An increase in demand increases both the equilibrium price and the equilibrium quantity; a decrease in demand has the opposite effect. An increase in supply reduces the equilibrium price and increases the equilibrium quantity; a decrease in supply has the opposite effect.

10. Shifts of the demand curve and the supply curve can happen simultaneously. When they shift in opposite directions, the change in price is predictable but the change in quantity is not. When they shift in the same direction, the change in quantity is predictable but the change in price is not. In general, the curve that shifts the greater distance has a greater effect on the changes in price and quantity.

11. Even when a market is efficient, governments often intervene to pursue greater fairness or to please a powerful interest group. Interventions can take the form of **price controls** or **quantity controls,** both of which generate predictable and undesirable side effects, consisting of various forms of inefficiency and illegal activity.

12. A **price ceiling,** a maximum market price below the equilibrium price, benefits successful buyers but creates persistent shortages. Because the price is maintained below the equilibrium price, the quantity demanded is increased and the quantity supplied is decreased compared to the equilibrium quantity. This leads to predictable problems including **inefficient allocation to consumers, wasted resources,** and **inefficiently low quality.** It also encourages illegal activity as people turn to **black markets** to get the good. Because of these problems, price ceilings have generally lost favor as an economic policy tool. But some governments continue to impose them either because they don't understand the effects or because the price ceilings benefit some influential group.

13. A **price floor,** a minimum market price above the equilibrium price, benefits successful sellers but creates a persistent surplus: because the price is maintained above the equilibrium price, the quantity demanded is decreased and the quantity supplied is increased compared to the equilibrium quantity. This leads to predictable problems: inefficiencies in the form of **inefficient allocation of sales among sellers,** wasted resources, and **inefficiently high quality.** It also encourages illegal activity and black markets. The most well known kind of price floor is the **minimum wage,** but price floors are also commonly applied to agricultural products.

14. Quantity controls, or **quotas,** limit the quantity of a good that can be bought or sold. The government issues **licenses** to individuals, the right to sell a given quantity of the good. The owner of a license earns a **quota rent,** earnings that accrue from ownership of the right to sell the good. It is equal to the difference between the **demand price** at the quota amount, what consumers are willing to pay for that amount, and the **supply price** at the quota amount, what suppliers are willing to accept for that amount. Economists say that a quota drives a **wedge** between the demand price and the supply price; this wedge is equal to the quota rent. By limiting mutually beneficial transactions, quantity controls generate inefficiency. Like price controls, quantity controls lead to **deadweight loss** and encourage illegal activity.

Key Terms

Problems

1. A survey indicated that chocolate ice cream is America's favorite ice-cream flavor. For each of the following, indicate the possible effects on the demand and/or supply, equilibrium price, and equilibrium quantity of chocolate ice cream.

   a. A severe drought in the Midwest causes dairy farmers to reduce the number of milk-producing cows in their herds by a third. These dairy farmers supply cream that is used to manufacture chocolate ice cream.

   b. A new report by the American Medical Association reveals that chocolate does, in fact, have significant health benefits.

   c. The discovery of cheaper synthetic vanilla flavoring lowers the price of vanilla ice cream.

   d. New technology for mixing and freezing ice cream lowers manufacturers' costs of producing chocolate ice cream.

2. In a supply and demand diagram, draw the change in demand for hamburgers in your hometown due to the following events. In each case show the effect on equilibrium price and quantity.

   a. The price of tacos increases.

   b. All hamburger sellers raise the price of their french fries.

   c. Income falls in town. Assume that hamburgers are a normal good for most people.

   d. Income falls in town. Assume that hamburgers are an inferior good for most people.

   e. Hot dog stands cut the price of hot dogs.

3. The market for many goods changes in predictable ways according to the time of year, in response to events such as holidays, vacation times, seasonal changes in production, and so on. Using supply and demand, explain the change in price in each of the following cases. Note that supply and demand may shift simultaneously.

   a. Lobster prices usually fall during the summer peak harvest season, despite the fact that people like to eat lobster during the summer months more than during any other time of year.

   b. The price of a Christmas tree is lower after Christmas than before and fewer trees are sold.

   c. The price of a round-trip ticket to Paris on Air France falls by more than $200 after the end of school vacation in September. This happens despite the fact that generally worsening weather increases the cost of operating flights to Paris, and Air France therefore reduces the number of flights to Paris at any given price.

4. Show in a diagram the effect on the demand curve, the supply curve, the equilibrium price, and the equilibrium quantity of each of the following events on the designated market.

   a. the market for newspapers in your town
   Case 1: The salaries of journalists go up.
   Case 2: There is a big news event in your town, which is reported in the newspapers, and residents want to learn more about it.

   b. the market for St. Louis Rams cotton T-shirts
   Case 1: The Rams win the national championship.
   Case 2: The price of cotton increases.

   c. the market for bagels
   Case 1: People realize how fattening bagels are.
   Case 2: People have less time to make themselves a cooked breakfast.

5. Find the flaws in reasoning in the following statements, paying particular attention to the distinction between changes in and movements along the supply and demand curves. Draw a diagram to illustrate what actually happens in each situation.

   a. "A technological innovation that lowers the cost of producing a good might seem at first to result in a reduction in the price of the good to consumers. But a fall in price will increase demand for the good, and higher demand will send the price up again. It is not certain, therefore, that an innovation will really reduce price in the end."

b. "A study shows that eating a clove of garlic a day can help prevent heart disease, causing many consumers to demand more garlic. This increase in demand results in a rise in the price of garlic. Consumers, seeing that the price of garlic has gone up, reduce their demand for garlic. This causes the demand for garlic to decrease and the price of garlic to fall. Therefore, the ultimate effect of the study on the price of garlic is uncertain."

6. In *Rolling Stone* magazine, several fans and rock stars, including Pearl Jam, were bemoaning the high price of concert tickets. One superstar argued, "It just isn't worth $75 to see me play. No one should have to pay that much to go to a concert." Assume this star sold out arenas around the country at an average ticket price of $75.

a. How would you evaluate the arguments that ticket prices are too high?

b. Suppose that due to this star's protests, ticket prices were lowered to $50. In what sense is this price too low? Draw a diagram using supply and demand curves to support your argument.

c. Suppose Pearl Jam really wanted to bring down ticket prices. Since the band controls the supply of its services, what do you recommend they do? Explain using a supply and demand diagram.

d. Suppose the band's next CD was a total dud. Do you think they would still have to worry about ticket prices being too high? Why or why not? Draw a supply and demand diagram to support your argument.

e. Suppose the group announced their next tour was going to be their last. What effect would this likely have on the demand for and price of tickets? Illustrate with a supply and demand diagram.

7. After several years of decline, the market for handmade acoustic guitars is making a comeback. These guitars are usually made in small workshops employing relatively few highly skilled luthiers. Assess the impact on the equilibrium price and quantity of handmade acoustic guitars as a result of each of the following events. In your answers, indicate which curve(s) shift(s) and in which direction.

a. Environmentalists succeed in having the use of Brazilian rosewood banned in the United States, forcing luthiers to seek out alternative, more costly woods.

b. A foreign producer reengineers the guitar-making process and floods the market with identical guitars.

c. Music featuring handmade acoustic guitars makes a comeback as audiences tire of heavy metal and grunge music.

d. The country goes into a deep recession and the income of the average American falls sharply.

8. Will Shakespeare is a struggling playwright in sixteenth-century London. As the price he receives for writing a play increases, he is willing to write more plays. For the following situations, use a diagram to illustrate how each event affects the equilibrium price and quantity in the market for Shakespeare's plays.

a. The playwright Christopher Marlowe, Shakespeare's chief rival, is killed in a bar brawl.

b. The bubonic plague, a deadly infectious disease, breaks out in London.

c. To celebrate the defeat of the Spanish Armada, Queen Elizabeth declares several weeks of festivities, which involves commissioning new plays.

9. The small town of Middling experiences a sudden doubling of the birth rate. After three years, the birth rate returns to normal. Use a diagram to illustrate the effect of these events on the following:

a. the market for an hour of babysitting services in Middling today

b. the market for an hour of babysitting services 14 years into the future, after the birth rate has returned to normal, by which time children born today are old enough to work as babysitters

c. the market for an hour of babysitting services 30 years into the future, when children born today are likely to be having children of their own

10. Use a diagram to illustrate how each of the following events affects the equilibrium price and quantity of pizza.

a. The price of mozzarella cheese rises.

b. The health hazards of hamburgers are widely publicized.

c. The price of tomato sauce falls.

d. The incomes of consumers rise and pizza is an inferior good.

e. Consumers expect the price of pizza to fall next week.

11. Although he was a prolific artist, Pablo Picasso painted only 1,000 canvases during his "Blue Period." Picasso is now dead, and all of his Blue Period works are currently on display in museums and private galleries throughout Europe and the United States.

a. Draw a supply curve for Picasso Blue Period works. Why is this supply curve different from ones you have seen?

b. Given the supply curve from part a, the price of a Picasso Blue Period work will be entirely dependent on what factor(s)? Draw a diagram showing how the equilibrium price of such a work is determined.

c. Suppose that rich art collectors decide that it is essential to acquire Picasso Blue Period art for their collections. Show the impact of this on the market for these paintings.

12. Draw the appropriate curve in each of the following cases. Is it like or unlike the curves you have seen so far? Explain.

a. the demand for cardiac bypass surgery, given that the government pays the full cost for any patient

b. the demand for elective cosmetic plastic surgery, given that the patient pays the full cost

c. the supply of Rembrandt paintings

d. the supply of reproductions of Rembrandt paintings

13. Suppose it is decided that rent control in New York City will be abolished and that market rents will now prevail. Assume that all rental units are identical and are therefore offered at the same rent. To address the plight of residents who may be unable to pay the market rent, an income supplement will be paid to all low-income households equal to the difference between the old controlled rent and the new market rent.

a. Use a diagram to show the effect on the rental market of the elimination of rent control. What will happen to the quality and quantity of rental housing supplied?

b. Now use a second diagram to show the additional effect of the income-supplement policy on the market. What effect does it have on the market rent and quantity of rental housing supplied in comparison to your answers to part a?

c. Are tenants better or worse off as a result of these policies? Are landlords better or worse off?

d. From a political standpoint, why do you think cities have been more likely to resort to rent control rather than a policy of income supplements to help low-income people pay for housing?

14. In the late eighteenth century, the price of bread in New York City was controlled, set at a predetermined price above the market price.

a. Draw a diagram showing the effect of the policy. Did the policy act as a price ceiling or a price floor?

b. What kinds of inefficiencies were likely to have arisen when the controlled price of bread was above the market price? Explain in detail.

One year during this period, a poor wheat harvest caused a leftward shift in the supply of bread and therefore an increase in its market price. New York bakers found that the controlled price of bread in New York was below the market price.

c. Draw a diagram showing the effect of the price control on the market for bread during this one-year period. Did the policy act as a price ceiling or a price floor?

d. What kinds of inefficiencies do you think occurred during this period? Explain in detail.

15. Suppose the U.S. government decides that the incomes of dairy farmers should be maintained at a level that allows the traditional family dairy farm to survive. It therefore implements a price floor of $1 per pint by buying surplus milk until the market price is $1 per pint. Use the accompanying diagram to answer the following questions.

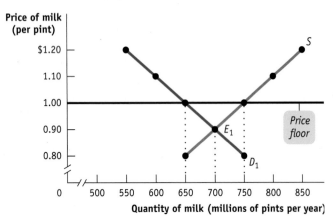

a. How much surplus milk will be produced as a result of this policy?

b. What will be the cost to the government of this policy?

c. Since milk is an important source of protein and calcium, the government decides to provide the surplus milk it purchases to elementary schools at a price of only $0.60 per pint. Assume that schools will buy any amount of milk available at this low price. But parents now reduce their purchases of milk at any price by 50 million pints per year because they

know their children are getting milk at school. How much will the dairy program now cost the government?

d. Give two examples of inefficiencies arising from wasted resources that are likely to result from this policy. What is the missed opportunity in each case?

16. As noted in the text, European governments tend to make greater use of price controls than does the U.S. government. For example, the French government sets minimum starting yearly wages for new hires who have completed *le bac*, certification roughly equivalent to a high school diploma. The demand schedule for new hires with *le bac* and the supply schedule for similarly credentialed new job seekers are given in the accompanying table. The price here—given in euros, the currency used in France—is the same as the yearly wage.

Wage (per year)	Quantity demanded (new job offers per year)	Quantity supplied (new job seekers per year)
€45,000	200,000	325,000
40,000	220,000	320,000
35,000	250,000	310,000
30,000	290,000	290,000
25,000	370,000	200,000

a. In the absence of government interference, what is the equilibrium wage and number of graduates hired per year? Illustrate with a diagram. Will there be anyone seeking a job at the equilibrium wage who is unable to find one—that is, will there be anyone who is involuntarily unemployed?

b. Suppose the French government sets a minimum yearly wage of 35,000 euros. Is there any involuntary unemployment at this wage? If so, how much? Illustrate with a diagram. What if the minimum wage is set at 40,000 euros? Also illustrate with a diagram.

c. Given your answer to part b and the information in the table, what do you think is the relationship between the level of involuntary unemployment and the level of the minimum wage? Who benefits from such a policy? Who loses? What is the missed opportunity here?

17. Until recently, the standard number of hours worked per week for a full-time job in France was 39 hours, similar to in the United States. But in response to social unrest over high levels of involuntary unemployment, the French government instituted a 35-hour workweek—a worker could not work more than 35 hours per week even if both the worker and employer wanted it. The motivation behind this policy was that if current employees worked fewer hours, employers would be forced to hire more new workers. Assume that it is costly for employers to train new workers. French employers were greatly opposed to this policy and threatened to move their operations to neighboring countries that did not have such employment restrictions. Can you explain their attitude? Give an example of both an inefficiency and an illegal activity that are likely to arise from this policy.

18. For the last 70 years, the U.S. government has used price supports to provide income assistance to U.S. farmers. At times the government has used price floors, which it maintains by

buying up the surplus farm products. At other times, it has used target prices, giving the farmer an amount equal to the difference between the market price and the target price for each unit sold. Use the accompanying diagram to answer the following questions.

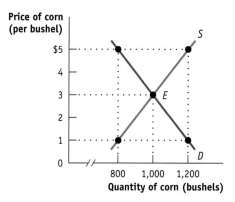

a. If the government sets a price floor of $5 per bushel, how many bushels of corn are produced? How many are purchased by consumers? by the government? How much does the program cost the government? How much revenue do corn farmers receive?

b. Suppose the government sets a target price of $5 per bushel for any quantity supplied up to 1,000 bushels. How many bushels of corn are purchased by consumers and at what price? by the government? How much does the program cost the government? How much revenue do corn farmers receive?

c. Which of these programs (in parts a and b) costs corn consumers more? Which program costs the government more? Explain.

d. What are the inefficiencies that arise in each of these cases (parts a and b)?

19. The waters off the north Atlantic coast were once teeming with fish. Now, due to overfishing by the commercial fishing industry, the stocks of fish are seriously depleted. In 1991, the National Marine Fishery Service of the U.S. government implemented a quota to allow fish stocks to recover. The quota limited the amount of swordfish caught per year by all U.S.-licensed fishing boats to 7 million pounds. As soon as the U.S. fishing fleet had met the quota, the swordfish catch was closed down for the rest of the year. The accompanying table gives the hypothetical demand and supply schedules for swordfish caught in the United States per year.

Price of swordfish (per pound)	Quantity of swordfish (millions of pounds per year)	
	Quantity demanded	Quantity supplied
$20	6	15
18	7	13
16	8	11
14	9	9
12	10	7

a. Use a diagram to show the effect of the quota on the market for swordfish in 1991.

b. How do you think fishermen will change how they fish in response to this policy?

Measurement of Economic Performance

In December 1975 the government of Portugal—a provisional government in the process of establishing a democracy—feared that it was facing an economic crisis. Business owners, alarmed by the rise of leftist political parties, issued dire warnings about plunging production. Newspapers speculated that the economy had shrunk 10 to 15% since the 1974 revolution that had overthrown the country's long-standing dictatorship.

In the face of these reports of economic collapse, some Portuguese were pronouncing democracy itself a failure. Others declared that capitalism was the culprit, demanding that the government seize control of the nation's factories and force them to produce more. But how bad was the situation, really?

To answer this question, Portugal's top monetary official invited his old friend Richard Eckaus, an economist at the Massachusetts Institute of Technology, and two other MIT economists to look at the country's national accounts, the set of data collected on the country's economic activity. The visiting experts had to engage in a lot of educated guesswork: Portugal's economic data collection had always been somewhat incomplete, and it had been further disrupted by political upheavals. For example, the country's statisticians normally tracked construction with data on the sales of structural steel and concrete. But in the somewhat chaotic situation of 1975, these indicators were moving in opposite directions

Guy LeQuerrec/Magnum

dpa photos/Newscom

because many builders were ignoring the construction regulations and using very little steel. (Travel tip: If you find yourself visiting Portugal, try to avoid being in a 1975-vintage building during an earthquake.)

Still, they went to work with the available data, and within a week they were able to make a rough estimate: aggregate output had declined only 3% from 1974 to 1975. The economy had indeed suffered a serious setback, but its decline was much less drastic than the calamity being portrayed in the newspapers. (While later revisions pushed the decline up to 4.5%, that was still much less than feared.) The Portuguese government certainly had work to do, but there was no need to abandon either democracy or a market economy. In fact, the economy soon began to recover. Over the past three decades, Portugal has, on the whole, been a success story. A once-backward dictatorship is now a fairly prosperous, solidly democratic member of the European Union.

What's the lesson of this story? It is that economic measurement matters. If the government of Portugal had believed the scare stories some were telling during 1975, it might have made major policy mistakes. Good macroeconomic policy depends on good measurement of what is happening in the economy as a whole. This section presents three of the most important macroeconomic measures: gross domestic product, unemployment, and inflation.

101

Module 10
The Circular Flow and Gross Domestic Product

The National Accounts

Almost all countries calculate a set of numbers known as the *national income and product accounts*. In fact, the accuracy of a country's accounts is a remarkably reliable indicator of its state of economic development—in general, the more reliable the accounts, the more economically advanced the country. When international economic agencies seek to help a less developed country, typically the first order of business is to send a team of experts to audit and improve the country's accounts.

In the United States, these numbers are calculated by the Bureau of Economic Analysis, a division of the U.S. government's Department of Commerce. The **national income and product accounts,** often referred to simply as the **national accounts,** keep track of the spending of consumers, sales of producers, business investment spending, government purchases, and a variety of other flows of money among different sectors of the economy. Let's see how they work.

The Circular-Flow Diagram

To understand the principles behind the national accounts, it helps to look at a graphic called a *circular-flow diagram*. This diagram is a simplified representation of the macroeconomy. It shows the flows of money, goods and services, and factors of production through the economy. It allows us to visualize the key concepts behind the national accounts. The underlying principle is that the flow of money into each market or sector is equal to the flow of money coming out of that market or sector.

The Simple Circular Flow Diagram The U.S. economy is a vastly complex entity, with more than a hundred million workers employed by millions of companies, producing millions of different goods and services. Yet you can learn some very important things about the economy by considering a simple diagram, shown in Figure 10.1.

National income and product accounts, or **national accounts,** keep track of the flows of money between different sectors of the economy.

figure 10.1

The Circular-Flow Diagram

This diagram represents the flows of money and goods and services in the economy. In the markets for goods and services, households purchase goods and services from firms, generating a flow of money to the firms and a flow of goods and services to the households. The money flows back to households as firms purchase factors of production from the households in factor markets.

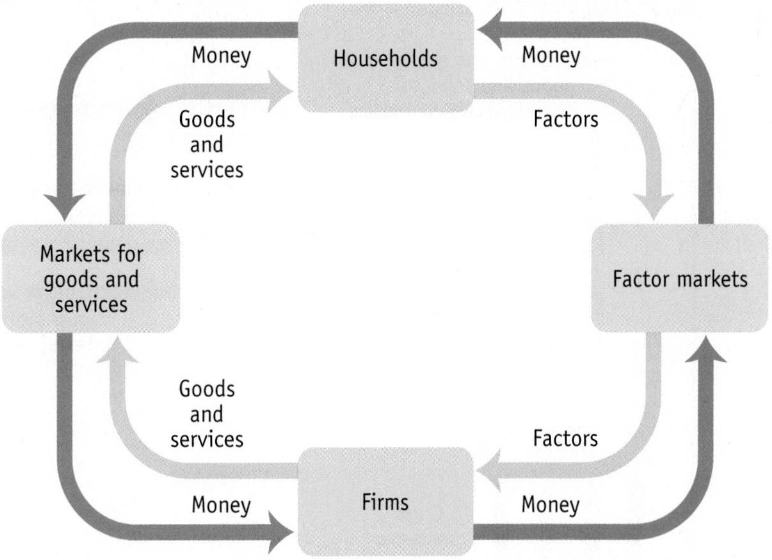

This simple model of the macroeconomy represents the transactions that take place by two kinds of flows around a circle: flows of physical things such as goods, services, labor, or raw materials in one direction, and flows of money that pay for these things in the opposite direction. In this case, the physical flows are shown in yellow, the money flows in green.

The simplest circular-flow diagram illustrates an economy that contains only two kinds of "inhabitants": households and firms. A **household** consists of either an individual or a group of people who share their income. A **firm** is an organization that produces goods and services for sale—and that employs members of households.

As you can see in Figure 10.1, there are two kinds of markets in this simple economy. On one side (here the left side) there are markets for goods and services (also known as **product markets**) in which households buy the goods and services they want from firms. This produces a flow of goods and services to the households and a return flow of money to firms.

On the other side, there are **factor markets** in which firms buy the resources they need to produce goods and services. The best known factor market is the *labor market,* in which workers are paid for their time. Besides labor, we can think of households as owning and selling the other factors of production to firms.

This simple circular-flow diagram omits a number of real-world complications in the interest of simplicity. However, it is a useful aid to thinking about the economy—and we can use it as the starting point for developing a more realistic (and therefore more complicated) circular-flow diagram.

The Expanded Circular-Flow Diagram Figure 10.2 on the next page is a revised and expanded circular-flow diagram. This diagram shows only the flows of money in the economy, but is expanded to include extra elements that were ignored in the interest of simplicity in the simple circular-flow diagram. The underlying principle that the inflow of money into each market or sector must equal the outflow of money coming from that market or sector still applies in this model.

In Figure 10.2, the circular flow of money between households and firms illustrated in Figure 10.1 remains. In the product markets, households engage in **consumer spending,** buying goods and services from domestic firms and from firms in the rest of the world. Households also own factors of production—land, labor, and capital.

A **household** is a person or group of people who share income.

A **firm** is an organization that produces goods and services for sale.

Product markets are where goods and services are bought and sold.

Factor markets are where resources, especially capital and labor, are bought and sold.

Consumer spending is household spending on goods and services.

figure 10.2

An Expanded Circular-Flow Diagram: How Money Flows Through the Economy

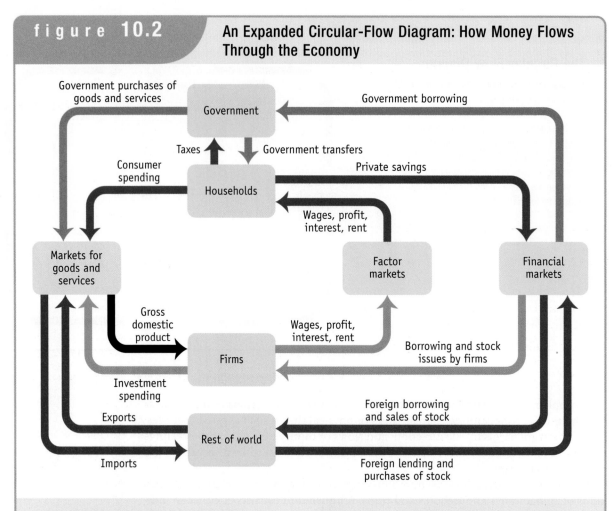

A circular flow of funds connects the four sectors of the economy—households, firms, government, and the rest of the world—via three types of markets: the factor markets, the markets for goods and services, and the *financial markets.* Funds flow from firms to households in the form of wages, profit, interest, and rent through the factor markets. After paying taxes to the government and receiving *government transfers,* households allocate the remaining income—*disposable income*—to private savings and consumer spending. Via the financial markets, *private savings* and funds from the rest of the world are channeled into investment spending by firms, government borrowing, foreign borrowing and lending, and foreign transactions of stocks. In turn, funds flow from the government and households to firms to pay for purchases of goods and services. Finally, exports to the rest of the world generate a flow of funds into the economy and imports lead to a flow of funds out of the economy. We can determine the total flow of funds by adding all spending—consumer spending on goods and services, investment spending by firms, government purchases of goods and services, and exports—and then subtracting the value of imports. This is the value of all the final goods and services produced in the United States—that is, the *gross domestic product* of the economy.

A **stock** is a share in the ownership of a company held by a shareholder.

A **bond** is a loan in the form of an IOU that pays interest.

They sell the use of these factors of production to firms, receiving rent, wages, and interest payments in return. Firms buy, and pay households for, the use of those factors of production in factor markets, represented to the right of center in the diagram. Most households derive the bulk of their income from wages earned by selling labor. Some households derive additional income from their indirect ownership of the physical capital used by firms, mainly in the form of **stocks**—shares in the ownership of a company—and **bonds**—loans to firms in the form of an IOU that pays interest. In other words, the income households receive from the factor markets includes profit distributed to company shareholders and the interest payments on any bonds that they hold. Finally, households receive rent from firms in exchange for the use of land or structures that the households own. So in factor markets, households receive income in the form of wages, profit, interest, and rent via factor markets.

Households spend most of the income received from factors of production on goods and services. However, in Figure 10.2 we see two reasons why the markets for goods and services don't in fact absorb *all* of a household's income. First, households don't get to keep all the income they receive via the factor markets. They must pay part of their income to the government in the form of taxes, such as income taxes and sales taxes. In addition, some households receive **government transfers**—payments that the government makes to individuals without expecting a good or service in return. Unemployment insurance payments are one example of a government transfer. The total income households have left after paying taxes and receiving government transfers is **disposable income.**

The second reason that the markets for goods and services do not absorb all household income is that many households set aside a portion of their income for **private savings.** These private savings go into **financial markets** where individuals, banks, and other institutions buy and sell stocks and bonds as well as make loans. As Figure 10.2 shows, the financial markets (on the far right of the circular flow diagram) also receive funds from the rest of the world and provide funds to the government, to firms, and to the rest of the world.

Before going further, we can use the box representing households to illustrate an important general characteristic of the circular-flow diagram: the total sum of flows of money out of a given box is equal to the total sum of flows of money into that box. It's simply a matter of accounting: what goes in must come out. So, for example, the total flow of money out of households—the sum of taxes paid, consumer spending, and private savings—must equal the total flow of money into households—the sum of wages, profit, interest, rent, and government transfers.

Now let's look at the other inhabitants in the circular-flow diagram, including the government and the rest of the world. The government returns a portion of the money it collects from taxes to households in the form of government transfers. However, it uses much of its tax revenue, plus additional funds borrowed in the financial markets through **government borrowing,** to buy goods and services. **Government purchases of goods and services,** the total of purchases made by federal, state, and local governments, includes everything from military spending on ammunition to your local public school's spending on chalk, erasers, and teacher salaries.

The rest of the world participates in the U.S. economy in three ways. First, some of the goods and services produced in the United States are sold to residents of other countries. For example, more than half of America's annual wheat and cotton crops are sold abroad. Goods and services sold to other countries are known as **exports.** Export sales lead to a flow of funds from the rest of the world into the United States to pay for them. Second, some of the goods and services purchased by residents of the United States are produced abroad. For example, many consumer goods are now made in China. Goods and services purchased from residents of other countries are known as **imports.** Import purchases lead to a flow of funds out of the United States to pay for them. Third, foreigners can participate in U.S. financial markets. Foreign lending—lending by foreigners to borrowers in the United States and purchases by foreigners of shares of stock in American companies—generates a flow of funds into the United States from the rest of the world. Conversely, foreign borrowing—borrowing by foreigners from U.S. lenders and purchases by Americans of stock in foreign companies—leads to a flow of funds out of the United States to the rest of the world.

Notice that like households, firms also buy goods and services in our economy. For example, an automobile company that is building a new factory will buy investment goods—machinery like stamping presses and welding robots—from companies that manufacture these items. It will also accumulate an inventory of finished cars in preparation for shipment to dealers. **Inventories,** then, are goods and raw materials that

Government transfers are payments that the government makes to individuals without expecting a good or service in return.

Disposable income, equal to income plus government transfers minus taxes, is the total amount of household income available to spend on consumption and to save.

Private savings, equal to disposable income minus consumer spending, is disposable income that is not spent on consumption.

The banking, stock, and bond markets, which channel private savings and foreign lending into investment spending, government borrowing, and foreign borrowing, are known as the **financial markets.**

Government borrowing is the amount of funds borrowed by the government in the financial markets.

Government purchases of goods and services are total expenditures on goods and services by federal, state, and local governments.

Goods and services sold to other countries are **exports.** Goods and services purchased from other countries are **imports.**

Inventories are stocks of goods and raw materials held to facilitate business operations.

Supplies used in public schools, such as the chalk shown here, are among the goods and services purchased by the government.

module **1 0** The Circular Flow and Gross Domestic Product **105** firms hold to facilitate their operations. The national accounts count this **investment spending**—spending on new productive physical capital, such as machinery and buildings, and on changes in *inventories*—as part of total spending on goods and services.

You might ask why changes in inventories are included in investment spending—finished cars aren't, after all, used to produce more cars. Changes in inventories of finished goods are counted as investment spending because, like machinery, they change the ability of a firm to make future sales. So spending on additions to inventories is a form of investment spending by a firm. Conversely, a drawing-down of inventories is counted as a fall in investment spending because it leads to lower future sales. It's also important to understand that investment spending includes spending on the construction of any structure, regardless of whether it is an assembly plant or a new house. Why include the construction of homes? Because, like a plant, a new house produces a future stream of output—housing services for its occupants.

Suppose we add up consumer spending on goods and services, investment spending, government purchases of goods and services, and the value of exports, then subtract the value of imports. This gives us a measure of the overall market value of the goods and services the economy produces. That measure has a name: it's a country's *gross domestic product*. But before we can formally define gross domestic product, or GDP, we have to examine an important distinction between classes of goods and services: the difference between *final goods and services* versus *intermediate goods and services*.

Gross Domestic Product

A consumer's purchase of a new car from a dealer is one example of a sale of **final goods and services:** goods and services sold to the final, or end, user. But an automobile manufacturer's purchase of steel from a steel foundry or glass from a glassmaker is an example of a sale of **intermediate goods and services:** goods and services that are inputs into the production of final goods and services. In the case of intermediate goods and services, the purchaser—another firm—is *not* the final user.

Gross domestic product, or **GDP,** is the total value of all *final goods and services* produced in an economy during a given period, usually a year. In 2009 the GDP of the United States was $14,259 billion, or about $46,372 per person.

There are three ways to calculate GDP. The first way is to *survey firms and add up the total value of their production of final goods and services*. The second way is to *add up* **aggregate spending** *on domestically produced final goods and services in the economy*—the sum of consumer spending, investment spending, government purchases of goods and services, and exports minus imports. The third way of calculating GDP is to *sum the total factor income earned by households from firms in the economy*.

Government statisticians use all three methods. To illustrate how they work, we will consider a hypothetical economy, shown in Figure 10.3. This economy consists of three firms—American Motors, Inc., which produces one car per year; American Steel, Inc., which produces the steel that goes into the car; and American Ore, Inc., which mines the iron ore that goes into the steel. GDP in this economy is $21,500, the value of the one car per year the economy produces. Let's look at how the three different methods of calculating GDP yield the same result.

Measuring GDP as the Value of Production of Final Goods and Services The first method for calculating GDP is to add up the value of all the final goods and services produced in the economy—a calculation that excludes the value of intermediate goods and services. Why are intermediate goods and services excluded? After all, don't they represent a very large and valuable portion of the economy?

To understand why only final goods and services are included in GDP, look at the simplified economy described in Figure 10.3. Should we measure the GDP of this economy by adding up the total sales of the iron ore producer, the steel producer, and the auto producer? If we did, we would in effect be counting the value of the steel twice—once when it is sold by the steel plant to the auto plant and again when the steel auto body is sold to a consumer as a finished car. And we would be counting the value of the

figure 10.3

Calculating GDP

In this hypothetical economy consisting of three firms, GDP can be calculated in three different ways: measuring GDP as the value of production of final goods and services by summing each firm's value added; measuring GDP as aggregate spending on domestically produced final goods and services; and measuring GDP as factor income earned by households from firms in the economy.

Aggregate spending on domestically produced final goods and services = $21,500

	American Ore, Inc.	American Steel, Inc.	American Motors, Inc.	Total factor income
Value of sales	$4,200 (ore)	$9,000 (steel)	$21,500 (car)	
Intermediate goods	0	4,200 (iron ore)	9,000 (steel)	
Wages	2,000	3,700	10,000	$15,700
Interest payments	1,000	600	1,000	2,600
Rent	200	300	500	1,000
Profit	1,000	200	1,000	2,200
Total expenditure by firm	4,200	9,000	21,500	
Value added per firm = Value of sales − cost of intermediate goods	4,200	4,800	12,500	

Total payments to factors = $21,500

Sum of value added = $21,500

iron ore *three* times—once when it is mined and sold to the steel company, a second time when it is made into steel and sold to the auto producer, and a third time when the steel is made into a car and sold to the consumer. So counting the full value of each producer's sales would cause us to count the same items several times and artificially inflate the calculation of GDP.

In Figure 10.3, the total value of all sales, intermediate and final, is $34,700: $21,500 from the sale of the car, plus $9,000 from the sale of the steel, plus $4,200 from the sale of the iron ore. Yet we know that GDP—the total value of all final goods and services in a given year—is only $21,500. To avoid double-counting, we count only each producer's **value added** in the calculation of GDP: the difference between the value of its sales and the value of the inputs it purchases from other businesses. That is, at each stage of the production process we subtract the cost of inputs—the intermediate goods—at that stage. In this case, the value added of the auto producer is the dollar value of the cars it manufactures *minus* the cost of the steel it buys, or $12,500. The value added of the steel producer is the dollar value of the steel it produces *minus* the cost of the ore it buys, or $4,800. Only the ore producer, who we have assumed doesn't buy any inputs, has value added equal to its total sales, $4,200. The sum of the three producers' value added is $21,500, equal to GDP.

Measuring GDP as Spending on Domestically Produced Final Goods and Services

Another way to calculate GDP is by adding up aggregate spending on domestically produced final goods and services. That is, GDP can be measured by the flow of funds into firms. Like the method that estimates GDP as the value of domestic production of final goods and services, this measurement must be carried out in a way that avoids double-counting. In terms of our steel and auto example, we don't want to count both consumer spending on a car (represented in Figure 10.3 by the sales price of the car) and the auto producer's

The **value added** of a producer is the value of its sales minus the value of its purchases of inputs.

Digitalvision

Steel is an intermediate good because it is sold to other product manufacturers like automakers or refrigerator makers, and rarely to the final consumer.

spending on steel (represented in Figure 10.3 by the price of a car's worth of steel). If we counted both, we would be counting the steel embodied in the car twice. We solve this problem by counting only the value of sales to *final buyers,* such as consumers, firms that purchase investment goods, the government, or foreign buyers. In other words, in order to avoid the double-counting of spending, we omit sales of inputs from one business to another when estimating GDP using spending data. You can see from Figure 10.3 that aggregate spending on final goods and services—the finished car—is $21,500.

As we've already pointed out, the national accounts *do* include investment spending by firms as a part of final spending. That is, an auto company's purchase of steel to make a car isn't considered a part of final spending, but the company's purchase of new machinery for its factory *is* considered a part of final spending. What's the difference? Steel is an input that is used up in production; machinery will last for a number of years. Since purchases of capital goods that will last for a considerable time aren't closely tied to current production, the national accounts consider such purchases a form of final sales.

What types of spending make up GDP? Look again at the markets for goods and services in Figure 10.2, and you will see that one source of sales revenue for firms is consumer spending. Let's denote consumer spending with the symbol C. Figure 10.2 shows three other components of sales: sales of investment goods to other businesses, or investment spending, which we will denote by I; government purchases of goods and services, which we will denote by G; and sales to foreigners—that is, exports—which we will denote by X.

In reality, not all of this final spending goes toward domestically produced goods and services. We must take account of spending on imports, which we will denote by IM. Income spent on imports is income not spent on domestic goods and services—it is income that has "leaked" across national borders. So to calculate domestic production using spending data, we must subtract spending on imports. Putting this all together gives us the following equation, which breaks GDP down by the four sources of aggregate spending:

(10-1) $GDP = C + I + G + X - IM$

where C = consumer spending, I = investment spending, G = government purchases of goods and services, X = sales to foreigners, or exports, and IM = spending on imports. Note that the value of $X - IM$—the difference between the value of exports and the value of imports—is known as **net exports.** We'll be seeing a lot of Equation 10-1 in later modules!

Measuring GDP as Factor Income Earned from Firms in the Economy A final way to calculate GDP is to add up all the income earned by factors of production in the economy—the wages earned by labor; the interest earned by those who lend their savings to firms and the government; the rent earned by those who lease their land or structures to firms; and the profit earned by the shareholders, the owners of the firms' physical capital. This is a valid measure because the money firms earn by selling goods and services must go somewhere; whatever isn't paid as wages, interest, or rent is profit. And part of profit is paid out to shareholders as *dividends.*

Figure 10.3 shows how this calculation works for our simplified economy. The shaded column at the far right shows the total wages, interest, and rent paid by all these firms as well as their total profit. Summing up all of these yields a total factor income of $21,500—again, equal to GDP.

We won't emphasize the income method as much as the other two methods of calculating GDP. It's important to keep in mind, however, that all the money spent on domestically produced goods and services generates factor income to households—that is, there really is a circular flow.

The Components of GDP Now that we know how GDP is calculated in principle, let's see what it looks like in practice.

Net exports are the difference between the value of exports and the value of imports ($X - IM$).

Figure 10.4 shows the first two methods of calculating GDP side by side. The height of each bar above the horizontal axis represents the GDP of the U.S. economy in 2009: $14,259 billion. Each bar is divided to show the breakdown of that total in terms of where the value was added and how the money was spent.

In the left bar in Figure 10.4, we see the breakdown of GDP by value added according to sector, the first method of calculating GDP. Of the $14,259 billion, $10,669 billion consisted of value added by businesses. Another $1,760 billion consisted of value added by government, in the form of military, education, and other government services. Finally, $1,830 billion of value added was added by households and institutions. For example, the value added by households includes the value of work performed in homes by professional gardeners, maids, and cooks.

The right bar in Figure 10.4 corresponds to the second method of calculating GDP, showing the breakdown by the four types of aggregate spending. The total length of the right bar is longer than the total length of the left bar, a difference of $390 billion (which, as you can see, extends below the horizontal axis). That's because the total length of the right bar represents total spending in the economy, spending on both domestically produced and foreign-produced—imported—final goods and services. Within the bar, consumer spending (C), which is 70. 8% of GDP, dominates the picture. But some of that spending was absorbed by foreign-produced goods and services. In 2009, the value of net exports, the difference between the value of exports and the value of imports ($X - IM$ in Equation 10-1), was negative—the United States was a net importer of foreign goods and services. The 2009 value of $X - IM$ was −$390 billion, or −2.7% of GDP. Thus, a portion of the right bar extends below the horizontal axis by $390 billion to represent the amount

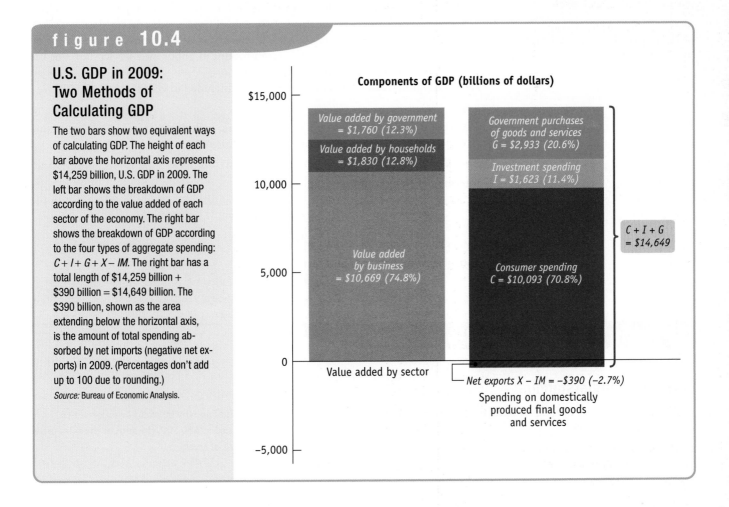

figure 10.4

U.S. GDP in 2009: Two Methods of Calculating GDP

The two bars show two equivalent ways of calculating GDP. The height of each bar above the horizontal axis represents $14,259 billion, U.S. GDP in 2009. The left bar shows the breakdown of GDP according to the value added of each sector of the economy. The right bar shows the breakdown of GDP according to the four types of aggregate spending: $C + I + G + X - IM$. The right bar has a total length of $14,259 billion + $390 billion = $14,649 billion. The $390 billion, shown as the area extending below the horizontal axis, is the amount of total spending absorbed by net imports (negative net exports) in 2009. (Percentages don't add up to 100 due to rounding.)

Source: Bureau of Economic Analysis.

Components of GDP (billions of dollars)

Value added by government = $1,760 (12.3%)
Value added by households = $1,830 (12.8%)
Value added by business = $10,669 (74.8%)

Government purchases of goods and services $G = $2,933 (20.6%)
Investment spending $I = $1,623 (11.4%)
Consumer spending $C = $10,093 (70.8%)

$C + I + G = $14,649

Value added by sector

Net exports $X - IM = -$390 (−2.7%)

Spending on domestically produced final goods and services

of total spending that was absorbed by net imports and so did not lead to higher U.S. GDP. Investment spending (*I*) constituted 11.4% of GDP; government purchases of goods and services (*G*) constituted 20.6% of GDP.

GDP: What's In and What's Out? It's easy to confuse what is included and what isn't included in GDP. So let's stop here and make sure the distinction is clear. Don't confuse investment spending with spending on inputs. Investment spending—spending on productive physical capital, the construction of structures (residential as well as commercial), and changes to inventories—is included in GDP. But spending on inputs is not. Why the difference? Recall the distinction between resources that are *used up* and those that are *not used up* in production. An input, like steel, is used up in production. A metal-stamping machine, an investment good, is not. It will last for many years and will be used repeatedly to make many cars. Since spending on productive physical capital—investment goods—and the construction of structures is not directly tied to current output, economists consider such spending to be spending on final goods. Spending on changes to inventories is considered a part of investment spending so it is also included in GDP. Why? Because, like a machine, additional inventory is an investment in future sales. And when a good is released for sale from inventories, its value is subtracted from the value of inventories and so from GDP. Used goods are not included in GDP because, as with inputs, to include them would be to double-count: counting them once when sold as new and again when sold as used.

Also, financial assets such as stocks and bonds are not included in GDP because they don't represent either the production or the sale of final goods and services. Rather, a bond represents a promise to repay with interest, and a stock represents a proof of ownership. And for obvious reasons, foreign-produced goods and services are not included in calculations of gross *domestic* product.

Here is a summary of what's included and not included in GDP:

Included

- Domestically produced final goods and services, including capital goods, new construction of structures, and changes to inventories

Not Included

- Intermediate goods and services
- Inputs
- Used goods
- Financial assets such as stocks and bonds
- Foreign-produced goods and services

The U.S. is a net importer of goods and services, such as these toys made on a production line in China.

Module 10 AP Review

Solutions appear at the back of the book.

Check Your Understanding

1. Explain why the three methods of calculating GDP produce the same estimate of GDP.

2. Identify each of the sectors to which firms make sales. What are the various ways in which households are linked with other sectors of the economy?

3. Consider Figure 10.3. Explain why it would be incorrect to calculate total value added as $30,500, the sum of the sales price of a car and a car's worth of steel.

Tackle the Test: Multiple-Choice Questions

1. Which of the following is true? The simple circular-flow diagram
    I. includes only the product markets.
    II. includes only the factor markets.
    III. is a simplified representation of the macroeconomy.
   a. I only
   b. II only
   c. III only
   d. I and III only
   e. none of the above

2. GDP is equal to
   a. the total value of all goods and services produced in an economy during a given period.
   b. $C + I + G + IM$.
   c. the total value of intermediate goods plus final goods.
   d. the total income received by producers of final goods and services.
   e. none of the above.

3. Which of the following is included in GDP?
   a. changes to inventories
   b. intermediate goods
   c. used goods
   d. financial assets (stocks and bonds)
   e. foreign-produced goods

4. Which of the following is *not* included in GDP?
   a. capital goods such as machinery
   b. imports
   c. the value of domestically produced services
   d. government purchases of goods and services
   e. the construction of structures

5. Which of the following components makes up the largest percentage of GDP measured by aggregate spending?
   a. consumer spending
   b. investment spending
   c. government purchases of goods and services
   d. exports
   e. imports

Tackle the Test: Free-Response Questions

1. Will each of the following transactions be included in GDP for the United States? Explain why or why not.
   a. Coca-Cola builds a new bottling plant in the United States.
   b. Delta sells one of its existing airplanes to Korean Air.
   c. Ms. Moneybags buys an existing share of Disney stock.
   d. A California winery produces a bottle of Chardonnay and sells it to a customer in Montreal, Canada.
   e. An American buys a bottle of French perfume in Tulsa.
   f. A book publisher produces too many copies of a new book; the books don't sell this year, so the publisher adds the surplus books to inventories.

2. Draw a correctly labeled circular-flow diagram showing the flows of funds between the markets for goods and services and the factor markets. Add the government to your diagram, and show how money leaks out of the economy to the government and how money is injected back into the economy by the government.

Answer (6 points)

1 point: Yes. New structures built in the United States are included in U.S. GDP.

1 point: No. The airplane is used, and sales of used goods are not included in GDP.

1 point: No. This is a transfer of ownership—not new production.

1 point: Yes. This is an export.

1 point: No. This is an import—it was not produced in the United States.

1 point: Yes. Additions to inventories are considered investments.

What you will learn in this Module:

- The difference between real GDP and nominal GDP

- Why real GDP is the appropriate measure of real economic activity

Module 11
Interpreting Real Gross Domestic Product

What GDP Tells Us

Now we've seen the various ways that gross domestic product is calculated. But what does the measurement of GDP tell us?

The most important use of GDP is as a measure of the size of the economy, providing us a scale against which to compare the economic performance of other years or other countries. For example, in 2009, as we've seen, U.S. GDP was $14,259 billion, Japan's GDP was $5,049 billion, and the combined GDP of the 25 countries that make up the European Union was $16,191 billion. This comparison tells us that Japan, although it has the world's second-largest national economy, carries considerably less economic weight than does the United States. When taken in aggregate, Europe's economy is larger than the U.S. economy.

Still, one must be careful when using GDP numbers, especially when making comparisons over time. That's because part of the increase in the value of GDP over time represents increases in the *prices* of goods and services rather than an increase in output. For example, U.S. GDP was $7,085 billion in 1994 and had approximately doubled to $14,259 billion by 2009. But U.S. production didn't actually double over that period. To measure actual changes in aggregate output, we need a modified version of GDP that is adjusted for price changes, known as *real GDP*. We'll see how real GDP is calculated next.

U.S. Department of Commerce

Real GDP: A Measure of Aggregate Output

At the beginning of this section we described the economic troubles that afflicted Portugal in 1975. While the economy wasn't in as bad shape as many people thought, output was declining. Strange to say, however, GDP was up. In fact, between 1974 and 1975 Portugal's GDP as measured in escudos (the national currency at the time, now replaced by the euro) rose 11 percent.

How was that possible? The answer is that Portugal had serious inflation. As a result, the escudo value of GDP rose even though output fell.

Creating the National Accounts

The national accounts, like modern macroeconomics, owe their creation to the Great Depression. As the economy plunged into depression, government officials found their ability to respond crippled not only by the lack of adequate economic theories but also by the lack of adequate information. All they had were scattered statistics: railroad freight car loadings, stock prices, and incomplete indexes of industrial production. They could only guess at what was happening to the economy as a whole.

In response to this perceived lack of information, the Department of Commerce commissioned Simon Kuznets, a young Russian-born economist, to develop a set of national income accounts. (Kuznets later won the Nobel Prize in Economics for his work.) The first version of these accounts was presented to Congress in 1937 and in a research report titled *National Income, 1929–35.*

Kuznets's initial estimates fell short of the full modern set of accounts because they focused on income, not production. The push to complete the national accounts came during World War II, when policy makers were in even more need of comprehensive measures of the economy's performance. The federal government began issuing estimates of gross domestic product and gross national product in 1942.

In January 2000, in its publication *Survey of Current Business,* the Department of Commerce ran an article titled "GDP: One of the Great Inventions of the 20th Century." This may seem a bit over the top, but national income accounting, invented in the United States, has since become a tool of economic analysis and policy making around the world.

The moral of this story is that the commonly cited GDP number is an interesting and useful statistic, one that provides a good way to compare the size of different economies, but it's not a good measure of the economy's growth over time. GDP can grow because the economy grows, but it can also grow simply because of inflation. Even if an economy's output doesn't change, GDP will go up if the prices of the goods and services the economy produces increase. Likewise, GDP can fall either because the economy is producing less or because prices have fallen.

To measure the economy's growth with accuracy, we need a measure of **aggregate output:** the total quantity of final goods and services the economy produces. The measure that is used for this purpose is known as *real GDP.* By tracking real GDP over time, we avoid the problem of changes in prices distorting the value of changes in production over time. Let's look first at how real GDP is calculated and then at what it means.

Aggregate output is the total quantity of final goods and services produced within an economy.

Calculating Real GDP

To understand how real GDP is calculated, imagine an economy in which only two goods, apples and oranges, are produced and in which both goods are sold only to final consumers. The outputs and prices of the two fruits for two consecutive years are shown in Table 11.1.

table **11.1**

Calculating GDP and Real GDP in a Simple Economy

	Year 1	Year 2
Quantity of apples (billions)	2,000	2,200
Price of an apple	$0.25	$0.30
Quantity of oranges (billions)	1,000	1,200
Price of an orange	$0.50	$0.70
GDP (billions of dollars)	$1,000	$1,500
Real GDP (billions of year 1 dollars)	$1,000	$1,150

The first thing we can say about these data is that the value of sales increased from year 1 to year 2. In the first year, the total value of sales was (2,000 billion × $0.25) + (1,000 billion × $0.50) = $1,000 billion; in the second, it was (2,200 billion × $0.30) + (1,200 billion × $0.70) = $1,500 billion, which is 50% larger. But it is also clear from the table that this increase in the dollar value of GDP overstates the real growth in the economy. Although the quantities of both apples and oranges increased, the prices of both apples and oranges also rose. So part of the 50% increase in the dollar value of GDP simply reflects higher prices, not higher production of output.

To estimate the true increase in aggregate output produced, we have to ask the following question: How much would GDP have gone up if prices had *not* changed? To answer this question, we need to find the value of output in year 2 expressed in year 1 prices. In year 1, the price of apples was $0.25 each and the price of oranges $0.50 each. So year 2 output *at year 1 prices* is (2,200 billion × $0.25) + (1,200 billion × $0.50) = $1,150 billion. And output in year 1 at year 1 prices was $1,000 billion. So in this example, GDP measured in year 1 prices rose 15%—from $1,000 billion to $1,150 billion.

Now we can define **real GDP:** it is the total value of final goods and services produced in the economy during a year, calculated as if prices had stayed constant at the level of some given base year. A real GDP number always comes with information about what the base year is. A GDP number that has not been adjusted for changes in prices is calculated using the prices in the year in which the output is produced. Economists call this measure **nominal GDP,** GDP at current prices. If we had used nominal GDP to measure the true change in output from year 1 to year 2 in our apples and oranges example, we would have overstated the true growth in output: we would have claimed it to be 50%, when in fact it was only 15%. By comparing output in the two years using a common set of prices—the year 1 prices in this example—we are able to focus solely on changes in the quantity of output by eliminating the influence of changes in prices.

Table 11.2 shows a real-life version of our apples and oranges example. The second column shows nominal GDP in 2001, 2005, and 2009. The third column shows real GDP for each year in 2005 dollars (that is, using the value of the dollar in the year 2005). For 2005 the nominal GDP and the real GDP are the same. But real GDP in 2001 expressed in 2005 dollars was higher than nominal GDP in 2001, reflecting the fact that prices were in general higher in 2005 than in 2001. Real GDP in 2009

Real GDP is the total value of all final goods and services produced in the economy during a given year, calculated using the prices of a selected base year.

Nominal GDP is the total value of all final goods and services produced in the economy during a given year, calculated with the prices current in the year in which the output is produced.

table **11.2**

Nominal versus Real GDP in 2001, 2005, and 2009

	Nominal GDP (billions of current dollars)	Real GDP (billions of 2005 dollars)
2001	$10,286	$11,347
2005	12,683	12,638
2009	14,259	12,989

Source: Bureau of Economic Analysis.

expressed in 2005 dollars, however, was less than nominal GDP in 2009 because prices in 2005 were lower than in 2009.

You might have noticed that there is an alternative way to calculate real GDP using the data in Table 11.1. Why not measure it using the prices of year 2 rather than year 1 as the base-year prices? This procedure seems equally valid. According to that calculation, real GDP in year 1 at year 2 prices is (2,000 billion × $0.30) + (1,000 billion × $0.70) = $1,300 billion; real GDP in year 2 at year 2 prices is $1,500 billion, the same as nominal GDP in year 2. So using year 2 prices as the base year, the growth rate of real GDP is equal to ($1,500 billion − $1,300 billion)/$1,300 billion = 0.154, or 15.4%. This is slightly higher than the figure we got from the previous calculation, in which year 1 prices were the base-year prices. In that calculation, we found that real GDP increased by 15%. Neither answer, 15.4% versus 15%, is more "correct" than the other. In reality, the government economists who put together the U.S. national accounts have adopted a method to measure the change in real GDP known as **chain-linking,** which uses the average between the GDP growth rate calculated using an early base year and the GDP growth rate calculated using a late base year. As a result, U.S. statistics on real GDP are always expressed in *chained dollars,* which splits the difference between using early and late base years.

Chain-linking is the method of calculating changes in real GDP using the average between the growth rate calculated using an early base year and the growth rate calculated using a late base year.

GDP per capita is GDP divided by the size of the population; it is equivalent to the average GDP per person.

What Real GDP Doesn't Measure

GDP is a measure of a country's aggregate output. Other things equal, a country with a larger population will have higher GDP simply because there are more people working. So if we want to compare GDP across countries but want to eliminate the effect of differences in population size, we use the measure **GDP per capita**—GDP divided by the size of the population, equivalent to the average GDP per person. Correspondingly, real GDP per capita is the average real GDP per person.

Real GDP per capita can be a useful measure in some circumstances, such as in a comparison of labor productivity between two countries. However, despite the fact that it is a rough measure of the average real output per person, real GDP per capita has well-known limitations as a measure of a country's living standards. Every once in a while economists are accused of believing that growth in real GDP per capita is the only thing that matters—that is, thinking that increasing real GDP per capita is a goal in itself. In fact, economists rarely make that mistake; the idea that economists care only about real GDP per capita is a sort of urban legend. Let's take a moment to be clear about why a country's real GDP per capita is not a sufficient measure of human welfare in that country and why growth in real GDP per capita is not an appropriate policy goal in itself.

Real GDP does not include many of the things that contribute to happiness, such as leisure time, volunteerism, housework, and natural beauty. And real GDP increases with expenditures on some things that make people unhappy, including disease, divorce, crime, and natural disasters.

Real GDP per capita is a measure of an economy's average aggregate output per person—and so of what it *can* do. A country with a high GDP can afford to be healthy, to be well

educated, and in general to have a good quality of life. But there is not a one-to-one match between real GDP and the quality of life. Real GDP doesn't address how a country uses that output to affect living standards, it doesn't include some sources of well-being, and it does include some things that are detriments to well-being.

Miracle in Venezuela?

The South American nation of Venezuela has a distinction that may surprise you: in recent years, it has had one of the world's fastest-growing nominal GDPs. Between 1997 and 2007, Venezuelan nominal GDP grew by an average of 28% each year—much faster than nominal GDP in the United States or even in booming economies like China.

So is Venezuela experiencing an economic miracle? No, it's just suffering from unusually high inflation. The figure shows Venezuela's nominal and real GDP from 1997 to 2007, with real GDP measured in 1997 prices. Real GDP did grow over the period, but at an annual rate of only 2.9%. That's about the same as the U.S. growth rate over the same period and far short of China's 9% growth.

Source: Banco Central de Venezuela.

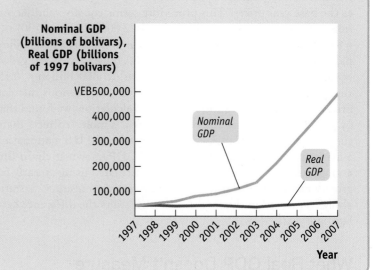

Module 11 AP Review

Solutions appear at the back of the book.

Check Your Understanding

1. Assume there are only two goods in the economy, french fries and onion rings. In 2009, 1,000,000 servings of french fries were sold for $0.40 each and 800,000 servings of onion rings were sold for $0.60 each. From 2009 to 2010, the price of french fries rose to $0.50 and the servings sold fell to 900,000; the price of onion rings fell to $0.51 and the servings sold rose to 840,000.
   a. Calculate nominal GDP in 2009 and 2010. Calculate real GDP in 2010 using 2009 prices.

   b. Why would an assessment of growth using nominal GDP be misguided?

2. From 1990 to 2000 the price of housing rose dramatically. What are the implications of this in deciding whether to use 1990 or 2000 as the base year in calculating 2010 real GDP?

Tackle the Test: Multiple-Choice Questions

1. Which of the following is true of real GDP?

   I. It is adjusted for changes in prices.

   II. It is always equal to nominal GDP.

   III. It increases whenever aggregate output increases.

   a. I only
   b. II only
   c. III only
   d. I and III
   e. I, II, and III

2. The best measure for comparing a country's aggregate output over time is
   a. nominal GDP.
   b. real GDP.

   c. nominal GDP per capita.
   d. real GDP per capita.
   e. average GDP per capita.

3. Use the information provided in the table below for an economy that produces only apples and oranges. Assume year 1 is the base year.

	Year 1	Year 2
Quantity of apples	3,000	4,000
Price of an apple	$0.20	$0.30
Quantity of oranges	2,000	3,000
Price of an orange	$0.40	$0.50

What was the value of real GDP in each year?

	Year 1	Year 2
a.	$1,400	$2,700
b.	1,900	2,700
c.	1,400	2,000
d.	1,900	2,000
e.	1,400	1,900

4. Real GDP per capita is an imperfect measure of the quality of life in part because it
   a. includes the value of leisure time.
   b. excludes expenditures on education.
   c. includes expenditures on natural disasters.
   d. excludes expenditures on entertainment.
   e. includes the value of housework.

5. Refer to the 2009 data in the table below.

	Nominal GDP in billions of dollars
United States	$14,259
Japan	5,049
European Union	16,191

Which of the following must be true?
   I. Residents of Japan were worse off than residents of the United States or the European Union.
   II. The European Union had a higher nominal GDP per capita than the United States.
   III. The European Union had a larger economy than the United States.
   a. I only
   b. II only
   c. III only
   d. II and III
   e. I, II, and III

Tackle the Test: Free-Response Questions

1. The economy of Britannica produces three goods: computers, DVDs, and pizza. The accompanying table shows the prices and output of the three goods for the years 2008, 2009, and 2010.

	Computers		DVDs		Pizza	
Year	Price	Quantity	Price	Quantity	Price	Quantity
2008	$900	10	$10	100	$15	2
2009	1,000	10.5	12	105	16	2
2010	1,050	12	14	110	17	3

   a. What is the percent change in computer production from 2008 to 2009?
   b. What is the percent change in the price of pizza from 2009 to 2010?
   c. Calculate nominal GDP in Britannica for 2008.
   d. Calculate real GDP in Britannica for 2008 using 2008 as the base year.
   e. Calculate real GDP in Britannica for 2010 using 2008 as the base year.

Answer (5 points)

1 point: $0.5/10 \times 100 = 5\%$

1 point: $\$1/\$16 \times 100 = 6.25\%$

1 point: $(\$900 \times 10) + (\$10 \times 100) + (\$15 \times 2) = \$9,000 + \$1,000 + \$30 = \$10,030$

1 point: Real GDP equals nominal GDP in the base year, so this answer is the same as in part c.

1 point: $(\$900 \times 12) + (\$10 \times 110) + (\$15 \times 3) = \$10,800 + \$1,100 + \$45 = \$11,945$

2. Use the information in the table below to answer the following questions.
   a. Calculate the percent increase in nominal GDP between 2005 and 2010 for each country.
   b. What happened to the price level in each country between 2005 and 2010?
   c. Calculate real GDP in each country in 2010, using 2005 as the base year.
   d. Calculate the percent increase in real GDP between 2005 and 2010 for each country.
   e. Compare the two countries' real GDP per capita in 2010 using 2005 as the base year.

Year	Nominal GDP	Price Level	Population
Country A			
2005	$2,000	$100	10
2010	4,000	100	20
Country B			
2005	$2,000	$100	10
2010	6,000	200	15

What you will learn in this **Module**:

- How unemployment is measured
- How the unemployment rate is calculated
- The significance of the unemployment rate for the economy
- The relationship between the unemployment rate and economic growth

Module 12
The Meaning and Calculation of Unemployment

The Unemployment Rate

One of the most important issues in the 2008 presidential election was the growing unemployment rate. Figure 12.1 shows the U.S. unemployment rate from 1948 to the early part of 2010; as you can see, the labor market hit a difficult patch starting in

figure 12.1

The U.S. Unemployment Rate, 1948–2010

The unemployment rate has fluctuated widely over time. It always rises during recessions, which are shown by the shaded bars. It usually, but not always, falls during periods of economic expansion.

Source: Bureau of Labor Statistics; National Bureau of Economic Research.

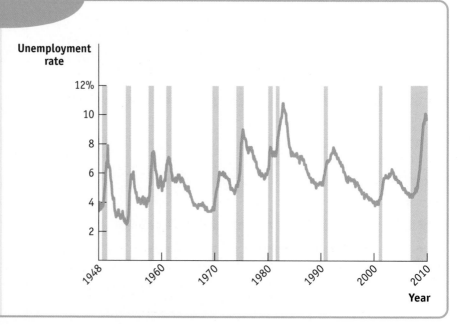

mid-2008, with the unemployment rate rising from 4.8% in February 2008 to 10.1% in October 2009. What did the rise in the unemployment rate mean, and why was it such a big factor in people's lives? To understand why policy makers pay so much attention to employment and unemployment, we need to understand how they are both defined and measured.

Defining and Measuring Unemployment

It's easy to define employment: you're **employed** if and only if you have a job.

Unemployment, however, is a more subtle concept. Just because a person isn't working doesn't mean that we consider that person unemployed. For example, in December 2008 there were 32 million retired workers in the United States receiving Social Security checks. Most of them were probably happy that they were no longer working, so we wouldn't consider someone who has settled into a comfortable, well-earned retirement to be unemployed. There were also 7 million disabled U.S. workers receiving benefits because they were unable to work. Again, although they weren't working, we wouldn't normally consider them to be unemployed.

The U.S. Census Bureau, the federal agency that collects data on unemployment, considers the unemployed to be those who are "jobless, looking for jobs, and available for work." Retired people don't count because they aren't looking for jobs; the disabled don't count because they aren't available for work. More specifically, an individual is considered unemployed if he or she doesn't currently have a job and has been actively seeking a job during the past four weeks. So the **unemployed** are people who are actively looking for work but aren't currently employed.

A country's **labor force** is the sum of the employed and the unemployed—that is, the people who are currently working and the people who are currently looking for work. The **labor force participation rate,** defined as the share of the working-age population that is in the labor force, is calculated as follows:

$$\textbf{(12-1)} \quad \text{Labor force participation rate} = \frac{\text{Labor force}}{\text{Population age 16 and older}} \times 100$$

The **unemployment rate,** defined as the percentage of the total number of people in the labor force who are unemployed, is calculated as follows:

$$\textbf{(12-2)} \quad \text{Unemployment rate} = \frac{\text{Number of unemployed workers}}{\text{Labor force}} \times 100$$

To estimate the numbers that go into calculating the unemployment rate, the U.S. Census Bureau carries out a monthly survey called the Current Population Survey, which involves interviewing a random sample of 60,000 American families. People are asked whether they are currently employed. If they are not employed, they are asked whether they have been looking for a job during the past four weeks. The results are then scaled up, using estimates of the total population, to estimate the total number of employed and unemployed Americans.

The Significance of the Unemployment Rate

In general, the unemployment rate is a good indicator of how easy or difficult it is to find a job given the current state of the economy. When the unemployment rate is low, nearly everyone who wants a job can find one. In 2000, when the unemployment rate averaged 4%, jobs were so abundant that employers spoke of a "mirror test" for getting a job: if you were breathing (therefore, your breath would fog a mirror), you could find work. By contrast, in 2009, the unemployment rate in 17 states rose to over 10% (over 15% in Michigan), with many highly qualified workers having lost their jobs and having a hard time finding new ones. Although the unemployment rate is a good indicator of current labor market conditions, it is not a perfect measure.

Employed people are currently holding a job in the economy, either full time or part time.

Unemployed people are actively looking for work but aren't currently employed.

The **labor force** is equal to the sum of the employed and the unemployed.

The **labor force participation rate** is the percentage of the population aged 16 or older that is in the labor force.

The **unemployment rate** is the percentage of the total number of people in the labor force who are unemployed.

How the Unemployment Rate Can Overstate the True Level of Unemployment

If you are searching for work, it's normal to take at least a few weeks to find a suitable job. Yet a worker who is quite confident of finding a job, but has not yet accepted a position, is counted as unemployed. As a consequence, the unemployment rate never falls to zero, even in boom times when jobs are plentiful. Even in the buoyant labor market of 2000, when it was easy to find work, the unemployment rate was still 4%. Later, we'll discuss in greater depth the reasons that measured unemployment persists even when jobs are abundant.

How the Unemployment Rate Can Understate the True Level of Unemployment

Frequently, people who would like to work but aren't working still don't get counted as unemployed. In particular, an individual who has given up looking for a job for the time being because there are no jobs available isn't counted as unemployed because he or she has not been searching for a job during the previous four weeks. Individuals who want to work but aren't currently searching because they see little prospect of finding a job given the state of the job market are known as **discouraged workers.** Because it does not count discouraged workers, the measured unemployment rate may understate the percentage of people who want to work but are unable to find jobs.

Discouraged workers are part of a larger group known as **marginally attached workers.** These are people who say they would like to have a job and have looked for work in the recent past but are not currently looking for work. They are also not included when calculating the unemployment rate.

Finally, another category of workers who are frustrated in their ability to find work but aren't counted as unemployed are the **underemployed:** workers who would like to find full-time jobs but are currently working part time "for economic reasons"—that is, they can't find a full-time job. Again, they aren't counted in the unemployment rate.

The Bureau of Labor Statistics is the federal agency that calculates the official unemployment rate. It also calculates broader "measures of labor underutilization" that include the three categories of frustrated workers. Figure 12.2 shows what happens to the measured unemployment rate once marginally attached workers (including discouraged workers) and the underemployed are counted. The broadest measure of unemployment and underemployment, known as *U6,* is the sum of these three measures plus the unemployed; it is substantially higher than the rate usually quoted by the news media. But U6 and the unemployment rate move very much in parallel, so changes in the unemployment rate remain a good guide to what's happening in the overall labor market.

Finally, it's important to realize that the unemployment rate varies greatly among demographic groups. Other things equal, jobs are generally easier to find for more experienced workers and for workers during their "prime" working years, from ages 25 to 54. For younger workers, as well as workers nearing retirement age, jobs are typically harder to find, other things equal. Figure 12.3 shows unemployment rates for different groups in August 2007, when the overall unemployment rate of 4.7% was low by historical standards. As you can see, in August 2007 the unemployment rate for African-American workers was much higher than the national average; the unemployment rate for White teenagers (ages 16–19) was more than three times the national average; and the unemployment rate for African-American teenagers, at more than 30%, was over six times the national average. (Bear in mind that a teenager isn't considered unemployed, even if he or she isn't working, unless that teenager is looking for work but can't find

figure 12.2

Alternative Measures of Unemployment, 1994–2010

The unemployment number usually quoted in the news media counts someone as unemployed only if he or she has been looking for work during the past four weeks. Broader measures also count discouraged workers, marginally attached workers, and the underemployed. These broader measures show a higher unemployment rate—but they move closely in parallel with the standard rate.

Source: Bureau of Labor Statistics.

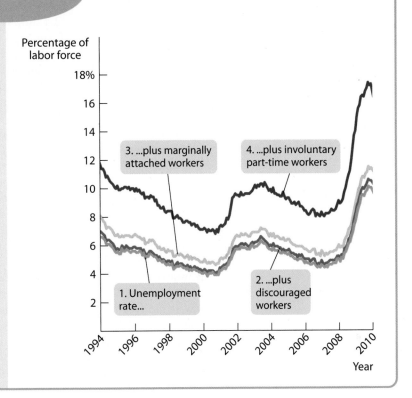

it.) So even at a time when the overall unemployment rate was relatively low, jobs were hard to find for some groups.

So although the unemployment rate is not an exact, literal measure of the percentage of people unable to find jobs, it is a good indicator of overall labor market conditions. The ups and downs of the unemployment rate closely reflect economic changes that have a significant impact on people's lives. Let's turn now to the causes of these fluctuations.

figure 12.3

Unemployment Rates of Different Groups, 2007

Unemployment rates vary greatly among different demographic groups. For example, although the overall unemployment rate in August 2007 was 4.7%, the unemployment rate among African-American teenagers was 31.2%. As a result, even during periods of low overall unemployment, unemployment remains a serious problem for some groups.

Source: Bureau of Labor Statistics.

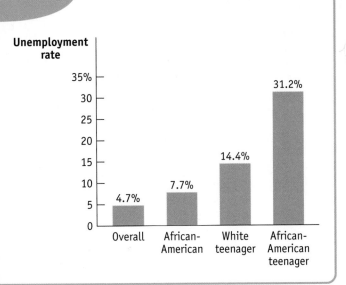

Growth and Unemployment

Compared to Figure 12.1, Figure 12.4 shows the U.S. unemployment rate over a somewhat shorter period, the 30 years from 1978 to 2010. The shaded bars represent periods of recession. As you can see, during every recession, without exception, the unemployment rate rose. The recession of 1981–1982, the most severe one shown, pushed the unemployment rate into double digits: unemployment peaked in November 1982 at 10.8%. And during the most recent recession shown, in late 2009 the unemployment rate rose to above 10%.

Correspondingly, during periods of economic expansion the unemployment rate usually falls. The long economic expansion of the 1990s eventually brought the unemployment rate below 4%. However, it's important to recognize that *economic expansions aren't always periods of falling unemployment.* Look at the periods immediately following two recent recessions, those of 1990–1991 and 2001. In each case the unemployment rate continued to rise for more than a year after the recession was officially over. The explanation in both cases is that although the economy was growing, it was not growing fast enough to reduce the unemployment rate.

Figure 12.5 is a scatter diagram showing U.S. data for the period from 1949 to 2009. The horizontal axis measures the annual rate of growth in real GDP—the percent by which each year's real GDP changed compared to the previous year's real GDP. (Notice that there were nine years in which growth was negative—that is, real GDP shrank.) The vertical axis measures the *change* in the unemployment rate over the previous year in percentage points. Each dot represents the observed growth rate of real GDP and change in the unemployment rate for a given year. For example, in 2000 the average unemployment rate fell to 4.0% from 4.2% in 1999; this is shown as a value of −0.2 along the vertical axis for the year 2000. Over the same period, real GDP grew by 4.1%; this is the value shown along the horizontal axis for the year 2000.

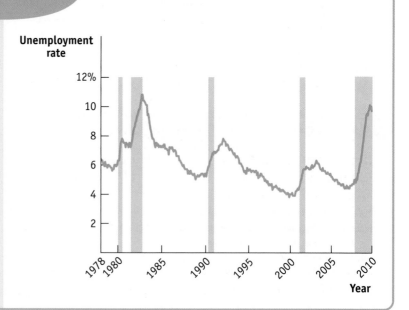

figure 12.4

Unemployment and Recessions, 1978–2010

This figure shows a close-up of the unemployment rate since the 1970s, with the shaded bars indicating recessions. It's clear that unemployment always rises during recessions and *usually* falls during expansions. But in both the early 1990s and the early 2000s, unemployment continued to rise for some time after the recession was officially declared over.

Source: Bureau of Labor Statistics; National Bureau of Economic Research.

figure 12.5   Growth and Changes in Unemployment, 1949–2009

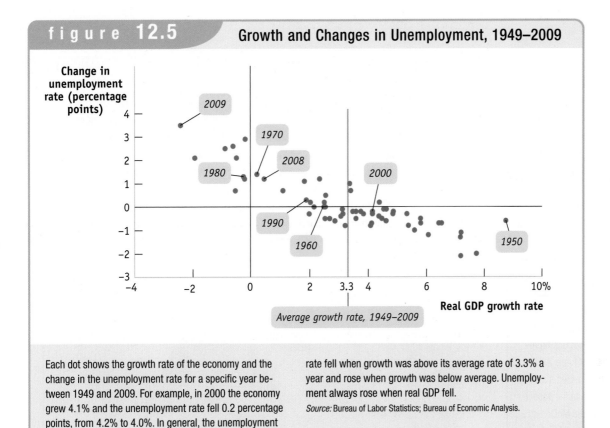

Each dot shows the growth rate of the economy and the change in the unemployment rate for a specific year between 1949 and 2009. For example, in 2000 the economy grew 4.1% and the unemployment rate fell 0.2 percentage points, from 4.2% to 4.0%. In general, the unemployment rate fell when growth was above its average rate of 3.3% a year and rose when growth was below average. Unemployment always rose when real GDP fell.

Source: Bureau of Labor Statistics; Bureau of Economic Analysis.

The downward trend of the scatter points in Figure 12.5 shows that there is a generally strong negative relationship between growth in the economy and the rate of unemployment. Years of high growth in real GDP were also years in which the unemployment rate fell, and years of low or negative growth in real GDP were years in which the unemployment rate rose. The green vertical line in Figure 12.5 at the value of 3.3% indicates the average growth rate of real GDP over the period from 1949 to 2009. Points lying to the right of the vertical line are years of above-average growth. In these years, the value on the vertical axis is usually negative, meaning that the unemployment rate fell. That is, years of above-average growth were usually years in which the unemployment rate was falling. Conversely, points lying to the left of the vertical line were years of below-average growth. In these years, the value on the vertical axis is usually positive, meaning that the unemployment rate rose. That is, years of below-average growth were usually years in which the unemployment rate was rising. There are periods in which GDP is growing, but at a below-average rate; these are periods in which the economy isn't in a recession but unemployment is still rising—sometimes called a "growth recession." But true recessions, periods when real GDP falls, are especially painful for workers. As illustrated by the points to the left of the vertical axis in Figure 12.5, falling real GDP is always associated with a rising rate of unemployment, causing a great deal of hardship to families.

Rocky Mountain Low

In addition to estimating the unemployment rate for the nation as a whole, the U.S. government also estimates unemployment rates for each state. These state unemployment rates often differ considerably—and the differences correspond to real differences in the condition of local labor markets. The figure shows how unemployment rates varied across the United States in July 2007.

As you can see from the figure, Montana had one of the lowest unemployment rates in the United States, only 2.7% in July 2007, mainly because the state's booming oil business was creating new jobs even as the state's aging population reduced the size of the labor force. And this low unemployment rate created a seller's market in labor. According to the Associated Press, the owner of the McDonald's franchise in Sidney, Montana, desperate to find workers, "tried advertising in the local newspaper and even offered up to $10 an hour to compete with higher-paying oil field jobs. Yet the only calls were from other business owners upset they would have to raise wages, too."

Michigan was at the opposite extreme. Layoffs by auto manufacturers, the traditional mainstay of Michigan's economy, had given the state the highest unemployment rate in the nation:

7.2% in July 2007. And this high unemployment rate did indeed correspond to a very poor labor market. A poll taken by the *Detroit Free Press* in early 2007 found that 3 out of every 10 young Michigan residents were considering leaving the state, including almost half of poor job prospects. These state-to-state comparisons show that the unemployment rate is indeed a good indicator of how easy or hard it is to find a job.

One thing you should know, however, is that differences in state unemployment rates don't tend to persist, in large part because, as that Michigan poll suggested, Americans tend to move to where the jobs are. As recently as 2000, Michigan had an unemployment rate of only 3.7%, well below the national average of 4.0%, while Montana had an unemployment rate of 4.8%, above the national average.

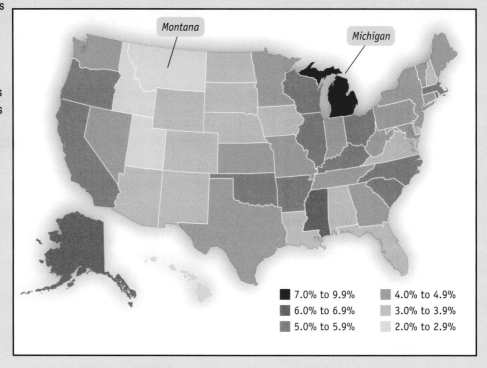

■ 7.0% to 9.9%	■ 4.0% to 4.9%
■ 6.0% to 6.9%	■ 3.0% to 3.9%
■ 5.0% to 5.9%	■ 2.0% to 2.9%

Module 12 AP Review

Solutions appear at the back of the book.

Check Your Understanding

1. Suppose that employment websites enable job-seekers to find suitable jobs more quickly. What effect will this have on the unemployment rate over time? Also suppose that these websites encourage job-seekers who had given up their searches to begin looking again. What effect will this have on the unemployment rate?

2. In which of the following cases would the worker be counted as unemployed? Explain.

   a. Rosa, an older worker, has been laid off and gave up looking for work months ago.
   b. Anthony, a schoolteacher, is not working during his three-month summer break.
   c. Grace, an investment banker, has been laid off and is currently searching for another position.
   d. Sergio, a classically trained musician, can only find work playing for local parties.

e. Natasha, a graduate student, went back to school because jobs were scarce.

3. Which of the following are consistent with the observed relationship between growth in real GDP and changes in the unemployment rate? Which are not?

a. A rise in the unemployment rate accompanies a fall in real GDP.
b. An exceptionally strong business recovery is associated with a greater percentage of the labor force being employed.
c. Negative real GDP growth is associated with a fall in the unemployment rate.

Tackle the Test: Multiple-Choice Questions

1. To be considered unemployed, a person must
   I. not be working.
   II. be actively seeking a job.
   III. be available for work.
   a. I only
   b. II only
   c. III only
   d. II and III
   e. I, II, and III

Use the information for a hypothetical economy presented in the following table to answer questions 2, 3, and 4.

Population age 16 and older = 200,000
Labor Force = 100,000
Number of people working part time = 20,000
Number of people working full time = 70,000

2. What is the labor force participation rate?
   a. 70%
   b. 50%
   c. 20%

d. 10%
e. 5%

3. How many people are unemployed?
   a. 10,000
   b. 20,000
   c. 30,000
   d. 100,000
   e. 110,000

4. What is the unemployment rate?
   a. 70%
   b. 50%
   c. 20%
   d. 10%
   e. 5%

5. The unemployment problem in an economy may be understated by the unemployment rate due to
   a. people lying about seeking a job.
   b. discouraged workers.
   c. job candidates with one offer but waiting for more.
   d. overemployed workers.
   e. none of the above.

Tackle the Test: Free-Response Questions

1. Use the data provided below to calculate each of the following. Show how you calculate each.
   a. the size of the labor force
   b. the labor force participation rate
   c. the unemployment rate

   Population age 16 and older = 12 million
   Employment = 5 million
   Unemployment = 1 million

   Answer (6 points)

   1 point: 6 million

   1 point: employment + unemployment = 5 million + 1 million = 6 million

   1 point: 50%

   1 point: (labor force/population) × 100 = ((5 million + 1 million)/12 million) × 100 = (6 million/12 million) × 100 = 50%

   1 point: 17%

   1 point: (unemployment/labor force) × 100 = (1 million/(5 million +1 million)) × 100 = (1 million/6 million) × 100 = 17%

2. What is the labor market classification of each of the following individuals? Be as specific as possible, and explain your answer.
   a. Julie has a graduate degree in mechanical engineering. She works full-time mowing lawns.
   b. Jeff was laid off from his previous job. He would very much like to work at any job, but, after looking for work for a year, has stopped looking for work.
   c. Ian is working 25 hours per week at a bookstore, and has no desire to work full time.
   d. Raj has decided to take a year off from work to stay home with his daughter.

Module 13
The Causes and Categories of Unemployment

What you will learn in this Module:

- The three different types of unemployment and their causes

- The factors that determine the natural rate of unemployment

The Natural Rate of Unemployment

Fast economic growth tends to reduce the unemployment rate. So how low can the unemployment rate go? You might be tempted to say zero, but that isn't feasible. Over the past half-century, the national unemployment rate has never dropped below 2.9%.

Can there be unemployment even when many businesses are having a hard time finding workers? To answer this question, we need to examine the nature of labor markets and why they normally lead to substantial measured unemployment even when jobs are plentiful. Our starting point is the observation that even in the best of times, jobs are constantly being created and destroyed.

Job Creation and Job Destruction

In early 2010 the unemployment rate hovered close to 10%. Even during good times, most Americans know someone who has lost his or her job. The U.S. unemployment rate in July 2007 was only 4.7%, relatively low by historical standards, yet in that month there were 4.5 million "job separations"—terminations of employment that occurred because a worker was either fired or quit voluntarily.

There are many reasons for such job loss. One is structural change in the economy: industries rise and fall as new technologies emerge and consumers' tastes change. For example, employment in high-tech industries such as telecommunications surged in the late 1990s but slumped severely after 2000. However, structural change also brings the creation of new jobs: since 2000, the number of jobs in the American healthcare sector has surged as new medical technologies have emerged and the aging of the population has increased the demand for medical care. Poor management performance or bad luck at individual companies also leads to job loss for their employees. For example, in 2005 General Motors announced plans to eliminate 30,000 jobs after several years of lagging sales, even as Japanese companies such as Toyota announced plans to open new plants in North America to meet growing demand for their cars.

This constant churning of the workforce is an inevitable feature of the modern economy. And this churning, in turn, is one source of *frictional unemployment*—one main reason that there is a considerable amount of unemployment even when jobs are abundant.

Frictional Unemployment

Workers who lose a job involuntarily due to job destruction often choose not to take the first new job offered. For example, suppose a skilled programmer, laid off because her software company's product line was unsuccessful, sees a help-wanted ad for clerical work in the local newspaper. She might respond to the ad and get the job—but that would be foolish. Instead, she should take the time to look for a job that takes advantage of her skills and pays accordingly. In addition, individual workers are constantly leaving jobs voluntarily, typically for personal reasons—family moves, dissatisfaction, and better job prospects elsewhere.

Economists say that workers who spend time looking for employment are engaged in **job search.** If all workers and all jobs were alike, job search wouldn't be necessary; if information about jobs and workers were perfect, job search would be very quick. In practice, however, it's normal for a worker who loses a job, or a young worker seeking a first job, to spend at least a few weeks searching.

Frictional unemployment is unemployment due to the time workers spend in job search. A certain amount of frictional unemployment is inevitable, for two reasons. One is the constant process of job creation and job destruction. The other is the fact that new workers are always entering the labor market. For example, in January 2010, when unemployment was high, out of 14.8 million workers counted as unemployed, 1.2 million were new entrants to the workforce and another 3.6 million were "re-entrants"—people who had come back after being out of the workforce for a time.

A limited amount of frictional unemployment is relatively harmless and may even be a good thing. The economy is more productive if workers take the time to find jobs that are well matched to their skills, and workers who are unemployed for a brief period while searching for the right job don't experience great hardship. In fact, when there is a low unemployment rate, periods of unemployment tend to be quite short, suggesting that much of the unemployment is frictional. Figure 13.1 shows the composition of unemployment in

Workers who spend time looking for employment are engaged in **job search.**

Frictional unemployment is unemployment due to the time workers spend in job search.

During the housing slump of 2009 when unemployment was running very high, many construction workers resorted to more traditional methods of finding work.

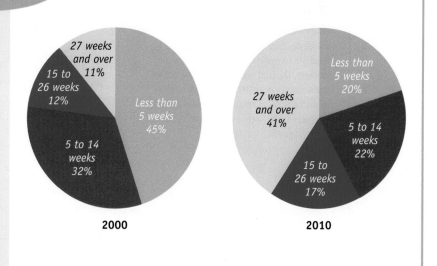

figure 13.1

Distribution of the Unemployed by Duration of Unemployment, 2000 and 2010

In years when the unemployment rate is low, most unemployed workers are unemployed for only a short period. In 2000, a year of low unemployment, 45% of the unemployed had been unemployed for less than 5 weeks and 77% for less than 15 weeks. The short duration of unemployment for most workers suggests that most unemployment in 2000 was frictional. In early 2010, by contrast, only 20% of the unemployed had been unemployed for less than 5 weeks, but 41% had been unemployed for 27 or more weeks, indicating that during periods of high unemployment, a smaller share of unemployment is frictional.

Source: Bureau of Labor Statistics.

2000

27 weeks and over 11%
15 to 26 weeks 12%
Less than 5 weeks 45%
5 to 14 weeks 32%

2010

Less than 5 weeks 20%
27 weeks and over 41%
5 to 14 weeks 22%
15 to 26 weeks 17%

2000, when the unemployment rate was only 4%. Forty-five percent of the unemployed had been unemployed for less than 5 weeks and only 23% had been unemployed for 15 or more weeks. Just 11% were considered to be "long-term unemployed"—unemployed for 27 or more weeks. The picture looked very different in January 2010, after unemployment had been high for an extended period of time.

In periods of higher unemployment, workers tend to be jobless for longer periods of time, suggesting that a smaller share of unemployment is frictional. By early 2010, when unemployment had been high for several months, for instance, the fraction of unemployed workers considered "long-term unemployed" had jumped to 41%.

Structural Unemployment

Frictional unemployment exists even when the number of people seeking jobs is equal to the number of jobs being offered—that is, the existence of frictional unemployment doesn't mean that there is a surplus of labor. Sometimes, however, there is a *persistent surplus* of job-seekers in a particular labor market. For example, there may be more workers with a particular skill than there are jobs available using that skill, or there may be more workers in a particular geographic region than there are jobs available in that region. **Structural unemployment** is unemployment that results when there are more people seeking jobs in a labor market than there are jobs available at the current wage rate.

The supply and demand model tells us that the price of a good, service, or factor of production tends to move toward an equilibrium level that matches the quantity supplied with the quantity demanded. This is equally true, in general, of labor markets. Figure 13.2 shows a typical market for labor. The labor demand curve indicates that when the price of labor—the wage rate—increases, employers demand less labor. The labor supply curve indicates that when the price of labor increases, more workers are willing to supply labor at the prevailing wage rate. These two forces coincide to lead to an equilibrium wage rate for any given type of labor in a particular location. That equilibrium wage rate is shown as W_E.

Even at the equilibrium wage rate, W_E, there will still be some frictional unemployment. That's because there will always be some workers engaged in job search even when the number of jobs available is equal to the number of workers seeking jobs. But there wouldn't be any structural unemployment in this labor market. *Structural unemployment*

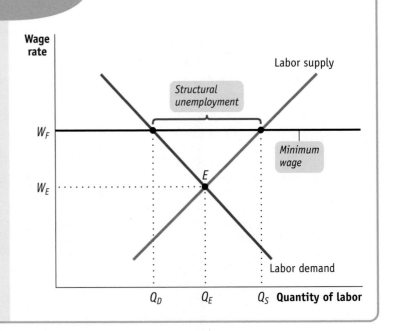

figure 13.2

The Effect of a Minimum Wage on the Labor Market

When the government sets a minimum wage, W_F, that exceeds the market equilibrium wage rate, W_E, the number of workers, Q_S, who would like to work at that minimum wage is greater than the number of workers, Q_D, demanded at that wage rate. This surplus of labor is considered structural unemployment.

occurs when the wage rate is, for some reason, persistently above W_E. Several factors can lead to a wage rate in excess of W_E, the most important being minimum wages, labor unions, *efficiency wages,* and the side effects of government policies.

Minimum Wages As explained in Module 8, a minimum wage is a government-mandated floor on the price of labor. In the United States, the national minimum wage in 2009 was $7.25 an hour. For many American workers, the minimum wage is irrelevant; the market equilibrium wage for these workers is well above this price floor. But for less skilled workers, the minimum wage may be binding—it affects the wages that people are actually paid and can lead to structural unemployment. In countries that have higher minimum wages, the range of workers for whom the minimum wage is binding is larger.

Figure 13.2 shows the effect of a binding minimum wage. In this market, there is a legal floor on wages, W_F, which is above the equilibrium wage rate, W_E. This leads to a persistent surplus in the labor market: the quantity of labor supplied, Q_S, is larger than the quantity demanded, Q_D. In other words, more people want to work than can find jobs at the minimum wage, leading to structural unemployment.

Given that minimum wages—that is, binding minimum wages—generally lead to structural unemployment, you might wonder why governments impose them. The rationale is to help ensure that people who work can earn enough income to afford at least a minimally comfortable lifestyle. However, this may come at a cost, because it may eliminate employment opportunities for some workers who would have willingly worked for lower wages. As illustrated in Figure 13.2, not only are there more sellers of labor than there are buyers, but there are also fewer people working at a minimum wage (Q_D) than there would have been with no minimum wage at all (Q_E).

Although economists broadly agree that a high minimum wage has the employment-reducing effects shown in Figure 13.2, there is some question about whether this is a good description of how the minimum wage actually works in the United States. The minimum wage in the United States is quite low compared with that in other wealthy countries. For three decades, from the 1970s to the mid-2000s, the U.S. minimum wage was so low that it was not binding for the vast majority of workers. In addition, some researchers have produced evidence that increases in the minimum wage actually lead to higher employment when, as was the case in the United States at one time, the minimum wage is low compared to average wages. They argue that firms that employ low-skilled workers sometimes restrict their hiring in order to keep wages low and that, as a result, the minimum wage can sometimes be increased without any loss of jobs. Most economists, however, agree that a sufficiently high minimum wage *does* lead to structural unemployment.

Labor Unions The actions of *labor unions* can have effects similar to those of minimum wages, leading to structural unemployment. By bargaining collectively for all of a firm's workers, unions can often win higher wages from employers than workers would have obtained by bargaining individually. This process, known as *collective bargaining,* is intended to tip the scales of bargaining power more toward workers and away from employers. Labor unions exercise bargaining power by threatening firms with a *labor strike,* a collective refusal to work. The threat of a strike can have very serious consequences for firms that have difficulty replacing striking workers. In such cases, workers acting collectively can exercise more power than they could if they acted individually.

When workers have greater bargaining power, they tend to demand and receive higher wages. Unions also bargain over benefits, such as health care and pensions, which we can think of as additional wages. Indeed, economists who study the effects of unions on wages find that unionized workers earn higher wages and more generous benefits than non-union workers with similar skills. The result of these increased wages can be the same as the result of a minimum wage: labor unions

Bill Pugliano/Stringer/Getty Images

Members of the United Auto Workers (UAW) union march on a picket line during a strike to protest unfair labor practices.

push the wage that workers receive above the equilibrium wage. Consequently, there are more people willing to work at the wage being paid than there are jobs available. Like a binding minimum wage, this leads to structural unemployment.

Efficiency Wages Actions by firms may also contribute to structural unemployment. Firms may choose to pay **efficiency wages**—wages that employers set above the equilibrium wage rate as an incentive for their workers to deliver better performance.

Employers may feel the need for such incentives for several reasons. For example, employers often have difficulty observing directly how hard an employee works. They can, however, elicit more work effort by paying above-market wages: employees receiving these higher wages are more likely to work harder to ensure that they aren't fired, which would cause them to lose their higher wages.

When many firms pay efficiency wages, the result is a pool of workers who want jobs but can't find them. So the use of efficiency wages by firms leads to structural unemployment.

Side Effects of Public Policy In addition, public policy designed to help workers who lose their jobs can lead to structural unemployment as an unintended side effect. Most economically advanced countries provide benefits to laid-off workers as a way to tide them over until they find a new job. In the United States, these benefits typically replace only a small fraction of a worker's income and expire after 26 weeks. In other countries, particularly in Europe, benefits are more generous and last longer. The drawback to this generosity is that it reduces the incentive to quickly find a new job, and by keeping more people searching for longer, the benefits increase structural and frictional unemployment. Generous unemployment benefits in some European countries are widely believed to be one of the main causes of "Eurosclerosis," the persistent high unemployment that afflicts a number of European economies.

The Natural Rate of Unemployment

Because some frictional unemployment is inevitable and because many economies also suffer from structural unemployment, a certain amount of unemployment is normal, or "natural. " Actual unemployment fluctuates around this normal level. The **natural rate of unemployment** is the normal unemployment rate around which the actual unemployment rate fluctuates. It is the rate of unemployment that arises from the effects of frictional plus structural unemployment. **Cyclical unemployment** is the deviation of the actual rate of unemployment from the natural rate; that is, it is the difference between the actual and natural rates of unemployment. As the name suggests, cyclical unemployment is the share of unemployment that arises from the business cycle. We'll see later that public policy cannot keep the unemployment rate persistently below the natural rate without leading to accelerating inflation.

We can summarize the relationships between the various types of unemployment as follows:

(13-1) Natural unemployment =
        Frictional unemployment + Structural unemployment

(13-2) Actual unemployment =
        Natural unemployment + Cyclical unemployment

Perhaps because of its name, people often imagine that the natural rate of unemployment is a constant that doesn't change over time and can't be affected by policy. Neither proposition is true. Let's take a moment to stress two facts: the natural rate of unemployment changes over time, and it can be affected by economic policies.

Changes in the Natural Rate of Unemployment

Private-sector economists and government agencies need estimates of the natural rate of unemployment both to make forecasts and to conduct policy analyses. Almost all these estimates show that the U.S. natural rate rises and falls over time. For example, the Congressional Budget Office, the independent agency that conducts budget and economic analyses for Congress, believes that the U.S. natural rate of unemployment was 5.3% in 1950, rose to 6.3% by the end of the 1970s, but has fallen to 4.8% today. European countries have experienced even larger swings in their natural rates of unemployment.

What causes the natural rate of unemployment to change? The most important factors are changes in the characteristics of the labor force, changes in labor market institutions, and changes in government policies. Let's look briefly at each factor.

Changes in Labor Force Characteristics In January 2010 the overall rate of unemployment in the United States was 9.7%. Young workers, however, had much higher unemployment rates: 26.4% for teenagers and 15.8% for workers aged 20 to 24. Workers aged 25 to 54 had an unemployment rate of only 8.6%.

In general, unemployment rates tend to be lower for experienced than for inexperienced workers. Because experienced workers tend to stay in a given job longer than do inexperienced ones, they have lower frictional unemployment. Also, because older workers are more likely than young workers to be family breadwinners, they have a stronger incentive to find and keep jobs.

One reason the natural rate of unemployment rose during the 1970s was a large rise in the number of new workers—children of the post–World War II baby boom entered the labor force, as did a rising percentage of married women. As Figure 13.3 shows, both the percentage of the labor force less than 25 years old and the percentage of women in the labor force surged in the 1970s. By the end of the 1990s, however, the share of women in the labor force had leveled off and the percentage of workers under 25 had fallen sharply. As a result, the labor force as a whole is more experienced today than it was in the 1970s, one likely reason that the natural rate of unemployment is lower today than in the 1970s.

Changes in Labor Market Institutions As we pointed out earlier, unions that negotiate wages above the equilibrium level can be a source of structural unemployment. Some economists believe that strong labor unions are one reason for the high natural rate of unemployment in Europe. In the United States, a sharp fall in union membership after 1980 may have been one reason the natural rate of unemployment fell between the 1970s and the 1990s.

Other institutional changes may also have been at work. For example, some labor economists believe that temporary employment agencies, which have proliferated in recent years, have reduced frictional unemployment by helping match workers to jobs. Furthermore, Internet websites such as monster.com may have reduced frictional unemployment.

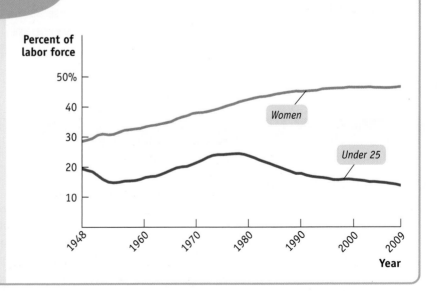

figure 13.3

The Changing Makeup of the U.S. Labor Force, 1948–2009

In the 1970s the percentage of the labor force consisting of women rose rapidly, as did the percentage under age 25. These changes reflected the entry of large numbers of women into the paid labor force for the first time and the fact that baby boomers were reaching working age. The natural rate of unemployment may have risen because many of these workers were relatively inexperienced. Today, the labor force is much more experienced, which is one possible reason the natural rate has fallen since the 1970s.

Source: Bureau of Labor Statistics.

Technological change, coupled with labor market institutions, can also affect the natural rate of unemployment.

Technological change probably leads to an increase in the demand for skilled workers who are familiar with the relevant technology and a reduction in the demand for unskilled workers. Economic theory predicts that wages should increase for skilled workers and decrease for unskilled workers. But if wages for unskilled workers cannot go down—say, due to a binding minimum wage—increased structural unemployment, and therefore a higher natural rate of unemployment, will result.

Changes in Government Policies A high minimum wage can cause structural unemployment. Generous unemployment benefits can increase both structural and frictional unemployment. So government policies intended to help workers can have the undesirable side effect of raising the natural rate of unemployment.

Some government policies, however, may reduce the natural rate. Two examples are job training and employment subsidies. Job-training programs are supposed to provide unemployed workers with skills that widen the range of jobs they can perform. Employment subsidies are payments either to workers or to employers that provide a financial incentive to accept or offer jobs.

fyi

Structural Unemployment in Eastern Germany

In one of the most dramatic events in world history, a spontaneous popular uprising in 1989 overthrew the communist dictatorship in East Germany. Citizens quickly tore down the wall that had divided Berlin, and in short order East and West Germany became a united, democratic nation.

Then the trouble started.

After reunification, employment in East Germany plunged and the unemployment rate soared. This high unemployment rate has persisted: despite receiving massive aid from the federal German government, the economy of the former East Germany has remained persist-

ently depressed, with an unemployment rate of 12.1% in December 2009, compared to West Germany's unemployment rate of 6.7%. Other parts of formerly communist Eastern Europe have done much better. For example, the Czech Republic, which was often cited along with East Germany as a relatively successful communist economy, had a comparatively lower unemployment rate of only 9.2% in December 2009. What went wrong in East Germany?

The answer is that, through nobody's fault, East Germany found itself suffering from severe structural unemployment. When Germany was reuni-

fied, it became clear that workers in East Germany were much less productive than their cousins in the west. Yet unions initially demanded wage rates equal to those in West Germany, and these wage rates have been slow to come down because East German workers don't want to be treated as inferior to their West German counterparts. Meanwhile, productivity in the former East Germany has remained well below West German levels, in part because of decades of misguided investment. The result has been a persistently large mismatch between the number of workers demanded and the number of those seeking jobs.

Module 13 APReview

Solutions appear at the back of the book.

Check Your Understanding

1. Explain the following.
   a. Frictional unemployment always exists.
   b. Frictional unemployment accounts for a larger share of total unemployment when the unemployment rate is low.

2. Why does collective bargaining have the same general effect on unemployment as a minimum wage? Illustrate your answer with a diagram.

3. Suppose the United States dramatically increases benefits for unemployed workers. Explain what will happen to the natural rate of unemployment.

Tackle the Test: Multiple-Choice Questions

1. A person who moved to a new state and took two months to find a new job experienced which type of unemployment?
   a. frictional
   b. structural
   c. cyclical
   d. natural
   e. none of the above

2. What type of unemployment is created by a recession?
   a. frictional
   b. structural
   c. cyclical
   d. natural
   e. none of the above

3. A person who is unemployed because of a mismatch between the quantity of labor supplied and the quantity of labor demanded is experiencing what type of unemployment?
   a. frictional
   b. structural
   c. cyclical
   d. natural
   e. none of the above

4. Which of the following is true of the natural rate of unemployment?
   I. It includes frictional unemployment.
   II. It includes structural unemployment.
   III. It is equal to 0%.
   a. I only
   b. II only
   c. III only
   d. I and II
   e. I, II, and III

5. Which of the following can affect the natural rate of unemployment in an economy over time?
   a. labor force characteristics such as age and work experience
   b. the existence of labor unions
   c. advances in technologies that help workers find jobs
   d. government job training programs
   e. all of the above

Tackle the Test: Free-Response Questions

1. a. Define the natural rate of unemployment.
   b. The natural rate of unemployment is made up of which of the types of unemployment?
   c. Explain how cyclical unemployment relates to the natural rate of unemployment.
   d. List three factors that can lead to a change in the natural rate of unemployment.

Answer (7 points)

1 point: The natural rate of unemployment is the normal unemployment rate around which the actual unemployment rate fluctuates.

1 point: The natural rate of unemployment is made up of frictional unemployment . . .

1 point: . . . plus structural unemployment.

1 point: Cyclical unemployment is the deviation of the actual rate of unemployment from the natural rate. *Or,* cyclical unemployment is the difference between the actual and natural rates of unemployment.

1 point: Changes in labor force characteristics

1 point: Changes in labor market institutions such as unions

1 point: Changes in government policies

2. In each of the following situations, what type of unemployment is Melanie facing? Explain.
   a. After completing a complex programming project, Melanie is laid off. Her prospects for a new job requiring similar skills are good, and she has signed up with a programmer placement service. She has passed up offers for low-paying jobs.
   b. When Melanie and her co-workers refused to accept pay cuts, her employer outsourced their programming tasks to workers in another country. This phenomenon is occurring throughout the programming industry.
   c. Due to the current slump in investment spending, Melanie has been laid off from her programming job. Her employer promises to rehire her when business picks up.

Module 14
Inflation: An Overview

Inflation and Deflation

In 1980 Americans were dismayed about the state of the economy for two reasons: the unemployment rate was high, and so was inflation. In fact, the high rate of inflation, not the high rate of unemployment, was the principal concern of policy makers at the time—so much so that Paul Volcker, the chairman of the Federal Reserve Board (which controls monetary policy), more or less deliberately created a deep recession in order to bring inflation under control. Only in 1982, after inflation had dropped sharply and the unemployment rate had risen to more than 10%, did fighting unemployment become the chief priority.

Why is inflation something to worry about? Why do policy makers even now get anxious when they see the inflation rate moving upward? The answer is that inflation can impose costs on the economy—but not in the way most people think.

The Level of Prices Doesn't Matter . . .

The most common complaint about inflation, an increase in the price level, is that it makes everyone poorer—after all, a given amount of money buys less. But inflation does *not* make everyone poorer. To see why, it's helpful to imagine what would happen if the United States did something other countries have done from time to time—replaced the dollar with a new currency.

A recent example of this kind of currency conversion happened in 2002, when France, like a number of other European countries, replaced its national currency, the franc, with the new Pan-European currency, the euro. People turned in their franc coins and notes, and received euro coins and notes in exchange, at a rate of precisely 6.55957 francs per euro. At the same time, all contracts were restated in euros at the same rate of exchange. For example, if a French citizen had a home mortgage debt of 500,000 francs, this became a debt of 500,000/6.55957 = 76,224.51 euros. If a worker's contract specified that he or she should be paid 100 francs per hour, it became a contract specifying a wage of 100/6.55957 = 15.2449 euros per hour, and so on.

You could imagine doing the same thing here, replacing the dollar with a "new dollar" at a rate of exchange of, say, 7 to 1. If you owed $140,000 on your home, that would become a debt of 20,000 new dollars. If you had a wage rate of $14 an hour, it would become 2 new dollars an hour, and so on. This would bring the overall U.S. price level back to about what it was when John F. Kennedy was president.

So would everyone be richer as a result because prices would be only one-seventh as high? Of course not. Prices would be lower, but so would wages and incomes in general. If you cut a worker's wage to one-seventh of its previous value, but also cut all prices to one-seventh of their previous level, the worker's **real wage**—the wage rate divided by the price level—doesn't change. In fact, bringing the overall price level back to what it was during the Kennedy administration would have no effect on overall purchasing power, because doing so would reduce income exactly as much as it reduced prices. Conversely, the rise in prices that has actually taken place since the early 1960s hasn't made America poorer, because it has also raised incomes by the same amount: **real income**—income divided by the price level—hasn't been affected by the rise in overall prices.

The moral of this story is that the *level* of prices doesn't matter: the United States would be no richer than it is now if the overall level of prices was still as low as it was in 1961; conversely, the rise in prices over the past 45 years hasn't made us poorer.

The **real wage** is the wage rate divided by the price level.

Real income is income divided by the price level.

The **inflation rate** is the percent change per year in a price index—typically the consumer price index.

. . . But the Rate of Change of Prices Does

The conclusion that the level of prices doesn't matter might seem to imply that the inflation rate doesn't matter either. But that's not true.

To see why, it's crucial to distinguish between the *level of prices* and the *inflation rate*. In the next module, we will discuss precisely how the level of prices in the economy is measured using price indexes such as the consumer price index. For now, let's look at the **inflation rate,** the percent increase in the overall level of prices per year. The inflation rate is calculated as follows:

$$\text{Inflation rate} = \frac{\text{Price level in year 2} - \text{Price level in year 1}}{\text{Price level in year 1}} \times 100$$

Figure 14.1 highlights the difference between the price level and the inflation rate in the United States since 1969, with the price level measured along the left vertical axis and the inflation rate measured along the right vertical axis. In the 2000s, the overall

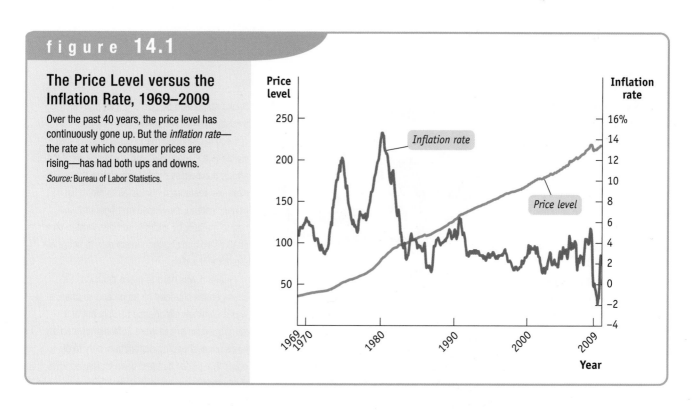

figure 14.1

The Price Level versus the Inflation Rate, 1969–2009

Over the past 40 years, the price level has continuously gone up. But the *inflation rate*—the rate at which consumer prices are rising—has had both ups and downs.
Source: Bureau of Labor Statistics.

level of prices in the United States was much higher than it was in 1969—but that, as we've learned, didn't matter. The inflation rate in the 2000s, however, was much lower than in the 1970s—and that almost certainly made the economy richer than it would have been if high inflation had continued.

Economists believe that high rates of inflation impose significant economic costs. The most important of these costs are *shoe-leather costs, menu costs,* and *unit-of-account costs.* We'll discuss each in turn.

Shoe-Leather Costs People hold money—cash in their wallets and bank deposits on which they can write checks—for convenience in making transactions. A high inflation rate, however, discourages people from holding money, because the purchasing power of the cash in your wallet and the funds in your bank account steadily erodes as the overall level of prices rises. This leads people to search for ways to reduce the amount of money they hold, often at considerable economic cost.

During the most famous of all inflations, the German *hyperinflation* of 1921–1923, merchants employed runners to take their cash to the bank many times a day to convert it into something that would hold its value, such as a stable foreign currency. In an effort to avoid having the purchasing power of their money eroded, people used up valuable resources—the time and labor of the runners—that could have been used productively elsewhere. During the German hyperinflation, so many banking transactions were taking place that the number of employees at German banks nearly quadrupled—from around 100,000 in 1913 to 375,000 in 1923. More recently, Brazil experienced hyperinflation during the early 1990s; during that episode, the Brazilian banking sector grew so large that it accounted for 15% of GDP, more than twice the size of the financial sector in the United States measured as a share of GDP. The large increase in the Brazilian banking sector that was needed to cope with the consequences of inflation represented a loss of real resources to its society.

fyi

Israel's Experience with Inflation

It's hard to see the costs of inflation clearly because serious inflation is often associated with other problems that disrupt the economy and life in general, notably war or political instability (or both). In the mid-1980s, however, Israel experienced a "clean" inflation: there was no war, the government was stable, and there was order in the streets. Yet a series of policy errors led to very high inflation, with prices often rising more than 10% a month.

As it happens, one of the authors spent a month visiting Tel Aviv University at the height of the inflation, so we can give a first-hand account of the effects.

First, the shoe-leather costs of inflation were substantial. At the time, Israelis spent a lot of time in lines at the bank, moving money in and

The shoe-leather costs of inflation in Israel: when the inflation rate hit 500% in 1985, people spent a lot of time in line at banks.

out of accounts that provided high enough interest rates to offset inflation. People walked around with very little cash in their wallets; they had to go to the bank whenever they needed to make even a moderately large cash payment.

Banks responded by opening a lot of branches, a costly business expense.

Second, although menu costs weren't that visible to a visitor, what you could see were the efforts businesses made to minimize them. For example, restaurant menus often didn't list prices. Instead, they listed numbers that you had to multiply by another number, written on a chalkboard and changed every day, to figure out the price of a dish.

Finally, it was hard to make decisions because prices changed so much and so often. It was a common experience to walk out of a store because prices were 25% higher than at one's usual shopping destination, only to discover that prices had just been increased 25% there, too.

Increased costs of transactions caused by inflation are known as **shoe-leather costs,** an allusion to the wear and tear caused by the extra running around that takes place when people are trying to avoid holding money. Shoe-leather costs are substantial in economies with very high inflation rates, as anyone who has lived in such an economy—say, one suffering inflation of 100% or more per year—can attest. Most estimates suggest, however, that the shoe-leather costs of inflation at the rates seen in the United States—which in peacetime has never had inflation above 15%—are quite small.

Menu Costs In a modern economy, most of the things we buy have a listed price. There's a price listed under each item on a supermarket shelf, a price printed on the front page of your newspaper, a price listed for each dish on a restaurant's menu. Changing a listed price has a real cost, called a **menu cost.** For example, to change a price in a supermarket may require a clerk to change the price listed under the item on the shelf and an office worker to change the price associated with the item's UPC code in the store's computer. In the face of inflation, of course, firms are forced to change prices more often than they would if the price level was more or less stable. This means higher costs for the economy as a whole.

In times of very high inflation rates, menu costs can be substantial. During the Brazilian inflation of the early 1990s, for instance, supermarket workers reportedly spent half of their time replacing old price stickers with new ones. When the inflation rate is high, merchants may decide to stop listing prices in terms of the local currency and use either an artificial unit—in effect, measuring prices relative to one another—or a more stable currency, such as the U.S. dollar. This is exactly what the Israeli real estate market began doing in the mid-1980s: prices were quoted in U.S. dollars, even though payment was made in Israeli shekels. And this is also what happened in Zimbabwe when, in May 2008, official estimates of the inflation rate reached 1,694,000%.

Menu costs are also present in low-inflation economies, but they are not severe. In low-inflation economies, businesses might update their prices only sporadically—not daily or even more frequently, as is the case in high-inflation or hyperinflation economies. Also, with technological advances, menu costs are becoming less and less important, since prices can be changed electronically and fewer merchants attach price stickers to merchandise.

Unit-of-Account Costs In the Middle Ages, contracts were often specified "in kind": a tenant might, for example, be obliged to provide his landlord with a certain number of cattle each year (the phrase *in kind* actually comes from an ancient word for *cattle*). This may have made sense at the time, but it would be an awkward way to conduct modern business. Instead, we state contracts in monetary terms: a renter owes a certain number of dollars per month, a company that issues a bond promises to pay the bondholder the dollar value of the bond when it comes due, and so on. We also tend to make our economic calculations in dollars: a family planning its budget, or a small business owner trying to figure out how well the business is doing, makes estimates of the amount of money coming in and going out.

This role of the dollar as a basis for contracts and calculation is called the *unit-of-account* role of money. It's an important aspect of the modern economy. Yet it's a role that can be degraded by inflation, which causes the purchasing power of a dollar to change over time—a dollar next year is worth less than a dollar this year. The effect, many economists argue, is to reduce the quality of economic decisions: the economy as a whole makes less efficient use of its resources because of the uncertainty caused by changes in the unit of account, the dollar. The **unit-of-account costs** of inflation are the costs arising from the way inflation makes money a less reliable unit of measurement.

Unit-of-account costs may be particularly important in the tax system, because inflation can distort the measures of income on which taxes are collected. Here's an example: Assume that the inflation rate is 10%, so that the overall level of prices rises 10% each year. Suppose that a business buys an asset, such as a piece of land, for $100,000 and then resells it a year later at a price of $110,000. In a fundamental sense, the business didn't make a profit on the deal: in real terms, it got no more for the land than it paid for it, because the $110,000 would purchase no more goods than the $100,000

Shoe-leather costs are the increased costs of transactions caused by inflation.

Menu costs are the real costs of changing listed prices.

Unit-of-account costs arise from the way inflation makes money a less reliable unit of measurement.

would have a year earlier. But U.S. tax law would say that the business made a capital gain of $10,000, and it would have to pay taxes on that phantom gain.

During the 1970s, when the United States had a relatively high inflation rate, the distorting effects of inflation on the tax system were a serious problem. Some businesses were discouraged from productive investment spending because they found themselves paying taxes on phantom gains. Meanwhile, some unproductive investments became attractive because they led to phantom losses that reduced tax bills. When the inflation rate fell in the 1980s—and tax rates were reduced—these problems became much less important.

Winners and Losers from Inflation

As we've just learned, a high inflation rate imposes overall costs on the economy. In addition, inflation can produce winners and losers within the economy. The main reason inflation sometimes helps some people while hurting others is that economic transactions, such as loans, often involve contracts that extend over a period of time and these contracts are normally specified in nominal—that is, in dollar—terms. In the case of a loan, the borrower receives a certain amount of funds at the beginning, and the loan contract specifies how much he or she must repay at some future date. But what that dollar repayment is worth in real terms—that is, in terms of purchasing power—depends greatly on the rate of inflation over the intervening years of the loan.

The *interest rate* on a loan is the percentage of the loan amount that the borrower must pay to the lender, typically on an annual basis, in addition to the repayment of the loan amount itself. Economists summarize the effect of inflation on borrowers and lenders by distinguishing between *nominal* interest rates and *real* interest rates. The **nominal interest rate** is the interest rate that is actually paid for a loan, unadjusted for the effects of inflation. For example, the interest rates advertised on student loans and every interest rate you see listed by a bank is a nominal rate. The **real interest rate** is the nominal interest rate adjusted for inflation. This adjustment is achieved by simply subtracting the inflation rate from the nominal interest rate. For example, if a loan carries a nominal interest rate of 8%, but the inflation rate is 5%, the real interest rate is 8% − 5% = 3%.

When a borrower and a lender enter into a loan contract, the contract normally specifies a nominal interest rate. But each party has an expectation about the future rate of inflation and therefore an expectation about the real interest rate on the loan. If the actual inflation rate is *higher* than expected, borrowers gain at the expense of lenders: borrowers will repay their loans with funds that have a lower real value than had been expected—they can purchase fewer goods and service than expected due to the surprisingly high inflation rate. Conversely, if the inflation rate is *lower* than expected, lenders will gain at the expense of borrowers: borrowers must repay their loans with funds that have a higher real value than had been expected.

Historically, the fact that inflation creates winners and losers has sometimes been a major source of political controversy. In 1896 William Jennings Bryan electrified the Democratic presidential convention with a speech in which he declared, "You shall not crucify mankind on a cross of gold." What he was actually demanding was an inflationary policy. At the time, the U.S. dollar had a fixed value in terms of gold. Bryan wanted the U.S. government to abandon the gold standard and print more money, which would have raised the level of prices and, he believed, helped the nation's farmers who were deeply in debt.

In modern America, home mortgages (loans for the purchase of homes) are the most important source of gains and losses from inflation. Americans who took out mortgages in the early 1970s quickly found their real payments reduced by higher-than-expected inflation: by 1983, the purchasing power of a dollar was only 45% of what it had been in 1973. Those who took out mortgages in the early 1990s were not so lucky, because the inflation rate fell to lower-than-expected levels in the following years: in 2003 the purchasing power of a dollar was 78% of what it had been in 1993.

Because gains for some and losses for others result from inflation that is either higher or lower than expected, yet another problem arises: uncertainty about the future inflation rate discourages people from entering into any form of long-term contract. This is an additional cost of high inflation, because high rates of inflation are usually unpredictable, too. In countries with high and uncertain inflation, long-term loans are rare. This, in turn, makes it difficult for people to commit to long-term investments.

One last point: unexpected deflation—a surprise fall in the price level—creates winners and losers, too. Between 1929 and 1933, as the U.S. economy plunged into the Great Depression, the price level fell by 35%. This meant that debtors, including many farmers and homeowners, saw a sharp rise in the real value of their debts, which led to widespread bankruptcy and helped create a banking crisis, as lenders found their customers unable to pay back their loans.

Disinflation is the process of bringing the inflation rate down.

Inflation Is Easy; Disinflation Is Hard

There is not much evidence that a rise in the inflation rate from, say, 2% to 5% would do a great deal of harm to the economy. Still, policy makers generally move forcefully to bring inflation back down when it creeps above 2% or 3%. Why? Because experience shows that bringing the inflation rate down—a process called **disinflation**—is very difficult and costly once a higher rate of inflation has become well established in the economy.

Figure 14.2 shows the inflation rate and the unemployment rate in the United States over a crucial decade, from 1978 to 1988. The decade began with an alarming rise in the inflation rate, but by the end of the period inflation averaged only about 4%. This was considered a major economic achievement—but it came at a high cost. Much of the fall in inflation probably resulted from the very severe recession of 1981–1982, which drove the unemployment rate to 10.8%—its highest level since the Great Depression.

Many economists believe that this period of high unemployment was necessary, because they believe that the only way to reduce inflation that has become deeply embedded in the economy is through policies that temporarily depress the economy. The best way to avoid having to put the economy through a wringer to reduce inflation, however, is to avoid having a serious inflation problem in the first place. So, policy makers respond forcefully to signs that inflation may be accelerating as a form of preventive medicine for the economy.

figure 14.2

The Cost of Disinflation

The U.S. inflation rate peaked in 1980 and then fell sharply. Progress against inflation was, however, accompanied by a temporary but very large increase in the unemployment rate, demonstrating the high cost of disinflation.

Source: Bureau of Labor Statistics.

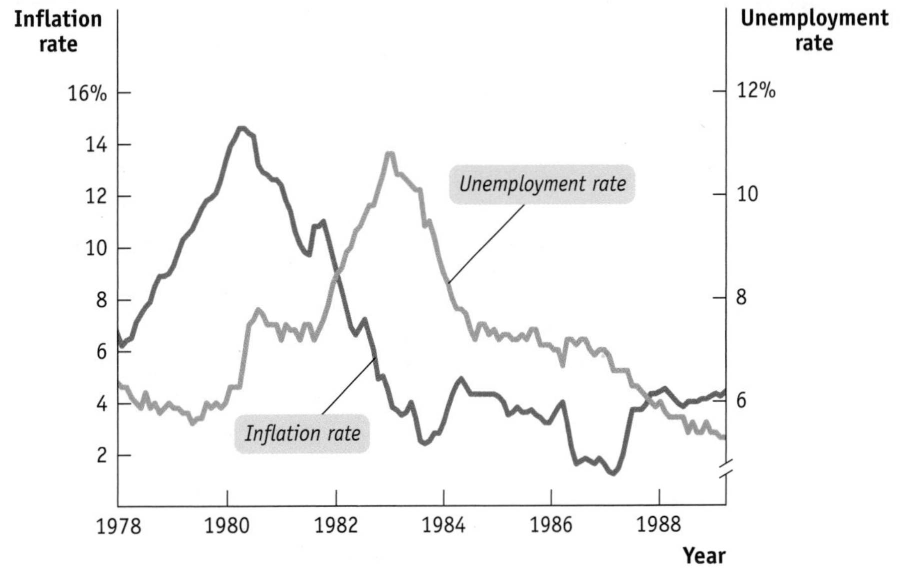

Solutions appear at the back of the book.

Check Your Understanding

1. The widespread use of technology has revolutionized the banking industry, making it much easier for customers to access and manage their assets. Does this mean that the shoe-leather costs of inflation are higher or lower than they used to be? Explain.

2. Most people in the United States have grown accustomed to a modest inflation rate of around 2-3%. Who would gain and who would lose if inflation came to a complete stop for several years? Explain.

Tackle the Test: Multiple-Choice Questions

1. Which of the following is true regarding prices in an economy?
   - I. An increase in the price level is called inflation.
   - II. The level of prices doesn't matter.
   - III. The rate of change in prices matters.
   - a. I only
   - b. II only
   - c. III only
   - d. II and III only
   - e. I, II, and III

2. If your nominal wage doubles at the same time as prices double, your real wage will
   - a. increase.
   - b. decrease
   - c. not change.
   - d. double.
   - e. be impossible to determine.

3. If inflation causes people to frequently convert their dollars into other assets, the economy experiences what type of cost?
   - a. price level
   - b. shoe-leather

   - c. menu
   - d. unit-of-account
   - e. monetary

4. Because dollars are used as the basis for contracts, inflation leads to which type of cost?
   - a. price level
   - b. shoe-leather
   - c. menu
   - d. unit-of-account
   - e. monetary

5. Changing the listed price when inflation leads to a price increase is an example of which type of cost?
   - a. price level
   - b. shoe-leather
   - c. menu
   - d. unit-of-account
   - e. monetary

Tackle the Test: Free-Response Questions

1. In the following examples, is inflation creating winners and losers at no net cost to the economy or is it imposing a net cost on the economy? Explain. If inflation is imposing a net cost on the economy, which type of cost is involved?
   a. When inflation is expected to be high, workers get paid more frequently and make more trips to the bank.
   b. Lanwei is reimbursed by her company for her work-related travel expenses. Sometimes, however, the company takes a long time to reimburse her. So when inflation is high, she is less willing to travel for her job.

   c. Hector Homeowner has a mortgage loan that he took out five years ago with a fixed 6% nominal interest rate. Over the years, the inflation rate has crept up unexpectedly to its present level of 7%.
   d. In response to unexpectedly high inflation, the manager of Cozy Cottages of Cape Cod must reprint and resend expensive color brochures correcting the price of rentals this season.

Answer (11 points)

1 point: There is a net cost to the economy.

1 point: This is an increase in the cost of financial transactions cost imposed by inflation.

1 point: This type of cost is called a shoe-leather cost.

1 point: There is a net cost to the economy.

1 point: Lanwei's forgone output is a cost to the economy.

1 point: This type of cost is called a unit-of-account cost.

1 point: There is no net cost to the economy.

1 point: Hector gains and the bank loses because the money Hector pays back is worth less than expected.

1 point: There is a net cost to the economy.

1 point: Cozy Cottages must reprint and resend the expensive brochure when inflation causes rental prices to rise.

1 point: This type of cost is called a menu cost.

2. You borrow $1,000 for one year at 5% interest to buy a couch. Although you did not anticipate any inflation, there is unexpected inflation of 5% over the life of your loan.
   a. What was the real interest rate on your loan?
   b. Explain how you gained from the inflation.
   c. Who lost as a result of the situation described? Explain.

- How the inflation rate is measured
- What a price index is and how it is calculated
- The importance of the consumer price index and other price indexes

Module 15
The Measurement and Calculation of Inflation

Price Indexes and the Aggregate Price Level

The **aggregate price level** is a measure of the overall level of prices in the economy.

A **market basket** is a hypothetical set of consumer purchases of goods and services.

In the summer of 2008, Americans were facing sticker shock at the gas pump: the price of a gallon of regular gasoline had risen from about $3 in late 2007 to more than $4 in most places. Many other prices were also up. Some prices, though, were heading down: the prices of some foods, like eggs, were coming down from a run-up earlier in the year, and virtually anything involving electronics was also getting cheaper. Yet practically everyone felt that the overall cost of living seemed to be rising. But how fast?

Clearly there was a need for a single number summarizing what was happening to consumer prices. Just as macroeconomists find it useful to have a single number to represent the overall level of output, they also find it useful to have a single number to represent the overall level of prices: the **aggregate price level.** Yet a huge variety of goods and services are produced and consumed in the economy. How can we summarize the prices of all these goods and services with a single number? The answer lies in the concept of a *price index*—a concept best introduced with an example.

Market Baskets and Price Indexes

Suppose that a frost in Florida destroys most of the citrus harvest. As a result, the price of oranges rises from $0.20 each to $0.40 each, the price of grapefruit rises from $0.60 to $1.00, and the price of lemons rises from $0.25 to $0.45. How much has the price of citrus fruit increased?

One way to answer that question is to state three numbers—the changes in prices for oranges, grapefruit, and lemons. But this is a very cumbersome method. Rather than having to recite three numbers in an effort to track changes in the prices of citrus fruit, we would prefer to have some kind of overall measure of the *average* price change.

To measure average price changes for consumer goods and services, economists track changes in the cost of a typical consumer's *consumption bundle*—the typical basket of goods and services purchased before the price changes. A hypothetical consumption bundle, used to measure changes in the overall price level, is known as a **market basket.** For our market basket in this example we will suppose that, before the frost, a

© PhotoAlto/Alamy

typical consumer bought 200 oranges, 50 grapefruit, and 100 lemons over the course of a year.

Table 15.1 shows the pre-frost and post-frost costs of this market basket. Before the frost, it cost $95; after the frost, the same basket of goods cost $175. Since $175/$95 = 1.842, the post-frost basket costs 1.842 times the cost of the pre-frost basket, a cost increase of 84.2%. In this example, the average price of citrus fruit has increased 84.2% since the base year as a result of the frost, where the base year is the initial year used in the measurement of the price change.

table 15.1

Calculating the Cost of a Market Basket

	Pre-frost	Post-frost
Price of orange	$0.20	$0.40
Price of grapefruit	0.60	1.00
Price of lemon	0.25	0.45
Cost of market basket (200 oranges, 50 grapefruit, 100 lemons)	(200 × $0.20) + (50 × $0.60) + (100 × $0.25) = $95.00	(200 × $0.40) + (50 × $1.00) + (100 × $0.45) = $175.00

Economists use the same method to measure changes in the overall price level: they track changes in the cost of buying a given market basket. Working with a market basket and a base year, we obtain what is known as a **price index,** a measure of the overall price level. It is always cited along with the year for which the aggregate price level is being measured and the base year. A price index can be calculated using the following formula:

$$\textbf{(15-1)} \quad \text{Price index in a given year} = \frac{\text{Cost of market basket in a given year}}{\text{Cost of market basket in base year}} \times 100$$

In our example, the citrus fruit market basket cost $95 in the base year, the year before the frost. So by applying Equation 15-1, we define the price index for citrus fruit as (cost of market basket in the current year/$95) × 100, yielding an index of 100 for the period before the frost and 184.2 after the frost. You should note that applying Equation 15-1 to calculate the price index for the base year always results in a price index of (cost of market basket in base year/cost of market basket in base year) × 100 = 100. Choosing a price index formula that always normalizes the index value to 100 in the base year avoids the need to keep track of the cost of the market basket, for example, $95, in such-and-such a year.

The price index makes it clear that the average price of citrus has risen 84.2% as a consequence of the frost. Because of its simplicity and intuitive appeal, the method we've just described is used to calculate a variety of price indexes to track average price changes among a variety of different groups of goods and services. Examples include the *consumer price index* and the *producer price index,* which we'll discuss shortly. Price indexes are also the basis for measuring inflation. The price level mentioned in the inflation rate formula in Module 14 is simply a price index value, and the inflation rate is determined as the annual percentage change in an official price index. The inflation rate from year 1 to year 2 is thus calculated using the following formula, with year 1 and year 2 being consecutive years.

$$\textbf{(15-2)} \quad \text{Inflation rate} = \frac{\text{Price index in year 2} - \text{Price index in year 1}}{\text{Price index in year 1}} \times 100$$

Typically, a news report that cites "the inflation rate" is referring to the annual percent change in the consumer price index.

A **price index** measures the cost of purchasing a given market basket in a given year. The index value is normalized so that it is equal to 100 in the selected base year.

The Consumer Price Index

The most widely used measure of the overall price level in the United States is the **consumer price index** (often referred to simply as the **CPI**), which is intended to show how the cost of all purchases by a typical urban family has changed over time. It is calculated by surveying market prices for a market basket that is constructed to represent the consumption of a typical family of four living in a typical American city. Rather than having a single base year, the CPI currently has a base period of 1982–1984.

The market basket used to calculate the CPI is far more complex than the three-fruit market basket we described above. In fact, to calculate the CPI, the Bureau of Labor Statistics sends its employees out to survey supermarkets, gas stations, hardware stores, and so on—some 23,000 retail outlets in 87 cities. Every month it tabulates about 80,000 prices, on everything from romaine lettuce to video rentals. Figure 15.1 shows the weight of major categories in the consumer price index as of December 2008. For example, motor fuel, mainly gasoline, accounted for 3% of the CPI in December 2008.

Figure 15.2 shows how the CPI has changed since measurement began in 1913. Since 1940, the CPI has risen steadily, although its annual percent increases in recent years have been much smaller than those of the 1970s and early 1980s. A logarithmic scale is used so that equal percent changes in the CPI appear the same.

Some economists believe that the consumer price index systematically overstates the actual rate of inflation. Why? Consider two families: one in 1985, with an after-tax income of $20,000, and another in 2010, with an after-tax income of $40,000. According to the CPI, prices in 2010 were about twice as high as in 1985, so those two families should have about the same standard of living. However, the 2010 family might have a higher standard of living for two reasons.

First, the CPI measures the cost of buying a given market basket. Yet, consumers typically alter the mix of goods and services they buy, reducing purchases of products

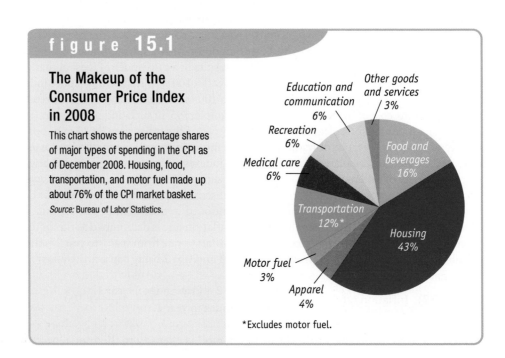

figure 15.1

The Makeup of the Consumer Price Index in 2008

This chart shows the percentage shares of major types of spending in the CPI as of December 2008. Housing, food, transportation, and motor fuel made up about 76% of the CPI market basket.

Source: Bureau of Labor Statistics.

- Other goods and services 3%
- Education and communication 6%
- Recreation 6%
- Medical care 6%
- Food and beverages 16%
- Transportation 12%*
- Housing 43%
- Motor fuel 3%
- Apparel 4%

*Excludes motor fuel.

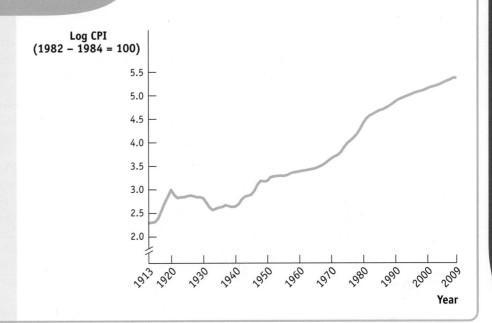

figure 15.2

The CPI, 1913–2009

Since 1940, the CPI has risen steadily. But the annual percentage increases in recent years have been much smaller than those of the 1970s and early 1980s. (The vertical axis is measured on a logarithmic scale so that equal percent changes in the CPI appear the same.)

Source: Bureau of Labor Statistics.

that have become relatively more expensive and increasing purchases of products that have become relatively cheaper. For example, suppose that the price of hamburgers suddenly doubled. Americans currently eat a lot of hamburgers, but in the face of such a price rise many of them would switch to cheaper foods. A price index based on a market basket with a lot of hamburgers in it would overstate the true rise in the cost of living.

The second reason arises from innovation. In 1985 many of the goods we now take for granted, especially those using information technology, didn't exist: there was no Internet and there were no iPhones. By widening the range of consumer choice, innovation makes a given amount of money worth more. That is, innovation is like a fall in consumer prices. For both of these reasons, many economists believe that the CPI somewhat overstates inflation when we think of inflation as measuring the actual change in the cost of living of a typical urban American family. But there is no consensus on how large the overstatement is, and for the time being, the official CPI remains the basis for most estimates of inflation.

The United States is not the only country that calculates a consumer price index. In fact, nearly every country calculates one. As you might expect, the market baskets that make up these indexes differ quite a lot from country to country. In poor countries, where people must spend a high proportion of their income just to feed themselves, food makes up a large share of the price index. Among high-income countries, differences in consumption patterns lead to differences in the price indexes: the Japanese price index puts a larger weight on raw fish and a smaller weight on beef than ours does, and the French price index puts a larger weight on wine.

Other Price Measures

There are two other price measures that are also widely used to track economy-wide price changes. One is the **producer price index** (or **PPI,** which used to be known as the *wholesale price index*). As its name suggests, the producer price index measures the cost of a typical basket of goods and services—containing raw commodities such as steel, electricity, coal, and so on—purchased by producers. Because commodity producers are relatively quick to raise prices when they perceive a change in overall demand for their

The **producer price index,** or **PPI,** measures changes in the prices of goods and services purchased by producers.

The **GDP deflator** for a given year is 100 times the ratio of nominal GDP to real GDP in that year.

goods, the PPI often responds to inflationary or deflationary pressures more quickly than the CPI. As a result, the PPI is often regarded as an "early warning signal" of changes in the inflation rate.

The other widely used price measure is the *GDP deflator;* it isn't exactly a price index, although it serves the same purpose. Recall how we distinguished between nominal GDP (GDP in current prices) and real GDP (GDP calculated using the prices of a base year). The **GDP deflator** for a given year is equal to 100 times the ratio of nominal GDP for that year to real GDP for that year expressed in prices of a selected base year. Since real GDP is currently expressed in 2005 dollars, the GDP deflator for 2005 is equal to 100. If nominal GDP doubles but real GDP does not change, the GDP deflator indicates that the aggregate price level doubled.

Perhaps the most important point about the different inflation rates generated by these three measures of prices is that they usually move closely together (although the producer price index tends to fluctuate more than either of the other two measures). Figure 15.3 shows the annual percent changes in the three indexes since 1930. By all three measures, the U.S. economy experienced deflation during the early years of the Great Depression, inflation during World War II, accelerating inflation during the 1970s, and a return to relative price stability in the 1990s. Notice, by the way, the large surge and subsequent drop in producer prices at the very end of the graph; this reflects a sharp rise in energy and food prices, during the second half of the 2000s, and the subsequent large drop in those prices as energy prices fell during the recession that began in 2007. And you can see these large changes in energy and food prices reflected most in the producer price index since they play a much bigger role in the PPI than they do in either the CPI or the GDP deflator.

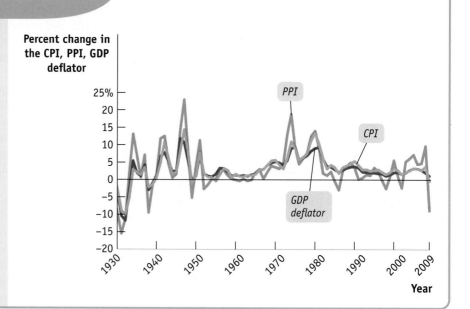

figure 15.3

The CPI, the PPI, and the GDP Deflator

As the figure shows, these three different measures of inflation usually move closely together. Each reveals a drastic acceleration of inflation during the 1970s and a return to relative price stability in the 1990s.

Source: Bureau of Labor Statistics; Bureau of Economic Analysis.

fyi

Indexing to the CPI

Although GDP is a very important number for shaping economic policy, official statistics on GDP don't have a direct effect on people's lives. The CPI, by contrast, has a direct and immediate impact on millions of Americans. The reason is that many payments are tied, or "indexed," to the CPI—the amount paid rises or falls when the CPI rises or falls.

The practice of indexing payments to consumer prices goes back to the dawn of the United States as a nation. In 1780 the Massachusetts State Legislature recognized that the pay of its soldiers fighting the British needed to be increased because of inflation that occurred during the Revolutionary War. The legislature adopted a formula that made a soldier's pay proportional to the cost of a market basket consisting of 5 bushels of corn, 68⁴⁄₇ pounds of beef, 10 pounds of sheep's wool, and 16 pounds of sole leather.

Today, 48 million people, most of them old or disabled, receive checks from Social Security, a national retirement program that accounts for almost a quarter of current total federal spending—more than the defense budget. The amount of an individual's check is

A small change in the CPI has large consequences for those dependent on Social Security payments.

determined by a formula that reflects his or her previous payments into the system as well as other factors. In addition, all Social Security payments are adjusted each year to offset any increase in consumer prices over the previous year. The CPI is used to calculate the official estimate of the inflation rate used to adjust these payments yearly. So every percentage point added to the official estimate of the rate

of inflation adds 1% to the checks received by tens of millions of individuals.

Other government payments are also indexed to the CPI. In addition, income tax brackets, the bands of income levels that determine a taxpayer's income tax rate, are indexed to the CPI. (An individual in a higher income bracket pays a higher income tax rate in a progressive tax system like ours.) Indexing also extends to the private sector, where many private contracts, including some wage settlements, contain cost-of-living allowances (called COLAs) that adjust payments in proportion to changes in the CPI.

Because the CPI plays such an important and direct role in people's lives, it's a politically sensitive number. The Bureau of Labor Statistics, which calculates the CPI, takes great care in collecting and interpreting price and consumption data. It uses a complex method in which households are surveyed to determine what they buy and where they shop, and a carefully selected sample of stores are surveyed to get representative prices. As explained in the preceding FYI, however, there is still considerable controversy about whether the CPI accurately measures inflation.

Module 15 AP Review

Solutions appear at the back of the book.

Check Your Understanding

1. Consider Table 15.1 but suppose that the market basket is composed of 100 oranges, 50 grapefruit, and 200 lemons. How does this change the pre-frost and post-frost consumer price indexes? Explain. Generalize your answer to explain how the construction of the market basket affects the CPI.

2. For each of the following events, explain how the use of a 10-year-old market basket would bias measurements of price changes over the past decade.

   a. A typical family owns more cars than it would have a decade ago. Over that time, the average price of a car has increased more than the average prices of other goods.
   b. Virtually no households had broadband Internet access a decade ago. Now many households have it, and the price has been falling.

3. The consumer price index in the United States (base period 1982–1984) was 201.6 in 2006 and 207.3 in 2007. Calculate the inflation rate from 2006 to 2007.

Tackle the Test: Multiple-Choice Questions

1. If the cost of a market basket of goods increases from $100 in year 1 to $108 in year 2, the consumer price index in year 2 equals _____ if year 1 is the base year.
   a. 8
   b. 10
   c. 100
   d. 108
   e. 110

2. If the consumer price index increases from 80 to 120 from one year to the next, the inflation rate over that time period was
   a. 20%
   b. 40%
   c. 50%
   d. 80%
   e. 120%

3. Which of the following is true of the CPI?
   I. It is the most common measure of the price level.
   II. It measures the price of a typical market basket of goods.
   III. It currently uses a base period of 1982–1984.

   a. I only
   b. II only
   c. III only
   d. I and II only
   e. I, II, and III

4. The value of a price index in the base year is
   a. 0.
   b. 100.
   c. 200.
   d. the inflation rate.
   e. the average cost of a market basket of goods.

5. If your wage doubles at the same time as the consumer price index goes from 100 to 300, your real wage
   a. doubles.
   b. falls.
   c. increases.
   d. stays the same.
   e. cannot be determined.

Tackle the Test: Free-Response Questions

1. Suppose the year 2000 is the base year for a price index. Between 2000 and 2020 prices double and at the same time your nominal income increases from $40,000 to $80,000.
   a. What is the value of the price index in 2000?
   b. What is the value of the price index in 2020?
   c. What is the percentage increase in your nominal income between 2000 and 2020?
   d. What has happened to your real income between 2000 and 2020? Explain.

> **Answer (5 points)**
>
> **1 point:** 100
>
> **1 point:** 200
>
> **1 point:** 100%
>
> **1 point:** It stayed the same.
>
> **1 point:** Real income is a measure of the purchasing power of my income, and because my income and the price level both doubled, the purchasing power of my income has not been affected: $40,000/100 = $80,000/200.

2. The accompanying table contains the values of two price indexes for the years 2004, 2005, and 2006: the GDP deflator and the CPI. For each price index, calculate the inflation rate from 2004 to 2005 and from 2005 to 2006.

Year	GDP deflator	CPI
2004	96.8	188.9
2005	100.0	195.3
2006	103.3	201.6

Section 3 Review

Summary

1. Economists keep track of the flows of money between sectors with the **national income and product accounts,** or **national accounts. Households** earn income via the **factor markets** from wages, interest on **bonds,** profit accruing to owners of **stocks,** and rent on land. In addition, they receive **government transfers.**

Disposable income, total household income minus taxes plus government transfers, is allocated to **consumer spending** (C) in the **product markets** and **private savings.** Via the **financial markets,** private savings and foreign lending are channeled to **investment spending** (I), government borrowing, and foreign borrowing. **Government purchases of goods and services** (G) are paid for by tax revenues and **government borrowing.** **Exports** (X) generate an inflow of funds into the country from the rest of the world, but **imports** (IM) lead to an outflow of funds to the rest of the world. Foreigners can also buy stocks and bonds in the U.S. financial markets.

2. **Gross domestic product,** or **GDP,** measures the value of all **final goods and services** produced in the economy. It does not include the value of **intermediate goods and services,** but it does include **inventories** and **net exports** $(X - IM)$. It can be calculated in three ways: add up the **value added** by all producers; add up all spending on domestically produced final goods and services, leading to the equation $GDP = C + I + G + X - IM$, also known as **aggregate spending;** or add up all the income paid by domestic **firms** to factors of production. These three methods are equivalent because in the economy as a whole, total income paid by domestic firms to factors of production must equal total spending on domestically produced final goods and services.

3. **Real GDP** is the value of the final goods and services produced calculated using the prices of a selected base year. Except in the base year, real GDP is not the same as **nominal GDP,** the value of **aggregate output** calculated using current prices. Analysis of the growth rate of aggregate output must use real GDP because doing so eliminates any change in the value of aggregate output due solely to price changes. Real **GDP per capita** is a measure of average aggregate output per person but is not in itself an appropriate policy goal. U.S. statistics on real GDP are always expressed in "chained dollars," which means they are calculated with the **chain-linking** method of averaging the GDP growth rate found using an early base year and the GDP growth rate found using a late base year.

4. **Employed** people currently hold a part-time or full-time job; **unemployed** people do not hold a job but are actively looking for work. Their sum is equal to the **labor force,** and the **labor force participation rate** is the percentage of the population age 16 or older that is in the labor force.

5. The **unemployment rate,** the percentage of the labor force that is unemployed and actively looking for work, can overstate or understate the true level of unemployment. It can overstate because it counts as unemployed those who are continuing to search for a job despite having been offered one (that is, workers who are frictionally unemployed). It can understate because it ignores frustrated workers, such as **discouraged workers, marginally attached workers,** and the **underemployed.** In addition, the unemployment rate varies greatly among different groups in the population; it is typically higher for younger workers and for workers near retirement age than for workers in their prime working years.

6. The unemployment rate is affected by the business cycle. The unemployment rate generally falls when the growth rate of real GDP is above average and generally rises when the growth rate of real GDP is below average.

7. Job creation and destruction, as well as voluntary job separations, lead to **job search** and **frictional unemployment.** In addition, a variety of factors such as minimum wages, unions, **efficiency wages,** and government policies designed to help laid-off workers result in a situation in which there is a surplus of labor at the market wage rate, creating **structural unemployment.** As a result, the **natural rate of unemployment,** the sum of frictional and structural unemployment, is well above zero, even when jobs are plentiful.

8. The actual unemployment rate is equal to the natural rate of unemployment, the share of unemployment that is independent of the business cycle, plus **cyclical unemployment,** the share of unemployment that depends on fluctuations in the business cycle.

9. The natural rate of unemployment changes over time, largely in response to changes in labor force characteristics, labor market institutions, and government policies.

10. Inflation does not, as many assume, make everyone poorer by raising the level of prices. That's because if wages and incomes are adjusted to take into account a rising price level, **real wages** and **real income** remain unchanged. However, a high inflation rate imposes overall costs on the economy: **shoe-leather costs, menu costs,** and **unit-of-account costs.**

11. Inflation can produce winners and losers within the economy, because long-term contracts are generally written in dollar terms. Loans typically specify a **nominal interest rate,** which differs from the **real interest rate** due to inflation. A higher-than-expected inflation rate is good for borrowers and bad for lenders. A lower-than-expected inflation rate is good for lenders and bad for borrowers.

12. It is very costly to create **disinflation,** so policy makers try to prevent inflation from becoming excessive in the first place.

13. To measure the **aggregate price level,** economists calculate the cost of purchasing a **market basket.** A **price index** is the ratio of the current cost of that market basket to the cost in a selected base year, multiplied by 100.

14. The **inflation rate** is the yearly percent change in a price index, typically based on the **consumer price index,** or **CPI,** the most common measure of the aggregate price level. A similar index for goods and services purchased by firms is the **producer price index,** or **PPI.** Finally, economists also use the **GDP deflator,** which measures the price level by calculating the ratio of nominal to real GDP times 100.

Key Terms

Problems

1. At right is a simplified circular-flow diagram for the economy of Micronia.

  a. What is the value of GDP in Micronia?

  b. What is the value of net exports?

  c. What is the value of disposable income?

  d. Does the total flow of money out of households—the sum of taxes paid and consumer spending—equal the total flow of money into households?

  e. How does the government of Micronia finance its purchases of goods and services?

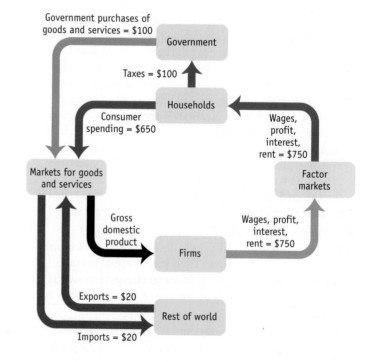

2. A more complex circular-flow diagram for the economy of Macronia is shown at right.

a. What is the value of GDP in Macronia?

b. What is the value of net exports?

c. What is the value of disposable income?

d. Does the total flow of money out of households—the sum of taxes paid, consumer spending, and private savings—equal the total flow of money into households?

e. How does the government finance its spending?

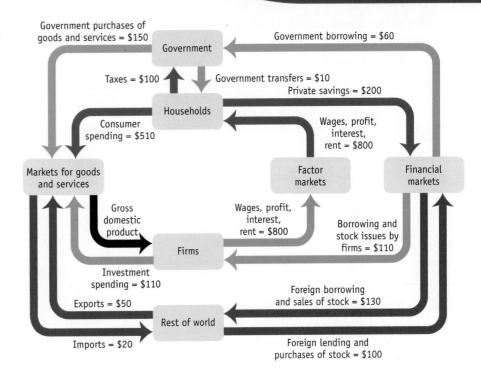

3. The components of GDP in the accompanying table were produced by the Bureau of Economic Analysis.

Category	Components of GDP in 2009 (billions of dollars)
Consumer spending	
Durable goods	$1,034.4
Nondurable goods	2,223.3
Services	6,835.0
Private investment spending	
Fixed investment spending	1,747.9
Nonresidential	1,386.6
Structures	480.7
Equipment and software	906
Residential	361.3
Change in private inventories	−125.0
Net exports	
Exports	1,560.0
Imports	1,950.1
Government purchases of goods and services and investment spending	
Federal	1,444.9
National defense	779.1
Nondefense	365.8
State and local	1,788.4

a. Calculate consumer spending.

b. Calculate private investment spending.

c. Calculate net exports.

d. Calculate government purchases of goods and services and investment spending.

e. Calculate gross domestic product.

f. Calculate consumer spending on services as a percentage of total consumer spending.

g. Calculate exports as a percentage of imports.

h. Calculate government purchases on national defense as a percentage of federal government purchases of goods and services.

4. The small economy of Pizzania produces three goods (bread, cheese, and pizza), each produced by a separate company. The bread and cheese companies produce all the inputs they need to make bread and cheese, respectively. The pizza company uses the bread and cheese from the other companies to make its pizzas. All three companies employ labor to help produce their goods, and the difference between the value of goods sold and the sum of labor and input costs is the firm's profit. The accompanying table summarizes the activities of the three companies when all the bread and cheese produced are sold to the pizza company as inputs in the production of pizzas.

	Bread company	Cheese company	Pizza company
Cost of inputs	$0	$0	$50 (Bread) 35 (Cheese)
Wages	15	20	75
Value of output	50	35	200

a. Calculate GDP as the value added in production.

b. Calculate GDP as spending on final goods and services.

c. Calculate GDP as factor income.

5. The economy of Pizzanistan resembles Pizzania (from Problem 4) except that bread and cheese are sold both to a pizza company as inputs in the production of pizzas and to consumers as final goods. The accompanying table summarizes the activities of the three companies.

	Bread company	Cheese company	Pizza company
Cost of inputs	$0	$0	$50 (Bread) 35 (Cheese)
Wages	25	30	75
Value of output	100	60	200

a. Calculate GDP as the value added in production.

b. Calculate GDP as spending on final goods and services.

c. Calculate GDP as factor income.

6. The accompanying table shows data on nominal GDP (in billions of dollars), real GDP (in billions of year 2000 dollars), and population (in thousands) of the United States in 1960, 1970, 1980, 1990, 2000, and 2007, years in which the U.S. price level consistently rose.

Year	Nominal GDP (billions of dollars)	Real GDP (billions of 2000 dollars)	Population (thousands)
1960	$526.4	$2,501.8	180,671
1970	1,038.5	3,771.9	205,052
1980	2,789.5	5,161.7	227,726
1990	5,803.1	7,112.5	250,132
2000	9,817.0	9,817.0	282,388
2007	13,841.3	11,566.8	301,140

a. Why is real GDP greater than nominal GDP for all years before 2000 and lower for 2007? Does nominal GDP have to equal real GDP in 2000?

b. Calculate the percent change in real GDP from 1960 to 1970, 1970 to 1980, 1980 to 1990, and 1990 to 2000. Which period had the highest growth rate?

c. Calculate real GDP per capita for each of the years in the table.

d. Calculate the percent change in real GDP per capita from 1960 to 1970, 1970 to 1980, 1980 to 1990, and 1990 to 2000. Which period had the highest growth rate?

e. How do the percent change in real GDP and the percent change in real GDP per capita compare? Which is larger? Do we expect them to have this relationship?

7. Eastland College is concerned about the rising price of textbooks that students must purchase. To better identify the increase in the price of textbooks, the dean asks you, the

Economics Department's star student, to create an index of textbook prices. The average student purchases three English, two math, and four economics textbooks. The prices of these books are given in the accompanying table.

	2008	2009	2010
English textbook	$50	$55	$57
Math textbook	70	72	74
Economics textbook	80	90	100

a. What is the percent change in the price of an English textbook from 2008 to 2010?

b. What is the percent change in the price of a math textbook from 2008 to 2010?

c. What is the percent change in the price of an economics textbook from 2008 to 2010?

d. Using 2008 as a base year, create a price index for these books for all years.

e. What is the percent change in the price index from 2008 to 2010?

8. The consumer price index, or CPI, measures the cost of living for a typical urban household by multiplying the price for each category of expenditure (housing, food, and so on) times a measure of the importance of that expenditure in the average consumer's market basket and summing over all categories. However, using data from the consumer price index, we can see that changes in the cost of living for different types of consumers can vary a great deal. Let's compare the cost of living for a hypothetical retired person and a hypothetical college student. Let's assume that the market basket of a retired person is allocated in the following way: 10% on housing, 15% on food, 5% on transportation, 60% on medical care, 0% on education, and 10% on recreation. The college student's market basket is allocated as follows: 5% on housing, 15% on food, 20% on transportation, 0% on medical care, 40% on education, and 20% on recreation. The accompanying table shows the December 2009 CPI for each of the relevant categories.

	CPI December 2009
Housing	215.5
Food	218.0
Transportation	188.3
Medical care	379.5
Education	128.9
Recreation	113.2

Calculate the overall CPI for the retired person and for the college student by multiplying the CPI for each of the categories by the relative importance of that category to the individual and then summing each of the categories. The CPI for all items in December 2009 was 215. How do your calculations for a CPI for the retired person and the college student compare to the overall CPI?

9. Each month the Bureau of Labor Statistics releases the Consumer Price Index Summary for the previous month. Go to www.bls.gov and find the latest report. (On the Bureau of Labor Statistics home page, click on "News Release" under "Latest Numbers—Consumer Price Index" and then choose "Consumer Price Index Summary.") What was the CPI for the previous month? How did it change from the month before? How did it change over the last year?

10. The accompanying table provides the annual real GDP (in billions of 2000 dollars) and nominal GDP (in billions of dollars) for the United States.

	2002	2003	2004	2005	2006
Real GDP (billions of 2000 dollars)	$10,048.8	10,301.0	10,675.8	11,003.4	11,319.4
Nominal GDP (billions of dollars)	$10,469.6	10,960.8	11,685.9	12,433.9	13,194.7

a. Calculate the GDP deflator for each year.

b. Use the GDP deflator to calculate the inflation rate for all years except 2002.

11. The cost of a college education in the United States is rising at a rate faster than inflation. The table below shows the average cost of a college education in the United States in 2006 and 2007 for public and private colleges. Assume the costs listed in the table are the only costs experienced by the various college students in a single year.

a. Calculate the cost of living for an average college student in each category for 2006 and 2007.

b. Assume the quantity of goods purchased in each category, that is, the market basket, is identical for 2006 and 2007. Calculate an inflation rate for each type of college student between 2006 and 2007.

	Cost of college education (averages in 2006 dollars)				
	Tuition and fees	Books and supplies	Room and board	Transportation	Other expenses
Two-year public college: commuter	$2,272	$850	$6,299	$1,197	$1,676
Four-year public college: resident	5,836	942	6,690	880	1,739
Four-year public college: commuter	5,836	942	6,917	1,224	2,048
Four-year public college: out-of-state	15,783	942	6,960	880	1,739
Four-year private college: resident	22,218	935	8,149	722	1,277
Four-year private college: commuter	22,218	935	7,211	1,091	1,630
	Cost of college education (averages in 2007 dollars)				
	Tuition and fees	Books and supplies	Room and board	Transportation	Other expenses
Two-year public college: commuter	$2,361	$921	$6,875	$1,270	$1,699
Four-year public college: resident	6,185	988	7,404	911	1,848
Four-year public college: commuter	6,185	988	7,419	1,284	2,138
Four-year public college: out-of-state	16,640	988	7,404	911	1,848
Four-year private college: resident	23,712	988	8,595	768	1,311
Four-year private college: commuter	23,712	988	7,499	1,138	1,664

12. Each month, usually on the first Friday of the month, the Bureau of Labor Statistics releases the Employment Situation Summary for the previous month. Go to www.bls.gov and find the latest report. (On the Bureau of Labor Statistics home page, on the left side of the page, find "Unemployment" and select "National Unemployment Rate. " You will find the Employment Situation Summary under "News Releases.") How does the unemployment rate compare to the rate one month earlier? How does the unemployment rate compare to the rate one year earlier?

13. In general, how do changes in the unemployment rate vary with changes in real GDP? After several quarters of a severe recession, explain why we might observe a decrease in the official unemployment rate. Could we see an increase in the official unemployment rate after several quarters of a strong expansion?

14. There is only one labor market in Profunctia. All workers have the same skills, and all firms hire workers with these skills. Use the accompanying diagram, which shows the supply of

and demand for labor, to answer the following questions. Illustrate each answer with a diagram.

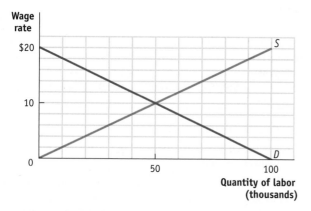

Wage rate

$20

10

0

50

100

Quantity of labor (thousands)

S

D

a. What is the equilibrium wage rate in Profunctia? At this wage rate, what are the level of employment, the size of the labor force, and the unemployment rate?

b. If the government of Profunctia sets a minimum wage equal to $12 per hour, what will be the level of employment, the size of the labor force, and the unemployment rate?

c. If unions bargain with the firms in Profunctia and set a wage rate equal to $14, what will be the level of employment, the size of the labor force, and the unemployment rate?

d. If the concern for retaining workers and encouraging high-quality work leads firms to set a wage rate equal to $16, what will be the level of employment, the size of the labor force, and the unemployment rate?

15. A country's labor force is the sum of the number of employed and unemployed workers. The accompanying table provides data on the size of the labor force and the number of unemployed workers for different regions of the United States.

Region	Labor force (thousands)		Unemployed (thousands)	
	March 2007	March 2008	March 2007	March 2008
Northeast	27,863.5	28,035.6	1,197.8	1,350.3
South	54,203.8	54,873.9	2,300.9	2,573.8
Midwest	34,824.3	35,048.6	1,718.2	1,870.8
West	35,231.8	35,903.3	1,588.0	1,914.4

a. Calculate the number of workers employed in each of the regions in March 2007 and March 2008. Use your answers to calculate the change in the total number of workers employed between March 2007 and March 2008.

b. For each region, calculate the growth in the labor force from March 2007 to March 2008.

c. Compute unemployment rates in the different regions of the country in March 2007 and March 2008.

d. What can you infer about the rise in unemployment rates over this period? Was it caused by a net loss in the number of jobs or by a large increase in the number of people seeking jobs?

16. In which of the following cases is it likely for efficiency wages to exist? Why?

a. Jane and her boss work as a team selling ice cream.

b. Jane sells ice cream without any direct supervision by her boss.

c. Jane speaks Korean and sells ice cream in a neighborhood in which Korean is the primary language. It is difficult to find another worker who speaks Korean.

17. How will the following changes affect the natural rate of unemployment?

a. The government reduces the time during which an unemployed worker can receive benefits.

b. More teenagers focus on their studies and do not look for jobs until after college.

c. Greater access to the Internet leads both potential employers and potential employees to use the Internet to list and find jobs.

d. Union membership declines.

18. With its tradition of a job for life for most citizens, Japan once had a much lower unemployment rate than that of the United States; from 1960 to 1995, the unemployment rate in Japan exceeded 3% only once. However, since the crash of its stock market in 1989 and slow economic growth in the 1990s, the job-for-life system has broken down and unemployment rose to more than 5% in 2003.

a. Explain the likely effect of the breakdown of the job-for-life system in Japan on the Japanese natural rate of unemployment.

b. As the accompanying diagram shows, the rate of growth of real GDP has picked up in Japan since 2001. Explain the likely effect of this increase in GDP growth on the unemployment rate. Is the likely cause of the change in the unemployment rate during this period a change in the natural rate of unemployment or a change in the cyclical unemployment rate?

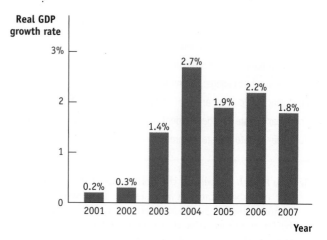

Real GDP growth rate

3%

2

1

0

0.2% 0.3% 1.4% 2.7% 1.9% 2.2% 1.8%

2001 2002 2003 2004 2005 2006 2007

Year

Source: OECD.

19. The accompanying diagram shows mortgage interest rates and inflation during 1990–2005 in the economy of Albernia. When would home mortgages have been especially attractive and why?

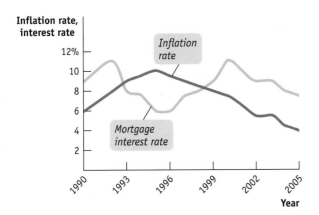

20. The accompanying table provides the inflation rate in the year 2000 and the average inflation rate over the period 2000–2007 for eight different countries.

    a. Given the expected relationship between average inflation and menu costs, rank the countries in descending order of menu costs using average inflation over the period 2000–2007.

    b. Rank the countries in order of inflation rates that most favored borrowers with seven-year loans that were taken out in 2000. Assume that the expected inflation rate was the inflation rate in 2000.

    c. Did borrowers who took out seven-year loans in Japan gain or lose overall versus lenders? Explain.

Country	Inflation rate in 2000	Average inflation rate, 2000–2007
Brazil	7.1%	7.3%
China	0.3	1.6
France	1.7	1.8
Indonesia	3.8	8.8
Japan	−0.7	−0.3
Turkey	56.4	27.8
United States	3.4	2.8
Zimbabwe	55.7	904.1

Source: IMF.

National Income and Price Determination

FROM BOOM TO BUST

Ft. Myers, Florida, was a boom town in 2003, 2004, and most of 2005. Jobs were plentiful: by 2005 the unemployment rate was less than 3%. The shopping malls were humming, and new stores were opening everywhere.

But then the boom went bust. Jobs became scarce, and by 2009 the unemployment rate had reached 14%. Stores had few customers, and many were closing. One new business was flourishing, however. Marc Joseph, a real estate agent, began offering "foreclosure tours": visits to homes that had been seized by banks after the owners were unable to make mortgage payments.

What happened? Ft. Myers boomed from 2003 to 2005 because of a surge in home construction, fueled in part by speculators who bought houses not to live in, but because they believed they could resell those houses at much higher prices. Home construction gave jobs to construction workers, electricians, real estate agents, and others. And these workers, in turn, spent money locally, creating jobs for sales workers, waiters, gardeners, pool cleaners, and more. These workers also spent money locally, creating further expansion, and so on.

The boom turned into a bust when home construction came to a virtual halt. It turned out that speculation had been feeding on itself: people were buying houses as investments, then selling them to other people who were also buying houses as investments, and the prices had risen to levels far beyond what people who actually wanted to live in houses were willing to pay.

The abrupt collapse of the housing market pulled the local economy down with it, as the process that had created the earlier boom operated in reverse.

The boom and bust in Ft. Myers illustrates, on a small scale, the way booms and busts often happen for the economy as a whole. The business cycle is often driven by ups or downs in investment spending—either residential investment spending (that is, spending on home construction) or nonresidential investment spending (such as spending on construction of office buildings, factories, and shopping malls). Changes in investment spending, in turn, indirectly lead to changes in consumer spending, which magnify—or *multiply*—the effect of the investment spending changes on the economy as a whole.

In this section we'll study how this process works on a grand scale. As a first step, we introduce *multiplier* analysis and show how it helps us understand the business cycle. In Module 17 we explain *aggregate demand* and its two most important components, consumer spending and investment spending. Module 18 introduces *aggregate supply,* the other half of the model used to analyze economic fluctuations. We will then be ready to explore how aggregate supply and aggregate demand determine the levels of prices and real output in an economy. Finally, we will use the aggregate demand-aggregate supply model to visualize the state of the economy and examine the effects of economic policy.

Courtesy of the Dallas Morning News

What you will learn in this **Module:**

- The nature of the multiplier, which shows how initial changes in spending lead to further changes

- The meaning of the aggregate consumption function, which shows how current disposable income affects consumer spending

- How expected future income and aggregate wealth affect consumer spending

- The determinants of investment spending

- Why investment spending is considered a leading indicator of the future state of the economy

Module 16
Income and Expenditure

The Multiplier: An Informal Introduction

The story of the boom and bust in Ft. Myers involves a sort of chain reaction in which an initial rise or fall in spending leads to changes in income, which lead to further changes in spending, and so on. Let's examine that chain reaction more closely, this time thinking through the effects of changes in spending in the economy as a whole.

For the sake of this analysis, we'll make four simplifying assumptions that we will have to reconsider in later modules.

1. We assume that *producers are willing to supply additional output at a fixed price.* That is, if consumers or businesses buying investment goods decide to spend an additional $1 billion, that will translate into the production of $1 billion worth of additional goods and services without driving up the overall level of prices. As a result, *changes in overall spending translate into changes in aggregate output,* as measured by real GDP. As we'll learn in this section, this assumption isn't too unrealistic in the short run, but it needs to be changed when we think about the long-run effects of changes in demand.

2. We take the interest rate as given.

3. We assume that there is no government spending and no taxes.

4. We assume that exports and imports are zero.

Given these simplifying assumptions, consider what happens if there is a change in investment spending. Specifically, imagine that for some reason home builders decide to spend an extra $100 billion on home construction over the next year.

The direct effect of this increase in investment spending will be to increase income and the value of aggregate output by the same amount. That's because each dollar spent on home construction translates into a dollar's worth of income for construction workers, suppliers of building materials, electricians, and so on. If the process stopped there, the increase in housing investment spending would raise overall income by exactly $100 billion.

But the process doesn't stop there. The increase in aggregate output leads to an increase in disposable income that flows to households in the form of profits and wages. The increase in households' disposable income leads to a rise in consumer spending, which, in turn, induces firms to increase output yet again. This generates another rise in disposable income, which leads to another round of consumer spending increases, and so on. So there are multiple rounds of increases in aggregate output.

How large is the total effect on aggregate output if we sum the effect from all these rounds of spending increases? To answer this question, we need to introduce the concept of the **marginal propensity to consume,** or **MPC:** the increase in consumer spending when disposable income rises by $1. When consumer spending changes because of a rise or fall in disposable income, MPC is the change in consumer spending divided by the change in disposable income:

$$(16\text{-}1) \quad MPC = \frac{\Delta \text{ Consumer spending}}{\Delta \text{ Disposable income}}$$

where the symbol Δ (delta) means "change in." For example, if consumer spending goes up by $6 billion when disposable income goes up by $10 billion, MPC is $6 billion/$10 billion = 0.6.

Because consumers normally spend part but not all of an additional dollar of disposable income, MPC is a number between 0 and 1. The additional disposable income that consumers don't spend is saved; the **marginal propensity to save,** or **MPS,** is the fraction of an additional dollar of disposable income that is saved. MPS is equal to $1 - MPC$.

With the assumption of no taxes and no international trade, each $1 increase in spending raises both real GDP and disposable income by $1. So the $100 billion increase in investment spending initially raises real GDP by $100 billion. The corresponding $100 billion increase in disposable income leads to a second-round increase in consumer spending, which raises real GDP by a further $MPC \times \$100$ billion. It is followed by a third-round increase in consumer spending of $MPC \times MPC \times \$100$ billion, and so on. After an infinite number of rounds, the total effect on real GDP is:

Increase in investment spending   = $100 billion
+ Second-round increase in consumer spending   = $MPC \times \$100$ billion
+ Third-round increase in consumer spending   = $MPC^2 \times \$100$ billion
+ Fourth-round increase in consumer spending   = $MPC^3 \times \$100$ billion
        •   •
        •   •
        •   •

Total increase in real GDP $= (1 + MPC + MPC^2 + MPC^3 + \ldots) \times \$100$ billion

So the $100 billion increase in investment spending sets off a chain reaction in the economy. The net result of this chain reaction is that a $100 billion increase in investment spending leads to a change in real GDP that is a *multiple* of the size of that initial change in spending.

How large is this multiple? It's a mathematical fact that an infinite series of the form $1 + x + x^2 + x^3 + \ldots$, where x is between 0 and 1, is equal to $1/(1 - x)$. So the total effect of a $100 billion increase in investment spending, I, taking into account all the subsequent increases in consumer spending (and assuming no taxes and no international trade), is given by:

$(16\text{-}2)$ Total increase in real GDP from $100 billion rise in $I =$

$$\frac{1}{(1 - MPC)} \times \$100 \text{ billion}$$

Juice Images/Alamy

Many businesses, such as those that support home improvement and interior design, benefit during housing booms.

The **marginal propensity to consume,** or **MPC,** is the increase in consumer spending when disposable income rises by $1.

The **marginal propensity to save,** or **MPS,** is the increase in household savings when disposable income rises by $1.

Let's consider a numerical example in which $MPC = 0.6$: each \$1 in additional disposable income causes a \$0.60 rise in consumer spending. In that case, a \$100 billion increase in investment spending raises real GDP by \$100 billion in the first round. The second-round increase in consumer spending raises real GDP by another $0.6 \times$ \$100 billion, or \$60 billion. The third-round increase in consumer spending raises real GDP by another $0.6 \times$ \$60 billion, or \$36 billion. This process goes on and on until the amount of spending in another round would be virtually zero. In the end, real GDP rises by \$250 billion as a consequence of the initial \$100 billion rise in investment spending:

$$\frac{1}{(1 - 0.6)} \times \$100 \text{ billion} = 2.5 \times \$100 \text{ billion} = \$250 \text{ billion}$$

Notice that even though there can be a nearly endless number of rounds of expansion of real GDP, the total rise in real GDP is limited to \$250 billion. The reason is that at each stage some of the rise in disposable income "leaks out" because it is saved, leaving less and less to be spent in the next round. How much of an additional dollar of disposable income is saved depends on MPS, the marginal propensity to save.

We've described the effects of a change in investment spending, but the same analysis can be applied to any other change in spending. The important thing is to distinguish between the initial change in aggregate spending, before real GDP rises, and the additional change in aggregate spending caused by the change in real GDP as the chain reaction unfolds. For example, suppose that a boom in housing prices makes consumers feel richer and that, as a result, they become willing to spend more at any given level of disposable income. This will lead to an initial rise in consumer spending, before real GDP rises. But it will also lead to second and later rounds of higher consumer spending as real GDP and disposable income rise.

An initial rise or fall in aggregate spending at a given level of real GDP is called an **autonomous change in aggregate spending.** It's autonomous—which means "self-governing"—because it's the cause, not the result, of the chain reaction we've just described. Formally, the **multiplier** is the ratio of the total change in real GDP caused by an autonomous change in aggregate spending to the size of that autonomous change. If we let ΔAAS stand for the autonomous change in aggregate spending and ΔY stand for the total change in real GDP, then the multiplier is equal to $\Delta Y/\Delta AAS$. We've already seen how to find the value of the multiplier. Assuming no taxes and no trade, the total change in real GDP caused by an autonomous change in aggregate spending is:

(16-3) $\quad \Delta Y = \dfrac{1}{(1 - MPC)} \times \Delta AAS$

So the multiplier is:

(16-4) $\quad \text{Multiplier} = \dfrac{\Delta Y}{\Delta AAS} = \dfrac{1}{(1 - MPC)}$

Notice that the size of the multiplier depends on MPC. If the marginal propensity to consume is high, so is the multiplier. This is true because the size of MPC determines how large each round of expansion is compared with the previous round. To put it another way, the higher MPC is, the less disposable income "leaks out" into savings at each round of expansion.

In later modules we'll use the concept of the multiplier to analyze the effects of fiscal and monetary policies. We'll also see that the formula for the multiplier changes when we introduce various complications, including taxes and foreign trade. First, however, we need to look more deeply at what determines consumer spending.

The Multiplier and the Great Depression

The concept of the multiplier was originally devised by economists trying to understand the greatest economic disaster in history, the collapse of output and employment from 1929 to 1933, which began the Great Depression. Most economists believe that the slump from 1929 to 1933 was driven by a collapse in investment spending. But as the economy shrank, consumer spending also fell sharply, multiplying the effect on real GDP.

The table shows what happened to investment spending, consumer spending, and GDP during those four terrible years. All data are in 2005 dollars. What we see is that investment spending imploded, falling by more than 80%. But consumer spending also fell drastically and actually accounted for more of the fall in real GDP. (The total fall in real GDP was larger than the combined fall in consumer and investment spending, mainly because of technical accounting issues.)

The numbers in the table suggest that at the time of the Great Depression, the multiplier was around 3. Most current estimates put the size of the multiplier considerably lower—but there's a reason for that change. In 1929, government in the United States was very small by modern standards: taxes were low and major government programs like Social Security and Medicare had not yet come into being. In the modern U.S. economy, taxes are much higher, and so is government spending. Why does this matter? Because taxes and some government programs act as *automatic stabilizers,* reducing the size of the multiplier. For example, when incomes are relatively high, tax payments are relatively high as well, thus moderating increases in expenditures. And when incomes are relatively low, the unemployment insurance program pays more money out to individuals, thus boosting expenditures higher than they would otherwise be.

Investment Spending, Consumer Spending, and Real GDP in the Great Depression (billions of 2005 dollars)

	1929	1933	Change
Investment spending	$101.7	$18.9	−$82.8
Consumer spending	736.6	601.1	−135.5
Real GDP	977.0	716.4	−260.6

Source: Bureau of Economic Analysis.

Consumer Spending

Should you splurge on a restaurant meal or save money by eating at home? Should you buy a new car and, if so, how expensive a model? Should you redo that bathroom or live with it for another year? In the real world, households are constantly confronted with such choices—not just about the consumption mix but also about how much to spend in total. These choices, in turn, have a powerful effect on the economy: consumer spending normally accounts for two-thirds of total spending on final goods and services. But what determines how much consumers spend?

Current Disposable Income and Consumer Spending

The most important factor affecting a family's consumer spending is its current disposable income—income after taxes are paid and government transfers are received. It's obvious from daily life that people with high disposable incomes on average drive more expensive cars, live in more expensive houses, and spend more on meals and clothing than people with lower disposable incomes. And the relationship between current disposable income and spending is clear in the data.

The Bureau of Labor Statistics (BLS) collects annual data on family income and spending. Families are grouped by levels of before-tax income; after-tax income for each group is also reported. Since the income figures include transfers from the government, what the BLS calls a household's after-tax income is equivalent to its current disposable income.

Figure 16.1 on the next page is a scatter diagram illustrating the relationship between household current disposable income and household consumer spending for

figure 16.1

Current Disposable Income and Consumer Spending for American Households in 2008

For each income group of households, average current disposable income in 2008 is plotted versus average consumer spending in 2008. For example, the middle income group, with an annual income of $36,271 to $59,086, is represented by point A, indicating a household average current disposable income of $46,936 and average household consumer spending of $42,659. The data clearly show a positive relationship between current disposable income and consumer spending: families with higher current disposable income have higher consumer spending.

Source: Bureau of Labor Statistics.

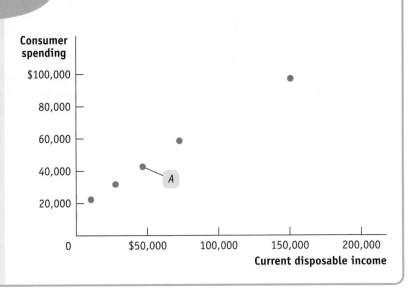

American households by income group in 2008. For example, point A shows that in 2008 the middle fifth of the population had an average current disposable income of $46,936 and average spending of $42,659. The pattern of the dots slopes upward from left to right, making it clear that households with higher current disposable income had higher consumer spending.

It's very useful to represent the relationship between an individual household's current disposable income and its consumer spending with an equation. The **consumption function** is an equation showing how an individual household's consumer spending varies with the household's current disposable income. The simplest version of a consumption function is a linear equation:

(16-5) $\quad c = a + MPC \times y_d$

where lowercase letters indicate variables measured for an individual household.

In this equation, c is individual household consumer spending and y_d is individual household current disposable income. Recall that MPC, the marginal propensity to consume, is the amount by which consumer spending rises if current disposable income rises by $1. Finally, a is a constant term—individual household **autonomous consumer spending**, the amount a household would spend if it had no disposable income. We assume that a is greater than zero because a household with no disposable income is able to fund some consumption by borrowing or using its savings. Notice, by the way, that we're using y for income. That's standard practice in macroeconomics, even though income isn't actually spelled "yncome." The reason is that I is reserved for investment spending.

Recall that we expressed MPC as the ratio of a change in consumer spending to the change in current disposable income. We've rewritten it for an individual household as Equation 16-6:

(16-6) $\quad MPC = \Delta c / \Delta y_d$

Multiplying both sides of Equation 16-6 by Δy_d, we get:

(16-7) $\quad MPC \times \Delta y_d = \Delta c$

Equation 16-7 tells us that when y_d goes up by $1, c goes up by $MPC \times$ $1.

The **consumption function** is an equation showing how an individual household's consumer spending varies with the household's current disposable income.

Autonomous consumer spending is the amount of money a household would spend if it had no disposable income.

figure 16.2

The Consumption Function

The consumption function relates a household's current disposable income to its consumer spending. The vertical intercept, *a*, is individual household autonomous consumer spending: the amount of a household's consumer spending if its current disposable income is zero. The slope of the consumption function line, *cf*, is the marginal propensity to consume, or *MPC*: of every additional $1 of current disposable income, $MPC \times \$1$ is spent.

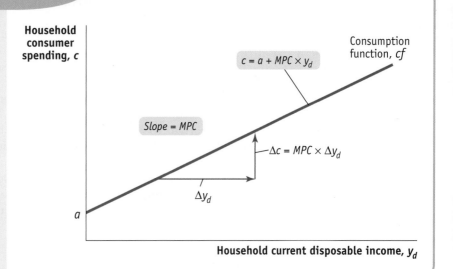

Figure 16.2 shows what Equation 16-5 looks like graphically, plotting y_d on the horizontal axis and *c* on the vertical axis. Individual household autonomous consumer spending, *a*, is the value of *c* when y_d is zero—it is the vertical *intercept* of the consumption function, *cf*. *MPC* is the *slope* of the line, measured by rise over run. If current disposable income rises by Δy_d, household consumer spending, *c*, rises by Δc. Since *MPC* is defined as $\Delta c / \Delta y_d$, the slope of the consumption function is:

(16-8) Slope of consumption function
= Rise over run
= $\Delta c / \Delta y_d$
= *MPC*

In reality, actual data never fit Equation 16-5 perfectly, but the fit can be pretty good. Figure 16.3 shows the data from Figure 16.1 again, together with a line drawn to fit the data as closely as possible. According to the data on households' consumer

figure 16.3

A Consumption Function Fitted to Data

The data from Figure 16.1 are reproduced here, along with a line drawn to fit the data as closely as possible. For American households in 2008, the best estimate of the average household's autonomous consumer spending, *a*, is $17,484 and the best estimate of *MPC* is 0.534, or approximately 0.53.

Source: Bureau of Labor Statistics.

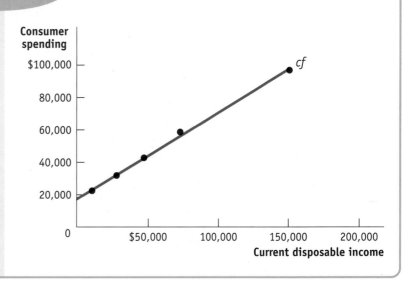

spending and current disposable income, the best estimate of a is \$17,484 and of MPC is 0.534. So the consumption function fitted to the data is:

$$c = \$17,484 + 0.534 \times y_d$$

That is, the data suggest a marginal propensity to consume of approximately 0.53. This implies that the marginal propensity to save (MPS)—the amount of an additional \$1 of disposable income that is saved—is approximately $1 - 0.53 = 0.47$, and the multiplier is $1/(1 - MPC) = 1/MPS =$ approximately $1/0.47 = 2.13$.

It's important to realize that Figure 16.3 shows a *microeconomic* relationship between the current disposable income of individual households and their spending on goods and services. However, macroeconomists assume that a similar relationship holds *for the economy as a whole:* that there is a relationship, called the **aggregate consumption function,** between aggregate current disposable income and aggregate consumer spending. We'll assume that it has the same form as the household-level consumption function:

(16-9) $C = A + MPC \times Y_D$

Here, C is aggregate consumer spending (called just "consumer spending"); Y_D is aggregate current disposable income (called, for simplicity, just "disposable income"); and A is aggregate autonomous consumer spending, the amount of consumer spending when Y_D equals zero. This is the relationship represented in Figure 16.4 by CF, analogous to cf in Figure 16.3.

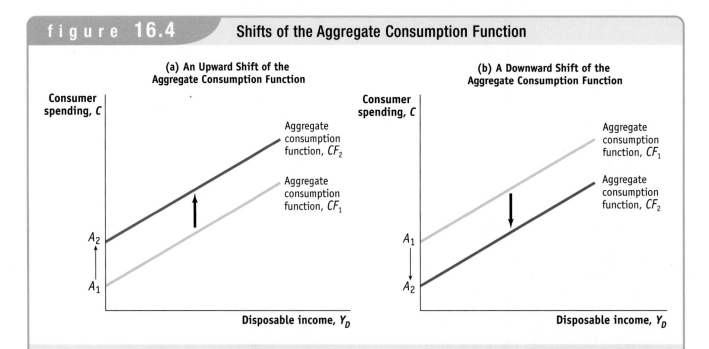

figure 16.4 — Shifts of the Aggregate Consumption Function

Panel (a) illustrates the effect of an increase in expected aggregate future disposable income. Consumers will spend more at every given level of aggregate current disposable income, Y_D. As a result, the initial aggregate consumption function CF_1, with aggregate autonomous consumer spending A_1, shifts up to a new position at CF_2 with aggregate autonomous consumer spending A_2. An increase in aggregate wealth will also shift the aggregate consumption function up. Panel (b), in contrast, illustrates the effect of a reduction in expected aggregate future disposable income. Consumers will spend less at every given level of aggregate current disposable income, Y_D. Consequently, the initial aggregate consumption function CF_1, with aggregate autonomous consumer spending A_1, shifts down to a new position at CF_2 with aggregate autonomous consumer spending A_2. A reduction in aggregate wealth will have the same effect.

Shifts of the Aggregate Consumption Function

The aggregate consumption function shows the relationship between disposable income and consumer spending for the economy as a whole, other things equal. When things other than disposable income change, the aggregate consumption function shifts. There are two principal causes of shifts of the aggregate consumption function: changes in expected future disposable income and changes in aggregate wealth.

Changes in Expected Future Disposable Income Suppose you land a really good, well-paying job on graduating from college—but the job, and the paychecks, won't start for several months. So your disposable income hasn't risen yet. Even so, it's likely that you will start spending more on final goods and services right away—maybe buying nicer work clothes than you originally planned—because you know that higher income is coming.

Conversely, suppose you have a good job but learn that the company is planning to downsize your division, raising the possibility that you may lose your job and have to take a lower-paying one somewhere else. Even though your disposable income hasn't gone down yet, you might well cut back on spending even while still employed, to save for a rainy day.

Both of these examples show how expectations about future disposable income can affect consumer spending. The two panels of Figure 16.4, which plot disposable income against consumer spending, show how changes in expected future disposable income affect the aggregate consumption function. In both panels, CF_1 is the initial aggregate consumption function. Panel (a) shows the effect of good news: information that leads consumers to expect higher disposable income in the future than they did before. Consumers will now spend more at any given level of current disposable income Y_D, corresponding to an increase in A, aggregate autonomous consumer spending, from A_1 to A_2. The effect is to shift the aggregate consumption function up, from CF_1 to CF_2. Panel (b) shows the effect of bad news: information that leads consumers to expect lower disposable income in the future than they did before. Consumers will now spend less at any given level of current disposable income, Y_D, corresponding to a fall in A from A_1 to A_2. The effect is to shift the aggregate consumption function down, from CF_1 to CF_2.

In a famous 1956 book, *A Theory of the Consumption Function*, Milton Friedman showed that taking the effects of expected future income into account explains an otherwise puzzling fact about consumer behavior. If we look at consumer spending during any given year, we find that people with high current income save a larger fraction of their income than those with low current income. (This is obvious from the data in Figure 16.3: people in the highest income group spend considerably less than their income; those in the lowest income group spend more than their income.) You might think this implies that the overall savings rate—the percentage of a country's disposable income that is saved—will rise as the economy grows and average current income rises; in fact, however, this hasn't happened.

Friedman pointed out that when we look at individual incomes in a given year, there are systematic differences between current and expected future income that create a positive relationship between current income and the savings rate. On one side, many of the people with low current income are having an unusually bad year. For example, they may be workers who have been laid off but will probably find new jobs eventually. They are people whose expected future income is higher than their current income, so it makes sense for them to have low or even negative savings. On the other side, many of the people with high current income in a given year are having an unusually good year. For example, they may have investments that happened to do extremely well. They are people whose expected future income is lower than their current income, so it makes sense for them to save most of their windfall.

When the economy grows, by contrast, current and expected future incomes rise together. Higher current income tends to lead to higher savings today, but higher

expected future income tends to lead to lower savings today. As a result, there's a weaker relationship between current income and the savings rate.

Friedman argued that consumer spending ultimately depends mainly on the income people expect to have over the long term rather than on their current income. This argument is known as the *permanent income hypothesis.*

Changes in Aggregate Wealth Imagine two individuals, Maria and Mark, both of whom expect to earn $30,000 this year. Suppose, however, that they have different histories. Maria has been working steadily for the past 10 years, owns her own home, and has $200,000 in the bank. Mark is the same age as Maria, but he has been in and out of work, hasn't managed to buy a house, and has very little in savings. In this case, Maria has something that Mark doesn't have: wealth. Even though they have the same disposable income, other things equal, you'd expect Maria to spend more on consumption than Mark. That is, *wealth* has an effect on consumer spending.

The effect of wealth on spending is emphasized by an influential economic model of how consumers make choices about spending versus saving called the *life-cycle hypothesis.* According to this hypothesis, consumers plan their spending over their lifetime, not just in response to their current disposable income. As a result, people try to *smooth* their consumption over their lifetimes—they save some of their current disposable income during their years of peak earnings (typically occurring during a worker's 40s and 50s) and during their retirement live off the wealth they accumulated while working. We won't go into the details of this hypothesis but will simply point out that it implies an important role for wealth in determining consumer spending. For example, a middle-aged couple who have accumulated a lot of wealth—who have paid off the mortgage on their house and already own plenty of stocks and bonds—will, other things equal, spend more on goods and services than a couple who have the same current disposable income but still need to save for their retirement.

Because wealth affects household consumer spending, changes in wealth across the economy can shift the aggregate consumption function. A rise in aggregate wealth—say, because of a booming stock market—increases the vertical intercept A, aggregate autonomous consumer spending. This, in turn, shifts the aggregate consumption function up in the same way as does an expected increase in future disposable income. A decline in aggregate wealth—say, because of a fall in housing prices as occurred in 2008—reduces A and shifts the aggregate consumption function down.

Investment Spending

Although consumer spending is much greater than investment spending, booms and busts in investment spending tend to drive the business cycle. In fact, most recessions originate as a fall in investment spending. Figure 16.5 illustrates this point; it shows the annual percent change of investment spending and consumer spending in the United States, both measured in 2005 dollars, during five recessions from 1973 to 2001. As you can see, swings in investment spending are much more dramatic than those in consumer spending. In addition, economists believe, due to the multiplier process, that declines in consumer spending are usually the result of a process that begins with a slump in investment spending. Soon we'll examine in more detail how a slump in investment spending generates a fall in consumer spending through the multiplier process.

Before we do that, however, let's analyze the factors that determine investment spending, which are somewhat different from those that determine consumer spending. **Planned investment spending** is the investment spending that firms *intend* to undertake during a given period. For reasons explained shortly, the level of investment

Planned investment spending is the investment spending that businesses intend to undertake during a given period.

figure 16.5

Fluctuations in Investment Spending and Consumer Spending

The bars illustrate the annual percent change in investment spending and consumer spending during five recent recessions. As the lengths of the bars show, swings in investment spending were much larger in percentage terms than those in consumer spending. The pattern has led economists to believe that recessions typically originate as a slump in investment spending.

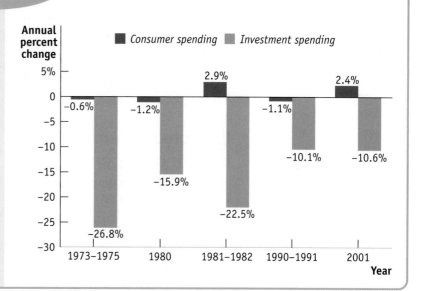

spending businesses *actually* carry out is sometimes not the same level as was planned. Planned investment spending depends on three principal factors: the interest rate, the expected future level of real GDP, and the current level of production capacity. First, we'll analyze the effect of the interest rate.

The Interest Rate and Investment Spending

Interest rates have their clearest effect on one particular form of investment spending: spending on residential construction—that is, on the construction of homes. The reason is straightforward: home builders only build houses they think they can sell, and houses are more affordable—and so more likely to sell—when the interest rate is low. Consider a potential home-buying family that needs to borrow $150,000 to buy a house. At an interest rate of 7.5%, a 30-year home mortgage will mean payments of $1,048 per month. At an interest rate of 5.5%, those payments would be only $851 per month, making houses significantly more affordable. Interest rates actually did drop from roughly 7.5% to 5.5% between the late 1990s and 2003, helping set off a housing boom.

Interest rates also affect other forms of investment spending. Firms with investment spending projects will go ahead with a project only if they expect a rate of return higher than the cost of the funds they would have to borrow to finance that project. If the interest rate rises, fewer projects will pass that test, and as a result investment spending will be lower.

You might think that the trade-off a firm faces is different if it can fund its investment project with its past profits rather than through borrowing. Past profits used to finance investment spending are called *retained earnings*. But even if a firm pays for investment spending out of retained earnings, the trade-off it must make in deciding whether or not to fund a project remains the same because it must take into account the opportunity cost of its funds. For example, instead of purchasing new equipment, the firm could lend out the funds and earn interest. The forgone interest earned is the opportunity cost of using retained earnings to fund an investment project. So the trade-off the firm faces when comparing a project's

Interest rates have a direct impact on whether or not construction companies decide to invest in the construction of new homes.

rate of return to the market interest rate has not changed when it uses retained earnings rather than borrowed funds. Either way, a rise in the market interest rate makes any given investment project less profitable. Conversely, a fall in the interest rate makes some investment projects that were unprofitable before profitable at the now lower interest rate. So some projects that had been unfunded before will be funded now.

So planned investment spending—spending on investment projects that firms voluntarily decide whether or not to undertake—is negatively related to the interest rate. Other things equal, a higher interest rate leads to a lower level of planned investment spending.

Expected Future Real GDP, Production Capacity, and Investment Spending

Suppose a firm has enough capacity to continue to produce the amount it is currently selling but doesn't expect its sales to grow in the future. Then it will engage in investment spending only to replace existing equipment and structures that wear out or are rendered obsolete by new technologies. But if, instead, the firm expects its sales to grow rapidly in the future, it will find its existing production capacity insufficient for its future production needs. So the firm will undertake investment spending to meet those needs. This implies that, other things equal, firms will undertake more investment spending when they expect their sales to grow.

Now suppose that the firm currently has considerably more capacity than necessary to meet current production needs. Even if it expects sales to grow, it won't have to undertake investment spending for a while—not until the growth in sales catches up with its excess capacity. This illustrates the fact that, other things equal, the current level of productive capacity has a negative effect on investment spending: other things equal, the higher the current capacity, the lower the investment spending.

If we put together the effects on investment spending of (1) growth in expected future sales and (2) the size of current production capacity, we can see one situation in which firms will most likely undertake high levels of investment spending: when they expect sales to grow rapidly. In that case, even excess production capacity will soon be used up, leading firms to resume investment spending.

What is an indicator of high expected growth in future sales? It's a high expected future growth rate of real GDP. A higher expected future growth rate of real GDP results in a higher level of planned investment spending, but a lower expected future growth rate of real GDP leads to lower planned investment spending.

Inventories and Unplanned Investment Spending

Most firms maintain **inventories,** stocks of goods held to satisfy future sales. Firms hold inventories so they can quickly satisfy buyers—a consumer can purchase an item off the shelf rather than waiting for it to be manufactured. In addition, businesses often hold inventories of their inputs to be sure they have a steady supply of necessary materials and spare parts. At the end of 2009, the overall value of inventories in the U.S. economy was estimated at $1.9 trillion, more than 13% of GDP.

A firm that increases its inventories is engaging in a form of investment spending. Suppose, for example, that the U.S. auto industry produces 800,000 cars per month but sells only 700,000. The remaining 100,000 cars are added to the inventory at auto company warehouses or car dealerships, ready to be sold in the future.

Inventory investment is the value of the change in total inventories held in the economy during a given period. Unlike other forms of investment spending, inventory investment can actually be negative. If, for example, the auto industry reduces its inventory over the course of a month, we say that it has engaged in negative inventory investment.

To understand inventory investment, think about a manager stocking the canned goods section of a supermarket. The manager tries to keep the store fully stocked so that shoppers can almost always find what they're looking for. But the manager does not want the shelves too heavily stocked because shelf space is limited and products can spoil. Similar considerations apply to many firms and typically lead them to manage

Inventories are stocks of goods held to satisfy future sales.

Inventory investment is the value of the change in total inventories held in the economy during a given period.

their inventories carefully. However, sales fluctuate. And because firms cannot always accurately predict sales, they often find themselves holding larger or smaller inventories than they had intended. When a firm's inventories are higher than intended due to an unforeseen decrease in sales, the result is **unplanned inventory investment.** An unexpected increase in sales depletes inventories and causes the value of unplanned inventory investment to be negative.

So in any given period, **actual investment spending** is equal to planned investment spending plus unplanned inventory investment. If we let $I_{Unplanned}$ represent unplanned inventory investment, $I_{Planned}$ represent planned investment spending, and I represent actual investment spending, then the relationship among all three can be represented as:

(16-10) $I = I_{Unplanned} + I_{Planned}$

Getty Images

Positive **unplanned inventory investment** occurs when actual sales are less than businesses expected, leading to unplanned increases in inventories. Sales in excess of expectations result in negative unplanned inventory investment.

Actual investment spending is the sum of planned investment spending and unplanned inventory investment.

fyi

Interest Rates and the U.S. Housing Boom

Interest rates dropped from roughly 7.5% to 5.5% between the late 1990s and 2003, helping set off a housing boom. The housing boom was part of a broader housing boom in the country as a whole. There is little question that this housing boom was caused, in the first instance, by low interest rates.

The figure shows the interest rate on 30-year home mortgages—the traditional way to borrow money for a home purchase—and the number of housing starts, the number of homes for which construction is started per month, from 1995 to the end of 2009 in the United

States. Panel (a), which shows the mortgage rate, gives you an idea of how much interest rates fell. In the second half of the 1990s, mortgage rates generally fluctuated between 7% and 8%; by 2003, they were down to between 5% and 6%. These lower rates were largely the result of Federal Reserve policy: the Fed cut rates in response to the 2001 recession and continued cutting them into 2003 out of concern that the economy's recovery was too weak to generate sustained job growth.

The low interest rates led to a large increase in residential investment spending, re-

flected in a surge of housing starts, shown in panel (b). This rise in investment spending drove an overall economic expansion, both through its direct effects and through the multiplier process.

Unfortunately, the housing boom eventually turned into too much of a good thing. By 2006, it was clear that the U.S. housing market was experiencing a bubble: people were buying housing based on unrealistic expectations about future price increases. When the bubble burst, housing—and the U.S. economy—took a fall.

(a) The Interest Rate on 30-Year Mortgages

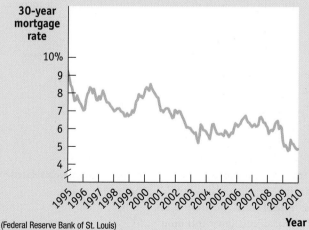

(Federal Reserve Bank of St. Louis)

Year

(b) Housing Starts

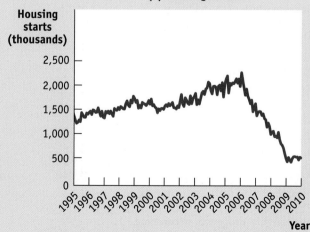

Year

To see how unplanned inventory investment can occur, let's continue to focus on the auto industry and make the following assumptions. First, let's assume that the industry must determine each month's production volume in advance, before it knows the volume of actual sales. Second, let's assume that it anticipates selling 800,000 cars next month and that it plans neither to add to nor subtract from existing inventories. In that case, it will produce 800,000 cars to match anticipated sales.

Now imagine that next month's actual sales are less than expected, only 700,000 cars. As a result, the value of 100,000 cars will be added to investment spending as unplanned inventory investment.

The auto industry will, of course, eventually adjust to this slowdown in sales and the resulting unplanned inventory investment. It is likely that it will cut next month's production volume in order to reduce inventories. In fact, economists who study macroeconomic variables in an attempt to determine the future path of the economy pay careful attention to changes in inventory levels. Rising inventories typically indicate positive unplanned inventory investment and a slowing economy, as sales are less than had been forecast. Falling inventories typically indicate negative unplanned inventory investment and a growing economy, as sales are greater than forecast. In the next section, we will see how production adjustments in response to fluctuations in sales and inventories ensure that the value of final goods and services actually produced is equal to desired purchases of those final goods and services.

Module 16 AP Review

Solutions appear at the back of the book.

Check Your Understanding

1. Explain why a decline in investment spending caused by a change in business expectations leads to a fall in consumer spending.

2. What is the multiplier if the marginal propensity to consume is 0.5? What is it if *MPC* is 0.8?

3. Suppose a crisis in the capital markets makes consumers unable to borrow and unable to save money. What implication does this have for the effects of expected future disposable income on consumer spending?

4. For each event, explain whether the initial effect is a change in planned investment spending or a change in unplanned inventory investment, and indicate the direction of the change.
   a. an unexpected increase in consumer spending
   b. a sharp rise in the cost of business borrowing
   c. a sharp increase in the economy's growth rate of real GDP
   d. an unanticipated fall in sales

Tackle the Test: Multiple-Choice Questions

1. Changes in which of the following leads to a shift of the aggregate consumption function?
   - I. expected future disposable income
   - II. aggregate wealth
   - III. current disposable income
   a. I only
   b. II only
   c. III only
   d. I and II only
   e. I, II, and III

2. The slope of a family's consumption function is equal to
   a. the real interest rate.
   b. the inflation rate.
   c. the marginal propensity to consume.

   d. the rate of increase in household current disposable income.
   e. the tax rate.

3. Given the consumption function $c = \$16,000 + 0.5\,y_d$, if individual household current disposable income is $20,000, individual household consumer spending will equal
   a. $36,000.
   b. $26,000.
   c. $20,000.
   d. $16,000.
   e. $6,000.

4. The level of planned investment spending is negatively related to the
   a. rate of return on investment.
   b. level of consumer spending.

c. level of actual investment spending.

d. interest rate.

e. all of the above.

5. Actual investment spending in any period is equal to

a. planned investment spending + unplanned inventory investment.

b. planned investment spending − unplanned inventory investment.

c. planned investment spending + inventory decreases.

d. unplanned inventory investment + inventory increases.

e. unplanned inventory investment − inventory increases.

Tackle the Test: Free-Response Questions

1. Use the consumption function provided to answer the following questions.

$$c = \$15{,}000 + 0.8 \times y_d$$

a. What is the value of the marginal propensity to consume?

b. If individual household current disposable income is $40,000, individual household consumer spending will equal how much?

c. Draw a correctly labeled graph showing this consumption function.

d. What is the slope of this consumption function?

e. On your graph from part c, show what would happen if expected future income decreased.

Answer (7 points)

1 point: 0.8

1 point: $47,000

1 point: Vertical axis labeled "Consumer spending" and horizontal axis labeled "Current disposable income"

1 point: Vertical intercept of $15,000

1 point: Upward sloping consumption function

1 point: 0.8

1 point: Consumption function shifts downward

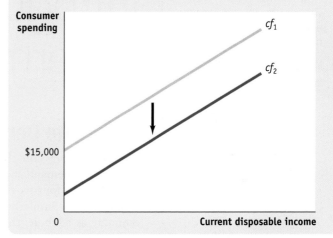

2. List the three most important factors affecting planned investment spending. Explain how each is related to actual investment spending.

- How the aggregate demand curve illustrates the relationship between the aggregate price level and the quantity of aggregate output demanded in the economy

- How the wealth effect and interest rate effect explain the aggregate demand curve's negative slope

- What factors can shift the aggregate demand curve

Module 17
Aggregate Demand: Introduction and Determinants

Aggregate Demand

The Great Depression, the great majority of economists agree, was the result of a massive negative demand shock. What does that mean? When economists talk about a fall in the demand for a particular good or service, they're referring to a leftward shift of the demand curve. Similarly, when economists talk about a negative demand shock to the economy as a whole, they're referring to a leftward shift of the **aggregate demand curve,** a curve that shows the relationship between the aggregate price level and the quantity of aggregate output demanded by households, firms, the government, and the rest of the world.

Figure 17.1 shows what the aggregate demand curve may have looked like in 1933, at the end of the 1929–1933 recession. The horizontal axis shows the total quantity of domestic goods and services demanded, measured in 2005 dollars. We use real GDP to measure aggregate output and will often use the two terms interchangeably. The vertical axis shows the aggregate price level, measured by the GDP deflator. With these variables on the axes, we can draw a curve, *AD,* showing how much aggregate output would have been demanded at any given aggregate price level. Since *AD* is meant to illustrate aggregate demand in 1933, one point on the curve corresponds to actual data for 1933, when the aggregate price level was 7.9 and the total quantity of domestic final goods and services purchased was $716 billion in 2005 dollars.

As drawn in Figure 17.1, the aggregate demand curve is downward sloping, indicating a negative relationship between the aggregate price level and the quantity of aggregate output demanded. A higher aggregate price level, other things equal, reduces the quantity of aggregate output demanded; a lower aggregate price level, other things equal, increases the quantity of aggregate output demanded. According to Figure 17.1, if the price level in 1933 had been 5.0 instead of 7.9, the total quantity of domestic final

The **aggregate demand curve** shows the relationship between the aggregate price level and the quantity of aggregate output demanded by households, businesses, the government, and the rest of the world.

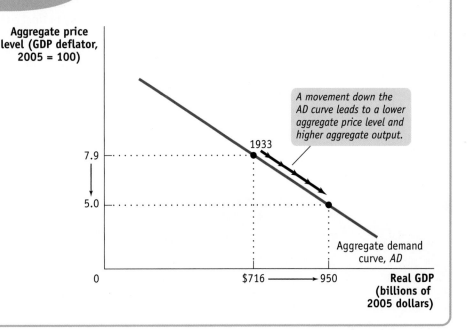

figure 17.1

The Aggregate Demand Curve

The aggregate demand curve shows the relationship between the aggregate price level and the quantity of aggregate output demanded. The curve is downward sloping due to the wealth effect of a change in the aggregate price level and the interest rate effect of a change in the aggregate price level. Corresponding to the actual 1933 data, here the total quantity of goods and services demanded at an aggregate price level of 7.9 is $716 billion in 2005 dollars. According to our hypothetical curve, however, if the aggregate price level had been only 5.0, the quantity of aggregate output demanded would have risen to $950 billion.

A movement down the AD curve leads to a lower aggregate price level and higher aggregate output.

goods and services demanded would have been $950 billion in 2005 dollars instead of $716 billion.

The first key question about the aggregate demand curve involves its negative slope.

Why Is the Aggregate Demand Curve Downward Sloping?

In Figure 17.1, the curve *AD* slopes downward. Why? Recall the basic equation of national income accounting:

(17-1) $GDP = C + I + G + X - IM$

where *C* is consumer spending, *I* is investment spending, *G* is government purchases of goods and services, *X* is exports to other countries, and *IM* is imports. If we measure these variables in constant dollars—that is, in prices of a base year—then $C + I + G + X - IM$ represents the quantity of domestically produced final goods and services demanded during a given period. *G* is decided by the government, but the other variables are private-sector decisions. To understand why the aggregate demand curve slopes downward, we need to understand why a rise in the aggregate price level reduces *C*, *I*, and *X − IM*.

You might think that the downward slope of the aggregate demand curve is a natural consequence of the *law of demand*. That is, since the demand curve for any one good is downward sloping, isn't it natural that the demand curve for aggregate output is also downward sloping? This turns out, however, to be a misleading parallel. The demand curve for any individual good shows how the quantity demanded depends on the price of that good, *holding the prices of other goods and services constant*. The main reason the quantity of a good demanded falls when the price of that good rises—that is, the quantity of a good demanded falls as we move up the demand curve—is that people switch their consumption to other goods and services that have become relatively less expensive.

But when we consider movements up or down the aggregate demand curve, we're considering *a simultaneous change in the prices of all final goods and services*. Furthermore, changes in the composition of goods and services in consumer spending aren't relevant to the aggregate demand curve: if consumers decide to buy fewer clothes but more cars, this doesn't necessarily change the total quantity of final goods and services they demand.

Why, then, does a rise in the aggregate price level lead to a fall in the quantity of all domestically produced final goods and services demanded? There are two main reasons: the *wealth effect* and the *interest rate effect* of a change in the aggregate price level.

The Wealth Effect An increase in the aggregate price level, other things equal, reduces the purchasing power of many assets. Consider, for example, someone who has $5,000 in a bank account. If the aggregate price level were to rise by 25%, that $5,000 would buy only as much as $4,000 would have bought previously. With the loss in purchasing power, the owner of that bank account would probably scale back his or her consumption plans. Millions of other people would respond the same way, leading to a fall in spending on final goods and services, because a rise in the aggregate price level reduces the purchasing power of everyone's bank account.

Correspondingly, a fall in the aggregate price level increases the purchasing power of consumers' assets and leads to more consumer demand. The **wealth effect of a change in the aggregate price level** is the change in consumer spending caused by the altered purchasing power of consumers' assets. Because of the wealth effect, consumer spending, C, falls when the aggregate price level rises, leading to a downward-sloping aggregate demand curve.

The Interest Rate Effect Economists use the term *money* in its narrowest sense to refer to cash and bank deposits on which people can write checks. People and firms hold money because it reduces the cost and inconvenience of making transactions. An increase in the aggregate price level, other things equal, reduces the purchasing power of a given amount of money holdings. To purchase the same basket of goods and services as before, people and firms now need to hold more money. So, in response to an increase in the aggregate price level, the public tries to increase its money holdings, either by borrowing more or by selling assets such as bonds. This reduces the funds available for lending to other borrowers and drives interest rates up. A rise in the interest rate reduces investment spending because it makes the cost of borrowing higher. It also reduces consumer spending because households save more of their disposable income. So a rise in the aggregate price level depresses investment spending, I, and consumer spending, C, through its effect on the purchasing power of money holdings, an effect known as the **interest rate effect of a change in the aggregate price level.** This also leads to a downward-sloping aggregate demand curve.

When the aggregate price level falls, the purchasing power of consumers' assets rises, leading shoppers to place more items in their carts.

The **wealth effect of a change in the aggregate price level** is the change in consumer spending caused by the altered purchasing power of consumers' assets.

The **interest rate effect of a change in the aggregate price level** is the change in investment and consumer spending caused by altered interest rates that result from changes in the demand for money.

Shifts of the Aggregate Demand Curve

When we introduced the analysis of supply and demand in the market for an individual good, we stressed the importance of the distinction between *movements along* the demand curve and *shifts of* the demand curve. The same distinction applies to the aggregate demand curve. Figure 17.1 shows a *movement along* the aggregate demand curve, a change in the aggregate quantity of goods and services demanded as the aggregate price level changes. But there can also be *shifts of* the aggregate demand curve, changes in the quantity of goods and services demanded at any given price level, as shown in Figure 17.2. When we talk about an increase in aggregate demand, we mean a shift of the aggregate demand curve to the right, as shown in panel (a) by the shift from AD_1 to AD_2. A rightward shift occurs when the quantity of aggregate output demanded increases at any given aggregate price level. A decrease in aggregate demand means that the AD curve shifts to the left, as in panel (b). A leftward

figure 17.2 Shifts of the Aggregate Demand Curve

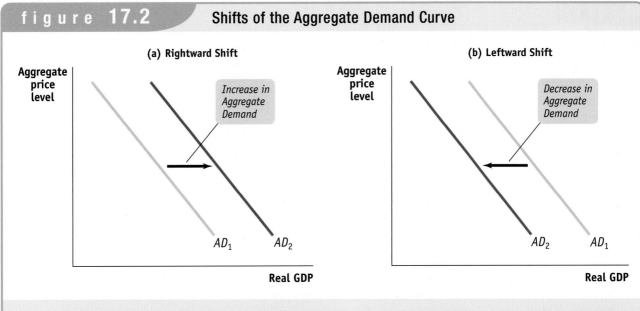

Panel (a) shows the effect of events that increase the quantity of aggregate output demanded at any given aggregate price level, for example, improvements in business and consumer expectations or increased government spending. Such changes shift the aggregate demand curve to the right, from AD_1 to AD_2. Panel (b) shows the effect of events that decrease the quantity of aggregate output demanded at any given aggregate price level, such as a fall in wealth caused by a stock market decline. This shifts the aggregate demand curve leftward from AD_1 to AD_2.

shift implies that the quantity of aggregate output demanded falls at any given aggregate price level.

A number of factors can shift the aggregate demand curve. Among the most important factors are changes in expectations, changes in wealth, and the size of the existing stock of physical capital. In addition, both fiscal and monetary policy can shift the aggregate demand curve. All five factors set the multiplier process in motion. By causing an initial rise or fall in real GDP, they change disposable income, which leads to additional changes in aggregate spending, which lead to further changes in real GDP, and so on. For an overview of factors that shift the aggregate demand curve, see Table 17.1 on the next page.

Changes in Expectations Both consumer spending and planned investment spending depend in part on people's expectations about the future. Consumers base their spending not only on the income they have now but also on the income they expect to have in the future. Firms base their planned investment spending not only on current conditions but also on the sales they expect to make in the future. As a result, changes in expectations can push consumer spending and planned investment spending up or down. If consumers and firms become more optimistic, aggregate spending rises; if they become more pessimistic, aggregate spending falls. In fact, short-run economic forecasters pay careful attention to surveys of consumer and business sentiment. In particular, forecasters watch the Consumer Confidence Index, a monthly measure calculated by the Conference Board, and the Michigan Consumer Sentiment Index, a similar measure calculated by the University of Michigan.

Changes in Wealth Consumer spending depends in part on the value of household assets. When the real value of these assets rises, the purchasing power they embody also rises, leading to an increase in aggregate spending. For example, in the 1990s, there was a significant rise in the stock market that increased aggregate demand. And when the real value of household assets falls—for example, because of a stock market

table **17.1**

Factors That Shift the Aggregate Demand Curve

Changes in expectations		
	If consumers and firms become more optimistic, . . .	. . . aggregate demand increases.
	If consumers and firms become more pessimistic, . . .	. . . aggregate demand decreases.
Changes in wealth		
	If the real value of household assets rises, . . .	. . . aggregate demand increases.
	If the real value of household assets falls, . . .	. . . aggregate demand decreases.
Size of the existing stock of physical capital		
	If the existing stock of physical capital is relatively small, . . .	. . . aggregate demand increases.
	If the existing stock of physical capital is relatively large, . . .	. . . aggregate demand decreases.
Fiscal policy		
	If the government increases spending or cuts taxes, . . .	. . . aggregate demand increases.
	If the government reduces spending or raises taxes, . . .	. . . aggregate demand decreases.
Monetary policy		
	If the central bank increases the quantity of money, . . .	. . . aggregate demand increases.
	If the central bank reduces the quantity of money, . . .	. . . aggregate demand decreases.

The loss of wealth resulting from the stock market crash of 1929 was a significant factor leading to the Great Depression.

crash—the purchasing power they embody is reduced and aggregate demand also falls. The stock market crash of 1929 was a significant factor leading to the Great Depression. Similarly, a sharp decline in real estate values was a major factor depressing consumer spending in 2008.

Size of the Existing Stock of Physical Capital Firms engage in planned investment spending to add to their stock of physical capital. Their incentive to spend depends in part on how much physical capital they already have: the more they have, the less they will feel a need to add more, other things equal. The same applies to other types of investment spending—for example, if a large number of houses have been built in recent years, this will depress the demand for new houses and as a result also tend to reduce residential investment spending. In fact, that's part of the reason for the deep slump in residential investment spending that began in 2006. The housing boom of the previous few years had created an oversupply of houses: by spring 2008, the inventory of unsold houses on the market was equal to more than 11 months of sales, and prices had fallen more than 20% from their peak. This gave the construction industry little incentive to build even more homes.

Government Policies and Aggregate Demand One of the key insights of macroeconomics is that the government can have a powerful influence on aggregate demand and that, in some circumstances, this influence can be used to improve economic performance.

The two main ways the government can influence the aggregate demand curve are through fiscal policy and monetary policy. We'll briefly discuss their influence on aggregate demand, leaving a full-length discussion for later.

Fiscal Policy **Fiscal policy** is the use of either government spending—government purchases of final goods and services and government transfers—or tax policy to stabilize the economy. In practice, governments often respond to recessions by increasing

Fiscal policy is the use of taxes, government transfers, or government purchases of goods and services to stabilize the economy.

spending, cutting taxes, or both. They often respond to inflation by reducing spending or increasing taxes.

The effect of government purchases of final goods and services, G, on the aggregate demand curve is *direct* because government purchases are themselves a component of aggregate demand. So an increase in government purchases shifts the aggregate demand curve to the right and a decrease shifts it to the left. History's most dramatic example of how increased government purchases affect aggregate demand was the effect of wartime government spending during World War II. Because of the war, U.S. federal purchases surged 400%. This increase in purchases is usually credited with ending the Great Depression. In the 1990s, Japan used large public works projects—such as government-financed construction of roads, bridges, and dams—in an effort to increase aggregate demand in the face of a slumping economy.

In contrast, changes in either tax rates or government transfers influence the economy *indirectly* through their effect on disposable income. A lower tax rate means that consumers get to keep more of what they earn, increasing their disposable income. An increase in government transfers also increases consumers' disposable income. In either case, this increases consumer spending and shifts the aggregate demand curve to the right. A higher tax rate or a reduction in transfers reduces the amount of disposable income received by consumers. This reduces consumer spending and shifts the aggregate demand curve to the left.

Monetary Policy In the next section, we will study the Federal Reserve System and monetary policy in detail. At this point, we just need to note that the Federal Reserve controls **monetary policy**—the use of changes in the quantity of money or the interest rate to stabilize the economy. We've just discussed how a rise in the aggregate price level, by reducing the purchasing power of money holdings, causes a rise in the interest rate. That, in turn, reduces both investment spending and consumer spending.

But what happens if the quantity of money in the hands of households and firms changes? In modern economies, the quantity of money in circulation is largely determined by the decisions of a *central bank* created by the government. As we'll learn in more detail later, the Federal Reserve, the U.S. central bank, is a special institution that is neither exactly part of the government nor exactly a private institution. When the central bank increases the quantity of money in circulation, households and firms have more money, which they are willing to lend out. The effect is to drive the interest rate down at any given aggregate price level, leading to higher investment spending and higher consumer spending. That is, increasing the quantity of money shifts the aggregate demand curve to the right. Reducing the quantity of money has the opposite effect: households and firms have less money holdings than before, leading them to borrow more and lend less. This raises the interest rate, reduces investment spending and consumer spending, and shifts the aggregate demand curve to the left.

> **Monetary policy** is the central bank's use of changes in the quantity of money or the interest rate to stabilize the economy.

Module 17 AP Review

Solutions appear at the back of the book.

Check Your Understanding

1. Determine the effect on aggregate demand of each of the following events. Explain whether it represents a movement along the aggregate demand curve (up or down) or a shift of the curve (leftward or rightward).

   a. a rise in the interest rate caused by a change in monetary policy

   b. a fall in the real value of money in the economy due to a higher aggregate price level

   c. news of a worse-than-expected job market next year

   d. a fall in tax rates

   e. a rise in the real value of assets in the economy due to a lower aggregate price level

   f. a rise in the real value of assets in the economy due to a surge in real estate values

Tackle the Test: Multiple-Choice Questions

1. Which of the following explains the slope of the aggregate demand curve?
   - I. the wealth effect of a change in the aggregate price level
   - II. the interest rate effect of a change in the aggregate price level
   - III. the product-substitution effect of a change in the aggregate price level
   a. I only
   b. II only
   c. III only
   d. I and II only
   e. I, II, and III

2. Which of the following will shift the aggregate demand curve to the right?
   a. a decrease in wealth
   b. pessimistic consumer expectations
   c. a decrease in the existing stock of capital
   d. contractionary fiscal policy
   e. a decrease in the quantity of money

3. The Consumer Confidence Index is used to measure which of the following?
   a. the level of consumer spending
   b. the rate of return on investments
   c. consumer expectations
   d. planned investment spending
   e. the level of current disposable income

4. Decreases in the stock market decrease aggregate demand by decreasing which of the following?
   a. consumer wealth
   b. the price level
   c. the stock of existing physical capital
   d. interest rates
   e. tax revenues

5. Which of the following government policies will shift the aggregate demand curve to the left?
   a. a decrease in the quantity of money
   b. an increase in government purchases of goods and services
   c. a decrease in taxes
   d. a decrease in interest rates
   e. an increase in government transfers

Tackle the Test: Free-Response Questions

1. a. Draw a correctly labeled graph showing aggregate demand.
   b. On your graph from part a, illustrate an increase in aggregate demand.
   c. List the four factors that shift aggregate demand.
   d. Describe a change in each determinant of aggregate demand that would lead to the shift you illustrated in part b.

Answer (12 points)

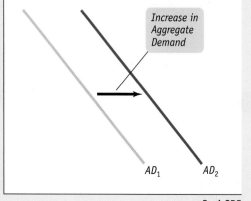

1 point: Vertical axis labeled "Aggregate price level" (or "Price level")

1 point: Horizontal axis labeled "Real GDP"

1 point: Downward sloping curve labeled "AD" (or "AD$_1$")

1 point: AD curve shifted to the right

1 point: Expectations

1 point: Wealth

1 point: Size of existing stock of physical capital

1 point: Government policies

1 point: Consumers/Producers more confident

1 point: Increase in wealth

1 point: Lower existing stock of physical capital

1 point: An increase in government spending or in the money supply

2. Identify the two effects that cause the aggregate demand curve to have a downward slope. Explain each.

Module 18
Aggregate Supply: Introduction and Determinants

Aggregate Supply

Between 1929 and 1933, there was a sharp fall in aggregate demand—a reduction in the quantity of goods and services demanded at any given price level. One consequence of the economy-wide decline in demand was a fall in the prices of most goods and services. By 1933, the GDP deflator (one of the price indexes) was 26% below its 1929 level, and other indexes were down by similar amounts. A second consequence was a decline in the output of most goods and services: by 1933, real GDP was 27% below its 1929 level. A third consequence, closely tied to the fall in real GDP, was a surge in the unemployment rate from 3% to 25%.

The association between the plunge in real GDP and the plunge in prices wasn't an accident. Between 1929 and 1933, the U.S. economy was moving down its **aggregate supply curve,** which shows the relationship between the economy's aggregate price level (the overall price level of final goods and services in the economy) and the total quantity of final goods and services, or aggregate output, producers are willing to supply. (As you will recall, we use real GDP to measure aggregate output, and we'll often use the two terms interchangeably.) More specifically, between 1929 and 1933, the U.S. economy moved down its *short-run aggregate supply curve.*

The Short-Run Aggregate Supply Curve

The period from 1929 to 1933 demonstrated that there is a positive relationship in the short run between the aggregate price level and the quantity of aggregate output supplied. That is, a rise in the aggregate price level is associated with a rise in the quantity of aggregate output supplied, other things equal; a fall in the aggregate price level is associated with a fall in the quantity of aggregate output supplied, other things equal. To understand why this positive relationship exists, consider the most basic

The **aggregate supply curve** shows the relationship between the aggregate price level and the quantity of aggregate output supplied in the economy.

question facing a producer: is producing a unit of output profitable or not? Let's define profit per unit:

(18-1)   Profit per unit of output =
Price per unit of output − Production cost per unit of output

Thus, the answer to the question depends on whether the price the producer receives for a unit of output is greater or less than the cost of producing that unit of output. At any given point in time, many of the costs producers face are fixed per unit of output and can't be changed for an extended period of time. Typically, the largest source of inflexible production cost is the wages paid to workers. *Wages* here refers to all forms of worker compensation, including employer-paid health care and retirement benefits in addition to earnings.

Wages are typically an inflexible production cost because the dollar amount of any given wage paid, called the **nominal wage,** is often determined by contracts that were signed some time ago. And even when there are no formal contracts, there are often informal agreements between management and workers, making companies reluctant to change wages in response to economic conditions. For example, companies usually will not reduce wages during poor economic times—unless the downturn has been particularly long and severe—for fear of generating worker resentment. Correspondingly, they typically won't raise wages during better economic times—until they are at risk of losing workers to competitors—because they don't want to encourage workers to routinely demand higher wages. As a result of both formal and informal agreements, then, the economy is characterized by **sticky wages:** nominal wages that are slow to fall even in the face of high unemployment and slow to rise even in the face of labor shortages. It's important to note, however, that nominal wages cannot be sticky forever: ultimately, formal contracts and informal agreements will be renegotiated to take into account changed economic circumstances. How long it takes for nominal wages to become flexible is an integral component of what distinguishes the short run from the long run.

To understand how the fact that many costs are fixed in nominal terms gives rise to an upward-sloping short-run aggregate supply curve, it's helpful to know that prices are set somewhat differently in different kinds of markets. In *perfectly competitive markets,* producers take prices as given; in *imperfectly competitive markets,* producers have some ability to choose the prices they charge. In both kinds of markets, there is a short-run positive relationship between prices and output, but for slightly different reasons.

Let's start with the behavior of producers in perfectly competitive markets; remember, they take the price as given. Imagine that, for some reason, the aggregate price level falls, which means that the price received by the typical producer of a final good or service falls. Because many production costs are fixed in the short run, production cost per unit of output doesn't fall by the same proportion as the fall in the price of output. So the profit per unit of output declines, leading perfectly competitive producers to reduce the quantity supplied in the short run.

On the other hand, suppose that for some reason the aggregate price level rises. As a result, the typical producer receives a higher price for its final good or service. Again, many production costs are fixed in the short run, so production cost per unit of output doesn't rise by the same proportion as the rise in the price of a unit. And since the typical perfectly competitive producer takes the price as given, profit per unit of output rises and output increases.

Now consider an imperfectly competitive producer that is able to set its own price. If there is a rise in the demand for this producer's product, it will be able to sell more at any given price. Given stronger demand for its products, it will probably choose to increase its prices as well as its output, as a way of increasing profit per unit of output. In

The **nominal wage** is the dollar amount of the wage paid.

Sticky wages are nominal wages that are slow to fall even in the face of high unemployment and slow to rise even in the face of labor shortages.

fact, industry analysts often talk about variations in an industry's "pricing power": when demand is strong, firms with pricing power are able to raise prices—and they do.

Conversely, if there is a fall in demand, firms will normally try to limit the fall in their sales by cutting prices.

Both the responses of firms in perfectly competitive industries and those of firms in imperfectly competitive industries lead to an upward-sloping relationship between aggregate output and the aggregate price level. The positive relationship between the aggregate price level and the quantity of aggregate output producers are willing to supply during the time period when many production costs, particularly nominal wages, can be taken as fixed is illustrated by the **short-run aggregate supply curve.** The positive relationship between the aggregate price level and aggregate output in the short run gives the short-run aggregate supply curve its upward slope. Figure 18.1 shows a hypothetical short-run aggregate supply curve, *SRAS,* that matches actual U.S. data for 1929 and 1933. On the horizontal axis is aggregate output (or, equivalently, real GDP)—the total quantity of final goods and services supplied in the economy—measured in 2005 dollars. On the vertical axis is the aggregate price level as measured by the GDP deflator, with the value for the year 2005 equal to 100. In 1929, the aggregate price level was 10.6 and real GDP was $977 billion. In 1933, the aggregate price level was 7.9 and real GDP was only $716 billion. The movement down the *SRAS* curve corresponds to the deflation and fall in aggregate output experienced over those years.

The **short-run aggregate supply curve** shows the relationship between the aggregate price level and the quantity of aggregate output supplied that exists in the short run, the time period when many production costs can be taken as fixed.

Shifts of the Short-Run Aggregate Supply Curve

Figure 18.1 shows a *movement along* the short-run aggregate supply curve, as the aggregate price level and aggregate output fell from 1929 to 1933. But there can also be *shifts of* the short-run aggregate supply curve, as shown in Figure 18.2 on the next page. Panel (a) shows a *decrease in short-run aggregate supply*—a leftward shift of the short-run aggregate supply curve. Aggregate supply decreases when producers reduce the quantity of aggregate output they are willing to supply at any given aggregate price level. Panel (b) shows an *increase in short-run aggregate supply*—a rightward shift of the short-run aggregate supply

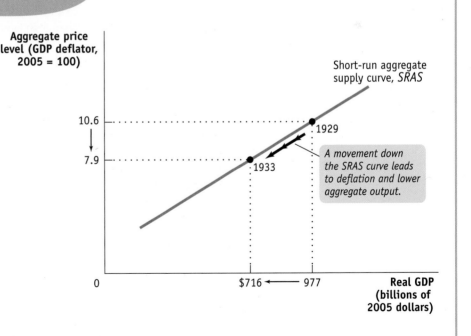

figure 18.1

The Short-Run Aggregate Supply Curve

The short-run aggregate supply curve shows the relationship between the aggregate price level and the quantity of aggregate output supplied in the short run, the period in which many production costs such as nominal wages are fixed. It is upward sloping because a higher aggregate price level leads to higher profit per unit of output and higher aggregate output given fixed nominal wages. Here we show numbers corresponding to the Great Depression, from 1929 to 1933: when deflation occurred and the aggregate price level fell from 10.6 (in 1929) to 7.9 (in 1933), firms responded by reducing the quantity of aggregate output supplied from $977 billion to $716 billion measured in 2005 dollars.

figure 18.2 — Shifts of the Short-Run Aggregate Supply Curve

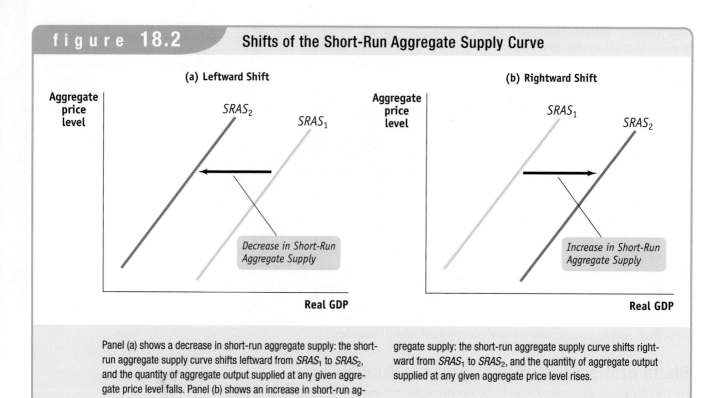

(a) Leftward Shift

Aggregate price level / Real GDP

SRAS₂ SRAS₁

Decrease in Short-Run Aggregate Supply

(b) Rightward Shift

Aggregate price level / Real GDP

SRAS₁ SRAS₂

Increase in Short-Run Aggregate Supply

Panel (a) shows a decrease in short-run aggregate supply: the short-run aggregate supply curve shifts leftward from *SRAS₁* to *SRAS₂*, and the quantity of aggregate output supplied at any given aggregate price level falls. Panel (b) shows an increase in short-run aggregate supply: the short-run aggregate supply curve shifts rightward from *SRAS₁* to *SRAS₂*, and the quantity of aggregate output supplied at any given aggregate price level rises.

curve. Aggregate supply increases when producers increase the quantity of aggregate output they are willing to supply at any given aggregate price level.

To understand why the short-run aggregate supply curve can shift, it's important to recall that producers make output decisions based on their profit per unit of output. The short-run aggregate supply curve illustrates the relationship between the aggregate price level and aggregate output: because some production costs are fixed in the short run, a change in the aggregate price level leads to a change in producers' profit per unit of output and, in turn, leads to a change in aggregate output. But other factors besides the aggregate price level can affect profit per unit and, in turn, aggregate output. It is changes in these other factors that will shift the short-run aggregate supply curve.

To develop some intuition, suppose that something happens that raises production costs—say, an increase in the price of oil. At any given price of output, a producer now earns a smaller profit per unit of output. As a result, producers reduce the quantity supplied at any given aggregate price level, and the short-run aggregate supply curve shifts to the left. If, in contrast, something happens that lowers production costs—say, a fall in the nominal wage—a producer now earns a higher profit per unit of output at any given price of output. This leads producers to increase the quantity of aggregate output supplied at any given aggregate price level, and the short-run aggregate supply curve shifts to the right.

Now we'll look more closely at the link between important factors that affect producers' profit per unit and shifts in the short-run aggregate supply curve.

Changes in Commodity Prices A surge in the price of oil caused problems for the U.S. economy in the 1970s and in early 2008. Oil is a *commodity,* a standardized input bought and sold in bulk quantities. An increase in the price of a commodity—oil—raised production costs across the economy and reduced the quantity of aggregate output supplied at any given aggregate price level, shifting the short-run aggregate supply curve to the left. Conversely, a decline in commodity prices reduces production costs, leading to an increase in the quantity supplied at any given aggregate price level and a rightward shift of the short-run aggregate supply curve.

Why isn't the influence of commodity prices already captured by the short-run aggregate supply curve? Because commodities—unlike, say, soft drinks—are not a final good, their prices are not included in the calculation of the aggregate price level. Furthermore, commodities represent a significant cost of production to most suppliers, just like nominal wages do. So changes in commodity prices have large impacts on production costs. And in contrast to noncommodities, the prices of commodities can sometimes change drastically due to industry-specific shocks to supply—such as wars in the Middle East or rising Chinese demand that leaves less oil for the United States.

Changes in Nominal Wages At any given point in time, the dollar wages of many workers are fixed because they are set by contracts or informal agreements made in the past. Nominal wages can change, however, once enough time has passed for contracts and informal agreements to be renegotiated. Suppose, for example, that there is an economy-wide rise in the cost of health care insurance premiums paid by employers as part of employees' wages. From the employers' perspective, this is equivalent to a rise in nominal wages because it is an increase in employer-paid compensation. So this rise in nominal wages increases production costs and shifts the short-run aggregate supply curve to the left. Conversely, suppose there is an economy-wide fall in the cost of such premiums. This is equivalent to a fall in nominal wages from the point of view of employers; it reduces production costs and shifts the short-run aggregate supply curve to the right.

An important historical fact is that during the 1970s, the surge in the price of oil had the indirect effect of also raising nominal wages. This "knock-on" effect occurred because many wage contracts included *cost-of-living allowances* that automatically raised the nominal wage when consumer prices increased. Through this channel, the surge in the price of oil—which led to an increase in overall consumer prices—ultimately caused a rise in nominal wages. So the economy, in the end, experienced two leftward shifts of the aggregate supply curve: the first generated by the initial surge in the price of oil, the second generated by the induced increase in nominal wages. The negative effect on the economy of rising oil prices was greatly magnified through the cost-of-living allowances in wage contracts. Today, cost-of-living allowances in wage contracts are rare.

Changes in Productivity An increase in productivity means that a worker can produce more units of output with the same quantity of inputs. For example, the introduction of bar-code scanners in retail stores greatly increased the ability of a single worker to stock, inventory, and resupply store shelves. As a result, the cost to a store of "producing" a dollar of sales fell and profit rose. And, correspondingly, the quantity supplied increased. (Think of Walmart and the increase in the number of its stores as an increase in aggregate supply.) So a rise in productivity, whatever the source, increases producers' profits and shifts the short-run aggregate supply curve to the right. Conversely, a fall in productivity—say, due to new regulations that require workers to spend more time filling out forms—reduces the number of units of output a worker can produce with the same quantity of inputs.

AP Photo/Paul Sakuma

Signs of the times: high oil prices caused high gasoline prices in 2008.

Almost every good purchased today has a UPC barcode on it, which allows stores to scan and track merchandise with great speed.

© Blend Images/Alamy

module **18** Aggregate Supply: Introduction and Determinants **183**

Consequently, the cost per unit of output rises, profit falls, and quantity supplied falls. This shifts the short-run aggregate supply curve to the left.

For a summary of the factors that shift the short-run aggregate supply curve, see Table 18.1.

table **18.1**

Factors that Shift the Short-Run Aggregate Supply Curve

Changes in commodity prices		
	If commodity prices fall, . . .	. . . short-run aggregate supply increases.
	If commodity prices rise, . . .	. . . short-run aggregate supply decreases.
Changes in nominal wages		
	If nominal wages fall, . . .	. . . short-run aggregate supply increases.
	If nominal wages rise, . . .	. . . short-run aggregate supply decreases.
Changes in productivity		
	If workers become more productive, . . .	. . . short-run aggregate supply increases.
	If workers become less productive, . . .	. . . short-run aggregate supply decreases.

The Long-Run Aggregate Supply Curve

We've just seen that in the short run, a fall in the aggregate price level leads to a decline in the quantity of aggregate output supplied. This is the result of nominal wages that are sticky in the short run. But as we mentioned earlier, contracts and informal agreements are renegotiated in the long run. So in the long run, nominal wages—like the aggregate price level—are flexible, not sticky. Wage flexibility greatly alters the long-run relationship between the aggregate price level and aggregate supply. In fact, in the long run the aggregate price level has *no* effect on the quantity of aggregate output supplied.

To see why, let's conduct a thought experiment. Imagine that you could wave a magic wand—or maybe a magic bar-code scanner—and cut *all prices* in the economy in half at the same time. By "all prices" we mean the prices of all inputs, including nominal wages, as well as the prices of final goods and services. What would happen to aggregate output, given that the aggregate price level has been halved and all input prices, including nominal wages, have been halved?

The answer is: nothing. Consider Equation 18-1 again: each producer would receive a lower price for its product, but costs would fall by the same proportion. As a result, every unit of output profitable to produce before the change in prices would still be profitable to produce after the change in prices. So a halving of *all* prices in the economy has no effect on the economy's aggregate output. In other words, changes in the aggregate price level now have no effect on the quantity of aggregate output supplied.

In reality, of course, no one can change all prices by the same proportion at the same time. But now, we'll consider the *long run,* the period of time over which all prices are fully flexible. In the long run, inflation or deflation has the same effect as someone changing all prices by the same proportion. As a result, changes in the aggregate price level do not change the quantity of aggregate output supplied in the long run. That's because changes in the aggregate price level will, in the long run, be accompanied by equal proportional changes in *all* input prices, including nominal wages.

The **long-run aggregate supply curve,** illustrated in Figure 18.3 by the curve *LRAS,* shows the relationship between the aggregate price level and the quantity of aggregate

The **long-run aggregate supply curve** shows the relationship between the aggregate price level and the quantity of aggregate output supplied that would exist if all prices, including nominal wages, were fully flexible.

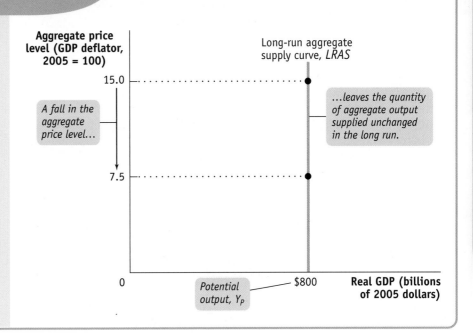

figure 18.3

The Long-Run Aggregate Supply Curve

The long-run aggregate supply curve shows the quantity of aggregate output supplied when all prices, including nominal wages, are flexible. It is vertical at potential output, Y_P, because in the long run a change in the aggregate price level has no effect on the quantity of aggregate output supplied.

output supplied that would exist if all prices, including nominal wages, were fully flexible. The long-run aggregate supply curve is vertical because changes in the aggregate price level have *no* effect on aggregate output in the long run. At an aggregate price level of 15.0, the quantity of aggregate output supplied is $800 billion in 2005 dollars. If the aggregate price level falls by 50% to 7.5, the quantity of aggregate output supplied is unchanged in the long run at $800 billion in 2005 dollars.

It's important to understand not only that the *LRAS* curve is vertical but also that its position along the horizontal axis marks an important benchmark for output. The horizontal intercept in Figure 18.3, where *LRAS* touches the horizontal axis ($800 billion in 2005 dollars), is the economy's **potential output,** Y_P: the level of real GDP the economy would produce if all prices, including nominal wages, were fully flexible.

In reality, the actual level of real GDP is almost always either above or below potential output. We'll see why later, when we discuss the *AD–AS* model. Still, an economy's potential output is an important number because it defines the trend around which actual aggregate output fluctuates from year to year.

In the United States, the Congressional Budget Office, or CBO, estimates annual potential output for the purpose of federal budget analysis. In Figure 18.4 on the next page, the CBO's estimates of U.S. potential output from 1989 to 2009 are represented by the black line and the actual values of U.S. real GDP over the same period are represented by the blue line. Years shaded purple on the horizontal axis correspond to periods in which actual aggregate output fell short of potential output, years shaded green to periods in which actual aggregate output exceeded potential output.

As you can see, U.S. potential output has risen steadily over time—implying a series of rightward shifts of the *LRAS* curve. What has caused these rightward shifts? The answer lies in the factors related to long-run growth:

- increases in the quantity of resources, including land, labor, capital, and entrepreneurship
- increases in the quality of resources, as with a better-educated workforce
- technological progress

Over the long run, as the size of the labor force and the productivity of labor both rise, for example, the level of real GDP that the economy is capable of producing also

Potential output is the level of real GDP the economy would produce if all prices, including nominal wages, were fully flexible.

figure 18.4 | **Actual and Potential Output from 1989 to 2009**

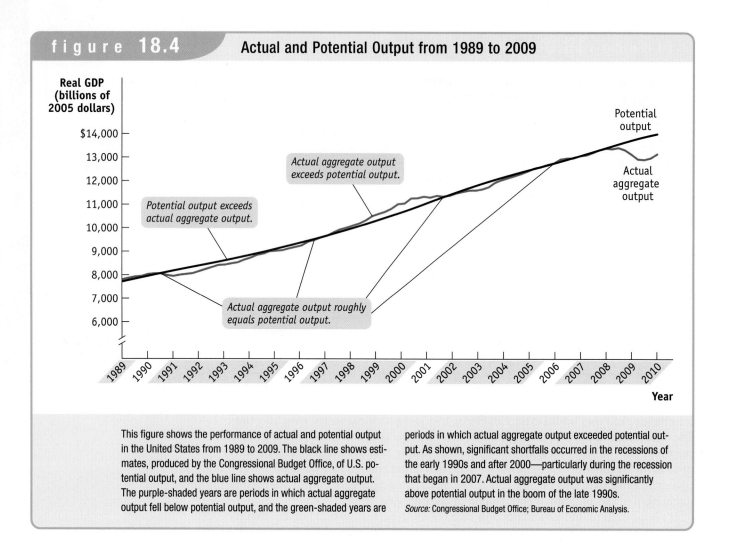

This figure shows the performance of actual and potential output in the United States from 1989 to 2009. The black line shows estimates, produced by the Congressional Budget Office, of U.S. potential output, and the blue line shows actual aggregate output. The purple-shaded years are periods in which actual aggregate output fell below potential output, and the green-shaded years are periods in which actual aggregate output exceeded potential output. As shown, significant shortfalls occurred in the recessions of the early 1990s and after 2000—particularly during the recession that began in 2007. Actual aggregate output was significantly above potential output in the boom of the late 1990s.

Source: Congressional Budget Office; Bureau of Economic Analysis.

rises. Indeed, one way to think about long-run economic growth is that it is the growth in the economy's potential output. We generally think of the long-run aggregate supply curve as shifting to the right over time as an economy experiences long-run growth.

From the Short Run to the Long Run

As you can see in Figure 18.4, the economy normally produces more or less than potential output: actual aggregate output was below potential output in the early 1990s, above potential output in the late 1990s, and below potential output for most of the 2000s. So the economy is normally on its short-run aggregate supply curve—but not on its long-run aggregate supply curve. Why, then, is the long-run curve relevant? Does the economy ever move from the short run to the long run? And if so, how?

The first step to answering these questions is to understand that the economy is always in one of only two states with respect to the short-run and long-run aggregate supply curves. It can be on both curves simultaneously by being at a point where the curves cross (as in the few years in Figure 18.4 in which actual aggregate output and potential output roughly coincided). Or it can be on the short-run aggregate supply curve but not the long-run aggregate supply curve (as in the years in which actual aggregate output and potential output *did not* coincide). But that is not the end of the story. If the economy is on the short-run but not the long-run aggregate supply curve, the short-run aggregate supply curve will shift over time until the economy is at a

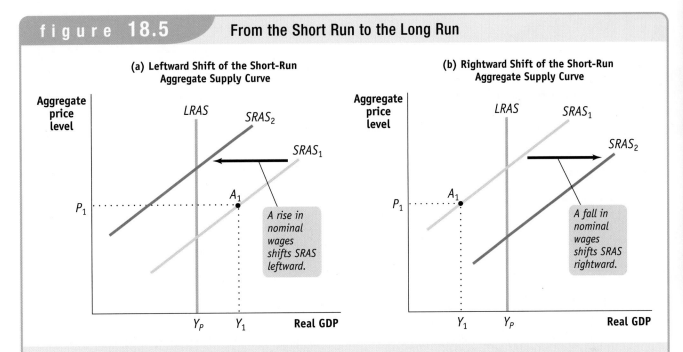

figure 18.5 — **From the Short Run to the Long Run**

(a) Leftward Shift of the Short-Run Aggregate Supply Curve

(b) Rightward Shift of the Short-Run Aggregate Supply Curve

In panel (a), the initial short-run aggregate supply curve is $SRAS_1$. At the aggregate price level, P_1, the quantity of aggregate output supplied, Y_1, exceeds potential output, Y_P. Eventually, low unemployment will cause nominal wages to rise, leading to a leftward shift of the short-run aggregate supply curve from $SRAS_1$ to $SRAS_2$. In panel (b), the reverse happens: at the aggregate price level, P_1, the quantity of aggregate output supplied is less than potential output. High unemployment eventually leads to a fall in nominal wages over time and a rightward shift of the short-run aggregate supply curve.

point where both curves cross—a point where actual aggregate output is equal to potential output.

Figure 18.5 illustrates how this process works. In both panels *LRAS* is the long-run aggregate supply curve, $SRAS_1$ is the initial short-run aggregate supply curve, and the aggregate price level is at P_1. In panel (a) the economy starts at the initial production point, A_1, which corresponds to a quantity of aggregate output supplied, Y_1, that is higher than potential output, Y_P. Producing an aggregate output level (such as Y_1) that is higher than potential output (Y_P) is possible only because nominal wages haven't yet fully adjusted upward. Until this upward adjustment in nominal wages occurs, producers are earning high profits and producing a high level of output. But a level of aggregate output higher than potential output means a low level of unemployment. Because jobs are abundant and workers are scarce, nominal wages will rise over time, gradually shifting the short-run aggregate supply curve leftward. Eventually, it will be in a new position, such as $SRAS_2$. (Later, we'll show where the short-run aggregate supply curve ends up. As we'll see, that depends on the aggregate demand curve as well.)

In panel (b), the initial production point, A_1, corresponds to an aggregate output level, Y_1, that is lower than potential output, Y_P. Producing an aggregate output level (such as Y_1) that is lower than potential output (Y_P) is possible only because nominal wages haven't yet fully adjusted downward. Until this downward adjustment occurs, producers are earning low (or negative) profits and producing a low level of output. An aggregate output level lower than potential output means high unemployment. Because workers are abundant and jobs are scarce, nominal wages will fall over time, shifting the short-run aggregate supply curve gradually to the right. Eventually, it will be in a new position, such as $SRAS_2$.

We'll see shortly that these shifts of the short-run aggregate supply curve will return the economy to potential output in the long run.

Prices and Output During the Great Depression

The figure shows the actual track of the aggregate price level, as measured by the GDP deflator, and real GDP, from 1929 to 1942. As you can see, aggregate output and the aggregate price level fell together from 1929 to 1933 and rose together from 1933 to 1937.

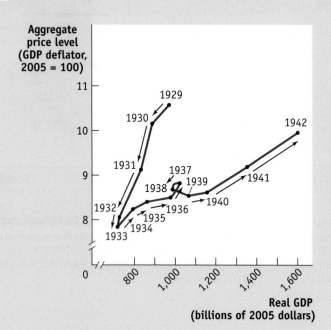

Aggregate price level (GDP deflator, 2005 = 100)

Real GDP (billions of 2005 dollars)

This is what we'd expect to see if the economy were moving down the short-run aggregate supply curve from 1929 to 1933 and moving up it (with a brief reversal in 1937–1938) thereafter.

But even in 1942 the aggregate price level was still lower than it was in 1929; yet real GDP was much higher. What happened?

The answer is that the short-run aggregate supply curve shifted to the right over time. This shift partly reflected rising productivity—a rightward shift of the underlying long-run aggregate supply curve. But since the U.S. economy was producing below potential output and had high unemployment during this period, the rightward shift of the short-run aggregate supply curve also reflected the adjustment process shown in panel (b) of Figure 18.5. So the movement of aggregate output from 1929 to 1942 reflected both movements along and shifts of the short-run aggregate supply curve.

Module 18 AP Review

Solutions appear at the back of the book.

Check Your Understanding

1. Determine the effect on short-run aggregate supply of each of the following events. Explain whether it represents a movement along the *SRAS* curve or a shift of the *SRAS* curve.
   a. A rise in the consumer price index (CPI) leads producers to increase output.
   b. A fall in the price of oil leads producers to increase output.
   c. A rise in legally mandated retirement benefits paid to workers leads producers to reduce output.

2. Suppose the economy is initially at potential output and the quantity of aggregate output supplied increases. What information would you need to determine whether this was due to a movement along the *SRAS* curve or a shift of the *LRAS* curve?

Tackle the Test: Multiple-Choice Questions

1. Which of the following will shift the short-run aggregate supply curve? A change in
   a. profit per unit at any given price level.
   b. commodity prices.
   c. nominal wages.
   d. productivity.
   e. all of the above

2. Because changes in the aggregate price level have no effect on aggregate output in the long run, the long-run aggregate supply curve is
   a. vertical.
   b. horizontal.
   c. fixed.
   d. negatively sloped.
   e. positively sloped.

3. The horizontal intercept of the long-run aggregate supply curve is
   a. at the origin.
   b. negative.
   c. at potential output.
   d. equal to the vertical intercept.
   e. always the same as the horizontal intercept of the short-run aggregate supply curve.

4. A decrease in which of the following will cause the short-run aggregate supply curve to shift to the left?
   a. commodity prices
   b. the cost of health care insurance premiums paid by employers
   c. nominal wages
   d. productivity
   e. the use of cost-of-living allowances in labor contracts

5. That employers are reluctant to decrease nominal wages during economic downturns and raise nominal wages during economic expansions leads nominal wages to be described as
   a. long-run.
   b. unyielding.
   c. flexible.
   d. real.
   e. sticky.

Tackle the Test: Free-Response Questions

1. a. Draw a correctly labeled graph illustrating a long-run aggregate supply curve.
   b On your graph from part a, label potential output.
   c. On your graph from part a, illustrate an increase in long-run aggregate supply.
   d. What could have caused the change you illustrated in part c? List three possible causes.

2. a. Draw a correctly labeled short-run aggregate supply curve.
   b. On your graph from part a, illustrate a decrease in short-run aggregate supply.
   c. List three types of changes, including the factor that changes and the direction of the change, that could lead to a decrease in aggregate supply.

Answer (8 points)

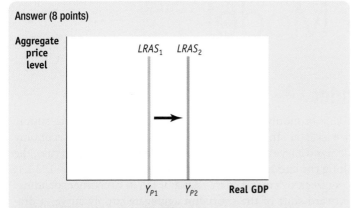

1 point: Vertical axis labeled "Aggregate price level" (or "Price level")

1 point: Horizontal axis labeled "Real GDP"

1 point: Vertical curve labeled "*LRAS*" (or "*LRAS*₁")

1 point: Potential output labeled Y_P (or Y_{P1}) on horizontal axis at intercept of long-run aggregate supply curve

1 point: Long-run aggregate supply curve shifted to the right

1 point: An increase in the quantity of resources (land, labor, capital, or entrepreneurship)

1 point: An increase in the quality of resources

1 point: Technological progress

Module 19
Equilibrium in the Aggregate Demand–Aggregate Supply Model

The *AD–AS* Model

From 1929 to 1933, the U.S. economy moved down the short-run aggregate supply curve as the aggregate price level fell. In contrast, from 1979 to 1980, the U.S. economy moved up the aggregate demand curve as the aggregate price level rose. In each case, the cause of the movement along the curve was a shift of the other curve. In 1929–1933, it was a leftward shift of the aggregate demand curve—a major fall in consumer spending. In 1979–1980, it was a leftward shift of the short-run aggregate supply curve—a dramatic fall in short-run aggregate supply caused by the oil *price shock*.

So to understand the behavior of the economy, we must put the aggregate supply curve and the aggregate demand curve together. The result is the *AD–AS* **model,** the basic model we use to understand economic fluctuations.

Short-Run Macroeconomic Equilibrium

We'll begin our analysis by focusing on the short run. Figure 19.1 shows the aggregate demand curve and the short-run aggregate supply curve on the same diagram. The point at which the *AD* and *SRAS* curves intersect, E_{SR}, is the **short-run macroeconomic equilibrium:** the point at which the quantity of aggregate output supplied is equal to the quantity demanded by domestic households, businesses, the government, and the rest of the world. The aggregate price level at E_{SR}, P_E, is the **short-run equilibrium aggregate price level.** The level of aggregate output at E_{SR}, Y_E, is the **short-run equilibrium aggregate output.**

In the *AD–AS* **model,** the aggregate supply curve and the aggregate demand curve are used together to analyze economic fluctuations.

The economy is in **short-run macroeconomic equilibrium** when the quantity of aggregate output supplied is equal to the quantity demanded.

The **short-run equilibrium aggregate price level** is the aggregate price level in the short-run macroeconomic equilibrium.

Short-run equilibrium aggregate output is the quantity of aggregate output produced in the short-run macroeconomic equilibrium.

figure 19.1

The *AD–AS* Model

The *AD–AS* model combines the aggregate demand curve and the short-run aggregate supply curve. Their point of intersection, E_{SR}, is the point of short-run macroeconomic equilibrium where the quantity of aggregate output demanded is equal to the quantity of aggregate output supplied. P_E is the short-run equilibrium aggregate price level, and Y_E is the short-run equilibrium level of aggregate output.

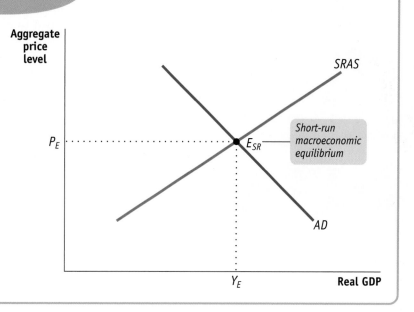

We have seen that a shortage of any individual good causes its market price to rise and a surplus of the good causes its market price to fall. These forces ensure that the market reaches equilibrium. The same logic applies to short-run macroeconomic equilibrium. If the aggregate price level is above its equilibrium level, the quantity of aggregate output supplied exceeds the quantity of aggregate output demanded. This leads to a fall in the aggregate price level and pushes it toward its equilibrium level. If the aggregate price level is below its equilibrium level, the quantity of aggregate output supplied is less than the quantity of aggregate output demanded. This leads to a rise in the aggregate price level, again pushing it toward its equilibrium level. In the discussion that follows, we'll assume that the economy is always in short-run macroeconomic equilibrium.

We'll also make another important simplification based on the observation that in reality there is a long-term upward trend in both aggregate output and the aggregate price level. We'll assume that a fall in either variable really means a fall compared to the long-run trend. For example, if the aggregate price level normally rises 4% per year, a year in which the aggregate price level rises only 3% would count, for our purposes, as a 1% decline. In fact, since the Great Depression there have been very few years in which the aggregate price level of any major nation actually declined—Japan's period of deflation from 1995 to 2005 is one of the few exceptions (which we will explain later). There have, however, been many cases in which the aggregate price level fell relative to the long-run trend.

The short-run equilibrium aggregate output and the short-run equilibrium aggregate price level can change because of shifts of either the *AD* curve or the *SRAS* curve. Let's look at each case in turn.

Shifts of Aggregate Demand: Short-Run Effects

An event that shifts the aggregate demand curve, such as a change in expectations or wealth, the effect of the size of the existing stock of physical capital, or the use of fiscal or monetary policy, is known as a **demand shock.** The Great Depression was caused by a negative demand shock, the collapse of wealth and of business and consumer confidence that followed the stock market crash of 1929 and the banking crises of 1930–1931. The Depression was ended by a positive demand shock—the huge increase

An event that shifts the aggregate demand curve is a **demand shock.**

in government purchases during World War II. In 2008, the U.S. economy experienced another significant negative demand shock as the housing market turned from boom to bust, leading consumers and firms to scale back their spending.

Figure 19.2 shows the short-run effects of negative and positive demand shocks. A negative demand shock shifts the aggregate demand curve, AD, to the left, from AD_1 to AD_2, as shown in panel (a). The economy moves down along the $SRAS$ curve from E_1 to E_2, leading to lower short-run equilibrium aggregate output and a lower short-run equilibrium aggregate price level. A positive demand shock shifts the aggregate demand curve, AD, to the right, as shown in panel (b). Here, the economy moves up along the $SRAS$ curve, from E_1 to E_2. This leads to higher short-run equilibrium aggregate output and a higher short-run equilibrium aggregate price level. Demand shocks cause aggregate output and the aggregate price level to move in the same direction.

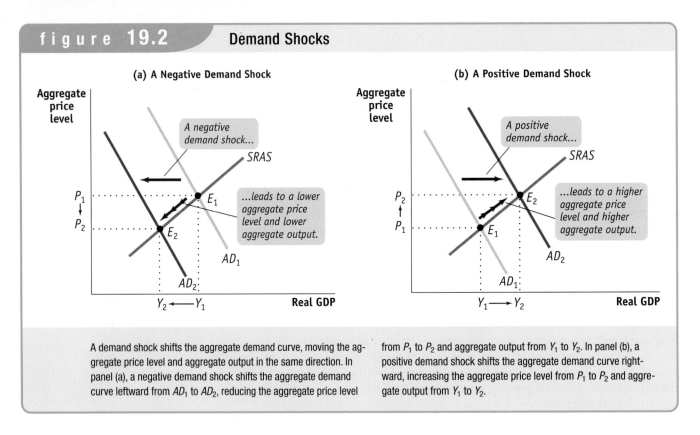

figure 19.2   Demand Shocks

A demand shock shifts the aggregate demand curve, moving the aggregate price level and aggregate output in the same direction. In panel (a), a negative demand shock shifts the aggregate demand curve leftward from AD_1 to AD_2, reducing the aggregate price level from P_1 to P_2 and aggregate output from Y_1 to Y_2. In panel (b), a positive demand shock shifts the aggregate demand curve rightward, increasing the aggregate price level from P_1 to P_2 and aggregate output from Y_1 to Y_2.

Shifts of the *SRAS* Curve

An event that shifts the short-run aggregate supply curve, such as a change in commodity prices, nominal wages, or productivity, is known as a **supply shock.** A *negative* supply shock raises production costs and reduces the quantity producers are willing to supply at any given aggregate price level, leading to a leftward shift of the short-run aggregate supply curve. The U.S. economy experienced severe negative supply shocks following disruptions to world oil supplies in 1973 and 1979. In contrast, a *positive* supply shock reduces production costs and increases the quantity supplied at any given aggregate price level, leading to a rightward shift of the short-run aggregate supply curve. The United States experienced a positive supply shock between 1995 and 2000, when the increasing use of the Internet and other information technologies caused productivity growth to surge.

An event that shifts the short-run aggregate supply curve is a **supply shock.**

The effects of a negative supply shock are shown in panel (a) of Figure 19.3. The initial equilibrium is at E_1, with aggregate price level P_1 and aggregate output Y_1. The disruption in the oil supply causes the short-run aggregate supply curve to shift to the left, from $SRAS_1$ to $SRAS_2$. As a consequence, aggregate output falls and the aggregate price level rises, an upward movement along the AD curve. At the new equilibrium, E_2, the short-run equilibrium aggregate price level, P_2, is higher, and the short-run equilibrium aggregate output level, Y_2, is lower than before.

Producers are vulnerable to dramatic changes in the price of oil, a cause of supply shocks.

The combination of inflation and falling aggregate output shown in panel (a) has a special name: **stagflation,** for "stagnation plus inflation." When an economy experiences stagflation, it's very unpleasant: falling aggregate output leads to rising unemployment, and people feel that their purchasing power is squeezed by rising prices. Stagflation in the 1970s led to a mood of national pessimism. It also, as we'll see shortly, poses a dilemma for policy makers.

A positive supply shock, shown in panel (b), has exactly the opposite effects. A rightward shift of the $SRAS$ curve, from $SRAS_1$ to $SRAS_2$ results in a rise in aggregate output and a fall in the aggregate price level, a downward movement along the AD curve. The favorable supply shocks of the late 1990s led to a combination of full employment and declining inflation. That is, the aggregate price level fell compared with the long-run trend. This combination produced, for a time, a great wave of national optimism.

The distinctive feature of supply shocks, both negative and positive, is that, unlike demand shocks, they cause the aggregate price level and aggregate output to move in *opposite* directions.

Stagflation is the combination of inflation and stagnating (or falling) aggregate output.

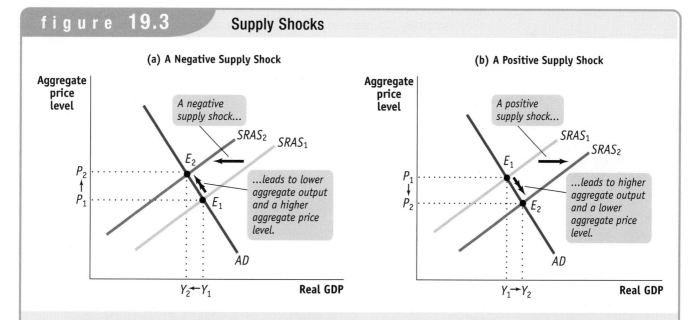

figure 19.3   **Supply Shocks**

(a) A Negative Supply Shock

A negative supply shock...

...leads to lower aggregate output and a higher aggregate price level.

(b) A Positive Supply Shock

A positive supply shock...

...leads to higher aggregate output and a lower aggregate price level.

A supply shock shifts the short-run aggregate supply curve, moving the aggregate price level and aggregate output in opposite directions. Panel (a) shows a negative supply shock, which shifts the short-run aggregate supply curve leftward and causes stagflation—lower aggregate output and a higher aggregate price level. Here the short-run aggregate supply curve shifts from $SRAS_1$ to $SRAS_2$, and the economy moves from E_1 to E_2. The aggregate price level rises from P_1 to P_2, and aggregate output falls from Y_1 to Y_2. Panel (b) shows a positive supply shock, which shifts the short-run aggregate supply curve rightward, generating higher aggregate output and a lower aggregate price level. The short-run aggregate supply curve shifts from $SRAS_1$ to $SRAS_2$, and the economy moves from E_1 to E_2. The aggregate price level falls from P_1 to P_2, and aggregate output rises from Y_1 to Y_2.

The economy is in **long-run macroeconomic equilibrium** when the point of short-run macroeconomic equilibrium is on the long-run aggregate supply curve.

There's another important contrast between supply shocks and demand shocks. As we've seen, monetary policy and fiscal policy enable the government to shift the *AD* curve, meaning that governments are in a position to create the kinds of shocks shown in Figure 19.2. It's much harder for governments to shift the *AS* curve. Are there good policy reasons to shift the *AD* curve? We'll turn to that question soon. First, however, let's look at the difference between short-run macroeconomic equilibrium and long-run macroeconomic equilibrium.

Long-Run Macroeconomic Equilibrium

Figure 19.4 combines the aggregate demand curve with both the short-run and long-run aggregate supply curves. The aggregate demand curve, *AD*, crosses the short-run aggregate supply curve, *SRAS*, at E_{LR}. Here we assume that enough time has elapsed that the economy is also on the long-run aggregate supply curve, *LRAS*. As a result, E_{LR} is at the intersection of all three curves—*SRAS, LRAS,* and *AD*. So short-run equilibrium aggregate output is equal to potential output, Y_P. Such a situation, in which the point of short-run macroeconomic equilibrium is on the long-run aggregate supply curve, is known as **long-run macroeconomic equilibrium.**

To see the significance of long-run macroeconomic equilibrium, let's consider what happens if a demand shock moves the economy away from long-run macroeconomic equilibrium. In Figure 19.5, we assume that the initial aggregate demand curve is AD_1 and the initial short-run aggregate supply curve is $SRAS_1$. So the initial macroeconomic equilibrium is at E_1, which lies on the long-run aggregate supply curve, *LRAS*. The economy, then, starts from a point of short-run and long-run macroeconomic equilibrium, and short-run equilibrium aggregate output equals potential output at Y_1.

Now suppose that for some reason—such as a sudden worsening of business and consumer expectations—aggregate demand falls and the aggregate demand curve shifts leftward to AD_2. This results in a lower equilibrium aggregate price level at P_2 and a lower equilibrium aggregate output level at Y_2 as the economy settles in the short run at E_2. The short-run effect of such a fall in aggregate demand is what the

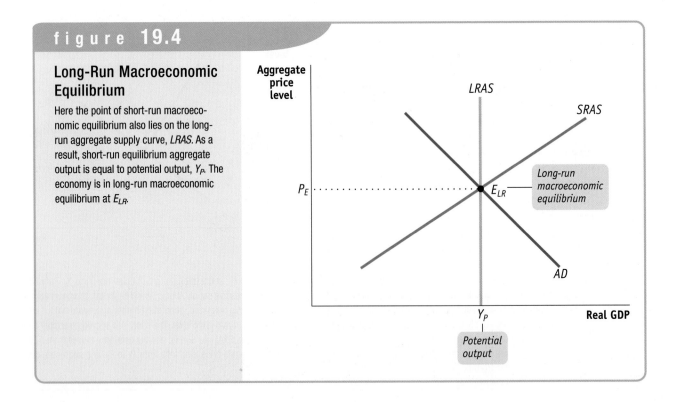

figure 19.4

Long-Run Macroeconomic Equilibrium

Here the point of short-run macroeconomic equilibrium also lies on the long-run aggregate supply curve, *LRAS.* As a result, short-run equilibrium aggregate output is equal to potential output, Y_P. The economy is in long-run macroeconomic equilibrium at E_{LR}.

figure 19.5

Short-Run Versus Long-Run Effects of a Negative Demand Shock

In the long run the economy is self-correcting: demand shocks have only a short-run effect on aggregate output. Starting at E_1, a negative demand shock shifts AD_1 leftward to AD_2. In the short run the economy moves to E_2 and a recessionary gap arises: the aggregate price level declines from P_1 to P_2, aggregate output declines from Y_1 to Y_2, and unemployment rises. But in the long run nominal wages fall in response to high unemployment at Y_2, and $SRAS_1$ shifts rightward to $SRAS_2$. Aggregate output rises from Y_2 to Y_1, and the aggregate price level declines again, from P_2 to P_3. Long-run macroeconomic equilibrium is eventually restored at E_3.

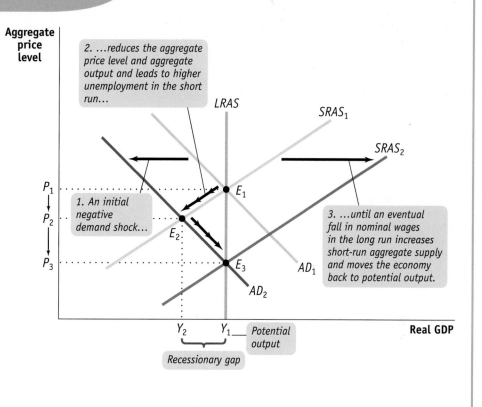

Aggregate price level

2. ...reduces the aggregate price level and aggregate output and leads to higher unemployment in the short run...

LRAS

SRAS₁

SRAS₂

P_1

P_2

1. An initial negative demand shock...

E_1

E_2

3. ...until an eventual fall in nominal wages in the long run increases short-run aggregate supply and moves the economy back to potential output.

P_3

E_3

AD_1

AD_2

Y_2 Y_1 Potential output

Real GDP

Recessionary gap

U.S. economy experienced in 1929–1933: a falling aggregate price level and falling aggregate output.

Aggregate output in this new short-run equilibrium, E_2, is below potential output. When this happens, the economy faces a **recessionary gap.** A recessionary gap inflicts a great deal of pain because it corresponds to high unemployment. The large recessionary gap that had opened up in the United States by 1933 caused intense social and political turmoil. And the devastating recessionary gap that opened up in Germany at the same time played an important role in Hitler's rise to power.

But this isn't the end of the story. In the face of high unemployment, nominal wages eventually fall, as do any other sticky prices, ultimately leading producers to increase output. As a result, a recessionary gap causes the short-run aggregate supply curve to gradually shift to the right. This process continues until $SRAS_1$ reaches its new position at $SRAS_2$, bringing the economy to equilibrium at E_3, where AD_2, $SRAS_2$, and $LRAS$ all intersect. At E_3, the economy is back in long-run macroeconomic equilibrium; it is back at potential output Y_1 but at a lower aggregate price level, P_3, reflecting a long-run fall in the aggregate price level. The economy is *self-correcting* in the long run.

What if, instead, there was an increase in aggregate demand? The results are shown in Figure 19.6 on the next page, where we again assume that the initial aggregate demand curve is AD_1 and the initial short-run aggregate supply curve is $SRAS_1$, so that the initial macroeconomic equilibrium, at E_1, lies on the long-run aggregate supply curve, $LRAS$. Initially, then, the economy is in long-run macroeconomic equilibrium.

Now suppose that aggregate demand rises, and the AD curve shifts rightward to AD_2. This results in a higher aggregate price level, at P_2, and a higher aggregate output level, at Y_2, as the economy settles in the short run at E_2. Aggregate output in this new short-run equilibrium is above potential output, and unemployment is low in order to

There is a **recessionary gap** when aggregate output is below potential output.

figure 19.6

Short-Run Versus Long-Run Effects of a Positive Demand Shock

Starting at E_1, a positive demand shock shifts AD_1 rightward to AD_2, and the economy moves to E_2 in the short run. This results in an inflationary gap as aggregate output rises from Y_1 to Y_2, the aggregate price level rises from P_1 to P_2, and unemployment falls to a low level. In the long run, $SRAS_1$ shifts leftward to $SRAS_2$ as nominal wages rise in response to low unemployment at Y_2. Aggregate output falls back to Y_1, the aggregate price level rises again to P_3, and the economy self-corrects as it returns to long-run macroeconomic equilibrium at E_3.

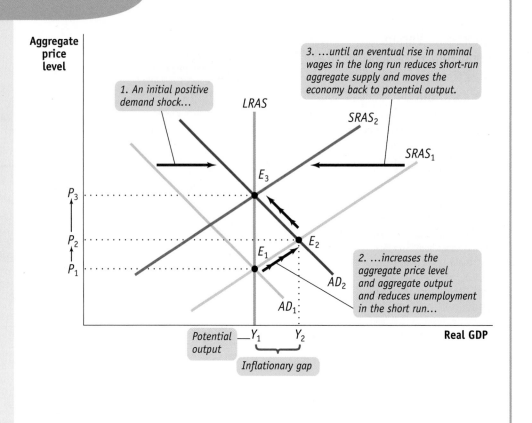

1. An initial positive demand shock...

3. ...until an eventual rise in nominal wages in the long run reduces short-run aggregate supply and moves the economy back to potential output.

2. ...increases the aggregate price level and aggregate output and reduces unemployment in the short run...

Inflationary gap

There is an **inflationary gap** when aggregate output is above potential output.

The **output gap** is the percentage difference between actual aggregate output and potential output.

The economy is **self-correcting** when shocks to aggregate demand affect aggregate output in the short run, but not the long run.

produce this higher level of aggregate output. When this happens, the economy experiences an **inflationary gap.** As in the case of a recessionary gap, this isn't the end of the story. In the face of low unemployment, nominal wages will rise, as will other sticky prices. An inflationary gap causes the short-run aggregate supply curve to shift gradually to the left as producers reduce output in the face of rising nominal wages. This process continues until $SRAS_1$ reaches its new position at $SRAS_2$, bringing the economy into equilibrium at E_3, where AD_2, $SRAS_2$, and $LRAS$ all intersect. At E_3, the economy is back in long-run macroeconomic equilibrium. It is back at potential output, but at a higher price level, P_3, reflecting a long-run rise in the aggregate price level. Again, the economy is self-correcting in the long run.

To summarize the analysis of how the economy responds to recessionary and inflationary gaps, we can focus on the **output gap,** the percentage difference between actual aggregate output and potential output. The output gap is calculated as follows:

$$(19\text{-}1) \quad \text{Output gap} = \frac{\text{Actual aggregate output} - \text{Potential output}}{\text{Potential output}} \times 100$$

Our analysis says that the output gap always tends toward zero.

If there is a recessionary gap, so that the output gap is negative, nominal wages eventually fall, moving the economy back to potential output and bringing the output gap back to zero. If there is an inflationary gap, so that the output gap is positive, nominal wages eventually rise, also moving the economy back to potential output and again bringing the output gap back to zero. So in the long run the economy is **self-correcting:** shocks to aggregate demand affect aggregate output in the short run but not in the long run.

Supply Shocks Versus Demand Shocks in Practice

How often do supply shocks and demand shocks, respectively, cause recessions? The verdict of most, though not all, macroeconomists is that recessions are mainly caused by demand shocks. But when a negative supply shock does happen, the resulting recession tends to be particularly severe.

Let's get specific. Officially there have been twelve recessions in the United States since World War II. However, two of these, in 1979–1980 and 1981–1982, are often treated as a single "double-dip" recession, bringing the total number down to 11. Of these 11 recessions, only two—the recession of 1973–1975 and the double-dip recession of 1979–1982—showed the distinctive combination of falling aggregate output and a surge in the price level that we call stagflation. In each case, the cause of the supply shock was political turmoil in the Middle East—the Arab–Israeli war of 1973 and the Iranian revolution of 1979—that disrupted world oil supplies and sent oil prices skyrocketing. In fact, economists sometimes refer to the two slumps as "OPEC I" and "OPEC II," after the Organization of Petroleum Exporting Countries, the world oil cartel. A third recession that began

in December 2007, and that had lasted for almost two years by the time this book went to press, was at least partially caused by a spike in oil prices.

So 8 of 11 postwar recessions were purely the result of demand shocks, not supply shocks. The few supply-shock recessions, however, were the worst as measured by the unemployment rate. The figure shows the U.S. unemployment rate since 1948, with

the dates of the 1973 Arab–Israeli war, the 1979 Iranian revolution, and the 2007 oil price shock marked on the graph. The three highest unemployment rates since World War II came after these big negative supply shocks.

There's a reason the aftermath of a supply shock tends to be particularly severe for the economy: macroeconomic policy has a much harder time dealing with supply shocks than with demand shocks.

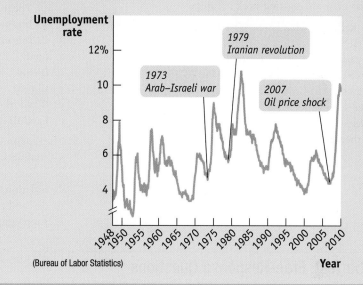

(Bureau of Labor Statistics)

M o d u l e 19 A P R e v i e w

Solutions appear at the back of the book.

Check Your Understanding

1. Describe the short-run effects of each of the following shocks on the aggregate price level and on aggregate output.
   a. The government sharply increases the minimum wage, raising the wages of many workers.
   b. Solar energy firms launch a major program of investment spending.
   c. Congress raises taxes and cuts spending.
   d. Severe weather destroys crops around the world.

2. A rise in productivity increases potential output, but some worry that demand for the additional output will be insufficient even in the long run. How would you respond?

Tackle the Test: Multiple-Choice Questions

1. Which of the following causes a negative supply shock?
   I. a technological advance
   II. increasing productivity
   III. an increase in oil prices
   a. I only
   b. II only
   c. III only
   d. I and III only
   e. I, II, and III

2. Which of the following causes a positive demand shock?
   a. an increase in wealth
   b. pessimistic consumer expectations
   c. a decrease in government spending
   d. an increase in taxes
   e. an increase in the existing stock of capital

3. During stagflation, what happens to the aggregate price level and real GDP?

	Aggregate price level	Real GDP
a.	decreases	increases
b.	decreases	decreases
c.	increases	increases
d.	increases	decreases
e.	stays the same	stays the same

Refer to the graph for questions 4 and 5.

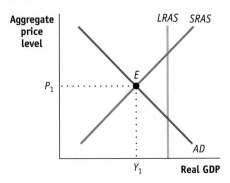

4. Which of the following statements is true if this economy is operating at P_1 and Y_1?
   I. The level of aggregate output equals potential output.
   II. It is in short-run macroeconomic equilibrium.
   III. It is in long-run macroeconomic equilibrium.
   a. I only
   b. II only
   c. III only
   d. II and III
   e. I and III

5. The economy depicted in the graph is experiencing a(n)
   a. contractionary gap.
   b. recessionary gap.
   c. inflationary gap.
   d. demand gap.
   e. supply gap.

Tackle the Test: Free-Response Questions

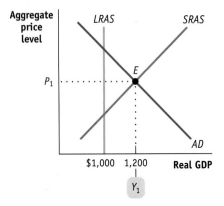

1. Refer to the graph above.
   a. Is the economy in short-run macroeconomic equilibrium? Explain.
   b. Is the economy in long-run macroeconomic equilibrium? Explain.
   c. What type of gap exists in this economy?
   d. Calculate the size of the output gap.
   e. What will happen to the size of the output gap in the long run?

Answer (7 points)

1 point: Yes

1 point: The economy is in short-run equilibrium because it operates at the point where short-run aggregate supply and aggregate demand intersect.

1 point: No

1 point: Short-run equilibrium occurs at a level of aggregate output that is not equal to potential output

1 point: Inflationary gap

1 point: [($1,200 − $1,000)/$1,000] × 100 = 20%

1 point: It will approach zero

2. Draw a correctly labeled aggregate demand and aggregate supply graph illustrating an economy in long-run macroeconomic equilibrium.

Module 20

Economic Policy and the Aggregate Demand–Aggregate Supply Model

What you will learn in this Module:

- How the *AD–AS* model is used to formulate macroeconomic policy
- The rationale for stabilization policy
- Why fiscal policy is an important tool for managing economic fluctuations
- Which policies constitute expansionary fiscal policy and which constitute contractionary fiscal policy

Macroeconomic Policy

We've just seen that the economy is self-correcting in the long run: it will eventually trend back to potential output. Most macro-economists believe, however, that the process of self-correction typically takes a decade or more. In particular, if aggregate output is below potential output, the economy can suffer an extended period of depressed aggregate output and high unemployment before it returns to normal.

This belief is the background to one of the most famous quotations in economics: John Maynard Keynes's declaration, "In the long run we are all dead." Economists usually interpret Keynes as having recommended that governments not wait for the economy to correct itself. Instead, it is argued by many economists, but not all, that the government should use fiscal policy to get the economy back to potential output in the aftermath of a shift of the aggregate demand curve. This is the rationale for active **stabilization policy,** which is the

Tim Gidal/ Picture Post/ Getty Images

Some people use *Keynesian economics* as a synonym for *left-wing economics*—but the truth is that the ideas of John Maynard Keynes have been accepted across a broad range of the political spectrum.

Stabilization policy is the use of government policy to reduce the severity of recessions and rein in excessively strong expansions.

use of government policy to reduce the severity of recessions and rein in excessively strong expansions.

Can stabilization policy improve the economy's performance? As we saw in Figure 18.4, the answer certainly appears to be yes. Under active stabilization policy, the U.S. economy returned to potential output in 1996 after an approximately five-year recessionary gap. Likewise, in 2001, it also returned to potential output after an approximately four-year inflationary gap. These periods are much shorter than the decade or more that economists believe it would take for the economy to self-correct in the absence of active stabilization policy. However, as we'll see shortly, the ability to improve the economy's performance is not always guaranteed. It depends on the kinds of shocks the economy faces.

Policy in the Face of Demand Shocks

Imagine that the economy experiences a negative demand shock, like the one shown by the shift from AD_1 to AD_2 in Figure 19.5. Monetary and fiscal policy shift the aggregate demand curve. If policy makers react quickly to the fall in aggregate demand, they can use monetary or fiscal policy to shift the aggregate demand curve back to the right. And if policy were able to perfectly anticipate shifts of the aggregate demand curve and counteract them, it could short-circuit the whole process shown in Figure 19.5. Instead of going through a period of low aggregate output and falling prices, the government could manage the economy so that it would stay at E_1.

Why might a policy that short-circuits the adjustment shown in Figure 19.5 and maintains the economy at its original equilibrium be desirable? For two reasons: First, the temporary fall in aggregate output that would happen without policy intervention is a bad thing, particularly because such a decline is associated with high unemployment. Second, *price stability* is generally regarded as a desirable goal. So preventing deflation—a fall in the aggregate price level—is a good thing.

Does this mean that policy makers should always act to offset declines in aggregate demand? Not necessarily. As we'll see, some policy measures to increase aggregate demand, especially those that increase budget deficits, may have long- term costs in terms of lower long-run growth. Furthermore, in the real world policy makers aren't perfectly informed, and the effects of their policies aren't perfectly predictable. This creates the danger that stabilization policy will do more harm than good; that is, attempts to stabilize the economy may end up creating more instability. We'll describe the long-running debate over macroeconomic policy in later modules. Despite these qualifications, most economists believe that a good case can be made for using macroeconomic policy to offset major negative shocks to the *AD* curve.

Should policy makers also try to offset positive shocks to aggregate demand? It may not seem obvious that they should. After all, even though inflation may be a bad thing, isn't more output and lower unemployment a good thing? Again, not necessarily. Most economists now believe that any short-run gains from an inflationary gap must be paid back later. So policy makers today usually try to offset positive as well as negative demand shocks. For reasons we'll explain later, attempts to eliminate recessionary gaps and inflationary gaps usually rely on monetary rather than fiscal policy. For now, let's explore how macroeconomic policy can respond to supply shocks.

Responding to Supply Shocks

In panel (a) of Figure 19.3 we showed the effects of a negative supply shock: in the short run such a shock leads to lower aggregate output but a higher aggregate price level. As we've noted, policy makers can respond to a negative *demand* shock by using monetary and fiscal policy to return aggregate demand to its original level. But what can or should they do about a negative *supply* shock?

In contrast to the case of a demand shock, there are no easy remedies for a supply shock. That is, there are no government policies that can easily counteract the changes in production costs that shift the short-run aggregate supply curve. So the policy response to a negative supply shock cannot aim to simply push the curve that shifted back to its original position.

And if you consider using monetary or fiscal policy to shift the aggregate demand curve in response to a supply shock, the right response isn't obvious. Two bad things are happening simultaneously: a fall in aggregate output, leading to a rise in unemployment, *and* a rise in the aggregate price level. Any policy that shifts the aggregate demand curve helps one problem only by making the other worse. If the government acts to increase aggregate demand and limit the rise in unemployment, it reduces the decline in output but causes even more inflation. If it acts to reduce aggregate demand, it curbs inflation but causes a further rise in unemployment.

It's a trade-off with no good answer. In the end, the United States and other economically advanced nations suffering from the supply shocks of the 1970s eventually chose to stabilize prices even at the cost of higher unemployment. But being an economic policy maker in the 1970s, or in early 2008, meant facing even harder choices than usual.

In 2008, *stagflation* made for difficult policy choices for Federal Reserve Chairman Ben Bernanke.

fyi

Is Stabilization Policy Stabilizing?

We've described the theoretical rationale for stabilization policy as a way of responding to demand shocks. But does stabilization policy actually stabilize the economy? One way we might try to answer this question is to look at the long-term historical record. Before World War II, the U.S. government didn't really have a stabilization policy, largely because macroeconomics as we know it didn't exist, and there was no consensus about what to do. Since World War II, and especially since 1960, active stabilization policy has become standard practice.

So here's the question: has the economy actually become more stable since the government began trying to stabilize it? The answer is a qualified yes. It's qualified because data from the pre–World War II era are less reliable than more modern data. But there still seems to be a clear reduction in the size of economic fluctuations.

The figure shows the number of unemployed as a percentage of the nonfarm labor force since 1890. (We focus on nonfarm workers because farmers, though they often suffer economic hardship, are rarely reported as un-

employed.) Even ignoring the huge spike in unemployment during the Great Depression, unemployment seems to have varied a lot more before World War II than after. It's also worth noticing that the peaks in postwar unemployment in 1975 and 1982 corresponded to major supply shocks—the kind of shock for which stabilization policy has no good answer.

It's possible that the greater stability of the economy reflects good luck rather than policy. But on the face of it, the evidence suggests that stabilization policy is indeed stabilizing.

Source: C. Romer, "Spurious Volititility in Historical Unemployment Data," *Journal of Political Economy* 94, no. 1 (1986): 1–37 (years 1890–1930); Bureau of Labor statistics (years 1931–2009).

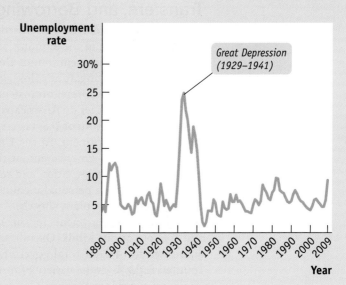

Fiscal Policy: The Basics

Let's begin with the obvious: modern governments spend a great deal of money and collect a lot in taxes. Figure 20.1 shows government spending and tax revenue as percentages of GDP for a selection of high-income countries in 2008. As you can see, the Swedish government sector is relatively large, accounting for more than half of the Swedish economy. The government of the United States plays a smaller role in the economy than those of Canada or most European countries. But that role is still sizable. As a result, changes in the federal budget—changes in government spending or in taxation—can have large effects on the American economy.

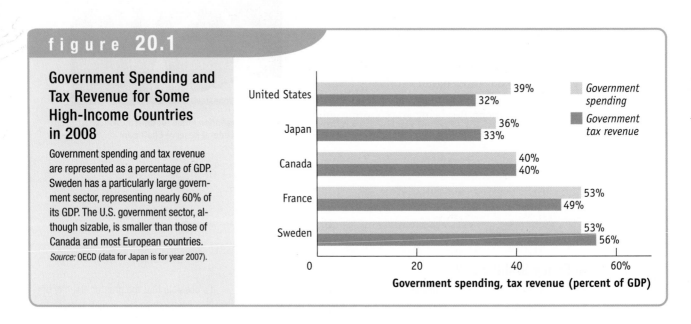

figure 20.1

Government Spending and Tax Revenue for Some High-Income Countries in 2008

Government spending and tax revenue are represented as a percentage of GDP. Sweden has a particularly large government sector, representing nearly 60% of its GDP. The U.S. government sector, although sizable, is smaller than those of Canada and most European countries.

Source: OECD (data for Japan is for year 2007).

To analyze these effects, we begin by showing how taxes and government spending affect the economy's flow of income. Then we can see how changes in spending and tax policy affect aggregate demand.

Taxes, Government Purchases of Goods and Services, Transfers, and Borrowing

In the circular flow diagram discussed in Module 10, we showed the circular flow of income and spending in the economy as a whole. One of the sectors represented in that figure was the government. Funds flow *into* the government in the form of taxes and government borrowing; funds flow *out* in the form of government purchases of goods and services and government transfers to households.

What kinds of taxes do Americans pay, and where does the money go? Figure 20.2 shows the composition of U.S. tax revenue in 2008. Taxes, of course, are required payments to the government. In the United States, taxes are collected at the national level by the federal government; at the state level by each state government; and at local levels by counties, cities, and towns. At the federal level, the main taxes are income taxes on both personal income and corporate profits as well as *social insurance* taxes, which we'll explain shortly. At the state and local levels, the picture is more complex: these governments rely on a mix of sales taxes, property taxes, income taxes, and fees of various kinds. Overall, taxes on personal income and corporate profits accounted for 44% of total government revenue in 2008; social insurance taxes accounted for 27%; and a variety of other taxes, collected mainly at the state and local levels, accounted for the rest.

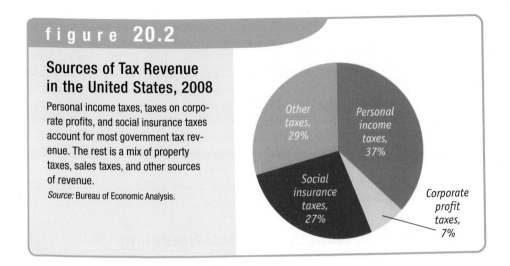

figure 20.2

Sources of Tax Revenue in the United States, 2008

Personal income taxes, taxes on corporate profits, and social insurance taxes account for most government tax revenue. The rest is a mix of property taxes, sales taxes, and other sources of revenue.

Source: Bureau of Economic Analysis.

Figure 20.3 shows the composition of 2008 total U.S. government spending, which takes two forms. One form is purchases of goods and services. This includes everything from ammunition for the military to the salaries of public schoolteachers (who are treated in the national accounts as providers of a service—education). The big items here are national defense and education. The large category labeled "Other goods and services" consists mainly of state and local spending on a variety of services, from police and firefighters to highway construction and maintenance.

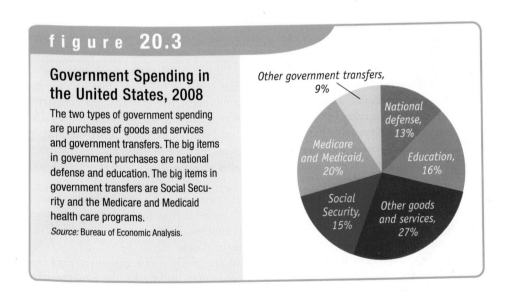

figure 20.3

Government Spending in the United States, 2008

The two types of government spending are purchases of goods and services and government transfers. The big items in government purchases are national defense and education. The big items in government transfers are Social Security and the Medicare and Medicaid health care programs.

Source: Bureau of Economic Analysis.

The other form of government spending is government transfers, which are payments by the government to households for which no good or service is provided in return. In the modern United States, as well as in Canada and Europe, government transfers represent a very large proportion of the budget. Most U.S. government spending on transfer payments is accounted for by three big programs:

- Social Security, which provides guaranteed income to older Americans, disabled Americans, and the surviving spouses and dependent children of deceased beneficiaries
- Medicare, which covers much of the cost of health care for Americans over age 65
- Medicaid, which covers much of the cost of health care for Americans with low incomes

Government transfers on their way: Social Security checks are run through a printer at the U.S. Treasury printing facility in Philadelphia, Pennsylvania.

The term **social insurance** is used to describe government programs that are intended to protect families against economic hardship. These include Social Security, Medicare, and Medicaid, as well as smaller programs such as unemployment insurance and food stamps. In the United States, social insurance programs are largely paid for with special, dedicated taxes on wages—the social insurance taxes we mentioned earlier.

But how do tax policy and government spending affect the economy? The answer is that taxation and government spending have a strong effect on total aggregate spending in the economy.

The Government Budget and Total Spending

Let's recall the basic equation of national income accounting:

(20-1) $GDP = C + I + G + X - IM$

The left-hand side of this equation is GDP, the value of all final goods and services produced in the economy. The right-hand side is aggregate spending, the total spending on final goods and services produced in the economy. It is the sum of consumer spending (C), investment spending (I), government purchases of goods and services (G), and the value of exports (X) minus the value of imports (IM). It includes all the sources of aggregate demand.

The government directly controls one of the variables on the right-hand side of Equation 20-1: government purchases of goods and services (G). But that's not the only effect fiscal policy has on aggregate spending in the economy. Through changes in taxes and transfers, it also influences consumer spending (C) and, in some cases, investment spending (I).

To see why the budget affects consumer spending, recall that *disposable income,* the total income households have available to spend, is equal to the total income they receive from wages, dividends, interest, and rent, *minus* taxes, *plus* government transfers. So either an increase in taxes or a decrease in government transfers *reduces* disposable income. And a fall in disposable income, other things equal, leads to a fall in consumer spending. Conversely, either a decrease in taxes or an increase in government transfers *increases* disposable income. And a rise in disposable income, other things equal, leads to a rise in consumer spending.

The government's ability to affect investment spending is a more complex story, which we won't discuss in detail. The important point is that the government taxes profits, and changes in the rules that determine how much a business owes can increase or reduce the incentive to spend on investment goods.

Because the government itself is one source of spending in the economy, and because taxes and transfers can affect spending by consumers and firms, the government can use changes in taxes or government spending to *shift the aggregate demand curve.* There are sometimes good reasons to shift the aggregate demand curve. In early 2008, there was bipartisan agreement that the U.S. government should act to prevent a fall in aggregate demand—that is, to move the aggregate demand curve to the right of where it would otherwise be. The 2008 stimulus package was a classic example of fiscal policy: the use of taxes, government transfers, or government purchases of goods and services to stabilize the economy by shifting the aggregate demand curve.

Expansionary and Contractionary Fiscal Policy

Why would the government want to shift the aggregate demand curve? Because it wants to close either a recessionary gap, created when aggregate output falls below potential output, or an inflationary gap, created when aggregate output exceeds potential output.

Social insurance programs are government programs intended to protect families against economic hardship.

figure 20.4

Expansionary Fiscal Policy Can Close a Recessionary Gap

At E_1 the economy is in short-run macroeconomic equilibrium where the aggregate demand curve, AD_1, intersects the *SRAS* curve. At E_1, there is a recessionary gap of $Y_P - Y_1$. An expansionary fiscal policy—an increase in government purchases of goods and services, a reduction in taxes, or an increase in government transfers—shifts the aggregate demand curve rightward. It can close the recessionary gap by shifting AD_1 to AD_2, moving the economy to a new short-run macroeconomic equilibrium, E_2, which is also a long-run macroeconomic equilibrium.

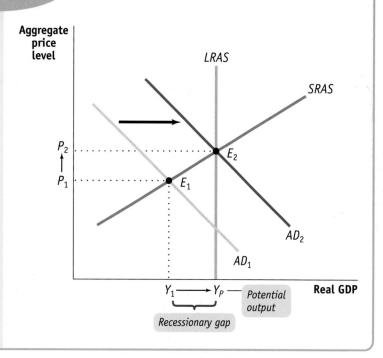

Figure 20.4 shows the case of an economy facing a recessionary gap. *SRAS* is the short-run aggregate supply curve, *LRAS* is the long-run aggregate supply curve, and AD_1 is the initial aggregate demand curve. At the initial short-run macroeconomic equilibrium, E_1, aggregate output is Y_1, below potential output, Y_P. What the government would like to do is increase aggregate demand, shifting the aggregate demand curve rightward to AD_2. This would increase aggregate output, making it equal to potential output. Fiscal policy that increases aggregate demand, called **expansionary fiscal policy,** normally takes one of three forms:

- an increase in government purchases of goods and services
- a cut in taxes
- an increase in government transfers

Figure 20.5 on the next page shows the opposite case—an economy facing an inflationary gap. At the initial equilibrium, E_1, aggregate output is Y_1, above potential output, Y_P. As we'll explain later, policy makers often try to head off inflation by eliminating inflationary gaps. To eliminate the inflationary gap shown in Figure 20.5, fiscal policy must reduce aggregate demand and shift the aggregate demand curve leftward to AD_2. This reduces aggregate output and makes it equal to potential output. Fiscal policy that reduces aggregate demand, called **contractionary fiscal policy,** is the opposite of expansionary fiscal policy. It is implemented by:

- a reduction in government purchases of goods and services
- an increase in taxes
- a reduction in government transfers

A classic example of contractionary fiscal policy occurred in 1968, when U.S. policy makers grew worried about rising inflation. President Lyndon Johnson imposed a temporary 10% surcharge on income taxes—everyone's income taxes were increased by 10%. He also tried to scale back government purchases of goods and services, which had risen dramatically because of the cost of the Vietnam War.

Expansionary fiscal policy increases aggregate demand.

Contractionary fiscal policy reduces aggregate demand.

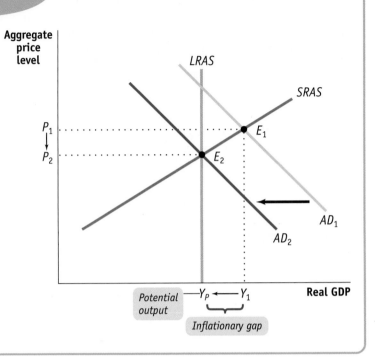

figure 20.5

Contractionary Fiscal Policy Can Close an Inflationary Gap

At E_1 the economy is in short-run macroeco-nomic equilibrium where the aggregate demand curve, AD_1, intersects the *SRAS* curve. At E_1, there is an inflationary gap of $Y_1 - Y_P$. A contrac-tionary fiscal policy—such as reduced govern-ment purchases of goods and services, an increase in taxes, or a reduction in government transfers—shifts the aggregate demand curve leftward. It closes the inflationary gap by shifting AD_1 to AD_2, moving the economy to a new short-run macroeconomic equilibrium, E_2, which is also a long-run macroeconomic equilibrium.

A Cautionary Note: Lags in Fiscal Policy

Looking at Figures 20.4 and 20.5, it may seem obvious that the government should ac-tively use fiscal policy—always adopting an expansionary fiscal policy when the econ-omy faces a recessionary gap and always adopting a contractionary fiscal policy when the economy faces an inflationary gap. But many economists caution against an ex-tremely active stabilization policy, arguing that a government that tries too hard to sta-bilize the economy—through either fiscal policy or monetary policy—can end up making the economy less stable.

We'll leave discussion of the warnings associated with monetary policy to later modules. In the case of fiscal policy, one key reason for caution is that there are important *time lags* in its use. To understand the nature of these lags, think about what has to happen before the government increases spending to fight a recessionary gap. First, the govern-ment has to realize that the recessionary gap exists: eco-nomic data take time to collect and analyze, and recessions are often recognized only months after they have begun. Second, the government has to develop a spending plan, which can itself take months, particularly if politicians take time debating how the money should be spent and passing legislation. Finally, it takes time to spend money. For example, a road construction project begins with activities such as surveying that don't in-volve spending large sums. It may be quite some time be-fore the big spending begins.

Because of these lags, an attempt to increase spending to fight a recessionary gap may take so long to get going that the economy has already recovered on its own. In fact, the recessionary gap may have turned into an inflationary gap by the time the fiscal policy takes effect. In that case, the fiscal policy will make things worse instead of better.

AP Photo/Ron Edmonds

Will the stimulus come in time to be worthwhile? President Barack Obama lis-tens to a question during a news confer-ence in the East Room of the White House in Washington D.C.

This doesn't mean that fiscal policy should never be actively used. In early 2008, there was good reason to believe that the U.S. economy had begun a lengthy slowdown caused by turmoil in the financial markets, so that a fiscal stimulus designed to arrive within a few months would almost surely push aggregate demand in the right direction. But the problem of lags makes the actual use of both fiscal and monetary policy harder than you might think from a simple analysis like the one we have just given.

Module 20 AP Review

Solutions appear at the back of the book.

Check Your Understanding

1. In each of the following cases, determine whether the policy is an expansionary or contractionary fiscal policy.
   a. Several military bases around the country, which together employ tens of thousands of people, are closed.
   b. The number of weeks an unemployed person is eligible for unemployment benefits is increased.
   c. The federal tax on gasoline is increased.

2. Explain why federal disaster relief, which quickly disburses funds to victims of natural disasters such as hurricanes, floods, and large-scale crop failures, will stabilize the economy more effectively after a disaster than relief that must be legislated.

3. Suppose someone says, "Using monetary or fiscal policy to pump up the economy is counterproductive—you get a brief high, but then you have the pain of inflation."
   a. Explain what this means in terms of the *AD–AS* model.
   b. Is this a valid argument against stabilization policy? Why or why not?

Tackle the Test: Multiple-Choice Questions

1. Which of the following contributes to the lag in implementing fiscal policy?
   I. It takes time for Congress and the President to pass spending and tax changes.
   II. Current economic data take time to collect and analyze.
   III. It takes time to realize an output gap exists.
   a. I only
   b. II only
   c. III only
   d. I and III only
   e. I, II, and III

2. Which of the following is a government transfer program?
   a. Social Security
   b. Medicare/Medicaid
   c. unemployment insurance
   d. food stamps
   e. all of the above

3. Which of the following is an example of expansionary fiscal policy?
   a. increasing taxes
   b. increasing government spending
   c. decreasing government transfers
   d. decreasing interest rates
   e. increasing the money supply

4. Which of the following is a fiscal policy that is appropriate to combat inflation?
   a. decreasing taxes
   b. decreasing government spending
   c. increasing government transfers
   d. increasing interest rates
   e. expansionary fiscal policy

5. An income tax rebate is an example of
   a. an expansionary fiscal policy.
   b. a contractionary fiscal policy.
   c. an expansionary monetary policy.
   d. a contractionary monetary policy.
   e. none of the above.

Tackle the Test: Free-Response Questions

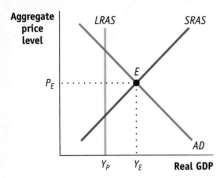

1. Refer to the graph above.
   a. What type of gap exists in this economy?
   b. What type of fiscal policy is appropriate in this situation?
   c. List the three variables the government can change to implement fiscal policy.
   d. How would the government change each of the three variables to implement the policy you listed in part b.

Answer (8 points)

1 point: Inflationary

1 point: Contractionary

1 point: Taxes

1 point: Government transfers

1 point: Government purchases of goods and services

1 point: Increase taxes

1 point: Decrease Government transfers

1 point: Decrease government purchases of goods and services

2. a. Draw a correctly labeled graph showing an economy experiencing a recessionary gap.
   b. What type of fiscal policy is appropriate in this situation?
   c. Give an example of what the government could do to implement the type of policy you listed in part b.

Module 21
Fiscal Policy
and the Multiplier

What you will learn
in this **Module**:

- Why fiscal policy has a multiplier effect

- How the multiplier effect is influenced by automatic stabilizers

Using the Multiplier to Estimate the Influence of Government Policy

An expansionary fiscal policy, like the American Recovery and Reinvestment Act, pushes the aggregate demand curve to the right. A contractionary fiscal policy, like Lyndon Johnson's tax surcharge, pushes the aggregate demand curve to the left. For policy makers, however, knowing the direction of the shift isn't enough: they need estimates of *how much* the aggregate demand curve is shifted by a given policy. To get these estimates, they use the concept of the multiplier.

Multiplier Effects of an Increase in Government Purchases of Goods and Services

Suppose that a government decides to spend $50 billion building bridges and roads. The government's purchases of goods and services will directly increase total spending on final goods and services by $50 billion. But there will also be an indirect effect because the government's purchases will start a chain reaction throughout the economy. The firms producing the goods and services purchased by the government will earn revenues that flow to households in the form of wages, profit, interest, and rent. This increase in disposable income will lead to a rise in consumer spending. The rise in consumer spending, in turn, will induce firms to increase output, leading to a further rise in disposable income, which will lead to another round of consumer spending increases, and so on.

In Module 16 we learned about the concept of the *multiplier*: the ratio of the change in real GDP caused by an autonomous change in aggregate spending to the size of that autonomous change. An increase in government purchases of goods and services is an example of an autonomous increase in aggregate spending. Any change in government purchases of goods and services will lead to an even greater change in real GDP. This chain reaction will cause the initial change in government purchases to multiply through the economy, resulting in an even larger final change in real GDP. The initial

When the government hires Boeing to build a space shuttle, Boeing employees spend their earnings on things like cars and the automakers spend their earnings on things like education, and so on, creating a multiplier effect.

change in spending, multiplied by the multiplier gives us the final change in real GDP.

Let's consider a simple case in which there are no taxes or international trade. In this case, any change in GDP accrues entirely to households. Assume that the aggregate price level is fixed, so that any increase in nominal GDP is also a rise in real GDP, and that the interest rate is fixed. In that case, the multiplier is $1/(1 - MPC)$. Recall that MPC is the *marginal propensity to consume*, the fraction of an additional dollar in disposable income that is spent. For example, if the marginal propensity to consume is 0.5, the multiplier is $1/(1 - 0.5) = 1/0.5 = 2$. Given a multiplier of 2, a $50 billion increase in government purchases of goods and services would increase real GDP by $100 billion. Of that $100 billion, $50 billion is the initial effect from the increase in G, and the remaining $50 billion is the subsequent effect of more production leading to more income which leads to more consumer spending, which leads to more production, and so on.

What happens if government purchases of goods and services are instead reduced? The math is exactly the same, except that there's a minus sign in front: if government purchases of goods and services fall by $50 billion and the marginal propensity to consume is 0.5, real GDP falls by $100 billion. This is the result of less production leading to less income, which leads to less consumption, which leads to less production, and so on.

Multiplier Effects of Changes in Government Transfers and Taxes

Expansionary or contractionary fiscal policy need not take the form of changes in government purchases of goods and services. Governments can also change transfer payments or taxes. In general, however, a change in government transfers or taxes shifts the aggregate demand curve by *less* than an equal-sized change in government purchases, resulting in a smaller effect on real GDP.

To see why, imagine that instead of spending $50 billion on building bridges, the government simply hands out $50 billion in the form of government transfers. In this case, there is no direct effect on aggregate demand as there was with government purchases of goods and services. Real GDP and income grow only because households spend some of that $50 billion—and they probably won't spend it all. In fact, they will spend additional income according to the MPC. If the MPC is 0.5, households will spend only 50 cents of every additional dollar they receive in transfers.

Table 21.1 shows a hypothetical comparison of two expansionary fiscal policies assuming an MPC equal to 0.5 and a multiplier equal to 2: one in which the government

table 21.1

Hypothetical Effects of a Fiscal Policy with a Multiplier of 2

Effect on real GDP	$50 billion rise in government purchases of goods and services	$50 billion rise in government transfer payments
First round	$50 billion	$25 billion
Second round	$25 billion	$12.5 billion
Third round	$12.5 billion	$6.25 billion
⋮	⋮	⋮
Eventual effect	$100 billion	$50 billion

directly purchases $50 billion in goods and services and one in which the government makes transfer payments instead, sending out $50 billion in checks to consumers. In each case, there is a first-round effect on real GDP, either from purchases by the government or from purchases by the consumers who received the checks, followed by a series of additional rounds as rising real GDP raises income (all of which is disposable under our assumption of no taxes), which raises consumption.

However, the first-round effect of the transfer program is smaller; because we have assumed that the *MPC* is 0.5, only $25 billion of the $50 billion is spent, with the other $25 billion saved. And as a result, all the further rounds are smaller, too. In the end, the transfer payment increases real GDP by only $50 billion. In comparison, a $50 billion increase in government purchases produces a $100 billion increase in real GDP.

Overall, when expansionary fiscal policy takes the form of a rise in transfer payments, real GDP may rise by either more or less than the initial government outlay—that is, the multiplier may be either more or less than 1. In Table 21.1, a $50 billion rise in transfer payments increases real GDP by $50 billion, so that the multiplier is exactly 1. If a smaller share of the initial transfer had been spent, the multiplier on that transfer would have been *less* than 1. If a larger share of the initial transfer had been spent, the multiplier would have been *more* than 1.

A tax cut has an effect similar to the effect of a transfer. It increases disposable income, leading to a series of increases in consumer spending. But the overall effect is smaller than that of an equal-sized increase in government purchases of goods and services: the autonomous increase in aggregate spending is smaller because households save part of the amount of the tax cut. They save a fraction of the tax cut equal to their *MPS* (or $1 - MPC$).

We should also note that taxes introduce a further complication: they typically change the size of the multiplier. That's because in the real world governments rarely impose **lump-sum taxes,** in which the amount of tax a household owes is independent of its income. Instead, the great majority of tax revenue is raised via taxes that depend positively on the level of real GDP. As we'll discuss shortly, taxes that depend positively on real GDP reduce the size of the multiplier.

In practice, economists often argue that it also matters *who* among the population gets tax cuts or increases in government transfers. For example, compare the effects of an increase in unemployment benefits with a cut in taxes on profits distributed to shareholders as dividends. Consumer surveys suggest that the average unemployed worker will spend a higher share of any increase in his or her disposable income than would the average recipient of dividend income. That is, people who are unemployed tend to have a higher *MPC* than people who own a lot of stocks because the latter tend to be wealthier and tend to save more of any increase in disposable income. If that's true, a dollar spent on unemployment benefits increases aggregate demand more than a dollar's worth of dividend tax cuts. Such arguments played an important role in the final provisions of the 2008 stimulus package.

How Taxes Affect the Multiplier

Government taxes capture some part of the increase in real GDP that occurs in each round of the multiplier process, since most government taxes depend positively on real GDP. As a result, disposable income increases by considerably less than $1 once we include taxes in the model.

The increase in government tax revenue when real GDP rises isn't the result of a deliberate decision or action by the government. It's a consequence of the way the tax laws are written, which causes most sources of government revenue to increase *automatically* when real GDP goes up. For example, income tax receipts increase when real GDP rises because the amount each individual owes in taxes depends positively on his

Lump-sum taxes are taxes that don't depend on the taxpayer's income.

Automatic stabilizers are government spending and taxation rules that cause fiscal policy to be automatically expansionary when the economy contracts and automatically contractionary when the economy expands.

Discretionary fiscal policy is fiscal policy that is the result of deliberate actions by policy makers rather than rules.

or her income, and households' taxable income rises when real GDP rises. Sales tax receipts increase when real GDP rises because people with more income spend more on goods and services. And corporate profit tax receipts increase when real GDP rises because profits increase when the economy expands.

The effect of these automatic increases in tax revenue is to reduce the size of the multiplier. Remember, the multiplier is the result of a chain reaction in which higher real GDP leads to higher disposable income, which leads to higher consumer spending, which leads to further increases in real GDP. The fact that the government siphons off some of any increase in real GDP means that at each stage of this process, the increase in consumer spending is smaller than it would be if taxes weren't part of the picture. The result is to reduce the multiplier.

Many macroeconomists believe it's a good thing that in real life taxes reduce the multiplier. Most, though not all, recessions are the result of negative demand shocks. The same mechanism that causes tax revenue to increase when the economy expands causes it to decrease when the economy contracts. Since tax receipts decrease when real GDP falls, the effects of these negative demand shocks are smaller than they would be if there were no taxes. The decrease in tax revenue reduces the adverse effect of the initial fall in aggregate demand. The automatic decrease in government tax revenue generated by a fall in real GDP—caused by a decrease in the amount of taxes households pay—acts like an automatic expansionary fiscal policy implemented in the face of a recession. Similarly, when the economy expands, the government finds itself automatically pursuing a contractionary fiscal policy—a tax increase. Government spending and taxation rules that cause fiscal policy to be automatically expansionary when the economy contracts and automatically contractionary when the economy expands, without requiring any deliberate action by policy makers, are called **automatic stabilizers.**

The rules that govern tax collection aren't the only automatic stabilizers, although they are the most important ones. Some types of government transfers also play a stabilizing role. For example, more people receive unemployment insurance when the economy is depressed than when it is booming. The same is true of Medicaid and food stamps. So transfer payments tend to rise when the economy is contracting and fall when the economy is expanding. Like changes in tax revenue, these automatic changes in transfers tend to reduce the size of the multiplier because the total change in disposable income that results from a given rise or fall in real GDP is smaller.

As in the case of government tax revenue, many macroeconomists believe that it's a good thing that government transfers reduce the multiplier. Expansionary and contractionary fiscal policies that are the result of automatic stabilizers are widely considered helpful to macroeconomic stabilization, because they blunt the extremes of the business cycle. But what about fiscal policy that *isn't* the result of automatic stabilizers? **Discretionary fiscal policy** is fiscal policy that is the direct result of deliberate actions by policy makers rather than automatic adjustment. For example, during a recession, the government may pass legislation that cuts taxes and increases government spending in order to stimulate the economy. In general, mainly due to problems with time lags as discussed in Module 10, economists tend to support the use of discretionary fiscal policy only in special circumstances, such as an especially severe recession.

AP Photo

A historical example of discretionary fiscal policy was the Works Progress Administration (WPA), a relief measure established during the Great Depression that put the unemployed to work building bridges, roads, buildings, and parks.

About That Stimulus Package . . .

In early 2008, there was broad bipartisan agreement that the U.S. economy needed a fiscal stimulus. There was, however, sharp partisan disagreement about what form that stimulus should take. The eventual bill was a compromise that left both sides unhappy and arguably made the stimulus less effective than it could have been.

Initially, there was little support for an increase in government purchases of goods and services—that is, neither party wanted to build bridges and roads to stimulate the economy. Both parties believed that the economy needed a quick boost, and ramping up spending would take too long. But there was a fierce debate over whether the stimulus should take the form of a tax cut, which would deliver its biggest benefits to those who paid the most taxes, or an increase in transfer payments targeted at Americans most in economic distress.

The eventual compromise gave most taxpayers a flat $600 rebate, $1,200 for married couples. Very high-income taxpayers were not entitled to a rebate; low earners who didn't make enough to pay income taxes, but did pay other taxes, re-

ceived $300. In effect, the plan was a combination of tax cuts for most Americans and transfer payments to Americans with low incomes.

How well designed was the stimulus plan? Many economists believed that only a fraction of the rebate checks would actually be spent, so that the eventual multiplier would be fairly low. White House economists appeared to agree: they estimated that the stimulus would raise employment by half a million jobs above what it would have been otherwise, the same number offered by independent economists who believed that the multiplier on the plan would be around 0.75. (Remember, the multiplier on changes in taxes or transfers can be less than 1.) Some economists were critical, arguing that Congress should have insisted on a plan that yielded more "bang for the buck."

Both Democratic and Republican economists working for Congress defended the plan, arguing that the perfect is the enemy of the good— that it was the best that could be negotiated on short notice and was likely to be of real help in fighting the economy's weakness. But by late summer 2008, with the U.S. economy still in the

doldrums, there was widespread agreement that the plan's results had been disappointing. And by late 2008, with the economy shrinking further, policy makers were working on a new, much larger stimulus plan that relied more heavily on government purchases. The American Recovery and Reinvestment Act was passed in February 2009. The bill called for $787 billion in expenditures on stimulus in three areas: help for the unemployed and those receiving Medicaid and food stamps; investments in infrastructure, energy, and health care; and tax cuts for families and small businesses.

Despite controversies over specifics, the general consensus about active stabilization policy is apparent: when at first you don't succeed, try, try again.

Module 21 AP Review

Solutions appear at the back of the book.

Check Your Understanding

1. Explain why a $500 million increase in government purchases of goods and services will generate a larger rise in real GDP than a $500 million increase in government transfers.

2. Explain why a $500 million reduction in government purchases of goods and services will generate a larger fall in real GDP than a $500 million tax increase.

3. The country of Boldovia has no unemployment insurance benefits and a tax system using only lump-sum taxes. The neighboring country of Moldovia has generous unemployment benefits and a tax system in which residents must pay a percentage of their income. Which country will experience greater variation in real GDP in response to demand shocks, positive and negative? Explain.

Tackle the Test: Multiple-Choice Questions

1. The marginal propensity to consume
     I. has a negative relationship to the multiplier.
     II. is equal to 1.
     III. represents the proportion of consumers' disposable
          income that is spent.
   a. I only
   b. II only
   c. III only
   d. I and III only
   e. I, II, and III

2. Assume that taxes and interest rates remain unchanged when
   government spending increases, and that both savings and
   consumer spending increase when income increases. The
   ultimate effect on real GDP of a $100 million increase in
   government purchases of goods and services will be
   a. an increase of $100 million.
   b. an increase of more than $100 million.
   c. an increase of less than $100 million.
   d. an increase of either more than or less than $100 million,
      depending on the *MPC*.
   e. a decrease of $100 million.

3. The presence of taxes has what effect on the multiplier? They
   a. increase it.
   b. decrease it.
   c. destabilize it.
   d. negate it.
   e. have no effect on it.

4. A lump-sum tax is
   a. higher as income increases.
   b. lower as income increases.
   c. independent of income.
   d. the most common form of tax.
   e. a type of business tax.

5. Which of the following is NOT an automatic stabilizer?
   a. income taxes
   b. unemployment insurance
   c. Medicaid
   d. food stamps
   e. monetary policy

Tackle the Test: Free-Response Questions

1. Assume the *MPC* in an economy is 0.8 and the government
   increases government purchases of goods and services by
   $50 million. Also assume the absence of taxes, international
   trade, and changes in the aggregate price level.
   a. What is the value of the multiplier?
   b. By how much will real GDP change as a result of the increase
      in government purchases?
   c. What would happen to the size of the effect on real GDP if
      the *MPC* fell? Explain.
   d. If we relax the assumption of no taxes, automatic changes in
      tax revenue as income changes will have what effect on the
      size of the multiplier?

2. A change in government purchases of goods and services results
   in a change in real GDP equal to $200 million. Assume the
   absence of taxes, international trade, and changes in the
   aggregate price level.
   a. Suppose that the *MPC* is equal to 0.75. What was the size of
      the change in government purchases of goods and services
      that resulted in the increase in real GDP of $200 million?
   b. Now suppose that the change in government purchases of
      goods and services was $20 million. What value of the
      multiplier would result in an increase in real GDP of
      $200 million?
   c. Given the value of the multiplier you calculated in part b,
      what marginal propensity to save would have led to that
      value of the multiplier?

Answer (5 points)

1 point: Multiplier = $1/(1 - MPC) = 1/(1 - 0.8) = 1/0.2 = 5$

1 point: $50 million × 5 = $250 million

1 point: It would decrease.

1 point: The multiplier is $1/(1 - MPC)$. A fall in *MPC* increases the denominator, $(1 - MPC)$, and therefore decreases the multiplier.

1 point: Decrease it

Summary

1. The **consumption function** shows how an individual household's consumer spending is determined by its current disposable income. The **aggregate consumption function** shows the relationship for the entire economy. According to the life-cycle hypothesis, households try to smooth their consumption over their lifetimes. As a result, the aggregate consumption function shifts in response to changes in expected future disposable income and changes in aggregate wealth.

2. **Planned investment spending** depends negatively on the interest rate and on existing production capacity; it depends positively on expected future real GDP.

3. Firms hold **inventories** of goods so that they can satisfy consumer demand quickly. **Inventory investment** is positive when firms add to their inventories, negative when they reduce them. Often, however, changes in inventories are not a deliberate decision but the result of mistakes in forecasts about sales. The result is **unplanned inventory investment,** which can be either positive or negative. **Actual investment spending** is the sum of planned investment spending and unplanned inventory investment.

4. The **aggregate demand curve** shows the relationship between the aggregate price level and the quantity of aggregate output demanded.

5. The aggregate demand curve is downward sloping for two reasons. The first is the **wealth effect of a change in the aggregate price level**—a higher aggregate price level reduces the purchasing power of households' wealth and reduces consumer spending. The second is the **interest rate effect of a change in the aggregate price level**—a higher aggregate price level reduces the purchasing power of households' and firms' money holdings, leading to a rise in interest rates and a fall in investment spending and consumer spending.

6. The aggregate demand curve shifts because of changes in expectations, changes in wealth not due to changes in the aggregate price level, and the effect of the size of the existing stock of physical capital. Policy makers can use **fiscal policy** and **monetary policy** to shift the aggregate demand curve.

7. The **aggregate supply curve** shows the relationship between the aggregate price level and the quantity of aggregate output supplied.

8. The **short-run aggregate supply curve** is upward sloping because **nominal wages** are **sticky** in the short run: a higher aggregate price level leads to higher profit per unit of output and increased aggregate output in the short run.

9. Changes in commodity prices, nominal wages, and productivity lead to changes in producers' profits and shift the short-run aggregate supply curve.

10. In the long run, all prices, including nominal wages, are flexible and the economy produces at its **potential output.** If actual aggregate output exceeds potential output, nominal wages will eventually rise in response to low unemployment and aggregate output will fall. If potential output exceeds actual aggregate output, nominal wages will eventually fall in response to high unemployment and aggregate output will rise. So the **long-run aggregate supply curve** is vertical at potential output.

11. In the *AD–AS* **model,** the intersection of the short-run aggregate supply curve and the aggregate demand curve is the point of **short-run macroeconomic equilibrium.** It determines the **short-run equilibrium aggregate price level** and the level of **short-run equilibrium aggregate output.**

12. Economic fluctuations occur because of a shift of the aggregate demand curve (a *demand shock*) or the short-run aggregate supply curve (a *supply shock*). A **demand shock** causes the aggregate price level and aggregate output to move in the same direction as the economy moves along the short-run aggregate supply curve. A **supply shock** causes them to move in opposite directions as the economy moves along the aggregate demand curve. A particularly nasty occurrence is **stagflation**—inflation and falling aggregate output—which is caused by a negative supply shock.

13. Demand shocks have only short-run effects on aggregate output because the economy is **self-correcting** in the long run. In a **recessionary gap,** an eventual fall in nominal wages moves the economy to **long-run macroeconomic equilibrium,** in which aggregate output is equal to potential output. In an **inflationary gap,** an eventual rise in nominal wages moves the economy to long-run macroeconomic equilibrium. We can use the **output gap,** the percentage difference between actual aggregate output and potential output, to summarize how the economy responds to recessionary and inflationary gaps. Because the economy tends to be self-correcting in the long run, the output gap always tends toward zero.

14. The high cost—in terms of unemployment—of a recessionary gap and the future adverse consequences of an inflationary gap lead many economists to advocate active **stabilization policy:** using fiscal or monetary policy to offset demand shocks. There can be drawbacks, however, because such policies may contribute to a long-term rise in the budget deficit, leading to lower

long-run growth. Also, poorly timed policies can increase economic instability.

15. Negative supply shocks pose a policy dilemma: a policy that counteracts the fall in aggregate output by increasing aggregate demand will lead to higher inflation, but a policy that counteracts inflation by reducing aggregate demand will deepen the output slump.

16. The government plays a large role in the economy, collecting a large share of GDP in taxes and spending a large share both to purchase goods and services and to make transfer payments, largely for **social insurance**. **Fiscal policy** is the use of taxes, government transfers, or government purchases of goods and services to shift the aggregate demand curve. But many economists caution that a very active fiscal policy may in fact make the economy less stable due to time lags in policy formulation and implementation.

17. Government purchases of goods and services directly affect aggregate demand, and changes in taxes and government transfers affect aggregate demand indirectly by changing households' disposable income. **Expansionary fiscal policy** shifts the aggregate demand curve rightward; **contractionary fiscal policy** shifts the aggregate demand curve leftward.

18. Fiscal policy has a multiplier effect on the economy, the size of which depends upon the fiscal policy. Except in the case of lump-sum taxes, taxes reduce the size of the multiplier. Expansionary fiscal policy leads to an increase in real GDP, while contractionary fiscal policy leads to a reduction in real GDP. Because part of any change in taxes or transfers is absorbed by savings in the first round of spending, changes in government purchases of goods and services have a more powerful effect on the economy than equal-size changes in taxes or transfers.

19. An **autonomous change in aggregate spending** leads to a chain reaction in which the total change in real GDP is equal to the multiplier times the initial change in aggregate spending. The size of the **multiplier**, $1/(1 - MPC)$, depends on the **marginal propensity to consume, MPC,** the fraction of an additional dollar of disposable income spent on consumption. The larger the *MPC*, the larger the multiplier and the larger the change in real GDP for any given autonomous change in aggregate spending. The fraction of an additional dollar of disposable income that is saved is called the **marginal propensity to save, MPS.**

20. Rules governing taxes—with the exception of **lump-sum taxes**—and some transfers act as **automatic stabilizers**, reducing the size of the multiplier and automatically reducing the size of fluctuations in the business cycle. In contrast, **discretionary fiscal policy** arises from deliberate actions by policy makers rather than from the business cycle.

Key Terms

Problems

1. A fall in the value of the dollar against other currencies makes U.S. final goods and services cheaper to foreigners even though the U.S. aggregate price level stays the same. As a result, foreigners demand more American aggregate output. Your study partner says that this represents a movement down the aggregate demand curve because foreigners are demanding more in response to a lower price. You, however, insist that this represents a rightward shift of the aggregate demand curve. Who is right? Explain.

2. Your study partner is confused by the upward-sloping short-run aggregate supply curve and the vertical long-run aggregate supply curve. How would you explain the shapes of these two curves?

3. Suppose that in Wageland all workers sign annual wage contracts each year on January 1. No matter what happens to prices of final goods and services during the year, all workers earn the wage specified in their annual contract. This year, prices of final goods and services fall unexpectedly after the contracts are signed. Answer the following questions using a diagram and assume that the economy starts at potential output.

   a. In the short run, how will the quantity of aggregate output supplied respond to the fall in prices?

   b. What will happen when firms and workers renegotiate their wages?

4. Determine whether, in the short run, each of the following events causes a shift of a curve or a movement along a curve. Also determine which curve is involved and the direction of the change.

   a. As a result of new discoveries of iron ore used to make steel, producers now pay less for steel, a major commodity used in production.

   b. An increase in the money supply by the Federal Reserve increases the quantity of money that people wish to lend, lowering interest rates.

   c. Greater union activity leads to higher nominal wages.

   d. A fall in the aggregate price level increases the purchasing power of households' and firms' money holdings. As a result, they borrow less and lend more.

5. Suppose that all households hold all their wealth in assets that automatically rise in value when the aggregate price level rises (an example of this is what is called an "inflation-indexed bond"—a bond for which the interest rate, among other things, changes one-for-one with the inflation rate). What happens to the wealth effect of a change in the aggregate price level as a result of this allocation of assets? What happens to the slope of the aggregate demand curve? Will it still slope downward? Explain.

6. Suppose that the economy is currently at potential output. Also suppose that you are an economic policy maker and that a college economics student asks you to rank, if possible, your most preferred to least preferred type of shock: positive demand shock, negative demand shock, positive supply shock, negative supply shock. For those shocks that can be ranked, how would you rank them and why?

7. Explain whether the following government policies affect the aggregate demand curve or the short-run aggregate supply curve and how.

   a. The government reduces the minimum nominal wage.

   b. The government increases Temporary Assistance to Needy Families (TANF) payments, government transfers to families with dependent children.

   c. To reduce the budget deficit, the government announces that households will pay much higher taxes beginning next year.

   d. The government reduces military spending.

8. In Wageland, all workers sign an annual wage contract each year on January 1. In late January, a new computer operating system is introduced that increases labor productivity dramatically. Explain how Wageland will move from one short-run macroeconomic equilibrium to another. Illustrate with a diagram.

9. The Conference Board publishes the Consumer Confidence Index (CCI) every month based on a survey of 5,000 representative U.S. households. It is used by many economists to track the state of the economy. A press release by the Board on April 29, 2008 stated: "The Conference Board Consumer Confidence Index, which had declined sharply in March, fell further in April. The Index now stands at 62.3 (1985 = 100), down from 65.9 in March."

   a. As an economist, is this news encouraging for economic growth?

   b. Explain your answer to part a with the help of the AD–AS model. Draw a typical diagram showing two equilibrium points (E_1) and (E_2). Label the vertical axis "Aggregate price level" and the horizontal axis "Real GDP." Assume that all other major macroeconomic factors remain unchanged.

   c. How should the government respond to this news? What are some policy measures that could be used to help neutralize the effect of falling consumer confidence?

10. There were two major shocks to the U.S. economy in 2007, leading to a severe economic slowdown. One shock was related to oil prices; the other was the slump in the housing market. This question analyzes the effect of these two shocks on GDP using the AD–AS framework.

    a. Draw typical aggregate demand and short-run aggregate supply curves. Label the horizontal axis "Real GDP" and the vertical axis "Aggregate price level." Label the equilibrium point E_1, the equilibrium quantity Y_1, and equilibrium price P_1.

    b. Data taken from the Department of Energy indicate that the average price of crude oil in the world increased from $54.63 per barrel on January 5, 2007, to $92.93 on December 28, 2007. Would an increase in oil prices cause a demand shock or a supply shock? Redraw the diagram from part a to illustrate the effect of this shock by shifting the appropriate curve.

    c. The Housing Price Index, published by the Office of Federal Housing Enterprise Oversight, calculates that U.S. home prices fell by an average of 3.0% in the 12 months between January 2007 and January 2008. Would the fall in home prices cause a supply shock or demand shock? Redraw the diagram from part b to illustrate the effect of this shock by shifting the appropriate curve. Label the new equilibrium point E_2, the equilibrium quantity Y_2, and equilibrium price P_2.

    d. Compare the equilibrium points E_1 and E_2 in your diagram for part c. What was the effect of the two shocks on real GDP and the aggregate price level (increase, decrease, or indeterminate)?

11. Using aggregate demand, short-run aggregate supply, and long-run aggregate supply curves, explain the process by which each of the following economic events will move the economy from one long-run macroeconomic equilibrium to another. Illustrate with diagrams. In each case, what are the short-run and long-run effects on the aggregate price level and aggregate output?

    a. There is a decrease in households' wealth due to a decline in the stock market.

    b. The government lowers taxes, leaving households with more disposable income, with no corresponding reduction in government purchases.

12. Using aggregate demand, short-run aggregate supply, and long-run aggregate supply curves, explain the process by which each of the following government policies will move the economy from one long-run macroeconomic equilibrium to another. Illustrate with diagrams. In each case, what are the short-run and long-run effects on the aggregate price level and aggregate output?

   a. There is an increase in taxes on households.

   b. There is an increase in the quantity of money.

   c. There is an increase in government spending.

13. The economy is in short-run macroeconomic equilibrium at point E_1 in the accompanying diagram. Based on the diagram, answer the following questions.

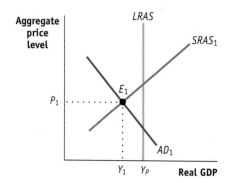

   a. Is the economy facing an inflationary or a recessionary gap?

   b. What policies can the government implement that might bring the economy back to long-run macroeconomic equilibrium? Illustrate with a diagram.

   c. If the government did not intervene to close this gap, would the economy return to long-run macroeconomic equilibrium? Explain and illustrate with a diagram.

   d. What are the advantages and disadvantages of the government implementing policies to close the gap?

14. In the accompanying diagram, the economy is in long-run macroeconomic equilibrium at point E_1 when an oil shock shifts the short-run aggregate supply curve to $SRAS_2$. Based on the diagram, answer the following questions.

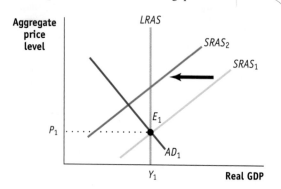

   a. How do the aggregate price level and aggregate output change in the short run as a result of the oil shock? What is this phenomenon known as?

   b. What fiscal policies can the government use to address the effects of the supply shock? Use a diagram that shows the effect of policies chosen to address the change in real GDP.

Use another diagram to show the effect of policies chosen to address the change in the aggregate price level.

   c. Why do supply shocks present a dilemma for government policy makers?

15. The late 1990s in the United States were characterized by substantial economic growth with low inflation; that is, real GDP increased with little, if any, increase in the aggregate price level. Explain this experience using aggregate demand and aggregate supply curves. Illustrate with a diagram.

16. In each of the following cases, either a recessionary or inflationary gap exists. Assume that the aggregate supply curve is horizontal, so that the change in real GDP arising from a shift of the aggregate demand curve equals the size of the shift of the curve. Calculate both the change in government purchases of goods and services, and, alternatively, the change in government transfers necessary to close the gap.

   a. Real GDP equals $100 billion, potential output equals $160 billion, and the marginal propensity to consume is 0.75.

   b. Real GDP equals $250 billion, potential output equals $200 billion, and the marginal propensity to consume is 0.5.

   c. Real GDP equals $180 billion, potential output equals $100 billion, and the marginal propensity to consume is 0.8.

17. Most macroeconomists believe it is a good thing that taxes act as automatic stabilizers and lower the size of the multiplier. However, a smaller multiplier means that the change in government purchases of goods and services, government transfers, or taxes necessary to close an inflationary or recessionary gap is larger. How can you explain this apparent inconsistency?

18. The accompanying table shows how consumers' marginal propensities to consume in a particular economy are related to their level of income.

Income range	Marginal propensity to consume
$0 – $20,000	0.9
$20,001 – $40,000	0.8
$40,001 – $60,000	0.7
$60,001 – $80,000	0.6
Above $80,000	0.5

   a. Suppose the government engages in increased purchases of goods and services. For each of the income groups in the accompanying table, what is the value of the multiplier—that is, what is the "bang for the buck" from each dollar the government spends on government purchases of goods and services in each income group?

   b. If the government needed to close a recessionary or inflationary gap, at which group should it primarily aim its fiscal policy of changes in government purchases of goods and services?

19. From 2003 to 2008, Eastlandia experienced large fluctuations in both aggregate consumer spending and disposable income, but wealth, the interest rate, and expected future disposable income did not change. The accompanying table shows the level of aggregate consumer spending and disposable income in

millions of dollars for each of these years. Use this information to answer the following questions.

Year	Disposable income (millions of dollars)	Consumer spending (millions of dollars)
2003	$100	$180
2004	350	380
2005	300	340
2006	400	420
2007	375	400
2008	500	500

a. Plot the aggregate consumption function for Eastlandia.

b. What is the marginal propensity to consume? What is the marginal propensity to save?

c. What is the aggregate consumption function?

20. From the end of 1995 to March 2000, the Standard and Poor's 500 (S&P 500) stock index, a broad measure of stock market prices, rose almost 150%, from 615.93 to a high of 1,527.46. From that time to September 10, 2001, the index fell 28.5% to 1,092.54. How do you think the movements in the stock index influenced both the growth in real GDP in the late 1990s and the concern about maintaining consumer spending after the terrorist attacks on September 11, 2001?

21. How will investment spending change as the following events occur?

a. The interest rate falls as a result of Federal Reserve policy.

b. The U.S. Environmental Protection Agency decrees that corporations must upgrade or replace their machinery in order to reduce their emissions of sulfur dioxide.

c. Baby boomers begin to retire in large numbers and reduce their savings, resulting in higher interest rates

22. Explain how each of the following actions will affect the level of investment spending and unplanned inventory investment.

a. The Federal Reserve raises the interest rate.

b. There is a rise in the expected growth rate of real GDP.

c. A sizable inflow of foreign funds into the country lowers the interest rate.

23. The accompanying diagram shows the current macroeconomic situation for the economy of Albernia. You have been hired as an economic consultant to help the economy move to potential output, Y_P.

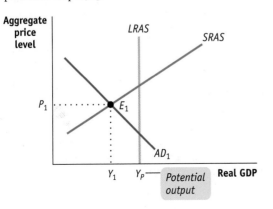

a. Is Albernia facing a recessionary or inflationary gap?

b. Which type of fiscal policy—expansionary or contractionary—would move the economy of Albernia to potential output, Y_P? What are some examples of such policies?

c. Use a diagram to illustrate the macroeconomic situation in Albernia after the successful fiscal policy has been implemented.

24. The accompanying diagram shows the current macroeconomic situation for the economy of Brittania; real GDP is Y_1, and the aggregate price level is P_1. You have been hired as an economic consultant to help the economy move to potential output, Y_P.

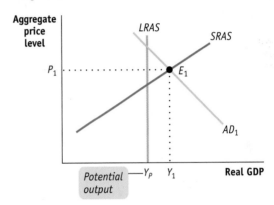

a. Is Brittania facing a recessionary or inflationary gap?

b. Which type of fiscal policy—expansionary or contractionary—would move the economy of Brittania to potential output, Y_P? What are some examples of such policies?

c. Illustrate the macroeconomic situation in Brittania with a diagram after the successful fiscal policy has been implemented.

25. An economy is in long-run macroeconomic equilibrium when each of the following aggregate demand shocks occurs. What kind of gap—inflationary or recessionary—will the economy face after the shock, and what type of fiscal policies would help move the economy back to potential output? How would your recommended fiscal policy shift the aggregate demand curve?

a. A stock market boom increases the value of stocks held by households.

b. Firms come to believe that a recession in the near future is likely.

c. Anticipating the possibility of war, the government increases its purchases of military equipment.

d. The quantity of money in the economy declines and interest rates increase.

The Financial Sector

FUNNY MONEY

On October 2, 2004, FBI and Secret Service agents seized a shipping container that had just arrived in Newark, New Jersey, on a ship from China. Inside the container, under cardboard boxes containing plastic toys, they found what they were looking for: more than $300,000 in counterfeit $100 bills. Two months later, another shipment with $3 million in counterfeit bills was intercepted. Government and law enforcement officials began alleging publicly that these bills—which were high-quality fakes, very hard to tell from the real thing—were being produced by the government of North Korea.

The funny thing is that elaborately decorated pieces of paper have little or no intrinsic value. Indeed, a $100 bill printed with blue or orange ink literally wouldn't be worth the paper it was printed on. But if the ink on that decorated piece of paper is just the right shade of green, people will think that it's *money* and will accept it as payment for very real goods and services. Why? Because they believe, correctly, that they can do the same thing: exchange that piece of green paper for real goods and services.

"The Atrain Is On the Banks," by James Flora, 1996, © Jim Flora Art LLC; Courtesy Irwin Chusid and Barbara Economon. www.JimFlora.

Money is the essential channel that links the various parts of the modern economy.

In fact, here's a riddle: If a fake $100 bill from North Korea enters the United States, and nobody ever realizes it's fake, who gets hurt? Accepting a fake $100 bill isn't like buying a car that turns out to be a lemon or a meal that turns out to be inedible; as long as the bill's counterfeit nature remains undiscovered, it will pass from hand to hand just like a real $100 bill. The answer to the riddle is that the real victims of North Korean counterfeiting are U.S. taxpayers because counterfeit dollars reduce the revenues available to pay for the operations of the U.S. government. Accordingly, the Secret Service diligently monitors the integrity of U.S. currency, promptly investigating any reports of counterfeit dollars.

The efforts of the Secret Service attest to the fact that money isn't like ordinary goods and services. In this section we'll look at the role money plays, the workings of a modern monetary system, and the institutions that sustain and regulate it. We'll then see how models of the money and loanable funds markets help us understand *monetary policy* as carried out by our central bank—the *Federal Reserve*.

- The relationship between savings and investment spending
- The purpose of the four principal types of financial assets: stocks, bonds, loans, and bank deposits
- How financial intermediaries help investors achieve diversification

Module 22
Saving, Investment, and the Financial System

Matching Up Savings and Investment Spending

Two instrumental sources of economic growth are increases in the skills and knowledge of the workforce, known as *human capital,* and increases in capital—goods used to make other goods—which can also be called *physical capital* to distinguish it from human capital. Human capital is largely provided by the government through public education. (In countries with a large private education sector, like the United States, private post-secondary education is also an important source of human capital.) But physical capital, with the exception of infrastructure such as roads and bridges, is mainly created through private investment spending—that is, spending by firms rather than by the government.

Who pays for private investment spending? In some cases it's the people or corporations who actually do the spending—for example, a family that owns a business might use its own savings to buy new equipment or a new building, or a corporation might reinvest some of its own profits to build a new factory. In the modern economy, however, individuals and firms who create physical capital often do it with other people's money—money that they borrow or raise by selling stock. If they borrow money to create physical capital, they are charged an interest rate. The **interest rate** is the price, calculated as a percentage of the amount borrowed, charged by lenders to borrowers for the use of their savings for one year.

To understand how investment spending is financed, we need to look first at how savings and investment spending are related for the economy as a whole.

The Savings–Investment Spending Identity

The most basic point to understand about savings and investment spending is that they are always equal. This is not a theory; it's a fact of accounting called the **savings–investment spending identity.**

To see why the savings–investment spending identity must be true, first imagine a highly simplified economy in which there is no government and no interaction with

The **interest rate** is the price, calculated as a percentage of the amount borrowed, charged by lenders to borrowers for the use of their savings for one year.

According to the **savings–investment spending identity,** savings and investment spending are always equal for the economy as a whole.

other countries. The overall income of this simplified economy would, by definition, be equal to total spending in the economy. Why? Because the only way people could earn income would be by selling something to someone else, and every dollar spent in the economy would create income for somebody. So in this simplified economy,

(22-1) Total income = Total spending

Now, what can people do with income? They can either spend it on consumption or save it. So it must be true that

(22-2) Total income = Consumer spending + Savings

Meanwhile, spending consists of either consumer spending or investment spending:

(22-3) Total spending = Consumer spending + Investment spending

Putting these together, we get:

(22-4) Consumer spending + Savings = Consumer spending + Investment spending

Subtract consumer spending from both sides, and we get:

(22-5) Savings = Investment spending

As we said, then, it's a basic accounting fact that savings equals investment spending for the economy as a whole.

So far, however, we've looked only at a simplified economy in which there is no government and no economic interaction with the rest of the world. Bringing these realistic complications back into the story changes things in two ways.

First, households are not the only parties that can save in an economy. In any given year the government can save, too, if it collects more tax revenue than it spends. When this occurs, the difference is called a **budget surplus** and is equivalent to savings by government. If, alternatively, government spending exceeds tax revenue, there is a **budget deficit**—a negative budget surplus. In this case we often say that the government is "dissaving": by spending more than its tax revenues, the government is engaged in the opposite of saving. We'll define the term **budget balance** to refer to both cases, with the understanding that the budget balance can be positive (a budget surplus) or negative (a budget deficit). **National savings** is equal to the sum of private savings and the budget balance, whereas private savings is disposable income (income after taxes) minus consumption.

Second, the fact that any one country is part of a wider world economy means that savings need not be spent on physical capital located in the same country in which the savings are generated. That's because the savings of people who live in any one country can be used to finance investment spending that takes place in other countries. So any given country can receive *inflows* of funds—foreign savings that finance investment spending in the country. Any given country can also generate *outflows* of funds—domestic savings that finance investment spending in another country.

The net effect of international inflows and outflows of funds on the total savings available for investment spending in any given country is known as the **capital inflow** into that country, equal to the total inflow of foreign funds minus the total outflow of domestic funds to other countries. Like the budget balance, a capital inflow can be negative—that is, more capital can flow out of a country than flows into it. In recent years the United States has experienced a consistent net inflow of capital from foreigners, who view our economy as an attractive place to put their savings. In 2008, for example, capital inflows into the United States were $707 billion.

The **budget surplus** is the difference between tax revenue and government spending when tax revenue exceeds government spending.

The **budget deficit** is the difference between tax revenue and government spending when government spending exceeds tax revenue.

The **budget balance** is the difference between tax revenue and government spending.

National savings, the sum of private savings and the budget balance, is the total amount of savings generated within the economy.

Capital inflow is the net inflow of funds into a country.

It's important to note that, from a national perspective, a dollar generated by national savings and a dollar generated by capital inflow are not equivalent. Yes, they can both finance the same dollar's worth of investment spending, but any dollar borrowed from a saver must eventually be repaid with interest. A dollar that comes from national savings is repaid with interest to someone domestically—either a private party or the government. But a dollar that comes as capital inflow must be repaid with interest to a foreigner. So a dollar of investment spending financed by a capital inflow comes at a higher *national* cost—the interest that must eventually be paid to a foreigner—than a dollar of investment spending financed by national savings.

istockphoto

The corner of Wall and Broad Streets is at the center of New York City's financial district.

So the application of the savings–investment spending identity to an economy that is open to inflows or outflows of capital means that investment spending is equal to savings, where savings is equal to national savings *plus* capital inflow. That is, in an economy with a positive capital inflow, some investment spending is funded by the savings of foreigners. And in an economy with a negative capital inflow (a net outflow), some portion of national savings is funding investment spending in other countries. In the United States in 2008, investment spending totaled $2,632 billion. Private savings were $2,506.9 billion, offset by a budget deficit of $683 billion and supplemented by capital inflows of $707 billion. Notice that these numbers don't quite add up; because data collection isn't perfect, there is a "statistical discrepancy" of $101 billion. But we know that this is an error in the data, not in the theory, because the savings–investment spending identity must hold in reality.

The Financial System

Financial markets are where households invest their current savings and their accumulated savings, or **wealth,** by purchasing *financial assets.*

A **financial asset** is a paper claim that entitles the buyer to future income from the seller. For example, when a saver lends funds to a company, the loan is a financial asset sold by the company that entitles the lender (the buyer) to future income from the company. A household can also invest its current savings or wealth by purchasing a **physical asset,** a claim on a tangible object, such as a preexisting house or preexisting piece of equipment. It gives the owner the right to dispose of the object as he or she wishes (for example, rent it or sell it).

If you were to go to your local bank and get a loan—say, to buy a new car—you and the bank would be creating a financial asset: your loan. A *loan* is one important kind of financial asset in the real world, one that is owned by the lender—in this case, your local bank. In creating that loan, you and the bank would also be creating a **liability,** a requirement to pay money in the future. So although your loan is a financial asset from the bank's point of view, it is a liability from your point of view: a requirement that you repay the loan, including any interest. In addition to loans, there are three other important kinds of financial assets: stocks, bonds, and *bank deposits.* Because a financial asset is a claim to future income that someone has to pay, it is also someone else's liability. We'll explain in detail shortly who bears the liability for each type of financial asset.

These four types of financial assets exist because the economy has developed a set of specialized markets, like the stock market and the bond market, and specialized institutions, like banks, that facilitate the flow of funds from lenders to borrowers. A well-functioning financial system is a critical ingredient in achieving long-run growth because it encourages greater savings and investment spending. It also ensures that savings and investment spending are undertaken efficiently. To understand how this occurs, we first need to know what tasks the financial system needs to accomplish. Then we can see how the job gets done.

A household's **wealth** is the value of its accumulated savings.

A **financial asset** is a paper claim that entitles the buyer to future income from the seller.

A **physical asset** is a claim on a tangible object that gives the owner the right to dispose of the object as he or she wishes.

A **liability** is a requirement to pay money in the future.

Three Tasks of a Financial System

There are three important problems facing borrowers and lenders: transaction costs, risk, and the desire for *liquidity*. The three tasks of a financial system are to reduce these problems in a cost-effective way. Doing so enhances the efficiency of financial markets: it makes it more likely that lenders and borrowers will make mutually beneficial trades—trades that make society as a whole richer.

Reducing Transaction Costs **Transaction costs** are the expenses of actually putting together and executing a deal. For example, arranging a loan requires spending time and money negotiating the terms of the deal, verifying the borrower's ability to pay, drawing up and executing legal documents, and so on. Suppose a large business decided that it wanted to raise $1 billion for investment spending. No individual would be willing to lend that much. And negotiating individual loans from thousands of different people, each willing to lend a modest amount, would impose very large total costs because each individual transaction would incur a cost. Total costs would be so large that the entire deal would probably be unprofitable for the business.

Fortunately, that's not necessary: when large businesses want to borrow money, they either get a loan from a bank or sell bonds in the bond market. Obtaining a loan from a bank avoids large transaction costs because it involves only a single borrower and a single lender. We'll explain more about how bonds work in the next section. For now, it is enough to know that the principal reason there is a bond market is that it allows companies to borrow large sums of money without incurring large transaction costs.

Reducing Risk A second problem that real-world borrowers and lenders face is **financial risk,** uncertainty about future outcomes that involve financial losses or gains. Financial risk (which from now on we'll simply call "risk") is a problem because the future is uncertain; it holds the potential for losses as well as gains.

Most people are risk-averse, although to differing degrees. A well-functioning financial system helps people reduce their exposure to risk. Suppose the owner of a business expects to make a greater profit if she buys additional capital equipment but isn't completely sure of this result. She could pay for the equipment by using her savings or selling her house. But if the profit is significantly less than expected, she will have lost her savings, or her house, or both. That is, she would be exposing herself to a lot of risk due to uncertainty about how well or poorly the business performs. So, being risk-averse, this business owner wants to share the risk of purchasing new capital equipment with someone, even if that requires sharing some of the profit if all goes well. How can she do this? By selling shares of her company to other people and using the money she receives from selling shares, rather than money from the sale of her other assets, to finance the equipment purchase. By selling shares in her company, she reduces her personal losses if the profit is less than expected: she won't have lost her other assets. But if things go well, the shareholders earn a share of the profit as a return on their investment.

By selling a share of her business, the owner has achieved *diversification:* she has been able to invest in several things in a way that lowers her total risk. She has maintained her investment in her bank account, a financial asset; in ownership of her house, a physical asset; and in ownership of the unsold portion of her business, also a physical asset. By engaging in **diversification**—investing in several assets with unrelated, or independent, risks—our business owner has lowered her total risk of loss. The desire of individuals to reduce their total risk by engaging in diversification is why we have stocks and a stock market.

Providing Liquidity The third and final task of the financial system is to provide investors with *liquidity,* which—like risk—becomes relevant because the future is uncertain. Suppose that, having made a loan, a lender suddenly finds himself in need of cash—say, to pay for a medical emergency. Unfortunately, if that loan was made to a business that used it to buy new equipment, the business cannot repay the loan on

Transaction costs are the expenses of negotiating and executing a deal.

Financial risk is uncertainty about future outcomes that involve financial losses and gains.

An individual can engage in **diversification** by investing in several different assets so that the possible losses are independent events.

short notice to satisfy the lender's need to recover his money. Knowing this in advance—that there is a danger of needing to get his money back before the term of the loan is up—our lender might be reluctant to lock up his money by lending it to a business.

An asset is **liquid** if it can be quickly converted into cash without much loss of value, **illiquid** if it cannot. As we'll see, stocks and bonds are a partial answer to the problem of liquidity. Banks provide a further way for individuals to hold liquid assets and still finance illiquid investments.

To help lenders and borrowers make mutually beneficial deals, then, the economy needs ways to reduce transaction costs, to reduce and manage risk through diversification, and to provide liquidity. How does it achieve these tasks? With a variety of financial assets.

Types of Financial Assets

In the modern economy there are four main types of financial assets: *loans,* bonds, stocks, and *bank deposits*. In addition, financial innovation has allowed the creation of a wide range of *loan-backed securities*. Each serves a somewhat different purpose. We'll explain loans, bonds, stocks, and loan-backed securities first. Then we'll turn to bank deposits when we explain the role banks play as financial intermediaries.

Loans A **loan** is a lending agreement between an individual lender and an individual borrower. Most people encounter loans in the form of bank loans to finance the purchase of a car or a house. And small businesses usually use bank loans to buy new equipment.

The good aspect of loans is that a given loan is usually tailored to the needs of the borrower. Before a small business can get a loan, it usually has to discuss its business plans, its profits, and so on with the lender. This results in a loan that meets the borrower's needs and ability to repay.

The bad aspect of loans is that making a loan to an individual person or a business typically involves a lot of transaction costs, such as the cost of negotiating the terms of the loan, investigating the borrower's credit history and ability to repay, and so on. To minimize these costs, large borrowers such as major corporations and governments often take a more streamlined approach: they sell (or issue) bonds.

Bonds A bond is an IOU issued by the borrower. Normally, the seller of the bond promises to pay a fixed sum of interest each year and to repay the principal—the value stated on the face of the bond—to the owner of the bond on a particular date. So a bond is a financial asset from its owner's point of view and a liability from its issuer's point of view. A bond issuer sells a number of bonds with a given interest rate and maturity date to whoever is willing to buy them, a process that avoids costly negotiation of the terms of a loan with many individual lenders.

Bond purchasers can acquire information free of charge on the quality of the bond issuer, such as the bond issuer's credit history, from *bond-rating agencies* rather than having to incur the expense of investigating it themselves. A particular concern for investors is the possibility of **default,** the risk that the bond issuer might fail to make payments as specified by the bond contract. Once a bond's risk of default has been rated, it can be sold on the bond market as a more or less standardized product—a product with clearly defined terms and quality. In general, bonds with a higher default risk must pay a higher interest rate to attract investors.

Another important advantage of bonds is that they are easy to resell. This provides liquidity to bond purchasers. Indeed, a bond will often pass through many hands before it finally comes due. Loans, in contrast, are much more difficult to resell because, unlike bonds, they are not standardized: they differ in size, quality, terms, and so on. This makes them a lot less liquid than bonds.

An asset is **liquid** if it can be quickly converted into cash without much loss of value.

An asset is **illiquid** if it cannot be quickly converted into cash without much loss of value.

A **loan** is a lending agreement between an individual lender and an individual borrower.

A **default** occurs when a borrower fails to make payments as specified by the loan or bond contract.

Loan-backed Securities **Loan-backed securities,** assets created by pooling individual loans and selling shares in that pool (a process called *securitization*), have become extremely popular over the past two decades. While mortgage-backed securities, in which thousands of individual home mortgages are pooled and shares sold to investors, are the best-known example, securitization has also been widely applied to student loans, credit card loans, and auto loans. These loan-backed securities trade on financial markets like bonds and are preferred by investors because they provide more diversification and liquidity than individual loans. However, with so many loans packaged together, it can be difficult to assess the true quality of the asset. That difficulty came to haunt investors during the financial crisis of 2007–2008, when the bursting of the housing bubble led to widespread defaults on mortgages and large losses for holders of "supposedly safe" mortgage-backed securities, causing pain that spread throughout the entire financial system.

Stocks A stock is a share in the ownership of a company. A share of stock is a financial asset from its owner's point of view and a liability from the company's point of view. Not all companies sell shares of their stock; "privately held" companies are owned by an individual or a few partners, who get to keep all of the company's profit. Most large companies, however, do sell stock. For example, as this book goes to press, Microsoft has nearly 9 billion shares outstanding; if you buy one of those shares, you are entitled to one-nine billionth of the company's profit, as well as 1 of 9 billion votes on company decisions.

© PhotoSpin, Inc/Alamy

Why does Microsoft, historically a very profitable company, allow you to buy a share in its ownership? Why don't Bill Gates and Paul Allen, the two founders of Microsoft, keep complete ownership for themselves and just sell bonds for their investment spending needs? The reason, as we have just learned, is risk: few individuals are risk-tolerant enough to face the risk involved in being the sole owner of a large company.

Reducing the risk that business owners face, however, is not the only way in which the existence of stocks improves society's welfare: it also improves the welfare of investors who buy stocks (that is, shareowners, or shareholders). Shareowners are able to enjoy the higher returns over time that stocks generally offer in comparison to bonds. Over the past century, stocks have typically yielded about 7% after adjusting for inflation; bonds have yielded only about 2%. But as investment companies warn you, "Past performance is no guarantee of future performance." And there is a downside: owning the stock of a given company is riskier than owning a bond issued by the same company. Why? Loosely speaking, a bond is a promise while a stock is a hope: by law, a company must pay what it owes its lenders (bondholders) before it distributes any profit to its shareholders. And if the company should fail (that is, be unable to pay its interest obligations and declare bankruptcy), its physical and financial assets go to its bondholders—its lenders—while its shareholders typically receive nothing. So, although a stock generally provides a higher return to an investor than a bond, it also carries higher risk.

The financial system has devised ways to help investors as well as business owners simultaneously manage risk and enjoy somewhat higher returns. It does that through the services of institutions known as *financial intermediaries.*

Financial Intermediaries

A **financial intermediary** is an institution that transforms funds gathered from many individuals into financial assets. The most important types of financial intermediaries are *mutual funds, pension funds, life insurance companies,* and *banks.* About three-quarters of the financial assets Americans own are held through these intermediaries rather than directly.

A **loan-backed security** is an asset created by pooling individual loans and selling shares in that pool.

A **financial intermediary** is an institution that transforms the funds it gathers from many individuals into financial assets.

Mutual Funds As we've explained, owning shares of a company entails risk in return for a higher potential reward. But it should come as no surprise that stock investors can lower their total risk by engaging in diversification. By owning a *diversified portfolio* of stocks—a group of stocks in which risks are unrelated to, or offset, one another—rather than concentrating investment in the shares of a single company or a group of related companies, investors can reduce their risk. In addition, financial advisers, aware that most people are risk-averse, almost always advise their clients to diversify not only their stock portfolio but also their entire wealth by holding other assets in addition to stock—assets such as bonds, real estate, and cash. (And, for good measure, to have plenty of insurance in case of accidental losses!)

However, for individuals who don't have a large amount of money to invest—say $1 million or more—building a diversified stock portfolio can incur high transaction costs (particularly fees paid to stockbrokers) because they are buying a few shares of a lot of companies. Fortunately for such investors, mutual funds help solve the problem of achieving diversification without high transaction costs. A **mutual fund** is a financial intermediary that creates a stock portfolio by buying and holding shares in companies and then selling *shares of the stock portfolio* to individual investors. By buying these shares, investors with a relatively small amount of money to invest can indirectly hold a diversified portfolio, achieving a better return for any given level of risk than they could otherwise achieve.

The daily performance of hundreds of different mutual funds is listed in the business section of most large city newspapers.

The mutual fund industry represents a huge portion of the modern U.S. economy, not just of the U.S. financial system. In total, U.S. mutual funds had assets of $10 trillion in late 2009. The largest mutual fund company at the end of 2009 was Fidelity Investments, which managed $1.5 trillion in funds.

We should mention, by the way, that mutual funds do charge fees for their services. These fees are quite small for mutual funds that simply hold a diversified portfolio of stocks, without trying to pick winners. But the fees charged by mutual funds that claim to have special expertise in investing your money can be quite high.

Pension Funds and Life Insurance Companies In addition to mutual funds, many Americans have holdings in **pension funds,** nonprofit institutions that collect the savings of their members and invest those funds in a wide variety of assets, providing their members with income when they retire. Although pension funds are subject to some special rules and receive special treatment for tax purposes, they function much like mutual funds. They invest in a diverse array of financial assets, allowing their members to achieve more cost-effective diversification and conduct more market research than they would be able to individually. At the end of 2009, pension funds in the United States held more than $9 trillion in assets.

Americans also have substantial holdings in the policies of **life insurance companies,** which guarantee a payment to the policyholder's beneficiaries (typically, the family) when the policyholder dies. By enabling policyholders to cushion their beneficiaries from financial hardship arising from their death, life insurance companies also improve welfare by reducing risk.

Banks Recall the problem of liquidity: other things equal, people want assets that can be readily converted into cash. Bonds and stocks are much more liquid than physical assets or loans, yet the transaction cost of selling bonds or stocks to meet a sudden expense can be large. Furthermore, for many small and moderate-size companies, the cost of issuing bonds and stocks is too large, given the modest amount of money they seek to raise. A *bank* is an institution that helps resolve the conflict between lenders' needs for liquidity and the financing needs of borrowers who don't want to use the stock or bond markets.

A bank works by first accepting funds from *depositors:* when you put your money in a bank, you are essentially becoming a lender by lending the bank your money. In return,

A **mutual fund** is a financial intermediary that creates a stock portfolio and then resells shares of this portfolio to individual investors.

A **pension fund** is a type of mutual fund that holds assets in order to provide retirement income to its members.

A **life insurance company** sells policies that guarantee a payment to a policyholder's beneficiaries when the policyholder dies.

Jay Brousseau/Getty Images

you receive credit for a **bank deposit**—a claim on the bank, which is obliged to give you your cash if and when you demand it. So a bank deposit is a financial asset owned by the depositor and a liability of the bank that holds it.

A bank, however, keeps only a fraction of its customers' deposits in the form of ready cash. Most of its deposits are lent out to businesses, buyers of new homes, and other borrowers. These loans come with a long-term commitment by the bank to the borrower: as long as the borrower makes his or her payments on time, the loan cannot be recalled by the bank and converted into cash. So a bank enables those who wish to borrow for long lengths of time to use the funds of those who wish to lend but simultaneously want to maintain the ability to get their cash back on demand. More formally, a **bank** is a financial intermediary that provides liquid financial assets in the form of deposits to lenders and uses their funds to finance the illiquid investment spending needs of borrowers.

In essence, a bank is engaging in a kind of mismatch: lending for long periods of time but also subject to the condition that its depositors could demand their funds back at any time. How can it manage that?

The bank counts on the fact that, on average, only a small fraction of its depositors will want their cash at the same time. On any given day, some people will make withdrawals and others will make new deposits; these will roughly cancel each other out. So the bank needs to keep only a limited amount of cash on hand to satisfy its depositors. In addition, if a bank becomes financially incapable of paying its depositors, individual bank deposits are currently guaranteed to depositors up to $250,000 by the Federal Deposit Insurance Corporation, or FDIC, a federal agency. This reduces the risk to a depositor of holding a bank deposit, in turn reducing the incentive to withdraw funds if concerns about the financial state of the bank should arise. So, under normal conditions, banks need hold only a fraction of their depositors' cash.

By reconciling the needs of savers for liquid assets with the needs of borrowers for long-term financing, banks play a key economic role.

A **bank deposit** is a claim on a bank that obliges the bank to give the depositor his or her cash when demanded.

A **bank** is a financial intermediary that provides liquid assets in the form of bank deposits to lenders and uses those funds to finance the illiquid investment spending needs of borrowers.

Module 22 AP Review

Solutions appear at the back of the book.

Check Your Understanding

1. Rank the following assets from the lowest level to the highest level of (i) transaction costs, (ii) risk, (iii) liquidity. Ties are acceptable for items that have indistinguishable rankings.
   a. a bank deposit with a guaranteed interest rate
   b. a share of a highly diversified mutual fund, which can be quickly sold
   c. a share of the family business, which can be sold only if you find a buyer and all other family members agree to the sale

2. What relationship would you expect to find between the level of development of a country's financial system and its level of economic development? Explain in terms of the country's levels of savings and investment spending.

Tackle the Test: Multiple-Choice Questions

1. Decreasing which of the following is a task of the financial system?
      I. transaction costs
      II. risk
      III. liquidity
   a. I only
   b. II only
   c. III only
   d. I and II only
   e. I, II, and III

2. Which of the following is NOT a type of financial asset?
   a. bonds
   b. stocks
   c. bank deposits
   d. loans
   e. houses

3. The federal government is said to be "dissaving" when
   a. there is a budget deficit.
   b. there is a budget surplus.
   c. there is no budget surplus or deficit.
   d. savings does not equal investment spending.
   e. national savings equals private savings.

4. A nonprofit institution collects the savings of its members and invests those funds in a wide variety of assets in order to provide its members with income after retirement. This describes a
   a. mutual fund.
   b. bank.

   c. savings and loan.
   d. pension fund.
   e. life insurance company.

5. A financial intermediary that provides liquid financial assets in the form of deposits to lenders and uses their funds to finance the illiquid investment spending needs of borrowers is called a
   a. mutual fund.
   b. bank.
   c. corporation.
   d. pension fund.
   e. life insurance company.

Tackle the Test: Free-Response Questions

1. Identify and describe the three tasks of a well-functioning financial system.

2. List and describe the four most important types of financial intermediaries.

> **Answer (6 points)**
>
> **1 point:** Decrease transaction costs
>
> **1 point:** A well-functioning financial system facilitates investment spending by allowing companies to borrow large sums of money without incurring large transaction costs.
>
> **1 point:** Decrease risk
>
> **1 point:** A well-functioning financial system helps people reduce their exposure to risk, so that they are more willing to engage in investment spending in the face of uncertainty in the economy.
>
> **1 point:** Provide liquidity
>
> **1 point:** A well-functioning financial system allows the fast, low-cost conversion of assets into cash.

Module 23
The Definition and Measurement of Money

What you will learn in this Module:

- The definition and functions of money

- The various roles money plays and the many forms it takes in the economy

- How the amount of money in the economy is measured

The Meaning of Money

In everyday conversation, people often use the word *money* to mean "wealth." If you ask, "How much money does Bill Gates have?" the answer will be something like, "Oh, $50 billion or so, but who's counting?" That is, the number will include the value of the stocks, bonds, real estate, and other assets he owns.

But the economist's definition of money doesn't include all forms of wealth. The dollar bills in your wallet are money; other forms of wealth—such as cars, houses, and stock certificates—aren't money. What, according to economists, distinguishes money from other forms of wealth?

What Is Money?

Money is defined in terms of what it does: **money** is any asset that can easily be used to purchase goods and services. In Module 22 we defined an asset as *liquid* if it can easily be converted into cash. Money consists of cash itself, which is liquid by definition, as well as other assets that are highly liquid.

You can see the distinction between money and other assets by asking yourself how you pay for groceries. The person at the cash register will accept dollar bills in return for milk and frozen pizza—but he or she won't accept stock certificates or a collection of vintage baseball cards. If you want to convert stock certificates or vintage baseball cards into groceries, you have to sell them—trade them for money—and then use the money to buy groceries.

Of course, many stores allow you to write a check on your bank account in payment for goods (or to pay with a debit card that is linked to your bank account). Does that make your bank account money, even if you haven't converted it into cash? Yes. **Currency in circulation**—actual cash in the hands of the public—is considered money. So are **checkable bank deposits**—bank accounts on which people can write checks.

Are currency and checkable bank deposits the only assets that are considered money? It depends. As we'll see later, there are two widely used definitions of the **money supply,**

Money is any asset that can easily be used to purchase goods and services.

Currency in circulation is cash held by the public.

Checkable bank deposits are bank accounts on which people can write checks.

The **money supply** is the total value of financial assets in the economy that are considered money.

the total value of financial assets in the economy that are considered money. The narrower definition considers only the most liquid assets to be money: currency in circulation, traveler's checks, and checkable bank deposits. The broader definition includes these three categories plus other assets that are "almost" checkable, such as savings account deposits that can be transferred into a checking account online with a few mouse clicks. Both definitions of the money supply, however, make a distinction between those assets that can easily be used to purchase goods and services, and those that can't.

Money plays a crucial role in generating *gains from trade* because it makes indirect exchange possible. Think of what happens when a cardiac surgeon buys a new refrigerator. The surgeon has valuable services to offer—namely, performing heart operations. The owner of the store has valuable goods to offer: refrigerators and other appliances. It would be extremely difficult for both parties if, instead of using money, they had to directly barter the goods and services they sell. In a barter system, a cardiac surgeon and an appliance store owner could trade only if the store owner happened to want a heart operation *and* the surgeon happened to want a new refrigerator. This is known as the problem of finding a "double coincidence of wants": in a barter system, two parties can trade only when each wants what the other has to offer. Money solves this problem: individuals can trade what they have to offer for money and trade money for what they want.

Because the ability to make transactions with money rather than relying on bartering makes it easier to achieve gains from trade, the existence of money increases welfare, even though money does not directly produce anything. As Adam Smith put it, money "may very properly be compared to a highway, which, while it circulates and carries to market all the grass and corn of the country, produces itself not a single pile of either."

Let's take a closer look at the roles money plays in the economy.

Roles of Money

Money plays three main roles in any modern economy: it is a *medium of exchange,* a *store of value,* and a *unit of account.*

Medium of Exchange Our cardiac surgeon/appliance store owner example illustrates the role of money as a **medium of exchange**—an asset that individuals use to trade for goods and services rather than for consumption. People can't eat dollar bills; rather, they use dollar bills to trade for edible goods and their accompanying services.

In normal times, the official money of a given country—the dollar in the United States, the peso in Mexico, and so on—is also the medium of exchange in virtually all transactions in that country. During troubled economic times, however, other goods or assets often play that role instead. For example, during economic turmoil people often turn to other countries' moneys as the medium of exchange: U.S. dollars have played this role in troubled Latin American countries, as have euros in troubled Eastern European countries. In a famous example, cigarettes functioned as the medium of exchange in World War II prisoner-of-war camps. Even nonsmokers traded goods and services for cigarettes because the cigarettes could in turn be easily traded for other items. During the extreme German inflation of 1923, goods such as eggs and lumps of coal became, briefly, mediums of exchange.

Gambling at the Stalag 383 prisoner of war camp during World War II was carried out using cigarettes as currency.

Store of Value In order to act as a medium of exchange, money must also be a **store of value**—a means of holding purchasing power over time. To see why this is necessary, imagine trying to operate an economy in which ice-cream cones were the medium of exchange. Such an economy would quickly suffer from, well, monetary meltdown: your medium of exchange would often turn into a sticky puddle before you could use it to buy something else. Of course, money is by no means the only store of value. Any asset that holds its purchasing power over time is a store of value. So the store-of-value role is a necessary but not distinctive feature of money.

Unit of Account Finally, money normally serves as the **unit of account**—the commonly accepted measure individuals use to set prices and make economic calculations. To understand the importance of this role, consider a historical fact: during the Middle Ages, peasants typically were required to provide landowners with goods and labor rather than money. A peasant might, for example, be required to work on the landowner's land one day a week and also hand over one-fifth of his harvest. Today, rents, like other prices, are almost always specified in money terms. That makes things much clearer: imagine how hard it would be to decide which apartment to rent if modern landowners followed medieval practice. Suppose, for example, that Mr. Smith says he'll let you have a place if you clean his house twice a week and bring him a pound of steak every day, whereas Ms. Jones wants you to clean her house just once a week but wants four pounds of chicken every day. Who's offering the better deal? It's hard to say. If, on the other hand, Smith wants $600 a month and Jones wants $700, the comparison is easy. In other words, without a commonly accepted measure, the terms of a transaction are harder to determine, making it more difficult to make transactions and achieve gains from trade.

A **unit of account** is a measure used to set prices and make economic calculations.

Commodity money is a good used as a medium of exchange that has intrinsic value in other uses.

Commodity-backed money is a medium of exchange with no intrinsic value whose ultimate value is guaranteed by a promise that it can be converted into valuable goods.

Types of Money

In some form or another, money has been in use for thousands of years. For most of that period, people used **commodity money:** the medium of exchange was a good, normally gold or silver, that had intrinsic value in other uses. These alternative uses gave commodity money value independent of its role as a medium of exchange. For example, the cigarettes that served as money in World War II POW camps were valuable because many prisoners smoked. Gold was valuable because it was used for jewelry and ornamentation, aside from the fact that it was minted into coins.

By 1776, the year in which the United States declared its independence and Adam Smith published *The Wealth of Nations,* there was widespread use of paper money in addition to gold or silver coins. Unlike modern dollar bills, however, this paper money consisted of notes issued by private banks, which promised to exchange their notes for gold or silver coins on demand. So the paper currency that initially replaced commodity money was **commodity-backed money,** a medium of exchange with no intrinsic value whose ultimate value was guaranteed by a promise that it could always be converted into valuable goods on demand.

The big advantage of commodity-backed money over simple commodity money, like gold and silver coins, was that it tied up fewer valuable resources. Although a note-issuing bank still had to keep some gold and silver on hand, it had to keep only enough to satisfy demands for redemption of its notes. And it could rely on the fact that on a normal day only a fraction of its paper notes would be redeemed. So the bank needed to keep only a portion of the total value of its notes in circulation in the form of gold and silver in its vaults. It could lend out the remaining gold and silver to those who wished to use it. This allowed society to use the remaining gold and silver for other purposes, all with no loss in the ability to achieve gains from trade.

In a famous passage in *The Wealth of Nations,* Adam Smith described paper money as a "waggon-way through the air." Smith was making an analogy between money and an imaginary highway that did not absorb valuable land beneath it. An actual highway provides a useful service but at a cost: land that could be used to grow crops is instead paved over. If the highway could be built through the air, it wouldn't destroy useful land. As Smith understood, when banks replaced gold and silver money with paper notes, they accomplished a similar feat: they reduced the amount of real resources used by society to provide the functions of money.

At this point you may ask, why make any use at all of gold and silver in the monetary system, even to back paper money? In fact, today's monetary system goes even further than the system Smith admired, having eliminated any role for gold and silver. A U.S. dollar bill isn't commodity money, and it isn't even commodity-backed. Rather, its value arises entirely from the fact that it is generally accepted as a means of payment, a

The History of the Dollar

U.S. dollar bills are pure fiat money: they have no intrinsic value, and they are not backed by anything that does. But American money wasn't always like that. In the early days of European settlement, the colonies that would become the United States used commodity money, partly consisting of gold and silver coins minted in Europe. But such coins were scarce on this side of the Atlantic, so the colonists relied on a variety of other forms of commodity money. For example, settlers in Virginia used tobacco as money and settlers in the Northeast used "wampum," a type of clamshell.

Later in American history, commodity-backed paper money came into widespread use. But this wasn't paper money as we now know it, issued by the U.S. government and bearing the signature of the Secretary of the Treasury. Before the Civil War, the U.S. government didn't issue any paper money. Instead, dollar bills were issued by private banks, which promised that their bills could be redeemed for silver coins on demand. These promises weren't always credible because banks sometimes failed, leaving holders of their bills with worthless pieces of paper. Understandably, people were reluctant to accept currency from any bank rumored to be in financial trouble. In other words, in this private money system, some dollars were less valuable than others.

A curious legacy of that time was notes issued by the Citizens' Bank of Louisiana, based in New Orleans They became among the most widely used bank notes in the southern states. These notes were printed in English on one side and French on the other. (At the time, many people in New Orleans, originally a colony of France, spoke French.) Thus, the $10 bill read *Ten* on one side and *Dix*, the French word for "ten," on the other. These $10 bills became known as "dixies," probably the source of the nickname of the U.S. South.

The U.S. government began issuing official paper money, called "greenbacks," during the Civil War, as a way to help pay for the war. At first greenbacks had no fixed value in terms of commodities. After 1873, the U.S. government guaranteed the value of a dollar in terms of gold, effectively turning dollars into commodity-backed money.

In 1933, when President Franklin D. Roosevelt broke the link between dollars and gold, his own federal budget director—who feared that the public would lose confidence in the dollar if it wasn't ultimately backed by gold—declared ominously, "This will be the end of Western civilization." It wasn't. The link between the dollar and gold was restored a few years later, and then dropped again—seemingly for good—in August 1971. Despite the warnings of doom, the U.S. dollar is still the world's most widely used currency.

The image of a valid U.S. five-dollar bill shows a pattern in the background of the Lincoln Memorial image as seen through a Document Security Systems, Inc. document verifier.

role that is ultimately decreed by the U.S. government. Money whose value derives entirely from its official status as a means of exchange is known as **fiat money** because it exists by government *fiat*, a historical term for a policy declared by a ruler.

Fiat money has two major advantages over commodity-backed money. First, it is even more of a "waggon-way through the air"—it doesn't tie up any real resources, except for the paper it's printed on. Second, the money supply can be managed based on the needs of the economy, instead of being determined by the amount of gold and silver prospectors happen to discover.

On the other hand, fiat money poses some risks. One such risk is counterfeiting. Counterfeiters usurp a privilege of the U.S. government, which has the sole legal right to print dollar bills. And the benefit that counterfeiters get by exchanging fake bills for real goods and services comes at the expense of the U.S. federal government, which covers a small but nontrivial part of its own expenses by issuing new currency to meet growing demand for money.

The larger risk is that government officials who have the authority to print money will be tempted to abuse the privilege by printing so much money that they create inflation.

Measuring the Money Supply

The Federal Reserve (an institution we'll talk about shortly) calculates the size of two **monetary aggregates,** overall measures of the money supply, which differ in how strictly money is defined. The two aggregates are known, rather cryptically, as M1 and M2. (There used to be a third aggregate named—you guessed it—M3, but in 2006 the Federal Reserve concluded that measuring it was no longer useful.) M1, the narrowest definition, contains only currency in circulation (also known as cash),

Fiat money is a medium of exchange whose value derives entirely from its official status as a means of payment.

A **monetary aggregate** is an overall measure of the money supply.

What's with All the Currency?

Alert readers may be a bit startled at one of the numbers in the money supply: $861.1 billion of currency in circulation in January 2010. That's $2,789 in cash for every man, woman, and child in the United States. How many people do you know who carry $2,789 in their wallets? Not many. So where is all that cash?

Part of the answer is that it isn't in individuals' wallets: it's in cash registers. Businesses as well as individuals need to hold cash.

Economists also believe that cash plays an important role in transactions that people want to keep hidden. Small businesses and the self-employed sometimes prefer to be paid in cash so they can avoid paying taxes by hiding income from the Internal Revenue Service. Also, drug dealers and other criminals obviously don't want bank records of their dealings. In fact, some analysts have tried to infer the amount of illegal activity in the economy from the total amount of cash holdings held by the public. The most important reason for those huge currency holdings, however, is foreign use of dollars. The Federal Reserve estimates that 60% of U.S. currency is actually held outside the United States—largely in countries in which residents are so distrustful of their national currencies that the U.S. dollar has become a widely accepted medium of exchange.

© S Meltzer/PhotoLink

traveler's checks, and checkable bank deposits. M2 starts with M1 and adds several other kinds of assets, often referred to as **near-moneys**—financial assets that aren't directly usable as a medium of exchange but can be readily converted into cash or checkable bank deposits, such as savings accounts. Examples are time deposits such as small denomination CDs, which aren't checkable but can be withdrawn at any time before their maturity date by paying a penalty. Because currency and checkable deposits are directly usable as a medium of exchange, M1 is the most liquid measure of money.

In January 2010, M1 was valued at $1,676.4 billion, with approximately 51% accounted for by currency in circulation, approximately 48% accounted for by checkable bank deposits, and a tiny slice accounted for by traveler's checks. In turn, M1 made up 20% of M2, valued at $8,462.9 billion. M2 consists of M1 plus other types of assets: two types of bank deposits, known as savings deposits and time deposits, both of which are considered noncheckable, plus money market funds, which are mutual funds that invest only in liquid assets and bear a close resemblance to bank deposits. These near-moneys pay interest while cash (currency in circulation) does not, and they typically pay higher interest rates than any offered on checkable bank deposits.

> **Near-moneys** are financial assets that can't be directly used as a medium of exchange but can be readily converted into cash or checkable bank deposits.

Module 23 AP Review

Solutions appear at the back of the book.

Check Your Understanding

1. Suppose you hold a gift certificate, good for certain products at participating stores. Is this gift certificate money? Why or why not?

2. Although most bank accounts pay some interest, depositors can get a higher interest rate by buying a certificate of deposit, or CD. The difference between a CD and a checking account is that the depositor pays a penalty for withdrawing the money before the CD comes due—a period of months or even years. Small CDs are counted in M2, but not in M1. Explain why they are not part of M1.

3. Explain why a system of commodity-backed money uses resources more efficiently than a system of commodity money.

Tackle the Test: Multiple-Choice Questions

1. When you use money to purchase your lunch, money is serving which role(s)?
   I. medium of exchange
   II. store of value
   III. unit of account
   a. I only
   b. II only
   c. III only
   d. I and III only
   e. I, II, and III

2. When you decide you want "$10 worth" of a product, money is serving which role(s)?
   I. medium of exchange
   II. store of value
   III. unit of account
   a. I only
   b. II only
   c. III only
   d. I and II only
   e. I, II, and III

3. In the United States, the dollar is
   a. backed by silver.
   b. backed by gold and silver.
   c. commodity-backed money.
   d. commodity money.
   e. fiat money.

4. Which of the following is the most liquid monetary aggregate?
   a. M1
   b. M2
   c. M3
   d. near-moneys
   e. dollar bills

5. Which of the following is the best example of using money as a store of value?
   a. A customer pays in advance for $10 worth of gasoline at a gas station.
   b. A babysitter puts her earnings in a dresser drawer while she saves to buy a bicycle.
   c. Travelers buy meals on board an airline flight.
   d. Foreign visitors to the United States convert their currency to dollars at the airport.
   e. You use $1 bills to purchase soda from a vending machine.

Tackle the Test: Free-Response Questions

1. a. What does it mean for an asset to be "liquid"?
   b. Which of the assets listed below is the most liquid? Explain.
      A Federal Reserve note (dollar bill)
      A savings account deposit
      A house
   c. Which of the assets listed above is the least liquid? Explain.
   d. In which monetary aggregate(s) calculated by the Federal Reserve are checkable deposits included?

2. a. The U.S. dollar derives its value from what? That is, what "backs" U.S. currency?
   b. What is the term used to describe the type of money used in the United States today?
   c. What other two types of money have been used throughout history? Define each.

> **Answer (6 points)**
>
> **1 point:** It can be easily converted into cash.
>
> **1 point:** A Federal Reserve note
>
> **1 point:** It is already cash.
>
> **1 point:** A house
>
> **1 point:** It takes time and resources to sell a house.
>
> **1 point:** M1 and M2

Module 24
The Time Value of Money

The Concept of Present Value

Individuals are often faced with financial decisions that will have consequences long into the future. For example, when you decide to attend college, you are committing yourself to years of study, which you expect will pay off for the rest of your life. So the decision to attend college is a decision to embark on a long-term project.

The basic rule in deciding whether or not to undertake a project is that you should compare the benefits of that project with its costs, implicit as well as explicit. But making these comparisons can sometimes be difficult because the benefits and costs of a project may not arrive at the same time. Sometimes the costs of a project come at an earlier date than the benefits. For example, going to college involves large immediate costs: tuition, income forgone because you are in school, and so on. The benefits, such as a higher salary in your future career, come later, often much later. In other cases, the benefits of a project come at an earlier date than the costs. If you take out a loan to pay for a vacation cruise, the satisfaction of the vacation will come immediately, but the burden of making payments will come later.

How, specifically is time an issue in economic decision-making?

Borrowing, Lending, and Interest

In general, having a dollar today is worth more than having a dollar a year from now. To see why, let's consider two examples.

First, suppose that you get a new job that comes with a $1,000 bonus, which will be paid at the end of the first year. But you would like to spend the extra money now—say, on new clothes for work. Can you do that?

The answer is yes—you can borrow money today and use the bonus to repay the debt a year from now. But if that is your plan, you cannot borrow the full $1,000 today. You must borrow *less* than that because a year from now you will have to repay the amount borrowed *plus interest*.

Now consider a different scenario. Suppose that you are paid a bonus of $1,000 today, and you decide that you don't want to spend the money until a year from now. What do you do with it? You put it in the bank; in effect, you are lending the $1,000 to the bank, which in turn lends it out to its customers who wish to borrow. At the end of a year, you will get *more* than $1,000 back—you will receive the $1,000 plus the interest earned.

All of this means that having $1,000 today is worth more than having $1,000 a year from now. As any borrower and lender know, this is what allows a lender to charge a borrower interest on a loan: borrowers are willing to pay interest in order to have money today rather than waiting until they acquire that money later on. Most interest rates are stated as the percentage of the borrowed amount that must be paid to the lender for each year of the loan. Whether money is actually borrowed for 1 month or 10 years, and regardless of the amount, the same principle applies: money in your pocket today is worth more than money in your pocket tomorrow. To keep things simple in the discussions that follow, we'll restrict ourselves to examples of 1-year loans of $1.

Because the value of money depends on when it is paid or received, you can't evaluate a project by simply adding up the costs and benefits when those costs and benefits arrive at different times. You must take time into account when evaluating the project because $1 that is paid to you today is worth more than $1 that is paid to you a year from now. Similarly, $1 that you must pay today is more burdensome than $1 that you must pay next year. Fortunately, there is a simple way to adjust for these complications so that we can correctly compare the value of dollars received and paid out at different times.

Next we'll see how the interest rate can be used to convert future benefits and costs into what economists call *present values*. By using present values when evaluating a project, you can evaluate a project *as if* all relevant costs and benefits were occurring today rather than at different times. This allows people to "factor out" the complications created by time. We'll start by defining the concept of present value.

Defining Present Value

The key to the concept of present value is to understand that you can use the interest rate to compare the value of a dollar realized today with the value of a dollar realized later. Why the interest rate? Because the interest rate correctly measures the cost to you of delaying the receipt of a dollar of benefit and, correspondingly, the benefit to you of delaying the payment of a dollar of cost. Let's illustrate this with some examples.

Suppose that you are evaluating whether or not to take a job in which your employer promises to pay you a bonus at the end of the first year. What is the value to you today of $1 of bonus money to be paid one year in the future? A slightly different way of asking the same question: what amount would you be willing to accept today as a substitute for receiving $1 one year from now?

To answer this question, begin by observing that you need *less* than $1 today in order to be assured of having $1 one year from now. Why? Because any money that you have today can be lent out at interest—say, by depositing it in a bank account so that the bank can then lend it out to its borrowers. This turns any amount you have today into a greater sum at the end of the year.

Let's work this out mathematically. We'll use the symbol r to represent the interest rate, expressed in decimal terms—that is, if the interest rate is 10%, then $r = 0.10$. If you lend out X, at the end of a year you will receive your X back, plus the interest on your X, which is $X \times r$. Thus, at the end of the year you will receive:

(24-1) Amount received one year from now as a result of lending X today $=$
$X + X \times r = X \times (1 + r)$

The next step is to find out how much you would have to lend out today to have $1 a year from now. To do that, we just need to set Equation 24-1 equal to $1 and solve for X. That is, we solve the following equation for X:

(24-2) Condition satisfied when $1 is received one year from now as a result of lending X today: $X \times (1 + r) = \$1$

Rearranging Equation 24-2 to solve for $X, the amount you need today in order to receive $1 one year from now is:

(24-3)   Amount lent today in order to receive $1 one year from now =
$$\$X = \$1/(1 + r)$$

The **present value** of $1 realized one year from now is equal to $1/(1 + r)$: the amount of money you must lend out today in order to have $1 in one year. It is the value to you today of $1 realized one year from now.

This means that you would be willing to accept today the amount $X defined by Equation 24-3 for every $1 to be paid to you one year from now. The reason is that if you were to lend out $X today, you would be assured of receiving $1 one year from now. Returning to our original question, this also means that if someone promises to pay you a sum of money one year in the future, you are willing to accept $X today in place of every $1 to be paid one year from now.

Now let's solve Equation 24-3 for the value of $X. To do this we simply need to use the actual value of r (a value determined by the financial markets). Let's assume that the actual value of r is 10%, which means that $r = 0.10$. In that case:

(24-4)   Value of $X when $r = 0.10$: $X = \$1/(1 + 0.10) = \$1/1.10 = \$0.91$

So you would be willing to accept $0.91 today in exchange for every $1 to be paid to you one year from now. Economists have a special name for $X—it's called the **present value** of $1. Note that the present value of any given amount will change as the interest rate changes.

To see that this technique works for evaluating future costs as well as evaluating future benefits, consider the following example. Suppose you enter into an agreement that obliges you to pay $1 one year from now—say, to pay off a car loan from your parents when you graduate in a year. How much money would you need today to ensure that you have $1 in a year? The answer is $X, the present value of $1, which in our example is $0.91. The reason $0.91 is the right answer is that if you lend it out for one year at an interest rate of 10%, you will receive $1 in return at the end. So if, for example, you must pay back $5,000 one year from now, then you need to deposit $5,000 × 0.91 = $4,550 into a bank account today earning an interest rate of 10% in order to have $5,000 one year from now. (There is a slight discrepancy due to rounding.) In other words, today you need to have the present value of $5,000, which equals $4,550, in order to be assured of paying off your debt in a year.

In the 1971 movie *Willy Wonka and the Chocolate Factory,* Veruca Salt appreciated the added value of having things in the present. She wanted a "golden-egg-laying-goose NOW!"

These examples show us that the present value concept provides a way to calculate the value today of $1 that is realized in a year—regardless of whether that $1 is realized as a benefit (the bonus) or a cost (the car loan payback). To evaluate a project today that has benefits, costs, or both to be realized in a year, we just use the relevant interest rate to convert those future dollars into their present values. In that way we have "factored out" the complication that time creates for decision making.

Below we will use the present value concept to evaluate a project. But before we do that, it is worthwhile to note that the present value method can be used for projects in which the $1 is realized more than a year later—say, two, three, or even more years. Suppose you are considering a project that will pay you $1 *two* years from today. What is the value to you today of $1 received two years into the future? We can find the answer to that question by expanding our formula for present value.

Let's call $V the amount of money you need to lend today at an interest rate of r in order to have $1 in two years. So if you lend $V today, you will receive $V \times (1 + r)$ in one year. And if you *re-lend* that sum for another year, you will receive $\$V \times (1 + r) \times (1 + r) = \$V \times (1 + r)^2$ at the end of the second year. At the end of two years, $V will be worth $\$V \times (1 + r)^2$. In other words:

(24-5)   Amount received in one year from lending $V = $V \times (1 + r)$

Amount received in two years from lending $\$V = \$V \times (1+r) \times (1+r) = \$V \times (1+r)^2$ and so on. For example, if $r = 0.10$, then $\$V \times (1.10)^2 = \$V \times 1.21$.

Now we are ready to answer the question of what $1 realized two years in the future is worth today. In order for the amount lent today, $\$V$, to be worth $1 two years from now, it must satisfy this formula:

(24-6) Condition satisfied when $1 is received two years from now as a result of lending $\$V$ today: $\$V \times (1+r)^2 = \$1$

Rearranging Equation 24-6, we can solve for $\$V$:

(24-7) Amount lent today in order to receive $1 two years from now = $\$V = \$1/(1+r)^2$

Given $r = 0.10$ and using Equation 24-7, we arrive at $\$V = \$1/1.21 = \$0.83$. So, when the interest rate is 10%, $1 realized two years from today is worth $0.83 today because by lending out $0.83 today you can be assured of having $1 in two years. And that means that the present value of $1 realized two years into the future is $0.83.

(24-8) Present value of $1 realized two years from now = $\$V = \$1/(1.10)^2 = \$1/1.21 = \$0.83$

From this example we can see how the present value concept can be expanded to a number of years even greater than two. If we ask what the present value is of $1 realized any number of years, represented by N, into the future, the answer is given by a generalization of the present value formula: it is equal to $\$1/(1+r)^N$.

Using Present Value

Suppose you have to choose one of three hypothetical projects to undertake. Project A costs nothing and has an immediate payoff to you of $100. Project B requires that you pay $10 today in order to receive $115 a year from now. Project C gives you an immediate payoff of $119 but requires that you pay $20 a year from now. We'll assume that the annual interest rate is 10%—that is, $r = 0.10$.

The problem in evaluating these three projects is that their costs and benefits are realized at different times. That is, of course, where the concept of present value becomes extremely helpful: by using present value to convert any dollars realized in the future into today's value, you factor out the issue of time. Appropriate comparisons can be made using the **net present value** of a project—the present value of current and future benefits minus the present value of current and future costs. The best project to undertake is the one with the highest net present value.

Table 24.1 shows how to calculate net present value for each of the three projects. The second and third columns show how many dollars are realized and when

table **24.1**

The Net Present Value of Three Hypothetical Projects

Project	Dollars realized today	Dollars realized one year from today	Present value formula	Net present value given $r = 0.10$
A	$100	—	$100	$100.00
B	−$10	$115	−$10 + $115/(1 + r)	$94.55
C	$119	−$20	$119 − $20/(1 + r)	$100.82

How Big Is That Jackpot, Anyway?

For a clear example of present value at work, consider the case of lottery jackpots.

On March 6, 2007, Mega Millions set the record for the largest jackpot ever in North America, with a payout of $390 million. Well, sort of. That $390 million was available only if you chose to take your winnings in the form of an "annuity," consisting of an annual payment for the next 26 years. If you wanted cash up front, the jackpot was only $233 million and change.

Why was Mega Millions so stingy about quick payoffs? It was all a matter of present value. If the winner had been willing to take the annuity, the lottery would have invested the jackpot money, buying U.S. government bonds (in effect lending the money to the federal government). The money would have been invested in such a way that the investments would pay just enough to cover the annuity. This worked, of course, because at the interest rates prevailing at the time, the present value of a $390 million annuity spread over 26 years was just about $233 million. To put it another way, the opportunity cost to the lottery of that annuity in present value terms was $233 million.

So why didn't they just call it a $233 million jackpot? Well, $390 million sounds more impressive! But receiving $390 million over 26 years is essentially the same as receiving $233 million today.

they are realized; costs are indicated by a minus sign. The fourth column shows the equations used to convert the flows of dollars into their present value, and the fifth column shows the actual amounts of the total net present value for each of the three projects.

For instance, to calculate the net present value of project B, we need to calculate the present value of $115 received in one year. The present value of $1 received in one year would be $1/(1 + r)$. So the present value of $115 is equal to $115 \times \$1/(1 + r)$; that is, $\$115/(1 + r)$. The net present value of project B is the present value of today's and future benefits minus the present value of today's and future costs: $-\$10 + \$115/(1 + r)$.

From the fifth column, we can immediately see which is the preferred project—it is project C. That's because it has the highest net present value, $100.82, which is higher than the net present value of project A ($100) and much higher than the net present value of project B ($94.55).

This example shows how important the concept of present value is. If we had failed to use the present value calculations and instead simply added up the dollars generated by each of the three projects, we could have easily been misled into believing that project B was the best project and project C was the worst.

Module 24 AP Review

Solutions appear at the back of the book.

Check Your Understanding

1. Consider the three hypothetical projects shown in Table 24.1. This time, however, suppose that the interest rate is only 2%.
   a. Calculate the net present values of the three projects. Which one is now preferred?
   b. Explain why the preferred choice is different with a 2% interest rate from with a 10% interest rate.

Tackle the Test: Multiple-Choice Questions

1. Suppose, for simplicity, that a bank uses a single interest rate for loans and deposits, there is no inflation, and all unspent money is deposited in the bank. The interest rate measures which of the following?

   I. the cost of using a dollar today rather than a year from now

   II. the benefit of delaying the use of a dollar from today until a year from now

   III. the price of borrowing money calculated as a percentage of the amount borrowed

   a. I only
   b. II only
   c. III only
   d. I and II only
   e. I, II, and III

2. If the interest rate is zero, then the present value of a dollar received at the end of the year is
   a. more than $1.
   b. equal to $1.
   c. less than $1.
   d. zero.
   e. infinite.

3. If the interest rate is 10%, the present value of $1 paid to you one year from now is
   a. $0.
   b. $0.89.
   c. $0.91.
   d. $1.
   e. more than $1.

4. If the interest rate is 5%, the amount received one year from now as a result of lending $100 today is
   a. $90.
   b. $95.
   c. $100.
   d. $105.
   e. $110.

5. What is the present value of $100 realized two years from now if the interest rate is 10%?
   a. $80
   b. $83
   c. $90
   d. $100
   e. $110

Tackle the Test: Free-Response Questions

1. a. Calculate the net present value of each of the three hypothetical projects described below. Assume the interest rate is 5%.
      Project A: You receive an immediate payoff of $1,000.
      Project B: You pay $100 today in order to receive $1,200 a year from now.
      Project C: You receive $1,200 today but must pay $200 one year from now.
   b. Which of the three projects would you choose to undertake based on your net present value calculations? Explain.

2. a. What is the amount you will receive in three years if you loan $1,000 at 5% interest?
   b. What is the present value of $1,000 received in three years if the interest rate is 5%?

Answer (5 points)

1 point: Project A net present value: $1,000

1 point: Project B net present value: −$100 + ($1,200/1.05) = $1,042.86

1 point: Project C net present value: $1,200 − ($200/1.05) = $1,009.52

1 point: Choose project B.

1 point: It has the highest net present value.

Module 25
Banking and Money Creation

What you will learn in this Module:

- The role of banks in the economy
- The reasons for and types of banking regulation
- How banks create money

The Monetary Role of Banks

More than half of M1, the narrowest definition of the money supply, consists of currency in circulation—$1 bills, $5 bills, and so on. It's obvious where currency comes from: it's printed by the U.S. Treasury. But the rest of M1 consists of bank deposits, and deposits account for the great bulk of M2, the broader definition of the money supply. By either measure, then, bank deposits are a major component of the money supply. And this fact brings us to our next topic: the monetary role of banks.

What Banks Do

A bank is a *financial intermediary* that uses liquid assets in the form of bank deposits to finance the illiquid investments of borrowers. Banks can create liquidity because it isn't necessary for a bank to keep all of the funds deposited with it in the form of highly liquid assets. Except in the case of a *bank run*—which we'll get to shortly—all of a bank's depositors won't want to withdraw their funds at the same time. So a bank can provide its depositors with liquid assets yet still invest much of the depositors' funds in illiquid assets, such as mortgages and business loans.

Banks can't, however, lend out all the funds placed in their hands by depositors because they have to satisfy any depositor who wants to withdraw his or her funds. In order to meet these demands, a bank must keep substantial quantities of liquid assets on hand. In the modern U.S. banking system, these assets take the form either of currency in the bank's vault or deposits held in the bank's own account at the Federal Reserve. As we'll see shortly, the latter can be converted into currency more or less instantly. Currency in bank vaults and bank deposits held at the Federal Reserve are called **bank reserves.** Because bank reserves are in bank vaults and at the Federal Reserve, not held by the public, they are not part of currency in circulation.

To understand the role of banks in determining the money supply, we start by introducing a simple tool for analyzing a bank's financial position: a **T-account.** A business's T-account summarizes its financial position by showing, in a single table, the

Bank reserves are the currency banks hold in their vaults plus their deposits at the Federal Reserve.

A **T-account** is a tool for analyzing a business's financial position by showing, in a single table, the business's assets (on the left) and liabilities (on the right).

figure 25.1

A T-Account for Samantha's Smoothies

A T-account summarizes a business's financial position. Its assets, in this case consisting of a building and some smoothie-making machinery, are on the left side. Its liabilities, consisting of the money it owes to a local bank, are on the right side.

Assets		Liabilities	
Building	$30,000	Loan from bank	$20,000
Smoothie-making machines	$15,000		

The **reserve ratio** is the fraction of bank deposits that a bank holds as reserves.

The **required reserve ratio** is the smallest fraction of deposits that the Federal Reserve allows banks to hold.

business's assets and liabilities, with assets on the left and liabilities on the right. Figure 25.1 shows the T-account for a hypothetical business that *isn't* a bank—Samantha's Smoothies. According to Figure 25.1, Samantha's Smoothies owns a building worth $30,000 and has $15,000 worth of smoothie-making equipment. These are assets, so they're on the left side of the table. To finance its opening, the business borrowed $20,000 from a local bank. That's a liability, so the loan is on the right side of the table. By looking at the T-account, you can immediately see what Samantha's Smoothies owns and what it owes. Oh, and it's called a T-account because the lines in the table make a T-shape.

Samantha's Smoothies is an ordinary, nonbank business. Now let's look at the T-account for a hypothetical bank, First Street Bank, which is the repository of $1 million in bank deposits.

Figure 25.2 shows First Street's financial position. The loans First Street has made are on the left side because they're assets: they represent funds that those who have borrowed from the bank are expected to repay. The bank's only other assets, in this simplified example, are its reserves, which, as we've learned, can take the form either of cash in the bank's vault or deposits at the Federal Reserve. On the right side we show the bank's liabilities, which in this example consist entirely of deposits made by customers at First Street. These are liabilities because they represent funds that must ultimately be repaid to depositors. Notice, by the way, that in this example First Street's assets are larger than its liabilities. That's the way it's supposed to be! In fact, as we'll see shortly, banks are required by law to maintain assets larger by a specific percentage than their liabilities.

In this example, First Street Bank holds reserves equal to 10% of its customers' bank deposits. The fraction of bank deposits that a bank holds as reserves is its **reserve ratio.**

In the modern American system, the Federal Reserve—which, among other things, regulates banks operating in the United States—sets a **required reserve ratio,** which is the smallest fraction of bank deposits that a bank must hold. To understand why banks are regulated, let's consider a problem banks can face: *bank runs.*

figure 25.2

Assets and Liabilities of First Street Bank

First Street Bank's assets consist of $1,000,000 in loans and $100,000 in reserves. Its liabilities consist of $1,000,000 in deposits—money owed to people who have placed funds in First Street's hands.

Assets		Liabilities	
Loans	$1,000,000	Deposits	$1,000,000
Reserves	$100,000		

The Problem of Bank Runs

A bank can lend out most of the funds deposited in its care because in normal times only a small fraction of its depositors want to withdraw their funds on any given day. But what would happen if, for some reason, all or at least a large fraction of its depositors *did* try to withdraw their funds during a short period of time, such as a couple of days?

The answer is that if a significant share of its depositors demanded their money back at the same time, the bank wouldn't be able to raise enough cash to meet those demands. The reason is that banks convert most of their depositors' funds into loans made to borrowers; that's how banks earn revenue—by charging interest on loans. Bank loans, however, are illiquid: they can't easily be converted into cash on short notice. To see why, imagine that First Street Bank has lent $100,000 to Drive-a-Peach Used Cars, a local dealership. To raise cash to meet demands for withdrawals, First Street can sell its loan to Drive-a-Peach to someone else—another bank or an individual investor. But if First Street tries to sell the loan quickly, potential buyers will be wary: they will suspect that First Street wants to sell the loan because there is something wrong and the loan might not be repaid. As a result, First Street Bank can sell the loan quickly only by offering it for sale at a deep discount—say, a discount of 50%, or $50,000.

The upshot is that if a significant number of First Street's depositors suddenly decided to withdraw their funds, the bank's efforts to raise the necessary cash quickly would force it to sell off its assets very cheaply. Inevitably, this leads to a *bank failure*: the bank would be unable to pay off its depositors in full.

What might start this whole process? That is, what might lead First Street's depositors to rush to pull their money out? A plausible answer is a spreading rumor that the bank is in financial trouble. Even if depositors aren't sure the rumor is true, they are likely to play it safe and get their money out while they still can. And it gets worse: a depositor who simply thinks that *other* depositors are going to panic and try to get

fyi

It's a Wonderful Banking System

Next Christmastime, it's a sure thing that at least one TV channel will show the 1946 film *It's a Wonderful Life,* featuring Jimmy Stewart as George Bailey, a small-town banker whose life is saved by an angel. The movie's climactic scene is a run on Bailey's bank, as fearful depositors rush to take their funds out.

When the movie was made, such scenes were still fresh in Americans' memories. There was a wave of bank runs in late 1930, a second wave in the spring of 1931, and a third wave in early 1933. By the end, more than a third of the nation's banks had failed. To bring the panic to an end, on March 6, 1933, the newly inaugurated president, Franklin Delano Roosevelt, closed all banks for a week to give bank regulators time to shut down unhealthy banks and certify healthy ones.

Gabriel Bouys/AFP/Getty Images

In July 2008, panicky IndyMac depositors lined up to pull their money out of the troubled California bank.

Since then, regulation has protected the United States and other wealthy countries against most bank runs. In fact, the scene in *It's a Wonderful Life* was already out of date when the movie was made. But the last decade has seen several waves of bank runs in developing countries. For example, bank runs played a

role in an economic crisis that swept Southeast Asia in 1997–1998 and in the severe economic crisis in Argentina, which began in late 2001.

Notice that we said "most bank runs." There are some limits on deposit insurance; in particular, currently only the first $250,000 of any bank account is insured. As a result, there can still be a rush to pull money out of a bank perceived as troubled. In fact, that's exactly what happened to IndyMac, a Pasadena-based lender that had made a large number of questionable home loans, in July 2008. As questions about IndyMac's financial soundness were raised, depositors began pulling out funds, forcing federal regulators to step in and close the bank. Unlike in the bank runs of the 1930s, however, most depositors got all their funds back—and the panic at IndyMac did not spread to other institutions.

their money out will realize that this could "break the bank." So he or she joins the rush. In other words, fear about a bank's financial condition can be a self-fulfilling prophecy: depositors who believe that other depositors will rush to the exit will rush to the exit themselves.

A **bank run** is a phenomenon in which many of a bank's depositors try to withdraw their funds due to fears of a bank failure. Moreover, bank runs aren't bad only for the bank in question and its depositors. Historically, they have often proved contagious, with a run on one bank leading to a loss of faith in other banks, causing additional bank runs. The FYI "It's a Wonderful Banking System" describes an actual case of just such a contagion, the wave of bank runs that swept across the United States in the early 1930s. In response to that experience and similar experiences in other countries, the United States and most other modern governments have established a system of bank regulations that protects depositors and prevents most bank runs.

Bank Regulation

Should you worry about losing money in the United States due to a bank run? No. After the banking crises of the 1930s, the United States and most other countries put into place a system designed to protect depositors and the economy as a whole against bank runs. This system has three main features: *deposit insurance, capital requirements,* and *reserve requirements.* In addition, banks have access to the *discount window,* a source of loans from the Federal Reserve when they're needed.

Deposit Insurance Almost all banks in the United States advertise themselves as a "member of the FDIC"—the Federal Deposit Insurance Corporation. The FDIC provides **deposit insurance,** a guarantee that depositors will be paid even if the bank can't come up with the funds, up to a maximum amount per account. Currently, the FDIC guarantees the first $250,000 of each account. This amount will be subject to change in 2014.

It's important to realize that deposit insurance doesn't just protect depositors if a bank actually fails. The insurance also eliminates the main reason for bank runs: since depositors know their funds are safe even if a bank fails, they have no incentive to rush to pull them out because of a rumor that the bank is in trouble.

Capital Requirements Deposit insurance, although it protects the banking system against bank runs, creates a well-known incentive problem. Because depositors are protected from loss, they have no incentive to monitor their bank's financial health, allowing risky behavior by the bank to go undetected. At the same time, the owners of banks have an incentive to engage in overly risky investment behavior, such as making questionable loans at high interest rates. That's because if all goes well, the owners profit; and if things go badly, the government covers the losses through federal deposit insurance.

To reduce the incentive for excessive risk-taking, regulators require that the owners of banks hold substantially more assets than the value of bank deposits. That way, the bank will still have assets larger than its deposits even if some of its loans go bad, and losses will accrue against the bank owners' assets, not the government. The excess of a bank's assets over its bank deposits and other liabilities is called the *bank's capital.* For example, First State Street Bank has capital of $100,000, equal to 9% of the total value of its assets. In practice, banks' capital is required to equal at least 7% of the value of their assets.

Reserve Requirements Another regulation used to reduce the risk of bank runs is **reserve requirements,** rules set by the Federal Reserve that establish the required reserve ratio for banks. For example, in the United States, the required reserve ratio for checkable bank deposits is 10%.

The Discount Window One final protection against bank runs is the fact that the Federal Reserve, which we'll discuss more thoroughly later, stands ready to lend money to banks, an arrangement known as the **discount window.** The ability to borrow money means a bank can avoid being forced to sell its assets at fire-sale prices in order to satisfy the demands of a sudden rush of depositors demanding cash. Instead, it can turn to the Federal Reserve and borrow the funds it needs to pay off depositors.

Determining the Money Supply

Without banks, there would be no checkable deposits, and so the quantity of currency in circulation would equal the money supply. In that case, the money supply would be determined solely by whoever controls government minting and printing presses. But banks do exist, and through their creation of checkable bank deposits, they affect the money supply in two ways. First, banks remove some currency from circulation: dollar bills that are sitting in bank vaults, as opposed to sitting in people's wallets, aren't part of the money supply. Second, and much more importantly, banks create money by accepting deposits and making loans—that is, they make the money supply larger than just the value of currency in circulation. Our next topic is how banks create money and what determines the amount of money they create.

How Banks Create Money

To see how banks create money, let's examine what happens when someone decides to deposit currency in a bank. Consider the example of Silas, a miser, who keeps a shoebox full of cash under his bed. Suppose Silas realizes that it would be safer, as well as more convenient, to deposit that cash in the bank and to use his debit card when shopping. Assume that he deposits $1,000 into a checkable account at First Street Bank. What effect will Silas's actions have on the money supply?

Panel (a) of Figure 25.3 shows the initial effect of his deposit. First Street Bank credits Silas with $1,000 in his account, so the economy's checkable bank deposits rise by $1,000. Meanwhile, Silas's cash goes into the vault, raising First Street's reserves by $1,000 as well.

This initial transaction has no effect on the money supply. Currency in circulation, part of the money supply, falls by $1,000; checkable bank deposits, also part of the money supply, rise by the same amount.

---

figure 25.3 — Effect on the Money Supply of Turning Cash into a Checkable Deposit at First Street Bank

(a) Initial Effect Before Bank Makes a New Loan

Assets		Liabilities	
Loans	No change	Checkable deposits	+$1,000
Reserves	+$1,000		

(b) Effect When Bank Makes a New Loan

Assets		Liabilities
Loans	+$900	No change
Reserves	−$900	

When Silas deposits $1,000 (which had been stashed under his bed) into a checkable bank account, there is initially no effect on the money supply: currency in circulation falls by $1,000, but checkable bank deposits rise by $1,000. The corresponding entries on the bank's T-account, depicted in panel (a), show deposits initially rising by $1,000 and the bank's reserves initially rising by $1,000. In the second stage, depicted in panel (b), the bank holds 10% of Silas's deposit ($100) as reserves and lends out the rest ($900) to Mary. As a result, its reserves fall by $900 and its loans increase by $900. Its liabilities, including Silas's $1,000 deposit, are unchanged. The money supply, the sum of checkable bank deposits and currency in circulation, has now increased by $900—the $900 now held by Mary.

But this is not the end of the story because First Street Bank can now lend out part of Silas's deposit. Assume that it holds 10% of Silas's deposit—$100—in reserves and lends the rest out in cash to Silas's neighbor, Mary. The effect of this second stage is shown in panel (b). First Street's deposits remain unchanged, and so does the value of its assets. But the composition of its assets changes: by making the loan, it reduces its reserves by $900, so that they are only $100 larger than they were before Silas made his deposit. In the place of the $900 reduction in reserves, the bank has acquired an IOU, its $900 cash loan to Mary. So by putting $900 of Silas's cash back into circulation by lending it to Mary, First Street Bank has, in fact, increased the money supply. That is, the sum of currency in circulation and checkable bank deposits has risen by $900 compared to what it had been when Silas's cash was still under his bed. Although Silas is still the owner of $1,000, now in the form of a checkable deposit, Mary has the use of $900 in cash from her borrowings.

And this may not be the end of the story. Suppose that Mary uses her cash to buy a television and a DVD player from Acme Merchandise. What does Anne Acme, the store's owner, do with the cash? If she holds on to it, the money supply doesn't increase any further. But suppose she deposits the $900 into a checkable bank deposit—say, at Second Street Bank. Second Street Bank, in turn, will keep only part of that deposit in reserves, lending out the rest, creating still more money.

Assume that Second Street Bank, like First Street Bank, keeps 10% of any bank deposit in reserves and lends out the rest. Then it will keep $90 in reserves and lend out $810 of Anne's deposit to another borrower, further increasing the money supply.

Table 25.1 shows the process of money creation we have described so far. At first the money supply consists only of Silas's $1,000. After he deposits the cash into a

table **25.1**

How Banks Create Money

	Currency in circulation	Checkable bank deposits	Money supply
First stage: Silas keeps his cash under his bed.	$1,000	$0	$1,000
Second stage: Silas deposits cash in First Street Bank, which lends out $900 to Mary, who then pays it to Anne Acme.	900	1,000	1,900
Third stage: Anne Acme deposits $900 in Second Street Bank, which lends out $810 to another borrower.	810	1,900	2,710

checkable bank deposit and the bank makes a loan, the money supply rises to $1,900. After the second deposit and the second loan, the money supply rises to $2,710. And the process will, of course, continue from there. (Although we have considered the case in which Silas places his cash in a checkable bank deposit, the results would be the same if he put it into any type of near-money.)

This process of money creation may sound familiar. Recall the *multiplier process* that we described in Module 16: an initial increase in real GDP leads to a rise in consumer spending, which leads to a further rise in real GDP, which leads to a further rise in consumer spending, and so on. What we have here is another kind of multiplier—the *money multiplier*. Next, we'll learn what determines the size of this multiplier.

Reserves, Bank Deposits, and the Money Multiplier

In tracing out the effect of Silas's deposit in Table 25.1, we assumed that the funds a bank lends out always end up being deposited either in the same bank or in another bank—so funds disbursed as loans come back to the banking system, even if not to the lending bank itself. In reality, some of these loaned funds may be held by borrowers in their wallets and not deposited in a bank, meaning that some of the loaned amount "leaks" out of the banking system. Such leaks reduce the size of the money multiplier, just as leaks of real income into savings reduce the size of the real GDP multiplier. (Bear in mind, however, that the "leak" here comes from the fact that borrowers keep some of their funds in currency, rather than the fact that consumers save some of their income.) But let's set that complication aside for a moment and consider how the money supply is determined in a "checkable-deposits-only" monetary system, in which funds are always deposited in bank accounts and none are held in wallets as currency. That is, in our checkable-deposits-only monetary system, any and all funds borrowed from a bank are immediately deposited into a checkable bank account. We'll assume that banks are required to satisfy a minimum reserve ratio of 10% and that every bank lends out all of its **excess reserves,** reserves over and above the amount needed to satisfy the minimum reserve ratio.

Excess reserves are a bank's reserves over and above its required reserves.

The **monetary base** is the sum of currency in circulation and bank reserves.

Now suppose that for some reason a bank suddenly finds itself with $1,000 in excess reserves. What happens? The answer is that the bank will lend out that $1,000, which will end up as a checkable bank deposit somewhere in the banking system, launching a money multiplier process very similar to the process shown in Table 25.1. In the first stage, the bank lends out its excess reserves of $1,000, which becomes a checkable bank deposit somewhere. The bank that receives the $1,000 deposit keeps 10%, or $100, as reserves and lends out the remaining 90%, or $900, which again becomes a checkable bank deposit somewhere. The bank receiving this $900 deposit again keeps 10%, which is $90, as reserves and lends out the remaining $810. The bank receiving this $810 keeps $81 in reserves and lends out the remaining $729, and so on. As a result of this process, the total increase in checkable bank deposits is equal to a sum that looks like:

$$\$1,000 + \$900 + \$810 + \$729 + \ldots$$

We'll use the symbol rr for the reserve ratio. More generally, the total increase in checkable bank deposits that is generated when a bank lends out $1,000 in excess reserves is the:

(25-1) Increase in checkable bank deposits from $1,000 in excess reserves = $\$1,000 + \$1,000 \times (1 - rr) + \$1,000 \times (1 - rr)^2 + \$1,000 \times (1 - rr)^3 + \ldots$

As we have seen, an infinite series of this form can be simplified to:

(25-2) Increase in checkable bank deposits from $1,000 in excess reserves = $\$1,000/rr$

Given a reserve ratio of 10%, or 0.1, a $1,000 increase in excess reserves will increase the total value of checkable bank deposits by $1,000/0.1 = $10,000. In fact, in a checkable-deposits-only monetary system, the total value of checkable bank deposits will be equal to the value of bank reserves divided by the reserve ratio. Or to put it a different way, if the reserve ratio is 10%, each $1 of reserves held by a bank supports $1/rr = $1/0.1 = $10 of checkable bank deposits.

The Money Multiplier in Reality

In reality, the determination of the money supply is more complicated than our simple model suggests because it depends not only on the ratio of reserves to bank deposits but also on the fraction of the money supply that individuals choose to hold in the form of currency. In fact, we already saw this in our example of Silas depositing the cash under his bed: when he chose to hold a checkable bank deposit instead of currency, he set in motion an increase in the money supply.

To define the money multiplier in practice, we need to understand that the Federal Reserve controls the **monetary base,** the sum of currency in circulation and the

reserves held by banks. The Federal Reserve does not determine how that sum is allocated between bank reserves and currency in circulation. Consider Silas and his deposit one more time: by taking the cash from under his bed and depositing it in a bank, he reduces the quantity of currency in circulation but increased bank reserves by an equal amount. So while the allocation of the monetary base changes—the amount in reserves grows and the amount in circulation shrinks—the total of these two, the monetary base, remains unchanged.

The monetary base is different from the money supply in two ways. First, bank reserves, which are part of the monetary base, aren't considered part of the money supply. A $1 bill in someone's wallet is considered money because it's available for an individual to spend, but a $1 bill held as bank reserves in a bank vault or deposited at the Federal Reserve isn't considered part of the money supply because it's not available for spending. Second, checkable bank deposits, which are part of the money supply because they are available for spending, aren't part of the monetary base.

Figure 25.4 shows the two concepts schematically. The circle on the left represents the monetary base, consisting of bank reserves plus currency in circulation. The circle on the right represents the money supply, consisting mainly of currency in circulation plus checkable or near-checkable bank deposits. As the figure indicates, currency in circulation is part of both the monetary base and the money supply. But bank reserves aren't part of the money supply, and checkable or near-checkable bank deposits aren't part of the monetary base. In normal times, most of the monetary base actually consists of currency in circulation, which also makes up about half of the money supply.

Now we can formally define the **money multiplier:** it's the ratio of the money supply to the monetary base. Most importantly, this tells us the total number of dollars created in the banking system by each $1 addition to the monetary base. In a simple situation in which banks hold no excess reserves and all cash is deposited in banks, the money multiplier is $1/rr$. So if the reserve requirement is 0.1 (the minimum required ratio for most checkable deposits in the United States), the money multiplier is $1/0.1 = 10$, and if the Federal Reserve adds $100 to the monetary base, the money supply will increase by $10 \times \$100 = \$1,000$. During normal times, the actual money multiplier in the United States, using M1 as our measure of money, is about 1.9. That's a lot smaller than 10. Normally, the reason the actual money multiplier is so small arises from the fact that people hold significant amounts of cash, and a dollar of currency in circulation, unlike a dollar in reserves, doesn't support multiple dollars of the money supply. In fact, currency in circulation normally accounts for more than 90% of the monetary base. But as this book went to press in early 2010, the money multiplier was even smaller, about 0.8. What was going on?

The **money multiplier** is the ratio of the money supply to the monetary base. It indicates the total number of dollars created in the banking system by each $1 addition to the monetary base.

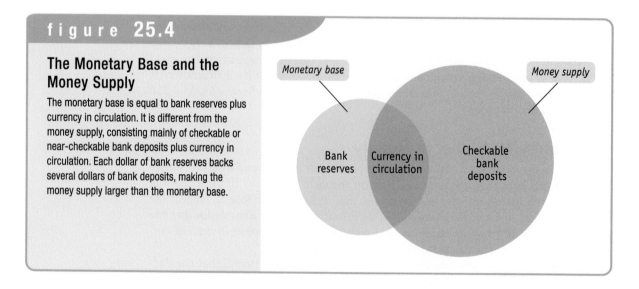

figure 25.4

The Monetary Base and the Money Supply

The monetary base is equal to bank reserves plus currency in circulation. It is different from the money supply, consisting mainly of checkable or near-checkable bank deposits plus currency in circulation. Each dollar of bank reserves backs several dollars of bank deposits, making the money supply larger than the monetary base.

Monetary base

Money supply

Bank reserves

Currency in circulation

Checkable bank deposits

The answer is that early 2010 was not a normal time: Starting in late 2008, legislation intended to stabilize the troubled U.S. economy made it much more attractive for banks to hold excess reserves. And banks responded by increasing their reserves tremendously, from $10 billion in 2008 to $1.2 trillion by January of 2010. And those large excess reserves—funds not lent out to potential borrowers—increased the monetary base without increasing the money supply. It was as if that money had "leaked" out of the money multiplier process and into excess reserves held by banks, reducing the size of the money multiplier.

Module 25 AP Review

Solutions appear at the back of the book.

Check Your Understanding

1. Suppose you are a depositor at First Street Bank. You hear a rumor that the bank has suffered serious losses on its loans. Every depositor knows that the rumor isn't true, but each thinks that most other depositors believe the rumor. Why, in the absence of deposit insurance, could this lead to a bank run? How does deposit insurance change the situation?

2. A con artist has a great idea: he'll open a bank without investing any capital and lend all the deposits at high interest rates to real estate developers. If the real estate market booms, the loans will be repaid and he'll make high profits. If the real estate market goes bust, the loans won't be repaid and the bank will fail—but he will not lose any of his own wealth. How would modern bank regulation frustrate his scheme?

3. Assume that total reserves are equal to $200 and total checkable bank deposits are equal to $1,000. Also assume that the public does not hold any currency and banks hold no excess reserves. Now suppose that the required reserve ratio falls from 20% to 10%. Trace out how this leads to an expansion in bank deposits.

4. Take the example of Silas depositing his $1,000 in cash into First Street Bank and assume that the required reserve ratio is 10%. But now assume that each recipient of a bank loan keeps half the loan in cash and deposits the rest. Trace out the resulting expansion in the money supply through at least three rounds of deposits.

Tackle the Test: Multiple-Choice Questions

1. Bank reserves include which of the following?
   I. currency in bank vaults
   II. bank deposits held in accounts at the Federal Reserve
   III. customer deposits in bank checking accounts
   a. I only
   b. II only
   c. III only
   d. I and II only
   e. I, II, and III

2. The fraction of bank deposits actually held as reserves is the
   a. reserve ratio.
   b. required reserve ratio.
   c. excess reserve ratio.
   d. reserve requirement.
   e. monetary base.

3. Bank regulation includes which of the following?
   I. deposit insurance
   II. capital requirements
   III. reserve requirements
   a. I only
   b. II only
   c. III only
   d. I and II
   e. I, II, and III

4. Which of the following changes would be the most likely to reduce the size of the money multiplier?
   a. a decrease in the required reserve ratio
   b. a decrease in excess reserves
   c. an increase in cash holding by consumers
   d. a decrease in bank runs
   e. an increase in deposit insurance

5. The monetary base equals
   a. currency in circulation.
   b. reserves held by banks.
   c. currency in circulation − reserves held by banks.
   d. currency in circulation + reserves held by banks.
   e. currency in circulation/reserves held by banks.

Tackle the Test: Free-Response Questions

1. How will each of the following affect the money supply through the money multiplier process? Explain.
   a. People hold more cash.
   b. Banks hold more excess reserves.
   c. The Fed increases the required reserve ratio.

2. The required reserve ratio is 5%.
   a. If a bank has deposits of $100,000 and holds $10,000 as reserves, how much are its excess reserves? Explain.
   b. If a bank holds no excess reserves and it receives a new deposit of $1,000, how much of that $1,000 can the bank lend out and how much is the bank required to add to its reserves? Explain.
   c. By how much can an increase in excess reserves of $2,000 change the money supply in a checkable-deposits-only system? Explain.

Module 26
The Federal Reserve System: History and Structure

What you will learn in this Module:

- The history of the Federal Reserve System
- The structure of the Federal Reserve System
- How the Federal Reserve has responded to major financial crises

The Federal Reserve System

Who's in charge of ensuring that banks maintain enough reserves? Who decides how large the monetary base will be? The answer, in the United States, is an institution known as the Federal Reserve (or, informally, as "the Fed"). The Federal Reserve is a **central bank**—an institution that oversees and regulates the banking system, and controls the monetary base. Other central banks include the Bank of England, the Bank of Japan, and the European Central Bank, or ECB.

An Overview of the Twenty-first Century American Banking System

Under normal circumstances, banking is a rather staid and unexciting business. Fortunately, bankers and their customers like it that way. However, there have been repeated episodes in which "sheer panic" would be the best description of banking conditions— the panic induced by a bank run and the specter of a collapse of a bank or multiple banks, leaving depositors penniless, bank shareholders wiped out, and borrowers unable to get credit. In this section, we'll give an overview of the behavior and regulation of the American banking system over the last century.

The creation of the Federal Reserve System in 1913 was largely a response to lessons learned in the Panic of 1907. In 2008, the United States found itself in the midst of a financial crisis that in many ways mirrored the Panic of 1907, which occurred almost exactly 100 years earlier.

A **central bank** is an institution that oversees and regulates the banking system and controls the monetary base.

Crisis in American Banking at the Turn of the Twentieth Century

The creation of the Federal Reserve System in 1913 marked the beginning of the modern era of American banking. From 1864 until 1913, American banking was dominated by a federally regulated system of national banks. They alone were allowed to issue currency, and the currency notes they issued were printed by the federal government with uniform size and design. How much currency a national bank could issue depended on its capital. Although this system was an improvement on the earlier period in which banks issued their own notes with no uniformity and virtually no regulation, the national banking regime still suffered numerous bank failures and major financial crises—at least one and often two per decade.

The main problem afflicting the system was that the money supply was not sufficiently responsive: it was difficult to shift currency around the country to respond quickly to local economic changes. (In particular, there was often a tug-of-war between New York City banks and rural banks for adequate amounts of currency.) Rumors that a bank had insufficient currency to satisfy demands for withdrawals would quickly lead to a bank run. A bank run would then spark a contagion, setting off runs at other nearby banks, sowing widespread panic and devastation in the local economy. In response, bankers in some locations pooled their resources to create local clearinghouses that would jointly guarantee a member's liabilities in the event of a panic, and some state governments began offering deposit insurance on their banks' deposits.

However, the cause of the Panic of 1907 was different from those of previous crises; in fact, its cause was eerily similar to the roots of the 2008 crisis. Ground zero of the 1907 panic was New York City, but the consequences devastated the entire country, leading to a deep four-year recession. The crisis originated in institutions in New York known as trusts, bank-like institutions that accepted deposits but that were originally intended to manage only inheritances and estates for wealthy clients. Because these trusts were supposed to engage only in low-risk activities, they were less regulated, had lower reserve requirements, and had lower cash reserves than national banks. However, as the American economy boomed during the first decade of the twentieth century, trusts began speculating in real estate and the stock market, areas of speculation forbidden to national banks. Being less regulated than national banks, trusts were able to pay their depositors higher returns. Yet trusts took a free ride on national banks' reputation for soundness, with depositors considering them equally safe. As a result, trusts grew

In both the Panic of 1907 and the financial crisis of 2008, large losses from risky speculation destabilized the banking system.

rapidly: by 1907, the total assets of trusts in New York City were as large as those of national banks. Meanwhile, the trusts declined to join the New York Clearinghouse, a consortium of New York City national banks that guaranteed one another's soundness; that would have required the trusts to hold higher cash reserves, reducing their profits. The Panic of 1907 began with the failure of the Knickerbocker Trust, a large New York City trust that failed when it suffered massive losses in unsuccessful stock market speculation. Quickly, other New York trusts came under pressure, and frightened depositors began queuing in long lines to withdraw their funds. The New York Clearinghouse declined to step in and lend to the trusts, and even healthy trusts came under serious assault. Within two days, a dozen major trusts had gone under. Credit markets froze, and the stock market fell dramatically as stock traders were unable to get credit to finance their trades, and business confidence evaporated.

Fortunately, one of New York City's wealthiest men, the banker J. P. Morgan, quickly stepped in to stop the panic. Understanding that the crisis was spreading and would soon engulf healthy institutions, trusts and banks alike, he worked with other bankers, wealthy men such as John D. Rockefeller, and the U.S. Secretary of the Treasury to shore up the reserves of banks and trusts so they could withstand the onslaught of withdrawals. Once people were assured that they could withdraw their money, the panic ceased. Although the panic itself lasted little more than a week, it and the stock market collapse decimated the economy. A four-year recession ensued, with production falling 11% and unemployment rising from 3% to 8%.

Responding to Banking Crises: The Creation of the Federal Reserve

Concerns over the frequency of banking crises and the unprecedented role of J. P. Morgan in saving the financial system prompted the federal government to initiate banking reform. In 1913 the national banking system was eliminated and the Federal Reserve System was created as a way to compel all deposit-taking institutions to hold adequate reserves and to open their accounts to inspection by regulators. The Panic of 1907 convinced many that the time for centralized control of bank reserves had come. The Federal Reserve was given the sole right to issue currency in order to make the money supply sufficiently responsive to satisfy economic conditions around the country.

The Structure of the Fed

The legal status of the Fed, which was created in 1913, is unusual: it is not exactly part of the U.S. government, but it is not really a private institution either. Strictly speaking, the Federal Reserve System consists of two parts: the Board of Governors and the 12 regional Federal Reserve Banks.

The Board of Governors, which oversees the entire system from its offices in Washington, D.C., is constituted like a government agency: its seven members are appointed by the president and must be approved by the Senate. However, they are appointed for 14-year terms, to insulate them from political pressure in their conduct of monetary policy. Although the chair is appointed more frequently—every four years—it is traditional for the chair to be reappointed and serve much longer terms. For example, William McChesney Martin was chair of the Fed from 1951 until 1970. Alan Greenspan, appointed in 1987, served as the Fed's chair until 2006.

The 12 Federal Reserve Banks each serve a region of the country, known as a *Federal Reserve district,* providing various banking and supervisory services. One of their jobs, for example, is to audit the books of private-sector banks to ensure their financial health. Each regional bank is run by a board of directors chosen from the local banking and business community. The Federal Reserve Bank of New York plays a special role: it carries out *open-market operations,* usually the main tool of monetary policy. Figure 26.1 on the next page shows the 12 Federal Reserve districts and the city in which each regional Federal Reserve Bank is located.

Decisions about monetary policy are made by the Federal Open Market Committee, which consists of the Board of Governors plus five of the regional bank presidents. The president of the Federal Reserve Bank of New York is always on the committee, and the other four seats rotate among the 11 other regional bank presidents. The chair of the Board of Governors normally also serves as the chair of the Federal Open Market Committee.

The effect of this complex structure is to create an institution that is ultimately accountable to the voting public because the Board of Governors is chosen by the president and confirmed by the Senate, all of whom are themselves elected officials. But the long terms served by board members, as well as the indirectness of their appointment process, largely insulate them from short-term political pressures.

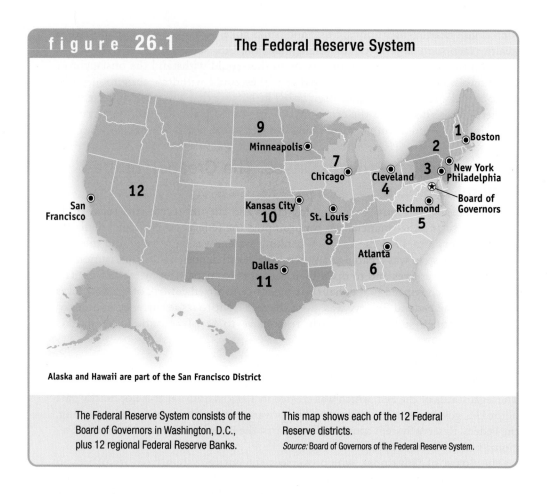

figure 26.1 The Federal Reserve System

Alaska and Hawaii are part of the San Francisco District

The Federal Reserve System consists of the Board of Governors in Washington, D.C., plus 12 regional Federal Reserve Banks.

This map shows each of the 12 Federal Reserve districts.
Source: Board of Governors of the Federal Reserve System.

The Effectiveness of the Federal Reserve System

Although the Federal Reserve System standardized and centralized the holding of bank reserves, it did not eliminate the potential for bank runs because banks' reserves were still less than the total value of their deposits. The potential for more bank runs became a reality during the Great Depression. Plunging commodity prices hit American farmers particularly hard, precipitating a series of bank runs in 1930, 1931, and 1933, each of which started at midwestern banks and then spread throughout the country. After the failure of a particularly large bank in 1930, federal officials realized that the economy-wide effects compelled them to take a less hands-off approach and to intervene more vigorously. In 1932, the Reconstruction Finance Corporation (RFC) was established and given the authority to make loans to banks in order to stabilize the banking sector. Also, the Glass-Steagall Act of 1932, which increased the ability of banks to borrow from the Federal Reserve System, was passed. A loan to a leading Chicago bank from the Federal Reserve appears to have stopped a major banking crisis in 1932. However, the beast had not yet been tamed. Banks became fearful of borrowing from the RFC because doing so signaled weakness to the public. During the midst of the catastrophic bank run of 1933, the new U.S. president, Franklin Delano Roosevelt, was inaugurated. He immediately declared a "bank holiday," closing all banks until regulators could get a handle on the problem. In March 1933, emergency measures were adopted that gave the RFC extraordinary powers to stabilize and restructure the banking industry by providing capital to banks either by loans or by outright purchases of bank shares. With the new regulations, regulators closed nonviable banks and recapitalized viable ones by allowing the RFC to buy preferred shares in banks (shares that gave the U.S. government more rights than regular shareholders) and by greatly expanding banks' ability to borrow from the Federal Reserve. By 1933, the RFC had invested over $16 billion (2008 dollars) in bank capital—one-third of the total capital of all banks in the United States at that time—and purchased shares in almost one-half of all banks. The RFC loaned more than $32 billion (2008 dollars) to banks during this period. Economic historians uniformly agree that the banking crises of the early 1930s greatly exacerbated the severity of the Great Depression, rendering monetary policy ineffective as the banking sector broke down and currency, withdrawn from banks and stashed under beds, reduced the money supply.

Although the powerful actions of the RFC stabilized the banking industry, new legislation was needed to prevent future banking crises. The Glass-Steagall Act of 1933 separated banks into two categories, **commercial banks,** depository banks that accepted deposits and were covered by deposit insurance, and **investment banks,** which engaged in creating and trading financial assets such as stocks and corporate bonds but were not covered by deposit insurance because their activities were considered more risky. Regulation Q prevented commercial banks from paying interest on checking accounts, in the belief that this would promote unhealthy competition between banks. In addition, investment banks were much more lightly regulated than commercial banks. The most important measure for the prevention of bank runs, however, was the adoption of federal deposit insurance (with an original limit of $2,500 per deposit).

These measures were clearly successful, and the United States enjoyed a long period of financial and banking stability. As memories of the bad old days dimmed, Depression-era bank regulations were lifted. In 1980 Regulation Q was eliminated, and by 1999, the Glass-Steagall Act had been so weakened that offering services like trading financial assets were no longer off-limits to commercial banks.

The Savings and Loan Crisis of the 1980s

Along with banks, the banking industry also included **savings and loans** (also called S&Ls or **thrifts**), institutions designed to accept savings and turn them into long-term mortgages for home-buyers. S&Ls were covered by federal deposit insurance and were tightly regulated for safety. However, trouble hit in the 1970s, as high inflation led savers to withdraw their funds from low-interest-paying S&L accounts and put them into higher-paying money market accounts. In addition, the high inflation rate severely eroded the value of the S&Ls' assets, the long-term mortgages they held on their books. In order to improve S&Ls' competitive position versus banks, Congress eased regulations to allow S&Ls to undertake much more risky investments in addition to long-term home mortgages. However, the new freedom did not bring with it increased oversight, leaving S&Ls with less oversight than banks. Not surprisingly, during the real estate boom of the 1970s and 1980s, S&Ls engaged in overly risky real estate lending. Also, corruption occurred as some S&L executives used their institutions as private piggy banks. Unfortunately, during the late 1970s and early 1980s, political interference from Congress kept insolvent S&Ls open when a bank in a comparable situation would have been quickly shut down by bank regulators. By the early 1980s, a large number of S&Ls had failed. Because accounts were covered by federal deposit insurance, the liabilities of a failed S&L were now liabilities of the federal government, and depositors had to be paid from taxpayer funds. From 1986 through 1995, the federal government closed over 1,000 failed S&Ls, costing U.S. taxpayers over $124 billion dollars.

In a classic case of shutting the barn door after the horse has escaped, in 1989 Congress put in place comprehensive oversight of S&L activities. It also empowered Fannie Mae and Freddie Mac to take over much of the home mortgage lending previously done by S&Ls. Fannie Mae and Freddie Mac are quasi-governmental agencies created during the Great Depression to make homeownership more affordable for low- and moderate-income households. It has been calculated that the S&L crisis helped cause a steep slowdown in the finance and real estate industries, leading to the recession of the early 1990s.

A **commercial bank** accepts deposits and is covered by deposit insurance.

An **investment bank** trades in financial assets and is not covered by deposit insurance.

A **savings and loan (thrift)** is another type of deposit-taking bank, usually specialized in issuing home loans.

Back to the Future: The Financial Crisis of 2008

The financial crisis of 2008 shared features of previous crises. Like the Panic of 1907 and the S&L crisis, it involved institutions that were not as strictly regulated as deposit-taking banks, as well as excessive speculation. Like the crises of the early 1930s, it involved a U.S. government that was reluctant to take aggressive action until the scale of the devastation became clear. In addition, by the late 1990s, advances in technology and financial innovation had created yet another systemic weakness that played a central role in 2008. The story of Long-Term Capital Management, or LTCM, highlights these problems.

Long-term Capital (Mis)Management Created in 1994, LTCM was a *hedge fund,* a private investment partnership open only to wealthy individuals and institutions. Hedge funds are virtually unregulated, allowing them to make much riskier investments than mutual funds, which are open to the average investor. Using vast amounts of **leverage**—that is, borrowed money—in order to increase its returns, LTCM used sophisticated computer models to make money by taking advantage of small differences in asset prices in global financial markets to buy at a lower price and sell at a higher price. In one year, LTCM made a return as high as 40%. LTCM was also heavily involved in *derivatives,* complex financial instruments that are constructed—derived—from the obligations of more basic financial assets. Derivatives are popular investment tools because they are cheaper to trade than basic financial assets and can be constructed to suit a buyer's or seller's particular needs. Yet their complexity can make it extremely hard to measure their value. LTCM believed that its computer models allowed it to accurately gauge the risk in the huge bets that it was undertaking in derivatives using borrowed money.

However, LTCM's computer models hadn't factored in a series of financial crises in Asia and in Russia during 1997 and 1998. Through its large borrowing, LTCM had become such a big player in global financial markets that attempts to sell its assets depressed the prices of what it was trying to sell. As the markets fell around the world and LTCM's panic-stricken investors demanded the return of their funds, LTCM's losses mounted as it tried to sell assets to satisfy those demands. Quickly, its operations collapsed because it could no longer borrow money and other parties refused to trade with it. Financial markets around the world froze in panic. The Federal Reserve realized that allowing LTCM's remaining assets to be sold at panic-stricken prices presented a grave risk to the entire financial system through the **balance sheet effect:** as sales of assets by LTCM depressed asset prices all over the world, other firms would see the value of their balance sheets fall as assets held on these balance sheets declined in value. Moreover, falling asset prices meant the value of assets held by borrowers on their balance sheet would fall below a critical threshold, leading to a default on the terms of their credit contracts and forcing creditors to call in their loans. This in turn would lead to more sales of assets as borrowers tried to raise cash to repay their loans, more credit defaults, and more loans called in, creating a **vicious cycle of deleveraging.** The Federal Reserve Bank of New York arranged a $3.625 billion bailout of LTCM in 1998, in which other private institutions took on shares of LTCM's assets and obligations, liquidated them in an orderly manner, and eventually turned a small profit. Quick action by the Federal Reserve Bank of New York prevented LTCM from sparking a contagion, yet virtually all of LTCM's investors were wiped out.

Subprime Lending and the Housing Bubble After the LTCM crisis, U.S. financial markets stabilized. They remained more or less stable even as stock prices fell sharply from 2000 to 2002 and the U.S. economy went into recession. During the recovery from the 2001 recession, however, the seeds for another financial crisis were planted.

The story begins with low interest rates: by 2003, U.S. interest rates were at historically low levels, partly because of Federal Reserve policy and partly because of large inflows of capital from other countries, especially China. These low interest rates helped cause a boom in housing, which in turn led the U.S. economy out of recession. As housing boomed, however, financial institutions began taking on growing risks—risks that were not well understood.

Traditionally, people were only able to borrow money to buy homes if they could show that they had sufficient income to meet the mortgage payments. Making home loans to people who didn't meet the usual criteria for borrowing, called **subprime lending,** was only a minor part of overall lending. But in the booming housing market of 2003–2006, subprime lending started to seem like a safe bet. Since housing prices kept rising, borrowers who couldn't make their mortgage payments could always pay off their mortgages, if necessary, by selling their homes. As a result, subprime lending exploded. Who was making these subprime loans? For the most part, it wasn't traditional banks lending out depositors' money. Instead, most of the loans were made by "loan originators," who quickly sold mortgages to other investors. These sales were made possible by a process known as **securitization:** financial institutions assembled pools of loans and sold shares in the income from these pools. These shares were considered relatively safe investments since it was considered unlikely that large numbers of home-buyers would default on their payments at the same time.

But that's exactly what happened. The housing boom turned out to be a bubble, and when home prices started falling in late 2006, many subprime borrowers were unable either to meet their mortgage payments or sell their houses for enough to pay off their mortgages. As a result, investors in securities backed by subprime mortgages started taking heavy losses. Many of the mortgage-backed assets were held by financial institutions, including banks and other institutions playing bank-like roles. Like the trusts that played a key role in the Panic of 1907, these "nonbank banks" were less regulated than commercial banks, which allowed them to offer higher returns to investors but left them extremely vulnerable in a crisis. Mortgage-related losses, in turn, led to a collapse of trust in the financial system. Figure 26.2 shows one measure of this loss of trust: the TED spread, which is the difference between the interest rate on three-month loans that banks make to each other and the interest rate the federal government pays on three-month bonds. Since government bonds are considered extremely safe, the TED spread shows how much risk banks think they're taking on when lending to each other. Normally, the spread is around a quarter of a percentage point, but it shot up in August 2007 and surged to an unprecedented 4.64 percentage points in October 2008.

Crisis and Response The collapse of trust in the financial system, combined with the large losses suffered by financial firms, led to a severe cycle of deleveraging and a credit crunch for the economy as a whole. Firms found it difficult to borrow, even for short-term operations; individuals found home loans unavailable and credit card

Subprime lending is lending to home buyers who don't meet the usual criteria for being able to afford their payments.

In **securitization** a pool of loans is assembled and shares of that pool are sold to investors.

---

figure **26.2**

The TED Spread

The TED spread is the difference between the interest rate at which banks lend to each other and the interest rate on U.S. government debt. It's widely used as a measure of financial stress. The TED spread soared as a result of the financial crisis that started in 2007.

Source: British Bankers' Association; Federal Reserve Bank of St. Louis.

Like FDR, Barack Obama, shown here with his team of economic advisers, was faced with a major financial crisis upon taking office.

limits reduced. Overall, the negative economic effect of the financial crisis bore a distinct and troubling resemblance to the effects of the banking crisis of the early 1930s, which helped cause the Great Depression. Policy makers noticed the resemblance and tried to prevent a repeat performance. Beginning in August 2007, the Federal Reserve engaged in a series of efforts to provide cash to the financial system, lending funds to a widening range of institutions and buying private-sector debt. The Fed and the Treasury Department also stepped in to rescue individual firms that were deemed too crucial to be allowed to fail, such as the investment bank Bear Stearns and the insurance company AIG.

In September 2008, however, policy makers decided that one major investment bank, Lehman Brothers, could be allowed to fail. They quickly regretted the decision. Within days of Lehman's failure, widespread panic gripped the financial markets, as illustrated by the late surge in the TED spread shown in Figure 26.2. In response to the intensified crisis, the U.S. government intervened further to support the financial system, as the U.S. Treasury began "injecting" capital into banks. Injecting capital, in practice, meant that the U.S. government would supply cash to banks in return for shares—in effect, partially nationalizing the financial system. This new rescue plan was still in its early stages when this book went to press, and it was too early to judge its success.

It is widely expected that the crisis of 2008 will lead to major changes in the financial system, probably the largest changes since the 1930s. Historically, it was considered enough to insure deposits and regulate commercial banks. The 2008 crisis raised new questions about the appropriate scope of safety nets and regulations. Like the crises preceding it, the financial crisis of 2008 exerted a powerful negative effect on the rest of the economy.

Module 26 AP Review

Solutions appear at the back of the book.

Check Your Understanding

1. What are the similarities between the Panic of 1907, the S&L crisis, and the crisis of 2008?

2. Why did the creation of the Federal Reserve fail to prevent the bank runs of the Great Depression? What measures did stop the bank runs?

3. Describe the balance sheet effect. Describe the vicious cycle of deleveraging. Why is it necessary for the government to step in to halt a vicious cycle of deleveraging?

Tackle the Test: Multiple-Choice Questions

1. Which of the following contributed to the creation of the Federal Reserve System?
     I. the bank panic of 1907
    II. the Great Depression
   III. the savings and loan crisis of the 1980s
   a. I only
   b. II only
   c. III only
   d. I and II only
   e. I, II, and III

2. Which of the following is a part of both the Federal Reserve System and the federal government?
   a. the Federal Reserve Board of Governors
   b. the 12 regional Federal Reserve Banks
   c. the Reconstruction Finance Corporation
   d. commercial banks
   e. the Treasury Department

3. Which of the following is NOT a role of the Federal Reserve System?
   a. controlling bank reserves
   b. printing currency (Federal Reserve notes)
   c. carrying out monetary policy
   d. supervising and regulating banks
   e. holding reserves for commercial banks

4. Who oversees the Federal Reserve System?
   a. the presidents of the Regional Federal Reserve Banks
   b. the president of the United States
   c. the Federal Open Market Committee
   d. the Board of Governors of the Federal Reserve System
   e. the Reconstruction Finance Corporation

5. Which of the following contributed to the financial crisis of 2008?
   a. subprime lending
   b. securitization
   c. deleveraging
   d. low interest rates leading to a housing boom
   e. all of the above

Tackle the Test: Free-Response Questions

1. a. What group determines monetary policy?
   b. How many members serve in this group?
   c. Who always serves in this group?
   d. Who sometimes serves in this group? Explain.

Answer (5 points)

1 point: The Federal Open Market Committee (FOMC)

1 point: 12

1 point: Members of the Board of Governors and the New York Federal Reserve bank president

1 point: 4 of the other 11 Federal Reserve bank presidents

1 point: The 11 other Federal Reserve bank presidents rotate their service on the FOMC.

2. a. What does the Board of Governors of the Federal Reserve System do?
   b. How many members serve on the group?
   c. Who appoints members?
   d. How long do members serve?
   e. Why do they serve a term of this length?
   f. How long does the chair serve?

What you will learn
in this **Module:**

- The functions of the Federal
  Reserve System
- The major tools the Federal
  Reserve uses to serve its
  functions

Module 27
The Federal Reserve:
Monetary Policy

The Federal Reserve System

In the previous module, we learned that the Federal Reserve System serves as the central bank of the United States. It has two parts: the Board of Governors, which is part of the U.S. government, and the 12 regional Federal Reserve Banks, which are privately owned. But what are the functions of the Federal Reserve System, and how does it serve them?

The Functions of the Federal Reserve System

Today, the Federal Reserve's functions fall into four basic categories: providing financial services to depository institutions, supervising and regulating banks and other financial institutions, maintaining the stability of the financial system, and conducting monetary policy. Let's look at each in turn.

Provide Financial Services The 12 regional Federal Reserve Banks provide financial services to depository institutions such as banks and other large institutions, including the U.S. government. The Federal Reserve is sometimes referred to as the "banker's bank" because it holds reserves, clears checks, provides cash, and transfers funds for commercial banks—all services that banks provide for their customers. The Federal Reserve also acts as the banker and fiscal agent for the federal government. The U.S. Treasury has its checking account with the Federal Reserve, so when the federal government writes a check, it is written on an account at the Fed.

Supervise and Regulate Banking Institutions The Federal Reserve System is charged with ensuring the safety and soundness of the nation's banking and financial system. The regional Federal Reserve Banks examine and regulate commercial banks in their district. The Board of Governors also engages in regulation and supervision of financial institutions.

Maintain the Stability of the Financial System As we have seen, one of the major reasons the Federal Reserve System was created was to provide the nation with a safe and stable monetary and financial system. The Fed is charged with maintaining the integrity of the financial system. As part of this function, Federal Reserve banks provide liquidity to financial institutions to ensure their safety and soundness.

Conduct Monetary Policy One of the Federal Reserve's most important functions is the conduct of monetary policy. As we will see, the Federal Reserve uses the tools of monetary policy to prevent or address extreme macroeconomic fluctuations in the U.S. economy.

What the Fed Does

How does the Fed go about performing its functions? The Federal Reserve has three main policy tools at its disposal: *reserve requirements,* the *discount rate,* and, perhaps most importantly, *open-market operations.* These tools play a part in how the Fed performs each of its functions as outlined below.

The Reserve Requirement

In our discussion of bank runs, we noted that the Fed sets a minimum required reserve ratio, currently equal to 10% for checkable bank deposits. Banks that fail to maintain at least the required reserve ratio on average over a two-week period face penalties.

What does a bank do if it looks as if it has insufficient reserves to meet the Fed's reserve requirement? Normally, it borrows additional reserves from other banks via the **federal funds market,** a financial market that allows banks that fall short of the reserve requirement to borrow reserves (usually just overnight) from banks that are holding excess reserves. The interest rate in this market is determined by supply and demand but the supply and demand for bank reserves are both strongly affected by Federal Reserve actions. Later we will see how the **federal funds rate,** the interest rate at which funds are borrowed and lent in the federal funds market, plays a key role in modern monetary policy.

In order to alter the money supply, the Fed can change reserve requirements. If the Fed reduces the required reserve ratio, banks will lend a larger percentage of their deposits, leading to more loans and an increase in the money supply via the money multiplier. Alternatively, if the Fed increases the required reserve ratio, banks are forced to reduce their lending, leading to a fall in the money supply via the money multiplier. Under current practice, however, the Fed doesn't use changes in reserve requirements to actively manage the money supply. The last significant change in reserve requirements was in 1992.

The Discount Rate

Banks in need of reserves can also borrow from the Fed itself via the *discount window.* The **discount rate** is the interest rate the Fed charges on those loans. Normally, the discount rate is set 1 percentage point above the federal funds rate in order to discourage banks from turning to the Fed when they are in need of reserves.

In order to alter the money supply, the Fed can change the discount rate. Beginning in the fall of 2007, the Fed reduced the spread between the federal funds rate and the discount rate as part of its response to an ongoing financial crisis, described later in this module. As a result, by the spring of 2008 the discount rate was only 0.25 percentage points above the federal funds rate.

If the Fed reduces the spread between the discount rate and the federal funds rate, the cost to banks of being short of reserves falls; banks respond by increasing their

The **federal funds market** allows banks that fall short of the reserve requirement to borrow funds from banks with excess reserves.

The **federal funds rate** is the interest rate determined in the federal funds market.

The **discount rate** is the interest rate the Fed charges on loans to banks.

A trader works on the floor of the New York Stock Exchange as the Federal Reserve announces that it will be keeping its key interest rate near zero.

Spencer Platt/Getty Images

An **open-market operation** is a purchase or sale of government debt by the Fed.

lending, and the money supply increases via the money multiplier. If the Fed increases the spread between the discount rate and the federal funds rate, bank lending falls—and so will the money supply via the money multiplier.

The Fed normally doesn't use the discount rate to actively manage the money supply. Although, as we mentioned earlier, there was a temporary surge in lending through the discount window in 2007 in response to a financial crisis. Today, normal monetary policy is conducted almost exclusively using the Fed's third policy tool: open-market operations.

Open-Market Operations

Like the banks it oversees, the Federal Reserve has assets and liabilities. The Fed's assets consist of its holdings of debt issued by the U.S. government, mainly short-term U.S. government bonds with a maturity of less than one year, known as U.S. Treasury bills. Remember, the Fed isn't exactly part of the U.S. government, so U.S. Treasury bills held by the Fed are a liability of the government but an asset of the Fed. The Fed's liabilities consist of currency in circulation and bank reserves. Figure 27.1 summarizes the normal assets and liabilities of the Fed in the form of a T-account.

figure 27.1

The Federal Reserve's Assets and Liabilities

The Federal Reserve holds its assets mostly in short-term government bonds called U.S. Treasury bills. Its liabilities are the monetary base—currency in circulation plus bank reserves.

Assets	Liabilities
Government debt (Treasury bills)	Monetary base (Currency in circulation + bank reserves)

In an **open-market operation** the Federal Reserve buys or sells U.S. Treasury bills, normally through a transaction with *commercial banks*—banks that mainly make business loans, as opposed to home loans. The Fed never buys U.S. Treasury bills directly from the federal government. There's a good reason for this: when a central bank buys government debt directly from the government, it is lending directly to the government—in effect, the central bank is issuing "printing money" to finance the government's budget deficit. As we'll see later in the book, this has historically been a formula for disastrous levels of inflation.

The two panels of Figure 27.2 show the changes in the financial position of both the Fed and commercial banks that result from open-market operations. When the Fed buys U.S. Treasury bills from a commercial bank, it pays by crediting the bank's reserve account by an amount equal to the value of the Treasury bills. This is illustrated in panel (a): the Fed buys $100 million of U.S. Treasury bills from commercial banks, which increases the monetary base by $100 million because it increases bank reserves by $100 million. When the Fed sells U.S. Treasury bills to commercial banks, it debits the banks' accounts, reducing their reserves. This is shown in panel (b), where the Fed sells $100 million of U.S. Treasury bills. Here, bank reserves and the monetary base decrease.

You might wonder where the Fed gets the funds to purchase U.S. Treasury bills from banks. The answer is that it simply creates them with a stroke of the pen—or, these days, a click of the mouse—that credits the banks' accounts with extra reserves. (The Fed issues currency to pay for Treasury bills only when banks want the additional reserves in the form of currency.) Remember, the modern dollar is fiat money, which isn't backed by anything. So the Fed can create additional monetary base at its own discretion.

figure 27.2 — Open-Market Operations by the Federal Reserve

(a) An Open-Market Purchase of $100 Million

	Assets		Liabilities	
Federal Reserve	Treasury bills	+$100 million	Monetary base	+$100 million

	Assets		Liabilities
Commercial banks	Treasury bills	−$100 million	No change
	Reserves	+$100 million	

(b) An Open-Market Sale of $100 Million

	Assets		Liabilities	
Federal Reserve	Treasury bills	−$100 million	Monetary base	−$100 million

	Assets		Liabilities
Commercial banks	Treasury bills	+$100 million	No change
	Reserves	−$100 million	

In panel (a), the Federal Reserve increases the monetary base by purchasing U.S. Treasury bills from private commercial banks in an open-market operation. Here, a $100 million purchase of U.S. Treasury bills by the Federal Reserve is paid for by a $100 million increase in the monetary base. This will ultimately lead to an increase in the money supply via the money multiplier as banks lend out some of these new reserves. In panel (b), the Federal Reserve reduces the monetary base by selling U.S. Treasury bills to private commercial banks in an open-market operation. Here, a $100 million sale of U.S. Treasury bills leads to a $100 million reduction in commercial bank reserves, resulting in a $100 million decrease in the monetary base. This will ultimately lead to a fall in the money supply via the money multiplier as banks reduce their loans in response to a fall in their reserves.

The change in bank reserves caused by an open-market operation doesn't directly affect the money supply. Instead, it starts the money multiplier in motion. After the $100 million increase in reserves shown in panel (a), commercial banks would lend out their additional reserves, immediately increasing the money supply by $100 million. Some of those loans would be deposited back into the banking system, increasing reserves

Who Gets the Interest on the Fed's Assets?

As we've just learned, the Fed owns a lot of assets—Treasury bills—which it bought from commercial banks in exchange for the monetary base in the form of credits to banks' reserve accounts. These assets pay interest. Yet the Fed's liabilities consist mainly of the monetary base, liabilities on which the Fed *doesn't* pay interest. So the Fed is, in effect, an institution that has the privilege of borrowing funds at a zero interest rate and lending them out at a positive interest rate. That sounds like a pretty profitable business. Who gets the profits?

You do—or rather, U.S. taxpayers do. The Fed keeps some of the interest it receives to finance its operations but turns most of it over to the U.S. Treasury. For example, in 2009 the Federal Reserve System received $52.1 billion in income—largely in interest on its holdings of Treasury bills, of which $46.1 billion was returned to the Treasury.

We can now finish the story of the impact of those forged $100 bills allegedly printed in North Korea. When a fake $100 bill enters circulation, it has the same economic effect as a real $100 bill printed by the U.S. government. That is, as long as nobody catches the forgery, the fake bill serves, for all practical purposes, as part of the monetary base. Meanwhile, the Fed decides on the size of the monetary base based on economic considerations—in particular, the Fed doesn't let the monetary base get too large because that can cause inflation. So every fake $100 bill that enters circulation basically means that the Fed prints one less real $100 bill. When the Fed prints a $100 bill legally, however, it gets Treasury bills in return—and the interest on those bills helps pay for the U.S. government's expenses. So a counterfeit $100 bill reduces the amount of Treasury bills the Fed can acquire and thereby reduces the interest payments going to the Fed and the U.S. Treasury. So taxpayers bear the real cost of counterfeiting.

again and permitting a further round of loans, and so on, leading to a rise in the money supply. An open-market sale has the reverse effect: bank reserves fall, requiring banks to reduce their loans, leading to a fall in the money supply.

Economists often say, loosely, that the Fed controls the money supply—checkable deposits plus currency in circulation. In fact, it controls only the monetary base—bank reserves plus currency in circulation. But by increasing or reducing the monetary base, the Fed can exert a powerful influence on both the money supply and interest rates. This influence is the basis of monetary policy, discussed in detail in Modules 28 and 29.

Module 27 AP Review

Solutions appear at the back of the book.

Check Your Understanding

1. Assume that any money lent by a bank is deposited back in the banking system as a checkable deposit and that the reserve ratio is 10%. Trace out the effects of a $100 million open-market purchase of U.S. Treasury bills by the Fed on the value of checkable bank deposits. What is the size of the money multiplier?

Tackle the Test: Multiple-Choice Questions

1. Which of the following is a function of the Federal Reserve System?
   - I. examine commercial banks
   - II. print Federal Reserve notes
   - III. conduct monetary policy
   a. I only
   b. II only
   c. III only
   d. I and III only
   e. I, II, and III

2. Which of the following financial services does the Federal Reserve provide for commercial banks?
   - I. clearing checks
   - II. holding reserves
   - III. making loans
   a. I only
   b. II only
   c. III only
   d. I and II
   e. I, II, and III

3. When the Fed makes a loan to a commercial bank, it charges
   a. no interest.
   b. the prime rate.
   c. the federal funds rate.
   d. the discount rate.
   e. the market interest rate.

4. If the Fed purchases U.S. Treasury bills from a commercial bank, what happens to bank reserves and the money supply?

	Bank reserves	Money supply
a.	increase	decrease
b.	increase	increase
c.	decrease	decrease
d.	decrease	increase
e.	increase	no change

5. When banks make loans to each other, they charge the
   a. prime rate.
   b. discount rate.
   c. federal funds rate.
   d. CD rate.
   e. mortgage rate.

Tackle the Test: Free-Response Questions

1. a. What are the three major tools of the Federal Reserve System?
   b. What would the Fed do with each tool to increase the money supply? Explain for each.

2. What are the four basic functions of the Federal Reserve System and what part of the system is responsible for each?

Answer (9 points)

1 point: The discount rate

1 point: The reserve requirement

1 point: Open-market operations

1 point: Decrease the discount rate

1 point: A lower discount rate makes it cheaper to borrow from the Fed so the money supply increases.

1 point: Decrease the reserve requirement

1 point: A lower reserve requirement allows banks to loan more, increasing the money supply.

1 point: Buy U.S. Treasury bills

1 point: When the Fed buys U.S. Treasury bills, banks' excess reserves increase. When lent out, these excess reserves increase the money supply with the assistance of the money multiplier.

What you will learn in this **Module**:

- What the money demand curve is

- Why the liquidity preference model determines the interest rate in the short run

Module 28
The Money Market

The Demand for Money

Remember that M1, the most commonly used definition of the money supply, consists of currency in circulation (cash), plus checkable bank deposits, plus traveler's checks. M2, a broader definition of the money supply, consists of M1 plus deposits that can easily be transferred into checkable deposits. We also learned why people hold money—to make it easier to purchase goods and services. Now we'll go deeper, examining what determines *how much* money individuals and firms want to hold at any given time.

The Opportunity Cost of Holding Money

Most economic decisions involve trade-offs at the margin. That is, individuals decide how much of a good to consume by determining whether the benefit they'd gain from consuming a bit more of any given good is worth the cost. The same decision process is used when deciding how much money to hold.

Individuals and firms find it useful to hold some of their assets in the form of money because of the convenience money provides: money can be used to make purchases directly, while other assets can't. But there is a price to be paid (an opportunity cost) for that convenience: money held in your wallet earns no interest.

As an example of how convenience makes it worth incurring some opportunity costs, consider the fact that even today—with the prevalence of credit cards, debit cards, and ATMs—people continue to keep cash in their wallets rather than leave the funds in an interest-bearing account. They do this because they don't want to have to go to an ATM to withdraw money every time they want to make a small purchase. In other words, the convenience of keeping some cash in your wallet is more valuable than the interest you would earn by keeping that money in the bank.

Even holding money in a checking account involves a trade-off between convenience and earning interest. That's because you can earn a higher interest rate by putting your money in assets other than a checking account. For example, many banks offer certificates of deposit, or CDs, which pay a higher interest rate than ordinary bank accounts. But CDs also carry a penalty if you withdraw the funds before a certain amount of time—say, six months—has elapsed. An individual who keeps funds in a checking account is forgoing the higher interest rate those funds would have earned if placed in a CD in return for the convenience of having cash readily available when needed.

Table 28.1 illustrates the opportunity cost of holding money in a specific month, June 2007. The first row shows the interest rate on one-month certificates of deposit—that is, the interest rate individuals could get if they were willing to tie their funds up for one month. In June 2007, one-month CDs yielded 5.30%. The second row shows the interest rate on interest-bearing bank accounts (specifically, those included in M1). Funds in these accounts were more accessible than those in CDs, but the price of that convenience was a much lower interest rate, only 2.478%. Finally, the last row shows the interest rate on currency—cash in your wallet—which was, of course, zero.

Table 28.1 shows the opportunity cost of holding money at one point in time, but the opportunity cost of holding money changes when the overall level of interest rates changes. Specifically, when the overall level of interest rates falls, the opportunity cost of holding money falls, too.

Table 28.2 illustrates this point by showing how selected interest rates changed between June 2007 and June 2008, a period when the Federal Reserve was slashing rates in an effort to fight off recession. Between June 2007 and June 2008, the federal funds rate, which is the rate the Fed controls most directly, fell by 3.25 percentage points. The interest rate on one-month CDs fell almost as much, 2.8 percentage points. That's not an accident: all **short-term interest rates**—rates on financial assets that come due, or mature, within less than a year—tend to move together, with rare exceptions. The reason short-term interest rates tend to move together is that CDs and other short-term assets (like one-month and three-month U.S. Treasury bills) are in effect competing for the same business. Any short-term asset that offers a lower-than-average interest rate will be sold by investors, who will move their wealth into a higher-yielding short-term asset. The selling of the asset, in turn, forces its interest rate up because investors must be rewarded with a higher rate in order to induce them to buy it. Conversely, investors will move their wealth into any short-term financial asset that offers an above-average interest rate. The purchase of the asset drives its interest rate down when sellers find they can lower the rate of return on the asset and still find willing buyers. So interest rates on short-term financial assets tend to be roughly the same because no asset will consistently offer a higher-than-average or a lower-than-average interest rate.

But as short-term interest rates fell between June 2007 and June 2008, the interest rates on money didn't fall by the same amount. The interest rate on currency, of course, remained at zero. The interest rate paid on demand deposits did fall, but by much less than short-term interest rates. As a result, the opportunity cost of holding money fell. The last two rows of Table 28.2 show the differences between the interest

table 28.1

Selected Interest Rates, June 2007

One-month CDs	5.30%
Interest-bearing demand deposits	2.478
Currency	0

Source: Federal Reserve Bank of St. Louis.

Short-term interest rates are the interest rates on financial assets that mature within less than a year.

table 28.2

Interest Rates and the Opportunity Cost of Holding Money

	June 2007	June 2008
Federal funds rate	5.25%	2.00%
One-month certificates of deposit (CD)	5.30	2.50
Interest-bearing demand deposits	2.773	1.353
Currency	0	0
CDs minus interest-bearing demand deposits	2.527	1.147
CDs minus currency	5.30	2.50

Source: Federal Reserve Bank of St. Louis.

Long-term Interest Rates

Long-term interest rates—rates on bonds or loans that mature in several years—don't necessarily move with short-term interest rates. How is that possible?

Consider the case of Millie, who has already decided to place $1,000 in CDs for the next two years. However, she hasn't decided whether to put the money in a one-year CD, at a 4% rate of interest, or a two-year CD, at a 5% rate of interest.

You might think that the two-year CD is a clearly better deal—but it may not be. Suppose that Millie expects the rate of interest on one-

year CDs to rise sharply next year. If she puts her funds in a one-year CD this year, she will be able to reinvest the money at a much higher rate next year. And this could give her a two-year rate of return that is higher than if she put her funds into the two-year CD. For example, if the rate of interest on one-year CDs rises from 4% this year to 8% next year, putting her funds in a one-year CD will give her an annual rate of return over the next two years of about 6%, better than the 5% rate on two-year CDs.

The same considerations apply to investors deciding between short-term and long-term

bonds. If they expect short-term interest rates to rise, investors may buy short-term bonds even if long-term bonds offer a higher interest rate. If they expect short-term interest rates to fall, investors may buy long-term bonds even if short-term bonds offer a higher interest rate.

In practice, long-term interest rates reflect the average expectation in the market about what's going to happen to short-term rates in the future. When long-term rates are higher than short-term rates, as they were in 2008, the market is signaling that it expects short-term rates to rise in the future.

Long-term interest rates are interest rates on financial assets that mature a number of years in the future.

The **money demand curve** shows the relationship between the quantity of money demanded and the interest rate.

rates on demand deposits and currency and the interest rate on CDs. These differences declined sharply between June 2007 and June 2008. This reflects a general result: the higher the short-term interest rate, the higher the opportunity cost of holding money; the lower the short-term interest rate, the lower the opportunity cost of holding money.

Table 28.2 contains only short-term interest rates. At any given moment, **long-term interest rates**—interest rates on financial assets that mature, or come due, a number of years into the future—may be different from short-term interest rates. The difference between short-term and long-term interest rates is sometimes important as a practical matter. Moreover, it's short-term rates rather than long-term rates that affect money demand, because the decision to hold money involves trading off the convenience of holding cash versus the payoff from holding assets that mature in the short-term—a year or less. For our current purposes, however, it's useful to ignore the distinction between short-term and long-term rates and assume that there is only one interest rate.

The Money Demand Curve

Because the overall level of interest rates affects the opportunity cost of holding money, the quantity of money individuals and firms want to hold is, other things equal, negatively related to the interest rate. In Figure 28.1, the horizontal axis shows the quantity of money demanded and the vertical axis shows the nominal interest rate, r, which you can think of as a representative short-term interest rate such as the rate on one-month CDs. Why do we place the nominal interest rate and not the real interest rate on the vertical axis? Because the opportunity cost of holding money includes both the real return that could be earned on a bank deposit and the erosion in purchasing power caused by inflation. The nominal interest rate includes both the forgone real return and the expected loss due to inflation. Hence, r in Figure 28.1 and all subsequent figures is the nominal interest rate.

The relationship between the interest rate and the quantity of money demanded by the public is illustrated by the **money demand curve,** *MD,* in Figure 28.1. The money demand curve slopes downward because, other things equal, a higher interest rate increases the opportunity cost of holding money, leading the public to reduce the quantity of money it demands. For example, if the interest rate is very low—say, 1%—the

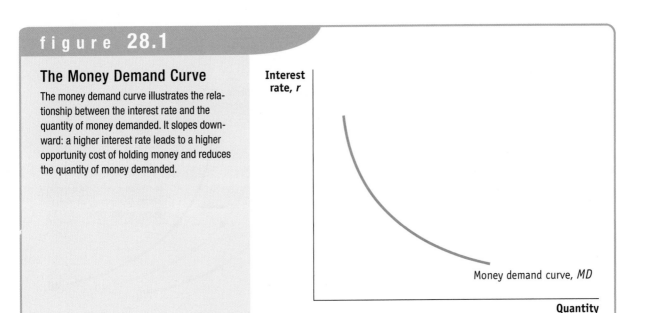

figure 28.1

The Money Demand Curve

The money demand curve illustrates the relationship between the interest rate and the quantity of money demanded. It slopes downward: a higher interest rate leads to a higher opportunity cost of holding money and reduces the quantity of money demanded.

Interest rate, *r*

Money demand curve, *MD*

Quantity of money

interest forgone by holding money is relatively small. As a result, individuals and firms will tend to hold relatively large amounts of money to avoid the cost and nuisance of converting other assets into money when making purchases. By contrast, if the interest rate is relatively high—say, 15%, a level it reached in the United States in the early 1980s—the opportunity cost of holding money is high. People will respond by keeping only small amounts in cash and deposits, converting assets into money only when needed.

You might ask why we draw the money demand curve with the interest rate—as opposed to rates of return on other assets, such as stocks or real estate—on the vertical axis. The answer is that for most people the relevant question in deciding how much money to hold is whether to put the funds in the form of other assets that can be turned fairly quickly and easily into money. Stocks don't fit that definition because there are significant broker's fees when you sell stock (which is why stock market investors are advised not to buy and sell too often); selling real estate involves even larger fees and can take a long time as well. So the relevant comparison is with assets that are "close to" money—fairly liquid assets like CDs. And as we've already seen, the interest rates on all these assets normally move closely together.

Shifts of the Money Demand Curve

Like the demand curve for an ordinary good, the money demand curve can be shifted by a number of factors. Figure 28.2 on the next page shows shifts of the money demand curve: an increase in the demand for money corresponds to a rightward shift of the *MD* curve, raising the quantity of money demanded at any given interest rate; a fall in the demand for money corresponds to a leftward shift of the *MD* curve, reducing the quantity of money demanded at any given interest rate. The most important factors causing the money demand curve to shift are changes in the aggregate price level, changes in real GDP, changes in banking technology, and changes in banking institutions.

Changes in the Aggregate Price Level Americans keep a lot more cash in their wallets and funds in their checking accounts today than they did in the 1950s. One reason is that they have to if they want to be able to buy anything: almost everything costs more now than it did when you could get a burger, fries, and a drink at McDonald's for

figure **28.2**

Increases and Decreases in the Demand for Money

A rise in money demand shifts the money demand curve to the right, from MD_1 to MD_2, and the quantity of money demanded rises at any given interest rate. A fall in money demand shifts the money demand curve to the left, from MD_1 to MD_3, and the quantity of money demanded falls at any given interest rate.

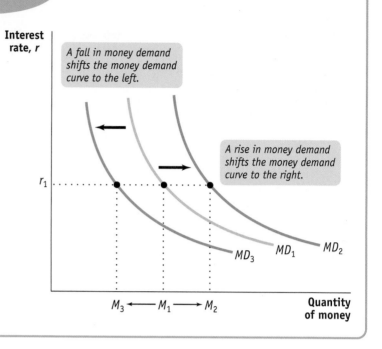

A fall in money demand shifts the money demand curve to the left.

A rise in money demand shifts the money demand curve to the right.

45 cents and a gallon of gasoline for 29 cents. So higher prices increase the demand for money (a rightward shift of the *MD* curve), and lower prices reduce the demand for money (a leftward shift of the *MD* curve).

We can actually be more specific than this: other things equal, the demand for money is *proportional* to the price level. That is, if the aggregate price level rises by 20%, the quantity of money demanded at any given interest rate, such as r_1 in Figure 28.2, also rises by 20%—the movement from M_1 to M_2. Why? Because if the price of everything rises by 20%, it takes 20% more money to buy the same basket of goods and services. And if the aggregate price level falls by 20%, at any given interest rate the quantity of money demanded falls by 20%—shown by the movement from M_1 to M_3 at the interest rate r_1. As we'll see later, the fact that money demand is proportional to the price level has important implications for the long-run effects of monetary policy.

Changes in Real GDP Households and firms hold money as a way to facilitate purchases of goods and services. The larger the quantity of goods and services they buy, the larger the quantity of money they will want to hold at any given interest rate. So an increase in real GDP—the total quantity of goods and services produced and sold in the economy—shifts the money demand curve rightward. A fall in real GDP shifts the money demand curve leftward.

Changes in Technology There was a time, not so long ago, when withdrawing cash from a bank account required a visit during the bank's hours of operation. And since most people tried to do their banking during lunch hour, they often found themselves standing in line. So people limited the number of times they needed to withdraw funds by keeping substantial amounts of cash on hand. Not surprisingly, this tendency diminished greatly with the advent of ATMs in the 1970s. As a result, the demand for money fell and the money demand curve shifted leftward.

These events illustrate how changes in technology can affect the demand for money. In general, advances in information technology have tended to reduce the demand for money by making it easier for the public to make purchases without

A re-creation of a McDonald's in the 1950s at the Ford Museum in Detroit, Michigan

holding significant sums of money. ATMs are only one example of how changes in technology have altered the demand for money. The ability of stores to process credit card and debit card transactions via the Internet has widened their acceptance and similarly reduced the demand for cash.

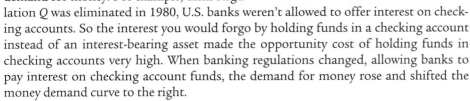

Changes in Institutions Changes in institutions can increase or decrease the demand for money. For example, until Regulation *Q* was eliminated in 1980, U.S. banks weren't allowed to offer interest on checking accounts. So the interest you would forgo by holding funds in a checking account instead of an interest-bearing asset made the opportunity cost of holding funds in checking accounts very high. When banking regulations changed, allowing banks to pay interest on checking account funds, the demand for money rose and shifted the money demand curve to the right.

Money and Interest Rates

The Federal Open Market Committee decided today to lower its target for the federal funds rate 75 basis points to 2¼ percent.

   Recent information indicates that the outlook for economic activity has weakened further. Growth in consumer spending has slowed and labor markets have softened. Financial markets remain under considerable stress, and the tightening of credit conditions and the deepening of the housing contraction are likely to weigh on economic growth over the next few quarters.

So read the beginning of a press release from the Federal Reserve issued on March 18, 2008. (A basis point is equal to 0.01 percentage point. So the statement implies that the Fed lowered the target from 3% to 2.25%.) The federal funds rate is the rate at which banks lend reserves to each other to meet the required reserve ratio. As the statement implies, at each of its eight-times-a-year meetings, the Federal Open Market Committee sets a target value for the federal funds rate. It's then up to Fed officials to achieve that target. This is done by the Open Market Desk at the Federal Reserve Bank of New York, which buys and sells short-term U.S. government debt, known as Treasury bills, to achieve that target.

   As we've already seen, other short-term interest rates, such as the rates on CDs, move with the federal funds rate. So when the Fed reduced its target for the federal funds rate from 3% to 2.25% in March 2008, many other short-term interest rates also fell by about three-quarters of a percentage point.

   How does the Fed go about achieving a *target federal funds rate*? And more to the point, how is the Fed able to affect interest rates at all?

The Equilibrium Interest Rate

Recall that, for simplicity, we've assumed that there is only one interest rate paid on nonmonetary financial assets, both in the short run and in the long run. To understand how the interest rate is determined, consider Figure 28.3 on the next page, which illustrates the **liquidity preference model of the interest rate;** this model says that the interest rate is determined by the supply and demand for money in the market for money. Figure 28.3 combines the money demand curve, *MD*, with the **money supply curve**, *MS*, which shows how the quantity of money supplied by the Federal Reserve varies with the interest rate.

   The Federal Reserve can increase or decrease the money supply: it usually does this through *open-market operations,* buying or selling Treasury bills, but it can also lend via the *discount window* or change *reserve requirements*. Let's assume for simplicity that the

According to the **liquidity preference model of the interest rate,** the interest rate is determined by the supply and demand for money.

The **money supply curve** shows how the quantity of money supplied varies with the interest rate.

figure 28.3

Equilibrium in the Money Market

The money supply curve, *MS,* is vertical at the money supply chosen by the Federal Reserve, $\overline{M}$. The money market is in equilibrium at the interest rate r_E: the quantity of money demanded by the public is equal to $\overline{M}$, the quantity of money supplied. At a point such as *L,* the interest rate, r_L, is below r_E and the corresponding quantity of money demanded, M_L, exceeds the money supply, $\overline{M}$. In an attempt to shift their wealth out of nonmoney interest-bearing financial assets and raise their money holdings, investors drive the interest rate up to r_E. At a point such as *H,* the interest rate r_H is above r_E and the corresponding quantity of money demanded, M_H, is less than the money supply, $\overline{M}$. In an attempt to shift out of money holdings into nonmoney interest-bearing financial assets, investors drive the interest rate down to r_E.

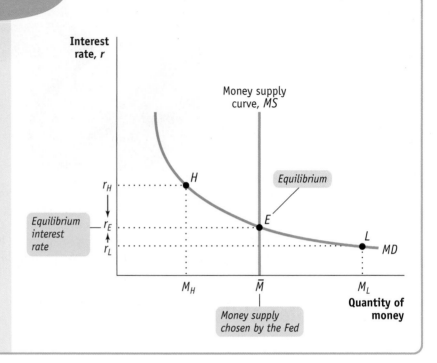

Fed, using one or more of these methods, simply chooses the level of the money supply that it believes will achieve its interest rate target. Then the money supply curve is a vertical line, *MS* in Figure 28.3, with a horizontal intercept corresponding to the money supply chosen by the Fed, $\overline{M}$. The money market equilibrium is at *E,* where *MS* and *MD* cross. At this point the quantity of money demanded equals the money supply, $\overline{M}$, leading to an equilibrium interest rate of r_E.

To understand why r_E is the equilibrium interest rate, consider what happens if the money market is at a point like *L,* where the interest rate, r_L, is below r_E. At r_L the public wants to hold the quantity of money M_L, an amount larger than the actual money supply, $\overline{M}$. This means that at point *L,* the public wants to shift some of its wealth out of interest-bearing assets such as high-denomination CDs (which aren't money) into money. This has two implications. One is that the quantity of money demanded is *more* than the quantity of money supplied. The other is that the quantity of interest-bearing nonmoney assets demanded is *less* than the quantity supplied. So those trying to sell nonmoney assets will find that they have to offer a higher interest rate to attract buyers. As a result, the interest rate will be driven up from r_L until the public wants to hold the quantity of money that is actually available, *M.* That is, the interest rate will rise until it is equal to r_E.

Now consider what happens if the money market is at a point such as *H* in Figure 28.3, where the interest rate r_H is above r_E. In that case the quantity of money demanded, M_H, is less than the quantity of money supplied, $\overline{M}$. Correspondingly, the quantity of interest-bearing nonmoney assets demanded is greater than the quantity supplied. Those trying to sell interest-bearing nonmoney assets will find that they can offer a lower interest rate and still find willing buyers. This leads to a fall in the interest rate from r_H. It falls until the public wants to hold the quantity of money that is actually available, $\overline{M}$. Again, the interest rate will end up at r_E.

Two Models of the Interest Rate

Here we have developed what is known as the liquidity preference model of the interest rate. In this model, the equilibrium interest rate is the rate at which the quantity of money demanded equals the quantity of money supplied. This model is different from, but consistent with, another model known as the loanable funds model of the interest rates, which is developed in the next module. In the loanable funds model, we will see that the interest rate matches the quantity of loanable funds supplied by savers with the quantity of loanable funds demanded for investment spending.

Module 28 AP Review

Solutions appear at the back of the book.

Check Your Understanding

1. Explain how each of the following would affect the quantity of money demanded, and indicate whether each change would cause a movement along the money demand curve or a shift of the money demand curve.
   a. Short-term interest rates rise from 5% to 30%.
   b. All prices fall by 10%.
   c. New wireless technology automatically charges supermarket purchases to credit cards, eliminating the need to stop at the cash register.
   d. In order to avoid paying taxes, a vast underground economy develops in which workers are paid their wages in cash rather than with checks.

2. How will each of the following affect the opportunity cost or benefit of holding cash? Explain.
   a. Merchants charge a 1% fee on debit/credit card transactions for purchases of less than $50.
   b. To attract more deposits, banks raise the interest paid on six-month CDs.
   c. Real estate prices fall significantly.
   d. The cost of food rises significantly.

Tackle the Test: Multiple-Choice Questions

1. A change in which of the following will shift the money demand curve?
   I. the aggregate price level
   II. real GDP
   III. the interest rate
   a. I only
   b. II only
   c. III only
   d. I and II only
   e. I, II, and III

2. Which of the following will decrease the demand for money?
   a. an increase in the interest rate
   b. inflation
   c. an increase in real GDP
   d. an increase in the availability of ATMs
   e. the adoption of Regulation Q

3. What will happen to the money supply and the equilibrium interest rate if the Federal Reserve sells Treasury securities?

Money supply	Equilibrium interest rate
a. increase	increase
b. decrease	increase
c. increase	decrease
d. decrease	decrease
e. decrease	no change

4. Which of the following is true regarding short-term and long-term interest rates?
   a. Short-term interest rates are always above long-term interest rates.
   b. Short-term interest rates are always below long-term interest rates.
   c. Short-term interest rates are always equal to long-term interest rates.
   d. Short-term interest rates are more important for determining the demand for money.
   e. Long-term interest rates are more important for determining the demand for money.

5. The quantity of money demanded rises (that is, there is a movement along the money demand curve) when
   a. the aggregate price level increases.
   b. the aggregate price level falls.
   c. real GDP increases.
   d. new technology makes banking easier.
   e. short-term interest rates fall.

Tackle the Test: Free-Response Questions

1. Draw three correctly labeled graphs of the money market. Show the effect of each of the following three changes on a separate graph.
   a. The aggregate price level increases.
   b. Real GDP falls.
   c. There is a dramatic increase in online banking.

Answer (6 points)

1 point: The vertical axis is labeled "Interest rate" or "r" and the horizontal axis is labeled "Quantity of money."

1 point: Money supply is vertical and labeled.

1 point: Money demand is negatively sloped and labeled.

1 point: a. Money demand shifts right.

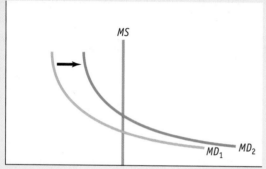

1 point: b. Money demand shifts left.

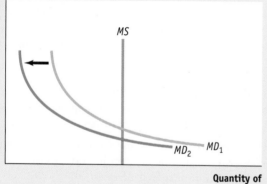

1 point: c. Money demand shifts left.

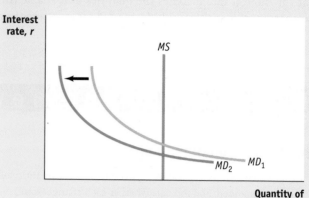

2. Draw a correctly labeled graph showing equilibrium in the money market. Select an interest rate below the equilibrium interest rate and explain what occurs in the market at that interest rate and how the market will eventually return to equilibrium.

Module 29
The Market for Loanable Funds

What you will learn in this Module:

- How the loanable funds market matches savers and investors
- The determinants of supply and demand in the loanable funds market
- How the two models of interest rates can be reconciled

The Market for Loanable Funds

Recall that, for the economy as a whole, savings always equals investment spending. In a closed economy, savings is equal to national savings. In an open economy, savings is equal to national savings plus capital inflow. At any given time, however, savers, the people with funds to lend, are usually not the same as borrowers, the people who want to borrow to finance their investment spending. How are savers and borrowers brought together?

Savers and borrowers are matched up with one another in much the same way producers and consumers are matched up: through markets governed by supply and demand. In the circular-flow diagram, we noted that the *financial markets* channel the savings of households to businesses that want to borrow in order to purchase capital equipment. It's now time to take a look at how those financial markets work.

The Equilibrium Interest Rate There are a large number of different financial markets in the financial system, such as the bond market and the stock market. However, economists often work with a simplified model in which they assume that there is just one market that brings together those who want to lend money (savers) and those who want to borrow (firms with investment spending projects). This hypothetical market is known as the **loanable funds market.** The price that is determined in the loanable funds market is the interest rate, denoted by *r*. It is the return a lender receives for allowing borrowers the use of a dollar for one year, calculated as a percentage of the amount borrowed.

Recall that in the money market, the *nominal* interest rate is of central importance and always serves as the "price" measured on the vertical axis. The interest rate in the loanable funds market can be measured in either real or nominal terms—with or without the inclusion of expected inflation that makes nominal rates differ from real rates. Investors and savers care about the *real* interest rate, which tells them the price paid for the use of money aside from the amount paid to keep up with inflation. However, in the real world neither borrowers nor lenders know what the future inflation rate will be when they make a deal, so actual loan contracts specify a nominal interest rate rather than a real interest rate. For this reason, and because it facilitates comparisons between

The **loanable funds market** is a hypothetical market that illustrates the market outcome of the demand for funds generated by borrowers and the supply of funds provided by lenders.

The **rate of return** on a project is the profit earned on the project expressed as a percentage of its cost.

the money market and the loanable funds market, the figures in this section are drawn with the vertical axis measuring the *nominal interest rate for a given expected future inflation rate*. As long as the expected inflation rate is unchanged, changes in the nominal interest rate also lead to changes in the real interest rate. We take up the influence of inflation later in this module.

We should also note at this point that there are, in reality, many different kinds of nominal interest rates because there are many different kinds of loans—short-term loans, long-term loans, loans made to corporate borrowers, loans made to governments, and so on. In the interest of simplicity, we'll ignore those differences and assume that there is only one type of loan. Figure 29.1 illustrates the hypothetical demand for loanable funds. On the horizontal axis we show the quantity of loanable funds demanded. On the vertical axis we show the interest rate, which is the "price" of borrowing. To see why the demand curve for loanable funds, *D*, slopes downward, imagine that there are many businesses, each of which has one potential investment project. How does a given business decide whether or not to borrow money to finance its project? The decision depends on the interest rate the business faces and the **rate of return** on its project—the profit earned on the project expressed as a percentage of its cost. This can be expressed in a formula as:

$$(29\text{-}1) \quad \text{Rate of return} = \frac{\text{Revenue from project–Cost of project}}{\text{Cost of project}} \times 100$$

A business will want a loan when the rate of return on its project is greater than or equal to the interest rate. So, for example, at an interest rate of 12%, only businesses with projects that yield a rate of return greater than or equal to 12% will want a loan. The demand curve in Figure 29.1 shows that if the interest rate is 12%, businesses will want to borrow $150 billion (point *A*); if the interest rate is only 4%, businesses will want to borrow a larger amount, $450 billion (point *B*). That's a consequence of our assumption that the demand curve slopes downward: the lower the interest rate, the larger the total quantity of loanable funds demanded. Why do we make that assumption? Because, in reality, the number of potential investment projects that yield at least 4% is always greater than the number that yield at least 12%.

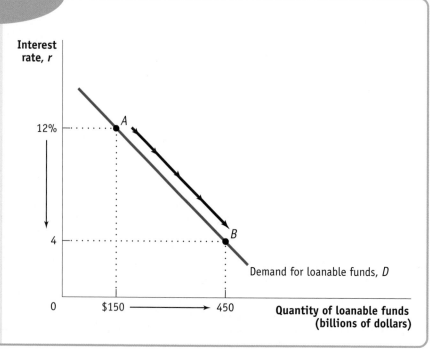

figure 29.1

The Demand for Loanable Funds

The demand curve for loanable funds slopes downward: the lower the interest rate, the greater the quantity of loanable funds demanded. Here, reducing the interest rate from 12% to 4% increases the quantity of loanable funds demanded from $150 billion to $450 billion.

figure 29.2

The Supply of Loanable Funds

The supply curve for loanable funds slopes upward: the higher the interest rate, the greater the quantity of loanable funds supplied. Here, increasing the interest rate from 4% to 12% increases the quantity of loanable funds supplied from $150 billion to $450 billion.

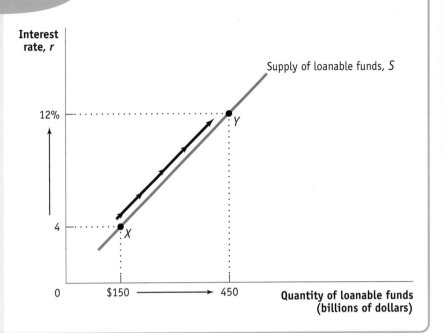

Figure 29.2 shows the hypothetical supply of loanable funds. Again, the interest rate plays the same role that the price plays in ordinary supply and demand analysis. Savers incur an opportunity cost when they lend to a business; the funds could instead be spent on consumption—say, a nice vacation. Whether a given individual becomes a lender by making funds available to borrowers depends on the interest rate received in return. By saving your money today and earning interest on it, you are rewarded with higher consumption in the future when your loan is repaid with interest. So it is a good assumption that more people are willing to forgo current consumption and make a loan when the interest rate is higher. As a result, our hypothetical supply curve of loanable funds slopes upward. In Figure 29.2, lenders will supply $150 billion to the loanable funds market at an interest rate of 4% (point *X*); if the interest rate rises to 12%, the quantity of loanable funds supplied will rise to $450 billion (point *Y*).

The equilibrium interest rate is the interest rate at which the quantity of loanable funds supplied equals the quantity of loanable funds demanded. As you can see in Figure 29.3 on the next page, the equilibrium interest rate, r_E, and the total quantity of lending, Q_E, are determined by the intersection of the supply and demand curves, at point *E*. Here, the equilibrium interest rate is 8%, at which $300 billion is lent and borrowed. Investment spending projects with a rate of return of 8% or more are funded; projects with a rate of return of less than 8% are not. Correspondingly, only lenders who are willing to accept an interest rate of 8% or less will have their offers to lend funds accepted.

Figure 29.3 shows how the market for loanable funds matches up desired savings with desired investment spending: in equilibrium, the quantity of funds that savers want to lend is equal to the quantity of funds that firms want to borrow. The figure also shows that this match-up is efficient, in two senses. First, the right investments get made: the investment spending projects that are actually financed have higher rates of return than those that do not get financed. Second, the right people do the saving: the potential savers who actually lend funds are willing to lend for lower interest rates than those who do not. The insight that the loanable funds market leads to an efficient use of savings, although drawn from a highly simplified model, has important implications for real life. As we'll see shortly, it is the reason that a well-functioning financial system increases an economy's long-run economic growth rate.

figure 29.3

Equilibrium in the Loanable Funds Market

At the equilibrium interest rate, the quantity of loanable funds supplied equals the quantity of loanable funds demanded. Here, the equilibrium interest rate is 8%, with $300 billion of funds lent and borrowed. Investment spending projects with a rate of return of 8% or higher receive funding; those with a lower rate of return do not. Lenders who demand an interest rate of 8% or lower have their offers of loans accepted; those who demand a higher interest rate do not.

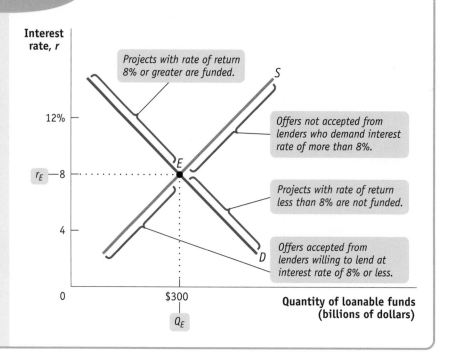

Before we get to that, however, let's look at how the market for loanable funds responds to shifts of demand and supply.

Shifts of the Demand for Loanable Funds The equilibrium interest rate changes when there are shifts of the demand curve for loanable funds, the supply curve for loanable funds, or both. Let's start by looking at the causes and effects of changes in demand.

The factors that can cause the demand curve for loanable funds to shift include the following:

- *Changes in perceived business opportunities:* A change in beliefs about the rate of return on investment spending can increase or reduce the amount of desired spending at any given interest rate. For example, during the 1990s there was great excitement over the business possibilities created by the Internet, which had just begun to be widely used. As a result, businesses rushed to buy computer equipment, put fiber-optic cables in the ground, and so on. This shifted the demand for loanable funds to the right. By 2001, the failure of many dot-com businesses led to disillusionment with technology-related investment; this shifted the demand for loanable funds back to the left.

- *Changes in the government's borrowing:* Governments that run budget deficits are major sources of the demand for loanable funds. As a result, changes in the budget deficit can shift the demand curve for loanable funds. For example, between 2000 and 2003, as the U.S. federal government went from a budget surplus to a budget deficit, net federal borrowing went from *minus* $189 billion—that is, in 2000 the federal government was actually providing loanable funds to the market because it was paying off some of its debt—to *plus* $416 billion because in 2003 the government had to borrow large sums to pay its bills. This change in the federal budget position had the effect, other things equal, of shifting the demand curve for loanable funds to the right.

Figure 29.4 shows the effects of an increase in the demand for loanable funds. S is the supply of loanable funds, and D_1 is the initial demand curve. The initial equilibrium interest rate is r_1. An increase in the demand for loanable funds means that the quantity of funds demanded rises at any given interest rate, so the demand curve shifts rightward to D_2. As a result, the equilibrium interest rate rises to r_2.

figure 29.4

An Increase in the Demand for Loanable Funds

If the quantity of funds demanded by borrowers rises at any given interest rate, the demand for loanable funds shifts rightward from D_1 to D_2. As a result, the equilibrium interest rate rises from r_1 to r_2.

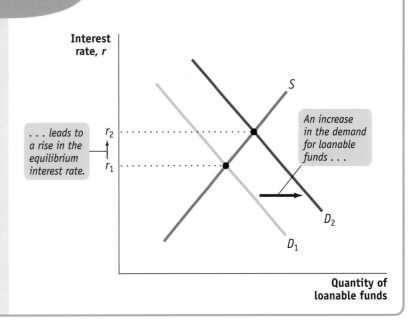

... leads to a rise in the equilibrium interest rate.

An increase in the demand for loanable funds ...

The fact that an increase in the demand for loanable funds leads, other things equal, to a rise in the interest rate has one especially important implication: beyond concern about repayment, there are other reasons to be wary of government budget deficits. As we've already seen, an increase in the government's deficit shifts the demand curve for loanable funds to the right, which leads to a higher interest rate. If the interest rate rises, businesses will cut back on their investment spending. So a rise in the government budget deficit tends to reduce overall investment spending. Economists call the negative effect of government budget deficits on investment spending **crowding out.** The threat of crowding out is a key source of concern about persistent budget deficits.

Crowding out occurs when a government deficit drives up the interest rate and leads to reduced investment spending.

Shifts of the Supply of Loanable Funds Like the demand for loanable funds, the supply of loanable funds can shift. Among the factors that can cause the supply of loanable funds to shift are the following:

- *Changes in private savings behavior:* A number of factors can cause the level of private savings to change at any given rate of interest. For example, between 2000 and 2006 rising home prices in the United States made many homeowners feel richer, making them willing to spend more and save less. This had the effect of shifting the supply of loanable funds to the left. The drop in home prices between 2006 and 2009 had the opposite effect, shifting the supply of loanable funds to the right.

- *Changes in capital inflows:* Capital flows into a country can change as investors' perceptions of that country change. For example, Argentina experienced large capital inflows during much of the 1990s because international investors believed that economic reforms early in the decade had made it a safe place to put their funds. By the late 1990s, however, there were signs of economic trouble, and investors lost confidence, causing the inflow of funds to dry up. As we've already seen, the United States has received large capital inflows in recent years, with much of the money coming from China and the Middle East. Those inflows helped fuel a big increase in residential investment spending—newly constructed homes—from 2003 to 2006. As a result of the worldwide slump, those inflows began to trail off in 2008.

figure 29.5

An Increase in the Supply of Loanable Funds

If the quantity of funds supplied by lenders rises at any given interest rate, the supply of loanable funds shifts rightward from S_1 to S_2. As a result, the equilibrium interest rate falls from r_1 to r_2.

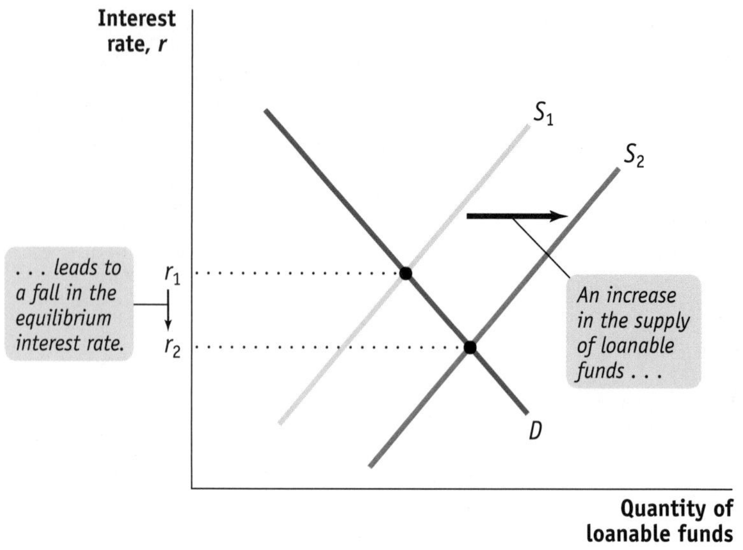

... leads to a fall in the equilibrium interest rate.

An increase in the supply of loanable funds ...

Figure 29.5 shows the effects of an increase in the supply of loanable funds. D is the demand for loanable funds, and S_1 is the initial supply curve. The initial equilibrium interest rate is r_1. An increase in the supply of loanable funds means that the quantity of funds supplied rises at any given interest rate, so the supply curve shifts rightward to S_2. As a result, the equilibrium interest rate falls to r_2.

Inflation and Interest Rates Anything that shifts either the supply of loanable funds curve or the demand for loanable funds curve changes the interest rate. Historically, major changes in interest rates have been driven by many factors, including changes in government policy and technological innovations that created new investment opportunities. However, arguably the most important factor affecting interest rates over time—the reason, for example, why interest rates today are much lower than they were in the late 1970s and early 1980s—is changing expectations about future inflation, which shift both the supply and the demand for loanable funds.

To understand the effect of expected inflation on interest rates, recall our discussion in Module 14 of the way inflation creates winners and losers—for example, the way that high U.S. inflation in the 1970s and 1980s reduced the real value of homeowners' mortgages, which was good for the homeowners but bad for the banks. We know that economists capture the effect of inflation on borrowers and lenders by distinguishing between the *nominal interest rate* and the *real interest rate,* where the distinction is as follows:

$$\text{Real interest rate} = \text{Nominal interest rate} - \text{Inflation rate}$$

The true cost of borrowing is the real interest rate, not the nominal interest rate. To see why, suppose a firm borrows $10,000 for one year at a 10% nominal interest rate. At the end of the year, it must repay $11,000—the amount borrowed plus the interest. But suppose that over the course of the year the average level of prices increases by 10%, so that the real interest rate is zero. Then the $11,000 repayment has the same purchasing power as the original $10,000 loan. In effect, the borrower has received a zero-interest loan.

Similarly, the true payoff to lending is the real interest rate, not the nominal rate. Suppose that a bank makes a $10,000 loan for one year at a 10% nominal interest rate. At the end of the year, the bank receives an $11,000 repayment. But if the average level of prices rises by 10% per year, the purchasing power of the money the bank gets back is no more than that of the money it lent out. In effect, the bank has made a zero-interest loan.

The expectations of borrowers and lenders about future inflation rates are normally based on recent experience. In the late 1970s, after a decade of high inflation, borrowers and lenders expected future inflation to be high. By the late 1990s, after a decade of fairly low inflation, borrowers and lenders expected future inflation to be low. And these changing expectations about future inflation had a strong effect on the nominal interest rate, largely explaining why interest rates were much lower in the early years of the twenty-first century than they were in the early 1980s.

Let's look at how changes in the expected future rate of inflation are reflected in the loanable funds model.

In Figure 29.6, the curves S_0 and D_0 show the supply and demand for loanable funds given that the expected future rate of inflation is 0%. In that case, equilibrium is at E_0 and the equilibrium nominal interest rate is 4%. Because expected future inflation is 0%, the equilibrium expected real interest rate over the life of the loan, the real interest rate expected by borrowers and lenders when the loan is contracted, is also 4%.

Now suppose that the expected future inflation rate rises to 10%. The demand curve for funds shifts upward to D_{10}: borrowers are now willing to borrow as much at a nominal interest rate of 14% as they were previously willing to borrow at 4%. That's because with a 10% inflation rate, a 14% nominal interest rate corresponds to a 4% real interest rate. Similarly, the supply curve of funds shifts upward to S_{10}: lenders require a nominal interest rate of 14% to persuade them to lend as much as they would previously have lent at 4%. The new equilibrium is at E_{10}: the result of an expected future inflation rate of 10% is that the equilibrium nominal interest rate rises from 4% to 14%.

This situation can be summarized as a general principle, known as the **Fisher effect** (after the American economist Irving Fisher, who proposed it in 1930): *the expected real interest rate is unaffected by the change in expected future inflation.* According to the Fisher effect, an increase in expected future inflation drives up nominal interest rates, where each additional percentage point of expected future inflation drives up the nominal interest rate by 1 percentage point. The central point is that both lenders and borrowers

According to the **Fisher effect,** an increase in expected future inflation drives up the nominal interest rate, leaving the expected real interest rate unchanged.

figure 29.6

The Fisher Effect

D_0 and S_0 are the demand and supply curves for loanable funds when the expected future inflation rate is 0%. At an expected inflation rate of 0%, the equilibrium nominal interest rate is 4%. An increase in expected future inflation pushes both the demand and supply curves upward by 1 percentage point for every percentage point increase in expected future inflation. D_{10} and S_{10} are the demand and supply curves for loanable funds when the expected future inflation rate is 10%. The 10 percentage point increase in expected future inflation raises the equilibrium nominal interest rate to 14%. The expected real interest rate remains at 4%, and the equilibrium quantity of loanable funds also remains unchanged.

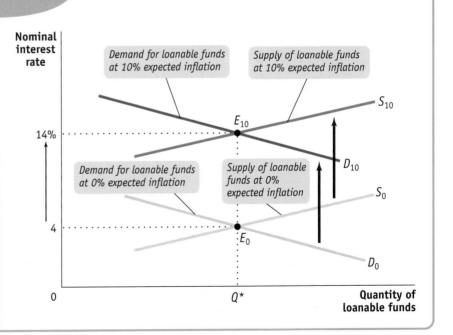

base their decisions on the expected real interest rate. As long as the level of inflation is expected, it does not affect the equilibrium quantity of loanable funds or the expected real interest rate; all it affects is the equilibrium nominal interest rate.

Reconciling the Two Interest Rate Models

In Module 28 we developed what is known as the liquidity preference model of the interest rate. In that model, the equilibrium interest rate is the rate at which the quantity of money demanded equals the quantity of money supplied. In the loanable funds model, we see that the interest rate matches the quantity of loanable funds supplied by savers with the quantity of loanable funds demanded for investment spending. How do the two compare?

The Interest Rate in the Short Run

As we explained using the liquidity preference model, a fall in the interest rate leads to a rise in investment spending, *I*, which then leads to a rise in both real GDP and consumer spending, *C*. The rise in real GDP doesn't lead only to a rise in consumer spending, however. It also leads to a rise in savings: at each stage of the multiplier process, part of the increase in disposable income is saved. How much do savings rise? According to the *savings–investment spending identity*, total savings in the economy is always equal to investment spending. This tells us that when a fall in the interest rate leads to higher investment spending, the resulting increase in real GDP generates exactly enough additional savings to match the rise in investment spending. To put it another way, after a fall in the interest rate, the quantity of savings supplied rises exactly enough to match the quantity of savings demanded.

Figure 29.7 shows how our two models of the interest rate are reconciled in the short run by the links among changes in the interest rate, changes in real GDP, and

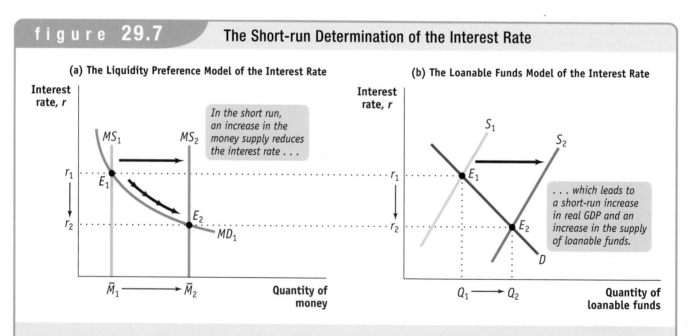

figure 29.7   **The Short-run Determination of the Interest Rate**

Panel (a) shows the liquidity preference model of the interest rate: the equilibrium interest rate matches the money supply to the quantity of money demanded. In the short run, the interest rate is determined in the money market, where an increase in the money supply, from $\bar{M}_1$ to $\bar{M}_2$, pushes the equilibrium interest rate down, from r_1 to r_2. Panel (b) shows the loanable funds model of the interest rate. The fall in the interest rate in the money market leads, through the multiplier effect, to an increase in real GDP and savings; to a rightward shift of the supply curve of loanable funds, from S_1 to S_2; and to a fall in the interest rate, from r_1 to r_2. As a result, the new equilibrium interest rate in the loanable funds market matches the new equilibrium interest rate in the money market at r_2.

changes in savings. Panel (a) represents the liquidity preference model of the interest rate. MS_1 and MD_1 are the initial supply and demand curves for money. According to the liquidity preference model, the equilibrium interest rate in the economy is the rate at which the quantity of money supplied is equal to the quantity of money demanded in the money market. Panel (b) represents the loanable funds model of the interest rate. S_1 is the initial supply curve and D is the demand curve for loanable funds. According to the loanable funds model, the equilibrium interest rate in the economy is the rate at which the quantity of loanable funds supplied is equal to the quantity of loanable funds demanded in the market for loanable funds.

In Figure 29.7 both the money market and the market for loanable funds are initially in equilibrium at E_1 with the same interest rate, r_1. You might think that this would happen only by accident, but in fact it will always be true. To see why, let's look at what happens when the Fed increases the money supply from $\overline{M}_1$ to $\overline{M}_2$. This pushes the money supply curve rightward to MS_2, causing the equilibrium interest rate in the market for money to fall to r_2, and the economy moves to a short-run equilibrium at E_2. What happens in panel (b), in the market for loanable funds? In the short run, the fall in the interest rate due to the increase in the money supply leads to a rise in real GDP, which generates a rise in savings through the multiplier process. This rise in savings shifts the supply curve for loanable funds rightward, from S_1 to S_2, moving the equilibrium in the loanable funds market from E_1 to E_2 and also reducing the equilibrium interest rate in the loanable funds market. And we know that savings rise by exactly enough to match the rise in investment spending. This tells us that the equilibrium rate in the loanable funds market falls to r_2, the same as the new equilibrium interest rate in the money market.

In the short run, then, the supply and demand for money determine the interest rate, and the loanable funds market follows the lead of the money market. When a change in the supply of money leads to a change in the interest rate, the resulting change in real GDP causes the supply of loanable funds to change as well. As a result, the equilibrium interest rate in the loanable funds market is the same as the equilibrium interest rate in the money market.

Notice our use of the phrase "in the short run." Changes in aggregate demand affect aggregate output only in the short run. In the long run, aggregate output is equal to potential output. So our story about how a fall in the interest rate leads to a rise in aggregate output, which leads to a rise in savings, applies only to the short run. In the long run, as we'll see next, the determination of the interest rate is quite different because the roles of the two markets are reversed. In the long run, the loanable funds market determines the equilibrium interest rate, and it is the market for money that follows the lead of the loanable funds market.

The Interest Rate in the Long Run

In the short run an increase in the money supply leads to a fall in the interest rate, and a decrease in the money supply leads to a rise in the interest rate. In the long run, however, changes in the money supply don't affect the interest rate.

Figure 29.8 on the next page shows why. As in Figure 29.7, panel (a) shows the liquidity preference model of the interest rate and panel (b) shows the supply and demand for loanable funds. We assume that in both panels the economy is initially at E_1, in long-run macroeconomic equilibrium at potential output with the money supply equal to $\overline{M}_1$. The demand curve for loanable funds is D, and the initial supply curve for loanable funds is S_1. The initial equilibrium interest rate in both markets is r_1.

Now suppose the money supply rises from $\overline{M}_1$ to $\overline{M}_2$. As we saw in Figure 29.7, this initially reduces the interest rate to r_2. However, in the long run the aggregate price level will rise by the same proportion as the increase in the money supply (due to the *neutrality of money*, a topic presented in detail in the next section). A rise in the aggregate price level increases money demand in the same proportion. So in the long run the money demand curve shifts out to MD_2, and the equilibrium interest rate rises back to its original level, r_1.

Panel (b) of Figure 29.8 shows what happens in the market for loanable funds. We saw earlier that an increase in the money supply leads to a short-run rise in real GDP and that

figure 29.8 — The Long-run Determination of the Interest Rate

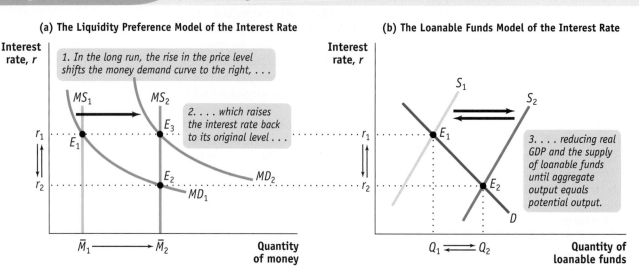

(a) The Liquidity Preference Model of the Interest Rate

1. In the long run, the rise in the price level shifts the money demand curve to the right, . . .

2. . . . which raises the interest rate back to its original level . . .

MS_1 MS_2 E_3 E_1 r_1 E_2 r_2 MD_1 MD_2

$\bar{M}_1 \longrightarrow \bar{M}_2$

Quantity of money

Interest rate, r

(b) The Loanable Funds Model of the Interest Rate

S_1 S_2 E_1 r_1 E_2 r_2 D

3. . . . reducing real GDP and the supply of loanable funds until aggregate output equals potential output.

$Q_1 \rightleftharpoons Q_2$

Quantity of loanable funds

Interest rate, r

Panel (a) shows the liquidity preference model long-run adjustment to an increase in the money supply from $\bar{M}_1$ to $\bar{M}_2$; panel (b) shows the corresponding long-run adjustment in the loanable funds market. As we discussed in Figure 29.7, the increase in the money supply reduces the interest rate from r_1 to r_2, increases real GDP, and increases savings in the short run. This is shown in panel (a) and panel (b) as the movement from E_1 to E_2. In the long run, however, the increase in the money supply raises wages and other nominal prices; this shifts

the money demand curve in panel (a) from MD_1 to MD_2, leading to an increase in the interest rate from r_1 to r_2 as the economy moves from E_2 to E_3. The rise in the interest rate causes a fall in real GDP and a fall in savings, shifting the loanable funds supply curve back to S_1 from S_2 and moving the loanable funds market from E_2 back to E_1. In the long run, the equilibrium interest rate is the rate that matches the supply and demand for loanable funds when real GDP equals potential output.

this shifts the supply of loanable funds rightward from S_1 to S_2. In the long run, however, real GDP falls back to its original level as wages and other nominal prices rise. As a result, the supply of loanable funds, S, which initially shifted from S_1 to S_2, shifts back to S_1.

In the long run, then, changes in the money supply do not affect the interest rate. So what determines the interest rate in the long run—that is, what determines r_1 in Figure 29.8? The answer is the supply and demand for loanable funds. More specifically, in the long run the equilibrium interest rate is the rate that matches the supply of loanable funds with the demand for loanable funds when real GDP equals potential output.

Module 29 AP Review

Solutions appear at the back of the book.

Check Your Understanding

1. Use a diagram of the loanable funds market to illustrate the effect of the following events on the equilibrium interest rate and quantity of loanable funds.
   a. An economy is opened to international movements of capital, and a capital inflow occurs.
   b. Retired people generally save less than working people at any interest rate. The proportion of retired people in the population goes up.

2. Explain what is wrong with the following statement: "Savings and investment spending may not be equal in the economy as a whole in equilibrium because when the interest rate rises, households will want to save more money than businesses will want to invest."

3. Suppose that expected inflation rises from 3% to 6%.
   a. How will the real interest rate be affected by this change?
   b. How will the nominal interest rate be affected by this change?
   c. What will happen to the equilibrium quantity of loanable funds?

Tackle the Test: Multiple-Choice Questions

1. A business will decide whether or not to borrow money to finance a project based on a comparison of the interest rate with the _____ from its project.
   a. expected revenue
   b. profit
   c. rate of return
   d. cost generated
   e. demand generated

2. The real interest rate equals the
   a. nominal interest rate plus the inflation rate.
   b. nominal interest rate minus the inflation rate.
   c. nominal interest rate divided by the inflation rate.
   d. nominal interest rate times the inflation rate.
   e. federal funds rate.

3. Which of the following will increase the demand for loanable funds?
   a. a federal government budget surplus
   b. an increase in perceived business opportunities
   c. a decrease in the interest rate
   d. positive capital inflows
   e. decreased private saving rates

4. Which of the following will increase the supply of loanable funds?
   a. an increase in perceived business opportunities
   b. decreased government borrowing
   c. an increased private saving rate
   d. an increase in the expected inflation rate
   e. a decrease in capital inflows

5. Both lenders and borrowers base their decisions on
   a. expected real interest rates.
   b. expected nominal interest rates.
   c. real interest rates.
   d. nominal interest rates.
   e. Nominal interest rates minus real interest rates.

Tackle the Test: Free-Response Questions

1. Draw a correctly labeled graph showing equilibrium in the loanable funds market.

2. Does each of the following affect either the supply or the demand for loanable funds, and if so, does the affected curve increase (shift to the right) or decrease (shift to the left)?
   a. There is an increase in capital inflows into the economy.
   b. Businesses are pessimistic about future business conditions.
   c. The government increases borrowing.
   d. The private savings rate decreases.

Answer (6 points)

1 point: Vertical axis labeled "Interest rate" or "r"

1 point: Horizontal axis labeled "Quantity of loanable funds"

1 point: Downward sloping demand curve for loanable funds (labeled)

1 point: Upward sloping supply curve for loanable funds (labeled)

1 point: Equilibrium quantity of loanable funds shown on horizontal axis below where curves intersect

1 point: Equilibrium interest rate shown on vertical axis across from where curves intersect

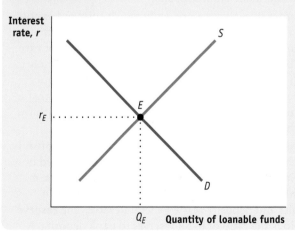

Summary

1. Investment in physical capital is necessary for long-run economic growth. So in order for an economy to grow, it must channel savings into investment spending.

2. According to the **savings–investment spending identity,** savings and investment spending are always equal for the economy as a whole. The government is a source of savings when it runs a positive **budget balance,** also known as a **budget surplus;** it is a source of dissavings when it runs a negative budget balance, also known as a **budget deficit.** In a closed economy, savings is equal to **national savings,** the sum of private savings plus the budget balance. In an open economy, savings is equal to national savings plus **capital inflow** of foreign savings. When a capital outflow, or negative capital inflow, occurs, some portion of national savings is funding investment spending in other countries.

3. Households invest their current savings or **wealth**—their accumulated savings—by purchasing assets. Assets come in the form of either a **financial asset,** a paper claim that entitles the buyer to future income from the seller, or a **physical asset,** a claim on a tangible object that gives the owner the right to dispose of it as desired. A financial asset is also a **liability** from the point of view of its seller. There are four main types of financial assets: loans, bonds, stocks, and **bank deposits.** Each of them serves a different purpose in addressing the three fundamental tasks of a financial system: reducing **transaction costs**—the cost of making a deal; reducing **financial risk**—uncertainty about future outcomes that involves financial gains and losses; and providing **liquid** assets—assets that can be quickly converted into cash without much loss of value (in contrast to **illiquid** assets, which are not easily converted).

4. Although many small and moderate-size borrowers use bank **loans** to fund investment spending, larger companies typically issue bonds. Bonds with a higher risk of **default** must typically pay a higher interest rate. Business owners reduce their risk by selling stock. Although stocks usually generate a higher return than bonds, investors typically wish to reduce their risk by engaging in **diversification,** owning a wide range of assets whose returns are based on unrelated, or independent, events. Most people are risk-averse, viewing the loss of a given amount of money as a significant hardship but viewing the gain of an equal amount of money as a much less significant benefit. **Loan-backed securities,** a recent innovation, are assets created by pooling individual loans and selling shares of that pool to investors. Because they are more diversified and more liquid than individual loans, trading on financial markets like bonds, they are preferred by investors. It can be difficult, however, to assess their quality.

5. **Financial intermediaries**—institutions such as **mutual funds, pension funds, life insurance companies,** and **banks**—are critical components of the financial system. Mutual funds and pension funds allow small investors to diversify and life insurance companies allow families to reduce risk.

6. A bank allows individuals to hold liquid bank deposits that are then used to finance illiquid loans. Banks can perform this mismatch because on average only a small fraction of depositors withdraw their savings at any one time. Banks are a key ingredient in long-run economic growth.

7. **Money** is any asset that can easily be used to purchase goods and services. **Currency in circulation** and **checkable bank deposits** are both considered part of the **money supply.** Money plays three roles: it is a **medium of exchange** used for transactions, a **store of value** that holds purchasing power over time, and a **unit of account** in which prices are stated.

8. Over time, **commodity money,** which consists of goods possessing value aside from their role as money, such as gold and silver coins, was replaced by **commodity-backed money,** such as paper currency backed by gold. Today the dollar is pure **fiat money,** whose value derives solely from its official role.

9. The Federal Reserve calculates two measures of the money supply. M1 is the narrowest **monetary aggregate;** it contains only currency in circulation, traveler's checks, and checkable bank deposits. M2 includes a wider range of assets called **near-moneys,** mainly other forms of bank deposits, that can easily be converted into checkable bank deposits.

10. In order to evaluate a project in which costs or benefits are realized in the future, you must first transform them into their **present values** using the **interest rate,** r. The present value of \$1 realized one year from now is $\$1/(1 + r)$, the amount of money you must lend out today to have \$1 one year from now. Once this transformation is done, you should choose the project with the highest **net present value.**

11. Banks allow depositors immediate access to their funds, but they also lend out most of the funds deposited in their care. To meet demands for cash, they maintain **bank reserves** composed of both currency held in vaults and deposits at the Federal Reserve. The **reserve ratio** is the ratio of bank reserves to bank deposits. A **T-account** summarizes a bank's financial position, with loans and reserves counted as assets, and deposits counted as liabilities.

12. Banks have sometimes been subject to **bank runs,** most notably in the early 1930s. To avert this danger, depositors are now protected by **deposit insurance,** bank owners face capital requirements that reduce the incentive to make overly risky loans with depositors' funds, and banks must satisfy **reserve requirements,** a legally mandated **required reserve ratio.**

13. When currency is deposited in a bank, it starts a multiplier process in which banks lend out **excess reserves,** leading to an increase in the money supply—so banks create money. If the entire money supply consisted of checkable bank deposits, the money supply would be equal to the value of reserves divided by the reserve ratio. In reality, much of the **monetary base** consists of currency in circulation, and the **money multiplier** is the ratio of the money supply to the monetary base.

14. In response to the Panic of 1907, the Fed was created to centralize holding of reserves, inspect banks' books, and make the money supply sufficiently responsive to varying economic conditions.

15. The Great Depression sparked widespread bank runs in the early 1930s, which greatly worsened and lengthened the depth of the Depression. Federal deposit insurance was created, and the government recapitalized banks by lending to them and by buying shares of banks. By 1933, banks had been separated into two categories: **commercial** (covered by deposit insurance) and **investment** (not covered). Public acceptance of deposit insurance finally stopped the bank runs of the Great Depression.

16. The **savings and loan (thrift)** crisis of the 1980s arose because insufficiently regulated S&Ls engaged in overly risky speculation and incurred huge losses. Depositors in failed S&Ls were compensated with taxpayer funds because they were covered by deposit insurance. However, the crisis caused steep losses in the financial and real estate sectors, resulting in a recession in the early 1990s.

17. During the mid-1990s, the hedge fund LTCM used huge amounts of **leverage** to speculate in global financial markets, incurred massive losses, and collapsed. LTCM was so large that, in selling assets to cover its losses, it caused **balance sheet effects** for firms around the world, leading to the prospect of a **vicious cycle of deleveraging.** As a result, credit markets around the world froze. The New York Fed coordinated a private bailout of LTCM and revived world credit markets.

18. **Subprime lending** during the U.S. housing bubble of the mid-2000s spread through the financial system via **securitization.** When the bubble burst, massive losses by banks and nonbank financial institutions led to widespread collapse in the financial system. To prevent another Great Depression, the Fed and the U.S. Treasury expanded lending to bank and nonbank institutions, provided capital through the purchase of bank shares, and purchased private debt. Because much of the crisis originated in nontraditional bank institutions, the crisis of 2008 raised the question of whether a wider safety net and broader regulation were needed in the financial sector.

19. The monetary base is controlled by the Federal Reserve, the **central bank** of the United States. The Fed regulates banks and sets reserve requirements. To meet those requirements, banks borrow and lend reserves in the **federal funds market** at the **federal funds rate.** Through the **discount window** facility, banks can borrow from the Fed at the **discount rate.**

20. **Open-market operations** by the Fed are the principal tool of monetary policy: the Fed can increase or reduce the monetary base by buying U.S. Treasury bills from banks or selling U.S. Treasury bills to banks.

21. The **money demand curve** arises from a trade-off between the opportunity cost of holding money and the liquidity that money provides. The opportunity cost of holding money depends on **short-term interest rates,** not **long-term interest rates.** Changes in the aggregate price level, real GDP, technology, and institutions shift the money demand curve.

22. According to the **liquidity preference model of the interest rate,** the interest rate is determined in the money market by the money demand curve and the **money supply curve.** The Federal Reserve can change the interest rate in the short run by shifting the money supply curve. In practice, the Fed uses open-market operations to achieve a target federal funds rate, which other short-term interest rates generally follow.

23. The hypothetical **loanable funds market** shows how loans from savers are allocated among borrowers with investment spending projects. In equilibrium, only those projects with a **rate of return** greater than or equal to the equilibrium interest rate will be funded. By showing how gains from trade between lenders and borrowers are maximized, the loanable funds market shows why a well-functioning financial system leads to greater long-run economic growth. Government budget deficits can raise the interest rate and can lead to **crowding out** of investment spending. Changes in perceived business opportunities and in government borrowing shift the demand curve for loanable funds; changes in private savings and capital inflows shift the supply curve.

24. Because neither borrowers nor lenders can know the future inflation rate, loans specify a nominal interest rate rather than a real interest rate. For a given expected future inflation rate, shifts of the demand and supply curves of loanable funds result in changes in the underlying real interest rate, leading to changes in the nominal interest rate. According to the **Fisher effect,** an increase in expected future inflation raises the nominal interest rate one-to-one so that the expected real interest rate remains unchanged.

Key Terms

Problems

1. Given the following information about the closed economy of Brittania, what is the level of investment spending and private savings, and what is the budget balance? What is the relationship among investment spending, private savings, and the budget balance? Is national savings equal to investment spending? There are no government transfers.

   GDP = $1,000 million T = $50 million

   C = $850 million G = $100 million

2. Which of the following are examples of investment spending, investing in financial assets, or investing in physical assets?

   a. Rupert Moneybucks buys 100 shares of existing Coca-Cola stock.

   b. Rhonda Moviestar spends $10 million to buy a mansion built in the 1970s.

   c. Ronald Basketballstar spends $10 million to build a new mansion with a view of the Pacific Ocean.

   d. Rawlings builds a new plant to make catcher's mitts.

   e. Russia buys $100 million in U.S. government bonds.

3. Explain how a well-functioning financial system increases savings and investment spending, holding the budget balance and any capital flows fixed.

4. What are the important types of financial intermediaries in the U.S. economy? What are the primary assets of these intermediaries, and how do they facilitate investment spending and saving?

5. For each of the following transactions, what is the initial effect (increase or decrease) on M1? or M2?

   a. You sell a few shares of stock and put the proceeds into your savings account.

   b. You sell a few shares of stock and put the proceeds into your checking account.

   c. You transfer money from your savings account to your checking account.

   d. You discover $0.25 under the floor mat in your car and deposit it in your checking account.

   e. You discover $0.25 under the floor mat in your car and deposit it in your savings account.

6. There are three types of money: commodity money, commodity-backed money, and fiat money. Which type of money is used in each of the following situations?

   a. Bottles of rum were used to pay for goods in colonial Australia.

b. Salt was used in many European countries as a medium of exchange.

c. For a brief time, Germany used paper money (the "Rye Mark") that could be redeemed for a certain amount of rye, a type of grain.

d. The town of Ithaca, New York, prints its own currency, Ithaca HOURS, which can be used to purchase local goods and services.

7. Indicate whether each of the following is part of M1, M2, or neither:

   a. $95 on your campus meal card

   b. $0.55 in the change cup of your car

   c. $1,663 in your savings account

   d. $459 in your checking account

   e. 100 shares of stock worth $4,000

   f. a $1,000 line of credit on your Sears credit card

8. You have won the state lottery. There are two ways in which you can receive your prize. You can either have $1 million in cash now, or you can have $1.2 million that is paid out as follows: $300,000 now, $300,000 in one year's time, $300,000 in two years' time, and $300,000 in three years' time. The interest rate is 20%. How would you prefer to receive your prize?

9. The drug company Pfizer is considering whether to invest in the development of a new cancer drug. Development will require an initial investment of $10 million now; beginning one year from now, the drug will generate annual profits of $4 million for three years.

   a. If the interest rate is 12%, should Pfizer invest in the development of the new drug? Why or why not?

   b. If the interest rate is 8%, should Pfizer invest in the development of the new drug? Why or why not?

10. Tracy Williams deposits $500 that was in her sock drawer into a checking account at the local bank.

    a. How does the deposit initially change the T-account of the local bank? How does it change the money supply?

    b. If the bank maintains a reserve ratio of 10%, how will it respond to the new deposit?

    c. If every time the bank makes a loan, the loan results in a new checkable bank deposit in a different bank equal to the amount of the loan, by how much could the total money supply in the economy expand in response to Tracy's initial cash deposit of $500?

    d. If every time the bank makes a loan, the loan results in a new checkable bank deposit in a different bank equal to the amount of the loan and the bank maintains a reserve ratio of 5%, by how much could the money supply expand in response to an initial cash deposit of $500?

11. Ryan Cozzens withdraws $400 from his checking account at the local bank and keeps it in his wallet.

    a. How will the withdrawal change the T-account of the local bank and the money supply?

    b. If the bank maintains a reserve ratio of 10%, how will the bank respond to the withdrawal? Assume that the bank responds to insufficient reserves by reducing the amount of

deposits it holds until its level of reserves satisfies its required reserve ratio. The bank reduces its deposits by calling in some of its loans, forcing borrowers to pay back these loans by taking cash from their checking deposits (at the same bank) to make repayment.

   c. If every time the bank decreases its loans, checkable bank deposits fall by the amount of the loan, by how much will the money supply in the economy contract in response to Ryan's withdrawal of $400?

   d. If every time the bank decreases its loans, checkable bank deposits fall by the amount of the loan and the bank maintains a reserve ratio of 20%, by how much will the money supply contract in response to a withdrawal of $400?

12. In Westlandia, the public holds 50% of M1 in the form of currency, and the required reserve ratio is 20%. Estimate how much the money supply will increase in response to a new cash deposit of $500 by completing the accompanying table. (*Hint:* The first row shows that the bank must hold $100 in minimum reserves—20% of the $500 deposit—against this deposit, leaving $400 in excess reserves that can be loaned out. However, since the public wants to hold 50% of the loan in currency, only $400 × 0.5 = $200 of the loan will be deposited in round 2 from the loan granted in round 1.) How does your answer compare to an economy in which the total amount of the loan is deposited in the banking system and the public doesn't hold any of the loan in currency? What does this imply about the relationship between the public's desire for holding currency and the money multiplier?

Round	Deposits	Required reserves	Excess reserves	Loans	Held as currency
1	$500.00	$100.00	$400.00	$400.00	$200.00
2	200.00	?	?	?	?
3	?	?	?	?	?
4	?	?	?	?	?
5	?	?	?	?	?
6	?	?	?	?	?
7	?	?	?	?	?
8	?	?	?	?	?
9	?	?	?	?	?
10	?	?	?	?	?
Total after 10 rounds	?	?	?	?	?

13. What will happen to the money supply under the following circumstances in a checkable-deposits-only system?

    a. The required reserve ratio is 25%, and a depositor withdraws $700 from his checkable bank deposit.

    b. The required reserve ratio is 5%, and a depositor withdraws $700 from his checkable bank deposit.

    c. The required reserve ratio is 20%, and a customer deposits $750 to her checkable bank deposit.

    d. The required reserve ratio is 10%, and a customer deposits $600 to her checkable bank deposit.

14. Although the U.S. Federal Reserve doesn't use changes in reserve requirements to manage the money supply, the central bank of Albernia does. The commercial banks of Albernia have $100 million in reserves and $1,000 million in checkable deposits; the initial required reserve ratio is 10%. The commercial banks follow a policy of holding no excess reserves. The public holds no currency, only checkable deposits in the banking system.

   a. How will the money supply change if the required reserve ratio falls to 5%?

   b. How will the money supply change if the required reserve ratio rises to 25%?

15. Using Figure 26.1 find the Federal Reserve district in which you live. Go to http://www.federalreserve.gov/bios/pres.htm, and click on your district to identify the president of the Federal Reserve Bank in your district. Go to http://www.federalreserve.gov/fomc/ and determine if the president of the Fed is currently a voting member of the Federal Open Market Committee (FOMC).

16. The Congressional Research Service estimates that at least $45 million of counterfeit U.S. $100 notes produced by the North Korean government are in circulation.

   a. Why do U.S. taxpayers lose because of North Korea's counterfeiting?

   b. As of September 2008, the interest rate earned on one-year U.S. Treasury bills was 2.2%. At a 2.2% rate of interest, what is the amount of money U.S. taxpayers are losing per year because of these $45 million in counterfeit notes?

17. The accompanying figure shows new U.S. housing starts, in thousands of units per month, between January 1980 and September 2008. The graph shows a large drop in new housing starts in 1984–1991 and 2006–2008. New housing starts are related to the availability of mortgages.

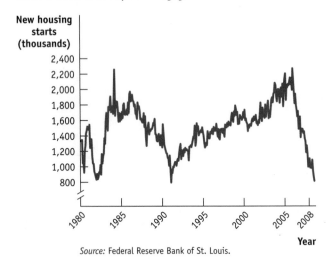

Source: Federal Reserve Bank of St. Louis.

   a. What caused the drop in new housing starts in 1984–1991?

   b. What caused the drop in new housing starts in 2006–2008?

   c. How could better regulation of financial institutions have prevented these two occurrences?

18. Use the market for loanable funds shown in the accompanying diagram to explain what happens to private savings, private investment spending, and the rate of interest if the following events occur. Assume that there are no capital inflows or outflows.

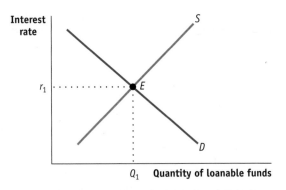

   a. The government reduces the size of its deficit to zero.

   b. At any given interest rate, consumers decide to save more. Assume the budget balance is zero.

   c. At any given interest rate, businesses become very optimistic about the future profitability of investment spending. Assume the budget balance is zero.

19. The government is running a budget balance of zero when it decides to increase education spending by $200 billion and finance the spending by selling bonds. The accompanying diagram shows the market for loanable funds before the government sells the bonds. Assume that there are no capital inflows or outflows. How will the equilibrium interest rate and the equilibrium quantity of loanable funds change? Is there any crowding out in the market?

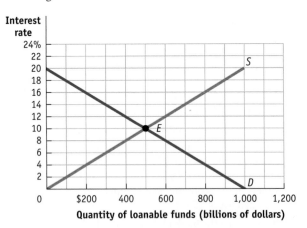

20. In 2006, Congress estimated that the cost of the Iraq War was approximately $100 billion a year. Since the U.S. government was running a budget deficit at the time, assume that the war was financed by government borrowing, which increases the demand for loanable funds without affecting supply. This question considers the likely effect of this government expenditure on the interest rate.

   a. Draw typical demand (D_1) and supply (S_1) curves for loanable funds without the cost of the war accounted for. Label the vertical axis "Interest rate" and the horizontal axis "Quantity of loanable funds." Label the equilibrium point (E_1) and the equilibrium interest rate (r_1).

b. Now consider a new diagram with the cost of the war included in the analysis. Shift the demand curve in the appropriate direction. Label the new equilibrium point (E_2) and the new equilibrium interest rate (r_2).

c. How does the equilibrium interest rate change in response to government expenditure on the war? Explain.

21. How would you respond to a friend who claims that the government should eliminate all purchases that are financed by borrowing because such borrowing crowds out private investment spending?

22. Boris Borrower and Lynn Lender agree that Lynn will lend Boris $10,000 and that Boris will repay the $10,000 with interest in one year. They agree to a nominal interest rate of 8%, reflecting a real interest rate of 3% on the loan and a commonly shared expected inflation rate of 5% over the next year.

a. If the inflation rate is actually 4% over the next year, how does that lower-than-expected inflation rate affect Boris and Lynn? Who is better off?

b. If the actual inflation rate is 7% over the next year, how does that affect Boris and Lynn? Who is better off?

23. Using the accompanying diagram, explain what will happen to the market for loanable funds when there is a fall of

2 percentage points in the expected future inflation rate. How will the change in the expected future inflation rate affect the equilibrium quantity of loanable funds?

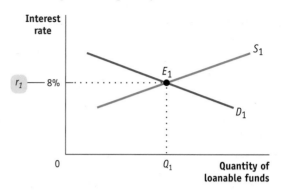

24. Using a figure similar to Figure 29.7, explain how the money market and the loanable funds market react to a reduction in the money supply in the short run.

25. Contrast the short-run effects of an increase in the money supply on the interest rate to the long-run effects of an increase in the money supply on the interest rate. Which market determines the interest rate in the short run? Which market does so in the long run? What are the implications of your answers for the effectiveness of monetary policy in influencing real GDP in the short run and the long run?

Inflation, Unemployment, and Stabilization Policies

THE FED IS ASLEEP!

Jim Cramer's *Mad Money* is one of the most popular shows on CNBC, a cable TV network that specializes in business and financial news. Cramer, who mostly offers investment advice, is known for his sense of showmanship. But few viewers were prepared for his outburst on August 3, 2007, when he began screaming about what he saw as inadequate action from the Federal Reserve:

"Bernanke is being an academic! It is no time to be an academic. . . . **He has no idea how bad it is out there. He has no idea! He has no idea!** . . . and Bill Poole? Has no idea what it's like out there! . . . They're nuts! **They know nothing!** . . . The Fed is asleep! Bill Poole is a shame! He's shameful!!"

Who are Bernanke and Bill Poole? In the previous chapter we described the role of the Federal Reserve System, the U.S. central bank. At the time of Cramer's tirade, Ben Bernanke, a former Princeton professor of economics, was the chair of the Fed's Board of Governors, and William Poole, also a former economics professor, was the president of the Federal Reserve Bank of St. Louis. Both men, because of their positions, are members of the Federal Open Market Committee, which meets eight times a year to set monetary policy. In August 2007, Cramer was crying out for the Fed to change monetary policy in order to address what he perceived to be a growing financial crisis.

In August 2007, an agitated Jim Cramer demanded that the Fed do something to address the growing financial crisis.

Why was Cramer screaming at the Federal Reserve rather than, say, the U.S. Treasury—or, for that matter, the president? The answer is that the Fed's control of monetary policy makes it the first line of response to macroeconomic difficulties—very much including the financial crisis that had Cramer so upset. Indeed, within a few weeks the Fed swung into action with a dramatic reversal of its previous policies.

In Section 4, we developed the aggregate demand and supply model and introduced the use of fiscal policy to stabilize the economy. In Section 5, we introduced money, banking, and the Federal Reserve System, and began to look at how monetary policy is used to stabilize the economy. In this section, we use the models introduced in Sections 4 and 5 to further develop our understanding of stabilization policies (both fiscal and monetary), including their long-run effects on the economy. In addition, we introduce the Phillips curve—a short-run trade-off between unexpected inflation and unemployment—and investigate the role of expectations in the economy. We end the section with a brief summary of the history of macroeconomic thought and how the modern consensus view of stabilization policy has developed.

What you will learn in this **Module:**

- Why governments calculate the cyclically adjusted budget balance
- Why a large public debt may be a cause for concern
- Why implicit liabilities of the government are also a cause for concern

Module 30
Long-run Implications of Fiscal Policy: Deficits and the Public Debt

In Module 20 we discussed how discretionary fiscal policy can be used to stabilize the economy in the short run. During a recession, an expansionary fiscal policy—raising government spending, lowering taxes, or both—can be used to shift the aggregate demand curve to the right. And when there are inflationary pressures in the economy, a contractionary fiscal policy—lowering government spending, raising taxes, or both— can be used to shift the aggregate demand curve to the left. But how do these policies affect the economy over a longer period of time? In this module we will look at some of the long-term effects of fiscal policy, including budget balance, debt, and liabilities.

The Budget Balance

Headlines about the government's budget tend to focus on just one point: whether the government is running a budget surplus or a budget deficit and, in either case, how big. People usually think of surpluses as good: when the federal government ran a record surplus in 2000, many people regarded it as a cause for celebration. Conversely, people usually think of deficits as bad: when the Congressional Budget Office projected a record federal deficit for 2009, many people regarded it as a cause for concern.

How do surpluses and deficits fit into the analysis of fiscal policy? Are deficits ever a good thing and surpluses a bad thing? To answer those questions, let's look at the causes and consequences of surpluses and deficits.

The Budget Balance as a Measure of Fiscal Policy

What do we mean by surpluses and deficits? The budget balance, which we have previously defined, is the difference between the government's tax revenue and its spending, both on goods and services and on government transfers, in a given year. That is, the budget balance—savings by government—is defined by Equation 30-1:

(30-1) $S_{Government} = T - G - TR$

where T is the value of tax revenues, G is government purchases of goods and services, and TR is the value of government transfers. A budget surplus is a positive budget balance, and a budget deficit is a negative budget balance.

Other things equal, expansionary fiscal policies—increased government purchases of goods and services, higher government transfers, or lower taxes—reduce the budget balance for that year. That is, expansionary fiscal policies make a budget surplus smaller or a budget deficit bigger. Conversely, contractionary fiscal policies—reduced government purchases of goods and services, lower government transfers, or higher taxes—increase the budget balance for that year, making a budget surplus bigger or a budget deficit smaller.

You might think this means that changes in the budget balance can be used to measure fiscal policy. In fact, economists often do just that: they use changes in the budget balance as a "quick-and-dirty" way to assess whether current fiscal policy is expansionary or contractionary. But they always keep in mind two reasons this quick-and-dirty approach is sometimes misleading:

- Two different changes in fiscal policy that have equal-size effects on the budget balance may have quite unequal effects on the economy. As we have already seen, changes in government purchases of goods and services have a larger effect on real GDP than equal-size changes in taxes and government transfers.

- Often, changes in the budget balance are themselves the result, not the cause, of fluctuations in the economy.

To understand the second point, we need to examine the effects of the business cycle on the budget.

The Business Cycle and the Cyclically Adjusted Budget Balance

Historically, there has been a strong relationship between the federal government's budget balance and the business cycle. The budget tends to move into deficit when the economy experiences a recession, but deficits tend to get smaller or even turn into surpluses when the economy is expanding. Figure 30.1 shows the federal budget deficit as a percentage of GDP from 1970 to 2009. Shaded areas indicate recessions; unshaded areas indicate expansions. As you can see, the federal budget deficit increased around the time of each recession and usually declined during expansions. In fact, in the late

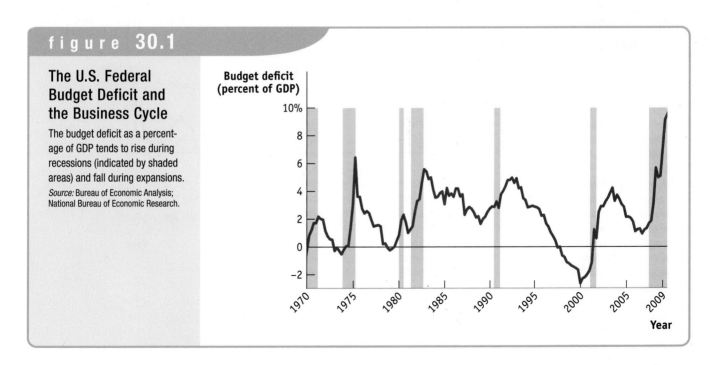

figure 30.1

The U.S. Federal Budget Deficit and the Business Cycle

The budget deficit as a percentage of GDP tends to rise during recessions (indicated by shaded areas) and fall during expansions.

Source: Bureau of Economic Analysis; National Bureau of Economic Research.

stages of the long expansion from 1991 to 2000, the deficit actually became negative—the budget deficit became a budget surplus.

The relationship between the business cycle and the budget balance is even clearer if we compare the budget deficit as a percentage of GDP with the unemployment rate, as we do in Figure 30.2. The budget deficit almost always rises when the unemployment rate rises and falls when the unemployment rate falls.

Is this relationship between the business cycle and the budget balance evidence that policy makers engage in discretionary fiscal policy? Not necessarily. It is largely automatic stabilizers that drive the relationship shown in Figure 30.2. As we learned in the discussion of automatic stabilizers in Module 21, government tax revenue tends to rise and some government transfers, like unemployment benefit payments, tend to fall when the economy expands. Conversely, government tax revenue tends to fall and some government transfers tend to rise when the economy contracts. So the budget tends to move toward surplus during expansions and toward deficit during recessions even without any deliberate action on the part of policy makers.

In assessing budget policy, it's often useful to separate movements in the budget balance due to the business cycle from movements due to discretionary fiscal policy changes. The former are affected by automatic stabilizers and the latter by deliberate changes in government purchases, government transfers, or taxes. It's important to realize that business-cycle effects on the budget balance are temporary: both recessionary gaps (in which real GDP is below potential output) and inflationary gaps (in which real GDP is above potential output) tend to be eliminated in the long run. Removing their effects on the budget balance sheds light on whether the government's taxing and spending policies are sustainable in the long run. In other words, do the government's tax policies yield enough revenue to fund its spending in the long run? As we'll learn shortly, this is a fundamentally more important question than whether the government runs a budget surplus or deficit in the current year.

To separate the effect of the business cycle from the effects of other factors, many governments produce an estimate of what the budget balance would be if there were neither a recessionary nor an inflationary gap. The **cyclically adjusted budget balance**

The **cyclically adjusted budget balance** is an estimate of what the budget balance would be if real GDP were exactly equal to potential output.

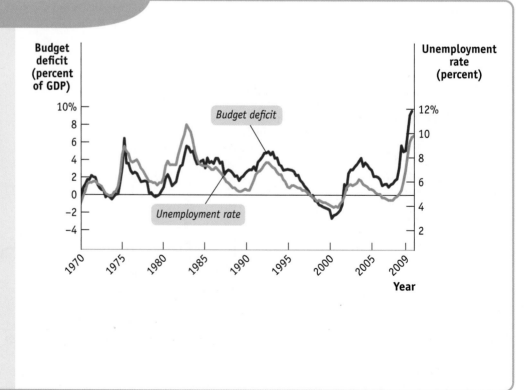

figure 30.2

The U.S. Federal Budget Deficit and the Unemployment Rate

There is a close relationship between the budget balance and the business cycle: a recession moves the budget balance toward deficit, but an expansion moves it toward surplus. Here, the unemployment rate serves as an indicator of the business cycle, and we should expect to see a higher unemployment rate associated with a higher budget deficit. This is confirmed by the figure: the budget deficit as a percentage of GDP moves closely in tandem with the unemployment rate.

Source: Bureau of Economic Analysis; Bureau of Labor Statistics.

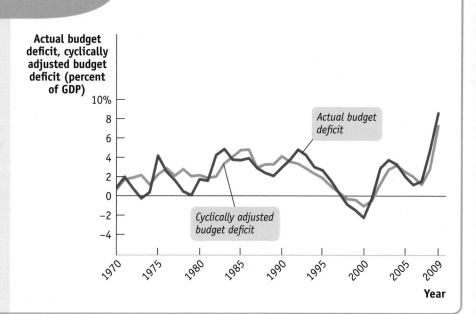

figure 30.3

The Actual Budget Deficit Versus the Cyclically Adjusted Budget Deficit

The cyclically adjusted budget deficit is an estimate of what the budget deficit would be if the economy were at potential output. It fluctuates less than the actual budget deficit, because years of large budget deficits also tend to be years when the economy has a large recessionary gap.

Source: Congressional Budget Office.

is an estimate of what the budget balance would be if real GDP were exactly equal to potential output. It takes into account the extra tax revenue the government would collect and the transfers it would save if a recessionary gap were eliminated—or the revenue the government would lose and the extra transfers it would make if an inflationary gap were eliminated.

Figure 30.3 shows the actual budget deficit and the Congressional Budget Office estimate of the cyclically adjusted budget deficit, both as a percentage of GDP, since 1970. As you can see, the cyclically adjusted budget deficit doesn't fluctuate as much as the actual budget deficit. In particular, large actual deficits, such as those of 1975 and 1983, are usually caused in part by a depressed economy.

Should the Budget Be Balanced?

Persistent budget deficits can cause problems for both the government and the economy. Yet politicians are always tempted to run deficits because this allows them to cater to voters by cutting taxes without cutting spending or by increasing spending without increasing taxes. As a result, there are occasional attempts by policy makers to force fiscal discipline by introducing legislation—even a constitutional amendment—forbidding the government from running budget deficits. This is usually stated as a requirement that the budget be "balanced"—that revenues at least equal spending each fiscal year. Would it be a good idea to require a balanced budget annually?

Most economists don't think so. They believe that the government should only balance its budget on average—that it should be allowed to run deficits in bad years, offset by surpluses in good years. They don't believe the government should be forced to run a balanced budget *every year* because this would undermine the role of taxes and transfers as automatic stabilizers. As we learned earlier, the tendency of tax revenue to fall and transfers to rise when the economy contracts helps to limit the size of recessions. But falling tax revenue and rising transfer payments push the budget toward deficit. If constrained by a balanced-budget rule, the government would have to respond to this deficit with contractionary fiscal policies that would tend to deepen a recession.

Colin Anderson/Brand X Pictures/Getty Images

Nonetheless, policy makers concerned about excessive deficits sometimes feel that rigid rules prohibiting—or at least setting an upper limit on—deficits are necessary.

Long-Run Implications of Fiscal Policy

During the 1990s, the Japanese government engaged in massive deficit spending in an effort to increase aggregate demand. That policy was partly successful: although Japan's economy was sluggish during the 1990s, it avoided a severe slump comparable to what happened to many countries in the 1930s. Yet the fact that Japan was running large deficits year after year made many observers uneasy, as Japan's debt—the accumulation of past deficits, net of surpluses—climbed to alarming levels. Now that we understand how government surpluses and deficits happen, let's take a closer look at their long-run effects on the economy.

Deficits, Surpluses, and Debt

When a family spends more than it earns over the course of a year, it has to raise the extra funds either by selling assets or by borrowing. And if a family borrows year after year, it will eventually end up with a lot of debt.

The same is true for governments. With a few exceptions, governments don't raise large sums by selling assets such as national parkland. Instead, when a government spends more than the tax revenue it receives—when it runs a budget deficit—it almost always borrows the extra funds. And governments that run persistent budget deficits end up with substantial debts.

To interpret the numbers that follow, you need to know a slightly peculiar feature of federal government accounting. For historical reasons, the U.S. government does not keep the books by calendar years. Instead, budget totals are kept by **fiscal years,** which run from October 1 to September 30 and are labeled by the calendar year in which they end. For example, fiscal 2009 began on October 1, 2008, and ended on September 30, 2009.

At the end of fiscal 2009, the U.S. federal government had total debt equal to $12 trillion. However, part of that debt represented special accounting rules specifying that the federal government as a whole owes funds to certain government programs, especially Social Security. We'll explain those rules shortly. For now, however, let's focus on **public debt:** government debt held by individuals and institutions outside the government. At the end of fiscal 2009, the federal government's public debt was "only" $7.6 trillion, or 53% of GDP. If we include the debts of state and local governments, total government public debt was approximately 69% of GDP.

U.S. federal government public debt at the end of fiscal 2009 was larger than it was at the end of fiscal 2008 because the federal government ran a budget deficit during fiscal 2009. A government that runs persistent budget deficits will experience a rising level of debt. Why is this a problem?

Problems Posed by Rising Government Debt

There are two reasons to be concerned when a government runs persistent budget deficits. We described one reason previously: when the government borrows funds in the financial markets, it is competing with firms that plan to borrow funds for investment spending. As a result, the government's borrowing may "crowd out" private investment spending, increasing interest rates and reducing the economy's long-run rate of growth.

The second reason: today's deficits, by increasing the government's debt, place financial pressure on future budgets. The impact of current deficits on future budgets is straightforward. Like individuals, governments must pay their bills, including interest payments on their accumulated debt. When a government is deeply in debt, those interest payments can be substantial. In fiscal 2009, the U.S. federal government paid

2.7% of GDP—$383 billion—in interest on its debt. And although this is a relatively large fraction of GDP, other countries pay even greater fractions of their GDP to service their debt. For example, in 2009, Greece paid interest of about 5.4% of GDP.

Other things equal, a government paying large sums in interest must raise more revenue from taxes or spend less than it would otherwise be able to afford—or it must borrow even more to cover the gap. And a government that borrows to pay interest on its outstanding debt pushes itself even deeper into debt. This process can eventually push a government to the point at which lenders question its ability to repay. Like consumers who have maxed out their credit cards, the government will find that lenders are unwilling to lend any more funds. The result can be that the government defaults on its debt—it stops paying what it owes. Default is often followed by deep financial and economic turmoil.

The idea of a government defaulting sounds far-fetched, but it is not impossible. In the 1990s, Argentina, a relatively high-income developing country, was widely praised for its economic policies—and it was able to borrow large sums from foreign lenders. By 2001, however, Argentina's interest payments were spiraling out of control, and the country stopped paying the sums that were due. Default creates havoc in a country's financial markets and badly shakes public confidence in both the government and the economy. Argentina's debt default was accompanied by a crisis in the country's banking system and a very severe recession. And even if a highly indebted government avoids default, a heavy debt burden typically forces it to slash spending or raise taxes, politically unpopular measures that can also damage the economy.

Lautario Palacios, 7, holds a sign that calls for politicians to stop robbing, during a January 9, 2002 demonstration in Buenos Aires, Argentina.

One question some people ask is: can't a government that has trouble borrowing just print money to pay its bills? Yes, it can, but this leads to another problem: inflation. In fact, budget problems are the main cause of very severe inflation, as we'll see later. The point for now is that governments do not want to find themselves in a position where the choice is between defaulting on their debts and inflating those debts away.

Concerns about the long-run effects of deficits need not rule out the use of fiscal policy to stimulate the economy when it is depressed. However, these concerns do mean that governments should try to offset budget deficits in bad years with budget surpluses in good years. In other words, governments should run a budget that is approximately balanced over time. Have they actually done so?

Deficits and Debt in Practice

Figure 30.4 on the next page shows how the U.S. federal government's budget deficit and its debt have evolved since 1940. Panel (a) shows the federal deficit as a percentage of GDP. As you can see, the federal government ran huge deficits during World War II. It briefly ran surpluses after the war, but it has normally run deficits ever since, especially after 1980. This seems inconsistent with the advice that governments should offset deficits in bad times with surpluses in good times.

However, panel (b) of Figure 30.4 shows that these deficits have not led to runaway debt. To assess the ability of governments to pay their debt, we often use the **debt–GDP ratio,** the government's debt as a percentage of GDP. We use this measure, rather than simply looking at the size of the debt because GDP, which measures the size of the economy as a whole, is a good indicator of the potential taxes the government can collect. If the government's debt grows more slowly than GDP, the burden of paying that debt is actually falling compared with the government's potential tax revenue.

What we see from panel (b) is that although the federal debt has grown in almost every year, the debt–GDP ratio fell for 30 years after the end of World War II. This shows that the debt–GDP ratio can fall, even when debt is rising, as long as GDP grows faster than debt. Growth and inflation sometimes allow a government that runs persistent budget deficits to nevertheless have a declining debt–GDP ratio.

The **debt–GDP ratio** is the government's debt as a percentage of GDP.

U.S. Federal Deficits and Debt

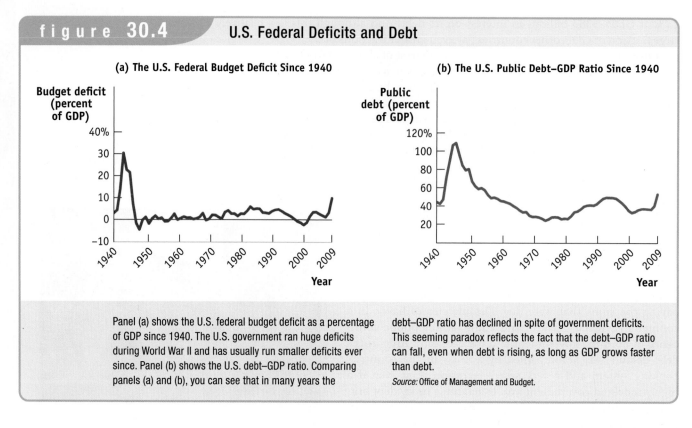

(a) The U.S. Federal Budget Deficit Since 1940

(b) The U.S. Public Debt–GDP Ratio Since 1940

Panel (a) shows the U.S. federal budget deficit as a percentage of GDP since 1940. The U.S. government ran huge deficits during World War II and has usually run smaller deficits ever since. Panel (b) shows the U.S. debt–GDP ratio. Comparing panels (a) and (b), you can see that in many years the debt–GDP ratio has declined in spite of government deficits. This seeming paradox reflects the fact that the debt–GDP ratio can fall, even when debt is rising, as long as GDP grows faster than debt.

Source: Office of Management and Budget.

Still, a government that runs persistent *large* deficits will have a rising debt–GDP ratio when debt grows faster than GDP. Panel (a) of Figure 30.5 shows Japan's budget deficit as a percentage of GDP, and panel (b) shows Japan's debt–GDP ratio, both since 1990. As we have already mentioned, Japan began running large deficits in the early 1990s, a by-product of its effort to prop up aggregate demand with

Japanese Deficits and Debt

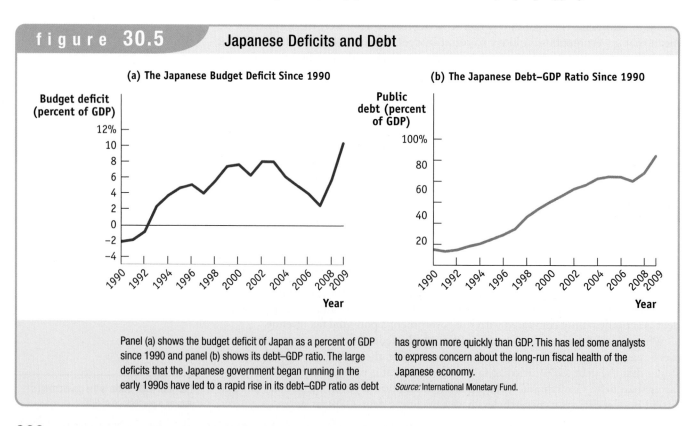

(a) The Japanese Budget Deficit Since 1990

(b) The Japanese Debt–GDP Ratio Since 1990

Panel (a) shows the budget deficit of Japan as a percent of GDP since 1990 and panel (b) shows its debt–GDP ratio. The large deficits that the Japanese government began running in the early 1990s have led to a rapid rise in its debt–GDP ratio as debt has grown more quickly than GDP. This has led some analysts to express concern about the long-run fiscal health of the Japanese economy.

Source: International Monetary Fund.

What Happened to the Debt from World War II?

As you can see from Figure 30.4, the government paid for World War II by borrowing on a huge scale. By the war's end, the public debt was more than 100% of GDP, and many people worried about how it could ever be paid off.

The truth is that it never was paid off. In 1946, the public debt was $242 billion; that number dipped slightly in the next few years, as the United States ran postwar budget surpluses, but the government budget went back into deficit in 1950 with the start of the Korean War. By 1962, the public debt was back up to $248 billion.

But by that time nobody was worried about the fiscal health of the U.S. government because the debt–GDP ratio had fallen by more than half. The reason? Vigorous economic growth, plus mild inflation, had led to a rapid rise in GDP. The experience was a clear lesson in the peculiar fact that modern governments can run deficits forever, as long as they aren't too large.

government spending. This has led to a rapid rise in the debt–GDP ratio. For this reason, some economic analysts are concerned about the long-run fiscal health of the Japanese economy.

Implicit Liabilities

Looking at Figure 30.4, you might be tempted to conclude that the U.S. federal budget is in fairly decent shape: the return to budget deficits after 2001, and large—but temporary—increases in government spending in response to the recession that began in 2007, caused the debt–GDP ratio to rise a bit, but that ratio is still low compared with both historical experience and some other wealthy countries. In fact, however, experts on long-run budget issues view the situation of the United States (and other countries with high public debt, such as Japan and Greece) with alarm. The reason is the problem of *implicit liabilities*. **Implicit liabilities** are spending promises made by governments that are effectively a debt despite the fact that they are not included in the usual debt statistics.

The largest implicit liabilities of the U.S. government arise from two transfer programs that principally benefit older Americans: Social Security and Medicare. The third-largest implicit liability, Medicaid, benefits low-income families. In each of these cases, the government has promised to provide transfer payments to future as well as current beneficiaries. So these programs represent a future debt that must be honored, even though the debt does not currently show up in the usual statistics. Together, these three programs currently account for almost 40% of federal spending.

The implicit liabilities created by these transfer programs worry fiscal experts. Figure 30.6 on the next page shows why. It shows actual spending on Social Security and on Medicare and Medicaid as percentages of GDP from 1962 to 2008, with Congressional Budget Office projections of spending through 2083. According to these projections, spending on Social Security will rise substantially over the next few decades and spending on the two health care programs will soar. Why?

In the case of Social Security, the answer is demography. Social Security is a "pay-as-you-go" system: current workers pay payroll taxes that fund the benefits of current retirees. So demography—specifically, the ratio of the number of retirees drawing benefits to the number of workers paying into Social Security—has a major impact on Social Security's finances. There was a huge surge in the U.S. birth rate between 1946 and 1964, the years of the baby boom. Baby boomers are currently of working age—which means they are paying taxes, not collecting benefits. As the baby boomers retire, they will stop earning income that is taxed and start collecting benefits. As a result, the ratio of retirees receiving benefits to workers paying into the Social Security system will rise. In 2008, there were 31 retirees receiving benefits for every 100 workers paying into

> **Implicit liabilities** are spending promises made by governments that are effectively a debt despite the fact that they are not included in the usual debt statistics.

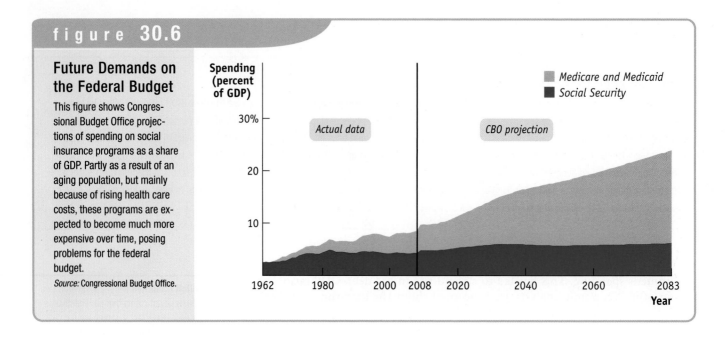

figure 30.6

Future Demands on the Federal Budget

This figure shows Congressional Budget Office projections of spending on social insurance programs as a share of GDP. Partly as a result of an aging population, but mainly because of rising health care costs, these programs are expected to become much more expensive over time, posing problems for the federal budget.

Source: Congressional Budget Office.

the system. By 2030, according to the Social Security Administration, that number will rise to 46; by 2050, it will rise to 48; and by 2080 that number will be 51. This will raise benefit payments relative to the size of the economy.

The aging of the baby boomers, by itself, poses only a moderately sized long-run fiscal problem. The projected rise in Medicare and Medicaid spending is a much more serious concern. The main story behind projections of higher Medicare and Medicaid spending is the long-run tendency of health care spending to rise faster than overall spending, both for government-funded and for private-funded health care.

To some extent, the implicit liabilities of the U.S. government are already reflected in debt statistics. We mentioned earlier that the government had a total debt of $12 trillion at the end of fiscal 2009, but that only $7.6 trillion of that total was owed to the public. The main explanation for that discrepancy is that both Social Security and part of Medicare (the hospital insurance program) are supported by *dedicated taxes:* their expenses are paid out of special taxes on wages. At times, these dedicated taxes yield more revenue than is needed to pay current benefits. In particular, since the mid-1980s the Social Security system has been taking in more revenue than it currently needs in order to prepare for the retirement of the baby boomers. This surplus in the Social Security system has been used to accumulate a *Social Security trust fund,* which was $2.5 trillion at the end of fiscal 2009.

The money in the trust fund is held in the form of U.S. government bonds, which are included in the $12 trillion in total debt. You could say that there's something funny about counting bonds in the Social Security trust fund as part of government debt. After all, these bonds are owed by one part of the government (the government outside the Social Security system) to another part of the government (the Social Security system itself). But the debt corresponds to a real, if implicit, liability: promises by the government to pay future retirement benefits. So many economists argue that the gross debt of $12 trillion, the sum of public debt and government debt held by Social Security and other trust funds, is a more accurate indication of the government's fiscal health than the smaller amount owed to the public alone.

Argentina's Creditors Take a Haircut

As we mentioned earlier, the idea that a government's debt can reach a level at which the government can't pay its creditors can seem far-fetched. In the United States, government debt is usually regarded as the safest asset there is.

But countries *do* default on their debts—they fail to repay the money they borrowed. In 1998, Russia defaulted on its bonds, triggering a worldwide panic in financial markets. In 2001, in the biggest default of modern times, the government of Argentina stopped making payments on $81 billion in debt.

How did the Argentine default happen? During much of the 1990s, the country was experiencing an economic boom and the government was easily able to borrow money from abroad. Although deficit spending led to rising government debt, few considered this a problem. In 1998, however, the country slid into an economic slump that reduced tax revenues, leading to much larger deficits. Foreign lenders, increasingly nervous about the country's ability to repay, became unwilling to lend more except at very high interest rates. By 2001, the country was caught in a vicious circle: to cover its deficits and pay off old loans as they came due, it was forced to borrow at much higher interest rates, and the escalating interest rates on new borrowing made the deficits even bigger.

Argentine officials tried to reassure lenders by raising taxes and cutting government spending. But they were never able to balance the budget due to the continuing recession and the negative multiplier impact of their contractionary fiscal policies. These strongly contractionary fiscal policies drove the country deeper into recession. Late in 2001, facing popular protests, the Argentine government collapsed, and the country defaulted on its debt.

Creditors can take individuals who fail to pay debts to court. The court, in turn, can seize the debtors' assets and force them to pay part of future earnings to their creditors. But when a country defaults, it's different. Its creditors can't send in the police to seize the country's assets. They must negotiate a deal with the country for partial repayment. The only leverage creditors have in these negotiations is the defaulting government's fear that if it fails to reach a settlement, its reputation will suffer and it will be unable to borrow in the future. (A report by Reuters, the news agency, on Argentina's debt negotiations was headlined "Argentina to unhappy bondholders: so sue.") It took three years for Argentina to reach an agreement with its creditors because the new Argentine government was determined to strike a hard bargain. And it did. Here's how Reuters described the settlement reached in March 2005: "The deal, which exchanged new paper valued at around

32 cents for every dollar in default, was the biggest 'haircut,' or loss on principal, for investors of any sovereign bond restructuring in modern times." Let's put this into English: Argentina forced its creditors to trade their "sovereign bonds"—debts of a sovereign nation, that is, Argentina—for new bonds worth only 32% as much. Such a reduction in the value of debt is known as a "haircut."

It's important to avoid two misconceptions about this "haircut." First, you might be tempted to think that because Argentina ended up paying only a fraction of the sums it owed, it paid a small price for default. In fact, Argentina's default accompanied one of the worst economic slumps of modern times, a period of mass unemployment, soaring poverty, and widespread unrest. Second, it's tempting to dismiss the Argentine story as being of little relevance to countries like the United States. After all, aren't we more responsible than that? But Argentina wouldn't have been able to borrow so much in the first place if its government hadn't been well regarded by international lenders. In fact, as late as 1998 Argentina was widely admired for its economic management. What Argentina's slide into default shows is that concerns about the long-run effects of budget deficits are not at all academic. Due to its large and growing debt–GDP ratio, one recession pushed Argentina over the edge into economic collapse.

Module 30 AP Review

Solutions appear at the back of the book.

Check Your Understanding

1. Why is the cyclically adjusted budget balance a better measure of the long-run sustainability of government policies than the actual budget balance?

2. Explain why states required by their constitutions to balance their budgets are likely to experience more severe economic fluctuations than states not held to that requirement.

3. Explain how each of the following events would affect the public debt or implicit liabilities of the U.S. government, other things equal. Would the public debt or implicit liabilities be greater or smaller?
   a. The growth rate of real GDP increases.
   b. Retirees live longer.

   c. Tax revenue decreases.
   d. The government borrows to pay interest on its current public debt.

4. Suppose the economy is in a slump and the current public debt is quite large. Explain the trade-off of short-run versus long-run objectives that policy makers face when deciding whether or not to engage in deficit spending.

Tackle the Test: Multiple-Choice Questions

1. If government spending exceeds tax revenues, which of the following is necessarily true? There is a
   - I. positive budget balance.
   - II. budget deficit.
   - III. recession.
   a. I only
   b. II only
   c. III only
   d. I and II only
   e. I, II, and III

2. Which of the following fiscal policies is expansionary?

	Taxes	Government spending
a.	increase by $100 million	increases by $100 million
b.	decrease by $100 million	decreases by $100 million
c.	increase by $100 million	decreases by $100 million
d.	decrease by $100 million	increases by $100 million
e.	both (a) and (d)	

3. The cyclically adjusted budget deficit is an estimate of what the budget balance would be if real GDP were
   a. greater than potential output.
   b. equal to nominal GDP.

   c. equal to potential output.
   d. falling.
   e. calculated during a recession.

4. During a recession in the United States, what happens automatically to tax revenues and government spending?

	Tax revenues	Government spending
a.	increase	increases
b.	decrease	decreases
c.	increase	decreases
d.	decrease	increases
e.	decrease	does not change

5. Which of the following is a reason to be concerned about persistent budget deficits?
   a. crowding out
   b. government default
   c. the opportunity cost of future interest payments
   d. higher interest rates leading to decreased long-run growth
   e. all of the above

Tackle the Test: Free-Response Questions

1. Consider the information provided below for the hypothetical country of Zeta.
   Tax revenues = 2,000
   Government purchases of goods and services = 1,500
   Government transfers = 1,000
   Real GDP = 20,000
   Potential output = 18,000
   a. Is the budget balance in Zeta positive or negative? What is the amount of the budget balance?
   b. Zeta is currently in what phase of the business cycle? Explain.
   c. Is Zeta implementing the appropriate fiscal policy given the current state of the economy? Explain.
   d. How does Zeta's cyclically adjusted budget deficit compare with its actual budget deficit? Explain.

Answer (8 points)

1 point: Negative

1 point: −500

1 point: Expansion

1 point: Real GDP > potential output

1 point: No

1 point: Zeta is running a budget deficit during an expansion.

1 point: It is larger.

1 point: Because if real GDP equaled potential output, tax revenues would be lower and government transfers would be higher.

2. In Module 29 you learned about the market for loanable funds, which is intimately related to our current topic of budget deficits. Use a correctly labeled graph of the market for loanable funds to illustrate the effect of a persistent budget deficit. Identify and explain the effect persistent budget deficits can have on private investment.

Module 31
Monetary Policy and the Interest Rate

What you will learn in this Module:

- How the Federal Reserve implements monetary policy, moving the interest rate to affect aggregate output

- Why monetary policy is the main tool for stabilizing the economy

In Modules 28 and 29 we developed models of the money market and the loanable funds market. We also saw how these two markets are consistent and related. In the short run, the interest rate is determined in the money market and the loanable funds market adjusts in response to changes in the money market. However, in the long run, the interest rate is determined by matching the supply and demand of loanable funds that arise when real GDP equals potential output. Now we are ready to use these models to explain how the Federal Reserve can use monetary policy to stabilize the economy in the short run.

Monetary Policy and the Interest Rate

Let's examine how the Federal Reserve can use changes in the money supply to change the interest rate. Figure 31.1 on the next page shows what happens when the Fed increases the money supply from $\overline{M}_1$ to $\overline{M}_2$. The economy is originally in equilibrium at E_1, with the equilibrium interest rate r_1 and the money supply $\overline{M}_1$. An increase in the money supply by the Fed to $\overline{M}_2$ shifts the money supply curve to the right, from MS_1 to MS_2, and leads to a fall in the equilibrium interest rate to r_2. Why? Because r_2 is the only interest rate at which the public is willing to hold the quantity of money actually supplied, $\overline{M}_2$. So an increase in the money supply drives the interest rate down. Similarly, a reduction in the money supply drives the interest rate up. By adjusting the money supply up or down, the Fed can set the interest rate.

In practice, at each meeting the Federal Open Market Committee decides on the interest rate to prevail for the next six weeks, until its next meeting. The Fed sets a **target federal funds rate,** a desired level for the federal funds rate. This target is then enforced by the Open Market Desk of the Federal Reserve Bank of New York, which adjusts the money supply through *open-market operations*—the purchase or sale of Treasury bills—until the actual federal funds rate equals the target rate. The other tools of monetary policy, lending through the discount window and changes in reserve requirements, aren't used on a regular basis (although the Fed used discount window lending in its efforts to address the 2008 financial crisis).

The Federal Reserve can move the interest rate through open-market operations that shift the money supply curve. In practice, the Fed sets a **target federal funds rate** and uses open-market operations to achieve that target.

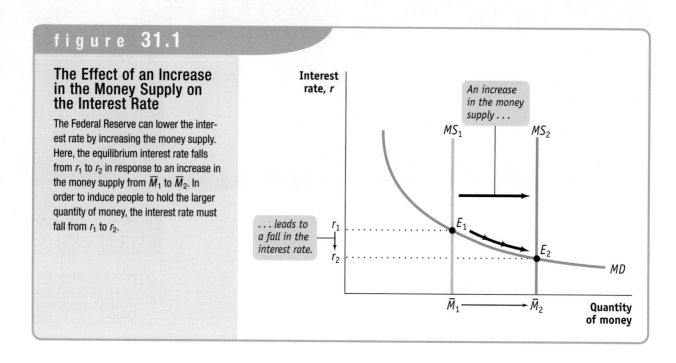

figure 31.1

The Effect of an Increase in the Money Supply on the Interest Rate

The Federal Reserve can lower the interest rate by increasing the money supply. Here, the equilibrium interest rate falls from r_1 to r_2 in response to an increase in the money supply from $\overline{M}_1$ to $\overline{M}_2$. In order to induce people to hold the larger quantity of money, the interest rate must fall from r_1 to r_2.

Figure 31.2 shows how interest rate targeting works. In both panels, r_T is the target federal funds rate. In panel (a), the initial money supply curve is MS_1 with money supply $\overline{M}_1$, and the equilibrium interest rate, r_1, is above the target rate. To lower the interest rate to r_T, the Fed makes an open-market purchase of Treasury bills, which leads to an increase in the money supply via the money multiplier. This is illustrated in

figure 31.2   Setting the Federal Funds Rate

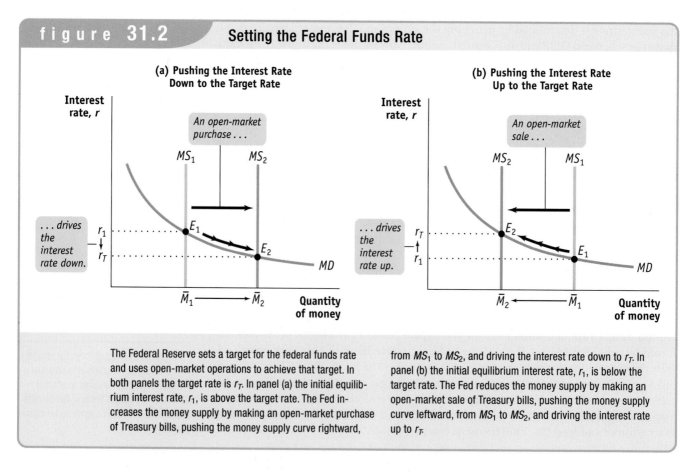

The Federal Reserve sets a target for the federal funds rate and uses open-market operations to achieve that target. In both panels the target rate is r_T. In panel (a) the initial equilibrium interest rate, r_1, is above the target rate. The Fed increases the money supply by making an open-market purchase of Treasury bills, pushing the money supply curve rightward, from MS_1 to MS_2, and driving the interest rate down to r_T. In panel (b) the initial equilibrium interest rate, r_1, is below the target rate. The Fed reduces the money supply by making an open-market sale of Treasury bills, pushing the money supply curve leftward, from MS_1 to MS_2, and driving the interest rate up to r_T.

The Fed Reverses Course

During the summer of 2007, many called for a change in Federal Reserve policy. At first the Fed remained unmoved. On August 7, 2007, the Federal Open Market Committee decided to stand pat, making no change in its interest rate policy. The official statement did, however, concede that "financial markets have been volatile in recent weeks" and that "credit conditions have become tighter for some households and businesses."

Just three days later, the Fed issued a special statement basically assuring market players that it was paying attention, and on August 17 it issued another statement declaring that it was "monitoring the situation," which is Fed-speak for "we're getting nervous." And on September 18, the Fed did what CNBC analyst Jim Cramer wanted: it cut the target federal funds rate "to help forestall some of the adverse effects on the broader economy that might otherwise arise from the disruptions in financial markets." In effect, it conceded that Cramer's worries were at least partly right.

It was the beginning of a major change in monetary policy. The figure shows two interest rates from the beginning of 2004 to early 2010: the target federal funds rate decided by the Federal Open Market Committee, which dropped in a series of steps starting in September 2007, and the aver-

age effective rate that prevailed in the market each day. The figure shows that the interest rate cut six weeks after Cramer's diatribe was only the first of several cuts. As you can see, this was a reversal of previous policy: previously the Fed had generally been raising rates, not reducing them, out of concern that inflation might become a problem. But starting in September 2007, fighting the financial crisis took priority. By the way, notice how beginning on December 16, 2008, it looks as if there are two target federal funds rates. What happened? The Federal

Open Market Committee set a target *range* for the federal funds rate, between 0% and 0.25%, starting on that date. That target range was still in effect at the time of writing.

The figure also shows that that the Fed doesn't always hit its target. There were a number of days, especially in 2008, when the actual federal funds rate was significantly above or below the target rate. But these episodes didn't last long, and overall the Fed got what it wanted, at least as far as short-term interest rates were concerned.

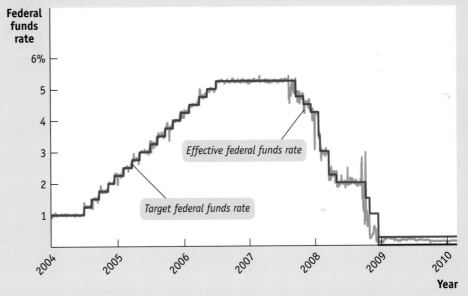

panel (a) by the rightward shift of the money supply curve from MS_1 to MS_2 and an increase in the money supply to $\overline{M}_2$. This drives the equilibrium interest rate *down* to the target rate, r_T.

Panel (b) shows the opposite case. Again, the initial money supply curve is MS_1 with money supply $\overline{M}_1$. But this time the equilibrium interest rate, r_1, is below the target federal funds rate, r_T. In this case, the Fed will make an open-market sale of Treasury bills, leading to a fall in the money supply to $\overline{M}_2$ via the money multiplier. The money supply curve shifts leftward from MS_1 to MS_2, driving the equilibrium interest rate *up* to the target federal funds rate, r_T.

Monetary Policy and Aggregate Demand

We have seen how fiscal policy can be used to stabilize the economy. Now we will see how monetary policy—changes in the money supply or the interest rate, or both—can play the same role.

Expansionary and Contractionary Monetary Policy

Previously we said that monetary policy shifts the aggregate demand curve. We can now explain how that works: through the effect of monetary policy on the interest rate.

Suppose that the Federal Reserve expands the money supply. As we've seen, this leads to a lower interest rate. A lower interest rate, in turn, will lead to more investment spending, which will lead to higher real GDP, which will lead to higher consumer spending, and so on through the multiplier process. So the total quantity of goods and services demanded at any given aggregate price level rises when the quantity of money increases, and the AD curve shifts to the right. Monetary policy that shifts the AD curve to the right, as illustrated in panel (a) of Figure 31.3, is known as **expansionary monetary policy.**

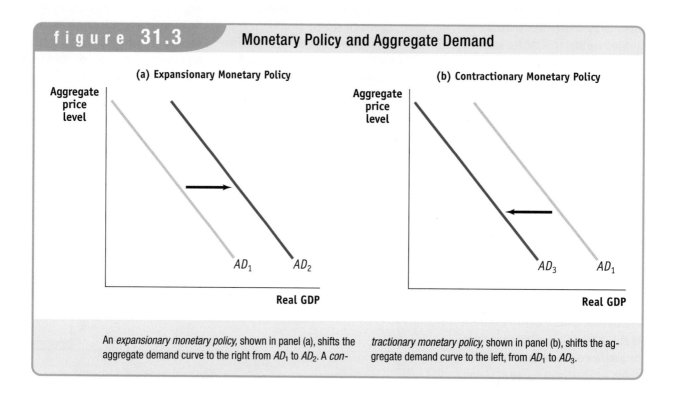

figure 31.3 · Monetary Policy and Aggregate Demand

An *expansionary monetary policy,* shown in panel (a), shifts the aggregate demand curve to the right from AD_1 to AD_2. A con- tractionary monetary policy, shown in panel (b), shifts the aggregate demand curve to the left, from AD_1 to AD_3.

Suppose, alternatively, that the Federal Reserve contracts the money supply. This leads to a higher interest rate. The higher interest rate leads to lower investment spending, which leads to lower real GDP, which leads to lower consumer spending, and so on. So the total quantity of goods and services demanded falls when the money supply is reduced, and the AD curve shifts to the left. Monetary policy that shifts the AD curve to the left, as illustrated in panel (b) of Figure 31.3, is called **contractionary monetary policy.**

Monetary Policy in Practice

We have learned that policy makers try to fight recessions. They also try to ensure *price stability*: low (though usually not zero) inflation. Actual monetary policy reflects a combination of these goals.

In general, the Federal Reserve and other central banks tend to engage in expansionary monetary policy when actual real GDP is below potential output. Panel (a) of Figure 31.4 shows the U.S. output gap, which we defined as the percentage difference between actual real GDP and potential output, versus the federal funds rate since 1985. (Recall that the output gap is positive when actual real GDP exceeds potential output.)

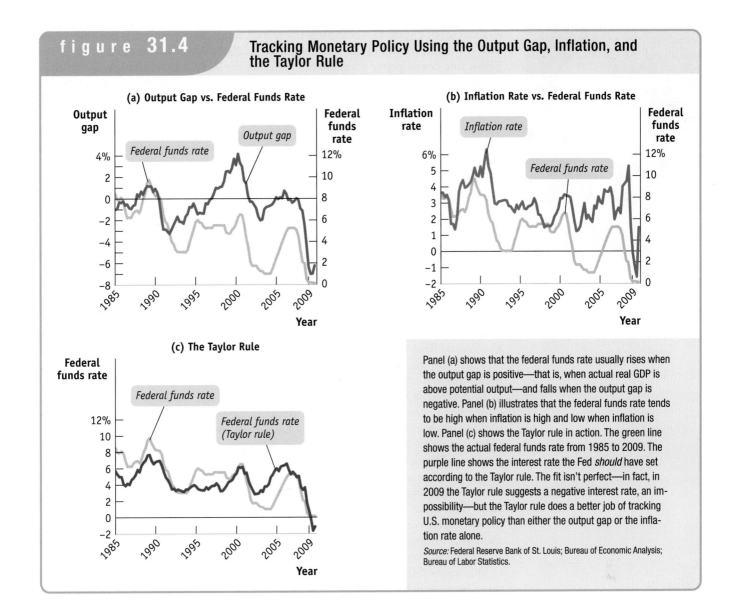

figure 31.4 Tracking Monetary Policy Using the Output Gap, Inflation, and the Taylor Rule

(a) Output Gap vs. Federal Funds Rate

(b) Inflation Rate vs. Federal Funds Rate

(c) The Taylor Rule

Panel (a) shows that the federal funds rate usually rises when the output gap is positive—that is, when actual real GDP is above potential output—and falls when the output gap is negative. Panel (b) illustrates that the federal funds rate tends to be high when inflation is high and low when inflation is low. Panel (c) shows the Taylor rule in action. The green line shows the actual federal funds rate from 1985 to 2009. The purple line shows the interest rate the Fed *should* have set according to the Taylor rule. The fit isn't perfect—in fact, in 2009 the Taylor rule suggests a negative interest rate, an impossibility—but the Taylor rule does a better job of tracking U.S. monetary policy than either the output gap or the inflation rate alone.

Source: Federal Reserve Bank of St. Louis; Bureau of Economic Analysis; Bureau of Labor Statistics.

As you can see, the Fed has tended to raise interest rates when the output gap is rising—that is, when the economy is developing an inflationary gap—and cut rates when the output gap is falling. The big exception was the late 1990s, when the Fed left rates steady for several years even as the economy developed a positive output gap (which went along with a low unemployment rate).

One reason the Fed was willing to keep interest rates low in the late 1990s was that inflation was low. Panel (b) of Figure 31.4 compares the inflation rate, measured as the rate of change in consumer prices excluding food and energy, with the federal funds rate. You can see how low inflation during the mid-1990s and early 2000s helped encourage loose monetary policy both in the late 1990s and in 2002–2003.

In 1993, Stanford economist John Taylor suggested that monetary policy should follow a simple rule that takes into account concerns about both the business cycle and inflation. The **Taylor rule for monetary policy** is a rule for setting the federal funds rate that takes into account both the inflation rate and the output gap. He also suggested that actual monetary policy often looks as if the Federal Reserve was, in fact, more or less following the proposed rule. The rule Taylor originally suggested was as follows:

Federal funds rate = 1 + (1.5 × inflation rate) + (0.5 × output gap)

The **Taylor rule for monetary policy** is a rule for setting the federal funds rate that takes into account both the inflation rate and the output gap.

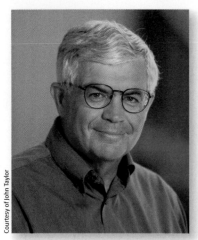

Stanford economist John Taylor suggested a simple rule for monetary policy.

Panel (c) of Figure 31.4 compares the federal funds rate specified by the Taylor rule with the actual federal funds rate from 1985 to 2009. With the exception of 2009, the Taylor rule does a pretty good job at predicting the Fed's actual behavior—better than looking at either the output gap alone or the inflation rate alone. Furthermore, the direction of changes in interest rates predicted by an application of the Taylor rule to monetary policy and the direction of changes in actual interest rates have always been the same—further evidence that the Fed is using some form of the Taylor rule to set monetary policy. But, what happened in 2009? A combination of low inflation and a large and negative output gap briefly put the Taylor's rule of prediction of the federal funds into negative territory. But a negative federal funds rate is, of course, impossible. So the Fed did the best it could—it cut rates aggressively and the federal funds rate fell to almost zero.

Monetary policy, rather than fiscal policy, is the main tool of stabilization policy. Like fiscal policy, it is subject to lags: it takes time for the Fed to recognize economic problems and time for monetary policy to affect the economy. However, since the Fed moves much more quickly than Congress, monetary policy is typically the preferred tool.

Inflation Targeting

The Federal Reserve tries to keep inflation low but positive. The Fed does not, however, explicitly commit itself to achieving any particular rate of inflation, although it is widely believed to prefer inflation at around 2% per year.

By contrast, a number of other central banks *do* have explicit inflation targets. So rather than using the Taylor rule to set monetary policy, they instead announce the inflation rate that they want to achieve—the *inflation target*—and set policy in an attempt to hit that target. This method of setting monetary policy is called **inflation targeting**. The central bank of New Zealand, which was the first country to adopt inflation targeting, specified a range for that target of 1% to 3%. Other central banks commit themselves to achieving a specific number. For example, the Bank of England is supposed to keep inflation at 2%. In practice, there doesn't seem to be much difference between these versions: central banks with a target range for inflation seem to aim for the middle of that range, and central banks with a fixed target tend to give themselves considerable wiggle room.

One major difference between inflation targeting and the Taylor rule is that inflation targeting is forward-looking rather than backward-looking. That is, the Taylor rule adjusts monetary policy in response to *past* inflation, but inflation targeting is based on a forecast of *future* inflation.

Advocates of inflation targeting argue that it has two key advantages, *transparency* and *accountability*. First, economic uncertainty is reduced because the public knows the objective of an inflation-targeting central bank. Second, the central bank's success can be judged by seeing how closely actual inflation rates have matched the inflation target, making central bankers accountable.

Critics of inflation targeting argue that it's too restrictive because there are times when other concerns—like the stability of the financial system—should take priority over achieving any particular inflation rate. Indeed, in late 2007 and early 2008 the Fed cut interest rates much more than either the Taylor rule or inflation targeting would have dictated because it feared that turmoil in the financial markets would lead to a major recession (which it did, in fact).

Many American macroeconomists have had positive things to say about inflation targeting—including Ben Bernanke, the current chair of the Federal Reserve. At the time of this writing, however, there were no moves to have the Fed adopt an explicit inflation target, and during normal times it still appears to set monetary policy by applying a loosely defined version of the Taylor rule.

Inflation targeting occurs when the central bank sets an explicit target for the inflation rate and sets monetary policy in order to hit that target.

fyi

What the Fed Wants, the Fed Gets

What's the evidence that the Fed can actually cause an economic contraction or expansion? You might think that finding such evidence is just a matter of looking at what happens to the economy when interest rates go up or down. But it turns out that there's a big problem with that approach: the Fed usually changes interest rates in an attempt to tame the business cycle, raising rates if the economy is expanding and reducing rates if the economy is slumping. So in the actual data, it often looks as if low interest rates go along with a weak economy and high rates go along with a strong economy.

In a famous 1994 paper titled "Monetary Policy Matters," the macroeconomists Christina Romer and David Romer solved this problem by focusing on episodes in which monetary policy *wasn't* a reaction to the business cycle. Specifically, they used minutes from the Federal Open Market Committee and other sources to identify episodes "in which the Federal Reserve in effect decided to attempt to create a recession to reduce inflation." Contractionary monetary policy is sometimes used to eliminate infla-

tion that has become *embedded* in the economy, rather than just as a tool of macroeconomic stabilization. In this case, the Fed needs to create a recessionary gap—not just eliminate an inflationary gap—to wring embedded inflation out of the economy.

The figure shows the unemployment rate between 1952 and 1984 (orange) and identifies five dates on which, according to Romer and

Romer, the Fed decided that it wanted a recession (vertical red lines). In four out of the five cases, the decision to contract the economy was followed, after a modest lag, by a rise in the unemployment rate. On average, Romer and Romer found, the unemployment rate rises by 2 percentage points after the Fed decides that unemployment needs to go up.

So yes, the Fed gets what it wants.

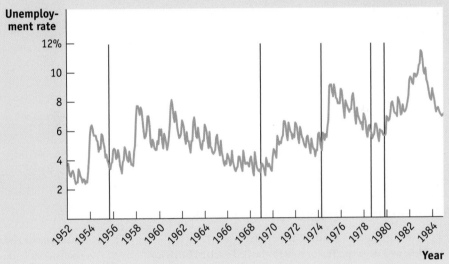

Module 31 AP Review

Solutions appear at the back of the book.

Check Your Understanding

1. Assume that there is an increase in the demand for money at every interest rate. Using a diagram, show what effect this will have on the equilibrium interest rate for a given money supply.

2. Now assume that the Fed is following a policy of targeting the federal funds rate. What will the Fed do in the situation described in question 1 to keep the federal funds rate unchanged? Illustrate with a diagram.

3. Suppose the economy is currently suffering from a recessionary gap and the Federal Reserve uses an expansionary monetary policy to close that gap. Describe the short-run effect of this policy on the following.
   a. the money supply curve
   b. the equilibrium interest rate
   c. investment spending
   d. consumer spending
   e. aggregate output

Tackle the Test: Multiple-Choice Questions

1. At each meeting of the Federal Open Market Committee, the Federal Reserve sets a target for which of the following?

    I. the federal funds rate

    II. the prime interest rate

    III. the market interest rate

    a. I only

    b. II only

    c. III only

    d. I and III only

    e. I, II, and III

2. Which of the following actions can the Fed take to decrease the equilibrium interest rate?

    a. increase the money supply

    b. increase money demand

    c. decrease the money supply

    d. decrease money demand

    e. both (a) and (d)

3. Contractionary monetary policy attempts to _____ aggregate demand by _____ interest rates.

    a. decrease   increasing

    b. increase   decreasing

    c. decrease   decreasing

    d. increase   increasing

    e. increase   maintaining

4. Which of the following is a goal of monetary policy?

    a. zero inflation

    b. deflation

    c. price stability

    d. increased potential output

    e. decreased actual real GDP

5. When implementing monetary policy, the Federal Reserve attempts to achieve

    a. an explicit target inflation rate.

    b. zero inflation.

    c. a low rate of deflation.

    d. a low, but positive inflation rate.

    e. 4–5% inflation.

Tackle the Test: Free-Response Questions

1. a. Give the equation for the Taylor rule.

    b. How well does the Taylor rule fit the Fed's actual behavior? Explain.

    c. What does the Taylor rule predict will happen when the inflation rate increases? Explain.

    d. What does the Taylor rule predict will happen if the economy sinks further into a recession? Explain.

Answer (7 points)

1 point: Federal funds rate = $1 + (1.5 \times \text{inflation rate}) + (0.5 \times \text{output gap})$

1 point: Not exactly, but fairly well

1 point: It does better than any one measure alone, and it has always correctly predicted the direction of change of interest rates.

1 point: The federal funds rate will increase.

1 point: According to the equation, the federal funds rate increases by 1.5 percentage points for every one percentage point increase in inflation. OR, the Taylor rule predicts contractionary monetary policy during periods of inflation.

1 point: The federal funds rate will decrease.

1 point: According to the equation, the federal funds rate decreases by 0.5 percentage points for every one percentage point decrease in the output gap, as from −1% to −2%, indicating a deeper recession. OR, the Taylor rule predicts expansionary monetary policy during periods of recession.

2. a. What can the Fed do with each of its tools to implement expansionary monetary policy during a recession?

    b. Use a correctly labeled graph of the money market to explain how the Fed's use of expansionary monetary policy affects interest rates in the short run.

    c. Explain how the interest rate changes you graphed in part b affect aggregate supply and demand in the short run.

    d. Use a correctly labeled aggregate demand and supply graph to illustrate how expansionary monetary policy affects aggregate output in the short run.

Module 32
Money, Output, and Prices in the Long Run

In the previous module we discussed how expansionary and contractionary monetary policy can be used to stabilize the economy. The Federal Reserve can use its monetary policy tools to change the money supply and cause the equilibrium interest rate in the money market to increase or decrease. But what if a central bank pursues a monetary policy that is not appropriate? That is, what if a central bank pursues expansionary policy during an expansion or contractionary policy during a recession? In this module we consider how a counter-productive action by a central bank can actually destabilize the economy in the short run. We also introduce the long-run effects of monetary policy. As we learned in the last section, the money market (where monetary policy has its effect on the money supply) determines the interest rate only in the short run. In the long run, the interest rate is determined in the market for loanable funds. Here we look at long-run adjustments and consider the long-run effects of monetary policy.

Money, Output, and Prices

Because of its expansionary and contractionary effects, monetary policy is generally the policy tool of choice to help stabilize the economy. However, not all actions by central banks are productive. In particular, as we'll see later, central banks sometimes print money not to fight a recessionary gap but to help the government pay its bills, an action that typically destabilizes the economy.

What happens when a change in the money supply pushes the economy away from, rather than toward, long-run equilibrium? The economy is self-correcting in the long run: a demand shock has only a temporary effect on aggregate output. If the demand shock is the result of a change in the money supply, we can make a stronger statement: in the long run, changes in the quantity of money affect the aggregate price level, but they do not change real aggregate output or the interest rate. To see why, let's look at what happens if the central bank permanently increases the money supply.

Short-Run and Long-Run Effects of an Increase in the Money Supply

To analyze the long-run effects of monetary policy, it's helpful to think of the central bank as choosing a target for the money supply rather than for the interest rate. In assessing the effects of an increase in the money supply, we return to the analysis of the long-run effects of an increase in aggregate demand.

Figure 32.1 shows the short-run and long-run effects of an increase in the money supply when the economy begins at potential output, Y_1. The initial short-run aggregate supply curve is $SRAS_1$, the long-run aggregate supply curve is $LRAS$, and the initial aggregate demand curve is AD_1. The economy's initial equilibrium is at E_1, a point of both short-run and long-run macroeconomic equilibrium because it is on both the short-run and the long-run aggregate supply curves. Real GDP is at potential output, Y_1.

Now suppose there is an increase in the money supply. Other things equal, an increase in the money supply reduces the interest rate, which increases investment spending, which leads to a further rise in consumer spending, and so on. So an increase in the money supply increases the quantity of goods and services demanded, shifting the AD curve rightward to AD_2. In the short run, the economy moves to a new short-run macroeconomic equilibrium at E_2. The price level rises from P_1 to P_2, and real GDP rises from Y_1 to Y_2. That is, both the aggregate price level and aggregate output increase in the short run.

But the aggregate output level Y_2 is above potential output. As a result, nominal wages will rise over time, causing the short-run aggregate supply curve to shift leftward. This process stops only when the $SRAS$ curve ends up at $SRAS_2$ and the economy ends up at point E_3, a point of both short-run and long-run macroeconomic equilibrium. The long-run effect of an increase in the money supply, then, is that the aggregate price level has increased from P_1 to P_3, but aggregate output is back at potential

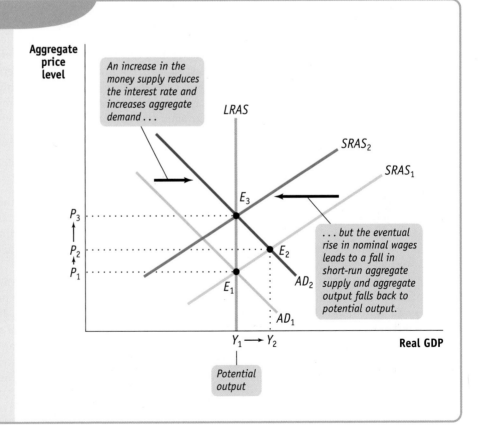

figure 32.1

The Short-Run and Long-Run Effects of an Increase in the Money Supply

An increase in the money supply generates a positive short-run effect, but no long-run effect, on real GDP. Here, the economy begins at E_1, a point of short-run and long-run macroeconomic equilibrium. An increase in the money supply shifts the AD curve rightward, and the economy moves to a new short-run equilibrium at E_2 and a new real GDP of Y_2. But E_2 is not a long-run equilibrium: Y_2 exceeds potential output, Y_1, leading over time to an increase in nominal wages. In the long run, the increase in nominal wages shifts the short-run aggregate supply curve leftward, to a new position at $SRAS_2$. The economy reaches a new short-run and long-run macroeconomic equilibrium at E_3 on the $LRAS$ curve, and output falls back to potential output, Y_1. The only long-run effect of an increase in the money supply is an increase in the aggregate price level from P_1 to P_3.

output, Y_1. In the long run, a monetary expansion raises the aggregate price level but has no effect on real GDP.

If the money supply decreases, the story we have just told plays out in reverse. Other things equal, a decrease in the money supply raises the interest rate, which decreases investment spending, which leads to a further decrease in consumer spending, and so on. So a decrease in the money supply decreases the quantity of goods and services demanded at any given aggregate price level, shifting the aggregate demand curve to the left. In the short run, the economy moves to a new short-run macroeconomic equilibrium at a level of real GDP below potential output and a lower aggregate price level. That is, both the aggregate price level and aggregate output decrease in the short run. But what happens over time? When the aggregate output level is below potential output, nominal wages fall. When this happens, the short-run aggregate supply curve shifts rightward. This process stops only when the *SRAS* curve ends up at a point of both short-run and long-run macroeconomic equilibrium. The long-run effect of a decrease in the money supply, then, is that the aggregate price level decreases, but aggregate output is back at potential output. In the long run, a monetary contraction decreases the aggregate price level but has no effect on real GDP.

Monetary Neutrality

How much does a change in the money supply change the aggregate price level in the long run? The answer is that a change in the money supply leads to a proportional change in the aggregate price level in the long run. For example, if the money supply falls 25%, the aggregate price level falls 25% in the long run; if the money supply rises 50%, the aggregate price level rises 50% in the long run.

How do we know this? Consider the following thought experiment: suppose all prices in the economy—prices of final goods and services and also factor prices, such as nominal wage rates—double. And suppose the money supply doubles at the same time. What difference does this make to the economy in real terms? None. All real variables in the economy—such as real GDP and the real value of the money supply (the amount of goods and services it can buy)—are unchanged. So there is no reason for anyone to behave any differently.

We can state this argument in reverse: if the economy starts out in long-run macroeconomic equilibrium and the money supply changes, restoring long-run macroeconomic equilibrium requires restoring all real values to their original values. This includes restoring the real value of the money supply to its original level. So if the money supply falls 25%, the aggregate price level must fall 25%; if the money supply rises 50%, the price level must rise 50%; and so on.

This analysis demonstrates the concept known as **monetary neutrality,** in which changes in the money supply have no real effects on the economy. In the long run, the only effect of an increase in the money supply is to raise the aggregate price level by an equal percentage. Economists argue that *money is neutral in the long run.*

· This is, however, a good time to recall the dictum of John Maynard Keynes: "In the long run we are all dead." In the long run, changes in the money supply don't have any effect on real GDP, interest rates, or anything else except the price level. But it would be foolish to conclude from this that the Fed is irrelevant. Monetary policy does have powerful real effects on the economy in the short run, often making the difference between recession and expansion. And that matters a lot for society's welfare.

Changes in the Money Supply and the Interest Rate in the Long Run

In the short run, an increase in the money supply leads to a fall in the interest rate, and a decrease in the money supply leads to a rise in the interest rate. Module 29 explained that in the long run it's a different story: changes in the money supply don't affect the interest rate at all. Here we'll review that story and discuss the reasons behind it in greater detail.

According to the concept of **monetary neutrality,** changes in the money supply have no real effects on the economy.

figure 32.2

The Long-Run Determination of the Interest Rate

In the short run, an increase in the money supply from $\overline{M}_1$ to $\overline{M}_2$ pushes the interest rate down from r_1 to r_2 and the economy moves to E_2, a short-run equilibrium. In the long run, however, the aggregate price level rises in proportion to the increase in the money supply, leading to an increase in money demand at any given interest rate in proportion to the increase in the aggregate price level, as shown by the shift from MD_1 to MD_2. The result is that the quantity of money demanded at any given interest rate rises by the same amount as the quantity of money supplied. The economy moves to long-run equilibrium at E_3 and the interest rate returns to r_1.

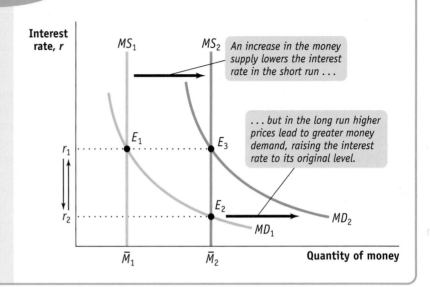

Figure 32.2 shows the money supply curve and the money demand curve before and after the Fed increases the money supply. We assume that the economy is initially at E_1, in long-run macroeconomic equilibrium at potential output, and with money supply $\overline{M}_1$. The initial equilibrium interest rate, determined by the intersection of the money demand curve MD_1 and the money supply curve MS_1, is r_1.

fyi

International Evidence of Monetary Neutrality

These days monetary policy is quite similar among wealthy countries. Each major nation (or, in the case of the euro, the eurozone) has a central bank that is insulated from political pressure. All of these central banks try to keep the aggregate price level roughly stable, which usually means inflation of at most 2% to 3% per year.

But if we look at a longer period and a wider group of countries, we see large differences in the growth of the money supply. Between 1970 and the present, the money supply rose only a few percentage points per year in countries such as Switzerland and the United States, but rose much more rapidly in some poorer countries, such as South Africa. These differences allow us to see whether it is really true that increases in the money supply lead, in the long run, to equal percentage increases in the aggregate price level.

The figure shows the annual percentage increases in the money supply and average annual increases in the aggregate price level—that is, the average rate of inflation—for a sample of

countries during the period 1970–2007, with each point representing a country. If the relationship between increases in the money supply and changes in the aggregate price level were exact, the points would lie precisely on a 45-degree line. In fact, the relationship isn't exact because other

factors besides money affect the aggregate price level. But the scatter of points clearly lies close to a 45-degree line, showing a more or less proportional relationship between money and the aggregate price level. That is, the data support the concept of monetary neutrality in the long run.

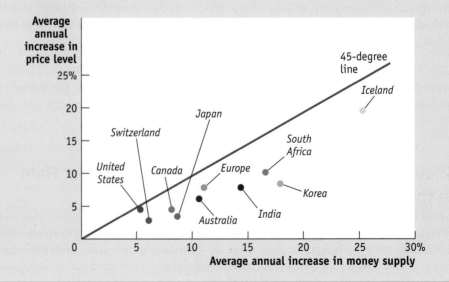

Now suppose the money supply increases from $\overline{M}_1$ to $\overline{M}_2$. In the short run, the economy moves from E_1 to E_2 and the interest rate falls from r_1 to r_2. Over time, however, the aggregate price level rises, and this raises money demand, shifting the money demand curve rightward from MD_1 to MD_2. The economy moves to a new long-run equilibrium at E_3, and the interest rate rises to its original level of r_1.

How do we know that the long-run equilibrium interest rate is the original interest rate, r_1? Because the eventual increase in money demand is proportional to the increase in money supply, thus counteracting the initial downward effect on interest rates. Let's follow the chain of events to see why. With monetary neutrality, an increase in the money supply is matched by a proportional increase in the price level in the long run. If the money supply rises by, say, 50%, the price level will also rise by 50%. Changes in the price level, in turn, cause proportional changes in the demand for money. So a 50% increase in the money supply raises the aggregate price level by 50%, which increases the quantity of money demanded at any given interest rate by 50%. Thus, at the initial interest rate of r_1, the quantity of money demanded rises exactly as much as the money supply, and r_1 is again the equilibrium interest rate. In the long run, then, changes in the money supply do not affect the interest rate.

Module 32 AP Review

Solutions appear at the back of the book.

Check Your Understanding

1. Suppose the economy begins in long-run macroeconomic equilibrium. What is the long-run effect on the aggregate price level of a 5% increase in the money supply? Explain.

2. Again supposing the economy begins in long-run macroeconomic equilibrium, what is the long-run effect on the interest rate of a 5% increase in the money supply? Explain.

Tackle the Test: Multiple-Choice Questions

1. In the long run, changes in the quantity of money affect which of the following?
   - I. real aggregate output
   - II. interest rates
   - III. the aggregate price level
   - a. I only
   - b. II only
   - c. III only
   - d. I and II only
   - e. I, II, and III

2. An increase in the money supply will lead to which of the following in the short run?
   - a. higher interest rates
   - b. decreased investment spending
   - c. decreased consumer spending
   - d. increased aggregate demand
   - e. lower real GDP

3. A 10% decrease in the money supply will change the aggregate price level in the long run by
   - a. zero.
   - b. less than 10%.
   - c. 10%.
   - d. 20%.
   - e. more than 20%.

4. Monetary neutrality means that, in the long run, changes in the money supply
   - a. can not happen.
   - b. have no effect on the economy.
   - c. have no real effect on the economy.
   - d. increase real GDP.
   - e. change real interest rates.

5. A graph of percentage increases in the money supply and average annual increases in the price level for various countries provides evidence that
   - a. changes in the two variables are exactly equal.
   - b. the money supply and aggregate price level are unrelated.
   - c. money neutrality holds only in wealthy countries.
   - d. monetary policy is ineffective.
   - e. money is neutral in the long run.

Tackle the Test: Free-Response Questions

1. Assume the central bank increases the quantity of money by 25%, even though the economy is initially in both short-run and long-run macroeconomic equilibrium. Describe the effects, in the short run and in the long run (giving numbers where possible), on the following:
   a. aggregate output
   b. the aggregate price level
   c. the real value of the money supply (its purchasing power for goods and services)
   d. the interest rate

2. a. Draw a correctly labeled graph of aggregate demand and supply showing an economy in long-run macroeconomic equilibrium.
   b. On your graph, show what happens in the short run if the central bank increases the money supply to pay off a government deficit. Explain.
   c. On your graph, show what will happen in the long run. Explain.

Answer (8 points)

1 point: Aggregate output rises in the short run.

1 point: Aggregate output falls back to potential output in the long run.

1 point: The aggregate price level rises in the short run (by less than 25%).

1 point: The aggregate price level rises by 25% in the long run.

1 point: The real value of the money supply increases in the short run.

1 point: The real value of the money supply does not change (relative to its original value) in the long run.

1 point: The interest rate falls in the short run.

1 point: The interest rate rises back to its original level in the long run.

Module 33
Types of Inflation, Disinflation, and Deflation

What you will learn in this Module:

- The classical model of the price level
- Why efforts to collect an inflation tax by printing money can lead to high rates of inflation and even hyperinflation
- The types of inflation: cost-push and demand-pull

We have seen that monetary policy affects economic welfare in the short-run. Let's take a closer look at two phenomena that involve monetary policy: inflation and deflation.

Money and Inflation

In the summer of 2008, the African nation of Zimbabwe achieved the unenviable distinction of having the world's highest inflation rate: 11 million percent a year. Although the United States has not experienced the inflation levels that some countries have seen, in the late 1970s and early 1980s, consumer prices were rising at an annual rate as high as 13%. The policies that the Federal Reserve instituted to reduce this high level led to the deepest recession since the Great Depression. As we'll see later, moderate levels of inflation such as those experienced in the United States—even the double-digit inflation of the late 1970s—can have complex causes. Very high inflation, the type suffered by Zimbabwe, is associated with rapid increases in the money supply while the causes of moderate inflation, the type experienced in the United States, are quite different.

To understand what causes inflation, we need to revisit the effect of changes in the money supply on the overall price level. Then we'll turn to the reasons why governments sometimes increase the money supply very rapidly.

The Classical Model of Money and Prices

We learned that in the short run an increase in the money supply increases real GDP by lowering the interest rate and stimulating investment spending and consumer spending. However, in the long run, as nominal wages and other sticky prices rise, real GDP falls back to its original level. So in the long run, an increase in the money supply does not change real GDP. Instead, other things equal, it leads to an equal percentage rise in the overall price level; that is, the prices of all goods and services in the economy, including nominal wages and the prices of intermediate goods, rise by the same percentage as

The Turkish currency is the *lira*. When Turkey made 1,000,000 "old" lira equivalent to 1 "new" lira, real GDP was unaffected because of the neutrality of money.

the money supply. And when the overall price level rises, the aggregate price level—the prices of all final goods and services—rises as well. As a result, a change in the *nominal* money supply, *M*, leads in the long run to a change in the aggregate price level, *P*, that leaves the *real* quantity of money, *M/P*, at its original level. As a result, there is no long-run effect on aggregate demand or real GDP. For example, when Turkey dropped six zeros from its currency, the Turkish lira, in January 2005, Turkish real GDP did not change. The only thing that changed was the number of zeros in prices: instead of something costing 2,000,000 lira, it cost 2 lira.

This is, to repeat, what happens in the long run. When analyzing large changes in the aggregate price level, however, macroeconomists often find it useful to ignore the distinction between the short run and the long run. Instead, they work with a simplified model in which the effect of a change in the money supply on the aggregate price level takes place instantaneously rather than over a long period of time. You might be concerned about this assumption given the emphasis we've placed on the difference between the short run and the long run. However, for reasons we'll explain shortly, this is a reasonable assumption to make in the case of high inflation.

The simplified model in which the real quantity of money, *M/P*, is always at its long-run equilibrium level is known as the **classical model of the price level** because it was commonly used by "classical" economists prior to the influence of John Maynard Keynes. To understand the classical model and why it is useful in the context of high inflation, let's revisit the *AD–AS* model and what it says about the effects of an increase in the money supply. (Unless otherwise noted, we will always be referring to changes in the *nominal* supply of money.)

Figure 33.1 reviews the effects of an increase in the money supply according to the *AD–AS* model. The economy starts at E_1, a point of short-run and long-run macroeconomic equilibrium. It lies at the intersection of the aggregate demand curve, AD_1, and the short-run aggregate supply curve, $SRAS_1$. It also lies on the long-run aggregate supply curve, *LRAS*. At E_1, the equilibrium aggregate price level is P_1.

Now suppose there is an increase in the money supply. This is an expansionary monetary policy, which shifts the aggregate demand curve to the right, to AD_2, and moves the economy to a new short-run macroeconomic equilibrium at E_2. Over time, however,

According to the **classical model of the price level,** the real quantity of money is always at its long-run equilibrium level.

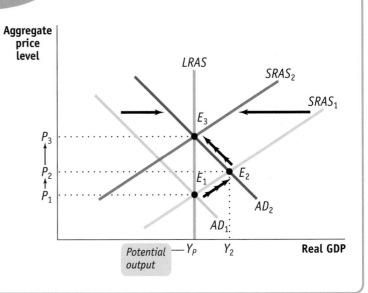

figure 33.1

The Classical Model of the Price Level

Starting at E_1, an increase in the money supply shifts the aggregate demand curve rightward, as shown by the movement from AD_1 to AD_2. There is a new short-run macroeconomic equilibrium at E_2 and a higher price level at P_2. In the long run, nominal wages adjust upward and push the *SRAS* curve leftward to $SRAS_2$. The total percent increase in the price level from P_1 to P_3 is equal to the percent increase in the money supply. In the *classical model of the price level*, we ignore the transition period and think of the price level as rising to P_3 immediately. This is a good approximation under conditions of high inflation.

nominal wages adjust upward in response to the rise in the aggregate price level, and the *SRAS* curve shifts to the left, to *SRAS*$_2$. The new long-run macroeconomic equilibrium is at E_3, and real GDP returns to its initial level. The long-run increase in the aggregate price level from P_1 to P_3 is proportional to the increase in the money supply. As a result, in the long run changes in the money supply have no effect on the real quantity of money, *M/P*, or on real GDP. In the long run, money—as we learned—is *neutral*.

The classical model of the price level ignores the short-run movement from E_1 to E_2, assuming that the economy moves directly from one long-run equilibrium to another long-run equilibrium. In other words, it assumes that the economy moves directly from E_1 to E_3 and that real GDP never changes in response to a change in the money supply. In effect, in the classical model the effects of money supply changes are analyzed as if the short-run as well as the long-run aggregate supply curves were vertical.

In reality, this is a poor assumption during periods of low inflation. With a low inflation rate, it may take a while for workers and firms to react to a monetary expansion by raising wages and prices. In this scenario, some nominal wages and the prices of some goods are sticky in the short run. As a result, under low inflation there is an upward-sloping *SRAS* curve, and changes in the money supply can indeed change real GDP in the short run.

But what about periods of high inflation? In the face of high inflation, economists have observed that the short-run stickiness of nominal wages and prices tends to vanish. Workers and businesses, sensitized to inflation, are quick to raise their wages and prices in response to changes in the money supply. This implies that under high inflation there is a quicker adjustment of wages and prices of intermediate goods than occurs in the case of low inflation. So the short-run aggregate supply curve shifts leftward more quickly and there is a more rapid return to long-run equilibrium under high inflation. As a result, the classical model of the price level is much more likely to be a good approximation of reality for economies experiencing persistently high inflation.

The consequence of this rapid adjustment of all prices in the economy is that in countries with persistently high inflation, changes in the money supply are quickly translated into changes in the inflation rate. Let's look at Zimbabwe. Figure 33.2 shows

Denise Bober

With a low inflation rate, it may take a while for workers and firms to react to a monetary expansion by raising wages and prices.

---

figure 33.2

Money Supply Growth and Inflation in Zimbabwe

This figure, drawn on a logarithmic scale, shows the annual rates of change of the money supply and the price level in Zimbabwe from 2003 through January 2008. The surges in the money supply were quickly reflected in a roughly equal surge in the price level.

Source: Reserve Bank of Zimbabwe.

Annual percent change

1,000,000%

100,000

Money supply

Consumer price index

10,000

1,000

2003   2004   2005   2006   2007   2008

Year

the annual rate of growth in the money supply and the annual rate of change of consumer prices from 2003 through January 2008. As you can see, the surge in the growth rate of the money supply coincided closely with a roughly equal surge in the inflation rate. Note that to fit these very large percentage increases—exceeding 100,000 percent—onto the figure, we have drawn the vertical axis using a logarithmic scale.

In late 2008, Zimbabwe's inflation rate reached 231 million percent. What leads a country to increase its money supply so much that the result is an inflation rate in the millions of percent?

The Inflation Tax

Modern economies use fiat money—pieces of paper that have no intrinsic value but are accepted as a medium of exchange. In the United States and most other wealthy countries, the decision about how many pieces of paper to issue is placed in the hands of a central bank that is somewhat independent of the political process. However, this independence can always be taken away if politicians decide to seize control of monetary policy.

So what is to prevent a government from paying for some of its expenses not by raising taxes or borrowing but simply by printing money? Nothing. In fact, governments, including the U.S. government, do it all the time. How can the U.S. government do this, given that the Federal Reserve, not the U.S. Treasury, issues money? The answer is that the Treasury and the Federal Reserve work in concert. The Treasury issues debt to finance the government's purchases of goods and services, and the Fed *monetizes* the debt by creating money and buying the debt back from the public through open-market purchases of Treasury bills. In effect, the U.S. government can and does raise revenue by printing money.

For example, in February 2010, the U.S. monetary base—bank reserves plus currency in circulation—was $559 billion larger than it had been a year earlier. This occurred because, over the course of that year, the Federal Reserve had issued $559 billion in money or its electronic equivalent and put it into circulation mainly through open-market operations. To put it another way, the Fed created money out of thin air and used it to buy valuable government securities from the private sector. It's true that the U.S. government pays interest on debt owned by the Federal Reserve—but the Fed, by law, hands the interest payments it receives on government debt back to the Treasury, keeping only enough to fund its own operations. In effect, then, the Federal Reserve's actions enabled the government to pay off $559 billion in outstanding government debt by printing money.

An alternative way to look at this is to say that the right to print money is itself a source of revenue. Economists refer to the revenue generated by the government's right to print money as *seignorage,* an archaic term that goes back to the Middle Ages. It refers to the right to stamp gold and silver into coins, and charge a fee for doing so, that medieval lords—seigneurs, in France—reserved for themselves.

Seignorage accounts for only a tiny fraction (less than 1%) of the U.S. government's budget. Furthermore, concerns about seignorage don't have any influence on the Federal Reserve's decisions about how much money to print; the Fed is worried about inflation and unemployment, not revenue. But this hasn't always been true, even in the United States: both sides relied on seignorage to help cover budget deficits during the Civil War. And there have been many occasions in history when governments turned to their printing presses as a crucial source of revenue. According to the usual scenario, a government finds itself running a large budget deficit—and lacks either the competence or the political will to eliminate this deficit by raising taxes or cutting spending. Furthermore, the government can't borrow to cover the gap because potential lenders won't extend loans, given the fear that the government's weakness will continue and leave it unable to repay its debts.

In such a situation, governments end up printing money to cover the budget deficit. But by printing money to pay its bills, a government increases the quantity of money in circulation. And as we've just seen, increases in the money supply translate into equally large increases in the aggregate price level. So printing money to cover a budget deficit leads to inflation.

Who ends up paying for the goods and services the government purchases with newly printed money? The people who currently hold money pay. They pay because inflation erodes the purchasing power of their money holdings. In other words, a government imposes an **inflation tax,** a reduction in the value of the money held by the public, by printing money to cover its budget deficit and creating inflation.

It's helpful to think about what this tax represents. If the inflation rate is 5%, then a year from now $1 will buy goods and services worth only about $0.95 today. So a 5% inflation rate in effect imposes a tax rate of 5% on the value of all money held by the public.

But why would any government push the inflation tax to rates of hundreds or thousands of percent? We turn next to the process by which high inflation turns into explosive hyperinflation.

The Logic of Hyperinflation

Inflation imposes a tax on individuals who hold money. And, like most taxes, it will lead people to change their behavior. In particular, when inflation is high, people will try to avoid holding money and will instead substitute real goods as well as interest-bearing assets for money. During the German hyperinflation, people began using eggs or lumps of coal as a medium of exchange. They did this because lumps of coal maintained their real value over time but money didn't. Indeed, during the peak of German hyperinflation, people often burned paper money, which was less valuable than wood. Moreover, people don't just reduce their nominal money holdings—they reduce their *real* money holdings, cutting the amount of money they hold so much that it actually has less purchasing power than the amount of money they would hold if inflation were low. Why? Because the more real money holdings they have, the greater the real amount of resources the government captures from them through the inflation tax.

We are now prepared to understand how countries can get themselves into situations of extreme inflation. High inflation arises when the government must print a large quantity of money, imposing a large inflation tax, to cover a large budget deficit.

Now, the seignorage collected by the government over a short period—say, one month—is equal to the change in the money supply over that period. Let's use M to represent the money supply and the symbol Δ to mean "monthly change in." Then:

(33-1) Seignorage $= \Delta M$

The money value of seignorage, however, isn't very informative by itself. After all, the whole point of inflation is that a given amount of money buys less and less over time. So it's more useful to look at *real* seignorage, the revenue created by printing money divided by the price level, P:

(33-2) Real seignorage $= \Delta M/P$

Equation 33-2 can be rewritten by dividing and multiplying by the current level of the money supply, M, giving us:

(33-3) Real seignorage $= (\Delta M/M) \times (M/P)$

or

Real seignorage $=$ Rate of growth of the money supply $\times$ Real money supply

An **inflation tax** is a reduction in the value of money held by the public caused by inflation.

Keystone/ Getty Images

In the 1920s, hyperinflation made German currency worth so little that children made kites from banknotes.

But as we've just explained, in the face of high inflation the public reduces the real amount of money it holds, so that the far right-hand term in Equation 33-3, M/P, gets smaller. Suppose that the government needs to print enough money to pay for a given quantity of goods and services—that is, it needs to collect a given *real* amount of seignorage. Then, as people hold smaller amounts of real money due to a high rate of inflation, the government has to respond by accelerating the rate of growth of the money supply, $\Delta M/M$. This will lead to an even higher rate of inflation. And people will respond to this new higher rate of inflation by reducing their real money holdings, M/P, yet again. As the process becomes self-reinforcing, it can easily spiral out of control. Although the amount of real seignorage that the government must ultimately collect to pay off its deficit does not change, the inflation rate the government needs to impose to collect that amount rises. So the government is forced to increase the money supply more rapidly, leading to an even higher rate of inflation, and so on.

Here's an analogy: imagine a city government that tries to raise a lot of money with a special fee on taxi rides. The fee will raise the cost of taxi rides, and this will cause people to turn to substitutes, such as walking or taking the bus. As taxi use declines, the government finds that its tax revenue declines and it must impose a higher fee to raise the same amount of revenue as before. You can imagine the ensuing vicious circle: the government imposes fees on taxi rides, which leads to less taxi use, which causes the government to raise the fee on taxi rides, which leads to even less taxi use, and so on.

Substitute the real money supply for taxi rides and the inflation rate for the increase in the fee on taxi rides, and you have the story of hyperinflation. A race develops

Zimbabwe's Inflation

Zimbabwe offers a recent example of a country experiencing very high inflation. Figure 33.2 showed that surges in Zimbabwe's money supply growth were matched by almost simultaneous surges in its inflation rate. But looking at rates of change doesn't give a true feel for just how much prices went up.

The figure here shows Zimbabwe's consumer price index from 1999 to June 2008, with the 2000 level set equal to 100. As in Figure 33.2, we use a logarithmic scale, which lets us draw equal-sized percent changes as the same size. Over the course of about nine years, consumer prices rose by approximately 4.5 trillion percent.

Why did Zimbabwe's government pursue policies that led to runaway inflation? The reason boils down to political instability, which in turn had its roots in Zimbabwe's history. Until the 1970s, Zimbabwe had been ruled by its small white minority; even after the shift to ma-

jority rule, many of the country's farms remained in the hands of whites. Eventually Robert Mugabe, Zimbabwe's president, tried to solidify his position by seizing these farms and turning them over to his political supporters. But because this seizure disrupted production, the result was to undermine the country's economy and its tax base. It became impossible for the country's government to balance its budget either by raising taxes or by cutting spending. At the same time, the regime's instability left Zimbabwe unable to borrow

money in world markets. Like many others before it, Zimbabwe's government turned to the printing press to cover the gap—leading to massive inflation.

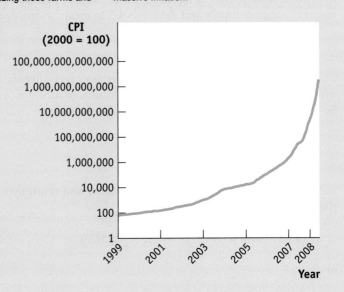

between the government printing presses and the public: the presses churn out money at a faster and faster rate to try to compensate for the fact that the public is reducing its real money holdings. At some point the inflation rate explodes into hyperinflation, and people are unwilling to hold any money at all (and resort to trading in eggs and lumps of coal). The government is then forced to abandon its use of the inflation tax and shut down the printing presses.

Moderate Inflation and Disinflation

The governments of wealthy, politically stable countries like the United States and Britain don't find themselves forced to print money to pay their bills. Yet over the past 40 years both countries, along with a number of other nations, have experienced uncomfortable episodes of inflation. In the United States, the inflation rate peaked at 13% in 1980. In Britain, the inflation rate reached 26% in 1975. Why did policy makers allow this to happen?

Using the aggregate demand and supply model, we can see that there are two possible changes that can lead to an increase in the aggregate price level: a decrease in aggregate supply or an increase in aggregate demand. Inflation that is caused by a significant increase in the price of an input with economy-wide importance is called **cost-push inflation.** For example, it is argued that the oil crisis in the 1970s led to an increase in energy prices in the United States, causing a leftward shift of the aggregate supply curve, increasing the aggregate price level. However, aside from crude oil, it is difficult to think of examples of inputs with economy-wide importance that experience significant price increases.

Inflation that is caused by an increase in aggregate demand is known as **demand-pull inflation**. When a rightward shift of the aggregate demand curve leads to an increase in the aggregate price level, the economy experiences demand-pull inflation. This is sometimes referred to by the phrase "too much money chasing too few goods," which means that the aggregate demand for goods and services is outpacing the aggregate supply and driving up the prices of goods.

In the short run, policies that produce a booming economy also tend to lead to higher inflation, and policies that reduce inflation tend to depress the economy. This creates both temptations and dilemmas for governments.

Imagine yourself as a politician facing an election in a year, and suppose that inflation is fairly low at the moment. You might well be tempted to pursue expansionary policies that will push the unemployment rate down, as a way to please voters, even if your economic advisers warn that this will eventually lead to higher inflation. You might also be tempted to find different economic advisers, who will tell you not to worry: in politics, as in ordinary life, wishful thinking often prevails over realistic analysis.

Conversely, imagine yourself as a politician in an economy suffering from inflation. Your economic advisers will probably tell you that the only way to bring inflation down is to push the economy into a recession, which will lead to temporarily higher unemployment. Are you willing to pay that price? Maybe not.

This political asymmetry—inflationary policies often produce short-term political gains, but policies to bring inflation down carry short-term political costs—explains how countries with no need to impose an inflation tax sometimes end up with serious inflation problems. For example, that 26% rate of inflation in Britain was largely the result of the British government's decision in 1971 to pursue highly expansionary monetary and fiscal policies. Politicians disregarded warnings that these policies would be inflationary and were extremely reluctant to reverse course even when it became clear that the warnings had been correct.

But why do expansionary policies lead to inflation? To answer that question, we need to look first at the relationship between output and unemployment.

Cost-push inflation is inflation that is caused by a significant increase in the price of an input with economy-wide importance.

Demand-pull inflation is inflation that is caused by an increase in aggregate demand.

The Output Gap and the Unemployment Rate

Earlier we introduced the concept of *potential output,* the level of real GDP that the economy would produce once all prices had fully adjusted. Potential output typically grows steadily over time, reflecting long-run growth. However, as we learned from the aggregate demand–aggregate supply model, actual aggregate output fluctuates around potential output in the short run: a recessionary gap arises when actual aggregate output falls short of potential output; an inflationary gap arises when actual aggregate output exceeds potential output. Recall that the percentage difference between the actual level of real GDP and potential output is called the *output gap.* A positive or negative output gap occurs when an economy is producing more than or less than what would be "expected" because all prices have not yet adjusted. And wages, as we've learned, are the prices in the labor market.

Meanwhile, we learned that the unemployment rate is composed of cyclical unemployment and natural unemployment, the portion of the unemployment rate unaffected by the business cycle. So there is a relationship between the unemployment rate and the output gap. This relationship is defined by two rules:

- When actual aggregate output is equal to potential output, the actual unemployment rate is equal to the natural rate of unemployment.

- When the output gap is positive (an inflationary gap), the unemployment rate is *below* the natural rate. When the output gap is negative (a recessionary gap), the unemployment rate is *above* the natural rate.

In other words, fluctuations of aggregate output around the long-run trend of potential output correspond to fluctuations of the unemployment rate around the natural rate.

This makes sense. When the economy is producing less than potential output—when the output gap is negative—it is not making full use of its productive resources. Among the resources that are not fully used is labor, the economy's most important resource. So we would expect a negative output gap to be associated with unusually high unemployment. Conversely, when the economy is producing more than potential output, it is temporarily using resources at higher-than-normal rates. With this positive output gap, we would expect to see lower-than-normal unemployment.

Figure 33.3 confirms this rule. Panel (a) shows the actual and natural rates of unemployment, as estimated by the Congressional Budget Office (CBO). Panel (b) shows two series. One is cyclical unemployment: the difference between the actual unemployment rate and the CBO estimate of the natural rate of unemployment, measured on the left. The other is the CBO estimate of the output gap, measured on the right. To make the relationship clearer, the output gap series is inverted—shown upside down—so that the line goes down if actual output rises above potential output and up if actual output falls below potential output. As you can see, the two series move together quite closely, showing the strong relationship between the output gap and cyclical unemployment. Years of high cyclical unemployment, like 1982 or 2009, were also years of a strongly negative output gap. Years of low cyclical unemployment, like the late 1960s or 2000, were also years of a strongly positive output gap.

figure 33.3

Cyclical Unemployment and the Output Gap

Panel (a) shows the actual U.S. unemployment rate from 1949 to 2009, together with the Congressional Budget Office estimate of the natural rate of unemployment. The actual rate fluctuates around the natural rate, often for extended periods. Panel (b) shows cyclical unemployment—the difference between the actual unemployment rate and the natural rate of unemployment—and the output gap, also estimated by the CBO. The unemployment rate is measured on the left vertical axis, and the output gap is measured with an inverted scale on the right vertical axis. With an inverted scale, it moves in the same direction as the unemployment rate: when the output gap is positive, the actual unemployment rate is below its natural rate; when the output gap is negative, the actual unemployment rate is above its natural rate. The two series track one another closely, showing the strong relationship between the output gap and cyclical unemployment.

Source: Congressional Budget Office; Bureau of Labor Statistics; Bureau of Economic Analysis.

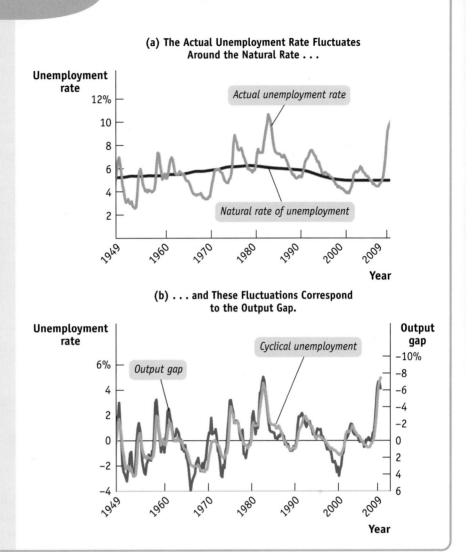

(a) The Actual Unemployment Rate Fluctuates Around the Natural Rate . . .

(b) . . . and These Fluctuations Correspond to the Output Gap.

Module 33 AP Review

Solutions appear at the back of the book.

Check Your Understanding

1. Suppose there is a large increase in the money supply in an economy that previously had low inflation. As a consequence, aggregate output expands in the short run. What does this say about situations in which the classical model of the price level applies?

2. Suppose that all wages and prices in an economy are indexed to inflation. Can there still be an inflation tax?

Tackle the Test: Multiple-Choice Questions

1. The real quantity of money is
   I. equal to M/P.
   II. the money supply adjusted for inflation.
   III. higher in the long run when the Fed buys government securities.
   a. I only
   b. II only
   c. III only
   d. I and II only
   e. I, II, and III

2. In the classical model of the price level
   a. only the short-run aggregate supply curve is vertical.
   b. both the short-run and long-run aggregate supply curves are vertical.
   c. only the long-run aggregate supply curve is vertical.
   d. both the short-run aggregate demand and supply curves are vertical.
   e. both the long-run aggregate demand and supply curves are vertical.

3. The classical model of the price level is most applicable in
   a. the United States.
   b. periods of high inflation.
   c. periods of low inflation.
   d. recessions.
   e. depressions.

4. An inflation tax is
   a. imposed by governments to offset price increases.
   b. paid directly as a percentage of the sale price on purchases.
   c. the result of a decrease in the value of money held by the public.
   d. generally levied by states rather than the federal government.
   e. higher during periods of low inflation.

5. Revenue generated by the government's right to print money is known as
   a. seignorage.
   b. an inflation tax.
   c. hyperinflation.
   d. fiat money.
   e. monetary funds.

Tackle the Test: Free-Response Questions

1. Use a correctly labeled aggregate supply and demand graph to illustrate cost-push inflation. Give an example of what might cause cost-push inflation in the economy.

Answer (9 points)

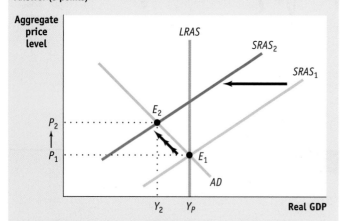

1 point: Aggregate price level on vertical axis and real GDP on horizontal axis

1 point: *AD* downward sloping and labeled

1 point: *SRAS* upward sloping and labeled

1 point: *LRAS* vertical and labeled

1 point: Potential output labeled at horizontal intercept of *LRAS*

1 point: Long-run macroeconomic equilibrium aggregate price level labeled on vertical axis at intersection of *SRAS, LRAS,* and *AD*

1 point: Leftward shift of the *SRAS* curve

1 point: Higher equilibrium aggregate price level at new intersection of *SRAS* and *AD*

1 point: This could be caused by anything that would shift the short-run aggregate supply curve to the left, such as an increase in the price of energy, labor, or another input with economy-wide importance.

2. Draw a correctly labeled aggregate demand and supply graph showing an economy in long-run macroeconomic equilibrium. On your graph, show the effect of an increase in the money supply, according to the classical model of the price level.

Module 34
Inflation and Unemployment: The Phillips Curve

What you will learn in this Module:

- What the Phillips curve is and the nature of the short-run trade-off between inflation and unemployment

- Why there is no long-run trade-off between inflation and unemployment

- Why expansionary policies are limited due to the effects of expected inflation

- Why even moderate levels of inflation can be hard to end

- Why deflation is a problem for economic policy and leads policy makers to prefer a low but positive inflation rate

The Short-Run Phillips Curve

We've just seen that expansionary policies lead to a lower unemployment rate. Our next step in understanding the temptations and dilemmas facing governments is to show that there is a short-run trade-off between unemployment and inflation—lower unemployment tends to lead to higher inflation, and vice versa. The key concept is that of the *Phillips curve.*

The origins of this concept lie in a famous 1958 paper by the New Zealand–born economist Alban W. H. Phillips. Looking at historical data for Britain, he found that when the unemployment rate was high, the wage rate tended to fall, and when the unemployment rate was low, the wage rate tended to rise. Using data from Britain, the United States, and elsewhere, other economists soon found a similar apparent relationship between the unemployment rate and the rate of inflation—that is, the rate of change in the aggregate price level. For example, Figure 34.1 on the next page shows the U.S. unemployment rate and the rate of consumer price inflation over each subsequent year from 1955 to 1968, with each dot representing one year's data.

Looking at evidence like Figure 34.1, many economists concluded that there is a negative short-run relationship between the unemployment rate and the inflation rate, represented by the **short-run Phillips curve,** or *SRPC.* (We'll explain the difference between the short-run and the long-run Phillips curve soon.) Figure 34.2 on the next page shows a hypothetical short-run Phillips curve.

Early estimates of the short-run Phillips curve for the United States were very simple: they showed a negative relationship between the unemployment rate and the inflation rate, without taking account of any other variables. During the 1950s and 1960s this simple approach seemed, for a while, to be adequate. And this simple relationship is clear in the data in Figure 34.1.

The **short-run Phillips curve** is the negative short-run relationship between the unemployment rate and the inflation rate.

figure **34.1**

Unemployment and Inflation, 1955–1968

Each dot shows the average U.S. unemployment rate for one year and the percentage increase in the consumer price index over the subsequent year. Data like this lay behind the initial concept of the Phillips curve.

Source: Bureau of Labor Statistics.

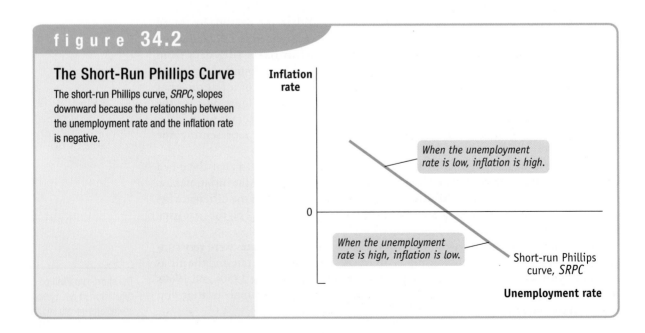

Even at the time, however, some economists argued that a more accurate short-run Phillips curve would include other factors. Previously, we discussed the effect of *supply shocks,* such as sudden changes in the price of oil, that shift the short-run aggregate supply curve. Such shocks also shift the short-run Phillips curve: surging oil prices were an important factor in the inflation of the 1970s and also played an important role in the acceleration of inflation in 2007–2008. In general, a negative supply shock shifts *SRPC* up, as the inflation rate increases for every level of the unemployment rate, and a positive supply shock shifts it down as the inflation rate falls for every level of the unemployment rate. Both outcomes are shown in Figure 34.3.

But supply shocks are not the only factors that can change the inflation rate. In the early 1960s, Americans had little experience with inflation as inflation rates had been low for decades. But by the late 1960s, after inflation had been steadily increasing for a number of years, Americans had come to expect future inflation. In 1968

figure **34.2**

The Short-Run Phillips Curve

The short-run Phillips curve, *SRPC,* slopes downward because the relationship between the unemployment rate and the inflation rate is negative.

When the unemployment rate is low, inflation is high.

When the unemployment rate is high, inflation is low.

Short-run Phillips curve, *SRPC*

Inflation rate

0

Unemployment rate

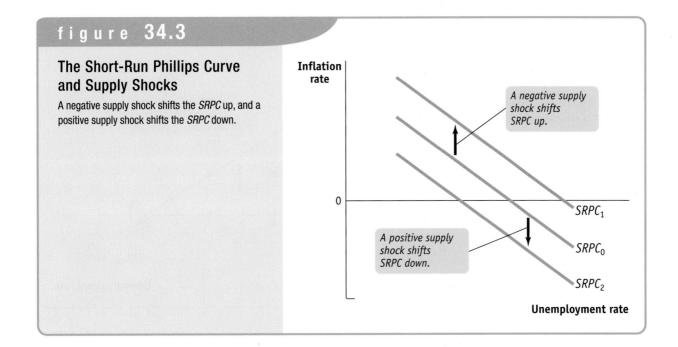

figure 34.3

The Short-Run Phillips Curve and Supply Shocks

A negative supply shock shifts the *SRPC* up, and a positive supply shock shifts the *SRPC* down.

two economists—Milton Friedman of the University of Chicago and Edmund Phelps of Columbia University—independently set forth a crucial hypothesis: that expectations about future inflation directly affect the present inflation rate. Today most economists accept that the *expected inflation rate*—the rate of inflation that employers and workers expect in the near future—is the most important factor, other than the unemployment rate, affecting inflation.

Inflation Expectations and the Short-Run Phillips Curve

The expected rate of inflation is the rate that employers and workers expect in the near future. One of the crucial discoveries of modern macroeconomics is that changes in the expected rate of inflation affect the short-run trade-off between unemployment and inflation and shift the short-run Phillips curve.

Why do changes in expected inflation affect the short-run Phillips curve? Put yourself in the position of a worker or employer about to sign a contract setting the worker's wages over the next year. For a number of reasons, the wage rate they agree to will be higher if everyone expects high inflation (including rising wages) than if everyone expects prices to be stable. The worker will want a wage rate that takes into account future declines in the purchasing power of earnings. He or she will also want a wage rate that won't fall behind the wages of other workers. And the employer will be more willing to agree to a wage increase now if hiring workers later will be even more expensive. Also, rising prices will make paying a higher wage rate more affordable for the employer because the employer's output will sell for more.

For these reasons, an increase in expected inflation shifts the short-run Phillips curve upward: the actual rate of inflation at any given unemployment rate is higher when the expected inflation rate is higher. In fact, macroeconomists believe that the relationship between changes in expected inflation and changes in actual inflation is one-to-one. That is, when the expected inflation rate increases, the actual inflation rate at any given unemployment rate will increase by the same amount. When the expected inflation rate falls, the actual inflation rate at any given level of unemployment will fall by the same amount.

Figure 34.4 on the next page shows how the expected rate of inflation affects the short-run Phillips curve. First, suppose that the expected rate of inflation is 0%. $SRPC_0$ is the short-run Phillips curve when the public expects 0% inflation. According to

Expected Inflation and the Short-Run Phillips Curve

An increase in expected inflation shifts the short-run Phillips curve up. $SRPC_0$ is the initial short-run Phillips curve with an expected inflation rate of 0%; $SRPC_2$ is the short-run Phillips curve with an expected inflation rate of 2%. Each additional percentage point of expected inflation raises the actual inflation rate at any given unemployment rate by 1 percentage point.

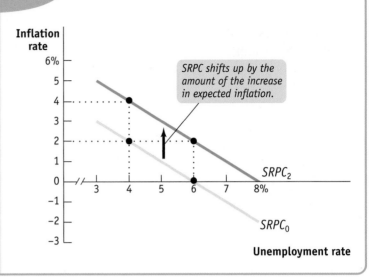

SRPC shifts up by the amount of the increase in expected inflation.

$SRPC_0$, the actual inflation rate will be 0% if the unemployment rate is 6%; it will be 2% if the unemployment rate is 4%.

Alternatively, suppose the expected rate of inflation is 2%. In that case, employers and workers will build this expectation into wages and prices: at any given unemployment rate, the actual inflation rate will be 2 percentage points higher than it would be

fyi

From the Scary Seventies to the Nifty Nineties

Figure 34.1 showed that the American experience during the 1950s and 1960s supported the belief in the existence of a short-run Phillips curve for the U.S. economy, with a short-run trade-off between unemployment and inflation.

After 1969, however, that relationship appeared to fall apart according to the data. The figure here plots the course of U.S. unemployment and inflation rates from 1961 to 1990. As you can see, the course looks more like a tangled piece of yarn than like a smooth curve.

Through much of the 1970s and early 1980s, the economy suffered from a combination of above-average unemployment rates coupled with inflation rates unprecedented in modern American history. This condition came to be known as *stagflation*—for stagnation combined with high inflation. In the late 1990s, by contrast, the economy was experiencing a blissful combination of low unemployment and low inflation. What explains these developments?

Part of the answer can be attributed to a series of negative supply shocks that the

U.S. economy suffered during the 1970s. The price of oil, in particular, soared as wars and revolutions in the Middle East led to a reduction in oil supplies and as oil-exporting countries deliberately curbed production to drive up prices. Compounding the oil price shocks, there was also a slowdown in labor productivity growth. Both of these factors shifted the short-run Phillips curve upward. During the 1990s, by contrast, supply shocks were positive. Prices of oil and other raw materials were generally falling, and productivity growth accelerated. As a result, the short-run Phillips curve shifted downward.

Equally important, however, was the role of expected inflation. As mentioned earlier, inflation accelerated during the 1960s. During the 1970s,

the public came to expect high inflation, and this also shifted the short-run Phillips curve up. It took a sustained and costly effort during the 1980s to get inflation back down. The result, however, was that expected inflation was very low by the late 1990s, allowing actual inflation to be low even with low rates of unemployment.

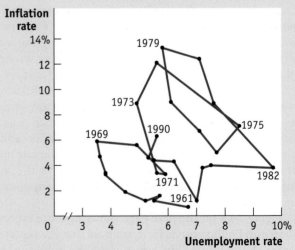

if people expected 0% inflation. $SRPC_2$, which shows the Phillips curve when the expected inflation rate is 2%, is $SRPC_0$ shifted upward by 2 percentage points at every level of unemployment. According to $SRPC_2$, the actual inflation rate will be 2% if the unemployment rate is 6%; it will be 4% if the unemployment rate is 4%.

What determines the expected rate of inflation? In general, people base their expectations about inflation on experience. If the inflation rate has hovered around 0% in the last few years, people will expect it to be around 0% in the near future. But if the inflation rate has averaged around 5% lately, people will expect inflation to be around 5% in the near future.

Since expected inflation is an important part of the modern discussion about the short-run Phillips curve, you might wonder why it was not in the original formulation of the Phillips curve. The answer lies in history. Think back to what we said about the early 1960s: at that time, people were accustomed to low inflation rates and reasonably expected that future inflation rates would also be low. It was only after 1965 that persistent inflation became a fact of life. So only then did it become clear that expected inflation would play an important role in price-setting.

Inflation and Unemployment in the Long Run

The short-run Phillips curve says that at any given point in time there is a trade-off between unemployment and inflation. According to this view, policy makers have a choice: they can choose to accept the price of high inflation in order to achieve low unemployment, or they can reject high inflation and pay the price of high unemployment. In fact, during the 1960s many economists believed that this trade-off represented a real choice.

However, this view was greatly altered by the later recognition that expected inflation affects the short-run Phillips curve. In the short run, expectations often diverge from reality. In the long run, however, any consistent rate of inflation will be reflected in expectations. If inflation is consistently high, as it was in the 1970s, people will come to expect more of the same; if inflation is consistently low, as it has been in recent years, that, too, will become part of expectations. So what does the trade-off between inflation and unemployment look like in the long run, when actual inflation is incorporated into expectations? Most macroeconomists believe that there is, in fact, no long-run trade-off. That is, it is not possible to achieve lower unemployment in the long run by accepting higher inflation. To see why, we need to introduce another concept: the *long-run Phillips curve*.

The Long-Run Phillips Curve

Figure 34.5 on the next page reproduces the two short-run Phillips curves from Figure 34.4, $SRPC_0$ and $SRPC_2$. It also adds an additional short-run Phillips curve, $SRPC_4$, representing a 4% expected rate of inflation. In a moment, we'll explain the significance of the vertical long-run Phillips curve, $LRPC$.

Suppose that the economy has, in the past, had a 0% inflation rate. In that case, the current short-run Phillips curve will be $SRPC_0$, reflecting a 0% expected inflation rate. If the unemployment rate is 6%, the actual inflation rate will be 0%.

Also suppose that policy makers decide to trade off lower unemployment for a higher rate of inflation. They use monetary policy, fiscal policy, or both to drive the unemployment rate down to 4%. This puts the economy at point A on $SRPC_0$, leading to an actual inflation rate of 2%.

Over time, the public will come to expect a 2% inflation rate. *This increase in inflationary expectations will shift the short-run Phillips curve upward* to $SRPC_2$. Now, when the unemployment rate is 6%, the actual inflation rate will be 2%. Given this new short-run Phillips curve, policies adopted to keep the unemployment rate at 4% will lead to a 4% actual inflation rate—point B on $SRPC_2$—rather than point A with a 2% actual inflation rate.

The NAIRU and the Long-Run Phillips Curve

SRPC$_0$ is the short-run Phillips curve when the expected inflation rate is 0%. At a 4% unemployment rate, the economy is at point *A* with an actual inflation rate of 2%. The higher inflation rate will be incorporated into expectations, and the *SRPC* will shift upward to *SRPC*$_2$. If policy makers act to keep the unemployment rate at 4%, the economy will be at *B* and the actual inflation rate will rise to 4%. Inflationary expectations will be revised upward again, and *SRPC* will shift to *SRPC*$_4$. At a 4% unemployment rate, the economy will be at *C* and the actual inflation rate will rise to 6%. Here, an unemployment rate of 6% is the NAIRU, or nonaccelerating inflation rate of unemployment. As long as unemployment is at the NAIRU, the actual inflation rate will match expectations and remain constant. An unemployment rate below 6% requires ever-accelerating inflation. The long-run Phillips curve, *LRPC*, which passes through *E*$_0$, *E*$_2$, and *E*$_4$, is vertical: no long-run trade-off between unemployment and inflation exists.

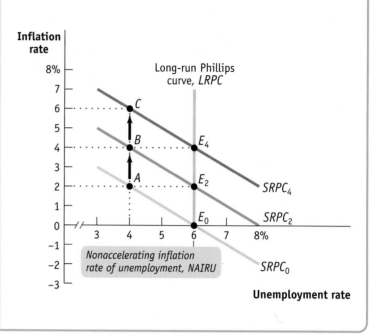

The **nonaccelerating inflation rate of unemployment,** or **NAIRU,** is the unemployment rate at which inflation does not change over time.

The **long-run Phillips curve** shows the relationship between unemployment and inflation after expectations of inflation have had time to adjust to experience.

The non-accelerating inflation rate of unemployment, or NAIRU, is the unemployment rate at which inflation does not change over time.

Eventually, the 4% actual inflation rate gets built into expectations about the future inflation rate, and the short-run Phillips curve shifts upward yet again to *SRPC*$_4$. To keep the unemployment rate at 4% would now require accepting a 6% actual inflation rate, point *C* on *SRPC*$_4$, and so on. In short, a persistent attempt to trade off lower unemployment for higher inflation leads to *accelerating* inflation over time.

To avoid accelerating inflation over time, the unemployment rate must be high enough that the actual rate of inflation matches the expected rate of inflation. This is the situation at *E*$_0$ on *SRPC*$_0$: when the expected inflation rate is 0% and the unemployment rate is 6%, the actual inflation rate is 0%. It is also the situation at *E*$_2$ on *SRPC*$_2$: when the expected inflation rate is 2% and the unemployment rate is 6%, the actual inflation rate is 2%. And it is the situation at *E*$_4$ on *SRPC*$_4$: when the expected inflation rate is 4% and the unemployment rate is 6%, the actual inflation rate is 4%. As we'll learn shortly, this relationship between accelerating inflation and the unemployment rate is known as the *natural rate hypothesis*.

The unemployment rate at which inflation does not change over time—6% in Figure 34.5—is known as the **nonaccelerating inflation rate of unemployment,** or **NAIRU** for short. Keeping the unemployment rate below the NAIRU leads to ever-accelerating inflation and cannot be maintained. Most macroeconomists believe that there is a NAIRU and that there is no long-run trade-off between unemployment and inflation.

We can now explain the significance of the vertical line *LRPC.* It is the **long-run Phillips curve,** the relationship between unemployment and inflation in the long run, after expectations of inflation have had time to adjust to experience. It is vertical because any unemployment rate below the NAIRU leads to ever-accelerating inflation. In other words, the long-run Phillips curve shows that there are limits to expansionary policies because an unemployment rate below the NAIRU cannot be maintained in the long run. Moreover there is a corresponding point we have not yet emphasized: any unemployment rate above the NAIRU leads to decelerating inflation.

The Natural Rate of Unemployment, Revisited

Recall the concept of the natural rate of unemployment, the portion of the unemployment rate unaffected by the swings of the business cycle. Now we have introduced the concept of the *NAIRU*. How do these two concepts relate to each other?

The answer is that the NAIRU is another name for the natural rate. The level of unemployment the economy "needs" in order to avoid accelerating inflation is equal to the natural rate of unemployment.

In fact, economists estimate the natural rate of unemployment by looking for evidence about the NAIRU from the behavior of the inflation rate and the unemployment rate over the course of the business cycle. For example, the way major European countries learned, to their dismay, that their natural rates of unemployment were 9% or more was through unpleasant experience. In the late 1980s, and again in the late 1990s, European inflation began to accelerate as European unemployment rates, which had been above 9%, began to fall, approaching 8%.

fyi

The Great Disinflation of the 1980s

As we've mentioned several times, the United States ended the 1970s with a high rate of inflation, at least by its own peacetime historical standards—13% in 1980. Part of this inflation was the result of one-time events, especially a world oil crisis. But expectations of future inflation at 10% or more per year appeared to be firmly embedded in the economy.

By the mid-1980s, however, inflation was running at about 4% per year. Panel (a) of the figure shows the annual rate of change in the "core" consumer price index (CPI)—also called the *core inflation rate*. This index, which excludes volatile energy and food prices, is widely regarded as a better indicator of underlying inflation trends than the overall CPI. By this measure, inflation fell from about 12% at the end of the 1970s to about 4% by the mid-1980s.

How was this disinflation achieved? At great cost. Beginning in late 1979, the Federal Reserve imposed strongly contractionary monetary policies, which pushed the economy into its worst recession since the Great Depression. Panel (b) shows the Congressional Budget Office estimate of the U.S. output gap from 1979 to 1989: by 1982, actual output was 7% below potential output, corresponding to an unemployment rate of more than 9%. Aggregate output didn't get back to potential output until 1987.

Our analysis of the Phillips curve tells us that a temporary rise in unemployment, like that of the 1980s, is needed to break the cycle of inflationary expectations. Once expectations of inflation are reduced, the economy can return to the natural rate of unemployment at a lower inflation rate. And that's just what happened.

At what cost? If you add up the output gaps over 1980–1987, you find that the economy sacrificed approximately 18% of an average year's output over the period. If we had to do the same thing today, that would mean giving up roughly $2.6 trillion worth of goods and services.

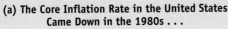

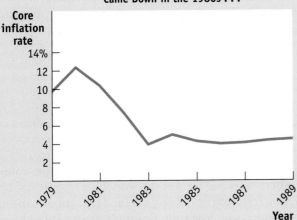

(a) The Core Inflation Rate in the United States Came Down in the 1980s . . .

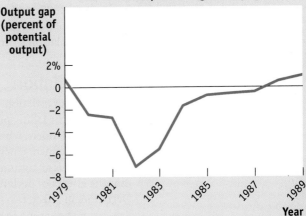

(b) . . . but Only at the Expense of a Huge Sacrifice of Output and High Unemployment.

In Figure 33.3 we cited Congressional Budget Office estimates of the U.S. natural rate of unemployment. The CBO has a model that predicts changes in the inflation rate based on the deviation of the actual unemployment rate from the natural rate. Given data on actual unemployment and inflation, this model can be used to deduce estimates of the natural rate—and that's where the CBO numbers come from.

The Costs of Disinflation

Through experience, policy makers have found that bringing inflation down is a much harder task than increasing it. The reason is that once the public has come to expect continuing inflation, bringing inflation down is painful.

A persistent attempt to keep unemployment below the natural rate leads to accelerating inflation that becomes incorporated into expectations. To reduce inflationary expectations, policy makers need to run the process in reverse, adopting contractionary policies that keep the unemployment rate above the natural rate for an extended period of time. The process of bringing down inflation that has become embedded in expectations is known as *disinflation*.

Disinflation can be very expensive. The U.S. retreat from high inflation at the beginning of the 1980s appears to have cost the equivalent of about 18% of a year's real GDP, the equivalent of roughly $2.6 trillion today. The justification for paying these costs is that they lead to a permanent gain. Although the economy does not recover the short-term production losses caused by disinflation, it no longer suffers from the costs associated with persistently high inflation. In fact, the United States, Britain, and other wealthy countries that experienced inflation in the 1970s eventually decided that the benefit of bringing inflation down was worth the required suffering—the large reduction in real GDP in the short term.

Some economists argue that the costs of disinflation can be reduced if policy makers explicitly state their determination to reduce inflation. A clearly announced, credible policy of disinflation, they contend, can reduce expectations of future inflation and so shift the short-run Phillips curve downward. Some economists believe that the clear determination of the Federal Reserve to combat the inflation of the 1970s was credible enough that the costs of disinflation, huge though they were, were lower than they might otherwise have been.

Deflation

Before World War II, *deflation*—a falling aggregate price level—was almost as common as inflation. In fact, the U.S. consumer price index on the eve of World War II was 30% lower than it had been in 1920. After World War II, inflation became the norm in all countries. But in the 1990s, deflation reappeared in Japan and proved difficult to reverse. Concerns about potential deflation played a crucial role in U.S. monetary policy in the early 2000s and again in late 2008. In fact, in late 2008, the U.S. experienced a brief period of deflation.

Why is deflation a problem? And why is it hard to end?

Debt Deflation

Deflation, like inflation, produces both winners and losers—but in the opposite direction. Due to the falling price level, a dollar in the future has a higher real value than a dollar today. So lenders, who are owed money, gain under deflation because the real value of borrowers' payments increases. Borrowers lose because the real burden of their debt rises.

In a famous analysis at the beginning of the Great Depression, Irving Fisher claimed that the effects of deflation on borrowers and lenders can worsen an economic slump. Deflation, in effect, takes real resources away from borrowers and redistributes them to lenders. Fisher argued that borrowers, who lose from deflation, are typically short of cash and will be forced to cut their spending sharply when their debt burden rises.

Lenders, however, are less likely to increase spending sharply when the values of the loans they own rise. The overall effect, said Fisher, is that deflation reduces aggregate demand, deepening an economic slump, which, in a vicious circle, may lead to further deflation. The effect of deflation in reducing aggregate demand, known as **debt deflation,** probably played a significant role in the Great Depression.

Debt deflation is the reduction in aggregate demand arising from the increase in the real burden of outstanding debt caused by deflation.

There is a **zero bound** on the nominal interest rate: it cannot go below zero.

A **liquidity trap** is a situation in which conventional monetary policy is ineffective because nominal interest rates are up against the zero bound.

Effects of Expected Deflation

Like expected inflation, expected deflation affects the nominal interest rate. Consider Figure 29.6 from Section 5 (repeated here as Figure 34.6), which demonstrates how expected inflation affects the equilibrium interest rate. As shown, the equilibrium nominal interest rate is 4% if the expected inflation rate is 0%. Clearly, if the expected inflation rate is −3%—if the public expects deflation at 3% per year—the equilibrium nominal interest rate will be 1%.

But what would happen if the expected rate of inflation were −5%? Would the nominal interest rate fall to −1%, meaning that lenders are paying borrowers 1% on their debt? No. Nobody would lend money at a negative nominal rate of interest because they could do better by simply holding cash. This illustrates what economists call the **zero bound** on the nominal interest rate: it cannot go below zero.

This zero bound can limit the effectiveness of monetary policy. Suppose the economy is depressed, with output below potential output and the unemployment rate above the natural rate. Normally, the central bank can respond by cutting interest rates so as to increase aggregate demand. If the nominal interest rate is already zero, however, the central bank cannot push it down any further. Banks refuse to lend and consumers and firms refuse to spend because, with a negative inflation rate and a 0% nominal interest rate, holding cash yields a positive real rate of return. Any further increases in the monetary base will either be held in bank vaults or held as cash by individuals and firms, without being spent.

A situation in which conventional monetary policy to fight a slump—cutting interest rates—can't be used because nominal interest rates are up against the zero bound is known as a **liquidity trap.** A liquidity trap can occur whenever there is a sharp reduction in demand for loanable funds—which is exactly what happened during the Great

---

figure 34.6

The Fisher Effect

D_0 and S_0 are the demand and supply curves for loanable funds when the expected future inflation rate is 0%. At an expected inflation rate of 0%, the equilibrium nominal interest rate is 4%. An increase in expected future inflation pushes both the demand and supply curves upward by 1 percentage point for every percentage point increase in expected future inflation. D_{10} and S_{10} are the demand and supply curves for loanable funds when the expected future inflation rate is 10%. The 10 percentage point increase in expected future inflation raises the equilibrium nominal interest rate to 14%. The expected real interest rate remains at 4%, and the equilibrium quantity of loanable funds also remains unchanged.

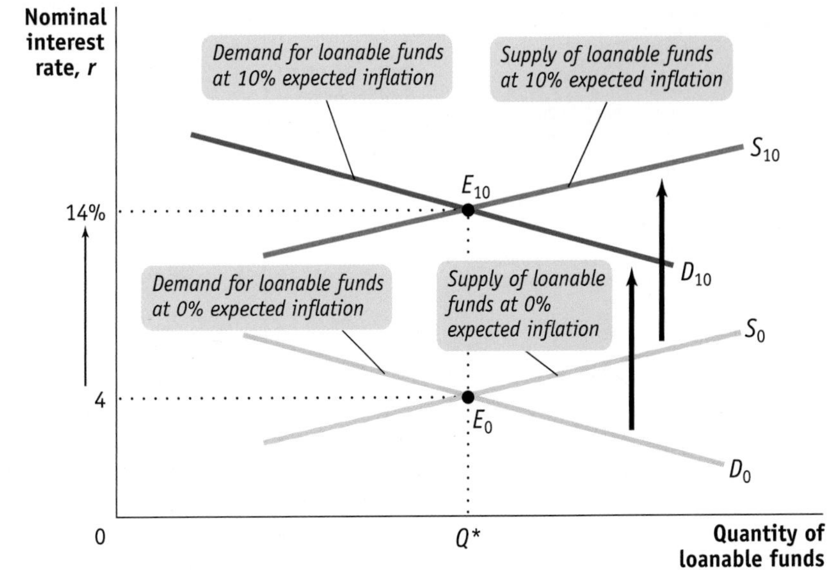

figure 34.7

The Zero Bound in U.S. History

This figure shows U.S. short-term interest rates, specifically the interest rate on three-month Treasury bills, since 1920. As shown by the shaded area at left, for much of the 1930s, interest rates were very close to zero, leaving little room for expansionary monetary policy. After World War II, persistent inflation generally kept rates well above zero. However, in late 2008, in the wake of the housing bubble bursting and the financial crisis, the interest rate on three-month Treasury bills was again virtually zero.

Source: Federal Reserve Bank of St. Louis.

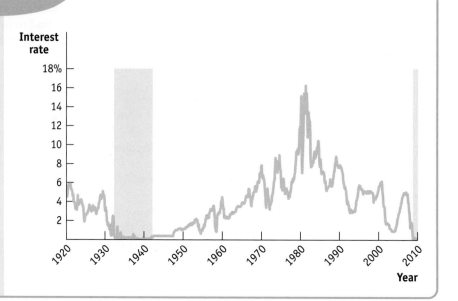

Depression. Figure 34.7 shows the interest rate on short-term U.S. government debt from 1920 to January 2010. As you can see, starting in 1933 and ending when World War II brought a full economic recovery, the U.S. economy was either close to or up against the zero bound. After World War II, when inflation became the norm around the world, the zero bound problem largely vanished as the public came to expect inflation rather than deflation.

However, the recent history of the Japanese economy, shown in Figure 34.8, provides a modern illustration of the problem of deflation and the liquidity trap. Japan experienced a huge boom in the prices of both stocks and real estate in the late 1980s, and then saw both bubbles burst. The result was a prolonged period of economic stagnation, the so-called Lost Decade, which gradually reduced the inflation rate and eventually led to persistent deflation. In an effort to fight the weakness of the economy, the

figure 34.8

Japan's Lost Decade

A prolonged economic slump in Japan led to deflation from the late 1990s on. The Bank of Japan responded by cutting interest rates—but eventually ran up against the zero bound.

Source: Japanese Ministry of Internal Affairs and Communications, Statistics Bureau; Bank of Japan.

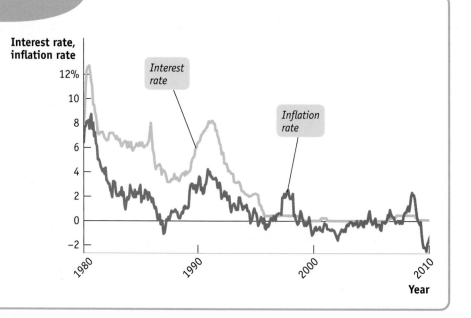

Bank of Japan—the equivalent of the Federal Reserve—repeatedly cut interest rates. Eventually, it arrived at the "ZIRP": the zero interest rate policy. The "call money rate," the equivalent of the U.S. federal funds rate, was literally set equal to zero. Because the economy was still depressed, it would have been desirable to cut interest rates even further. But that wasn't possible: Japan was up against the zero bound.

In 2008 and 2009, the Federal Reserve also found itself up against the zero bound. In the aftermath of the bursting of the housing bubble and the ensuing financial crisis, the interest on short-term U.S. government debt had fallen to virtually zero.

Module 34 AP Review

Solutions appear at the back of the book.

Check Your Understanding

1. Explain how the short-run Phillips curve illustrates the negative relationship between cyclical unemployment and the actual inflation rate for a given level of the expected inflation rate.

2. Why is there no long-run trade-off between unemployment and inflation?

3. Why is disinflation so costly for an economy? Are there ways to reduce these costs?

4. Why won't anyone lend money at a negative nominal rate of interest? How can this pose problems for monetary policy?

Tackle the Test: Multiple-Choice Questions

1. The long-run Phillips curve is
   - I. the same as the short-run Phillips curve.
   - II. vertical.
   - III. the short-run Phillips curve plus expected inflation.
   - a. I only
   - b. II only
   - c. III only
   - d. I and II only
   - e. I, II, and III

2. The short-run Phillips curve shows a _____ relationship between _____.
   - a. negative   the aggregate price level and aggregate output
   - b. positive   the aggregate price level and aggregate output
   - c. negative   unemployment and inflation
   - d. positive   unemployment and aggregate output
   - e. positive   unemployment and the aggregate price level

3. An increase in expected inflation will shift
   - a. the short-run Phillips curve downward.
   - b. the short-run Phillips curve upward.
   - c. the long-run Phillips curve upward.
   - d. the long-run Phillips curve downward.
   - e. neither the short-run nor the long-run Phillips curve.

4. Bringing down inflation that has become embedded in expectations is called
   - a. deflation.
   - b. negative inflation.
   - c. anti-inflation.
   - d. unexpected inflation.
   - e. disinflation.

5. Debt deflation is
   - a. the effect of deflation in decreasing aggregate demand.
   - b. an idea proposed by Irving Fisher.
   - c. a contributing factor in causing the Great Depression.
   - d. due to differences in how borrowers/lenders respond to inflation losses/gains.
   - e. all of the above.

Tackle the Test: Free-Response Questions

1. a. Draw a correctly labeled graph showing a short-run Phillips curve with an expected inflation rate of 0% and the corresponding long-run Phillips curve.
   b. On your graph, label the nonaccelerating inflation rate of unemployment.
   c. On your graph, show what happens in the long run if the government decides to decrease the unemployment rate below the nonaccelerating inflation rate of unemployment. Explain.

Answer (8 points)

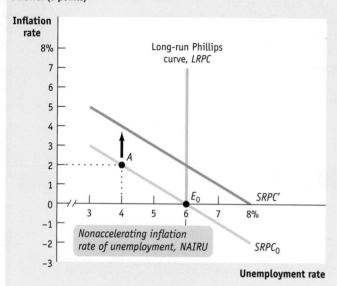

1 point: Vertical axis labeled "Inflation rate"

1 point: Horizontal axis labeled "Unemployment rate"

1 point: Downward sloping curve labeled "$SRPC_0$"

1 point: Vertical curve labeled "$LRPC$"

1 point: $SRPC_0$ crosses horizontal axis where it crosses $LRPC$

1 point: $NAIRU$ is labeled where $SRPC_0$ crosses $LRPC$ and horizontal axis

1 point: New $SRPC$ is labeled, for example as "$SRAS'$", and shown above the original $SRPC_0$

1 point: When the unemployment rate moves below the $NAIRU$, it creates inflation and moves the economy to a point such as A. This leads to positive inflationary expectations, which shift the $SRPC$ up as shown by $SRPC'$.

2. Consider the accompanying diagram.

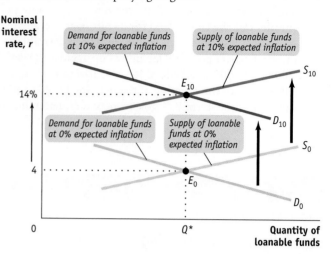

a. What is the nominal interest rate if expected inflation is 0%?

b. What would the nominal interest rate be if the expected inflation rate were −2%? Explain.

c. What would the nominal interest rate be if the expected inflation rate were −6%? Explain.

d. What would a negative nominal interest rate mean for lenders? How much lending would take place at a negative nominal interest rate? Explain.

e. What effect does a nominal interest rate of zero have on monetary policy? What is this situation called?

Module 35
History and Alternative Views of Macroeconomics

What you will learn in this **Module:**

- Why classical macroeconomics wasn't adequate for the problems posed by the Great Depression

- How Keynes and the experience of the Great Depression legitimized macroeconomic policy activism

- What monetarism is and its views about the limits of discretionary monetary policy

- How challenges led to a revision of Keynesian ideas and the emergence of the new classical macroeconomics

Classical Macroeconomics

The term *macroeconomics* appears to have been coined in 1933 by the Norwegian economist Ragnar Frisch. The timing, during the worst year of the Great Depression, was no accident. Still, there were economists analyzing what we now consider macroeconomic issues—the behavior of the aggregate price level and aggregate output—before then.

Money and the Price Level

Previously, we described the *classical model of the price level.* According to the classical model, prices are flexible, making the aggregate supply curve vertical even in the short run. In this model, an increase in the money supply leads, other things equal, to a proportional rise in the aggregate price level, with no effect on aggregate output. As a result, increases in the money supply lead to inflation, and that's all. Before the 1930s, the classical model of the price level dominated economic thinking about the effects of monetary policy.

Did classical economists really believe that changes in the money supply affected only aggregate prices, without any effect on aggregate output? Probably not. Historians of economic thought argue that before 1930 most economists were aware that changes in the money supply affected aggregate output as well as aggregate prices in the short run—or, to use modern terms, they were aware that the short-run aggregate supply curve sloped upward. But they regarded such short-run effects as unimportant, stressing the long run instead. It was this attitude that led John Maynard Keynes to scoff at the focus on the long run, in which, as he said, "we are all dead."

The Business Cycle

Classical economists were, of course, also aware that the economy did not grow smoothly. The American economist Wesley Mitchell pioneered the quantitative study of business cycles. In 1920, he founded the National Bureau of Economic Research, an independent, nonprofit organization that to this day has the official role of declaring the beginnings of recessions and expansions. Thanks to Mitchell's work, the *measurement* of business cycles was well advanced by 1930. But there was no widely accepted *theory* of business cycles.

In the absence of any clear theory, views about how policy makers should respond to a recession were conflicting. Some economists favored expansionary monetary and fiscal policies to fight a recession. Others believed that such policies would worsen the slump or merely postpone the inevitable. For example, in 1934 Harvard's Joseph Schumpeter, now famous for his early recognition of the importance of technological change, warned that any attempt to alleviate the Great Depression with expansionary monetary policy "would, in the end, lead to a collapse worse than the one it was called in to remedy." When the Great Depression hit, the policy making process was paralyzed by this lack of consensus. In many cases, economists now believe, policy makers took steps in the wrong direction.

Necessity was, however, the mother of invention. As we'll explain next, the Great Depression provided a strong incentive for economists to develop theories that could serve as a guide to policy—and economists responded.

The Great Depression and the Keynesian Revolution

The Great Depression demonstrated, once and for all, that economists cannot safely ignore the short run. Not only was the economic pain severe, it threatened to destabilize societies and political systems. In particular, the economic plunge helped Adolf Hitler rise to power in Germany.

The whole world wanted to know how this economic disaster could be happening and what should be done about it. But because there was no widely accepted theory of the business cycle, economists gave conflicting and, we now believe, often harmful advice. Some believed that only a huge change in the economic system—such as having the government take over much of private industry and replace markets with a command economy—could end the slump. Others argued that slumps were natural—even beneficial—and that nothing should be done.

Some economists, however, argued that the slump both could have and should have been cured—without giving up on the basic idea of a market economy. In 1930, the British economist John Maynard Keynes compared the problems of the U.S. and British economies to those of a car with a defective alternator. Getting the economy running, he argued, would require only a modest repair, not a complete overhaul.

Nice metaphor. But what was the nature of the trouble?

Keynes's Theory

In 1936, Keynes presented his analysis of the Great Depression—his explanation of what was wrong with the economy's alternator—in a book titled *The General Theory of Employment, Interest, and Money.* In 1946, the great American economist Paul Samuelson wrote that "it is a badly written book, poorly organized. . . . Flashes of insight and intuition intersperse tedious algebra. . . . We find its analysis to be obvious and at the same time new. In short, it is a work of genius." *The General Theory* isn't easy reading, but it stands with Adam Smith's *The Wealth of Nations* as one of the most influential books on economics ever written.

As Samuelson's description suggests, Keynes's book is a vast stew of ideas. Keynesian economics mainly reflected two innovations. First, Keynes emphasized the short-run

Some people use *Keynesian economics* as a synonym for *left-wing economics*—but the truth is that the ideas of John Maynard Keynes have been accepted across a broad part of the political spectrum.

effects of shifts in aggregate demand on aggregate output, rather than the long-run determination of the aggregate price level. As Keynes's famous remark about being dead in the long run suggests, until his book appeared most economists had treated short-run macroeconomics as a minor issue. Keynes focused the attention of economists on situations in which the short-run aggregate supply curve slopes upward and shifts in the aggregate demand curve affect aggregate output and employment as well as aggregate prices.

Figure 35.1 illustrates the difference between Keynesian and classical macroeconomics. Both panels of the figure show the short-run aggregate supply curve, *SRAS*; in both it is assumed that for some reason the aggregate demand curve shifts leftward from AD_1 to AD_2—let's say in response to a fall in stock market prices that leads households to reduce consumer spending.

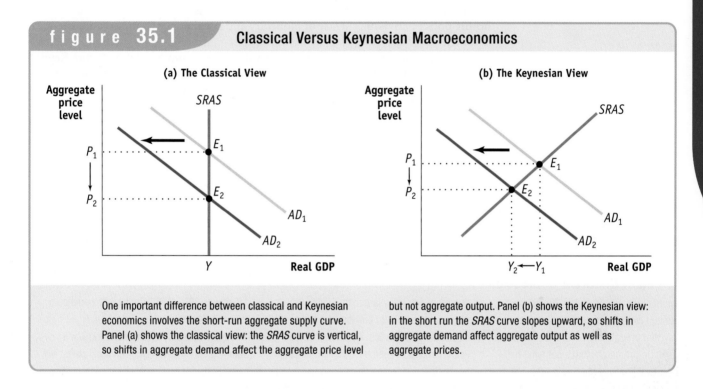

figure 35.1 **Classical Versus Keynesian Macroeconomics**

(a) The Classical View

(b) The Keynesian View

One important difference between classical and Keynesian economics involves the short-run aggregate supply curve. Panel (a) shows the classical view: the *SRAS* curve is vertical, so shifts in aggregate demand affect the aggregate price level but not aggregate output. Panel (b) shows the Keynesian view: in the short run the *SRAS* curve slopes upward, so shifts in aggregate demand affect aggregate output as well as aggregate prices.

Panel (a) shows the classical view: the short-run aggregate supply curve is vertical. The decline in aggregate demand leads to a fall in the aggregate price level, from P_1 to P_2, but no change in aggregate output. Panel (b) shows the Keynesian view: the short-run aggregate supply curve slopes upward, so the decline in aggregate demand leads to both a fall in the aggregate price level, from P_1 to P_2, and a fall in aggregate output, from Y_1 to Y_2. As we've already explained, many classical macroeconomists would have agreed that panel (b) was an accurate story in the short run—but they regarded the short run as unimportant. Keynes disagreed. (Just to be clear, there isn't any diagram that looks like panel (b) of Figure 35.1 in Keynes's *General Theory*. But Keynes's discussion of aggregate supply, translated into modern terminology, clearly implies an upward-sloping *SRAS* curve.)

Second, classical economists emphasized the role of changes in the money supply in shifting the aggregate demand curve, paying little attention to other factors. Keynes, however, argued that other factors, especially changes in "animal spirits"—these days usually referred to with the bland term *business confidence*—are mainly responsible for business cycles. Before Keynes, economists often argued that a decline in business confidence would have no effect on either the aggregate price level or aggregate output, as long as the money supply stayed constant. Keynes offered a very different picture.

Keynes's ideas have penetrated deeply into the public consciousness, to the extent that many people who have never heard of Keynes, or have heard of him but think they disagree with his theory, use Keynesian ideas all the time. For example, suppose that a business commentator says something like this: "Because of a decline in business confidence, investment spending slumped, causing a recession." Whether the commentator knows it or not, that statement is pure Keynesian economics.

Keynes himself more or less predicted that his ideas would become part of what "everyone knows." In another famous passage, this from the end of *The General Theory*, he wrote: "Practical men, who believe themselves to be quite exempt from any intellectual influences, are usually the slaves of some defunct economist."

Policy to Fight Recessions

The main practical consequence of Keynes's work was that it legitimized **macroeconomic policy activism**—the use of monetary and fiscal policy to smooth out the business cycle.

Macroeconomic policy activism wasn't something completely new. Before Keynes, many economists had argued for using monetary expansion to fight economic downturns—though others were fiercely opposed. Some economists had even argued that temporary budget deficits were a good thing in times of recession—though others disagreed strongly. In practice, during the 1930s many governments followed policies that we would now call Keynesian. In the United States, the administration of Franklin Roosevelt engaged in modest deficit spending in an effort to create jobs.

But these efforts were half-hearted. Roosevelt's advisers were deeply divided over the appropriate policies to adopt. In fact, in 1937 Roosevelt gave in to advice from

fyi

The End of the Great Depression

It would make a good story if Keynes's ideas had led to a change in economic policy that brought the Great Depression to an end. Unfortunately, that's not what happened. Still, the way the Depression ended did a lot to convince economists that Keynes was right.

The basic message many of the young economists who adopted Keynes's ideas in the 1930s took from his work was that economic recovery requires aggressive fiscal expansion—deficit spending on a large scale to create jobs. And that is what they eventually got, but it wasn't because politicians were persuaded. Instead, what happened was a very large and expensive war, World War II.

The figure here shows the U.S. unemployment rate and the federal budget deficit as a share of GDP from 1930 to 1947. As you can see, deficit spending during the 1930s was on a modest scale. In 1940, as

the risk of war grew larger, the United States began a large military buildup, and the budget moved deep into deficit. After the attack on Pearl Harbor on December 7, 1941, the country began deficit spending on an enormous scale: in fiscal 1943, which began in July 1942, the

deficit was 30% of GDP. Today that would be a deficit of $4.3 trillion.

And the economy recovered. World War II wasn't intended as a Keynesian fiscal policy, but it demonstrated that expansionary fiscal policy can, in fact, create jobs in the short run.

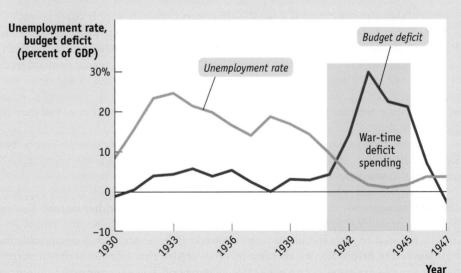

non-Keynesian economists who urged him to balance the budget and raise interest rates, even though the economy was still depressed. The result was a renewed slump.

Today, by contrast, there is broad consensus about the useful role monetary and fiscal policy can play in fighting recessions. The 2004 Economic Report of the President was issued by a conservative Republican administration that was generally opposed to government intervention in the economy. Yet its view on economic policy in the face of recession was far more like that of Keynes than like that of most economists before 1936.

It would be wrong, however, to suggest that Keynes's ideas have been fully accepted by modern macroeconomists. In the decades that followed the publication of *The General Theory,* Keynesian economics faced a series of challenges, some of which succeeded in modifying the macroeconomic consensus in important ways.

Challenges to Keynesian Economics

Keynes's ideas fundamentally changed the way economists think about business cycles. They did not, however, go unquestioned. In the decades that followed the publication of *The General Theory,* Keynesian economics faced a series of challenges. As a result, the consensus of macroeconomists retreated somewhat from the strong version of Keynesianism that prevailed in the 1950s. In particular, economists became much more aware of the limits to macroeconomic policy activism.

The Revival of Monetary Policy

Keynes's *General Theory* suggested that monetary policy wouldn't be very effective in depression conditions. Many modern macroeconomists agree: earlier we introduced the concept of a *liquidity trap,* a situation in which monetary policy is ineffective because the interest rate is down against the zero bound. In the 1930s, when Keynes wrote, interest rates were, in fact, very close to 0%. (The term *liquidity trap* was first introduced by the British economist John Hicks in a 1937 paper, "Mr. Keynes and the Classics: A Suggested Interpretation," that summarized Keynes's ideas.)

But even when the era of near-0% interest rates came to an end after World War II, many economists continued to emphasize fiscal policy and downplay the usefulness of monetary policy. Eventually, however, macroeconomists reassessed the importance of monetary policy. A key milestone in this reassessment was the 1963 publication of *A Monetary History of the United States, 1867–1960* by Milton Friedman, of the University of Chicago, and Anna Schwartz, of the National Bureau of Economic Research. Friedman and Schwartz showed that business cycles had historically been associated with fluctuations in the money supply. In particular, the money supply fell sharply during the onset of the Great Depression. Friedman and Schwartz persuaded many, though not all, economists that the Great Depression could have been avoided if the Federal Reserve had acted to prevent that monetary contraction. They persuaded most economists that monetary policy should play a key role in economic management.

The revival of interest in monetary policy was significant because it suggested that the burden of managing the economy could be shifted away from fiscal policy—meaning that economic management could largely be taken out of the hands of politicians. Fiscal policy, which must involve changing tax rates or government spending, necessarily involves political choices. If the government tries to stimulate the economy by cutting taxes, it must decide whose taxes will be cut. If it tries to stimulate the economy with government spending, it must decide what to spend the money on.

Milton Friedman and his co-author Anna Schwartz played a key role in convincing macroeconomists of the importance of monetary policy.

Monetary policy, in contrast, does not involve such choices: when the central bank cuts interest rates to fight a recession, it cuts everyone's interest rate at the same time. So a shift from relying on fiscal policy to relying on monetary policy makes macroeconomics a more technical, less political issue. In fact, monetary policy in most major economies is set by an independent central bank that is insulated from the political process.

Monetarism

After the publication of *A Monetary History,* Milton Friedman led a movement, called *monetarism,* that sought to eliminate macroeconomic policy activism while maintaining the importance of monetary policy. **Monetarism** asserted that GDP will grow steadily if the money supply grows steadily. The monetarist policy prescription was to have the central bank target a constant rate of growth of the money supply, such as 3% per year, and maintain that target regardless of any fluctuations in the economy.

It's important to realize that monetarism retained many Keynesian ideas. Like Keynes, Friedman asserted that the short run is important and that short-run changes in aggregate demand affect aggregate output as well as aggregate prices. Like Keynes, he argued that policy should have been much more expansionary during the Great Depression.

Monetarists argued, however, that most of the efforts of policy makers to smooth out the business cycle actually make things worse. We have already discussed concerns over the usefulness of *discretionary fiscal policy*—changes in taxes or government spending, or both—in response to the state of the economy. As we explained, government perceptions about the economy often lag behind reality, and there are further lags in changing fiscal policy and in its effects on the economy. As a result, discretionary fiscal policies intended to fight a recession often end up feeding a boom, and vice versa. According to monetarists, **discretionary monetary policy,** changes in the interest rate or the money supply by the central bank in order to stabilize the economy, faces the same problem of lags as fiscal policy, but to a lesser extent.

Friedman also argued that if the central bank followed his advice and refused to change the money supply in response to fluctuations in the economy, fiscal policy would be much less effective than Keynesians believed. Earlier we analyzed the phenomenon of *crowding out,* in which government deficits drive up interest rates and lead to reduced investment spending. Friedman and others pointed out that if the money supply is held fixed while the government pursues an expansionary fiscal policy, crowding out will limit the effect of the fiscal expansion on aggregate demand.

Figure 35.2 illustrates this argument. Panel (a) shows aggregate output and the aggregate price level. AD_1 is the initial aggregate demand curve and $SRAS$ is the short-run aggregate supply curve. At the initial equilibrium, E_1, the level of aggregate output is Y_1 and the aggregate price level is P_1. Panel (b) shows the money market. MS is the money supply curve and MD_1 is the initial money demand curve, so the initial interest rate is r_1.

Now suppose the government increases purchases of goods and services. We know that this will shift the AD curve rightward, as illustrated by the shift from AD_1 to AD_2; that aggregate output will rise, from Y_1 to Y_2, and that the aggregate price level will rise, from P_1 to P_2. Both the rise in aggregate output and the rise in the aggregate price level will, however, increase the demand for money, shifting the money demand curve rightward from MD_1 to MD_2. This drives up the equilibrium interest rate to r_2. Friedman's point was that this rise in the interest rate reduces investment spending, partially offsetting the initial rise in government spending. As a result, the rightward shift of the AD curve is smaller than multiplier analysis indicates. And Friedman argued that with a constant money supply, the multiplier is so small that there's not much point in using fiscal policy.

But Friedman didn't favor activist monetary policy either. He argued that the problem of time lags that limit the ability of discretionary fiscal policy to stabilize the

figure 35.2 — Fiscal Policy with a Fixed Money Supply

(a) The increase in aggregate demand from an expansionary fiscal policy is limited when the money supply is fixed...

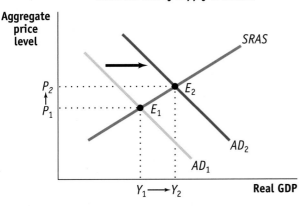

(b) ...because the increase in money demand drives up the interest rate, crowding out some investment spending.

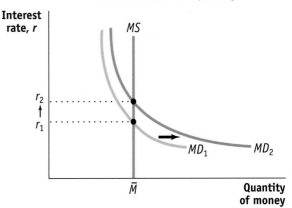

In panel (a) an expansionary fiscal policy shifts the *AD* curve rightward, driving up both the aggregate price level and aggregate output. However, this leads to an increase in the demand for money. If the money supply is held fixed, as in panel (b), the increase in money demand drives up the interest rate, reducing investment spending and offsetting part of the fiscal expansion. So the shift of the *AD* curve is less than it would otherwise be: fiscal policy becomes less effective when the money supply is held fixed.

economy also apply to discretionary monetary policy. Friedman's solution was to put monetary policy on "autopilot." The central bank, he argued, should follow a **monetary policy rule,** a formula that determines its actions and leaves it relatively little discretion. During the 1960s and 1970s, most monetarists favored a monetary policy rule of slow, steady growth in the money supply. Underlying this view was the **Quantity Theory of Money,** which relies on the concept of the **velocity of money,** the ratio of nominal GDP to the money supply. Velocity is a measure of the number of times the average dollar bill in the economy turns over per year between buyers and sellers (e.g., I tip the Starbucks barista a dollar, she uses it to buy lunch, and so on). This concept gives rise to the *velocity equation:*

(35-1) $M \times V = P \times Y$

Where M is the money supply, V is velocity, P is the aggregate price level, and Y is real GDP.

Monetarists believed, with considerable historical justification, that the velocity of money was stable in the short run and changed only slowly in the long run. As a result, they claimed, steady growth in the money supply by the central bank would ensure steady growth in spending, and therefore in GDP.

Monetarism strongly influenced actual monetary policy in the late 1970s and early 1980s. It quickly became clear, however, that steady growth in the money supply didn't ensure steady growth in the economy: the velocity of money wasn't stable enough for such a simple policy rule to work. Figure 35.3 shows how events eventually undermined the monetarists' view. The figure shows the velocity of money, as measured by the ratio of nominal GDP to M1, from 1960 to the middle of 2009. As you can see, until 1980, velocity followed a fairly smooth, seemingly predictable trend. After the Fed began to adopt monetarist ideas in the late 1970s and early 1980s, however, the velocity of money began moving erratically—probably due to financial market innovations.

A **monetary policy rule** is a formula that determines the central bank's actions.

The **Quantity Theory of Money** emphasizes the positive relationship between the price level and the money supply. It relies on the velocity equation ($M \times V = P \times Y$).

The **velocity of money** is the ratio of nominal GDP to the money supply. It is a measure of the number of times the average dollar bill is spent per year.

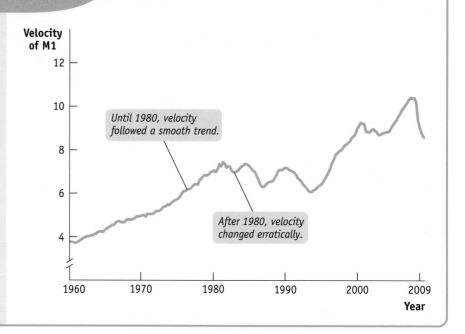

figure 35.3

The Velocity of Money

From 1960 to 1980, the velocity of money was stable, leading monetarists to believe that steady growth in the money supply would lead to a stable economy. After 1980, however, velocity began moving erratically, undermining the case for traditional monetarism. As a result, traditional monetarism fell out of favor.

Source: Bureau of Economic Analysis; Federal Reserve Bank of St. Louis.

Until 1980, velocity followed a smooth trend.

After 1980, velocity changed erratically.

Traditional monetarists are hard to find among today's macroeconomists. As we'll see later, however, the concern that originally motivated the monetarists—that too much discretionary monetary policy can actually destabilize the economy—has become widely accepted.

Inflation and the Natural Rate of Unemployment

At the same time that monetarists were challenging Keynesian views about how macroeconomic policy should be conducted, other economists—some, but not all, monetarists—were emphasizing the limits to what activist macroeconomic policy could achieve.

In the 1940s and 1950s, many Keynesian economists believed that expansionary fiscal policy could be used to achieve full employment on a permanent basis. In the 1960s, however, many economists realized that expansionary policies could cause problems with inflation, but they still believed policy makers could choose to trade off low unemployment for higher inflation even in the long run.

In 1968, however, Edmund Phelps of Columbia University and Milton Friedman, working independently, proposed the concept of the natural rate of unemployment. In Module 34 we saw that the natural rate of unemployment is also the nonaccelerating inflation rate of unemployment, or NAIRU. According to the **natural rate hypothesis,** because inflation is eventually embedded in expectations, to avoid accelerating inflation over time, the unemployment rate must be high enough that the actual inflation rate equals the expected rate of inflation. Attempts to keep the unemployment rate below the natural rate will lead to an ever-rising inflation rate.

The natural rate hypothesis limits the role of activist macroeconomic policy compared to earlier theories. Because the government can't keep unemployment below the natural rate, its task is not to keep unemployment low but to keep it *stable*—to prevent large fluctuations in unemployment in either direction.

The Friedman-Phelps hypothesis made a strong prediction: that the apparent trade-off between unemployment and inflation would not survive an extended period of rising prices. Once inflation was embedded in the public's expectations, inflation would continue even in the face of high unemployment. Sure enough, that's exactly what happened in the 1970s. This accurate prediction was one of the triumphs of

According to the **natural rate hypothesis,** to avoid accelerating inflation over time, the unemployment rate must be high enough that the actual inflation rate equals the expected inflation rate.

macroeconomic analysis, and it convinced the great majority of economists that the natural rate hypothesis was correct. In contrast to traditional monetarism, which declined in influence as more evidence accumulated, the natural rate hypothesis has become almost universally accepted among macroeconomists, with a few qualifications. (Some macroeconomists believe that at very low or negative rates of inflation the hypothesis doesn't work.)

The Political Business Cycle

One final challenge to Keynesian economics focused not on the validity of the economic analysis but on its political consequences. A number of economists and political scientists pointed out that activist macroeconomic policy lends itself to political manipulation.

Statistical evidence suggests that election results tend to be determined by the state of the economy in the months just before the election. In the United States, if the economy is growing rapidly and the unemployment rate is falling in the six months or so before Election Day, the incumbent party tends to be re-elected even if the economy performed poorly in the preceding three years.

This creates an obvious temptation to abuse activist macroeconomic policy: pump up the economy in an election year, and pay the price in higher inflation and/or higher unemployment later. The result can be unnecessary instability in the economy, a **political business cycle** caused by the use of macroeconomic policy to serve political ends.

An often-cited example is the combination of expansionary fiscal and monetary policy that led to rapid growth in the U.S. economy just before the 1972 election and a sharp acceleration in inflation after the election. Kenneth Rogoff, a respected macroeconomist who served as chief economist at the International Monetary Fund, proclaimed Richard Nixon, the president at the time, "the all-time hero of political business cycles."

One way to avoid a political business cycle is to place monetary policy in the hands of an independent central bank, insulated from political pressure. The political business cycle is also a reason to limit the use of discretionary fiscal policy to extreme circumstances.

Election results tend to be determined by the state of the economy in the months just before the election.

Rational Expectations, Real Business Cycles, and New Classical Macroeconomics

As we have seen, one key difference between classical economics and Keynesian economics is that classical economists believed that the short-run aggregate supply curve is vertical, but Keynes emphasized the idea that the aggregate supply curve slopes upward in the short run. As a result, Keynes argued that demand shocks—shifts in the aggregate demand curve—can cause fluctuations in aggregate output.

The challenges to Keynesian economics that arose in the 1950s and 1960s—the renewed emphasis on monetary policy and the natural rate hypothesis—didn't question the view that an increase in aggregate demand leads to a rise in aggregate output in the short run nor that a decrease in aggregate demand leads to a fall in aggregate output in the short run. In the 1970s and 1980s, however, some economists developed an approach to the business cycle known as **new classical macroeconomics,** which returned to the classical view that shifts in the aggregate demand curve affect only the aggregate price level, not aggregate output. The new approach evolved in two steps. First, some economists challenged traditional arguments about the slope of the short-run aggregate supply curve based on the concept of *rational expectations*. Second, some economists suggested that changes in productivity caused economic fluctuations, a view known as *real business cycle theory*.

A **political business cycle** results when politicians use macroeconomic policy to serve political ends.

New classical macroeconomics is an approach to the business cycle that returns to the classical view that shifts in the aggregate demand curve affect only the aggregate price level, not aggregate output.

Rational Expectations

In the 1970s, a concept known as *rational expectations* had a powerful impact on macroeconomics. **Rational expectations,** a theory originally introduced by John Muth in 1961, is the view that individuals and firms make decisions optimally, using all available information.

For example, workers and employers bargaining over long-term wage contracts need to estimate the inflation rate they expect over the life of that contract. Rational expectations says that in making estimates of future inflation, they won't just look at past rates of inflation; they will also take into account available information about monetary and fiscal policy. Suppose that prices didn't rise last year, but that the monetary and fiscal policies announced by policy makers made it clear to economic analysts that there would be substantial inflation over the next few years. According to rational expectations, long-term wage contracts will be adjusted today to reflect this future inflation, even though prices didn't rise in the past.

Rational expectations can make a major difference to the effects of government policy. According to the original version of the natural rate hypothesis, a government attempt to trade off higher inflation for lower unemployment would work in the short run but would eventually fail because higher inflation would get built into expectations. According to rational expectations, we should remove the word *eventually*: if it's clear that the government intends to trade off higher inflation for lower unemployment, the public will understand this, and expected inflation will immediately rise.

In the 1970s, Robert Lucas of the University of Chicago, in a series of highly influential papers, used this logic to argue that monetary policy can change the level of unemployment only if it comes as a surprise to the public. If his analysis was right, monetary policy isn't useful in stabilizing the economy after all. In 1995 Lucas won the Nobel Prize in economics for this work, which remains widely admired. However, many—perhaps most—macroeconomists, especially those advising policy makers, now believe that his conclusions were overstated. The Federal Reserve certainly thinks that it can play a useful role in economic stabilization.

Why, in the view of many macroeconomists, doesn't the rational expectations hypothesis accurately describe how the economy behaves? **New Keynesian economics,** a set of ideas that became influential in the 1990s, provides an explanation. It argues that market imperfections interact to make many prices in the economy temporarily sticky. For example, one new Keynesian argument points out that monopolists don't have to be too careful about setting prices exactly "right": if they set a price a bit too high, they'll lose some sales but make more profit on each sale; if they set the price too low, they'll reduce the profit per sale but sell more. As a result, even small costs to changing prices can lead to substantial price stickiness and make the economy as a whole behave in a Keynesian fashion.

Over time, new Keynesian ideas combined with actual experience have reduced the practical influence of the rational expectations concept. Nonetheless, the idea of rational expectations served as a useful caution for macroeconomists who had become excessively optimistic about their ability to manage the economy.

Real Business Cycles

Earlier we introduced the concept of *total factor productivity,* the amount of output that can be generated with a given level of factor inputs. Total factor productivity grows over time, but that growth isn't smooth. In the 1980s, a number of economists argued that slowdowns in productivity growth, which they attributed to pauses in technological progress, are the main cause of recessions. **Real business cycle theory** claims that fluctuations in the rate of growth of total factor productivity cause the business cycle. Believing that the aggregate supply curve is vertical, real business cycle theorists attribute the source of business cycles to shifts of the aggregate supply curve: a recession occurs when a slowdown in productivity growth shifts the aggregate supply curve leftward, and a recovery occurs when a pickup in productivity growth shifts the aggregate supply curve rightward. In the early days of real business cycle theory, the theory's proponents denied that changes in aggregate demand had any effect on aggregate output.

This theory was strongly influential, as shown by the fact that two of the founders of real business cycle theory, Finn Kydland of Carnegie Mellon University and Edward Prescott of the Federal Reserve Bank of Minneapolis, won the 2004 Nobel Prize in economics. The current status of real business cycle theory, however, is somewhat similar to that of rational expectations. The theory is widely recognized as having made valuable contributions to our understanding of the economy, and it serves as a useful caution against too much emphasis on aggregate demand. But many of the real business cycle theorists themselves now acknowledge that their models need an upward-sloping aggregate supply curve to fit the economic data—and that this gives aggregate demand a potential role in determining aggregate output. And as we have seen, policy makers strongly believe that aggregate demand policy has an important role to play in fighting recessions.

Module 35 AP Review

Solutions appear at the back of the book.

Check Your Understanding

1. The figure below shows the behavior of M1 before, during, and after the 2001 recession. What would a classical economist have said about the Fed's policy?

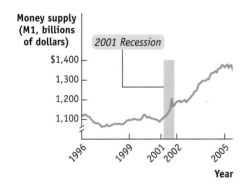

2. What would the figure above have looked like if the Fed had been following a monetarist policy since 1996?

3. Now look at Figure 35.3, which shows the path of the velocity of money. What problems do you think the United States would have had since 1996 if the Fed had followed a monetarist policy?

4. In addition to praising aggressive monetary policy, the 2004 Economic Report of the President says that "tax cuts can boost economic activity by raising after-tax income and enhancing incentives to work, save, and invest." Which part is a Keynesian statement and which part is not? Explain your answer.

5. In early 2001, as it became clear that the United States was experiencing a recession, the Fed stated that it would fight the recession with an aggressive monetary policy. By 2004, most observers concluded that this aggressive monetary expansion should be given credit for ending the recession.
   a. What would rational expectations theorists say about this conclusion?
   b. What would real business cycle theorists say?

Tackle the Test: Multiple-Choice Questions

1. Which of the following was an important point emphasized in Keynes's influential work?

    I. In the short run, shifts in aggregate demand affect aggregate output.

    II. Animal spirits are an important determinant of business cycles.

    III. In the long run we're all dead.

    a. I only
    b. II only
    c. III only
    d. I and II only
    e. I, II, and III

2. Which of the following is a central point of monetarism?
    a. Business cycles are associated with fluctuations in money demand.
    b. Activist monetary policy is the best way to address business cycles.
    c. Discretionary monetary policy is effective while discretionary fiscal policy is not.
    d. The Fed should follow a monetary policy rule.
    e. All of the above.

3. The natural rate hypothesis says that the unemployment rate should be
    a. below the NAIRU.

    b. high enough that the actual rate of inflation equals the expected rate.
    c. as close to zero as possible.
    d. 5%.
    e. left wherever the economy sets it.

4. The main difference between the classical model of the price level and Keynesian economics is that
    a. the classical model assumes a vertical short-run aggregate supply curve.
    b. Keynesian economics assumes a vertical short-run aggregate supply curve.
    c. the classical model assumes an upward sloping long-run aggregate supply curve.
    d. Keynesian economics assumes a vertical long-run aggregate supply curve.
    e. the classical model assumes aggregate demand can not change in the long run.

5. That fluctuations in total factor productivity growth cause the business cycle is the main tenet of which theory?
    a. Keynesian
    b. classical
    c. rational expectations
    d. real business cycle
    e. natural rate

Tackle the Test: Free-Response Questions

1. a. According to monetarism, business cycles are associated with fluctuations in what?
    b. Does monetarism advocate discretionary fiscal policy? Discretionary monetary policy?
    c. What monetary policy does monetarism suggest?
    d. What is the velocity equation? Define each of the terms in the velocity equation.
    e. Use the velocity equation to explain the major conclusion of monetarism.

2. For each of the following economic theories, identify its fundamental conclusion.
    a. the classical model of the price level
    b. Keynesian economics
    c. monetarism
    d. the natural rate hypothesis
    e. rational expectations
    f. real business cycle theory

Answer (10 points)

1 point: The money supply

1 point: No

1 point: No

1 point: A monetary policy rule

1 point: $M \times V = P \times Y$

1 point: M is the money supply.

1 point: V is the velocity of money.

1 point: P is the aggregate price level.

1 point: Y is real GDP.

1 point: Since V is stable, a steady growth of M will lead to a steady growth in GDP.

Module 36
The Modern Macroeconomic Consensus

What you will learn in this **Module:**

- The elements of the modern macroeconomic consensus
- The main remaining disputes

The Modern Consensus

As we've seen, there were intense debates about macroeconomics in the 1960s, 1970s, and 1980s. More recently, however, things have settled down. The age of macroeconomic controversy is by no means over, but there is now a broad consensus about several crucial macroeconomic issues.

To understand the modern consensus, where it came from, and what still remains in dispute, we'll look at how macroeconomists have changed their answers to five key questions about macroeconomic policy. The five questions, and the answers given by macroeconomists over the past 70 years, are summarized in Table 36.1 on the next page. (In the table, new classical economics is subsumed under classical economics, and new Keynesian economics is subsumed under the modern consensus.) Notice that classical macroeconomics said no to each question; basically, classical macroeconomists didn't think macroeconomic policy could accomplish very much. But let's go through the questions one by one.

Is Expansionary Monetary Policy Helpful in Fighting Recessions?

As we've seen, classical macroeconomists generally believed that expansionary monetary policy was ineffective or even harmful in fighting recessions. In the early years of Keynesian economics, macroeconomists weren't against monetary expansion during recessions, but they tended to believe that it was of doubtful effectiveness. Milton Friedman and his followers convinced economists that monetary policy was effective after all.

Nearly all macroeconomists now agree that monetary policy can be used to shift the aggregate demand curve and to reduce economic instability. The classical view that

table **36.1**

Five Key Questions About Macroeconomic Policy

	Classical macroeconomics	Keynesian macroeconomics	Monetarism	Modern consensus
Is expansionary monetary policy helpful in fighting recessions?	No	Not very	Yes	Yes, except in special circumstances
Is expansionary fiscal policy effective in fighting recessions?	No	Yes	No	Yes
Can monetary and/or fiscal policy reduce unemployment in the long run?	No	Yes	No	No
Should fiscal policy be used in a discretionary way?	No	Yes	No	No, except in special circumstances
Should monetary policy be used in a discretionary way?	No	Yes	No	Still in dispute

changes in the money supply affect only aggregate prices, not aggregate output, has few supporters today. The view once held by some Keynesian economists—that changes in the money supply have little effect—has equally few supporters. Now, it is generally agreed that monetary policy is ineffective only in the case of a liquidity trap.

Is Expansionary Fiscal Policy Effective in Fighting Recessions?

Classical macroeconomists were, if anything, even more opposed to fiscal expansion than to monetary expansion. Keynesian economists, on the other hand, gave fiscal policy a central role in fighting recessions. Monetarists argued that fiscal policy was ineffective as long as the money supply was held constant. But that strong view has become relatively rare.

Most macroeconomists now agree that fiscal policy, like monetary policy, can shift the aggregate demand curve. Most macroeconomists also agree that the government should not seek to balance the budget regardless of the state of the economy: they agree that the role of the budget as an automatic stabilizer helps keep the economy on an even keel.

Can Monetary and/or Fiscal Policy Reduce Unemployment in the Long Run?

Classical macroeconomists didn't believe the government could do anything about unemployment. Some Keynesian economists moved to the opposite extreme, arguing that expansionary policies could be used to achieve a permanently low unemployment rate, perhaps at the cost of some inflation. Monetarists believed that unemployment could not be kept below the natural rate.

Almost all macroeconomists now accept the natural rate hypothesis and agree on the limitations of monetary and fiscal policy. They believe that effective monetary and fiscal policy can limit the size of fluctuations of the actual unemployment rate around the natural rate but can't keep unemployment below the natural rate.

Should Fiscal Policy Be Used in a Discretionary Way?

As we've already seen, views about the effectiveness of fiscal policy have gone back and forth, from rejection by classical macroeconomists, to a positive view by Keynesian economists, to a negative view once again by monetarists. Today, most macroeconomists believe that tax cuts and spending increases are at least somewhat effective in increasing aggregate demand.

Many, but not all, macroeconomists, believe that *discretionary fiscal policy* is usually counterproductive: the lags in adjusting fiscal policy mean that, all too often, policies intended to fight a slump end up intensifying a boom.

As a result, the macroeconomic consensus gives monetary policy the lead role in economic stabilization. Discretionary fiscal policy plays the leading role only in special circumstances when monetary policy is ineffective, such as those facing Japan during the 1990s when interest rates were at or near the zero bound and the economy was in a liquidity trap.

Should Monetary Policy Be Used in a Discretionary Way?

Classical macroeconomists didn't think that monetary policy should be used to fight recessions; Keynesian economists didn't oppose discretionary monetary policy, but they were skeptical about its effectiveness. Monetarists argued that discretionary monetary policy was doing more harm than good. Where are we today? This remains an area of dispute. Today there is a broad consensus among macroeconomists on these points:

- Monetary policy should play the main role in stabilization policy.
- The central bank should be independent, insulated from political pressures, in order to avoid a political business cycle.
- Discretionary fiscal policy should be used sparingly, both because of policy lags and because of the risks of a political business cycle.

There are, however, debates over how the central bank should set its policy. Should the central bank be given a simple, clearly defined target for its policies, or

fyi

Supply-Side Economics

During the 1970s, a group of economic writers began propounding a view of economic policy that came to be known as "supply-side economics." The core of this view was the belief that reducing tax rates, and so increasing the incentives to work and invest, would have a powerful positive effect on the growth rate of potential output. The supply-siders urged the government to cut taxes without worrying about matching spending cuts: economic growth, they argued, would offset any negative effects from budget deficits. Some supply-siders even argued that a cut in tax *rates* would have such a miraculous effect on economic growth that tax *revenues*—the total amount taxpayers pay to the government—would actually rise. That is, some supply-siders argued that the United States was on the wrong side of the *Laffer*

curve, a hypothetical relationship between tax rates and total tax revenue that slopes upward (meaning higher taxes bring higher tax revenues) at low tax rates but turns downward (meaning higher taxes bring lower tax revenues) when tax rates are very high.

In the 1970s, supply-side economics was enthusiastically supported by the editors of the *Wall Street Journal* and other figures in the media, and it became popular with politicians. In 1980, Ronald Reagan made supply-side economics the basis of his presidential campaign.

Because supply-side economics emphasizes supply rather than demand, and because the supply-siders themselves are harshly critical of Keynesian economics, it might seem as if supply-side theory belongs in our discussion of

new classical macroeconomics. But unlike rational expectations and real business cycle theory, supply-side economics is generally dismissed by economic researchers.

The main reason for this dismissal is lack of evidence. Almost all economists agree that tax cuts increase incentives to work and invest, but attempts to estimate these incentive effects indicate that at current U.S. tax levels they aren't nearly strong enough to support the strong claims made by supply-siders. In particular, the supply-side doctrine implies that large tax cuts, such as those implemented by Ronald Reagan in the early 1980s, should sharply raise potential output. Yet estimates of potential output by the Congressional Budget Office and others show no sign of an acceleration in growth after the Reagan tax cuts.

should it be given discretion to manage the economy as it sees fit? Should the central bank consider the management of asset prices, such as stock prices and real estate prices, part of its responsibility? And what actions should the central bank undertake when interest rates have hit the zero bound and conventional monetary policy has reached its limits?

Central Bank Targets It may sound funny to say this, but it's often not clear exactly what the Federal Reserve, the central bank of the United States, is trying to achieve. Clearly it wants a stable economy with price stability, but there isn't any document setting out the Fed's official view about exactly how stable the economy should be or what the inflation rate should be.

This is not necessarily a bad thing. Experienced staff at the Fed generally believe that the absence of specific guidelines gives the central bank flexibility in coping with economic events and that history proves the Fed uses that flexibility well. In practice, chairs of the Fed tend to stay in office for a long time—William McChesney Martin was chair from 1951 to 1970, and Alan Greenspan, appointed in 1987, served as chair until 2006. These long-serving chairs acquire personal credibility that reassures the public that the central bank's power will be used well.

Central banks in some other countries have adopted formal guidelines. Some American economists—including some members of the Federal Reserve Board of Governors—believe that the United States should follow suit. The best-known example of a central bank using formal guidelines is the Bank of England. Until 1997, the Bank of England was simply an arm of the British Treasury Department, with no independence. When it became an independent organization like the Federal Reserve, it was given a mandate to achieve an inflation target of 2.5%. (In 2003, that target was changed to 2%.)

While inflation targeting is now advocated by many macroeconomists, others believe that such a rule can limit the ability of the central bank to respond to events, such as a stock market crash or a world financial crisis.

Unlike the Bank of England, the Fed doesn't have an explicit inflation target. However, it is widely believed to want an inflation rate of about 2%. Once the economy has moved past the current recession and financial crisis, there is likely to be renewed debate about whether the Fed should adopt an explicit inflation target.

The Bank of England has a mandate to keep inflation at around 2%.

Asset Prices During the 1990s, many economists warned that the U.S. stock market was losing touch with reality—share prices were much higher than could be justified given realistic forecasts of companies' future profits. Among these economists was Alan Greenspan, then chair of the Federal Reserve, who warned about "irrational exuberance" in a famous speech. In 2000, the stock market headed downward, taking the economy with it. Americans who had invested in the stock market suddenly felt poorer and so cut back on spending, helping push the economy into a recession.

Just a few years later the same thing happened in the housing market, as home prices climbed above levels that were justified by the incomes of home buyers and the cost of renting rather than buying. This time, however, Alan Greenspan dismissed concerns about a bubble as "most unlikely." But it turned out that there was indeed a bubble, which popped in 2006, leading to a financial crisis, and which pushed the economy into yet another recession.

These events highlighted a long-standing debate over monetary policy: should the central bank restrict its concerns to inflation and possibly unemployment, or should it also try to prevent extreme movements in asset prices, such as the average price of stocks or the average price of houses?

When the housing market fell in 2006, people began to question whether the central bank should concern itself with extreme movements in asset prices such as homes.

One view is that the central bank shouldn't try to second-guess the value investors place on assets like stocks or houses, even if it suspects that those prices are getting out of line. That is, the central bank shouldn't raise interest rates to curb stock prices or housing prices if overall consumer price inflation remains low. If an overvalued stock market eventually falls and depresses aggregate demand, the central bank can deal with that by cutting interest rates.

The alternative view warns that after a bubble bursts—after overvalued asset prices fall to earth—it may be difficult for monetary and fiscal policy to offset the effects on aggregate demand. After having seen the Japanese economy struggle for years with deflation in the aftermath of the collapse of its bubble economy, proponents of this view argue that the central bank should act to rein in irrational exuberance when it is happening, even if consumer price inflation isn't a problem.

The 2001 recession and the recession that started in 2007 gave ammunition to both sides in this debate, which shows no sign of ending.

Unconventional Monetary Policies In 2008, responding to a growing financial crisis, the Federal Reserve began engaging in highly unconventional monetary policy. The Fed normally conducts monetary policy through open-market operations in which it buys and sells short-term U.S. government debt in order to influence interest rates. We have also seen that in 2008, faced with severe problems in the financial markets, the Fed vastly expanded its operations. It lent huge sums to a wide variety of financial institutions, and it began large-scale purchases of private assets, including commercial paper (short-term business debts) and assets backed by home mortgages.

These actions and similar actions by other central banks, such as the Bank of Japan, were controversial. Supporters of the moves argued that extraordinary action was necessary to deal with the financial crisis and to cope with the liquidity trap that the economy had fallen into. But skeptics questioned both the effectiveness of the moves and whether the Fed was taking on dangerous risks. However, with interest rates up against the zero bound, it's not clear that the Fed had any other alternative but to turn unconventional. Future attitudes toward unconventional monetary policy will probably depend on how the Fed's efforts play out.

The Clean Little Secret of Macroeconomics

It's important to keep the debates we have just described in perspective. Macroeconomics has always been a contentious field, much more so than microeconomics. There will always be debates about appropriate policies. But the striking thing about current debates is how modest the differences among macroeconomists really are. The clean little secret of modern macroeconomics is how much consensus economists have reached over the past 70 years.

fyi

After the Bubble

In the 1990s, many economists worried that stock prices were irrationally high, and these worries proved justified. Starting in 2000, the NASDAQ, an index made up largely of technology stocks, began declining, ultimately losing two-thirds of its peak value. And in 2001 the plunge in stock prices helped push the United States into recession.

The Fed responded with large, rapid interest rate cuts. But should it have tried to burst the stock bubble when it was happening?

Many economists expected the aftermath of the 1990s stock market bubble to settle, once and for all, the question of whether central banks should concern themselves about asset prices. But the test results came out ambiguous, failing to settle the issue.

If the Fed had been unable to engineer a recovery—if the U.S. economy had slid into a liquidity trap like that of Japan—critics of the Fed's previous inaction would have had a very strong case. But the recession was, in fact, short: the National Bureau of Economic Research says that the recession began in March 2001 and ended in November 2001.

Furthermore, if the Fed had been able to produce a quick, strong recovery, its inaction during the 1990s would have been strongly vindicated. Unfortunately, that didn't happen either. Although the economy began recovering in late 2001, the recovery was initially weak—so weak that employment continued to drop until the summer of 2003. Also, the fact that the Fed had to cut the federal funds rate to only 1%—uncomfortably close to 0%—suggested that the U.S. economy had come dangerously close to a liquidity trap.

In other words, the events of 2001–2003 probably intensified the debate over monetary policy and asset prices, rather than resolving it.

Check Your Understanding

1. What debates has the modern consensus resolved? What debates has it not resolved?

Tackle the Test: Multiple-Choice Questions

1. Which of the following is an example of an opinion on which economists have reached a broad consensus?

    I. The natural rate hypothesis holds true.

    II. Discretionary fiscal policy is usually counterproductive.

    III. Monetary policy is effective, especially in a liquidity trap.

    a. I only

    b. II only

    c. III only

    d. I and II only

    e. I, II, and III

2. In the first FYI box of this module (p. 357) you learned about supply-side economics. Which of the following is stressed by supply siders?

    a. Taxes should be increased.

    b. Lower taxes will lead to lower tax revenues.

    c. It is important to increase incentives to work, save, and invest.

    d. The economy operates on the upward-sloping section of the Laffer curve.

    e. Supply side views are widely supported by empirical evidence.

3. Which of the following is true regarding central bank targets?

    a. The Fed has an explicit inflation target.

    b. All central banks have explicit inflation targets.

    c. No central banks have explicit inflation targets.

    d. The Fed clearly does not have an implicit inflation target.

    e. Economists are split regarding the need for explicit inflation targets.

4. The Fed's main concerns are

    a. inflation and unemployment.

    b. inflation and asset prices.

    c. inflation, asset prices, and unemployment.

    d. asset prices and unemployment.

    e. inflation and the value of the dollar.

5. The "clean little secret of macroeconomics" is that

    a. microeconomics is even more contentious than macroeconomics.

    b. debate among macroeconomists has ended.

    c. economists have reached a significant consensus.

    d. macroeconomics has progressed much more than microeconomics in the past 70 years.

    e. economists have identified how to prevent future business cycles.

Tackle the Test: Free-Response Questions

1. What is the consensus view of macroeconomists on each of the following:

    a. monetary policy and aggregate demand

    b. when monetary policy is ineffective

    c. fiscal policy and aggregate demand

    d. a balanced budget mandate

    e. the effectiveness of discretionary fiscal policy

2. On the basis of the description of the Laffer curve in the FYI box on supply-side economics on page 357, draw a correctly labeled graph of the Laffer curve. Use an "x" to identify a point on the curve at which a reduction in tax rates would lead to increased tax revenue.

Answer (5 points)

1 point: Monetary policy can shift aggregate demand in the short run.

1 point: Monetary policy is ineffective when in a liquidity trap.

1 point: Fiscal policy can shift aggregate demand.

1 point: This is not a good idea. Fluctuations in the budget act as an automatic stabilizer for the economy.

1 point: It is usually counterproductive (for example, due to lags in implementation).

Section ⑥ Review

Summary

1. Some of the fluctuations in the budget balance are due to the effects of the business cycle. In order to separate the effects of the business cycle from the effects of discretionary fiscal policy, governments estimate the **cyclically adjusted budget balance,** an estimate of the budget balance if the economy were at potential output.

2. U.S. government budget accounting is calculated on the basis of **fiscal years.** Persistent budget deficits have long-run consequences because they lead to an increase in **public debt.** This can be a problem for two reasons. Public debt may crowd out investment spending, which reduces long-run economic growth. And in extreme cases, rising debt may lead to government default, resulting in economic and financial turmoil.

3. A widely used measure of fiscal health is the **debt–GDP ratio.** This number can remain stable or fall even in the face of moderate budget deficits if GDP rises over time. However, a stable debt–GDP ratio may give a misleading impression that all is well because modern governments often have large **implicit liabilities.** The largest implicit liabilities of the U.S. government come from Social Security, Medicare, and Medicaid, the costs of which are increasing due to the aging of the population and rising medical costs.

4. **Expansionary monetary policy** reduces the interest rate by increasing the money supply. This increases investment spending and consumer spending, which in turn increases aggregate demand and real GDP in the short run. **Contractionary monetary policy** raises the interest rate by reducing the money supply. This reduces investment spending and consumer spending, which in turn reduces aggregate demand and real GDP in the short run.

5. The Federal Reserve and other central banks try to stabilize their economies, limiting fluctuations of actual output to around potential output, while also keeping inflation low but positive. Under the **Taylor rule for monetary policy,** the target interest rate rises when there is inflation, or a positive output gap, or both; the target interest rate falls when inflation is low or negative, or when the output gap is negative, or both. Some central banks engage in **inflation targeting,** which is a forward-looking policy rule, whereas the Taylor rule is a backward-looking policy rule. In practice, the Fed appears to operate on a loosely defined version of the Taylor rule. Because monetary policy is subject to fewer implementation lags than fiscal policy, it is the preferred policy tool for stabilizing the economy.

6. In the long run, changes in the money supply affect the aggregate price level but not real GDP or the interest rate. Data show that the concept of **monetary neutrality** holds: changes in the money supply have no real effect on the economy in the long run.

7. In analyzing high inflation, economists use the **classical model of the price level,** which says that changes in the money supply lead to proportional changes in the aggregate price level even in the short run.

8. Governments sometimes print money in order to finance budget deficits. When they do, they impose an **inflation tax,** generating tax revenue equal to the inflation rate times the money supply, on those who hold money. Revenue from the real inflation tax, the inflation rate times the real money supply, is the real value of resources captured by the government. In order to avoid paying the inflation tax, people reduce their real money holdings and force the government to increase inflation to capture the same amount of real inflation tax revenue. In some cases, this leads to a vicious circle of a shrinking real money supply and a rising rate of inflation, leading to hyperinflation and a fiscal crisis.

9. A positive output gap is associated with lower-than-normal unemployment; a negative output gap is associated with higher-than-normal unemployment.

10. Countries that don't need to print money to cover government deficits can still stumble into moderate inflation, either because of political opportunism or because of wishful thinking.

11. At a given point in time, there is a downward-sloping relationship between unemployment and inflation known as the **short-run Phillips curve.** This curve is shifted by changes in the expected rate of inflation. The **long-run Phillips curve,** which shows the relationship between unemployment and inflation once expectations have had time to adjust, is vertical. It defines the **nonaccelerating inflation rate of unemployment,** or **NAIRU,** which is equal to the natural rate of unemployment.

12. Once inflation has become embedded in expectations, getting inflation back down can be difficult because **disinflation** can be very costly, requiring the sacrifice of large amounts of aggregate output and imposing high levels of unemployment. However, policy makers in the United States and other wealthy countries were willing to pay that price of bringing down the high inflation of the 1970s.

13. Deflation poses several problems. It can lead to **debt deflation,** in which a rising real burden of outstanding debt intensifies an economic downturn. Also, interest rates are more likely to run up against the **zero bound** in an economy experiencing deflation. When this happens, the economy enters a **liquidity trap,** rendering conventional monetary policy ineffective.

14. Classical macroeconomics asserted that monetary policy affected only the aggregate price level, not aggregate output, and that the short run was unimportant. By the 1930s, measurement of business cycles was a well-established subject, but there was no widely accepted theory of business cycles.

15. **Keynesian economics** attributed the business cycle to shifts of the aggregate demand curve, often the result of changes in business confidence. Keynesian economics also offered a rationale for **macroeconomic policy activism.**

16. In the decades that followed Keynes's work, economists came to agree that monetary policy as well as fiscal policy is effective under certain conditions. **Monetarism** is a doctrine that called for a **monetary policy rule** as opposed to **discretionary monetary policy.** The argument of monetarists—based on a belief that the **velocity of money** was stable—that GDP would grow steadily if the money supply grew steadily, was influential for a time but was eventually rejected by many macroeconomists.

17. The **natural rate hypothesis** became almost universally accepted, limiting the role of macroeconomic policy to stabilizing the economy rather than seeking a perma-nently low unemployment rate. Fears of a **political business cycle** led to a consensus that monetary policy should be insulated from politics.

18. **Rational expectations** suggests that even in the short run there might not be a tradeoff between inflation and unemployment because expected inflation would change immediately in the face of expected changes in policy. **Real business cycle theory** claims that changes in the rate of growth of total factor productivity are the main cause of business cycles. Both of these versions of **new classical macroeconomics** received wide attention and respect, but policy makers and many economists haven't accepted the conclusion that monetary and fiscal policy are ineffective in changing aggregate output.

19. **New Keynesian economics** argues that market imperfections can lead to price stickiness, so that changes in aggregate demand have effects on aggregate output after all.

20. The modern consensus is that monetary and fiscal policy are both effective in the short run but that neither can reduce the unemployment rate in the long run. Discretionary fiscal policy is considered generally unadvisable, except in special circumstances.

21. There are continuing debates about the appropriate role of monetary policy. Some economists advocate the explicit use of an inflation target, but others oppose it. There's also a debate about whether monetary policy should take steps to manage asset prices and what kind of unconventional monetary policy, if any, should be adopted to address a liquidity trap.

Key Terms

Problems

1. The government's budget surplus in Macroland has risen consistently over the past five years. Two government policy makers disagree as to why this has happened. One argues that a rising budget surplus indicates a growing economy; the other argues that it shows that the government is using contractionary fiscal policy. Can you determine which policy maker is correct? If not, why not?

2. You are an economic adviser to a candidate for national office. She asks you for a summary of the economic consequences of a balanced-budget rule for the federal government and for your recommendation on whether she should support such a rule. How do you respond?

3. In which of the following cases does the size of the government's debt and the size of the budget deficit indicate potential problems for the economy?

   a. The government's debt is relatively low, but the government is running a large budget deficit as it builds a high-speed rail system to connect the major cities of the nation.

   b. The government's debt is relatively high due to a recently ended deficit-financed war, but the government is now running only a small budget deficit.

   c. The government's debt is relatively low, but the government is running a budget deficit to finance the interest payments on the debt.

4. Unlike households, governments are often able to sustain large debts. For example, in September 2007, the U.S. government's total debt reached $9 trillion, approximately 64% of GDP. At the time, according to the U.S. Treasury, the average interest rate paid by the government on its debt was 5.0%. However, running budget deficits becomes hard when very large debts are outstanding.

   a. Calculate the dollar cost of the annual interest on the government's total debt assuming the interest rate and debt figures cited above.

   b. If the government operates on a balanced budget before interest payments are taken into account, at what rate must GDP grow in order for the debt–GDP ratio to remain unchanged?

   c. Calculate the total increase in national debt if the government incurs a deficit of $200 billion in fiscal year 2008. Assume that the only other change to the government's total debt arises from interest payments on the current debt of $9 trillion.

   d. At what rate must GDP grow in order for the debt–GDP ratio to remain unchanged when the deficit in fiscal year 2008 is $200 billion?

   e. Why is the debt–GDP ratio the preferred measure of a country's debt rather than the dollar value of the debt? Why is it important for a government to keep this number under control?

5. In the economy of Eastlandia, the money market is initially in equilibrium when the economy begins to slide into a recession.

   a. Using the accompanying diagram, explain what will happen to the interest rate if the central bank of Eastlandia keeps the money supply constant at $\overline{M}_1$.

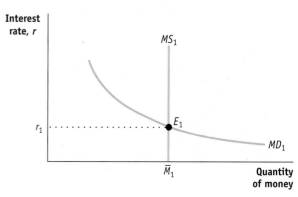

   b. If the central bank is instead committed to maintaining an interest rate target of r_1, then as the economy slides into recession, how should the central bank react? Using your diagram from part a, demonstrate the central bank's reaction.

6. Continuing from equilibrium E_1 in the previous problem, now suppose that in the economy of Eastlandia the central bank decides to decrease the money supply.

   a. Using the diagram in problem 5, explain what will happen to the interest rate in the short run.

   b. What will happen to the interest rate in the long run?

7. An economy is in long-run macroeconomic equilibrium with an unemployment rate of 5% when the government passes a law requiring the central bank to use monetary policy to lower the unemployment rate to 3% and keep it there. How could the central bank achieve this goal in the short run? What would happen in the long run? Illustrate with a diagram.

8. In the following examples, would the classical model of the price level be relevant?

   a. There is a great deal of unemployment in the economy and no history of inflation.

   b. The economy has just experienced five years of hyperinflation.

   c. Although the economy experienced inflation in the 10% to 20% range three years ago, prices have recently been stable and the unemployment rate has approximated the natural rate of unemployment.

9. Answer the following questions about the (real) inflation tax, assuming that the price level starts at 1.

   a. Maria Moneybags keeps $1,000 in her sock drawer for a year. Over the year, the inflation rate is 10%. What is the real inflation tax paid by Maria for this year?

b. Maria continues to keep the $1,000 in her drawer for a second year. What is the real value of this $1,000 at the beginning of the second year? Over the year, the inflation rate is again 10%. What is the real inflation tax paid by Maria for the second year?

c. For a third year, Maria keeps the $1,000 in the drawer. What is the real value of this $1,000 at the beginning of the third year? Over the year, the inflation rate is again 10%. What is the real inflation tax paid by Maria for the third year?

d. After three years, what is the cumulative real inflation tax paid?

e. Redo parts a through d with an inflation rate of 25%. Why is hyperinflation such a problem?

10. Concerned about the crowding-out effects of government borrowing on private investment spending, a candidate for president argues that the United States should just print money to cover the government's budget deficit. What are the advantages and disadvantages of such a plan?

11. The accompanying table provides data from the United States on the average annual rates of unemployment and inflation. Use the numbers to construct a scatter plot similar to Figure 34.1. Discuss why, in the short run, the unemployment rate rises when inflation falls.

Year	Unemployment rate	Inflation rate
2000	4.0%	3.4%
2001	4.7	2.8
2002	5.8	1.6
2003	6.0	2.3
2004	5.5	2.7
2005	5.1	3.4
2006	4.6	3.2
2007	4.6	2.9

Source: IMF.

12. In the modern world, central banks are free to increase or reduce the money supply as they see fit. However, some people harken back to the "good old days" of the gold standard. Under the gold standard, the money supply could expand only when the amount of available gold increased.

a. Under the gold standard, if the velocity of money was stable when the economy was expanding, what would have had to happen to keep prices stable?

b. Why would modern macroeconomists consider the gold standard a bad idea?

13. Monetarists believed for a period of time that the velocity of money was stable within a country. However, with financial innovation, the velocity began shifting around erratically after 1980. As would be expected, the velocity of money is different across countries depending upon the sophistication of their financial systems—velocity of money tends to be higher in countries with developed financial systems. The accompanying table provides money supply and GDP information in 2005 for six countries.

Country	National currency	M1 (billions in national currency)	Nominal GDP (billions in national currency)
Egypt	Egyptian pounds	101	539
South Korea	Korean won	77,274	806,622
Thailand	Thai baht	863	7,103
United States	U.S. dollars	1,369	12,456
Kenya	Kenyan pounds	231	1,415
India	Indian rupees	7,213	35,314

Source: Datastream.

a. Calculate the velocity of money for each of the countries. The accompanying table shows GDP per capita for each of these countries in 2005 in U.S. dollars.

Country	Nominal GDP per capita (U.S. dollars)
Egypt	$1,270
South Korea	16,444
Thailand	2,707
United States	41,886
Kenya	572
India	710

Source: IMF.

b. Rank the countries in descending order of per capita income and velocity of money. Do wealthy countries or poor countries tend to "turn over" their money more times per year? Would you expect that wealthy countries have more sophisticated financial systems?

14. Module 35 explains that Kenneth Rogoff proclaimed Richard Nixon "the all-time hero of political business cycles." Using the table of data below from the *Economic Report of the President*, explain why Nixon may have earned that title. (*Note:*

Nixon entered office in January 1969 and was reelected in November 1972. He resigned in August 1974.)

Year	Government receipts (billions of dollars)	Government spending (billions of dollars)	Government budget balance (billions of dollars)	M1 growth	M2 growth	3-month Treasury bill rate
1969	$186.9	$183.6	$3.2	3.3%	3.7%	6.68%
1970	192.8	195.6	−2.8	5.1	6.6	6.46
1971	187.1	210.2	−23.0	6.5	13.4	4.35
1972	207.3	230.7	−23.4	9.2	13.0	4.07
1973	230.8	245.7	−14.9	5.5	6.6	7.04

15. The economy of Albernia is facing a recessionary gap, and the leader of that nation calls together five of its best economists representing the classical, Keynesian, monetarist, real business cycle, and modern consensus views of the macroeconomy. Explain what policies each economist would recommend and why.

16. Which of the following policy recommendations, if any, are consistent with the classical, Keynesian, monetarist, and/or modern consensus views of the macroeconomy?

    a. Since the long-run growth of GDP is 2%, the money supply should grow at 2%.

    b. Decrease government spending in order to decrease inflationary pressure.

    c. Increase the money supply in order to alleviate a recessionary gap.

    d. Always maintain a balanced budget.

    e. Decrease the budget deficit as a percent of GDP when facing a recessionary gap.

17. Using a set of graphs as in Figure 35.2, show how a monetarist can argue that a contractionary fiscal policy may not lead to the desired fall in real GDP given a fixed money supply. Explain.

Economic Growth and Productivity

China is growing—and so are the Chinese. According to official statistics, children in China are almost 2½ inches taller now than they were 30 years ago. The average Chinese citizen is still a lot shorter than the average American, but at the current rate of growth the difference may be largely gone in a couple of generations.

If that does happen, China will be following in Japan's footsteps. Older Americans tend to think of the Japanese as short, but today young Japanese men are more than 5 inches taller on average than they were in 1900, which makes them almost as tall as their American counterparts.

There's no mystery about why the Japanese grew taller—it's because they grew richer. In the early twentieth century, Japan was a relatively poor country in which many families couldn't afford to give their children adequate nutrition. As a result, their children grew up to be short adults. However, since World War II, Japan has become an economic powerhouse in which food is ample and young adults are much taller than before.

The same phenomenon is now happening in China. Although it continues to be a relatively poor country, China has made great economic strides over the past 30 years. Its recent history is probably the world's most dramatic example of economic growth—a sustained increase in the productive capacity of an economy. Yet despite its impressive performance, China is currently playing catch-up with economically advanced countries like the United States and Japan. It's still relatively poor because these other nations began their own processes of economic growth many decades ago—and in the case of the United States and European countries, more than a century ago.

Unlike a short-run increase in real GDP caused by an increase in aggregate demand or short-run aggregate supply, we'll see that economic growth pushes the production possibilities curve outward and shifts the long-run aggregate supply curve to the right. Because economic growth is a long-run concept, we often refer to it as *long-run economic growth* for clarity. Many economists have argued that long-run economic growth—why it happens and how to achieve it—is the single most important issue in macroeconomics. In this section, we present some facts about long-run growth, look at the factors that economists believe determine its pace, examine how government policies can help or hinder growth, and address questions about the environmental sustainability of growth.

AP Photo/EyePress

Module 37
Long-run
Economic Growth

Comparing Economies Across Time and Space

Before we analyze the sources of long-run economic growth, it's useful to have a sense of just how much the U.S. economy has grown over time and how large the gaps are between wealthy countries like the United States and countries that have yet to achieve a comparable standard of living. So let's take a look at the numbers.

Real GDP per Capita

The key statistic used to track economic growth is *real GDP per capita*—real GDP divided by the population size. We focus on GDP because, as we have learned, GDP measures the total value of an economy's production of final goods and services as well as the income earned in that economy in a given year. We use *real* GDP because we want to separate changes in the quantity of goods and services from the effects of a rising price level. We focus on real GDP *per capita* because we want to isolate the effect of changes in the population. For example, other things equal, an increase in the population lowers the standard of living for the average person—there are now more people to share a given amount of real GDP. An increase in real GDP that only matches an increase in population leaves the average standard of living unchanged.

Although we learned that growth in real GDP per capita should not be a policy goal in and of itself, it does serve as a very useful summary measure of a country's economic progress over time. Figure 37.1 shows real GDP per capita for the United States, India, and China, measured in 1990 dollars, from 1908 to 2008. (We'll talk about India and China in a moment.) The vertical axis is drawn on a logarithmic scale so that equal percent changes in real GDP per capita across countries are the same size in the graph.

To give a sense of how much the U.S. economy grew during the last century, Table 37.1 shows real GDP per capita at 20-year intervals, expressed two ways: as a percentage of the 1908 level and as a percentage of the 2008 level. In 1928, the U.S. economy already produced 144% as much per person as it did in 1908. In 2008, it produced 684% as much per

What you will learn in this Module:

- How we measure long-run economic growth
- How real GDP has changed over time
- How real GDP varies across countries
- The sources of long-run economic growth
- How productivity is driven by physical capital, human capital, and technological progress

figure 37.1

Economic Growth in the United States, India, and China over the Past Century

Real GDP per capita from 1908 to 2008, measured in 1990 dollars, is shown for the United States, India, and China. Equal percent changes in real GDP per capita are drawn the same size. India and China currently have a much higher growth rate than the United States. However, China has only just attained the standard of living achieved in the United States in 1908, while India is still poorer than the United States was in 1908.

Sources: Angus Maddison, *Statistics on World Population, GDP, and Per Capita GDP, 1–2008AD,* http://www.ggdc.net/maddison.

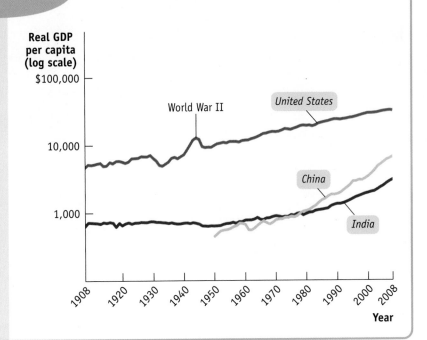

person as it did in 1908. Alternatively, in 1908, the U.S. economy produced only 15% as much per person as it did in 2008.

The income of the typical family normally grows more or less in proportion to per capita income. For example, a 1% increase in real GDP per capita corresponds, roughly, to a 1% increase in the income of the median or typical family—a family at the center of the income distribution. In 2008, the median American household had an income of about $50,000. Since Table 37.1 tells us that real GDP per capita in 1908 was only 15% of its 2008 level, a typical family in 1908 probably had purchasing power only 15% as large as the purchasing power of a typical family in 2008. That's around $8,000 in today's dollars, representing a standard of living that we would now consider severe poverty. Today's typical American family, if transported back to the United States of 1908, would feel quite a lot of deprivation.

Yet many people in the world have a standard of living equal to or lower than that of the United States a century ago. That's the message about China and India in Figure 37.1: despite dramatic economic growth in China over the last three decades and the less dramatic acceleration of economic growth in India, China has only just attained the standard of living that the United States enjoyed in 1908, while India is still poorer than the United States was in 1908. And much of the world today is poorer than China or India.

You can get a sense of how poor much of the world remains by looking at Figure 37.2 on the next page, a map of the world in which countries are classified according to their 2008 levels of GDP per capita, in U.S. dollars. As you can see, large parts of the world have very low incomes. Generally speaking, the countries of Europe and North America, as well as a few in the Pacific, have high incomes. The rest of the world, containing most of its population, is dominated by countries with GDP less than $5,000 per capita—and often much less. In fact, today more than 50% of the world's people live in countries with a lower standard of living than the United States had a century ago.

table 37.1

U.S. Real GDP per Capita

Year	Percentage of 1908 real GDP per capita	Percentage of 2008 real GDP per capita
1908	100%	15%
1928	144	21
1948	199	29
1968	326	48
1988	493	72
2008	684	100

Source: Angus Maddison, *Statistics on World Population, GDP, and Per Capita GDP, 1–2008AD,* http://www.ggdc.net/maddison.

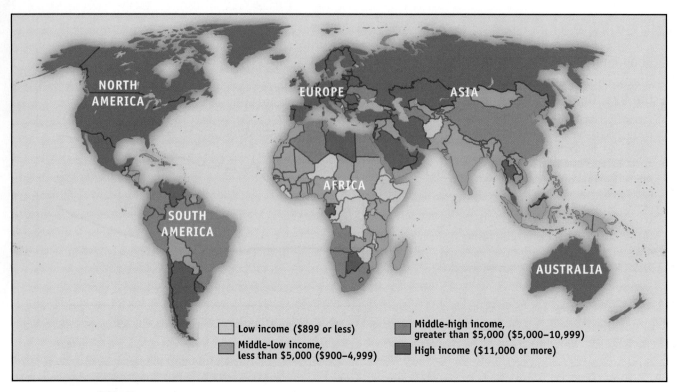

figure 37.2
Incomes Around the World, 2008

Although the countries of Europe and North America—along with a few in East Asia—have high incomes, much of the world is still very poor. Today, more than 50% of the world's population lives in countries with a lower standard of living than the United States had a century ago.

Source: International Monetary Fund.

fyi

India Takes Off

India achieved independence from Great Britain in 1947, becoming the world's most populous democracy—a status it has maintained to this day. For more than three decades after independence, however, this happy political story was partly overshadowed by economic disappointment. Despite ambitious economic development plans, India's performance was consistently sluggish. In 1980, India's real GDP per capita was only about 50% higher than it had been in 1947; the gap between Indian living standards and those in wealthy countries like the United States had been growing rather than shrinking.

Since then, however, India has done much better. As Figure 37.3 shows, real GDP per capita has grown at an average rate of 4.1% a year, tripling between 1980 and 2008. India now has a large and rapidly growing middle class. And yes, the well-fed children of that middle class are much taller than their parents.

What went right in India after 1980? Many economists point to policy reforms. For decades after independence, India had a tightly controlled, highly regulated economy. Today, things are very different: a series of reforms opened the economy to international trade and freed up domestic competition. Some economists, however, argue that this can't be the main story because the big policy reforms weren't adopted until 1991, yet growth accelerated around 1980.

Regardless of the explanation, India's economic rise has transformed it into a major new

India's high rate of economic growth since 1980 has raised living standards and led to the emergence of a rapidly growing middle class.

economic power—and allowed hundreds of millions of people to have a much better life, better than their grandparents could have dreamed.

Growth Rates

How did the United States manage to produce nearly seven times more per person in 2008 than in 1908? A little bit at a time. Long-run economic growth is normally a gradual process in which real GDP per capita grows at most a few percent per year. From 1908 to 2008, real GDP per capita in the United States increased an average of 1.9% each year.

To have a sense of the relationship between the annual growth rate of real GDP per capita and the long-run change in real GDP per capita, it's helpful to keep in mind the **Rule of 70,** a mathematical formula that tells us how long it takes real GDP per capita, or any other variable that grows gradually over time, to double. The approximate answer is:

$$\text{(37-1)} \quad \text{Number of years for variable to double} = \frac{70}{\text{Annual growth rate of variable}}$$

(Note that the Rule of 70 can be applied to only a positive growth rate.) So if real GDP per capita grows at 1% per year, it will take 70 years to double. If it grows at 2% per year, it will take only 35 years to double. Applying the Rule of 70 to the 1.9% average growth rate in the United States implies that it should have taken 37 years for real GDP per capita to double; it would have taken 111 years—three periods of 37 years each—for U.S. real GDP per capita to double three times. That is, the Rule of 70 implies that over the course of 111 years, U.S. real GDP per capita should have increased by a factor of $2 \times 2 \times 2 = 8$. And this does turn out to be a pretty good approximation of reality. Between 1890 and 2008—a period of 118 years—real GDP per capita rose just about eightfold.

Figure 37.3 shows the average annual rate of growth of real GDP per capita for selected countries from 1980 to 2008. Some countries were notable success stories: we've already mentioned China, which has made spectacular progress. India, although not matching China's performance, has also achieved impressive growth.

Some countries, though, have had very disappointing growth. Argentina was once considered a wealthy nation. In the early years of the twentieth century, it was in the same league as the United States and Canada. But since then it has

The **Rule of 70** tells us that the time it takes a variable that grows gradually over time to double is approximately 70 divided by that variable's annual growth rate.

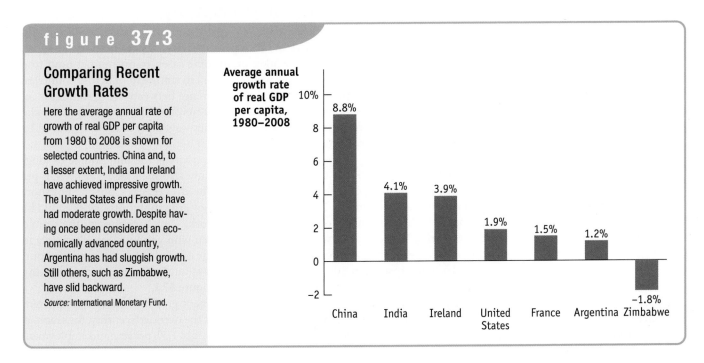

figure 37.3

Comparing Recent Growth Rates

Here the average annual rate of growth of real GDP per capita from 1980 to 2008 is shown for selected countries. China and, to a lesser extent, India and Ireland have achieved impressive growth. The United States and France have had moderate growth. Despite having once been considered an economically advanced country, Argentina has had sluggish growth. Still others, such as Zimbabwe, have slid backward.

Source: International Monetary Fund.

The Walmart Effect

After 20 years of being sluggish, U.S. productivity growth accelerated sharply in the late 1990s. What caused that acceleration? Was it the rise of the Internet?

Not according to analysts at McKinsey and Co., a famous business consulting firm. They found that a major source of productivity improvement after 1995 was a surge in output per worker in retailing—stores were selling much more merchandise per worker. And why did productivity surge in retailing in the United States? "The reason can be explained in just two syllables: Walmart," wrote McKinsey.

Walmart has been a pioneer in using modern technology to improve productivity. For example, it was one of the first companies to use computers to track inventory, to use bar-code scanners, to establish direct electronic links with suppliers, and so on. It continued to set the pace in the 1990s, but, increasingly, other companies have imitated Walmart's business practices.

There are two lessons from the "Walmart effect," as McKinsey calls it. One is that how you apply a technology makes all the difference: everyone in the retail business knew about computers, but Walmart figured out what to do

with them. The other is that a lot of economic growth comes from everyday improvements rather than glamorous new technologies.

lagged far behind more dynamic economies. And still others, like Zimbabwe, have slid backward.

What explains these differences in growth rates? To answer that question, we need to examine the sources of long-run growth.

The Sources of Long-run Growth

Long-run economic growth depends almost entirely on one ingredient: rising *productivity*. However, a number of factors affect the growth of productivity. Let's look first at why productivity is the key ingredient. After that, we'll examine what affects it.

The Crucial Importance of Productivity

Sustained growth in real GDP per capita occurs only when the amount of output produced by the average worker increases steadily. The term **labor productivity,** or **productivity** for short, is used to refer either to output per worker or, in some cases, to output per hour (the number of hours worked by an average worker differs to some extent across countries, although this isn't an important factor in the difference between living standards in, say, India and the United States). In this book we'll focus on output per worker. For the economy as a whole, productivity—output per worker—is simply real GDP divided by the number of people working.

You might wonder why we say that higher productivity is the only source of long-run growth in real GDP per capita. Can't an economy also increase its real GDP per capita by putting more of the population to work? The answer is, yes, but .... For short periods of time, an economy can experience a burst of growth in output per capita by putting a higher percentage of the population to work. That happened in the United States during World War II, when millions of women who previously worked only in the home entered the paid workforce. The percentage of adult civilians employed outside the home rose from 50% in 1941 to 58% in 1944, and you can see the resulting bump in real GDP per capita during those years in Figure 37.1.

Over the longer run, however, the rate of employment growth is never very different from the rate of population growth. Over the course of the twentieth century, for example, the population of the United States rose at an average rate of 1.3% per year and employment

Labor productivity, often referred to simply as **productivity,** is output per worker.

rose 1.5% per year. Real GDP per capita rose 1.9% per year; of that, 1.7%—that is, almost 90% of the total—was the result of rising productivity. In general, overall real GDP can grow because of population growth, but any large increase in real GDP *per capita* must be the result of increased output *per worker.* That is, it must be due to higher productivity.

We have just seen that increased productivity is the key to long-run economic growth. But what leads to higher productivity?

Explaining Growth in Productivity

There are three main reasons why the average U.S. worker today produces far more than his or her counterpart a century ago. First, the modern worker has far more *physical capital,* such as tools and office space, to work with. Second, the modern worker is much better educated and so possesses much more *human capital.* Finally, modern firms have the advantage of a century's accumulation of technical advancements reflecting a great deal of *technological progress.*

Let's look at each of these factors in turn.

Physical Capital Module 22 explained that capital—manufactured goods used to produce other goods and services—is often described as **physical capital** to distinguish it from human capital and other types of capital. Physical capital such as buildings and machinery makes workers more productive. For example, a worker operating a backhoe can dig a lot more feet of trench per day than one equipped with only a shovel.

The average U.S. private-sector worker today makes use of around $130,000 worth of physical capital—far more than a U.S. worker had 100 years ago and far more than the average worker in most other countries has today.

Human Capital It's not enough for a worker to have good equipment—he or she must also know what to do with it. **Human capital** refers to the improvement in labor created by the education and knowledge embodied in the workforce.

The human capital of the United States has increased dramatically over the past century. A century ago, although most Americans were able to read and write, very few had an extensive education. In 1910, only 13.5% of Americans over 25 had graduated from high school and only 3% had four-year college degrees. By 2008, the percentages were 86% and 27%, respectively. It would be impossible to run today's economy with a population as poorly educated as that of a century ago.

Analyses based on *growth accounting,* described later in this section, suggest that education—and its effect on productivity—is an even more important determinant of growth than increases in physical capital.

Technology Probably the most important driver of productivity growth is progress in **technology,** which is broadly defined as the technical means for the production of goods and services. We'll see shortly how economists measure the impact of technology on growth.

Workers today are able to produce more than those in the past, even with the same amount of physical and human capital, because technology has advanced over time. It's important to realize that economically important technological progress need not be flashy or rely on cutting-edge science. Historians have noted that past economic growth has been driven not only by major inventions, such as the railroad or the semiconductor chip, but also by thousands of modest innovations, such as the flat-bottomed paper bag, patented in 1870, which made packing groceries and many other goods much easier, and the Post-it note, introduced in 1981, which has had surprisingly large benefits for office productivity. Experts attribute much of the productivity surge that took place in the United States late in the twentieth century to new technology adopted by retail companies like Walmart rather than to high-technology companies.

Jon Feingersch/Corbis

If you've ever had doubts about attending college, consider this: factory workers with only high school degrees will make much less than college grads. The present discounted value of the difference in lifetime earnings is as much as $300,000.

Corbis Super RF/Alamy

Physical capital consists of human-made goods such as buildings and machines used to produce other goods and services.

Human capital is the improvement in labor created by the education and knowledge of members of the workforce.

Technology is the technical means for the production of goods and services.

Check Your Understanding

1. Why do economists focus on real GDP per capita as a measure of economic progress rather than on some other measure, such as nominal GDP per capita or real GDP?

2. Apply the Rule of 70 to the data in Figure 37.3 to determine how long it will take each of the countries listed there to double its real GDP per capita. Would India's real GDP per capita exceed that of the United States in the future if growth rates remained the same? Why or why not?

3. Although China and India currently have growth rates much higher than the U.S. growth rate, the typical Chinese or Indian household is far poorer than the typical American household. Explain why.

Tackle the Test: Multiple-Choice Questions

1. Which of the following is true regarding growth rates for countries around the world compared to the United States?
   I. Fifty percent of the world's people live in countries with a lower standard of living than the U.S. in 1908.
   II. The U.S. growth rate is six times the growth rate in the rest of the world.
   III. China has only just attained the same standard of living the U.S. had in 1908.
   a. I only
   b. II only
   c. III only
   d. I and III only
   e. I, II, and III

2. Which of the following is the key statistic used to track economic growth?
   a. GDP
   b. real GDP
   c. real GDP per capita
   d. median real GDP
   e. median real GDP per capita

3. According to the "Rule of 70," if a country's real GDP per capita grows at a rate of 2% per year, it will take how many years for real GDP per capita to double?
   a. 3.5
   b. 20
   c. 35
   d. 70
   e. It will never double at that rate.

4. If a country's real GDP per capita doubles in 10 years, what was its average annual rate of growth of real GDP per capita?
   a. 3.5%
   b. 7%
   c. 10%
   d. 70%
   e. 700%

5. Long-run economic growth depends almost entirely on
   a. technological change.
   b. rising productivity.
   c. increased labor force participation.
   d. rising real GDP per capita.
   e. population growth.

Tackle the Test: Free-Response Questions

1. Refer to Figure 37.3.

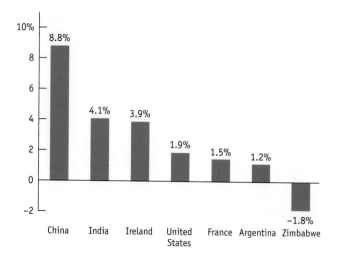

   a. If growth continues at the rates shown in Figure 37.3, which of the seven countries will have a lower real GDP per capita in 2009 than in 2008? Explain.
   b. If growth continues at the rates shown in Figure 37.3, which of the seven countries will have the highest real GDP per capita in 2009? Explain.
   c. If growth continues at the rates shown in Figure 37.3, real GDP per capita for which of the seven countries will at least double over the next 10 years? Explain.

Answer (6 points)

1 point: Zimbabwe

1 point: It has a negative average annual growth rate of real GDP per capita.

1 point: It cannot be determined.

1 point: The figure provides data for growth rates, but not for the level of real GDP per capita. Higher growth rates do not indicate higher levels.

1 point: China

1 point: A country has to have an average annual growth rate of 7% or higher for real GDP to at least double in 10 years. China has a growth rate of 8.8%.

2. Increases in real GDP per capita result mostly from changes in what variable? Define that variable. What other factor could also lead to increased real GDP per capita? Why is this other factor not as significant?

What you will learn in this **Module:**

- How changes in productivity are illustrated using an aggregate production function

- How growth has varied among several important regions of the world and why the convergence hypothesis applies to economically advanced countries

Module 38
Productivity and Growth

Accounting for Growth: The Aggregate Production Function

Productivity is higher, other things equal, when workers are equipped with more physical capital, more human capital, better technology, or any combination of the three. But can we put numbers to these effects? To do this, economists make use of estimates of the **aggregate production function,** which shows how productivity depends on the quantities of physical capital per worker and human capital per worker as well as the state of technology. In general, all three factors tend to rise over time, as workers are equipped with more machinery, receive more education, and benefit from technological advances. What the aggregate production function does is allow economists to disentangle the effects of these three factors on overall productivity.

A recent example of an aggregate production function applied to real data comes from a comparative study of Chinese and Indian economic growth conducted by the economists Barry Bosworth and Susan Collins of the Brookings Institution. They used the following aggregate production function:

$$\text{GDP per worker} = T \times (\text{physical capital per worker})^{0.4} \times (\text{human capital per worker})^{0.6}$$

> The **aggregate production function** is a hypothetical function that shows how productivity (output per worker) depends on the quantities of physical capital per worker and human capital per worker as well as the state of technology.
>
> An aggregate production function exhibits **diminishing returns to physical capital** when, holding the amount of human capital per worker and the state of technology fixed, each successive increase in the amount of physical capital per worker leads to a smaller increase in productivity.

where T represented an estimate of the level of technology and they assumed that each year of education raised workers' human capital by 7%. Using this function, they tried to explain why China grew faster than India between 1978 and 2004. About half the difference, they found, was due to China's higher levels of investment spending, which raised its level of physical capital per worker faster than India's. The other half was due to faster Chinese technological progress.

In analyzing historical economic growth, economists have discovered a crucial fact about the estimated aggregate production function: it exhibits **diminishing returns to physical capital.** That is, when the amount of human capital per worker and the state of technology are held fixed, each successive increase in the amount of physical capital per worker leads to a smaller increase in productivity. Table 38.1 gives a hypothetical example of how the level of physical capital per worker might affect the level of

table 38.1

A Hypothetical Example: How Physical Capital per Worker Affects Productivity, Holding Human Capital and Technology Fixed

Physical capital investment per worker	Real GDP per worker
$0	$0
15,000	30,000
30,000	45,000
45,000	55,000

real GDP per worker, holding human capital per worker and the state of technology fixed. In this example, we measure the quantity of physical capital in terms of the dollars worth of investment.

As you can see from the table, there is a big payoff from the first $15,000 invested in physical capital: real GDP per worker rises by $30,000. The second $15,000 worth of physical capital also raises productivity, but not by as much: real GDP per worker goes up by only $15,000. The third $15,000 worth of physical capital raises real GDP per worker by only $10,000.

To see why the relationship between physical capital per worker and productivity exhibits diminishing returns, think about how having farm equipment affects the productivity of farm workers. A little bit of equipment makes a big difference: a worker equipped with a tractor can do much more than a worker without one. And a worker using more expensive equipment will, other things equal, be more productive: a worker with a $30,000 tractor will normally be able to cultivate more farmland in a given amount of time than a worker with a $15,000 tractor because the more expensive machine will be more powerful, perform more tasks, or both.

But will a worker with a $30,000 tractor, holding human capital and technology constant, be twice as productive as a worker with a $15,000 tractor? Probably not: there's a huge difference between not having a tractor at all and having even an inexpensive tractor; there's much less difference between having an inexpensive tractor and having a better tractor. And we can be sure that a worker with a $150,000 tractor won't be 10 times as productive: a tractor can be improved only so much. Because the same is true of other kinds of equipment, the aggregate production function shows diminishing returns to physical capital.

Figure 38.1 on the next page is a graphical representation of the aggregate production function with diminishing returns to physical capital. As the *productivity curve* illustrates, more physical capital per worker leads to more output per worker. But each $30,000 increment in physical capital per worker adds less to productivity. By comparing points *A*, *B*, and *C*, you can also see that as physical capital per worker rises, output per worker also rises—but at a diminishing rate. Going from point *A* to point *B*, representing a $30,000 increase in physical capital per worker, leads to an increase of $20,000 in real GDP per worker. Going from point *B* to point *C*, a second $30,000 increase in physical capital per worker, leads to an increase of only $10,000 in real GDP per worker.

It's important to realize that diminishing returns to physical capital is an "other things equal" phenomenon: additional amounts of physical capital are less productive *when the amount of human capital per worker and the technology are held fixed*. Diminishing returns may disappear if we increase the amount of human capital per worker, or improve the technology, or both when the amount of physical capital per worker is increased. For example, a worker with a $30,000 tractor who has also been trained in the most advanced cultivation techniques may in fact be more than twice

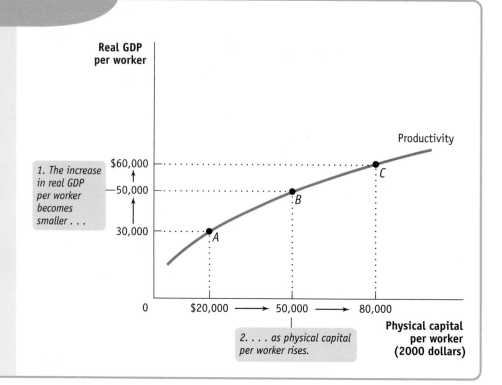

figure **38.1**

Physical Capital and Productivity

Other things equal, a greater quantity of physical capital per worker leads to higher real GDP per worker but is subject to diminishing returns: each successive addition to physical capital per worker produces a smaller increase in productivity. Starting at point *A*, with $20,000 in physical capital per worker, a $30,000 increase in physical capital per worker leads to an increase of $20,000 in real GDP per worker. At point *B*, with $50,000 in physical capital per worker, a $30,000 increase in physical capital per worker leads to an increase of only $10,000 in real GDP per worker.

Economists use **growth accounting** to estimate the contribution of each major factor in the aggregate production function to economic growth.

as productive as a worker with only a $15,000 tractor and no additional human capital. But diminishing returns to any one input—regardless of whether it is physical capital, human capital, or labor—is a pervasive characteristic of production. Typical estimates suggest that, in practice, a 1% increase in the quantity of physical capital per worker increases output per worker by only one-third of 1%, or 0.33%.

In practice, all the factors contributing to higher productivity rise during the course of economic growth: both physical capital and human capital per worker increase, and technology advances as well. To disentangle the effects of these factors, economists use **growth accounting** to estimate the contribution of each major factor in the aggregate production function to economic growth. For example, suppose the following are true:

- The amount of physical capital per worker grows 3% a year.

- According to estimates of the aggregate production function, each 1% rise in physical capital per worker, holding human capital and technology constant, raises output per worker by one-third of 1%, or 0.33%.

In that case, we would estimate that growing physical capital per worker is responsible for 1 percentage point (3% × 0.33) of productivity growth per year. A similar but more complex procedure is used to estimate the effects of growing human capital. The procedure is more complex because there aren't simple dollar measures of the quantity of human capital.

Growth accounting allows us to calculate the effects of greater physical and human capital on economic growth. But how can we estimate the effects of technological progress? We can do so by estimating what is left over after the effects of physical and human capital have been taken into account. For example, let's imagine that there was no increase in human capital per worker so that we can focus on changes in physical capital and in technology. In Figure 38.2, the lower curve shows the same hypothetical relationship between physical capital per worker and output per worker shown in Figure 38.1. Let's assume that this was the relationship given the technology available in 1940. The upper curve also shows a relationship between physical capital per worker

figure 38.2

Technological Progress and Productivity Growth

Technological progress shifts the productivity curve upward. Here we hold human capital per worker fixed. We assume that the lower curve (the same curve as in Figure 38.1) reflects technology in 1940 and the upper curve reflects technology in 2010. Holding technology and human capital fixed, quadrupling physical capital per worker from $20,000 to $80,000 leads to a doubling of real GDP per worker, from $30,000 to $60,000. This is shown by the movement from point *A* to point *C*, reflecting an approximately 1% per year rise in real GDP per worker. In reality, technological progress shifted the productivity curve upward and the actual rise in real GDP per worker is shown by the movement from point *A* to point *D*. Real GDP per worker grew 2% per year, leading to a quadrupling during the period. The extra 1% in growth of real GDP per worker is due to higher total factor productivity.

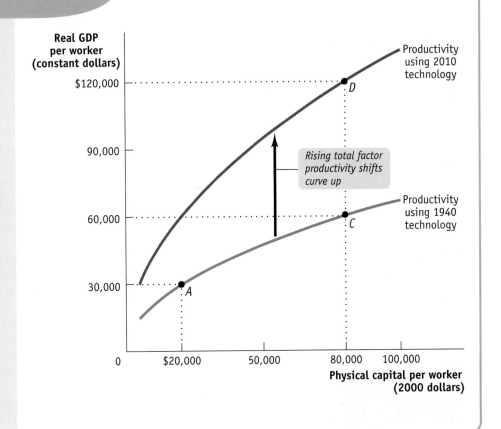

and productivity, but this time given the technology available in 2010. (We've chosen a 70-year stretch to allow us to use the Rule of 70.) The 2010 curve is shifted up compared to the 1940 curve because technologies developed over the previous 70 years make it possible to produce more output for a given amount of physical capital per worker than was possible with the technology available in 1940. (Note that the two curves are measured in constant dollars.)

Let's assume that between 1940 and 2010 the amount of physical capital per worker rose from $20,000 to $80,000. If this increase in physical capital per worker had taken place without any technological progress, the economy would have moved from *A* to *C*: output per worker would have risen, but only from $30,000 to $60,000, or 1% per year (using the Rule of 70 tells us that a 1% growth rate over 70 years doubles output). In fact, however, the economy moved from *A* to *D*: output rose from $30,000 to $120,000, or 2% per year. There was an increase in both physical capital per worker and technological progress, which shifted the aggregate production function.

In this case, 50% of the annual 2% increase in productivity—that is, 1% in annual productivity growth—is due to higher **total factor productivity,** the amount of output that can be produced with a given amount of factor inputs. So when total factor productivity increases, the economy can produce more output with the same quantity of physical capital, human capital, and labor.

Most estimates find that increases in total factor productivity are central to a country's economic growth. We believe that observed increases in total factor productivity in fact measure the economic effects of technological progress. All of this implies that technological change is crucial to

Total factor productivity is the amount of output that can be achieved with a given amount of factor inputs.

economic growth. The Bureau of Labor Statistics estimates the growth rate of both labor productivity and total factor productivity for nonfarm business in the United States. According to the Bureau's estimates, over the period from 1948 to 2008 American labor productivity rose 2.6% per year. Only 46% of that rise is explained by increases in physical and human capital per worker; the rest is explained by rising total factor productivity—that is, by technological progress.

What About Natural Resources?

In our discussion so far, we haven't mentioned natural resources, which certainly have an effect on productivity. Other things equal, countries that are abundant in valuable natural resources, such as highly fertile land or rich mineral deposits, have higher real GDP per capita than less fortunate countries. The most obvious modern example is the Middle East, where enormous oil deposits have made a few sparsely populated countries very rich. For instance, Kuwait has about the same level of real GDP per capita as South Korea, but Kuwait's wealth is based on oil, not manufacturing, the source of South Korea's high output per worker.

But other things are often not equal. In the modern world, natural resources are a much less important determinant of productivity than human or physical capital for the great majority of countries. For example, some nations with very high real GDP per capita, such as Japan, have very few natural resources. Some resource-rich nations, such as Nigeria (which has sizable oil deposits), are very poor.

Mark Shenley/Alamy

The offerings at markets such as this one in Lagos, Nigeria, are shaped by the available natural resources, human and physical capital, and technology.

Historically, natural resources played a much more prominent role in determining productivity. In the nineteenth century, the countries with the highest real GDP per capita were those abundant in rich farmland and mineral deposits: the United States, Canada, Argentina, and Australia. As a consequence, natural resources figured prominently in the development of economic thought. In a famous book published in 1798, *An Essay on the Principle of Population*, the English economist Thomas Malthus made the fixed quantity of land in the world the basis of a pessimistic prediction about future productivity. As population grew, he pointed out, the amount of land per worker would decline. And this, other things equal, would cause productivity to fall. His view, in fact, was that improvements in technology or increases in physical capital would lead only to temporary improvements in productivity because they would always be offset by the pressure of rising population and more workers on the supply of land. In the long run, he concluded, the great majority of people were condemned to living on the edge of starvation. Only then would death rates be high enough and birth rates low enough to prevent rapid population growth from outstripping productivity growth.

It hasn't turned out that way, although many historians believe that Malthus's prediction of falling or stagnant productivity was valid for much of human history. Population pressure probably did prevent large productivity increases until the eighteenth century. But in the time since Malthus wrote his book, any negative effects on productivity from population growth have been far outweighed by other, positive factors—advances in technology, increases in human and physical capital, and the opening up of enormous amounts of cultivatable land in the New World.

It remains true, however, that we live on a finite planet, with limited supplies of resources such as oil and limited ability to absorb environmental damage. We address the concerns these limitations pose for economic growth later in this section.

The Information Technology Paradox

From the early 1970s through the mid-1990s, the United States went through a slump in total factor productivity growth. The figure shows Bureau of Labor Statistics estimates of annual total factor productivity growth since 1949. As you can see, there was a large fall in the productivity growth rate beginning in the early 1970s. Because higher total factor productivity plays such a key role in long-run growth, the economy's overall growth was also disappointing, leading to a widespread sense that economic progress had ground to a halt.

Many economists were puzzled by the slowdown in total factor productivity growth after 1973, since in other ways the era seemed to be one of rapid technological progress. Modern information technology really began with the development of the first microprocessor—a computer on a chip—in 1971. In the 25 years that followed, a series of inventions that seemed revolutionary became standard equipment in the business world: fax machines, desktop computers, cell phones, and e-mail. Yet the rate of growth of productivity remained stagnant. In a famous remark, MIT economics professor and Nobel laureate Robert Solow, a pioneer in the analysis of economic growth, declared that the infor-

mation technology revolution could be seen everywhere except in the economic statistics.

Why didn't information technology show large rewards? Paul David, a Stanford University economic historian, offered a theory and a prediction. He pointed out that 100 years earlier another miracle technology—electric power—had spread through the economy, again with surprisingly little impact on productivity growth at first. The reason, he suggested, was that a new technology doesn't yield its full potential if you use it in old ways.

For example, a traditional factory around 1900 was a multistory building, with the machinery tightly crowded together and designed to be powered by a steam engine in the basement. This design had problems: it was very difficult to move people and materials around. Yet owners who electrified their factories initially maintained the multistory, tightly packed layout. Only with the switch to spread-out, one-story factories that took advantage of the flexibility of

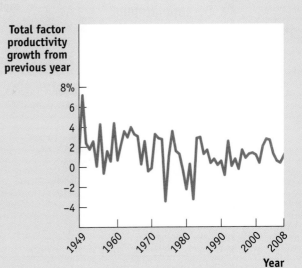

electric power—most famously Henry Ford's auto assembly line—did productivity take off.

David suggested that the same phenomenon was happening with information technology. Productivity, he predicted, would take off when people really changed their way of doing business to take advantage of the new technology—such as replacing letters and phone calls with e-mail. Sure enough, productivity growth accelerated dramatically in the second half of the 1990s. And, a lot of that may have been due to the discovery by companies like Walmart of how to effectively use information technology.

Success, Disappointment, and Failure

Rates of long-run economic growth differ markedly around the world. Let's look at three regions that have had quite different experiences with economic growth over the last few decades.

Figure 38.3 on the next page shows trends since 1960 in real GDP per capita in 2000 dollars for three countries: Argentina, Nigeria, and South Korea. (As in Figure 37.1, the vertical axis is drawn in logarithmic scale.) We have chosen these countries because each is a particularly striking example of what has happened in its region. South Korea's amazing rise is part of a larger success story in East Asia. Argentina's slow progress, interrupted by repeated setbacks, is more or less typical of the disappointment that has characterized Latin America. And Nigeria's unhappy story—real GDP per capita is barely higher now than it was in 1960—is, unfortunately, an experience shared by many African countries.

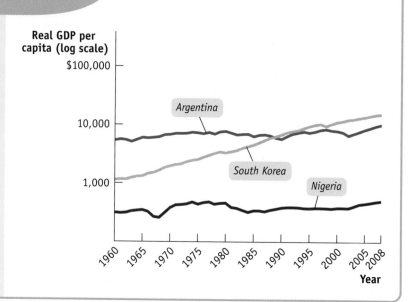

figure 38.3

Success and Disappointment

Real GDP per capita from 1960 to 2008, measured in 2000 dollars, is shown for Argentina, South Korea, and Nigeria, using a logarithmic scale. South Korea and some other East Asian countries have been highly successful at achieving economic growth. Argentina, like much of Latin America, has had several setbacks, slowing its growth. Nigeria's standard of living in 2008 was only barely higher than it had been in 1960, an experience shared by many African countries.

Source: World Bank.

East Asia's Miracle

In 1960, South Korea was a very poor country. In fact, in 1960 its real GDP per capita was lower than that of India today. But, as you can see from Figure 38.3, beginning in the early 1960s, South Korea began an extremely rapid economic ascent: real GDP per capita grew about 7% per year for more than 30 years. Today South Korea, though still somewhat poorer than Europe or the United States, looks very much like an economically advanced country.

South Korea's economic growth is unprecedented in history: it took the country only 35 years to achieve growth that required centuries elsewhere. Yet South Korea is only part of a broader phenomenon, often referred to as the East Asian economic miracle. High growth rates first appeared in South Korea, Taiwan, Hong Kong, and Singapore but then spread across the region, most notably to China. Since 1975, the whole region has increased real GDP per capita by 6% per year, three times America's historical rate of growth.

How have the Asian countries achieved such high growth rates? The answer is that all of the sources of productivity growth have been firing on all cylinders. Very high savings rates, the percentage of GDP that is saved nationally in any given year, have allowed the countries to significantly increase the amount of physical capital per worker. Very good basic education has permitted a rapid improvement in human capital. And these countries have experienced substantial technological progress.

Why hasn't any economy achieved this kind of growth in the past? Most economic analysts think that East Asia's growth spurt was possible because of its *relative* backwardness. That is, by the time that East Asian economies began to move into the modern world, they could benefit from adopting the technological advances that had been generated in technologically advanced countries such as the United States. In 1900, the United States could not have moved quickly to a modern level of productivity because much of the technology that powers the modern economy, from jet planes to computers, hadn't been invented yet. In 1970, South Korea probably still had lower labor productivity than the United States had in 1900, but it could rapidly upgrade

Countries in East Asia have enjoyed unprecedented growth since the 1970s, thanks largely to the adoption of modern technology and the accumulation of human capital.

its productivity by adopting technology that had been developed in the United States, Europe, and Japan over the previous century. This was aided by a huge investment in human capital through widespread schooling.

The East Asian experience demonstrates that economic growth can be especially fast in countries that are playing catch-up to other countries with higher GDP per capita. On this basis, many economists have suggested a general principle known as the **convergence hypothesis.** It says that differences in real GDP per capita among countries tend to narrow over time because countries that start with lower real GDP per capita tend to have higher growth rates. We'll look at the evidence for the convergence hypothesis later in this section.

Even before we get to that evidence, however, we can say right away that starting with a relatively low level of real GDP per capita is no guarantee of rapid growth, as the examples of Latin America and Africa both demonstrate.

Latin America's Disappointment

In 1900, Latin America was not regarded as an economically backward region. Natural resources, including both minerals and cultivable land, were abundant. Some countries, notably Argentina, attracted millions of immigrants from Europe in search of a better life. Measures of real GDP per capita in Argentina, Uruguay, and southern Brazil were comparable to those in economically advanced countries.

Since about 1920, however, growth in Latin America has been disappointing. As Figure 38.3 shows in the case of Argentina, it has remained disappointing to this day. The fact that South Korea is now much richer than Argentina would have seemed inconceivable a few generations ago.

Why has Latin America stagnated? Comparisons with East Asian success stories suggest several factors. The rates of savings and investment spending in Latin America have been much lower than in East Asia, partly as a result of irresponsible government policy that has eroded savings through high inflation, bank failures, and other disruptions. Education—especially broad basic education—has been underemphasized: even Latin American nations rich in natural resources often failed to channel that wealth into their educational systems. And political instability, leading to irresponsible economic policies, has taken a toll.

In the 1980s, many economists came to believe that Latin America was suffering from excessive government intervention in markets. They recommended opening the economies to imports, selling off government-owned companies, and, in general, freeing up individual initiative. The hope was that this would produce an East Asian–type economic surge. So far, however, only one Latin American nation, Chile, has achieved rapid growth. It now seems that pulling off an economic miracle is harder than it looks.

Relatively low rates of savings, investment spending, and education, along with political instability, have hampered economic growth in Latin America.

Africa's Troubles

Africa south of the Sahara is home to about 780 million people, more than 2½ times the population of the United States. On average, they are very poor, nowhere close to U.S. living standards 100 or even 200 years ago. And economic progress has been both slow and uneven, as the example of Nigeria, the most populous nation in the region, suggests. In fact, real GDP per capita in sub-Saharan Africa actually fell 13 percent from 1980 to 1994, although it has recovered since then. The consequence of this poor growth performance has been intense and continuing poverty.

This is a very disheartening picture. What explains it?

Perhaps first and foremost is the problem of political instability. In the years since 1975, large parts of Africa have experienced savage civil wars (often with outside powers

According to the **convergence hypothesis,** international differences in real GDP per capita tend to narrow over time.

Are Economies Converging?

In the 1950s, much of Europe seemed quaint and backward to American visitors, and Japan seemed very poor. Today, a visitor to Paris or Tokyo sees a city that looks about as rich as New York. Although real GDP per capita is still somewhat higher in the United States, the differences in the standards of living among the United States, Europe, and Japan are relatively small.

Many economists have argued that this convergence in living standards is normal; the convergence hypothesis says that relatively poor countries should have higher rates of growth of real GDP per capita than relatively rich countries. And if we look at today's relatively well-off countries, the convergence hypothesis seems to be true. Panel (a) of the figure shows data for a number of today's wealthy economies measured in 1990 dollars. On the horizontal axis is real GDP per capita in 1955; on the vertical axis is the average annual growth rate of real GDP per capita from 1955 to 2008. There is a clear negative relationship. The

United States was the richest country in this group in 1955 and had the slowest rate of growth. Japan and Spain were the poorest countries in 1955 and had the fastest rates of growth. These data suggest that the convergence hypothesis is true.

But economists who looked at similar data realized that these results depended on the countries selected. If you look at successful economies that have a high standard of living today, you find that real GDP per capita has converged. But looking across the world as a whole, including countries that remain poor, there is little evidence of convergence. Panel (b) of the figure illustrates this point using data for regions rather than individual countries (other than the United States). In 1955, East Asia and Africa were both very poor regions. Over the next 53 years, the East Asian regional economy grew quickly, as the convergence hypothesis would have predicted, but the African regional economy grew very slowly. In 1955, Western Europe had substantially higher real GDP per capita

than Latin America. But, contrary to the convergence hypothesis, the Western European regional economy grew more quickly over the next 53 years, widening the gap between the regions.

So is the convergence hypothesis all wrong? No: economists still believe that countries with relatively low real GDP per capita tend to have higher rates of growth than countries with relatively high real GDP per capita, *other things equal.* But other things—education, infrastructure, rule of law, and so on—are often not equal. Statistical studies find that when you adjust for differences in these other factors, poorer countries do tend to have higher growth rates. This result is known as *conditional convergence.*

Because other factors differ, however, there is no clear tendency toward convergence in the world economy as a whole. Western Europe, North America, and parts of Asia are becoming more similar in real GDP per capita, but the gap between these regions and the rest of the world is growing.

(a) Convergence among Wealthy Countries...

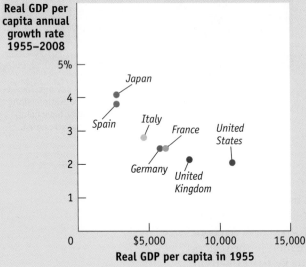

(b) ... But Not for the World as a Whole

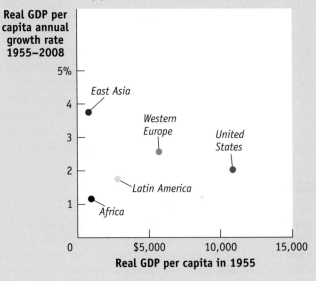

backing rival sides) that have killed millions of people and made productive investment spending impossible. The threat of war and general anarchy has also inhibited other important preconditions for growth, such as education and provision of necessary infrastructure.

Property rights are also a problem. The lack of legal safeguards means that property owners are often subject to extortion because of government corruption, making them averse to owning property or improving it. This is especially damaging in a country that is very poor.

While many economists see political instability and government corruption as the leading causes of underdevelopment in Africa, some—most notably Jeffrey Sachs of Columbia University and the United Nations—believe the opposite. They argue that Africa is politically unstable because Africa is poor. And Africa's poverty, they go on to claim, stems from its extremely unfavorable geographic conditions—much of the continent is landlocked, hot, infested with tropical diseases, and cursed with poor soil.

Sachs, along with economists from the World Health Organization, has highlighted the importance of health problems in Africa. In poor countries, worker productivity is often severely hampered by malnutrition and disease. In particular, tropical diseases such as malaria can be controlled only with an effective public health infrastructure, something that is lacking in much of Africa. At the time of this writing, economists are studying certain regions of Africa to determine whether modest amounts of aid given directly to residents for the purposes of increasing crop yields, reducing malaria, and increasing school attendance can produce self-sustaining gains in living standards.

Although the example of African countries represents a warning that long-run economic growth cannot be taken for granted, there are some signs of hope. Mauritius has developed a successful textile industry. Several African countries that are dependent on exporting commodities such as coffee and oil have benefited from the higher prices of those commodities. And Africa's economic performance since the mid-1990s has been generally much better than it was in preceding decades.

Module 38 AP Review

Solutions appear at the back of the book.

Check Your Understanding

1. Explain the effect of each of the following on the growth rate of productivity.
   a. The amounts of physical and human capital per worker are unchanged, but there is significant technological progress.
   b. The amount of physical capital per worker grows, but the level of human capital per worker and technology are unchanged.

2. The economy of Erehwon has grown 3% per year over the past 30 years. The labor force has grown at 1% per year, and the quantity of physical capital has grown at 4% per year. The average education level hasn't changed. Estimates by economists say that each 1% increase in physical capital per worker, other things equal, raises productivity by 0.3%.
   a. How fast has productivity in Erehwon grown?
   b. How fast has physical capital per worker grown?

   c. How much has growing physical capital per worker contributed to productivity growth? What percentage of total productivity growth is that?
   d. How much has technological progress contributed to productivity growth? What percentage of total productivity growth is that?

3. Multinomics, Inc., is a large company with many offices around the country. It has just adopted a new computer system that will affect virtually every function performed within the company. Why might a period of time pass before employees' productivity is improved by the new computer system? Why might there be a temporary decrease in employees' productivity?

Tackle the Test: Multiple-Choice Questions

1. Which of the following is a source of increased productivity growth?
    - I. increased physical capital
    - II. increased human capital
    - III. technological progress
    - a. I only
    - b. II only
    - c. III only
    - d. I and II only
    - e. I, II, and III

2. Which of the following is an example of physical capital?
    - a. machinery
    - b. healthcare
    - c. education
    - d. money
    - e. all of the above

3. The following statement describes which area of the world? "This area has experienced growth rates unprecedented in history and now looks like an economically advanced country."
    - a. North America
    - b. Latin America
    - c. Europe
    - d. East Asia
    - e. Africa

4. Which of the following is cited as an important factor preventing long-run economic growth in Africa?
    - a. political instability
    - b. lack of property rights
    - c. unfavorable geographic conditions
    - d. poor health
    - e. all of the above

5. The "convergence hypothesis"
    - a. states that differences in real GDP per capita among countries widen over time.
    - b. states that low levels of real GDP per capita are associated with higher growth rates.
    - c. states that low levels of real GDP per capita are associated with lower growth rates.
    - d. contradicts the "Rule of 70."
    - e. has been proven by evidence from around the world.

Tackle the Test: Free-Response Questions

1. a. Draw a correctly labeled graph of an aggregate production function that illustrates diminishing returns to physical capital.
    b. Explain how your aggregate production function illustrates diminishing returns to physical capital.
    c. On your graph, illustrate the effect of technological progress.
    d. How is the level of human capital per worker addressed on your graph?

Answer (7 points)

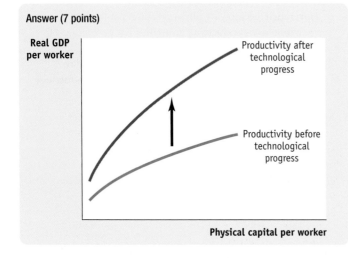

1 point: Vertical axis is labeled "Real GDP per worker."

1 point: Horizontal axis is labeled physical capital per worker.

1 point: Upward-sloping curve is labeled "Aggregate production function" or "Productivity."

1 point: Curve increases at a decreasing rate (the slope is positive and decreasing).

1 point: Equal increases in physical capital per worker lead to smaller increases in real GDP per worker.

1 point: Upward shift of production function is labeled to indicate technological progress.

1 point: Human capital per worker is held constant.

2. Assume that between 1940 and 2010:

    The amount of physical capital per worker grows at 2% per year.

    Each 1% rise in physical capital per worker (holding human capital and technology constant) raises output per worker by ½ of a percent, or 0.5%.

    There is no growth in human capital.

    Real GDP per capita rises from $30,000 to $60,000.

    a. Growing physical capital per worker is responsible for how much productivity growth per year? Show your calculation.
    b. By how much did total factor productivity grow over the time period? Explain.

Module 39
Growth Policy:
Why Economic
Growth Rates Differ

What you will learn in this **Module:**

- The factors that explain why long-run growth rates differ so much among countries
- The challenges to growth posed by scarcity of natural resources, environmental degradation, and efforts to make growth sustainable

Why Growth Rates Differ

In 1820, according to estimates by the economic historian Angus Maddison, Mexico had somewhat higher real GDP per capita than Japan. Today, Japan has higher real GDP per capita than most European nations and Mexico is a poor country, though by no means among the poorest. The difference? Over the long run, real GDP per capita grew at 1.9% per year in Japan but at only 1.2% per year in Mexico.

As this example illustrates, even small differences in growth rates have large consequences over the long run. So why do growth rates differ across countries and across periods of time?

Capital, Technology, and Growth Differences

As one might expect, economies with rapid growth tend to be economies that add physical capital, increase their human capital, or experience rapid technological progress. Striking economic success stories, like Japan in the 1950s and 1960s or China today, tend to be countries that do all three: that rapidly add to their physical capital, upgrade their educational level, and make fast technological progress.

Adding to Physical Capital One reason for differences in growth rates among countries is that some countries are increasing their stock of physical capital much more rapidly than others, through high rates of investment spending. In the 1960s, Japan was the fastest-growing major economy; it also spent a much higher share of its GDP on investment goods than other major economies. Today, China is the fastest-growing major economy, and it similarly spends a very large share of its GDP on investment goods. In 2009, investment spending was 44% of China's GDP, compared with only 18% in the United States.

Where does the money for high investment spending come from? We have already analyzed how financial markets channel savings into investment spending. The key point is that investment spending must be paid for either out of savings from domestic households or by an inflow of foreign capital—that is, savings from foreign households. Foreign capital has played an important role in the long-run economic growth of some countries, including the United States, which relied heavily on foreign funds during its early industrialization. For the most part, however, countries that invest a large share of their GDP are able to do so because they have high domestic savings. One reason for differences in growth rates, then, is that countries have different rates of savings and investment spending.

Adding to Human Capital Just as countries differ substantially in the rate at which they add to their physical capital, there have been large differences in the rate at which countries add to their human capital through education.

A case in point is the comparison between Latin America and East Asia. In both regions the average educational level has risen steadily over time, but it has risen much faster in East Asia. As shown in Table 39.1, East Asia had a significantly less educated population than Latin America in 1960. By 2000, that gap had been closed: East Asia still had a slightly higher fraction of adults with no education—almost all of them elderly—but had moved well past Latin America in terms of secondary and higher education.

table 39.1

Human Capital in Latin America and East Asia

	Latin America		East Asia	
	1960	2000	1960	2000
Percentage of population with no schooling	37.9%	14.6%	52.5%	19.8%
Percentage of population with high school or above	5.9	19.5	4.4	26.5

Source: Barro, Robert J. and Lee, Jong-Wha (2001) "International Data on Educational Attainment: Updates and Implications," *Oxford Economic Papers* vol. 53(3), p. 541–563.

Technological Progress The advance of technology is a key force behind economic growth. What drives technology?

Scientific advances make new technologies possible. To take the most spectacular example in today's world, the semiconductor chip—which is the basis for all modern information technology—could not have been developed without the theory of quantum mechanics in physics.

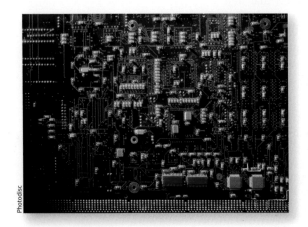

But science alone is not enough: scientific knowledge must be translated into useful products and processes. And that often requires devoting a lot of resources to **research and development,** or **R&D,** spending to create new technologies and prepare them for practical use.

Although some research and development is conducted by governments, much R&D is paid for by the private sector, as discussed below. The United States became the world's leading economy in large part because American businesses were among the first to make systematic research and development a part of their operations.

Developing new technology is one thing; applying it is another. There have often been notable differences in the pace at which different countries take advantage of new technologies. America's surge in productivity growth after 1995, as firms learned to make use of information technology, was at least initially not matched in Europe.

Inventing R&D

Thomas Edison is best known as the inventor of the light bulb and the phonograph. But his biggest invention may surprise you: he invented research and development.

Before Edison's time, there had, of course, been many inventors. Some of them worked in teams. But in 1875 Edison created something new: his Menlo Park, New Jersey, laboratory. It employed 25 men full-time to generate new products and processes for business. In other words, he did not set out to pursue a particular idea and then cash in. He created an organization whose purpose was to create new ideas year after year.

Edison's Menlo Park lab is now a museum. "To name a few of the products that were developed in Menlo Park," says the museum's website, "we can list the following: the carbon button mouthpiece for the telephone, the phonograph, the incandescent light bulb and the electrical distribution system, the electric train, ore separation, the Edison effect bulb, early experiments in wireless, the grasshopper telegraph, and improvements in telegraphic transmission."

You could say that before Edison's lab, technology just sort of happened: people came up with ideas, but businesses didn't plan to make continuous technological progress. Now R&D

Thomas Alva Edison in his laboratory in East Orange, New Jersey, in 1901.

operations, often much bigger than Edison's original team, are standard practice throughout the business world.

The Role of Government in Promoting Economic Growth

Governments can play an important role in promoting—or blocking—all three sources of long-term economic growth: physical capital, human capital, and technological progress.

Governments and Physical Capital Governments play an important direct role in building **infrastructure:** roads, power lines, ports, information networks, and other parts of an economy's physical capital that provide an underpinning, or foundation, for economic activity. Although some infrastructure is provided by private companies, much of it is either provided by the government or requires a great deal of government regulation and support. Ireland, whose economy really took off in the 1990s, is often cited as an example of the importance of government-provided infrastructure: the government invested in an excellent telecommunications infrastructure in the 1980s, and this helped make Ireland a favored location for high-technology companies.

Poor infrastructure—for example, a power grid that often fails, cutting off electricity to homes and businesses—is a major obstacle to economic growth in some countries. To provide good infrastructure, an economy must be able to afford it, but it must also have the political discipline to maintain it and provide for the future.

Perhaps the most crucial infrastructure is something we rarely think about: basic public health measures in the form of a clean water supply and disease control. As we'll see in the next section, poor health infrastructure is a major obstacle to economic growth in poor countries, especially those in Africa.

Governments also play an important indirect role in making high rates of private investment spending possible. Both the amount of savings and the ability of an economy to direct savings into productive investment spending depend on the economy's institutions, notably its financial system. In particular, a well-functioning banking system is very important for economic growth because in most countries it is the principal way in which savings are channeled into business investment spending. If a country's citizens trust their banks, they will place their savings in bank deposits, which the banks will then lend to their business customers. But if people don't

Roads, power lines, ports, information networks, and other underpinnings for economic activity are known as **infrastructure.**

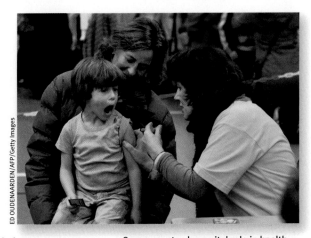

Governments play a vital role in health maintenance. A child is vaccinated against the influenza A (H1N1) virus during a mass vaccination in Schiedam, Netherlands, in late 2009.

trust their banks, they will hoard gold or foreign currency, keeping their savings in safe deposit boxes or under their mattresses, where it cannot be turned into productive investment spending. A well-functioning financial system requires appropriate government regulation that assures depositors that their funds are protected.

Governments and Human Capital An economy's physical capital is created mainly through investment spending by individuals and private companies. Much of an economy's human capital, in contrast, is the result of government spending on education. Governments pay for the great bulk of primary and secondary education, although individuals pay a significant share of the costs of higher education.

As a result, differences in the rate at which countries add to their human capital largely reflect government policy. As we saw in Table 39.1, East Asia now has a more educated population than Latin America. This isn't because East Asia is richer than Latin America and so can afford to spend more on education. Until very recently, East Asia was, on average, poorer than Latin America. Instead, it reflects the fact that Asian governments made broad education of the population a higher priority.

Governments and Technology Technological progress is largely the result of private initiative. But much important R&D is done by government agencies. For example, Brazil's agricultural boom was made possible by government researchers who discovered that adding crucial nutrients to the soil would allow crops to be grown on previously unusable land. They also developed new varieties of soybeans and breeds of cattle that flourish in Brazil's tropical climate.

Political Stability, Property Rights, and Excessive Government Intervention There's not much point in investing in a business if rioting mobs are likely to destroy it. And why save your money if someone with political connections can steal it? Political stability and protection of property rights are crucial ingredients in long-run economic growth.

Long-run economic growth in successful economies, like that of the United States, has been possible because there are good laws, institutions that enforce those laws, and a stable political system that maintains those institutions. The law must say that your property is really yours so that someone else can't take it away. The courts and the police must be honest so that they can't be bribed to ignore the law. And the political system must be stable so that the law doesn't change capriciously.

Americans take these preconditions for granted, but they are by no means guaranteed. Aside from the disruption caused by war or revolution, many countries find that

fyi

The Brazilian Breadbasket

A wry Brazilian joke says that "Brazil is the country of the future—and always will be." The world's fifth most populous country has often been considered a possible major economic power yet has never fulfilled that promise.

In recent years, however, Brazil's economy has made a better showing, especially in agriculture. This success depends on exploiting a natural resource, the tropical savanna land known as the *cerrado*. Until a quarter century ago, the land was considered unsuitable for farming. A combination of three factors changed that: technological progress due to research and development, improved economic policies, and greater physical capital.

The Brazilian Enterprise for Agricultural and Livestock Research, a government-run agency, developed the crucial technologies. It showed that adding lime and phosphorus made *cerrado* land productive, and it developed breeds of cattle and varieties of soybeans suited for the climate. (Now they're working on wheat.) Also, until the 1980s, Brazilian international trade policies discouraged exports, as did an overvalued exchange rate that made the country's goods more expensive to foreigners. After economic reform, investing in Brazilian agriculture became much more profitable and companies began putting in place the farm machinery, buildings, and other forms of physical capital needed to exploit the land.

What still limits Brazil's growth? Infrastructure. According to a report in the *New York Times,* Brazilian farmers are "concerned about the lack of reliable highways, railways and barge routes, which adds to the cost of doing business." Recognizing this, the Brazilian government is investing in infrastructure, and Brazilian agriculture is continuing to expand. The country has already overtaken the United States as the world's largest beef exporter and may not be far behind in soybeans.

their economic growth suffers due to corruption among the government officials who should be enforcing the law. For example, until 1991 the Indian government imposed many bureaucratic restrictions on businesses, which often had to bribe government officials to get approval for even routine activities—a tax on business, in effect. Economists have argued that a reduction in this burden of corruption is one reason Indian growth has been much faster in recent years than it was in the first 40 years after India gained independence in 1947.

Even when governments aren't corrupt, excessive government intervention can be a brake on economic growth. If large parts of the economy are supported by government subsidies, protected from imports, or otherwise insulated from competition, productivity tends to suffer because of a lack of incentives. As we saw in Module 38, excessive government intervention is one often-cited explanation for slow growth in Latin America.

Long-run economic growth is **sustainable** if it can continue in the face of the limited supply of natural resources and the impact of growth on the environment.

Is World Growth Sustainable?

Earlier we described the views of Thomas Malthus, the nineteenth-century economist who warned that the pressure of population growth would tend to limit the standard of living. Malthus was right—about the past: for around 58 centuries, from the origins of civilization until his own time, limited land supplies effectively prevented any large rise in real incomes per capita. Since then, however, technological progress and rapid accumulation of physical and human capital have allowed the world to defy Malthusian pessimism.

But will this always be the case? Some skeptics have expressed doubt about whether long-run economic growth is **sustainable**—whether it can continue in the face of the limited supply of natural resources and the impact of growth on the environment.

Natural Resources and Growth, Revisited

In 1972, a group of scientists called the Club of Rome made a big splash with a book titled *The Limits to Growth*, which argued that long-run economic growth wasn't sustainable due to limited supplies of nonrenewable resources such as oil and natural gas. These "neo-Malthusian" concerns at first seemed to be validated by a sharp rise in resource prices in the 1970s, then came to seem foolish when resource prices fell sharply in the 1980s. After 2005, however, resource prices rose sharply again, leading to renewed concern about resource limitations to growth. Figure 39.1 shows the real price

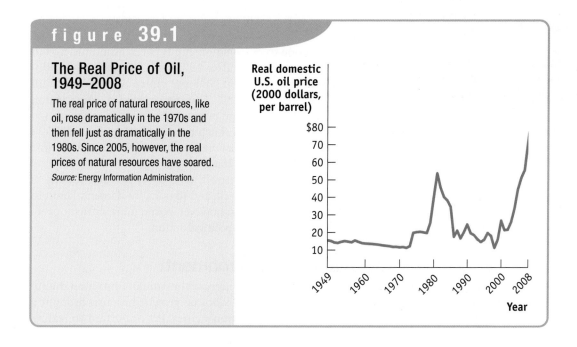

figure 39.1

The Real Price of Oil, 1949–2008

The real price of natural resources, like oil, rose dramatically in the 1970s and then fell just as dramatically in the 1980s. Since 2005, however, the real prices of natural resources have soared.

Source: Energy Information Administration.

of oil—the price of oil adjusted for inflation in the rest of the economy. The rise and fall of concerns about resource-based limits to growth have more or less followed the rise and fall of oil prices shown in the figure.

Differing views about the impact of limited natural resources on long-run economic growth turn on the answers to three questions:

- How large are the supplies of key natural resources?
- How effective will technology be at finding alternatives to natural resources?
- Can long-run economic growth continue in the face of resource scarcity?

It's mainly up to geologists to answer the first question. Unfortunately, there's wide disagreement among the experts, especially about the prospects for future oil production. Some analysts believe that there is so much untapped oil in the ground that world oil production can continue to rise for several decades. Others—including a number of oil company executives—believe that the growing difficulty of finding new oil fields will cause oil production to plateau—that is, stop growing and eventually begin a gradual decline—in the fairly near future. Some analysts believe that we have already reached that plateau.

The answer to the second question, whether there are alternatives to certain natural resources, will come from engineers. There's no question that there are many alternatives to the natural resources currently being depleted, some of which are already being exploited. For example, "unconventional" oil extracted from Canadian tar sands is already making a significant contribution to world oil supplies, and electricity generated by wind turbines is rapidly becoming big business in the United States—a development highlighted by the fact that in 2009 the United States surpassed Germany to become the world's largest producer of wind energy.

The third question, whether economies can continue to grow in the face of resource scarcity, is mainly a question for economists. And most, though not all, economists are optimistic: they believe that modern economies can find ways to work around limits on the supply of natural resources. One reason for this optimism is the fact that resource scarcity leads to high resource prices. These high prices in turn provide strong incentives to conserve the scarce resource and to find alternatives.

The Tehachapi Wind Farm, in Tehachapi, California, is the second largest collection of wind generators in the world. The turbines are operated by several private companies and collectively produce enough electricity to meet the needs of 350,000 people every year.

For example, after the sharp oil price increases of the 1970s, American consumers turned to smaller, more fuel-efficient cars, and U.S. industry also greatly intensified its efforts to reduce energy bills. The result is shown in Figure 39.2, which compares the growth rates of real GDP per capita and oil consumption before and after the 1970s energy crisis. Before 1973, there seemed to be a more or less one-to-one relationship between economic growth and oil consumption, but after 1973 the U.S. economy continued to deliver growth in real GDP per capita even as it substantially reduced its use of oil. This move toward conservation paused after 1990, as low real oil prices encouraged consumers to shift back to gas-greedy larger cars and SUVs. A sharp rise in oil prices from 2005 to 2008 encouraged renewed shifts toward oil conservation, although these shifts lost some steam as prices started falling again in late 2008.

Given such responses to prices, economists generally tend to see resource scarcity as a problem that modern economies handle fairly well, and so not a fundamental limit to long-run economic growth. Environmental issues, however, pose a more difficult problem because dealing with them requires effective political action.

Economic Growth and the Environment

Economic growth, other things equal, tends to increase the human impact on the environment. For example, China's spectacular economic growth has also brought a spectacular increase in air pollution in that nation's cities. It's important to realize,

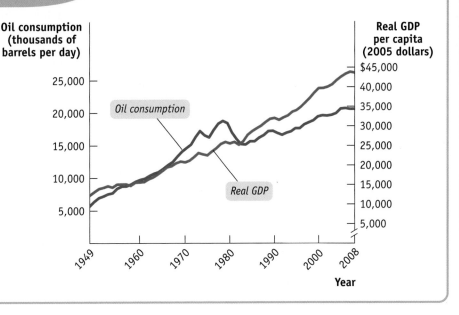

figure 39.2

U.S. Oil Consumption and Growth over Time

Until 1973, the real price of oil was relatively cheap and there was a more or less one-to-one relationship between economic growth and oil consumption. Conservation efforts increased sharply after the spike in the real price of oil in the mid-1970s. Yet the U.S. economy was still able to grow despite cutting back on oil consumption.

Sources: Energy Information Administration; Bureau of Economic Analysis.

however, that other things aren't necessarily equal: countries can and do take action to protect their environments. In fact, air and water quality in today's advanced countries is generally much better than it was a few decades ago. London's famous "fog"—actually a form of air pollution, which killed 4,000 people during a two-week episode in 1952—is gone, thanks to regulations that virtually eliminated the use of coal heat. The equally famous smog of Los Angeles, although not extinguished, is far less severe than it was in the 1960s and early 1970s, again thanks to pollution regulations.

Despite these past environmental success stories, there is widespread concern today about the environmental impacts of continuing economic growth, reflecting a change in the scale of the problem. Environmental success stories have mainly involved dealing with *local* impacts of economic growth, such as the effect of widespread car ownership on air quality in the Los Angeles basin. Today, however, we are faced with *global* environmental issues—the adverse impacts on the environment of the Earth as a whole by

fyi

Coal Comfort on Resources

Those who worry that exhaustion of natural resources will bring an end to economic growth can take some comfort from the story of William Stanley Jevons, a nineteenth-century British economist best known today for his role in the development of marginal analysis. In addition to his work in economic theory, Jevons worked on the real-world economic problems of the day, and in 1865 he published an influential book, *The Coal*

Question, that foreshadowed many modern concerns about resources and growth. But his pessimism was proved wrong.

The Industrial Revolution was launched in Britain, and in 1865 Britain still had the world's richest major economy. But Jevons argued that Britain's economic success had depended on the availability of cheap coal and that the gradual exhaustion of Britain's coal resources, as miners were forced to dig ever

deeper, would threaten the nation's long-run prosperity.

He was right about the exhaustion of Britain's coal: production peaked in 1913, and today the British coal industry is a shadow of its former self. But Britain was able to turn to alternative sources of energy, including imported coal and oil. And economic growth did not collapse: real GDP per capita in Britain today is about seven times its level in 1865.

worldwide economic growth. The biggest of these issues involves the impact of fossil-fuel consumption on the world's climate.

Burning coal and oil releases carbon dioxide into the atmosphere. There is broad scientific consensus that rising levels of carbon dioxide and other gases are causing a greenhouse effect on the Earth, trapping more of the sun's energy and raising the planet's overall temperature. And rising temperatures may impose high human and economic costs: rising sea levels may flood coastal areas; changing climate may disrupt agriculture, especially in poor countries; and so on.

The problem of climate change is clearly linked to economic growth. Figure 39.3 shows carbon dioxide emissions from the United States, Europe, and China since 1980. Historically, the wealthy nations have been responsible for the bulk of these emissions because they have consumed far more energy per person than poorer countries. As China and other emerging economies have grown, however, they have begun to consume much more energy and emit much more carbon dioxide.

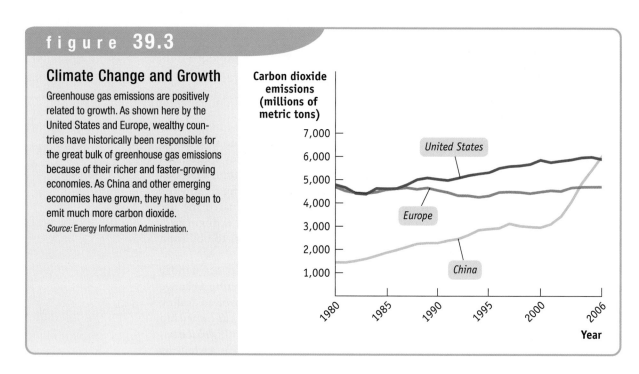

figure 39.3

Climate Change and Growth

Greenhouse gas emissions are positively related to growth. As shown here by the United States and Europe, wealthy countries have historically been responsible for the great bulk of greenhouse gas emissions because of their richer and faster-growing economies. As China and other emerging economies have grown, they have begun to emit much more carbon dioxide.

Source: Energy Information Administration.

Is it possible to continue long-run economic growth while curbing the emissions of greenhouse gases? The answer, according to most economists who have studied the issue, is yes. It should be possible to reduce greenhouse gas emissions in a wide variety of ways, ranging from the use of non-fossil-fuel energy sources such as wind, solar, and nuclear power; to preventive measures such as carbon sequestration (capturing carbon dioxide and storing it); to simpler things like designing buildings so that they're easier to keep warm in winter and cool in summer. Such measures would impose costs on the economy, but the best available estimates suggest that even a large reduction in greenhouse gas emissions over the next few decades would only modestly dent the long-term rise in real GDP per capita.

The problem is how to make all of this happen. Unlike resource scarcity, environmental problems don't automatically provide incentives for changed behavior. Pollution is an example of a *negative externality,* a cost that individuals or firms impose on others without having to offer compensation. In the absence of government intervention, individuals and firms have no incentive to reduce negative externalities, which is why it took regulation to reduce air pollution in America's cities. And as Nicholas Stern, the author of an influential report on climate change, put it, greenhouse gas emissions are "the mother of all externalities."

So there is a broad consensus among economists—although there are some dissenters—that government action is needed to deal with climate change. There is also broad consensus that this action should take the form of market-based incentives, either in the form of a carbon tax—a tax per unit of carbon emitted—or a cap and trade system in which the total amount of emissions is capped, and producers must buy licenses to emit greenhouse gases. There is, however, considerable dispute about how much action is appropriate, reflecting both uncertainty about the costs and benefits and scientific uncertainty about the pace and extent of climate change.

There are also several aspects of the climate change problem that make it much more difficult to deal with than, say, smog in Los Angeles. One is the problem of taking the long view. The impact of greenhouse gas emissions on the climate is very gradual: carbon dioxide put into the atmosphere today won't have its full effect on the climate for several generations. As a result, there is the political problem of persuading voters to accept pain today in return for gains that will benefit their children, grandchildren, or even great-grandchildren.

The added problem of international burden sharing presents a stumbling block for consensus, as it did at the United Nations Climate Change Conference in 2009. As Figure 39.3 shows, today's rich countries have historically been responsible for most greenhouse gas emissions, but newly emerging economies like China are responsible for most of the recent growth. Inevitably, rich countries are reluctant to pay the price of reducing emissions only to have their efforts frustrated by rapidly growing emissions from new players. On the other hand, countries like China, which are still relatively poor, consider it unfair that they should be expected to bear the burden of protecting an environment threatened by the past actions of rich nations.

Despite political issues and the need for compromise, the general moral of this story is that it is possible to reconcile long-run economic growth with environmental protection. The main question is one of getting political consensus around the necessary policies.

fyi

The Cost of Climate Protection

At the time of this writing, there were a number of bills before the U.S. Congress, some of them with bipartisan sponsorship, calling for ambitious, long-term efforts to reduce U.S. emissions of greenhouse gases. For example, a bill sponsored by Senators Joseph Lieberman and John McCain would use a cap and trade system to gradually reduce emissions over time, eventually—by 2050—reducing them to 60% below their 1990 level. Another bill, sponsored by Senators Barbara Boxer and Bernie Sanders, called for an 80% reduction by 2050.

Would implementing these bills put a stop to long-run economic growth? Not according to a comprehensive study by a team at MIT, which found that reducing emissions would impose significant but not overwhelming costs. Using an elaborate model of the interaction between environmental policy and the economy, the MIT group estimated that the Lieberman–McCain proposal would reduce real GDP per capita in 2050 by 1.11% and the more stringent Sanders–Boxer proposal would reduce real GDP per capita by 1.79%.

These may sound like big numbers—they would amount to between $200 billion and $250 billion today—but they would hardly make a dent in the economy's long-run growth rate. Remember that over the long run the U.S. economy has on average seen real GDP per capita rise by almost 2% a year. If the MIT group's estimates are correct, even a strong policy to avert climate change would, in effect, require that we give up less than one year's growth over the next four decades.

Check Your Understanding

1. Explain the link between a country's growth rate, its investment spending as a percent of GDP, and its domestic savings.

2. Which of the following is the better predictor of a future high long-run growth rate: a high standard of living today or high levels of savings and investment spending? Explain your answer.

3. Some economists think the best way to help African countries is for wealthier countries to provide more funds for basic infrastructure. Others think this policy will have no long-run effect unless African countries have the financial and political means to maintain this infrastructure. What policies would you suggest?

4. What is the link between greenhouse gas emissions and growth? What is the expected effect on growth from emissions reduction? Why is international burden sharing of greenhouse gas emissions reduction a contentious problem?

Tackle the Test: Multiple-Choice Questions

1. Economies experience more rapid economic growth when they do which of the following?
   I. add physical capital
   II. promote technological progress
   III. limit human capital
   a. I only
   b. II only
   c. III only
   d. I and II only
   e. I, II, and III

2. Which of the following can lead to increases in physical capital in an economy?
   a. increased investment spending
   b. increased savings by domestic households
   c. increased savings from foreign households
   d. an inflow of foreign capital
   e. all of the above

3. Which of the following is true of sustainable long-run economic growth?
   a. Long-run growth can continue in the face of the limited supply of natural resources.
   b. It was predicted by Thomas Malthus.
   c. Modern economies handle resource scarcity problems poorly.
   d. It is less likely when we find alternatives to natural resources.
   e. All of the above are true.

4. Which of the following statements is true of environmental quality?
   a. It is typically not affected by government policy.
   b. Other things equal, it tends to improve with economic growth.
   c. There is broad scientific consensus that rising levels of carbon dioxide and other gases are raising the planet's overall temperature.
   d. Most economists believe it is not possible to reduce greenhouse gas emissions while economic growth continues.
   e. Most environmental success stories involve dealing with global, rather than local impacts.

5. According to the MIT study discussed in the module, a cap and trade system to reduce greenhouse gas emissions in the United States would lead to
   a. no significant costs.
   b. significant but not overwhelming costs.
   c. a loss of roughly three year's real GDP over the next 40 years.
   d. a reduction in real GDP per capita of over 10%.
   e. a loss of 5 years' worth of economic growth over the next 40 years.

Tackle the Test: Free-Response Questions

1. List and explain five different actions the government can take to promote long-run economic growth.

Answer (10 points)—10 points for 5 of the 6 possible actions/descriptions

1 point: Build infrastructure.

1 point: The government can provide roads, power lines, ports, rail lines, and related systems to support economic activity.

1 point: Invest in human capital.

1 point: The government can improve access to quality education.

1 point: Invest in research and development.

1 point: The government can promote technological progress by having government agencies support and participate in R&D.

1 point: Provide political stability.

1 point: The government can create and maintain institutions that make and enforce laws that promote stability.

1 point: Establish and protect property rights.

1 point: Growth is promoted by laws that define what property belongs to whom and by institutions that defend those property rights.

1 point: Minimize government intervention.

1 point: The government can limit its intervention in the economy and promote competition.

2. What roles do physical capital, human capital, technology, and natural resources play in influencing long-run economic growth of aggregate output per capita?

What you will learn in this **Module:**

- How long-run economic growth is represented in macroeconomic models

- How to model the effects of economic growth policies

Module 40

Economic Growth in Macroeconomic Models

Long-run economic growth is fundamental to solving many of today's most pressing economic problems. It is even more critical in poorer, less developed countries. But the policies we have studied in earlier sections to address short-run fluctuations and the business cycle may not encourage long-run economic growth. For example, an increase in household consumption can help an economy to recover from a recession. However, when households increase consumption, they decrease their savings, which leads to decreased investment spending and slows long-run economic growth.

In addition to understanding short-run stabilization policies, we need to understand the factors that influence economic growth and how choices by governments and individuals can promote or retard that growth in the long-run.

Long-run economic growth is the sustained rise in the quantity of goods and services the economy produces, as opposed to the short-run ups and downs of the business cycle. In Module 18, we looked at actual and potential output in the United States from 1989 to 2009. As shown in Figure 40.1, increases in potential output during that time represent long-run economic growth in the economy. The fluctuations of actual output compared to potential output are the result of the business cycle.

As we have seen throughout this section, long-run economic growth depends almost entirely on rising productivity. Good macroeconomic policy strives to foster increases in productivity, which in turn leads to long-run economic growth. In this module, we will learn how to evaluate the effects of long-run growth policies using the production possibilities curve and the aggregate demand and supply model.

Long-run Economic Growth and the Production Possibilities Curve

Recall from Section 1 that we defined the production possibilities curve as a graph that illustrates the trade-offs facing an economy that produces only two goods. In our example, we developed the production possibilities curve for Tom, a castaway facing a figure **40.1** Actual and Potential Output from 1989 to 2009

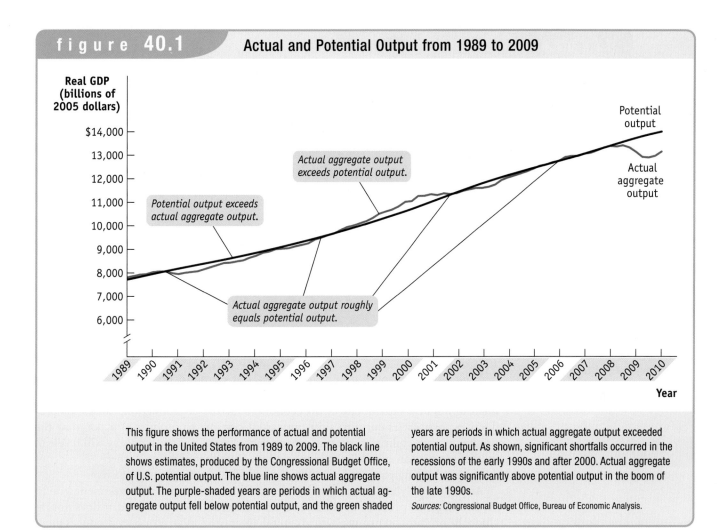

This figure shows the performance of actual and potential output in the United States from 1989 to 2009. The black line shows estimates, produced by the Congressional Budget Office, of U.S. potential output. The blue line shows actual aggregate output. The purple-shaded years are periods in which actual aggregate output fell below potential output, and the green shaded years are periods in which actual aggregate output exceeded potential output. As shown, significant shortfalls occurred in the recessions of the early 1990s and after 2000. Actual aggregate output was significantly above potential output in the boom of the late 1990s.

Sources: Congressional Budget Office, Bureau of Economic Analysis.

trade-off between producing fish and coconuts. Looking at Figure 40.2 on the next page, we see that economic growth is shown as an outward shift of the production possibilities curve. Now let's return to the production possibilities curve model and use a different example to illustrate how economic growth policies can lead to long-run economic growth.

Figure 40.3 on the next page shows a hypothetical production possibilities curve for a fictional country we'll call Kyland. In our previous production possibilities examples, the trade-off was between producing quantities of two different goods. In this example, our production possibilities curve illustrates Kyland's trade-off between two different *categories* of goods. The production possibilities curve shows the alternative combinations of investment goods and consumer goods that Kyland can produce. The consumer goods category includes everything purchased for consumption by households, such as food, clothing, and sporting goods. Investment goods include all forms of physical capital. That is, goods that are used to produce other goods. Kyland's production possibilities curve shows the trade-off between the production of consumer goods and the production of investment goods. Recall that the bowed-out shape of the production possibilities curve reflects increasing opportunity cost.

Kyland's production possibilities curve shows all possible combinations of consumer and investment goods that can be produced with full and efficient use of all of Kyland's resources. However, the production possibilities curve model does not tell us which of the possible points Kyland *should* select.

figure 40.2

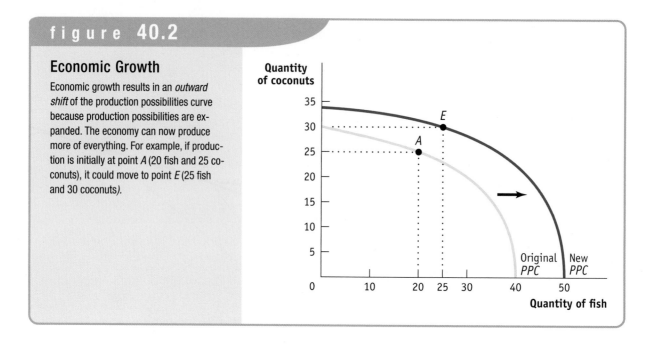

Economic Growth

Economic growth results in an *outward shift* of the production possibilities curve because production possibilities are expanded. The economy can now produce more of everything. For example, if production is initially at point *A* (20 fish and 25 coconuts), it could move to point *E* (25 fish and 30 coconuts).

Figure 40.3 illustrates four points on Kyland's production possibilities curve. At point *A*, Kyland is producing all investment goods and no consumer goods. Investment in physical capital, one of the economy's factors of production, causes the production possibilities curve to shift outward. Choosing to produce at a point on the production possibilities curve that creates more capital for the economy will result in greater production possibilities in the future. Note that at point *A*, there are no consumer goods being produced, a situation which the economy cannot survive.

At point *D*, Kyland is producing all consumer goods and no investment goods. While this point provides goods and services for consumers in Kyland, it does not include the production of any physical capital. Over time, as an economy produces more goods and services, some of its capital is used up in that production. A loss in the value of physical capital due to wear, age, or obsolescence is called **depreciation.** If Kyland were to produce at point *D* year after year, it would soon find its stock of physical

Depreciation occurs when the value of an asset is reduced by wear, age, or obsolescence.

---

figure 40.3

The Trade-off Between Investment and Consumer Goods

This production possibilities curve illustrates Kyland's trade-off between the production of investment goods and consumer goods. At point *A*, Kyland produces all investment goods and no consumer goods. At point *D*, Kyland produces all consumer goods and no investment goods.

capital depreciating and its production possibilities curve would shift inward over time, indicating a decrease in production possibilities. Points *B* and *C* represent a mix of consumer and investment goods for the economy. While we can see that points *A* and *D* would not be acceptable choices over a long period of time, the choice between points *B* and *C* would depend on the values, politics, and other details related to the economy and people of Kyland. What we do know is that the choice made by Kyland each year will affect the position of the production possibilities curve in the future. An emphasis on the production of consumer goods will make consumers better off in the short run but will prevent the production possibilities curve from moving farther out in the future. An emphasis on investment goods will lead the production possibilities curve to shift out farther in the future but will decrease the quantity of consumer goods available in the short run.

So what does the production possibilities curve tell us about economic growth? Since long-run economic growth depends almost entirely on rising productivity, a country's decision regarding investment in physical capital, human capital, and technology affects its long-run economic growth. Governments can promote long-run economic growth, shifting the country's production possibilities curve outward over time, by investing in physical capital such as infrastructure. They can also encourage high rates of private investment in physical capital by promoting a well-functioning financial system, property rights, and political stability.

© Rosenfeld/Corbis

Investments in capital help the economy reach new heights of productivity.

Long-run Economic Growth and the Aggregate Demand-Aggregate Supply Model

The aggregate demand and supply model we developed in Section 4 is another useful tool for understanding long-run economic growth. Recall that in the aggregate demand-aggregate supply model, the long-run aggregate supply curve shows the relationship between the aggregate price level and the quantity of aggregate output supplied when all prices, including nominal wages, are flexible. As shown in Figure 40.4, the

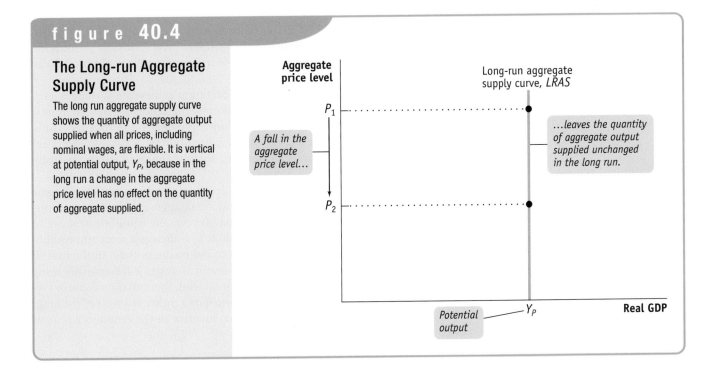

figure 40.4

The Long-run Aggregate Supply Curve

The long run aggregate supply curve shows the quantity of aggregate output supplied when all prices, including nominal wages, are flexible. It is vertical at potential output, Y_P, because in the long run a change in the aggregate price level has no effect on the quantity of aggregate supplied.

Aggregate price level

Long-run aggregate supply curve, *LRAS*

P_1

A fall in the aggregate price level...

...leaves the quantity of aggregate output supplied unchanged in the long run.

P_2

Potential output — Y_P

Real GDP

module **40** Economic Growth in Macroeconomic Models **401** long-run aggregate supply curve is vertical at the level of potential output. While actual real GDP is almost always above or below potential output, reflecting the current phase of the business cycle, potential output is the level of output around which actual aggregate output fluctuates. Potential output in the United States has risen steadily over time. This corresponds to a rightward shift of the long-run aggregate supply curve, as shown in Figure 40.5. Thus, the same government policies that promote an outward shift of the production possibilities curve promote a rightward shift of the long-run aggregate supply curve.

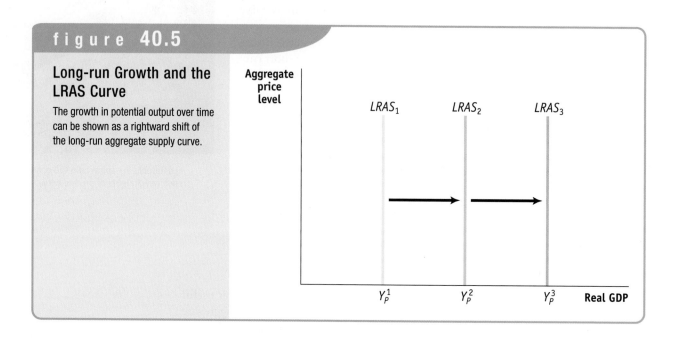

figure 40.5

Long-run Growth and the LRAS Curve

The growth in potential output over time can be shown as a rightward shift of the long-run aggregate supply curve.

Distinguishing Between Long-run Growth and Short-run Fluctuations

When considering changes in real GDP, it is important to distinguish long-run growth from short-run fluctuations due to the business cycle. Both the production possibilities curve model and the aggregate demand-aggregate supply model can help us do this.

The points along a production possibilities curve are achievable if there is efficient use of the economy's resources. If the economy experiences a macroeconomic fluctuation due to the business cycle, such as unemployment due to a recession, production falls to a point inside the production possibilities curve. On the other hand, long-run growth will appear as an outward shift of the production possibilities curve.

In the aggregate demand-aggregate supply model, fluctuations of actual aggregate output around potential output are illustrated by shifts of aggregate demand or short-run aggregate supply that result in a short-run macroeconomic equilibrium above or below potential output. In both panels of Figure 40.6, E_1 indicates a short-run equilibrium that differs from long-run equilibrium due to the business cycle. In the case of short-run fluctuations like these, adjustments in nominal wages will eventually bring the equilibrium level of real GDP back to the potential level. By contrast, we saw in Figure 40.5 that long-run economic growth is represented by a rightward shift of the long-run aggregate supply curve and corresponds to an increase in the economy's level of potential output.

figure 40.6

From the Short Run to the Long Run

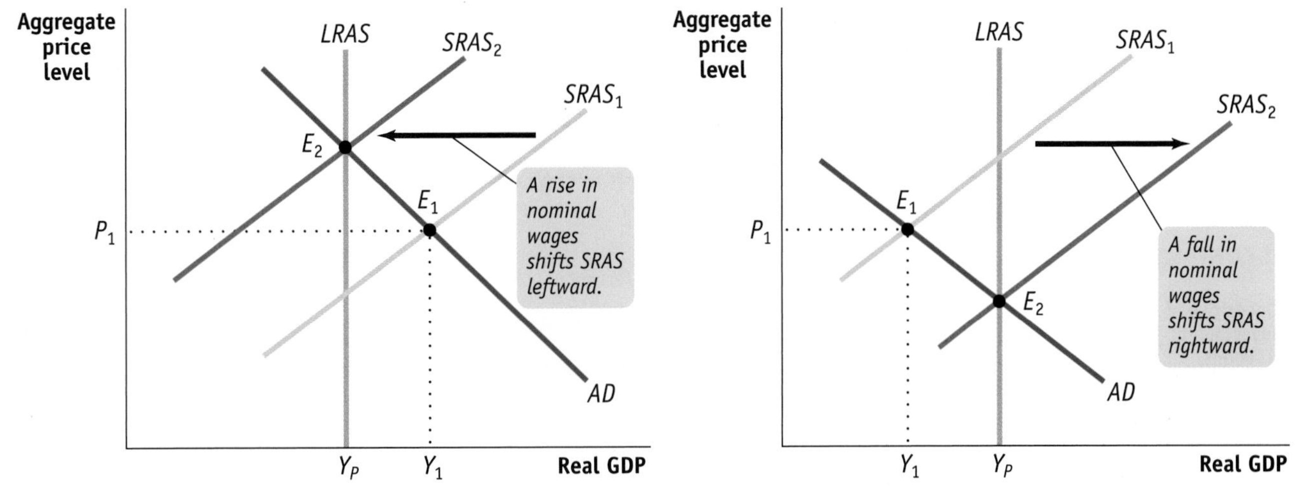

In panel (a), the initial equilibrium is E_1. At the aggregate price level, P_1, the quantity of aggregate output supplied, Y_1, exceeds potential output, Y_P. Eventually, low unemployment will cause nominal wages to rise, leading to a leftward shift of the short-run aggregate supply curve from $SRAS_1$ to $SRAS_2$ and a long-run equilibrium at E_2. In

panel (b), the reverse happens: at the short-run equilibrium, E_1, the quantity of aggregate output supplied is less than potential output. High unemployment eventually leads to a fall in nominal wages over time and a rightward shift of the short-run aggregate supply curve. The end result is long-run equilibrium at E_2.

Module 40 AP Review

Solutions appear at the back of the book.

Check Your Understanding

1. How are long-run economic growth and short-run fluctuations during a business cycle represented using the production possibilities curve model?

2. How are long-run economic growth and short-run fluctuations during a business cycle represented using the aggregate demand–aggregate supply model?

Tackle the Test: Multiple-Choice Questions

1. Which of the following will shift the production possibilities curve outward?
   I. an increase in the production of investment goods
   II. an increase in the production of consumer goods
   III. technological progress
   a. I only
   b. II only
   c. III only
   d. I and III only
   e. I, II, and III

2. In the production possibilities curve (PPC) model, long-run economic growth is shown by a(n)
   a. outward shift of the PPC.
   b. inward shift of the PPC.

   c. movement from a point below the PPC to a point on the PPC.
   d. movement from a point on the PPC to a point below the PPC.
   e. movement from a point on the PPC to a point beyond the PPC.

3. The reduction in the value of an asset due to wear and tear is known as
   a. depreciation.
   b. negative investment.
   c. economic decline.
   d. disinvestment.
   e. net investment.

4. In the aggregate demand-aggregate supply model, long-run economic growth is shown by a
   a. leftward shift of the aggregate demand curve.
   b. rightward shift of the aggregate demand curve.
   c. rightward shift of the long-run aggregate supply curve.
   d. rightward shift of the short-run aggregate supply curve.
   e. leftward shift of the short-run aggregate supply curve.

5. Which of the following is listed among the key sources of growth in potential output?
   a. expansionary fiscal policy
   b. expansionary monetary policy
   c. a rightward shift of the short-run aggregate supply curve
   d. investment in human capital
   e. both a and b

Tackle the Test: Free-Response Questions

1. Refer to the graph provided.

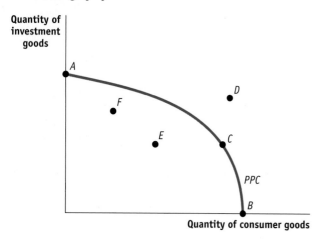

Quantity of investment goods

A

D

F

E

C

PPC

B

Quantity of consumer goods

a. Which point(s) could represent a downturn in the business cycle?
b. Which point(s) represent efficient production?
c. Which point(s) are attainable only after long-run economic growth?
d. How would long-run economic growth be represented on this graph?
e. Policy that results in an increase in the production of consumer goods without reducing the production of investment goods is represented by a movement from point _____ to point _____.
f. Producing at which efficient point this year would lead to the most economic growth next year?

Answer (9 points)

2 points: A downturn could be represented by points E or F

3 points: Points A, B, and C represent efficient production.

1 point: Point D is attainable only after long-run economic growth.

1 point: Long-run economic growth would be represented by an outward shift of the curve.

1 point: Consumer goods increase and investment goods remain unchanged when moving from point E to point C.

1 point: Producing at point A would lead to the most economic growth.

2. Draw a separate, correctly labeled aggregate demand and supply graph to illustrate each of the following situations. On each of your graphs, include the short-run aggregate supply curve(s), long-run aggregate supply curve(s), and aggregate demand curve(s).
   a. Expansionary fiscal policy moves the economy out of a recession.
   b. Investment in infrastructure by the government leads to long-run economic growth.

Section 7 Review

Summary

1. Economic growth is a sustained increase in the productive capacity of an economy and can be measured as changes in real GDP per capita. This measurement eliminates the effects of changes in both the price level and population size. Levels of real GDP per capita vary greatly around the world: more than half of the world's population lives in countries that are still poorer than the United States was in 1908.

2. Growth rates of real GDP per capita also vary widely. According to the **Rule of 70,** the number of years it takes for real GDP per capita to double is equal to 70 divided by the annual growth rate of real GDP per capita.

3. The key to long-run economic growth is rising **labor productivity,** or just **productivity,** which is output per worker. Increases in productivity arise from increases in **physical capital** per worker and **human capital** per worker as well as advances in **technology.** The **aggregate production function** shows how real GDP per worker depends on these three factors. Other things equal, there are **diminishing returns to physical capital:** holding human capital per worker and technology fixed, each successive addition to physical capital per worker yields a smaller increase in productivity than the one before. Similarly, there are diminishing returns to human capital among other inputs. With **growth accounting,** which involves estimates of each factor's contribution to economic growth, economists have shown that rising **total factor productivity,** the amount of output produced from a given amount of factor inputs, is key to long-run growth. Rising total factor productivity is usually interpreted as the effect of technological progress. In most countries, natural resources are a less significant source of productivity growth today than in earlier times.

4. The world economy contains examples of success and failure in the effort to achieve long-run economic growth. East Asian economies have done many things right and achieved very high growth rates. In Latin America, where some important conditions are lacking, growth has generally been disappointing. In Africa, real GDP per capita declined for several decades, although there are recent signs of progress. The growth rates of economically advanced countries have converged, but the growth rates of countries across the world have not. This has led economists to believe that the **convergence hypothesis** fits the data only when factors that affect growth, such as education, infrastructure, and favorable policies and institutions, are held equal across countries.

5. The large differences in countries' growth rates are largely due to differences in their rates of accumulation of physical and human capital as well as differences in technological progress. A prime factor is differences in savings and investment rates, since most countries that have high investment in physical capital finance it by high domestic savings. Technological progress is largely a result of **research and development,** or **R&D.**

6. Government actions that contribute to growth include the building of **infrastructure,** particularly for transportation and public health; the creation and regulation of a well-functioning banking system that channels savings into investment spending; and the financing of both education and R&D. Government actions that slow growth are corruption, political instability, excessive government intervention, and the neglect or violation of property rights.

7. In regard to making economic growth **sustainable,** economists generally believe that environmental degradation poses a greater problem than natural resource scarcity does. Addressing environmental degradation requires effective governmental intervention, but the problem of natural resource scarcity is often well handled by the incentives created by market prices.

8. The emission of greenhouse gases is clearly linked to growth, and limiting emissions will require some reduction in growth. However, the best available estimates suggest that a large reduction in emissions would require only a modest reduction in the growth rate.

9. There is broad consensus that government action to address climate change and greenhouse gases should be in the form of market-based incentives, like a carbon tax or a cap and trade system. It will also require rich and poor countries to come to some agreement on how the cost of emissions reductions will be shared.

10. Long-run economic growth can be analyzed using the production possibilities curve and the aggregate demand-aggregate supply model. In these models, long-run economic growth is represented by an outward shift of the production possibilities curve and a rightward shift of the long-run aggregate supply curve.

11. Physical capital **depreciates** with use. Therefore, over time, the production possibilities curve will shift inward and the long-run aggregate supply curve will shift to the left if the stock of capital is not replaced.

Key Terms

Problems

1. The accompanying table shows data on real GDP per capita for several countries between 1960 and 2000. (*Source:* The Penn World Table, Version 6.2.)

	Argentina			Ghana			South Korea			United States		
	Real GDP per capita (2000 dollars)	Percentage of		Real GDP per capita (2000 dollars)	Percentage of		Real GDP per capita (2000 dollars)	Percentage of		Real GDP per capita (2000 dollars)	Percentage of	
Year		1960 real GDP per capita	2000 real GDP per capita		1960 real GDP per capita	2000 real GDP per capita		1960 real GDP per capita	2000 real GDP per capita		1960 real GDP per capita	2000 real GDP per capita
1960	$7,838	?	?	$412	?	?	$1,458	?	?	$12,892	?	?
1970	9,821	?	?	1,052	?	?	2,552	?	?	17,321	?	?
1980	10,921	?	?	1,142	?	?	4,497	?	?	21,606	?	?
1990	8,195	?	?	1,153	?	?	9,593	?	?	27,097	?	?
2000	11,332	?	?	1,392	?	?	15,702	?	?	34,365	?	?

a. Complete the table by expressing each year's real GDP per capita as a percentage of its 1960 and 2000 levels.

b. How does the growth in living standards from 1960 to 2000 compare across these four nations? What might account for these differences?

2. The accompanying table shows the average annual growth rate in real GDP per capita for several countries between 1960 and 2000. (*Source:* The Penn World Table, Version 6.2)

	Average annual growth rate of real GDP per capita		
Years	Argentina	Ghana	South Korea
1960–1970	2.53%	15.54%	7.50%
1970–1980	1.12	0.85	7.62
1980–1990	−2.50	0.10	11.33
1990–2000	3.83	2.08	6.37

a. For each decade and for each country, use the Rule of 70 where possible to calculate how long it would take for that country's real GDP per capita to double.

b. Suppose that the average annual growth rate that each country achieved over the period 1990–2000 continues indefinitely into the future. Starting from 2000, use the Rule of 70 to calculate, where possible, the year in which a country will have doubled its real GDP per capita.

3. The accompanying table provides approximate statistics on per capita income levels and growth rates for regions defined by income levels. According to the Rule of 70, the high-income countries are projected to double their per capita GDP in approximately 37 years, in 2042. Throughout this question, assume constant growth rates for each of the regions that are fixed at their average value between 2000 and 2005.

Region	GDP per capita (2005)	Average GDP per capita growth (2000–2005)
High-income countries	$28,612	1.9%
Middle-income countries	2,196	5.7
Low-income countries	494	3.6

Source: World Bank.

a. Calculate the ratio of per capita GDP in 2005 for each of the following:
   I. middle-income to high-income countries
   II. low-income to high-income countries
   III. low-income to middle-income countries

b. Calculate the number of years it will take the low-income and middle-income countries to double their per capita GDP.

c. Calculate the per capita GDP of each of the regions in 2042. (*Hint:* How many times does their per capita GDP double in 37 years?)

d. Repeat part a with the projected per capita GDP in 2042.

e. Compare your answers to parts a and d. Comment on the change in economic inequality between the regions.

4. You are hired as an economic consultant to the countries of Albernia and Brittania. Each country's current relationship between physical capital per worker and output per worker is given by the curve labeled Productivity$_1$ in the

accompanying diagram. Albernia is at point *A* and Brittania is at point *B*.

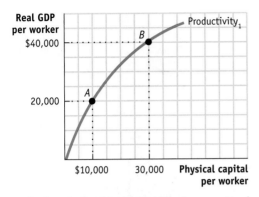

a. In the relationship depicted by the curve Productivity$_1$, what factors are held fixed? Do these countries experience diminishing returns to physical capital per worker?

b. Assuming that the amount of human capital per worker and the technology are held fixed in each country, can you recommend a policy to generate a doubling of real GDP per capita in Albernia?

c. How would your policy recommendation change if the amount of human capital per worker and the technology were not fixed? Draw a curve on the diagram that represents this policy for Albernia.

5. The country of Androde is currently using Method 1 for its production function. By chance, scientists stumble on a technological breakthrough that will enhance Androde's productivity. This technological breakthrough is reflected in another production function, Method 2. The accompanying table shows combinations of physical capital per worker and output per worker for both methods, assuming that human capital per worker is fixed.

Method 1		Method 2	
Physical capital per worker	Real GDP per worker	Physical capital per worker	Real GDP per worker
0	0.00	0	0.00
50	35.36	50	70.71
100	50.00	100	100.00
150	61.24	150	122.47
200	70.71	200	141.42
250	79.06	250	158.11
300	86.60	300	173.21
350	93.54	350	187.08
400	100.00	400	200.00
450	106.07	450	212.13
500	111.80	500	223.61

a. Using the data in the accompanying table, draw the two production functions in one diagram. Androde's current amount of physical capital per worker is 100 using Method 1. In your figure, label that point *A*.

b. Starting from point *A*, over a period of 70 years, the amount of physical capital per worker in Androde rises to 400. Assuming Androde still uses Method 1, in your diagram, label the resulting point of production *B*. Using the Rule of 70, calculate by how many percent per year output per worker has grown.

c. Now assume that, starting from point *A*, over the same 70 years, the amount of physical capital per worker in Androde rises to 400, but that during that time, Androde switches to Method 2. In your diagram, label the resulting point of production *C*. Using the Rule of 70, calculate by how many percent per year output per worker has grown now.

d. As the economy of Androde moves from point *A* to point *C*, which percentage of the annual productivity growth is due to higher total factor productivity?

6. The Bureau of Labor Statistics regularly releases the "Productivity and Costs" report for the previous month. Go to www.bls.gov and find the latest report. (On the Bureau of Labor Statistics home page, under Latest Numbers, find "Productivity" and click on "News Release.") What were the percent changes in business and nonfarm business productivity for the previous quarter (on the basis of annualized rates for output per hour of all persons)? How does the percent change in that quarter's productivity compare to data from the previous quarter?

7. How have U.S. policies and institutions influenced the country's long-run economic growth?

8. Over the next 100 years, real GDP per capita in Groland is expected to grow at an average annual rate of 2.0%. In Sloland, however, growth is expected to be somewhat slower, at an average annual growth rate of 1.5%. If both countries have a real GDP per capita today of $20,000, how will their real GDP per capita differ in 100 years? [*Hint:* A country that has a real GDP today of x and grows at y% per year will achieve a real GDP of $x \times (1 + 0.0y)^z$ in z years. We assume that $0 \le y < 10$.]

9. The accompanying table shows data on real GDP per capita in 2000 U.S. dollars for several countries in 1950 and 2004. (*Source:* The Penn World Table, Version 6.2) Complete the table. Have these countries converged economically?

	1950		2004	
	Real GDP per capita (2000 dollars)	Percentage of U.S. real GDP per capita	Real GDP per capita (2000 dollars)	Percentage of U.S. real GDP per capita
France	$5,921	?	$26,168	?
Japan	2,188	?	24,661	?
United Kingdom	8,082	?	26,762	?
United States	11,233	?	36,098	?

10. The accompanying table shows data on real GDP per capita in 2000 U.S. dollars for several countries in 1960 and 2003. (*Source:* The Penn World Table, Version 6.2.) Complete the table. Have these countries converged economically?

	1960		2003	
	Real GDP per capita (2000 dollars)	Percentage of U.S. real GDP per capita	Real GDP per capita (2000 dollars)	Percentage of U.S. real GDP per capita
Argentina	$7,838	?	$10,170	?
Ghana	412	?	1,440	?
South Korea	1,458	?	17,597	?
United States	12,892	?	34,875	?

11. Why would you expect real GDP per capita in California and Pennsylvania to exhibit convergence but not in California and Baja California, a state of Mexico that borders the United States? What changes would allow California and Baja California to converge?

12. According to the *Oil & Gas Journal*, the proven oil reserves of the top 12 oil producers was 1,137 billion barrels of oil in 2007. In that year, the U.S. Energy Information Administration reported that the daily oil production from these nations was 48.2 million barrels a day.

    a. At this rate, how many years will the proven oil reserves of the top 12 oil producers last? Discuss the Malthusian view in the context of the number you just calculated.

    b. What are some important assumptions implicit in your calculations that challenge the Malthusian view on this issue?

    c. Discuss how market forces may affect the amount of time the proven oil reserves will last, assuming that no new oil reserves are discovered and that the demand curve for oil remains unchanged.

13. The accompanying table shows the percent change in verified emissions of carbon dioxide (CO_2) and the percent change in real GDP per capita for selected EU countries.

Country	Percent change in real GDP per capita 2005–2007	Percent change in CO_2 emissions 2005–2007
Austria	6.30%	−4.90%
Belgium	4.19	−4.60
Cyprus	5.56	6.20
Finland	9.23	28.50
France	2.76	−3.50
Germany	5.79	2.50
Greece	8.09	2.00
Ireland	6.56	−5.30
Italy	2.28	0.20
Luxembourg	8.55	−1.40
Netherlands	4.61	−0.60
Portugal	2.67	−14.40
Slovenia	11.79	3.80
Spain	4.28	1.60

Sources: European Commission Press Release, May 23, 2008; International Monetary Fund, *World Factbook* 2008.

a. Rank the countries in terms of percentage increase in CO_2 emissions, from highest to lowest. What five countries have the highest percentage increase in emissions? What five countries have the lowest percentage increase in emissions?

b. Now rank the countries in terms of the percentage increase in real GDP per person, from highest to lowest. What five countries have the highest percentage increase? What five countries have the lowest percentage increase?

c. Would you infer from your results that CO_2 emissions are linked to growth in output per person?

d. Do high growth rates necessarily lead to high CO_2 emissions?

The Open Economy: International Trade and Finance

"You should see, when they come in the door, the shopping bags they hand off to the coat check. I mean, they're just spending. It's Monopoly money to them." So declared a New York restaurant manager, describing the European tourists who, in the summer of 2008, accounted for a large share of her business. Meanwhile, American tourists in Europe were suffering sticker shock. One American, whose family of four was visiting Paris, explained his changing vacation plans: "We might not stay as long. We might eat cheese sandwiches."

It was quite a change from 2000, when an article in the *New York Times* bore the headline: "Dollar makes the good life a tourist bargain in Europe." What happened? The answer is that there was a large shift in the relative values of the euro, the currency used by much of Europe, and the U.S. dollar. At its low point in 2000, a euro was worth only about

Bloomberg via Getty Images

85 cents. By mid-2008 it was worth more than $1.50, and in early 2010 it's value had fallen again, to less than $1.28.

What causes the relative value of the dollar and the euro to change? What are the effects of such changes? These are among the questions addressed by *open-economy macroeconomics,* the branch of macroeconomics that deals with the relationships between national economies. In this section we'll learn about some of the key issues in open-economy macroeconomics: the determinants of a country's *balance of payments,* the factors affecting *exchange rates,* the different forms of *exchange rate policy* adopted by various countries, and the relationship between exchange rates and macroeconomic policy. In the final module we will apply what we have learned about macroeconomic modeling to conduct policy analysis.

Module 41
Capital Flows and the Balance of Payments

Capital Flows and the Balance of Payments

In 2008, people living in the United States sold about $3.5 trillion worth of stuff to people living in other countries and bought about $3.5 trillion worth of stuff in return. What kind of stuff? All kinds. Residents of the United States (including employees of firms operating in the United States) sold airplanes, bonds, wheat, and many other items to residents of other countries. Residents of the United States bought cars, stocks, oil, and many other items from residents of other countries.

How can we keep track of these transactions? Earlier we learned that economists keep track of the domestic economy using the national income and product accounts. Economists keep track of international transactions using a different but related set of numbers, the *balance of payments accounts*.

> A country's **balance of payments accounts** are a summary of the country's transactions with other countries.

Balance of Payments Accounts

A country's **balance of payments accounts** are a summary of the country's transactions with other countries.

To understand the basic idea behind the balance of payments accounts, let's consider a small-scale example: not a country, but a family farm. Let's say that we know the following about how last year went financially for the Costas, who own a small artichoke farm in California:

- They made $100,000 by selling artichokes.

- They spent $70,000 on running the farm, including purchases of new farm machinery, and another $40,000 buying food, paying utility bills for their home, replacing their worn-out car, and so on.

- They received $500 in interest on their bank account but paid $10,000 in interest on their mortgage.

- They took out a new $25,000 loan to help pay for farm improvements but didn't use all the money immediately. So they put the extra in the bank.

table 41.1

The Costas' Financial Year

	Sources of cash	Uses of cash	Net
Purchases or sales of goods and services	Artichoke sales: $100,000	Farm operation and living expenses: $110,000	–$10,000
Interest payments	Interest received on bank account: $500	Interest paid on mortgage: $10,000	–$9,500
Loans and deposits	Funds received from new loan: $25,000	Funds deposited in bank: $5,500	+$19,500
Total	$125,500	$125,500	$0

How could we summarize the Costas' year? One way would be with a table like Table 41.1, which shows sources of cash coming in and money going out, characterized under a few broad headings. The first row of Table 41.1 shows sales and purchases of goods and services: sales of artichokes; purchases of groceries, heating oil, that new car, and so on. The second row shows interest payments: the interest the Costas received from their bank account and the interest they paid on their mortgage. The third row shows cash coming in from new borrowing versus money deposited in the bank.

In each row we show the net inflow of cash from that type of transaction. So the net in the first row is –$10,000 because the Costas spent $10,000 more than they earned. The net in the second row is –$9,500, the difference between the interest the Costas received on their bank account and the interest they paid on the mortgage. The net in the third row is $19,500: the Costas brought in $25,000 with their new loan but put only $5,500 of that sum in the bank.

The last row shows the sum of cash coming in from all sources and the sum of all cash used. These sums are equal, by definition: every dollar has a source, and every dollar received gets used somewhere. (What if the Costas hid money under the mattress? Then that would be counted as another "use" of cash.)

A country's balance of payments accounts summarize its transactions with the world using a table similar to the one we just used to summarize the Costas' financial year.

Table 41.2 on the next page shows a simplified version of the U.S. balance of payments accounts for 2008. Where the Costa family's accounts show sources and uses of cash, the balance of payments accounts show payments from foreigners—in effect, sources of cash for the United States as a whole—and payments to foreigners.

Row 1 of Table 41.2 shows payments that arise from sales and purchases of goods and services. For example, the value of U.S. wheat exports and the fees foreigners pay to U.S. consulting companies appear in the second column of row 1; the value of U.S. oil imports and the fees American companies pay to Indian call centers—the people who often answer your 1-800 calls—appear in the third column of row 1.

Row 2 shows *factor income*—payments for the use of factors of production owned by residents of other countries. Mostly this means investment income: interest paid on loans from overseas, the profits of foreign-owned corporations, and so on. For example, the profits earned by Disneyland Paris, which is owned by the U.S.-based Walt Disney Company, appear in the second column of row 2; the profits earned by the U.S. operations of Japanese auto companies appear in the third column. Factor income also includes labor income. For example, the wages of an American engineer who works temporarily on a construction site in Dubai are counted in the second column of row 2.

Row 3 shows *international transfers*—funds sent by residents of one country to residents of another. The main element here is the remittances that immigrants, such as the millions of Mexican-born workers employed in the United States,

table 41.2

The U.S. Balance of Payments in 2008 (billions of dollars)

	Payments from foreigners	Payments to foreigners	Net
1 Sales and purchases of goods and services	$1,827	$2,523	−$696
2 Factor income	765	646	119
3 Transfers	—	—	−128
Current account (1 + 2 + 3)			−705
4 Official asset sales and purchases	487	530	−43
5 Private sales and purchases of assets	47	−534	581
Financial account (4 + 5)			538
Total	—	—	−167

Source: Bureau of Economic Analysis.

send to their families in their country of origin. Notice that Table 41.2 shows only the net value of transfers. That's because the U.S. government provides only an estimate of the net, not a breakdown between payments to foreigners and payments from foreigners.

The next two rows of Table 41.2 show payments resulting from sales and purchases of assets, broken down by who is doing the buying and selling. Row 4 shows transactions that involve governments or government agencies, mainly central banks. As we'll learn later, in 2008, most of the U.S. sales in this category involved the accumulation of *foreign exchange reserves* by the central banks of China and oil-exporting countries. Row 5 shows private sales and purchases of assets. For example, the 2008 purchase of Budweiser, an American brewing company, by the Belgian corporation InBev showed up in the second column of row 5; purchases of European stocks by U.S. investors show up as positive values in the third column. However, because U.S. residents sold more foreign assets than they purchased in 2008, the value for this category is negative.

In laying out Table 41.2, we have separated rows 1, 2, and 3 into one group and rows 4 and 5 into another. This reflects a fundamental difference in how these two groups of transactions affect the future.

When a U.S. resident sells a good, such as wheat, to a foreigner, that's the end of the transaction. But a financial asset, such as a bond, is different. Remember, a bond is a promise to pay interest and principal in the future. So when a U.S. resident sells a bond to a foreigner, that sale creates a liability: the U.S. resident will have to pay interest and repay principal in the future. The balance of payments accounts distinguish between transactions that don't create liabilities and those that do.

Transactions that don't create liabilities are considered part of the **balance of payments on the current account,** often referred to simply as the **current account:** the balance of payments on goods and services plus factor income and net international transfer payments. The balance of row 1 of Table 41.2, −$696 billion, corresponds to the most important part of the current account: **the balance of payments on goods and services,** the difference between the value of exports and the value of imports during a given period.

By the way, if you read news reports on the economy, you may well see references to another measure, the **merchandise trade balance,** sometimes referred to as the **trade balance** for short. This is the difference between a country's exports and imports of

A country's **balance of payments on the current account,** or the **current account,** is its balance of payments on goods and services plus net international transfer payments and factor income.

A country's **balance of payments on goods and services** is the difference between its exports and its imports during a given period.

The **merchandise trade balance,** or **trade balance,** is the difference between a country's exports and imports of goods.

goods alone—not including services. Economists sometimes focus on the merchandise trade balance, even though it's an incomplete measure, because data on international trade in services aren't as accurate as data on trade in physical goods, and they are also slower to arrive.

The current account, as we've just learned, consists of international transactions that don't create liabilities. Transactions that involve the sale or purchase of assets, and therefore do create future liabilities, are considered part of the **balance of payments on the financial account,** or the **financial account** for short. (Until a few years ago, economists often referred to the financial account as the *capital account*. We'll use the modern term, but you may run across the older term.)

So how does it all add up? The shaded rows of Table 41.2 show the bottom lines: the overall U.S. current account and financial account for 2008. As you can see, in 2008, the United States ran a current account deficit: the amount it paid to foreigners for goods, services, factors, and transfers was greater than the amount it received. Simultaneously, it ran a financial account surplus: the value of the assets it sold to foreigners was greater than the value of the assets it bought from foreigners.

In the official data, the U.S. current account deficit and financial account surplus almost, but not quite, offset each other: the financial account surplus was $167 billion smaller than the current account deficit. But that's just a statistical error, reflecting the imperfection of official data. (And a $167 billion error when you're measuring inflows and outflows of $3.5 trillion isn't bad!) In fact, it's a basic rule of balance of payments accounting that the current account and the financial account must sum to zero:

(41-1) Current account (CA) + Financial account (FA) = 0

or

$$CA = -FA$$

Why must Equation 41-1 be true? We already saw the fundamental explanation in Table 41.1, which showed the accounts of the Costa family: in total, the sources of cash must equal the uses of cash. The same applies to balance of payments accounts. Figure 41.1 on the next page, a variant on the circular-flow diagram we have found useful in discussing domestic macroeconomics, may help you visualize how this adding up works.

Instead of showing the flow of money *within* a national economy, Figure 41.1 shows the flow of money *between* national economies. Money flows into the United States from the rest of the world as payment for U.S. exports of goods and services, as payment for the use of U.S.-owned factors of production, and as transfer payments. These flows (indicated by the lower green arrow) are the positive components of the U.S. current account. Money also flows into the United States from foreigners who purchase U.S. assets (as shown by the lower red arrow)—the positive component of the U.S. financial account.

At the same time, money flows from the United States to the rest of the world as payment for U.S. imports of goods and services, as payment for the use of foreign-owned factors of production, and as transfer payments. These flows, indicated by the upper green arrow, are the negative components of the U.S. current account. Money also flows from the United States to purchase foreign assets, as shown by the upper red arrow—the negative component of the U.S. financial account. As in all circular-flow diagrams, the flow into a box and the flow out of a box are equal. This means

A country's **balance of payments on the financial account,** or simply the **financial account,** is the difference between its sales of assets to foreigners and its purchases of assets from foreigners during a given period.

The Balance of Payments

The green arrows represent payments that are counted in the current account. The red arrows represent payments that are counted in the financial account. Because the total flow into the United States must equal the total flow out of the United States, the sum of the current account plus the financial account is zero.

Payments to the rest of the world for assets

Payments to the rest of the world for goods and services, factor income, and transfers

United States

Rest of world

Payments to the United States for goods and services, factor income, and transfers

Payments to the United States for assets

that the sum of the red and green arrows going into the United States is equal to the sum of the red and green arrows going out of the United States. That is,

(41-2) Positive entries on the current account (lower green arrow) + Positive entries on the financial account (lower red arrow) = Negative entries on the current account (upper green arrow) + Negative entries on the financial account (upper red arrow)

Equation 41-2 can be rearranged as follows:

(41-3) Positive entries on the current account − Negative entries on the current account + Positive entries on the financial account − Negative entries on the financial account = 0

fyi

GDP, GNP, and the Current Account

When we discussed national income accounting, we derived the basic equation relating GDP to the components of spending:

$$Y = C + I + G + X - IM$$

where X and IM are exports and imports, respectively, of goods and services. But as we've learned, the balance of payments on goods and services is only one component of the current account balance. Why doesn't the national income equation use the current account as a whole?

The answer is that gross domestic product, which is the value of goods and services produced in a country, doesn't include two sources of income that are included in calculating the current account balance: international factor income and international transfers. The profits of Ford Motors

U.K. aren't included in America's GDP, and the funds Latin American immigrants send home to their families aren't subtracted from GDP.

Shouldn't we have a broader measure that does include these sources of income? Actually, gross national product—GNP—does include international factor income. Estimates of U.S. GNP differ slightly from estimates of GDP because GNP adds in items such as the earnings of U.S. companies abroad and subtracts items such as the interest payments on bonds owned by residents of China and Japan. There isn't, however, any regularly calculated measure that includes transfer payments.

Why do economists use GDP rather than a broader measure? Two reasons. First, the original purpose of the national accounts was to track

The funds Latin American immigrants send home through Western Union wires, as advertised on this billboard, aren't subtracted from GDP.

production rather than income. Second, data on international factor income and transfer payments are generally considered somewhat unreliable. So if you're trying to keep track of movements in the economy, it makes sense to focus on GDP, which doesn't rely on these unreliable data.

Equation 41-3 is equivalent to Equation 41-1: the current account plus the financial account—both equal to positive entries minus negative entries—is equal to zero.

But what determines the current account and the financial account?

Modeling the Financial Account

A country's financial account measures its net sales of assets, such as currencies, securities, and factories, to foreigners. Those assets are exchanged for a type of capital called *financial capital,* which is funds from savings that are available for investment spending. We can thus think of the financial account as a measure of *capital inflows* in the form of foreign savings that become available to finance domestic investment spending.

What determines these capital inflows?

Part of our explanation will have to wait for a little while because some international capital flows are created by governments and central banks, which sometimes act very differently from private investors. But we can gain insight into the motivations for capital flows that are the result of private decisions by using the *loanable funds model* we developed previously. In using this model, we make two important simplifications:

■ We simplify the reality of international capital flows by assuming that all flows are in the form of loans. In reality, capital flows take many forms, including purchases of shares of stock in foreign companies and foreign real estate as well as *foreign direct investment,* in which companies build factories or acquire other productive assets abroad.

■ We also ignore the effects of expected changes in *exchange rates,* the relative values of different national currencies. We'll analyze the determination of exchange rates later.

Figure 41.2 recaps the loanable funds model for a closed economy. Equilibrium corresponds to point *E,* at an interest rate of 4%, at which the supply of loanable funds (*S*) intersects the demand (*D*). If international capital flows are possible, this diagram changes and *E* may no longer be the equilibrium. We can analyze the causes and effects of international capital flows using Figure 41.3 on the next page, which places the loanable funds market diagrams for two countries side by side.

Figure 41.3 illustrates a world consisting of only two countries, the United States and Britain. Panel (a) shows the loanable funds market in the United States, where

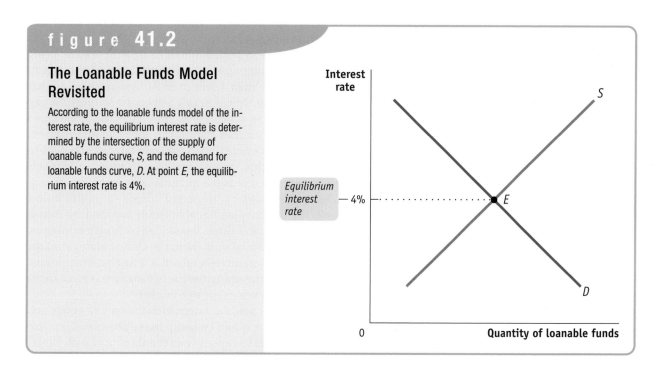

figure 41.2

The Loanable Funds Model Revisited

According to the loanable funds model of the interest rate, the equilibrium interest rate is determined by the intersection of the supply of loanable funds curve, *S,* and the demand for loanable funds curve, *D.* At point *E,* the equilibrium interest rate is 4%.

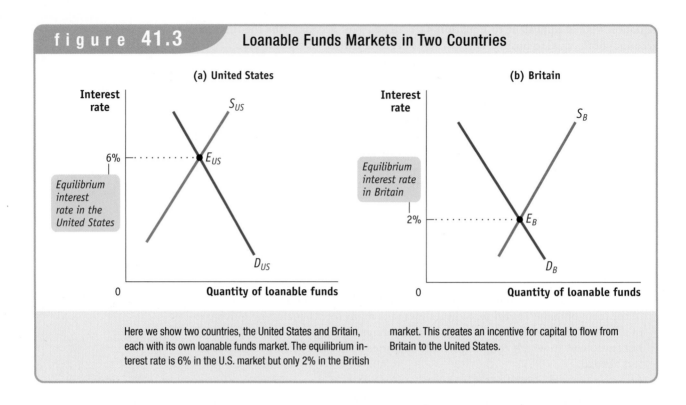

figure 41.3 | Loanable Funds Markets in Two Countries

(a) United States

Interest rate

S_{US}

6% .... E_{US}

D_{US}

Equilibrium interest rate in the United States

0   Quantity of loanable funds

(b) Britain

Interest rate

S_B

Equilibrium interest rate in Britain

2% .... E_B

D_B

0   Quantity of loanable funds

Here we show two countries, the United States and Britain, each with its own loanable funds market. The equilibrium interest rate is 6% in the U.S. market but only 2% in the British market. This creates an incentive for capital to flow from Britain to the United States.

the equilibrium in the absence of international capital flows is at point E_{US} with an interest rate of 6%. Panel (b) shows the loanable funds market in Britain, where the equilibrium in the absence of international capital flows is at point E_B with an interest rate of 2%.

Will the actual interest rate in the United States remain at 6% and that in Britain at 2%? Not if it is easy for British residents to make loans to Americans. In that case, British lenders, attracted by high American interest rates, will send some of their loanable funds to the United States. This capital inflow will increase the quantity of loanable funds supplied to American borrowers, pushing the U.S. interest rate down. At the same time, it will reduce the quantity of loanable funds supplied to British borrowers, pushing the British interest rate up. So international capital flows will narrow the gap between U.S. and British interest rates.

Let's further suppose that British lenders regard a loan to an American as being just as good as a loan to one of their own compatriots, and American borrowers regard a debt to a British lender as no more costly than a debt to an American lender. In that case, the flow of funds from Britain to the United States will continue until the gap between their interest rates is eliminated. In other words, international capital flows will equalize the interest rates in the two countries. Figure 41.4 shows an international equilibrium in the loanable funds markets where the equilibrium interest rate is 4% in both the United States and Britain. At this interest rate, the quantity of loanable funds demanded by American borrowers exceeds the quantity of loanable funds supplied by American lenders. This gap is filled by "imported" funds—a capital inflow from Britain. At the same time, the quantity of loanable funds supplied by British lenders is greater than the quantity of loanable funds demanded by British borrowers. This excess is "exported" in the form of a capital outflow to the United States. And the two markets are in equilibrium at a common interest rate of 4%. At that interest rate, the total quantity of loans demanded by borrowers across the two markets is equal to the total quantity of loans supplied by lenders across the two markets.

In short, international flows of capital are like international flows of goods and services. Capital moves from places where it would be cheap in the absence of international capital flows to places where it would be expensive in the absence of such flows.

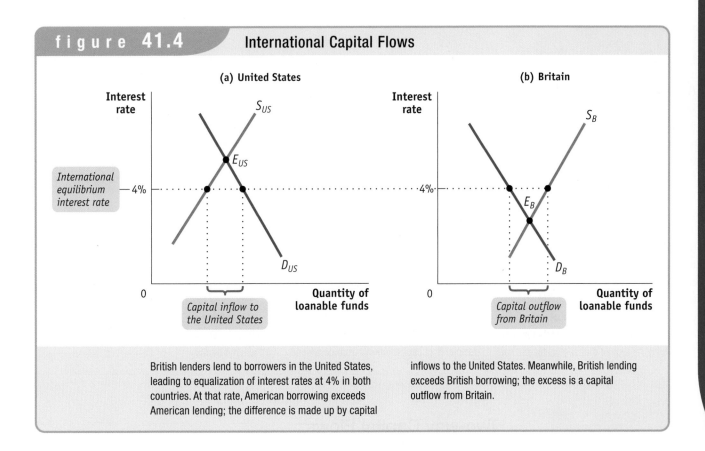

figure 41.4   **International Capital Flows**

British lenders lend to borrowers in the United States, leading to equalization of interest rates at 4% in both countries. At that rate, American borrowing exceeds American lending; the difference is made up by capital inflows to the United States. Meanwhile, British lending exceeds British borrowing; the excess is a capital outflow from Britain.

Underlying Determinants of International Capital Flows

The open-economy version of the loanable funds model helps us understand international capital flows in terms of the supply and demand for funds. But what underlies differences across countries in the supply and demand for funds? And why, in the absence of international capital flows, would interest rates differ internationally, creating an incentive for international capital flows?

International differences in the demand for funds reflect underlying differences in investment opportunities. In particular, a country with a rapidly growing economy, other things equal, tends to offer more investment opportunities than a country with a slowly growing economy. So a rapidly growing economy typically—though not always—has a higher demand for capital and offers higher returns to investors than a slowly growing economy in the absence of capital flows. As a result, capital tends to flow from slowly growing to rapidly growing economies.

The classic example is the flow of capital from Britain to the United States, among other countries, between 1870 and 1914. During that era, the U.S. economy was growing rapidly as the population increased and spread westward and as the nation industrialized. This created a demand for investment spending on railroads, factories, and so on. Meanwhile, Britain had a much more slowly growing population, was already industrialized, and already had a railroad network covering the country. This left Britain with savings to spare, much of which were lent to the United States and other New World economies.

International differences in the supply of funds reflect differences in savings across countries. These may be the result of differences in private savings rates, which vary widely among countries. For example, in 2006, private savings were 26.5% of Japan's GDP but only 14.8% of U.S. GDP. They may also reflect differences in savings by governments. In particular, government budget deficits, which reduce overall national savings, can lead to capital inflows.

A Global Savings Glut?

In the early years of the twenty-first century, the United States entered into a massive current account deficit, which meant that it became the recipient of huge capital inflows from the rest of the world, especially China, other Asian countries, and the Middle East. Why did that happen?

In an influential speech early in 2005, Ben Bernanke—who was at that time a governor of the Federal Reserve and who would soon become the Fed's chair—offered a hypothesis: the United States wasn't responsible. The "principal causes of the U.S. current account deficit," he declared, lie "outside the country's borders." Specifically, he argued that special factors had created a "global savings glut" that had pushed down interest rates worldwide and thereby led to an excess of investment spending over savings in the United States.

What caused this global savings glut? According to Bernanke, the main cause was the series of financial crises that began in Thailand in 1997, ricocheted across much of Asia, and then hit Russia in 1998, Brazil in 1999, and Argentina in 2002. The ensuing fear and economic devastation led to a fall in investment spending and a rise in savings in many relatively poor countries. As a result, a number of these countries, which had previously been the recipients of capital inflows from developed countries like the United States, began experiencing large capital outflows. For the most part, the capital flowed to the United States, perhaps because "the depth and sophistication of the country's financial markets" made it an attractive destination.

When Bernanke gave his speech, it was viewed as reassuring: basically, he argued that the United States was responding in a sensible way to the availability of cheap money in world financial markets. Later, however, it would become clear that the cheap money from abroad helped fuel a housing bubble, which caused widespread financial and economic damage when it burst.

Two-way Capital Flows

The loanable funds model helps us understand the direction of *net* capital flows—the excess of inflows into a country over outflows, or vice versa. As we saw in Table 41.2, however, *gross* flows take place in both directions: for example, the United States both sells assets to foreigners and buys assets from foreigners. Why does capital move in both directions?

The answer to this question is that in the real world, as opposed to the simple model we've just constructed, there are other motives for international capital flows besides seeking a higher rate of interest. Individual investors often seek to diversify against risk by buying stocks in a number of countries. Stocks in Europe may do well when stocks in the United States do badly, or vice versa, so investors in Europe try to reduce their risk by buying some U.S. stocks, even as investors in the United States try to reduce their risk by buying some European stocks. The result is capital flows in both directions. Meanwhile, corporations often engage in international investment as part of their business strategy—for example, auto companies may find that they can compete better in a national market if they assemble some of their cars locally. Such business investments can also lead to two-way capital flows, as, say, European carmakers build plants in the United States even as U.S. computer companies open facilities in Europe.

Finally, some countries, including the United States, are international banking centers: people from all over the world put money in U.S. financial institutions, which then invest many of those funds overseas.

Nike, like many other companies, has opened plants in China to take advantage of low labor costs and to gain better access to the large Chinese market. Here, two Chinese employees assemble running shoes in a Nike factory in China.

The result of these two-way flows is that modern economies are typically both debtors (countries that owe money to the rest of the world) and creditors (countries to which the rest of the world owes money). Due to years of both capital inflows and outflows, at the end of 2008, the United States had accumulated foreign assets worth $19.9 trillion and foreigners had accumulated assets in the United States worth $23.3 trillion.

The Golden Age of Capital Flows

Technology, it's often said, shrinks the world. Jet planes have put most of the world's cities within a few hours of one another; modern telecommunications transmit information instantly around the globe. So you might think that international capital flows must now be larger than ever.

But if capital flows are measured as a share of world savings and investment, that belief turns out not to be true. The golden age of capital flows actually preceded World War I—it lasted from 1870 to 1914.

These capital flows went mainly from European countries, especially Britain, to what were then known as "zones of recent settlement," countries that were attracting large numbers of European immigrants. Among the big recipients of capital inflows were Australia, Argentina, Canada, and the United States.

The large capital flows reflected differences in investment opportunities. Britain, a mature industrial economy with limited natural resources and a slowly growing population, offered relatively limited opportunities for new investment. The zones of recent settlement, with rapidly growing populations and abundant natural resources, offered investors a higher return and attracted capital inflows. Estimates suggest that over this period Britain sent about 40% of its savings abroad, largely to finance railroads and other large projects. No country has matched that record in modern times.

Why can't we match the capital flows of our great-great-grandfathers? Economists aren't completely sure, but they have pointed to two causes: migration restrictions and political risks.

During the golden age of capital flows, capital movements were complementary to population movements: the big recipients of capital from Europe were also places to which large numbers of Europeans were moving. These large-scale population movements were possible before World War I because there were few legal restrictions on immigration. In today's world, by contrast, migration is limited by extensive legal barriers, as anyone considering a move to the United States or Europe can tell you.

The other factor that has changed is political risk. Modern governments often limit foreign investment because they fear it will diminish their national autonomy. And due to political or security concerns, governments sometimes seize foreign property, a risk that deters investors from sending more than a relatively modest share of their wealth abroad. In the nineteenth century such actions were rare, partly because some major destinations of investment were still European colonies and partly because in those days governments had a habit of sending troops and gunboats to enforce the claims of their investors.

Module 41 AP Review

Solutions appear at the back of the book.

Check Your Understanding

1. Which of the balance of payments accounts do the following events affect?
   a. Boeing, a U.S.-based company, sells a newly built airplane to China.
   b. Chinese investors buy stock in Boeing from Americans.
   c. A Chinese company buys a used airplane from American Airlines and ships it to China.
   d. A Chinese investor who owns property in the United States buys a corporate jet, which he will keep in the United States so he can travel around America.

Tackle the Test: Multiple-Choice Questions

1. The current account includes which of the following?
   I. payments for goods and services
   II. transfer payments
   III. factor income
   a. I only
   b. II only
   c. III only
   d. I and II only
   e. I, II, and III

2. The balance of payments on the current account plus the balance of payments on the financial account is equal to
   a. zero.
   b. one.
   c. the trade balance.
   d. net capital flows.
   e. the size of the trade deficit.

3. The financial account was previously known as the
   a. gross national product.
   b. capital account.
   c. trade deficit.
   d. investment account.
   e. trade balance.

4. The trade balance includes which of the following?
      I. imports and exports of goods
      II. imports and exports of services
      III. net capital flows
   a. I only
   b. II only
   c. III only
   d. I and II only
   e. I, II, and III

5. Which of the following will increase the demand for loanable funds in a country?
   a. economic growth
   b. decreased investment opportunities
   c. a recession
   d. decreased private savings rates
   e. government budget surpluses

Tackle the Test: Free-Response Questions

1. a. How would a decrease in real income in the United States affect the U.S. current account balance? Explain.
   b. Suppose China decides that it needs a huge program of infrastructure spending, which it will finance by borrowing. How will this program affect the U.S. balance of payments? Explain.

2. Use two correctly labeled side-by-side graphs of the loanable funds market in the United States and China to show how a higher interest rate in the United States will lead to capital flows between the two countries. On your graphs, be sure to label the starting and ending interest rates and the size of the capital inflows and outflows.

Answer (4 points)

1 point: The current account balance will increase (or move toward a surplus).

1 point: The decrease in income will cause imports to decrease.

1 point: The increase in infrastructure spending in China will reduce the surplus in the U.S. financial account and reduce the deficit in the U.S. current account.

1 point: Because China is financing the program by borrowing, it is likely that other countries will increase their lending to China, decreasing their lending to the United States. These capital outflows from the United States will reduce the U.S. surplus in the financial account and reduce the deficit in the current account.

Module 42
The Foreign Exchange Market

The Role of the Exchange Rate

We've just seen how differences in the supply of loanable funds from savings and the demand for loanable funds for investment spending lead to international capital flows. We've also learned that a country's balance of payments on the current account plus its balance of payments on the financial account add up to zero: a country that receives net capital inflows must run a matching current account deficit, and a country that generates net capital outflows must run a matching current account surplus.

The behavior of the financial account—reflecting inflows or outflows of capital—is best described as equilibrium in the international loanable funds market. At the same time, the balance of payments on goods and services, the main component of the current account, is determined by decisions in the international markets for goods and services. So given that the financial account reflects the movement of capital and the current account reflects the movement of goods and services, what ensures that the balance of payments really does balance? That is, what ensures that the two accounts actually offset each other?

The answer lies in the role of the *exchange rate,* which is determined in the *foreign exchange market.*

Understanding Exchange Rates

In general, goods, services, and assets produced in a country must be paid for in that country's currency. American products must be paid for in dollars; European products must be paid for in euros; Japanese products must be paid for in yen. Occasionally, sellers will accept payment in foreign currency, but they will then exchange that currency for domestic money.

International transactions, then, require a market—the **foreign exchange market**— in which currencies can be exchanged for each other. This market determines **exchange rates,** the prices at which currencies trade. (The foreign exchange market is, in fact, not located in any one geographic spot. Rather, it is a global electronic market that traders around the world use to buy and sell currencies.)

Currencies are traded in the **foreign exchange market.**

The prices at which currencies trade are known as **exchange rates.**

table **42.1**

Exchange Rates, April 30, 2010, 9:40 A.M.

	U.S. dollars	Yen	Euros
One U.S. dollar exchanged for	1	94.20	0.7479
One yen exchanged for	0.010616	1	0.00796
One euro exchanged for	1.3371	125.6	1

Table 42.1 shows exchange rates among the world's three most important currencies as of 9:40 A.M., EST, on April 30, 2010. Each entry shows the price of the "row" currency in terms of the "column" currency. For example, at that time US$1 exchanged for €0.7479, so it took €0.7479 to buy US$1. Similarly, it took US$1.3371 to buy €1. These two numbers reflect the same rate of exchange between the euro and the U.S. dollar: 1/1.3371 = €0.7479.

There are two ways to write any given exchange rate. In this case, there were €0.7479 to US$1 and US$1.3371 to €1. Which is the correct way to write it? The answer is that there is no fixed rule. In most countries, people tend to express the exchange rate as the price of a dollar in domestic currency. However, this rule isn't universal, and the U.S. dollar–euro rate is commonly quoted both ways. The important thing is to be sure you know which one you are using!

When discussing movements in exchange rates, economists use specialized terms to avoid confusion. When a currency becomes more valuable in terms of other currencies, economists say that the currency **appreciates.** When a currency becomes less valuable in terms of other currencies, it **depreciates.** Suppose, for example, that the value of €1 went from $1 to $1.25, which means that the value of US$1 went from €1 to €0.80 (because 1/1.25 = 0.80). In this case, we would say that the euro appreciated and the U.S. dollar depreciated.

Movements in exchange rates, other things equal, affect the relative prices of goods, services, and assets in different countries. Suppose, for example, that the price of an American hotel room is US$100 and the price of a French hotel room is €100. If the exchange rate is €1 = US$1, these hotel rooms have the same price. If the exchange rate is €1.25 = US$1, the French hotel room is 20% cheaper than the American hotel room. If the exchange rate is €0.80 = US$1, the French hotel room is 25% more expensive than the American hotel room.

But what determines exchange rates? Supply and demand in the foreign exchange market.

The Equilibrium Exchange Rate

Imagine, for the sake of simplicity, that there are only two currencies in the world: U.S. dollars and euros. Europeans who want to purchase American goods, services, and assets come to the foreign exchange market to exchange euros for U.S. dollars. That is, Europeans demand U.S. dollars from the foreign exchange market and, correspondingly, supply euros to that market. Americans who want to buy European goods, services, and assets come to the foreign exchange market to exchange U.S. dollars for euros. That is, Americans supply U.S. dollars to the foreign exchange market and, correspondingly, demand euros from that market. (International transfers and payments of factor income also enter into the foreign exchange market, but to make things simple, we'll ignore these.)

Figure 42.1 shows how the foreign exchange market works. The quantity of dollars demanded and supplied at any given euro–U.S. dollar exchange rate is shown on the horizontal axis, and the euro–U.S. dollar exchange rate is shown on the vertical axis. The exchange rate plays the same role as the price of a good or service in an ordinary supply and demand diagram.

The figure shows two curves, the demand curve for U.S. dollars and the supply curve for U.S. dollars. The key to understanding the slopes of these curves is that the level of the exchange rate affects exports and imports. When a country's currency appreciates (becomes more valuable), exports fall and imports rise. When a country's currency depreciates (becomes less valuable), exports rise and imports fall. To understand why the demand curve for U.S. dollars slopes downward, recall that the exchange rate, other things equal, determines the prices of American goods, services, and assets relative to those of European goods, services, and assets. If the U.S. dollar rises against the euro

When a currency becomes more valuable in terms of other currencies, it **appreciates.**

When a currency becomes less valuable in terms of other currencies, it **depreciates.**

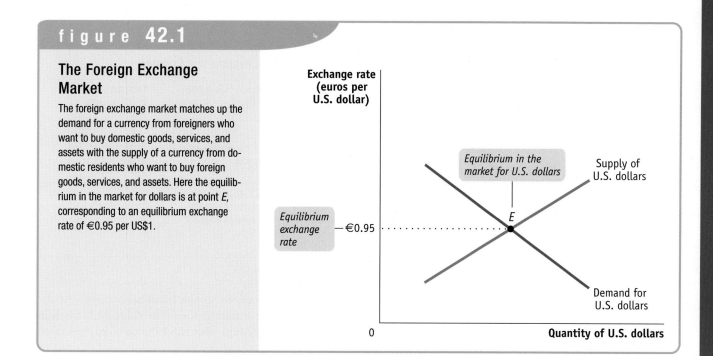

figure 42.1

The Foreign Exchange Market

The foreign exchange market matches up the demand for a currency from foreigners who want to buy domestic goods, services, and assets with the supply of a currency from domestic residents who want to buy foreign goods, services, and assets. Here the equilibrium in the market for dollars is at point *E*, corresponding to an equilibrium exchange rate of €0.95 per US$1.

(the dollar appreciates), American products will become more expensive to Europeans relative to European products. So Europeans will buy less from the United States and will acquire fewer dollars in the foreign exchange market: the quantity of U.S. dollars demanded falls as the number of euros needed to buy a U.S. dollar rises. If the U.S. dollar falls against the euro (the dollar depreciates), American products will become relatively cheaper for Europeans. Europeans will respond by buying more from the United States and acquiring more dollars in the foreign exchange market: the quantity of U.S. dollars demanded rises as the number of euros needed to buy a U.S. dollar falls.

A similar argument explains why the supply curve of U.S. dollars in Figure 42.1 slopes upward: the more euros required to buy a U.S. dollar, the more dollars Americans will supply. Again, the reason is the effect of the exchange rate on relative prices. If the U.S. dollar rises against the euro, European products look cheaper to Americans—who will demand more of them. This will require Americans to convert more dollars into euros.

The **equilibrium exchange rate** is the exchange rate at which the quantity of U.S. dollars demanded in the foreign exchange market is equal to the quantity of U.S. dollars supplied. In Figure 42.1, the equilibrium is at point *E*, and the equilibrium exchange rate is 0.95. That is, at an exchange rate of €0.95 per US$1, the quantity of U.S. dollars supplied to the foreign exchange market is equal to the quantity of U.S. dollars demanded.

To understand the significance of the equilibrium exchange rate, it's helpful to consider a numerical example of what equilibrium in the foreign exchange market looks like. Such an example is shown in Table 42.2 on the next page. (This is a hypothetical table that isn't intended to match real numbers.) The first row shows European purchases of U.S. dollars, either to buy U.S. goods and services or to buy U.S. assets such as real estate or shares of stock in U.S. companies. The second row shows U.S. sales of U.S. dollars, either to buy European goods and services or to buy European assets. At the equilibrium exchange rate, the total quantity of U.S. dollars Europeans want to buy is equal to the total quantity of U.S. dollars Americans want to sell.

Remember that the balance of payments accounts divide international transactions into two types. Purchases and sales of goods and services are counted in the current account. (Again, we're leaving out transfers and factor income to keep things

The **equilibrium exchange rate** is the exchange rate at which the quantity of a currency demanded in the foreign exchange market is equal to the quantity supplied.

table **42.2**

Equilibrium in the Foreign Exchange Market: A Hypothetical Example

European purchases of U.S. dollars (trillions of U.S. dollars)	To buy U.S. goods and services: 1.0	To buy U.S. assets: 1.0	Total purchases of U.S. dollars: 2.0
U.S. sales of U.S. dollars (trillions of U.S. dollars)	To buy European goods and services: 1.5	To buy European assets: 0.5	Total sales of U.S. dollars: 2.0
	U.S. balance of payments on the current account: −0.5	U.S. balance of payments on the financial account: +0.5	

simple.) Purchases and sales of assets are counted in the financial account. At the equilibrium exchange rate, then, we have the situation shown in Table 42.2: the sum of the balance of payments on the current account plus the balance of payments on the financial account is zero.

Now let's briefly consider how a shift in the demand for U.S. dollars affects equilibrium in the foreign exchange market. Suppose that for some reason capital flows from Europe to the United States increase—say, due to a change in the preferences of European investors. The effects are shown in Figure 42.2. The demand for U.S. dollars in the foreign exchange market increases as European investors convert euros into dollars to fund their new investments in the United States. This is shown by the shift of the demand curve from D_1 to D_2. As a result, the U.S. dollar appreciates: the number of euros per U.S. dollar at the equilibrium exchange rate rises from XR_1 to XR_2.

What are the consequences of this increased capital inflow for the balance of payments? The total quantity of U.S. dollars supplied to the foreign exchange market still must equal the total quantity of U.S. dollars demanded. So the increased capital inflow to the United States—an increase in the balance of payments on the financial

---

figure **42.2**

An Increase in the Demand for U.S. Dollars

An increase in the demand for U.S. dollars might result from a change in the preferences of European investors. The demand curve for U.S. dollars shifts from D_1 to D_2. So the equilibrium number of euros per U.S. dollar rises—the dollar *appreciates*. As a result, the balance of payments on the current account falls as the balance of payments on the financial account rises.

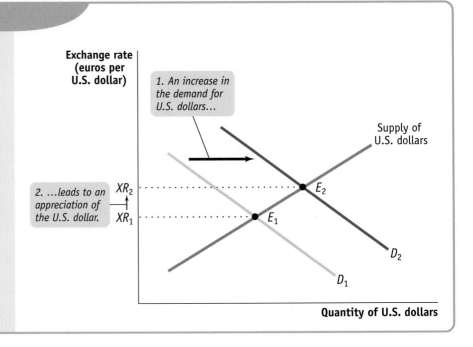

account—must be matched by a decline in the balance of payments on the current account. What causes the balance of payments on the current account to decline? The appreciation of the U.S. dollar. A rise in the number of euros per U.S. dollar leads Americans to buy more European goods and services and Europeans to buy fewer American goods and services.

Table 42.3 shows how this might work. Europeans are buying more U.S. assets, increasing the balance of payments on the financial account from 0.5 to 1.0. This is offset by a reduction in European purchases of U.S. goods and services and a rise in U.S. purchases of European goods and services, both the result of the dollar's appreciation. *So any change in the U.S. balance of payments on the financial account generates an equal and opposite reaction in the balance of payments on the current account.* Movements in the exchange rate ensure that changes in the financial account and in the current account offset each other.

table 42.3

Effects of Increased Capital Inflows

European purchases of U.S. dollars (trillions of U.S. dollars)	To buy U.S. goods and services: 0.75 (down 0.25)	To buy U.S. assets: 1.5 (up 0.5)	Total purchases of U.S. dollars: 2.25
U.S. sales of U.S. dollars (trillions of U.S. dollars)	To buy European goods and services: 1.75 (up 0.25)	To buy European assets: 0.5 (no change)	Total sales of U.S. dollars: 2.25
	U.S. balance of payments on the current account: −1.0 (down 0.5)	U.S. balance of payments on the financial account: +1.0 (up 0.5)	

Let's briefly run this process in reverse. Suppose there is a reduction in capital flows from Europe to the United States—again due to a change in the preferences of European investors. The demand for U.S. dollars in the foreign exchange market falls, and the dollar depreciates: the number of euros per U.S. dollar at the equilibrium exchange rate falls. This leads Americans to buy fewer European products and Europeans to buy more American products. Ultimately, this generates an increase in the U.S. balance of payments on the current account. So a fall in capital flows into the United States leads to a weaker dollar, which in turn generates an increase in U.S. net exports.

Real exchange rates are exchange rates adjusted for international differences in aggregate price levels.

Inflation and Real Exchange Rates

In 1990, one U.S. dollar exchanged, on average, for 2.8 Mexican pesos. By 2010, the peso had fallen against the dollar by more than 75%, with an average exchange rate in early 2010 of 12.8 pesos per dollar. Did Mexican products also become much cheaper relative to U.S. products over that 20-year period? Did the price of Mexican products expressed in terms of U.S. dollars also fall by more than 75%? The answer is no because Mexico had much higher inflation than the United States over that period. In fact, the relative price of U.S. and Mexican products changed little between 1990 and 2010, although the exchange rate changed a lot.

To take account of the effects of differences in inflation rates, economists calculate **real exchange rates,** exchange rates adjusted for international differences in aggregate price levels. Suppose that the exchange rate we are looking at is the number of Mexican pesos per U.S. dollar. Let P_{US} and P_{Mex} be indexes of the aggregate price levels in the United States and Mexico, respectively.

Keith Dannemiller/Alamy

The exchange rates listed at currency exchange booths are nominal exchange rates. The current account responds only to changes in real exchange rates, which have been adjusted for differing levels of inflation.

module **4 2** The Foreign Exchange Market **425**

Then the real exchange rate between the Mexican peso and the U.S. dollar is defined as:

(42-1) $\text{Real exchange rate} = \text{Mexican pesos per U.S. dollar} \times \dfrac{P_{US}}{P_{Mex}}$

To distinguish it from the real exchange rate, the exchange rate unadjusted for aggregate price levels is sometimes called the *nominal* exchange rate.

To understand the significance of the difference between the real and nominal exchange rates, let's consider the following example. Suppose that the Mexican peso depreciates against the U.S. dollar, with the exchange rate going from 10 pesos per U.S. dollar to 15 pesos per U.S. dollar, a 50% change. But suppose that at the same time the price of everything in Mexico, measured in pesos, increases by 50%, so that the Mexican price index rises from 100 to 150. We'll assume that there is no change in U.S. prices, so that the U.S. price index remains at 100. The initial real exchange rate is:

$$\text{Pesos per dollar} \times \frac{P_{US}}{P_{Mex}} = 10 \times \frac{100}{100} = 10$$

After the peso depreciates and the Mexican price level increases, the real exchange rate is:

$$\text{Pesos per dollar} \times \frac{P_{US}}{P_{Mex}} = 15 \times \frac{100}{150} = 10$$

In this example, the peso has depreciated substantially in terms of the U.S. dollar, but the *real* exchange rate between the peso and the U.S. dollar hasn't changed at all. And because the real peso–U.S. dollar exchange rate hasn't changed, the nominal depreciation of the peso against the U.S. dollar will have no effect either on the quantity of goods and services exported by Mexico to the United States or on the quantity of goods and services imported by Mexico from the United States. To see why, consider again the example of a hotel room. Suppose that this room initially costs 1,000 pesos per night, which is $100 at an exchange rate of 10 pesos per dollar. After both Mexican prices and the number of pesos per dollar rise by 50%, the hotel room costs 1,500 pesos per night—but 1,500 pesos divided by 15 pesos per dollar is $100, so the Mexican hotel room still costs $100. As a result, a U.S. tourist considering a trip to Mexico will have no reason to change plans.

The same is true for all goods and services that enter into trade: *the current account responds only to changes in the real exchange rate, not the nominal exchange rate.* A country's products become cheaper to foreigners only when that country's currency depreciates in real terms, and those products become more expensive to foreigners only when the currency appreciates in real terms. As a consequence, economists who analyze movements in exports and imports of goods and services focus on the real exchange rate, not the nominal exchange rate.

Figure 42.3 illustrates just how important it can be to distinguish between nominal and real exchange rates. The line labeled "Nominal exchange rate" shows the number of pesos it took to buy a U.S. dollar from 1990 to 2009. As you can see, the peso depreciated massively over that period. But the line labeled "Real exchange rate" shows the real exchange rate: it was calculated using Equation 42.1, with price indexes for both Mexico and the United States set so that the value in 1990 was 100. In real terms, the

PhotoSpin, Inc/Alamy

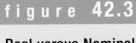

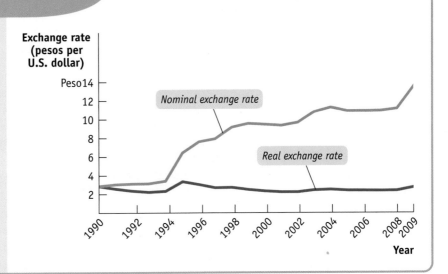

Real versus Nominal Exchange Rates, 1990–2009

Between 1990 and 2009, the price of a dollar in Mexican pesos increased dramatically. But because Mexico had higher inflation than the United States, the real exchange rate, which measures the relative price of Mexican goods and services, ended up roughly where it started.

Source: OECD.

peso depreciated between 1994 and 1995, and again in 2008, but not by nearly as much as the nominal depreciation. By 2009, the real peso–U.S. dollar exchange rate was just about back where it started.

The **purchasing power parity** between two countries' currencies is the nominal exchange rate at which a given basket of goods and services would cost the same amount in each country.

Purchasing Power Parity

A useful tool for analyzing exchange rates, closely connected to the concept of the real exchange rate, is known as *purchasing power parity*. The **purchasing power parity** between two countries' currencies is the nominal exchange rate at which a given basket of goods and services would cost the same amount in each country. Suppose, for example, that a basket of goods and services that costs $100 in the United States costs 1,000 pesos in Mexico. Then the purchasing power parity is 10 pesos per U.S. dollar: at that exchange rate, 1,000 pesos = $100, so the market basket costs the same amount in both countries.

Calculations of purchasing power parities are usually made by estimating the cost of buying broad market baskets containing many goods and services—everything from automobiles and groceries to housing and telephone calls. But once a year the magazine *The Economist* publishes a list of purchasing power parities based on the cost of buying a market basket that contains only one item—a McDonald's Big Mac.

Nominal exchange rates almost always differ from purchasing power parities. Some of these differences are systematic: in general, aggregate price levels are lower in poor countries than in rich countries because services tend to be cheaper in poor countries. But even among countries at roughly the same level of economic development, nominal exchange rates vary quite a lot from purchasing power parity. Figure 42.4 shows the nominal exchange rate between the Canadian dollar and the U.S. dollar, measured as the number of Canadian dollars per U.S. dollar, from 1990 to 2008, together with an estimate of the purchasing power parity exchange rate between the United States and Canada over the same period. The purchasing power parity didn't change much over the whole period because the United States and Canada had about the same rate of inflation. But at the beginning of the period the nominal exchange rate was below purchasing power parity, so a given market basket was more expensive in Canada than in the United States. By 2002, the nominal exchange rate was far above the purchasing power parity, so a market basket was much cheaper in Canada than in the United States.

Burgernomics

For a number of years the British magazine *The Economist* has produced an annual comparison of the cost in different countries of one particular consumption item that is found around the world—a McDonald's Big Mac. The magazine finds the price of a Big Mac in local currency, then computes two numbers: the price of a Big Mac in U.S. dollars using the prevailing exchange rate, and the exchange rate at which the price of a Big Mac would equal the U.S. price. If purchasing power parity held for Big Macs, the dollar price of a Big Mac would be the same everywhere. If purchasing power parity is a good theory for the long run, the exchange rate at which a Big Mac's price matches the

U.S. price should offer some guidance about where the exchange rate will eventually end up.

In the July 2009 version of the Big Mac index, there were some wide variations in the dollar price of a Big Mac. In the U.S., the price was $3.57. In China, converting at the official

exchange rate, a Big Mac cost only $1.83. In Switzerland, though, the price was $5.98.

The Big Mac index suggested that the euro would eventually fall against the dollar: a Big Mac on average cost €3.31, so that the purchasing power parity was $1.08 per €1 versus an actual market exchange rate of $1.39.

Serious economic studies of purchasing power parity require data on the prices of many goods and services. It turns out, however, that estimates of purchasing power parity based on the Big Mac index usually aren't that different from more elaborate measures. Fast food seems to make for pretty good fast research.

Over the long run, however, purchasing power parities are pretty good at predicting actual changes in nominal exchange rates. In particular, nominal exchange rates between countries at similar levels of economic development tend to fluctuate around levels that lead to similar costs for a given market basket. In fact, by July 2005, the nominal exchange rate between the United States and Canada was C$1.22 per US$1—just about the purchasing power parity. And by 2008, the cost of living was once again higher in Canada than in the United States.

figure 42.4

Purchasing Power Parity versus the Nominal Exchange Rate, 1990–2008

The purchasing power parity between the United States and Canada—the exchange rate at which a basket of goods and services would have cost the same amount in both countries—changed very little over the period shown, staying near C$1.20 per US$1. But the nominal exchange rate fluctuated widely.

Source: OECD.

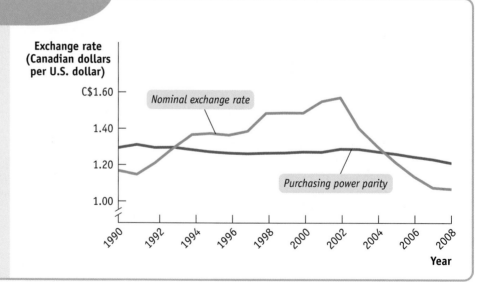

fyi

Low-Cost America

Does the exchange rate matter for business decisions? And how. Consider what European auto manufacturers were doing in 2008. One report from the University of Iowa summarized the situation as follows:

While luxury German carmakers BMW and Mercedes have maintained plants in the American South since the 1990s, BMW aims to expand U.S. manufacturing in South Carolina by 50% during the next five years. Volvo of Sweden is in negotiations to build a plant in New Mexico. Analysts at Italian carmaker Fiat determined that it needs to build a North American factory to profit from the upcoming re-launch of its Alfa Romeo model. Tennessee recently closed a deal with Volkswagen to build a $1 billion factory by offering $577 million in incentives.

Why were European automakers flocking to America? To some extent because they were being offered special incentives, as the case of Volkswagen in Tennessee illustrates. But the big factor was the exchange rate. In the early 2000s, one euro was, on average, worth less than a dollar; by the summer of 2008 the exchange rate was around €1 = $1.50. This change in the ex-

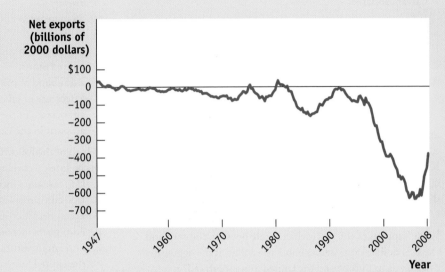

change rate made it substantially cheaper for European car manufacturers to produce in the United States than at home—especially if the cars were intended for the U.S. market.

Automobile manufacturing wasn't the only U.S. industry benefiting from the weak dollar; across the board, U.S. exports surged after 2006 while import growth fell off. The figure shows one measure of U.S. trade performance,

real net exports of goods and services: exports minus imports, both measured in 2000 dollars. As you can see, this balance, after a long slide, turned sharply upward in 2006.

The positive effects of the weak dollar on net exports were good news for the U.S. economy. The collapse of the housing bubble after 2006 was a big drag on aggregate demand; rising net exports were a welcome offsetting boost.

Module 42 AP Review

Solutions appear at the back of the book.

Check Your Understanding

1. Suppose Mexico discovers huge reserves of oil and starts exporting oil to the United States. Describe how this would affect the following:
   a. the nominal peso–U.S. dollar exchange rate
   b. Mexican exports of other goods and services
   c. Mexican imports of goods and services

2. Suppose a basket of goods and services that costs $100 in the United States costs 800 pesos in Mexico and the current nominal exchange rate is 10 pesos per U.S. dollar. Over the next five years, the cost of that market basket rises to $120 in the United States and to 1,200 pesos in Mexico, although the nominal exchange rate remains at 10 pesos per U.S. dollar. Calculate the following:
   a. the real exchange rate now and five years from now, if today's price index in both countries is 100
   b. purchasing power parity today and five years from now

Tackle the Test: Multiple-Choice Questions

1. When the U.S. dollar buys more Japanese yen, the U.S. dollar has
    I. become more valuable in terms of the yen.
    II. appreciated.
    III. depreciated
   a. I only
   b. II only
   c. III only
   d. I and II only
   e. I and III only

2. The nominal exchange rate at which a given basket of goods and services would cost the same in each country describes
   a. the international consumer price index (ICPI).
   b. appreciation.
   c. depreciation.
   d. purchasing power parity.
   e. the balance of payments on the current account.

3. What happens to the real exchange rate between the euro and the U.S. dollar (expressed as euros per dollar) if the aggregate price levels in Europe and the United States both fall? It
   a. is unaffected.
   b. increases.
   c. decreases.
   d. may increase, decrease, or stay the same.
   e. cannot be calculated.

4. Which of the following would cause the real exchange rate between pesos and U.S. dollars (in terms of pesos per dollar) to decrease?
   a. an increase in net capital flows from Mexico to the United States
   b. an increase in the real interest rate in Mexico relative to the United States
   c. a doubling of prices in both Mexico and the United States
   d. a decrease in oil exports from Mexico to the United States
   e. an increase in the balance of payments on the current account in the United States

5. Which of the following will decrease the supply of U.S. dollars in the foreign exchange market?
   a. U.S. residents increase their travel abroad.
   b. U.S. consumers demand fewer imports.
   c. Foreigners increase their demand for U.S. goods.
   d. Foreigners increase their travel to the United States.
   e. Foreign investors see increased investment opportunities in the United States.

Tackle the Test: Free-Response Questions

1. Draw a correctly labeled graph of the foreign exchange market showing the effect on the equilibrium exchange rate between the U.S. and Japan (the number of yen per U.S. dollar) if capital flows from Japan to the United States decrease due to a change in the preferences of Japanese investors. Has the U.S. dollar appreciated or depreciated?

Answer (7 points)

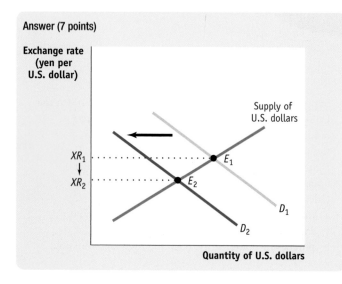

1 point: The axes are labeled "Exchange rate (yen per U.S. dollar)" and "Quantity of U.S. dollars".

1 point: The supply of U.S. dollars is labeled and slopes upward.

1 point: The demand for U.S. dollars is labeled and slopes downward.

1 point: The initial equilibrium exchange rate is found at the intersection of the initial supply and demand curves and is shown on the vertical axis.

1 point: The new demand for U.S. dollars is to the left of the initial demand.

1 point: The new equilibrium exchange rate is found where the initial supply curve and new demand curve intersect and is shown on the vertical axis.

1 point: The U.S. dollar has depreciated.

2. Use a correctly labeled graph of the foreign exchange market between the U.S. and Europe to illustrate what would happen to the value of the U.S. dollar if there were an increase in the U.S. demand for imports from Europe.

Module 43
Exchange Rate Policy

What you will learn in this **Module**:

- The difference between fixed exchange rates and floating exchange rates

- Considerations that lead countries to choose different exchange rate regimes.

Exchange Rate Policy

The nominal exchange rate, like other prices, is determined by supply and demand. Unlike the price of wheat or oil, however, the exchange rate is the price of a country's money (in terms of another country's money). Money isn't a good or service produced by the private sector; it's an asset whose quantity is determined by government policy. As a result, governments have much more power to influence nominal exchange rates than they have to influence ordinary prices.

The nominal exchange rate is a very important price for many countries: the exchange rate determines the price of imports; it determines the price of exports; in economies where exports and imports are large relative to GDP, movements in the exchange rate can have major effects on aggregate output and the aggregate price level. What do governments do with their power to influence this important price?

The answer is, it depends. At different times and in different places, governments have adopted a variety of *exchange rate regimes*. Let's talk about these regimes, how they are enforced, and how governments choose a regime. (From now on, we'll adopt the convention that we mean the nominal exchange rate when we refer to the exchange rate.)

Exchange Rate Regimes

An **exchange rate regime** is a rule governing policy toward the exchange rate. There are two main kinds of exchange rate regimes. A country has a **fixed exchange rate** when the government keeps the exchange rate against some other currency at or near a particular target. For example, Hong Kong has an official policy of setting an exchange rate of HK$7.80 per US$1. A country has a **floating exchange rate** when the government lets the exchange rate go wherever the market takes it. This is the policy followed by Britain, Canada, and the United States.

Fixed exchange rates and floating exchange rates aren't the only possibilities. At various times, countries have adopted compromise policies that lie somewhere between fixed and floating exchange rates. These include exchange rates that are fixed at any given time but are adjusted frequently, exchange rates that aren't fixed but are "managed" by the government to avoid wide swings, and exchange rates that float within a "target zone" but are prevented from leaving that zone. In this book, however, we'll focus on the two main exchange rate regimes.

An **exchange rate regime** is a rule governing policy toward the exchange rate.

A country has a **fixed exchange rate** when the government keeps the exchange rate against some other currency at or near a particular target.

A country has a **floating exchange rate** when the government lets the exchange rate go wherever the market takes it.

Government purchases or sales of currency in the foreign exchange market constitute **exchange market intervention.**

Foreign exchange reserves are stocks of foreign currency that governments maintain to buy their own currency on the foreign exchange market.

The immediate question about a fixed exchange rate is how it is possible for governments to fix the exchange rate when the exchange rate is determined by supply and demand.

How Can an Exchange Rate Be Held Fixed?

To understand how it is possible for a country to fix its exchange rate, let's consider a hypothetical country, Genovia, which for some reason has decided to fix the value of its currency, the geno, at US$1.50.

The obvious problem is that $1.50 may not be the equilibrium exchange rate in the foreign exchange market: the equilibrium rate may be either higher or lower than the target exchange rate. Figure 43.1 shows the foreign exchange market for genos, with the quantities of genos supplied and demanded on the horizontal axis and the exchange rate of the geno, measured in U.S. dollars per geno, on the vertical axis. Panel (a) shows the case in which the equilibrium value of the geno is *below* the target exchange rate. Panel (b) shows the case in which the equilibrium value of the geno is *above* the target exchange rate.

Consider first the case in which the equilibrium value of the geno is below the target exchange rate. As panel (a) shows, at the target exchange rate there is a surplus of genos in the foreign exchange market, which would normally push the value of the geno down. How can the Genovian government support the value of the geno to keep the rate where it wants? There are three possible answers, all of which have been used by governments at some point.

One way the Genovian government can support the geno is to "soak up" the surplus of genos by buying its own currency in the foreign exchange market. Government purchases or sales of currency in the foreign exchange market are called **exchange market intervention.** To buy genos in the foreign exchange market, of course, the Genovian government must have U.S. dollars to exchange for genos. In fact, most countries maintain **foreign exchange reserves,** stocks of foreign currency (usually U.S. dollars or euros) that they can use to buy their own currency to support its price.

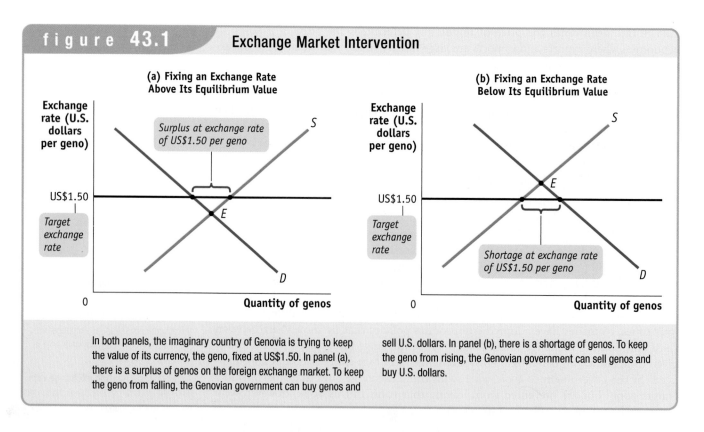

figure 43.1   **Exchange Market Intervention**

In both panels, the imaginary country of Genovia is trying to keep the value of its currency, the geno, fixed at US$1.50. In panel (a), there is a surplus of genos on the foreign exchange market. To keep the geno from falling, the Genovian government can buy genos and sell U.S. dollars. In panel (b), there is a shortage of genos. To keep the geno from rising, the Genovian government can sell genos and buy U.S. dollars.

We mentioned earlier that an important part of international capital flows is the result of purchases and sales of foreign assets by governments and central banks. Now we can see why governments sell foreign assets: they are supporting their currency through exchange market intervention. As we'll see in a moment, governments that keep the value of their currency *down* through exchange market intervention must *buy* foreign assets. First, however, let's talk about the other ways governments fix exchange rates.

A second way for the Genovian government to support the geno is to try to shift the supply and demand curves for the geno in the foreign exchange market. Governments usually do this by changing monetary policy. For example, to support the geno, the Genovian central bank can raise the Genovian interest rate. This will increase capital flows into Genovia, increasing the demand for genos, at the same time that it reduces capital flows out of Genovia, reducing the supply of genos. So, other things equal, an increase in a country's interest rate will increase the value of its currency.

Third, the Genovian government can support the geno by reducing the supply of genos to the foreign exchange market. It can do this by requiring domestic residents who want to buy foreign currency to get a license and giving these licenses only to people engaging in approved transactions (such as the purchase of imported goods the Genovian government thinks are essential). Licensing systems that limit the right of individuals to buy foreign currency are called **foreign exchange controls.** Other things equal, foreign exchange controls increase the value of a country's currency.

Foreign exchange controls are licensing systems that limit the right of individuals to buy foreign currency.

So far we've been discussing a situation in which the government is trying to prevent a depreciation of the geno. Suppose, instead, that the situation is as shown in panel (b) of Figure 43.1, where the equilibrium value of the geno is *above* the target exchange rate and there is a shortage of genos. To maintain the target exchange rate, the Genovian government can apply the same three basic options in the reverse direction. It can intervene in the foreign exchange market, in this case *selling* genos and acquiring U.S. dollars, which it can add to its foreign exchange reserves. It can *reduce* interest rates to increase the supply of genos and reduce the demand. Or it can impose foreign exchange controls that limit the ability of foreigners to buy genos. All of these actions, other things equal, will reduce the value of the geno.

As we said, all three techniques have been used to manage fixed exchange rates. But we haven't said whether fixing the exchange rate is a good idea. In fact, the choice of exchange rate regime poses a dilemma for policy makers because fixed and floating exchange rates each have both advantages and disadvantages.

The Exchange Rate Regime Dilemma

Few questions in macroeconomics produce as many arguments as that of whether a country should adopt a fixed or a floating exchange rate. The reason there are so many arguments is that both sides have a case.

To understand the case for a fixed exchange rate, consider for a moment how easy it is to conduct business across state lines in the United States. There are a number of things that make interstate commerce trouble-free, but one of them is the absence of any uncertainty about the value of money: a dollar is a dollar, in both New York City and Los Angeles.

By contrast, a dollar isn't a dollar in transactions between New York City and Toronto. The exchange rate between the Canadian dollar and the U.S. dollar fluctuates, sometimes widely. If a U.S. firm promises to pay a Canadian firm a given number of U.S. dollars a year from now, the value of that promise in Canadian currency can vary by 10% or more. This uncertainty has the effect of deterring trade between the two countries. So one benefit of a fixed exchange rate is certainty about the future value of a currency.

Once you cross the border into Canada, a dollar is no longer worth a dollar.

There is also, in some cases, an additional benefit to adopting a fixed exchange rate: by committing itself to a fixed rate, a country is also committing itself not to engage in inflationary policies because such policies would destabilize the exchange rate. For example, in 1991, Argentina, which has a long history of irresponsible policies leading to severe inflation, adopted a fixed exchange rate of US$1 per Argentine peso in an attempt to commit itself to non-inflationary policies in the future. (Argentina's fixed exchange rate regime collapsed disastrously in late 2001. But that's another story.)

The point is that there is some economic value in having a stable exchange rate. Indeed, the presumed benefits of stable exchange rates motivated the international system of fixed exchange rates created after World War II. It was also a major reason for the creation of the euro.

However, there are also costs to fixing the exchange rate. To stabilize an exchange rate through intervention, a country must keep large quantities of foreign currency on hand, and that currency is usually a low-return investment. Furthermore, even large reserves can be quickly exhausted when there are large capital flows out of a country. If a country chooses to stabilize an exchange rate by adjusting monetary policy rather than through intervention, it must divert monetary policy from other goals, notably stabilizing the economy and managing the inflation rate. Finally, foreign exchange controls, like import quotas and tariffs, distort incentives for importing and exporting goods and services. They can also create substantial costs in terms of red tape and corruption.

So there's a dilemma. Should a country let its currency float, which leaves monetary policy available for macroeconomic stabilization but creates uncertainty for everyone affected by trade? Or should it fix the exchange rate, which eliminates the uncertainty but means giving up monetary policy, adopting exchange controls, or both? Different countries reach different conclusions at different times. Most European countries, except for Britain, have long believed that exchange rates among major European economies, which do most of their international trade with each other, should be fixed. But Canada seems happy with a floating exchange rate with the United States, even though the United States accounts for most of Canada's trade.

In the next module we'll consider macroeconomic policy under each type of exchange rate regime.

fyi

China Pegs the Yuan

In the early years of the twenty-first century, China provided a striking example of the lengths to which countries sometimes go to maintain a fixed exchange rate. Here's the background: China's spectacular success as an exporter led to a rising surplus on the current account. At the same time, non-Chinese private investors became increasingly eager to shift funds into China, to take advantage of its growing domestic economy. These capital flows were somewhat limited by foreign exchange controls—but kept coming in anyway. As a result of the current account surplus and private capital inflows, China found itself in the position described by panel (b) of Figure 43.1: at the target exchange rate, the demand for yuan exceeded the supply. Yet the Chinese government was determined to keep the exchange rate fixed (although it began allowing gradual appreciation in 2005).

To keep the rate fixed, China had to engage in large-scale exchange market intervention, selling yuan, buying up other countries' currencies (mainly U.S. dollars) on the foreign exchange market, and adding them to its reserves. During 2008, China added $418 billion to its foreign exchange reserves, bringing the year-end total to $1.9 trillion.

To get a sense of how big these totals are, you have to know that in 2008 China's nominal GDP, converted into U.S. dollars at the prevailing exchange rate, was $4.25 trillion. So in 2008, China bought U.S. dollars and other currencies equal to about 10% of its GDP. That's as if the U.S. government had bought $1.4 trillion worth

China has a history of intervention in the foreign exchange market that kept its currency, and therefore its exports, relatively cheap for foreign consumers to buy.

of yen and euros in just a single year—and was continuing to buy yen and euros even though it was already sitting on a $7 trillion pile of foreign currencies.

Module 43 AP Review

Solutions appear at the back of the book.

Check Your Understanding

1. Draw a diagram, similar to Figure 43.1, representing the foreign exchange situation of China when it kept the exchange rate fixed at a target rate of $0.121 per yuan and the market equilibrium rate was higher than the target rate. Then show with a diagram how each of the following policy changes might eliminate the disequilibrium in the market.

   a. allowing the exchange rate to float more freely
   b. placing restrictions on foreigners who want to invest in China
   c. removing restrictions on Chinese who want to invest abroad
   d. imposing taxes on Chinese exports, such as clothing

Tackle the Test: Multiple-Choice Questions

1. Which of the following methods can be used to fix a country's exchange rate at a predetermined level?
   I. using foreign exchange reserves to buy its own currency
   II. using monetary policy to change interest rates
   III. implementing foreign exchange controls
   a. I only
   b. II only
   c. III only
   d. I and II only
   e. I, II, and III

2. Changes in exchange rates affect which of the following?
   a. the price of imports
   b. the price of exports
   c. aggregate demand
   d. aggregate output
   e. all of the above

3. The United States has which of the following exchange rate regimes?
   a. fixed
   b. floating
   c. fixed, but adjusted frequently
   d. fixed, but managed
   e. floating within a target zone

4. Which of the following interventions would be required to keep a country's exchange rate fixed if the equilibrium exchange rate in the foreign exchange market were below the fixed exchange rate (measured as units of foreign currency per unit of domestic currency)? The government/ central bank
   a. buys the domestic currency.
   b. sells the domestic currency.
   c. buys the foreign currency.
   d. lowers domestic interest rates.
   e. removes foreign exchange controls.

5. Which of the following is a benefit of a fixed exchange rate regime?
   a. certainty about the value of domestic currency
   b. commitment to inflationary policies
   c. no need for foreign exchange reserves
   d. allows unrestricted use of monetary policy
   e. all of the above

Tackle the Test: Free-Response Questions

1. Suppose the United States and India were the only two countries in the world.
   a. Draw a correctly labeled graph of the foreign exchange market for U.S. dollars showing the equilibrium in the market.
   b. On your graph, indicate a fixed exchange rate set above the equilibrium exchange rate. Does the fixed exchange rate lead to a surplus or shortage of U.S. dollars? Explain and show the amount of the surplus/shortage on your graph.
   c. To bring the foreign exchange market back to an equilibrium at the fixed exchange rate, would the U.S. government need to buy or sell dollars? On your graph, illustrate how the government's buying or selling of dollars would bring the equilibrium exchange rate back to the desired fixed rate.

Answer (9 points)

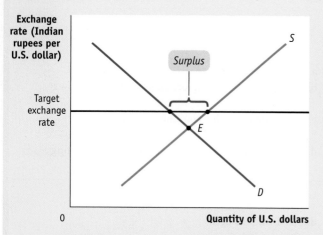

1 point: The vertical axis is labeled "Exchange rate (Indian rupees per U.S. dollar)" and the horizontal axis is labeled "Quantity of U.S. dollars."

1 point: Demand is downward sloping and labeled, supply is upward sloping and labeled.

1 point: The equilibrium exchange rate and the equilibrium quantity of dollars are labeled on the axes at the point where the supply and demand curves intersect.

1 point: The fixed exchange rate level is depicted above the equilibrium exchange rate.

1 point: Surplus

1 point: The quantity supplied exceeds the quantity demanded at the higher fixed exchange rate.

1 point: The surplus is labeled as the horizontal distance between the supply and demand curves at the fixed exchange rate.

1 point: Buy

1 point: The new demand curve is shown to the right of the old demand curve, crossing the supply curve at the fixed exchange rate.

2. List three tools used to fix exchange rates and explain the major costs resulting from their use.

Module 44
Exchange Rates and Macroeconomic Policy

Exchange Rates and Macroeconomic Policy

When the euro was created in 1999, there were celebrations across the nations of Europe—with a few notable exceptions. You see, some countries chose not to adopt the new currency. The most important of these was Britain, but other European countries, such as Switzerland and Sweden, also decided that the euro was not for them.

Why did Britain say no? Part of the answer was national pride: for example, if Britain gave up the pound, it would also have to give up currency that bears the portrait of the queen. But there were also serious economic concerns about giving up the pound in favor of the euro. British economists who favored adoption of the euro argued that if Britain used the same currency as its neighbors, the country's international trade would expand and its economy would become more productive. But other economists pointed out that adopting the euro would take away Britain's ability to have an independent monetary policy and might lead to macroeconomic problems.

As this discussion suggests, the fact that modern economies are open to international trade and capital flows adds a new level of complication to our analysis of macroeconomic policy. Let's look at three policy issues raised by open-economy macroeconomics.

Devaluation and Revaluation of Fixed Exchange Rates

Historically, fixed exchange rates haven't been permanent commitments. Sometimes countries with a fixed exchange rate switch to a floating rate. In other cases, they retain a fixed exchange rate regime but change the target exchange rate. Such adjustments in the target were common during the Bretton Woods era. For example, in 1967 Britain changed the exchange rate of the pound against the U.S. dollar from US$2.80 per £1 to US$2.40 per £1. A modern example is Argentina, which maintained a fixed exchange rate against the dollar from 1991 to 2001, but switched to a floating exchange rate at the end of 2001.

From Bretton Woods to the Euro

In 1944, while World War II was still raging, representatives of the Allied nations met in Bretton Woods, New Hampshire, to establish a postwar international monetary system of fixed exchange rates among major currencies. The system was highly successful at first, but it broke down in 1971. After a confusing interval during which policy makers tried unsuccessfully to establish a new fixed exchange rate system, by 1973 most economically advanced countries had moved to floating exchange rates.

In Europe, however, many policy makers were unhappy with floating exchange rates, which they believed created too much uncertainty for business. From the late 1970s onward they tried several times to create a system of more or less fixed exchange rates in Europe, culminating in an arrangement known as the Exchange Rate Mechanism. (The Exchange Rate Mechanism was, strictly speaking, a "target zone" system—exchange rates were free to move within a narrow band, but not outside it.) And in 1991 they agreed to move to the ultimate in fixed exchange rates: a common European currency, the euro. To the surprise of many analysts, they pulled it off: today most of Europe has abandoned national currencies for euros.

The accompanying figure illustrates the history of European exchange rate arrangements. It shows the exchange rate between the French franc and the German mark, measured as francs per mark, since 1971. The exchange rate fluctuated widely at first. The "plateaus" you can see in the data—eras when the exchange rate fluctuated only modestly—are periods when attempts to restore fixed exchange rates were in process. The Exchange Rate Mechanism, after a couple of false starts, became effective in 1987, stabilizing the exchange rate at about 3.4 francs per mark. (The wobbles in the early 1990s reflect two currency crises—episodes in which widespread expectations of imminent devaluations led to large but temporary capital flows.)

In 1999 the exchange rate was "locked"—no further fluctuations were allowed as the countries prepared to switch from francs and marks to euros. At the end of 2001, the franc and the mark ceased to exist.

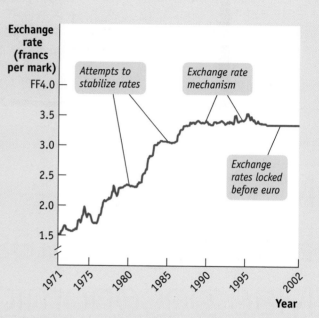

The transition to the euro has not been without costs. With most of Europe sharing the same currency, it must also share the same monetary policy. Yet economic conditions in the different countries aren't always the same.

Indeed, as this book went to press, there were serious stresses within the eurozone because the world financial crisis was hitting some countries, such as Greece, Portugal, Spain and Ireland, much more severely than it was hitting others, notably Germany.

A **devaluation** is a reduction in the value of a currency that is set under a fixed exchange rate regime.

A **revaluation** is an increase in the value of a currency that is set under a fixed exchange rate regime.

A reduction in the value of a currency that is set under a fixed exchange rate regime is called **devaluation**. As we've already learned, a *depreciation* is a downward move in a currency. A devaluation is a depreciation that is due to a revision in a fixed exchange rate target. An increase in the value of a currency that is set under a fixed exchange rate regime is called a **revaluation.**

A devaluation, like any depreciation, makes domestic goods cheaper in terms of foreign currency, which leads to higher exports. At the same time, it makes foreign goods more expensive in terms of domestic currency, which reduces imports. The effect is to increase the balance of payments on the current account. Similarly, a revaluation makes domestic goods more expensive in terms of foreign currency, which reduces exports, and makes foreign goods cheaper in domestic currency, which increases imports. So a revaluation reduces the balance of payments on the current account.

Devaluations and revaluations serve two purposes under a fixed exchange rate regime. First, they can be used to eliminate shortages or surpluses in the foreign exchange market. For example, in 2010, some economists were urging China to revalue the yuan so that it would not have to buy up so many U.S. dollars on the foreign exchange market.

Second, devaluation and revaluation can be used as tools of macroeconomic policy. A devaluation, by increasing exports and reducing imports, increases aggregate demand. So a devaluation can be used to reduce or eliminate a recessionary gap. A revaluation has the opposite effect, reducing aggregate demand. So a revaluation can be used to reduce or eliminate an inflationary gap.

Monetary Policy Under a Floating Exchange Rate Regime

Under a floating exchange rate regime, a country's central bank retains its ability to pursue independent monetary policy: it can increase aggregate demand by cutting the interest rate or decrease aggregate demand by raising the interest rate. But the exchange rate adds another dimension to the effects of monetary policy. To see why, let's return to the hypothetical country of Genovia as discussed in Module 43 and ask what happens if the central bank cuts the interest rate.

Just as in a closed economy, a lower interest rate leads to higher investment spending and higher consumer spending. But the decline in the interest rate also affects the foreign exchange market. Foreigners have less incentive to move funds into Genovia because they will receive a lower rate of return on their loans. As a result, they have less need to exchange U.S. dollars for genos, so the demand for genos falls. At the same time, Genovians have *more* incentive to move funds abroad because the rate of return on loans at home has fallen, making investments outside the country more attractive. Thus, they need to exchange more genos for U.S. dollars and the supply of genos rises.

Figure 44.1 shows the effect of an interest rate reduction on the foreign exchange market. The demand curve for genos shifts leftward, from D_1 to D_2, and the supply curve shifts rightward, from S_1 to S_2. The equilibrium exchange rate, as measured in U.S. dollars per geno, falls from XR_1 to XR_2. That is, a reduction in the Genovian interest rate causes the geno to *depreciate*.

The depreciation of the geno, in turn, affects aggregate demand. We've already seen that a devaluation—a depreciation that is the result of a change in a fixed exchange

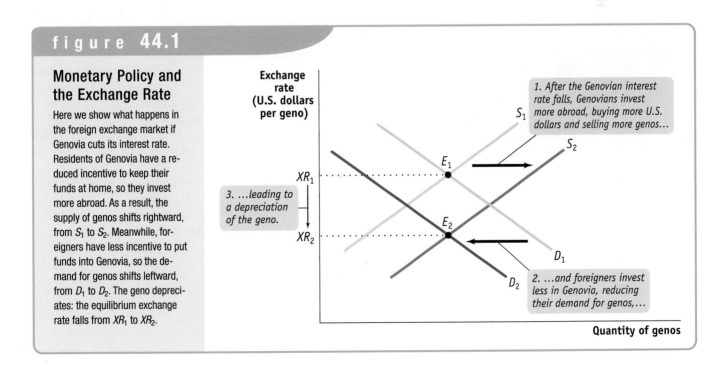

figure 44.1

Monetary Policy and the Exchange Rate

Here we show what happens in the foreign exchange market if Genovia cuts its interest rate. Residents of Genovia have a reduced incentive to keep their funds at home, so they invest more abroad. As a result, the supply of genos shifts rightward, from S_1 to S_2. Meanwhile, foreigners have less incentive to put funds into Genovia, so the demand for genos shifts leftward, from D_1 to D_2. The geno depreciates: the equilibrium exchange rate falls from XR_1 to XR_2.

Exchange rate (U.S. dollars per geno)

1. After the Genovian interest rate falls, Genovians invest more abroad, buying more U.S. dollars and selling more genos...

3. ...leading to a depreciation of the geno.

2. ...and foreigners invest less in Genovia, reducing their demand for genos,...

Quantity of genos

module **44** Exchange Rates and Macroeconomic Policy **439** rate—increases exports and reduces imports, thereby increasing aggregate demand. A depreciation that results from an interest rate cut has the same effect: it increases exports and reduces imports, increasing aggregate demand.

In other words, monetary policy under floating rates has effects beyond those we've described in looking at closed economies. In a closed economy, a reduction in the interest rate leads to a rise in aggregate demand because it leads to more investment spending and consumer spending. In an open economy with a floating exchange rate, the interest rate reduction leads to increased investment spending and consumer spending, but it also increases aggregate demand in another way: it leads to a currency depreciation, which increases exports and reduces imports, further increasing aggregate demand.

International Business Cycles

Up to this point, we have discussed macroeconomics, even in an open economy, as if all demand changes or *shocks* originated from the domestic economy. In reality, however, economies sometimes face shocks coming from abroad. For example, recessions in the United States have historically led to recessions in Mexico.

The key point is that changes in aggregate demand affect the demand for goods and services produced abroad as well as at home: other things equal, a recession leads to a fall in imports and an expansion leads to a rise in imports. And one country's imports are another country's exports. This link between aggregate demand in different national economies is one reason business cycles in different countries sometimes—but not always—seem to be synchronized. The prime example is the Great Depression, which affected countries around the world.

The extent of this link depends, however, on the exchange rate regime. To see why, think about what happens if a recession abroad reduces the demand for Genovia's exports. A reduction in foreign demand for Genovian goods and services is also a reduction in demand for genos on the foreign exchange market. If Genovia has a fixed exchange rate, it responds to this decline with exchange market intervention. But if Genovia has a floating exchange rate, the geno depreciates. Because Genovian goods and services become cheaper to foreigners when the demand for exports falls, the quantity of goods and services exported doesn't fall by as much as it would under a fixed rate. At the same time, the fall in the geno makes imports more expensive to Genovians, leading to a fall in imports. Both effects limit the decline in Genovia's aggregate demand compared to what it would have been under a fixed exchange rate regime.

One of the virtues of floating exchange rates, according to their advocates, is that they help insulate countries from recessions originating abroad. This theory looked pretty good in the early 2000s: Britain, with a floating exchange rate, managed to stay out of a recession that affected the rest of Europe, and Canada, which also has a floating rate, suffered a less severe recession than the United States.

For better or worse, trading partners tend to import each other's business cycles in addition to each other's goods.

In 2008, however, a financial crisis that began in the United States seemed to be producing a recession in virtually every country. In this case, it appears that the international linkages between financial markets were much stronger than any insulation from overseas disturbances provided by floating exchange rates.

fyi

The Joy of a Devalued Pound

The Exchange Rate Mechanism is the system of European fixed exchange rates that paved the way for the creation of the euro in 1999. Britain joined that system in 1990 but dropped out in 1992. The story of Britain's exit from the Exchange Rate Mechanism is a classic example of open-economy macroeconomic policy.

Britain originally fixed its exchange rate for both the reasons we described earlier: British leaders believed that a fixed exchange rate would help promote international trade, and they also hoped that it would help fight inflation. But by 1992 Britain was suffering from high unemployment: the unemployment rate in September 1992 was over 10%. And as long as the country had a fixed exchange rate, there wasn't much the government could do. In particular, the government wasn't able to cut interest rates because it was using high interest rates to help support the value of the pound.

In the summer of 1992, investors began speculating against the pound—selling pounds in the expectation that the currency would drop in value. As its foreign reserves dwindled, this speculation forced the British government's hand. On September 16, 1992, Britain abandoned its fixed exchange rate. The pound promptly dropped 20% against the German mark, the most important European currency at the time.

At first, the devaluation of the pound greatly damaged the prestige of the British government. But the Chancellor of the Exchequer—the equivalent of the U.S. Treasury Secretary—claimed to be happy about it. "My wife has never before heard me singing in the bath," he told reporters. There were several reasons for his joy. One was that the British government would no longer have to engage in large-scale exchange market intervention to support the pound's value. Another was that devaluation increases aggregate demand, so the pound's fall would help reduce British unemployment. Finally, because Britain no longer had a fixed exchange rate, it was free to pursue an expansionary monetary policy to fight its slump.

Indeed, events made it clear that the chancellor's joy was well founded. British unemployment fell over the next two years, even as the unemployment rate rose in France and Germany. One person who did not share in the improving employment picture, however, was the chancellor himself. Soon after his remark about singing in the bath, he was fired.

Module 44 AP Review

Solutions appear at the back of the book.

Check Your Understanding

1. Look at the graph in the FYI section on page 438. Where do you see devaluations and revaluations of the franc against the mark?

2. In the late 1980s, Canadian economists argued that the high interest rate policies of the Bank of Canada weren't just causing high unemployment—they were also making it hard for Canadian manufacturers to compete with U.S. manufacturers. Explain this complaint, using our analysis of how monetary policy works under floating exchange rates.

Tackle the Test: Multiple-Choice Questions

1. Devaluation of a currency occurs when which of the following happens?
   - I. The supply of a currency with a floating exchange rate increases.
   - II. The demand for a currency with a floating exchange rate decreases.
   - III. The government decreases the fixed exchange rate.

   a. I only
   b. II only
   c. III only
   d. I and II only
   e. I, II, and III

2. Devaluation of a currency will lead to which of the following?
   a. appreciation of the currency
   b. an increase in exports
   c. an increase in imports
   d. a decrease in exports
   e. floating exchange rates

3. Devaluation of a currency is used to achieve which of the following?
   a. an elimination of a surplus in the foreign exchange market
   b. an elimination of a shortage in the foreign exchange market
   c. a reduction in aggregate demand
   d. a lower inflation rate
   e. a floating exchange rate

4. Monetary policy that reduces the interest rate will do which of the following?
   a. appreciate the domestic currency
   b. decrease exports
   c. increase imports
   d. depreciate the domestic currency
   e. prevent inflation

5. Which of the following will happen in a country if a trading partner's economy experiences a recession?
   a. It will experience an expansion.
   b. Exports will decrease.
   c. The demand for the country's currency will increase.
   d. The country's currency will appreciate.
   e. All of the above will occur.

Tackle the Test: Free-Response Questions

1. Suppose the United States and Australia were the only two countries in the world, and that both countries pursued a floating exchange rate regime. Note that the currency in Australia is the Australian dollar.
   a. Draw a correctly labeled graph showing equilibrium in the foreign exchange market for U.S. dollars.
   b. If the Federal Reserve pursues expansionary monetary policy, what will happen to the U.S. interest rate and international capital flows? Explain.
   c. On your graph of the foreign exchange market, illustrate the effect of the Fed's policy on the supply of U.S. dollars, the demand for U.S. dollars, and the equilibrium exchange rate.
   d. How does the Fed's monetary policy affect U.S. aggregate demand? Explain.

1 point: The equilibrium exchange rate and equilibrium quantity of dollars are labeled on the axes at the point where the supply and demand curves intersect.

1 point: The U.S. interest rate falls.

1 point: There is an increase in the capital flow into Australia and an increase in the capital flow out of the United States.

1 point: The lower interest rate in the United States reduces the incentive to invest in the United States and increases the incentive to invest in Australia.

1 point: The supply of U.S. dollars increases.

1 point: The demand for U.S. dollars decreases.

1 point: The exchange rate falls (the U.S. dollar depreciates).

1 point: The lower exchange rate leads to more exports from the United States to Australia (they are cheaper now) and fewer imports into the United States from Australia (they are more expensive now). When exports increase and imports decrease, U.S. aggregate demand increases.

2. Explain how a floating exchange rate system can help insulate a country from recessions abroad.

Answer (10 points)

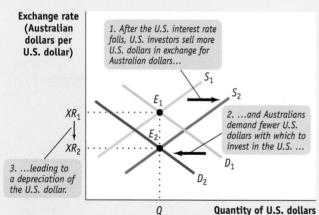

1 point: The vertical axis is labeled "Exchange rate (Australian dollars per U.S. dollar)" and the horizontal axis is labeled "Quantity of U.S. dollars."

1 point: Demand is downward sloping and labeled; supply is upward sloping and labeled.

What you will learn
in this **Module:**

● How to use macroeconomic
models to conduct policy
analysis

● How to approach
free-response
macroeconomics questions

Module 45
Putting It All Together

Having completed our study of the basic macroeconomic models, we can use them to analyze scenarios and evaluate policy recommendations. In this module we develop a step-by-step approach to macroeconomic analysis. You can adapt this approach to problems involving any macroeconomic model, including models of aggregate demand and supply, production possibilities, money markets, and the Phillips curve. By the end of this module you will be able to combine mastery of the principles of macroeconomics with problem solving skills to analyze a new scenario on your own.

A Structure for Macroeconomic Analysis

In our study of macroeconomics we have seen questions about the macroeconomy take many different forms. No matter what the specific question, most macroeconomic problems have the following components:

1) A *starting point.* To analyze any situation, you have to know where to start.

2) A *pivotal event.* This might be a change in the economy or a policy response to the initial situation.

3) *Initial effects of the event.* An event will generally have some initial, short-run effects.

4) *Secondary and long-run effects of the event.* After the short-run effects run their course, there are typically secondary effects and the economy will move toward its long-run equilibrium.

For example, you might be asked to consider the following scenario and answer the associated questions.

> Assume the U.S. economy is currently operating at an aggregate output level above potential output. Draw a correctly labeled graph showing aggregate demand, short-run aggregate supply, long-run aggregate supply, equilibrium output, and the aggregate price level. Now assume that the Federal Reserve conducts contractionary monetary policy. Identify the open-market operation the Fed would conduct, and draw a correctly labeled graph of the money market to show the effect of the monetary policy on the nominal interest rate.
>
> Show and explain how the Fed's actions will affect equilibrium in the aggregate demand and supply graph you drew previously. Indicate the new aggregate price level on your graph.
>
> Assume Canada is the largest trading partner of the United States. Draw a correctly labeled graph of the foreign exchange market for the U.S. dollar showing how the change in the aggregate price level

How will the Fed's monetary policy change nominal interest rates?

you indicate on your graph above will affect the foreign exchange market. What will happen to the value of the U.S. dollar relative to the Canadian dollar?

How will the Federal Reserve's contractionary monetary policy affect the real interest rate in the United States? Explain.

Taken as a whole, this scenario and the associated questions can seem overwhelming. Let's start by breaking down our analysis into four components.

1. The starting point

Assume the U.S. economy is currently operating at an aggregate output level above potential output.

2. The pivotal event

Now assume that the Federal Reserve conducts contractionary monetary policy.

3. Initial effects of the event

Show and explain how the Fed's actions will affect equilibrium.

4. Secondary and long-run effects of the event

Assume Canada is the largest trading partner of the United States. What will happen to the value of the U.S. dollar relative to the Canadian dollar?

How will the Federal Reserve's contractionary monetary policy affect the real interest rate in the United States? Explain.

Now we are ready to look at each of the steps and untangle this scenario.

The Starting Point

Assume the U.S. economy is currently operating at an aggregate output level above potential output. Draw a correctly labeled graph showing aggregate demand, short-run aggregate supply, long-run aggregate supply, equilibrium output, and the aggregate price level.

To analyze a situation, you have to know where to start. You will most often use the aggregate demand-aggregate supply model to evaluate macroeconomic scenarios. In this model, there are three possible starting points: long-run macroeconomic equilibrium, a recessionary gap, and an inflationary gap. This means that there are three possible "starting-point" graphs, as shown in Figure 45.1. The economy can be in long-run macroeconomic equilibrium with production at potential output as in panel (a), it can be in short-run macroeconomic equilibrium at an aggregate output level below potential output (creating a recessionary gap) as in panel (b), or it can be in short-run macroeconomic equilibrium at an aggregate output level above potential output (creating an inflationary gap) as in panel (c) and in our scenario.

The Pivotal Event

Now assume that the Federal Reserve conducts contractionary monetary policy.

It is the events in a scenario that make it interesting. Perhaps a country goes into or recovers from a recession, inflation catches consumers off guard or becomes expected, consumers or businesses become more or less confident, holdings of money or wealth change, trading partners prosper or falter, or oil prices plummet or spike. The event can also be expansionary or contractionary monetary or fiscal policy. With the infinite number of possible changes in policy, politics, the economy, and markets around the world, don't expect to analyze a familiar scenario on the exam.

While it's impossible to foresee all of the scenarios you might encounter, we can group the determinants of change into a reasonably small set of major factors that influence macroeconomic models. Table 45.1 matches major factors with the curves they affect. With these influences in mind, it is relatively easy to proceed through a problem by identifying how the given events affect these factors. Most hypothetical scenarios involve changes in just one or two major factors. Although the real world is more complex, it is largely the same factors that change—there are just more of them changing at once.

figure 45.1   Analysis Starting Points

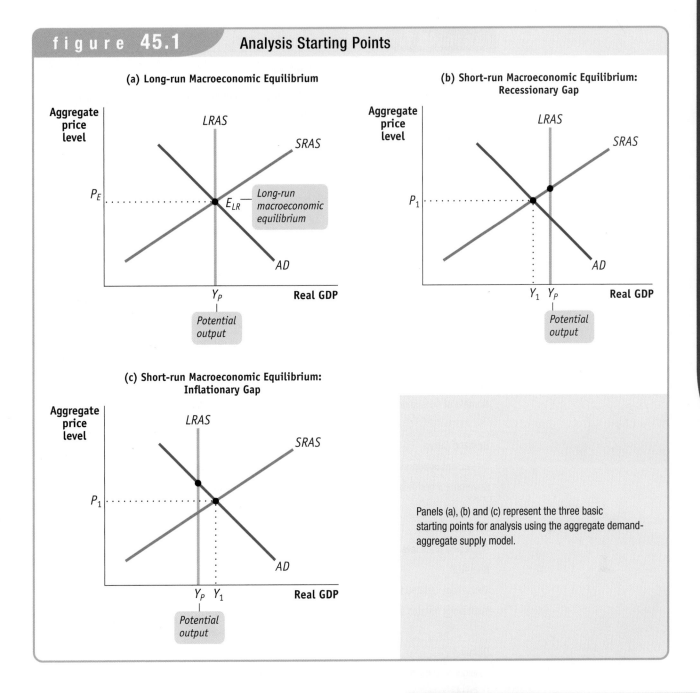

(a) Long-run Macroeconomic Equilibrium

(b) Short-run Macroeconomic Equilibrium: Recessionary Gap

(c) Short-run Macroeconomic Equilibrium: Inflationary Gap

Panels (a), (b) and (c) represent the three basic starting points for analysis using the aggregate demand-aggregate supply model.

As shown in Table 45.1 on the next page, many curves are shifted by changes in only two or three major factors. Even for the aggregate demand curve, which has the largest number of associated factors, you can simplify the task further by asking yourself, "Does the event influence consumer spending, investment spending, government spending, or net exports?" If so, aggregate demand shifts. A shift of the long-run aggregate supply curve is caused only by events that affect labor productivity or the number of workers.

In the supply and demand model there are five major factors that shift the demand curve and five major factors that shift the supply curve. Most examples using this model will represent a change in one of these ten factors. The loanable funds market, money market, and foreign exchange market

You've seen the speech, now, how would you analyze the proposed policy?

table **45.1**

Major Factors that Shift Curves in Each Model

Aggregate Demand and Aggregate Supply		
Aggregate Demand Curve	Short-run Aggregate Supply Curve	Long-run Aggregate Supply Curve
Expectations	Commodity prices	Productivity
Wealth	Nominal wages	Physical capital
Size of existing capital stock	Productivity	Human capital
Fiscal and monetary policy	Business taxes	Technology
Net Exports		Quantity of resources
Interest rates		
Investment spending		

Supply and Demand	
Demand Curve	Supply Curve
Income	Input prices
Prices of substitutes and complements	Prices of substitutes and complements in production
Tastes	Technology
Consumer expectations	Producer expectations
Number of consumers	Number of producers

Loanable Funds Market	
Demand Curve	Supply Curve
Investment opportunities	Private saving behavior
Government borrowing	Capital inflows

Money Market	
Demand Curve	Supply Curve
Aggregate price level	Set by the Federal Reserve
Real GDP	
Technology (related to money market)	
Institutions (related to money market)	

Foreign Exchange Market	
Demand	Supply
Foreigners' purchases of domestic	Domestic residents' purchases of foreign
Goods	Goods
Services	Services
Assets	Assets

Note: It is the *real* exchange rate (adjusted for international differences in aggregate price levels) that affects imports and exports.

have their own clearly identified factors that affect supply or demand. With this information you can link specific events to relevant factors in the models to see what changes will occur. Remember that having correctly labeled axes on your graphs is crucial to a correct analysis.

Often, as in our scenario, the event is a policy response to an undesirable starting point such as a recessionary or inflationary gap. Expansionary policy is used to combat a recession, and contractionary policy is used to combat inflationary pressures. To begin analyzing a policy response, you need to fully understand how the Federal Reserve can implement each type of monetary policy (e.g., increase or decrease the money supply) and how that policy eventually affects the economy. You also need to understand how the government can implement expansionary or contractionary fiscal policy by raising or lowering taxes or government spending.

The Initial Effect of the Event

Show and explain how the Fed's actions will affect equilibrium.

We have seen that events will create short-run effects in our models. In the short-run, fiscal and monetary policy both affect the economy by shifting the aggregate demand curve. As shown in panel (a) of Figure 45.2, expansionary policy shifts aggregate demand to the right, and as shown in panel (b), contractionary policy shifts aggregate demand to the left. To illustrate the effect of a policy response, shift the aggregate demand curve on your starting point graph and indicate the effects of the shift on the aggregate price level and aggregate output.

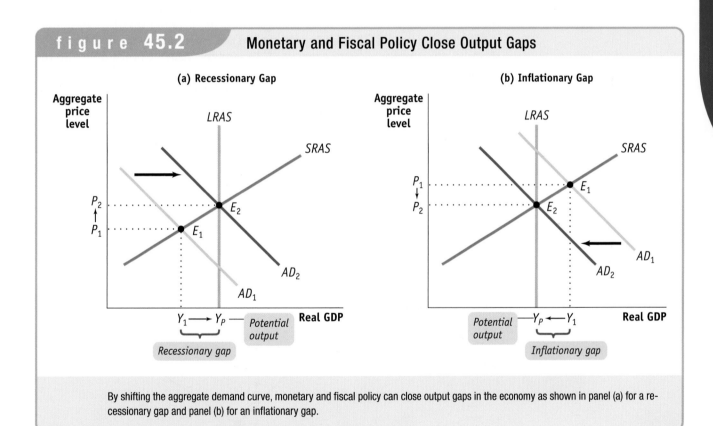

figure 45.2 **Monetary and Fiscal Policy Close Output Gaps**

By shifting the aggregate demand curve, monetary and fiscal policy can close output gaps in the economy as shown in panel (a) for a recessionary gap and panel (b) for an inflationary gap.

Secondary and Long-Run Effects of the Event

Assume Canada is the largest trading partner of the United States. What will happen to the value of the U.S. dollar relative to the Canadian dollar?

How will the Federal Reserve's contractionary monetary policy affect the real interest rate in the United States? Explain.

Secondary Effects In addition to the initial, short-run effects of any event, there will be secondary effects and the economy will move to its long-run equilibrium after the short-run effects run their course.

We have seen that negative or positive demand shocks (including those created by inappropriate monetary or fiscal policy) move the economy away from long-run macroeconomic equilibrium. As explained in Module 18, in the absence of policy responses, such events will eventually be offset through changes in short-run aggregate supply resulting from changes in nominal wage rates. This will move the economy back to long-run macroeconomic equilibrium.

If the short-run effects of an action result in changes in the aggregate price level or real interest rate, there will also be secondary effects throughout the open economy. International capital flows and international trade will be affected as a result of the initial effects experienced in the economy. A price level decrease, as in our scenario, will encourage exports and discourage imports, causing an appreciation in the domestic currency on the foreign exchange market. A change in the interest rate affects aggregate demand through changes in investment spending and consumer spending. Interest rate changes also affect aggregate demand through changes in imports or exports caused by currency appreciation and depreciation. These secondary effects act to reinforce the effects of monetary policy.

Long-run Effects While deviations from potential output are ironed out in the long run, other effects remain. For example, in the long run the use of fiscal policy affects the federal budget. Changes in taxes or government spending that lead to budget deficits (and increased federal debt) can "crowd out" private investment spending in the long run. The government's increased demand for loanable funds drives up the interest rate, decreases investment spending, and partially offsets the initial increase in aggregate demand. Of course, the deficit could be addressed by printing money, but that would lead to problems with inflation in the long run.

We know that in the long run, monetary policy affects only the aggregate price level, not real GDP. Because money is neutral, changes in the money supply have no effect on the real economy. The aggregate price level and nominal values will be affected by the same proportion, leaving real values (including the real interest rate as mentioned in our scenario) unchanged.

Analyzing Our Scenario

Now let's address the specific demands of our problem.

✔ *Draw a correctly labeled graph showing aggregate demand, short-run aggregate supply, long-run aggregate supply, equilibrium output, and the aggregate price level.*

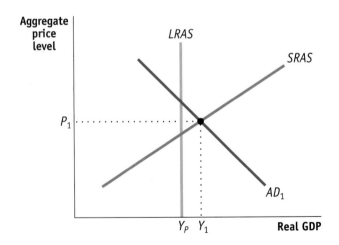

✔ *Identify the open-market operation the Fed would conduct.*

The Fed would sell U.S. Treasury securities (bonds, bills, or notes).

✔ *Draw a correctly labeled graph of the money market to show the effect of the monetary policy on the nominal interest rate.*

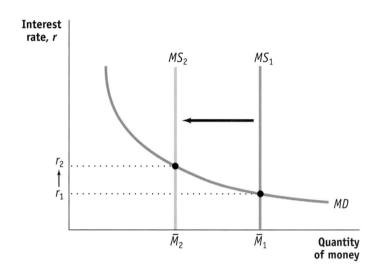

✔ *Show and explain how the Fed's actions will affect equilibrium in the aggregate demand and supply graph you drew previously. Indicate the new aggregate price level on your graph.*

A higher interest rate will lead to decreased investment and consumer spending, decreasing aggregate demand. The equilibrium price level and real GDP will fall.

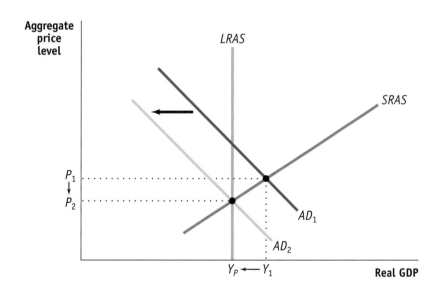

✔ *Draw a correctly labeled graph of the foreign exchange market for the U.S. dollar showing how the change in the aggregate price level you indicate on your graph above will affect the foreign exchange market.*

The decrease in the U.S. price level will make U.S. exports relatively inexpensive for Canadians to purchase and lead to an increase in demand for U.S. dollars with which to purchase those exports.

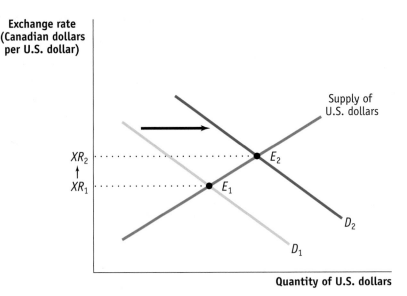

Exchange rate
(Canadian dollars
per U.S. dollar)

Quantity of U.S. dollars

✔ *What will happen to the U.S. dollar relative to the Canadian dollar?*

The U.S. dollar will appreciate.

✔ *How will the Federal Reserve's contractionary monetary policy affect the real interest rate in the United States? Explain.*

There will be no effect on the real interest rate in the long run because, due to the neutrality of money, changes in the money supply do not affect real values in the long run.

Module 45 AP Review

Solutions appear at the back of the book.

Check Your Understanding

1. The economy is operating in long-run macroeconomic equilibrium.
   a. Illustrate this situation using a correctly labeled aggregate demand-aggregate supply graph.
   b. Use your graph to show the short-run effect on real GDP and the aggregate price level if there is a decrease in government spending.
   c. What will happen to the aggregate price level and real GDP in the long run? Explain.
   d. Suppose the government is experiencing a persistent budget deficit. How will the decrease in government spending affect that deficit? Use a correctly labeled graph of the loanable funds market to show the effect of a decrease in government spending on the interest rate.

Tackle the Test: Multiple-Choice Questions

Questions 1–5 refer to the following scenario:

The United States and Mexico are trading partners. Suppose a flu outbreak significantly decreases U.S. tourism in Mexico and causes the Mexican economy to enter a recession. Assume that the money that would have been spent by U.S. tourists in Mexico is, instead, not spent at all.

1. Which of the following occurs as a result of the recession in Mexico?
   I. Output in Mexico decreases.
   II. Aggregate demand in the United States decreases.
   III. Output in the United States decreases.
   a. I only
   b. II only
   c. III only
   d. I and II only
   e. I, II, and III

2. What is the effect of Mexico's falling income on the demand for money and the nominal interest rate in Mexico?

Demand for money	Nominal interest rate
a. increases	decreases
b. decreases	decreases
c. increases	increases
d. decreases	increases
e. increases	unchanged

3. If the aggregate price level in Mexico decreases, what will happen to the real interest rate?
   a. It will increase.
   b. It will decrease.
   c. It will be unchanged.
   d. It will stabilize.
   e. It cannot be determined.

4. Suppose the aggregate price level in Mexico decreases relative to that in the United States. What is the effect of this price level change on the demand and on the exchange rate, for Mexican pesos?

Demand for pesos	Exchange rate
a. increases	appreciates
b. increases	depreciates
c. decreases	appreciates
d. decreases	depreciates
e. decreases	is unchanged

5. If the Mexican government pursues expansionary fiscal policy in response to the recession, what will happen to aggregate demand and aggregate supply in the short-run?

Aggregate demand	Short-run aggregate supply
a. increase	increase
b. increase	decrease
c. decrease	increase
d. decrease	decrease
e. increase	no change

Tackle the Test: Free-Response Questions

1. Suppose the U.S. economy is experiencing a recession.
   a. Draw a correctly labeled aggregate demand-aggregate supply graph showing the aggregate demand, short-run aggregate supply, long-run aggregate supply, equilibrium output, and aggregate price level.
   b. Assume that energy prices increase in the United States. Show the effects of this increase on the equilibrium in your graph from part a.
   c. According to your graph, how does the increase in energy prices affect unemployment and inflation in the economy?
   d. Assume the United States and Canada are the only two countries in an open economy and that energy prices have remained unchanged in Canada. Draw a correctly labeled graph of the foreign exchange market for U.S. dollars, and use it to show the effect of increased U.S. energy prices on the demand for U.S. dollars. Explain.

Answer (12 points)

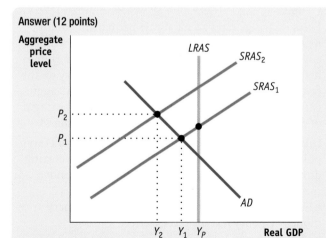

1 point: The vertical axis is labeled "Aggregate price level" and the horizontal axis is labeled "Aggregate output" or "Real GDP."

1 point: The AD curve slopes downward, the SRAS curve slopes upward, and the LRAS curve is vertical.

1 point: The equilibrium is found where the SRAS curve crosses the AD curve, and the equilibrium aggregate price level and aggregate output are shown on the axes at this point.

1 point: The equilibrium is to the left of the LRAS curve.

1 point: The SRAS curve shifts to the left.

1 point: The equilibrium aggregate price level and output are shown on the axes at the new equilibrium (increased aggregate price level, decreased aggregate output).

1 point: It increases unemployment.

1 point: It increases the aggregate price level (inflation).

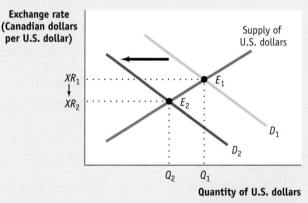

1 point: The vertical axis is labeled "Exchange rate (Canadian dollars per U.S. dollar)," horizontal axis is labeled "Quantity of U.S. dollars." Demand for U.S. dollars slopes downward and is labeled, supply of U.S. dollars slopes upward and is labeled.

1 point: The equilibrium exchange rate and quantity of U.S. dollars are shown on the axes at the intersection of the demand and supply curves.

1 point: The demand for U.S. dollars will decrease.

1 point: The inflation in the United States will lead to a decrease in the demand for U.S. exports (which must be purchased with U.S. dollars).

2. Assume the United States is operating below potential output.
   a. Draw a correctly labeled aggregate demand and supply graph showing equilibrium in the economy.
   b. Suppose the government decreases taxes. On your graph, show how the decrease in taxes will affect *AD, SRAS, LRAS,* equilibrium aggregate price level, and output.
   c. Assume the decrease in taxes led to an increased budget deficit and that the deficit spending was funded through government borrowing from the public. Use a correctly labeled graph of the market for loanable funds to show the effect of increased borrowing on the interest rate.
   d. Given the effect on the interest rate from part c, draw a correctly labeled graph of the foreign exchange market showing the effect of the change in the interest rate on the supply of U.S. dollars. Explain how the interest rate affects the supply of U.S. dollars.
   e. According to your graph from part d, what has happened to the value of the U.S. dollar? How will this affect U.S. exports and aggregate demand?

Section ⑧ Review

Summary

1. A country's **balance of payments accounts** summarize its transactions with the rest of the world. The **balance of payments on the current account,** or the **current account,** includes the **balance of payments on goods and services** together with balances on factor income and transfers. The **merchandise trade balance,** or **trade balance,** is a frequently cited component of the balance of payments on goods and services. The **balance of payments on the financial account,** or **the financial account,** measures capital flows. By definition, the balance of payments on the current account plus the balance of payments on the financial account is zero.

2. Capital flows respond to international differences in interest rates and other rates of return; they can be usefully analyzed using an international version of the loanable funds model, which shows how a country where the interest rate would be low in the absence of capital flows sends funds to a country where the interest rate would be high in the absence of capital flows. The underlying determinants of capital flows are international differences in savings and opportunities for investment spending.

3. Currencies are traded in the **foreign exchange market;** the prices at which they are traded are **exchange rates.** When a currency rises against another currency, it **appreciates;** when it falls, it **depreciates.** The **equilibrium exchange rate** matches the quantity of that currency supplied to the foreign exchange market to the quantity demanded.

4. To correct for international differences in inflation rates, economists calculate **real exchange rates,** which multiply the exchange rate between two countries' respective currencies by the ratio of the countries' price levels. The current account responds only to changes in the real exchange rate, not the nominal exchange rate. **Purchasing power parity** is the exchange rate that makes the cost of a basket of goods and services equal in two countries. While purchasing power parity and the nominal exchange rate almost always differ, purchasing power parity is a good predictor of actual changes in the nominal exchange rate.

5. Countries adopt different **exchange rate regimes,** rules governing exchange rate policy. The main types are **fixed exchange rates,** where the government takes action to keep the exchange rate at a target level, and **floating exchange rates,** where the exchange rate is free to fluctuate. Countries can fix exchange rates using **exchange market intervention,** which requires them to hold **foreign exchange reserves** that they use to buy any surplus of their currency. Alternatively, they can change domestic policies, especially monetary policy, to shift the demand and supply curves in the foreign exchange market. Finally, they can use **foreign exchange controls.**

6. Exchange rate policy poses a dilemma: there are economic payoffs to stable exchange rates, but the policies used to fix the exchange rate have costs. Exchange market intervention requires large reserves, and exchange controls distort incentives. If monetary policy is used to help fix the exchange rate, it isn't available to use for domestic policy.

7. Fixed exchange rates aren't always permanent commitments: countries with a fixed exchange rate sometimes engage in **devaluations** or **revaluations.** In addition to helping eliminate a surplus of domestic currency on the foreign exchange market, a devaluation increases aggregate demand. Similarly, a revaluation reduces shortages of domestic currency and reduces aggregate demand.

8. Under floating exchange rates, expansionary monetary policy works in part through the exchange rate: cutting domestic interest rates leads to a depreciation, and through that to higher exports and lower imports, which increases aggregate demand. Contractionary monetary policy has the reverse effect.

9. The fact that one country's imports are another country's exports creates a link between the business cycles in different countries. Floating exchange rates, however, may reduce the strength of that link.

Key Terms

Balance of payments accounts, p. 410

Balance of payments on the current account (the current account), p. 412

Balance of payments on goods and services, p. 412

Merchandise trade balance (trade balance), p. 412

Balance of payments on the financial account (the financial account), p. 413

Foreign exchange market, p. 421

Exchange rates, p. 421

Appreciates, p. 422

Depreciates, p. 422

Equilibrium exchange rate, p. 423

Real exchange rate, p. 425

Purchasing power parity, p. 427

Exchange rate regime, p. 431

Fixed exchange rate, p. 431

Floating exchange rate, p. 431

Exchange market intervention, p. 432

Foreign exchange reserves, p. 432

Foreign exchange controls, p. 433

Devaluation, p. 438

Revaluation, p. 438

Problems

1. How would the following transactions be categorized in the U.S. balance of payments accounts? Would they be entered in the current account (as a payment to or from a foreigner) or the financial account (as a sale to or purchase of assets from a foreigner)? How will the balance of payments on the current and financial accounts change?

   a. A French importer buys a case of California wine for $500.

   b. An American who works for a French company deposits her paycheck, drawn on a Paris bank, into her San Francisco bank.

   c. An American buys a bond from a Japanese company for $10,000.

   d. An American charity sends $100,000 to Africa to help local residents buy food after a harvest shortfall.

2. The accompanying diagram shows the assets of the rest of the world that are in the United States and U.S. assets abroad, both as a percentage of rest-of-the-world GDP. As you can see from the diagram, both have increased nearly fivefold since 1980.

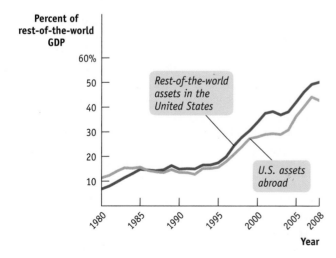

   a. As U.S. assets abroad have increased as a percentage of rest-of-the-world GDP, does this mean that the United States, over the period, has experienced net capital outflows?

   b. Does this diagram indicate that world economies were more tightly linked in 2007 than they were in 1980?

3. In the economy of Scottopia in 2008, exports equaled $400 billion of goods and $300 billion of services, imports equaled $500 billion of goods and $350 billion of services, and the rest of the world purchased $250 billion of Scottopia's assets. What was the merchandise trade balance for Scottopia? What was the balance of payments on the current account in Scottopia? What was the balance of payments on the financial account? What was the value of Scottopia's purchases of assets from the rest of the world?

4. In the economy of Popania in 2008, total Popanian purchases of assets in the rest of the world equaled $300 billion, purchases of Popanian assets by the rest of the world equaled $400 billion, and Popania exported goods and services equaled $350 billion. What was Popania's balance of payments on the financial account in 2008? What was its balance of payments on the current account? What was the value of its imports?

5. Suppose that Northlandia and Southlandia are the only two trading countries in the world, that each nation runs a balance of payments on both current and financial accounts equal to zero, and that each nation sees the other's assets as identical to its own. Using the accompanying diagrams, explain how the demand and supply of loanable funds, the interest rate, and the balance of payments on the current and

financial accounts will change in each country if international capital flows are possible.

(a) Northlandia

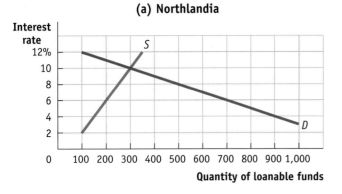

(b) Southlandia

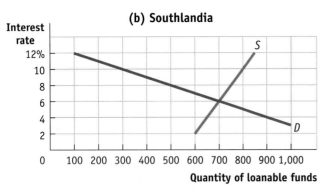

6. Based on the exchange rates for the first trading days of 2009 and 2010 shown in the accompanying table, did the U.S. dollar appreciate or depreciate during 2009? Did the movement in the value of the U.S. dollar make American goods and services more or less attractive to foreigners?

January 2, 2009	January 4, 2010
US$1.45 to buy 1 British pound sterling	US$1.61 to buy 1 British pound sterling
32.82 Taiwan dollars to buy US$1	31.74 Taiwan dollars to buy US$1
US$0.82 to buy 1 Canadian dollar	US$0.96 to buy 1 Canadian dollar
90.98 Japanese yen to buy US$1	92.35 Japanese yen to buy US$1
US$1.39 to buy 1 euro	US$1.44 to buy 1 euro
1.07 Swiss francs to buy US$1	1.03 Swiss francs to buy US$1

7. Go to http://fx.sauder.ubc.ca. Using the table labeled "The Most Recent Cross-Rates of Major Currencies," determine whether the British pound (GBP), the Canadian dollar (CAD), the Japanese yen (JPY), the euro (EUR), and the Swiss franc (CHF) have appreciated or depreciated against the U.S. dollar (USD) since January 4, 2010. The exchange rates on January 4, 2010, are listed in the table in Problem 6 above.

8. Suppose the United States and Japan are the only two trading countries in the world. What will happen to the value of the U.S. dollar if the following occur, other things equal?

a. Japan relaxes some of its import restrictions.

b. The United States imposes some import tariffs on Japanese goods.

c. Interest rates in the United States rise dramatically.

d. A report indicates that Japanese cars are much safer than previously thought, especially compared with American cars.

9. From January 1, 2001, to June 30, 2003, the U.S. federal funds rate decreased from 6.5% to 1%. During the same period, the analogous interest rate in Europe decreased from 5.75% to 3%.

a. Considering the change in interest rates over the period and using the loanable funds model, would you have expected funds to flow from the United States to Europe or from Europe to the United States over this period?

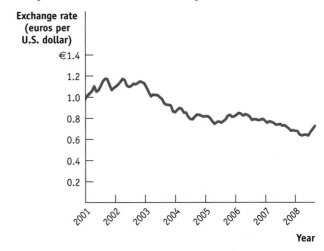

b. The accompanying diagram shows the exchange rate between the euro and the U.S. dollar from January 1, 2001, through September 30, 2008. Is the eventual decrease in the exchange rate over the period from January 2001 to June 2003 consistent with the movement in funds predicted in part a?

10. In each of the following scenarios, suppose that the two nations are the only trading nations in the world. Given inflation and the change in the nominal exchange rate, which nation's goods become more attractive?

a. Inflation is 10% in the United States and 5% in Japan; the U.S. dollar–Japanese yen exchange rate remains the same.

b. Inflation is 3% in the United States and 8% in Mexico; the price of the U.S. dollar falls from 12.50 to 10.25 Mexican pesos.

c. Inflation is 5% in the United States and 3% in the eurozone; the price of the euro falls from $1.30 to $1.20.

d. Inflation is 8% in the United States and 4% in Canada; the price of the Canadian dollar rises from US$0.60 to US$0.75.

11. Starting from a position of equilibrium in the foreign exchange market under a fixed exchange rate regime, how must a government react to an increase in the demand for the nation's goods and services by the rest of the world to keep the exchange rate at its fixed value?

12. Suppose that Albernia's central bank has fixed the value of its currency, the bern, to the U.S. dollar (at a rate of US$1.50 to 1 bern) and is committed to that exchange rate. Initially, the foreign exchange market for the bern is also in equilibrium, as shown in the accompanying diagram. However, both Albernians and Americans begin to believe that there are big risks in holding Albernian assets; as a result, they become unwilling to hold Albernian assets unless they receive a higher rate of return on them than they do on U.S. assets. How would this affect the diagram? If the Albernian central bank tries to keep the exchange rate fixed using monetary policy, how will this affect the Albernian economy?

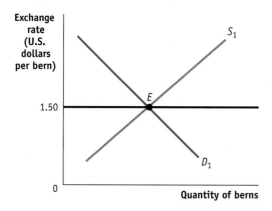

13. Your study partner asks you, "If central banks lose the ability to use discretionary monetary policy under fixed exchange rates, why would nations agree to a fixed exchange rate system?" How do you respond?

section 9

Behind the Demand Curve: Consumer Choice

Panic was the only word to describe the situation at hospitals, clinics, and nursing homes across America in October 2004. Early that month, Chiron Corporation, one of only two suppliers of flu vaccine for the entire U.S. market, announced that contamination problems would force the closure of its manufacturing plant. With that closure, the U.S. supply of vaccine for the 2004–2005 flu season was suddenly cut in half, from 100 million to 50 million doses. Because making flu vaccine is a costly and time-consuming process, no more doses could be made to replace Chiron's lost output. And since every country jealously guards its supply of flu vaccine for its own citizens, none could be obtained from other countries.

If you've ever had a real case of the flu, you know just how unpleasant an experience it is. And it can be worse than unpleasant: every year the flu kills around 36,000 Americans and sends another 200,000 to the hospital. Victims are most commonly children, seniors, or those with compromised immune systems. In a normal flu season, this part of the population, along with health care workers, are immunized first.

But the flu vaccine shortfall of 2004 upended those plans. As news of it spread, there was a rush to get the shots. People lined up in the middle of the night at the few locations that had somehow obtained the vaccine and were offering it at a reasonable price: the crowds included seniors with oxygen tanks, parents with sleeping children, and others in wheelchairs. Meanwhile, some pharmaceutical distributors—the companies that obtain vaccine from manufacturers and then distribute it to hospitals and pharmacies—detected a profit-making opportunity in the frenzy. One company, Med-Stat, which normally charged $8.50 for a dose, began charging $90, more than 10 times the normal price.

A survey of pharmacists found that price-gouging was fairly widespread.

Although many people refused or were unable to pay such a high price for the vaccine, many others undoubtedly did. Med-Stat judged, correctly, that consumers of the vaccine were relatively *unresponsive* to price; that is, the large increase in the price of the vaccine left the quantity demanded by consumers relatively unchanged.

Clearly, the demand for flu vaccine is unusual in this respect. For many, getting vaccinated meant the difference between life and death. Let's consider a very different and less urgent scenario. Suppose, for example, that the supply of a particular type of breakfast cereal was halved due to manufacturing problems. It would be extremely unlikely, if not impossible, to find a consumer willing to pay 10 times the original price for a box of this particular cereal. In other words, consumers of breakfast cereal are much more responsive to price than consumers of flu vaccine. But how do we define *responsiveness*? Economists measure consumers' responsiveness to price with a particular number, called the *price elasticity of demand*.

In this section we take a closer look at the supply and demand model developed in Section 2 and present several economic concepts used to evaluate market results. We will see how the price elasticity of demand is calculated and why it is the best measure of how the quantity demanded responds to changes in price. We will then discover that the price elasticity of demand is only one of a family of related concepts, including the *income elasticity of demand* and the *price elasticity of supply*. We will look at how the price and the quantity bought and sold in a market affect consumer, producer, and overall welfare. And we will consider how consumers make choices to maximize their individual *utility*, the term economists use to describe "satisfaction."

AP Photo/Will Kincaid

Because consumers are relatively unresponsive to the price of flu vaccine, the price depends largely on availability.

457

Module 46
Income Effects, Substitution Effects, and Elasticity

What you will learn in this **Module:**

- How the income and substitution effects explain the law of demand

- The definition of elasticity, a measure of responsiveness to changes in prices or incomes

- The importance of the price elasticity of demand, which measures the responsiveness of the quantity demanded to changes in price

- How to calculate the price elasticity of demand

Explaining the Law of Demand

In Section 2 we introduced the demand curve and the law of demand. To this point, we have accepted that the demand curve has a negative slope. And we have drawn demand curves that are somewhere in the middle between flat and steep (with a negative slope). In this module, we present more detail about why demand curves slope downward and what the slope of the demand curve tells us. We begin with the *income* and *substitution effects,* which explain why the demand curve has a negative slope.

The Substitution Effect

When the price of a good increases, an individual will normally consume less of that good and more of other goods. Correspondingly, when the price of a good decreases, an individual will normally consume more of that good and less of other goods. This explains why the individual demand curve, which relates an individual's consumption of a good to the price of that good, normally slopes downward—that is, it obeys the law of demand.

An alternative way to think about why demand curves slope downward is to focus on opportunity costs. For simplicity, let's suppose there are only two goods between which to choose. When the price of one good decreases, an individual doesn't have to give up as many units of the other good in order to buy one more unit of the first good. That makes it attractive to buy more of the good whose price has gone down. Conversely, when the price of one good increases, one must give up more units of the other good to buy one more unit of the first good, so consuming that good becomes less attractive and the consumer buys fewer. The change in the quantity demanded as the good that has become relatively cheaper is substituted for the good that has become relatively more expensive is known as the **substitution effect.** When a good absorbs only a small share of the typical consumer's income, as with pillow cases and swim

The **substitution effect** of a change in the price of a good is the change in the quantity of that good demanded as the consumer substitutes the good that has become relatively cheaper for the good that has become relatively more expensive.

goggles, the substitution effect is essentially the sole explanation of why the market demand curve slopes downward. There are, however, some goods, like food and housing, that account for a substantial share of many consumers' incomes. In such cases another effect, called the *income effect,* also comes into play.

The Income Effect

Consider the case of a family that spends half of its income on rental housing. Now suppose that the price of housing increases everywhere. This will have a substitution effect on the family's demand: other things equal, the family will have an incentive to consume less housing—say, by moving to a smaller apartment—and more of other goods. But the family will also, in a real sense, be made poorer by that higher housing price—its income will buy less housing than before. When income is adjusted to reflect its true purchasing power, it is called *real income,* in contrast to *money income* or *nominal income,* which has not been adjusted. And this reduction in a consumer's real income will have an additional effect, beyond the substitution effect, on the family's consumption choices, including its consumption of housing. The **income effect** is the change in the quantity of a good demanded that results from a change in the overall purchasing power of the consumer's income due to a change in the price of that good.

It's possible to give more precise definitions of the substitution effect and the income effect of a price change, but for most purposes, there are only two things you need to know about the distinction between these two effects.

First, for the majority of goods and services, the income effect is not important and has no significant effect on individual consumption. Thus, most market demand curves slope downward solely because of the substitution effect—end of story.

Second, when it matters at all, the income effect usually reinforces the substitution effect. That is, when the price of a good that absorbs a substantial share of income rises, consumers of that good become a bit poorer because their purchasing power falls. And the vast majority of goods are *normal* goods, goods for which demand decreases when income falls. So this effective reduction in income leads to a reduction in the quantity demanded and reinforces the substitution effect.

> The **income effect** of a change in the price of a good is the change in the quantity of that good demanded that results from a change in the consumer's purchasing power when the price of the good changes.

fyi

Giffen Goods

Back when Ireland was a desperately poor country—not the prosperous "Celtic Tiger" it has lately become—it was claimed that the Irish would eat *more* potatoes when the price of potatoes went up. That is, some observers claimed that Ireland's demand curve for potatoes sloped upward, not downward.

Can this happen? In theory, yes. If Irish demand for potatoes actually sloped upward, it would have been a real-life case of a "Giffen good," named after a nineteenth-century statistician who thought (probably wrongly) that he saw an upward-sloping demand curve in some data he was studying.

Here's the story. Suppose that there is some good that absorbs a large share of consumers'

budgets and that this good is also *inferior*—people demand less of it when their income rises. The classic supposed example was, as you might guess, potatoes in Ireland, back when potatoes were an inferior good—they were what poor people ate—and when the Irish were very poor.

Now suppose that the price of potatoes increases. This would, *other things equal,* cause people to substitute other goods for potatoes. But other things are not equal: given the higher price of potatoes, people are poorer. And this *increases* the demand for potatoes, because potatoes are an inferior good.

If this income effect outweighs the substitution effect, a rise in the price of potatoes would

increase the quantity demanded; the law of demand would not hold.

In a way the point of this story—which has never been validated in any real situation, nineteenth-century Ireland included—is how unlikely such an event is. The law of demand really is a law, with few exceptions.

However, in the case of an *inferior* good, a good for which demand increases when income falls, the income and substitution effects work in opposite directions. Although the substitution effect decreases the quantity of any good demanded as its price increases, the income effect of a price increase for an inferior good is an *increase* in the quantity demanded. This makes sense because the price increase lowers the real income of the consumer, and as real income falls, the demand for an inferior good increases.

If a good were so inferior that the income effect exceeded the substitution effect, a price increase would lead to an increase in the quantity demanded. There is controversy over whether such goods, known as "Giffen goods," exist at all. If they do, they are very rare. You can generally assume that the income effect for an inferior good is smaller than the substitution effect, and so a price increase will lead to a decrease in the quantity demanded.

Defining and Measuring Elasticity

As we saw in Section 1, *dependent variables* respond to changes in *independent variables*. For example, if two variables are negatively related and the independent variable increases, the dependent variable will respond by decreasing. But often the important question is not whether the variables are negatively or positively related, but how responsive the dependent variable is to changes in the independent variable (that is, **by how much** will the dependent variable change?). If price increases, we know that quantity demanded will decrease (that is the *law of demand*). The question in this context is *by how much* will quantity demanded decrease if price goes up?

Economists use the concept of *elasticity* to measure the responsiveness of one variable to changes in another. For example, *price elasticity of demand* measures the responsiveness of quantity demanded to changes in price—something a firm considering changing its price would certainly want to know! Elasticity can be used to measure responsiveness using any two related variables. We will start by looking at the price elasticity of demand and then move on to other examples of elasticities commonly used by economists.

Think back to the opening example of the 2004 flu shot panic. In order for Flunomics, a hypothetical flu vaccine distributor, to know whether it could raise its revenue by significantly raising the price of its flu vaccine during the 2004 flu vaccine panic, it would have to know whether the price increase would decrease the quantity demanded by a lot or a little. That is, it would have to know the price elasticity of demand for flu vaccinations.

Calculating the Price Elasticity of Demand

Figure 46.1 shows a hypothetical demand curve for flu vaccinations. At a price of $20 per vaccination, consumers would demand 10 million vaccinations per year (point *A*); at a price of $21, the quantity demanded would fall to 9.9 million vaccinations per year (point *B*).

Figure 46.1, then, tells us the change in the quantity demanded for a particular change in the price. But how can we turn this into a measure of price responsiveness? The answer is to calculate the price elasticity of demand. The **price elasticity of demand** compares the *percent change in quantity demanded* to the *percent change in price* as we move along the demand curve. As we'll see later, the reason economists use percent changes is to get a measure that doesn't depend on the units in which a good is measured (say, a child-size dose versus an adult-size dose of vaccine). But before we get to that, let's look at how elasticity is calculated.

To calculate the price elasticity of demand, we first calculate the *percent change in the quantity demanded* and the corresponding *percent change in the price* as we move along the demand curve. These are defined as follows:

(46-1) % change in quantity demanded $= \dfrac{\text{Change in quantity demanded}}{\text{Initial quantity demanded}} \times 100$

The **price elasticity of demand** is the ratio of the percent change in the quantity demanded to the percent change in the price as we move along the demand curve (dropping the minus sign).

figure 46.1

The Demand for Vaccinations

At a price of $20 per vaccination, the quantity of vaccinations demanded is 10 million per year (point *A*). When price rises to $21 per vaccination, the quantity demanded falls to 9.9 million vaccinations per year (point *B*).

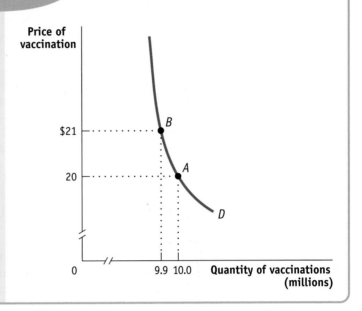

and

(46-2)   % change in price $= \dfrac{\text{Change in price}}{\text{Initial price}} \times 100$

In Figure 46.1, we see that when the price rises from $20 to $21, the quantity demanded falls from 10 million to 9.9 million vaccinations, yielding a change in the quantity demanded of 0.1 million vaccinations. So the percent change in the quantity demanded is

% change in quantity demanded $= \dfrac{-0.1 \text{ million vaccinations}}{10 \text{ million vaccinations}} \times 100 = -1\%$

The initial price is $20 and the change in the price is $1, so the percent change in the price is

% change in price $= \dfrac{\$1}{\$20} \times 100 = 5\%$

To calculate the price elasticity of demand, we find the ratio of the percent change in the quantity demanded to the percent change in the price:

(46-3)   Price elasticity of demand $= \dfrac{\text{\% change in quantity demanded}}{\text{\% change in price}}$

In Figure 46.1, the price elasticity of demand is therefore

Price elasticity of demand $= \dfrac{1\%}{5\%} = 0.2$

The *law of demand* says that demand curves slope downward, so price and quantity demanded always move in opposite directions. In other words, a positive percent change in price (a rise in price) leads to a negative percent change in the quantity demanded; a negative percent change in price (a fall in price) leads to a positive percent change in the quantity demanded. This means that the price elasticity of demand is, in strictly mathematical terms, a negative number. However, it is inconvenient to repeatedly write a minus sign. So when economists talk about the price elasticity of demand, they usually drop the minus sign and report the absolute value of the price elasticity of demand. In this case, for example, economists would usually say "the price elasticity of demand is 0.2," taking it for granted that you understand they mean *minus* 0.2. We follow this convention here.

The larger the price elasticity of demand, the more responsive the quantity demanded is to the price. When the price elasticity of demand is large—when consumers change their quantity demanded by a large percentage compared with the percent change in the price—economists say that demand is highly elastic.

As we'll see shortly, a price elasticity of 0.2 indicates a small response of quantity demanded to price. That is, the quantity demanded will fall by a relatively small amount when price rises. This is what economists call *inelastic* demand. And inelastic demand was exactly what Flunomics needed for its strategy to increase revenue by raising the price of its flu vaccines.

An Alternative Way to Calculate Elasticities: The Midpoint Method

We've seen that price elasticity of demand compares the *percent change in quantity demanded* with the *percent change in price*. When we look at some other elasticities, which we will do shortly, we'll see why it is important to focus on percent changes. But at this point we need to discuss a technical issue that arises when you calculate percent changes in variables and how economists deal with it.

The best way to understand the issue is with a real example. Suppose you were trying to estimate the price elasticity of demand for gasoline by comparing gasoline prices and consumption in different countries. Because of high taxes, gasoline usually costs about three times as much per gallon in Europe as it does in the United States. So what is the percent difference between American and European gas prices?

Well, it depends on which way you measure it. Because the price of gasoline in Europe is approximately three times higher than in the United States, it is 200 percent higher. Because the price of gasoline in the United States is one-third as high as in Europe, it is 66.7 percent lower.

This is a nuisance: we'd like to have a percent measure of the difference in prices that doesn't depend on which way you measure it. A good way to avoid computing different elasticities for rising and falling prices is to use the *midpoint method* (sometimes called the *arc method*).

The **midpoint method** replaces the usual definition of the percent change in a variable, X, with a slightly different definition:

$$\text{(46-4)} \quad \text{\% change in } X = \frac{\text{Change in } X}{\text{Average value of } X} \times 100$$

where the average value of X is defined as

$$\text{Average value of } X = \frac{\text{Starting value of } X + \text{Final value of } X}{2}$$

When calculating the price elasticity of demand using the midpoint method, both the percent change in the price and the percent change in the quantity demanded are found using average values in this way. To see how this method works, suppose you have the following data for some good:

The **midpoint method** is a technique for calculating the percent change. In this approach, we calculate changes in a variable compared with the average, or midpoint, of the initial and final values.

	Price	Quantity demanded
Situation A	$0.90	1,100
Situation B	$1.10	900

To calculate the percent change in quantity going from situation A to situation B, we compare the change in the quantity demanded—a fall of 200 units—with the *average* of the quantity demanded in the two situations. So we calculate

$$\% \text{ change in quantity demanded} = \frac{-200}{(1{,}100 + 900)/2} \times 100 = \frac{-200}{1{,}000} \times 100 = -20\%$$

In the same way, we calculate the percentage change in price as

$$\% \text{ change in price} = \frac{\$0.20}{(\$0.90 + \$1.10)/2} \times 100 = \frac{\$0.20}{\$1.00} \times 100 = 20\%$$

So in this case we would calculate the price elasticity of demand to be

$$\text{Price elasticity of demand} = \frac{\% \text{ change in quantity demanded}}{\% \text{ change in price}} = \frac{20\%}{20\%} = 1$$

again dropping the minus sign.

The important point is that we would get the same result, a price elasticity of demand of 1, whether we went up the demand curve from situation A to situation B or down from situation B to situation A.

To arrive at a more general formula for price elasticity of demand, suppose that we have data for two points on a demand curve. At point 1 the quantity demanded and

fyi

Estimating Elasticities

You might think it's easy to estimate price elasticities of demand from real-world data: just compare percent changes in prices with percent changes in quantities demanded. Unfortunately, it's rarely that simple because changes in price aren't the only thing affecting changes in the quantity demanded: other factors—such as changes in income, changes in population, and changes in the prices of other goods—shift the demand curve, thereby changing the quantity demanded at any given price. To estimate price elasticities of demand, economists must use careful statistical analysis to separate the influence of these different factors, holding other things equal.

The most comprehensive effort to estimate price elasticities of demand was a mammoth study by the economists Hendrik S. Houthakker and Lester D. Taylor. Some of their results are summarized in Table 46.1. These estimates show a wide range of price elasticities. There are some goods, like eggs, for which demand hardly responds at all to changes in the price; there are other goods, most notably foreign travel, for which the quantity demanded is very sensitive to the price.

Notice that Table 46.1 is divided into two parts: inelastic and elastic demand. We'll explain in the next section the significance of that division.

table 46.1

Some Estimated Price Elasticities of Demand

Good	Price elasticity of demand
Inelastic demand	
Eggs	0.1
Beef	0.4
Stationery	0.5
Gasoline	0.5
Elastic demand	
Housing	1.2
Restaurant meals	2.3
Airline travel	2.4
Foreign travel	4.1

Source: Hendrick S. Houthakker and Lester D. Taylor, *Consumer Demand in the United States, 1929–1970* (Cambridge: Harvard University Press, 1970)

price are (Q_1, P_1); at point 2 they are (Q_2, P_2). Then the formula for calculating the price elasticity of demand is:

$$(46\text{-}5) \quad \text{Price elasticity of demand} = \frac{\dfrac{Q_2 - Q_1}{(Q_1 + Q_2)/2}}{\dfrac{P_2 - P_1}{(P_1 + P_2)/2}}$$

As before, when reporting a price elasticity of demand calculated by the midpoint method, we drop the minus sign and report the absolute value.

Module 46 AP Review

Solutions appear at the back of the book.

Check Your Understanding

1. In each of the following cases, state whether the income effect, the substitution effect, or both are significant. In which cases do they move in the same direction? In opposite directions? Why?
   a. Orange juice represents a small share of Clare's spending. She buys more lemonade and less orange juice when the price of orange juice goes up. She does not change her spending on other goods.
   b. Apartment rents have risen dramatically this year. Since rent absorbs a major part of her income, Delia moves to a smaller apartment. Assume that rental housing is a normal good.
   c. The cost of a semester-long meal ticket at the student cafeteria rises, representing a significant increase in living costs. As a result, many students have less money to spend on weekend meals at restaurants and eat in the cafeteria instead. Assume that cafeteria meals are an inferior good.

2. The price of strawberries falls from $1.50 to $1.00 per carton, and the quantity demanded goes from 100,000 to 200,000 cartons. Use the midpoint method to find the price elasticity of demand.

3. At the present level of consumption, 4,000 movie tickets, and at the current price, $5 per ticket, the price elasticity of demand for movie tickets is 1. Using the midpoint method, calculate the percentage by which the owners of movie theaters must reduce the price in order to sell 5,000 tickets.

4. The price elasticity of demand for ice-cream sandwiches is 1.2 at the current price of $0.50 per sandwich and the current consumption level of 100,000 sandwiches. Calculate the change in the quantity demanded when price rises by $0.05. Use Equations 46-1 and 46-2 to calculate percent changes and Equation 46-3 to relate price elasticity of demand to the percent changes.

Tackle the Test: Multiple-Choice Questions

1. Which of the following statements is true?
   I. When a good absorbs only a small share of consumer spending, the income effect explains the demand curve's negative slope.
   II. A change in consumption brought about by a change in purchasing power describes the income effect.
   III. In the case of an inferior good, the income and substitution effects work in opposite directions.
   a. I only
   b. II only
   c. III only
   d. II and III only
   e. I, II, and III

2. The income effect is most likely to come into play for which of the following goods?
   a. water
   b. clothing
   c. housing
   d. transportation
   e. entertainment

3. If a decrease in price from $2 to $1 causes an increase in quantity demanded from 100 to 120, using the midpoint method, price elasticity of demand equals
   a. 0.17.
   b. 0.27.
   c. 0.40.
   d. 2.5.
   e. 3.72.

4. Which of the following is likely to have the highest price elasticity of demand?
   a. eggs
   b. beef
   c. housing
   d. gasoline
   e. foreign travel

5. If a 2% change in the price of a good leads to a 10% change in the quantity demanded of a good, what is the value of price elasticity of demand?

    a. 0.02
    b. 0.2
    c. 5
    d. 10
    e. 20

Tackle the Test: Free-Response Questions

1. a. Define the price elasticity of demand and provide the formula for calculating the price elasticity of demand using the midpoint method.
   b. Refer to the table provided. Using the midpoint method, calculate the price elasticity of demand for good X.
   c. Based on your calculation of price elasticity of demand in part b, if price increases by 10%, in what direction and by what percentage will quantity demanded change?

Good X

Price	Quantity demanded
$2	800
$4	500

2. Assume the price of an inferior good increases.
   a. In what direction will the substitution effect change the quantity demanded? Explain.
   b. In what direction will the income effect change the quantity demanded? Explain.
   c. Given that the demand curve for the good slopes downward, what is true of the relative sizes of the income and substitution effects for the inferior good? Explain.

Answer (5 points)

1 point: The price elasticity of demand measures the responsiveness of the quantity demanded to price changes.

1 point: (Change in quantity demanded/average quantity demanded)/(change in price/average price)

1 point: 0.69

1 point: Decrease

1 point: 6.9%

Module 47
Interpreting Price Elasticity of Demand

Interpreting the Price Elasticity of Demand

Med-Stat and other pharmaceutical distributors believed they could sharply drive up flu vaccine prices in the face of a shortage because the price elasticity of vaccine demand was low. But what does that mean? How low does a price elasticity have to be for us to classify it as low? How high does it have to be for us to consider it high? And what determines whether the price elasticity of demand is high or low, anyway? To answer these questions, we need to look more deeply at the price elasticity of demand.

How Elastic Is Elastic?

As a first step toward classifying price elasticities of demand, let's look at the extreme cases.

First, consider the demand for a good when people pay no attention to the price of, say, shoelaces. Suppose that consumers would buy 1 billion pairs of shoelaces per year regardless of the price. If that were true, the demand curve for shoelaces would look like the curve shown in panel (a) of Figure 47.1: it would be a vertical line at 1 billion pairs of shoelaces. Since the percent change in the quantity demanded is zero for *any* change in the price, the price elasticity of demand in this case is zero. The case of a zero price elasticity of demand is known as **perfectly inelastic** demand.

The opposite extreme occurs when even a tiny rise in the price will cause the quantity demanded to drop to zero or even a tiny fall in the price will cause the quantity demanded to get extremely large. Panel (b) of Figure 47.1 shows the case of pink tennis balls; we suppose that tennis players really don't care what color their balls are and that other colors, such as neon green and vivid yellow, are available at $5 per dozen balls. In this case, consumers will buy no pink balls if they cost more than $5 per dozen but will buy only pink balls if they cost less than $5. The demand curve will therefore be a horizontal line at a price of $5 per dozen balls. As you move back and forth along this line, there is a change in the quantity demanded but no change in the price. When you divide a number by zero, you get infinity, denoted by the symbol ∞.

Demand is **perfectly inelastic** when the quantity demanded does not respond at all to changes in the price. When demand is perfectly inelastic, the demand curve is a vertical line.

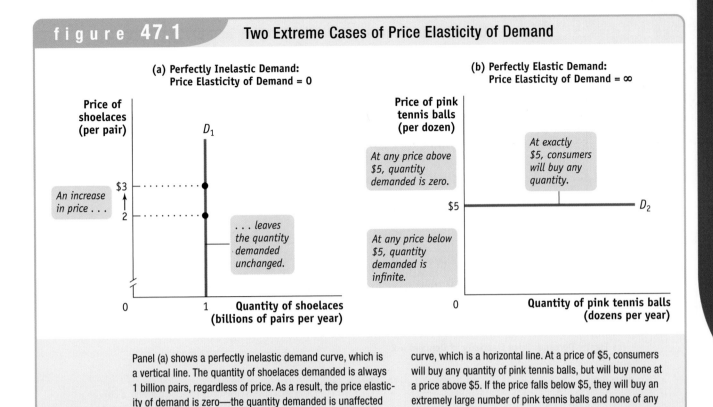

figure 47.1 — Two Extreme Cases of Price Elasticity of Demand

(a) Perfectly Inelastic Demand:
Price Elasticity of Demand = 0

Price of shoelaces (per pair)

D_1

$3

An increase in price . . .

2

. . . leaves the quantity demanded unchanged.

0   1   Quantity of shoelaces (billions of pairs per year)

(b) Perfectly Elastic Demand:
Price Elasticity of Demand = ∞

Price of pink tennis balls (per dozen)

At any price above $5, quantity demanded is zero.

At exactly $5, consumers will buy any quantity.

$5 D_2

At any price below $5, quantity demanded is infinite.

0   Quantity of pink tennis balls (dozens per year)

Panel (a) shows a perfectly inelastic demand curve, which is a vertical line. The quantity of shoelaces demanded is always 1 billion pairs, regardless of price. As a result, the price elasticity of demand is zero—the quantity demanded is unaffected by the price. Panel (b) shows a perfectly elastic demand curve, which is a horizontal line. At a price of $5, consumers will buy any quantity of pink tennis balls, but will buy none at a price above $5. If the price falls below $5, they will buy an extremely large number of pink tennis balls and none of any other color.

So a horizontal demand curve implies an infinite price elasticity of demand. When the price elasticity of demand is infinite, economists say that demand is **perfectly elastic.**

The price elasticity of demand for the vast majority of goods is somewhere between these two extreme cases. Economists use one main criterion for classifying these intermediate cases: they ask whether the price elasticity of demand is greater or less than 1. When the price elasticity of demand is greater than 1, economists say that demand is **elastic.** When the price elasticity of demand is less than 1, they say that demand is **inelastic.** The borderline case is **unit-elastic** demand, where the price elasticity of demand is—surprise—exactly 1.

To see why a price elasticity of demand equal to 1 is a useful dividing line, let's consider a hypothetical example: a toll bridge operated by the state highway department. Other things equal, the number of drivers who use the bridge depends on the toll, the price the highway department charges for crossing the bridge: the higher the toll, the fewer the drivers who use the bridge.

Figure 47.2 on the next page shows three hypothetical demand curves—one in which demand is unit-elastic, one in which it is inelastic, and one in which it is elastic. In each case, point A shows the quantity demanded if the toll is $0.90 and point B shows the quantity demanded if the toll is $1.10. An increase in the toll from $0.90 to $1.10 is an increase of 20% if we use the midpoint method to calculate percent changes.

Panel (a) shows what happens when the toll is raised from $0.90 to $1.10 and the demand curve is unit-elastic. Here the 20% price rise leads to a fall in the quantity of cars using the bridge each day from 1,100 to 900, which is a 20% decline (again using the midpoint method). So the price elasticity of demand is 20%/20% = 1.

Panel (b) shows a case of inelastic demand when the toll is raised from $0.90 to $1.10. The same 20% price rise reduces the quantity demanded from 1,050 to 950. That's only a 10% decline, so in this case the price elasticity of demand is 10%/20% = 0.5.

Demand is **perfectly elastic** when any price increase will cause the quantity demanded to drop to zero. When demand is perfectly elastic, the demand curve is a horizontal line.

Demand is **elastic** if the price elasticity of demand is greater than 1, **inelastic** if the price elasticity of demand is less than 1, and **unit-elastic** if the price elasticity of demand is exactly 1.

Photodisc

When the Bay Area Toll Authority deliberated a toll increase from $4 to $6 for San Francisco's Bay Bridge in 2010, at issue was the price elasticity of demand, which would determine the resulting drop in use.

figure 47.2   Unit-Elastic Demand, Inelastic Demand, and Elastic Demand

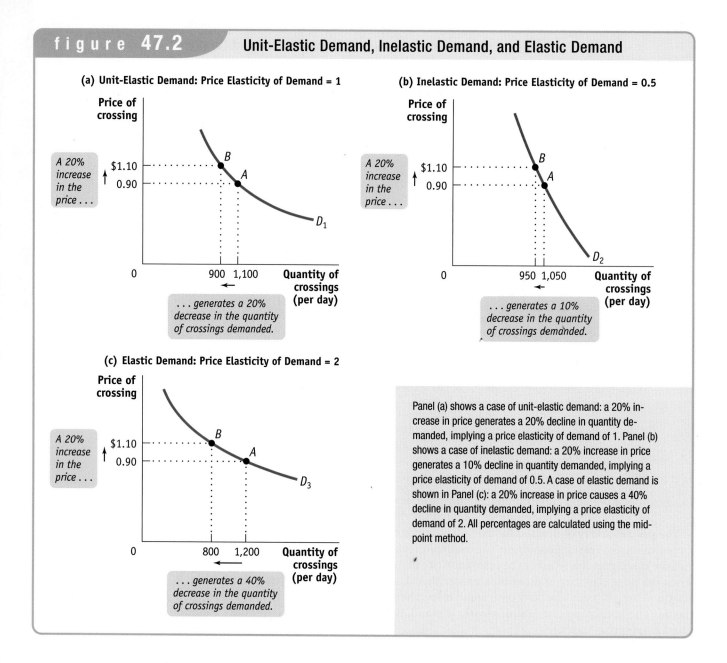

(a) Unit-Elastic Demand: Price Elasticity of Demand = 1

A 20% increase in the price... *generates a 20% decrease in the quantity of crossings demanded.*

(b) Inelastic Demand: Price Elasticity of Demand = 0.5

A 20% increase in the price... *generates a 10% decrease in the quantity of crossings demanded.*

(c) Elastic Demand: Price Elasticity of Demand = 2

A 20% increase in the price... *generates a 40% decrease in the quantity of crossings demanded.*

Panel (a) shows a case of unit-elastic demand: a 20% increase in price generates a 20% decline in quantity demanded, implying a price elasticity of demand of 1. Panel (b) shows a case of inelastic demand: a 20% increase in price generates a 10% decline in quantity demanded, implying a price elasticity of demand of 0.5. A case of elastic demand is shown in Panel (c): a 20% increase in price causes a 40% decline in quantity demanded, implying a price elasticity of demand of 2. All percentages are calculated using the midpoint method.

Panel (c) shows a case of elastic demand when the toll is raised from $0.90 to $1.10. The 20% price increase causes the quantity demanded to fall from 1,200 to 800, a 40% decline, so the price elasticity of demand is 40%/20% = 2.

Why does it matter whether demand is unit-elastic, inelastic, or elastic? Because this classification predicts how changes in the price of a good will affect the *total revenue* earned by producers from the sale of that good. In many real-life situations, such as the one faced by Med-Stat, it is crucial to know how price changes affect total revenue. **Total revenue** is defined as the total value of sales of a good or service: the price multiplied by the quantity sold.

(47-1)   Total revenue = Price × Quantity sold

Total revenue has a useful graphical representation that can help us understand why knowing the price elasticity of demand is crucial when we ask whether a price rise will increase or reduce total revenue. Panel (a) of Figure 47.3 shows the same demand curve as panel (a) of Figure 47.2. We see that 1,100 drivers will use the bridge if the toll

Total revenue is the total value of sales of a good or service. It is equal to the price multiplied by the quantity sold.

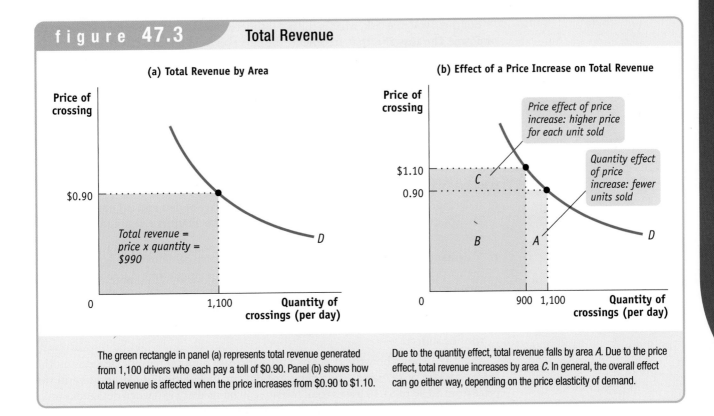

figure 47.3   Total Revenue

(a) Total Revenue by Area

Price of crossing

$0.90

Total revenue =
price x quantity =
$990

D

0   1,100   Quantity of crossings (per day)

(b) Effect of a Price Increase on Total Revenue

Price of crossing

Price effect of price increase: higher price for each unit sold

Quantity effect of price increase: fewer units sold

$1.10

0.90

C

B   *A*

D

0   900   1,100   Quantity of crossings (per day)

The green rectangle in panel (a) represents total revenue generated from 1,100 drivers who each pay a toll of $0.90. Panel (b) shows how total revenue is affected when the price increases from $0.90 to $1.10.

Due to the quantity effect, total revenue falls by area *A*. Due to the price effect, total revenue increases by area *C*. In general, the overall effect can go either way, depending on the price elasticity of demand.

is $0.90. So the total revenue at a price of $0.90 is $0.90 × 1,100 = $990. This value is equal to the area of the green rectangle, which is drawn with the bottom left corner at the point (0, 0) and the top right corner at (1,100, 0.90). In general, the total revenue at any given price is equal to the area of a rectangle whose height is the price and whose width is the quantity demanded at that price.

To get an idea of why total revenue is important, consider the following scenario. Suppose that the toll on the bridge is currently $0.90 but that the highway department must raise extra money for road repairs. One way to do this is to raise the toll on the bridge. But this plan might backfire, since a higher toll will reduce the number of drivers who use the bridge. And if traffic on the bridge dropped a lot, a higher toll would actually reduce total revenue instead of increasing it. So it's important for the highway department to know how drivers will respond to a toll increase.

We can see graphically how the toll increase affects total bridge revenue by examining panel (b) of Figure 47.3. At a toll of $0.90, total revenue is given by the sum of the areas *A* and *B*. After the toll is raised to $1.10, total revenue is given by the sum of areas *B* and *C*. So when the toll is raised, revenue represented by area *A* is lost but revenue represented by area *C* is gained. These two areas have important interpretations. Area *C* represents the revenue gain that comes from the additional $0.20 paid by drivers who continue to use the bridge. That is, the 900 who continue to use the bridge contribute an additional $0.20 × 900 = $180 per day to total revenue, represented by area *C*. But 200 drivers who would have used the bridge at a price of $0.90 no longer do so, generating a loss to total revenue of $0.90 × 200 = $180 per day, represented by area *A*. (In this particular example, because demand is unit-elastic—the same as in panel (a) of Figure 47.2—the rise in the toll has no effect on total revenue; areas *A* and *B* are the same size.)

Except in the rare case of a good with perfectly elastic or perfectly inelastic demand, when a seller raises the price of a good, two countervailing effects are present:

- *A price effect.* After a price increase, each unit sold sells at a higher price, which tends to raise revenue.

- *A quantity effect.* After a price increase, fewer units are sold, which tends to lower revenue.

But then, you may ask, what is the net ultimate effect on total revenue: does it go up or down? The answer is that, in general, the effect on total revenue can go either way—a price rise may either increase total revenue or lower it. If the price effect, which tends to raise total revenue, is the stronger of the two effects, then total revenue goes up. If the quantity effect, which tends to reduce total revenue, is the stronger, then total revenue goes down. And if the strengths of the two effects are exactly equal—as in our toll bridge example, where a $180 gain offsets a $180 loss—total revenue is unchanged by the price increase.

The price elasticity of demand tells us what happens to total revenue when price changes: its size determines which effect—the price effect or the quantity effect—is stronger. Specifically:

- If demand for a good is *unit-elastic* (the price elasticity of demand is 1), an increase in price does not change total revenue. In this case, the quantity effect and the price effect exactly offset each other.

- If demand for a good is *inelastic* (the price elasticity of demand is less than 1), a higher price increases total revenue. In this case, the price effect is stronger than the quantity effect.

- If demand for a good is *elastic* (the price elasticity of demand is greater than 1), an increase in price reduces total revenue. In this case, the quantity effect is stronger than the price effect.

Table 47.1 shows how the effect of a price increase on total revenue depends on the price elasticity of demand, using the same data as in Figure 47.2. An increase in the price from $0.90 to $1.10 leaves total revenue unchanged at $990 when demand is unit-elastic. When demand is inelastic, the price effect dominates the quantity effect; the same price increase leads to an increase in total revenue from $945 to $1,045. And when demand is elastic, the quantity effect dominates the price effect; the price increase leads to a decline in total revenue from $1,080 to $880.

table 47.1

Price Elasticity of Demand and Total Revenue

	Price of crossing = $0.90	Price of crossing = $1.10
Unit-elastic demand (price elasticity of demand = 1)		
Quantity demanded	1,100	900
Total revenue	$990	$990
Inelastic demand (price elasticity of demand = 0.5)		
Quantity demanded	1,050	950
Total revenue	$945	$1,045
Elastic demand (price elasticity of demand = 2)		
Quantity demanded	1,200	800
Total revenue	$1,080	$880

The price elasticity of demand also predicts the effect of a *fall* in price on total revenue. When the price falls, the same two countervailing effects are present, but they work in the opposite directions as compared to the case of a price rise. There is the price effect of a lower price per unit sold, which tends to lower revenue. This is countered by the quantity effect of more units sold, which tends to raise revenue. Which effect dominates depends on the price elasticity. Here is a quick summary:

- When demand is *unit-elastic,* the two effects exactly balance each other out; so a fall in price has no effect on total revenue.
- When demand is *inelastic,* the price effect dominates the quantity effect; so a fall in price reduces total revenue.
- When demand is *elastic,* the quantity effect dominates the price effect; so a fall in price increases total revenue.

Price Elasticity Along the Demand Curve

Suppose an economist says that "the price elasticity of demand for coffee is 0.25." What he or she means is that *at the current price* the elasticity is 0.25. In the previous discussion of the toll bridge, what we were really describing was the elasticity *at the price* of $0.90. Why this qualification? Because for the vast majority of demand curves, the price elasticity of demand at one point along the curve is different from the price elasticity of demand at other points along the same curve.

To see this, consider the table in Figure 47.4, which shows a hypothetical demand schedule. It also shows in the last column the total revenue generated at each price and quantity combination in the demand schedule. The upper panel of the graph in Figure

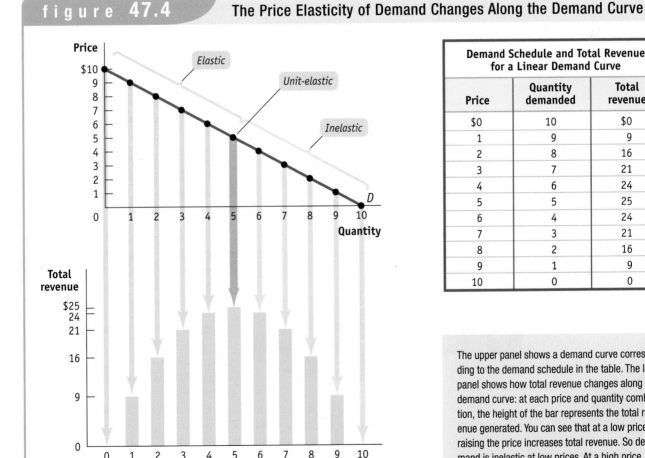

figure 47.4   The Price Elasticity of Demand Changes Along the Demand Curve

Demand Schedule and Total Revenue for a Linear Demand Curve		
Price	Quantity demanded	Total revenue
$0	10	$0
1	9	9
2	8	16
3	7	21
4	6	24
5	5	25
6	4	24
7	3	21
8	2	16
9	1	9
10	0	0

The upper panel shows a demand curve corresponding to the demand schedule in the table. The lower panel shows how total revenue changes along that demand curve: at each price and quantity combination, the height of the bar represents the total revenue generated. You can see that at a low price, raising the price increases total revenue. So demand is inelastic at low prices. At a high price, however, a rise in price reduces total revenue. So demand is elastic at high prices.

Demand is elastic: a higher price reduces total revenue.

Demand is inelastic: a higher price increases total revenue.

47.4 shows the corresponding demand curve. The lower panel illustrates the same data on total revenue: the height of a bar at each quantity demanded—which corresponds to a particular price—measures the total revenue generated at that price.

In Figure 47.4, you can see that when the price is low, raising the price increases total revenue: starting at a price of $1, raising the price to $2 increases total revenue from $9 to $16. This means that when the price is low, demand is inelastic. Moreover, you can see that demand is inelastic on the entire section of the demand curve from a price of $0 to a price of $5.

When the price is high, however, raising it further reduces total revenue: starting at a price of $8, for example, raising the price to $9 reduces total revenue, from $16 to $9. This means that when the price is high, demand is elastic. Furthermore, you can see that demand is elastic over the section of the demand curve from a price of $5 to $10.

For the vast majority of goods, the price elasticity of demand changes along the demand curve. So whenever you measure a good's elasticity, you are really measuring it at a particular point or section of the good's demand curve.

What Factors Determine the Price Elasticity of Demand?

The flu vaccine shortfall of 2004–2005 allowed vaccine distributors to significantly raise their prices for two important reasons: there were no substitutes, and for many people the vaccine was a medical necessity. People responded in various ways. Some paid the high prices, and some traveled to Canada and other countries to get vaccinated. Some simply did without (and over time often changed their habits to avoid catching the flu, such as eating out less often and avoiding mass transit). This experience illustrates the four main factors that determine elasticity: whether close substitutes are available, whether the good is a necessity or a luxury, the share of income a consumer spends on the good, and how much time has elapsed since the price change. We'll briefly examine each of these factors.

Whether Close Substitutes Are Available The price elasticity of demand tends to be high if there are other goods that consumers regard as similar and would be willing to consume instead. The price elasticity of demand tends to be low if there are no close substitutes.

Whether the Good Is a Necessity or a Luxury The price elasticity of demand tends to be low if a good is something you must have, like a life-saving medicine. The price elasticity of demand tends to be high if the good is a luxury—something you can easily live without.

Share of Income Spent on the Good The price elasticity of demand tends to be low when spending on a good accounts for a small share of a consumer's income. In that case, a significant change in the price of the good has little impact on how much the consumer spends. In contrast, when a good accounts for a significant share of a consumer's spending, the consumer is likely to be very responsive to a change in price. In this case, the price elasticity of demand is high.

Time In general, the price elasticity of demand tends to increase as consumers have more time to adjust to a price change. This means that the long-run price elasticity of demand is often higher than the short-run elasticity.

A good illustration of the effect of time on the elasticity of demand is drawn from the 1970s, the first time gasoline prices increased dramatically in the United States. Initially, consumption fell very little because there were no close substitutes for gasoline and because driving their cars was necessary for people to carry out the ordinary tasks of life. Over time, however, Americans changed their habits in ways that enabled them to gradually reduce their gasoline consumption. The result was a steady decline in gasoline consumption over the next decade, even though the price of gasoline did not continue to rise, confirming that the long-run price elasticity of demand for gasoline was indeed much larger than the short-run elasticity.

fyi

Responding to Your Tuition Bill

College costs more than ever—and not just because of overall inflation. Tuition has been rising faster than the overall cost of living for years. But does rising tuition keep people from going to college? Two studies found that the answer depends on the type of college. Both studies assessed how responsive the decision to go to college is to a change in tuition.

A 1988 study found that a 3% increase in tuition led to an approximately 2% fall in the number of students enrolled at four-year institutions, giving a price elasticity of demand of 0.67 (2%/3%). In the case of two-year institutions, the study found a significantly higher response: a 3% increase in tuition led to a 2.7% fall in enrollments, giving a price elasticity of demand of 0.9. In other words, the enrollment decision for

students at two-year colleges was significantly more responsive to price than for students at four-year colleges. The result: students at two-year colleges are more likely to forgo getting a degree because of tuition costs than students at four-year colleges.

A 1999 study confirmed this pattern. In comparison to four-year colleges, it found that two-year college enrollment rates were significantly more responsive to changes in state financial aid (a decline in aid leading to a decline in enrollments), a predictable effect given these students' greater sensitivity to the cost of tuition. Another piece of evidence suggests that students at two-year colleges are more likely to be paying their own way and making a trade-off between attending college and working: the

study found that enrollments at two-year colleges are much more responsive to changes in the unemployment rate (an increase in the unemployment rate leading to an increase in enrollments) than enrollments at four-year colleges. So is the cost of tuition a barrier to getting a college degree in the United States? Yes, but more so at two-year colleges than at four-year colleges.

Interestingly, the 1999 study found that for both two-year and four-year colleges, price sensitivity of demand had fallen somewhat since the 1988 study. One possible explanation is that because the value of a college education has risen considerably over time, fewer people forgo college, even if tuition goes up. (See source note on copyright page.)

Module 47 AP Review

Solutions appear at the back of the book.

Check Your Understanding

1. For each case, choose the condition that characterizes demand: elastic demand, inelastic demand, or unit-elastic demand.
   a. Total revenue decreases when price increases.
   b. When price falls, the additional revenue generated by the increase in the quantity sold is exactly offset by the revenue lost from the fall in the price received per unit.
   c. Total revenue falls when output increases.

   d. Producers in an industry find they can increase their total revenues by working together to reduce industry output.

2. For the following goods, is demand elastic, inelastic, or unit-elastic? Explain. What is the shape of the demand curve?
   a. demand by a snake-bite victim for an antidote
   b. demand by students for blue pencils

Tackle the Test: Multiple-Choice Questions

1. A perfectly elastic demand curve is
   a. upward sloping.
   b. vertical.
   c. not a straight line.
   d. horizontal.
   e. downward sloping.

2. Which of the following would cause the demand for a good to be relatively inelastic?
   a. The good has a large number of close substitutes.
   b. Expenditures on the good represent a large share of consumer income.
   c. There is ample time to adjust to price changes.
   d. The good is a necessity.
   e. The price of the good is in the upper left section of a linear demand curve.

3. Which of the following is true if the price elasticity of demand for a good is zero?
   a. The slope of the demand curve is zero.
   b. The slope of the demand curve is one.
   c. The demand curve is vertical.
   d. The demand curve is horizontal.
   e. The price of the good is high.

4. Which of the following is correct for a price increase? When demand is _____, total revenue will _____.

	Demand	Total Revenue
a.	inelastic	decrease
b.	elastic	decrease
c.	unit-elastic	increase
d.	unit-elastic	decrease
e.	elastic	increase

5. Total revenue is maximized when demand is
   a. elastic.
   b. inelastic.
   c. unit-elastic.
   d. zero.
   e. infinite.

Tackle the Test: Free-Response Questions

1. Draw a correctly labeled graph of a perfectly inelastic demand curve.
   a. What is the price elasticity of demand for this good?
   b. What is the slope of the demand curve for this good?
   c. Is this good more likely to be a luxury or a necessity? Explain.

2. Draw a correctly labeled graph illustrating a demand curve that is a straight line and is neither perfectly elastic nor perfectly inelastic.
   a. On your graph, indicate the half of the demand curve along which demand is elastic.
   b. In the elastic range, how will an increase in price affect total revenue? Explain.

Answer (5 points)

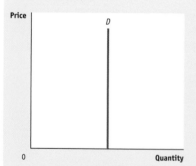

1 point: A graph with "Price" (or "*P*") on the vertical axis, "Quantity" (or "*Q*") on the horizontal axis, and a vertical line labeled "Demand" (or "*D*")

1 point: Zero

1 point: Infinite or undefined

1 point: Necessity

1 point: Since you have to have a necessity (such as a life-saving medicine), you do not change the quantity you purchase when price changes.

Module 48
Other Elasticities

What you will learn in this **Module:**

- How the cross-price elasticity of demand measures the responsiveness of demand for one good to changes in the price of another good

- The meaning and importance of the income elasticity of demand, a measure of the responsiveness of demand to changes in income

- The significance of the price elasticity of supply, which measures the responsiveness of the quantity supplied to changes in price

- The factors that influence the size of these various elasticities

Other Elasticities

We stated earlier that economists use the concept of *elasticity* to measure the responsiveness of one variable to changes in another. However, up to this point we have focused on the price elasticity of demand. Now that we have used elasticity to measure the responsiveness of quantity demanded to changes in price, we can go on to look at how elasticity is used to understand the relationship between other important variables in economics.

The quantity of a good demanded depends not only on the price of that good but also on other variables. In particular, demand curves shift because of changes in the prices of related goods and changes in consumers' incomes. It is often important to have a measure of these other effects, and the best measures are—you guessed it—elasticities. Specifically, we can best measure how the demand for a good is affected by prices of other goods using a measure called the *cross-price elasticity of demand,* and we can best measure how demand is affected by changes in income using the *income elasticity of demand.*

Finally, we can also use elasticity to measure supply responses. The *price elasticity of supply* measures the responsiveness of the quantity supplied to changes in price.

The Cross-Price Elasticity of Demand

The demand for a good is often affected by the prices of other, related goods—goods that are substitutes or complements. A change in the price of a related good shifts the demand curve of the original good, reflecting a change in the quantity demanded at any given price. The strength of such a "cross" effect on demand can be measured by the **cross-price elasticity of demand,** defined as the ratio of the percent change in the quantity demanded of one good to the percent change in the price of another.

(48-1) Cross-price elasticity of demand between goods A and B

$$= \frac{\% \text{ change in quantity of A demanded}}{\% \text{ change in price of B}}$$

When two goods are substitutes, like hot dogs and hamburgers, the cross-price elasticity of demand is positive: a rise in the price of hot dogs increases the demand for hamburgers—that is, it causes a rightward shift of the demand curve for hamburgers. If the goods are close substitutes, the cross-price elasticity will be positive and large;

The **cross-price elasticity of demand** between two goods measures the effect of the change in one good's price on the quantity demanded of the other good. It is equal to the percent change in the quantity demanded of one good divided by the percent change in the other good's price.

if they are not close substitutes, the cross-price elasticity will be positive and small. So when the cross-price elasticity of demand is positive, its size is a measure of how closely substitutable the two goods are.

When two goods are complements, like hot dogs and hot dog buns, the cross-price elasticity is negative: a rise in the price of hot dogs decreases the demand for hot dog buns—that is, it causes a leftward shift of the demand curve for hot dog buns. As with substitutes, the size of the cross-price elasticity of demand between two complements tells us how strongly complementary they are: if the cross-price elasticity is only slightly below zero, they are weak complements; if it is very negative, they are strong complements.

Note that in the case of the cross-price elasticity of demand, the sign (plus or minus) is very important: it tells us whether the two goods are complements or substitutes. So we cannot drop the minus sign as we did for the price elasticity of demand.

Our discussion of the cross-price elasticity of demand is a useful place to return to a point we made earlier: elasticity is a *unit-free* measure—that is, it doesn't depend on the units in which goods are measured.

To see the potential problem, suppose someone told you that "if the price of hot dog buns rises by $0.30, Americans will buy 10 million fewer hot dogs this year." If you've ever bought hot dog buns, you'll immediately wonder: is that a $0.30 increase in the price *per bun,* or is it a $0.30 increase in the price *per package* of buns? It makes a big difference what units we are talking about! However, if someone says that the cross-price elasticity of demand between buns and hot dogs is –0.3, it doesn't matter whether buns are sold individually or by the package. So elasticity is defined as a ratio of percent changes, which avoids confusion over units.

The Income Elasticity of Demand

The **income elasticity of demand** measures how changes in income affect the demand for a good. It indicates whether a good is normal or inferior and specifies how responsive demand for the good is to changes in income. Having learned the price and cross-price elasticity formulas, the income elasticity formula will look familiar:

$$(48\text{-}2) \quad \text{Income elasticity of demand} = \frac{\%\ \text{change in quantity demanded}}{\%\ \text{change in income}}$$

Just as the cross-price elasticity of demand between two goods can be either positive or negative, depending on whether the goods are substitutes or complements, the income elasticity of demand for a good can also be either positive or negative. Recall that goods can be either *normal goods,* for which demand increases when income rises, or *inferior goods,* for which demand decreases when income rises. These definitions relate directly to the sign of the income elasticity of demand:

- When the income elasticity of demand is positive, the good is a normal good—that is, the quantity demanded at any given price increases as income increases.

- When the income elasticity of demand is negative, the good is an inferior good—that is, the quantity demanded at any given price decreases as income increases.

Economists often use estimates of the income elasticity of demand to predict which industries will grow most rapidly as the incomes of consumers grow over time. In doing this, they often find it useful to make a further distinction among normal goods, identifying which are *income-elastic* and which are *income-inelastic.*

The demand for a good is **income-elastic** if the income elasticity of demand for that good is greater than 1. When income rises, the demand for income-elastic goods rises *faster* than income. Luxury goods such as second homes and international travel tend to be income-elastic. The demand for a good is **income-inelastic** if the income elasticity of demand for that good is positive but less than 1. When income rises, the demand for income-inelastic goods rises, but more slowly than income. Necessities such as food and clothing tend to be income-inelastic.

The **income elasticity of demand** is the percent change in the quantity of a good demanded when a consumer's income changes divided by the percent change in the consumer's income.

The demand for a good is **income-elastic** if the income elasticity of demand for that good is greater than 1.

The demand for a good is **income-inelastic** if the income elasticity of demand for that good is positive but less than 1.

Where Have All the Farmers Gone?

What percentage of Americans live on farms? Sad to say, the U.S. government no longer publishes that number. In 1991 the official percentage was 1.9, but in that year the government decided it was no longer a meaningful indicator of the size of the agricultural sector because a large proportion of those who live on farms actually make their living doing something else. But in the days of the Founding Fathers, the great majority of Americans lived on farms. As recently as the 1940s, one American in six—or approximately 17%—still did.

Why do so few people now live and work on farms in the United States? There are two main reasons, both involving elasticities.

First, the income elasticity of demand for food is much less than 1—food demand is income-inelastic. As consumers grow richer, other things equal, spending on food rises less than in proportion to income. As a result, as the U.S. econ-

omy has grown, the share of income spent on food—and therefore the share of total U.S. income earned by farmers—has fallen.

Second, agriculture has been a technologically progressive sector for approximately 150 years in the United States, with steadily increasing yields over time. You might think that technological progress would be good for farmers. But competition among farmers means that technological progress leads to lower food prices. Meanwhile, the demand for food is price-inelastic, so falling prices of agricultural goods, other things equal, reduce the total revenue of farmers. That's right: progress in farming is good for consumers but bad for farmers.

The combination of these effects explains the relative decline of farming. Even if farming weren't such a technologically progressive sector, the low income elasticity of demand for food

would ensure that the income of farmers grows more slowly than the economy as a whole. The combination of rapid technological progress in farming with price-inelastic demand for farm products reinforces this effect, further reducing the growth of farm income. In short, the U.S. farm sector has been a victim of success—the U.S. economy's success as a whole (which reduces the importance of spending on food) and its own success in increasing yields.

The Price Elasticity of Supply

In the wake of the flu vaccine shortfall of 2004, attempts by vaccine distributors to drive up the price of vaccines would have been much less effective if a higher price had induced a large increase in the output of flu vaccines by flu vaccine manufacturers other than Chiron. In fact, if the rise in price had precipitated a significant increase in flu vaccine production, the price would have been pushed back down. But that didn't happen because, as we mentioned earlier, it would have been far too costly and technically difficult to produce more vaccine for the 2004–2005 flu season. (In reality, the production of flu vaccine is begun a year before it is to be distributed.) This was another critical element in the ability of some flu vaccine distributors, like Med-Stat, to get significantly higher prices for their product: a low responsiveness in the quantity of output supplied to the higher price of flu vaccine by flu vaccine producers. To measure the response of producers to price changes, we need a measure parallel to the price elasticity of demand—the *price elasticity of supply*.

Measuring the Price Elasticity of Supply

The **price elasticity of supply** is defined the same way as the price elasticity of demand (although there is no minus sign to be eliminated here):

$$(48\text{-}3) \quad \text{Price elasticity of supply} = \frac{\%\ \text{change in quantity supplied}}{\%\ \text{change in price}}$$

The **price elasticity of supply** is a measure of the responsiveness of the quantity of a good supplied to the price of that good. It is the ratio of the percent change in the quantity supplied to the percent change in the price as we move along the supply curve.

The only difference is that here we consider movements along the supply curve rather than movements along the demand curve.

Suppose that the price of tomatoes rises by 10%. If the quantity of tomatoes supplied also increases by 10% in response, the price elasticity of supply of tomatoes is

1 (10%/10%) and supply is unit-elastic. If the quantity supplied increases by 5%, the price elasticity of supply is 0.5 and supply is inelastic; if the quantity increases by 20%, the price elasticity of supply is 2 and supply is elastic.

As in the case of demand, the extreme values of the price elasticity of supply have a simple graphical representation. Panel (a) of Figure 48.1 shows the supply of cell phone frequencies, the portion of the radio spectrum that is suitable for sending and receiving cell phone signals. Governments own the right to sell the use of this part of the radio spectrum to cell phone operators inside their borders. But governments can't increase or decrease the number of cell phone frequencies they have to offer—for technical reasons, the quantity of frequencies suitable for cell phone operation is fixed. So the supply curve for cell phone frequencies is a vertical line, which we have assumed is set at the quantity of 100 frequencies. As you move up and down that curve, the change in the quantity supplied by the government is zero, whatever the change in price. So panel (a) illustrates a case of **perfectly inelastic supply,** meaning that the price elasticity of supply is zero.

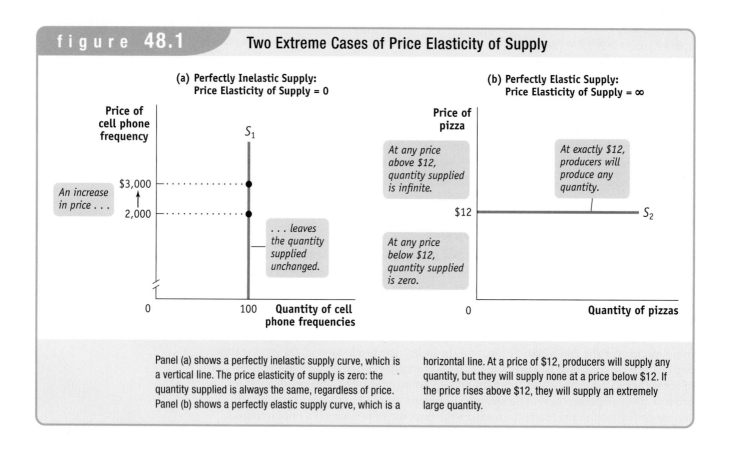

figure 48.1   **Two Extreme Cases of Price Elasticity of Supply**

Panel (a) shows a perfectly inelastic supply curve, which is a vertical line. The price elasticity of supply is zero: the quantity supplied is always the same, regardless of price. Panel (b) shows a perfectly elastic supply curve, which is a horizontal line. At a price of $12, producers will supply any quantity, but they will supply none at a price below $12. If the price rises above $12, they will supply an extremely large quantity.

Panel (b) shows the supply curve for pizza. We suppose that it costs $12 to produce a pizza, including all opportunity costs. At any price below $12, it would be unprofitable to produce pizza and all the pizza parlors would go out of business. At a price of $12 or more, there are many producers who could operate pizza parlors. The ingredients— flour, tomatoes, cheese—are plentiful. And if necessary, more tomatoes could be grown, more milk could be produced to make mozzarella cheese, and so on. So by allowing profits, any price above $12 would elicit the supply of an extremely large quantity of pizzas. The implied supply curve is therefore a horizontal line at $12. Since even a tiny increase in the price would lead to an enormous increase in the quantity supplied, the price elasticity of supply would be virtually infinite. A horizontal supply curve such as this represents a case of **perfectly elastic supply.**

As our cell phone frequencies and pizza examples suggest, real-world instances of both perfectly inelastic and perfectly elastic supply are easier to find than their counterparts in demand.

What Factors Determine the Price Elasticity of Supply?
Our examples tell us the main determinant of the price elasticity of supply: the availability of inputs. In addition, as with the price elasticity of demand, time may also play a role in the price elasticity of supply. Here we briefly summarize the two factors.

The Availability of Inputs
The price elasticity of supply tends to be large when inputs are readily available and can be shifted into and out of production at a relatively low cost. It tends to be small when inputs are available only in a more-or-less fixed quantity or can be shifted into and out of production only at a relatively high cost.

Time
The price elasticity of supply tends to grow larger as producers have more time to respond to a price change. This means that the long-run price elasticity of supply is often higher than the short-run elasticity. In the case of the flu vaccine shortfall, time was the crucial element because flu vaccine must be grown in cultures over many months.

The price elasticity of pizza supply is very high because the inputs needed to make more pizza are readily available. The price elasticity of cell phone frequencies is zero because an essential input—the radio spectrum—cannot be increased at all.

Many industries are like pizza and have large price elasticities of supply: they can be

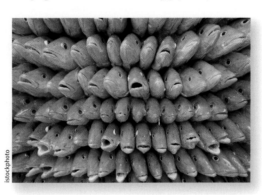

readily expanded because they don't require any special or unique resources. On the other hand, the price elasticity of supply is usually substantially less than perfectly elastic for goods that involve limited natural resources: minerals like gold or copper, agricultural products like coffee that flourish only on certain types of land, and renewable resources like ocean fish that can be exploited only up to a point without destroying the resource.

But given enough time, producers are often able to significantly change the amount they produce in response to a price change, even when production involves a limited natural resource. For example, consider again the effects of a surge in flu vaccine prices, but this time focus on the supply response. If the price were to rise to $90 per vaccination and stay there for a number of years, there would almost certainly be a substantial increase in flu vaccine production. Producers such as Chiron would eventually respond by increasing the size of their manufacturing plants, hiring more lab technicians, and so on. But significantly enlarging the capacity of a biotech manufacturing lab takes several years, not weeks or months or even a single year.

For this reason, economists often make a distinction between the short-run elasticity of supply, usually referring to a few weeks or months, and the long-run elasticity of supply, usually referring to several years. In most industries, the long-run elasticity of supply is larger than the short-run elasticity.

An Elasticity Menagerie

We've just run through quite a few different types of elasticity. Keeping them all straight can be a challenge. So in Table 48.1 on the next page we provide a summary of all the types of elasticity we have discussed and their implications.

There is **perfectly elastic supply** if the quantity supplied is zero below some price and infinite above that price. A perfectly elastic supply curve is a horizontal line.

table **48.1**

An Elasticity Menagerie

Name	Possible values	Significance
Price elasticity of demand $= \dfrac{\text{\% change in quantity demanded}}{\text{\% change in price}}$ (dropping the minus sign)		
Perfectly inelastic demand	0	Price has no effect on quantity demanded (vertical demand curve).
Inelastic demand	Between 0 and 1	A rise in price increases total revenue.
Unit-elastic demand	Exactly 1	Changes in price have no effect on total revenue.
Elastic demand	Greater than 1, less than ∞	A rise in price reduces total revenue.
Perfectly elastic demand	∞	A rise in price causes quantity demanded to fall to 0. A fall in price leads to an infinite quantity demanded (horizontal demand curve).
Cross-price elasticity of demand $= \dfrac{\text{\% change in quantity } of\ one\ good \text{ demanded}}{\text{\% change in price } of\ another\ good}$		
Complements	Negative	Quantity demanded of one good falls when the price of another rises.
Substitutes	Positive	Quantity demanded of one good rises when the price of another rises.
Income elasticity of demand $= \dfrac{\text{\% change in quantity demanded}}{\text{\% change in income}}$		
Inferior good	Negative	Quantity demanded falls when income rises.
Normal good, income-inelastic	Positive, less than 1	Quantity demanded rises when income rises, but not as rapidly as income.
Normal good, income-elastic	Greater than 1	Quantity demanded rises when income rises, and more rapidly than income.
Price elasticity of supply $= \dfrac{\text{\% change in quantity supplied}}{\text{\% change in price}}$		
Perfectly inelastic supply	0	Price has no effect on quantity supplied (vertical supply curve).
	Greater than 0, less than ∞	Ordinary upward-sloping supply curve.
Perfectly elastic supply	∞	Any fall in price causes quantity supplied to fall to 0. Any rise in price elicits an infinite quantity supplied (horizontal supply curve).

Module 48 AP Review

Solutions appear at the back of the book.

Check Your Understanding

1. After Chelsea's income increased from $12,000 to $18,000 a year, her purchases of CDs increased from 10 to 40 CDs a year. Calculate Chelsea's income elasticity of demand for CDs using the midpoint method.

2. As the price of margarine rises by 20%, a manufacturer of baked goods increases its quantity of butter demanded by 5%. Calculate the cross-price elasticity of demand between butter and margarine. Are butter and margarine substitutes or complements for this manufacturer?

3. Using the midpoint method, calculate the price elasticity of supply for web-design services when the price per hour rises from $100 to $150 and the number of hours supplied increases from 300,000 hours to 500,000. Is supply elastic, inelastic, or unit-elastic?

Tackle the Test: Multiple-Choice Questions

1. If the cross-price elasticity between two goods is negative, this means that the two goods are
   a. substitutes.
   b. complements.
   c. normal.
   d. inferior.
   e. luxuries.

2. If Kylie buys 200 units of good X when her income is $20,000 and 300 units of good X when her income increases to $25,000, her income elasticity of demand, using the midpoint method, is
   a. 0.06.
   b. 0.5.
   c. 1.65.
   d. 1.8.
   e. 2.00.

3. The income elasticity of demand for a normal good is
   a. zero.
   b. 1.
   c. infinite.
   d. positive.
   e. negative.

4. A perfectly elastic supply curve is
   a. positively sloped.
   b. negatively sloped.
   c. vertical.
   d. horizontal.
   e. U-shaped

5. Which of the following leads to a more inelastic price elasticity of supply?
   I. the use of inputs that are easily obtained
   II. a high degree of substitutability between inputs
   III. a shorter time period in which to supply the good
   a. I only
   b. II only
   c. III only
   d. I and II only
   e. I, II, and III

Tackle the Test: Free-Response Questions

1. Refer to the table below to answer the following questions.

Price of Good A	Quantity of Good A Demanded	Quantity of Good B Demanded
$10	100	5
8	110	10

   a. Using the midpoint method, calculate the price elasticity of demand for good A.
   b. Give the formula for calculating the cross-price elasticity of demand between good A and good B.
   c. Using the midpoint method, calculate the cross-price elasticity of demand between good A and good B.
   d. What does your answer for part c tell you about the relationship between the two goods? Explain.

2. Assume the price of corn rises by 20% and this causes suppliers to increase the quantity of corn supplied by 40%.
   a. Calculate the price elasticity of supply.
   b. In this case, is supply elastic or inelastic?
   c. Draw a correctly labeled graph of a supply curve illustrating the most extreme case of the category of elasticity you found in part b (either perfectly elastic or perfectly inelastic supply).
   d. What would likely be true of the availability of inputs for a firm with the supply curve you drew in part c? Explain.

Answer (5 points)

1 point: 0.43

1 point: % change in quantity of good B/% change in price of good A or (change in Q_B/average Q_B)/(change in P_A/average P_A)

1 point: −3

1 point: They are complements.

1 point: Cross-price elasticity is negative—when the price of good A goes down, in addition to buying more of good A, people buy more of good B to go along with it.

- The meaning of consumer
  surplus and its relationship to
  the demand curve
- The meaning of producer
  surplus and its relationship to
  the supply curve

Module 49
Consumer and
Producer Surplus

There is a lively market in second-hand college textbooks. At the end of each term, some students who took a course decide that the money they can make by selling their used books is worth more to them than keeping the books. And some students who are taking the course next term prefer to buy a somewhat battered but less expensive used textbook rather than pay full price for a new one.

Textbook publishers and authors are not happy about these transactions because they cut into sales of new books. But both the students who sell used books and those who buy them clearly benefit from the existence of the market. That is why many college bookstores facilitate their trade, buying used textbooks and selling them alongside the new books.

But can we put a number on what used textbook buyers and sellers gain from these transactions? Can we answer the question "*How much* do the buyers and sellers of textbooks gain from the existence of the used-book market?"

Yes, we can. In this module we will see how to measure benefits, such as those to buyers of used textbooks, from being able to purchase a good—known as *consumer surplus*. And we will see that there is a corresponding measure, *producer surplus*, of the benefits sellers receive from being able to sell a good.

The concepts of consumer surplus and producer surplus are useful for analyzing a wide variety of economic issues. They let us calculate how much benefit producers and consumers receive from the existence of a market. They also allow us to calculate how the welfare of consumers and producers is affected by changes in market prices. Such calculations play a crucial role in evaluating many economic policies.

What information do we need to calculate consumer and producer surplus? Surprisingly, all we need are the demand and supply curves for a good. That is, the supply and demand model isn't just a model of how a competitive market works—it's also a model of how much consumers and producers gain from participating in that market. So our first step will be to learn how consumer and producer surplus can be derived from the demand and supply curves. We will then see how these concepts can be applied to actual economic issues.

Consumer Surplus and the Demand Curve

First-year college students are often surprised by the prices of the textbooks required for their classes. The College Board estimates that in 2006-2007 students at four-year schools spent, on average, $942 for books and supplies. But at the end of the semester, students might again be surprised to find out that they can sell back at least some of the textbooks they used for the semester for a percentage of the purchase price (offsetting some of the cost of textbooks). The ability to purchase used textbooks at the start of the semester and to sell back used textbooks at the end of the semester is beneficial to students on a budget. In fact, the market for used textbooks is a big business in terms of dollars and cents—approximately $1.9 billion in 2004-2005. This market provides a convenient starting point for us to develop the concepts of consumer and producer surplus. We'll use the concepts of consumer and producer surplus to understand exactly how buyers and sellers benefit from a competitive market and how big those benefits are. In addition, these concepts assist in the analysis of what happens when competitive markets don't work well or there is interference in the market.

So let's begin by looking at the market for used textbooks, starting with the buyers. The key point, as we'll see in a minute, is that the demand curve is derived from their tastes or preferences—and that those same preferences also determine how much they gain from the opportunity to buy used books.

Willingness to Pay and the Demand Curve

A used book is not as good as a new book—it will be battered and coffee-stained, may include someone else's highlighting, and may not be completely up to date. How much this bothers you depends on your preferences. Some potential buyers would prefer to buy the used book even if it is only slightly cheaper than a new one, while others would buy the used book only if it is considerably cheaper. Let's define a potential buyer's **willingness to pay** as the maximum price at which he or she would buy a good, in this case a used textbook. An individual won't buy the good if it costs more than this amount but is eager to do so if it costs less. If the price is just equal to an individual's willingness to pay, he or she is indifferent between buying and not buying. For the sake of simplicity, we'll assume that the individual buys the good in this case.

The table in Figure 49.1 on the next page shows five potential buyers of a used book that costs $100 new, listed in order of their willingness to pay. At one extreme is Aleisha, who will buy a second-hand book even if the price is as high as $59. Brad is less willing to have a used book and will buy one only if the price is $45 or less. Claudia is willing to pay only $35 and Darren, only $25. Edwina, who really doesn't like the idea of a used book, will buy one only if it costs no more than $10.

How many of these five students will actually buy a used book? It depends on the price. If the price of a used book is $55, only Aleisha buys one; if the price is $40, Aleisha and Brad both buy used books, and so on. So the information in the table can be used to construct the *demand schedule* for used textbooks.

We can use this demand schedule to derive the market demand curve shown in Figure 49.1. Because we are considering only a small number of consumers, this curve doesn't look like the smooth demand curves we have seen previously, for markets that contained hundreds or thousands of consumers. This demand curve is step-shaped, with alternating horizontal and vertical segments. Each horizontal segment—each step—corresponds to one potential buyer's willingness to pay. However, we'll see shortly that for the analysis of consumer surplus it doesn't matter whether the demand curve is step-shaped, as in this figure, or whether there are many consumers, making the curve smooth.

A consumer's **willingness to pay** for a good is the maximum price at which he or she would buy that good.

figure 49.1

The Demand Curve for Used Textbooks

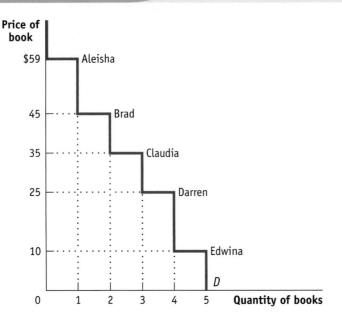

Potential buyers	Willingness to pay
Aleisha	$59
Brad	45
Claudia	35
Darren	25
Edwina	10

With only five potential consumers in this market, the demand curve is step-shaped. Each step represents one consumer, and its height indicates that consumer's willingness to pay—the maximum price at which each will buy a used textbook—as indicated in the table. Aleisha has the highest willingness to pay at $59, Brad has the next highest at $45, and so on down to Edwina with the lowest willingness to pay at $10. At a price of $59, the quantity demanded is one (Aleisha); at a price of $45, the quantity demanded is two (Aleisha and Brad); and so on until you reach a price of $10, at which all five students are willing to purchase a book.

Willingness to Pay and Consumer Surplus

Suppose that the campus bookstore makes used textbooks available at a price of $30. In that case Aleisha, Brad, and Claudia will buy books. Do they gain from their purchases, and if so, how much?

The answer, shown in Table 49.1, is that each student who purchases a book does achieve a net gain but that the amount of the gain differs among students.

Aleisha would have been willing to pay $59, so her net gain is $59 − $30 = $29. Brad would have been willing to pay $45, so his net gain is $45 − $30 = $15. Claudia would

table 49.1

Consumer Surplus When the Price of a Used Textbook Is $30

Potential buyer	Willingness to pay	Price paid	Individual consumer surplus = Willingness to pay − Price paid
Aleisha	$59	$30	$29
Brad	45	30	15
Claudia	35	30	5
Darren	25	—	—
Edwina	10	—	—
All buyers			Total consumer surplus = $49

have been willing to pay $35, so her net gain is $35 − $30 = $5. Darren and Edwina, however, won't be willing to buy a used book at a price of $30, so they neither gain nor lose.

The net gain that a buyer achieves from the purchase of a good is called that buyer's **individual consumer surplus.** What we learn from this example is that whenever a buyer pays a price less than his or her willingness to pay, the buyer achieves some individual consumer surplus.

The sum of the individual consumer surpluses achieved by all the buyers of a good is known as the **total consumer surplus** achieved in the market. In Table 49.1, the total consumer surplus is the sum of the individual consumer surpluses achieved by Aleisha, Brad, and Claudia: $29 + $15 + $5 = $49.

Economists often use the term **consumer surplus** to refer to both individual and total consumer surplus. We will follow this practice; it will always be clear in context whether we are referring to the consumer surplus achieved by an individual or by all buyers.

Total consumer surplus can be represented graphically. Figure 49.2 reproduces the demand curve from Figure 49.1. Each step in that demand curve is one book wide and represents one consumer. For example, the height of Aleisha's step is $59, her willingness to pay. This step forms the top of a rectangle, with $30—the price she actually pays for a book—forming the bottom. The area of Aleisha's rectangle, ($59 − $30) × 1 = $29, is her consumer surplus from purchasing one book at $30. So the individual consumer surplus Aleisha gains is the *area of the dark blue rectangle* shown in Figure 49.2.

In addition to Aleisha, Brad and Claudia will also each buy a book when the price is $30. Like Aleisha, they benefit from their purchases, though not as much, because they each have a lower willingness to pay. Figure 49.2 also shows the consumer surplus gained by Brad and Claudia; again, this can be measured by the areas of the appropriate rectangles. Darren and Edwina, because they do not buy books at a price of $30, receive no consumer surplus.

The total consumer surplus achieved in this market is just the sum of the individual consumer surpluses received by Aleisha, Brad, and Claudia. So total consumer surplus is equal to the combined area of the three rectangles—the entire shaded area in Figure 49.2. Another way to say this is that total consumer surplus is equal to the area below the demand curve but above the price.

Individual consumer surplus is the net gain to an individual buyer from the purchase of a good. It is equal to the difference between the buyer's willingness to pay and the price paid.

Total consumer surplus is the sum of the individual consumer surpluses of all the buyers of a good in a market.

The term **consumer surplus** is often used to refer to both individual and to total consumer surplus.

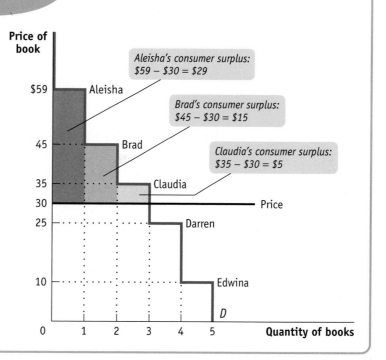

figure 49.2

Consumer Surplus in the Used-Textbook Market

At a price of $30, Aleisha, Brad, and Claudia each buy a book but Darren and Edwina do not. Aleisha, Brad, and Claudia get individual consumer surpluses equal to the difference between their willingness to pay and the price, illustrated by the areas of the shaded rectangles. Both Darren and Edwina have a willingness to pay less than $30, so they are unwilling to buy a book in this market; they receive zero consumer surplus. The total consumer surplus is given by the entire shaded area—the sum of the individual consumer surpluses of Aleisha, Brad, and Claudia— equal to $29 + $15 + $5 = $49.

Aleisha's consumer surplus: $59 − $30 = $29

Brad's consumer surplus: $45 − $30 = $15

Claudia's consumer surplus: $35 − $30 = $5

This is worth repeating as a general principle: *The total consumer surplus generated by purchases of a good at a given price is equal to the area below the demand curve but above that price.* The same principle applies regardless of the number of consumers.

When we consider large markets, this graphical representation becomes particularly helpful. Consider, for example, the sales of personal computers to millions of potential buyers. Each potential buyer has a maximum price that he or she is willing to pay. With so many potential buyers, the demand curve will be smooth, like the one shown in Figure 49.3.

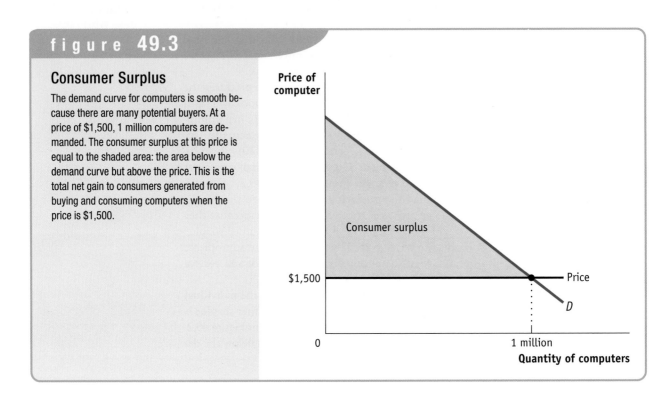

figure 49.3

Consumer Surplus

The demand curve for computers is smooth because there are many potential buyers. At a price of $1,500, 1 million computers are demanded. The consumer surplus at this price is equal to the shaded area: the area below the demand curve but above the price. This is the total net gain to consumers generated from buying and consuming computers when the price is $1,500.

Suppose that at a price of $1,500, a total of 1 million computers are purchased. How much do consumers gain from being able to buy those 1 million computers? We could answer that question by calculating the individual consumer surplus of each buyer and then adding these numbers up to arrive at a total. But it is much easier just to look at Figure 49.3 and use the fact that total consumer surplus is equal to the shaded area below the demand curve but above the price.

How Changing Prices Affect Consumer Surplus

It is often important to know how price *changes* affect consumer surplus. For example, we may want to know the harm to consumers from a frost in Florida that drives up orange prices or consumers' gain from the introduction of fish farming that makes salmon steaks less expensive. The same approach we have used to derive consumer surplus can be used to answer questions about how changes in prices affect consumers.

Let's return to the example of the market for used textbooks. Suppose that the bookstore decided to sell used textbooks for $20 instead of $30. By how much would this fall in price increase consumer surplus?

The answer is illustrated in Figure 49.4. As shown in the figure, there are two parts to the increase in consumer surplus. The first part, shaded dark blue, is the gain of those who would have bought books even at the higher price of $30. Each of the students who would have bought books at $30—Aleisha, Brad, and Claudia—now pays $10 less, and therefore each gains $10 in consumer surplus from the fall in price to $20. So

figure 49.4

Consumer Surplus and a Fall in the Price of Used Textbooks

There are two parts to the increase in consumer surplus generated by a fall in price from $30 to $20. The first is given by the dark blue rectangle: each person who would have bought at the original price of $30—Aleisha, Brad, and Claudia—receives an increase in consumer surplus equal to the total reduction in price, $10. So the area of the dark blue rectangle corresponds to an amount equal to 3 × $10 = $30. The second part is given by the light blue area: the increase in consumer surplus for those who would *not* have bought at the original price of $30 but who buy at the new price of $20—namely, Darren. Darren's willingness to pay is $25, so he now receives consumer surplus of $5. The total increase in consumer surplus is 3 × $10 + $5 = $35, represented by the sum of the shaded areas. Likewise, a rise in price from $20 to $30 would decrease consumer surplus by an amount equal to the sum of the shaded areas.

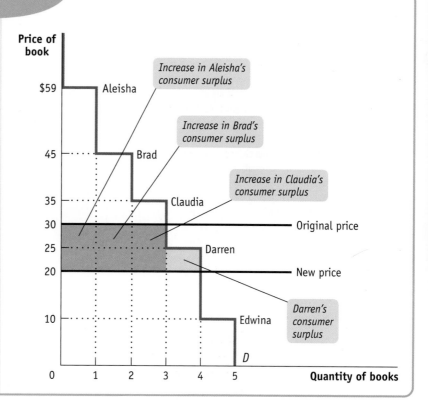

the dark blue area represents the $10 × 3 = $30 increase in consumer surplus to those three buyers. The second part, shaded light blue, is the gain to those who would not have bought a book at $30 but are willing to pay more than $20. In this case that gain goes to Darren, who would not have bought a book at $30 but does buy one at $20. He gains $5—the difference between his willingness to pay of $25 and the new price of $20. So the light blue area represents a further $5 gain in consumer surplus. The total increase in consumer surplus is the sum of the shaded areas, $35. Likewise, a rise in price from $20 to $30 would decrease consumer surplus by an amount equal to the sum of the shaded areas.

Figure 49.4 illustrates that when the price of a good falls, the area under the demand curve but above the price—the total consumer surplus—increases. Figure 49.5 on the next page shows the same result for the case of a smooth demand curve for personal computers. Here we assume that the price of computers falls from $5,000 to $1,500, leading to an increase in the quantity demanded from 200,000 to 1 million units. As in the used-textbook example, we divide the gain in consumer surplus into two parts. The dark blue rectangle in Figure 49.5 corresponds to the dark blue area in Figure 49.4: it is the gain to the 200,000 people who would have bought computers even at the higher price of $5,000. As a result of the price reduction, each receives additional surplus of $3,500. The light blue triangle in Figure 49.5 corresponds to the light blue area in Figure 49.4: it is the gain to people who would not have bought the good at the higher price but are willing to do so at a price of $1,500. For example, the light blue triangle includes the gain to someone who would have been willing to pay $2,000 for a computer and therefore gains $500 in consumer surplus when it is possible to buy a computer for only $1,500. As before, the total gain in consumer surplus is the sum of the shaded areas, the increase in the area under the demand curve but above the price.

What would happen if the price of a good were to rise instead of fall? We would do the same analysis in reverse. Suppose, for example, that for some reason the price of

figure 49.5

A Fall in the Price Increases Consumer Surplus

A fall in the price of a computer from $5,000 to $1,500 leads to an increase in the quantity demanded and an increase in consumer surplus. The change in total consumer surplus is given by the sum of the shaded areas: the total area below the demand curve and between the old and new prices. Here, the dark blue area represents the increase in consumer surplus for the 200,000 consumers who would have bought a computer at the original price of $5,000; they each receive an increase in consumer surplus of $3,500. The light blue area represents the increase in consumer surplus for those willing to buy at a price equal to or greater than $1,500 but less than $5,000. Similarly, a rise in the price of a computer from $1,500 to $5,000 generates a decrease in consumer surplus equal to the sum of the two shaded areas.

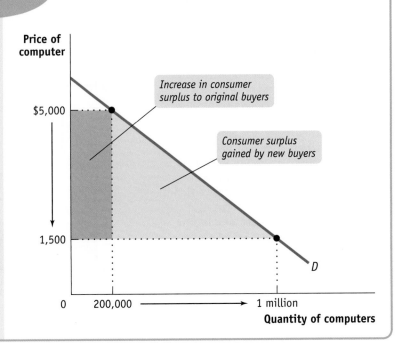

computers rises from $1,500 to $5,000. This would lead to a fall in consumer surplus equal to the sum of the shaded areas in Figure 49.5. This loss consists of two parts. The dark blue rectangle represents the loss to consumers who would still buy a computer, even at a price of $5,000. The light blue triangle represents the loss to consumers who decide not to buy a computer at the higher price.

fyi

A Matter of Life and Death

Each year about 4,000 people in the United States die while waiting for a kidney transplant. In 2009, some 80,000 were on the waiting list. Since the number of those in need of a kidney far exceeds availability, what is the best way to allocate available organs? A market isn't feasible. For understandable reasons, the sale of human body parts is illegal in this country. So the task of establishing a protocol for these situations has fallen to the nonprofit group United Network for Organ Sharing (UNOS).

Under current UNOS guidelines, a donated kidney goes to the person who has been waiting the longest. According to this system, an available kidney would go to a 75-year-old who has been waiting for 2 years instead of to a 25-year-old who has been waiting 6 months, even though the 25-year-old will likely live longer and benefit from the transplanted organ for a longer period of time.

To address this issue, UNOS is devising a new set of guidelines based on a concept it calls "net benefit." According to these new guidelines, kidneys would be allocated on the basis of who will receive the greatest net benefit, where net benefit is measured as the expected increase in lifespan from the transplant. And age is by far the biggest predictor of how long someone will live after a transplant. For example, a typical 25-year-old diabetic will gain an extra 8.7 years of life from a transplant, but a typical 55-year-old diabetic will gain only 3.6 extra years. Under the current system, based on waiting times, transplants lead to about 44,000 extra years of life for recipients; under the new system, that number would jump to 55,000 extra years. The share of kidneys going to those in their 20s would triple; the share going to those 60 and older would be halved.

What does this have to do with consumer surplus? As you may have guessed, the UNOS

concept of "net benefit" is a lot like individual consumer surplus—the individual consumer surplus generated from getting a new kidney. In essence, UNOS has devised a system that allocates donated kidneys according to who gets the greatest individual consumer surplus. In terms of results, then, its proposed "net benefit" system operates a lot like a competitive market.

Producer Surplus and the Supply Curve

Just as some buyers of a good would have been willing to pay more for their purchase than the price they actually pay, some sellers of a good would have been willing to sell it for less than the price they actually receive. We can therefore carry out an analysis of producer surplus and the supply curve that is almost exactly parallel to that of consumer surplus and the demand curve.

Cost and Producer Surplus

Consider a group of students who are potential sellers of used textbooks. Because they have different preferences, the various potential sellers differ in the price at which they are willing to sell their books. The table in Figure 49.6 shows the prices at which several different students would be willing to sell. Andrew is willing to sell the book as long as he can get at least $5; Betty won't sell unless she can get at least $15; Carlos requires $25; Donna requires $35; Engelbert $45.

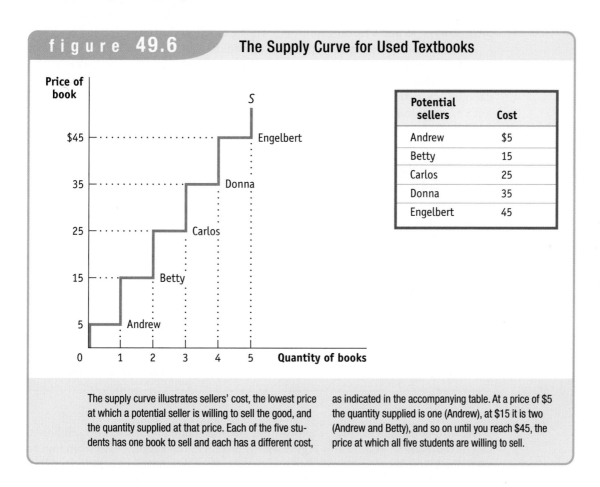

figure 49.6 **The Supply Curve for Used Textbooks**

Potential sellers	Cost
Andrew	$5
Betty	15
Carlos	25
Donna	35
Engelbert	45

The supply curve illustrates sellers' cost, the lowest price at which a potential seller is willing to sell the good, and the quantity supplied at that price. Each of the five students has one book to sell and each has a different cost, as indicated in the accompanying table. At a price of $5 the quantity supplied is one (Andrew), at $15 it is two (Andrew and Betty), and so on until you reach $45, the price at which all five students are willing to sell.

The lowest price at which a potential seller is willing to sell is called the seller's **cost.** So Andrew's cost is $5, Betty's is $15, and so on.

Using the term *cost,* which people normally associate with the monetary cost of producing a good, may sound a little strange when applied to sellers of used textbooks. The students don't have to manufacture the books, so it doesn't cost the student who sells a book anything to make that book available for sale, does it?

Yes, it does. A student who sells a book won't have it later, as part of his or her personal collection. So there is an *opportunity* cost to selling a textbook, even if the owner has completed the course for which it was required. And remember that one of the basic principles of economics is that the true measure of the cost of doing something is

A seller's **cost** is the lowest price at which he or she is willing to sell a good.

always its opportunity cost. That is, the real cost of something is what you must give up to get it.

So it is good economics to talk of the minimum price at which someone will sell a good as the "cost" of selling that good, even if he or she doesn't spend any money to make the good available for sale. Of course, in most real-world markets the sellers are also those who produce the good and therefore *do* spend money to make the good available for sale. In this case the cost of making the good available for sale *includes* monetary costs, but it may also include other opportunity costs.

Getting back to the example, suppose that Andrew sells his book for $30. Clearly he has gained from the transaction: he would have been willing to sell for only $5, so he has gained $25. This net gain, the difference between the price he actually gets and his cost—the minimum price at which he would have been willing to sell—is known as his **individual producer surplus.**

Just as we derived the demand curve from the willingness to pay of different consumers, we can derive the supply curve from the cost of different producers. The step-shaped curve in Figure 49.6 shows the supply curve implied by the costs shown in the accompanying table. At a price less than $5, none of the students are willing to sell; at a price between $5 and $15, only Andrew is willing to sell, and so on.

As in the case of consumer surplus, we can add the individual producer surpluses of sellers to calculate the **total producer surplus,** the total net gain to all sellers in the market. Economists use the term **producer surplus** to refer to either total or individual producer surplus. Table 49.2 shows the net gain to each of the students who would sell a used book at a price of $30: $25 for Andrew, $15 for Betty, and $5 for Carlos. The total producer surplus is $25 + $15 + $5 = $45.

table 49.2

Producer Surplus When the Price of a Used Textbook Is $30

Potential seller	Cost	Price received	Individual producer surplus = Price received – Cost
Andrew	$5	$30	$25
Betty	15	30	15
Carlos	25	30	5
Donna	35	—	—
Engelbert	45	—	—
All sellers			**Total producer surplus = $45**

As with consumer surplus, the producer surplus gained by those who sell books can be represented graphically. Figure 49.7 reproduces the supply curve from Figure 49.6. Each step in that supply curve is one book wide and represents one seller. The height of Andrew's step is $5, his cost. This forms the bottom of a rectangle, with $30, the price he actually receives for his book, forming the top. The area of this rectangle, ($30 − $5) × 1 = $25, is his producer surplus. So the producer surplus Andrew gains from selling his book is the *area of the dark red rectangle* shown in the figure.

Let's assume that the campus bookstore is willing to buy all the used copies of this book that students are willing to sell at a price of $30. Then, in addition to Andrew, Betty and Carlos will also sell their books. They will also benefit from their sales, though not as much as Andrew, because they have higher costs. Andrew, as we have seen, gains $25. Betty gains a smaller amount: since her cost is $15, she gains only $15. Carlos gains even less, only $5.

figure 49.7

Producer Surplus in the Used-Textbook Market

At a price of $30, Andrew, Betty, and Carlos each sell a book but Donna and Engelbert do not. Andrew, Betty, and Carlos get individual producer surpluses equal to the difference between the price and their cost, illustrated here by the shaded rectangles. Donna and Engelbert each have a cost that is greater than the price of $30, so they are unwilling to sell a book and so receive zero producer surplus. The total producer surplus is given by the entire shaded area, the sum of the individual producer surpluses of Andrew, Betty, and Carlos, equal to $25 + $15 + $5 = $45.

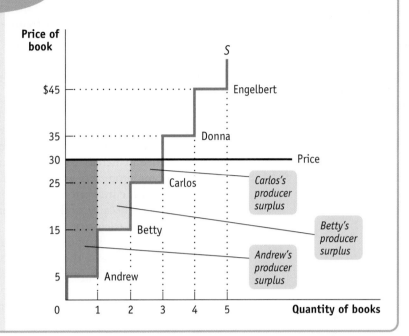

Again, as with consumer surplus, we have a general rule for determining the total producer surplus from sales of a good: *The total producer surplus from sales of a good at a given price is the area above the supply curve but below that price.*

This rule applies both to examples like the one shown in Figure 49.7, where there are a small number of producers and a step-shaped supply curve, and to more realistic examples, where there are many producers and the supply curve is more or less smooth.

Consider, for example, the supply of wheat. Figure 49.8 shows how producer surplus depends on the price per bushel. Suppose that, as shown in

figure 49.8

Producer Surplus

Here is the supply curve for wheat. At a price of $5 per bushel, farmers supply 1 million bushels. The producer surplus at this price is equal to the shaded area: the area above the supply curve but below the price. This is the total gain to producers—farmers in this case—from supplying their product when the price is $5.

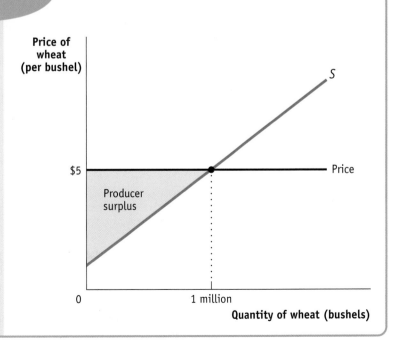

module **4 9** Consumer and Producer Surplus **491**

the figure, the price is $5 per bushel and farmers supply 1 million bushels. What is the benefit to the farmers from selling their wheat at a price of $5? Their producer surplus is equal to the shaded area in the figure—the area above the supply curve but below the price of $5 per bushel.

How Changing Prices Affect Producer Surplus

As in the case of consumer surplus, a change in price alters producer surplus. However, although a fall in price increases consumer surplus, it reduces producer surplus. Similarly, a rise in price reduces consumer surplus but increases producer surplus.

To see this, let's first consider a rise in the price of the good. Producers of the good will experience an increase in producer surplus, though not all producers gain the same amount. Some producers would have produced the good even at the original price; they will gain the entire price increase on every unit they produce. Other producers will enter the market because of the higher price; they will gain only the difference between the new price and their cost.

Figure 49.9 is the supply counterpart of Figure 49.5. It shows the effect on producer surplus of a rise in the price of wheat from $5 to $7 per bushel. The increase in producer surplus is the sum of the shaded areas, which consists of two parts. First, there is a dark red rectangle corresponding to the gains to those farmers who would have supplied wheat even at the original $5 price. Second, there is an additional light red triangle that corresponds to the gains to those farmers who would not have supplied wheat at the original price but are drawn into the market by the higher price.

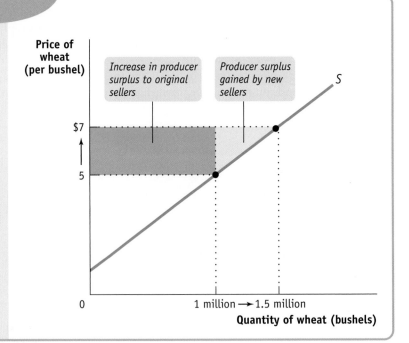

figure 49.9

A Rise in the Price Increases Producer Surplus

A rise in the price of wheat from $5 to $7 leads to an increase in the quantity supplied and an increase in producer surplus. The change in total producer surplus is given by the sum of the shaded areas: the total area above the supply curve but between the old and new prices. The dark red area represents the gain to the farmers who would have supplied 1 million bushels at the original price of $5; they each receive an increase in producer surplus of $2 for each of those bushels. The triangular light red area represents the increase in producer surplus achieved by the farmers who supply the additional 500,000 bushels because of the higher price. Similarly, a fall in the price of wheat generates a reduction in producer surplus equal to the sum of the shaded areas.

If the price were to fall from $7 to $5 per bushel, the story would run in reverse. The sum of the shaded areas would now be the decline in producer surplus, the decrease in the area above the supply curve but below the price. The loss would consist of two parts, the loss to farmers who would still grow wheat at a price of $5 (the dark red rectangle) and the loss to farmers who decide to no longer grow wheat because of the lower price (the light red triangle).

Module 49 AP Review

Solutions appear at the back of the book.

Check Your Understanding

1. Consider the market for cheese-stuffed jalapeno peppers. There are two consumers, Casey and Josey, and their willingness to pay for each pepper is given in the accompanying table. (Neither is willing to consume more than 4 peppers at any price.) Use the table (i) to construct the demand schedule for peppers for prices of $0.00, $0.10, and so on, up to $0.90, and (ii) to calculate the total consumer surplus when the price of a pepper is $0.40.

Quantity of peppers	Casey's willingness to pay	Josey's willingness to pay
1st pepper	$0.90	$0.80
2nd pepper	0.70	0.60
3rd pepper	0.50	0.40
4th pepper	0.30	0.30

2. Again consider the market for cheese-stuffed jalapeno peppers. There are two producers, Cara and Jamie, and their costs of producing each pepper are given in the accompanying table. (Neither is willing to produce more than 4 peppers at any price.) Use the table (i) to construct the supply schedule for peppers for prices of $0.00, $0.10, and so on, up to $0.90, and (ii) to calculate the total producer surplus when the price of a pepper is $0.70.

Quantity of peppers	Cara's cost	Jamie's cost
1st pepper	$0.10	$0.30
2nd pepper	0.10	0.50
3rd pepper	0.40	0.70
4th pepper	0.60	0.90

Tackle the Test: Multiple-Choice Questions

1. Refer to the graph below. What is the value of consumer surplus when the market price is $40?

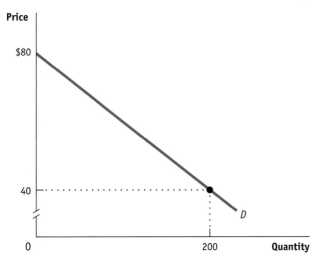

a. $400
b. $800
c. $4,000
d. $8,000
e. $16,000

2. Refer to the graph below. What is the value of producer surplus when the market price is $60?

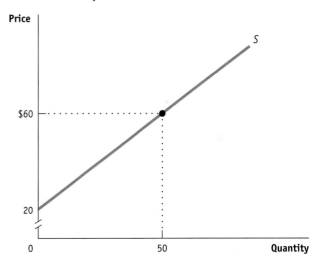

a. $100
b. $150
c. $1,000
d. $1,500
e. $3,000

3. Other things equal, a rise in price will result in which of the following?
a. Producer surplus will rise; consumer surplus will rise.
b. Producer surplus will fall; consumer surplus will fall.
c. Producer surplus will rise; consumer surplus will fall.
d. Producer surplus will fall; consumer surplus will rise.
e. Producer surplus will not change; consumer surplus will rise.

4. Consumer surplus is found as the area
   a. above the supply curve and below the price.
   b. below the demand curve and above the price.
   c. above the demand curve and below the price.
   d. below the supply curve and above the price.
   e. below the supply curve and above the demand curve.

5. Allocating kidneys to those with the highest net benefit (where net benefit is measured as the expected increase in lifespan from a transplant) is an attempt to maximize
   a. consumer surplus.
   b. producer surplus.
   c. profit.
   d. equity.
   e. respect for elders.

Tackle the Test: Free-Response Questions

1. Refer to the graph provided.

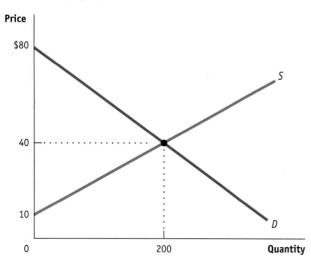

a. Calculate consumer surplus.
b. Calculate producer surplus.
c. If supply increases, what will happen to consumer surplus? Explain.
d. If demand decreases, what will happen to producer surplus? Explain.

Answer (6 points)

1 point: $4,000

1 point: $3,000

1 point: Consumer surplus will increase.

1 point: An increase in supply lowers the equilibrium price, which causes consumer surplus to increase.

1 point: Producer surplus will decrease.

1 point: A decrease in demand decreases the equilibrium price, which causes producer surplus to decrease.

2. Draw a correctly labeled graph showing a competitive market in equilibrium. On your graph, clearly indicate and label the area of consumer surplus and the area of producer surplus.

Module 50
Efficiency and Deadweight Loss

What you will learn
in this **Module:**

- The meaning and importance
  of total surplus and how it
  can be used to illustrate
  efficiency in markets

- How taxes affect total
  surplus and can create
  deadweight loss

Consumer Surplus, Producer Surplus, and Efficiency

Markets are a remarkably effective way to organize economic activity: under the right conditions, they can make society as well off as possible given the available resources. The concepts of consumer and producer surplus can help us deepen our understanding of why this is so.

The Gains from Trade

Let's return to the market for used textbooks, but now consider a much bigger market—say, one at a large state university. There are many potential buyers and sellers, so the market is competitive. Let's line up incoming students who are potential buyers of a book in order of their willingness to pay, so that the entering student with the highest willingness to pay is potential buyer number 1, the student with the next highest willingness to pay is number 2, and so on. Then we can use their willingness to pay to derive a demand curve like the one in Figure 50.1 on the next page. Similarly, we can line up outgoing students, who are potential sellers of the book, in order of their cost, starting with the student with the lowest cost, then the student with the next lowest cost, and so on, to derive a supply curve like the one shown in the same figure.

As we have drawn the curves, the market reaches equilibrium at a price of $30 per book, and 1,000 books are bought and sold at that price. The two shaded triangles show the consumer surplus (blue) and the producer surplus (red) generated by this market. The sum of consumer and producer surplus is known as **total surplus.**

The striking thing about this picture is that both consumers and producers gain—that is, both consumers and producers are better off because there is a market in this good. But this should come as no surprise—it illustrates another core principle of economics: *There are gains from trade.* These gains from trade are the reason everyone is better off participating in a market economy than they would be if each individual tried to be self-sufficient.

Total surplus is the total net gain to consumers and producers from trading in a market. It is the sum of producer and consumer surplus.

figure **50.1**

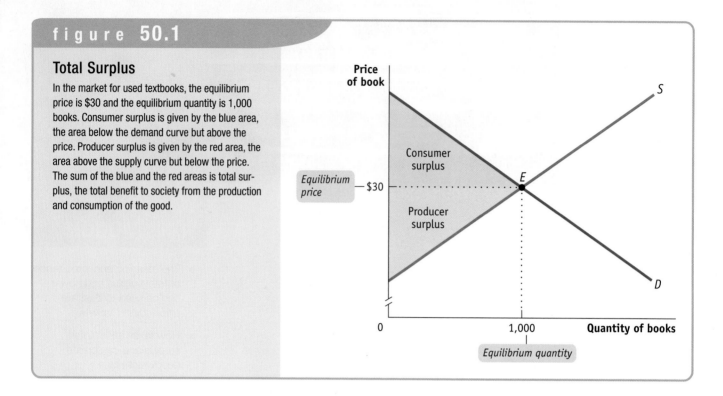

Total Surplus

In the market for used textbooks, the equilibrium price is $30 and the equilibrium quantity is 1,000 books. Consumer surplus is given by the blue area, the area below the demand curve but above the price. Producer surplus is given by the red area, the area above the supply curve but below the price. The sum of the blue and the red areas is total surplus, the total benefit to society from the production and consumption of the good.

But are we as well off as we could be? This brings us to the question of the efficiency of markets.

The Efficiency of Markets

A market is *efficient* if, once the market has produced its gains from trade, there is no way to make some people better off without making other people worse off. Note that market equilibrium is just *one* way of deciding who consumes a good and who sells a good. To better understand how markets promote efficiency, let's examine some alternatives. Consider the example of kidney transplants discussed earlier in an FYI box. There is not a market for kidneys, and available kidneys currently go to whoever has been on the waiting list the longest. Of course, those who have been waiting the longest aren't necessarily those who would benefit the most from a new kidney.

Similarly, imagine a committee charged with improving on the market equilibrium by deciding who gets and who gives up a used textbook. The committee's ultimate goal would be to bypass the market outcome and come up with another arrangement that would increase total surplus.

Let's consider three approaches the committee could take:

1. It could reallocate consumption among consumers.

2. It could reallocate sales among sellers.

3. It could change the quantity traded.

The Reallocation of Consumption Among Consumers The committee might try to increase total surplus by selling books to different consumers. Figure 50.2 shows why this will result in lower surplus compared to the market equilibrium outcome. Points *A* and *B* show the positions on the demand curve of two potential buyers of used books, Ana and Bob. As we can see from the figure, Ana is willing to pay $35 for a book, but Bob is willing to pay only $25. Since the market equilibrium price is $30, under the market outcome Ana gets a book and Bob does not.

Now suppose the committee reallocates consumption. This would mean taking the book away from Ana and giving it to Bob. Since the book is worth $35 to Ana but only $25 to Bob, this change *reduces total consumer surplus* by $35 − $25 = $10. Moreover, this result

figure 50.2

Reallocating Consumption Lowers Consumer Surplus

Ana (point A) has a willingness to pay of $35. Bob (point B) has a willingness to pay of only $25. At the market equilibrium price of $30, Ana purchases a book but Bob does not. If we rearrange consumption by taking a book from Ana and giving it to Bob, consumer surplus declines by $10 and, as a result, total surplus declines by $10. The market equilibrium generates the highest possible consumer surplus by ensuring that those who consume the good are those who most value it.

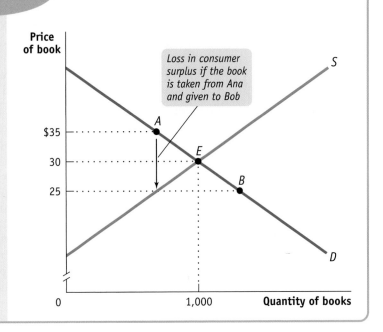

doesn't depend on which two students we pick. Every student who buys a book at the market equilibrium price has a willingness to pay of $30 or more, and every student who doesn't buy a book has a willingness to pay of less than $30. So reallocating the good among consumers always means taking a book away from a student who values it more and giving it to one who values it less. This necessarily reduces total consumer surplus.

The Reallocation of Sales Among Sellers The committee might try to increase total surplus by altering who sells their books, taking sales away from sellers who would have sold their books in the market equilibrium and instead compelling those who would not have sold their books in the market equilibrium to sell them. Figure 50.3 shows why this will result in lower surplus. Here points X and Y show the positions on the supply

figure 50.3

Reallocating Sales Lowers Producer Surplus

Yvonne (point Y) has a cost of $35, $10 more than Xavier (point X), who has a cost of $25. At the market equilibrium price of $30, Xavier sells a book but Yvonne does not. If we rearrange sales by preventing Xavier from selling his book and compelling Yvonne to sell hers, producer surplus declines by $10 and, as a result, total surplus declines by $10. The market equilibrium generates the highest possible producer surplus by assuring that those who sell the good are those who most value the right to sell it.

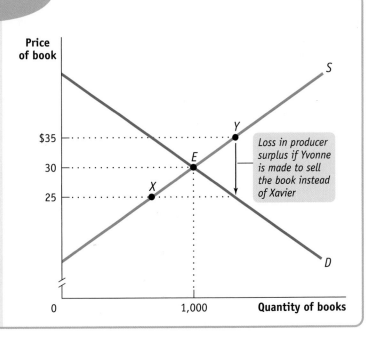

module **50** Efficiency and Deadweight Loss **497**

curve of Xavier, who has a cost of $25, and Yvonne, who has a cost of $35. At the equilibrium market price of $30, Xavier would sell his book but Yvonne would not sell hers. If the committee reallocated sales, forcing Xavier to keep his book and Yvonne to sell hers, total producer surplus would be reduced by $35 − $25 = $10. Again, it doesn't matter which two students we choose. Any student who sells a book at the market equilibrium price has a lower cost than any student who keeps a book. So reallocating sales among sellers necessarily increases total cost and reduces total producer surplus.

Changes in the Quantity Traded The committee might try to increase total surplus by compelling students to trade either more books or fewer books than the market equilibrium quantity. Figure 50.4 shows why this will result in lower surplus. It shows all four students: potential buyers Ana and Bob, and potential sellers Xavier and Yvonne. To reduce sales, the committee will have to prevent a transaction that would have occurred in the market equilibrium—that is, prevent Xavier from selling to Ana. Since Ana is willing to pay $35 and Xavier's cost is $25, preventing this transaction reduces total surplus by $35 − $25 = $10. Once again, this result doesn't depend on which two students we pick: any student who would have sold the book in the market equilibrium has a cost of $30 or less, and any student who would have purchased the book in the market equilibrium has a willingness to pay of $30 or more. So preventing any sale that would have occurred in the market equilibrium necessarily reduces total surplus.

figure 50.4

Changing the Quantity Lowers Total Surplus

If Xavier (point *X*) were prevented from selling his book to someone like Ana (point *A*), total surplus would fall by $10, the difference between Ana's willingness to pay ($35) and Xavier's cost ($25). This means that total surplus falls whenever fewer than 1,000 books—the equilibrium quantity—are transacted. Likewise, if Yvonne (point *Y*) were compelled to sell her book to someone like Bob (point *B*), total surplus would also fall by $10, the difference between Yvonne's cost ($35) and Bob's willingness to pay ($25). This means that total surplus falls whenever more than 1,000 books are transacted. These two examples show that at market equilibrium, all mutually beneficial transactions—and only mutually beneficial transactions—occur.

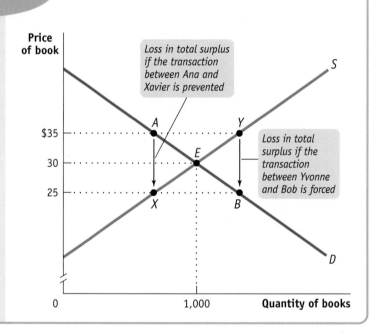

Finally, the committee might try to increase sales by forcing Yvonne, who would not have sold her book in the market equilibrium, to sell it to someone like Bob, who would not have bought a book in the market equilibrium. Because Yvonne's cost is $35, but Bob is only willing to pay $25, this transaction reduces total surplus by $10. And once again it doesn't matter which two students we pick—anyone who wouldn't have bought the book has a willingness to pay of less than $30, and anyone who wouldn't have sold has a cost of more than $30.

The key point to remember is that once this market is in equilibrium, there is no way to increase the gains from trade. Any other outcome reduces total surplus. We can summarize our results by stating that an efficient market performs four important functions:

1. It allocates consumption of the good to the potential buyers who most value it, as indicated by the fact that they have the highest willingness to pay.

2. It allocates sales to the potential sellers who most value the right to sell the good, as indicated by the fact that they have the lowest cost.

3. It ensures that every consumer who makes a purchase values the good more than every seller who makes a sale, so that all transactions are mutually beneficial.

4. It ensures that every potential buyer who doesn't make a purchase values the good less than every potential seller who doesn't make a sale, so that no mutually beneficial transactions are missed.

There are three caveats, however. First, although a market may be efficient, it isn't necessarily *fair*. In fact, fairness, or *equity*, is often in conflict with efficiency. We'll discuss this next.

The second caveat is that markets sometimes *fail*. Under some well-defined conditions, markets can fail to deliver efficiency. When this occurs, markets no longer maximize total surplus. We'll take a closer look at market failures in later modules.

Third, even when the market equilibrium maximizes total surplus, this does not mean that it results in the best outcome for every *individual* consumer and producer. Other things equal, each buyer would like to pay a lower price and each seller would like to receive a higher price. So if the government were to intervene in the market—say, by lowering the price below the equilibrium price to make consumers happy or by raising the price above the equilibrium price to make producers happy—the outcome would no longer be efficient. Although some people would be happier, society as a whole would be worse off because total surplus would be lower.

Equity and Efficiency

It's easy to get carried away with the idea that markets are always good and that economic policies that interfere with efficiency are bad. But that would be misguided because there is another factor to consider: society cares about equity, or what's "fair." There is often a trade-off between equity and efficiency: policies that promote equity often come at the cost of decreased efficiency, and policies that promote efficiency often result in decreased equity. So it's important to realize that a society's choice to sacrifice some efficiency for the sake of equity, however it defines equity, may well be a valid one. And it's important to understand that fairness, unlike efficiency, can be very hard to define. Fairness is a concept about which well-intentioned people often disagree.

In fact, the debate about equity and efficiency is at the core of most debates about taxation. Proponents of taxes that redistribute income from the rich to the poor often argue for the fairness of such redistributive taxes. Opponents of taxation often argue that phasing out certain taxes would make the economy more efficient.

Because taxes are ultimately paid out of income, economists classify taxes according to how they vary with the income of individuals. A tax that rises more than in proportion to income, so that high-income taxpayers pay a larger percentage of their income than low-income taxpayers, is a **progressive tax.** A tax that rises less than in proportion to income, so that high-income taxpayers pay a smaller percentage of their income than low-income taxpayers, is a **regressive tax.** A tax that rises in proportion to income, so that all taxpayers pay the same percentage of their income, is a **proportional tax.** The U.S. tax system contains a mixture of progressive and regressive taxes, though it is somewhat progressive overall.

A **progressive tax** rises more than in proportion to income. A **regressive tax** rises less than in proportion to income. A **proportional tax** rises in proportion to income.

An **excise tax** is a tax on sales of a particular good or service.

The Effects of Taxes on Total Surplus

To understand the economics of taxes, it's helpful to look at a simple type of tax known as an **excise tax**—a tax charged on each unit of a good or service that is sold. Most tax revenue in the United States comes from other kinds of taxes, but excise taxes are common. For example, there are excise taxes on gasoline, cigarettes, and foreign-made trucks, and many local governments impose excise taxes on services such as hotel room rentals. The lessons we'll learn from studying excise taxes apply to other, more complex taxes as well.

The Effect of an Excise Tax on Quantities and Prices

Suppose that the supply and demand for hotel rooms in the city of Potterville are as shown in Figure 50.5. We'll make the simplifying assumption that all hotel rooms are the same. In the absence of taxes, the equilibrium price of a room is $80 per night and the equilibrium quantity of hotel rooms rented is 10,000 per night.

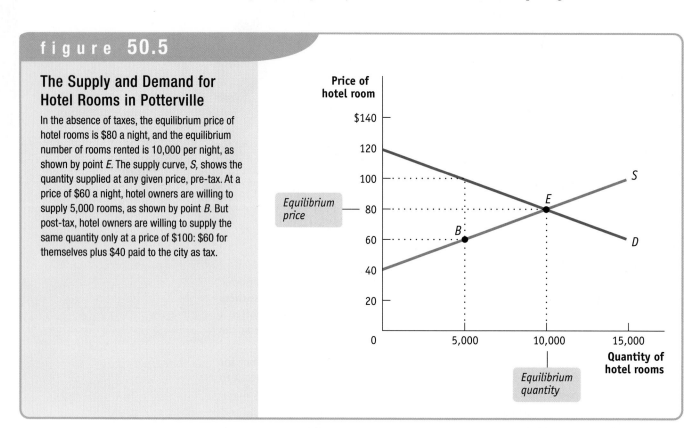

figure 50.5

The Supply and Demand for Hotel Rooms in Potterville

In the absence of taxes, the equilibrium price of hotel rooms is $80 a night, and the equilibrium number of rooms rented is 10,000 per night, as shown by point *E*. The supply curve, *S*, shows the quantity supplied at any given price, pre-tax. At a price of $60 a night, hotel owners are willing to supply 5,000 rooms, as shown by point *B*. But post-tax, hotel owners are willing to supply the same quantity only at a price of $100: $60 for themselves plus $40 paid to the city as tax.

Now suppose that Potterville's government imposes an excise tax of $40 per night on hotel rooms—that is, every time a room is rented for the night, the owner of the hotel must pay the city $40. For example, if a customer pays $80, $40 is collected as a tax, leaving the hotel owner with only $40. As a result, hotel owners are less willing to supply rooms at any given price.

What does this imply about the supply curve for hotel rooms in Potterville? To answer this question, we must compare the incentives of hotel owners *pre-tax* (before the tax is levied) to their incentives *post-tax* (after the tax is levied). From Figure 50.5 we know that pre-tax, hotel owners are willing to supply 5,000 rooms per night at a price of $60 per room. But after the $40 tax per room is levied, they are willing to supply the same amount, 5,000 rooms, only if they receive $100 per room—$60 for themselves plus $40 paid to the city as tax. In other words, in order for hotel owners to be willing to supply the same quantity post-tax as they would have pre-tax, they must receive an additional $40 per room, the amount of the tax. This implies that the post-tax supply curve shifts up by the amount of the tax compared to the pre-tax supply curve. At every quantity supplied, the supply price—the price that producers must receive to produce a given quantity—has increased by $40.

The upward shift of the supply curve caused by the tax is shown in Figure 50.6, where S_1 is the pre-tax supply curve and S_2 is the post-tax supply curve. As you can see, the market equilibrium moves from E, at the equilibrium price of $80 per room and 10,000 rooms rented each night, to A, at a market price of $100 per room and only 5,000 rooms rented each night. A is, of course, on both the demand curve D and the new supply curve S_2. In this case, $100 is the demand price of 5,000 rooms—but in effect hotel owners receive only $60, when you account for the fact that they have to pay the $40 tax. From the point of view of hotel owners, it is as if they were on their original supply curve at point B.

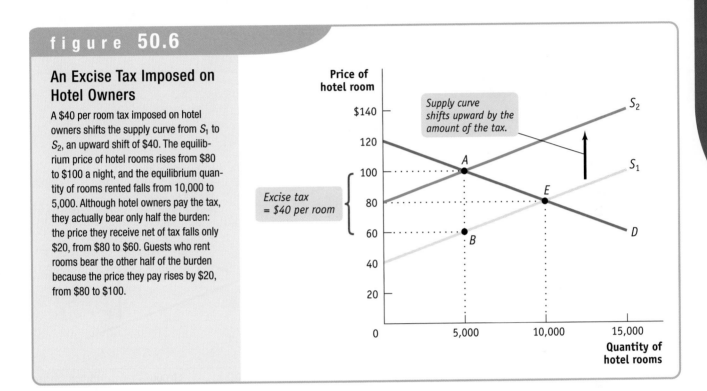

figure 50.6

An Excise Tax Imposed on Hotel Owners

A $40 per room tax imposed on hotel owners shifts the supply curve from S_1 to S_2, an upward shift of $40. The equilibrium price of hotel rooms rises from $80 to $100 a night, and the equilibrium quantity of rooms rented falls from 10,000 to 5,000. Although hotel owners pay the tax, they actually bear only half the burden: the price they receive net of tax falls only $20, from $80 to $60. Guests who rent rooms bear the other half of the burden because the price they pay rises by $20, from $80 to $100.

Let's check this again. How do we know that 5,000 rooms will be supplied at a price of $100? Because the price *net of tax* is $60, and according to the original supply curve, 5,000 rooms will be supplied at a price of $60, as shown by point B in Figure 50.6.

An excise tax *drives a wedge* between the price paid by consumers and the price received by producers. As a result of this wedge, consumers pay more and producers receive less. In our example, consumers—people who rent hotel rooms—end up paying $100 a night, $20 more than the pre-tax price of $80. At the same time, producers—the hotel owners—receive a price net of tax of $60 per room, $20 less than the pre-tax price. In addition, the tax creates missed opportunities: 5,000 potential consumers who would have rented hotel rooms—those willing to pay $80 but not $100 per night—are discouraged from renting rooms. Correspondingly, 5,000 rooms that would have been made available by hotel owners when they receive $80 are not offered when they receive only $60. Like a quota on sales as discussed in Module 9, this tax leads to inefficiency by distorting incentives and creating missed opportunities for mutually beneficial transactions.

It's important to recognize that as we've described it, Potterville's hotel tax is a tax on the hotel owners, not their guests—it's a tax on the producers, not the consumers. Yet the price received by producers, net of tax, is down by only $20, half the amount of the tax, and the price paid by consumers is up by $20. In effect, half the tax is being paid by consumers.

What would happen if the city levied a tax on consumers instead of producers? That is, suppose that instead of requiring hotel owners to pay $40 a night for each room they rent, the city required hotel *guests* to pay $40 for each night they stayed in a hotel. The answer is shown in Figure 50.7. If a hotel guest must pay a tax of $40 per night, then the price for a room paid by that guest must be reduced by $40 in order for the quantity of hotel rooms demanded post-tax to be the same as that demanded pre-tax. So the demand curve shifts *downward*, from D_1 to D_2, by the amount of the tax. At every quantity demanded, the demand price—the price that consumers must be offered to demand a given quantity—has fallen by $40. This shifts the equilibrium from E to B, where the market price of hotel rooms is $60 and 5,000 hotel rooms are bought and sold. In effect, hotel guests pay $100 when you include the tax. So from the point of view of guests, it is as if they were on their original demand curve at point A.

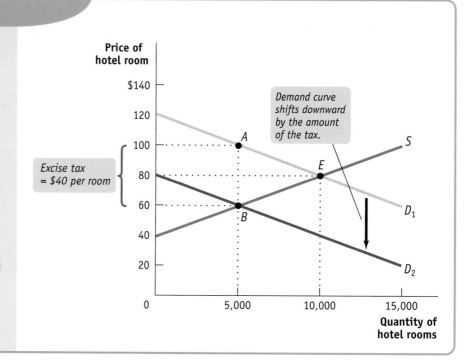

figure 50.7

An Excise Tax Imposed on Hotel Guests

A $40 per room tax imposed on hotel guests shifts the demand curve from D_1 to D_2, a downward shift of $40. The equilibrium price of hotel rooms falls from $80 to $60 a night, and the quantity of rooms rented falls from 10,000 to 5,000. Although in this case the tax is officially paid by consumers, while in Figure 50.6 the tax was paid by producers, the outcome is the same: after taxes, hotel owners receive $60 per room but guests pay $100. This illustrates a general principle: *The incidence of an excise tax doesn't depend on whether consumers or producers officially pay the tax.*

If you compare Figures 50.6 and 50.7, you will notice that the effects of the tax are the same even though different curves are shifted. In each case, consumers pay $100 per unit (including the tax, if it is their responsibility), producers receive $60 per unit (after paying the tax, if it is their responsibility), and 5,000 hotel rooms are bought and sold. *In fact, it doesn't matter who officially pays the tax—the equilibrium outcome is the same.*

This example illustrates a general principle of **tax incidence,** a measure of who really pays a tax: the burden of a tax cannot be determined by looking at who writes the check to the government. In this particular case, a $40 tax on hotel rooms brings about a $20 increase in the price paid by consumers and a $20 decrease in the price received by producers. Regardless of whether the tax is levied on consumers or producers, the incidence of the tax is the same. As we will see next, the burden of a tax depends on the price elasticities of supply and demand.

Price Elasticities and Tax Incidence

We've just learned that the incidence of an excise tax doesn't depend on who officially pays it. In the example shown in Figures 50.5 through 50.7, a tax on hotel rooms falls equally on consumers and producers, no matter on whom the tax is

Tax incidence is the distribution of the tax burden.

levied. But it's important to note that this 50–50 split between consumers and producers is a result of our assumptions in this example. In the real world, the incidence of an excise tax usually falls unevenly between consumers and producers: one group bears more of the burden than the other.

What determines how the burden of an excise tax is allocated between consumers and producers? The answer depends on the shapes of the supply and the demand curves. *More specifically, the incidence of an excise tax depends on the price elasticity of supply and the price elasticity of demand.* We can see this by looking first at a case in which consumers pay most of an excise tax, and then at a case in which producers pay most of the tax.

When an Excise Tax Is Paid Mainly by Consumers Figure 50.8 shows an excise tax that falls mainly on consumers: an excise tax on gasoline, which we set at $1 per gallon. (There really is a federal excise tax on gasoline, though it is actually only about $0.18 per gallon in the United States. In addition, states impose excise taxes between $0.08 and $0.37 per gallon.) According to Figure 50.8, in the absence of the tax, gasoline would sell for $2 per gallon.

figure 50.8

An Excise Tax Paid Mainly by Consumers

The relatively steep demand curve here reflects a low price elasticity of demand for gasoline. The relatively flat supply curve reflects a high price elasticity of supply. The pre-tax price of a gallon of gasoline is $2.00, and a tax of $1.00 per gallon is imposed. The price paid by consumers rises by $0.95 to $2.95, reflecting the fact that most of the burden of the tax falls on consumers. Only a small portion of the tax is borne by producers: the price they receive falls by only $0.05 to $1.95.

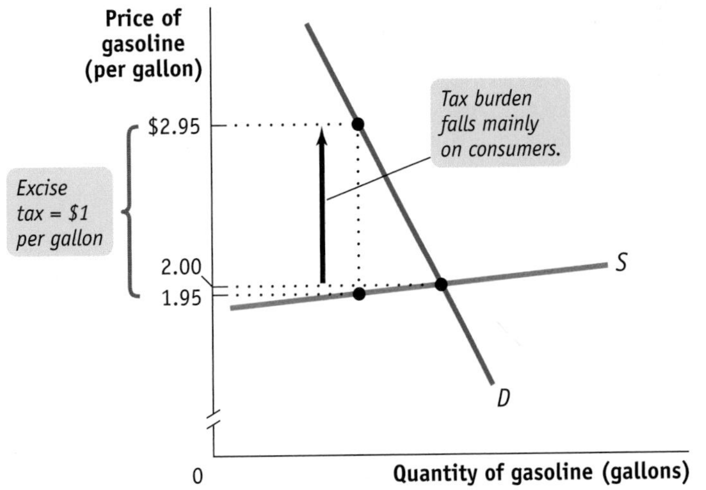

Two key assumptions are reflected in the shapes of the supply and demand curves in Figure 50.8. First, the price elasticity of demand for gasoline is assumed to be very low, so the demand curve is relatively steep. Recall that a low price elasticity of demand means that the quantity demanded changes little in response to a change in price. Second, the price elasticity of supply of gasoline is assumed to be very high, so the supply curve is relatively flat. A high price elasticity of supply means that the quantity supplied changes a lot in response to a change in price.

We have just learned that an excise tax drives a wedge, equal to the size of the tax, between the price paid by consumers and the price received by producers. This wedge drives the price paid by consumers up and the price received by producers down. But as we can see from Figure 50.8, in this case those two effects are very unequal in size. The price received by producers falls only slightly, from $2.00 to $1.95, but the price paid by consumers rises by a lot, from $2.00 to $2.95. This means that consumers bear the greater share of the tax burden.

This example illustrates another general principle of taxation: *When the price elasticity of demand is low and the price elasticity of supply is high, the burden of an excise tax falls mainly on consumers.* Why? A low price elasticity of demand means that consumers have few substitutes and so little alternative to buying higher-priced gasoline. In contrast, a high price elasticity of supply results from the fact that producers have many production substitutes for their gasoline (that is, other uses for the crude oil from which gasoline is refined). This gives producers much greater flexibility in refusing to accept lower prices for their gasoline. And, not surprisingly, the party with the least flexibility—in this case, consumers—gets stuck paying most of the tax. This is a good description of how the burden of the main excise taxes actually collected in the United States today, such as those on cigarettes and alcoholic beverages, is allocated between consumers and producers.

When an Excise Tax Is Paid Mainly by Producers Figure 50.9 shows an example of an excise tax paid mainly by producers, a $5.00 per day tax on downtown parking in a small city. In the absence of the tax, the market equilibrium price of parking is $6.00 per day.

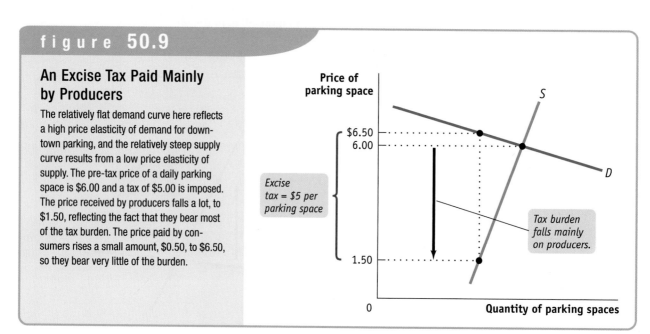

figure 50.9

An Excise Tax Paid Mainly by Producers

The relatively flat demand curve here reflects a high price elasticity of demand for downtown parking, and the relatively steep supply curve results from a low price elasticity of supply. The pre-tax price of a daily parking space is $6.00 and a tax of $5.00 is imposed. The price received by producers falls a lot, to $1.50, reflecting the fact that they bear most of the tax burden. The price paid by consumers rises a small amount, $0.50, to $6.50, so they bear very little of the burden.

We've assumed in this case that the price elasticity of supply is very low because the lots used for parking have very few alternative uses. This makes the supply curve for parking spaces relatively steep. The price elasticity of demand, however, is assumed to be high: consumers can easily switch from the downtown spaces to other parking spaces a few minutes' walk from downtown, spaces that are not subject to the tax. This makes the demand curve relatively flat.

The tax drives a wedge between the price paid by consumers and the price received by producers. In this example, however, the tax causes the price paid by consumers to rise only slightly, from $6.00 to $6.50, but the price received by producers falls a lot, from $6.00 to $1.50. In the end, a consumer bears only $0.50 of the $5 tax burden, with a producer bearing the remaining $4.50.

Again, this example illustrates a general principle: *When the price elasticity of demand is high and the price elasticity of supply is low, the burden of an excise tax falls mainly on producers.* A real-world example is a tax on purchases of existing houses. In many American towns, house prices in desirable locations have risen as well-off outsiders have moved in and purchased homes from the less well-off original occupants, a phenomenon called gentrification. Some of these towns have imposed taxes on house sales intended to extract money from the new arrivals. But this ignores the fact that the price elasticity of demand for houses in a particular town is often high because potential buyers can choose to move to other towns. Furthermore, the price elasticity of supply is often low because most sellers must sell their houses due to job transfers or to provide funds for their retirement. So taxes on home purchases are actually paid mainly by the less well-off sellers—not, as town officials imagine, by wealthy buyers.

The Benefits and Costs of Taxation

When a government is considering whether to impose a tax or how to design a tax system, it has to weigh the benefits of a tax against its costs. We may not think of a tax as something that provides benefits, but governments need money to provide things people want, such as streets, schools, national defense, and health care for those unable to afford it. The benefit of a tax is the revenue it raises for the government to pay for these services. Unfortunately, this benefit comes at a cost—a cost that is normally larger than the amount consumers and producers pay. Let's look first at what determines how much money a tax raises and then at the costs a tax imposes.

istockphoto

The Revenue from an Excise Tax

How much revenue does the government collect from an excise tax? In our hotel tax example, the revenue is equal to the area of the shaded rectangle in Figure 50.10.

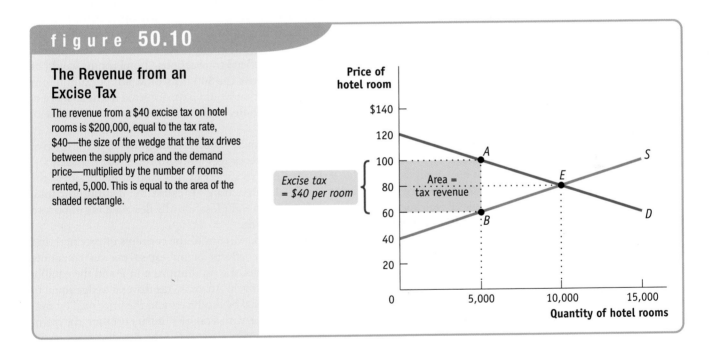

figure 50.10

The Revenue from an Excise Tax

The revenue from a $40 excise tax on hotel rooms is $200,000, equal to the tax rate, $40—the size of the wedge that the tax drives between the supply price and the demand price—multiplied by the number of rooms rented, 5,000. This is equal to the area of the shaded rectangle.

To see why this area represents the revenue collected by a $40 tax on hotel rooms, notice that the *height* of the rectangle is $40, equal to the tax per room. It is also, as we've seen, the size of the wedge that the tax drives between the supply price (the price received by producers) and the demand price (the price paid by consumers). Meanwhile, the *width* of the rectangle is 5,000 rooms, equal to the equilibrium quantity of rooms given the $40 tax. With that information, we can make the following calculations.

The tax revenue collected is:

$$\text{Tax revenue} = \$40 \text{ per room} \times 5,000 \text{ rooms} = \$200,000$$

module **50** Efficiency and Deadweight Loss **505**

The area of the shaded rectangle is:

$$\text{Area} = \text{Height} \times \text{Width} = \$40 \text{ per room} \times 5{,}000 \text{ rooms} = \$200{,}000,$$

or

$$\text{Tax revenue} = \text{Area of shaded rectangle}$$

This is a general principle: *The revenue collected by an excise tax is equal to the area of a rectangle with the height of the tax wedge between the supply price and the demand price and the width of the quantity sold under the tax.*

The Costs of Taxation

What is the cost of a tax? You might be inclined to answer that it is the amount of money taxpayers pay to the government—the tax revenue collected. But suppose the government uses the tax revenue to provide services that taxpayers want. Or suppose that the government simply hands the tax revenue back to taxpayers. Would we say in those cases that the tax didn't actually cost anything?

No—because a tax, like a quota, prevents mutually beneficial transactions from occurring. Consider Figure 50.10 once more. Here, with a $40 tax on hotel rooms, guests pay $100 per room but hotel owners receive only $60 per room. Because of the wedge created by the tax, we know that some transactions didn't occur that would have occurred without the tax. More specifically, we know from the supply and demand curves that there are some potential guests who would be willing to pay up to $90 per night and some hotel owners who would be willing to supply rooms if they received at least $70 per night. If these two sets of people were allowed to trade with each other without the tax, they would engage in mutually beneficial transactions—hotel rooms would be rented. But such deals would be illegal because the $40 tax would not be paid. In our example, 5,000 potential hotel room rentals that would have occurred in the absence of the tax, to the mutual benefit of guests and hotel owners, do not take place because of the tax.

So an excise tax imposes costs over and above the tax revenue collected in the form of inefficiency, which occurs because the tax discourages mutually beneficial transactions. You may recall from Module 9 that the cost to society of this kind of inefficiency—the value of the forgone mutually beneficial transactions—is called the **deadweight loss.** While all real-world taxes impose some deadweight loss, a badly designed tax imposes a larger deadweight loss than a well-designed one.

To measure the deadweight loss from a tax, we turn to the concepts of producer and consumer surplus. Figure 50.11 shows the effects of an excise tax on consumer and producer surplus. In the absence of the tax, the equilibrium is at E and the equilibrium price and quantity are P_E and Q_E, respectively. An excise tax drives a wedge equal to the amount of the tax between the price received by producers and the price paid by consumers, reducing the quantity sold. In this case, with a tax of T dollars per unit, the quantity sold falls to Q_T. The price paid by consumers rises to P_C, the demand price of the reduced quantity, Q_T, and the price received by producers falls to P_P, the supply price of that quantity. The difference between these prices, $P_C - P_P$, is equal to the excise tax, T.

Using the concepts of producer and consumer surplus, we can show exactly how much surplus producers and consumers lose as a result of the tax. We learned previously that a fall in the price of a good generates a gain in consumer surplus that is equal to the sum of the areas of a rectangle and a triangle. Similarly, a price increase causes a loss to consumers that is represented by the sum of the areas of a rectangle and a triangle. So it's not surprising that in the case of an excise tax, the rise in the price paid by consumers causes a loss equal to the sum of the areas of a rectangle and a triangle: the dark blue rectangle labeled A and the area of the light blue triangle labeled B in Figure 50.11.

The **deadweight loss** (from a tax) is the decrease in total surplus resulting from the tax, minus the tax revenues generated.

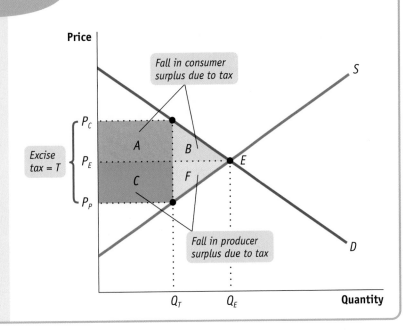

figure 50.11

A Tax Reduces Consumer and Producer Surplus

Before the tax, the equilibrium price and quantity are P_E and Q_E, respectively. After an excise tax of T per unit is imposed, the price to consumers rises to P_C and consumer surplus falls by the sum of the dark blue rectangle, labeled A, and the light blue triangle, labeled B. The tax also causes the price to producers to fall to P_P; producer surplus falls by the sum of the dark red rectangle, labeled C, and the light red triangle, labeled F. The government receives revenue from the tax, $Q_T \times T$, which is given by the sum of the areas A and C. Areas B and F represent the losses to consumer and producer surplus that are not collected by the government as revenue; they are the deadweight loss to society of the tax.

Meanwhile, the fall in the price received by producers leads to a fall in producer surplus. This, too, is equal to the sum of the areas of a rectangle and a triangle. The loss in producer surplus is the sum of the areas of the dark red rectangle labeled C and the light red triangle labeled F in Figure 50.11.

Of course, although consumers and producers are hurt by the tax, the government gains revenue. The revenue the government collects is equal to the tax per unit sold, T, multiplied by the quantity sold, Q_T. This revenue is equal to the area of a rectangle Q_T wide and T high. And we already have that rectangle in the figure: it is the sum of rectangles A and C. So the government gains part of what consumers and producers lose from an excise tax.

But a portion of the loss to producers and consumers from the tax is not offset by a gain to the government—specifically, the two triangles B and F. The deadweight loss caused by the tax is equal to the combined area of these two triangles. It represents the total surplus lost to society because of the tax—that is, the amount of surplus that would have been generated by transactions that now do not take place because of the tax.

Figure 50.12 on the next page is a version of Figure 50.11 that leaves out rectangles A (the surplus shifted from consumers to the government) and C (the surplus shifted from producers to the government) and shows only the deadweight loss, drawn here as a triangle shaded yellow. The base of that triangle is equal to the tax wedge, T; the height of the triangle is equal to the reduction in the quantity transacted due to the tax, $Q_E - Q_T$. Clearly, the larger the tax wedge and the larger the reduction in the quantity transacted, the greater the inefficiency from the tax. But also note an important, contrasting point: if the excise tax somehow *didn't* reduce the quantity bought and sold in this market—if Q_T remained equal to Q_E after the tax was levied—the yellow triangle would disappear and the deadweight loss from the tax would be zero. So if a tax does *not* discourage transactions, it causes no deadweight loss. In this case, the tax simply shifts surplus straight from consumers and producers to the government.

Using a triangle to measure deadweight loss is a technique used in many economic applications. For example, triangles are used to measure the deadweight loss produced by types of taxes other than excise taxes. They are also used to measure the deadweight loss produced by monopoly, another kind of market distortion. And deadweight-loss triangles are often used to evaluate the benefits and costs of public policies besides taxation—such as whether to impose stricter safety standards on a product.

figure 50.12

The Deadweight Loss of a Tax

A tax leads to a deadweight loss because it creates inefficiency: some mutually beneficial transactions never take place because of the tax, namely the transactions $Q_E - Q_T$. The yellow area here represents the value of the deadweight loss: it is the total surplus that would have been gained from the $Q_E - Q_T$ transactions. If the tax had not discouraged transactions—had the number of transactions remained at Q_E—no deadweight loss would have been incurred.

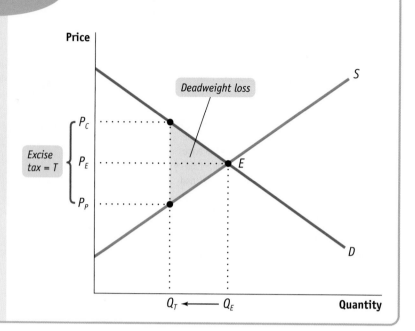

In considering the total amount of inefficiency caused by a tax, we must also take into account something not shown in Figure 50.12: the resources actually used by the government to collect the tax, and by taxpayers to pay it, over and above the amount of the tax. These lost resources are called the **administrative costs** of the tax. The most familiar administrative cost of the U.S. tax system is the time individuals spend filling out their income tax forms or the money they spend on accountants to prepare their tax forms for them. (The latter is considered an inefficiency from the point of view of society because accountants could instead be performing other, non-tax-related services.) Included in the administrative costs that taxpayers incur are resources used to evade the tax, both legally and illegally. The costs of operating the Internal Revenue Service, the arm of the federal government tasked with collecting the federal income tax, are actually quite small in comparison to the administrative costs paid by taxpayers. The total inefficiency caused by a tax is the sum of its deadweight loss and its administrative costs.

Some extreme forms of taxation, such as the *poll tax* instituted by the government of British Prime Minister Margaret Thatcher in 1989, are notably unfair but very efficient. A poll tax is an example of a **lump-sum tax,** a tax that is the same for everyone regardless of any actions people take. The poll tax in Britain was widely perceived as much less fair than the tax structure it replaced, in which local taxes were proportional to property values.

Under the old system, the highest local taxes were paid by the people with the most expensive houses. Because these people tended to be wealthy, they were also best able to bear the burden. But the old system definitely distorted incentives to engage in mutually beneficial transactions and created deadweight loss. People who were considering home improvements knew that such improvements, by making their property more valuable, would increase their tax bills. The result, surely, was that some home improvements that would have taken place without the tax did not take place because of it. In contrast, a lump-sum tax does not distort incentives. Because under a lump-sum tax people have to pay the same amount of tax regardless of their actions, it does not cause them to substitute untaxed goods for a good whose price has been artificially inflated by a tax, as occurs with an excise tax. So lump-sum taxes, although unfair, are better than other taxes at promoting economic efficiency.

The **administrative costs** of a tax are the resources used by government to collect the tax, and by taxpayers to pay (or to evade) it, over and above the amount collected.

A **lump-sum tax** is a tax of a fixed amount paid by all taxpayers.

Module 50 AP Review

Solutions appear at the back of the book.

Check Your Understanding

1. Using the tables in Check Your Understanding Module 49, find the equilibrium price and quantity in the market for cheese-stuffed jalapeno peppers. What is the total surplus in the equilibrium in this market, and who receives it?

2. Consider the market for butter, shown in the accompanying figure. The government imposes an excise tax of $0.30 per pound of butter. What is the price paid by consumers post-tax? What is the price received by producers post-tax? What is the quantity of butter sold? How is the incidence of the tax allocated between consumers and producers? Show this on the figure.

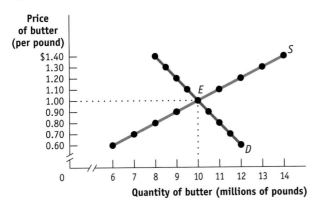

3. The accompanying table shows five consumers' willingness to pay for one can of diet soda each as well as five producers' costs of selling one can of diet soda each. Each consumer buys at most one can of soda; each producer sells at most one can of soda. The government asks your advice about the effects of an

excise tax of $0.40 per can of diet soda. Assume that there are no administrative costs from the tax.

	Consumer Willingness to Pay		Producer Cost
Ana	$0.70	Zhang	$0.10
Bernice	0.60	Yves	0.20
Chizuko	0.50	Xavier	0.30
Dagmar	0.40	Walter	0.40
Ella	0.30	Vern	0.50

a. Without the excise tax, what is the equilibrium price and the equilibrium quantity of soda?

b. The excise tax raises the price paid by consumers post-tax to $0.60 and lowers the price received by producers post-tax to $0.20. With the excise tax, what is the quantity of soda sold?

c. Without the excise tax, how much individual consumer surplus does each of the consumers gain? How much individual consumer surplus does each consumer gain with the tax? How much total consumer surplus is lost as a result of the tax?

d. Without the excise tax, how much individual producer surplus does each of the producers gain? How much individual producer surplus does each producer gain with the tax? How much total producer surplus is lost as a result of the tax?

e. How much government revenue does the excise tax create?

f. What is the deadweight loss from the imposition of this excise tax?

Tackle the Test: Multiple-Choice Questions

1. At market equilibrium in a competitive market, which of the following is necessarily true?

   I. Consumer surplus is maximized.
   II. Producer surplus is maximized.
   III. Total surplus is maximized.

   a. I only
   b. II only
   c. III only
   d. I and II only
   e. I, II, and III

2. When a competitive market is in equilibrium, total surplus can be increased by

   I. reallocating consumption among consumers.
   II. reallocating sales among sellers.
   III. changing the quantity traded.

   a. I only
   b. II only
   c. III only
   d. I, II, and III
   e. None of the above

3. Which of the following is true regarding equity and efficiency in competitive markets?

   a. Competitive markets ensure equity and efficiency.
   b. There is often a trade-off between equity and efficiency.
   c. Competitive markets lead to neither equity nor efficiency.
   d. There is generally agreement about the level of equity and efficiency in a market.
   e. None of the above.

4. An excise tax imposed on sellers in a market will result in which of the following?

    I. an upward shift of the supply curve

    II. a downward shift of the demand curve

    III. deadweight loss

    a. I only

    b. II only

    c. III only

    d. I and III only

    e. I, II, and III

5. An excise tax will be paid mainly by producers when

    a. it is imposed on producers.

    b. it is imposed on consumers.

    c. the price elasticity of supply is low and the price elasticity of demand is high.

    d. the price elasticity of supply is high and the price elasticity of demand is low.

    e. the price elasticity of supply is perfectly elastic.

Tackle the Test: Free-Response Questions

1. Refer to the graph provided. Assume the government has imposed an excise tax of $60 on producers in this market.

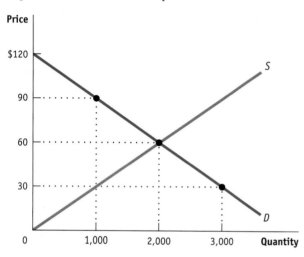

a. What quantity will be sold in the market?

b. What price will consumers pay in the market?

c. By how much will consumer surplus change as a result of the tax?

d. By how much will producer surplus change as a result of the tax?

e. How much revenue will the government collect from this excise tax?

f. Calculate the deadweight loss created by the tax.

Answer (8 points)

1 point: 1,000

1 point: $90

1 point: Consumer surplus will decrease by $45,000, from $60,000 before the tax to $15,000 after the tax.

1 point: Producer surplus will decrease by $45,000, from $60,000 before the tax to $15,000 after the tax.

1 point: $60 × 1,000 = $60,000

1 point: $30,000

2. Draw a correctly labeled graph of a competitive market in equilibrium. Use your graph to illustrate the effect of an excise tax imposed on consumers. Indicate each of the following on your graph:

a. the equilibrium price and quantity without the tax, labeled P_E and Q_E

b. the quantity sold in the market post-tax, labeled Q_T

c. the price paid by consumers post-tax, labeled P_C

d. the price received by producers post-tax, labeled P_P

e. the tax revenue generated by the tax, labeled "Tax revenue"

f. The deadweight loss resulting from the tax, labeled "DWL."

Module 51
Utility Maximization

We have used the demand curve to study consumer responsiveness to changes in prices and discovered its usefulness in predicting how consumers will gain from the availability of goods and services in a market. But where does the demand curve come from? In other words, what lies behind the demand curve? The demand curve represents the tastes, preferences, and resulting choices of individual consumers. Its shape reflects the additional satisfaction, or *utility,* people receive from consuming more and more of a good or service.

What you will learn in this Module:

- How consumers make choices about the purchase of goods and services
- Why consumers' general goal is to maximize utility
- Why the principle of diminishing marginal utility applies to the consumption of most goods and services
- How to use marginal analysis to find the optimal consumption bundle

Utility: It's All About Getting Satisfaction

When analyzing consumer behavior, we're looking into how people pursue their needs and wants and the subjective feelings that motivate purchases. Yet there is no simple way to measure subjective feelings. How much satisfaction do I get from my third cookie? Is it less or more than the satisfaction you receive from your third cookie? Does it even make sense to ask that question?

Luckily, we don't need to make comparisons between your feelings and mine. The analysis of consumer behavior that follows requires only the assumption that individuals try to maximize some personal measure of the satisfaction gained from consumption. That measure of satisfaction is known as **utility,** a concept we use to understand behavior but don't expect to measure in practice.

Utility is a measure of personal satisfaction.

Utility and Consumption

We can think of consumers as using consumption to "produce" utility, much in the same way that producers use inputs to produce output. As consumers, we do not make explicit calculations of the utility generated by consumption choices, but we must make choices, and we usually base them on at least a rough attempt to achieve greater satisfaction. I can have either soup or salad with my dinner. Which will I enjoy more? I can go to Disney World this year or put the money toward buying a new car. Which will make me happier? These are the types of questions that go into utility maximization.

The concept of utility offers a way to study choices that are made in a more or less rational way.

A **util** is a unit of utility.

How do we measure utility? For the sake of simplicity, it is useful to suppose that we can measure utility in hypothetical units called—what else?—**utils.** A *utility function* shows the relationship between a consumer's utility and the combination of goods and services—the *consumption bundle*—he or she consumes.

Figure 51.1 illustrates a utility function. It shows the total utility that Cassie, who likes fried clams, gets from an all-you-can-eat clam dinner. We suppose that her consumption bundle consists of a side of coleslaw, which comes with the meal, plus a number of clams to be determined. The table that accompanies the figure shows how Cassie's total utility depends on the number of clams; the curve in panel (a) of the figure shows that same information graphically.

Cassie's utility function slopes upward over most of the range shown, but it gets flatter as the number of clams consumed increases. And in this example it eventually turns downward. According to the information in the table in Figure 51.1, nine clams is a clam too far. Adding that additional clam actually makes Cassie worse off: it would lower her total utility. If she's rational, of course, Cassie will realize that and not consume the ninth clam.

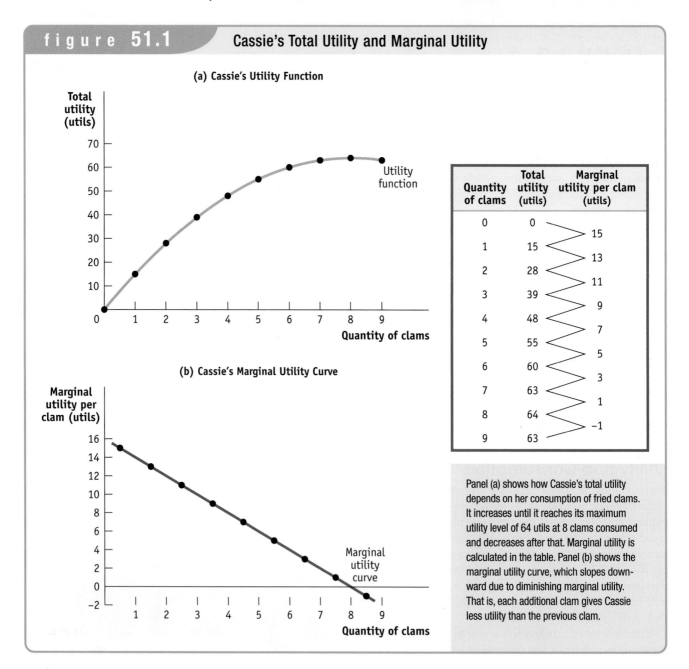

figure 51.1

Cassie's Total Utility and Marginal Utility

(a) Cassie's Utility Function

(b) Cassie's Marginal Utility Curve

Quantity of clams	Total utility (utils)	Marginal utility per clam (utils)
0	0	
		15
1	15	
		13
2	28	
		11
3	39	
		9
4	48	
		7
5	55	
		5
6	60	
		3
7	63	
		1
8	64	
		−1
9	63	

Panel (a) shows how Cassie's total utility depends on her consumption of fried clams. It increases until it reaches its maximum utility level of 64 utils at 8 clams consumed and decreases after that. Marginal utility is calculated in the table. Panel (b) shows the marginal utility curve, which slopes downward due to diminishing marginal utility. That is, each additional clam gives Cassie less utility than the previous clam.

So when Cassie chooses how many clams to consume, she will make this decision by considering the *change* in her total utility from consuming one more clam. This illustrates the general point: to maximize *total* utility, consumers must focus on *marginal* utility.

The Principle of Diminishing Marginal Utility

In addition to showing how Cassie's total utility depends on the number of clams she consumes, the table in Figure 51.1 also shows the **marginal utility** generated by consuming each additional clam—that is, the *change* in total utility from consuming one additional clam. The **marginal utility curve** is constructed by plotting points at the midpoint between the numbered quantities since marginal utility is found as consumption levels change. For example, when consumption rises from 1 to 2 clams, marginal utility is 13. Therefore, we place the point corresponding to marginal utility of 13 halfway between 1 and 2 clams.

The marginal utility curve slopes downward because each successive clam adds less to total utility than the previous clam. This is reflected in the table: marginal utility falls from a high of 15 utils for the first clam consumed to −1 for the ninth clam consumed. The fact that the ninth clam has negative marginal utility means that consuming it actually reduces total utility. (Restaurants that offer all-you-can-eat meals depend on the proposition that you can have too much of a good thing.) Not all marginal utility curves eventually become negative. But it is generally accepted that marginal utility curves do slope downward—that consumption of most goods and services is subject to *diminishing marginal utility*.

The basic idea behind the **principle of diminishing marginal utility** is that the additional satisfaction a consumer gets from one more unit of a good or service declines as the amount of that good or service consumed rises. Or, to put it slightly differently, the more of a good or service you consume, the closer you are to being satiated—reaching a point at which an additional unit of the good adds nothing to your satisfaction. For someone who almost never gets to eat a banana, the occasional banana is a marvelous treat (as it was in Eastern Europe before the fall of communism, when bananas were very hard to find). For someone who eats them all the time, a banana is just, well, a banana.

The **marginal utility** of a good or service is the change in total utility generated by consuming one additional unit of that good or service. The **marginal utility curve** shows how marginal utility depends on the quantity of a good or service consumed.

According to the **principle of diminishing marginal utility,** each successive unit of a good or service consumed adds less to total utility than does the previous unit.

fyi

Is Marginal Utility Really Diminishing?

Are all goods really subject to diminishing marginal utility? Of course not; there are a number of goods for which, at least over some range, marginal utility is surely *increasing.*

For example, there are goods that require some experience to enjoy. The first time you do it, downhill skiing involves a lot more fear than enjoyment—or so they say: two of the authors have never tried it! It only becomes a pleasurable activity if you do it enough to become reasonably competent. And even some less strenuous forms of consumption take practice; people who are not accustomed to drinking coffee say it has a bitter taste and can't understand its appeal. (The authors, on the other hand, regard coffee as one of the basic food groups.)

Another example would be goods that only deliver positive utility if you buy enough. The great Victorian economist Alfred Marshall, who more or less invented the supply and demand model, gave the example of wallpaper: buying only enough to do half a room is worse than useless. If you need two rolls of wallpaper to finish a room, the marginal utility of the second roll is larger than the marginal utility of the first roll.

So why does it make sense to assume diminishing marginal utility? For one thing, most goods don't suffer from these qualifications: nobody needs to learn to like ice cream. Also, although most people don't ski and some people don't drink coffee, those who do ski or drink coffee do enough of it that the marginal utility of one more ski run or one more cup is less than that of the last. So *in the relevant range* of consumption, marginal utility is still diminishing.

The principle of diminishing marginal utility doesn't always apply, but it does apply in the great majority of cases, enough to serve as a foundation for our analysis of consumer behavior.

Budgets and Optimal Consumption

The principle of diminishing marginal utility explains why most people eventually reach a limit, even at an all-you-can-eat buffet where the cost of another clam is measured only in future indigestion. Under ordinary circumstances, however, it costs some additional resources to consume more of a good, and consumers must take that cost into account when making choices.

What do we mean by cost? As always, the fundamental measure of cost is *opportunity cost*. Because the amount of money a consumer can spend is limited, a decision to consume more of one good is also a decision to consume less of some other good.

Budget Constraints and Budget Lines

Consider Sammy, whose appetite is exclusively for clams and potatoes. (There's no accounting for tastes.) He has a weekly income of $20 and since, given his appetite, more of either good is better than less, he spends all of it on clams and potatoes. We will assume that clams cost $4 per pound and potatoes cost $2 per pound. What are his possible choices?

Whatever Sammy chooses, we know that the cost of his consumption bundle cannot exceed the amount of money he has to spend. That is,

(51-1)   Expenditure on clams + Expenditure on potatoes ≤ Total income

Consumers always have limited income, which constrains how much they can consume. So the requirement illustrated by Equation 51-1—that a consumer must choose a consumption bundle that costs no more than his or her income—is known as the consumer's **budget constraint.** It's a simple way of saying that a consumer can't spend more than the total amount of income available to him or her. In other words, consumption bundles are affordable when they obey the budget constraint. We call the set of all of Sammy's affordable consumption bundles his **consumption possibilities.** In general, whether or not a particular consumption bundle is included in a consumer's consumption possibilities depends on the consumer's income and the prices of goods and services.

Figure 51.2 shows Sammy's consumption possibilities. The quantity of clams in his consumption bundle is measured on the horizontal axis and the quantity of potatoes on the vertical axis. The downward-sloping line connecting points *A* through *F* shows which consumption bundles are affordable and which are not. Every bundle on or inside this line (the shaded area) is affordable; every bundle outside this line is unaffordable. As an example of one of the points, let's look at point *C*, representing 2 pounds of clams and 6 pounds of potatoes, and check whether it satisfies Sammy's budget constraint. The cost of bundle *C* is 6 pounds of potatoes × $2 per pound + 2 pounds of clams × $4 per pound = $12 + $8 = $20. So bundle *C* does indeed satisfy Sammy's budget constraint: it costs no more than his weekly income of $20. In fact, bundle *C* costs exactly as much as Sammy's income. By doing the arithmetic, you can check that all the other points lying on the downward-sloping line are also bundles at which Sammy spends all of his income.

The downward-sloping line has a special name, the **budget line.** It shows all the consumption bundles available to Sammy when he spends all of his income. It's downward-sloping because when Sammy is spending all of his income, say by consuming at point *A* on the budget line, then in order to consume more clams he must consume fewer potatoes—that is, he must move to a point like *B*. In other words, when

A **budget constraint** limits the cost of a consumer's consumption bundle to no more than the consumer's income.

A consumer's **consumption possibilities** is the set of all consumption bundles that are affordable, given the consumer's income and prevailing prices.

A consumer's **budget line** shows the consumption bundles available to a consumer who spends all of his or her income.

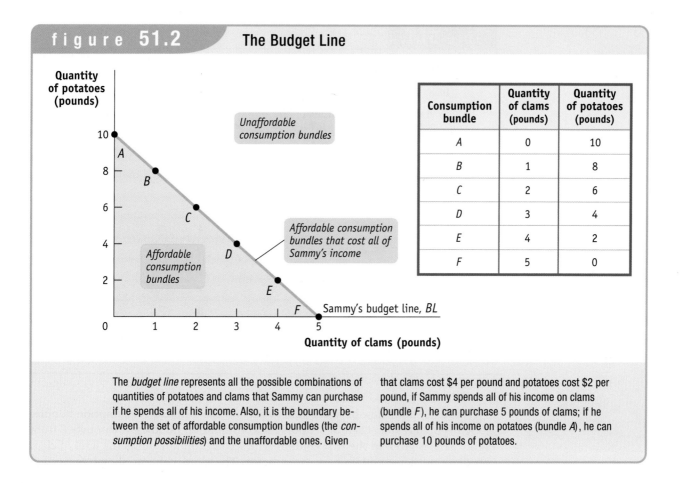

figure 51.2 **The Budget Line**

The *budget line* represents all the possible combinations of quantities of potatoes and clams that Sammy can purchase if he spends all of his income. Also, it is the boundary between the set of affordable consumption bundles (the *consumption possibilities*) and the unaffordable ones. Given that clams cost $4 per pound and potatoes cost $2 per pound, if Sammy spends all of his income on clams (bundle *F*), he can purchase 5 pounds of clams; if he spends all of his income on potatoes (bundle *A*), he can purchase 10 pounds of potatoes.

Sammy is on his budget line, the opportunity cost of consuming more clams is consuming fewer potatoes, and vice versa. As Figure 51.2 indicates, any consumption bundle that lies above the budget line is unaffordable.

Do we need to consider the other bundles in Sammy's consumption possibilities, the ones that lie *within* the shaded region in Figure 51.2 bounded by the budget line? The answer is, for all practical situations, no: as long as Sammy doesn't get satiated—that is, as long as his marginal utility from consuming either good is always positive—and he doesn't get any utility from saving income rather than spending it, then he will always choose to consume a bundle that lies on his budget line.

Given that $20 per week budget, next we can consider the culinary dilemma of what point on his budget line Sammy will choose.

The Optimal Consumption Bundle

Because Sammy's budget constrains him to a consumption bundle somewhere along the budget line, a choice to consume a given quantity of clams also determines his potato consumption, and vice versa. We want to find the consumption bundle—represented by a point on the budget line—that maximizes Sammy's total utility. This bundle is Sammy's **optimal consumption bundle**.

Table 51.1 on the next page shows how much utility Sammy gets from different levels of consumption of clams and potatoes, respectively. According to the table, Sammy has a healthy appetite; the more of either good he consumes, the higher his utility. But because he has a limited budget, he must make a trade-off: the more pounds of clams he consumes, the fewer pounds of potatoes, and vice versa. That is, he must choose a point on his budget line.

A consumer's **optimal consumption bundle** is the consumption bundle that maximizes the consumer's total utility given his or her budget constraint.

table **51.1**

Sammy's Utility from Clam and Potato Consumption

Utility from clam consumption		Utility from potato consumption	
Quantity of clams (pounds)	Utility from clams (utils)	Quantity of potatoes (pounds)	Utility from potatoes (utils)
0	0	0	0
1	15	1	11.5
2	25	2	21.4
3	31	3	29.8
4	34	4	36.8
5	36	5	42.5
		6	47.0
		7	50.5
		8	53.2
		9	55.2
		10	56.7

Table 51.2 shows how his total utility varies for the different consumption bundles along his budget line. Each of six possible consumption bundles, *A* through *F* from Figure 51.2, is given in the first column. The second column shows the level of clam consumption corresponding to each choice. The third column shows the utility Sammy gets from consuming those clams. The fourth column shows the quantity of potatoes Sammy can afford *given* the level of clam consumption; this quantity goes down as his clam consumption goes up because he is sliding down the budget line. The fifth column shows the utility he gets from consuming those potatoes. And the final column shows his *total utility*. In this example, Sammy's total utility is the sum of the utility he gets from clams and the utility he gets from potatoes.

Figure 51.3 gives a visual representation of the data shown in Table 51.2. Panel (a) shows Sammy's budget line, to remind us that when he decides to consume more clams he is also deciding to consume fewer potatoes. Panel (b) then shows how his total utility depends on that choice. The horizontal axis in panel (b) has two sets of labels: it shows both the quantity of clams, increasing from left to right, and the quantity of

table **51.2**

Sammy's Budget and Total Utility

Consumption bundle	Quantity of clams (pounds)	Utility from clams (utils)	Quantity of potatoes (pounds)	Utility from potatoes (utils)	Total utility (utils)
A	0	0	10	56.7	56.7
B	1	15	8	53.2	68.2
C	2	25	6	47.0	72.0
D	3	31	4	36.8	67.8
E	4	34	2	21.4	55.4
F	5	36	0	0	36.0

figure 51.3

Optimal Consumption Bundle

Panel (a) shows Sammy's budget line and his six possible consumption bundles. Panel (b) shows how his total utility is affected by his consumption bundle, which must lie on his budget line. The quantity of clams is measured from left to right on the horizontal axis, and the quantity of potatoes is measured from right to left. His total utility is maximized at bundle *C*, where he consumes 2 pounds of clams and 6 pounds of potatoes. This is Sammy's *optimal consumption bundle.*

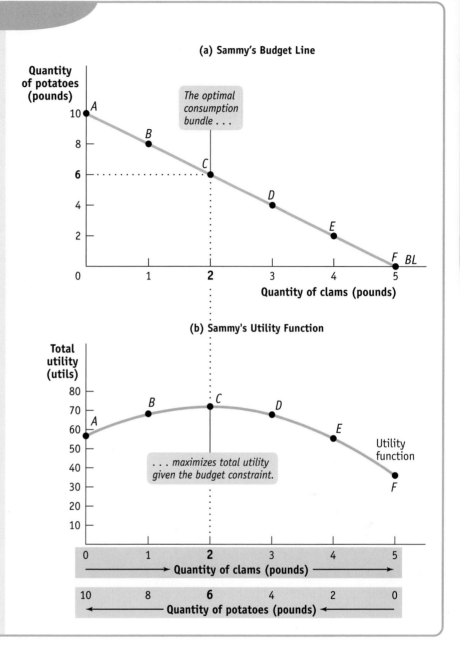

potatoes, increasing from right to left. The reason we can use the same axis to represent consumption of both goods is, of course, that he is constrained by the budget line: the more pounds of clams Sammy consumes, the fewer pounds of potatoes he can afford, and vice versa.

Clearly, the consumption bundle that makes the best of the trade-off between clam consumption and potato consumption, the optimal consumption bundle, is the one that maximizes Sammy's total utility. That is, Sammy's optimal consumption bundle puts him at the top of the total utility curve.

As always, we can find the top of the curve by direct observation. We can see from Figure 51.3 that Sammy's total utility is maximized at point *C*—that his optimal consumption bundle contains 2 pounds of clams and 6 pounds of potatoes. But we know that we usually gain more insight into "how much" problems when we use marginal analysis. So in the next section we turn to representing and solving the optimal consumption choice problem with marginal analysis.

Spending the Marginal Dollar

As we've just seen, we can find Sammy's optimal consumption choice by finding the total utility he receives from each consumption bundle on his budget line and then choosing the bundle at which total utility is maximized. But we can use marginal analysis instead, turning Sammy's problem of finding his optimal consumption choice into a "how much" problem. How do we do this? By thinking about choosing an optimal consumption bundle as a problem of *how much to spend on each good.* That is, to find the optimal consumption bundle with marginal analysis we ask the question of whether Sammy can make himself better off by spending a little bit more of his income on clams and less on potatoes, or by doing the opposite—spending a little bit more on potatoes and less on clams. In other words, the marginal decision is a question of how to *spend the marginal dollar*—how to allocate an additional dollar between clams and potatoes in a way that maximizes utility.

Our first step in applying marginal analysis is to ask if Sammy is made better off by spending an additional dollar on either good; and if so, by how much is he better off. To answer this question we must calculate the **marginal utility per dollar** spent on either clams or potatoes—how much additional utility Sammy gets from spending an additional dollar on either good.

Marginal Utility per Dollar

We've already introduced the concept of marginal utility, the additional utility a consumer gets from consuming one more unit of a good or service; now let's see how this concept can be used to derive the related measure of marginal utility per dollar.

Table 51.3 shows how to calculate the marginal utility per dollar spent on clams and potatoes, respectively.

table **51.3**

Sammy's Marginal Utility per Dollar

(a) Clams (price of clams = $4 per pound)				(b) Potatoes (price of potatoes = $2 per pound)			
Quantity of clams (pounds)	Utility from clams (utils)	Marginal utility per pound of clams (utils)	Marginal utility per dollar (utils)	Quantity of potatoes (pounds)	Utility from potatoes (utils)	Marginal utility per pound of potatoes (utils)	Marginal utility per dollar (utils)
0	0			0	0		
		15	3.75			11.5	5.75
1	15			1	11.5		
		10	2.50			9.9	4.95
2	25			2	21.4		
		6	1.50			8.4	4.20
3	31			3	29.8		
		3	0.75			7.0	3.50
4	34			4	36.8		
		2	0.50			5.7	2.85
5	36			5	42.5		
						4.5	2.25
				6	47.0		
						3.5	1.75
				7	50.5		
						2.7	1.35
				8	53.2		
						2.0	1.00
				9	55.2		
						1.5	0.75
				10	56.7		

In panel (a) of the table, the first column shows different possible amounts of clam consumption. The second column shows the utility Sammy derives from each amount of clam consumption; the third column then shows the marginal utility, the increase in utility Sammy gets from consuming an additional pound of clams. Panel (b) provides the same information for potatoes. The next step is to derive marginal utility *per dollar* for each good. To do this, we just divide the marginal utility of the good by its price in dollars.

To see why we divide by the price, compare the third and fourth columns of panel (a). Consider what happens if Sammy increases his clam consumption from 2 pounds to 3 pounds. This raises his total utility by 6 utils. But he must spend $4 for that additional pound, so the increase in his utility per additional dollar spent on clams is 6 utils/$4 = 1.5 utils per dollar. Similarly, if he increases his clam consumption from 3 pounds to 4 pounds, his marginal utility is 3 utils but his marginal utility per dollar is 3 utils/$4 = 0.75 utils per dollar. Notice that because of diminishing marginal utility, Sammy's marginal utility per pound of clams falls as the quantity of clams he consumes rises. As a result, his marginal utility per dollar spent on clams also falls as the quantity of clams he consumes rises.

So the last column of panel (a) shows how Sammy's marginal utility per dollar spent on clams depends on the quantity of clams he consumes. Similarly, the last column of panel (b) shows how his marginal utility per dollar spent on potatoes depends on the quantity of potatoes he consumes. Again, marginal utility per dollar spent on each good declines as the quantity of that good consumed rises because of diminishing marginal utility.

We will use the symbols MU_C and MU_P to represent the marginal utility per pound of clams and potatoes, respectively. And we will use the symbols P_C and P_P to represent the price of clams (per pound) and the price of potatoes (per pound). Then the marginal utility per dollar spent on clams is MU_C/P_C and the marginal utility per dollar spent on potatoes is MU_P/P_P. In general, the additional utility generated from an additional dollar spent on a good is equal to:

(51-2) Marginal utility per dollar spent on a good
   = Marginal utility of one unit of the good/Price of one unit of the good
   = MU_{good}/P_{good}

Next we'll see how this concept helps us determine a consumer's optimal consumption bundle using marginal analysis.

Optimal Consumption

Let's consider Figure 51.4 on the next page. As in Figure 51.3, we can measure both the quantity of clams and the quantity of potatoes on the horizontal axis due to the budget constraint. Along the horizontal axis of Figure 51.4—also as in Figure 51.3—the quantity of clams increases as you move from left to right, and the quantity of potatoes increases as you move from right to left. The curve labeled MU_C/P_C in Figure 51.4 shows Sammy's marginal utility per dollar spent on clams as derived in Table 51.3. Likewise, the curve labeled MU_P/P_P shows his marginal utility per dollar spent on potatoes. Notice that the two curves, MU_C/P_C and MU_P/P_P, cross at the optimal consumption bundle, point *C*, consisting of 2 pounds of clams and 6 pounds of potatoes. Moreover, Figure 51.4 illustrates an important feature of Sammy's optimal consumption bundle: when Sammy consumes 2 pounds of clams and 6 pounds of potatoes, his marginal utility per dollar spent is the same, 2, for both goods. That is, at the optimal consumption bundle, $MU_C/P_C = MU_P/P_P = 2$.

This isn't an accident. Consider another one of Sammy's possible consumption bundles—say, *B* in Figure 51.3, at which he consumes 1 pound of clams and 8 pounds of potatoes. The marginal utility per dollar spent on each good is shown by points B_C and B_P in Figure 51.4. At that consumption bundle, Sammy's marginal utility per

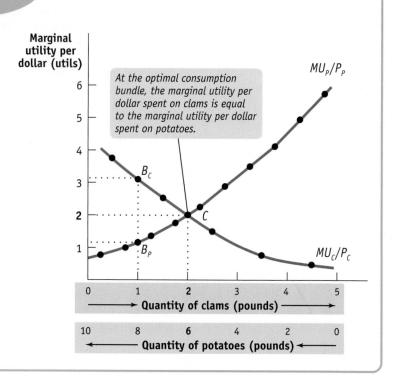

figure 51.4

Marginal Utility per Dollar

Sammy's optimal consumption bundle is at point C, where his marginal utility per dollar spent on clams, MU_C/P_C, is equal to his marginal utility per dollar spent on potatoes, MU_P/P_P. This illustrates the optimal consumption rule: *at the optimal consumption bundle, the marginal utility per dollar spent on each good and service is the same.* At any other consumption bundle on Sammy's budget line, such as bundle B in Figure 51.3, represented here by points B_C and B_P, consumption is not optimal: Sammy can increase his utility at no additional cost by reallocating his spending.

dollar spent on clams would be approximately 3, but his marginal utility per dollar spent on potatoes would be only approximately 1. This shows that he has made a mistake: he is consuming too many potatoes and not enough clams.

How do we know this? If Sammy's marginal utility per dollar spent on clams is higher than his marginal utility per dollar spent on potatoes, he has a simple way to make himself better off while staying within his budget: spend $1 less on potatoes and $1 more on clams. By spending an additional dollar on clams, he adds about 3 utils to his total utility; meanwhile, by spending $1 less on potatoes, he subtracts only about 1 util from his total utility. Because his marginal utility per dollar spent is higher for clams than for potatoes, reallocating his spending toward clams and away from potatoes would increase his total utility. On the other hand, if his marginal utility per dollar spent on potatoes is higher, he can increase his utility by spending less on clams and more on potatoes. So if Sammy has in fact chosen his optimal consumption bundle, his marginal utility per dollar spent on clams and potatoes must be equal.

This is a general principle, known as the **optimal consumption rule:** *when a consumer maximizes utility in the face of a budget constraint, the marginal utility per dollar spent on each good or service in the consumption bundle is the same.* That is, for any two goods C and P, the optimal consumption rule says that at the optimal consumption bundle

$$(51\text{-}3) \quad \frac{MU_C}{P_C} = \frac{MU_P}{P_P}$$

It's easiest to understand this rule using examples in which the consumption bundle contains only two goods, but it applies no matter how many goods or services a consumer buys: the marginal utilities per dollar spent for each and every good or service in the optimal consumption bundle are equal.

The main reason for studying consumer behavior is to look behind the market demand curve. In Module 46 we explained how the *substitution effect* leads consumers to buy less of a good when its price increases. We used the substitution effect to explain,

The **optimal consumption rule** says that in order to maximize utility, a consumer must equate the marginal utility per dollar spent on each good and service in the consumption bundle.

in general, why the individual demand curve obeys the law of demand. Marginal analysis adds clarity to the utility-maximizing behavior of individuals and explains more precisely how an increase in price leads to less marginal utility per dollar and therefore a decrease in the quantity demanded.

Module 51 AP Review

Solutions appear at the back of the book.

Check Your Understanding

1. Explain why a rational consumer who has diminishing marginal utility for a good would not consume an additional unit when it generates negative marginal utility, even when that unit is free.

2. In the following two examples, find all the consumption bundles that lie on the consumer's budget line. Illustrate these consumption possibilities in a diagram, and draw the budget line through them.
   a. The consumption bundle consists of movie tickets and buckets of popcorn. The price of each ticket is $10.00, the price of each bucket of popcorn is $5.00, and the consumer's income is $20.00. In your diagram, put movie tickets on the vertical axis and buckets of popcorn on the horizontal axis.

   b. The consumption bundle consists of underwear and socks. The price of each pair of underwear is $4.00, the price of each pair of socks is $2.00, and the consumer's income is $12.00. In your diagram, put pairs of socks on the vertical axis and pairs of underwear on the horizontal axis.

3. In Table 51.3 you can see that the marginal utility per dollar spent on clams and the marginal utility per dollar spent on potatoes are equal when Sammy increases his consumption of clams from 3 pounds to 4 pounds and his consumption of potatoes from 9 pounds to 10 pounds. Explain why this is not Sammy's optimal consumption bundle. Illustrate your answer using a budget line like the one in Figure 51.3.

Tackle the Test: Multiple-Choice Questions

1. Generally, each successive unit of a good consumed will cause marginal utility to
   a. increase at an increasing rate.
   b. increase at a decreasing rate.
   c. increase at a constant rate.
   d. decrease.
   e. either increase or decrease.

2. Assume there are two goods, good X and good Y. Good X costs $5 and good Y costs $10. If your income is $200, which of the following combinations of good X and good Y is on your budget line?
   a. 0 units of good X and 18 units of good Y
   b. 0 units of good X and 20 units of good Y
   c. 20 units of good X and 0 units of good Y
   d. 10 units of good X and 12 units of good Y
   e. all of the above

3. The optimal consumption rule states that total utility is maximized when all income is spent and
   a. MU/P is equal for all goods.
   b. MU is equal for all goods.
   c. P/MU is equal for all goods.
   d. MU is as high as possible for all goods.
   e. The amount spent on each good is equal.

4. A consumer is spending all of her income and receiving 100 utils from the last unit of good A and 80 utils from the last unit of good B. If the price of good A is $2 and the price of good B is $1, to maximize total utility the consumer should buy
   a. more of good A.
   b. more of good B.
   c. less of good B.
   d. more of both goods.
   e. less of both goods.

5. The optimal consumption bundle is always represented by a point
   a. inside the consumer's budget line.
   b. outside the consumer's budget line.
   c. at the highest point on the consumer's budget line.
   d. on the consumer's budget line.
   e. at the horizontal intercept of the consumer's budget line.

Tackle the Test: Free-Response Questions

1. Refer to the table provided. Assume you have $20 to spend.

Snacks (price = $4)		Drinks (price = $2)	
Quantity	Total Utility (utils)	Quantity	Total Utility (utils)
1	15	1	12
2	25	2	21
3	31	3	29
4	34	4	36
5	36	5	42
		6	47
		7	50
		8	52

a. Draw a correctly labeled budget line.
b. Determine the marginal utility and the marginal utility per dollar spent on the fourth drink.
c. What is the optimal consumption rule?
d. How many drinks and snacks should you purchase to maximize your total utility?

Answer (6 points)

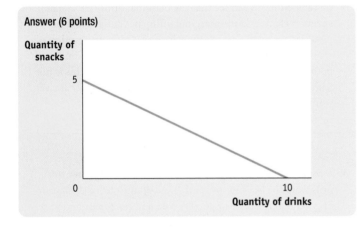

1 point: Graph with "Quantity of snacks" and "Quantity of drinks" as axis labels.

1 point: Straight budget line with intercepts at 5 snacks and 0 drinks and at 0 snacks and 10 drinks.

1 point: MU = 7 utils

1 point: MU/P = 3.5 utils per dollar

1 point: Total utility is maximized when the marginal utility per dollar is equal for all goods.

1 point: 6 drinks, 2 snacks

2. Assume you have an income of $100. The price of good X is $5, and the price of good Y is $20.
   a. Draw a correctly labeled budget line with "Quantity of good X" on the horizontal axis and "Quantity of good Y" on the vertical axis. Be sure to correctly label the horizontal and vertical intercepts.
   b. With your current consumption bundle, you receive 100 utils from consuming your last unit of good X and 400 utils from consuming your last unit of good Y. Are you maximizing your total utility? Explain.
   c. What will happen to the total and marginal utility you receive from consuming good X if you decide to consume another unit of good X? Explain.

Section 9 Review

Summary

1. Changes in the price of a good affect the quantity consumed as a result of the **substitution effect,** and in some cases the **income effect.** Most goods absorb only a small share of a consumer's spending; for these goods, only the substitution effect—buying less of the good that has become relatively more expensive and more of the good that has become relatively cheaper—is significant. The income effect becomes substantial when there is a change in the price of a good that absorbs a large share of a consumer's spending, thereby changing the purchasing power of the consumer's income.

2. Many economic questions depend on the size of consumer or producer responses to changes in prices or other variables. *Elasticity* is a general measure of responsiveness that can be used to answer such questions.

3. The **price elasticity of demand**—the percent change in the quantity demanded divided by the percent change in the price (dropping the minus sign)—is a measure of the responsiveness of the quantity demanded to changes in the price. In practical calculations, it is usually best to use the **midpoint method,** which calculates percent changes in prices and quantities based on the average of the initial and final values.

4. Demand can fall anywhere in the range from **perfectly inelastic,** meaning the quantity demanded is unaffected by the price, to **perfectly elastic,** meaning there is a unique price at which consumers will buy as much

or as little as they are offered. When demand is perfectly inelastic, the demand curve is a vertical line; when it is perfectly elastic, the demand curve is a horizontal line.

5. The price elasticity of demand is classified according to whether it is more or less than 1. If it is greater than 1, demand is **elastic;** if it is less than 1, demand is **inelastic;** if it is exactly 1, demand is **unit-elastic.** This classification determines how **total revenue,** the total value of sales, changes when the price changes. If demand is elastic, total revenue falls when the price increases and rises when the price decreases. If demand is inelastic, total revenue rises when the price increases and falls when the price decreases.

6. The price elasticity of demand depends on whether there are close substitutes for the good in question, whether the good is a necessity or a luxury, the share of income spent on the good, and the length of time that has elapsed since the price change.

7. The **cross-price elasticity of demand** measures the effect of a change in one good's price on the quantity of another good demanded. The cross-price elasticity of demand can be positive, in which case the goods are substitutes, or negative, in which case they are complements.

8. The **income elasticity of demand** is the percent change in the quantity of a good demanded when a consumer's income changes divided by the percent change in income. The income elasticity of demand indicates how intensely the demand for a good responds to changes in income. It can be negative; in that case the good is an inferior good. Goods with positive income elasticities of demand are normal goods. If the income elasticity is greater than 1, a good is **income-elastic;** if it is positive and less than 1, the good is **income-inelastic.**

9. The **price elasticity of supply** is the percent change in the quantity of a good supplied divided by the percent change in the price. If the quantity supplied does not change at all, we have an instance of **perfectly inelastic supply;** the supply curve is a vertical line. If the quantity supplied is zero below some price but infinite above that price, we have an instance of **perfectly elastic supply;** the supply curve is a horizontal line.

10. The price elasticity of supply depends on the availability of resources to expand production and on time. It is higher when inputs are available at relatively low cost and when more time has elapsed since the price change.

11. The **willingness to pay** of each individual consumer determines the shape of the demand curve. When price is less than or equal to the willingness to pay, the potential consumer purchases the good. The difference between willingness to pay and price is the net gain to the consumer, the **individual consumer surplus.**

12. **Total consumer surplus** in a market, which is the sum of all individual consumer surpluses in a market, is equal to the area below the market demand curve but

above the price. A rise in the price of a good reduces consumer surplus; a fall in the price increases consumer surplus. The term **consumer surplus** is often used to refer to both individual and total consumer surplus.

13. The **cost** of each potential producer of a good, the lowest price at which he or she is willing to supply a unit of that good, determines the supply curve. If the price of a good is above a producer's cost, a sale generates a net gain to the producer, known as the **individual producer surplus.**

14. **Total producer surplus** in a market, the sum of the individual producer surpluses in a market, is equal to the area above the market supply curve but below the price. A rise in the price of a good increases producer surplus; a fall in the price reduces producer surplus. The term **producer surplus** is often used to refer to both individual and total producer surplus.

15. **Total surplus,** the total gain to society from the production and consumption of a good, is the sum of consumer and producer surplus.

16. Usually, markets are efficient and achieve the maximum total surplus. Any possible reallocation of consumption or sales, or change in the quantity bought and sold, reduces total surplus. However, society also cares about equity. So government intervention in a market that reduces efficiency but increases equity can be a valid choice by society.

17. A tax that rises more than in proportion to income is a **progressive tax.** A tax that rises less than in proportion to income is a **regressive tax.** A taxes that rises in proportion to income is, you guessed it, a **proportional tax.**

18. An **excise tax**—a tax on the purchase or sale of a good—raises the price paid by consumers and reduces the price received by producers, driving a wedge between the two. The **incidence** of the tax—how the burden of the tax is divided between consumers and producers—does not depend on who officially pays the tax.

19. The incidence of an excise tax depends on the price elasticities of supply and demand. If the price elasticity of demand is higher than the price elasticity of supply, the tax falls mainly on producers; if the price elasticity of supply is higher than the price elasticity of demand, the tax falls mainly on consumers.

20. The tax revenue generated by a tax depends on the **tax rate** and on the number of units sold with the tax. Excise taxes cause inefficiency in the form of deadweight loss because they discourage some mutually beneficial transactions. Taxes also impose **administrative costs:** resources used to collect the tax, to pay it (over and above the amount of the tax), and to evade it.

21. An excise tax generates revenue for the government but lowers total surplus. The loss in total surplus exceeds the tax revenue, resulting in a deadweight loss to society. This deadweight loss is represented by a triangle, the area of which equals the value of the transactions

discouraged by the tax. The greater the elasticity of demand or supply, or both, the larger the deadweight loss from a tax. If either demand or supply is perfectly inelastic, there is no deadweight loss from a tax.

22. A **lump-sum tax** is a tax of a fixed amount paid by all taxpayers. Because a lump-sum tax does not depend on the behavior of taxpayers, it does not discourage mutually beneficial transactions and therefore causes no deadweight loss.

23. Consumers maximize a measure of satisfaction called **utility.** We measure utility in hypothetical units called **utils.**

24. A good's or service's **marginal utility** is the additional utility generated by consuming one more unit of the good or service. We usually assume that the **principle of diminishing marginal utility** holds: consumption of another unit of a good or service yields less additional utility than the previous unit. As a result, the **marginal utility curve** slopes downward.

25. A **budget constraint** limits a consumer's spending to no more than his or her income. It defines the consumer's **consumption possibilities,** the set of all affordable consumption bundles. A consumer who spends all of his or her income will choose a consumption bundle on the **budget line.** An individual chooses the consumption bundle that maximizes total utility, the **optimal consumption bundle.**

26. We use marginal analysis to find the optimal consumption bundle by analyzing how to allocate the marginal dollar. According to the **optimal consumption rule,** with the optimal consumption bundle, the **marginal utility per dollar** spent on each good and service—the marginal utility of a good divided by its price—is the same.

Key Terms

Problems

1. Nile.com, the online bookseller, wants to increase its total revenue. One strategy is to offer a 10% discount on every book it sells. Nile.com knows that its customers can be divided into two distinct groups according to their likely responses to the discount. The accompanying table shows how the two groups respond to the discount.

	Group A (sales per week)	Group B (sales per week)
Volume of sales before the 10% discount	1.55 million	1.50 million
Volume of sales after the 10% discount	1.65 million	1.70 million

a. Using the midpoint method, calculate the price elasticities of demand for group A and group B.

b. Explain how the discount will affect total revenue from each group.

c. Suppose Nile.com knows which group each customer belongs to when he or she logs on and can choose whether or not to offer the 10% discount. If Nile.com wants to increase its total revenue, should discounts be offered to group A or to group B, to neither group, or to both groups?

2. Do you think the price elasticity of demand for Ford sport-utility vehicles (SUVs) will increase, decrease, or remain the same when each of the following events occurs? Explain your answer.

a. Other car manufacturers, such as General Motors, decide to make and sell SUVs.

b. SUVs produced in foreign countries are banned from the American market.

c. Due to ad campaigns, Americans believe that SUVs are much safer than ordinary passenger cars.

d. The time period over which you measure the elasticity lengthens. During that longer time, new models such as four-wheel-drive cargo vans appear.

3. The accompanying table gives part of the supply schedule for personal computers in the United States.

Price per computer	Quantity of computers supplied
$1,100	12,000
900	8,000

a. Using the midpoint method, calculate the price elasticity of supply when the price increases from $900 to $1,100.

b. Suppose firms produce 1,000 more computers at any given price due to improved technology. As price increases from $900 to $1,100, is the price elasticity of supply now greater than, less than, or the same as it was in part a?

c. Suppose a longer time period under consideration means that the quantity supplied at any given price is 20% higher than the figures given in the table. As price increases from $900 to $1,100, is the price elasticity of supply now greater than, less than, or the same as it was in part a?

4. The accompanying table lists the cross-price elasticities of demand for several goods, where the percent quantity change is measured for the first good of the pair, and the percent price change is measured for the second good.

Good	Cross-price elasticities of demand
Air-conditioning units and kilowatts of electricity	−0.34
Coke and Pepsi	+0.63
High-fuel-consuming sport-utility vehicles (SUVs) and gasoline	−0.28
McDonald's burgers and Burger King burgers	+0.82
Butter and margarine	+1.54

a. Explain the sign of each of the cross-price elasticities. What does it imply about the relationship between the two goods in question?

b. Compare the absolute values of the cross-price elasticities and explain their magnitudes. For example, why is the cross-price elasticity of McDonald's burgers and Burger King burgers less than the cross-price elasticity of butter and margarine?

c. Use the information in the table to calculate how a 5% increase in the price of Pepsi affects the quantity of Coke demanded.

d. Use the information in the table to calculate how a 10% decrease in the price of gasoline affects the quantity of SUVs demanded.

5. The accompanying table shows the price and yearly quantity sold of souvenir T-shirts in the town of Crystal Lake according to the average income of the tourists visiting.

Price of T-shirt	Quantity of T-shirts demanded when average tourist income is $20,000	Quantity of T-shirts demanded when average tourist income is $30,000
$4	3,000	5,000
5	2,400	4,200
6	1,600	3,000
7	800	1,800

a. Using the midpoint method, calculate the price elasticity of demand when the price of a T-shirt rises from $5 to $6 and the average tourist income is $20,000. Also calculate it when the average tourist income is $30,000.

b. Using the midpoint method, calculate the income elasticity of demand when the price of a T-shirt is $4 and the average tourist income increases from $20,000 to $30,000. Also calculate it when the price is $7.

6. In each of the following cases, do you think the price elasticity of supply is (i) perfectly elastic; (ii) perfectly inelastic; (iii) elastic, but not perfectly elastic; or (iv) inelastic, but not perfectly inelastic? Explain using a diagram.

a. An increase in demand this summer for luxury cruises leads to a huge jump in the sales price of a cabin on the Queen Mary 2.

b. The price of a kilowatt of electricity is the same during periods of high electricity demand as during periods of low electricity demand.

c. Fewer people want to fly during February than during any other month. The airlines cancel about 10% of their flights as ticket prices fall about 20% during this month.

d. Owners of vacation homes in Maine rent them out during the summer. Due to a soft economy, a 30% decline in the price of a vacation rental leads more than half of homeowners to occupy their vacation homes themselves during the summer.

7. Worldwide, the average coffee grower has increased the amount of acreage under cultivation over the past few years. The result has been that the average coffee plantation produces significantly more coffee than it did 10 to 20 years ago. Unfortunately for the growers, however, this has also been a period in which their total revenues have plunged. In terms of an elasticity, what must be true for these events to have occurred? Illustrate these events with a diagram, indicating the quantity effect and the price effect that gave rise to these events.

8. Determine the amount of consumer surplus generated in each of the following situations.

a. Leon goes to the clothing store to buy a new T-shirt, for which he is willing to pay up to $10. He picks out one he likes with a price tag of exactly $10. When he is paying for it, he learns that the T-shirt has been discounted by 50%.

b. Alberto goes to the CD store hoping to find a used copy of *Nirvana's Greatest Hits* for up to $10. The store has one copy selling for $10, which he purchases.

c. After soccer practice, Stacey is willing to pay $2 for a bottle of mineral water. The 7-Eleven sells mineral water for $2.25 per bottle, so she declines to purchase it.

9. Determine the amount of producer surplus generated in each of the following situations.

a. Gordon lists his old Lionel electric trains on eBay. He sets a minimum acceptable price, known as his *reserve price,* of $75. After five days of bidding, the final high bid is exactly $75. He accepts the bid.

b. So-Hee advertises her car for sale in the used-car section of the student newspaper for $2,000, but she is willing to sell the car for any price higher than $1,500. The best offer she gets is $1,200, which she declines.

c. Sanjay likes his job so much that he would be willing to do it for free. However, his annual salary is $80,000.

10. You are the manager of Fun World, a small amusement park. The accompanying diagram shows the demand curve of a typical customer at Fun World.

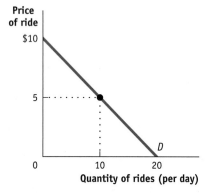

a. Suppose that the price of each ride is $5. At that price, how much consumer surplus does an individual consumer get? (Recall that the area of a right triangle is ½ × the height of the triangle × the base of the triangle.)

b. Suppose that Fun World considers charging an admission fee, even though it maintains the price of each ride at $5. What is the maximum admission fee it could charge? (Assume that all potential customers have enough money to pay the fee.)

c. Suppose that Fun World lowered the price of each ride to zero. How much consumer surplus does an individual consumer get? What is the maximum admission fee Fun World could charge?

11. The accompanying diagram illustrates a taxi driver's individual supply curve. (Assume that each taxi ride is the same distance.)

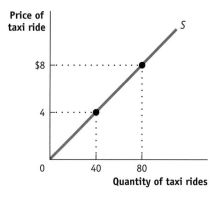

a. Suppose the city sets the price of taxi rides at $4 per ride, and at $4 the taxi driver is able to sell as many taxi rides as he desires. What is this taxi driver's producer surplus? (Recall that the area of a right triangle is ½ × the height of the triangle × the base of the triangle.)

b. Suppose that the city keeps the price of a taxi ride set at $4, but it decides to charge taxi drivers a "licensing fee." What is the maximum licensing fee the city could extract from this taxi driver?

c. Suppose that the city allowed the price of taxi rides to increase to $8 per ride. Again assume that, at this price, the taxi driver sells as many rides as he is willing to offer. How much producer surplus does an individual taxi driver now get? What is the maximum licensing fee the city could charge this taxi driver?

12. Consider the original market for pizza in Collegetown, illustrated in the accompanying table. Collegetown officials decide to impose an excise tax on pizza of $4 per pizza.

Price of pizza	Quantity of pizza demanded	Quantity of pizza supplied
10	0	6
9	1	5
8	2	4
7	3	3
6	4	2
5	5	1
4	6	0
3	7	0
2	8	0
1	9	0

a. What is the quantity of pizza bought and sold after the imposition of the tax? What is the price paid by consumers? What is the price received by producers?

b. Calculate the consumer surplus and the producer surplus after the imposition of the tax. By how much has the imposition of the tax reduced consumer surplus? By how much has it reduced producer surplus?

c. How much tax revenue does Collegetown earn from this tax?

d. Calculate the deadweight loss from this tax.

13. The state needs to raise money, and the governor has a choice of imposing an excise tax of the same amount on one of two previously untaxed goods: either restaurant meals or gasoline. Both the demand for and the supply of restaurant meals are more elastic than the demand for and the supply of gasoline. If the governor wants to minimize the deadweight loss caused by the tax, which good should be taxed? For each good, draw a diagram that illustrates the deadweight loss from taxation.

14. For each of the following situations, decide whether Al has increasing, constant, or diminishing marginal utility.

a. The more economics classes Al takes, the more he enjoys the subject. And the more classes he takes, the easier each one gets, making him enjoy each additional class even more than the one before.

b. Al likes loud music. In fact, according to him, "the louder, the better." Each time he turns the volume up a notch, he adds 5 utils to his total utility.

c. Al enjoys watching reruns of the old sitcom *Friends*. He claims that these episodes are always funny, but he does admit that the more times he sees an episode, the less funny it gets.

d. Al loves toasted marshmallows. The more he eats, however, the fuller he gets and the less he enjoys each additional marshmallow. And there is a point at which he becomes satiated: beyond that point, more marshmallows actually make him feel worse rather than better.

15. Use the concept of marginal utility to explain the following: Newspaper vending machines are designed so that once you have paid for one paper, you could take more than one paper at a time. But soda vending machines, once you have paid for one soda, dispense only one soda at a time.

16. Brenda likes to have bagels and coffee for breakfast. The accompanying table shows Brenda's total utility from various consumption bundles of bagels and coffee.

Consumption bundle		Total utility (utils)
Quantity of bagels	Quantity of coffee (cups)	
0	0	0
0	2	28
0	4	40
1	2	48
1	3	54
2	0	28
2	2	56
3	1	54
3	2	62
4	0	40
4	2	66

Suppose Brenda knows she will consume 2 cups of coffee for sure. However, she can choose to consume different quantities of bagels: she can choose either 0, 1, 2, 3, or 4 bagels.

a. Calculate Brenda's marginal utility from bagels as she goes from consuming 0 bagel to 1 bagel, from 1 bagel to 2 bagels, from 2 bagels to 3 bagels, and from 3 bagels to 4 bagels.

b. Draw Brenda's marginal utility curve of bagels. Does Brenda have increasing, diminishing, or constant marginal utility of bagels?

17. Bernie loves notebooks and Beyoncé CDs. The accompanying table shows the utility Bernie receives from each product.

Quantity of notebooks	Utility from notebooks (utils)	Quantity of CDs	Utility from CDs (utils)
0	0	0	0
2	70	1	80
4	130	2	150
6	180	3	210
8	220	4	260
10	250	5	300

The price of a notebook is $5, the price of a CD is $10, and Bernie has $50 of income to spend.

a. Which consumption bundles of notebooks and CDs can Bernie consume if he spends all his income? Illustrate Bernie's budget line with a diagram, putting notebooks on the horizontal axis and CDs on the vertical axis.

b. Calculate the marginal utility of each notebook and the marginal utility of each CD. Then calculate the marginal utility per dollar spent on notebooks and the marginal utility per dollar spent on CDs.

c. Draw a diagram like Figure 51.4 in which both the marginal utility per dollar spent on notebooks and the marginal utility per dollar spent on CDs are illustrated. Using this diagram and the optimal consumption rule, predict which bundle—from all the bundles on his budget line—Bernie will choose.

18. For each of the following situations, decide whether the bundle Lakshani is considering is optimal or not. If it is not optimal, how could Lakshani improve her overall level of utility? That is, determine which good she should spend more on and which good she should spend less on.

a. Lakshani has $200 to spend on sneakers and sweaters. Sneakers cost $50 per pair, and sweaters cost $20 each. She is thinking about buying 2 pairs of sneakers and 5 sweaters. She tells her friend that the additional utility she would get from the second pair of sneakers is the same as the additional utility she would get from the fifth sweater.

b. Lakshani has $5 to spend on pens and pencils. Each pen costs $0.50 and each pencil costs $0.10. She is thinking about buying 6 pens and 20 pencils. The last pen would add five times as much to her total utility as the last pencil.

c. Lakshani has $50 per season to spend on tickets to football games and tickets to soccer games. Each football ticket costs $10, and each soccer ticket costs $5. She is thinking about buying 3 football tickets and 2 soccer tickets. Her marginal utility from the third football ticket is twice as much as her marginal utility from the second soccer ticket.

section 10

Behind the Supply Curve: Profit, Production, and Costs

In Section 9 we examined the factors that affect consumer choice—the demand side of the supply and demand model. In this section we turn our attention to the factors that affect producer choice and the supply side of the supply and demand model. We'll begin with the concept of profit and examine profit maximization as the goal of a firm. We will then investigate the firm's production function, which shows the relationship between the inputs used for production and the output that is produced. Next we'll consider the costs that influence firms' decisions about supply. The final module in this section introduces the models of market structure used to understand how the supply side of the economy works.

Brand-X Pictures

Module 52
Defining Profit

Understanding Profit

The primary goal of most firms is to maximize profit. Other goals, such as maximizing market share or protecting the environment, may also figure into a firm's mission. But economic models generally start with the assumption that firms attempt to maximize profit. So we will begin with an explanation of how economists define and calculate profit. In the next module we will look at how firms go about maximizing their profit.

In general, a firm's profit equals its *total revenue*—which is equal to the price of the output times the quantity sold, or $P \times Q$—minus the cost of all the inputs used to produce its output, its *total cost*. That is,

$$\text{Profit} = \text{Total Revenue} - \text{Total Cost}$$

However, there are different types of costs that may be used to calculate different types of profit. To start the discussion of how to calculate profit, we'll look at two different types of costs, *explicit costs* and *implicit costs*.

Explicit versus Implicit Costs

Suppose that, after graduating from high school, you have two options: to go to college or to take a job immediately. You would like to continue your education but are concerned about the cost.

But what exactly is the cost of attending college? Here is where it is important to remember the concept of opportunity cost: the cost of the time spent getting a degree is what you forgo by not taking a job for the years you go to college. The opportunity cost of additional education, like any cost, can be broken into two parts: the *explicit cost* and the *implicit cost*.

An **explicit cost** is a cost that requires an outlay of money. For example, the explicit cost of a year of college includes tuition. An **implicit cost,** though, does not involve an outlay of money; instead, it is measured by the value, in dollar terms, of the benefits that are forgone. For example, the implicit cost of a year spent in college includes the income you would have earned if you had taken a job instead.

A common mistake, both in economic analysis and in real business situations, is to ignore implicit costs and focus exclusively on explicit costs. But often the implicit cost

What you will learn in this Module:

- The difference between explicit and implicit costs and their importance in decision making
- The different types of profit, including economic profit, accounting profit, and normal profit
- How to calculate profit

An **explicit cost** is a cost that involves actually laying out money. An **implicit cost** does not require an outlay of money; it is measured by the value, in dollar terms, of benefits that are forgone.

of an activity is quite substantial—indeed, sometimes it is much larger than the explicit cost.

Table 52.1 gives a breakdown of hypothetical explicit and implicit costs associated with spending a year in college instead of taking a job. The explicit cost consists of tuition, books, supplies, and a computer for doing assignments—all of which require you to spend money. The implicit cost is the salary you would have earned if you had taken a job instead. As you can see, the forgone salary is $35,000 and the explicit cost is $19,500, making the implicit cost more than the explicit cost in this example. So ignoring the implicit cost of an action can lead to a seriously misguided decision.

> The **accounting profit** of a business is the business's total revenue minus the explicit cost and depreciation.

table 52.1

Opportunity Cost of an Additional Year of School

Explicit cost		Implicit cost	
Tuition	$17,000	Forgone salary	$35,000
Books and supplies	1,000		
Computer	1,500		
Total explicit cost	19,500	Total implicit cost	35,000
Total opportunity cost = Total explicit cost + Total implicit cost = $54,500			

A slightly different way of looking at the implicit cost in this example can deepen our understanding of opportunity cost. The forgone salary is the cost of using your own resources—your time—in going to college rather than working. The use of your *time* for more education, despite the fact that you don't have to spend any money, is still costly to you. This illustrates an important aspect of opportunity cost: in considering the cost of an activity, you should include the cost of using any of your own resources for that activity. You can calculate the cost of using your own resources by determining what they would have earned in their next best alternative use.

Accounting Profit versus Economic Profit

As the example of going to college suggests, taking account of implicit as well as explicit costs can be very important when making decisions. This is true whether the decisions affect individuals, groups, governments, or businesses.

Consider the case of Babette's Cajun Café, a small restaurant in New Orleans. This year Babette brought in $100,000 in revenue. Out of that revenue, she paid her expenses: the cost of food ingredients and other supplies, the cost of wages for her employees, and the rent for her restaurant space. This year her expenses were $60,000. We assume that Babette owns her restaurant equipment—items such as appliances and furnishings. The question is: Is Babette's restaurant profitable?

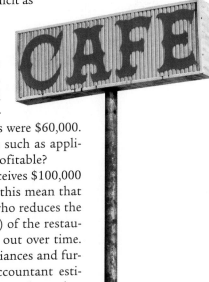

At first it might seem that the answer is obviously yes: she receives $100,000 from her customers and has expenses of only $60,000. Doesn't this mean that she has a profit of $40,000? Not according to her accountant, who reduces the number by $5,000 for the yearly *depreciation* (reduction in value) of the restaurant equipment. Depreciation occurs because equipment wears out over time. As a consequence, every few years Babette must replace her appliances and furnishings. The yearly depreciation amount reflects what an accountant estimates to be the reduction in the value of the machines due to wear and tear that year. This leaves $35,000, which is the business's **accounting profit.** That is,

The **economic profit** of a business is the business's total revenue minus the opportunity cost of its resources. It is usually less than the accounting profit.

The **implicit cost of capital** is the opportunity cost of the capital used by a business—the income the owner could have realized from that capital if it had been used in its next best alternative way.

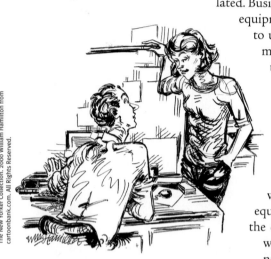

"I've done the numbers, and I will marry you."

the accounting profit of a business is its total revenue minus its *explicit* cost and depreciation. The accounting profit is the number that Babette has to report on her income tax forms and that she would be obliged to report to anyone thinking of investing in her business.

Accounting profit is a very useful number, but suppose that Babette wants to decide whether to keep her restaurant open or do something else. To make this decision, she will need to calculate her **economic profit**—the total revenue she receives minus her *opportunity* cost, which includes implicit as well as explicit costs. In general, when economists use the simple term *profit,* they are referring to economic profit. (We adopt this simplification in this book.)

Why does Babette's economic profit differ from her accounting profit? Because she may have an implicit cost over and above the explicit cost her accountant has calculated. Businesses can face an implicit cost for two reasons. First, a business's capital—its equipment, buildings, tools, inventory, and financial assets—could have been put to use in some other way. If the business owns its capital, it does not pay any money for its use, but it pays an implicit cost because it does not use the capital in some other way. Second, the owner devotes time and energy to the business that could have been used elsewhere—a particularly important factor in small businesses, whose owners tend to put in many long hours.

If Babette had rented her appliances and furnishings instead of owning them, her rent would have been an explicit cost. But because Babette owns her own equipment, she does not pay rent on them and her accountant deducts an estimate of their depreciation in the profit statement. However, this does not account for the opportunity cost of the equipment—what Babette forgoes by owning it. Suppose that instead of using the equipment in her own restaurant, the best alternative Babette has is to sell the equipment for $50,000 and put the money into a bank account where it would earn yearly interest of $3,000. This $3,000 is an implicit cost of running the business. The **implicit cost of capital** is the opportunity cost of the capital used by a business; it reflects the income that could have been earned if the capital had been used in its next best alternative way. It is just as much a true cost as if Babette had rented her equipment instead of owning it.

Finally, Babette should take into account the opportunity cost of her own time. Suppose that instead of running her own restaurant, she could earn $34,000 as a chef in someone else's restaurant. That $34,000 is also an implicit cost of her business.

Table 52.2, in the column titled Case 1, summarizes the accounting for Babette's Cajun Café, taking both explicit and implicit costs into account. It turns out, unfortunately, that

table **52.2**

Profit at Babette's Cajun Café

	Case 1	Case 2
Revenue	$100,000	$100,000
Explicit cost	−60,000	−60,000
Depreciation	−5,000	−5,000
Accounting profit	**35,000**	**35,000**
Implicit cost of business		
Income Babette could have earned on capital used in the next best way	−3,000	−3,000
Income Babette could have earned as a chef in someone else's restaurant	−34,000	−30,000
Economic profit	**−2,000**	**+2,000**

although the business makes an accounting profit of $35,000, its economic profit is actually negative. This means that Babette would be better off financially if she closed the restaurant and devoted her time and capital to something else. If, however, some of Babette's cost should fall sufficiently, she could earn a positive economic profit. In that case, she would be better off financially if she continued to operate the restaurant. For instance, consider the column titled Case 2: here we assume that what Babette could earn as a chef employed by someone else has dropped to $30,000 (say, due to a soft labor market). In this case, her economic profit is positive: she is earning more than her explicit and implicit costs and she should keep her restaurant open.

In real life, discrepancies between accounting profit and economic profit are extremely common. As the FYI above explains, this is a message that has found a receptive audience among real-world businesses.

Normal Profit

In the example above, when Babette is earning an economic profit, her total revenue is higher than the sum of her implicit and explicit costs. This means that operating her restaurant makes Babette better off financially than she would be using her resources in any other activity. When Babette earns a negative economic profit (which can also be described as a *loss*), it means that Babette would be better off financially if she devoted her resources to her next best alternative. As this example illustrates, economic profits signal the best use of resources. A positive economic profit indicates that the current use is the best use of resources. A negative economic profit indicates that there is a better alternative use for resources.

An economic profit equal to zero is also known as a **normal profit.** It is an economic profit just high enough to keep a firm engaged in its current activity.

But what about an economic profit *equal to* zero? Most of us would generally think earning zero profit was a bad thing. After all, a firm's goal is to maximize profit—profit is what firms are after! However, an economic profit equal to zero is not bad at all. An economic profit of zero means that the firm could not do any better using its resources in any alternative activity. Another name for an economic profit of zero is a **normal profit.** A firm earning a normal profit is earning just enough to keep it using its resources in its current activity. After all, it can't do any better in any other activity!

Module 52 AP Review

Solutions appear at the back of the book.

Check Your Understanding

1. Karma and Don run a furniture-refinishing business from their home. Which of the following represent an explicit cost of the business and which represent an implicit cost?
   a. supplies such as paint stripper, varnish, polish, sandpaper, and so on
   b. basement space that has been converted into a workroom
   c. wages paid to a part-time helper
   d. a van that they inherited and use only for transporting furniture
   e. the job at a larger furniture restorer that Karma gave up in order to run the business

2. a. Suppose you are in business earning an accounting profit of $25,000. What is your economic profit if the implicit cost of your capital is $2,000 and the opportunity cost of your time is $23,000? Explain your answer.
   b. What does your answer to part a tell you about the advisability of devoting your time and capital to this business?

Tackle the Test: Multiple-Choice Questions

1. Which of the following is an example of an *implicit* cost of going out for lunch?
   a. the amount of the tip you leave the waiter
   b. the total bill you charge to your credit card
   c. the cost of gas to drive to the restaurant
   d. the value of the time you spent eating lunch
   e. all of the above

2. Which of the following is an *implicit* cost of attending college?
   a. tuition
   b. books
   c. laptop computer
   d. lab fees
   e. forgone salary

3. Which of the following is the best definition of accounting profit? Accounting profit equals total revenue minus depreciation and total
   a. explicit cost only.
   b. implicit cost only.
   c. explicit cost plus implicit cost.
   d. opportunity cost.
   e. explicit cost plus opportunity cost.

4. Which of the following is considered when calculating economic profit but not accounting profit?
   a. implicit cost
   b. explicit cost
   c. total revenue
   d. marginal cost
   e. All of the above are considered when calculating accounting profit.

5. You sell T-shirts at your school's football games. Each shirt costs $5 to make and sells for $10. Each game lasts two hours and you sell 100 shirts per game. You could always be earning $8 per hour at your other job. Which of the following is correct? Your accounting profit from selling shirts at a game is
   a. $1,000 and your economic profit is $500.
   b. $500 and your economic profit is $1,000.
   c. $500 and your economic profit is $484.
   d. $484 and your economic profit is $500.
   e. $500 and your economic profit is also $500.

Tackle the Test: Free-Response Questions

1. Your firm is selling 10,000 units of output at a price of $10 per unit. Your firm's total explicit cost is $70,000. Your firm's implicit cost of capital is $10,000, and your opportunity cost is $20,000.
   a. Calculate total revenue.
   b. Calculate total implicit cost.
   c. Calculate your accounting profit.
   d. Calculate your economic profit.
   e. What does the value of your economic profit calculated in part d tell you?

Answer (5 points)

1 point: Total revenue = $100,000

1 point: Total implicit cost = $30,000

1 point: Accounting profit = $30,000

1 point: Economic profit = $0

1 point: Because your firm earns normal profit, there is no better alternative use for your resources.

---

2. Sunny owns and operates Sunny's Sno Cone Stand. Use the data in the table provided to answer the questions below.

Sunny's Sno Cone Stand: January

Price of Sno Cone	$2
Sno Cones sold	2,000
Explicit cost	$400
Depreciation	$100
Implicit cost of capital	$200

   a. Calculate Sunny's Sno Cone Stand's total revenue for January.
   b. Calculate Sunny's Sno Cone Stand's accounting profit for January.
   c. What additional information would Sunny need in order to determine whether or not to continue operating the Sno Cone Stand?
   d. Explain how Sunny would determine whether or not to continue operating the business on the basis of these numbers.

- The principle of marginal analysis

- How to determine the profit-maximizing level of output using the optimal output rule

Module 53
Profit Maximization

Maximizing Profit

In the previous module we learned about different types of profit, how to calculate profit, and how firms can use profit calculations to make decisions—for instance to determine whether to continue using resources for the same activity or not. In this module we ask the question: what quantity of output would maximize the producer's profit? First we will find the profit-maximizing quantity by calculating the total profit at each quantity for comparison. Then we will use marginal analysis to determine the *optimal output rule,* which turns out to be simple: as our discussion of marginal analysis in Module 1 suggested, a producer should produce up until marginal benefit equals marginal cost.

Consider Jennifer and Jason, who run an organic tomato farm. Suppose that the market price of organic tomatoes is $18 per bushel and that Jennifer and Jason can sell as many as they would like at that price. Then we can use the data in Table 53.1 to find their profit-maximizing level of output.

The first column shows the quantity of output in bushels, and the second column shows Jennifer and Jason's total revenue from their output: the market value of their output. Total revenue, *TR*, is equal to the market price multiplied by the quantity of output:

(53-1) $TR = P \times Q$

In this example, total revenue is equal to $18 per bushel times the quantity of output in bushels.

The third column of Table 53.1 shows Jennifer and Jason's total cost, *TC*. The fourth column shows their profit, equal to total revenue minus total cost:

(53-2) $\text{Profit} = TR - TC$

As indicated by the numbers in the table, profit is maximized at an output of five bushels, where profit is equal to $18. But we can gain more insight into the profit-maximizing choice of output by viewing it as a problem of marginal analysis, a task we'll dive into next.

table 53.1

Profit for Jennifer and Jason's Farm When Market Price Is $18

Quantity of tomatoes Q (bushels)	Total revenue TR	Total cost TC	Profit $TR - TC$
0	$0	$14	−$14
1	18	30	−12
2	36	36	0
3	54	44	10
4	72	56	16
5	90	72	18
6	108	92	16
7	126	116	10

Using Marginal Analysis to Choose the Profit-Maximizing Quantity of Output

The **principle of marginal analysis** provides a clear message about when to stop doing anything: proceed until *marginal benefit* equals *marginal cost*. To apply this principle, consider the effect on a producer's profit of increasing output by one unit. The marginal benefit of that unit is the additional revenue generated by selling it; this measure has a name—it is called the **marginal revenue** of that output. The general formula for marginal revenue is:

$$(53\text{-}3) \quad \text{Marginal revenue} = \frac{\text{Change in total revenue generated by one additional unit of output}}{} = \frac{\text{Change in total revenue}}{\text{Change in quantity of output}}$$

or

$$MR = \Delta TR / \Delta Q$$

In this equation, the Greek uppercase delta (the triangular symbol) represents the change in a variable.

The application of the principle of marginal analysis to the producer's decision of how much to produce is called the **optimal output rule,** which states that profit is maximized by producing the quantity at which the marginal revenue of the last unit produced is equal to its marginal cost. As this rule suggests, we will see that Jennifer and Jason maximize their profit by equating marginal revenue and marginal cost.

Note that there may not be any particular quantity at which marginal revenue exactly equals marginal cost. In this case the producer should produce until one more unit would cause marginal benefit to fall below marginal cost. As a common simplification, we can think of marginal cost as rising steadily, rather than jumping from one level at one quantity to a different level at the next quantity. This ensures that marginal cost will equal marginal revenue at some quantity. We employ this simplified approach in what follows.

Consider Table 53.2 on the next page, which provides cost and revenue data for Jennifer and Jason's farm. The second column contains the farm's total cost of output.

According to the **principle of marginal analysis,** every activity should continue until marginal benefit equals marginal cost.

Marginal revenue is the change in total revenue generated by an additional unit of output.

The **optimal output rule** says that profit is maximized by producing the quantity of output at which the marginal revenue of the last unit produced is equal to its marginal cost.

table **53.2**

Short-Run Costs for Jennifer and Jason's Farm

Quantity of tomatoes Q (bushels)	Total cost TC	Marginal cost of bushel $MC = \Delta TC/\Delta Q$	Marginal revenue of bushel MR	Net gain of bushel = $MR - MC$
0	$14			
		$16	$18	$2
1	30			
		6	18	12
2	36			
		8	18	10
3	44			
		12	18	6
4	56			
		16	18	2
5	72			
		20	18	−2
6	92			
		24	18	−6
7	116			

The third column shows their marginal cost. Notice that, in this example, marginal cost initially falls as output rises but then begins to increase, so that the marginal cost curve has a "swoosh" shape. (Later it will become clear that this shape has important implications for short-run production decisions.)

The fourth column contains the farm's marginal revenue, which has an important feature: Jennifer and Jason's marginal revenue is assumed to be constant at $18 for every output level. The assumption holds true for a particular type of market—perfectly competitive markets—which we will study in Modules 58–60, but for now it is just to make the calculations easier. The fifth and final column shows the calculation of the net gain per bushel of tomatoes, which is equal to marginal revenue minus marginal cost. As you can see, it is positive for the first through fifth bushels; producing each of these bushels raises Jennifer and Jason's profit. For the sixth and seventh bushels, however, net gain is negative: producing them would decrease, not increase, profit. (You can verify this by reexamining Table 53.1.) So five bushels are Jennifer and Jason's profit-maximizing output; it is the level of output at which marginal cost is equal to the market price, $18.

Figure 53.1 shows that Jennifer and Jason's profit-maximizing quantity of output is, indeed, the number of bushels at which the marginal cost of production is equal to marginal revenue (which is equivalent to price in perfectly competitive markets). The figure shows the **marginal cost curve,** MC, drawn from the data in the third column of Table 53.2. We plot the marginal cost of increasing output from one to two bushels halfway between one and two, and so on. The horizontal line at $18 is Jennifer and Jason's **marginal revenue curve.** Note that marginal revenue stays the same regardless of how much Jennifer and Jason sell because we have assumed marginal revenue is constant.

Does this mean that the firm's production decision can be entirely summed up as "produce up to the point where the marginal cost of production is equal to the price"? No, not quite. Before applying the principle of marginal analysis to determine how much to produce, a potential producer must, as a first step, answer an "either–or" question: Should I produce at all? If the answer to that question is yes, the producer then proceeds to the second step—a "how much" decision: maximizing profit by choosing the quantity of output at which marginal cost is equal to price.

The **marginal cost curve** shows how the cost of producing one more unit depends on the quantity that has already been produced.

The **marginal revenue curve** shows how marginal revenue varies as output varies.

The Firm's Profit-Maximizing Quantity of Output

At the profit-maximizing quantity of output, marginal revenue is equal to marginal cost. It is located at the point where the marginal cost curve crosses the marginal revenue curve, which is a horizontal line at the market price. Here, the profit-maximizing point is at an output of 5 bushels of tomatoes, the output quantity at point *E*.

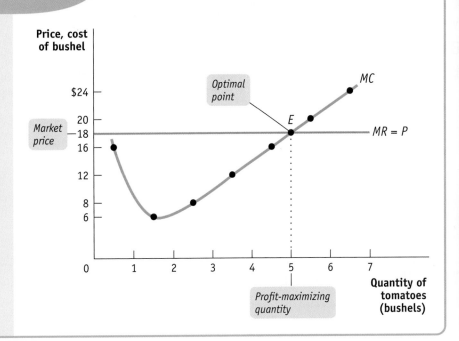

To understand why the first step in the production decision involves an "either–or" question, we need to ask how we determine whether it is profitable or unprofitable to produce at all.

When Is Production Profitable?

Recall that a firm's decision whether or not to stay in a given business depends on its *economic profit*—a measure based on the opportunity cost of resources used in the business. To put it a slightly different way: in the calculation of economic profit, a firm's total cost incorporates the implicit cost—the benefits forgone in the next best use of the firm's resources—as well as the explicit cost in the form of actual cash outlays. In contrast, *accounting profit* is profit calculated using only the explicit costs incurred by the firm. This means that economic profit incorporates the opportunity cost of resources owned by the firm and used in the production of output, while accounting profit does not. As in the example of Babette's Cajun Café, a firm may make positive accounting profit while making zero or even negative economic profit. It's important to understand clearly that a firm's decision to produce or not, to stay in business or to close down permanently, should be based on economic profit, not accounting profit.

So we will assume, as we always do, that the cost numbers given in Tables 53.1 and 53.2 include all costs, implicit as well as explicit, and that the profit numbers in Table 53.1 are economic profit. What determines whether Jennifer and Jason's farm earns a profit or generates a loss? The answer is that whether or not it is profitable depends on the market price of tomatoes—specifically, *whether selling the firm's optimal quantity of output at the market price results in at least a normal profit.*

In the next modules, we look in detail at the two components used to calculate profit; firm revenue (which is determined by the level of production) and firm cost.

Photodisc

module **53** Profit Maximization **539**

Section 10 Behind the Supply Curve: Profit, Production, and Costs

Check Your Understanding

1. Suppose a firm can sell as many units of output as it wants for a price of $15 per unit and faces total costs as indicated in the table below. Use the optimal output rule to determine the profit-maximizing level of output for the firm.

Q	TC
0	$2
1	10
2	20
3	33
4	50
5	71

2. Use the data from Question 1 to graph the firm's *MC* and *MR* curves and show the profit-maximizing level of output.

Tackle the Test: Multiple-Choice Questions

Use the data in the table provided to answer questions 1–3.

Quantity	Total Revenue	Total Cost
Q	TR	TC
0	$0	$14
1	18	30
2	36	36
3	54	44
4	72	56
5	90	72
6	108	92
7	126	116

1. What is the marginal revenue of the third unit of output?
   a. $8
   b. $14
   c. $18
   d. $44
   e. $54

2. What is the marginal cost of the first unit of output?
   a. $0
   b. $14
   c. $16
   d. $18
   e. $30

3. At what level of output is profit maximized?
   a. 0
   b. 1
   c. 3
   d. 5
   e. 7

4. A firm should continue to produce as long as its
   a. total revenue is less than its total costs.
   b. total revenue is greater than its total explicit costs.
   c. accounting profit is greater than its economic profit.
   d. accounting profit is not negative.
   e. economic profit is at least zero.

5. A firm earns a normal profit when its
   a. accounting profit equals 0.
   b. economic profit is positive.
   c. total revenue equals its total costs.
   d. accounting profit equals its economic profit.
   e. economic profit equals its total explicit and implicit costs.

Tackle the Test: Free-Response Questions

1. Use the data in the table provided.

Quantity	Total Revenue	Total Cost
Q	TR	TC
0	$0	$7
1	18	23
2	36	29
3	54	37
4	72	49
5	90	65
6	108	87
7	126	112

a. What is the marginal revenue of the fourth unit?

b. Calculate profit at a quantity of two. Explain how you calculated the profit.

c. What is the profit-maximizing level of output? Explain how to use the optimal output rule to determine the profit-maximizing level of output.

Answer (5 points)

1 point: $18

1 point: $7

1 point: $36 – $29 or TR – TC

1 point: 5 units

1 point: The optimal output rule states that profit is maximized when $MC = MR$. Here, MC never exactly equals MR. When this occurs, the firm should produce the largest quantity at which MR exceeds MC. At a quantity of 5, $MC = 16 and $MR = 18. For the sixth unit, $MC = 22 and $MR = 18, and because $MC > MR$, the sixth unit would add more to total cost than it would to total revenue, and it therefore should not be produced.

---

2. Use a graph to illustrate the typical shape of the two curves used to find a firm's profit-maximizing level of output on the basis of the optimal output rule. Assume all units of output can be sold for $5. Indicate the profit-maximizing level of output with a "Q^*" on the appropriate axis. (You don't have enough information to provide a specific numerical answer.)

What you will learn in this **Module:**

- The importance of the firm's production function, the relationship between the quantity of inputs and the quantity of output

- Why production is often subject to diminishing returns to inputs

Module 54
The Production Function

The Production Function

A *firm* produces goods or services for sale. To do this, it must transform inputs into output. The quantity of output a firm produces depends on the quantity of inputs; this relationship is known as the firm's **production function.** As we'll see, a firm's production function underlies its *cost curves.* As a first step, let's look at the characteristics of a hypothetical production function.

Inputs and Output

To understand the concept of a production function, let's consider a farm that we assume, for the sake of simplicity, produces only one output, wheat, and uses only two inputs, land and labor. This particular farm is owned by a couple named George and Martha. They hire workers to do the actual physical labor on the farm. Moreover, we will assume that all potential workers are of the same quality—they are all equally knowledgeable and capable of performing farmwork.

George and Martha's farm sits on 10 acres of land; no more acres are available to them, and they are currently unable to either increase or decrease the size of their farm by selling, buying, or leasing acreage. Land here is what economists call a **fixed input**— an input whose quantity is fixed for a period of time and cannot be varied. George and Martha are, however, free to decide how many workers to hire. The labor provided by these workers is called a **variable input**—an input whose quantity the firm can vary at any time.

In reality, whether or not the quantity of an input is really fixed depends on the time horizon. In the **long run**—that is, given that a long enough period of time has elapsed— firms can adjust the quantity of any input. So there are no fixed inputs in the long run. In contrast, the **short run** is defined as the time period during which at least one input is fixed. Later, we'll look more carefully at the distinction between the short run and the long run. But for now, we will restrict our attention to the short run and assume that at least one input (land) is fixed.

A **production function** is the relationship between the quantity of inputs a firm uses and the quantity of output it produces.

A **fixed input** is an input whose quantity is fixed for a period of time and cannot be varied.

A **variable input** is an input whose quantity the firm can vary at any time.

The **long run** is the time period in which all inputs can be varied.

The **short run** is the time period in which at least one input is fixed.

George and Martha know that the quantity of wheat they produce depends on the number of workers they hire. Using modern farming techniques, one worker can cultivate the 10-acre farm, albeit not very intensively. When an additional worker is added, the land is divided equally among all the workers: each worker has 5 acres to cultivate when 2 workers are employed, each cultivates 3⅓ acres when 3 are employed, and so on. So as additional workers are employed, the 10 acres of land are cultivated more intensively and more bushels of wheat are produced. The relationship between the quantity of labor and the quantity of output, for a given amount of the fixed input, constitutes the farm's production function. The production function for George and Martha's farm, where land is the fixed input and labor is the variable input, is shown in the first two columns of the table in Figure 54.1; the diagram there shows the same information graphically. The curve in Figure 54.1 shows how the quantity of output depends on the quantity of the variable input for a given quantity of the fixed input; it is called the farm's **total product curve.** The physical quantity of output, bushels of wheat, is measured on the vertical axis; the quantity of the variable input, labor (that is, the number of workers employed), is measured on the horizontal axis. The total product curve here slopes upward, reflecting the fact that more bushels of wheat are produced as more workers are employed.

Although the total product curve in Figure 54.1 slopes upward along its entire length, the slope isn't constant: as you move up the curve to the right, it flattens out. To understand this changing slope, look at the third column of the table in Figure 54.1, which shows the *change in the quantity of output* generated by adding one more worker. That is, it shows the **marginal product** of labor, or *MPL*: the additional quantity of output from using one more unit of labor (one more worker).

The **total product curve** shows how the quantity of output depends on the quantity of the variable input, for a given quantity of the fixed input.

The **marginal product** of an input is the additional quantity of output produced by using one more unit of that input.

| figure 54.1 | Production Function and Total Product Curve for George and Martha's Farm |

Quantity of labor *L* (workers)	Quantity of wheat *Q* (bushels)	Marginal product of labor $MPL = \Delta Q/\Delta L$ (bushels per worker)
0	0	
		19
1	19	
		17
2	36	
		15
3	51	
		13
4	64	
		11
5	75	
		9
6	84	
		7
7	91	
		5
8	96	

The table shows the production function, the relationship between the quantity of the variable input (labor, measured in number of workers) and the quantity of output (wheat, measured in bushels) for a given quantity of the fixed input. It also shows the marginal product of labor on George and Martha's farm.

The total product curve shows the production function graphically. It slopes upward because more wheat is produced as more workers are employed. It also becomes flatter because the marginal product of labor declines as more and more workers are employed.

In this example, we have data at intervals of 1 worker—that is, we have information on the quantity of output when there are 3 workers, 4 workers, and so on. Sometimes data aren't available in increments of 1 unit—for example, you might have information on the quantity of output only when there are 40 workers and when there are 50 workers. In this case, you can use the following equation to calculate the marginal product of labor:

$$\text{(54-1)} \quad \begin{matrix} \text{Marginal} \\ \text{product} \\ \text{of labor} \end{matrix} = \begin{matrix} \text{Change in quantity of} \\ \text{output produced by one} \\ \text{additional unit of labor} \end{matrix} = \frac{\text{Change in quantity of output}}{\text{Change in quantity of labor}}$$

or

$$MPL = \frac{\Delta Q}{\Delta L}$$

Recall that Δ, the Greek uppercase delta, represents the change in a variable. Now we can explain the significance of the slope of the total product curve: it is equal to the marginal product of labor. The slope of a line is equal to "rise" over "run." This implies that the slope of the total product curve is the change in the quantity of output (the "rise") divided by the change in the quantity of labor (the "run"). And this, as we can see from Equation 54-1, is simply the marginal product of labor. So in Figure 54.1, the fact that the marginal product of the first worker is 19 also means that the slope of the total product curve in going from 0 to 1 worker is 19. Similarly, the slope of the total product curve in going from 1 to 2 workers is the same as the marginal product of the second worker, 17, and so on.

In this example, the marginal product of labor steadily declines as more workers are hired—that is, each successive worker adds less to output than the previous worker. So as employment increases, the total product curve gets flatter.

Figure 54.2 shows how the marginal product of labor depends on the number of workers employed on the farm. The marginal product of labor, *MPL*, is measured on the vertical axis in units of physical output—bushels of wheat—produced per additional worker, and the number of workers employed is measured on the horizontal axis. You can see from the table in Figure 54.1 that if 5 workers are employed instead of 4, output rises from 64 to 75 bushels; in this case the marginal product of labor is

figure 54.2

Marginal Product of Labor Curve for George and Martha's Farm

The marginal product of labor curve plots each worker's marginal product, the increase in the quantity of output generated by each additional worker. The change in the quantity of output is measured on the vertical axis and the number of workers employed on the horizontal axis. The first worker employed generates an increase in output of 19 bushels, the second worker generates an increase of 17 bushels, and so on. The curve slopes downward due to diminishing returns to labor.

11 bushels—the same number found in Figure 54.2. To indicate that 11 bushels is the marginal product when employment rises from 4 to 5, we place the point corresponding to that information halfway between 4 and 5 workers.

In this example the marginal product of labor falls as the number of workers increases. That is, there are *diminishing returns to labor* on George and Martha's farm. In general, there are **diminishing returns to an input** when an increase in the quantity of that input, holding the quantity of all other inputs fixed, reduces that input's marginal product. Due to diminishing returns to labor, the *MPL* curve is negatively sloped.

To grasp why diminishing returns can occur, think about what happens as George and Martha add more and more workers without increasing the number of acres. As the number of workers increases, the land is farmed more intensively and the number of bushels increases. But each additional worker is working with a smaller share of the 10 acres—the fixed input—than the previous worker. As a result, the additional worker cannot produce as much output as the previous worker. So it's not surprising that the marginal product of the additional worker falls.

The crucial point to emphasize about diminishing returns is that, like many propositions in economics, it is an "other things equal" proposition: each successive unit of an input will raise production by less than the last *if the quantity of all other inputs is held fixed.*

What would happen if the levels of other inputs were allowed to change? You can see the answer illustrated in Figure 54.3. Panel (a) shows two total product curves, TP_{10} and TP_{20}. TP_{10} is the farm's total product curve when its total area is 10 acres (the same curve as in Figure 54.1). TP_{20} is the total product curve when the farm's area has increased to 20 acres. Except when 0 workers are employed, TP_{20} lies everywhere above TP_{10} because with more acres available, any given number of workers produces more output. Panel (b) shows the corresponding marginal product of labor curves.

There are **diminishing returns to an input** when an increase in the quantity of that input, holding the levels of all other inputs fixed, leads to a decline in the marginal product of that input.

Photodisc

With diminishing marginal returns to labor, as more and more workers are added to a fixed amount of land, each worker adds less to total output than the previous worker.

---

figure 54.3   Total Product, Marginal Product, and the Fixed Input

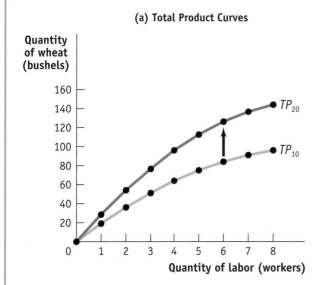

(a) Total Product Curves

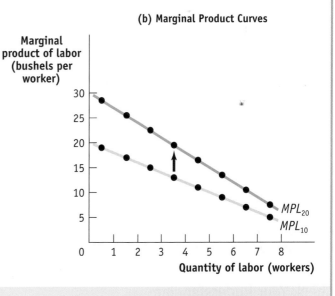

(b) Marginal Product Curves

This figure shows how the quantity of output—illustrated by the total product curve—and marginal product depend on the level of the fixed input. Panel (a) shows two total product curves for George and Martha's farm, TP_{10} when their farm is 10 acres and TP_{20} when it is 20 acres. With more land, each worker can produce more wheat. So an increase in the fixed input shifts the total product curve up from TP_{10} to TP_{20}. This also implies that the marginal product of each worker is higher when the farm is 20 acres than when it is 10 acres. As a result, an increase in acreage also shifts the marginal product of labor curve up from MPL_{10} to MPL_{20}. Panel (b) shows the marginal product of labor curves. Note that both marginal product of labor curves still slope downward due to diminishing returns to labor.

Was Malthus Right?

In 1798, Thomas Malthus, an English pastor, authored the book *An Essay on the Principle of Population,* which introduced the principle of diminishing returns to an input. Malthus's writings were influential in his own time and continue to provoke heated argument to this day.

Malthus argued that as a country's population grew but its land area remained fixed, it would become increasingly difficult to grow enough food. Though more intensive cultivation of the land could increase yields, as the marginal product of labor declined, each successive farmer would add less to the total than the last.

From this argument, Malthus drew a powerful conclusion—that misery was the normal condition of humankind. In a country with a small population and abundant land (a description of the United States at the time), he argued, families would be large and the population would grow rapidly. Ultimately, the pressure of population on the land would reduce the condi-

tion of most people to a level at which starvation and disease held the population in check. (Arguments like this led the historian Thomas Carlyle to dub economics the "dismal science.")

Happily, over the long term, Malthus's predictions have turned out to be wrong. World population has increased from about 1 billion when Malthus wrote to more than 6.8 billion in 2010, but in most of the world people eat better now than ever before. So was Malthus completely wrong? And do his incorrect predictions refute the idea of diminishing returns? No, on both counts.

First, the Malthusian story is a pretty accurate description of 57 of the last 59 centuries: peasants in eighteenth-century France probably did not live much better than Egyptian peasants in the age of the pyramids. Yet diminishing returns does not mean that using more labor to grow food on a given amount of land will lead to a decline in the marginal product of labor—*if*

there is also a radical improvement in farming technology. Fortunately, since the eighteenth century, technological progress has been so rapid that it has alleviated much of the limits imposed by diminishing returns. Diminishing returns implies that the marginal product declines when *all* other things—including technology—remain the same. So the happy fact that Malthus's predictions were wrong does not invalidate the concept of diminishing returns.

Typically, however, technological progress relaxes the limits imposed by diminishing returns only over the very long term. This was demonstrated in 2008 when bad weather, an ethanol-driven increase in the demand for corn, and a brisk rise in world income led to soaring world grain prices. As farmers scrambled to plant more acreage, they ran up against limits in the availability of inputs like land and fertilizer. Hopefully, we can prove Malthus wrong again before long.

MPL_{10} is the marginal product of labor curve given 10 acres to cultivate (the same curve as in Figure 54.2), and MPL_{20} is the marginal product of labor curve given 20 acres. Both curves slope downward because, in each case, the amount of land is fixed, albeit at different levels. But MPL_{20} lies everywhere above MPL_{10}, reflecting the fact that the marginal product of the same worker is higher when he or she has more of the fixed input to work with.

Figure 54.3 demonstrates a general result: the position of the total product curve depends on the quantities of other inputs. If you change the quantities of the other inputs, both the total product curve and the marginal product curve of the remaining input will shift. The importance of the "other things equal" assumption in discussing diminishing returns is illustrated in the FYI above.

Module 54 AP Review

Solutions appear at the back of the book.

Check Your Understanding

1. Bernie's ice-making company produces ice cubes using a 10-ton machine and electricity (along with water, which we will ignore as an input for simplicity). The quantity of output, measured in pounds of ice, is given in the accompanying table.

   a. What is the fixed input? What is the variable input?

   b. Construct a table showing the marginal product of the variable input. Does it show diminishing returns?

   c. Suppose a 50% increase in the size of the fixed input increases output by 100% for any given amount of the variable input. What is the fixed input now? Construct a table showing the quantity of output and the marginal product in this case.

Quantity of electricity (kilowatts)	Quantity of ice (pounds)
0	0
1	1,000
2	1,800
3	2,400
4	2,800

Tackle the Test: Multiple-Choice Questions

1. A production function shows the relationship between inputs and
   a. fixed costs.
   b. variable costs.
   c. total revenue.
   d. output.
   e. profit.

2. Which of the following defines the short run?
   a. less than a year
   b. when all inputs are fixed
   c. when no inputs are variable
   d. when only one input is variable
   e. when at least one input is fixed

3. The slope of the total product curve is also known as
   a. marginal product.
   b. marginal cost.
   c. average product.
   d. average revenue.
   e. profit.

4. Diminishing returns to an input ensures that as a firm continues to produce, the total product curve will have what kind of slope?
   a. negative decreasing
   b. positive decreasing
   c. negative increasing
   d. positive increasing
   e. positive constant

5. Historically, the limits imposed by diminishing returns have been alleviated by
   a. investment in capital.
   b. increases in the population.
   c. discovery of more land.
   d. Thomas Malthus.
   e. economic models.

Tackle the Test: Free-Response Questions

1. Draw a correctly labeled graph of a production function that exhibits diminishing returns to labor. Assume labor is the variable input and capital is the fixed input. Explain how your graph illustrates diminishing returns to labor.

Answer (4 points)

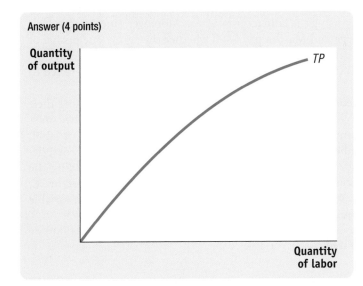

1 point: Graph with vertical axis labeled "Quantity of output" or "Q" and horizontal axis labeled "Quantity of labor" or "L"

1 point: Upward sloping curve labeled "Total product" or "TP"

1 point: The slope of the total product curve is positive and decreasing

1 point: Explanation that a positive and decreasing slope illustrates diminishing returns to labor because each additional unit of labor increases total product by less than the previous unit of labor

2. Use the data in the table below to graph the production function and the marginal product of labor. Do the data illustrate diminishing returns to labor? Explain.

Quantity of labor L	Quantity of output Q
0	0
1	19
2	36
3	51
4	64
5	75
6	84
7	91
8	96

What you will learn in this Module:

- The various types of cost a firm faces, including fixed cost, variable cost, and total cost

- How a firm's costs generate marginal cost curves and average cost curves

Module 55
Firm Costs

From the Production Function to Cost Curves

Now that we have learned about the firm's production function, we can use that knowledge to develop its cost curves. To see how a firm's production function is related to its cost curves, let's turn once again to George and Martha's farm. Once George and Martha know their production function, they know the relationship between inputs of labor and land and output of wheat. But if they want to maximize their profits, they need to translate this knowledge into information about the relationship between the quantity of output and cost. Let's see how they can do this.

To translate information about a firm's production function into information about its cost, we need to know how much the firm must pay for its inputs. We will assume that George and Martha face either an explicit or an implicit cost of $400 for the use of the land. As we learned previously, it is irrelevant whether George and Martha must rent the land for $400 from someone else or whether they own the land themselves and forgo earning $400 from renting it to someone else. Either way, they pay an opportunity cost of $400 by using the land to grow wheat. Moreover, since the land is a fixed input for which George and Martha pay $400 whether they grow one bushel of wheat or one hundred, its cost is a **fixed cost,** denoted by *FC*—a cost that does not depend on the quantity of output produced. In business, a fixed cost is often referred to as an "overhead cost."

We also assume that George and Martha must pay each worker $200. Using their production function, George and Martha know that the number of workers they must hire depends on the amount of wheat they intend to produce. So the cost of labor, which is equal to the number of workers multiplied by $200, is a **variable cost,** denoted by *VC*—a cost that depends on the quantity of output produced. Adding the fixed cost and the variable cost of a given quantity of output gives the **total cost,** or *TC,* of that quantity of output. We can express the relationship among fixed cost, variable cost, and total cost as an equation:

(55-1)   Total cost = Fixed cost + Variable cost

or

$$TC = FC + VC$$

A **fixed cost** is a cost that does not depend on the quantity of output produced. It is the cost of the fixed input.

A **variable cost** is a cost that depends on the quantity of output produced. It is the cost of the variable input.

The **total cost** of producing a given quantity of output is the sum of the fixed cost and the variable cost of producing that quantity of output.

The table in Figure 55.1 shows how total cost is calculated for George and Martha's farm. The second column shows the number of workers employed, L. The third column shows the corresponding level of output, Q, taken from the table in Figure 54.1. The fourth column shows the variable cost, VC, equal to the number of workers multiplied by $200. The fifth column shows the fixed cost, FC, which is $400 regardless of the quantity of wheat produced. The sixth column shows the total cost of output, TC, which is the variable cost plus the fixed cost.

The first column labels each row of the table with a letter, from A to I. These labels will be helpful in understanding our next step: drawing the **total cost curve,** a curve that shows how total cost depends on the quantity of output.

George and Martha's total cost curve is shown in the diagram in Figure 55.1, where the horizontal axis measures the quantity of output in bushels of wheat and the vertical axis measures total cost in dollars. Each point on the curve corresponds to one row of the table in Figure 55.1. For example, point A shows the situation when 0 workers are employed: output is 0, and total cost is equal to fixed cost, $400. Similarly, point B shows the situation when 1 worker is employed: output is 19 bushels, and total cost is $600, equal to the sum of $400 in fixed cost and $200 in variable cost.

Like the total product curve, the total cost curve slopes upward: due to the increasing variable cost, the more output produced, the higher the farm's total cost.

The **total cost curve** shows how total cost depends on the quantity of output.

figure 55.1

Total Cost Curve for George and Martha's Farm

The table shows the variable cost, fixed cost, and total cost for various output quantities on George and Martha's 10-acre farm. The total cost curve shows how total cost (measured on the vertical axis) depends on the quantity of output (measured on the horizontal axis). The labeled points on the curve correspond to the rows of the table. The total cost curve slopes upward because the number of workers employed, and hence total cost, increases as the quantity of output increases. The curve gets steeper as output increases due to diminishing returns to labor.

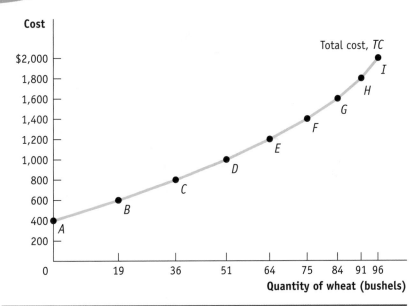

Point on graph	Quantity of labor L (workers)	Quantity of wheat Q (bushels)	Variable cost VC	Fixed cost FC	Total cost TC = FC + VC
A	0	0	$0	$400	$400
B	1	19	200	400	600
C	2	36	400	400	800
D	3	51	600	400	1,000
E	4	64	800	400	1,200
F	5	75	1,000	400	1,400
G	6	84	1,200	400	1,600
H	7	91	1,400	400	1,800
I	8	96	1,600	400	2,000

But unlike the total product curve, which gets flatter as employment rises, the total cost curve gets *steeper*. That is, the slope of the total cost curve is greater as the amount of output produced increases. As we will soon see, the steepening of the total cost curve is also due to diminishing returns to the variable input. Before we can see why, we must first look at the relationships among several useful measures of cost.

Two Key Concepts: Marginal Cost and Average Cost

We've just learned how to derive a firm's total cost curve from its production function. Our next step is to take a deeper look at total cost by deriving two extremely useful measures: *marginal cost* and *average cost*. As we'll see, these two measures of the cost of production have a somewhat surprising relationship to each other. Moreover, they will prove to be vitally important in later modules, where we will use them to analyze the firm's output decision and the market supply curve.

Marginal Cost

Module 53 explained that marginal cost is the added cost of doing something one more time. In the context of production, marginal cost is the change in total cost generated by producing one more unit of output. We've already seen that marginal product is easiest to calculate if data on output are available in increments of one unit of input. Similarly, marginal cost is easiest to calculate if data on total cost are available in increments of one unit of output because the increase in total cost for each unit is clear. When the data come in less convenient increments, it's still possible to calculate marginal cost over each interval. But for the sake of simplicity, let's work with an example in which the data come in convenient one-unit increments.

Selena's Gourmet Salsas produces bottled salsa; Table 55.1 shows how its costs per day depend on the number of cases of salsa it produces per day. The firm has a fixed

table **55.1**

Costs at Selena's Gourmet Salsas

Quantity of salsa Q (cases)	Fixed cost FC	Variable cost VC	Total cost $TC = FC + VC$	Marginal cost of case $MC = \Delta TC/\Delta Q$
0	$108	$0	$108	
				$12
1	108	12	120	
				36
2	108	48	156	
				60
3	108	108	216	
				84
4	108	192	300	
				108
5	108	300	408	
				132
6	108	432	540	
				156
7	108	588	696	
				180
8	108	768	876	
				204
9	108	972	1,080	
				228
10	108	1,200	1,308	

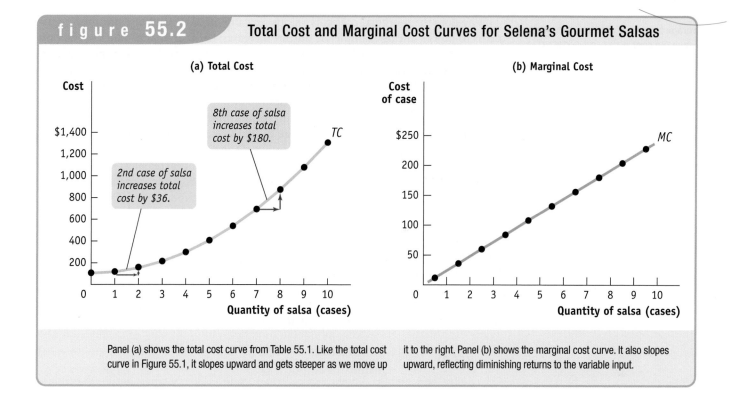

figure 55.2 Total Cost and Marginal Cost Curves for Selena's Gourmet Salsas

(a) Total Cost

8th case of salsa increases total cost by $180.

2nd case of salsa increases total cost by $36.

TC

(b) Marginal Cost

MC

Panel (a) shows the total cost curve from Table 55.1. Like the total cost curve in Figure 55.1, it slopes upward and gets steeper as we move up

it to the right. Panel (b) shows the marginal cost curve. It also slopes upward, reflecting diminishing returns to the variable input.

cost of $108 per day, shown in the second column, which is the daily rental cost of its food-preparation equipment. The third column shows the variable cost, and the fourth column shows the total cost. Panel (a) of Figure 55.2 plots the total cost curve. Like the total cost curve for George and Martha's farm in Figure 55.1, this curve slopes upward, getting steeper as quantity increases.

The significance of the slope of the total cost curve is shown by the fifth column of Table 55.1, which indicates marginal cost—the additional cost of each additional unit. The general formula for marginal cost is:

(55-2) $\text{Marginal cost} = \dfrac{\text{Change in total cost generated by one additional unit of output}}{} = \dfrac{\text{Change in total cost}}{\text{Change in quantity of output}}$

or

$$MC = \frac{\Delta TC}{\Delta Q}$$

As in the case of marginal product, marginal cost is equal to "rise" (the increase in total cost) divided by "run" (the increase in the quantity of output). So just as marginal product is equal to the slope of the total product curve, marginal cost is equal to the slope of the total cost curve.

Now we can understand why the total cost curve gets steeper as it increases from left to right: as you can see in Table 55.1, marginal cost at Selena's Gourmet Salsas rises as output increases. And because marginal cost equals the slope of the total cost curve, a higher marginal cost means a steeper slope. Panel (b) of Figure 55.2 shows the marginal cost curve corresponding to the data in Table 55.1. Notice that, as in Figure 53.1, we plot the marginal cost for increasing output from 0 to 1 case of salsa halfway between 0 and 1, the marginal cost for increasing output from 1 to 2 cases of salsa halfway between 1 and 2, and so on.

iStockphoto

Why does the marginal cost curve slope upward? Because there are diminishing returns to inputs in this example. As output increases, the marginal product of the variable input declines. This implies that more and more of the variable input must be used to produce each additional unit of output as the amount of output already produced rises. And since each unit of the variable input must be paid for, the additional cost per additional unit of output also rises.

Recall that the flattening of the total product curve is also due to diminishing returns: if the quantities of other inputs are fixed, the marginal product of an input falls as more of that input is used. The flattening of the total product curve as output increases and the steepening of the total cost curve as output increases are just flip-sides of the same phenomenon. That is, as output increases, the marginal cost of output also increases because the marginal product of the variable input decreases. Our next step is to introduce another measure of cost: *average cost.*

Average Cost

In addition to total cost and marginal cost, it's useful to calculate **average total cost,** often simply called **average cost.** The average total cost is total cost divided by the quantity of output produced; that is, it is equal to total cost per unit of output. If we let *ATC* denote average total cost, the equation looks like this:

$$\text{(55-3)} \quad ATC = \frac{\text{Total cost}}{\text{Quantity of output}} = \frac{TC}{Q}$$

Average total cost is important because it tells the producer how much the *average* or *typical* unit of output costs to produce. Marginal cost, meanwhile, tells the producer how much *one more* unit of output costs to produce. Although they may look very similar, these two measures of cost typically differ. And confusion between them is a major source of error in economics, both in the classroom and in real life. Table 55.2 uses data from Selena's Gourmet Salsas to calculate average total cost. For example, the total cost of producing 4 cases of salsa is $300, consisting of $108 in fixed cost and $192 in variable cost (from Table 55.1). So the average total cost of producing 4 cases of salsa is

table 55.2

Average Costs for Selena's Gourmet Salsas

Quantity of salsa Q (cases)	Total cost TC	Average total cost of case $ATC = TC/Q$	Average fixed cost of case $AFC = FC/Q$	Average variable cost of case $AVC = VC/Q$
1	$120	$120.00	$108.00	$12.00
2	156	78.00	54.00	24.00
3	216	72.00	36.00	36.00
4	300	75.00	27.00	48.00
5	408	81.60	21.60	60.00
6	540	90.00	18.00	72.00
7	696	99.43	15.43	84.00
8	876	109.50	13.50	96.00
9	1,080	120.00	12.00	108.00
10	1,308	130.80	10.80	120.00

$300/4 = $75. You can see from Table 55.2 that as the quantity of output increases, average total cost first falls, then rises.

Figure 55.3 plots that data to yield the *average total cost curve*, which shows how average total cost depends on output. As before, cost in dollars is measured on the vertical axis and quantity of output is measured on the horizontal axis. The average total cost curve has a distinctive U shape that corresponds to how average total cost first falls and then rises as output increases. Economists believe that such **U-shaped average total cost curves** are the norm for firms in many industries.

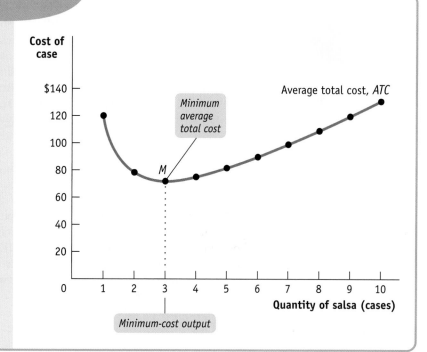

figure 55.3

Average Total Cost Curve for Selena's Gourmet Salsas

The average total cost curve at Selena's Gourmet Salsas is U-shaped. At low levels of output, average total cost falls because the "spreading effect" of falling average fixed cost dominates the "diminishing returns effect" of rising average variable cost. At higher levels of output, the opposite is true and average total cost rises. At point *M*, corresponding to an output of three cases of salsa per day, average total cost is at its minimum level, the minimum average total cost.

To help our understanding of why the average total cost curve is U-shaped, Table 55.2 breaks average total cost into its two underlying components, *average fixed cost* and *average variable cost*. **Average fixed cost,** or *AFC,* is fixed cost divided by the quantity of output, also known as the fixed cost per unit of output. For example, if Selena's Gourmet Salsas produces 4 cases of salsa, average fixed cost is $108/4 = $27 per case. **Average variable cost,** or *AVC,* is variable cost divided by the quantity of output, also known as variable cost per unit of output. At an output of 4 cases, average variable cost is $192/4 = $48 per case. Writing these in the form of equations:

(55-4) $AFC = \dfrac{\text{Fixed cost}}{\text{Quantity of output}} = \dfrac{FC}{Q}$

$AVC = \dfrac{\text{Variable cost}}{\text{Quantity of output}} = \dfrac{VC}{Q}$

Average total cost is the sum of average fixed cost and average variable cost; it has a U shape because these components move in opposite directions as output rises.

Average fixed cost falls as more output is produced because the numerator (the fixed cost) is a fixed number but the denominator (the quantity of output) increases as more is produced. Another way to think about this relationship is that, as more output is produced, the fixed cost is spread over more units of output; the end result is that the

A **U-shaped average total cost curve** falls at low levels of output and then rises at higher levels.

Average fixed cost is the fixed cost per unit of output.

Average variable cost is the variable cost per unit of output.

fixed cost *per unit of output*—the average fixed cost—falls. You can see this effect in the fourth column of Table 55.2: average fixed cost drops continuously as output increases. Average variable cost, however, rises as output increases. As we've seen, this reflects diminishing returns to the variable input: each additional unit of output adds more to variable cost than the previous unit because increasing amounts of the variable input are required to make another unit.

So increasing output has two opposing effects on average total cost—the "spreading effect" and the "diminishing returns effect":

- *The spreading effect.* The larger the output, the greater the quantity of output over which fixed cost is spread, leading to lower average fixed cost.

- *The diminishing returns effect.* The larger the output, the greater the amount of variable input required to produce additional units, leading to higher average variable cost.

At low levels of output, the spreading effect is very powerful because even small increases in output cause large reductions in average fixed cost. So at low levels of output, the spreading effect dominates the diminishing returns effect and causes the average total cost curve to slope downward. But when output is large, average fixed cost is already quite small, so increasing output further has only a very small spreading effect. Diminishing returns, however, usually grow increasingly important as output rises. As a result, when output is large, the diminishing returns effect dominates the spreading effect, causing the average total cost curve to slope upward. At the bottom of the U-shaped average total cost curve, point *M* in Figure 55.3, the two effects exactly balance each other. At this point average total cost is at its minimum level, the minimum average total cost.

Figure 55.4 brings together in a single picture the four other cost curves that we have derived from the total cost curve for Selena's Gourmet Salsas: the marginal cost curve (*MC*), the average total cost curve (*ATC*), the average variable cost curve (*AVC*), and the average fixed cost curve (*AFC*). All are based on the information in Tables 55.1 and 55.2. As before, cost is measured on the vertical axis and the quantity of output is measured on the horizontal axis.

figure 55.4

Marginal Cost and Average Cost Curves for Selena's Gourmet Salsas

Here we have the family of cost curves for Selena's Gourmet Salsas: the marginal cost curve (*MC*), the average total cost curve (*ATC*), the average variable cost curve (*AVC*), and the average fixed cost curve (*AFC*). Note that the average total cost curve is U-shaped and the marginal cost curve crosses the average total cost curve at the bottom of the U, point *M*, corresponding to the minimum average total cost from Table 55.2 and Figure 55.3.

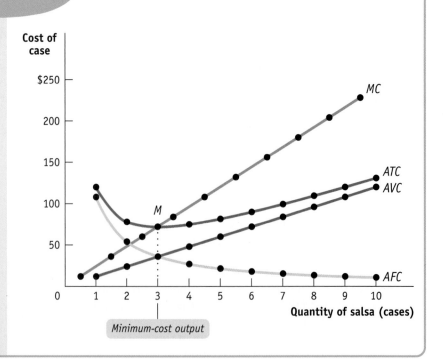

Let's take a moment to note some features of the various cost curves. First of all, marginal cost slopes upward—the result of diminishing returns that make an additional unit of output more costly to produce than the one before. Average variable cost also slopes upward—again, due to diminishing returns—but is flatter than the marginal cost curve. This is because the higher cost of an additional unit of output is averaged across all units, not just the additional unit, in the average variable cost measure. Meanwhile, average fixed cost slopes downward because of the spreading effect.

Finally, notice that the marginal cost curve intersects the average total cost curve from below, crossing it at its lowest point, point *M* in Figure 55.4. This last feature is our next subject of study.

> The **minimum-cost output** is the quantity of output at which average total cost is lowest—it corresponds to the bottom of the U-shaped average total cost curve.

Minimum Average Total Cost

For a U-shaped average total cost curve, average total cost is at its minimum level at the bottom of the U. Economists call the quantity of output that corresponds to the minimum average total cost the **minimum-cost output.** In the case of Selena's Gourmet Salsas, the minimum-cost output is three cases of salsa per day.

In Figure 55.4, the bottom of the U is at the level of output at which the marginal cost curve crosses the average total cost curve from below. Is this an accident? No—it reflects general principles that are always true about a firm's marginal cost and average total cost curves:

- At the minimum-cost output, average total cost *is equal to* marginal cost.

- At output less than the minimum-cost output, marginal cost *is less than* average total cost and average total cost is falling.

- And at output greater than the minimum-cost output, marginal cost *is greater than* average total cost and average total cost is rising.

To understand these principles, think about how your grade in one course—say, a 3.0 in physics—affects your overall grade point average. If your GPA before receiving that grade was more than 3.0, the new grade lowers your average.

Similarly, if marginal cost—the cost of producing one more unit—is less than average total cost, producing that extra unit lowers average total cost. This is shown in Figure 55.5 by the movement from A_1 to A_2. In this case, the marginal cost of producing

figure **55.5**

The Relationship Between the Average Total Cost and the Marginal Cost Curves

To see why the marginal cost curve (*MC*) must cut through the average total cost curve at the minimum average total cost (point *M*), corresponding to the minimum-cost output, we look at what happens if marginal cost is different from average total cost. If marginal cost is *less* than average total cost, an increase in output must reduce average total cost, as in the movement from A_1 to A_2. If marginal cost is *greater* than average total cost, an increase in output must increase average total cost, as in the movement from B_1 to B_2.

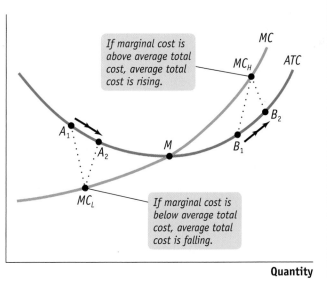

an additional unit of output is low, as indicated by the point MC_L on the marginal cost curve. When the cost of producing the next unit of output is less than average total cost, increasing production reduces average total cost. So any quantity of output at which marginal cost is less than average total cost must be on the downward-sloping segment of the U.

But if your grade in physics is more than the average of your previous grades, this new grade raises your GPA. Similarly, if marginal cost is greater than average total cost, producing that extra unit raises average total cost. This is illustrated by the movement from B_1 to B_2 in Figure 55.5, where the marginal cost, MC_H, is higher than average total cost. So any quantity of output at which marginal cost is greater than average total cost must be on the upward-sloping segment of the U.

Finally, if a new grade is exactly equal to your previous GPA, the additional grade neither raises nor lowers that average—it stays the same. This corresponds to point M in Figure 55.5: when marginal cost equals average total cost, we must be at the bottom of the U because only at that point is average total cost neither falling nor rising.

Does the Marginal Cost Curve Always Slope Upward?

Up to this point, we have emphasized the importance of diminishing returns, which lead to a marginal product curve that always slopes downward and a marginal cost curve that always slopes upward. In practice, however, economists believe that marginal cost curves often slope *downward* as a firm increases its production from zero up to some low level, sloping upward only at higher levels of production: marginal cost curves look like the curve labeled MC in Figure 55.6.

This initial downward slope occurs because a firm often finds that, when it starts with only a very small number of workers, employing more workers and expanding output allows its workers to specialize in various tasks. This, in turn, lowers the firm's marginal cost as it expands output. For example, one individual producing salsa would have to perform all the tasks involved: selecting and preparing the ingredients, mixing the salsa, bottling and labeling it, packing it into cases, and so on. As more workers are employed, they can divide the tasks, with each worker specializing in one or a few aspects of salsa-making. This specialization leads to *increasing returns* to the hiring of additional workers and results in a marginal cost curve that initially slopes downward.

figure 55.6

More Realistic Cost Curves

A realistic marginal cost curve has a "swoosh" shape. Starting from a very low output level, marginal cost often falls as the firm increases output. That's because hiring additional workers allows greater specialization of their tasks and leads to increasing returns. Once specialization is achieved, however, diminishing returns to additional workers set in and marginal cost rises. The corresponding average variable cost curve is now U-shaped, like the average total cost curve.

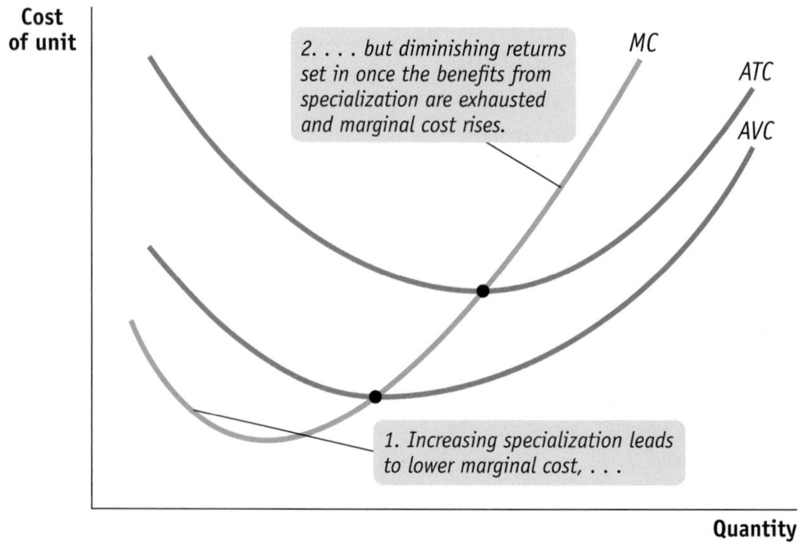

2. . . . but diminishing returns set in once the benefits from specialization are exhausted and marginal cost rises.

1. Increasing specialization leads to lower marginal cost, . . .

But once there are enough workers to have completely exhausted the benefits of further specialization, diminishing returns to labor set in and the marginal cost curve changes direction and slopes upward. So typical marginal cost curves actually have the "swoosh" shape shown by *MC* in Figure 55.6. For the same reason, average variable cost curves typically look like *AVC* in Figure 55.6: they are U-shaped rather than strictly upward sloping.

However, as Figure 55.6 also shows, the key features we saw from the example of Selena's Gourmet Salsas remain true: the average total cost curve is U-shaped, and the marginal cost curve passes through the point of minimum average total cost.

Module 55 AP Review

Solutions appear at the back of the book.

Check Your Understanding

1. Alicia's Apple Pies is a roadside business. Alicia must pay $9.00 in rent each day. In addition, it costs her $1.00 to produce the first pie of the day, and each subsequent pie costs 50% more to produce than the one before. For example, the second pie costs $1.00 × 1.5 = $1.50 to produce, and so on.
   a. Calculate Alicia's marginal cost, variable cost, average fixed cost, average variable cost, and average total cost as her daily pie output rises from 0 to 6. (*Hint:* The variable cost of two pies is just the marginal cost of the first pie, plus the marginal cost of the second, and so on.)

   b. Indicate the range of pies for which the spreading effect dominates and the range for which the diminishing returns effect dominates.
   c. What is Alicia's minimum-cost output? Explain why making one more pie lowers Alicia's average total cost when output is lower than the minimum-cost output. Similarly, explain why making one more pie raises Alicia's average total cost when output is greater than the minimum-cost output.

Tackle the Test: Multiple-Choice Questions

1. When a firm is producing zero output, total cost equals
   a. zero.
   b. variable cost.
   c. fixed cost.
   d. average total cost.
   e. marginal cost.

2. Which of the following statements is true?
   I. Marginal cost is the change in total cost generated by one additional unit of output.
   II. Marginal cost is the change in variable cost generated by one additional unit of output.
   III. The marginal cost curve must cross the minimum of the average total cost curve.
   a. I only
   b. II only
   c. III only
   d. I and II only
   e. I, II, and III

3. Which of the following is correct?
   a. AVC is the change in total cost generated by one additional unit of output.
   b. MC = TC/Q
   c. The average cost curve crosses at the minimum of the marginal cost curve.

   d. The AFC curve slopes upward.
   e. AVC = ATC − AFC

4. The slope of the total cost curve equals
   a. variable cost.
   b. average variable cost.
   c. average total cost.
   d. average fixed cost.
   e. marginal cost.

5.
Q	VC	TC
0	$0	$40
1	20	60
2	50	90
3	90	130
4	140	180
5	200	240

   On the basis of the data in the table above, what is the marginal cost of the third unit of output?
   a. 40
   b. 50
   c. 60
   d. 90
   e. 130

Tackle the Test: Free-Response Questions

1. Use the information in the table below to answer the following questions.

Q	VC	TC
0	$0	$40
1	20	60
2	50	90
3	90	130
4	140	180
5	200	240

   a. What is the firm's level of fixed cost? Explain how you know.
   b. Draw one correctly labeled graph showing the firm's marginal and average total cost curves.

2. Draw a correctly labeled graph showing a firm with an upward sloping MC curve and typically shaped ATC, AVC, and AFC curves.

Answer (6 points)

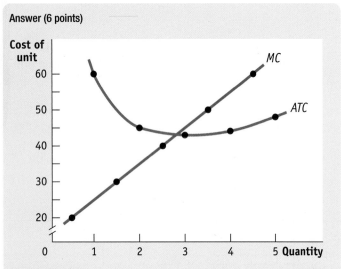

1 point: FC = $40

1 point: We can identify the fixed cost as $40 because when the firm is not producing, it still incurs a cost of $40. This could only be the result of a fixed cost because variable cost is zero when output is zero.

1 point: Graph with correct labels ("Cost of unit" on vertical axis; "Quantity" on horizontal axis)

1 point: Upward sloping MC curve plotted according to data, labeled "MC"

1 point: U-shaped ATC curve plotted according to the provided data, labeled "ATC"

1 point: MC curve crossing at minimum of ATC curve (Note: We have simplified this graph by drawing smooth lines between discrete points. If we had drawn the MC curve as a step function instead, the MC curve would have crossed the ATC curve exactly at its minimum point.)

Module 56
Long-Run Costs and Economies of Scale

Up to this point, we have treated fixed cost as completely outside the control of a firm because we have focused on the short run. But all inputs are variable in the long run: this means that in the long run, even "fixed cost" may change. *In the long run, in other words, a firm's fixed cost becomes a variable it can choose.* For example, given time, Selena's Gourmet Salsas can acquire additional food-preparation equipment or dispose of some of its existing equipment. In this module, we will examine how a firm's costs behave in the short run and in the long run. We will also see that the firm will choose its fixed cost in the long run based on the level of output it expects to produce.

Short-Run versus Long-Run Costs

Let's begin by supposing that Selena's Gourmet Salsas is considering whether to acquire additional food-preparation equipment. Acquiring additional machinery will affect its total cost in two ways. First, the firm will have to either rent or buy the additional equipment; either way, that will mean a higher fixed cost in the short run. Second, if the workers have more equipment, they will be more productive: fewer workers will be needed to produce any given output, so variable cost for any given output level will be reduced.

The table in Figure 56.1 on the next page shows how acquiring an additional machine affects costs. In our original example, we assumed that Selena's Gourmet Salsas had a fixed cost of \$108. The left half of the table shows variable cost as well as total cost and average total cost assuming a fixed cost of \$108. The average total cost curve for this level of fixed cost is given by ATC_1 in Figure 56.1. Let's compare that to a situation in which the firm buys additional food-preparation equipment, doubling its fixed cost to \$216 but reducing its variable cost at any given level of output. The right half of the table shows the firm's variable cost, total cost, and average total cost with this higher level of fixed cost. The average total cost curve corresponding to \$216 in fixed cost is given by ATC_2 in Figure 56.1.

figure 56.1

Choosing the Level of Fixed Cost for Selena's Gourmet Salsas

There is a trade-off between higher fixed cost and lower variable cost for any given output level, and vice versa. ATC_1 is the average total cost curve corresponding to a fixed cost of $108; it leads to lower fixed cost and higher variable cost. ATC_2 is the average total cost curve corresponding to a higher fixed cost of $216 but lower variable cost. At low output levels, at 4 or fewer cases of salsa per day, ATC_1 lies below ATC_2: average total cost is lower with only $108 in fixed cost. But as output goes up, average total cost is lower with the higher amount of fixed cost, $216: at more than 4 cases of salsa per day, ATC_2 lies below ATC_1.

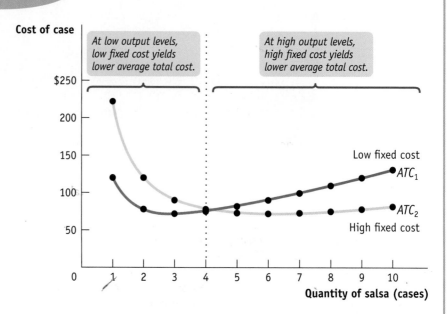

	Low fixed cost (FC = $108)			High fixed cost (FC = $216)		
Quantity of salsa (cases)	High variable cost	Total cost	Average total cost of case ATC_1	Low variable cost	Total cost	Average total cost of case ATC_2
1	$12	$120	$120.00	$6	$222	$222.00
2	48	156	78.00	24	240	120.00
3	108	216	72.00	54	270	90.00
4	192	300	75.00	96	312	78.00
5	300	408	81.60	150	366	73.20
6	432	540	90.00	216	432	72.00
7	588	696	99.43	294	510	72.86
8	768	876	109.50	384	600	75.00
9	972	1,080	120.00	486	702	78.00
10	1,200	1,308	130.80	600	816	81.60

From the figure you can see that when output is small, 4 cases of salsa per day or fewer, average total cost is smaller when Selena forgoes the additional equipment and maintains the lower fixed cost of $108: ATC_1 lies below ATC_2. For example, at 3 cases per day, average total cost is $72 without the additional machinery and $90 with the additional machinery. But as output increases beyond 4 cases per day, the firm's average total cost is lower if it acquires the additional equipment, raising its fixed cost to $216. For example, at 9 cases of salsa per day, average total cost is $120 when fixed cost is $108 but only $78 when fixed cost is $216.

Why does average total cost change like this when fixed cost increases? When output is low, the increase in fixed cost from the additional equipment outweighs the reduction in variable cost from higher worker productivity—that is, there are too few units of output over which to spread the additional fixed cost. So if Selena plans to produce 4 or fewer cases per day, she would be better off choosing the lower level of fixed cost, $108, to achieve a lower average total cost of production. When planned output is high, however, she should acquire the additional machinery.

In general, for each output level there is some choice of fixed cost that minimizes the firm's average total cost for that output level. So when the firm has a desired output level that it expects to maintain over time, it should choose the optimal fixed cost for that level—that is, the level of fixed cost that minimizes its average total cost.

Now that we are studying a situation in which fixed cost can change, we need to take *time* into account when discussing average total cost. All of the average total cost curves we have considered until now are defined for a given level of fixed cost—that is, they are defined for the short run, the period of time over which fixed cost doesn't vary. To reinforce that distinction, for the rest of this module we will refer to these average total cost curves as "short-run average total cost curves."

For most firms, it is realistic to assume that there are many possible choices of fixed cost, not just two. The implication: for such a firm, many possible short-run average total cost curves will exist, each corresponding to a different choice of fixed cost and so giving rise to what is called a firm's "family" of short-run average total cost curves.

At any given time, a firm will find itself on one of its short-run cost curves, the one corresponding to its current level of fixed cost; a change in output will cause it to move along that curve. If the firm expects that change in output level to be long-standing, then it is likely that the firm's current level of fixed cost is no longer optimal. Given sufficient time, it will want to adjust its fixed cost to a new level that minimizes average total cost for its new output level. For example, if Selena had been producing 2 cases of salsa per day with a fixed cost of $108 but found herself increasing her output to 8 cases per day for the foreseeable future, then in the long run she should purchase more equipment and increase her fixed cost to a level that minimizes average total cost at the 8-cases-per-day output level.

Suppose we do a thought experiment and calculate the lowest possible average total cost that can be achieved for each output level if the firm were to choose its fixed cost for each output level. Economists have given this thought experiment a name: the *long-run average total cost curve*. Specifically, the **long-run average total cost curve,** or *LRATC,* is the relationship between output and average total cost when fixed cost has been chosen to minimize average total cost *for each level of output*. If there are many possible choices of fixed cost, the long-run average total cost curve will have the familiar, smooth U shape, as shown by *LRATC* in Figure 56.2.

The **long-run average total cost curve** shows the relationship between output and average total cost when fixed cost has been chosen to minimize average total cost for each level of output.

figure 56.2

Short-Run and Long-Run Average Total Cost Curves

Short-run and long-run average total cost curves differ because a firm can choose its fixed cost in the long run. If Selena has chosen the level of fixed cost that minimizes short-run average total cost at an output of 6 cases, and actually produces 6 cases, then she will be at point *C* on *LRATC* and *ATC₆*. But if she produces only 3 cases, she will move to point *B*. If she expects to produce only 3 cases for a long time, in the long run she will reduce her fixed cost and move to point *A* on *ATC₃*. Likewise, if she produces 9 cases (putting her at point *Y*) and expects to continue this for a long time, she will increase her fixed cost in the long run and move to point *X*.

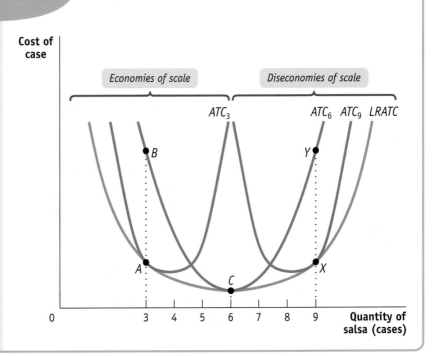

We can now draw the distinction between the short run and the long run more fully. In the long run, when a producer has had time to choose the fixed cost appropriate for its desired level of output, that producer will be at some point on the long-run average total cost curve. But if the output level is altered, the firm will no longer be on its long-run average total cost curve and will instead be moving along its current short-run average total cost curve. It will not be on its long-run average total cost curve again until it readjusts its fixed cost for its new output level.

Figure 56.2 illustrates this point. The curve ATC_3 shows short-run average total cost if Selena has chosen the level of fixed cost that minimizes average total cost at an output of 3 cases of salsa per day. This is confirmed by the fact that at 3 cases·per day, ATC_3 touches $LRATC$, the long-run average total cost curve. Similarly, ATC_6 shows short-run average total cost if Selena has chosen the level of fixed cost that minimizes average total cost if her output is 6 cases per day. It touches $LRATC$ at 6 cases per day. And ATC_9 shows short-run average total cost if Selena has chosen the level of fixed cost that minimizes average total cost if her output is 9 cases per day. It touches $LRATC$ at 9 cases per day.

Suppose that Selena initially chose to be on ATC_6. If she actually produces 6 cases of salsa per day, her firm will be at point C on both its short-run and long-run average total cost curves. Suppose, however, that Selena ends up producing only 3 cases of salsa per day. In the short run, her average total cost is indicated by point B on ATC_6; it is no longer on $LRATC$. If Selena had known that she would be producing only 3 cases per day, she would have been better off choosing a lower level of fixed cost, the one corresponding to ATC_3, thereby achieving a lower average total cost. Then her firm would have found itself at point A on the long-run average total cost curve, which lies below point B.

Suppose, conversely, that Selena ends up producing 9 cases per day even though she initially chose to be on ATC_6. In the short run her average total cost is indicated by point Y on ATC_6. But she would be better off purchasing more equipment and incurring a higher fixed cost in order to reduce her variable cost and move to ATC_9. This would allow her to reach point X on the long-run average total cost curve, which lies below Y. The distinction between short-run and long-run average total costs is extremely important in making sense of how real firms operate over time. A company that has to increase output suddenly to meet a surge in demand will typically find that in the short run its average total cost rises sharply because it is hard to get extra production out of existing facilities. But given time to build new factories or add machinery, short-run average total cost falls.

Returns to Scale

What determines the shape of the long-run average total cost curve? It is the influence of *scale*, the size of a firm's operations, on its long-run average total cost of production. Firms that experience *scale effects* in production find that their long-run average total cost changes substantially depending on the quantity of output they produce. There are **economies of scale** when long-run average total cost declines as output increases. As you can see in Figure 56.2, Selena's Gourmet Salsas experiences economies of scale over output levels ranging from 0 up to 6 cases of salsa per day—the output levels over which the long-run average total cost curve is declining. Economies of scale can result from **increasing returns to scale,** which exist when output increases more than in proportion to an increase in all inputs. For example, if Selena could double all of her inputs and make more than twice as much salsa, she would be experiencing increasing returns to scale. With twice the inputs (and costs) and more than twice the salsa, she would be enjoying decreasing long-run average total costs, and thus economies of scale. Increasing returns to scale therefore imply economies of scale, although economies of scale exist whenever long-run average total cost is falling, whether or not all inputs are increasing by the same proportion.

In contrast, there are **diseconomies of scale** when long-run average total cost increases as output increases. For Selena's Gourmet Salsas, decreasing returns to scale occur at output levels greater than 6 cases, the output levels over which its long-run

There are **economies of scale** when long-run average total cost declines as output increases.

There are **increasing returns to scale** when output increases more than in proportion to an increase in all inputs. For example, with increasing returns to scale, doubling all inputs would cause output to more than double.

There are **diseconomies of scale** when long-run average total cost increases as output increases.

average total cost curve is rising. Diseconomies of scale can result from **decreasing returns to scale,** which exist when output increases less than in proportion to an increase in all inputs—doubling the inputs results in less than double the output. When output increases directly in proportion to an increase in all inputs—doubling the inputs results in double the output—the firm is experiencing **constant returns to scale.**

What explains these scale effects in production? The answer ultimately lies in the firm's technology of production. Economies of scale often arise from the increased *specialization* that larger output levels allow—a larger scale of operation means that individual workers can limit themselves to more specialized tasks, becoming more skilled and efficient at doing them. Another source of economies of scale is a very large initial setup cost; in some industries—such as auto manufacturing, electricity generating, and petroleum refining—it is necessary to pay a high fixed cost in the form of plant and equipment before producing any output. A third source of economies of scale, found in certain high-tech industries such as software development, is *network externalities,* a topic covered in a later module. As we'll see when we study monopoly, increasing returns have very important implications for how firms and industries behave and interact.

Diseconomies of scale—the opposite scenario—typically arise in large firms due to problems of coordination and communication: as a firm grows in size, it becomes ever more difficult and therefore costly to communicate and to organize activities. Although economies of scale induce firms to grow larger, diseconomies of scale tend to limit their size.

There are **decreasing returns to scale** when output increases less than in proportion to an increase in all inputs.

There are **constant returns to scale** when output increases directly in proportion to an increase in all inputs.

A **sunk cost** is a cost that has already been incurred and is nonrecoverable. A sunk cost should be ignored in a decision about future actions.

Sunk Costs

To complete our discussion of costs, we need to include the concept of sunk costs. When making decisions, knowing what to ignore is important. Although we have devoted much attention to costs that are important to take into account when making a decision, some costs should be ignored when doing so. This section presents the kind of costs that people should ignore when making decisions—what economists call *sunk costs*—and explains why they should be ignored.

To gain some intuition, consider the following scenario. You own a car that is a few years old, and you have just replaced the brake pads at a cost of $250. But then you find out that the entire brake system is defective and also must be replaced. This will cost you an additional $1,500. Alternatively, you could sell the car and buy another of comparable quality, but with no brake defects, by spending an additional $1,600. What should you do: fix your old car, or sell it and buy another?

Some might say that you should take the latter option. After all, this line of reasoning goes, if you repair your car, you will end up having spent $1,750: $1,500 for the brake system and $250 for the brake pads. If you were instead to sell your old car and buy another, you would spend only $1,600.

© Greatstock Photographic Library / Alamy

But this reasoning, although it sounds plausible, is wrong. It ignores the fact that you have *already* spent $250 on brake pads, and that $250 is *nonrecoverable.* That is, having already been spent, the $250 cannot be recouped. Therefore, it should be ignored and should have no effect on your decision whether to repair your car and keep it or not. From a rational viewpoint, the real cost at this time of repairing and keeping your car is $1,500, not $1,750. So the correct decision is to repair your car and keep it rather than spend $1,600 on a new car.

In this example, the $250 that has already been spent and cannot be recovered is what economists call a **sunk cost.** Sunk costs should be ignored in making decisions because they have no influence on future costs and benefits. It's like the old saying, "There's no use crying over spilled milk": once something can't be recovered, it is irrelevant in making decisions about what to do in the future. This applies equally to individuals, firms, and governments—regardless of how much has been spent on a project in the past, if the future costs exceed the future benefits, the project should not continue.

It is often psychologically hard to ignore sunk costs. And if, in fact, you haven't yet incurred the costs, then you should take them into consideration. That is, if you had known

There's No Business Like Snow Business

Anyone who has lived both in a snowy city, like Chicago, and in a city that only occasionally experiences significant snowfall, like Washington, D.C., is aware of the differences in total cost that arise from making different choices about fixed cost.

In Washington, even a minor snowfall—say, an inch or two overnight—is enough to create chaos during the next morning's commute. The same snowfall in Chicago has hardly any effect at all. The reason is not that Washingtonians are wimps and Chicagoans are made of sterner stuff; it is that Washington, where it rarely snows, has only a fraction as many snowplows

and other snow-clearing equipment as cities where heavy snow is a fact of life.

In this sense Washington and Chicago are like two producers who expect to produce different levels of output, where the "output" is snow removal. Washington, which rarely has significant snow, has chosen a low level of fixed cost in the form of snow-clearing equipment. This makes sense under normal circumstances but leaves the city unprepared when major snow does fall. Chicago, which knows that it will face lots of snow, chooses to accept the higher fixed cost that leaves it in a position to respond effectively.

A lesson in returns to scale: cities with higher average annual snowfall maintain larger snowplow fleets.

at the beginning that it would cost $1,750 to repair your car, then the right choice *at that time* would have been to buy a new car for $1,600. But once you have already paid the $250 for brake pads, you should no longer include it in your decision making about your next actions. It may be hard to "let bygones be bygones," but it is the right way to make a decision.

Summing Up Costs: The Short and Long of It

If a firm is to make the best decisions about how much to produce, it has to understand how its costs relate to the quantity of output it chooses to produce. Table 56.1 provides a quick summary of the concepts and measures of cost you have learned about.

table 56.1

Concepts and Measures of Cost

	Measurement	Definition	Mathematical term
Short run	Fixed cost	Cost that does not depend on the quantity of output produced	FC
	Average fixed cost	Fixed cost per unit of output	$AFC = FC/Q$
Short run and long run	Variable cost	Cost that depends on the quantity of output produced	VC
	Average variable cost	Variable cost per unit of output	$AVC = VC/Q$
	Total cost	The sum of fixed cost (short run) and variable cost	$TC = FC$ (short run) $+ VC$
	Average total cost (average cost)	Total cost per unit of output	$ATC = TC/Q$
	Marginal cost	The change in total cost generated by producing one more unit of output	$MC = \Delta TC/\Delta Q$
Long run	Long-run average total cost	Average total cost when fixed cost has been chosen to minimize average total cost for each level of output	$LRATC$

Module 56 AP Review

Solutions appear at the back of the book.

Check Your Understanding

1. The accompanying table shows three possible combinations of fixed cost and average variable cost. Average variable cost is constant in this example. (It does not vary with the quantity of output produced.)

Choice	Fixed cost	Average variable cost
1	$8,000	$1.00
2	12,000	0.75
3	24,000	0.25

   a. For each of the three choices, calculate the average total cost of producing 12,000, 22,000, and 30,000 units. For each of these quantities, which choice results in the lowest average total cost?

   b. Suppose that the firm, which has historically produced 12,000 units, experiences a sharp, permanent increase in demand that leads it to produce 22,000 units. Explain how its average total cost will change in the short run and in the long run.

   c. Explain what the firm should do instead if it believes the change in demand is temporary.

2. In each of the following cases, explain whether the firm is likely to experience economies of scale or diseconomies of scale and why.

   a. an interior design firm in which design projects are based on the expertise of the firm's owner

   b. a diamond-mining company

Tackle the Test: Multiple-Choice Questions

1. In the long run,
   a. all inputs are variable.
   b. all inputs are fixed.
   c. some inputs are variable and others are fixed.
   d. a firm will go out of business.
   e. firms increase in size.

2. Which of the following is always considered the long run?
   a. 1 month
   b. 1 year
   c. 5 years
   d. 10 years
   e. none of the above

3. Which of the following statements is generally correct?
   I. The long-run average total cost curve is U-shaped.
   II. The short-run average total cost curve is U-shaped.
   III. Firms tend to experience economies of scale at low levels of production and diseconomies of scale at high levels of production.
   a. I only
   b. II only
   c. III only
   d. I and II only
   e. I, II, and III

4. When making decisions, which of the following costs should be ignored?
   a. average costs
   b. total costs
   c. marginal costs
   d. sunk costs
   e. None—no costs should be ignored.

5. Economies of scale will allow which of the following types of cities to lower their average total cost of clearing snow by investing in larger snow plow fleets? Cities with
   a. more people.
   b. more existing snow plows.
   c. less snowfall.
   d. larger budgets.
   e. more snowfall.

Tackle the Test: Free-Response Questions

1. Refer to the graph provided to answer the following questions.

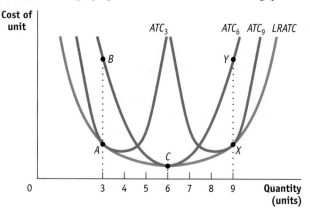

a. The same level of fixed cost that puts the firm at point B when the quantity is 3 minimizes short-run average total cost for what output level?

b. At an output level of 3, is the firm experiencing economies or diseconomies of scale? Explain.

c. In the long run, if the firm expects to produce an output of 9, the firm will produce on which short-run average total cost curve and at which point on the graph?

2. Draw a correctly labeled graph showing a short-run average total cost curve and the corresponding long-run average total cost curve. On your graph, identify the areas of economies and diseconomies of scale.

Module 57
Introduction to Market Structure

What you will learn in this **Module:**

- The meaning and dimensions of market structure
- The four principal types of market structure—perfect competition, monopoly, oligopoly, and monopolistic competition

You may have noticed that this section is titled "Behind the Supply Curve," but we have yet to mention any supply curve. The reason is that to discuss the supply curve in a market, we need to identify the type of market we are looking at. In this module we will learn about the basic characteristics of the four major types of markets in the economy.

Types of Market Structure

The real world holds a mind-boggling array of different markets. Patterns of firm behavior vary as widely as the markets themselves: in some markets firms are extremely competitive; in others, they seem somehow to coordinate their actions to limit competition; and some markets are monopolies in which there is no competition at all. In order to develop principles and make predictions about markets and firm behavior, economists have developed four primary models of market structure: *perfect competition, monopoly, oligopoly,* and *monopolistic competition.*

This system of market structure is based on two dimensions:

- the number of firms in the market (one, few, or many)
- whether the goods offered are identical or *differentiated*

Differentiated goods are goods that are different but considered at least somewhat substitutable by consumers (think Coke versus Pepsi).

Figure 57.1 on the next page provides a simple visual summary of the types of market structure classified according to the two dimensions. In *perfect competition* many firms each sell an identical product. In *monopoly,* a single firm sells a single, undifferentiated product. In *oligopoly,* a few firms—more than one but not a large number—sell products that may be either identical or differentiated. And in *monopolistic competition,* many firms each sell a differentiated product (think of producers of economics textbooks).

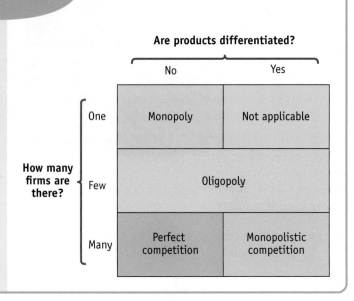

figure 57.1

Types of Market Structure

The behavior of any given firm and the market it occupies are analyzed using one of four models of market structure—monopoly, oligopoly, perfect competition, or monopolistic competition. This system for categorizing market structure is based on two dimensions: (1) whether products are differentiated or identical and (2) the number of firms in the industry—one, a few, or many.

Are products differentiated?

	No	Yes
One	Monopoly	Not applicable
Few	Oligopoly	
Many	Perfect competition	Monopolistic competition

How many firms are there?

Perfect Competition

Suppose that Yves and Zoe are neighboring farmers, both of whom grow organic tomatoes. Both sell their output to the same grocery store chains that carry organic foods; so, in a real sense, Yves and Zoe compete with each other.

Does this mean that Yves should try to stop Zoe from growing tomatoes or that Yves and Zoe should form an agreement to grow fewer? Almost certainly not: there are hundreds or thousands of organic tomato farmers (let's not forget Jennifer and Jason from Module 53!), and Yves and Zoe are competing with all those other growers as well as with each other. Because so many farmers sell organic tomatoes, if any one of them produced more or fewer, there would be no measurable effect on market prices.

When people talk about business competition, they often imagine a situation in which two or three rival firms are struggling for advantage. But economists know that when a business focuses on a few main competitors, it's actually a sign that competition is fairly limited. As the example of organic tomatoes suggests, when the number of competitors is large, it doesn't even make sense to identify rivals and engage in aggressive competition because each firm is too small within the scope of the market to make a significant difference.

We can put it another way: Yves and Zoe are *price-takers*. A firm is a **price-taker** when its actions cannot affect the market price of the good or service it sells. As a result, a price-taking firm takes the market price as given. When there is enough competition—when competition is what economists call "perfect"—then every firm is a price-taker. There is a similar definition for consumers: a **price-taking consumer** is a consumer who cannot influence the market price of the good or service by his or her actions. That is, the market price is unaffected by how much or how little of the good the consumer buys.

Defining Perfect Competition

In a **perfectly competitive market,** all market participants, both consumers and producers, are price-takers. That is, neither consumption decisions by individual consumers nor production decisions by individual producers affect the market price of the good.

The supply and demand model is a model of a perfectly competitive market. It depends fundamentally on the assumption that no individual buyer or seller of a good,

A **price-taking firm** is a firm whose actions have no effect on the market price of the good or service it sells.

A **price-taking consumer** is a consumer whose actions have no effect on the market price of the good or service he or she buys.

A **perfectly competitive market** is a market in which all market participants are price-takers.

such as coffee beans or organic tomatoes, believes that it is possible to individually affect the price at which he or she can buy or sell the good. For a firm, being a price-taker means that the demand curve is a horizontal line at the market price. If the firm charged more than the market price, buyers would go to any of the many alternative sellers of the same product. And it is unnecessary to charge a lower price because, as an insignificantly small part of the perfectly competitive market, the firm can sell all that it wants at the market price.

As a general rule, consumers are indeed price-takers. Instances in which consumers are able to affect the prices they pay are rare. It is, however, quite common for producers to have a significant ability to affect the prices they receive, a phenomenon we'll address later. So the model of perfect competition is appropriate for some but not all markets. An industry in which firms are price-takers is called a **perfectly competitive industry.** Clearly, some industries aren't perfectly competitive; in later modules we'll focus on industries that don't fit the perfectly competitive model.

Under what circumstances will all firms be price-takers? As we'll discover next, there are two necessary conditions for a perfectly competitive industry and a third condition is often present as well.

Two Necessary Conditions for Perfect Competition

The markets for major grains, such as wheat and corn, are perfectly competitive: individual wheat and corn farmers, as well as individual buyers of wheat and corn, take market prices as given. In contrast, the markets for some of the food items made from these grains—in particular, breakfast cereals—are by no means perfectly competitive. There is intense competition among cereal brands, but not *perfect* competition. To understand the difference between the market for wheat and the market for shredded wheat cereal is to understand the two necessary conditions for perfect competition.

First, for an industry to be perfectly competitive, it must contain many firms, none of whom have a large **market share.** A firm's market share is the fraction of the total industry output accounted for by that firm's output. The distribution of market share constitutes a major difference between the grain industry and the breakfast cereal industry. There are thousands of wheat farmers, none of whom account for more than a tiny fraction of total wheat sales. The breakfast cereal industry, however, is dominated by four firms: Kellogg's, General Mills, Post, and Quaker Foods. Kellogg's alone accounts for about one-third of all cereal sales. Kellogg's executives know that if they try to sell more corn flakes, they are likely to drive down the market price of corn flakes. That is, they know that their actions influence market prices—due to their tremendous size, changes in their production will significantly affect the overall quantity supplied. It makes sense to assume that firms are price-takers only when they are numerous and relatively small.

Second, an industry can be perfectly competitive only if consumers regard the products of all firms as equivalent. This clearly isn't true in the breakfast cereal market: consumers don't consider Cap'n Crunch to be a good substitute for Wheaties. As a result, the maker of Wheaties has some ability to increase its price without fear that it will lose all its customers to the maker of Cap'n Crunch. Contrast this with the case of a **standardized product,** sometimes known as a **commodity,** which is a product that consumers regard as the same good even when it comes from different firms. Because wheat is a standardized product, consumers regard the output of one wheat producer as a perfect substitute for that of another producer. Consequently, one farmer cannot increase the price for his or her wheat without losing all sales to other wheat farmers. So the second necessary condition for a perfectly competitive industry is that the industry output is a standardized product. (See the FYI that follows.)

A **perfectly competitive industry** is an industry in which firms are price-takers.

A firm's **market share** is the fraction of the total industry output accounted for by that firm's output.

A good is a **standardized product,** also known as a **commodity,** when consumers regard the products of different firms as the same good.

Scott Bauer/ARS/USDA

What's a Standardized Product?

A perfectly competitive industry must produce a standardized product. But is it enough for the products of different firms actually to be the same? No: people must also *think* that they are the same. And producers often go to great lengths to convince consumers that they have a distinctive, or *differentiated,* product, even when they don't.

Consider, for example, champagne—not the super-expensive premium champagnes, but the more ordinary stuff. Most people cannot tell the difference between champagne actually produced in the Champagne

region of France, where the product originated, and similar products from Spain or California. But the French government has sought and obtained legal protection for the winemakers of Champagne, ensuring that around the world only bubbly wine from that region can be called champagne. If it's from someplace else, all the seller can do is say that it was produced using the *méthode Champenoise.* This creates a differentiation in the minds of consumers and lets the champagne producers of Champagne charge higher prices.

Similarly, Korean producers of *kimchi,* the spicy fermented cabbage that is the Korean national side dish, are doing their best to convince consumers that the same product packaged by Japanese firms is just not the real thing. The purpose is, of course, to ensure higher prices for Korean *kimchi.*

So is an industry perfectly competitive if it sells products that are indistinguishable except in name but that consumers, for whatever reason, don't think are standardized? No. When it comes to defining the nature of competition, the consumer is always right.

An industry has **free entry and exit** when new firms can easily enter into the industry and existing firms can easily leave the industry.

Free Entry and Exit

All perfectly competitive industries have many firms with small market shares, producing a standardized product. Most perfectly competitive industries are also characterized by one more feature: it is easy for new firms to enter the industry or for firms that are currently in the industry to leave. That is, no obstacles in the form of government regulations or limited access to key resources prevent new firms from entering the market. And no additional costs are associated with shutting down a company and leaving the industry. Economists refer to the arrival of new firms into an industry as *entry;* they refer to the departure of firms from an industry as *exit.* When there are no obstacles to entry into or exit from an industry, we say that the industry has **free entry and exit.**

Free entry and exit is not strictly necessary for perfect competition. However, it ensures that the number of firms in an industry can adjust to changing market conditions. And, in particular, it ensures that firms in an industry cannot act to keep other firms out.

To sum up, then, perfect competition depends on two necessary conditions. First, the industry must contain many firms, each having a small market share. Second, the industry must produce a standardized product. In addition, perfectly competitive industries are normally characterized by free entry and exit.

Monopoly

The De Beers monopoly of South Africa was created in the 1880s by Cecil Rhodes, a British businessman. By 1880, mines in South Africa already dominated the world's supply of diamonds. There were, however, many mining companies, all competing with each other. During the 1880s Rhodes bought the great majority of those mines and consolidated them into a single company, De Beers. By 1889, De Beers controlled almost all of the world's diamond production.

De Beers, in other words, became a *monopolist.* But what does it mean to be a monopolist? And what do monopolists do?

Paul Katz/Digital Vision/Getty Images

Defining Monopoly

As we mentioned earlier, the supply and demand model of a market is not universally valid. Instead, it's a model of perfect competition, which is only one of several types of market structure. A market will be perfectly competitive only if there are many firms, all of which produce the same good. Monopoly is the most extreme departure from perfect competition.

A **monopolist** is a firm that is the only producer of a good that has no close substitutes. An industry controlled by a monopolist is known as a **monopoly.**

In practice, true monopolies are hard to find in the modern American economy, partly because of legal obstacles. A contemporary entrepreneur who tried to consolidate all the firms in an industry the way Rhodes did would soon find himself in court, accused of breaking *antitrust* laws, which are intended to prevent monopolies from emerging. Monopolies do, however, play an important role in some sectors of the economy.

Why Do Monopolies Exist?

A monopolist making profits will not go unnoticed by others. (Recall that this is "economic profit," revenue over and above the opportunity costs of the firm's resources.) But won't other firms crash the party, grab a piece of the action, and drive down prices and profits in the long run? If possible, yes, they will. For a profitable monopoly to persist, something must keep others from going into the same business; that "something" is known as a **barrier to entry.** There are four principal types of barriers to entry: control of a scarce resource or input, economies of scale, technological superiority, and government-created barriers.

Control of a Scarce Resource or Input A monopolist that controls a resource or input crucial to an industry can prevent other firms from entering its market. Cecil Rhodes made De Beers into a monopolist by establishing control over the mines that produced the great bulk of the world's diamonds.

Economies of Scale Many Americans have natural gas piped into their homes for cooking and heating. Invariably, the local gas company is a monopolist. But why don't rival companies compete to provide gas?

In the early nineteenth century, when the gas industry was just starting up, companies did compete for local customers. But this competition didn't last long; soon local gas companies became monopolists in almost every town because of the large fixed cost of providing a town with gas lines. The cost of laying gas lines didn't depend on how much gas a company sold, so a firm with a larger volume of sales had a cost advantage: because it was able to spread the fixed cost over a larger volume, it had a lower average total cost than smaller firms.

The natural gas industry is one in which average total cost falls as output increases, resulting in economies of scale and encouraging firms to grow larger. In an industry characterized by economies of scale, larger firms are more profitable and drive out smaller ones. For the same reason, established firms have a cost advantage over any potential entrant—a potent barrier to entry. So economies of scale can both give rise to and sustain a monopoly.

A monopoly created and sustained by economies of scale is called a **natural monopoly.** The defining characteristic of a natural monopoly is that it possesses economies of scale over the range of output that is relevant for the industry. The source of this condition is large fixed costs: when large fixed costs are required to operate, a given quantity of output is produced at lower average total cost by one large firm than by two or more smaller firms.

The most visible natural monopolies in the modern economy are local utilities—water, gas, electricity, local land-line phone service, and, in most locations, cable television. As we'll see later, natural monopolies pose a special challenge to public policy.

A **monopolist** is the only [producer of] a good that has no close substitutes. [The] industry controlled by a monopolist is known as a **monopoly.**

To earn economic profits, a monopolist must be protected by a **barrier to entry**—something that prevents other firms from entering the industry.

A **natural monopoly** exists when economies of scale provide a large cost advantage to a single firm that produces all of an industry's output.

Technological Superiority A firm that maintains a consistent technological advantage over potential competitors can establish itself as a monopolist. For example, from the 1970s through the 1990s, the chip manufacturer Intel was able to maintain a consistent advantage over potential competitors in both the design and production of microprocessors, the chips that run computers. But technological superiority is typically not a barrier to entry over the longer term: over time competitors will invest in upgrading their technology to match that of the technology leader. In fact, in the last few years Intel found its technological superiority eroded by a competitor, Advanced Micro Devices (also known as AMD), which now produces chips approximately as fast and as powerful as Intel chips.

Photodisc

We should note, however, that in certain high-tech industries, technological superiority is not a guarantee of success against competitors. Some high-tech industries are characterized by *network externalities,* a condition that arises when the value of a good to a consumer rises as the number of other people who also use the good rises. In these industries, the firm possessing the largest network—the largest number of consumers currently using its product—has an advantage over its competitors in attracting new customers, an advantage that may allow it to become a monopolist. Microsoft is often cited as an example of a company with a technologically inferior product—its computer operating system—that grew into a monopolist through the phenomenon of network externalities.

Government-Created Barriers In 1998 the pharmaceutical company Merck introduced Propecia, a drug effective against baldness. Despite the fact that Propecia was very profitable and other drug companies had the know-how to produce it, no other firms challenged Merck's monopoly. That's because the U.S. government had given Merck the sole legal right to produce the drug in the United States. Propecia is an example of a monopoly protected by government-created barriers.

The most important legally created monopolies today arise from *patents* and *copyrights*. A **patent** gives an inventor the sole right to make, use, or sell that invention for a period that in most countries lasts between 16 and 20 years. Patents are given to the creators of new products, such as drugs or mechanical devices. Similarly, a **copyright** gives the creator of a literary or artistic work the sole right to profit from that work, usually for a period equal to the creator's lifetime plus 70 years.

The justification for patents and copyrights is a matter of incentives. If inventors were not protected by patents, they would gain little reward from their efforts: as soon as a valuable invention was made public, others would copy it and sell products based on it. And if inventors could not expect to profit from their inventions, then there would be no incentive to incur the costs of invention in the first place. Likewise for the creators of literary or artistic works. So the law allows a monopoly to exist temporarily by granting property rights that encourage invention and creation. Patents and copyrights are temporary because the law strikes a compromise. The higher price for the good that holds while the legal protection is in effect compensates inventors for the cost of invention; conversely, the lower price that results once the legal protection lapses benefits consumers.

Because the lifetime of the temporary monopoly cannot be tailored to specific cases, this system is imperfect and leads to some missed opportunities. In some cases there can be significant welfare issues. For example, the violation of American drug patents by pharmaceutical companies in poor countries has been a major source of controversy, pitting the needs of poor patients who cannot afford to pay retail drug prices against the interests of drug manufacturers who have incurred high research costs to discover these drugs. To solve this problem, some American drug companies and poor countries have negotiated deals in which the patents are honored but the American companies sell their drugs at deeply discounted prices. (This is an example of *price discrimination,* which we'll learn more about later.)

A **patent** gives an inventor a temporary monopoly in the use or sale of an invention.

A **copyright** gives the creator of a literary or artistic work the sole right to profit from that work.

Oligopoly

An industry with only a few firms is known as an **oligopoly;** a producer in such an industry is known as an **oligopolist.**

Oligopolists compete with each other for sales. But oligopolists aren't like producers in a perfectly competitive industry, who take the market as given. Oligopolists know their decisions about how much to produce will affect the market price. That is, like monopolists, oligopolists have some *market power.* Economists refer to a situation in which firms compete but also possess market power—which enables them to affect market prices—as **imperfect competition.** There are two important forms of imperfect competition: oligopoly and *monopolistic competition.* Of these, oligopoly is probably the more important in practice.

Many familiar goods and services are supplied by only a few competing sellers, which means the industries in question are oligopolies. For example, most air routes are served by only two or three airlines: in recent years, regularly scheduled shuttle service between New York and either Boston or Washington, D.C., has been provided only by Delta and US Airways. Three firms—Chiquita, Dole, and Del Monte, which own huge banana plantations in Central America—control 65% of world banana exports. Most cola beverages are sold by Coca-Cola and Pepsi. This list could go on for many pages.

It's important to realize that an oligopoly isn't necessarily made up of large firms. What matters isn't size per se; the question is how many competitors there are. When a small town has only two grocery stores, grocery service there is just as much an oligopoly as air shuttle service between New York and Washington.

Why are oligopolies so prevalent? Essentially, an oligopoly is the result of the same factors that sometimes produce a monopoly, but in somewhat weaker form. Probably the most important source of oligopolies is the existence of economies of scale, which give bigger firms a cost advantage over smaller ones. When these effects are very strong, as we have seen, they lead to a monopoly; when they are not that strong, they lead to an industry with a small number of firms. For example, larger grocery stores typically have lower costs than smaller stores. But the advantages of large scale taper off once grocery stores are reasonably large, which is why two or three stores often survive in small towns.

Is It an Oligopoly or Not?

In practice, it is not always easy to determine an industry's market structure just by looking at the number of sellers. Many oligopolistic industries contain a number of small "niche" firms, which don't really compete with the major players. For example, the U.S. airline industry includes a number of regional airlines such as New Mexico Airlines, which flies propeller planes between Albuquerque and Carlsbad, New Mexico; if you count these carriers, the U.S. airline industry contains nearly one hundred firms, which doesn't sound like competition among a small group. But there are only a handful of national competitors like American and United, and on many routes, as we've seen, there are only two or three competitors.

To get a better picture of market structure, economists often use two measures of market power: **concentration ratios** and the **Herfindahl–Hirschman Index.** Concentration ratios measure the percentage of industry sales accounted for by the "X" largest firms, where "X" can equal any number of firms. For example, the four-firm concentration ratio is the percentage of sales accounted for by the four largest firms and the eight-firm concentration ratio is the percentage of industry sales accounted for by the eight largest firms. Let's say that the largest four firms account for 25%, 20%, 15%, and10% of industry sales, then the four-firm concentration ratios would equal 70 (25+20+15+10). And if the next largest four firms in that industry account for 9%, 8%, 6%, and 2% of sales, the eight-firm concentration ratio would equal 95 (70 +9+8+6+2). The

An **oligopoly** is an industry with only a small number of firms. A producer in such an industry is known as an **oligopolist.**

When no one firm has a monopoly, but producers nonetheless realize that they can affect market prices, an industry is characterized by **imperfect competition.**

Concentration ratios measure the percentage of industry sales accounted for by the "X" largest firms, for example the four-firm concentration ratio or the eight-firm concentration ratio.

Herfindahl–Hirschman Index, or HHI, is the square of each firm's share of market sales summed over the industry. It gives a picture of the industry market structure.

Courtesy of Henry M. Trotter

four- and eight-firm concentration ratios are the most commonly used. A higher concentration ratio signals a market is more concentrated and thus is more likely to be an oligopoly.

Another measure of market concentration is the Herfindahl-Hirschman index, or HHI. The HHI for an industry is the square of each firm's share of market sales summed over the firms in the industry. Unlike concentration ratios, the HHI takes into account the distribution of market sales among the top firms by squaring each firm's market share, thereby giving more weight to larger firms. For example, if an industry contains only 3 firms and their market shares are 60%, 25%, and 15%, then the HHI for the industry is:

$$HHI = 60^2 + 25^2 + 15^2 = 4,450$$

By squaring each market share, the HHI calculation produces numbers that are much larger when a larger share of an industry output is dominated by fewer firms. This is confirmed by the data in Table 57.1. Here, the indices for industries dominated by a small number of firms, like the personal computer operating systems industry or the wide-body aircraft industry, are many times larger than the index for the retail grocery industry, which has numerous firms of approximately equal size.

table **57.1**

The HHI for Some Oligopolistic Industries

Industry	HHI	Largest firms
PC operating systems	9,182	Microsoft, Linux
Wide-body aircraft	5,098	Boeing, Airbus
Diamond mining	2,338	De Beers, Alrosa, Rio Tinto
Automobiles	1,432	GM, Ford, Chrysler, Toyota, Honda, Nissan, VW
Movie distributors	1,096	Buena Vista, Sony Pictures, 20th Century Fox, Warner Bros., Universal, Paramount, Lionsgate
Internet service providers	750	SBC, Comcast, AOL, Verizon, Road Runner, Earthlink, Charter, Qwest
Retail grocers	321	Walmart, Kroger, Sears, Target, Costco, Walgreens, Ahold, Albertsons

Sources: Canadian Government; Diamond Facts 2006; www.w3counter.com; Planet retail; Autodata; Reuters; ISP Planet; Swivel. Data cover 2006–2007.

Monopolistic Competition

Leo manages the Wonderful Wok stand in the food court of a big shopping mall. He offers the only Chinese food there, but there are more than a dozen alternatives, from Bodacious Burgers to Pizza Paradise. When deciding what to charge for a meal, Leo knows that he must take those alternatives into account: even people who normally prefer stir-fry won't order a $15 lunch from Leo when they can get a burger, fries, and drink for $4.

But Leo also knows that he won't lose all his business even if his lunches cost a bit more than the alternatives. Chinese food isn't the same thing as burgers or pizza. Some people will really be in the mood for Chinese that day, and they will buy from Leo even if they could have dined more cheaply on burgers. Of course, the reverse is also true: even if Chinese is a bit cheaper, some people will choose burgers instead. In other words, Leo does have some market power: he has *some* ability to set his own price.

So how would you describe Leo's situation? He definitely isn't a price-taker, so he isn't in a situation of perfect competition. But you wouldn't exactly call him a monopolist, either. Although he's the only seller of Chinese food in that food court, he does face competition from other food vendors.

Yet it would also be wrong to call him an oligopolist. Oligopoly, remember, involves competition among a small number of interdependent firms in an industry protected by some—albeit limited—barriers to entry and whose profits are highly interdependent. Because their profits are highly interdependent, oligopolists have an incentive to collude, tacitly or explicitly. But in Leo's case there are *lots* of vendors in the shopping mall, too many to make tacit collusion feasible.

Economists describe Leo's situation as one of **monopolistic competition.** Monopolistic competition is particularly common in service industries such as the restaurant and gas station industries, but it also exists in some manufacturing industries. It involves three conditions:

- a large number of competing firms,
- differentiated products, and
- free entry into and exit from the industry in the long run.

In a monopolistically competitive industry, each producer has some ability to set the price of her differentiated product. But exactly how high she can set it is limited by the competition she faces from other existing and potential firms that produce close, but not identical, products.

Defining Monopolistic Competition Large Numbers
In a monopolistically competitive industry there are many firms. Such an industry does not look either like a monopoly, where the firm faces no competition, or like an oligopoly, where each firm has only a few rivals. Instead, each seller has many competitors. For example, there are many vendors in a big food court, many gas stations along a major highway, and many hotels at a popular beach resort.

Differentiated Products
In a monopolistically competitive industry, each firm has a product that consumers view as somewhat distinct from the products of competing firms. Such product differentiation can come in the form of different styles or types, different locations, or different levels of quality. At the same time, though, consumers see these competing products as close substitutes. If Leo's food court contained 15 vendors selling exactly the same kind and quality of food, there would be perfect competition: any seller who tried to charge a higher price would have no customers. But suppose that Wonderful Wok is the only Chinese food vendor, Bodacious Burgers is the only hamburger stand, and so on. The result of this differentiation is that each vendor has some ability to set his or her own price: each firm has some—albeit limited—market power.

Free Entry and Exit in the Long Run
In monopolistically competitive industries, new firms, with their own distinct products, can enter the industry freely in the long run. For example, other food vendors would open outlets in the food court if they thought it would be profitable to do so. In addition, firms will exit the industry if they find they are not covering their costs in the long run.

Monopolistic competition, then, differs from the three market structures we have examined so far. It's not the same as perfect competition: firms have some power to set prices. It's not pure monopoly: firms face some competition. And it's not the same as oligopoly: there are many firms and free entry, which eliminates the potential for collusion that is so important in oligopoly. As we'll see in modules 66 and 67, competition among the sellers of differentiated products is the key to understanding how monopolistic competition works.

Now that we have introduced the idea of market structure and presented the four principal models of market structure, we can proceed in the next two sections to use the cost curves we have developed to build each of the four market structure models. These models will allow us to explain and predict firm behavior (e.g., price and quantity determination) and analyze individual markets.

Monopolistic competition is a market structure in which there are many competing firms in an industry, each firm sells a differentiated product, and there is free entry into and exit from the industry in the long run.

Solutions appear at the back of the book.

Check Your Understanding

1. In each of the following situations, what type of market structure do you think the industry represents?
   a. There are three producers of aluminum in the world, a good sold in many places.
   b. There are thousands of farms that produce indistinguishable soybeans to thousands of buyers.
   c. Many designers sell high-fashion clothes. Each designer has a distinctive style and a somewhat loyal clientele.
   d. A small town in the middle of Alaska has one bicycle shop.

Tackle the Test: Multiple-Choice Questions

1. Which of the following is true for a perfectly competitive industry?
   I. There are many firms, each with a large market share.
   II. The firms in the industry produce a standardized product.
   III. There are barriers to entry and exit.
   a. I only
   b. II only
   c. III only
   d. I and II only
   e. I, II, and III

2. Which of the following is true for a monopoly?
   I. There is only one firm.
   II. The firm produces a product with many close substitutes.
   III. The industry has free entry and exit.
   a. I only
   b. II only
   c. III only
   d. I and II only
   e. I, II, and III

3. Which of the following is true for an oligopoly?
   I. There are a few firms, each with a large market share.
   II. The firms in the industry are interdependent.
   III. The industry experiences diseconomies of scale.

   a. I only
   b. II only
   c. III only
   d. I and II only
   e. I, II, and III

4. Which of the following is true for a monopolistically competitive industry?
   I. There are many firms, each with a small market share.
   II. The firms in the industry produce a standardized product.
   III. Firms are price-takers.
   a. I only
   b. II only
   c. III only
   d. I and II only
   e. I, II, and III

5. Which of the following is an example of differentiated products?
   a. Coke and Pepsi
   b. automobiles and bicycles
   c. trucks and gasoline
   d. stocks and bonds
   e. gold and silver

Tackle the Test: Free-Response Questions

1. For each of the following characteristics, indicate which market structure(s) exhibit that characteristic.
   a. many sellers
   b. price-takers
   c. barriers to entry
   d. differentiated product

Answer (7 points)

a. 1 point: perfect competition

 1 point: monopolistic competition

b. 1 point: perfect competition

c. 1 point: monopoly

 1 point: oligopoly

d. 1 point: oligopoly

 1 point: monopolistic competition

2. a. Draw a correctly labeled graph of a perfectly competitive firm's demand curve if the market price is $10.
   b. What does the firm's marginal revenue equal any time it sells one more unit of its output?

Section 10 Review

Summary

1. The cost of using a resource for a particular activity is the opportunity cost of that resource. Some opportunity costs are **explicit costs;** they involve a direct payment of cash. Other opportunity costs, however, are **implicit costs;** they involve no outlay of money but represent the inflows of cash that are forgone. Both explicit and implicit costs should be taken into account when making decisions. Firms use capital and their owners' time, so firms should base decisions on **economic profit,** which takes into account implicit costs such as the opportunity cost of the owners' time and the **implicit cost of capital. Accounting profit,** which firms calculate for the purposes of taxes and public reporting, is often considerably larger than economic profit because it includes only explicit costs and depreciation, not implicit costs. Finally, **normal profit** is a term used to describe an economic profit equal to zero—a profit just high enough to justify the use of resources in an activity.

2. A producer chooses output according to the **optimal output rule:** produce the quantity at which marginal revenue equals marginal cost. The **marginal revenue** for each unit of output is shown by the **marginal revenue curve.** More generally, the **principle of marginal analysis** suggests that every activity should continue until marginal benefit equals marginal cost.

3. The relationship between inputs and output is represented by a firm's **production function.** In the **short run,** the quantity of a **fixed input** cannot be varied but the quantity of a **variable input,** by definition, can. In the **long run,** the quantities of all inputs can be varied. For a given amount of the fixed input, the **total product curve** shows how the quantity of output changes as the quantity of the variable input changes. The **marginal product** of an input is the increase in output that results from using one more unit of that input.

4. There are **diminishing returns to an input** when its marginal product declines as more of the input is used, holding the quantity of all other inputs fixed.

5. **Total cost,** represented by the **total cost curve,** is equal to the sum of **fixed cost,** which does not depend on output, and **variable cost,** which does depend on output. Due to diminishing returns, marginal cost, the increase in total cost generated by producing one more unit of output, normally increases as output increases.

6. **Average total cost** (also known as **average cost**) is the total cost divided by the quantity of output. Economists believe that U-**shaped average total cost curves** are typical because average total cost consists of two parts: **average fixed cost,** which falls when output increases (the

spreading effect), and **average variable cost,** which rises with output (the diminishing returns effect).

7. When average total cost is U-shaped, the bottom of the U is the level of output at which average total cost is minimized, the point of **minimum-cost output.** This is also the point at which the **marginal cost curve** crosses the average total cost curve from below. Due to gains from specialization, the marginal cost curve may slope downward initially before sloping upward, giving it a "swoosh" shape.

8. In the long run, a firm can change its fixed input and its level of fixed cost. By accepting higher fixed cost, a firm can lower its variable cost for any given output level, and vice versa. The **long-run average total cost curve** shows the relationship between output and average total cost when fixed cost has been chosen to minimize average total cost at each level of output. A firm moves along its short-run average total cost curve as it changes the quantity of output, and it returns to a point on both its short-run and long-run average total cost curves once it has adjusted fixed cost to its new output level.

9. As output increases, there are **economies of scale** if long-run average total cost decreases and **diseconomies of scale** if long-run average total cost increases. As all inputs are increased by the same proportion, there are **increasing returns to scale** if output increases by a larger proportion than the inputs; **decreasing returns to scale** if output increases by a smaller proportion; and **constant returns to scale** if output increases by the same proportion.

10. **Sunk costs** are expenditures that have already been made and cannot be recovered. Sunk costs should be ignored in making decisions about future actions because what is important is a comparison of future costs and future benefits.

11. There are four main types of market structure based on the number of firms in the industry and product differentiation: perfect competition, monopoly, oligopoly, and monopolistic competition.

12. A **monopolist** is a producer who is the sole supplier of a good without close substitutes. An industry controlled by a monopolist is a **monopoly.**

13. To persist, a monopoly must be protected by a **barrier to entry.** This can take the form of control of a natural resource or input, increasing returns to scale that give rise to a **natural monopoly,** technological superiority, or government rules that prevent entry by other firms, such as **patents** or **copyrights.**

14. In a **perfectly competitive market** all firms are **price-taking firms** and all consumers are **price-taking consumers**—no one's actions can influence the market price. Consumers are normally price-takers, but firms often are not. In a **perfectly competitive industry,** every firm in the industry is a price-taker.

15. There are two necessary conditions for a perfectly competitive industry: there are many firms, none of which has a large **market share,** and the industry produces a **standardized product** or **commodity**—goods that consumers regard as equivalent. A third condition is often satisfied as well: **free entry and exit** into and from the industry.

16. Many industries are **oligopolies:** there are only a few sellers. Oligopolies exist for more or less the same reasons that monopolies exist, but in weaker form. They are characterized by **imperfect competition:** firms compete but possess some market power.

17. **Monopolistic competition** is a market structure in which there are many competing firms, each producing a differentiated product, and there is free entry and exit in the long run. Product differentiation takes three main forms: by style or type, by location, and by quality. The extent of imperfect competition can be measured by the **concentration ratio,** or the **Herfindahl–Hirschman Index.**

Key Terms

Explicit cost, p. 530
Implicit cost, p. 530
Accounting profit, p. 531
Economic profit, p. 532
Implicit cost of capital, p. 532
Normal profit, p. 534
Principle of marginal analysis, p. 537
Marginal revenue, p. 537
Optimal output rule, p. 537
Marginal cost curve, p. 538
Marginal revenue curve, p. 538
Production function, p. 542
Fixed input, p. 542
Variable input, p. 542
Long run, p. 542
Short run, p. 542
Total product curve, p. 543
Marginal product, p. 543
Diminishing returns to an input, p. 545

Fixed cost, p. 548
Variable cost, p. 548
Total cost, p. 548
Total cost curve, p. 549
Average total cost, p. 552
Average cost, p. 552
U-shaped average total cost curve, p. 553
Average fixed cost, p. 553
Average variable cost, p. 553
Minimum-cost output, p. 555
Long-run average total cost curve, p. 561
Economies of scale, p. 562
Increasing returns to scale, p. 562
Diseconomies of scale, p. 562
Decreasing returns to scale, p. 563
Constant returns to scale, p. 563
Sunk cost, p. 563
Price-taking firm, p. 568
Price-taking consumer, p. 568

Perfectly competitive market, p. 568
Perfectly competitive industry, p. 569
Market share, p. 569
Standardized product, p. 569
Commodity, p. 569
Free entry and exit, p. 570
Monopolist, p. 571
Monopoly, p. 571
Barrier to entry, p. 571
Natural monopoly, p. 571
Patent, p. 572
Copyright, p. 572
Oligopoly, p. 573
Oligopolist, p. 573
Imperfect competition, p. 573
Concentration ratios, p. 573
Herfindahl–Hirschman Index, p. 573
Monopolistic competition, p. 575

Problems

1. Hiro owns and operates a small business that provides economic consulting services. During the year he spends $55,000 on traveling to clients and other expenses, and the computer that he owns depreciates by $2,000. If he didn't use the computer, he could sell it and earn yearly interest of $100 on the money created through this sale. Hiro's total revenue for the year is $100,000. Instead of working as a consultant for the year, he could teach economics at a small local college and make a salary of $50,000.

   a. What is Hiro's accounting profit?

   b. What is Hiro's economic profit?

   c. Should Hiro continue working as a consultant, or should he teach economics instead?

2. Jackie owns and operates a Web-design business. Her computing equipment depreciates by $5,000 per year. She runs the business out of a room in her home. If she didn't use the room as her business office, she could rent it out for $2,000 per year. Jackie knows that if she didn't run her own business, she could return to her previous job at a large software company that would pay her a salary of $60,000 per year. Jackie has no other expenses.

   a. How much total revenue does Jackie need to make in order to break even in the eyes of her accountant? That is, how much total revenue would give Jackie an accounting profit of just zero?

   b. How much total revenue does Jackie need to make in order for her to want to remain self-employed? That is, how much total revenue would give Jackie an economic profit of just zero?

3. You own and operate a bike store. Each year, you receive revenue of $200,000 from your bike sales, and it costs you $100,000 to obtain the bikes. In addition, you pay $20,000 for electricity, taxes, and other expenses per year. Instead of running the bike store, you could become an accountant and receive a yearly salary of $40,000. A large clothing retail chain wants to expand and offers to rent the store from you for $50,000 per year. How do you explain to your friends that despite making a profit, it is too costly for you to continue running your store?

4. Suppose you have just paid a nonrefundable fee of $1,000 for your meal plan for this academic term. This allows you to eat dinner in the cafeteria every evening.

   a. You are offered a part-time job in a restaurant where you can eat for free each evening. Your parents say that you should eat dinner in the cafeteria anyway, since you have already paid for those meals. Are your parents right? Explain why or why not.

   b. You are offered a part-time job in a different restaurant where, rather than being able to eat for free, you receive only a large discount on your meals. Each meal there will cost you $2; if you eat there each evening this semester, it will add up to $200. Your roommate says that you should eat in the restaurant since it costs less than the $1,000 that you paid for the meal plan. Is your roommate right? Explain why or why not.

5. You have bought a $10 ticket in advance for the college soccer game, a ticket that cannot be resold. You know that going to the soccer game will give you a benefit equal to $20. After you have bought the ticket, you hear that there will be a professional baseball post-season game at the same time. Tickets to the baseball game cost $20, and you know that going to the baseball game will give you a benefit equal to $35. You tell your friends the following: "If I had known about the baseball game before buying the ticket to the soccer game, I would have gone to the baseball game instead. But now that I already have the ticket to the soccer game, it's better for me to just go to the soccer game." Are you making the correct decision? Justify your answer by calculating the benefits and costs of your decision.

6. You are the manager of a gym, and you have to decide how many customers to admit each hour. Assume that each customer stays exactly one hour. Customers are costly to admit because they inflict wear and tear on the exercise equipment. Moreover, each additional customer generates more wear and tear than the customer before. As a result, the gym faces increasing marginal cost. The accompanying table shows the marginal cost associated with each number of customers per hour.

Quantity of customers per hour	Marginal cost of customer
0	
	$14.00
1	
	14.50
2	
	15.00
3	
	15.50
4	
	16.00
5	
	16.50
6	
	17.00
7	

   a. Suppose that each customer pays $15.25 for a one-hour workout. Use the principle of marginal analysis to find the optimal number of customers that you should admit per hour.

   b. You increase the price of a one-hour workout to $16.25. What is the optimal number of customers per hour that you should admit now?

7. Georgia and Lauren are economics students who go to a karate class together. Both have to choose how many classes to go to per week. Each class costs $20. The accompanying table shows Georgia's and Lauren's estimates of the marginal benefit that each of them gets from each class per week.

Quantity of Classes	Lauren's marginal benefit of each class	Georgia's marginal benefit of each class
0		
	$23	$28
1		
	19	22
2		
	14	15
3		
	8	7
4		

   a. Use marginal analysis to find Lauren's optimal number of karate classes per week. Explain your answer.

   b. Use marginal analysis to find Georgia's optimal number of karate classes per week. Explain your answer.

8. Changes in the prices of key commodities can have a significant impact on a company's bottom line. According to a September 27, 2007, article in the *Wall Street Journal,* "Now, with oil, gas and electricity prices soaring, companies are beginning to realize that saving energy can translate into dramatically lower costs." Another *Wall Street Journal* article, dated September 9, 2007, states, "Higher grain prices are taking an increasing financial toll." Energy is an input into virtually all types of production; corn is an input into the production of beef, chicken, high-fructose corn syrup, and ethanol (the gasoline substitute fuel).

   a. Explain how the cost of energy can be both a fixed cost and a variable cost for a company.

   b. Suppose energy is a fixed cost and energy prices rise. What happens to the company's average total cost curve? What happens to its marginal cost curve? Illustrate your answer with a diagram.

   c. Explain why the cost of corn is a variable cost but not a fixed cost for an ethanol producer.

   d. When the cost of corn goes up, what happens to the average total cost curve of an ethanol producer? What happens to its marginal cost curve? Illustrate your answer with a diagram.

9. Marty's Frozen Yogurt is a small shop that sells cups of frozen yogurt in a university town. Marty owns three frozen-yogurt machines. His other inputs are refrigerators, frozen-yogurt mix, cups, sprinkle toppings, and, of course, workers. He estimates that his daily production function when he varies the number of workers employed (and at the same

time, of course, yogurt mix, cups, and so on) is as shown in the accompanying table.

Quantity of labor (workers)	Quantity of frozen yogurt (cups)
0	0
1	110
2	200
3	270
4	300
5	320
6	330

a. What are the fixed inputs and variable inputs in the production of cups of frozen yogurt?

b. Draw the total product curve. Put the quantity of labor on the horizontal axis and the quantity of frozen yogurt on the vertical axis.

c. What is the marginal product of the first worker? The second worker? The third worker? Why does marginal product decline as the number of workers increases?

10. The production function for Marty's Frozen Yogurt is given in Problem 9. Marty pays each of his workers $80 per day. The cost of his other variable inputs is $0.50 per cup of yogurt. His fixed cost is $100 per day.

a. What is Marty's variable cost and total cost when he produces 110 cups of yogurt? 200 cups? Calculate variable and total cost for every level of output given in Problem 9.

b. Draw Marty's variable cost curve. On the same diagram, draw his total cost curve.

c. What is the marginal cost per cup for the first 110 cups of yogurt? For the next 90 cups? Calculate the marginal cost for all remaining levels of output.

11. The production function for Marty's Frozen Yogurt is given in Problem 9. The costs are given in Problem 10.

a. For each of the given levels of output, calculate the average fixed cost (*AFC*), average variable cost (*AVC*), and average total cost (*ATC*) per cup of frozen yogurt.

b. On one diagram, draw the *AFC*, *AVC*, and *ATC* curves.

c. What principle explains why the *AFC* declines as output increases? What principle explains why the *AVC* increases as output increases? Explain your answers.

d. How many cups of frozen yogurt are produced when average total cost is minimized?

12. The accompanying table shows a car manufacturer's total cost of producing cars.

Quantity of cars	TC
0	$500,000
1	540,000
2	560,000
3	570,000
4	590,000
5	620,000
6	660,000
7	720,000
8	800,000
9	920,000
10	1,100,000

a. What is this manufacturer's fixed cost?

b. For each level of output, calculate the variable cost (*VC*). For each level of output except zero, calculate the average variable cost (*AVC*), average total cost (*ATC*), and average fixed cost (*AFC*). What is the minimum-cost output?

c. For each level of output, calculate this manufacturer's marginal cost (*MC*).

d. On one diagram, draw the manufacturer's *AVC, ATC,* and *MC* curves.

13. Labor costs represent a large percentage of total costs for many firms. According to a September 1, 2007, *Wall Street Journal* article, U.S. labor costs were up 0.9% during the preceding three months and 0.8% over the three months preceding those.

a. When labor costs increase, what happens to average total cost and marginal cost? Consider a case in which labor costs are only variable costs and a case in which they are both variable and fixed costs.

An increase in labor productivity means each worker can produce more output. Recent data on productivity show that labor productivity in the U.S. nonfarm business sector grew 2% for each of the years 2005, 2006, and 2007. Annual growth in labor productivity averaged 1.5% from the mid-1970s to mid-1990s, 2.6% in the past decade, and 4% for a couple of years in the early 2000s.

b. When productivity growth is positive, what happens to the total product curve and the marginal product of labor curve? Illustrate your answer with a diagram.

c. When productivity growth is positive, what happens to the marginal cost curve and the average total cost curve? Illustrate your answer with a diagram.

d. If labor costs are rising over time on average, why would a company want to adopt equipment and methods that increase labor productivity?

14. Magnificent Blooms is a florist specializing in floral arrangements for weddings, graduations, and other events. The firm has a fixed cost associated with space and equipment of $100 per day. Each worker is paid $50 per day. The daily production function for Magnificent Blooms is shown in the accompanying table.

Quantity of labor (workers)	Quantity of floral arrangements
0	0
1	5
2	9
3	12
4	14
5	15

a. Calculate the marginal product of each worker. What principle explains why the marginal product per worker declines as the number of workers employed increases?

b. Calculate the marginal cost of each level of output. What principle explains why the marginal cost per floral arrangement increases as the number of arrangements increases?

15. You have the information shown in the accompanying table about a firm's costs. Complete the missing data.

Quantity	TC	MC	ATC	AVC
0	$20		—	—
		$20		
1	?		?	?
		10		
2	?		?	?
		16		
3	?		?	?
		20		
4	?		?	?
		24		
5	?		?	?

16. Evaluate each of the following statements. If a statement is true, explain why; if it is false, identify the mistake and try to correct it.

a. A decreasing marginal product tells us that marginal cost must be rising.

b. An increase in fixed cost increases the minimum-cost output.

c. An increase in fixed cost increases marginal cost.

d. When marginal cost is above average total cost, average total cost must be falling.

17. Mark and Jeff operate a small company that produces souvenir footballs. Their fixed cost is $2,000 per month. They can hire workers for $1,000 per worker per month. Their monthly production function for footballs is as given in the accompanying table.

Quantity of labor (workers)	Quantity of footballs
0	0
1	300
2	800
3	1,200
4	1,400
5	1,500

a. For each quantity of labor, calculate average variable cost (AVC), average fixed cost (AFC), average total cost (ATC), and marginal cost (MC).

b. On one diagram, draw the AVC, ATC, and MC curves.

c. At what level of output is Mark and Jeff's average total cost minimized?

18. You produce widgets. Currently you produce 4 widgets at a total cost of $40.

a. What is your average total cost?

b. Suppose you could produce one more (the fifth) widget at a marginal cost of $5. If you do produce that fifth widget, what will your average total cost be? Has your average total cost increased or decreased? Why?

c. Suppose instead that you could produce one more (the fifth) widget at a marginal cost of $20. If you do produce that fifth widget, what will your average total cost be? Has your average total cost increased or decreased? Why?

Market Structures: Perfect Competition and Monopoly

Section 10 explained how factors including the number of firms in the industry, the type of product sold, and the existence of barriers to entry determine the market power of firms. We learned about the four basic market structures—perfect competition, monopoly, oligopoly, and monopolistic competition. We can think about these structures as falling along a spectrum from perfect competition at one end to monopoly at the other, with monopolistic competition and oligopoly lying in between. To shed more light on the market structure spectrum, consider two very different markets introduced in previous sections: the market for organic tomatoes and the market for diamonds.

In the United States, a growing interest in healthy living has steadily increased the demand for products such as organically grown fruits and vegetables. Over the past decade, the markets for these products have been healthy as well, with an average growth rate of 20% per year. It costs a bit more to grow crops without chemical fertilizers and pesticides, but consumers are willing to pay higher prices for the benefits of fruits and vegetables grown the natural way. The farmers in each area who pioneered organic farming techniques had little competition and many prospered thanks to these higher prices.

But with profits as a lure for expanded production, the high prices were unlikely to persist. Over time, farmers already producing organically would increase their capacity, and conventional farmers would enter the organic food fray, increasing supply and driving down price. With a large and growing number of buyers and sellers, undifferentiated products, and few barriers to entry, the organic food market increasingly resembles a *perfectly competitive* market.

In contrast, the market for diamonds is dominated by one supplier, De Beers. For generations, diamonds have been valued not just for their attractive appearance, but also for their rarity. But geologists will tell you that diamonds aren't all that rare. In fact, they are fairly common and only seem rare compared to other gem-quality stones. This is because De Beers *makes* them rare: the company controls most of the world's diamond mines and limits the quantity supplied to the market. This makes De Beers resemble a *monopolist,* the sole (or almost sole) producer of a good. Because De Beers controls so much of the world's diamond supply, other firms have considerable difficulty trying to enter the diamond market and increase the quantity of the gems available.

In this section we will study how markets like those for organic tomatoes and diamonds differ, and how these markets respond to market conditions. We will see how firms positioned at opposite ends of the spectrum of market power—from perfect competition to monopoly—make key decisions about output and prices. Then, in Section 12, we will complete our exploration of market structure with a closer look at oligopoly and monopolistic competition.

Module 58
Introduction to Perfect Competition

Recall the example of the market for organic tomatoes from our discussions in Section 10. Jennifer and Jason run an organic tomato farm. But many other organic tomato farmers, such as Yves and Zoe, sell their output to the same grocery store chains. Since organic tomatoes are a standardized product, consumers don't care which farmer produces the organic tomatoes they buy. And because so many farmers sell organic tomatoes, no individual farmer has a large market share, which means that no individual farmer can have a measurable effect on market prices. These farmers are price-taking producers and their customers are price-taking consumers. The market for organic tomatoes meets the two necessary conditions for perfect competition: there are many producers each with a small market share, and the firms produce a standardized product. In this module, we build the model of perfect competition and use it to look at a representative firm in the market.

Production and Profits

Jennifer and Jason's tomato farm will maximize its profit by producing bushels of tomatoes up to the point at which marginal revenue equals marginal cost. We know this from the producer's *optimal output rule* introduced in Module 53—profit is maximized by producing the quantity at which the marginal revenue of the last unit produced is equal to its marginal cost. Always remember, $MR = MC$ at the optimal quantity of output. This will be true for any profit-maximizing firm in any market structure.

We can review how to apply the optimal output rule with the help of Table 58.1, which provides various short-run cost measures for Jennifer and Jason's farm. The second column contains the farm's variable cost, and the third column shows its total cost of output based on the assumption that the farm incurs a fixed cost of $14. The fourth column shows their marginal cost. Notice that, in this example, the marginal cost initially falls as output rises but then begins to increase, so that the marginal cost curve has the familiar "swoosh" shape.

The fifth column contains the farm's marginal revenue, which has an important feature: Jennifer and Jason's marginal revenue is constant at $18 for every output level.

table 58.1

Short-Run Costs for Jennifer and Jason's Farm

Quantity of tomatoes Q (bushels)	Variable cost VC	Total cost TC	Marginal cost of bushel $MC = \Delta TC/\Delta Q$	Marginal revenue of bushel MR	Net gain of bushel = $MR - MC$
0	$0	$14			
			$16	$18	$2
1	16	30			
			6	18	12
2	22	36			
			8	18	10
3	30	44			
			12	18	6
4	42	56			
			16	18	2
5	58	72			
			20	18	−2
6	78	92			
			24	18	−6
7	102	116			

The sixth and final column shows the calculation of the net gain per bushel of tomatoes, which is equal to marginal revenue minus marginal cost—or, equivalently in this case, market price minus marginal cost. As you can see, it is positive for the 1st through 5th bushels; producing each of these bushels raises Jennifer and Jason's profit. For the 6th bushel, however, net gain is negative: producing it would decrease, not increase, profit. So 5 bushels are Jennifer and Jason's profit-maximizing output; it is the level of output at which marginal cost rises from a level below market price to a level above market price, passing through the market price of $18 along the way.

This example illustrates an application of the optimal output rule to the particular case of a price-taking firm—the **price-taking firm's optimal output rule:** *price equals marginal cost at the price-taking firm's optimal quantity of output.* That is, a price-taking firm's profit is maximized by producing the quantity of output at which the market price is equal to the marginal cost of the last unit produced. Why? Because *in the case of a price-taking firm, marginal revenue is equal to the market price.* A price-taking firm cannot influence the market price by its actions. It always takes the market price as given because it cannot lower the market price by selling more or raise the market price by selling less. So, for a price-taking firm, the additional revenue generated by producing one more unit is always the market price. We will need to keep this fact in mind in future modules, in which we will learn that in the three other market structures, firms are *not* price takers. Therefore, marginal revenue is *not* equal to the market price.

Figure 58.1 on the next page shows Jennifer and Jason's profit-maximizing quantity of output. The figure shows the marginal cost curve, *MC,* drawn from the data in the fourth column of Table 58.1. We plot the marginal cost of increasing output from 1 to 2 bushels halfway between 1 and 2, and likewise for each incremental change. The horizontal line at $18 is Jennifer and Jason's marginal revenue curve. Remember from Module 53 that whenever a firm is a price-taker, its marginal revenue curve is a horizontal line at the market price: it can sell as much as it likes at the market price. Regardless of whether it sells more or less, the market price is unaffected. In effect, the individual firm faces a horizontal, perfectly elastic demand curve for its output—an individual demand curve that is equivalent to its marginal revenue curve. In fact, the horizontal line with the height of the market price represents the perfectly competitive

The **price-taking firm's optimal output rule** says that a price-taking firm's profit is maximized by producing the quantity of output at which the market price is equal to the marginal cost of the last unit produced.

figure 58.1

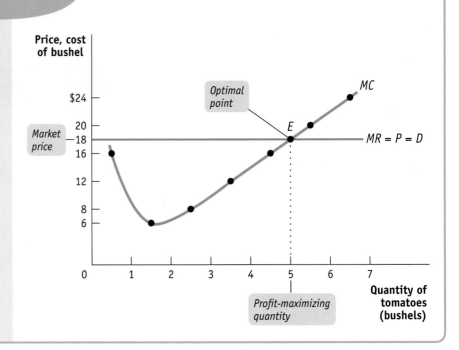

The Price-Taking Firm's Profit-Maximizing Quantity of Output

At the profit-maximizing quantity of output, the market price is equal to marginal cost. It is located at the point where the marginal cost curve crosses the marginal revenue curve, which is a horizontal line at the market price and represents the firm's demand curve. Here, the profit-maximizing point is at an output of 5 bushels of tomatoes, the output quantity at point *E*.

firm's demand, marginal revenue, and *average revenue*—the average amount of revenue taken in per unit—because price equals average revenue whenever every unit is sold for the same price. The marginal cost curve crosses the marginal revenue curve at point *E*. Sure enough, the quantity of output at *E* is 5 bushels.

Does this mean that the price-taking firm's production decision can be entirely summed up as "produce up to the point where the marginal cost of production is equal to the price"? No, not quite. Before applying the principle of marginal analysis to determine how much to produce, a potential producer must as a first step answer an "either-or" question: should it produce at all? If the answer to that question is yes, it then proceeds to the second step—a "how much" decision: maximizing profit by choosing the quantity of output at which marginal cost is equal to price.

To understand why the first step in the production decision involves an "either-or" question, we need to ask how we determine whether it is profitable or unprofitable to produce at all. In the next module we'll see that unprofitable firms shut down in the long run, but tolerate losses in the short run up to a certain point.

When Is Production Profitable?

Remember from Module 52 that firms make their production decisions with the goal of maximizing *economic profit*—a measure based on the opportunity cost of resources used by the firm. In the calculation of economic profit, a firm's total cost incorporates the implicit cost—the benefits forgone in the next best use of the firm's resources—as well as the explicit cost in the form of actual cash outlays. In contrast, *accounting profit* is profit calculated using only the explicit costs incurred by the firm. This means that economic profit incorporates all of the opportunity cost of resources owned by the firm and used in the production of output, while accounting profit does not. A firm may make positive accounting profit while making zero or even negative economic profit. It's important to understand that a firm's decisions of how much to produce, and whether or not to stay in business, should be based on economic profit, not accounting profit.

So we will assume, as usual, that the cost numbers given in Table 58.1 include all costs, implicit as well as explicit. What determines whether Jennifer

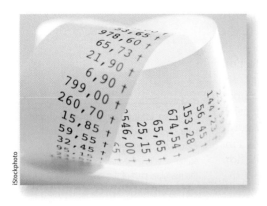

table 58.2

Short-Run Average Costs for Jennifer and Jason's Farm

Quantity of tomatoes Q (bushels)	Variable cost VC	Total cost TC	Short-run average variable cost of bushel AVC = VC/Q	Short-run average total cost of bushel ATC = TC/Q
1	$16.00	$30.00	$16.00	$30.00
2	22.00	36.00	11.00	18.00
3	30.00	44.00	10.00	14.67
4	42.00	56.00	10.50	14.00
5	58.00	72.00	11.60	14.40
6	78.00	92.00	13.00	15.33
7	102.00	116.00	14.57	16.57

and Jason's farm earns a profit or generates a loss? This depends on the market price of tomatoes—specifically, *whether the market price is more or less than the farm's minimum average total cost.*

In Table 58.2 we calculate short-run average variable cost and short-run average total cost for Jennifer and Jason's farm. These are short-run values because we take fixed cost as given. (We'll turn to the effects of changing fixed cost shortly.) The short-run average total cost curve, *ATC*, is shown in Figure 58.2, along with the marginal cost curve, *MC*, from Figure 58.1. As you can see, average total cost is minimized at point *C*, corresponding to an output of 4 bushels—the *minimum-cost output*—and an average total cost of $14 per bushel.

figure 58.2

Costs and Production in the Short Run

This figure shows the marginal cost curve, *MC*, and the short-run average total cost curve, *ATC*. When the market price is $14, output will be 4 bushels of tomatoes (the minimum-cost output), represented by point *C*. The price of $14 is equal to the firm's minimum average total cost, so at this price the firm breaks even.

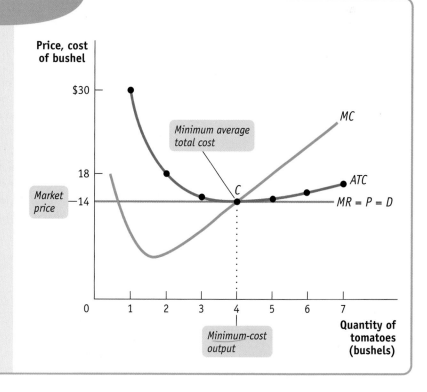

module 5 8 Introduction to Perfect Competition **587**

To see how these curves can be used to decide whether production is profitable or unprofitable, recall that profit is equal to total revenue minus total cost, $TR - TC$. This means:

- If the firm produces a quantity at which $TR > TC$, the firm is profitable.
- If the firm produces a quantity at which $TR = TC$, the firm breaks even.
- If the firm produces a quantity at which $TR < TC$, the firm incurs a loss.

We can also express this idea in terms of revenue and cost per unit of output. If we divide profit by the number of units of output, Q, we obtain the following expression for profit per unit of output:

(58-1) $\text{Profit}/Q = TR/Q - TC/Q$

TR/Q is average revenue, which is the market price. TC/Q is average total cost. So a firm is profitable if the market price for its product is more than the average total cost of the quantity the firm produces; a firm experiences losses if the market price is less than the average total cost of the quantity the firm produces. This means:

- If the firm produces a quantity at which $P > ATC$, the firm is profitable.
- If the firm produces a quantity at which $P = ATC$, the firm breaks even.
- If the firm produces a quantity at which $P < ATC$, the firm incurs a loss.

In summary, in the short run a firm will maximize profit by producing the quantity of output at which $MC = MR$. A perfectly competitive firm is a price-taker, so it can sell as many units of output as it would like at the market price. This means that for a perfectly competitive firm it is always true that $MR = P$. The firm is profitable, or breaks even, as long as the market price is greater than, or equal to, average total cost. In the next module, we develop the perfect competition model using graphs to analyze the firm's level of profit.

Module 58 AP Review

Solutions appear at the back of the book.

Check Your Understanding

1. Refer to the graph provided.

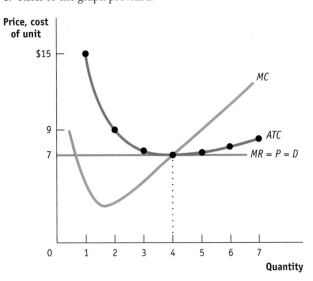

a. At what level of output does the firm maximize profit? Explain how you know.
b. At the profit-maximizing quantity of output, is the firm profitable, does it just break even, or does it earn a loss? Explain.

2. If a firm has a total cost of $500 at a quantity of 50 units, and it is at that quantity that average total cost is minimized for the firm, what is the lowest price that would allow the firm to break even (that is, earn a normal profit)? Explain.

Tackle the Test: Multiple-Choice Questions

1. A perfectly competitive firm will maximize profit at the quantity at which the firm's marginal revenue equals
   a. price.
   b. average revenue.
   c. total cost.
   d. marginal cost.
   e. demand.

2. Which of the following is correct for a perfectly competitive firm?
   - I. The marginal revenue curve is the demand curve.
   - II. The firm maximizes profit when price equals marginal cost.
   - III. The market demand curve is horizontal.
   a. I only
   b. II only
   c. III only
   d. I and II only
   e. I, II, and III

3. A firm is profitable if
   a. $TR < TC$.
   b. $AR < ATC$.
   c. $MC < ATC$.
   d. $ATC < P$.
   e. $ATC > MC$.

4. If a firm has a total cost of $200, its profit-maximizing level of output is 10 units, and it is breaking even (that is, earning a normal profit), what is the market price?
   a. $200
   b. $100
   c. $20
   d. $10
   e. $2

5. What is the firm's profit if the price of its product is $5 and it produces 500 units of output at a total cost of $1,000?
   a. $5,000
   b. $2,500
   c. $1,500
   d. −$1,500
   e. −$2,500

Tackle the Test: Free-Response Questions

1. Draw a correctly labeled graph showing a profit-maximizing perfectly competitive firm producing at its minimum average total cost.

Answer (6 points)

1 point: Vertical axis and horizontal axis labels are correct ("Price, cost of unit" on vertical axis; "Quantity" on horizontal axis).

1 point: The line representing demand, marginal revenue, and price is horizontal and correctly labeled.

1 point: Marginal cost is "swoosh" shaped or upward sloping and correctly labeled.

1 point: Average total cost is U-shaped and correctly labeled.

1 point: Quantity is found where $MC = MR$.

1 point: Average total cost reaches its minimum point at the profit-maximizing level of output.

2. Refer to the table provided. Price is equal to $14.
   a. Calculate the firm's marginal cost at each quantity.
   b. Determine the firm's profit-maximizing level of output.
   c. Calculate the firm's profit at the profit-maximizing level of output.

Short-Run Costs for Jennifer and Jason's Farm

Quantity of tomatoes Q (bushels)	Variable cost VC	Total cost TC
0	$0	$14
1	16	30
2	22	36
3	30	44
4	42	56
5	58	72
6	78	92
7	102	116

- How to evaluate a perfectly competitive firm's situation using a graph
- How to determine a perfect competitor's profit or loss
- How a firm decides whether to produce or shut down in the short run

Module 59
Graphing Perfect Competition

We have just learned that for a perfectly competitive firm, a comparison of the market price to the firm's average total cost determines whether the firm is earning a profit, taking a loss, or breaking even with a normal profit of zero. Now we can evaluate the profitability of perfectly competitive firms in a variety of situations.

Interpreting Perfect Competition Graphs

Figure 59.1 illustrates how the market price determines whether a firm is profitable. It also shows how profits are depicted graphically. Each panel shows the marginal cost curve, *MC*, and the short-run average total cost curve, *ATC*. Average total cost is minimized at point *C*. Panel (a) shows the case in which the market price of tomatoes is $18 per bushel. Panel (b) shows the case in which the market price of tomatoes is lower, $10 per bushel.

In panel (a), we see that at a price of $18 per bushel the profit-maximizing quantity of output is 5 bushels, indicated by point *E*, where the marginal cost curve, *MC*, intersects the marginal revenue curve, *MR*—which for a price-taking firm is a horizontal line at the market price. At that quantity of output, average total cost is $14.40 per bushel, indicated by point *Z*. Since the price per bushel exceeds the average total cost per bushel, Jennifer and Jason's farm is profitable.

Jennifer and Jason's total profit when the market price is $18 is represented by the area of the shaded rectangle in panel (a). To see why, notice that total profit can be expressed in terms of profit per unit:

(59-1) $\text{Profit} = TR - TC = (TR/Q - TC/Q) \times Q$

or, equivalently, because *P* is equal to *TR/Q* and *ATC* is equal to *TC/Q*,

$$\text{Profit} = (P - ATC) \times Q$$

figure 59.1

Profitability and the Market Price

In panel (a) the market price is $18. The farm is profitable because price exceeds minimum average total cost, the break-even price, $14. The farm's optimal output choice is indicated by point *E*, corresponding to an output of 5 bushels. The average total cost of producing 5 bushels is indicated by point *Z* on the *ATC* curve, corresponding to an amount of $14.40. The vertical distance between *E* and *Z* corresponds to the farm's per-unit profit, $18.00 − $14.40 = $3.60. Total profit is given by the area of the shaded rectangle, 5 × $3.60 = $18.00. In panel (b) the market price is $10; the farm is unprofitable because the price falls below the minimum average total cost, $14. The farm's optimal output choice when producing is indicated by point *A*, corresponding to an output of 3 bushels. The farm's per-unit loss, $14.67 − $10.00 = $4.67, is represented by the vertical distance between *A* and *Y*. The farm's total loss is represented by the shaded rectangle, 3 × $4.67 = $14.00 (adjusted for rounding error).

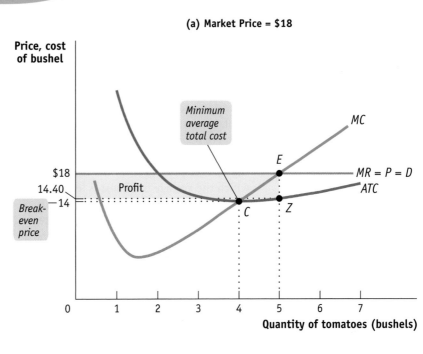

(a) Market Price = $18

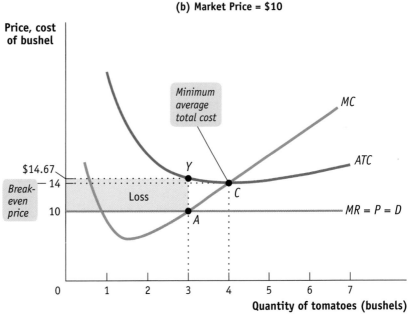

(b) Market Price = $10

The height of the shaded rectangle in panel (a) corresponds to the vertical distance between points *E* and *Z*. It is equal to *P* − *ATC* = $18.00 − $14.40 = $3.60 per bushel. The shaded rectangle has a width equal to the output: *Q* = 5 bushels. So the area of that rectangle is equal to Jennifer and Jason's profit: 5 bushels × $3.60 profit per bushel = $18.

What about the situation illustrated in panel (b)? Here the market price of tomatoes is $10 per bushel. Producing until price equals marginal cost leads to a profit-maximizing output of 3 bushels, indicated by point *A*. At this output, Jennifer and Jason have an average total cost of $14.67 per bushel, indicated by point *Y*. At their

The **break-even price** of a price-taking firm is the market price at which it earns zero profits.

profit-maximizing output quantity—3 bushels—average total cost exceeds the market price. This means that Jennifer and Jason's farm generates a loss, not a profit.

How much do they lose by producing when the market price is $10? On each bushel they lose $ATC - P = \$14.67 - \$10.00 = \$4.67$, an amount corresponding to the vertical distance between points A and Y. And they produce 3 bushels, which corresponds to the width of the shaded rectangle. So the total value of the losses is $\$4.67 \times 3 = \$14.00$ (adjusted for rounding error), an amount that corresponds to the area of the shaded rectangle in panel (b).

But how does a producer know, in general, whether or not its business will be profitable? It turns out that the crucial test lies in a comparison of the market price to the firm's *minimum average total cost*. On Jennifer and Jason's farm, average total cost reaches its minimum, $14, at an output of 4 bushels, indicated by point C. Whenever the market price exceeds the minimum average total cost, there are output levels for which the average total cost is less than the market price. In other words, the producer can find a level of output at which the firm makes a profit. So Jennifer and Jason's farm will be profitable whenever the market price exceeds $14. And they will achieve the highest possible profit by producing the quantity at which marginal cost equals price.

Conversely, if the market price is less than the minimum average total cost, there is no output level at which price exceeds average total cost. As a result, the firm will be unprofitable at any quantity of output. As we saw, at a price of $10—an amount less than the minimum average total cost—Jennifer and Jason did indeed lose money. By producing the quantity at which marginal cost equaled price, Jennifer and Jason did the best they could, but the best they could do was a loss of $14. Any other quantity would have increased the size of their loss.

The minimum average total cost of a price-taking firm is called its **break-even price,** the price at which it earns zero economic profit (which we now know as a *normal profit*). A firm will earn positive profit when the market price is above the break-even price, and it will suffer losses when the market price is below the break-even price. Jennifer and Jason's break-even price of $14 is the price at point C in Figure 59.1.

So the rule for determining whether a firm is profitable depends on a comparison of the market price of the good to the firm's break-even price—its minimum average total cost:

- Whenever the market price exceeds the minimum average total cost, the producer is profitable.

- Whenever the market price equals the minimum average total cost, the producer breaks even.

- Whenever the market price is less than the minimum average total cost, the producer is unprofitable.

The Short-Run Production Decision

You might be tempted to say that if a firm is unprofitable because the market price is below its minimum average total cost, it shouldn't produce any output. In the short run, however, this conclusion isn't right. In the short run, sometimes the firm should produce even if price falls below minimum average total cost. The reason is that total cost includes *fixed cost*—cost that does not depend on the amount of output produced and can be altered only in the long run. In the short run, fixed cost must still be paid, regardless of whether or not a firm produces. For example, if Jennifer and Jason have rented a tractor for the year, they have to pay the rent on the tractor regardless of whether they produce any tomatoes. *Since it cannot be changed in the short run, their fixed cost is irrelevant to their decision about whether to produce or shut down in the short run.* Although fixed cost should play no role in the decision about whether to produce in the short run, another type of cost—variable cost—does matter. Part of the variable cost for Jennifer and Jason is the wage cost of workers who must be hired to help with planting and harvesting. Variable cost can be eliminated by *not* producing, which makes it a critical consideration when determining whether or not to produce in the short run.

Let's turn to Figure 59.2: it shows both the short-run average total cost curve, *ATC*, and the short-run average variable cost curve, *AVC*, drawn from the information in Table 59.1. Recall that the difference between the two curves—the vertical distance between them—represents average fixed cost, the fixed cost per unit of output, *FC/Q*. Because the marginal cost curve has a "swoosh" shape—falling at first before rising—the short-run average variable cost curve is U-shaped: the initial fall in marginal cost causes average variable cost to fall as well, and then the rise in marginal cost eventually pulls average variable cost up again. The short-run average variable cost curve reaches its minimum value of $10 at point *A*, at an output of 3 bushels.

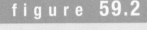

The Short-Run Individual Supply Curve

When the market price equals or exceeds Jennifer and Jason's *shut-down price* of $10, the minimum average variable cost indicated by point *A*, they will produce the output quantity at which marginal cost is equal to price. So at any price equal to or above the minimum average *variable* cost, the short-run individual supply curve is the firm's marginal cost curve; this corresponds to the upward-sloping segment of the individual supply curve. When market price falls below minimum average variable cost, the firm ceases operation in the short run. This corresponds to the vertical segment of the individual supply curve along the vertical axis.

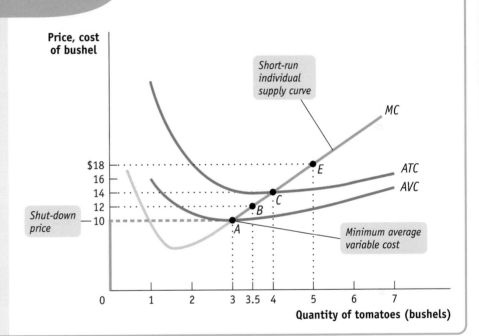

The Shut-Down Price

We are now prepared to analyze the optimal production decision in the short run. We have two cases to consider:

- When the market price is below the minimum average *variable* cost
- When the market price is greater than or equal to the minimum average *variable* cost

When the market price is below the minimum average variable cost, the price the firm receives per unit is not covering its variable cost per unit. A firm in this situation should cease production immediately. Why? Because there is no level of output at which the firm's total revenue covers its variable cost—the cost it can avoid by not operating. In this case the firm maximizes its profit by not producing at all—by, in effect, minimizing its loss. It will still incur a fixed cost in the short run, but it will no longer incur any variable cost. This means that the minimum average variable cost determines the **shut-down price,** the price at which the firm ceases production in the short run.

When price is greater than minimum average variable cost, however, the firm should produce in the short run. In this case, the firm maximizes profit—or minimizes loss—by choosing the output level at which its marginal cost is equal to the market price. For example, if the market price of tomatoes is $18 per bushel, Jennifer and Jason should

A firm will cease production in the short run if the market price falls below the **shut-down price,** which is equal to minimum average variable cost.

produce at point E in Figure 59.2, corresponding to an output of 5 bushels. Note that point C in Figure 59.2 corresponds to the farm's break-even price of $14 per bushel. Since E lies above C, Jennifer and Jason's farm will be profitable; they will generate a per-bushel profit of $18.00 - $14.40 = $3.60 when the market price is $18.

But what if the market price lies between the shut-down price and the break-even price—that is, between the minimum average *variable* cost and the minimum average *total* cost? In the case of Jennifer and Jason's farm, this corresponds to prices anywhere between $10 and $14—say, a market price of $12. At $12, Jennifer and Jason's farm is not profitable; since the market price is below the minimum average total cost, the farm is losing (on average) the difference between price and average total cost on every unit produced. Yet even though the market price isn't covering Jennifer and Jason's average total cost, it is covering their average variable cost and some—but not all—of the average fixed cost. If a firm in this situation shuts down, it will incur no variable cost but it will incur the *full* fixed cost. As a result, shutting down will generate an even greater loss than continuing to operate.

This means that whenever price falls between minimum average total cost and minimum average variable cost, the firm is better off producing some output in the short run. The reason is that by producing, it can cover its variable cost and at least some of its fixed cost, even though it is incurring a loss. In this case, the firm maximizes profit—that is, minimizes loss—by choosing the quantity of output at which its marginal cost is equal to the market price. So if Jennifer and Jason face a market price of $12 per bushel, their profit-maximizing output is given by point B in Figure 59.2, corresponding to an output of 3.5 bushels.

It's worth noting that the decision to produce when the firm is covering its variable cost but not all of its fixed cost is similar to the decision to ignore a *sunk cost*, a concept we studied previously. You may recall that a sunk cost is a cost that has already been incurred and cannot be recouped; and because it cannot be changed, it should have no effect on any current decision. In the short-run production decision, fixed cost is, in effect, like a sunk cost—it has been spent, and it can't be recovered in the short run. This comparison also illustrates why variable cost does indeed matter in the short run: it can be avoided by not producing.

And what happens if the market price is exactly equal to the shut-down price, the minimum average variable cost? In this instance, the firm is indifferent between producing 3 units or 0 units. As we'll see shortly, this is an important point when looking at the behavior of an industry as a whole. For the sake of clarity, we'll assume that the firm, although indifferent, does indeed produce output when price is equal to the shut-down price.

Putting everything together, we can now draw the **short-run individual supply curve** of Jennifer and Jason's farm, the red line in Figure 59.2; it shows how the profit-maximizing quantity of output in the short run depends on the price. As you can see, the curve is in two segments. The upward-sloping red segment starting at point A shows the short-run profit-maximizing output when market price is equal to or above the shut-down price of $10 per bushel. As long as the market price is equal to or above the shut-down price, Jennifer and Jason will produce the quantity of output at which marginal cost is equal to the market price. So at market prices equal to or above the shut-down price, the firm's short-run supply curve corresponds to its marginal cost curve. But at any market price below the minimum average variable cost, in this case, $10 per bushel—the firm shuts down and output drops to zero in the short run. This corresponds to the vertical segment of the curve that lies on top of the vertical axis.

Do firms sometimes shut down temporarily without going out of business? Yes. In fact, in some industries temporary shut-downs are routine. The most common examples are industries in which demand is highly seasonal, like outdoor amusement parks

Muntz/Stone/Getty Images

in climates with cold winters. Such parks would have to offer very low prices to entice customers during the colder months—prices so low that the owners would not cover their variable cost (principally wages and electricity). The wiser choice economically is to shut down until warm weather brings enough customers who are willing to pay a higher price.

Changing Fixed Cost

Although fixed cost cannot be altered in the short run, in the long run firms can acquire or get rid of machines, buildings, and so on. In the long run the level of fixed cost is a matter of choice, and a firm will choose the level of fixed cost that minimizes the average total cost for its desired output level. Now we will focus on an even bigger question facing a firm when choosing its fixed cost: whether to incur *any* fixed cost at all by continuing to operate.

In the long run, a firm can always eliminate fixed cost by selling off its plant and equipment. If it does so, of course, it can't produce any output—it has exited the industry. In contrast, a new firm can take on some fixed cost by acquiring machines and other resources, which puts it in a position to produce—it can enter the industry. In most perfectly competitive industries the set of firms, although fixed in the short run, changes in the long run as some firms enter or exit the industry.

Consider Jennifer and Jason's farm once again. In order to simplify our analysis, we will sidestep the issue of choosing among several possible levels of fixed cost. Instead, we will assume that if they operate at all, Jennifer and Jason have only one possible choice of fixed cost: $14. Alternatively, they can choose a fixed cost of zero if they exit the industry. It is changes in fixed cost that cause short-run average total cost curves to differ from long-run total cost curves, so with this assumption, Jennifer and Jason's short-run and long-run average total cost curves are one and the same.

Suppose that the market price of organic tomatoes is consistently less than the break-even price of $14 over an extended period of time. In that case, Jennifer and Jason never fully cover their total cost: their business runs at a persistent loss. In the long run, then, they can do better by closing their business and leaving the industry. In other words, *in the long run* firms will exit an industry if the market price is consistently less than their break-even price—their minimum average total cost.

Conversely, suppose that the price of organic tomatoes is consistently above the break-even price, $14, for an extended period of time. Because their farm is profitable, Jennifer and Jason will remain in the industry and continue producing. But things won't stop there. The organic tomato industry meets the criterion of *free entry*: there are many potential organic tomato producers because the necessary inputs are easy to obtain. And the cost curves of those potential producers are likely to be similar to those of Jennifer and Jason, since the technology used by other producers is likely to be very similar to that used by Jennifer and Jason. If the price is high enough to generate profits for existing producers, it will also attract some of these potential producers into the industry. So *in the long run* a price in excess of $14 should lead to entry: new producers will come into the organic tomato industry.

As we will see shortly, exit and entry lead to an important distinction between the *short-run industry supply curve* and the *long-run industry supply curve*.

Summing Up: The Perfectly Competitive Firm's Profitability and Production Conditions

In this module we've studied what's behind the supply curve for a perfectly competitive, price-taking firm. A perfectly competitive firm maximizes profit, or minimizes loss, by producing the quantity that equates price and marginal cost. The exception is if price is below minimum average variable cost in the short run, or below minimum average total cost in the long run, in which case the firm is better off shutting down.

table **59.1**

Summary of the Perfectly Competitive Firm's Profitability and Production Conditions

Profitability condition (minimum *ATC* = break-even price)	Result
P > minimum *ATC*	Firm profitable. Entry into industry in the long run.
P = minimum *ATC*	Firm breaks even. No entry into or exit from industry in the long run.
P < minimum *ATC*	Firm unprofitable. Exit from industry in the long run.

Production condition (minimum *AVC* = shut-down price)	Result
P > minimum *AVC*	Firm produces in the short run. If *P* < minimum *ATC*, firm covers variable cost and some but not all of fixed cost. If *P* > minimum *ATC*, firm covers all variable cost and fixed cost.
P = minimum *AVC*	Firm indifferent between producing in the short run or not. Just covers variable cost.
P < minimum *AVC*	Firm shuts down in the short run. Does not cover variable cost.

Table 59.1 summarizes the perfectly competitive firm's profitability and production conditions. It also relates them to entry into and exit from the industry in the long run. Now that we understand how a perfectly competitive *firm* makes its decisions, we can go on to look at the supply curve for a perfectly competitive *market* and the long-run equilibrium in perfect competition.

fyi

Prices Are Up . . . but So Are Costs

In 2005 Congress passed the Energy Policy Act, mandating that by the year 2012, 7.5 billion gallons of alternative fuel—mostly corn-based ethanol—be added to the American fuel supply with the goal of reducing gasoline consumption. The unsurprising result of this mandate: the demand for corn skyrocketed, along with its price. In spring 2007, the price of corn was 50% higher than it had been a year earlier.

This development caught the eye of American farmers like Ronnie Gerik of Aquilla, Texas, who, in response to surging corn prices, reduced the size of his cotton crop and increased his corn acreage by 40%. He was not alone; within a year, the amount of U.S. acreage planted in corn increased by 15%.

Although this sounds like a sure way to make a profit, Gerik was actually taking a big gamble: even though the price of corn increased, so did the cost of the raw materials needed to grow it—by 20%. Consider the cost of just two inputs:

fertilizer and fuel. Corn requires more fertilizer than other crops and, with more farmers planting corn, the increased demand for fertilizer led to a price increase. Corn also has to be transported farther away from the farm than cotton; at the same time that Gerik began shifting to greater corn production, diesel fuel became very expensive. Moreover, corn is much more sensitive to the amount of rainfall than a crop like cotton. So farmers who plant corn in drought-prone places like Texas are increasing their risk of loss. Gerik had to incorporate into his calculations his best guess of what a dry spell would cost him.

Despite all of this, what Gerik did made complete economic sense. By planting more corn, he was moving up his individual short-run supply curve for corn production. And because his individual supply curve is his marginal cost curve, his costs also went up because he had to use more inputs—inputs that had become more expensive to obtain.

Courtesy of Ronnie Gerik.

Although Gerik was taking a big gamble when he cut the size of his cotton crop to plant more corn, his decision made good economic sense.

So the moral of this story is that farmers will increase their corn acreage until the marginal cost of producing corn is approximately equal to the market price of corn—which shouldn't come as a surprise because corn production satisfies all the requirements of a perfectly competitive industry.

Module 59 AP Review

Solutions appear at the back of the book.

Check Your Understanding

1. Draw a short-run diagram showing a U-shaped average total cost curve, a U-shaped average variable cost curve, and a "swoosh"-shaped marginal cost curve. On it, indicate the range of prices for which the following actions are optimal.
   a. The firm shuts down immediately.
   b. The firm operates in the short run despite sustaining a loss.
   c. The firm operates while making a profit.

2. The state of Maine has a very active lobster industry, which harvests lobsters during the summer months. During the rest of the year, lobsters can be obtained by restaurants from producers in other parts of the world, but at a much higher price. Maine is also full of "lobster shacks," roadside restaurants serving lobster dishes that are open only during the summer. Supposing that the market demand for lobster dishes remains the same throughout the year, explain why it is optimal for lobster shacks to operate only during the summer.

Tackle the Test: Multiple-Choice Questions

For questions 1–3, refer to the graph provided.

Market Price = $20

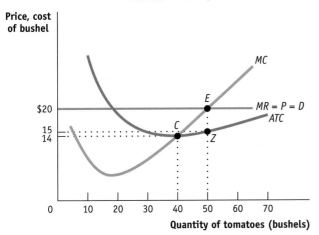

1. The firm's total revenue is equal to
   a. $14.
   b. $20.
   c. $560.
   d. $750.
   e. $1,000.

2. The firm's total cost is equal to
   a. $14.
   b. $15.
   c. $560.
   d. $750.
   e. $1,000.

3. The firm is earning a
   a. profit equal to $5.
   b. profit equal to $250.
   c. loss equal to $15.
   d. loss equal to $750.
   e. loss equal to $250.

4. A firm should continue to produce in the short run as long as price is at least equal to
   a. *MR*.
   b. *MC*.
   c. minimum *ATC*.
   d. minimum *AVC*.
   e. *AFC*.

5. At prices that motivate the firm to produce at all, the short-run supply curve for a perfect competitor corresponds to which curve?
   a. the *ATC* curve
   b. the *AVC* curve
   c. the *MC* curve
   d. the *AFC* curve
   e. the *MR* curve

Tackle the Test: Free-Response Questions

Draw a correctly labeled graph showing a perfectly competitive firm producing and incurring a loss in the short run.

Answer (10 points)

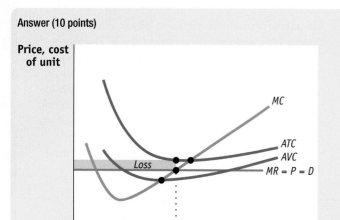

1 point: Vertical axis is labeled "Price, cost of unit" or "Dollars per unit"; horizontal axis labeled "Quantity" or "Q."

1 point: Demand curve is horizontal and labeled with some combination of *"P," "MR,"* or *"D."*

1 point: *MC* is labeled and slopes upward in the shape of a swoosh.

1 point: Profit-maximizing quantity is labeled (for example, as *"Q*"*) on the horizontal axis where *MC = MR.*

1 point: *ATC* is labeled and U-shaped.

1 point: *ATC* is above price at the profit-maximizing output.

1 point: *MC* crosses *ATC* at the lowest point on *ATC.*

1 point: *AVC* is labeled and U-shaped.

1 point: *AVC* is below price at the profit-maximizing output.

1 point: Loss rectangle is correctly located and identified.

2. Refer to the graph provided.

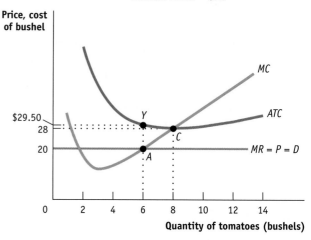

a. Assuming it is appropriate for the firm to produce in the short run, what is the firm's profit-maximizing level of output?

b. Calculate the firm's total revenue.

c. Calculate the firm's total cost.

d. Calculate the firm's profit or loss.

e. If *AVC* were $22 at the profit-maximizing level of output, would the firm produce in the short run? Explain why or why not.

Module 60
Long-Run Outcomes in Perfect Competition

What you will learn in this Module:

- Why industry behavior differs between the short run and the long run

- What determines the industry supply curve in both the short run and the long run

Up to this point we have been discussing the perfectly competitive firm's short-run situation—whether to produce or not, and if so, whether the firm earns a positive profit, breaks even with a normal profit, or takes a loss. In this module, we look at the long-run situation in a perfectly competitive market. We will see that perfect competition leads to some interesting and desirable market outcomes. Later, we will contrast these outcomes with the outcomes in monopolistic and imperfectly competitive markets.

The Industry Supply Curve

Why will an increase in the demand for organic tomatoes lead to a large price increase at first but a much smaller increase in the long run? The answer lies in the behavior of the **industry supply curve**—the relationship between the price and the total output of an industry as a whole. The industry supply curve is what we referred to in earlier modules as the supply curve or the market supply curve. But here we take some extra care to distinguish between the *individual supply curve* of a single firm and the supply curve of the industry as a whole.

As you might guess from the previous module, the industry supply curve must be analyzed in somewhat different ways for the short run and the long run. Let's start with the short run.

The Short-Run Industry Supply Curve

Recall that in the short run the number of firms in an industry is fixed—there is no entry or exit. And you may also remember that the industry supply curve is the horizontal sum of the individual supply curves of all firms—you find it by summing the total output across all suppliers at every given price. We will do that exercise here under the assumption that all the firms are alike—an assumption that makes the derivation particularly simple. So let's assume that there are 100 organic tomato farms, each with the same costs as Jennifer and Jason's farm. Each of these 100 farms will have an individual short-run supply curve like the one in Figure 59.2 from the previous module, which is reprinted on the next page for your convenience.

The **industry supply curve** shows the relationship between the price of a good and the total output of the industry as a whole.

figure 59.2

The Short-Run Individual Supply Curve

When the market price equals or exceeds Jennifer and Jason's *shut-down price* of $10, the minimum average variable cost indicated by point *A*, they will produce the output quantity at which marginal cost is equal to price. So at any price equal to or above the minimum average *variable* cost, the short-run individual supply curve is the firm's marginal cost curve; this corresponds to the upward-sloping segment of the individual supply curve. When market price falls below minimum average variable cost, the firm ceases operation in the short run. This corresponds to the vertical segment of the individual supply curve along the vertical axis.

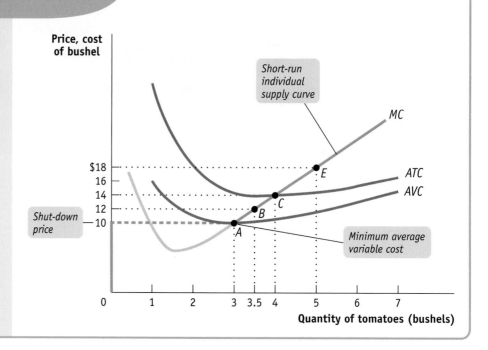

The **short-run industry supply curve** shows how the quantity supplied by an industry depends on the market price, given a fixed number of firms.

At a price below $10, no farms will produce. At a price of more than $10, each farm will produce the quantity of output at which its marginal cost is equal to the market price. As you can see from Figure 59.2, this will lead each farm to produce 4 bushels if the price is $14 per bushel, 5 bushels if the price is $18, and so on. So if there are 100 organic tomato farms and the price of organic tomatoes is $18 per bushel, the industry as a whole will produce 500 bushels, corresponding to 100 farms × 5 bushels per farm. The result is the **short-run industry supply curve,** shown as *S* in Figure 60.1. This curve shows the quantity that producers will supply at each price, *taking the number of farms as given.*

figure 60.1

The Short-Run Market Equilibrium

The short-run industry supply curve, *S*, is the industry supply curve taking the number of producers—here, 100—as given. It is generated by adding together the individual supply curves of the 100 producers. Below the shut-down price of $10, no producer wants to produce in the short run. Above $10, the short-run industry supply curve slopes upward, as each producer increases output as price increases. It intersects the demand curve, *D*, at point E_{MKT}, the point of short-run market equilibrium, corresponding to a market price of $18 and a quantity of 500 bushels.

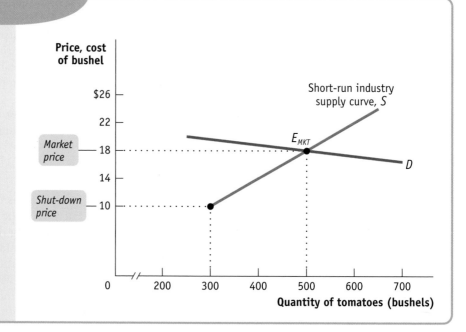

The market demand curve, labeled D in Figure 60.1, crosses the short-run industry supply curve at E_{MKT}, corresponding to a price of $18 and a quantity of 500 bushels. Point E_{MKT} is a **short-run market equilibrium:** the quantity supplied equals the quantity demanded, taking the number of farms as given. But the long run may look quite different because in the long run farms may enter or exit the industry.

There is a **short-run market equilibrium** when the quantity supplied equals the quantity demanded, taking the number of producers as given.

The Long-Run Industry Supply Curve

Suppose that in addition to the 100 farms currently in the organic tomato business, there are many other potential organic tomato farms. Suppose also that each of these potential farms would have the same cost curves as existing farms, like the one owned by Jennifer and Jason, upon entering the industry.

When will additional farms enter the industry? Whenever existing farms are making a profit—that is, whenever the market price is above the break-even price of $14 per bushel, the minimum average total cost of production. For example, at a price of $18 per bushel, new farms will enter the industry.

What will happen as additional farms enter the industry? Clearly, the quantity supplied at any given price will increase. The short-run industry supply curve will shift to the right. This will, in turn, alter the market equilibrium and result in a lower market price. Existing farms will respond to the lower market price by reducing their output, but the total industry output will increase because of the larger number of farms in the industry.

Figure 60.2 illustrates the effects of this chain of events on an existing farm and on the market; panel (a) shows how the market responds to entry, and panel (b) shows

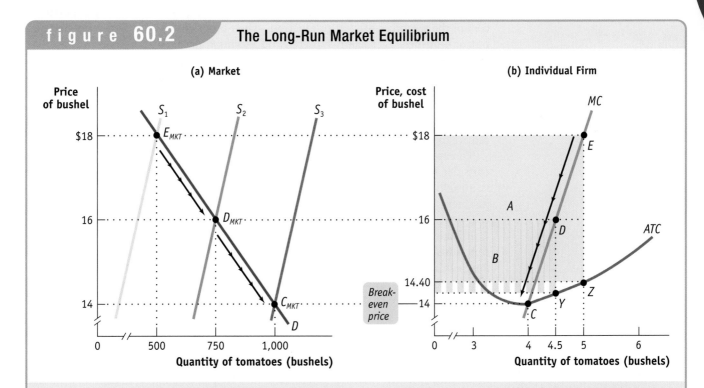

figure 60.2   The Long-Run Market Equilibrium

Point E_{MKT} of panel (a) shows the initial short-run market equilibrium. Each of the 100 existing producers makes an economic profit, illustrated in panel (b) by the green rectangle labeled A, the profit of an existing firm. Profits induce entry by additional producers, shifting the short-run industry supply curve outward from S_1 to S_2 in panel (a), resulting in a new short-run equilibrium at point D_{MKT}, at a lower market price of $16 and higher industry output. Existing firms re-duce output and profit falls to the area given by the striped rectangle labeled B in panel (b). Entry continues to shift out the short-run industry supply curve, as price falls and industry output increases yet again. Entry ceases at point C_{MKT} on supply curve S_3 in panel (a). Here market price is equal to the break-even price; existing producers make zero economic profits and there is no incentive for entry or exit. Therefore C_{MKT} is also a long-run market equilibrium.

how an individual existing farm responds to entry. (Note that these two graphs have been rescaled in comparison to Figures 59.2 and 60.1 to better illustrate how profit changes in response to price.) In panel (a), S_1 is the initial short-run industry supply curve, based on the existence of 100 producers. The initial short-run market equilibrium is at E_{MKT}, with an equilibrium market price of $18 and a quantity of 500 bushels. At this price existing farms are profitable, which is reflected in panel (b): an existing farm makes a total profit represented by the green shaded rectangle labeled A when the market price is $18.

These profits will induce new producers to enter the industry, shifting the short-run industry supply curve to the right. For example, the short-run industry supply curve when the number of farms has increased to 167 is S_2. Corresponding to this supply curve is a new short-run market equilibrium labeled D_{MKT}, with a market price of $16 and a quantity of 750 bushels. At $16, each farm produces 4.5 bushels, so that industry output is $167 \times 4.5 = 750$ bushels (rounded). From panel (b) you can see the effect of the entry of 67 new farms on an existing farm: the fall in price causes it to reduce its output, and its profit falls to the area represented by the striped rectangle labeled B.

Although diminished, the profit of existing farms at D_{MKT} means that entry will continue and the number of farms will continue to rise. If the number of farms rises to 250, the short-run industry supply curve shifts out again to S_3, and the market equilibrium is at C_{MKT}, with a quantity supplied and demanded of 1,000 bushels and a market price of $14 per bushel.

Like E_{MKT} and D_{MKT}, C_{MKT} is a short-run equilibrium. But it is also something more. Because the price of $14 is each farm's break-even price, an existing producer makes zero economic profit—neither a profit nor a loss, earning only the opportunity cost of the resources used in production—when producing its profit-maximizing output of 4 bushels. At this price there is no incentive either for potential producers to enter or for existing producers to exit the industry. So C_{MKT} corresponds to a **long-run market equilibrium**—a situation in which the quantity supplied equals the quantity demanded, given that sufficient time has elapsed for producers to either enter or exit the industry. In a long-run market equilibrium, all existing and potential producers have fully adjusted to their optimal long-run choices; as a result, no producer has an incentive to either enter or exit the industry.

To explore further the difference between short-run and long-run equilibrium, consider the effect of an increase in demand on an industry with free entry that is initially in long-run equilibrium. Panel (b) in Figure 60.3 shows the market adjustment; panels (a) and (c) show how an existing individual firm behaves during the process.

In panel (b) of Figure 60.3, D_1 is the initial demand curve and S_1 is the initial short-run industry supply curve. Their intersection at point X_{MKT} is both a short-run and a long-run market equilibrium because the equilibrium price of $14 leads to zero economic profit—and therefore neither entry nor exit. It corresponds to point X in panel (a), where an individual existing firm is operating at the minimum of its average total cost curve.

Now suppose that the demand curve shifts out for some reason to D_2. As shown in panel (b), in the short run, industry output moves along the short-run industry supply curve, S_1, to the new short-run market equilibrium at Y_{MKT}, the intersection of S_1 and D_2. The market price rises to $18 per bushel, and industry output increases from Q_X to Q_Y. This corresponds to an existing firm's movement from X to Y in panel (a) as the firm increases its output in response to the rise in the market price.

But we know that Y_{MKT} is not a long-run equilibrium because $18 is higher than minimum average total cost, so existing firms are making economic profits. This will lead additional firms to enter the industry. Over time entry will cause the short-run industry supply curve to shift to the right. In the long run, the short-run industry supply curve will have shifted out to S_2, and the equilibrium will be at Z_{MKT}—with the price

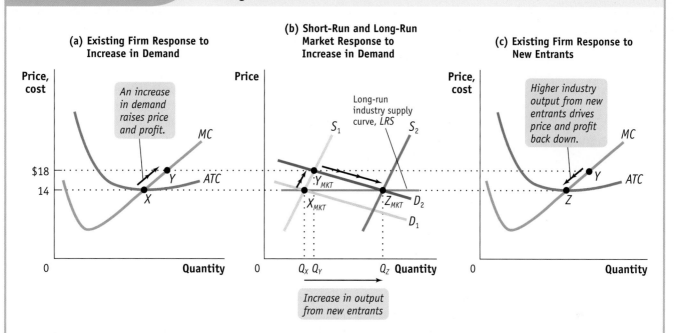

figure 60.3

The Effect of an Increase in Demand in the Short Run and the Long Run

(a) Existing Firm Response to Increase in Demand

(b) Short-Run and Long-Run Market Response to Increase in Demand

(c) Existing Firm Response to New Entrants

Panel (b) shows how an industry adjusts in the short and long run to an increase in demand; panels (a) and (c) show the corresponding adjustments by an existing firm. Initially the market is at point X_{MKT} in panel (b), a short-run and long-run equilibrium at a price of \$14 and industry output of Q_X. An existing firm makes zero economic profit, operating at point X in panel (a) at minimum average total cost. Demand increases as D_1 shifts rightward to D_2, in panel (b), raising the market price to \$18. Existing firms increase their output, and industry output moves along the short-run industry supply curve S_1 to a short-run equilibrium at Y_{MKT}. Correspondingly, the existing firm in panel (a) moves from point X to point Y. But at a price of \$18 existing firms are profitable. As shown in panel (b), in the long run

new entrants arrive and the short-run industry supply curve shifts rightward, from S_1 to S_2. There is a new equilibrium at point Z_{MKT}, at a lower price of \$14 and higher industry output of Q_Z. An existing firm responds by moving from Y to Z in panel (c), returning to its initial output level and zero economic profit. Production by new entrants accounts for the total increase in industry output, $Q_Z - Q_X$. Like X_{MKT}, Z_{MKT} is also a short-run and long-run equilibrium: with existing firms earning zero economic profit, there is no incentive for any firms to enter or exit the industry. The horizontal line passing through X_{MKT} and Z_{MKT}, LRS, is the *long-run industry supply curve:* at the break-even price of \$14, producers will produce any amount that consumers demand in the long run.

falling back to \$14 per bushel and industry output increasing yet again, from Q_Y to Q_Z. Like X_{MKT} before the increase in demand, Z_{MKT} is both a short-run and a long-run market equilibrium.

The effect of entry on an existing firm is illustrated in panel (c), in the movement from Y to Z along the firm's individual supply curve. The firm reduces its output in response to the fall in the market price, ultimately arriving back at its original output quantity, corresponding to the minimum of its average total cost curve. In fact, every firm that is now in the industry—the initial set of firms and the new entrants—will operate at the minimum of its average total cost curve, at point Z. This means that the entire increase in industry output, from Q_X to Q_Z, comes from production by new entrants.

The line LRS that passes through X_{MKT} and Z_{MKT} in panel (b) is the **long-run industry supply curve.** It shows how the quantity supplied by an industry responds to the price, given that firms have had time to enter or exit the industry.

In this particular case, the long-run industry supply curve is horizontal at \$14. In other words, in this industry supply is *perfectly elastic* in the long run: given time to enter or exit, firms will supply any quantity that consumers demand at a price of \$14.

The **long-run industry supply curve** shows how the quantity supplied responds to the price once producers have had time to enter or exit the industry.

Perfectly elastic long-run supply is actually a good assumption for many industries. In this case we speak of there being *constant costs across the industry*: each firm, regardless of whether it is an incumbent or a new entrant, faces the same cost structure (that is, they each have the same cost curve). Industries that satisfy this condition are industries in which there is a perfectly elastic supply of inputs—industries like agri-

culture or bakeries. In other industries, however, even the long-run industry supply curve slopes upward. The usual reason for this is that producers must use some input that is in limited supply (that is, their supply is at least somewhat inelastic). As the industry expands, the price of that input is driven up. Consequently, the cost structure for firms becomes higher than it was when the industry was smaller. An example is beach front resort hotels, which must compete for a limited quantity of prime beachfront property. Industries that behave like this are said to have *increasing costs across the industry*. Finally, it is possible for the long-run industry supply curve to slope downward, a condition that occurs when the cost structure for firms becomes lower as the industry expands. This is the case in industries such as the electric car industry, in which increased output allows for economies of scale in the production of lithium batteries and other specialized inputs, and thus lower input prices. A downward-sloping industry supply curve indicates *decreasing costs across the industry*.

Regardless of whether the long-run industry supply curve is horizontal, upward sloping, or downward sloping, the long-run price elasticity of supply is *higher* than the short-run price elasticity whenever there is free entry and exit. As shown in Figure 60.4, the long-run industry supply curve is always flatter than the short-run industry supply curve. The reason is entry and exit: a high price caused by an increase in demand attracts entry by new firms, resulting in a rise in industry output and an eventual fall in price; a low price caused by a decrease in demand induces existing firms to exit, leading to a fall in industry output and an eventual increase in price.

The distinction between the short-run industry supply curve and the long-run industry supply curve is very important in practice. We often see a sequence of events like that shown in Figure 60.3: an increase in demand initially leads to a large price

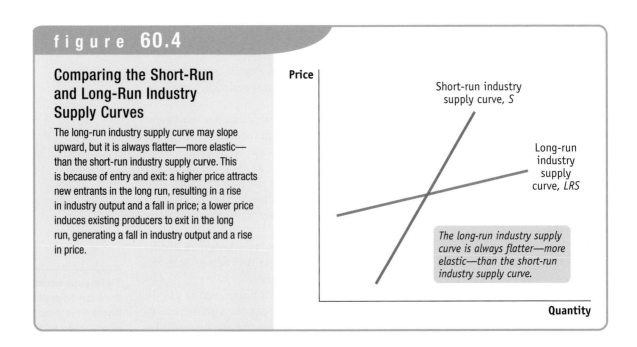

figure 60.4

Comparing the Short-Run and Long-Run Industry Supply Curves

The long-run industry supply curve may slope upward, but it is always flatter—more elastic—than the short-run industry supply curve. This is because of entry and exit: a higher price attracts new entrants in the long run, resulting in a rise in industry output and a fall in price; a lower price induces existing producers to exit in the long run, generating a fall in industry output and a rise in price.

Price

Short-run industry supply curve, *S*

Long-run industry supply curve, *LRS*

The long-run industry supply curve is always flatter—more elastic—than the short-run industry supply curve.

Quantity

increase, but prices return to their initial level once new firms have entered the industry. Or we see the sequence in reverse: a fall in demand reduces prices in the short run, but they return to their initial level as producers exit the industry.

The Cost of Production and Efficiency in Long-Run Equilibrium

Our analysis leads us to three conclusions about the cost of production and efficiency in the long-run equilibrium of a perfectly competitive industry. These results will be important in our upcoming discussion of how monopoly gives rise to inefficiency.

First, in a perfectly competitive industry in equilibrium, the value of marginal cost is the same for all firms. That's because all firms produce the quantity of output at which marginal cost equals the market price, and as price-takers they all face the same market price.

Second, in a perfectly competitive industry with free entry and exit, each firm will have zero economic profit in the long-run equilibrium. Each firm produces the quantity of output that minimizes its average total cost—corresponding to point Z in panel (c) of Figure 60.3. So the total cost of producing the industry's output is minimized in a perfectly competitive industry.

The third and final conclusion is that the long-run market equilibrium of a perfectly competitive industry is efficient: no mutually beneficial transactions go unexploited. To understand this, recall a fundamental requirement for efficiency: all consumers who are willing to pay an amount greater than or equal to the sellers' cost actually get the good. We also learned that when a market is efficient (except under certain, well-defined conditions), the market price matches all consumers willing to pay at least the market price with all sellers who have a cost of production that is less than or equal to the market price.

So in the long-run equilibrium of a perfectly competitive industry, production is efficient: costs are minimized and no resources are wasted. In addition, the allocation of goods to consumers is efficient: every consumer willing to pay the cost of producing the good gets it. Indeed, no mutually beneficial transaction is left unexploited. Moreover, this condition tends to persist over time as the environment changes: the force of competition makes producers responsive to changes in consumers' desires and to changes in technology.

fyi

A Crushing Reversal

For some reason, starting in the mid-1990s, Americans began drinking a lot more wine. Part of this increase in demand may have reflected a booming economy, but the surge in wine consumption continued even after the economy stumbled in 2001. By 2006, Americans were consuming 59% more wine than they did in 1993—a total of 2.4 gallons of wine per year per U.S. resident.

At first, the increase in wine demand led to sharply higher prices; between 1993 and 2000, the price of red wine grapes rose approximately 50%, and California grape growers earned high profits. Then, as the discussions of long-run supply foretell, there was a rapid expansion of the industry, both because existing grape growers expanded their capacity and because new growers entered the industry. Between 1994 and 2002, production of red wine grapes almost doubled. The result was predictable: the price of grapes fell as the supply curve shifted out. As demand growth slowed in 2002, prices plunged by 17%. The effect was to end the California wine industry's expansion. In fact, some grape producers began to exit the industry. By 2004, U.S. grape production had fallen by 20% compared to 2002.

John Lee/Aurora Photos

Solutions appear at the back of the book.

Check Your Understanding

1. Which of the following events will induce firms to enter an industry? Which will induce firms to exit? When will entry or exit cease? Explain your answer.
   a. A technological advance lowers the fixed cost of production of every firm in the industry.
   b. The wages paid to workers in the industry go up for an extended period of time.
   c. A permanent change in consumer tastes increases demand for the good.
   d. The price of a key input rises due to a long-term shortage of that input.

2. Assume that the egg industry is perfectly competitive and is in long-run equilibrium with a perfectly elastic long-run industry supply curve. Health concerns about cholesterol then lead to a decrease in demand. Construct a figure similar to Figure 60.3, showing the short-run behavior of the industry and how long-run equilibrium is reestablished.

Tackle the Test: Multiple-Choice Questions

1. In the long run, a perfectly competitive firm will earn
   a. a negative market return.
   b. a positive profit.
   c. a loss.
   d. a normal profit.
   e. excess profit.

2. With perfect competition, efficiency is generally attained in
   a. the short run but not the long run.
   b. the long run but not the short run.
   c. both the short run and the long run.
   d. neither the short run nor the long run.
   e. specific firms only.

3. Compared to the short-run industry supply curve, the long-run industry supply curve will be more
   a. elastic.
   b. inelastic.
   c. steeply sloped.
   d. profitable.
   e. accurate.

4. Which of the following is generally true for perfect competition?
   I. There is free entry and exit.
   II. Long-run market equilibrium is efficient.
   III. Firms maximize profits at the output level where $P = MC$.
   a. I only
   b. II only
   c. III only
   d. I and II only
   e. I, II, and III

5. Which of the following will happen in response if perfectly competitive firms are earning positive economic profit?
   a. Firms will exit the industry.
   b. The short-run industry supply curve will shift right.
   c. The short-run industry supply curve will shift left.
   d. Firm output will increase.
   e. Market price will increase.

Tackle the Test: Free-Response Questions

1. Draw a correctly labeled graph showing a perfectly competitive firm in long-run equilibrium.

2. Draw correctly labeled side-by-side graphs to show the long-run adjustment that would take place if perfectly competitive firms were earning a profit.

Answer (7 points)

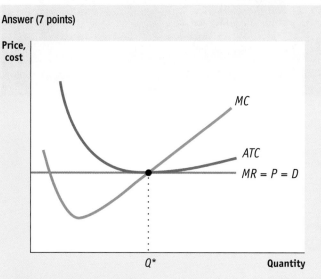

1 point: Axes are correctly labeled.

1 point: Demand curve is horizontal and labeled with some combination of "*P,*" "*MR,*" or "*D.*"

1 point: Marginal cost curve is labeled and slopes upward.

1 point: Profit-maximizing quantity is labeled on horizontal axis where $MC = MR$.

1 point: Average total cost curve is labeled and U–shaped.

1 point: Average total cost is equal to price at the profit-maximizing output

1 point: Marginal cost curve crosses the average total cost curve at the lowest point on the average total cost curve

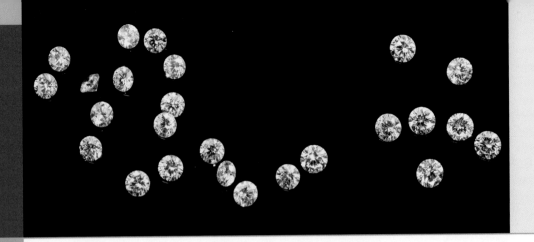

• How a monopolist
determines the
profit-maximizing price and
quantity

• How to determine whether a
monopoly is earning a profit
or a loss

Module 61
Introduction
to Monopoly

In this module we turn to monopoly, the market structure at the opposite end of the spectrum from perfect competition. A monopolist's profit-maximizing decision is subtly different from that of a price-taking producer, but it has large implications for the output produced and the welfare created. We will see the crucial role that market demand plays in leading a monopolist to behave differently from a firm in a perfectly competitive industry.

The Monopolist's Demand Curve and Marginal Revenue

Recall the firm's optimal output rule: a profit-maximizing firm produces the quantity of output at which the marginal cost of producing the last unit of output equals marginal revenue—the change in total revenue generated by the last unit of output. That is, $MR = MC$ at the profit-maximizing quantity of output. Although the optimal output rule holds for *all* firms, decisions about price and the quantity of output differ between monopolies and perfectly competitive industries due to differences in the demand curves faced by monopolists and perfectly competitive firms.

We have learned that even though the *market* demand curve always slopes downward, each of the firms that make up a perfectly competitive industry faces a horizontal, *perfectly elastic* demand curve, like D_C in panel (a) of Figure 61.1. Any attempt by an individual firm in a perfectly competitive industry to charge more than the going market price will cause the firm to lose all its sales. It can, however, sell as much as it likes at the market price. We saw that the marginal revenue of a perfectly competitive firm is simply the market price. As a result, the price-taking firm's optimal output rule is to produce the output level at which the marginal cost of the last unit produced is equal to the market price.

A monopolist, in contrast, is the sole supplier of its good. So its demand curve is simply the market demand curve, which slopes downward, like D_M in panel (b) of

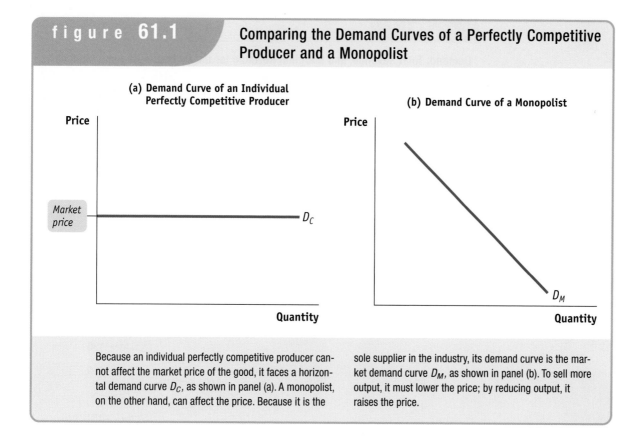

figure 61.1

Comparing the Demand Curves of a Perfectly Competitive Producer and a Monopolist

(a) Demand Curve of an Individual Perfectly Competitive Producer

Price

Market price — D_C

Quantity

(b) Demand Curve of a Monopolist

Price

D_M

Quantity

Because an individual perfectly competitive producer cannot affect the market price of the good, it faces a horizontal demand curve D_C, as shown in panel (a). A monopolist, on the other hand, can affect the price. Because it is the sole supplier in the industry, its demand curve is the market demand curve D_M, as shown in panel (b). To sell more output, it must lower the price; by reducing output, it raises the price.

Figure 61.1. This downward slope creates a "wedge" between the price of the good and the marginal revenue of the good. Table 61.1 on the next page shows how this wedge develops. The first two columns of Table 61.1 show a hypothetical demand schedule for De Beers diamonds. For the sake of simplicity, we assume that all diamonds are exactly alike. And to make the arithmetic easy, we suppose that the number of diamonds sold is far smaller than is actually the case. For instance, at a price of $500 per diamond, we assume that only 10 diamonds are sold. The demand curve implied by this schedule is shown in panel (a) of Figure 61.2 on page 611.

The third column of Table 61.1 shows De Beers's total revenue from selling each quantity of diamonds—the price per diamond multiplied by the number of diamonds sold. The last column shows marginal revenue, the change in total revenue from producing and selling another diamond.

Clearly, after the 1st diamond, the marginal revenue a monopolist receives from selling one more unit is less than the price at which that unit is sold. For example, if De Beers sells 10 diamonds, the price at which the 10th diamond is sold is $500. But the marginal revenue—the change in total revenue in going from 9 to 10 diamonds—is only $50.

Why is the marginal revenue from that 10th diamond less than the price? Because an increase in production by a monopolist has two opposing effects on revenue:

- *A quantity effect.* One more unit is sold, increasing total revenue by the price at which the unit is sold (in this case, +$500).

- *A price effect.* In order to sell that last unit, the monopolist must cut the market price on *all* units sold. This decreases total revenue (in this case, by $9 \times -\$50 = -\$450$).

The quantity effect and the price effect are illustrated by the two shaded areas in panel (a) of Figure 61.2. Increasing diamond sales from 9 to 10 means moving down the demand curve from A to B, reducing the price per diamond from $550 to $500. The green-shaded area represents the quantity effect: De Beers sells the 10th diamond at a price of $500. This is offset, however, by the price effect, represented by the orange-shaded area. In order to

table 61.1

Demand, Total Revenue, and Marginal Revenue for the De Beers Diamond Monopoly

Price of diamond P	Quantity of diamonds demanded Q	Total revenue $TR = P \times Q$	Marginal revenue $MR = \Delta TR / \Delta Q$
$1,000	0	$0	
			$950
950	1	950	
			850
900	2	1,800	
			750
850	3	2,550	
			650
800	4	3,200	
			550
750	5	3,750	
			450
700	6	4,200	
			350
650	7	4,550	
			250
600	8	4,800	
			150
550	9	4,950	
			50
500	10	5,000	
			−50
450	11	4,950	
			−150
400	12	4,800	
			−250
350	13	4,550	
			−350
300	14	4,200	
			−450
250	15	3,750	
			−550
200	16	3,200	
			−650
150	17	2,550	
			−750
100	18	1,800	
			−850
50	19	950	
			−950
0	20	0	

sell that 10th diamond, De Beers must reduce the price on all its diamonds from $550 to $500. So it loses 9 × $50 = $450 in revenue, the orange-shaded area. So, as point C indicates, the total effect on revenue of selling one more diamond—the marginal revenue—derived from an increase in diamond sales from 9 to 10 is only $50.

Point C lies on the monopolist's marginal revenue curve, labeled MR in panel (a) of Figure 61.2 and taken from the last column of Table 61.1. The crucial point about the monopolist's marginal revenue curve is that it is always *below* the demand curve. That's because of the price effect, which means that a monopolist's marginal revenue from selling an additional unit is always less than the price the monopolist receives for that unit. It is the price effect that creates the wedge between the monopolist's marginal revenue curve and the demand curve: in order to sell an additional diamond, De Beers must cut the market price on all units sold.

In fact, this wedge exists for any firm that possesses market power, such as an oligopolist, except in the case of price discrimination as explained in Module 63. Having market

figure 61.2

A Monopolist's Demand, Total Revenue, and Marginal Revenue Curves

Panel (a) shows the monopolist's demand and marginal revenue curves for diamonds from Table 61.1. The marginal revenue curve lies below the demand curve. To see why, consider point *A* on the demand curve, where 9 diamonds are sold at $550 each, generating total revenue of $4,950. To sell a 10th diamond, the price on all 10 diamonds must be cut to $500, as shown by point *B*. As a result, total revenue increases by the green area (the quantity effect: +$500) but decreases by the orange area (the price effect: –$450). So the marginal revenue from the 10th diamond is $50 (the difference between the green and orange areas), which is much lower than its price, $500. Panel (b) shows the monopolist's total revenue curve for diamonds. As output goes from 0 to 10 diamonds, total revenue increases. It reaches its maximum at 10 diamonds—the level at which marginal revenue is equal to 0—and declines thereafter. The quantity effect dominates the price effect when total revenue is rising; the price effect dominates the quantity effect when total revenue is falling.

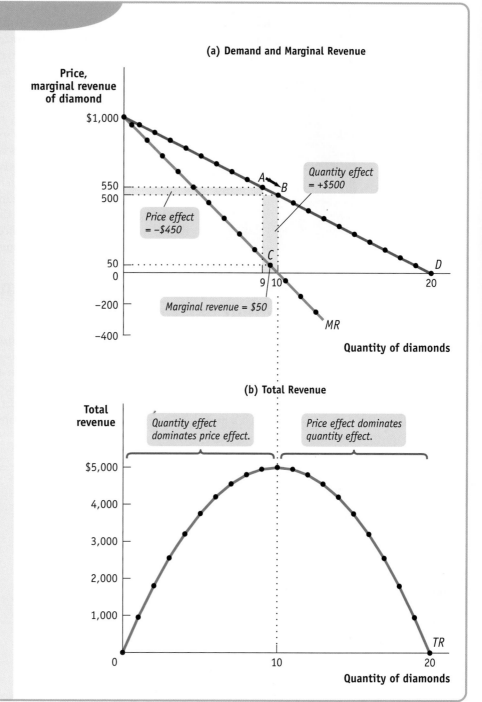

(a) Demand and Marginal Revenue

Price, marginal revenue of diamond

Quantity effect = +$500

Price effect = –$450

Marginal revenue = $50

Quantity of diamonds

(b) Total Revenue

Total revenue

Quantity effect dominates price effect.

Price effect dominates quantity effect.

Quantity of diamonds

power means that the firm faces a downward-sloping demand curve. As a result, there will always be a price effect from an increase in output for a firm with market power that charges every customer the same price. So for such a firm, the marginal revenue curve always lies below the demand curve.

Take a moment to compare the monopolist's marginal revenue curve with the marginal revenue curve for a perfectly competitive firm, which has no market power. For such a firm there is no price effect from an increase in output: its marginal revenue curve is simply its horizontal demand curve. So for a perfectly competitive firm, market price and marginal revenue are always equal.

module **61** Introduction to Monopoly **611**

To emphasize how the quantity and price effects offset each other for a firm with market power, De Beers's total revenue curve is shown in panel (b) of Figure 61.2. Notice that it is hill-shaped: as output rises from 0 to 10 diamonds, total revenue increases. This reflects the fact that *at low levels of output, the quantity effect is stronger than the price effect*: as the monopolist sells more, it has to lower the price on only very few units, so the price effect is small. As output rises beyond 10 diamonds, total revenue actually falls. This reflects the fact that *at high levels of output, the price effect is stronger than the quantity effect*: as the monopolist sells more, it now has to lower the price on many units of output, making the price effect very large. Correspondingly, the marginal revenue curve lies below zero at output levels above 10 diamonds. For example, an increase in diamond production from 11 to 12 yields only $400 for the 12th diamond, simultaneously reducing the revenue from diamonds 1 through 11 by $550. As a result, the marginal revenue of the 12th diamond is −$150.

The Monopolist's Profit-Maximizing Output and Price

To complete the story of how a monopolist maximizes profit, we now bring in the monopolist's marginal cost. Let's assume that there is no fixed cost of production; we'll also assume that the marginal cost of producing an additional diamond is constant at $200, no matter how many diamonds De Beers produces. Then marginal cost will always equal average total cost, and the marginal cost curve (and the average total cost curve) is a horizontal line at $200, as shown in Figure 61.3.

figure 61.3

The Monopolist's Profit-Maximizing Output and Price

This figure shows the demand, marginal revenue, and marginal cost curves. Marginal cost per diamond is constant at $200, so the marginal cost curve is horizontal at $200. According to the optimal output rule, the profit-maximizing quantity of output for the monopolist is at $MR = MC$, shown by point A, where the marginal cost and marginal revenue curves cross at an output of 8 diamonds. The price De Beers can charge per diamond is found by going to the point on the demand curve directly above point A, which is point B here—a price of $600 per diamond. It makes a profit of $400 × 8 = $3,200. A perfectly competitive industry produces the output level at which $P = MC$, given by point C, where the demand curve and marginal cost curves cross. So a competitive industry produces 16 diamonds, sells at a price of $200, and makes zero profit.

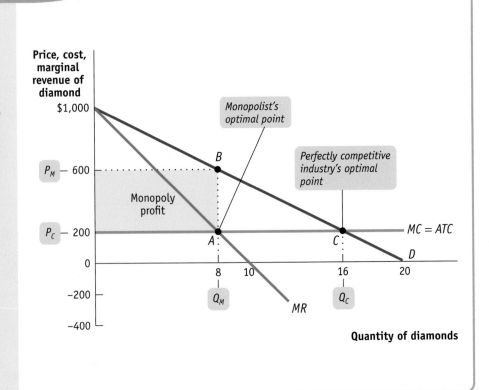

To maximize profit, the monopolist compares marginal cost with marginal revenue. If marginal revenue exceeds marginal cost, De Beers increases profit by producing more; if marginal revenue is less than marginal cost, De Beers increases profit by producing less. So the monopolist maximizes its profit by using the optimal output rule:

(61-1) $MR = MC$ at the monopolist's profit-maximizing quantity of output

The monopolist's optimal point is shown in Figure 61.3. At *A*, the marginal cost curve, *MC*, crosses the marginal revenue curve, *MR*. The corresponding output level, 8 diamonds, is the monopolist's profit-maximizing quantity of output, Q_M. The price at which consumers demand 8 diamonds is $600, so the monopolist's price, P_M, is $600—corresponding to point *B*. The average total cost of producing each diamond is $200, so the monopolist earns a profit of $600 − $200 = $400 per diamond, and total profit is $8 \times \$400 = \$3,200$, as indicated by the shaded area.

Monopoly versus Perfect Competition

When Cecil Rhodes consolidated many independent diamond producers into De Beers, he converted a perfectly competitive industry into a monopoly. We can now use our analysis to see the effects of such a consolidation.

Let's look again at Figure 61.3 and ask how this same market would work if, instead of being a monopoly, the industry were perfectly competitive. We will continue to assume that there is no fixed cost and that marginal cost is constant, so average total cost and marginal cost are equal.

If the diamond industry consists of many perfectly competitive firms, each of those producers takes the market price as given. That is, each producer acts as if its marginal revenue is equal to the market price. So each firm within the industry uses the price-taking firm's optimal output rule:

(61-2) $P = MC$ at the perfectly competitive firm's profit-maximizing quantity of output.

In Figure 61.3, this would correspond to producing at *C*, where the price per diamond, P_C, is $200, equal to the marginal cost of production. So the profit-maximizing output of an industry under perfect competition, Q_C, is 16 diamonds.

But does the perfectly competitive industry earn any profit at *C*? No: the price of $200 is equal to the average total cost per diamond. So there is no economic profit for this industry when it produces at the perfectly competitive output level.

We've already seen that once the industry is consolidated into a monopoly, the result is very different. The monopolist's marginal revenue is influenced by the price effect, so that marginal revenue is less than the price. That is,

(61-3) $P > MR = MC$ at the monopolist's profit-maximizing quantity of output

As we've already seen, the monopolist produces less than the competitive industry—8 diamonds rather than 16. The price under monopoly is $600, compared with only $200 under perfect competition. The monopolist earns a positive profit, but the competitive industry does not.

So, we can see that compared with a competitive industry, a monopolist does the following:

- produces a smaller quantity: $Q_M < Q_C$
- charges a higher price: $P_M > P_C$
- earns a profit

Monopoly Behavior and the Price Elasticity of Demand

A monopolist faces marginal revenue that is lower than the market price. But how much lower? The answer depends on the *price elasticity of demand.*

Remember that the price elasticity of demand determines how total revenue from sales changes when the price changes. If the price elasticity is greater than 1 (demand is elastic), a fall in the price increases total revenue because the rise in the quantity demanded outweighs the lower price of each unit sold. If the price elasticity is less than 1 (demand is inelastic), a lower price reduces total revenue.

When a monopolist increases output by one unit, it must reduce the market price in order to sell that unit. If the price elasticity of demand is

less than 1, this will actually reduce revenue—that is, marginal revenue will be negative. The monopolist can increase revenue by producing more only if the price elasticity of demand is greater than 1; the higher the elasticity, the closer the additional revenue is to the initial market price.

What this tells us is that the difference between monopoly behavior and perfectly competitive behavior depends on the price elasticity of demand. A monopolist that faces highly elastic demand will behave almost like a firm in a perfectly competitive industry.

For example, Amtrak has a monopoly on intercity passenger service in the Northeast Corridor, but it has very little ability to raise prices: potential train travelers will switch to cars and

KAREN BLEIER/AFP/Getty Images

planes. In contrast, a monopolist that faces less elastic demand—like most cable TV companies—will behave very differently from a perfect competitor: it will charge much higher prices and restrict output more.

Monopoly: The General Picture

Figure 61.3 involved specific numbers and assumed that marginal cost was constant, there was no fixed cost, and therefore, that the average total cost curve was a horizontal line. Figure 61.4 shows a more general picture of monopoly in action: D is the market demand curve; MR, the marginal revenue curve; MC, the marginal cost curve; and ATC, the average total cost curve. Here we return to the usual assumption that the marginal cost curve has a "swoosh" shape and the average total cost curve is U-shaped.

figure 61.4

The Monopolist's Profit

In this case, the marginal cost curve has a "swoosh" shape and the average total cost curve is U-shaped. The monopolist maximizes profit by producing the level of output at which $MR = MC$, given by point A, generating quantity Q_M. It finds its monopoly price, P_M, from the point on the demand curve directly above point A, point B here. The average total cost of Q_M is shown by point C. Profit is given by the area of the shaded rectangle.

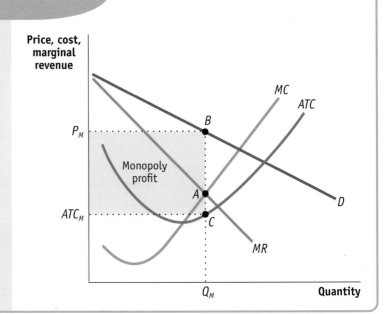

Applying the optimal output rule, we see that the profit-maximizing level of output, identified as the quantity at which marginal revenue and marginal cost intersect (see point A), is Q_M. The monopolist charges the highest price possible for this quantity, P_M, found at the height of the demand curve at Q_M (see point B). At the profit-maximizing level of output, the monopolist's average total cost is ATC_M (see point C).

Recalling how we calculated profit in Equation 59-1, profit is equal to the difference between total revenue and total cost. So we have

(61-4) $\text{Profit} = TR - TC$
$$= (P_M \times Q_M) - (ATC_M \times Q_M)$$
$$= (P_M - ATC_M) \times Q_M.$$

Profit is equal to the area of the shaded rectangle in Figure 61.4, with a height of $P_M - ATC_M$ and a width of Q_M.

We learned that a perfectly competitive industry can have profits *in the short run but not in the long run.* In the short run, price can exceed average total cost, allowing a perfectly competitive firm to make a profit. But we also know that this cannot persist. In the long run, any profit in a perfectly competitive industry will be competed away as new firms enter the market. In contrast, while a monopoly can earn a profit or a loss in the short run, barriers to entry make it possible for a monopolist to make positive profits in the long run.

Reprinted with special permission of King Feature Syndicate.

Module 61 AP Review

Solutions appear at the back of the book.

Check Your Understanding

1. Use the accompanying total revenue schedule of Emerald, Inc., a monopoly producer of 10-carat emeralds, to calculate the items listed in parts a–d. Then answer part e.

Quantity of emeralds demanded	Total revenue
1	$100
2	186
3	252
4	280
5	250

   a. the demand schedule (Hint: the average revenue at each quantity indicates the price at which that quantity would be demanded.)
   b. the marginal revenue schedule
   c. the quantity effect component of marginal revenue at each output level
   d. the price effect component of marginal revenue at each output level
   e. What additional information is needed to determine Emerald, Inc.'s profit-maximizing output?

2. Replicate Figure 61.3 and use your graph to show what happens to the following when the marginal cost of diamond production rises from $200 to $400. Use the information in Table 61.1 to identify specific numbers for prices and quantities on your graph.
   a. the marginal cost curve
   b. the profit-maximizing price and quantity
   c. the profit of the monopolist
   d. the quantity that would be produced if the diamond industry were perfectly competitive, and the associated profit

Tackle the Test: Multiple-Choice Questions

Refer to the graph provided for questions 1–4.

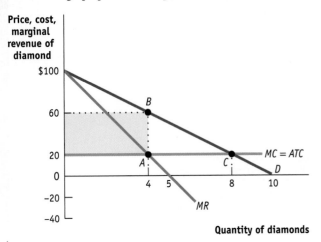

Quantity of diamonds

1. The monopolist's profit-maximizing output is
   a. 0.
   b. 4.
   c. 5.
   d. 8.
   e. 10.

2. The monopolist's total revenue equals
   a. $80.
   b. $160.
   c. $240.

   d. $300.
   e. $480.

3. The monopolist's total cost equals
   a. $20.
   b. $80.
   c. $160.
   d. $240.
   e. $480.

4. The monopolist is earning a profit equal to
   a. $0.
   b. $40.
   c. $80.
   d. $160.
   e. $240.

5. How does a monopoly differ from a perfectly competitive industry with the same costs?
   I. It produces a smaller quantity.
   II. It charges a higher price.
   III. It earns normal profits in the long run.
   a. I only
   b. II only
   c. III only
   d. I and II only
   e. I, II, and III

Tackle the Test: Free-Response Questions

1. a. Draw a correctly labeled graph showing a monopoly incurring a loss in the short run.
   b. How can the monopolist determine whether to shut down or produce at a loss in the short run?

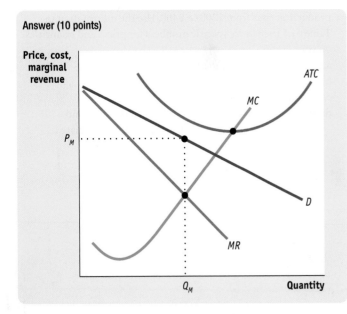

Answer (10 points)

1 point: Axes are correctly labeled.

1 point: The demand curve is labeled and negatively sloped.

1 point: The marginal revenue curve is labeled, negatively sloped, and below the demand curve.

1 point: The marginal cost curve is labeled and slopes upward in the shape of a swoosh.

1 point: The profit-maximizing quantity is labeled on the horizontal axis where $MC = MR$.

1 point: Price is determined on the demand curve above the point where $MC = MR$.

1 point: The average total cost curve is labeled and U–shaped.

1 point: Average total cost is above price at the profit-maximizing output.

1 point: The marginal cost curve crosses the average total cost curve at the lowest point on the average total cost curve.

1 point: The firm will produce despite a loss in the short run if $P \geq AVC$.

2. a. Draw a graph showing a monopoly earning a normal profit in the short run.
   b. Can a monopoly earn a normal profit in the long run? Explain.

Module 62
Monopoly and Public Policy

It's good to be a monopolist, but it's not so good to be a monopolist's customer. A monopolist, by reducing output and raising prices, benefits at the expense of consumers. But buyers and sellers always have conflicting interests. Is the conflict of interest under monopoly any different from what it is under perfect competition?

The answer is yes, because monopoly is a source of inefficiency: the losses to consumers from monopoly behavior are larger than the gains to the monopolist. Because monopoly leads to net losses for the economy, governments often try either to prevent the emergence of monopolies or to limit their effects. In this module, we will see why monopoly leads to inefficiency and examine the policies governments adopt in an attempt to prevent this inefficiency.

Welfare Effects of Monopoly

By holding output below the level at which marginal cost is equal to the market price, a monopolist increases its profit but hurts consumers. To assess whether this is a net benefit or loss to society, we must compare the monopolist's gain in profit to the consumers' loss. And what we learn is that the consumers' loss is larger than the monopolist's gain. Monopoly causes a net loss for society.

To see why, let's return to the case in which the marginal cost curve is horizontal, as shown in the two panels of Figure 62.1 on the next page. Here the marginal cost curve is MC, the demand curve is D, and, in panel (b), the marginal revenue curve is MR.

Panel (a) shows what happens if this industry is perfectly competitive. Equilibrium output is Q_C; the price of the good, P_C, is equal to marginal cost, and marginal cost is also equal to average total cost because there is no fixed cost and marginal cost is constant. Each firm is earning exactly its average total cost per unit of output, so there is no producer surplus in this equilibrium. The consumer surplus generated by the market is equal to the area of the blue-shaded triangle CS_C shown in panel (a). Since there is no producer surplus when the industry is perfectly competitive, CS_C also represents the total surplus.

figure 62.1

Monopoly Causes Inefficiency

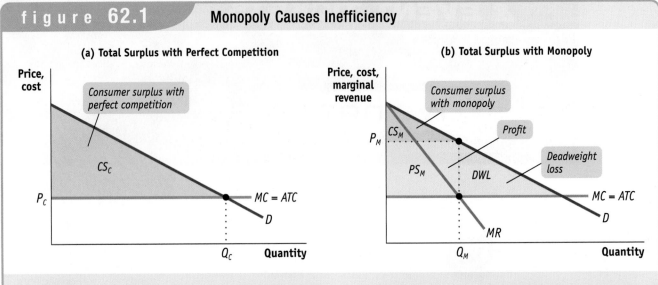

(a) Total Surplus with Perfect Competition

Price, cost

Consumer surplus with perfect competition

CS_C

P_C — MC = ATC

D

Q_C — Quantity

(b) Total Surplus with Monopoly

Price, cost, marginal revenue

Consumer surplus with monopoly

P_M — CS_M

Profit

PS_M

Deadweight loss

DWL

MC = ATC

D

MR

Q_M — Quantity

Panel (a) depicts a perfectly competitive industry: output is Q_C, and market price, P_C, is equal to MC. Since price is exactly equal to each producer's average total cost of production per unit, there is no producer surplus. So total surplus is equal to consumer surplus, the entire shaded area. Panel (b) depicts the industry under monopoly: the mo-

nopolist decreases output to Q_M and charges P_M. Consumer surplus (blue area) has shrunk: a portion of it has been captured as profit (green area), and a portion of it has been lost to deadweight loss (yellow area), the value of mutually beneficial transactions that do not occur because of monopoly behavior. As a result, total surplus falls.

Panel (b) shows the results for the same market, but this time assuming that the industry is a monopoly. The monopolist produces the level of output, Q_M, at which marginal cost is equal to marginal revenue, and it charges the price, P_M. The industry now earns profit—which is also the producer surplus in this case—equal to the area of the green rectangle, PS_M. Note that this profit is part of what was consumer surplus in the perfectly competitive market, and consumer surplus with the monopoly shrinks to the area of the blue triangle, CS_M.

By comparing panels (a) and (b), we see that in addition to the redistribution of surplus from consumers to the monopolist, another important change has occurred: the sum of profit and consumer surplus—total surplus—is *smaller* under monopoly than under perfect competition. That is, the sum of CS_M and PS_M in panel (b) is less than the area CS_C in panel (a). Previously, we analyzed how taxes could cause *deadweight loss* for society. Here we show that a monopoly creates deadweight loss equal to the area of the yellow triangle, *DWL*. So monopoly produces a net loss for society.

This net loss arises because some mutually beneficial transactions do not occur. There are people for whom an additional unit of the good is worth more than the marginal cost of producing it but who don't consume it because they are not willing to pay the monopoly price, P_M. Indeed, by driving a wedge between price and marginal cost, a monopoly acts much like a tax on consumers and produces the same kind of inefficiency.

So monopoly power detracts from the welfare of society as a whole and is a source of market failure. Is there anything government policy can do about it?

Preventing Monopoly Power

Policy toward monopolies depends crucially on whether or not the industry in question is a natural monopoly, one in which increasing returns to scale ensure that a bigger producer has lower average total cost. If the industry is *not* a natural monopoly, the best policy is to prevent a monopoly from arising or break it up if it already exists.

Government policy used to prevent or eliminate monopolies is known as *antitrust policy,* which we will discuss in Module 77. For now, let's focus on the more difficult problem of dealing with a natural monopoly.

Dealing with a Natural Monopoly

Breaking up a monopoly that isn't natural is clearly a good idea: the gains to consumers outweigh the loss to the producer. But it's not so clear whether a natural monopoly, one in which large producers have lower average total costs than small producers, should be broken up, because this would raise average total cost. For example, a town government that tried to prevent a single company from dominating local gas supply—which, as we've discussed, is almost surely a natural monopoly—would raise the cost of providing gas to its residents.

Yet even in the case of a natural monopoly, a profit-maximizing monopolist acts in a way that causes inefficiency—it charges consumers a price that is higher than marginal cost and, by doing so, prevents some potentially beneficial transactions. Also, it can seem unfair that a firm that has managed to establish a monopoly position earns a large profit at the expense of consumers.

What can public policy do about this? There are two common answers.

Public Ownership

In many countries, the preferred answer to the problem of natural monopoly has been **public ownership.** Instead of allowing a private monopolist to control an industry, the government establishes a public agency to provide the good and protect consumers' interests.

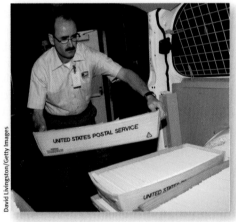

The advantage of public ownership, in principle, is that a publicly owned natural monopoly can set prices based on the criterion of efficiency rather than profit maximization. In a perfectly competitive industry, profit-maximizing behavior *is* efficient because producers set price equal to marginal cost; that is why there is no economic argument for public ownership of, say, wheat farms.

Experience suggests, however, that public ownership as a solution to the problem of natural monopoly often works badly in practice. One reason is that publicly owned firms are often less eager than private companies to keep costs down or offer high-quality products. Another is that publicly owned companies all too often end up serving political interests—providing contracts or jobs to people with the right connections.

Regulation

In the United States, the more common answer has been to leave the industry in private hands but subject it to regulation. In particular, most local utilities, like electricity, telephone service, natural gas, and so on, are covered by **price regulation** that limits the prices they can charge.

Figure 62.2 on the next page shows an example of price regulation of a natural monopoly—a highly simplified version of a local gas company. The company faces a demand curve, *D,* with an associated marginal revenue curve, *MR.* For simplicity, we assume that the firm's total cost consists of two parts: a fixed cost and a variable cost that is the same for every unit. So marginal cost is constant in this case, and the marginal cost curve (which here is also the average variable cost curve) is the horizontal line *MC.* The average total cost curve is the downward-sloping curve *ATC;* it slopes downward because the higher the output, the lower the average fixed cost (the fixed cost per unit of output). Because average total cost slopes downward over the range of output relevant for market demand, this is a natural monopoly.

In **public ownership** of a monopoly, the good is supplied by the government or by a firm owned by the government.

Price regulation limits the price that a monopolist is allowed to charge.

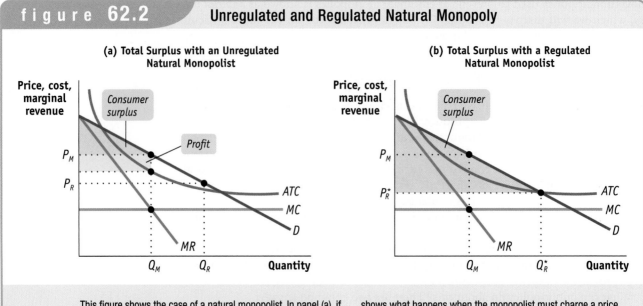

figure 62.2 — Unregulated and Regulated Natural Monopoly

(a) Total Surplus with an Unregulated Natural Monopolist

(b) Total Surplus with a Regulated Natural Monopolist

This figure shows the case of a natural monopolist. In panel (a), if the monopolist is allowed to charge P_M, it makes a profit, shown by the green area; consumer surplus is shown by the blue area. If it is regulated and must charge the lower price, P_R, output increases from Q_M to Q_R and consumer surplus increases. Panel (b) shows what happens when the monopolist must charge a price equal to average total cost, the price P_R^*. Output expands to Q_R^*, and consumer surplus is now the entire blue area. The monopolist makes zero profit. This is the greatest total surplus possible without the monopoly incurring losses.

Panel (a) illustrates a case of natural monopoly without regulation. The unregulated natural monopolist chooses the monopoly output Q_M and charges the price P_M. Since the monopolist receives a price greater than average total cost, she or he earns a profit, represented by the green-shaded rectangle in panel (a). Consumer surplus is given by the blue-shaded triangle.

Now suppose that regulators impose a price ceiling on local gas deliveries—one that falls below the monopoly price P_M but above average total cost, say, at P_R in panel (a). At that price the quantity demanded is Q_R.

Does the company have an incentive to produce that quantity? Yes. If the price the monopolist can charge is fixed at P_R by regulators, the firm can sell any quantity between zero and Q_R for the same price, P_R. Because it doesn't have to lower its price to sell more (up to Q_R), there is no price effect to bring marginal revenue below price, so the regulated price becomes the marginal revenue for the monopoly just like the market price is the marginal revenue for a perfectly competitive firm. With marginal revenue being above marginal cost and price exceeding average cost, the firm expands output to meet the quantity demanded, Q_R. This policy has appeal because at the regulated price, the monopolist produces more at a lower price.

Of course, the monopolist will not be willing to produce at all in the long run if the regulated price means producing at a loss. That is, the price ceiling has to be set high enough to allow the firm to cover its average total cost. Panel (b) shows a situation in which regulators have pushed the price down as far as possible, at the level where the average total cost curve crosses the demand curve. At any lower price the firm loses money. The price here, P_R^*, is the best regulated price: the monopolist is just willing to operate and produces Q_R^*, the quantity demanded at that price. Consumers and society gain as a result.

The welfare effects of this regulation can be seen by comparing the shaded areas in the two panels of Figure 62.2. Consumer surplus is increased by the regulation, with the gains coming from two sources. First, profits are eliminated and added instead to consumer surplus. Second, the larger output and lower price leads to an overall welfare gain—an increase in total surplus. In fact, panel (b) illustrates the largest total surplus possible.

Must Monopoly Be Controlled?

Sometimes the cure is worse than the disease. Some economists have argued that the best solution, even in the case of a natural monopoly, may be to live with it. The case for doing nothing is that attempts to control monopoly will, one way or another, do more harm than good.

The following FYI describes the case of cable television, a natural monopoly that has been alternately regulated and deregulated as politicians change their minds about the appropriate policy.

fyi

Cable Dilemmas

Most price regulation in the United States goes back a long way: electricity, local phone service, water, and gas have been regulated in most places for generations. But cable television is a relatively new industry. Until the late 1970s, only rural areas too remote to support local broadcast stations were served by cable. After 1972, new technology and looser rules made it profitable to offer cable service to major metropolitan areas; new networks like HBO and CNN emerged to take advantage of the possibilities.

Until recently, local cable TV was a natural monopoly: running cable through a town entails large fixed costs that don't depend on how many people actually subscribe. Having more than one cable company would involve a lot of wasteful duplication. But if the local cable company is a monopoly, should its prices be regulated?

At first, most local governments thought so, and cable TV was subject to price regulation. In 1984, however, Congress passed a law prohibiting most local governments from regulating cable prices. (The law was the result both of

widespread skepticism about whether price regulation was actually a good idea and of intensive lobbying by the cable companies.)

After the law went into effect, however, cable television rates increased sharply. The resulting consumer backlash led to a new law, in 1992, which once again allowed local governments to set limits on cable prices.

Was the second round of regulation a success? As measured by the prices of "basic" cable service, it was: after rising rapidly during the period of deregulation, the cost of basic service leveled off.

However, price regulation in cable applies only to "basic" service. Cable operators can try to evade the restrictions by charging more for premium channels like HBO or by offering fewer channels in the "basic" package. So some skeptics have questioned whether current regulation has actually been effective.

Yet technological change has begun providing relief to consumers in some areas. Although cable TV is a natural monopoly, there is now another means of delivering video programs to

homes: over a high-speed fiber-optic Internet connection. In some locations, fiber-optic Internet providers have begun competing aggressively with traditional cable TV companies. Studies have shown that when a second provider enters a market, prices can drop significantly, as much as 30%. In fact, the United States is currently behind on this front: today 60% of households in Hong Kong watch TV programs delivered over the Internet. What will these changes mean for the cable TV monopolies? Stay tuned.

Module 62 AP Review

Solutions appear at the back of the book.

Check Your Understanding

1. What policy should the government adopt in the following cases? Explain.
   a. Internet service in Anytown, OH, is provided by cable. Customers feel they are being overcharged, but the cable company claims it must charge prices that let it recover the costs of laying cable.
   b. The only two airlines that currently fly to Alaska need government approval to merge. Other airlines wish to fly to Alaska but need government-allocated landing slots to do so.

2. True or false? Explain your answer.
   a. Society's welfare is lower under monopoly because some consumer surplus is transformed into profit for the monopolist.
   b. A monopolist causes inefficiency because there are consumers who are willing to pay a price greater than or equal to marginal cost but less than the monopoly price.

3. Suppose a monopolist mistakenly believes that her or his marginal revenue is always equal to the market price. Assuming constant marginal cost and no fixed cost, draw a diagram comparing the level of profit, consumer surplus, total surplus, and deadweight loss for this misguided monopolist compared to a smart monopolist.

Tackle the Test: Multiple-Choice Questions

1. Which of the following statements is true of a monopoly as compared to a perfectly competitive market with the same costs?
   I. Consumer surplus is smaller.
   II. Profit is smaller.
   III. Deadweight loss is smaller.
   a. I only
   b. II only
   c. III only
   d. I and II only
   e. I, II, and III

2. Which of the following is true of a natural monopoly?
   a. It experiences diseconomies of scale.
   b. ATC is lower if there is a single firm in the market.
   c. It occurs in a market that relies on natural resources for its production.
   d. There are decreasing returns to scale in the industry.
   e. The government must provide the good or service to achieve efficiency.

3. Which of the following government actions is the most common for a natural monopoly in the United States?
   a. prevent its formation
   b. break it up using antitrust laws

   c. use price regulation
   d. public ownership
   e. elimination of the market

4. Which of the following markets is an example of a regulated natural monopoly?
   a. local cable TV
   b. gasoline
   c. cell phone service
   d. organic tomatoes
   e. diamonds

5. Which of the following is most likely to be higher for a regulated natural monopoly than for an unregulated natural monopoly?
   a. product variety
   b. quantity
   c. price
   d. profit
   e. deadweight loss

Tackle the Test: Free-Response Questions

1. Draw a correctly labeled graph showing a profit-making natural monopoly. On your graph, indicate each of the following:
   a. the monopoly's profit-maximizing output (Q_M)
   b. the monopoly's price (P_M)
   c. the monopoly's profit
   d. the regulated price that would maximize consumer surplus without creating losses for the firm (P_R)

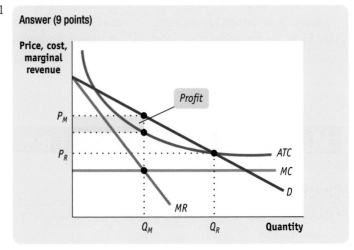

Answer (9 points)

1 point: The axes are correctly labeled.

1 point: The demand curve is labeled and sloped downward.

1 point: The marginal revenue curve is labeled, sloped downward, and below the demand curve.

1 point: The average total cost curve is labeled and downward sloping (not U-shaped!).

1 point: The marginal cost curve is labeled and below the average total cost curve.

1 point: The profit-maximizing output, Q_M, is shown on the horizontal axis where $MC = MR$.

1 point: The profit-maximizing price is found on the demand curve above the point where $MC = MR$.

1 point: The monopoly profit area is correctly shaded and identified.

1 point: The regulated price is labeled on the vertical axis to the left of the point where the demand curve crosses the average total cost curve.

2. Draw a correctly labeled graph of a natural monopoly. Use your graph to identify each of the following:
   a. consumer surplus if the market were somehow able to operate as a perfectly competitive market
   b. consumer surplus with the monopoly
   c. monopoly profit
   d. deadweight loss with the monopoly

What you will learn in this **Module:**

- The meaning of price discrimination
- Why price discrimination is so prevalent when producers have market power

Module 63
Price Discrimination

Up to this point, we have considered only the case of a monopolist who charges all consumers the same price. However, monopolists want to maximize their profits and often they do so by charging different prices for the same product. In this module we look at how monopolists increase their profits by engaging in *price discrimination*.

Price Discrimination Defined

A monopolist who charges everyone the same price is known as a **single-price monopolist.** As the term suggests, not all monopolists do this. In fact, many monopolists find that they can increase their profits by selling the same good to different customers for different prices: they practice **price discrimination.**

An example of price discrimination that travelers encounter regularly involves airline tickets. Although there are a number of airlines, most routes in the United States are serviced by only one or two carriers, which, as a result, have market power and can influence prices. So any regular airline passenger quickly becomes aware that the simple question "How much will it cost me to fly there?" rarely has a simple answer. If you are willing to buy a nonrefundable ticket a month in advance and stay over a Saturday night, the round trip may cost only $150—or less if you are a senior citizen or a student. But if you have to go on a business trip tomorrow, which happens to be Tuesday, and want to come back on Wednesday, the same round trip might cost $550. Yet the business traveler and the visiting grandparent receive the same product.

You might object that airlines are not usually monopolies—that in most flight markets the airline industry is an oligopoly. In fact, price discrimination takes place under oligopoly and monopolistic competition as well as monopoly. But it doesn't happen under perfect competition. And once we've seen why monopolists sometimes price-discriminate, we'll be in a good position to understand why it happens in other cases, too.

The Logic of Price Discrimination

To get a preliminary view of why price discrimination might be more profitable than charging all consumers the same price, imagine that Air Sunshine offers the only non-stop flights between Bismarck, North Dakota, and Ft. Lauderdale, Florida. Assume

A **single-price monopolist** charges all consumers the same price.

Sellers engage in **price discrimination** when they charge different prices to different consumers for the same good.

that there are no capacity problems—the airline can fly as many planes as the number of passengers warrants. Also assume that there is no fixed cost. The marginal cost to the airline of providing a seat is $125 however many passengers it carries.

Further assume that the airline knows there are two kinds of potential passengers. First, there are business travelers, 2,000 of whom want to travel between the destinations each week. Second, there are high school students, 2,000 of whom also want to travel each week.

Will potential passengers take the flight? It depends on the price. The business travelers, it turns out, really need to fly; they will take the plane as long as the price is no more than $550. Since they are flying purely for business, we assume that cutting the price below $550 will not lead to any increase in business travel. The students, however, have less money and more time; if the price goes above $150, they will take the bus. The implied demand curve is shown in Figure 63.1.

figure 63.1

Two Types of Airline Customers

Air Sunshine has two types of customers, business travelers willing to pay at most $550 per ticket and students willing to pay at most $150 per ticket. There are 2,000 of each kind of customer. Air Sunshine has constant marginal cost of $125 per seat. If Air Sunshine could charge these two types of customers different prices, it would maximize its profit by charging business travelers $550 and students $150 per ticket. It would capture all of the consumer surplus as profit.

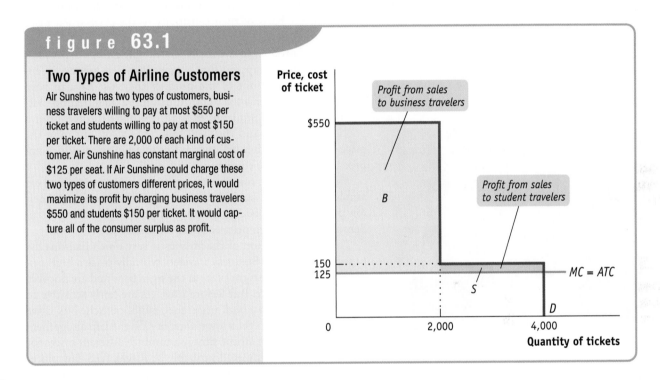

So what should the airline do? If it has to charge everyone the same price, its options are limited. It could charge $550; that way it would get as much as possible out of the business travelers but lose the student market. Or it could charge only $150; that way it would get both types of travelers but would make significantly less money from sales to business travelers.

We can quickly calculate the profits from each of these alternatives. If the airline charged $550, it would sell 2,000 tickets to the business travelers, earning a total revenue of 2,000 × $550 = $1.1 million and incurring costs of 2,000 × $125 = $250,000; so its profit would be $850,000, illustrated by the shaded area B in Figure 63.1. If the airline charged only $150, it would sell 4,000 tickets, receiving revenue of 4,000 × $150 = $600,000 and incurring costs of 4,000 × $125 = $500,000; so its profit would be $100,000. If the airline must charge everyone the same price, charging the higher price and forgoing sales to students is clearly more profitable.

What the airline would really like to do, however, is charge the business travelers the full $550 but offer $150 tickets to the students. That's a lot less than the price paid by business travelers, but it's still above marginal cost; so if the airline could sell those extra 2,000 tickets to students, it would make an additional $50,000 in profit. That is, it would make a profit equal to the areas B plus S in Figure 63.1.

It would be more realistic to suppose that there is some "give" in the demand of each group: at a price below $550, there would be some increase in business travel; and at a price above $150, some students would still purchase tickets. But this, it turns out, does not do away with the argument for price discrimination. The important point is that the two groups of consumers differ in their *sensitivity to price*—that a high price has a larger effect in discouraging purchases by students than by business travelers. As long as different groups of customers respond differently to the price, a monopolist will find that it can capture more consumer surplus and increase its profit by charging them different prices.

Price Discrimination and Elasticity

A more realistic description of the demand that airlines face would not specify particular prices at which different types of travelers would choose to fly. Instead, it would distinguish between the groups on the basis of their sensitivity to the price—their price elasticity of demand.

Suppose that a company sells its product to two easily identifiable groups of people—business travelers and students. It just so happens that business travelers are very insensitive to the price: there is a certain amount of the product they just have to have whatever the price, but they cannot be persuaded to buy much more than that no matter how cheap it is. Students, though, are more flexible: offer a good enough price and they will buy quite a lot, but raise the price too high and they will switch to something else. Which approach is best for the company in this case?

The answer is the one already suggested by our simplified example: the company should charge business travelers, with their low price elasticity of demand, a higher price than it charges students, with their high price elasticity of demand.

The actual situation of the airlines is very much like this hypothetical example. Business travelers typically place a high priority on being in the right place at the right time and are not very sensitive to the price. But leisure travelers are fairly sensitive to the price: faced with a high price, they might take the bus, drive to another airport to get a lower fare, or skip the trip altogether.

On many airline routes, the fare you pay depends on the type of traveler you are.

So why doesn't an airline simply announce different prices for business and leisure customers? First, this would probably be illegal. (U.S. law places some limits on the ability of companies to practice blatant price discrimination.) Second, even if it were legal, it would be a hard policy to enforce: business travelers might be willing to wear casual clothing and claim they were visiting family in Ft. Lauderdale in order to save $400.

So what the airlines do—quite successfully—is impose rules that indirectly have the effect of charging business and leisure travelers different fares. Business travelers usually travel during the week and want to be home on the weekend, so the round-trip fare is much higher if you don't stay over a Saturday night. The requirement of a weekend stay for a cheap ticket effectively separates business travelers from leisure travelers. Similarly, business travelers often visit several cities in succession rather than make a simple round trip; so round-trip fares are much lower than twice the one-way fare. Many business trips are scheduled on short notice, so fares are much lower if you book far in advance. Fares are also lower if you travel standby, taking your chances on whether you actually get a seat—business travelers have to make it to that meeting; people visiting their relatives don't. And because customers must show their ID at check-in, airlines make sure there are no resales of tickets between the two groups that would undermine their ability to price-discriminate—students can't buy cheap tickets and resell them to business travelers. Look at the rules that govern ticket pricing, and you will see an ingenious implementation of profit-maximizing price discrimination.

Perfect Price Discrimination

Let's return to the example of business travelers and students traveling between Bismarck and Ft. Lauderdale, illustrated in Figure 63.1, and ask what would happen if the airline could distinguish between the two groups of customers in order to charge each a different price.

Clearly, the airline would charge each group its *willingness to pay*—that is, the maximum that each group is willing to pay. For business travelers, the willingness to pay is $550; for students, it is $150. As we have assumed, the marginal cost is $125 and does not depend on output, making the marginal cost curve a horizontal line. And as we noted earlier, we can easily determine the airline's profit: it is the sum of the areas of rectangle *B* and rectangle *S*.

In this case, the consumers do not get any consumer surplus! The entire surplus is captured by the monopolist in the form of profit. When a monopolist is able to capture the entire surplus in this way, we say that the monopolist achieves **perfect price discrimination.**

In general, the greater the number of different prices charged, the closer the monopolist is to perfect price discrimination. Figure 63.2 on the next page shows a monopolist facing a downward-sloping demand curve, a monopolist who we assume is able to charge different prices to different groups of consumers, with the consumers who are willing to pay the most being charged the most. In panel (a) the monopolist charges two different prices; in panel (b) the monopolist charges three different prices. Two things are apparent:

- The greater the number of prices the monopolist charges, the lower the lowest price—that is, some consumers will pay prices that approach marginal cost.

- The greater the number of prices the monopolist charges, the more money extracted from consumers.

With a very large number of different prices, the picture would look like panel (c), a case of perfect price discrimination. Here, every consumer pays the most he or she is willing to pay, and the entire consumer surplus is extracted as profit.

Both our airline example and the example in Figure 63.2 can be used to make another point: a monopolist who can engage in perfect price discrimination doesn't cause any inefficiency! The reason is that the source of inefficiency is eliminated: all potential consumers who are willing to purchase the good at a price equal to or above marginal cost are able to do so. The perfectly price-discriminating monopolist manages to "scoop up" all consumers by offering some of them lower prices than others.

Perfect price discrimination is almost never possible in practice. At a fundamental level, the inability to achieve perfect price discrimination is a problem of prices as economic signals. When prices work as economic signals, they convey the information needed to ensure that all mutually beneficial transactions will indeed occur: the market price signals the seller's cost, and a consumer signals willingness to pay by purchasing the good whenever that willingness to pay is at least as high as the market price. The problem in reality, however, is that prices are often not perfect signals: a consumer's true willingness to pay can be disguised, as by a business traveler who claims to be a student when buying a ticket in order to obtain a lower fare. When such disguises work, a monopolist cannot achieve perfect price discrimination. However, monopolists do try to move in the direction of perfect price discrimination through a variety of pricing strategies. Common techniques for price discrimination include the following:

- *Advance purchase restrictions.* Prices are lower for those who purchase well in advance (or in some cases for those who purchase at the last minute). This separates those who are likely to shop for better prices from those who won't.

- *Volume discounts.* Often the price is lower if you buy a large quantity. For a consumer who plans to consume a lot of a good, the cost of the last unit—the marginal cost to the consumer—is considerably less than the average price. This separates those who plan to buy a lot, and so are likely to be more sensitive to price, from those who don't.

Perfect price discrimination takes place when a monopolist charges each consumer his or her willingness to pay—the maximum that the consumer is willing to pay.

Section 11 Market Structures: Perfect Competition and Monopoly

figure 63.2   Price Discrimination

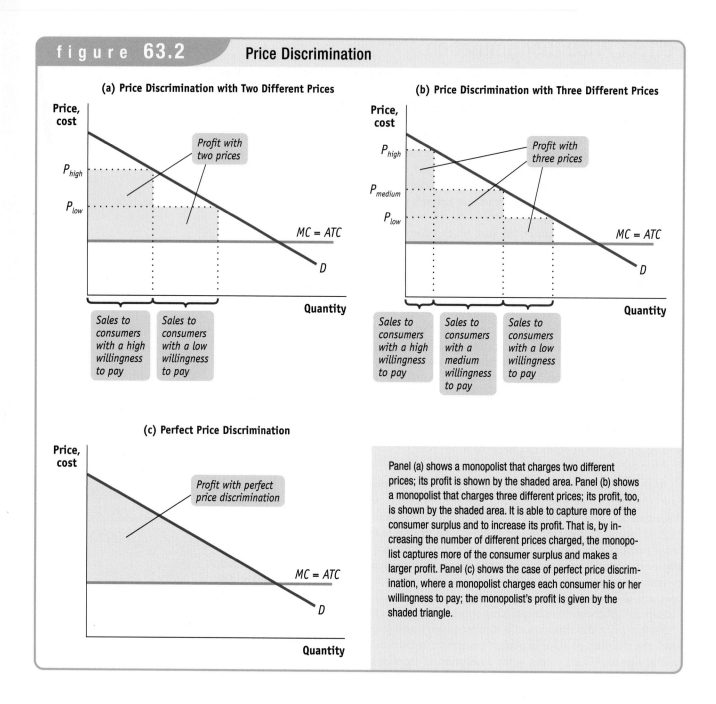

(a) Price Discrimination with Two Different Prices

Profit with two prices

Sales to consumers with a high willingness to pay

Sales to consumers with a low willingness to pay

(b) Price Discrimination with Three Different Prices

Profit with three prices

Sales to consumers with a high willingness to pay

Sales to consumers with a medium willingness to pay

Sales to consumers with a low willingness to pay

(c) Perfect Price Discrimination

Profit with perfect price discrimination

Panel (a) shows a monopolist that charges two different prices; its profit is shown by the shaded area. Panel (b) shows a monopolist that charges three different prices; its profit, too, is shown by the shaded area. It is able to capture more of the consumer surplus and to increase its profit. That is, by increasing the number of different prices charged, the monopolist captures more of the consumer surplus and makes a larger profit. Panel (c) shows the case of perfect price discrimination, where a monopolist charges each consumer his or her willingness to pay; the monopolist's profit is given by the shaded triangle.

■ *Two-part tariffs.* In a discount club like Costco or Sam's Club (which are not monopolists but monopolistic competitors), you pay an annual fee (the first part of the tariff) in addition to the price of the item(s) you purchase (the second part of the tariff). So the full price of the first item you buy is in effect much higher than that of subsequent items, making the two-part tariff behave like a volume discount.

Our discussion also helps explain why government policies on monopoly typically focus on preventing deadweight loss, not preventing price discrimination—unless it causes serious issues of equity. Compared to a single-price monopolist, price discrimination—even when it is not perfect—can increase the efficiency of the market. When a single, medium-level price is replaced by a high price and a low price, some consumers who were formerly priced out of the market will be able to purchase the good. The price discrimination increases efficiency because more of the units for which the willingness to pay (as indicated by the height of the demand curve) exceeds the marginal cost are produced and sold. Consider a drug that is disproportionately prescribed to senior citizens, who are often on fixed incomes and so are very sensitive to price. A policy that allows a drug company to charge senior citizens a low price and everyone else a high price will serve more consumers and create more total surplus than a situation in which everyone is charged the same price. But price discrimination that creates serious concerns about equity is likely to be prohibited—for example, an ambulance service that charges patients based on the severity of their emergency.

M o d u l e 63 A P R e v i e w

Solutions appear at the back of the book.

Check Your Understanding

1. True or false? Explain your answer.
   a. A single-price monopolist sells to some customers that would not find the product affordable if purchasing from a price-discriminating monopolist.
   b. A price-discriminating monopolist creates more inefficiency than a single-price monopolist because it captures more of the consumer surplus.
   c. Under price discrimination, a customer with highly elastic demand will pay a lower price than a customer with inelastic demand.

2. Which of the following are cases of price discrimination and which are not? In the cases of price discrimination, identify the consumers with high price elasticity of demand and those with low price elasticity of demand.
   a. Damaged merchandise is marked down.
   b. Restaurants have senior citizen discounts.
   c. Food manufacturers place discount coupons for their merchandise in newspapers.
   d. Airline tickets cost more during the summer peak flying season.

Tackle the Test: Multiple-Choice Questions

1. Which of the following characteristics is necessary in order for a firm to price discriminate?
   a. free entry and exit
   b. differentiated product
   c. many sellers
   d. some control over price
   e. horizontal demand curve

2. Price discrimination
   a. is the opposite of volume discounts.
   b. is a practice limited to movie theaters and the airline industry.
   c. can lead to increased efficiency in the market.
   d. rarely occurs in the real world.
   e. helps to increase the profits of perfect competitors.

3. With perfect price discrimination, consumer surplus
   a. is maximized.
   b. equals zero.
   c. is increased.
   d. cannot be determined.
   e. is the area below the demand curve above MC.

4. Which of the following is a technique used by price discriminating monopolists?
   I. advance purchase restrictions
   II. two-part tariffs
   III. volume discounts
   a. I only
   b. II only
   c. III only
   d. I and II only
   e. I, II, and III

5. A price discriminating monopolist will charge a higher price to consumers with
   a. a more inelastic demand.
   b. a less inelastic demand.
   c. higher income.
   d. lower willingness to pay.
   e. less experience in the market.

Tackle the Test: Free-Response Questions

1. a. Define price discrimination.
   b. Why do firms price discriminate?
   c. In which market structures can firms price discriminate? Explain why.
   d. Give an example of price discrimination.

2. Draw a correctly labeled graph showing a monopoly practicing perfect price discrimination. On your graph, identify the monopoly's profit. What does consumer surplus equal in this case? Explain.

Answer (5 points)

1 point: Price discrimination is the practice of charging different prices to different customers for the same product.

1 point: Firms price discriminate to increase their profits.

1 point: In order to price discriminate, firms must be in the monopoly, oligopoly, or monopolistic competition market structure.

1 point: Because rather than being price-takers, firms in these market structures have some degree of market power, which gives them the ability to charge more than one price.

1 point: An example is different prices for movie tickets charged for people of different ages.

Section ⑪ Review

Summary

1. A producer chooses output according to the **price-taking firm's optimal output rule:** produce the quantity at which price equals marginal cost. However, a firm that produces the optimal quantity may not be profitable.

2. A firm is profitable if total revenue exceeds total cost or, equivalently, if the market price exceeds its **break-even price**—minimum average total cost. If market price exceeds the break-even price, the firm is profitable. If market price is less than minimum average total cost, the firm is unprofitable. If market price is equal to minimum average total cost, the firm breaks even. When profitable, the firm's per-unit profit is $P - ATC$; when unprofitable, its per-unit loss is $ATC - P$.

3. Fixed cost is irrelevant to the firm's optimal short-run production decision. The short-run production decision depends on the firm's **shut-down price**—its minimum average variable cost—and the market price. When

the market price is equal to or exceeds the shut-down price, the firm produces the output quantity at which marginal cost equals the market price. When the market price falls below the shut-down price, the firm ceases production in the short run. This generates the firm's **short-run individual supply curve.**

4. Fixed cost matters over time. If the market price is below minimum average total cost for an extended period of time, firms will exit the industry in the long run. If market price is above minimum average total cost, existing firms are profitable and new firms will enter the industry in the long run.

5. The **industry supply curve** depends on the time period (short run or long run). When the number of firms is fixed, the **short-run industry supply curve** applies. The **short-run market equilibrium** occurs where the short-run industry supply curve and the demand curve intersect.

6. With sufficient time for entry into and exit from an industry, the **long-run industry supply curve** applies. The **long-run market equilibrium** occurs at the intersection of the long-run industry supply curve and the demand curve. At this point, no producer has an incentive to enter or exit. The long-run industry supply curve is often horizontal. It may slope upward if there is limited supply of an input, resulting in increasing costs across the industry. It may even slope downward, as in the case of decreasing costs across the industry. But the long-run industry supply curve is always more elastic than the short-run industry supply curve.

7. In the long-run market equilibrium of a competitive industry, profit maximization leads each firm to produce at the same marginal cost, which is equal to the market price. Free entry and exit means that each firm earns zero economic profit—producing the output corresponding to its minimum average total cost. So the total cost of production of an industry's output is minimized. The outcome is efficient because every consumer with willingness to pay greater than or equal to marginal cost gets the good.

8. The key difference between a monopoly and a perfectly competitive industry is that a single, perfectly competitive firm faces a horizontal demand curve but a monopolist faces a downward-sloping demand curve. This gives the monopolist market power, the ability to raise the market price by reducing output.

9. The marginal revenue of a monopolist is composed of a quantity effect (the price received from the additional unit) and a price effect (the reduction in the price at which all units are sold). Because of the price effect, a monopolist's marginal revenue is always less than the market price, and the marginal revenue curve lies below the demand curve.

10. At the monopolist's profit-maximizing output level, marginal cost equals marginal revenue, which is less than market price. At the perfectly competitive firm's profit-maximizing output level, marginal cost equals the market price. So in comparison to perfectly competitive industries, monopolies produce less, charge higher prices, and can earn profits in both the short run and the long run.

11. A monopoly creates deadweight losses by charging a price above marginal cost: the loss in consumer surplus exceeds the monopolist's profit. This makes monopolies a source of market failure and governments often make policies to prevent or end them.

12. Natural monopolies also cause deadweight losses. To limit these losses, governments sometimes impose **public ownership** and at other times impose **price regulation.** A price ceiling on a monopolist, as opposed to a perfectly competitive industry, need not cause shortages and can increase total surplus.

13. Not all monopolists are **single-price monopolists.** Monopolists, as well as oligopolists and monopolistic competitors, often engage in **price discrimination** to make higher profits, using various techniques to differentiate consumers based on their sensitivity to price and charging those with less elastic demand higher prices. A monopolist that achieves **perfect price discrimination** charges each consumer a price equal to his or her willingness to pay and captures the total surplus in the market. Although perfect price discrimination creates no inefficiency, it is practically impossible to implement.

Key Terms

Price-taking firm's optimal output rule, p. 585
Break-even price, p. 592
Shut-down price, p. 593
Short-run individual supply curve, p. 594
Industry supply curve, p. 599

Short-run industry supply curve, p. 600
Short-run market equilibrium, p. 601
Long-run market equilibrium, p. 602
Long-run industry supply curve, p. 603
Public ownership, p. 619

Price regulation, p. 619
Single-price monopolist, p. 624
Price discrimination, p. 624
Perfect price discrimination, p. 627

Problems

1. For each of the following, is the industry perfectly competitive? Referring to market share, standardization of the product, and/or free entry and exit, explain your answers.

   a. aspirin

   b. Alicia Keys concerts

   c. SUVs

2. Kate's Katering provides catered meals, and the catered meals industry is perfectly competitive. Kate's machinery costs $100 per day and is the only fixed input. Her variable cost consists of the wages paid to the cooks and the food ingredients. The variable cost per day associated with each level of output is given in the accompanying table.

Quantity of meals	VC
0	$0
10	200
20	300
30	480
40	700
50	1,000

   a. Calculate the total cost, the average variable cost, the average total cost, and the marginal cost for each quantity of output.

   b. What is the break-even price? What is the shut-down price?

   c. Suppose that the price at which Kate can sell catered meals is $21 per meal. In the short run, will Kate earn a profit? In the short run, should she produce or shut down?

   d. Suppose that the price at which Kate can sell catered meals is $17 per meal. In the short run, will Kate earn a profit? In the short run, should she produce or shut down?

   e. Suppose that the price at which Kate can sell catered meals is $13 per meal. In the short run, will Kate earn a profit? In the short run, should she produce or shut down?

3. Bob produces DVD movies for sale, which requires a building and a machine that copies the original movie onto a DVD. Bob rents a building for $30,000 per month and rents a machine for $20,000 a month. Those are his fixed costs. His variable costs per month are given in the accompanying table.

Quantity of DVDs	VC
0	$0
1,000	5,000
2,000	8,000
3,000	9,000
4,000	14,000
5,000	20,000
6,000	33,000
7,000	49,000
8,000	72,000
9,000	99,000
10,000	150,000

   a. Calculate Bob's average variable cost, average total cost, and marginal cost for each quantity of output.

   b. There is free entry into the industry, and anyone who enters will face the same costs as Bob. Suppose that currently the price of a DVD is $25. What will Bob's profit be? Is this a long-run equilibrium? If not, what will the price of DVD movies be in the long run?

4. Consider Bob's DVD company described in Problem 3. Assume that DVD production is a perfectly competitive industry. For each of the following questions, explain your answers.

   a. What is Bob's break-even price? What is his shut-down price?

   b. Suppose the price of a DVD is $2. What should Bob do in the short run?

   c. Suppose the price of a DVD is $7. What is the profit-maximizing quantity of DVDs that Bob should produce? What will his total profit be? Will he produce or shut down in the short run? Will he stay in the industry or exit in the long run?

   d. Suppose instead that the price of DVDs is $20. Now what is the profit-maximizing quantity of DVDs that Bob should produce? What will his total profit be now? Will he produce or shut down in the short run? Will he stay in the industry or exit in the long run?

5. Consider again Bob's DVD company described in Problem 3.

  a. Draw Bob's marginal cost curve.

  b. Over what range of prices will Bob produce no DVDs in the short run?

  c. Draw Bob's individual supply curve.

6. a. A profit-maximizing business incurs an economic loss of $10,000 per year. Its fixed cost is $15,000 per year. Should it produce or shut down in the short run? Should it stay in the industry or exit in the long run?

  b. Suppose instead that this business has a fixed cost of $6,000 per year. Should it produce or shut down in the short run? Should it stay in the industry or exit in the long run?

7. The first sushi restaurant opens in town. Initially, people are very cautious about eating tiny portions of raw fish, as this is a town where large portions of grilled meat have always been popular. Soon, however, an influential health report warns consumers against grilled meat and suggests that they increase their consumption of fish, especially raw fish. The sushi restaurant becomes very popular and its profit increases.

  a. What will happen to the short-run profit of the sushi restaurant? What will happen to the number of sushi restaurants in town in the long run? Will the first sushi restaurant be able to sustain its short-run profit over the long run? Explain your answers.

  b. Local steakhouses suffer from the popularity of sushi and start incurring losses. What will happen to the number of steakhouses in town in the long run? Explain your answer.

8. A perfectly competitive firm has the following short-run total costs:

Quantity	TC
0	$5
1	10
2	13
3	18
4	25
5	34
6	45

Market demand for the firm's product is given by the following market demand schedule:

Price	Quantity demanded
$12	300
10	500
8	800
6	1,200
4	1,800

  a. Calculate this firm's marginal cost and, for all output levels except zero, the firm's average variable cost and average total cost.

  b. There are 100 firms in this industry that all have costs identical to those of this firm. Draw the short-run industry supply curve. In the same diagram, draw the market demand curve.

  c. What is the market price, and how much profit will each firm make?

9. A new vaccine against a deadly disease has just been discovered. Presently, 55 people die from the disease each year. The new vaccine will save lives, but it is not completely safe. Some recipients of the shots will die from adverse reactions. The projected effects of the inoculation are given in the accompanying table:

Percent of population inoculated	Total deaths due to disease	Total deaths due to inoculation	Marginal benefit of inoculation	Marginal cost of inoculation	"Profit" of inoculation
0	55	0	—	—	—
10	45	0	—	—	—
20	36	1	—	—	—
30	28	3	—	—	—
40	21	6	—	—	—
50	15	10	—	—	—
60	10	15	—	—	—
70	6	20	—	—	—
80	3	25	—	—	—
90	1	30	—	—	—
100	0	35	—	—	—

  a. What are the interpretations of "marginal benefit" and "marginal cost" here? Calculate marginal benefit and marginal cost per each 10% increase in the rate of inoculation. Write your answers in the table.

  b. What proportion of the population should optimally be inoculated?

  c. What is the interpretation of "profit" here? Calculate the profit for all levels of inoculation.

10. The production of agricultural products like wheat is one of the few examples of a perfectly competitive industry. In this question, we analyze results from a study released by the U.S. Department of Agriculture about wheat production in the United States in 1998 and make some comparisons to wheat production in 2010.

  a. The average variable cost per acre planted with wheat was $107 per acre. Assuming a yield of 50 bushels per acre, calculate the average variable cost per bushel of wheat.

b. The average price of wheat received by a farmer in 1998 was $2.65 per bushel. Do you think the average farm would have exited the industry in the short run? Explain.

c. With a yield of 50 bushels of wheat per acre, the average total cost per farm was $3.80 per bushel. The harvested acreage for rye (a type of wheat) in the United States fell from 418,000 acres in 1998 to 250,000 in 2010. Using the information on prices and costs here and in parts a and b, explain why this might have happened.

d. Using the above information, do you think the prices of wheat were higher or lower prior to 1998? Why?

11. Skyscraper City has a subway system for which a one-way fare is $1.50. There is pressure on the mayor to reduce the fare by one-third, to $1.00. The mayor is dismayed, thinking that this will mean Skyscraper City is losing one-third of its revenue from sales of subway tickets. The mayor's economic adviser reminds her that she is focusing only on the price effect and ignoring the quantity effect. Explain why the mayor's estimate of a one-third loss of revenue is likely to be an overestimate. Illustrate with a diagram.

12. Consider an industry with the demand curve (*D*) and marginal cost curve (*MC*) shown in the accompanying diagram. There is no fixed cost. If the industry is a single-price monopoly, the monopolist's marginal revenue curve would be *MR*. Answer the following questions by naming the appropriate points or areas.

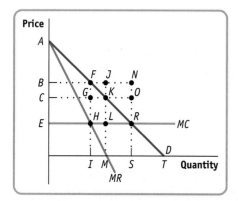

a. If the industry is perfectly competitive, what will be the total quantity produced? At what price?

b. Which area reflects consumer surplus under perfect competition?

c. If the industry is a single-price monopoly, what quantity will the monopolist produce? Which price will it charge?

d. Which area reflects the single-price monopolist's profit?

e. Which area reflects consumer surplus under single-price monopoly?

f. Which area reflects the deadweight loss to society from single-price monopoly?

g. If the monopolist can price-discriminate perfectly, what quantity will the perfectly price-discriminating monopolist produce?

13. Bob, Bill, Ben, and Brad Baxter have just made a documentary movie about their basketball team. They are thinking about making the movie available for download on the Internet, and they can act as a single-price monopolist if they choose to. Each time the movie is downloaded, their Internet service provider charges them a fee of $4. The Baxter brothers are arguing about which price to charge customers per download. The accompanying table shows the demand schedule for their film.

Price of download	Quantity of downloads demanded
$10	0
8	1
6	3
4	6
2	10
0	15

a. Calculate the total revenue and the marginal revenue per download.

b. Bob is proud of the film and wants as many people as possible to download it. Which price would he choose? How many downloads would be sold?

c. Bill wants as much total revenue as possible. Which price would he choose? How many downloads would be sold?

d. Ben wants to maximize profit. Which price would he choose? How many downloads would be sold?

e. Brad wants to charge the efficient price. Which price would he choose? How many downloads would be sold?

14. Suppose that De Beers is a single-price monopolist in the market for diamonds. De Beers has five potential customers: Raquel, Jackie, Joan, Mia, and Sophia. Each of these customers will buy at most one diamond—and only if the price is just equal to, or lower than, her willingness to pay. Raquel's willingness to pay is $400; Jackie's, $300; Joan's, $200; Mia's, $100; and Sophia's, $0. De Beers's marginal cost per diamond is $100. This leads to the demand schedule for diamonds shown in the accompanying table.

Price of diamond	Quantity of diamonds demanded
$500	0
400	1
300	2
200	3
100	4
0	5

a. Calculate De Beers's total revenue and its marginal revenue. From your calculation, draw the demand curve and the marginal revenue curve.

b. Explain why De Beers faces a downward-sloping demand curve.

c. Explain why the marginal revenue from an additional diamond sale is less than the price of the diamond.

d. Suppose De Beers currently charges $200 for its diamonds. If it lowers the price to $100, how large is the price effect? How large is the quantity effect?

e. Add the marginal cost curve to your diagram from part a, and determine which quantity maximizes the company's profit and which price De Beers will charge.

15. Use the demand schedule for diamonds given in Problem 14. The marginal cost of producing diamonds is constant at $100. There is no fixed cost.

a. If De Beers charges the monopoly price, how large is the individual consumer surplus that each buyer experiences? Calculate total consumer surplus by summing the individual consumer surpluses. How large is producer surplus?

Suppose that upstart Russian and Asian producers enter the market and the market becomes perfectly competitive.

b. What is the perfectly competitive price? What quantity will be sold in this perfectly competitive market?

c. At the competitive price and quantity, how large is the consumer surplus that each buyer experiences? How large is total consumer surplus? How large is producer surplus?

d. Compare your answer to part c to your answer to part a. How large is the deadweight loss associated with monopoly in this case?

16. Use the demand schedule for diamonds given in Problem 14. De Beers is a monopolist, but it can now price-discriminate perfectly among all five of its potential customers. De Beers's marginal cost is constant at $100. There is no fixed cost.

a. If De Beers can price-discriminate perfectly, to which customers will it sell diamonds and at what prices?

b. How large is each individual consumer surplus? How large is total consumer surplus? Calculate producer surplus by summing the producer surplus generated by each sale.

17. Download Records decides to release an album by the group Mary and the Little Lamb. It produces the album with no fixed cost, but the total cost of downloading an album to a CD and paying Mary her royalty is $6 per album. Download Records can act as a single-price monopolist. Its marketing division finds that the demand schedule for the album is as shown in the accompanying table.

Price of album	Quantity of albums demanded
$22	0
20	1,000
18	2,000
16	3,000
14	4,000
12	5,000
10	6,000
8	7,000

a. Calculate the total revenue and the marginal revenue per album.

b. The marginal cost of producing each album is constant at $6. To maximize profit, what level of output should Download Records choose, and which price should it charge for each album?

c. Mary renegotiates her contract and now needs to be paid a higher royalty per album. So the marginal cost rises to be constant at $14. To maximize profit, what level of output should Download Records now choose, and which price should it charge for each album?

18. The accompanying diagram illustrates your local electricity company's natural monopoly. The diagram shows the demand curve for kilowatt-hours (kWh) of electricity, the company's marginal revenue (*MR*) curve, its marginal cost (*MC*) curve, and its average total cost (*ATC*) curve. The government wants to regulate the monopolist by imposing a price ceiling.

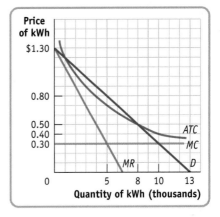

a. If the government does not regulate this monopolist, which price will it charge? Illustrate the inefficiency this creates by shading the deadweight loss from monopoly.

b. If the government imposes a price ceiling equal to the marginal cost, $0.30, will the monopolist make a profit or lose money? Shade the area of profit (or loss) for the monopolist. If the government does impose this price ceiling, do you think the firm will continue to produce in the long run?

c. If the government imposes a price ceiling of $0.50, will the monopolist make a profit, lose money, or break even?

19. The movie theater in Collegetown serves two kinds of customers: students and professors. There are 900 students and 100 professors in Collegetown. Each student's willingness to pay for a movie ticket is $5. Each professor's willingness to pay for a movie ticket is $10. Each will buy at most one ticket. The movie theater's marginal cost per ticket is constant at $3, and there is no fixed cost.

a. Suppose the movie theater cannot price-discriminate and needs to charge both students and professors the same price per ticket. If the movie theater charges $5, who will buy tickets and what will the movie theater's profit be? How large is consumer surplus?

b. If the movie theater charges $10, who will buy movie tickets and what will the movie theater's profit be? How large is consumer surplus?

c. Now suppose that, if it chooses to, the movie theater can price-discriminate between students and professors by requiring students to show their student ID. If the movie theater charges students $5 and professors $10, how much profit will the movie theater make? How large is consumer surplus?

20. A monopolist knows that in order to expand the quantity of output it produces from 8 to 9 units, it must lower the price of its output from $2 to $1. Calculate the quantity effect and the price effect. Use these results to calculate the monopolist's marginal revenue of producing the 9th unit. The marginal cost of producing the 9th unit is positive. Is it a good idea for the monopolist to produce the 9th unit?

Market Structures: Imperfect Competition

The agricultural products company Archer Daniels Midland (also known as ADM) has often described itself as "supermarket to the world." In 1993, executives from ADM and its Japanese competitor Ajinomoto met to discuss the market for lysine, an additive used in animal feed. In this and subsequent meetings, the two companies joined with several other producers to set targets for the price of lysine, behavior known as *price-fixing*. Each company agreed to limit its production to achieve the price targets, with the goal of raising industry profits. But what the companies were doing was illegal, and the FBI had bugged the meeting room with a camera hidden in a lamp. Over the past few years, there have been numerous investigations and some convictions for price-fixing in a variety of industries, from insurance to college education to computer chips. Despite its illegality, some firms continue to attempt to fix the price of their products.

In the fast food market, it is the legal practice of *product differentiation* that occupies the minds of marketing executives. Fast-food producers go to great lengths to convince

you they have something special to offer beyond the ordinary burger: it's flame broiled or 100% beef or super-thick or lathered with special sauce. Or maybe they offer chicken or fish or roast beef. And the differentiation dance goes on in the pizza industry as well. Pizza Hut offers cheese in the crust. Papa John's claims "better ingredients." Dominoes has a "new recipe," and if you don't want thin crust, the alternative isn't "regular," it's "hand tossed"! The slogans and logos for fast-food restaurants often seem to differ more than the food itself.

To understand why ADM engaged in illegal price-fixing and why fast-food joints go to great lengths to differentiate their patties and pizzas, we need to understand the two market structures in between perfect competition and monopoly in the spectrum of market power—oligopoly and monopolistic competition. The models of these two market structures are at the same time more complicated and more realistic than those we studied in the previous section. Indeed, they describe the behavior of most of the firms in the real world.

Module 64 Introduction to Oligopoly

In Module 57 we learned that an oligopoly is an industry with only a few sellers. But what number constitutes a "few"? There is no universal answer, and it is not always easy to determine an industry's market structure just by looking at the number of sellers. Economists use various measures to gain a better picture of market structure, including concentration ratios and the Herfindahl-Hirschman Index, as explained in Module 57.

In addition to having a small number of sellers in the industry, an oligopoly is characterized by **interdependence,** a relationship in which the outcome (profit) of each firm depends on the actions of the other firms in the market. This is not true for monopolies because, by definition, they have no other firms to consider. On the other hand, competitive markets contain so many firms that no one firm has a significant effect on the outcome of the others. However, in an oligopoly, an industry with few sellers, the outcome for each seller depends on the behavior of the others. Interdependence makes studying a market much more interesting because firms must observe and predict the behavior of other firms. But it is also more complicated. To understand the strategies of oligopolists, we must do more than find the point where the *MC* and *MR* curves intersect!

Understanding Oligopoly

How much will a firm produce? Up to this point, we have always answered: the quantity that maximizes its profit. When a firm is a perfect competitor or a monopolist, we can assume that the firm will use its cost curves to determine its profit-maximizing output. When it comes to oligopoly, however, we run into some difficulties.

A Duopoly Example

Let's begin looking at the puzzle of oligopoly with the simplest version, an industry in which there are only two firms—a **duopoly**—and each is known as a **duopolist.**

Firms are **interdependent** when the outcome (profit) of each firm depends on the actions of the other firms in the market.

An oligopoly consisting of only two firms is a **duopoly.** Each firm is known as a **duopolist.**

Imagine that there are only two producers of lysine (the animal feed additive mentioned in the section opener). To make things even simpler, suppose that once a company has incurred the fixed cost needed to produce lysine, the marginal cost of producing another pound is zero. So the companies are concerned only with the revenue they receive from sales.

Table 64.1 shows a hypothetical demand schedule for lysine and the total revenue of the industry at each price–quantity combination.

table 64.1

Demand Schedule for Lysine

Price of lysine (per pound)	Quantity of lysine demanded (millions of pounds)	Total revenue (millions)
$12	0	$0
11	10	110
10	20	200
9	30	270
8	40	320
7	50	350
6	60	360
5	70	350
4	80	320
3	90	270
2	100	200
1	110	110
0	120	0

If this were a perfectly competitive industry, each firm would have an incentive to produce more as long as the market price was above marginal cost. Since the marginal cost is assumed to be zero, this would mean that at equilibrium, lysine would be provided for free. Firms would produce until price equals zero, yielding a total output of 120 million pounds and zero revenue for both firms.

However, with only two firms in the industry, it would seem foolish to allow price and revenue to plummet to zero. Each would realize that with more production comes a lower market price. So each firm would, like a monopolist, see that profits would be higher if it and its rival limited their production.

So how much will the two firms produce?

One possibility is that the two companies will engage in **collusion**—they will cooperate to raise their joint profits. The strongest form of collusion is a **cartel,** a group of producers with an agreement to work together to limit output and increase price, and therefore profit. The world's most famous cartel is the Organization of Petroleum Exporting Countries (OPEC).

As its name indicates, OPEC is actually a cartel made up of governments rather than firms. There's a reason for this: cartels among firms are illegal in the United States and many other jurisdictions. But let's ignore the law for a moment. Suppose the firms producing lysine were to form a cartel and that this cartel decided to act

OPEC representatives discuss the cartel's policies of cooperation.

as if it were a monopolist, maximizing total industry profits. It's obvious from Table 64.1 that in order to maximize the combined profits of the firms, this cartel should set total industry output at 60 million pounds of lysine, which would sell at a price of $6 per pound, leading to revenue of $360 million, the maximum possible. Then the only question would be how much of that 60 million pounds each firm gets to produce. A "fair" solution might be for each firm to produce 30 million pounds and receive revenues of $180 million.

But even if the two firms agreed on such a deal, they might have a problem: each of the firms would have an incentive to break its word and produce more than the agreed-upon quantity.

Collusion and Competition

Suppose that the presidents of the two lysine producers were to agree that each would produce 30 million pounds of lysine over the next year. Both would understand that this plan maximizes their combined profits. And both would have an incentive to cheat.

To see why, consider what would happen if one firm honored its agreement, producing only 30 million pounds, but the other ignored its promise and produced 40 million pounds. This increase in total output would drive the price down from $6 to $5 per pound, the price at which 70 million pounds are demanded. The industry's total revenue would fall from $360 million ($6 × 60 million pounds) to $350 million ($5 × 70 million pounds). However, the cheating firm's revenue would *rise*, from $180 million to $200 million. Since we are assuming a marginal cost of zero, this would mean a $20 million increase in profits.

But both firms' presidents might make exactly the same calculation. And if *both* firms were to produce 40 million pounds of lysine, the price would drop to $4 per pound. So each firm's profits would fall, from $180 million to $160 million.

The incentive to cheat motivates the firms to produce more than the quantity that maximizes their joint profits rather than limiting output as a true monopolist would. We know that a profit-maximizing monopolist sets marginal cost (which in this case is zero) equal to marginal revenue. But what is marginal revenue? Recall that producing an additional unit of a good has two effects:

1. A positive *quantity* effect: one more unit is sold, increasing total revenue by the price at which that unit is sold.

2. A negative *price* effect: in order to sell one more unit, the monopolist must cut the market price on *all* units sold.

The negative price effect is the reason marginal revenue for a monopolist is less than the market price. But when considering the effect of increasing production, a firm is concerned only with the price effect on its *own* units of output, not on those of its fellow oligopolists. In the lysine example, both duopolists suffer a negative price effect if one firm decides to produce extra lysine and so drives down the price. But each firm cares only about the portion of the negative price effect that falls on the lysine it produces.

This tells us that an individual firm in an oligopolistic industry faces a smaller price effect from an additional unit of output than a monopolist; therefore, the marginal revenue that such a firm calculates is higher. So it will seem to be profitable for any one firm in an oligopoly to increase production, even if that increase reduces the profits of the industry as a whole. But if everyone thinks that way, the result is that everyone earns a lower profit!

Until now, we have been able to analyze producer behavior by asking what a producer should do to maximize profits. But even if the duopolists are both trying to maximize profits, what does this predict about their behavior? Will they engage in collusion, reaching and holding to an agreement that maximizes their combined profits? Or will they engage in **noncooperative behavior,** with each firm acting in its own self-interest, even though this has the effect of driving down everyone's profits? Both strategies can be carried out with a goal of profit maximization. Which will actually describe their behavior?

When firms ignore the effects of their actions on each other's profits, they engage in **noncooperative behavior.**

Now you see why oligopoly presents a puzzle: there are only a small number of players, making collusion a real possibility. If there were dozens or hundreds of firms, it would be safe to assume they would behave noncooperatively. Yet, when there are only a handful of firms in an industry, it's hard to determine whether collusion will actually occur.

Since collusion is ultimately more profitable than noncooperative behavior, firms have an incentive to collude if they can. One way to do so is to formalize it—sign an agreement (maybe even make a legal contract) or establish some financial incentives for the companies to set their prices high. But in the United States and many other nations, firms can't do that—at least not legally. A contract among firms to keep prices high would be unenforceable, and it could be a one-way ticket to jail. The same goes for an informal agreement. In fact, executives from rival firms rarely meet without lawyers present, who make sure that the conversation does not stray into inappropriate territory. Even hinting at how nice it would be if prices were higher can bring an unwelcome interview with the Justice Department or the Federal Trade Commission. For example, in 2003 the Justice Department launched a price-fixing case against Monsanto and other large producers of genetically modified seed. The Justice Department was alerted by a series of meetings held between Monsanto and Pioneer Hi-Bred International, two companies that account for 60% of the U.S. market in maize and soybean seed. These companies, parties to a licensing agreement involving genetically modified seed, claimed that no illegal discussions of price-fixing occurred in those meetings. But the fact that the two firms discussed prices as part of the licensing agreement was enough to trigger action by the Justice Department.

Bryan Smith/Zuma Press

Competing with Prices versus Competing with Quantities

Sometimes, as we've seen, oligopolistic firms just ignore the rules. But more often they develop strategies for making the best of the situation depending on what they know, or assume, about the other firms' behavior. The uncertainties of oligopoly behavior make it harder to model than the behavior of monopolists or perfectly competitive firms, but models do exist. One such model is an example of *price competition* developed by French economist Joseph Bertrand. According to the *Bertrand model,* oligopolists repeatedly undercut each others' prices—charging a bit less than the others to steal their customers—until price reaches the level of marginal cost, as under perfect competition. Another French economist, Augustin Cournot, focused instead on *quantity competition,* which had oligopolists choosing quantities and charging as much as possible for those quantities, rather than choosing prices and selling as much as possible at those prices. According to the *Cournot model,* each oligopolist treats the output of its competitors as fixed, and restricts output to that quantity that will maximize profit given the fixed output of others. The firms' restriction of output in the Cournot model results in lower overall output levels, and higher prices, than under perfect competition, and each firm earns a positive economic profit.

Consider American Airlines and British Airways, which we will assume are duopolists with exclusive rights to fly the Chicago–London route. When the economy is strong and lots of people want to fly between Chicago and London, American Airlines and British Airways might assume the number of passengers the other can carry is constrained, for example by the number of landing slots or terminal gates available. In this environment they are likely to behave according to the Cournot model and price above marginal cost—say, charging $800 per round trip. But when the business climate is poor, the two airlines are likely to find that they have lots of empty seats at a fare of $800 and that capacity constraints are no longer an issue. What will they do?

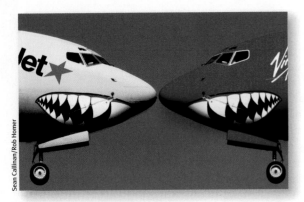
In the absence of collusion, price competition among oligopolists can be intense, as with the airfare war between Jetstar and Virgin Blue that has led to $300 fares to Bali.

Recent history tells us they will engage in a price war by slashing ticket prices. If American Airlines were to try to maintain a price of $800, it would soon find itself undercut by British Airways, which would charge $750 and steal its customers. In turn, American Airlines would undercut British Airways by charging $700—and so on. As long as each firm finds that it can capture the customers by cutting price, each will continue cutting until price is equal to marginal cost. (Going any lower would cause them to incur an avoidable loss.) This is the outcome Bertrand predicted.

Oligopolists would, understandably, prefer to avoid Bertrand behavior because it earns them zero profits. Lacking an environment that imposes constraints on their output capacity, firms try other means of avoiding direct price competition—such as producing products that are not perfect substitutes but are instead differentiated. We'll examine this strategy in more detail in Module 68. For now, we note that producing differentiated products allows oligopolists to cultivate a loyal set of customers and to charge prices higher than marginal cost.

Collusion is another approach to dodging the profit-suppressing effects of competition. In the next module, we'll see why informal collusion often works but sometimes fails.

fyi

The Great Vitamin Conspiracy

It was a bitter pill to swallow. In the late 1990s, some of the world's largest drug companies (mainly European and Japanese) agreed to pay billions of dollars in damages to customers after being convicted of a huge conspiracy to rig the world vitamin market.

The conspiracy began in 1989 when the Swiss company Roche and the German company BASF began secret talks about raising prices for vitamins. Soon a French company, Rhone-Poulenc, joined in, followed by several Japanese companies and other companies around the world. The members of the group, which referred to itself as "Vitamins, Inc.," met regularly—sometimes at hotels, sometimes at

the private homes of executives—to set prices and divide up markets for "bulk" vitamins (like vitamin A, vitamin C, and so on). These bulk vitamins are sold mainly to other companies, such as animal feed makers, food producers, and so on, which include them in their products. Indeed, it was the animal feed companies that grew suspicious about the prices they were being charged, which led to a series of investigations. The case eventually broke open when Rhone-Poulenc made a deal with U.S. officials to provide evidence of the conspiracy. The French company was concerned that rumors about price-fixing would lead U.S. officials to block its planned merger with another company.

How could it have happened?

The main answer probably lies in different national traditions about how to treat oligopolists. The United States has a long tradition of taking tough legal action against price-fixing. European governments, however, have historically been much less stringent. Indeed, in the past some European governments have actually encouraged major companies to form cartels. But European antitrust law has changed recently to become more like U.S. antitrust law. Despite this change, however, the cultural tradition of forming cartels as normal business practice lingers within the boardrooms of some European companies.

Module 64 AP Review

Solutions appear at the back of the book.

Check Your Understanding

1. Explain whether each of the following characteristics will increase or decrease the likelihood that a firm will collude with other firms in an oligopoly to restrict output.
   a. The firm's initial market share is small. (Hint: Think about the price effect.)
   b. The firm has a cost advantage over its rivals.
   c. The firm's customers face additional costs when they switch from one firm's product to another firm's product.
   d. The firm and its rivals are currently operating at maximum production capacity, which cannot be altered in the short run.

Tackle the Test: Multiple-Choice Questions

1. When firms cooperate to raise their joint profits, they are necessarily
   a. colluding.
   b. in a cartel.
   c. a monopoly.
   d. in a duopoly.
   e. in a competitive industry.

2. Use the information in the table below on market shares in the search engine industry and measures of market power (defined in Section 10) to determine which of the following statements are correct.

Search Engine	Market share
Google	44%
Yahoo	29
MSN	13
AOL	6
Ask	5
Other	3

   I. The 4-firm concentration ratio is 92.
   II. The Herfindahl-Hirschman index is 3,016.
   III. The industry is likely to be an oligopoly.
   a. I only
   b. II only
   c. III only
   d. I and II only
   e. I, II, and III

3. An agreement among several producers to restrict output and increase profit is necessary for
   a. cooperation.
   b. collusion.
   c. monopolization.
   d. a cartel.
   e. competition.

4. Oligopolists engage in which of the following types of behavior?
   I. quantity competition
   II. price competition
   III. cooperative behavior
   a. I only
   b. II only
   c. III only
   d. I and II only
   e. I, II, and III

5. Which of the following will make it easier for firms in an industry to maintain positive economic profit?
   a. a ban on cartels
   b. a small number of firms in the industry
   c. a lack of product differentiation
   d. low start-up costs for new firms
   e. the assumption by firms that other firms have variable output levels

Tackle the Test: Free-Response Questions

1. Refer to the table provided to answer the following questions. Assume that marginal cost is zero.

   Demand Schedule

Price	Quantity
$24	0
22	1
20	2
18	3
16	4
14	5
12	6
10	7
8	8
6	9
4	10
2	11
0	12

   a. If the market is perfectly competitive, what will the market equilibrium price and quantity be in the long run? Explain.
   b. If the market is a duopoly and the firms collude to maximize joint profits, what will market price and quantity be? Explain.
   c. If the market is a duopoly and the firms collude to maximize joint profits, what is each firm's total revenue if the firms split the market equally?

   Answer (7 points)

   1 point: If the market is perfectly competitive, price will be zero.

   1 point: If the market is perfectly competitive, quantity will be 12.

   1 point: Price equals marginal cost in the long-run equilibrium of a perfectly competitive market, so price will be zero, at which price the quantity is 12.

   1 point: If the market is a duopoly, price will be $12.

   1 point: If the market is a duopoly, quantity will be 6.

   1 point: In order to maximize joint profits, the two firms would act as a monopoly, setting marginal revenue equal to marginal cost and finding price on the demand curve above the profit-maximizing quantity. Marginal revenue passes through zero (going from 2 to – 2) after the 6th unit, making 6 the profit-maximizing quantity. The most consumers would pay for 6 units is $12, so that is the profit-maximizing price.

   1 point: Total revenue is $12 × 6 = $72. By dividing this equally, each firm receives $36.

2. a. What are the two major reasons we don't see cartels among oligopolistic industries in the United States?
   b. Explain the difference between behavior under the Cournot model and behavior under the Bertrand model.

- How our understanding of oligopoly can be enhanced by using game theory
- The concept of the prisoners' dilemma
- How repeated interactions among oligopolists can result in collusion in the absence of any formal agreement

Module 65
Game Theory

Games Oligopolists Play

In our duopoly example and in real life, each oligopolistic firm realizes both that its profit depends on what its competitor does and that its competitor's profit depends on what it does. That is, the two firms are in a situation of interdependence, whereby each firm's decision significantly affects the profit of the other firm (or firms, in the case of more than two).

In effect, the two firms are playing a "game" in which the profit of each player depends not only on its own actions but on those of the other player (or players). In order to understand more fully how oligopolists behave, economists, along with mathematicians, developed the area of study of such games, known as **game theory.** It has many applications, not just to economics but also to military strategy, politics, and other social sciences.

Let's see how game theory helps us understand oligopoly.

The Prisoners' Dilemma

Game theory deals with any situation in which the reward to any one player—the **payoff**—depends not only on his or her own actions but also on those of other players in the game. In the case of oligopolistic firms, the payoff is simply the firm's profit.

When there are only two players, as in a lysine duopoly, the interdependence between the players can be represented with a **payoff matrix** like that shown in Figure 65.1. Each row corresponds to an action by one player; each column corresponds to an action by the other. For simplicity, let's assume that each firm can pick only one of two alternatives: produce 30 million pounds of lysine or produce 40 million pounds.

The matrix contains four boxes, each divided by a diagonal line. Each box shows the payoff to the two firms that results from a pair of choices; the number below the diagonal shows Firm 1's profits, the number above the diagonal shows Firm 2's profits.

These payoffs show what we concluded from our earlier analysis: the combined profit of the two firms is maximized if they each produce 30 million pounds. Either firm can, however, increase its own profits by producing 40 million pounds if the other produces only 30 million pounds. But if both produce the larger quantity, both will have lower profits than if they had both held their output down.

The study of behavior in situations of interdependence is known as **game theory.**

The reward received by a player in a game, such as the profit earned by an oligopolist, is that player's **payoff.**

A **payoff matrix** shows how the payoff to each of the participants in a two-player game depends on the actions of both. Such a matrix helps us analyze situations of interdependence.

figure 65.1

A Payoff Matrix

Two firms must decide how much lysine to produce. The profits of the two firms are *interdependent:* each firm's profit depends not only on its own decision but also on the other's decision. Each row represents an action by Firm 1, each column one by Firm 2. Both firms will be better off if they both choose the lower output; but it is in each firm's individual interest to choose the higher output.

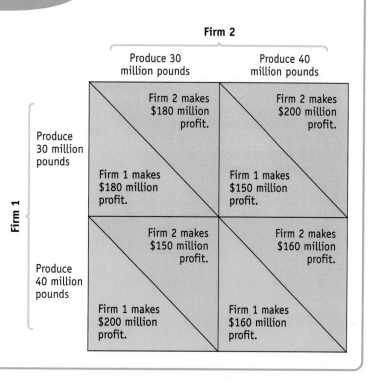

The particular situation shown here is a version of a famous—and seemingly paradoxical—case of interdependence that appears in many contexts. Known as the **prisoners' dilemma,** it is a type of game in which the payoff matrix implies the following:

- Each player has an incentive, regardless of what the other player does, to cheat—to take an action that benefits it at the other's expense.

- When both players cheat, both are worse off than they would have been if neither had cheated.

The original illustration of the prisoners' dilemma occurred in a fictional story about two accomplices in crime—let's call them Thelma and Louise—who have been caught by the police. The police have enough evidence to put them behind bars for 5 years. They also know that the pair have committed a more serious crime, one that carries a 20-year sentence; unfortunately, they don't have enough evidence to convict the women on that charge. To do so, they would need each of the prisoners to implicate the other in the second crime.

So the police put the miscreants in separate cells and say the following to each: "Here's the deal: if neither of you confesses, you know that we'll send you to jail for 5 years. If you confess and implicate your partner, and she doesn't do the same, we reduce your sentence from 5 years to 2. But if your partner confesses and you don't, you'll get the maximum 20 years. And if both of you confess, we'll give you both 15 years."

Figure 65.2 on the next page shows the payoffs that face the prisoners, depending on the decision of each to remain silent or to confess. (Usually the payoff matrix reflects the players' payoffs, and higher payoffs are better than lower payoffs. This case is an exception: a higher number of years in prison is bad, not good!) Let's assume that the prisoners have no way to communicate and that they have not sworn an oath not to harm each other or anything of that sort. So each acts in her own self-interest. What will they do?

The prisoners' dilemma is a game based on two premises: (1) Each player has an incentive to choose an action that benefits itself at the other player's expense; and (2) When both players act in this way, both are worse off than if they had acted cooperatively.

The Kobal Collection

The critically acclaimed 1991 movie *Thelma and Louise* was innovative in depicting two female characters running from the law.

figure 65.2

The Prisoners' Dilemma

Each of two prisoners, held in separate cells, is offered a deal by the police—a light sentence if she confesses and implicates her accomplice but her accomplice does not do the same, a heavy sentence if she does not confess but her accomplice does, and so on. It is in the joint interest of both prisoners not to confess; it is in each one's individual interest to confess.

	Louise	
Thelma	**Don't confess**	**Confess**
Don't confess	Louise gets 5-year sentence. / Thelma gets 5-year sentence.	Louise gets 2-year sentence. / Thelma gets 20-year sentence.
Confess	Louise gets 20-year sentence. / Thelma gets 2-year sentence.	Louise gets 15-year sentence. / Thelma gets 15-year sentence.

An action is a **dominant strategy** when it is a player's best action regardless of the action taken by the other player.

A **Nash equilibrium,** also known as a **noncooperative equilibrium,** is the result when each player in a game chooses the action that maximizes his or her payoff, given the actions of other players.

Mathematician and Nobel Laureate John Forbes Nash proposed one of the key ideas in game theory.

The answer is clear: both will confess. Look at it first from Thelma's point of view: she is better off confessing, regardless of what Louise does. If Louise doesn't confess, Thelma's confession reduces her own sentence from 5 years to 2. If Louise *does* confess, Thelma's confession reduces her sentence from 20 to 15 years. Either way, it's clearly in Thelma's interest to confess. And because she faces the same incentives, it's clearly in Louise's interest to confess, too. To confess in this situation is a type of action that economists call a *dominant strategy*. An action is a **dominant strategy** when it is the player's best action regardless of the action taken by the other player. It's important to note that not all games have a dominant strategy—it depends on the structure of payoffs in the game. But in the case of Thelma and Louise, it is clearly in the interest of the police to structure the payoffs so that confessing is a dominant strategy for each person. As long as the two prisoners have no way to make an enforceable agreement that neither will confess (something they can't do if they can't communicate, and the police certainly won't allow them to do so because the police want to compel each one to confess), the dominant strategy exists as the best alternative.

So if each prisoner acts rationally in her own interest, both will confess. Yet if neither of them had confessed, both would have received a much lighter sentence! In a prisoners' dilemma, each player has a clear incentive to act in a way that hurts the other player—but when both make that choice, it leaves both of them worse off.

When Thelma and Louise both confess, they reach an *equilibrium* of the game. We have used the concept of equilibrium many times in this book; it is an outcome in which no individual or firm has any incentive to change his or her action. In game theory, this kind of equilibrium, in which each player takes the action that is best for her, given the actions taken by other players, is known as a **Nash equilibrium,** after the mathematician and Nobel Laureate John Nash. (Nash's life was chronicled in the best-selling biography *A Beautiful Mind,* which was made into a movie.) Because the players in a Nash equilibrium do not take into account the effect of their actions on others, this is also known as a **noncooperative equilibrium.**

In the prisoners' dilemma, the Nash equilibrium happens to be an equilibrium of two dominant strategies—a *dominant strategy equilibrium*—but Nash equilibria can exist when there is no dominant strategy at all. For example, suppose that after serving time in jail, Thelma and Louise are disheartened by the mutual distrust that led them to confess, and each wants nothing more than to avoid seeing the other. On a Saturday night, they might each have to choose between going to the nightclub and going to the movie theater. Neither has a dominant strategy because the best strategy for each depends on what the other is doing. However, Thelma going to the nightclub and Louise going to the movie theater is a Nash equilibrium because each player takes the action that is best given the action of the other. Thelma going to the movie theater and Louise going to the nightclub is also a Nash equilibrium, because again, neither wants to change her behavior given what the other is doing.

Now look back at Figure 65.1: the two firms face a prisoners' dilemma just like Thelma and Louise did after the crimes. Each firm is better off producing the higher output, regardless of what the other firm does. Yet if both produce 40 million pounds, both are worse off than if they had followed their agreement and produced only 30 million pounds. In both cases, then, the pursuit of individual self-interest—the effort to maximize profits or to minimize jail time—has the perverse effect of hurting both players.

Prisoners' dilemmas appear in many situations. The upcoming FYI describes an example from the days of the Cold War. Clearly, the players in any prisoners' dilemma would be better off if they had some way of enforcing cooperative behavior: if Thelma and Louise had both sworn to a code of silence, or if the two firms had signed an enforceable agreement not to produce more than 30 million pounds of lysine.

But we know that in the United States an agreement setting the output levels of two oligopolists isn't just unenforceable, it's illegal. So it seems that a noncooperative equilibrium is the only possible outcome. Or is it?

Overcoming the Prisoners' Dilemma: Repeated Interaction and Tacit Collusion

Thelma and Louise are playing what is known as a *one-shot* game—they play the game with each other only once. They get to choose once and for all whether to confess or deny, and that's it. However, most of the games that oligopolists play aren't one-shot games; instead, the players expect to play the game repeatedly with the same rivals. An oligopolist usually expects to be in business for many years, and knows that a decision today about whether to cheat is likely to affect the decisions of other firms in the future. So a smart oligopolist doesn't just decide what to do based on the effect on profit in the short run. Instead, it engages in **strategic behavior,** taking into account the effects of its action on the future actions of other players. And under some conditions oligopolists that behave strategically can manage to behave as if they had a formal agreement to collude.

Suppose that our two firms expect to be in the lysine business for many years and therefore expect to play the game of cheat versus collude shown in Figure 65.1 many times. Would they really betray each other time and again?

Probably not. Suppose that each firm considers two strategies. In one strategy it always cheats, producing 40 million pounds of lysine each year, regardless of what the other firm does. In the other strategy, it starts with good behavior, producing only 30 million pounds in the first year, and watches to see what its rival does. If the other firm also keeps its production down, each firm will stay cooperative, producing 30 million pounds again for the next year. But if one firm produces 40 million pounds, the other firm will take the gloves off and also produce 40 million pounds next year. This latter strategy—start by behaving cooperatively, but thereafter do whatever the other player did in the previous period—is generally known as **tit for tat.**

Playing "tit for tat" is a form of strategic behavior because it is intended to influence the future actions of other players. The "tit for tat" strategy offers a reward to

A firm engages in **strategic behavior** when it attempts to influence the future behavior of other firms.

A strategy of **tit for tat** involves playing cooperatively at first, then doing whatever the other player did in the previous period.

the other player for cooperative behavior—if you behave cooperatively, so will I. It also provides a punishment for cheating—if you cheat, don't expect me to be nice in the future.

The payoff to each firm of each of these strategies would depend on which strategy the other chooses. Consider the four possibilities, shown in Figure 65.3:

1. If one firm plays "tit for tat" and so does the other, both firms will make a profit of $180 million each year.

2. If one firm plays "always cheat" but the other plays "tit for tat," one makes a profit of $200 million the first year but only $160 million per year thereafter.

3. If one firm plays "tit for tat" but the other plays "always cheat," one makes a profit of only $150 million in the first year but $160 million per year thereafter.

4. If one firm plays "always cheat" and the other does the same, both firms will make a profit of $160 million each year.

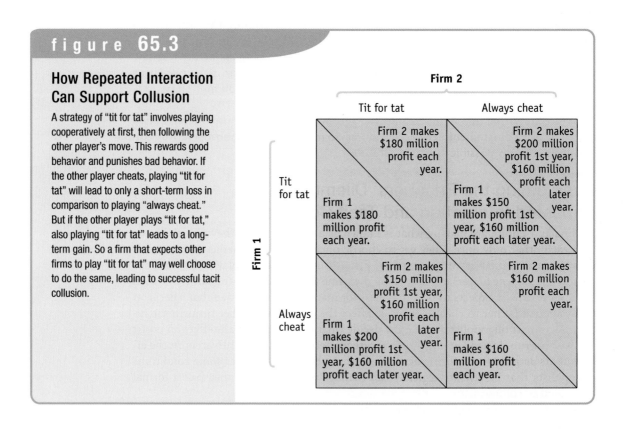

figure 65.3

How Repeated Interaction Can Support Collusion

A strategy of "tit for tat" involves playing cooperatively at first, then following the other player's move. This rewards good behavior and punishes bad behavior. If the other player cheats, playing "tit for tat" will lead to only a short-term loss in comparison to playing "always cheat." But if the other player plays "tit for tat," also playing "tit for tat" leads to a long-term gain. So a firm that expects other firms to play "tit for tat" may well choose to do the same, leading to successful tacit collusion.

Which strategy is better? In the first year, one firm does better playing "always cheat," whatever its rival's strategy: it assures itself that it will get either $200 million or $160 million. (Which of the two payoffs it actually receives depends on whether the other plays "tit for tat" or "always cheat.") This is better than what it would get in the first year if it played "tit for tat": either $180 million or $150 million. But by the second year, a strategy of "always cheat" gains the firm only $160 million per year for the second and all subsequent years, regardless of the other firm's actions. Over time, the total amount gained by playing "always cheat" is less than the amount gained by playing "tit for tat": for the second and all subsequent years, it would never get any less than $160 million and would get as much as $180 million if the other firm played "tit for tat" as well. Which strategy, "always cheat" or "tit for tat," is more profitable depends on two things: how many years each firm expects to play the game and what strategy its rival follows.

If the firm expects the lysine business to end in the near future, it is in effect playing a one-shot game. So it might as well cheat and grab what it can. Even if the firm expects to remain in the lysine business for many years (therefore to find itself repeatedly playing this game) and, for some reason, expects the other firm will always cheat, it should also always cheat. That is, the firm should follow the old rule, "Do unto others before they do unto you."

But if the firm expects to be in the business for a long time and thinks the other firm is likely to play "tit for tat," it will make more profits over the long run by playing "tit for tat," too. It could have made some extra short-term profit by cheating at the beginning, but this would provoke the other firm into cheating, too, and would, in the end, mean less profit.

The lesson of this story is that when oligopolists expect to compete with each other over an extended period of time, each individual firm will often conclude that it is in its own best interest to be helpful to the other firms in the industry. So it will restrict its output in a way that raises the profit of the other firms, expecting them to return the favor. Despite the fact that firms have no way of making an enforceable agreement to limit output and raise prices (and are in legal jeopardy if they even discuss prices), they manage to act "as if" they had such an agreement. When this type of unspoken agreement comes about, we say that the firms are engaging in **tacit collusion.**

> When firms limit production and raise prices in a way that raises each other's profits, even though they have not made any formal agreement, they are engaged in **tacit collusion.**

fyi

Prisoners of the Arms Race

Between World War II and the late 1980s, the United States and the Soviet Union were locked in a seemingly endless struggle that never broke out into open war. During this Cold War, both countries spent huge sums on arms, sums that were a significant drain on the U.S. economy and eventually proved a crippling burden for the Soviet Union, whose underlying economic base was much weaker. Yet neither country was ever able to achieve a decisive military advantage.

As many people pointed out, both nations would have been better off if they had both spent less on arms. Yet the arms race continued for 40 years.

Why? As political scientists were quick to notice, one way to explain the arms race was to suppose that the two countries were locked in a classic prisoners' dilemma. Each government would have liked to achieve decisive mil-

itary superiority, and each feared military inferiority. But both would have preferred a stalemate with low military spending to one with high spending. However, each government rationally chose to engage in high spending. If its rival did not spend heavily, this would lead to military superiority; not spending heavily would lead to inferiority if the other government continued its arms buildup. So the countries were trapped.

The answer to this trap could have been an agreement not to spend as much; indeed, the two sides tried repeatedly to negotiate limits on some kinds of weapons. But these agreements weren't very effective. In the end the issue was resolved as heavy military spending hastened the collapse of the Soviet Union in 1991.

Unfortunately, the logic of an arms race has not disappeared. A nuclear arms race has devel-

TASS/Soufoto

oped between Pakistan and India, neighboring countries with a history of mutual antagonism. In 1998 the two countries confirmed the unrelenting logic of the prisoners' dilemma: both publicly tested their nuclear weapons in a tit-for-tat sequence, each seeking to prove to the other that it could inflict just as much damage as its rival.

Solutions appear at the back of the book.

Check Your Understanding

1. Suppose world leaders Nikita and Margaret are engaged in an arms race and face the decision of whether to build a missile. Answer the following questions using the information in the payoff matrix below, which shows how each set of actions will affect the utility of the players (the numbers represent utils gained or lost).

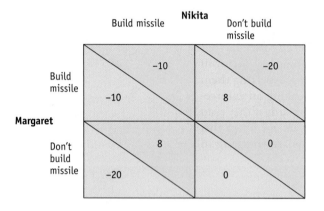

a. Identify any Nash equilibria that exist in this game, and explain why they do or do not exist.

b. Which set of actions maximizes the total payoff for Nikita and Margaret?

c. Why is it unlikely that they will choose the payoff-maximizing set of actions without some communication?

2. For each of the following characteristics of an industry, explain whether the characteristic makes it more likely that oligopolists will play noncooperatively rather than engaging in tacit collusion.

a. Each oligopolist expects several new firms to enter the market in the future.

b. It is very difficult for a firm to detect whether another firm has raised output.

c. The firms have coexisted while maintaining high prices for a long time.

Tackle the Test: Multiple-Choice Questions

1. Each player has an incentive to choose an action that, when both players choose it, makes them both worse off. This situation describes

   a. a dominant strategy.
   b. the prisoners' dilemma.
   c. interdependence.
   d. Nash equilibrium.
   e. tit for tat.

2. Which of the following types of oligopoly behavior is/are illegal?

   I. tacit collusion
   II. cartel formation
   III. tit for tat

   a. I only
   b. II only
   c. III only
   d. I and II only
   e. I, II, and III

3. A situation in which each player in a game chooses the action that maximizes his or her payoff, given the actions of the other players, ignoring the effects of his or her action on the payoffs received by others, is known as a:

   a. dominant strategy.
   b. cooperative equilibrium.
   c. Nash equilibrium.
   d. strategic situation.
   e. prisoners' dilemma.

4. In the context of the Thelma and Louise story in the module, suppose that Louise discovers Thelma's action (confess or don't confess) before choosing her own action.

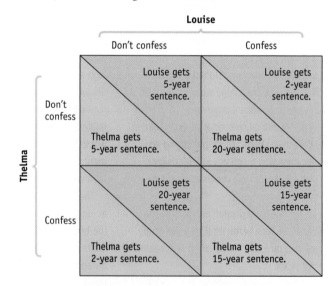

Based on the payoff matrix provided, Louise will

a. confess whether or not Thelma confessed.
b. not confess only if Thelma confessed.
c. not confess only if Thelma didn't confess.
d. not confess regardless of whether or not Thelma confessed.
e. confess only if Thelma did not confess.

5. Which of the following is true on the basis of the payoff matrix provided in Question 4?
   a. Louise has no dominant strategy, but Thelma does.
   b. Thelma has no dominant strategy, but Louise does.
   c. Both Thelma and Louise have a dominant strategy.
   d. Neither Thelma nor Louise has a dominant strategy.
   e. Louise has a dominant strategy only if Thelma confesses.

Tackle the Test: Free-Response Questions

1. Refer to the payoff matrix provided. You and your competitor must decide whether or not to market a new product.

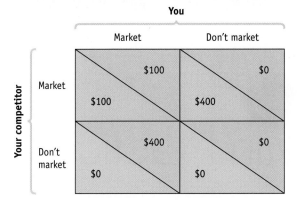

You

	Market	Don't market

Your competitor — Market: $100 / $100 ; $0 / $400

Your competitor — Don't market: $400 / $0 ; $0 / $0

   a. If you market the new product and your competitor does not, how much profit will you earn?
   b. If you market the new product, what should your competitor do?
   c. Do you have a dominant strategy? Explain.
   d. Does this situation have a Nash equilibrium? Explain.

Answer (6 points)

1 point: $400

1 point: Market the new product.

1 point: Yes

1 point: Profits are greater (either $100 or $400 versus $0) if I market the new product, regardless of what my competitor does.

1 point: Yes

1 point: Both players marketing the product is a Nash equilibrium because neither side wants to change to not marketing, given what the other side is doing. (In fact, in this case both sides want to market the product regardless of what the other side is doing, so it is a dominant strategy equilibrium as well as a Nash equilibrium.)

2. Draw a clearly labeled payoff matrix illustrating the following situation. There are two firms, "Firm A" and "Firm B." Each firm must decide whether to charge a high price or a low price. If one firm charges a high price and the other a low price, the firm charging the high price will earn low profits while the firm charging the low price will earn high profits. If both firms charge a high price, both earn high profits and if both firms charge low prices, both earn low profits.

Module 66
Oligopoly in Practice

Previously, we described the cartel known as "Vitamins, Inc.," which effectively sustained collusion for many years. The conspiratorial dealings of the vitamin makers were not, fortunately, the norm. But how do oligopolies usually work in practice? The answer depends both on the legal framework that limits what firms can do and on the underlying ability of firms in a given industry to cooperate without formal agreements. In this module we will explore a variety of oligopoly behaviors and how antitrust laws limit oligopolists' attempts to maximize their profits.

The Legal Framework

To understand oligopoly pricing in practice, we must be familiar with the legal constraints under which oligopolistic firms operate. In the United States, oligopoly first became an issue during the second half of the nineteenth century, when the growth of railroads—themselves an oligopolistic industry—created a national market for many goods. Large firms producing oil, steel, and many other products soon emerged. The industrialists quickly realized that profits would be higher if they could limit price competition. So many industries formed cartels—that is, they signed formal agreements to limit production and raise prices. Until 1890, when the first federal legislation against such cartels was passed, this was perfectly legal.

However, although these cartels were legal, their agreements weren't legally *enforceable*—members of a cartel couldn't ask the courts to force a firm that was violating its agreement to reduce its production. And firms often did violate their agreements, for the reason already suggested by our duopoly example in Module 65: there is always a temptation for each firm in a cartel to produce more than it is supposed to.

In 1881 clever lawyers at John D. Rockefeller's Standard Oil Company came up with a solution—the so-called *trust*. In a trust, shareholders of all the major companies in an industry placed their shares in the hands of a board of trustees who controlled the companies. This, in effect, merged the companies into a single firm that could then engage in monopoly pricing. In this way, the Standard Oil Trust established what was essentially a monopoly of the oil industry, and it was soon followed by trusts in sugar, whiskey, lead, cottonseed oil, and linseed oil.

Eventually, there was a public backlash, driven partly by concern about the economic effects of the trust movement and partly by fear that the owners of the trusts were simply becoming too powerful. The result was the Sherman Antitrust Act of 1890, which was intended both to prevent the creation of more monopolies and to break up existing ones. At first this law went largely unenforced. But over the decades that followed, the federal government became increasingly committed to making it difficult for oligopolistic industries either to become monopolies or to behave like them. Such efforts are known to this day as **antitrust policy.**

One of the most striking early actions of antitrust policy was the breakup of Standard Oil in 1911. Its components formed the nuclei of many of today's large oil companies—Standard Oil of New Jersey became Exxon, Standard Oil of New York became Mobil, and so on. In the 1980s a long-running case led to the breakup of Bell Telephone, which once had a monopoly on both local and long-distance phone service in the United States. As we mentioned earlier, the Justice Department reviews proposed mergers between companies in the same industry and will bar mergers that it believes will reduce competition.

Among advanced countries, the United States is unique in its long tradition of antitrust policy. Until recently, other advanced countries did not have policies against price-fixing, and some even supported the creation of cartels, believing that it would help their own firms compete against foreign rivals. But the situation has changed radically over the past 20 years, as the European Union (EU)—an international body with the duty of enforcing antitrust policy for its member countries—has converged toward U.S. practices. Today, EU and U.S. regulators often target the same firms because price-fixing has "gone global" as international trade has expanded. During the early 1990s, the United States instituted an amnesty program in which a price-fixer receives a much-reduced penalty if it provides information on its co-conspirators. (Remember that the Great Vitamin Conspiracy was busted when a French company, Rhone-Poulenc, revealed the cartel in order to get favorable treatment from U.S. regulators.) In addition, Congress substantially increased maximum fines levied upon conviction. These two new policies clearly made informing on cartel partners a dominant strategy, and it has paid off: in recent years, executives from Belgium, Britain, Canada, France, Germany, Italy, Mexico, the Netherlands, South Korea, and Switzerland, as well as from the United States, have been convicted in U.S. courts of cartel crimes. As one lawyer commented, "You get a race to the courthouse" as each conspirator seeks to be the first to come clean.

Life has gotten much tougher over the past few years if you want to operate a cartel. So what's an oligopolist to do?

> **Antitrust policy** involves efforts by the government to prevent oligopolistic industries from becoming or behaving like monopolies.

In 1911, Standard Oil was broken up into 34 separate companies, 3 of which later became Chevron, Conoco, and Exxon.

Tacit Collusion and Price Wars

If real life were as simple as our lysine story, it probably wouldn't be necessary for the company presidents to meet or do anything that could land them in jail. Both firms would realize that it was in their mutual interest to restrict output to 30 million pounds each and that any short-term gains to either firm from producing more would be much less than the later losses as the other firm retaliated. So even without any explicit agreement, the firms would probably have achieved the tacit collusion needed to maximize their combined profits.

Real industries are nowhere near that simple; nonetheless, in most oligopolistic industries, most of the time, the sellers do appear to succeed in keeping prices above their noncooperative level. Tacit collusion, in other words, is the normal state of oligopoly.

Although tacit collusion is common, it rarely allows an industry to push prices all the way up to their monopoly level; collusion is usually far from perfect. A variety of factors make it hard for an industry to coordinate on high prices.

Large Numbers

Suppose that there were three instead of two firms in the lysine industry and that each was currently producing only 20 million pounds. In that case any one firm that decided to produce an extra 10 million pounds would gain more in short-term profits—and lose less once another firm responded in kind—than in our original example because it has fewer units on which to feel the price effect. The general point is that the more firms there are in an oligopoly, the less is the incentive of any one firm to behave cooperatively, taking into account the impact of its actions on the profits of the other firms. Large numbers of firms in an industry also make the monitoring of price and output levels more difficult, and typically indicate low barriers to entry.

Complex Products and Pricing Schemes

In our simplified lysine example the two firms produce only one product. In reality, however, oligopolists often sell thousands or even tens of thousands of different products. A Walmart Supercenter sells over 100,000 items! Under these circumstances, as when there are a large number of firms, keeping track of what other firms are producing and what prices they are charging is difficult. This makes it hard to determine whether a firm is cheating on the tacit agreement.

Differences in Interests

In the lysine example, a tacit agreement for the firms to split the market equally is a natural outcome, probably acceptable to both firms. In other situations, however, firms often differ both in their perceptions about what is fair and in their real interests.

For example, suppose that one firm in a duopoly was a long-established producer and the other a more recent entrant into the industry. The long-established firm might feel that it deserved to continue producing more than the newer firm, but the newer firm might feel that it was entitled to 50% of the business.

Alternatively, suppose that the newer firm's marginal costs were lower than the long-established firm's. Even if they could agree on market shares, they would then disagree about the profit-maximizing level of output.

Bargaining Power of Buyers

Often oligopolists sell not to individual consumers but to large buyers—other industrial enterprises, nationwide chains of stores, and so on. These large buyers are in a position to bargain for lower prices from the oligopolists: they can ask for a discount from an oligopolist, and warn that they will go to a competitor if they don't get it. An important reason large retailers like Target are able to offer lower prices to customers than small retailers is precisely their ability to use their size to extract lower prices from their suppliers.

These difficulties in enforcing tacit collusion have sometimes led companies to defy the law and create illegal cartels. We've already examined the cases of the lysine industry and the bulk vitamin industry. An older, classic example was the U.S. electrical equipment conspiracy of the 1950s, which led to the indictment of and jail sentences for some executives. The industry was one in which tacit collusion was especially difficult because of all the reasons just mentioned. There were many firms—40 companies were indicted. They produced a very complex array of products, often more or less custom-built for particular clients. They differed greatly in size, from giants like General Electric to family firms with only a few dozen employees. And the customers in many cases were large buyers like electrical utilities, which would normally try to force suppliers to compete for their business. Tacit collusion just didn't seem practical—so executives met secretly and illegally to decide who would bid what price for which contract.

The FYI describes yet another price-fixing conspiracy: the one between the very posh auction houses Sotheby's and Christie's.

Because tacit collusion is often hard to achieve, most oligopolies charge prices that are well below what the same industry would charge if it were controlled by a monopolist—or what they would charge if they were able to collude explicitly. In addition, sometimes tacit collusion breaks down and aggressive price competition amounts to a **price war**. A price war sometimes precipitates a collapse of prices to their noncooperative level, or even lower, as sellers try to put each other out of business or at least punish what they regard as cheating.

A **price war** occurs when tacit collusion breaks down and aggressive price competition causes prices to collapse.

Product Differentiation and Price Leadership

In many oligopolies, however, firms produce products that consumers regard as similar but not identical. A $10 difference in the price won't make many customers switch from a Ford to a Chrysler, or vice versa. Sometimes the differences between products are real, like differences between Froot Loops and Wheaties; sometimes, they exist mainly in the minds of consumers, like differences between brands of vodka (which is *supposed* to be tasteless). Either way, the effect is to reduce the intensity of competition among the firms: consumers will not all rush to buy whichever product is cheapest.

As you might imagine, oligopolists welcome the extra market power that comes when consumers think that their product is different from that of competitors. So in many oligopolistic industries, firms make considerable efforts to create the perception that their product is different—that is, they engage in **product differentiation.**

A firm that tries to differentiate its product may do so by altering what it actually produces, adding "extras," or choosing a different design. It may also use advertising and marketing campaigns to create a differentiation in the minds of consumers, even though its product is more or less identical to the products of rivals.

A classic case of how products may be perceived as different even when they are really pretty much the same is over-the-counter medication. For many years there were only three widely sold pain relievers—aspirin, ibuprofen, and acetaminophen. Yet each of these generic pain relievers were marketed under a number of brand names. And each brand used a marketing campaign implying some special superiority.

Whatever the nature of product differentiation, oligopolists producing differentiated products often reach a tacit understanding not to compete on price. For example, during the years when the great majority of cars sold in the United States were produced by the Big Three auto companies (General Motors, Ford, and Chrysler), there was an unwritten rule that none of the three companies would try to gain market share by making its cars noticeably cheaper than those of the other two.

But then who would decide on the overall price of cars? The answer was normally General Motors: as the biggest of the three, it would announce its prices for the year

Product differentiation is an attempt by a firm to convince buyers that its product is different from the products of other firms in the industry.

In **price leadership,** one firm sets its price first, and other firms then follow.

Firms that have a tacit understanding not to compete on price often engage in intense **nonprice competition,** using advertising and other means to try to increase their sales.

first; and the other companies would adopt similar prices. This pattern of behavior, in which one company tacitly sets prices for the industry as a whole, is known as **price leadership.**

Interestingly, firms that have a tacit agreement not to compete on price often engage in vigorous **nonprice competition**—adding new features to their products, spending large sums on ads that proclaim the inferiority of their rivals' offerings, and so on.

Perhaps the best way to understand the mix of cooperation and competition in such industries is with a political analogy. During the long Cold War between the United States and the Soviet Union, the two countries engaged in intense rivalry for global influence. They not only provided financial and military aid to their allies; they sometimes supported forces trying to overthrow governments allied with their rival (as the Soviet Union did in Vietnam in the 1960s and early 1970s, and as the United States did in Afghanistan from 1979 until the collapse of the Soviet Union in 1991). They even sent their own soldiers to support allied governments against rebels (as the United States did in Vietnam and the Soviet Union did in Afghanistan). But they did not get into direct military confrontations with each other; open warfare between the two superpowers was regarded by both as too dangerous—and tacitly avoided.

Price wars aren't as serious as shooting wars, but the principle is the same.

How Important Is Oligopoly?

We have seen that, across industries, oligopoly is far more common than either perfect competition or monopoly. When we try to analyze oligopoly, the economist's usual way of thinking—asking how self-interested individuals would behave, then analyzing their interaction—does not work as well as we might hope because we do not know whether rival firms will engage in noncooperative behavior or manage to engage in some kind of collusion. Given the prevalence of oligopoly, then, is the analysis we developed in earlier modules, which was based on perfect competition, still useful?

The conclusion of the great majority of economists is yes. For one thing, important parts of the economy are fairly well described by perfect competition. And even though many industries are oligopolistic, in many cases the limits to collusion keep prices relatively close to marginal costs—in other words, the industry behaves "almost" as if it were perfectly competitive.

It is also true that predictions from supply and demand analysis are often valid for oligopolies. For example, we saw that price controls will produce shortages. Strictly speaking, this conclusion is certain only for perfectly competitive industries. But in the 1970s, when the U.S. government imposed price controls on the definitely oligopolistic oil industry, the result was indeed to produce shortages and lines at the gas pumps.

So how important is it to take account of oligopoly? Most economists adopt a pragmatic approach. As we have seen here, the analysis of oligopoly is far more difficult and messy than that of perfect competition; so in situations where they do not expect the complications associated with oligopoly to be crucial, economists prefer to adopt the working assumption of perfectly competitive markets. They always keep in mind the possibility that oligopoly might be important; they recognize that there are important issues, from antitrust policies to price wars, that make trying to understand oligopolistic behavior crucial.

Cars line up for gasoline in 1973 after the U.S. government imposed price controls.

Module 66 AP Review

Solutions appear at the back of the book.

Check Your Understanding

1. For each of the following industry practices, explain whether the practice supports the conclusion that there is tacit collusion in this industry.
   a. For many years the price in the industry has changed infrequently, and all the firms in the industry charge the same price. The largest firm publishes a catalog containing a "suggested" retail price. Changes in price coincide with changes in the catalog.
   b. There has been considerable variation in the market shares of the firms in the industry over time.
   c. Firms in the industry build into their products unnecessary features that make it hard for consumers to switch from one company's products to another's.
   d. Firms meet yearly to discuss their annual sales forecasts.
   e. Firms tend to adjust their prices upward at the same times.

Tackle the Test: Multiple-Choice Questions

1. Having which of the following makes it easier for oligopolies to coordinate on raising prices?
   a. a large number of firms
   b. differentiated products
   c. buyers with bargaining power
   d. identical perceptions of fairness
   e. complex pricing schemes

2. Which of the following led to the passage of the first antitrust laws?
      I. growth of the railroad industry
      II. the emergence of the Standard Oil Company
      III. increased competition in agricultural industries
   a. I only
   b. II only
   c. III only
   d. I and II only
   e. I, II, and III

3. When was the first federal legislation against cartels passed?
   a. 1776
   b. 1800
   c. 1890
   d. 1900
   e. 1980

4. Which of the following industries has been prosecuted for creating an illegal cartel?
   a. the lysine industry
   b. the art auction house industry
   c. the U.S. electrical equipment industry
   d. the bulk vitamin industry
   e. all of the above

5. Oligopolists engage in tacit collusion in order to
   a. raise prices.
   b. increase output.
   c. share profits.
   d. increase market share.
   e. all of the above.

Tackle the Test: Free-Response Questions

1. Like other firms, universities face temptations to collude in order to limit the effects of competition and avoid price wars. (In fact, the U.S. Department of Justice formally accused a group of universities of price-fixing in 1991.) Answer the following questions about behavior in the market for higher education.
   a. Describe one factor of the market for higher education that invites tacit collusion.
   b. Describe one factor of the market for higher education that works against tacit collusion.
   c. Explain one way in which universities could engage in illegal collusion.
   d. What are three ways in which universities engage in product differentiation?
   e. Explain how price leadership might work in the university setting.
   f. What forms of nonprice competition do you see universities engaged in?

Answer (6 points)

1 point: The fact that universities offer a small number of products—enrollment into a small number of programs—invites tacit collusion. They may also have similar perceptions of fairness.

1 point: Factors that work against tacit collusion in the market for higher education include the large number of universities and the bargaining power of the better applicants.

1 point: Universities could engage in illegal collusion by holding meetings to establish uniform tuition rates, divvying up applicants so that each is accepted by a limited number of schools (to avoid competition), or sharing information on scholarship offerings so that applicants will receive similar offers from the competing schools.

1 point: Universities seek product differentiation in regard to athletic programs, facilities, academic standards, location, overseas programs, faculty, graduation requirements, and class size, among other areas.

1 point: Price leadership could be achieved in the university setting if one school, perhaps a large or prestigious university, announced its tuition early and then other schools based their tuition on that announcement.

1 point: Universities can engage in nonprice competition by offering better food, bigger dorm rooms, more accomplished faculty members, plush student centers, and similar amenities.

2. List four factors that make it difficult for firms to form a cartel. Explain each.

Module 67
Introduction to Monopolistic Competition

What you will learn in this Module:

- How prices and profits are determined in monopolistic competition, both in the short run and in the long run

- How monopolistic competition can lead to inefficiency and excess capacity

Understanding Monopolistic Competition

Suppose an industry is monopolistically competitive: it consists of many producers, all competing for the same consumers but offering differentiated products. How does such an industry behave?

As the term *monopolistic competition* suggests, this market structure combines some features typical of monopoly with others typical of perfect competition. Because each firm is offering a distinct product, it is in a way like a monopolist: it faces a downward-sloping demand curve and has some market power—the ability within limits to determine the price of its product. However, unlike a pure monopolist, a monopolistically competitive firm does face competition: the amount of its product it can sell depends on the prices and products offered by other firms in the industry.

The same, of course, is true of an oligopoly. In a monopolistically competitive industry, however, there are *many* producers, as opposed to the small number that defines an oligopoly. This means that the "puzzle" of oligopoly—whether firms will collude or behave noncooperatively—does not arise in the case of monopolistically competitive industries. True, if all the gas stations or all the restaurants in a town could agree—explicitly or tacitly—to raise prices, it would be in their mutual interest to do so. But such collusion is virtually impossible when the number of firms is large and, by implication, there are no barriers to entry. So in situations of monopolistic competition, we can safely assume that firms behave noncooperatively and ignore the potential for collusion.

Monopolistic Competition in the Short Run

We introduced the distinction between short-run and long-run equilibrium when we studied perfect competition. The short-run equilibrium of an industry takes the number of firms as given. The long-run equilibrium, by contrast, is reached only after enough time has elapsed for firms to enter or exit the industry. To analyze monopolistic competition, we focus first on the short run and then on how an industry moves from the short run to the long run.

Panels (a) and (b) of Figure 67.1 show two possible situations that a typical firm in a monopolistically competitive industry might face in the short run. In each case, the firm looks like any monopolist: it faces a downward-sloping demand curve, which implies a downward-sloping marginal revenue curve.

We assume that every firm has an upward-sloping marginal cost curve but that it also faces some fixed costs, so that its average total cost curve is U-shaped. This assumption doesn't matter in the short run; but, as we'll see shortly, it is crucial to understanding the long-run equilibrium.

In each case the firm, in order to maximize profit, sets marginal revenue equal to marginal cost. So how do these two figures differ? In panel (a) the firm is profitable; in panel (b) it is unprofitable. (Recall that we are referring always to economic profit and not accounting profit—that is, a profit given that all factors of production are earning their opportunity costs.)

In panel (a) the firm faces the demand curve D_P and the marginal revenue curve MR_P. It produces the profit-maximizing output Q_P, the quantity at which marginal revenue is equal to marginal cost, and sells it at the price P_P. This price is above the average total cost at this output, ATC_P. The firm's profit is indicated by the area of the shaded rectangle.

In panel (b) the firm faces the demand curve D_U and the marginal revenue curve MR_U. It chooses the quantity Q_U at which marginal revenue is equal to marginal cost.

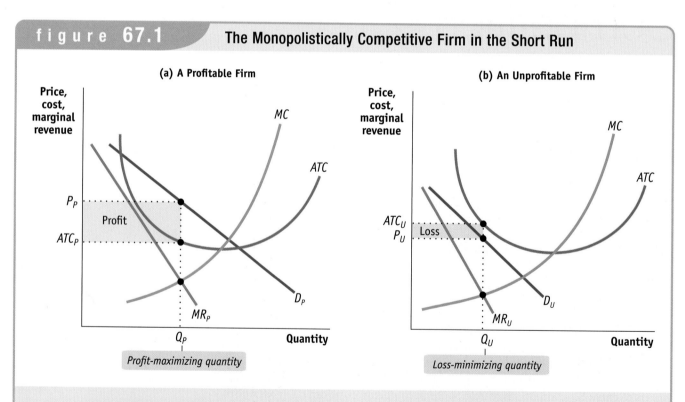

figure 67.1   The Monopolistically Competitive Firm in the Short Run

(a) A Profitable Firm

(b) An Unprofitable Firm

The firm in panel (a) can be profitable for some output quantities: the quantities for which its average total cost curve, *ATC*, lies below its demand curve, D_P. The profit-maximizing output quantity is Q_P, the output at which marginal revenue, MR_P, is equal to marginal cost, *MC*. The firm charges price P_P and earns a profit, represented by the area of the green shaded rectangle. The firm in panel (b), however, can never be profitable because its average total cost curve lies above its demand curve, D_U, for every output quantity. The best that it can do if it produces at all is to produce quantity Q_U and charge price P_U. This generates a loss, indicated by the area of the yellow shaded rectangle. Any other output quantity results in a greater loss.

However, in this case the price P_U is *below* the average total cost ATC_U; so at this quantity the firm loses money. Its loss is equal to the area of the shaded rectangle. Since Q_U is the profit-maximizing quantity—which means, in this case, the loss-minimizing quantity—there is no way for a firm in this situation to make a profit. We can confirm this by noting that at any quantity of output, the average total cost curve in panel (b) lies above the demand curve D_U. Because $ATC > P$ at all quantities of output, this firm always suffers a loss.

As this comparison suggests, the key to whether a firm with market power is profitable or unprofitable in the short run lies in the relationship between its demand curve and its average total cost curve. In panel (a) the demand curve D_P crosses the average total cost curve, meaning that some of the demand curve lies above the average total cost curve. So there are some price–quantity combinations available at which price is higher than average total cost, indicating that the firm can choose a quantity at which it makes positive profit.

In panel (b), by contrast, the demand curve D_U does not cross the average total cost curve—it always lies below it. So the price corresponding to each quantity demanded is always less than the average total cost of producing that quantity. There is no quantity at which the firm can avoid losing money.

These figures, showing firms facing downward-sloping demand curves and their associated marginal revenue curves, look just like ordinary monopoly graphs. The "competition" aspect of monopolistic competition comes into play, however, when we move from the short run to the long run.

Monopolistic Competition in the Long Run

Obviously, an industry in which existing firms are losing money, like the one in panel (b) of Figure 67.1, is not in long-run equilibrium. When existing firms are losing money, some firms will *exit* the industry. The industry will not be in long-run equilibrium until the persistent losses have been eliminated by the exit of some firms.

It may be less obvious that an industry in which existing firms are earning profits, like the one in panel (a) of Figure 67.1, is also not in long-run equilibrium. Given there is *free entry* into the industry, persistent profits earned by the existing firms will lead to the entry of additional producers. The industry will not be in long-run equilibrium until the persistent profits have been eliminated by the entry of new producers.

How will entry or exit by other firms affect the profit of a typical existing firm? Because the differentiated products offered by firms in a monopolistically competitive industry are available to the same set of customers, entry or exit by other firms will affect the demand curve facing every existing producer. If new gas stations open along a highway, each of the existing gas stations will no longer be able to sell as much gas as before at any given price. So, as illustrated in panel (a) of Figure 67.2 on the next page, entry of additional producers into a monopolistically competitive industry will lead to a *leftward* shift of the demand curve and the marginal revenue curve facing a typical existing producer.

Conversely, suppose that some of the gas stations along the highway close. Then each of the remaining stations will be able to sell more gasoline at any given price. So as illustrated in panel (b), exit of firms from an industry leads to a *rightward* shift of the demand curve and marginal revenue curve facing a typical remaining producer.

The industry will be in long-run equilibrium when there is neither entry nor exit. This will occur only when every firm earns zero profit. So in the long run, a monopolistically competitive industry will end up in **zero-profit equilibrium,** in which firms just manage to cover their costs at their profit-maximizing output quantities.

We have seen that a firm facing a downward-sloping demand curve will earn positive profit if any part of that demand curve lies above its average total cost curve; it

In the long-run, profit lures new firms to enter an industry.

In the long run, a monopolistically competitive industry ends up in **zero-profit equilibrium:** each firm makes zero profit at its profit-maximizing quantity.

figure **67.2**

Entry and Exit Shift Existing Firms' Demand Curves and Marginal Revenue Curves

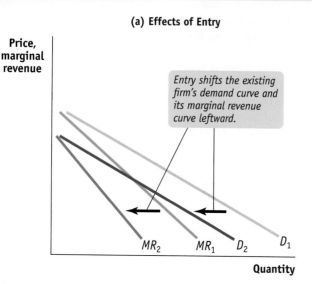

(a) Effects of Entry

Entry shifts the existing firm's demand curve and its marginal revenue curve leftward.

MR_2 MR_1 D_2 D_1

Quantity

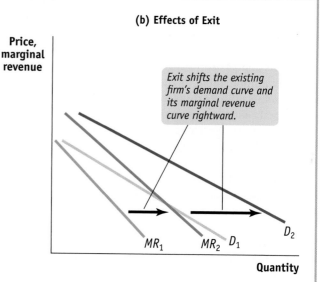

(b) Effects of Exit

Exit shifts the existing firm's demand curve and its marginal revenue curve rightward.

MR_1 MR_2 D_1 D_2

Quantity

Entry will occur in the long run when existing firms are profitable. In panel (a), entry causes each existing firm's demand curve and marginal revenue curve to shift to the left. The firm receives a lower price for every unit it sells, and its profit falls. Entry will cease when firms make zero profit. Exit will occur in the long run when existing firms are unprofitable. In panel (b), exit from the industry shifts each remaining firm's demand curve and marginal revenue curve to the right. The firm receives a higher price for every unit it sells, and profit rises. Exit will cease when the remaining firms make zero profit.

will incur a loss if its entire demand curve lies below its average total cost curve. So in zero-profit equilibrium, the firm must be in a borderline position between these two cases; its demand curve must just touch its average total cost curve. That is, the demand curve must be just *tangent* to the average total cost curve at the firm's profit-maximizing output quantity—the output quantity at which marginal revenue equals marginal cost.

If this is not the case, the firm operating at its profit-maximizing quantity will find itself making either a profit or loss, as illustrated in the panels of Figure 67.1. But we also know that free entry and exit means that this cannot be a long-run equilibrium. Why? In the case of a profit, new firms will enter the industry, shifting the demand curve of every existing firm leftward until all profit is eliminated. In the case of a loss, some existing firms exit and so shift the demand curve of every remaining firm to the right until all losses are eliminated. All entry and exit ceases only when every existing firm makes zero profit at its profit-maximizing quantity of output.

Figure 67.3 shows a typical monopolistically competitive firm in such a zero-profit equilibrium. The firm produces Q_{MC}, the output at which $MR_{MC} = MC$, and charges price P_{MC}. At this price and quantity, represented by point Z, the demand curve is just tangent to its average total cost curve. The firm earns zero profit because price, P_{MC}, is equal to average total cost, ATC_{MC}.

The normal long-run condition of a monopolistically competitive industry, then, is that each producer is in the situation shown in Figure 67.3. Each producer acts like a monopolist, facing a downward-sloping demand curve and setting marginal cost equal to marginal revenue so as to maximize profit. But this is just enough to achieve zero economic profit. The producers in the industry are like monopolists without monopoly profit.

figure 67.3

The Long-Run Zero-Profit Equilibrium

If existing firms are profitable, entry will occur and shift each existing firm's demand curve leftward. If existing firms are unprofitable, each remaining firm's demand curve shifts rightward as some firms exit the industry. Entry and exit will cease when every existing firm makes zero profit at its profit-maximizing quantity. So, in long-run zero-profit equilibrium, the demand curve of each firm is tangent to its average total cost curve at its profit-maximizing quantity: at the profit-maximizing quantity, Q_{MC}, price, P_{MC}, equals average total cost, ATC_{MC}. A monopolistically competitive firm is like a monopolist without monopoly profits.

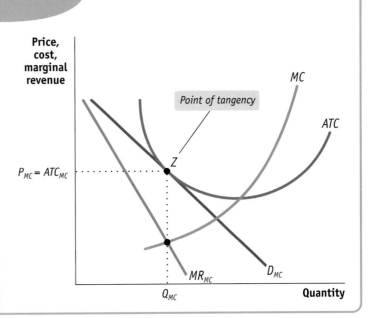

fyi

Hits and Flops

On the face of it, the movie business seems to meet the criteria for monopolistic competition. Movies compete for the same consumers; each movie is different from the others; new companies can and do enter the business. But where's the zero-profit equilibrium? After all, some movies are enormously profitable.

The key is to realize that for every successful blockbuster, there are several flops—and that the movie studios don't know in advance which will be which. (One observer of Hollywood summed up his conclusions as follows: "Nobody knows anything.") And by the time it becomes clear that a movie will be a flop, it's too late to cancel it.

The difference between movie-making and the type of monopolistic competition we model in this section is that the fixed costs of making a movie are also *sunk costs*—once they've been incurred, they can't be recovered.

Yet there is still, in a way, a zero-profit equilibrium. If movies on average were highly profitable, more studios would enter the industry and more movies would be made. If movies on average lost money, fewer movies would be made. In fact, as you might expect, the movie industry on average earns just about enough to cover the cost of production—that is, it earns roughly zero economic profit.

This kind of situation—in which firms earn zero profit on average but have a mixture of highly profitable hits and money-losing

flops—can be found in other industries characterized by high up-front sunk costs. A notable example is the pharmaceutical industry, in which many research projects lead nowhere but a few lead to highly profitable drugs.

Monopolistic Competition versus Perfect Competition

In a way, long-run equilibrium in a monopolistically competitive industry looks a lot like long-run equilibrium in a perfectly competitive industry. In both cases, there are many firms; in both cases, profits have been competed away; in both cases, the price received by every firm is equal to the average total cost of production.

However, the two versions of long-run equilibrium are different—in ways that are economically significant.

Price, Marginal Cost, and Average Total Cost

Figure 67.4 compares the long-run equilibrium of a typical firm in a perfectly competitive industry with that of a typical firm in a monopolistically competitive industry. Panel (a) shows a perfectly competitive firm facing a market price equal to its minimum average total cost; panel (b) reproduces Figure 67.3. Comparing the panels, we see two important differences.

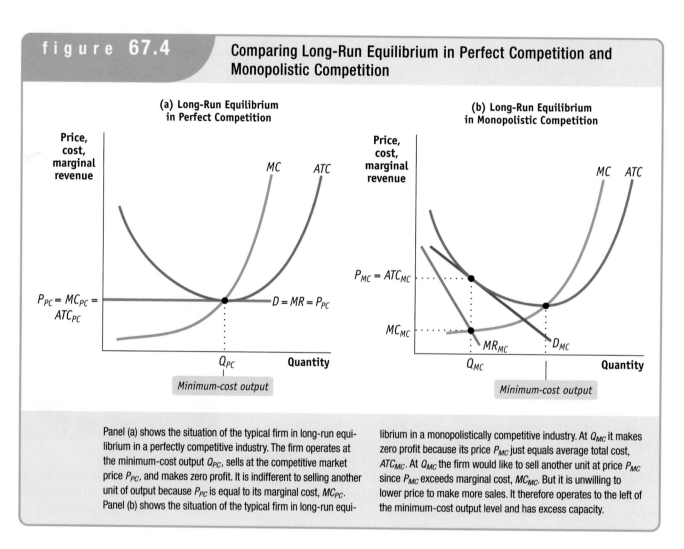

figure 67.4

Comparing Long-Run Equilibrium in Perfect Competition and Monopolistic Competition

Panel (a) shows the situation of the typical firm in long-run equilibrium in a perfectly competitive industry. The firm operates at the minimum-cost output Q_{PC}, sells at the competitive market price P_{PC}, and makes zero profit. It is indifferent to selling another unit of output because P_{PC} is equal to its marginal cost, MC_{PC}. Panel (b) shows the situation of the typical firm in long-run equilibrium in a monopolistically competitive industry. At Q_{MC} it makes zero profit because its price P_{MC} just equals average total cost, ATC_{MC}. At Q_{MC} the firm would like to sell another unit at price P_{MC} since P_{MC} exceeds marginal cost, MC_{MC}. But it is unwilling to lower price to make more sales. It therefore operates to the left of the minimum-cost output level and has excess capacity.

First, in the case of the perfectly competitive firm shown in panel (a), the price, P_{PC}, received by the firm at the profit-maximizing quantity, Q_{PC}, is equal to the firm's marginal cost of production, MC_{PC}, at that quantity of output. By contrast, at the profit-maximizing quantity chosen by the monopolistically competitive firm in panel (b), Q_{MC}, the price, P_{MC}, is *higher* than the marginal cost of production, MC_{MC}.

This difference translates into a difference in the attitude of firms toward consumers. A wheat farmer, who can sell as much wheat as he likes at the going market price, would not get particularly excited if you offered to buy some more wheat at the market price. Since he has no desire to produce more at that price and can sell the wheat to someone else, you are not doing him a favor.

But if you decide to fill up your tank at Jamil's gas station rather than at Katy's, you are doing Jamil a favor. He is not willing to cut his price to get more customers—he's already made the best of that trade-off. But if he gets a few more customers than he expected at the posted price, that's good news: an additional sale at the *posted* price increases his revenue more than it increases his cost because the posted price exceeds marginal cost.

The fact that monopolistic competitors, unlike perfect competitors, want to sell more at the going price is crucial to understanding why they engage in activities like advertising that help increase sales.

The other difference between monopolistic competition and perfect competition that is visible in Figure 67.4 involves the position of each firm on its average total cost curve. In panel (a), the perfectly competitive firm produces at point Q_{PC}, at the bottom of the U-shaped *ATC* curve. That is, each firm produces the quantity at which average total cost is minimized—the *minimum-cost output*. As a consequence, the total cost of industry output is also minimized.

Under monopolistic competition, in panel (b), the firm produces at Q_{MC}, on the *downward-sloping* part of the U-shaped *ATC* curve: it produces less than the quantity that would minimize average total cost. This failure to produce enough to minimize average total cost is sometimes described as the **excess capacity** issue. The typical vendor in a food court or a gas station along a road is not big enough to take maximum advantage of available cost savings. So the total cost of industry output is not minimized in the case of a monopolistically competitive industry.

Some people have argued that, because every monopolistic competitor has excess capacity, monopolistically competitive industries are inefficient. But the issue of efficiency under monopolistic competition turns out to be a subtle one that does not have a clear answer.

Is Monopolistic Competition Inefficient?

A monopolistic competitor, like a monopolist, charges a price that is above marginal cost. As a result, some people who are willing to pay at least as much for an egg roll at Wonderful Wok as it costs to produce it are deterred from doing so. In monopolistic competition, some mutually beneficial transactions go unexploited.

Furthermore, it is often argued that monopolistic competition is subject to a further kind of inefficiency: that the excess capacity of every monopolistic competitor implies *wasteful duplication* because monopolistically competitive industries offer too many varieties. According to this argument, it would be better if there were only two or three vendors in the food court, not six or seven. If there were fewer vendors, they would each have lower average total costs and so could offer food more cheaply.

Is this argument against monopolistic competition right—that it lowers total surplus by causing inefficiency? Not necessarily. It's true that if there were fewer gas stations along a highway, each gas station would sell more gasoline and so would have a lower cost per gallon. But there is a drawback: motorists would be inconvenienced because gas stations would be farther apart. The point is that the diversity of products offered in a monopolistically competitive industry is beneficial to consumers. So the higher price consumers pay because of excess capacity is offset to some extent by the value they receive from greater diversity.

There is, in other words, a trade-off: more producers mean higher average total costs but also greater product diversity. Does a monopolistically competitive industry arrive at the socially optimal point in this trade-off? Probably not—but it is hard to say whether there are too many firms or too few! Most economists now believe that duplication of effort and excess capacity in monopolistically competitive industries are not large problems in practice.

Firms in a monopolistically competitive industry have **excess capacity:** they produce less than the output at which average total cost is minimized.

Check Your Understanding

1. Suppose a monopolistically competitive industry composed of firms with U-shaped average total cost curves is in long-run equilibrium. For each of the following changes, explain how the industry is affected in the short run and how it adjusts to a new long-run equilibrium.
   a. a technological change that increases fixed cost for every firm in the industry
   b. a technological change that decreases marginal cost for every firm in the industry

2. Why is it impossible for firms in a monopolistically competitive industry to join together to form a monopoly that is capable of maintaining positive economic profit in the long run?

3. Indicate whether the following statements are true or false, and explain your answers.
   a. Like a firm in a perfectly competitive industry, a firm in a monopolistically competitive industry is willing to sell a good at any price that equals or exceeds marginal cost.
   b. Suppose there is a monopolistically competitive industry in long-run equilibrium that possesses excess capacity. All the firms in the industry would be better off if they merged into a single firm and produced a single product, but whether consumers would be made better off by this is ambiguous.
   c. Fads and fashions are more likely to arise in industries characterized by monopolistic competition or oligopoly than in those characterized by perfect competition or monopoly.

Tackle the Test: Multiple-Choice Questions

1. Which of the following is a characteristic of monopolistic competition?
   a. a standardized product
   b. many sellers
   c. barriers to entry
   d. positive long-run profits
   e. a perfectly elastic demand curve

2. Which of the following results is possible for a monopolistic competitor in the short run?
   I. positive economic profit
   II. normal profit
   III. loss
   a. I only
   b. II only
   c. III only
   d. I and II only
   e. I, II, and III

3. Which of the following results is possible for a monopolistic competitor in the long run?
   I. positive economic profit
   II. normal profit
   III. loss
   a. I only
   b. II only
   c. III only
   d. I and II only
   e. I, II, and III

4. Which of the following best describes a monopolistic competitor's demand curve?
   a. upward sloping
   b. downward sloping
   c. U-shaped
   d. horizontal
   e. vertical

5. The long-run outcome in a monopolistically competitive industry results in
   a. inefficiency because firms earn positive economic profits.
   b. efficiency due to excess capacity.
   c. inefficiency due to product diversity.
   d. efficiency because price exceeds marginal cost.
   e. a trade-off between higher average total cost and more product diversity.

Tackle the Test: Free-Response Questions

1. Draw a correctly labeled graph for a monopolistically competitive firm that is unprofitable in the short run. Shade the area that represents the firm's losses.

2. Draw a correctly labeled graph for a monopolistically competitive firm in long-run equilibrium. Label the distance on the quantity axis that represents excess capacity.

Answer (7 points)

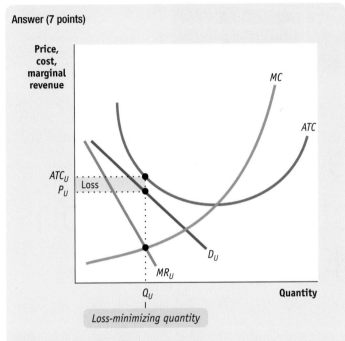

Loss-minimizing quantity

1 point: Correctly labeled axes

1 point: Downward-sloping demand curve

1 point: Marginal revenue curve below the demand curve

1 point: Loss-minimizing quantity where $MC = MR$

1 point: Loss-minimizing price on demand curve above where $MC = MR$

1 point: U-shaped average total cost curve above the demand curve at every quantity

1 point: Correct loss area shaded

Module 68
Product Differentiation and Advertising

In Module 66 we saw that product differentiation often plays an important role in oligopolistic industries. In such industries, product differentiation reduces the intensity of competition between firms when tacit collusion cannot be achieved. Product differentiation plays an even more crucial role in monopolistically competitive industries. Because tacit collusion is virtually impossible when there are many producers, product differentiation is the only way monopolistically competitive firms can acquire some market power. In this module, we look at how oligopolists and monopolistic competitors differentiate their products in order to maximize profits.

How Firms Differentiate Their Products

How do firms in the same industry—such as fast-food vendors, gas stations, or chocolate makers—differentiate their products? Sometimes the difference is mainly in the minds of consumers rather than in the products themselves. We'll discuss the role of advertising and the importance of brand names in achieving this kind of product differentiation later. But, in general, firms differentiate their products by—surprise!—actually making them different.

The key to product differentiation is that consumers have different preferences and are willing to pay somewhat more to satisfy those preferences. Each producer can carve out a market niche by producing something that caters to the particular preferences of some group of consumers better than the products of other firms. There are three important forms of product differentiation: differentiation by style or type, differentiation by location, and differentiation by quality.

Differentiation by Style or Type

The sellers in Leo's food court offer different types of fast food: hamburgers, pizza, Chinese food, Mexican food, and so on. Each consumer arrives at the food court with some preference for one or another of these offerings. This preference may depend on the consumer's mood, her diet, or what she has already eaten that day. These preferences will not make consumers indifferent to price: if Wonderful Wok were to charge $15 for an egg roll, everybody would go to Bodacious Burgers or Pizza Paradise instead. But some people will choose a more expensive meal if that type of food is closer to their preference. So the products of the different vendors are substitutes, but they aren't *perfect* substitutes—they are *imperfect substitutes*.

Vendors in a food court aren't the only sellers who differentiate their offerings by type. Clothing stores concentrate on women's or men's clothes, on business attire or sportswear, on trendy or classic styles, and so on. Auto manufacturers offer sedans, minivans, sport-utility vehicles, and sports cars, each type aimed at drivers with different needs and tastes.

Books offer yet another example of differentiation by type and style. Mysteries are differentiated from romances; among mysteries, we can differentiate among hard-boiled detective stories, whodunits, and police procedurals. And no two writers of hard-boiled detective stories are exactly alike: Raymond Chandler and Sue Grafton each have their devoted fans.

In fact, product differentiation is characteristic of most consumer goods. As long as people differ in their tastes, producers find it possible and profitable to offer variety.

Differentiation by Location

Gas stations along a road offer differentiated products. True, the gas may be exactly the same. But the location of the stations is different, and location matters to consumers: it's more convenient to stop for gas near your home, near your workplace, or near wherever you are when the gas gauge gets low.

In fact, many monopolistically competitive industries supply goods differentiated by location. This is especially true in service industries, from dry cleaners to hair-dressers, where customers often choose the seller who is closest rather than cheapest.

Differentiation by Quality

Do you have a craving for chocolate? How much are you willing to spend on it? You see, there's chocolate and then there's chocolate: although ordinary chocolate may not be very expensive, gourmet chocolate can cost several dollars per bite.

With chocolate, as with many goods, there is a range of possible qualities. You can get a usable bicycle for less than $100; you can get a much fancier bicycle for 10 times as much. It all depends on how much the additional quality matters to you and how much you will miss the other things you could have purchased with that money.

Because consumers vary in what they are willing to pay for higher quality, producers can differentiate their products by quality—some offering lower-quality, inexpensive products and others offering higher-quality products at a higher price.

Product differentiation, then, can take several forms. Whatever form it takes, however, there are two important features of industries with differentiated products: *competition among sellers* and *value in diversity*.

Competition among sellers means that even though sellers of differentiated products are not offering identical goods, they are to some extent competing for a limited market. If more businesses enter the market, each will find that it sells a lower quantity at any given price. For example, if a new gas station opens along a road, each of the existing gas stations will sell a bit less.

Value in diversity refers to the gain to consumers from the proliferation of differentiated products. A food court with eight vendors makes consumers happier than one with only six vendors, even if the prices are the same, because some customers will get a meal that is closer to what they had in mind. A road on which there is a gas station every two miles is more convenient for motorists than a road where gas stations are five miles apart. When a product is available in many different qualities, fewer people are forced to pay for more quality than they need or to settle for lower quality than they want. There are, in other words, benefits to consumers from a greater diversity of available products.

As we'll see next, competition among the sellers of differentiated products is the key to understanding how monopolistic competition works.

Controversies About Product Differentiation

Up to this point, we have assumed that products are differentiated in a way that corresponds to some real desire of consumers. There is real convenience in having a gas station in your neighborhood; Chinese food and Mexican food are really different from each other.

In the real world, however, some instances of product differentiation can seem puzzling if you think about them. What is the real difference between Crest and Colgate toothpaste? Between Energizer and Duracell batteries? Or a Marriott and a Hilton hotel room? Most people would be hard-pressed to answer any of these questions. Yet the producers of these goods make considerable efforts to convince consumers that their products are different from and better than those of their competitors.

No discussion of product differentiation is complete without spending at least a bit of time on the two related issues—and puzzles—of *advertising* and *brand names*.

The Role of Advertising

Wheat farmers don't advertise their wares on TV, but car dealers do. That's not because farmers are shy and car dealers are outgoing; it's because advertising is worthwhile only in industries in which firms have at least some market power. The purpose of advertisements is to persuade people to buy more of a seller's product at the going price. A perfectly competitive firm, which can sell as much as it likes at the going market price, has no incentive to spend money persuading consumers to buy more. Only a firm that has some market power, and which therefore charges a price that is above marginal cost, can gain from advertising. (Industries that are more or less perfectly competitive, like the milk industry, do advertise—but these ads are sponsored by an association on behalf of the industry as a whole, not on behalf of a particular farm.)

Given that advertising "works," it's not hard to see why firms with market power would spend money on it. But the big question about advertising is, *why* does it work? A related question is whether advertising is, from society's point of view, a waste of resources.

Not all advertising poses a puzzle. Much of it is straightforward: it's a way for sellers to inform potential buyers about what they have to offer (or, occasionally, for buyers to inform potential sellers about what they want). Nor is there much controversy about the economic usefulness of ads that provide information: the real estate ad that declares "sunny, charming, 2 bedrooms, 1 bath, a/c" tells you things you need to know (even if a few euphemisms are involved—"charming," of course, means "small").

But what information is being conveyed when a TV actress proclaims the virtues of one or another toothpaste or a sports hero declares that some company's batteries are better than those inside that pink mechanical rabbit? Surely nobody believes that the sports star is an expert on batteries—or that he chose the company that he personally believes makes the best batteries, as opposed to the company that offered to pay him the most. Yet companies believe, with good reason, that money spent on such promotions increases their sales—and that they would be in big trouble if they stopped advertising but their competitors continued to do so.

Why are consumers influenced by ads that do not really provide any information about the product? One answer is that consumers are not as rational as economists typically assume. Perhaps consumers' judgments, or even their tastes, can be influenced by things that economists think ought to be irrelevant, such as which company has hired the most charismatic celebrity to endorse its product. And there is surely some truth to this. Consumer rationality is a useful working assumption; it is not an absolute truth.

However, another answer is that consumer response to advertising is not entirely irrational because ads can serve as indirect "signals" in a world where consumers don't have good information about products. Suppose, to take a common example, that you need to avail yourself of some local service that you don't use regularly—body work on your car, say, or furniture moving. You turn to the Yellow Pages, where you see a number of small listings and several large display ads. You know that those display ads are large because the firms paid extra for them; still, it may be quite rational to call one of the firms with a big display ad. After all, the big ad probably means that it's a relatively large, successful company—otherwise, the company wouldn't have found it worth spending the money for the larger ad.

The same principle may partly explain why ads feature celebrities. You don't really believe that the supermodel prefers that watch; but the fact that the watch manufacturer is willing and able to pay her fee tells you that it is a major company that is likely to stand behind its product. According to this reasoning, an expensive advertisement serves to establish the quality of a firm's products in the eyes of consumers.

The possibility that it is rational for consumers to respond to advertising also has some bearing on the question of whether advertising is a waste of resources. If ads work by manipulating only the weak-minded, the $149 billion U.S. businesses spent on advertising in 2007 would have been an economic waste—except to the extent that ads sometimes provide entertainment. To the extent that advertising conveys important information, however, it is an economically productive activity after all.

Brand Names

You've been driving all day, and you decide that it's time to find a place to sleep. On your right, you see a sign for the Bates Motel; on your left, you see a sign for a Motel 6, or a Best Western, or some other national chain. Which one do you choose?

A **brand name** is a name owned by a particular firm that distinguishes its products from those of other firms.

Unless they were familiar with the area, most people would head for the chain. In fact, most motels in the United States are members of major chains; the same is true of most fast-food restaurants and many, if not most, stores in shopping malls.

Motel chains and fast-food restaurants are only one aspect of a broader phenomenon: the role of **brand names,** names owned by particular companies that differentiate their products in the minds of consumers. In many cases, a company's brand name is the most important asset it possesses: clearly, McDonald's is worth far more than the sum of the deep-fat fryers and hamburger grills the company owns.

In fact, companies often go to considerable lengths to defend their brand names, suing anyone else who uses them without permission. You may talk about blowing your nose on a kleenex or xeroxing a term paper, but unless the product in question comes from Kleenex or Xerox, legally the seller must describe it as a facial tissue or a photocopier.

As with advertising, with which they are closely linked, the social usefulness of brand names is a source of dispute. Does the preference of consumers for known brands reflect consumer irrationality? Or do brand names convey real information? That is, do brand names create unnecessary market power, or do they serve a real purpose?

As in the case of advertising, the answer is probably some of both. On the one hand, brand names often do create unjustified market power. Consumers often pay more for brand-name goods in the supermarket even though consumer experts assure us that the cheaper store brands are equally good. Similarly, many common medicines, like aspirin, are cheaper—with no loss of quality—in their generic form.

On the other hand, for many products the brand name does convey information. A traveler arriving in a strange town can be sure of what awaits in a Holiday Inn or a McDonald's; a tired and hungry traveler may find this preferable to trying an independent hotel or restaurant that might be better—but might be worse.

In addition, brand names offer some assurance that the seller is engaged in repeated interaction with its customers and so has a reputation to protect. If a traveler eats a bad meal at a restaurant in a tourist trap and vows never to eat there again, the restaurant owner may not care, since the chance is small that the traveler will be in the same area again in the future. But if that traveler eats a bad meal at McDonald's and vows never to eat at a McDonald's again, that matters to the company. This gives McDonald's an incentive to provide consistent quality, thereby assuring travelers that quality controls are in place.

Module 68 AP Review

Solutions appear at the back of the book.

Check Your Understanding

1. For each of the following types of advertising, explain whether it is likely to be useful or wasteful from the standpoint of consumers.
   a. advertisements explaining the benefits of aspirin
   b. advertisements for Bayer aspirin
   c. advertisements that state how long a plumber or an electrician has been in business

2. Some industry analysts have stated that a successful brand name is like a barrier to entry. Explain why this might be true.

Tackle the Test: Multiple-Choice Questions

1. Which of the following is a form of product differentiation?
   - I. style or type
   - II. location
   - III. quality
   - a. I only
   - b. II only
   - c. III only
   - d. I and II only
   - e. I, II, and III

2. In which of the following market structures will individual firms advertise?
   - I. perfect competition
   - II. oligopoly
   - III. monopolistic competition
   - a. I only
   - b. II only
   - c. III only
   - d. II and III only
   - e. I, II, and III

3. Advertising is an attempt to affect which of the following?
   - a. consumer tastes and preferences
   - b. consumer income
   - c. the price of complements
   - d. the price of substitutes
   - e. input prices

4. Brand names generally serve to
   - a. waste resources.
   - b. decrease firm profits.
   - c. confuse consumers.
   - d. decrease information.
   - e. signal quality.

5. Which of the following is true of advertising expenditures in monopolistic competition? Monopolistic competitors
   - a. will not advertise.
   - b. use only informational advertising.
   - c. waste resources on advertising.
   - d. attempt to create popular brand names.
   - e. earn long-run profits through advertising.

Tackle the Test: Free-Response Questions

1. Refer to the table below showing the effects of running television commercials on a firm's total revenue. Assume that each commercial costs $1,000 to run.

Number of Commercials	Total revenue
0	$20,000
1	30,000
2	38,000
3	44,000
4	48,000
5	50,000
6	50,500

   a. What is the marginal revenue from running the second commercial?
   b. Should the firm run a third commercial? Explain.
   c. If the firm has no variable costs aside from the cost of commercials, how many commercials should the firm run to maximize profits? Explain.

Answer (5 points)

1 point: $8,000

1 point: Yes.

1 point: Because the marginal revenue of $6,000 exceeds the marginal cost of $1,000.

1 point: 5

1 point: Marginal revenue exceeds marginal cost for the first 5 commercials. Marginal revenue is less than marginal cost for the 6th commercial.

2. When is product differentiation socially efficient? Explain. When is it not socially efficient? Explain.

Section 12 Review

Summary

1. Many industries are oligopolies, characterized by a small number of sellers. The smallest type of oligopoly, a **duopoly,** has only two sellers. Oligopolies exist for more or less the same reasons that monopolies exist, but in weaker form. They are characterized by imperfect competition: firms compete but possess market power.

2. Predicting the behavior of oligopolists poses something of a puzzle. The firms in an oligopoly could maximize their combined profits by acting as a **cartel,** setting output levels for each firm as if they were a single monopolist; to the extent that firms manage to do this, they engage in **collusion.** But each individual

firm has an incentive to produce more than the agreed upon quantity of output—to engage in **noncooperative behavior.** Informal collusion is likely to be easier to achieve in industries in which firms face capacity constraints.

3. The situation of **interdependence,** in which each firm's profit depends noticeably on what other firms do, is the subject of **game theory.** In the case of a game with two players, the **payoff** of each player depends on both its own actions and on the actions of the other; this interdependence can be shown in a **payoff matrix.** Depending on the structure of payoffs in the payoff matrix, a player may have a **dominant strategy**—an action that is always the best regardless of the other player's actions.

4. Some **duopolists** face a particular type of game known as a **prisoners' dilemma;** if each acts independently on its own interest, the resulting **Nash equilibrium** or **noncooperative equilibrium** will be bad for both. However, firms that expect to play a game repeatedly tend to engage in **strategic behavior,** trying to influence each other's future actions. A particular strategy that seems to work well in such situations is **tit for tat,** which often leads to **tacit collusion.**

5. In order to limit the ability of oligopolists to collude and act like monopolists, most governments pursue **antitrust policy** designed to make collusion more difficult. In practice, however, tacit collusion is widespread.

6. A variety of factors make tacit collusion difficult: a large numbers of firms, complex products and pricing, differences in interests, and buyers with bargaining power. When tacit collusion breaks down, there can be a **price war.** Oligopolists try to avoid price wars in various ways, such as through **product differentiation** and through **price leader-**

ship, in which one firm sets prices for the industry. Another approach is **nonprice competition,** such as advertising.

7. Monopolistic competition is a market structure in which there are many competing producers, each producing a differentiated product, and there is free entry and exit in the long run.

8. Short-run profits will attract the entry of new firms in the long run. This reduces the quantity each existing producer sells at any given price and shifts its demand curve to the left. Short-run losses will induce exit by some firms in the long run. This shifts the demand curve of each remaining firm to the right.

9. In the long run, a monopolistically competitive industry is in **zero-profit equilibrium:** at its profit-maximizing quantity, the demand curve for each existing firm is tangent to its average total cost curve. There are zero profits in the industry and no entry or exit.

10. In long-run equilibrium, firms in a monopolistically competitive industry sell at a price greater than marginal cost. They also have **excess capacity** because they produce less than the minimum-cost output; as a result, they have higher costs than firms in a perfectly competitive industry. Whether or not monopolistic competition is inefficient is ambiguous because consumers value the product diversity that it creates.

11. Product differentiation takes three main forms: style or type, location, or quality. Firms will engage in advertising to increase demand for their products and enhance their market power. Advertising and **brand names** that provide useful information to consumers are valuable to society. Advertisements can be wasteful from a societal standpoint when their only purpose is to create market power.

Key Terms

Interdependence, p. 638
Duopoly, p. 638
Duopolist, p. 638
Collusion, p. 639
Cartel, p. 639
Noncooperative behavior, p. 640
Game theory, p. 644
Payoff, p. 644

Payoff matrix, p. 644
Prisoners' dilemma, p. 645
Dominant strategy, p. 646
Nash equilibrium, p. 646
Noncooperative equilibrium, p. 646
Strategic behavior, p. 647
Tit for tat, p. 647
Tacit collusion, p. 649

Antitrust policy, p. 653
Price war, p. 654
Product differentiation, p. 655
Price leadership, p. 656
Nonprice competition, p. 656
Zero-profit equilibrium, p. 661
Excess capacity, p. 665
Brand name, p. 672

Problems

1. The accompanying table presents market share data for the U.S. breakfast cereal market in 2006.

Company	Market Share
Kellogg	30%
General Mills	26
PepsiCo (Quaker Oats)	14
Kraft	13
Private Label	11
Other	6

Source: Advertising Age

a. Use the data provided to calculate the Herfindahl–Hirschman Index (HHI) for the market.

b. Based on this HHI, what type of market structure is the U.S. breakfast cereal market?

2. The accompanying table shows the demand schedule for vitamin D. Suppose that the marginal cost of producing vitamin D is zero.

Price of vitamin D (per ton)	Quantity of vitamin D demanded (tons)
$8	0
7	10
6	20
5	30
4	40
3	50
2	60
1	70

a. Assume that BASF is the only producer of vitamin D and acts as a monopolist. It currently produces 40 tons of vitamin D at $4 per ton. If BASF were to produce 10 more tons, what would be the price effect for BASF? What would be the quantity effect? Would BASF have an incentive to produce those 10 additional tons?

b. Now assume that Roche enters the market by also producing vitamin D and the market is now a duopoly. BASF and Roche agree to produce 40 tons of vitamin D in total, 20 tons each. BASF cannot be punished for deviating from the agreement with Roche. If BASF, on its own, were to deviate from that agreement and produce 10 more tons, what would be the price effect for BASF? What would be the quantity effect for BASF? Would BASF have an incentive to produce those 10 additional tons?

3. The market for olive oil in New York City is controlled by two families, the Sopranos and the Contraltos. Both families will ruthlessly eliminate any other family that attempts to enter the New York City olive oil market. The marginal cost of producing olive oil is constant and equal to $40 per gallon. There is no fixed cost. The accompanying table gives the market demand schedule for olive oil.

Price of olive oil (per gallon)	Quantity of olive oil demanded (gallons)
$100	1,000
90	1,500
80	2,000
70	2,500
60	3,000
50	3,500
40	4,000
30	4,500
20	5,000
10	5,500

a. Suppose the Sopranos and the Contraltos form a cartel. For each of the quantities given in the table, calculate the total revenue for their cartel and the marginal revenue for each additional gallon. How many gallons of olive oil would the cartel sell in total and at what price? The two families share the market equally (each produces half of the total output of the cartel). How much profit does each family make?

b. Uncle Junior, the head of the Soprano family, breaks the agreement and sells 500 more gallons of olive oil than under the cartel agreement. Assuming the Contraltos maintain the agreement, how does this affect the price for olive oil and the profits earned by each family?

c. Anthony Contralto, the head of the Contralto family, decides to punish Uncle Junior by increasing his sales by 500 gallons as well. How much profit does each family earn now?

4. In France, the market for bottled water is controlled by two large firms, Perrier and Evian. Each firm has a fixed cost of €1 million and a constant marginal cost of €2 per liter of bottled water (€1 = 1 euro). The following table gives the market demand schedule for bottled water in France.

Price of bottled water (per liter)	Quantity of bottled water demanded (millions of liters)
€10	0
9	1
8	2
7	3
6	4
5	5
4	6
3	7
2	8
1	9

a. Suppose the two firms form a cartel and act as a monopolist. Calculate marginal revenue for the cartel. What will the monopoly price and output be? Assuming the firms divided the output evenly, how much will each produce and what will each firm's profits be?

b. Now suppose Perrier decides to increase production by 1 million liters. Evian doesn't change its production. What will the new market price and output be? What is Perrier's profit? What is Evian's profit?

c. What if Perrier increases production by 3 million liters? Evian doesn't change its production. What would its output and profits be relative to those in part b?

d. What do your results tell you about the likelihood of cheating on such agreements?

5. To preserve the North Atlantic fish stocks, it is decided that only two fishing fleets, one from the United States and the other from the European Union (EU), can fish in those waters. The accompanying table shows the market demand schedule per week for fish from these waters. The only costs are fixed costs, so fishing fleets maximize profit by maximizing revenue.

Price of fish (per pound)	Quantity of fish demanded (pounds)
$17	1,800
16	2,000
15	2,100
14	2,200
12	2,300

a. If both fishing fleets collude, what is the revenue-maximizing output for the North Atlantic fishery? What price will a pound of fish sell for?

b. If both fishing fleets collude and share the output equally, what is the revenue to the EU fleet? To the U.S. fleet?

c. Suppose the EU fleet cheats by expanding its own catch by 100 pounds per week. The U.S. fleet doesn't change its catch. What is the revenue to the U.S. fleet? To the EU fleet?

d. In retaliation for the cheating by the EU fleet, the U.S. fleet also expands its catch by 100 pounds per week. What is the revenue to the U.S. fleet? To the EU fleet?

6. Suppose that the fisheries agreement in Problem 5 breaks down, so that the fleets behave noncooperatively. Assume that the United States and the EU each can send out either one or two fleets. The more fleets in the area, the more fish they catch in total but the lower the catch of each fleet. The accompany-

ing matrix shows the profit (in dollars) per week earned by the two sides.

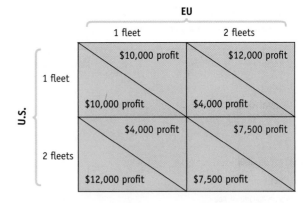

a. What is the noncooperative Nash equilibrium? Will each side choose to send out one or two fleets?

b. Suppose that the fish stocks are being depleted. Each region considers the future and comes to a "tit-for-tat" agreement whereby each side will send only one fleet out as long as the other does the same. If either of them breaks the agreement and sends out a second fleet, the other will also send out two and will continue to do so until its competitor sends out only one fleet. If both play this "tit-for-tat" strategy, how much profit will each make every week?

7. Untied and Air "R" Us are the only two airlines operating flights between Collegeville and Bigtown. That is, they operate in a duopoly. Each airline can charge either a high price or a low price for a ticket. The accompanying matrix shows their payoffs, in profits per seat (in dollars), for any choice that the two airlines can make.

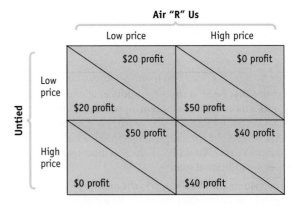

a. Suppose the two airlines play a one-shot game—that is, they interact only once and never again. What will be the Nash equilibrium in this one-shot game?

b. Now suppose the two airlines play this game twice. And suppose each airline can play one of two strategies: it can play either "always charge the low price" or "tit for tat"—that is, start off charging the high price in the first period, and then in the second period do whatever the other airline did in the previous period. Write down the payoffs to Untied from the following four possibilities:

  i. Untied plays "always charge the low price" when Air "R" Us also plays "always charge the low price."

  ii. Untied plays "always charge the low price" when Air "R" Us plays "tit for tat."

  iii. Untied plays "tit for tat" when Air "R" Us plays "always charge the low price."

  iv. Untied plays "tit for tat" when Air "R" Us also plays "tit for tat."

8. Suppose that Coke and Pepsi are the only two producers of cola drinks, making them duopolists. Both companies have zero marginal cost and a fixed cost of $100,000.

  a. Assume first that consumers regard Coke and Pepsi as perfect substitutes. Currently both are sold for $0.20 per can, and at that price each company sells 4 million cans per day.

  i. How large is Pepsi's profit?

  ii. If Pepsi were to raise its price to $0.30 cents per can, and Coke did not respond, what would happen to Pepsi's profit?

  b. Now suppose that each company advertises to differentiate its product from the other company's. As a result of advertising, Pepsi realizes that if it raises or lowers its price, it will sell less or more of its product, as shown by the demand schedule in the accompanying table.

Price of Pepsi (per can)	Quantity of Pepsi demanded (millions of cans)
$0.10	5
0.20	4
0.30	3
0.40	2
0.50	1

  If Pepsi now were to raise its price to $0.30 per can, what would happen to its profit?

  c. Comparing your answer to part a(i) and to part b, what is the maximum amount Pepsi would be willing to spend on advertising?

9. Philip Morris and R.J. Reynolds spend huge sums of money each year to advertise their tobacco products in an attempt to steal customers from each other. Suppose each year Philip Morris and R.J. Reynolds have to decide whether or not they want to spend money on advertising. If neither firm advertises, each will earn a profit of $2 million. If they both advertise, each will earn a profit of $1.5 million. If one firm advertises and the other does not, the firm that advertises will earn a profit of $2.8 million and the other firm will earn $1 million.

  a. Use a payoff matrix to depict this problem.

  b. Suppose Philip Morris and R.J. Reynolds can write an enforceable contract about what they will do. What is the cooperative solution to this game?

  c. What is the Nash equilibrium without an enforceable contract? Explain why this is the likely outcome.

10. Use the three conditions for monopolistic competition discussed in this section to decide which of the following firms are likely to be operating as monopolistic competitors. If they are not monopolistically competitive firms, are they monopolists, oligopolists, or perfectly competitive firms?

  a. a local band that plays for weddings, parties, and so on

  b. Minute Maid, a producer of individual-serving juice boxes

  c. your local dry cleaner

  d. a farmer who produces soybeans

11. You are thinking of setting up a coffee shop. The market structure for coffee shops is monopolistic competition. There are three Starbucks shops, and two other coffee shops very much like Starbucks, in your town already. In order for you to have some degree of market power, you may want to differentiate your coffee shop. Thinking about the three different ways in which products can be differentiated, explain how you would decide whether you should copy Starbucks or whether you should sell coffee in a completely different way.

12. The restaurant business in town is a monopolistically competitive industry in long-run equilibrium. One restaurant owner asks for your advice. She tells you that, each night, not all tables in her restaurant are full. She also tells you that if she lowered the prices on her menu, she would attract more customers and that doing so would lower her average total cost. Should she lower her prices? Draw a diagram showing the demand curve, marginal revenue curve, marginal cost curve, and average total cost curve for this restaurant to explain your advice. Show in your diagram what would happen to the restaurant owner's profit if she were to lower the price so that she sells the minimum-cost output.

13. The market structure of the local gas station industry is monopolistic competition. Suppose that currently each gas station incurs a loss. Draw a diagram for a typical gas station to show this short-run situation. Then, in a separate diagram, show what will happen to the typical gas station in the long run. Explain your reasoning.

14. The local hairdresser industry has the market structure of monopolistic competition. Your hairdresser boasts that he is making a profit and that if he continues to do so, he will be able to

retire in five years. Use a diagram to illustrate your hairdresser's current situation. Do you expect this to last? In a separate diagram, draw what you expect to happen in the long run. Explain your reasoning.

15. Magnificent Blooms is a florist in a monopolistically competitive industry. It is a successful operation, producing the quantity that minimizes its average total cost and making a profit. The owner also says that at its current level of output, its marginal cost is above marginal revenue. Illustrate the current situation of Magnificent Blooms in a diagram. Answer the following questions by illustrating with a diagram.

   a. In the short run, could Magnificent Blooms increase its profit?

   b. In the long run, could Magnificent Blooms increase its profit?

16. "In both the short run and in the long run, the typical firm in monopolistic competition and a monopolist each make a profit." Do you agree with this statement? Explain your reasoning.

17. The market for clothes has the structure of monopolistic competition. What impact will fewer firms in this industry have on you as a consumer? Address the following issues:

   a. variety of clothes

   b. differences in quality of service

   c. price

18. For each of the following situations, decide whether advertising is directly informative about the product or simply an indirect signal of its quality. Explain your reasoning.

   a. Golf champion Tiger Woods drives a Buick in a TV commercial and claims that he prefers it to any other car.

   b. A newspaper ad states, "For sale: 1999 Honda Civic, 160,000 miles, new transmission."

   c. McDonald's spends millions of dollars on an advertising campaign that proclaims: "I'm lovin' it."

   d. Subway advertises one of its sandwiches by claiming that it contains 6 grams of fat and fewer than 300 calories.

19. In each of the following cases, explain how the advertisement functions as a signal to a potential buyer. Explain what information the buyer lacks that is being supplied by the advertisement and how the information supplied by the advertisement is likely to affect the buyer's willingness to buy the good.

   a. "Looking for work. Excellent references from previous employers available."

   b. "Electronic equipment for sale. All merchandise carries a one-year, no-questions-asked warranty."

   c. "Car for sale by original owner. All repair and maintenance records available."

20. The accompanying table shows the Herfindahl-Hirschman Index (HHI) for the restaurant, cereal, movie, and laundry detergent industries as well as the advertising expenditures of the top 10 firms in each industry in 2006. Use the information in the table to answer the following questions.

Industry	HHI	Advertising expenditures (millions)
Restaurants	179	$1,784
Cereal	2,098	732
Movie studios	918	3,324
Laundry detergent	2,068	132

   a. Which market structure—oligopoly or monopolistic competition—best characterizes each of the industries?

   b. Based on your answer to part a, which type of market structure has higher advertising expenditures? Use the characteristics of each market structure to explain why this relationship might exist.

Factor Markets

Does higher education pay? Yes, it does: In the modern economy, employers are willing to pay a premium for workers with more education. And the size of that premium has increased a lot over the last few decades. Back in 1973 workers with advanced degrees, such as law degrees or MBAs, earned only 76% more than those who had only graduated from high school. By 2009, the premium for an advanced degree had risen to over 112%.

Who decided that the wages of workers with advanced degrees would rise so much compared with those of high school grads? The answer, of course, is that nobody decided it. Wage rates are prices, the prices of different kinds of labor; and they are decided, like other prices, by supply and demand.

Still, there is a qualitative difference between the wage rate of high school grads and the price of used textbooks: the wage rate isn't the price of a *good*; it's the price of a *factor of production*. And although markets for factors of production are in many ways similar to those for goods, there are also some important differences.

In this section, we examine *factor markets*, the markets in which the factors of production such as labor, land, and capital are traded. Factor markets, like goods markets, play a crucial role in the economy: they allocate productive resources to firms and help ensure that those resources are used efficiently.

If you've ever had doubts about attending college, consider this: factory workers with only high school degrees will make much less than college grads. The present discounted value of the difference in lifetime earnings is as much as $300,000.

679

Module 69 Introduction and Factor Demand

The Economy's Factors of Production

You may recall that we have already defined a factor of production in the context of the circular-flow diagram; it is any resource that is used by firms to produce goods and services, items that are consumed by households. The markets in which factors of production are bought and sold are called *factor markets*, and the prices in factor markets are known as *factor prices*.

What are these factors of production, and why do factor prices matter?

The Factors of Production

Economists divide factors of production into four principal classes. The first is *labor*, the work done by human beings. The second is *land*, which encompasses resources provided by nature. The third is capital, which can be divided into two categories: **physical capital**—often referred to simply as "capital"—consists of manufactured resources such as equipment, buildings, tools, and machines. In the modern economy, **human capital**, the improvement in labor created by education and knowledge, and embodied in the workforce, is at least equally significant. Technological progress has boosted the importance of human capital and made technical sophistication essential to many jobs, thus helping to create the premium for workers with advanced degrees. The final factor of production, *entrepreneurship*, is a unique resource that is not purchased in an easily identifiable factor market like the other three. It refers to risk-taking activities that bring together resources for innovative production.

Why Factor Prices Matter: The Allocation of Resources

The factor prices determined in factor markets play a vital role in the important process of allocating resources among firms.

Consider the example of Mississippi and Louisiana in the aftermath of Hurricane Katrina, the costliest hurricane ever to hit the U.S. mainland. The states had an urgent

Physical capital—often referred to simply as "capital"—consists of manufactured productive resources such as equipment, buildings, tools, and machines.

Human capital is the improvement in labor created by education and knowledge that is embodied in the workforce.

need for workers in the building trades—everything from excavation to roofing—to repair or replace damaged structures. What ensured that those needed workers actually came? The factor market: the high demand for workers drove up wages. During 2005, the average U.S. wage grew at a rate of around 6%. But in areas heavily affected by Katrina, the average wage during the fall of 2005 grew by 30% more than the national rate, and some areas saw twice that rate of increase. Over time, these higher wages led large numbers of workers with the right skills to move temporarily to these states to do the work.

In other words, the market for a factor of production—construction workers—allocated that factor of production to where it was needed.

In this sense factor markets are similar to goods markets, which allocate goods among consumers. But there are two features that make factor markets special. Unlike in a goods market, demand in a factor market is what we call **derived demand.** That is, demand for the factor is derived from demand for the firm's output. The second feature is that factor markets are where most of us get the largest shares of our income (government transfers being the next largest source of income in the economy).

In the months after Hurricane Katrina, home repair signs like these were abundant throughout New Orleans.

Factor Incomes and the Distribution of Income

Most American families get most of their income in the form of wages and salaries—that is, they get their income by selling labor. Some people, however, get most of their income from physical capital: when you own stock in a company, what you really own is a share of that company's physical capital. Some people get much of their income from rents earned on land they own. And successful entrepreneurs earn income in the form of profits.

Obviously, then, the prices of factors of production have a major impact on how the economic "pie" is sliced among different groups. For example, a higher wage rate, other things equal, means that a larger proportion of the total income in the economy goes to people who derive their income from labor and less goes to those who derive their income from capital, land, or entrepreneurship. Economists refer to how the economic pie is sliced as the "distribution of income." Specifically, factor prices determine the **factor distribution of income**—how the total income of the economy is divided among labor, land, capital, and entrepreneurship.

The factor distribution of income in the United States has been quite stable over the past few decades. In other times and places, however, large changes have taken place in the factor distribution. One notable example: during the Industrial Revolution, the share of total income earned by landowners fell sharply, while the share earned by capital owners rose.

The Factor Distribution of Income in the United States

When we talk about the factor distribution of income, what are we talking about in practice?

In the United States, as in all advanced economies, payments to labor account for most of the economy's total income. Figure 69.1 on the next page shows the factor distribution of income in the United States in 2009: in that year, 70.9% of total income in the economy took the form of "compensation of employees"—a number that includes

The demand for a factor is a **derived demand.** It results from (that is, it is derived from) the demand for the output being produced.

The **factor distribution of income** is the division of total income among land, labor, capital, and entrepreneurship.

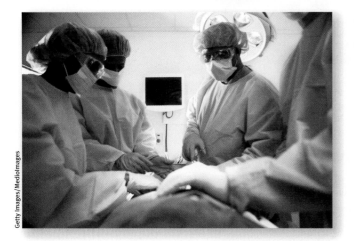

figure 69.1

Factor Distribution of Income in the United States in 2009

In 2009, compensation of employees accounted for most income earned in the United States—70.9% of the total. Most of the remainder—consisting of earnings paid in the form of interest, corporate profits, and rent—went to owners of physical capital. Finally, proprietors' income—9.2% of the total—went to individual owners of businesses as compensation for their labor, entrepreneurship, and capital expended in their businesses.

Source: Bureau of Economic Analysis.

Interest
11.1%

Corporate profits
6.3%

Compensation of employees
70.9%

Rent
2.5%

Proprietors' income
9.2%

both wages and benefits such as health insurance. This number has been quite stable over the long run; 37 years earlier, in 1972, compensation of employees was very similar, at 72.2% of total income.

Much of what we call compensation of employees is really a return on human capital. A surgeon isn't just supplying the services of a pair of ordinary hands (at least the patient hopes not!): that individual is also supplying the result of many years and hundreds of thousands of dollars invested in training and experience. We can't directly measure what fraction of wages is really a payment for education and training, but many economists believe that labor resources created through additional human capital has become *the* most important factor of production in modern economies.

Marginal Productivity and Factor Demand

All economic decisions are about comparing costs and benefits—and usually about comparing marginal costs and marginal benefits. This goes both for a consumer, deciding whether to buy more goods or services, and for a firm, deciding whether to hire an additional worker.

Although there are some important exceptions, most factor markets in the modern American economy are perfectly competitive. This means that most buyers and sellers of factors are price-takers because they are too small relative to the market to do anything but accept the market price. And in a competitive labor market, it's clear how to define the marginal cost an employer pays for a worker: it is simply the worker's wage rate. But what is the marginal benefit of that worker? To answer that question, we return to the production function, which relates inputs to output. For now we assume that all firms are price-takers in their output markets—that is, they operate in a perfectly competitive industry.

Value of the Marginal Product

Figure 69.2 shows the production function for wheat on George and Martha's farm, as introduced in Module 54. Panel (a) uses the total product curve to show how total wheat production depends on the number of workers employed on the farm; panel (b) shows how the *marginal product of labor,* the increase in output from employing one more worker, depends on the number of workers employed. Table 69.1 shows the

figure 69.2   The Production Function for George and Martha's Farm

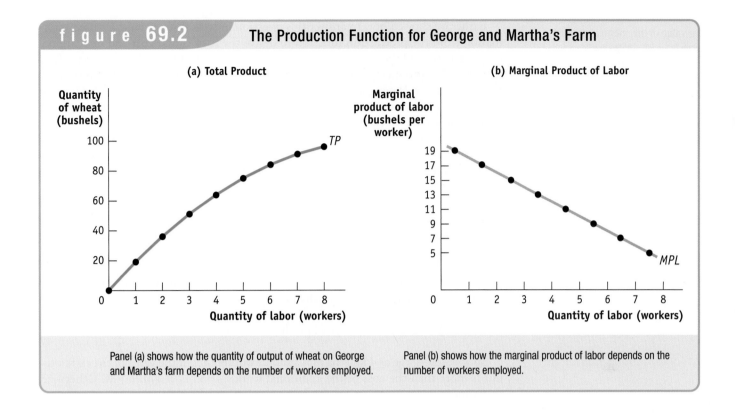

(a) Total Product

(b) Marginal Product of Labor

Panel (a) shows how the quantity of output of wheat on George and Martha's farm depends on the number of workers employed.

Panel (b) shows how the marginal product of labor depends on the number of workers employed.

numbers behind the figure. Note: sometimes the marginal product (*MP*) is called the *marginal physical product* or *MPP*. These two terms are the same; the extra "P" just emphasizes that the term refers to the quantity of physical output being produced, not the monetary value of that output.

If workers are paid $200 each and wheat sells for $20 per bushel, how many workers should George and Martha employ to maximize profit?

table 69.1

Employment and Output for George and Martha's Farm

Quantity of labor L (workers)	Quantity of wheat Q (bushels)	Marginal product of labor $MPL = \frac{\Delta Q}{\Delta L}$ (bushels per worker)
0	0	
		19
1	19	
		17
2	36	
		15
3	51	
		13
4	64	
		11
5	75	
		9
6	84	
		7
7	91	
		5
8	96	

The **value of the marginal product** of a factor is the value of the additional output generated by employing one more unit of that factor.

The **value of the marginal product curve** of a factor shows how the value of the marginal product of that factor depends on the quantity of the factor employed.

Earlier we showed how to answer this question in several steps. First, we used information from the production function to derive the firm's total cost and its marginal cost. Then we used the *price-taking firm's optimal output rule:* a price-taking firm's profit is maximized by producing the quantity of output at which the marginal cost is equal to the market price. Having determined the optimal quantity of output, we went back to the production function to find the optimal number of workers—which was simply the number of workers needed to produce the optimal quantity of output.

As you might have guessed, marginal analysis provides a more direct way to find the number of workers that maximizes a firm's profit. This alternative approach is just a different way of looking at the same thing. But it gives us more insight into the demand for factors as opposed to the supply of goods.

To see how this alternative approach works, suppose that George and Martha are deciding whether to employ another worker. The increase in *cost* from employing another worker is the wage rate, *W*. The *benefit* to George and Martha from employing another worker is the value of the extra output that worker can produce. What is this value? It is the marginal product of labor, *MPL*, multiplied by the price per unit of output, *P*. This amount—the extra value of output generated by employing one more unit of labor—is known as the **value of the marginal product** of labor, or *VMPL*:

(69-1) Value of the marginal product of labor $= VMPL = P \times MPL$

So should George and Martha hire another worker? Yes, if the value of the extra output is more than the cost of the additional worker—that is, if *VMPL* > *W*. Otherwise, they should not.

The hiring decision is made using marginal analysis, by comparing the marginal benefit from hiring another worker (*VMPL*) with the marginal cost (*W*). And as with any decision that is made on the margin, the optimal choice is made by equating marginal benefit with marginal cost (or if they're never equal, by continuing to hire until the marginal cost of one more unit would exceed the marginal benefit). That is, to maximize profit, George and Martha will employ workers up to the point at which, for the last worker employed,

(69-2) $VMPL = W.$

This rule isn't limited to labor; it applies to any factor of production. The value of the marginal product of any factor is its marginal product times the price of the good it produces. And as a general rule, profit-maximizing, price-taking firms will keep adding more units of each factor of production until the value of the marginal product of the last unit employed is equal to the factor's price.

This rule is consistent with our previous analysis. We saw that a profit-maximizing firm chooses the level of output at which the price of the good it produces equals the marginal cost of producing that good. It turns out that if the level of output is chosen so that price equals marginal cost, then it is also true that with the amount of labor required to produce that output level, the value of the marginal product of labor will equal the wage rate.

Now let's look more closely at why choosing the level of employment to equate *VMPL* and *W* works, and at how it helps us understand factor demand.

Value of the Marginal Product and Factor Demand

Table 69.2 shows the value of the marginal product of labor on George and Martha's farm when the price of wheat is $20 per bushel. In Figure 69.3, the horizontal axis shows the number of workers employed; the vertical axis measures the value of the marginal product of labor *and* the wage rate. The curve shown is the **value of the marginal product curve** of labor. This curve, like the marginal product of labor curve, slopes downward because of diminishing returns to labor in production. That is, the value of the

table 69.2

Value of the Marginal Product of Labor for George and Martha's Farm

Quantity of labor *L* (workers)	Marginal product of labor *MPL* (bushels per worker)	Value of the marginal product of labor *VMPL = P × MPL*
0		
	19	$380
1		
	17	340
2		
	15	300
3		
	13	260
4		
	11	220
5		
	9	180
6		
	7	140
7		
	5	100
8		

marginal product of each worker is less than that of the preceding worker because the marginal product of each worker is less than that of the preceding worker.

We have just seen that to maximize profit, George and Martha hire workers until the wage rate is equal to the value of the marginal product of the last worker employed. Let's use the example to see how this principle really works.

figure 69.3

The Value of the Marginal Product Curve

This curve shows how the value of the marginal product of labor depends on the number of workers employed. It slopes downward because of diminishing returns to labor in production. To maximize profit, George and Martha choose the level of employment at which the value of the marginal product of labor is equal to the market wage rate. For example, at a wage rate of $200 the profit-maximizing level of employment is 5 workers, shown by point *A*. The value of the marginal product curve of a factor is the producer's individual demand curve for that factor.

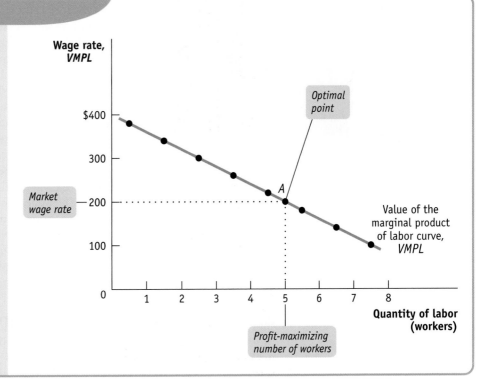

Assume that George and Martha currently employ 3 workers and that these workers must be paid the market wage rate of $200. Should they employ an additional worker?

Looking at Table 69.2, we see that if George and Martha currently employ 3 workers, the value of the marginal product of an additional worker is $260. So if they employ an additional worker, they will increase the value of their production by $260 but increase their cost by only $200, yielding an increased profit of $60. In fact, a firm can always increase profit by employing one more unit of a factor of production as long as the value of the marginal product produced by that unit exceeds the factor price.

Alternatively, suppose that George and Martha employ 8 workers. By reducing the number of workers to 7, they can save $200 in wages. In addition, the value of the marginal product of the 8th worker is only $100. So, by reducing employment by one worker, they can increase profit by $200 − $100 = $100. In other words, a firm can always increase profit by employing one less unit of a factor of production as long as the value of the marginal product produced by that unit is less than the factor price.

Using this method, we can see from Table 69.2 that the profit-maximizing employment level is 5 workers, given a wage rate of $200. The value of the marginal product of the 5th worker is $220, so adding the 5th worker results in $20 of additional profit. But George and Martha should not hire more than 5 workers: the value of the marginal product of the 6th worker is only $180, $20 less than the cost of that worker. So, to maximize profit, George and Martha should employ workers up to but not beyond the point at which the value of the marginal product of the last worker employed is equal to the wage rate.

Look again at the value of the marginal product curve in Figure 69.3. To determine the profit-maximizing level of employment, we set the value of the marginal product of labor equal to the price of labor—a wage rate of $200 per worker. This means that the profit-maximizing level of employment is at point *A*, corresponding to an employment level of 5 workers. If the wage rate were higher, we would simply move up the curve and decrease the number of workers employed: if the wage rate were lower than $200, we would move down the curve and increase the number of workers employed.

In this example, George and Martha have a small farm in which the potential employment level varies from 0 to 8 workers, and they hire workers up to the point at which the value of the marginal product of another worker would fall below the wage rate. For a larger farm with many employees, the value of the marginal product of labor falls only slightly when an additional worker is employed. As a result, there will be some worker whose value of the marginal product almost exactly equals the wage rate. (In keeping with the George and Martha example, this means that some worker generates a value of the marginal product of approximately $200.) In this case, the firm maximizes profit by choosing a level of employment at which the value of the marginal product of the last worker hired *equals* (to a very good approximation) the wage rate.

Firms keep hiring more workers until the value of the marginal product of labor equals the wage rate.

In the interest of simplicity, we will assume from now on that firms use this rule to determine the profit-maximizing level of employment. *This means that the value of the marginal product of labor curve is the individual firm's labor demand curve.* And in general, a firm's value of the marginal product curve for any factor of production is that firm's individual demand curve for that factor of production.

Shifts of the Factor Demand Curve

As in the case of ordinary demand curves, it is important to distinguish between movements along the factor demand curve and shifts of the factor demand curve. What causes factor demand curves to shift? There are three main causes:

- Changes in the prices of goods
- Changes in the supply of other factors
- Changes in technology

Changes in the Prices of Goods Remember that factor demand is derived demand: if the price of the good that is produced with a factor changes, so will the value of the marginal product of the factor. That is, in the case of labor demand, if P changes, $VMPL = P \times MPL$ will change at any given level of employment.

Figure 69.4 illustrates the effects of changes in the price of wheat, assuming that $200 is the current wage rate. Panel (a) shows the effect of an *increase* in the price of wheat. This shifts the value of the marginal product of labor curve upward because $VMPL$ rises at any given level of employment. If the wage rate remains unchanged at $200, the optimal point moves from point A to point B: the profit-maximizing level of employment rises.

Panel (b) shows the effect of a *decrease* in the price of wheat. This shifts the value of the marginal product of labor curve downward. If the wage rate remains unchanged at $200, the optimal point moves from point A to point C: the profit-maximizing level of employment falls.

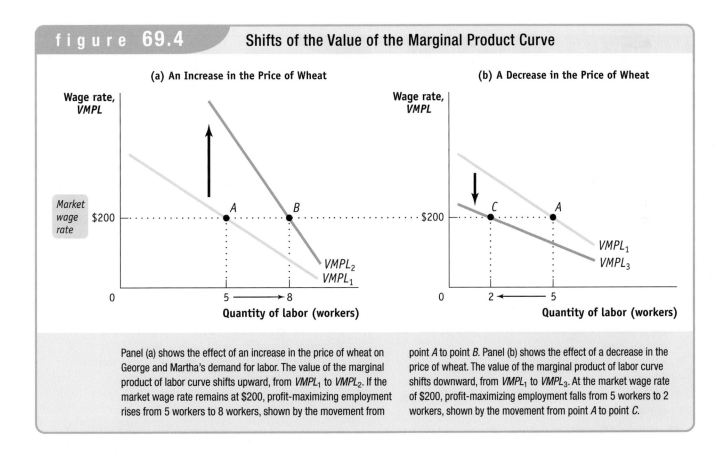

figure 69.4   Shifts of the Value of the Marginal Product Curve

Panel (a) shows the effect of an increase in the price of wheat on George and Martha's demand for labor. The value of the marginal product of labor curve shifts upward, from $VMPL_1$ to $VMPL_2$. If the market wage rate remains at $200, profit-maximizing employment rises from 5 workers to 8 workers, shown by the movement from point A to point B. Panel (b) shows the effect of a decrease in the price of wheat. The value of the marginal product of labor curve shifts downward, from $VMPL_1$ to $VMPL_3$. At the market wage rate of $200, profit-maximizing employment falls from 5 workers to 2 workers, shown by the movement from point A to point C.

Changes in the Supply of Other Factors Suppose that George and Martha acquire more land to cultivate—say, by clearing a woodland on their property. Each worker now produces more wheat because each one has more land to work with. As a result, the marginal product of labor on the farm rises at any given level of employment. This has the same effect as an increase in the price of wheat, which is illustrated in panel (a) of Figure 69.4: the value of the marginal product of labor curve shifts upward, and at any given wage rate the profit-maximizing level of employment rises. Similarly, suppose

George and Martha cultivate less land. This leads to a fall in the marginal product of labor at any given employment level. Each worker produces less wheat because each has less land to work with. As a result, the value of the marginal product of labor curve shifts downward—as in panel (b) of Figure 69.4—and the profit-maximizing level of employment falls.

Changes in Technology In general, the effect of technological progress on the demand for any given factor can go either way: improved technology can either increase or decrease the demand for a given factor of production.

How can technological progress decrease factor demand? Consider horses, which were once an important factor of production. The development of substitutes for horse power, such as automobiles and tractors, greatly reduced the demand for horses.

The usual effect of technological progress, however, is to increase the demand for a given factor, often because it raises the marginal product of the factor. In particular, although there have been persistent fears that machinery would reduce the demand for labor, over the long run the U.S. economy has seen both large wage increases and large increases in employment, suggesting that technological progress has greatly increased labor demand.

Module 69 AP Review

Solutions appear at the back of the book.

Check Your Understanding

1. Suppose that the government places price controls on the market for college professors, imposing a wage that is lower than the market wage. Describe the effect of this policy on the production of college degrees. What sectors of the economy do you think would be adversely affected by this policy? What sectors of the economy might benefit?

2. a. Suppose service industries, such as retailing and banking, experience an increase in demand. These industries use relatively more labor than nonservice industries. Does the demand curve for labor shift to the right, shift to the left, or remain unchanged?

   b. Suppose diminishing fish populations off the coast of Maine lead to policies restricting the use of the most productive types of nets in that area. The result is a decrease in the number of fish caught per day by commercial fishers in Maine. The price of fish is unaffected. Does the demand curve for fishers in Maine shift to the right, shift to the left, or remain unchanged?

Tackle the Test: Multiple-Choice Questions

1. Which of the following is an example of *physical* capital?
   a. manual labor
   b. welding equipment
   c. farm land
   d. lumber
   e. education

2. Which of the following can shift the factor demand curve to the right?
   I. an increase in the price of the good being produced
   II. an increase in the factor's marginal productivity
   III. a technological advance
   a. I only
   b. II only
   c. III only
   d. I and II only
   e. I, II, and III

3. Factor market demand is called a *derived* demand because it
   a. derives its name from the Latin *factorus*.
   b. is derived from the market wage received by workers.
   c. is derived from the productivity of workers.
   d. is derived from the product market.
   e. derives its shape from the price of the factor.

4. Which factor of production receives the largest portion of income in the United States?
   a. land
   b. labor
   c. physical capital
   d. entrepreneurship
   e. interest

5. The individual firm's demand curve for labor is
   a. the *VMPL* curve.
   b. upward sloping.
   c. horizontal at the level of the product price.
   d. vertical.
   e. equal to the *MPL* curve.

Tackle the Test: Free-Response Questions

1. Refer to the table below. Assume the firm can sell all of the output it produces at a price of $15.

Quantity of labor (workers)	Quantity of output
0	0
1	300
2	550
3	700
4	800
5	850
6	890

   a. What is the value of the marginal product of labor of the 3rd worker?
   b. Draw a correctly labeled graph showing the firm's demand curve for labor.
   c. What happens to the demand curve for labor if the price of the product increases to $20? Show the result on your graph from part b.
   d. Assume that a technological advance doubles the productivity of workers. Calculate the total quantity that will now be produced with each quantity of workers.

   1 point: Axes are correctly labeled.

   1 point: *VMPL* is downward sloping and labeled.

   1 point: *VMPL* is plotted using correct numbers (see graph).

   1 point: The demand curve for labor shifts to the right.

   1 point: *VMPL* curve is shown shifted to the right.

   1 point: The new quantities produced are 600; 1,100; 1,400; 1,600; 1,700; and 1,780.

2. Draw a separate, correctly labeled graph illustrating the effect of each of the following changes on the demand for labor. Adopt the usual *ceteris paribus* assumption that all else remains unchanged in each case.
   a. The price of the product being produced decreases.
   b. Worker productivity increases.
   c. Firms invest in more capital to be used by workers.

Answer (7 points)

1 point: *VMPL* = 150 × $15 = $2,250

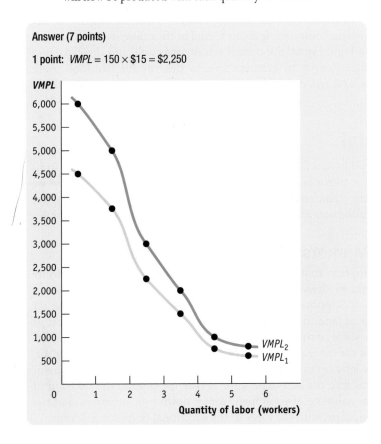

Module 70
The Markets for Land and Capital

In Figure 69.1 we saw the factor distribution of income and found that approximately 70% of total income in the economy took the form of compensation for employees. Because labor is such an important resource, it is often used as the example in discussions of factor markets. But land and capital are critical resources as well, and their markets have unique characteristics worthy of examination. In this module we look more closely at the markets for land and capital before moving on to discuss the labor market further in Module 71.

Land and Capital

In the previous module we used a labor market example to explain why a firm's individual demand curve for a factor is its value of the marginal product curve. Now we look at the distinguishing characteristics of demand and supply in land and capital markets, and how the equilibrium price and quantity of these factors are determined.

Demand in the Markets for Land and Capital

If we maintain the assumption that the markets for goods and services are perfectly competitive, the result that we derived for demand in the labor market also applies to other factors of production. Suppose, for example, that a farmer is considering whether to rent an additional acre of land for the next year. He or she will compare the cost of renting that acre with the value of the additional output generated by employing an additional acre—the value of the marginal product of an acre of land. To maximize profit, the farmer will rent more land up until the value of the marginal product of an acre of land is equal to the rental rate per acre. The same is true for capital: the decision of whether to rent an additional piece of equipment comes down to a comparison of the additional cost of the equipment with the value of the additional output it generates.

What if the farmer already owns the land or the firm already owns the equipment? As discussed in Module 52 in the context of Babette's Cajun Café, even if you own land or capital, there is an implicit cost—the opportunity cost—of using it for a given activity because it could be used for something else, such as renting it out to other firms at the market rental rate. So a profit-maximizing firm employs additional units of land and capital until the cost of the last unit employed, explicit or implicit, is equal to the value of the marginal product of that unit. We call the explicit cost of renting a unit of land or capital for a set period of time its **rental rate.**

As with labor, due to diminishing returns, the value of the marginal product curve and therefore the individual firm's demand curves for land and capital slope downward.

> The **rental rate** of either land or capital is the cost, explicit or implicit, of using a unit of that asset for a given period of time.

Supply in the Markets for Land and Capital

Figure 70.1 illustrates the markets for land and capital. The red curve in panel (a) is the supply curve for land. As we have drawn it, the supply curve for land is relatively steep and therefore relatively inelastic. This reflects the fact that finding new supplies of land for production is typically difficult and expensive—for example, creating new farmland through expensive irrigation.

The red curve in panel (b) is the supply curve for capital. In contrast to the supply curve for land, the supply curve for capital is relatively flat and therefore relatively elastic. That's because the supply of capital is relatively responsive to price: capital is typically paid for with the savings of investors, and the amount of savings that investors make available is relatively responsive to the rental rate for capital.

As in the case of supply curves for goods and services, the supply curve for a factor of production will shift as the factor becomes more or less available. For example, the supply of farmland could decrease as a result of a drought or the supply of capital could increase as a result of a government policy to promote investment. Because of diminishing returns, when the supply of land or capital changes, its marginal product will change.

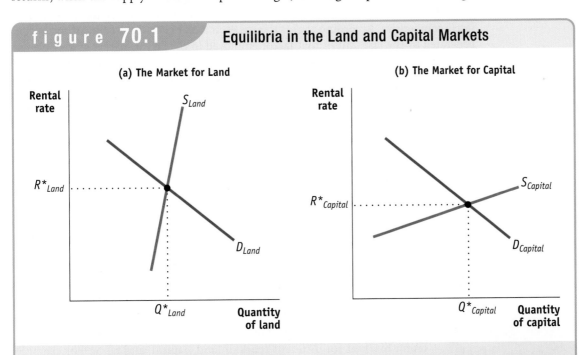

figure 70.1 **Equilibria in the Land and Capital Markets**

Panel (a) illustrates equilibrium in the market for land; panel (b) illustrates equilibrium in the market for capital. The supply curve for land is relatively steep, reflecting the high cost of increasing the quantity of productive land. The supply curve for capital, in contrast, is relatively flat, due to the relatively high responsiveness of savings to changes in the rental rate for capital. The equilibrium rental rates for land and capital, as well as the equilibrium quantities transacted, are given by the intersections of the demand and supply curves. In a competitive land market, each unit of land will be paid the equilibrium value of the marginal product of land, R^*_{Land}. Likewise, in a competitive capital market, each unit of capital will be paid the equilibrium value of the marginal product of capital, $R^*_{Capital}$.

When the supply of land or capital decreases, the marginal product and rental rate increase. For example, if the number of available delivery trucks decreased, the additional benefit from the last truck used would be higher than before—it would serve more critical delivery needs—and firms would pay more for it. Likewise, when the supply of land or capital increases, the marginal product and rental rate decrease.

Equilibrium in Land and Capital Markets

The equilibrium rental rate and quantity in the land and capital markets are found at the intersection of the supply and demand curves in Figure 70.1. Panel (a) shows the equilibrium in the market for land. Summing all of the firm demand curves for land gives us the market demand curve for land. The equilibrium rental rate for land is R^*_{Land}, and the equilibrium quantity of land employed in production is Q^*_{Land}. In a competitive land market, each unit of land will be paid the equilibrium value of the marginal product of land.

Panel (b) shows the equilibrium in the market for capital. The equilibrium rental rate for capital is $R^*_{Capital}$, and the equilibrium quantity of capital employed in production is $Q^*_{Capital}$. In a competitive capital market, each unit of capital will be paid the equilibrium value of the marginal product of capital.

Now that we know how equilibrium rental rates and quantities are determined in land and capital markets, we can learn how these markets influence the factor distribution of income. To do this, we look more closely at marginal productivity in factor markets.

Marginal Productivity Theory

The **marginal productivity theory of income distribution** sums up what we have learned about payments to factors when goods markets and factor markets are perfectly competitive. According to this theory, each factor is paid the value of the output generated by the last unit of that factor employed in the factor market as a whole—its equilibrium value of the marginal product. To understand why the marginal productivity theory of income distribution is important, look back at Figure 69.1, which shows the factor distribution of income in the United States, and ask yourself this question: who or what determined that labor would get 70.9% of total U.S. income? Why not 90% or 50%?

The answer, according to this theory, is that the division of income among the economy's factors of production isn't arbitrary: in the economy-wide factor market, the price paid for each factor is equal to the increase in the value of output generated by the last unit of that factor employed in the market. If a unit of labor is paid more than a unit of capital, it is because at the equilibrium quantity of each factor, the value of the marginal product of labor exceeds the value of the marginal product of capital.

Ariel Skelley/Blend Images/Getty Images

So far we have treated factor markets as if every unit of each factor were identical. That is, as if all land were identical, all labor were identical, and all capital were identical. But in reality factors differ considerably with respect to productivity. For instance, land resources differ in their ability to produce crops and workers have different skills and abilities. Rather than thinking of one land market for all land resources in an economy, and similarly one capital market and one labor market, we can instead think of different markets for different types of land, capital, and labor. For example, the market for computer programmers is different from the market for pastry chefs.

When we consider that there are separate factor markets for different types of factors, the marginal productivity theory of income distribution still holds. That is, when the labor market for computer programmers is in equilibrium, the wage rate earned by all computer programmers is equal to the market's equilibrium value of the marginal product—the value of the marginal product of the last computer programmer hired in that market. The

Help Wanted!

Hamill Manufacturing of Pennsylvania makes precision components for military helicopters and nuclear submarines. Their highly skilled senior machinists are well paid compared to other workers in manufacturing, earning nearly $70,000 in 2006, excluding benefits. Like most skilled machinists in the United States, Hamill's machinists are very productive: according to the National Mechanists Association, in 2006 each skilled American machinist generated approximately $120,000 in yearly revenue.

But there is a $50,000 difference between the salary paid to Hamill machinists and the revenue they generate. Does this mean that the marginal productivity theory of income distribution doesn't hold? Doesn't the theory imply that machinists should be paid $120,000, the average revenue that each one generates? The answer is no, for two reasons. First, the $120,000 figure is averaged over *all machinists currently employed*. The theory says that machinists will be paid the value

of the marginal product of the *last machinist hired,* and due to diminishing returns to labor, that value will be lower than the average over all machinists currently employed. Second, a worker's equilibrium wage rate includes other costs, such as employee benefits, that have to be added to the $70,000 salary. The marginal productivity theory of income distribution says that workers are paid a wage rate, *including all benefits,* equal to the value of the marginal product. At Hamill, the machinists have job security and good benefits, which add to their salary. Including these benefits, machinists' total compensation will be equal to the value of the marginal product of the last machinist employed.

In Hamill's case, there is yet another factor that explains the $50,000 gap: there are not enough machinists at the current wage rate. Although the company increased the number of employees from 85 in 2004 to 110 in 2006, they would like to hire more. Why doesn't Hamill

Source: Courtesy U.S. Air Force

raise its wages in order to attract more skilled machinists? The problem is that the work they do is so specialized that it is hard to hire from the outside, even when the company raises wages as an inducement. To address this problem, Hamill is now spending a significant amount of money training each new hire. In the end, it does appear that the marginal productivity theory of income distribution holds.

marginal productivity theory can explain the distribution of income among different types of land, labor, and capital as well as the distribution of income among the factors of production. In Module 73 we look more closely at the distribution of income between different types of labor and the extent to which the marginal productivity theory of income distribution explains differences in workers' wages.

Module 70 AP Review

Solutions appear at the back of the book.

Check Your Understanding

1. Explain how each of the following events would affect the equilibrium rental rate and the equilibrium quantity in the land market.
   a. Developers improve the process of filling in coastal waters with rocks and soil to form large new areas of land.
   b. New fertilizers improve the productivity of each acre of farmland.

2. Explain the following statement: "When firms in different industries all compete for the same land, the value of the marginal product of the last unit of land rented will be equal across all firms, regardless of whether they are in different industries."

Tackle the Test: Multiple-Choice Questions

1. The implicit cost of capital that you own is
   a. the rental rate.
   b. greater than the rental rate.
   c. the original purchase price of the capital.
   d. greater than the original purchase price of the capital.
   e. zero because you already own it.

2. Which of the following is true in relation to a very steep supply curve for land?
   - I. It is relatively elastic.
   - II. The quantity of land is very responsive to price changes.
   - III. Finding new supplies of land is relatively expensive and difficult.
   a. I only
   b. II only
   c. III only
   d. I and II only
   e. I, II, and III

3. The explicit cost of land you don't own is equal to the
   a. rental rate.
   b. interest rate.
   c. profit received from using that land.
   d. market wage rate.
   e. marginal product of land.

4. A firm will continue to employ more land until its value of the marginal product of land is
   a. zero.
   b. maximized.
   c. equal to the rental rate.
   d. equal to the wage rate.
   e. equal to the value of the marginal product of labor and capital.

5. According to the marginal productivity theory of income distribution,
   a. each unit of a factor will be paid the value of its marginal product.
   b. as more of a factor is used, its marginal productivity increases.
   c. factors that receive higher payments are less productive.
   d. capital should receive the highest portion of factor income.
   e. each factor is paid the equilibrium value of its marginal product.

Tackle the Test: Free-Response Questions

1. Refer to the table below. Assume that the price of the product is $10 and the rental rate for capital is $100 per unit.

Quantity of capital (units)	Quantity of output
0	0
1	30
2	55
3	70
4	78
5	85
6	89

   a. What is the VMP of the 2nd unit of capital?
   b. Will the firm employ the 2nd unit of capital? Explain.
   c. How many units of capital will the firm hire? Explain.

   Answer (5 points)

   1 point: $VMP = 25 \times \$10 = \$250$

   1 point: Yes

   1 point: Because the VMP of $250 is greater than the rental rate of $100

   1 point: 3

   1 point: Because the VMP exceeds the rental rate for the first 3 units

2. Draw a correctly labeled graph showing how the market rental rate and quantity of land are determined in the land market. On your graph, be sure to include each of the following: the supply and demand curves for land, the equilibrium rental rate, the equilibrium quantity of land employed, and correct labels on the axes.

Here, to hire an additional worker, the monopolist has to raise the wage, so the marginal factor cost is the wage plus the wage increase for those workers who could otherwise be hired at the lower wage.

Equilibrium in the Imperfectly Competitive Labor Market

In a perfectly competitive labor market, firms hire labor until the value of the marginal product of labor equals the market wage. With imperfect competition in a factor market, a firm will hire additional workers until the marginal revenue product of labor equals the marginal factor cost of labor. Note that the marginal revenue product of labor for a perfectly competitive firm is the same as the value of the marginal product of labor and that the marginal factor cost of labor for a perfectly competitive firm is the market wage. The terms *marginal revenue product* and *marginal factor cost* are generally applicable to the analysis of any market structure. The terms we used previously, *value of the marginal product* and *wage,* refer to the specific cases of perfect competition in the product market and labor market respectively. Thus, we can generalize and say that every firm hires workers up to the point at which the marginal revenue product of labor equals the marginal factor cost of labor:

(71-2)   Hire workers until $MRPL = MFCL$

Equilibrium in the labor market with imperfect competition is shown in Figure 71.6. Once an imperfectly competitive firm has determined the optimal number of workers to hire, L^*, it finds the wage necessary to hire that number of workers by starting at the point on the labor supply curve above the optimal number of workers, and looking straight to the left to see the wage level at that point, W^*.

Let's put the information we just learned together, again referring to Figure 71.6: The labor demand curve is the marginal revenue product curve. In an imperfectly competitive labor market, the firm must offer a higher wage to hire more workers, so

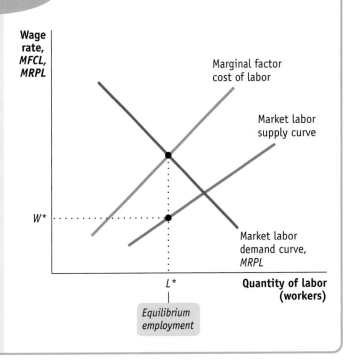

figure 71.6

Equilibrium in the Labor Market with Imperfect Competition

The equilibrium quantity of labor is found where the marginal revenue product of labor equals the marginal factor cost, at L^*. The equilibrium wage, W^*, is found on the vertical axis at the height of the market supply curve directly above L^*.

the marginal factor cost curve is above the labor supply curve. The equilibrium quantity of labor is found where the marginal revenue product equals the marginal factor cost, as represented by L^* on the graph. The firm will pay the wage required to hire L^* workers, which is found on the supply curve above L^*. The labor supply curve shows that the quantity of labor supplied is equal to L^* at a wage of W^*. The equilibrium wage in the market is thus W^*. Note that, unlike the wage in a perfectly competitive labor market, the wage in the imperfectly competitive labor market is less than the marginal factor cost of labor.

In Modules 69–71 we have learned how firms determine the optimal amount of land, labor, or capital to hire in factor markets. But often there are different combinations of factors that a firm can use to produce the same level of output. In the next module, we look at how a firm chooses between alternative input combinations for producing a given level of output.

Module 71 AP Review

Solutions appear at the back of the book.

Check Your Understanding

1. Formerly, Clive was free to work as many or as few hours per week as he wanted. But a new law limits the maximum number of hours he can work per week to 35. Explain under what circumstances, if any, he is made
   a. worse off.
   b. equally well off.
   c. better off.

2. Explain in terms of the income and substitution effects how a fall in Clive's wage rate can induce him to work more hours than before.

Tackle the Test: Multiple-Choice Questions

1. Which of the following is necessarily true if you work more when your wage rate increases?
   a. The income effect is large.
   b. The substitution effect is small.
   c. The income effect dominates the substitution effect.
   d. The substitution effect dominates the income effect.
   e. The income effect equals the substitution effect.

2. Which of the following will cause you to work more as your wage rate decreases?
   I. the income effect
   II. the substitution effect
   III. a desire for leisure
   a. I only
   b. II only
   c. III only
   d. I and II only
   e. I, II, and III

3. Which of the following will shift the supply curve for labor to the right?
   a. a decrease in the labor force participation rate of women
   b. a decrease in population
   c. an increase in wealth

   d. a decrease in the opportunity cost of leisure
   e. an increase in labor market opportunities for women

4. An increase in the wage rate will
   a. shift the labor supply curve to the right.
   b. shift the labor supply curve to the left.
   c. cause an upward movement along the labor supply curve.
   d. cause a downward movement along the labor supply curve.
   e. have no effect on the quantity of labor supplied.

5. The factor demand curve for a firm in an imperfectly competitive factor market is the same as which of the following curves?
   a. *VMP*
   b. *MPP*
   c. *MFC*
   d. *MRP*
   e. *MP*

Tackle the Test: Free-Response Questions

1. Assume the demand curve for a firm's product is as shown below and that the firm can hire as many workers as it wants for a wage of $80 per day.

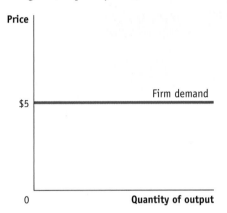

a. What is the market structure of the factor market in which the firm hires labor? Explain.
b. What is the market structure of the product market in which the firm sells its good? Explain.
c. Define marginal factor cost. What is the marginal factor cost of labor for this firm?
d. If the last worker hired produces an additional 20 units of output, what is the last worker's *MRPL*? Explain.

Answer (8 points)

1 point: The firm hires labor in a perfectly competitive labor market.

1 point: The firm is a price-taker in the labor market. (It can hire all that it wants for $80 per day.)

1 point: The firm sells its good in a perfectly competitive product market.

1 point: The horizontal demand curve indicates that the firm is a price-taker in the product market (it can sell all the output it wants at the market price of $5).

1 point: the additional cost of hiring one more unit of a factor

1 point: $80

1 point: $100

1 point: $MRPL = MPL \times MR$, $MPL = 20$, $MR = \$5$, so $MRPL = 20 \times \$5 = \$100$.

2. a. Draw a correctly labeled graph showing a perfectly competitive labor market in equilibrium. On your graph, be sure to label the labor demand curve, the labor supply curve, marginal revenue product of labor, the equilibrium wage (W^*), and the equilibrium quantity of labor (L^*).
b. On your graph, illustrate how a decrease in the price of the product made by the firm would affect the equilibrium wage and quantity of labor. Label the resulting wage rate W_2 and the resulting quantity of labor L_2.

What you will learn in this **Module:**

- How firms determine the optimal input mix
- The cost-minimizing rule for hiring inputs

Module 72
The Cost-Minimizing Input Combination

In the past three modules we discussed the markets for factors of production—land, capital, and labor—and how firms determine the optimal quantity of each factor to hire. But firms don't determine how much of each input to hire separately. Production requires multiple inputs, and firms must decide what *combination* of inputs to use to produce their output. In this module, we will look at how firms decide the optimal combination of factors for producing the desired level of output.

Alternative Input Combinations

In many instances a firm can choose among a number of alternative combinations of inputs that will produce a given level of output. For example, on George and Martha's wheat farm, the decision might involve labor and capital. To produce their optimal quantity of wheat, they could choose to have a relatively *capital-intensive* operation by investing in several tractors and other mechanized farm equipment and hiring relatively little labor. Alternatively, they could have a more *labor-intensive* operation by hiring a lot of workers to do much of the planting and harvesting by hand. The same amount of wheat can be produced using many different combinations of capital and labor. George and Martha must determine which combination of inputs will maximize their profits.

To begin our study of the optimal combination of inputs, we'll look at the relationship between the inputs used for production. Depending on the situation, inputs can be either substitutes or complements.

Substitutes and Complements in Factor Markets

In Section 2 we discussed substitutes and complements in the context of the supply and demand model. Two goods are *substitutes* if a rise in the price of one good makes consumers more willing to buy the other good. For example, an increase in the price of oranges will cause some buyers to switch from purchasing oranges to purchasing tangerines. When buyers tend to consume two goods together, the goods are known as *complements*. For example, cereal and milk are considered complements because many people consume them together. If the price of cereal increases, people will buy less cereal and therefore need less milk. The decision about how much of a good to buy is influenced by the prices of related goods.

The concepts of substitutes and complements also apply to a firm's purchase of inputs. And just as the price of related goods affects consumers' purchasing decisions, the price of other inputs can affect a firm's decision about how much of an input it will use. In some situations, capital and labor are substitutes. For example, George and Martha can produce the same amount of wheat by substituting more tractors for fewer farm workers. Likewise, ATM machines can substitute for bank tellers.

Capital and labor can also be complements when more of one increases the marginal product of the other. For example, a farm worker is more productive when George and Martha buy a tractor, and each tractor requires a worker to drive it. Office workers are more productive when they can use faster computers, and doctors are more productive with modern X-ray machines. In these cases the quantity and quality of capital available affect the marginal product of labor, and thus the demand for labor. Given the relationship between inputs, how does a firm determine which of the possible combinations to use?

istockphoto

Determining the Optimal Input Mix

If several alternative input combinations can be used to produce the optimal level of output, a profit-maximizing firm will select the input combination with the lowest cost. This process is known as cost minimization.

Cost Minimization

How does a firm determine the combination of inputs that maximizes profits? Let's consider this question using an example.

Imagine you manage a grocery store chain and you need to decide the right combination of self-checkout stations and cashiers at a new store. Table 72.1 shows the alternative combinations of capital (self-checkout stations) and labor (cashiers) you can hire to check out customers shopping at the store. If the store puts in 20 self-checkout stations, you will need to hire 1 cashier to monitor every 5 stations for a total of 4 cashiers. However, trained cashiers are faster than customers at scanning goods, so the store could check out the same number of customers using 10 cashiers and only 10 self-checkout stations.

If you can check out the same number of customers using either of these combinations of capital and labor, how do you decide which combination of inputs to use? By finding the input combination that costs the least—the cost-minimizing input combination.

table 72.1

Cashiers and Self-Checkout Stations

Capital (self-checkout stations)	Labor (cashiers)
Rental rate = $1,000/month	Wage rate = $1,600/month
a. 20	4
b. 10	10

Assume that the cost to rent, operate, and maintain a self-checkout station for a month is $1,000 and hiring a cashier costs $1,600 per month. The cost of each input combination from Table 72.1 is shown below.

a. cost of capital $20 \times \$1,000 = \$20,000$
    cost of labor $4 \times \$1,600 = \underline{\$\ 6,400}$
    TOTAL $\$26,400$

b. cost of capital $10 \times \$1,000 = \$10,000$
    cost of labor $10 \times \$1,600 = \underline{\$16,000}$
    TOTAL $\$26,000$

Clearly, your firm would choose the lower cost combination, combination b, and hire 10 cashiers and put in 10 self-checkout stations.

When firms must choose between alternative combinations of inputs, they evaluate the cost of each combination and select the one that minimizes the cost of production. This can be done by calculating the total cost of each alternative combination of inputs, as shown in this example. However, because the number of possible combinations can be very large, it is more practical to use marginal analysis to find the cost-minimizing level of output–which brings us to the cost-minimization rule.

The Cost-Minimization Rule

We already know that the additional output that results from hiring an additional unit of an input is the marginal product (*MP*) of that input. Firms want to receive the highest possible marginal product from each dollar spent on inputs. To do this, firms adjust their hiring of inputs until the marginal product per dollar is equal for all inputs. This is the **cost-minimization rule.** When the inputs are labor and capital, this amounts to equating the marginal product of labor (*MPL*) per dollar spent on wages to the marginal product of capital (*MPK*) per dollar spent to rent capital:

(72-1) $MPL/\text{Wage} = MPK/\text{Rental rate}$

To understand why cost minimization occurs when the marginal product per dollar is equal for all inputs, let's start by looking at two counterexamples. Consider a situation in which the marginal product of labor per dollar is greater than the marginal product of capital per dollar. This situation is described by Equation 72-2:

(72-2) $MPL/\text{Wage} > MPK/\text{Rental rate}$

Suppose the marginal product of labor is 20 units and the marginal product of capital is 100 units. If the wage is $10 and the rental rate for capital is $100, then the marginal product per dollar will be 20/$10 = 2 units of output per dollar for labor and 100/$100 = 1 units of output per dollar for capital. The firm is receiving 2 additional units of output for each dollar spent on labor and only 1 additional unit of output for each dollar spent on capital. In this case, the firm gets more additional output for its money by hiring labor, so it should hire more labor and less capital. Because of diminishing returns, as the firm hires more labor, the marginal product of labor falls and as it hires less capital, the marginal product of capital rises. The firm will continue to substitute labor for capital until the falling marginal product of labor per dollar meets the rising marginal product of capital per dollar and the two are equivalent. That is, the firm will adjust its hiring of capital and labor until the marginal product per dollar spent on each input is equal, as in Equation 72-1.

Next, consider a situation in which the marginal product of capital per dollar is greater than the marginal product of labor per dollar. This situation is described by Equation 72-3:

(72-3) $MPL/\text{Wage} < MPK/\text{Rental rate}$

Self-checkout lines have reduced the need for many stores to hire extra cashiers.

A firm determines the cost-minimizing combination of inputs using the **cost-minimization rule:** hire factors so that the marginal product per dollar spent on each factor is the same.

Let's continue with the assumption that the marginal product of labor for the last unit of labor hired is 20 units and the marginal product of capital for the last unit of capital hired is 100 units. If the wage is $10 and the rental rate for capital is $25, then the marginal product per dollar will be 20/$10 = 2 units of output per dollar for labor and 100/$25 = 4 units of output per dollar for capital. The firm is receiving 4 additional units of output for each dollar spent on capital and only 2 additional units of output for each dollar spent on labor. In this case, the firm gets more additional output for its money by hiring capital, so it should hire more capital and less labor. Because of diminishing returns, as the firm hires more capital, the marginal product of capital falls, and as it hires less labor, the marginal product of labor rises. The firm will continue to hire more capital and less labor until the falling marginal product of capital per dollar meets the rising marginal product of labor per dollar to satisfy the cost-minimization rule. That is, the firm will adjust its hiring of capital and labor until the marginal product per dollar spent on each input is equal.

The cost-minimization rule is analogous to the optimal consumption rule (introduced in Module 51), which has consumers maximize their utility by choosing the combination of goods so that the marginal utility per dollar is equal for all goods.

So far in this section we have learned how factor markets determine the equilibrium price and quantity in the markets for land, labor, and capital and how firms determine the combination of inputs they will hire. But how well do these models of factor markets explain the distribution of factor incomes in our economy? In Module 70 we considered how the marginal productivity theory of income distribution explains the factor distribution of income. In the final module in this section we look at the distribution of income in *labor* markets and consider to what extent the marginal productivity theory of income distribution explains wage differences.

Module 72 APReview

Solutions appear at the back of the book.

Check Your Understanding

1. A firm produces its output using only capital and labor. Labor costs $100 per worker per day and capital costs $200 per unit per day. If the marginal product of the last worker employed is 500 and the marginal product of the last unit of capital employed is 1,000, is the firm employing the cost-minimizing combination of inputs? Explain.

Tackle the Test: Multiple-Choice Questions

1. An automobile factory employs either assembly line workers or robotic arms to produce automobile engines. In this case, labor and capital are considered
   a. independent.
   b. complements.
   c. substitutes.
   d. supplements.
   e. human capital.

2. If an increase in the amount of capital employed by a firm leads to an increase in the marginal product of labor, labor and capital are considered
   a. independent.
   b. complements.
   c. substitutes.
   d. supplements.
   e. human capital.

3. If the marginal product of labor per dollar is greater than the marginal product of capital per dollar, which of the following is true? The firm should
   a. not change its employment of capital and labor.
   b. hire more capital.
   c. hire more labor.
   d. hire less labor.
   e. hire more capital and labor.

4. The cost-minimization rule states that costs are minimized when
   a. *MP* per dollar is equal for all factors.
   b. $(MP \times P)$ is equal for all factors.
   c. each factor's *MP* is the same.
   d. *MRP* is maximized.
   e. *MFC* is minimized.

5. A firm currently produces its desired level of output. Its marginal product of labor is 400, its marginal product of capital is 1,000, the wage rate is $20 and the rental rate of capital is $100. In that case, the firm should

a. employ more capital and more labor.
b. employ less labor and less capital.
c. employ less labor and more capital.
d. employ less capital and more labor.
e. not change its allocation of capital and labor.

Tackle the Test: Free-Response Questions

1. Answer the following questions under the assumption that firms use only two inputs and seek to maximize profit.
   a. Would it be wise for a firm that does not have the cost-minimizing combination of inputs to hire more of the input with the highest marginal product and less of the input with the lowest marginal product? Explain.
   b. What is the cost-minimization rule?
   c. When a firm hires more labor and less capital, what happens to the marginal product of labor per dollar and the marginal product of capital per dollar? Explain.

2. Refer to the table below. Assume that the wage is $10 per day and the price of pencils is $1.

Quantity of labor (workers)	Quantity of pencils produced
0	0
1	40
2	90
3	120
4	140
5	150
6	160
7	166

   a. What is the MPL of the 4th worker?
   b. What is the MPL per dollar of the 5th worker?
   c. How many workers would the firm hire if it hired every worker for whom the marginal product per dollar is greater than or equal to 1 pencil per dollar?
   d. If the marginal product per dollar spent on labor is 1 pencil per dollar, the marginal product of the last unit of capital hired is 100 pencils per dollar, and the rental rate is $50 per day, is the firm minimizing its cost? Explain.

What you will learn
in this **Module:**

- Labor market applications of the marginal productivity theory of income distribution
- Sources of wage disparities and the role of discrimination

Module 73
Theories of Income Distribution

In Module 70, we introduced the factor distribution of income and explained how the *marginal productivity theory of income distribution* helps to explain how income is divided among factors of production in an economy. We also considered how the markets for factors of production are broken down. There are different markets for different types of factors. For example, there are different labor markets for different types of labor, such as for computer programmers, pastry chefs, and economists. In this module, we look at the marginal productivity theory of income distribution and the extent to which it explains wage disparities between workers.

The Marginal Productivity Theory of Income Distribution

According to the marginal productivity theory of income distribution, the division of income among the economy's factors of production is determined by each factor's marginal productivity at the market equilibrium. If we consider an economy-wide factor market, the price paid for *all* factors in the economy is equal to the increase in the value of output generated by the last unit of the factor employed in the market. But what about the distribution of income among different labor markets and workers? Does the marginal productivity theory of income distribution help to explain why some workers earn more than others?

Marginal Productivity and Wage Inequality

A large part of the observed inequality in wages can be explained by considerations that are consistent with the marginal productivity theory of income distribution. In particular, there are three well-understood sources of wage differences across occupations and individuals.

The first is the existence of **compensating differentials:** across different types of jobs, wages are often higher or lower depending on how attractive or unattractive the

Compensating differentials are wage differences across jobs that reflect the fact that some jobs are less pleasant or more dangerous than others.

Arthur S. Aubry/Photodisc/Getty Images

job is. Workers in unpleasant or dangerous jobs receive a higher wage than workers in jobs that require the same skill, training, and effort but lack the unpleasant or dangerous qualities. For example, truckers who haul hazardous chemicals are paid more than truckers who haul bread. For any *particular* job, the marginal productivity theory of income distribution generally holds true. For example, hazardous-load truckers are paid a wage equal to the **equilibrium value of the marginal product** of the last person employed in the market for hazardous-load truckers.

A second reason for wage inequality that is clearly consistent with marginal productivity theory is differences in talent. People differ in their abilities: a high-ability person, by producing a better product that commands a higher price compared to a lower-ability person, generates a higher value of the marginal product. And these differences in the value of the marginal product translate into differences in earning potential. We all know that this is true in sports: practice is important, but 99.99% (at least) of the population just doesn't have what it takes to control a soccer ball like Lionel Messi or hit a tennis ball like Serena Williams. The same is true, though less obvious, in other fields of endeavor.

A third, very important reason for wage differences is differences in the quantity of *human capital*. Recall that human capital—education and training—is at least as important in the modern economy as physical capital in the form of buildings and machines. Different people "embody" quite different quantities of human capital, and a person with more human capital typically generates a higher value of the marginal product by producing more or better products. So differences in human capital account for substantial differences in wages. People with high levels of human capital, such as surgeons or engineers, generally receive high wages.

The most direct way to see the effect of human capital on wages is to look at the relationship between education levels and earnings. Figure 73.1 shows earnings differentials by gender, ethnicity, and three education levels for people 25 years or older in 2009. As you can see, regardless of gender or ethnicity, higher education is associated with higher median earnings. For example, in 2009 white females with 9 to 12 years of

figure 73.1

Earnings Differentials by Education, Gender, and Ethnicity, 2009

It is clear that, regardless of gender or ethnicity, education pays: those with a high school diploma earn more than those without one, and those with a college degree earn substantially more than those with only a high school diploma. Other patterns are evident as well: for any given education level, white males earn more than every other group, and males earn more than females for any given ethnic group.
Source: Bureau of Labor Statistics.

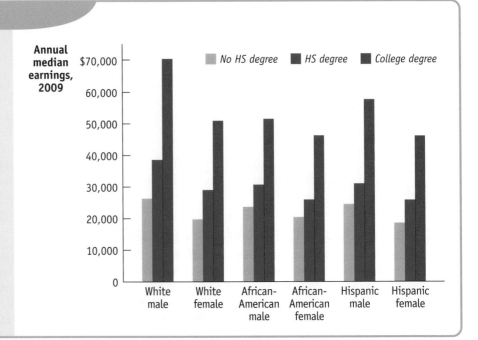

schooling but without a high school diploma had median earnings 30% less than those with a high school diploma and 60% less than those with a college degree—and similar patterns exist for the other five groups. Additional data show that surgeons—an occupation that requires steady hands and many years of formal training—earned an average of $219,770 in 2009.

Because even now men typically have had more years of education than women and whites more years than non-whites, differences in education level are part of the explanation for earnings differences.

It's also important to realize that formal education is not the only source of human capital; on-the-job training and experience are also very important. This point was highlighted by a 2003 National Science Foundation report on earnings differences between male and female scientists and engineers. The study was motivated by concerns over the male–female earnings gap: the median salary for women in science and engineering is about 24% less than the median salary for men. The study found that women in these occupations are, on average, younger than men and have considerably less experience than their male counterparts. This difference in age and experience, according to the study, explained most of the earnings differential. Differences in job tenure and experience can partly explain one notable aspect of Figure 73.1: that, across all ethnicities, women's median earnings are less than men's median earnings for any given education level.

But it's also important to emphasize that earnings differences arising from differences in human capital are not necessarily "fair." A society in which non-white children typically receive a poor education because they live in underfunded school districts, and then go on to earn low wages because they are poorly educated, may have labor markets that are well described by marginal productivity theory (and earnings consistent with the earnings differentials across ethnic groups shown in Figure 73.1). Yet many people would still consider the resulting distribution of income unfair.

Still, many observers think that actual wage differentials cannot be entirely explained by compensating differentials, differences in talent, and differences in human capital. They believe that market power, *efficiency wages,* and discrimination also play an important role. We will examine these forces next.

Unions are organizations of workers that try to raise wages and improve working conditions for their members by bargaining collectively.

Market Power

The marginal productivity theory of income distribution is based on the assumption that factor markets are perfectly competitive. In such markets we can expect workers to be paid the equilibrium value of their marginal product, regardless of who they are. But how valid is this assumption?

We studied markets that are *not* perfectly competitive in previous modules; now let's touch briefly on the ways in which labor markets may deviate from the competitive assumption.

One undoubted source of differences in wages between otherwise similar workers is **unions**—organizations that try to raise wages and improve working conditions for their members. Labor unions, when successful, replace one-on-one wage deals between workers and employers with "collective bargaining," in which the employer negotiates wages with union representatives. Without question, this leads to higher wages for those workers who are represented by unions. In 2009, the median weekly earnings of union members in the United States were $908, compared with $710 for workers not represented by unions—about a 22% difference.

Just as workers can sometimes organize to demand higher wages than they would otherwise receive, employers can sometimes organize to pay *lower* wages than would result from competition. For example, health care workers—doctors, nurses, and so on—sometimes argue that health maintenance organizations (HMOs) are engaged in a collective effort to hold down their wages.

Union members rally to demand higher wages.

Collective action, either by workers or by employers, is less common in the United States than it used to be. Several decades ago, around 30% of U.S. workers were union members. Today, however, union membership in the United States is relatively limited: less than 7.2% of the employees of private businesses are represented by unions. And although there are fields like health care in which a few large firms account for a sizable share of employment in certain geographical areas, the sheer size of the U.S. labor market and the ease with which most workers can move in search of higher-paying jobs probably mean that concerted efforts to hold wages below the unrestrained market equilibrium level rarely occur and even more rarely succeed.

Efficiency Wages

A second source of wage inequality is the phenomenon of *efficiency wages*—a type of incentive scheme used by employers to motivate workers to work hard and to reduce worker turnover. Suppose a worker performs a job that is extremely important but that the employer can observe how well the job is being performed only at infrequent intervals. This would be true, for example, for childcare providers. Then it often makes sense for the employer to pay more than the worker could earn in an alternative job—that is, more than the equilibrium wage. Why? Because earning a premium makes losing this job and having to take the alternative job quite costly for the worker. So a worker who happens to be observed performing poorly and is therefore fired is now worse off for having to accept a lower-paying job. The threat of losing a job that pays a premium motivates the worker to perform well and avoid being fired. Likewise, paying a premium also reduces worker turnover—the frequency with which an employee leaves a job voluntarily. Despite the fact that it may take no more effort and skill to be a childcare provider than to be an office worker, efficiency wages show why it often makes economic sense for a parent to pay a caregiver more than the equilibrium wage of an office worker.

The **efficiency-wage model** explains why we may observe wages offered above their equilibrium level. Like the price floors we studied in Module 8—and, in particular, much like the minimum wage—this phenomenon leads to a surplus of labor in labor markets that are characterized by the efficiency-wage model. This surplus of labor translates into unemployment—some workers are actively searching for a high-paying efficiency-wage job but are unable to get one, and other more fortunate but no more deserving workers are able to find work. As a result, two workers with exactly the same profile—the same skills and job history—may earn different wages: the worker who is lucky enough to get an efficiency-wage job earns more than the worker who gets a standard job (or who remains unemployed while searching for a higher-paying job). Efficiency wages are a response to a type of market failure that arises from the fact that some employees don't always perform as well as they should and are able to hide that fact. As a result, employers use above-equilibrium wages to motivate their employees, leading to an inefficient outcome.

Discrimination

It is an ugly fact that throughout history there has been discrimination against workers who are considered to be of the wrong race, ethnicity, gender, or other characteristics. How does this fit into our economic models?

The main insight economic analysis offers is that discrimination is *not* a natural consequence of market competition. On the contrary, market forces tend to work against discrimination. To see why, consider the incentives that would exist if social convention dictated that women be paid, say, 30% less than men with equivalent qualifications and experience. A company whose management was itself unbiased would then be able to reduce its costs by hiring women rather than men—and such companies would have an advantage over other companies that hired men despite their higher cost. The result would be to create an excess demand for female workers, which would tend to drive up their wages.

According to the **efficiency-wage model,** some employers pay an above-equilibrium wage as an incentive for better performance and loyalty.

But if market competition works against discrimination, how is it that so much discrimination has taken place? The answer is twofold. First, when labor markets don't work well, employers may have the ability to discriminate without hurting their profits. For example, market interferences (such as unions or minimum-wage laws) or market failures (such as efficiency wages) can lead to wages that are above their equilibrium levels. In these cases, there are more job applicants than there are jobs, leaving employers free to discriminate among applicants. In research published in the *American Economic Review,* two economists, Marianne Bertrand and Sendhil Mullainathan, documented discrimination in hiring by sending fictitious résumés to prospective employers on a random basis. Applicants with "white-sounding" names such as Emily Walsh were 50% more likely to be contacted than applicants with "African-American-sounding" names such as Lakisha Washington. Also, applicants with white-sounding names and good credentials were much more likely to be contacted than those without such credentials. By contrast, potential employers seemed to ignore the credentials of applicants with African-American-sounding names.

Second, discrimination has sometimes been institutionalized in government policy. This institutionalization has made it easier to maintain discrimination against market pressure. For example, at one time in the United States, African-Americans were barred from attending "whites-only" public schools and universities in many parts of the country and forced to attend inferior schools. Although market competition tends to work against *current* discrimination, it is not a remedy for past discrimination, which typically has had an impact on the education and experience of its victims and thereby reduces their income. The following FYI illustrates the way in which government policy enforced discrimination in the world's most famous racist regime, that of the former government of South Africa.

Wage Disparities in Practice

Wage rates in the United States cover a very wide range. In 2009, hundreds of thousands of workers received the legal federal minimum of $7.25 per hour. At the other extreme, the chief executives of several companies were paid more than $100 million for

fyi

The Economics of Apartheid

The Republic of South Africa is the richest nation in Africa, but it also has a harsh political history. Until the peaceful transition to majority rule in 1994, the country was controlled by its white minority, Afrikaners, the descendants of European (mainly Dutch) immigrants. This minority imposed an economic system known as apartheid, which overwhelmingly favored white interests over those of native Africans and other groups considered "non-white," such as Asians.

The origins of apartheid go back to the early years of the twentieth century, when large numbers of white farmers began moving into South Africa's growing cities. There they discovered, to their horror, that they did not automatically earn higher wages than other races. But they had the

right to vote—and non-whites did not. And so the South African government instituted "job-reservation" laws designed to ensure that only whites got jobs that paid well. The government also set about creating jobs for whites in government-owned industries. As Allister Sparks notes in *The Mind of South Africa* (1990), in its efforts to provide high-paying jobs for whites, the country "eventually acquired the largest amount of nationalized industry of any country outside the Communist bloc."

In other words, racial discrimination was possible because it was backed by the power of the government, which prevented markets from following their natural course. A postscript: in 1994, in one of the political miracles of modern times, the white regime

ceded power and South Africa became a full-fledged democracy. Apartheid was abolished. Unfortunately, large racial differences in earnings remain. The main reason is that apartheid created huge disparities in human capital, which will persist for many years to come.

the year, which works out to $20,000 per hour even if they worked 100-hour weeks. Leaving out these extremes, there is still a huge range of wage rates. Are people really that different in their marginal productivities?

A particular source of concern is the existence of systematic wage differences across gender and ethnicity. Figure 73.2 compares annual median earnings in 2009 of workers 25 years or older classified by gender and ethnicity. As a group, white males had the highest earnings. Women (averaging across all ethnicities) earned only about 76% as much; African-American workers (male and female combined) only 69% as much; and Hispanic workers only 64% as much.

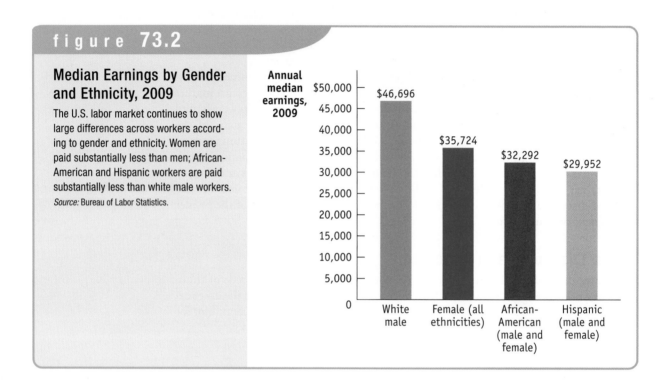

figure 73.2

Median Earnings by Gender and Ethnicity, 2009

The U.S. labor market continues to show large differences across workers according to gender and ethnicity. Women are paid substantially less than men; African-American and Hispanic workers are paid substantially less than white male workers.

Source: Bureau of Labor Statistics.

We are a nation founded on the belief that all men are created equal—and if the Constitution were rewritten today, we would say that *all people* are created equal. So why do they receive such unequal pay? In part, the pay differences may be due to differences in marginal productivity, but we also must allow for the possible effects of other influences.

Is the Marginal Productivity Theory of Income Distribution Really True?

Although the marginal productivity theory of income distribution is a well-established part of economic theory, closely linked to the analysis of markets in general, it is a source of some controversy. There are two main objections to it.

First, in the real world we see large disparities in income between workers who, in the eyes of some observers, should receive the same payment. Perhaps the most conspicuous examples in the United States are the large differences in the average wages between women and men and among various racial and ethnic groups. Do these wage differences really reflect differences in marginal productivity, or is something else going on?

Second, many people wrongly believe that the marginal productivity theory of income distribution gives a *moral* justification for the distribution of income, implying that the existing distribution is fair and appropriate. This misconception sometimes leads other people, who believe that the current distribution of income is unfair, to reject marginal productivity theory.

So Does Marginal Productivity Theory Work?

The main conclusion you should draw from this discussion is that the marginal productivity theory of income distribution is not a perfect description of how factor incomes are determined but that it works pretty well. The deviations are important. But, by and large, in a modern economy with well-functioning labor markets, factors of production are paid the equilibrium value of the marginal product—the value of the marginal product of the last unit employed in the market as a whole.

It's important to emphasize, once again, that this does not mean that the factor distribution of income is morally justified.

Module 73 AP Review

Solutions appear at the back of the book.

Check Your Understanding

1. Assess each of the following statements. Do you think they are true, false, or ambiguous? Explain.
   a. The marginal productivity theory of income distribution is inconsistent with the presence of income disparities associated with gender, race, or ethnicity.
   b. Companies that engage in workplace discrimination but whose competitors do not are likely to earn less profit as a result of their actions.
   c. Workers who are paid less because they have less experience are not the victims of discrimination.

Tackle the Test: Multiple-Choice Questions

1. Which group of U.S. workers had the highest median earnings in 2009?
   a. white males
   b. females (all ethnicities)
   c. African-Americans (males and female)
   d. Hispanics
   e. African-American males

2. Which of the following sources of wage differences is/are consistent with the marginal productivity theory of income distribution?
   I. talent
   II. discrimination
   III. efficiency wages
   a. I only
   b. II only
   c. III only
   d. I and II only
   e. I, II, and III

3. Compensating differentials mean that which of the following leads to higher wages for some jobs?
   a. danger
   b. discrimination
   c. marginal productivity
   d. market power
   e. a surplus of labor

4. Which of the following is a result in the efficiency-wage model?
   a. compensating differentials
   b. surpluses of labor
   c. shortages of labor
   d. discrimination
   e. increased productivity

5. Which of the following statements regarding the marginal productivity theory of income distribution is correct?
   a. Each worker should earn a wage based on his or her marginal productivity.
   b. The wage rate should equal the rental rate.
   c. Workers with higher marginal products always receive a higher wage than workers with lower marginal products.
   d. The factor distribution of income is morally justified.
   e. With well-functioning labor markets, each factor is paid the equilibrium value of the marginal product of that factor.

Tackle the Test: Free-Response Questions

1. For each of the following situations in which similar workers are paid different wages, provide the most likely reason for the differences and explain why that reason applies.
   a. Test pilots for new jet aircraft earn higher wages than airline pilots.
   b. College graduates usually have higher earnings in their first year on the job than workers without college degrees have in their first year on the job.
   c. Experienced AP teachers command higher salaries than new AP teachers for teaching the same class.

2. List three different economic concepts that explain wage differences when the marginal productivity theory of income distribution does not. Explain each.

Section 13 Review

Summary

1. Just as there are markets for goods and services, there are markets for factors of production, including labor, land, and both **physical capital** and **human capital.** These markets determine the **factor distribution of income.**

2. A profit-maximizing, price-taking firm will keep employing more units of a factor until the factor's price is equal to the **value of the marginal product**—the marginal product of the factor multiplied by the price of the output it produces. The **value of the marginal product curve** is therefore the price-taking firm's demand curve for a factor. Factor demand is often referred to as a **derived demand** because it is derived from the demand for the producer's output.

3. The market demand curve for labor is the horizontal sum of the individual demand curves of firms in that market. It shifts for three main reasons: changes in output price, changes in the supply of other factors, and technological changes.

4. When a competitive labor market is in equilibrium, the market wage is equal to the **equilibrium value of the marginal product** of labor, the additional value produced by the last worker hired in the labor market as a whole. The same principle applies to other factors of production: the **rental rate** of land or capital is equal to the equilibrium value of the marginal product. This insight leads to the **marginal productivity theory of income distribution,** according to which each factor is paid the value of the marginal product of the last unit of that factor employed in the factor market as a whole.

5. Labor supply is the result of decisions about **time allocation,** with each worker facing a trade-off between

leisure and work. An increase in the hourly wage rate tends to increase work hours via the substitution effect but decrease work hours via the income effect. If the net result is that a worker increases the quantity of labor supplied in response to a higher wage, the **individual labor supply curve** slopes upward. If the net result is that a worker decreases work hours, the individual labor supply curve—unlike supply curves for goods and services—slopes downward.

6. The market labor supply curve is the horizontal sum of the individual labor supply curves of all workers in that market. It shifts for four main reasons: changes in preferences and social norms, changes in population, changes in opportunities, and changes in wealth.

7. When a firm is not a price-taker in a factor market, the firm will consider the **marginal revenue product** and the **marginal factor cost** when determining how much of a factor to hire. These concepts are equivalent to the value of the marginal product and the wage (or the price of the factor) in a perfectly competitive market.

8. A **monopsonist** is the single buyer of a factor. A market in which there is a monopsonist is a **monopsony.**

9. Firms will determine the optimal input combination using the **cost-minimization rule:** When a firm uses the cost-minimizing combination of inputs, the marginal product of labor divided by the wage rate is equal to the marginal product of capital divided by the rental rate.

10. Large disparities in wages raise questions about the validity of the marginal productivity theory of income distribution. Many disparities can be explained by

compensating differentials and by differences in talent, job experience, and human capital across workers. Market interference in the forms of **unions** and collective action by employers also creates wage disparities. The **efficiency-wage model,** which arises from a type of market failure, shows how wage disparities can result from employers' attempts to increase worker performance. Free markets tend to diminish discrimination, but discrimination remains a real source of wage disparity. Discrimination is typically maintained either through problems in labor markets or (historically) through institutionalization in government policies.

Key Terms

Physical capital, p. 680
Human capital, p. 680
Derived demand, p. 681
Factor distribution of income, p. 681
Value of the marginal product, p. 684
Value of the marginal product curve, p. 684
Rental rate, p. 691

Marginal productivity theory of income distribution, p. 692
Time allocation, p. 695
Leisure, p. 696
Individual labor supply curve, p. 696
Marginal revenue product of labor, p. 700
Marginal factor cost of labor, p. 700

Monopsonist, p. 701
Monopsony, p. 701
Cost-minimization rule, p. 708
Compensating differentials, p. 711
Equilibrium value of the marginal product, p. 712
Unions, p. 713
Efficiency-wage model, p. 714

Problems

1. In 2007, national income in the United States was $11,186.9 billion. In the same year, 137 million workers were employed, at an average wage of $57,526 per worker per year.

   a. How much compensation of employees was paid in the United States in 2007?

   b. Analyze the factor distribution of income. What percentage of national income was received in the form of compensation to employees in 2007?

   c. Suppose that a huge wave of corporate downsizing leads many terminated employees to open their own businesses. What is the effect on the factor distribution of income?

   d. Suppose the supply of labor rises due to an increase in the retirement age. What happens to the percentage of national income received in the form of compensation of employees?

2. Marty's Frozen Yogurt has the production function per day shown in the accompanying table. The equilibrium wage rate for a worker is $80 per day. Each cup of frozen yogurt sells for $2.

Quantity of labor (workers)	Quantity of frozen yogurt (cups)
0	0
1	110
2	200
3	270
4	300
5	320
6	330

   a. Calculate the marginal product of labor for each worker and the value of the marginal product of labor per worker.

   b. How many workers should Marty employ?

3. Patty's Pizza Parlor has the production function per hour shown in the accompanying table. The hourly wage rate for each worker is $10. Each pizza sells for $2.

Quantity of labor (workers)	Quantity of pizza
0	0
1	9
2	15
3	19
4	22
5	24

   a. Calculate the marginal product of labor for each worker and the value of the marginal product of labor per worker.

   b. Draw the value of the marginal product of labor curve. Use your diagram to determine how many workers Patty should employ.

   c. Now the price of pizza increases to $4. Calculate the value of the marginal product of labor per worker, and draw the new value of the marginal product of labor curve in your diagram. Use your diagram to determine how many workers Patty should employ now.

4. The production function for Patty's Pizza Parlor is given in the table in Problem 3. The price of pizza is $2, but the hourly wage rate rises from $10 to $15. Use a diagram to determine how Patty's demand for workers responds as a result of this wage rate increase.

5. Patty's Pizza Parlor initially had the production function given in the table in Problem 3. A worker's hourly wage rate was $10, and pizza sold for $2. Now Patty buys a new high-tech pizza oven that allows her workers to become twice as productive as before. That is, the first worker now produces 18 pizzas per hour instead of 9, and so on.

a. Calculate the new marginal product of labor and the new value of the marginal product of labor.

b. Use a diagram to determine how Patty's hiring decision responds to this increase in the productivity of her workforce.

6. Jameel runs a driver education school. The more driving instructors he hires, the more driving lessons he can sell. But because he owns a limited number of training automobiles, each additional driving instructor adds less to Jameel's output of driving lessons. The accompanying table shows Jameel's production function per day. Each driving lesson can be sold at $35 per hour.

Quantity of labor (driving instructors)	Quantity of driving lessons (hours)
0	0
1	8
2	15
3	21
4	26
5	30
6	33

Determine Jameel's labor demand schedule (his demand schedule for driving instructors) for each of the following daily wage rates for driving instructors: $160, $180, $200, $220, $240, and $260.

7. Dale and Dana work at a self-service gas station and convenience store. Dale opens up every day, and Dana arrives later to help stock the store. They are both paid the current market wage of $9.50 per hour. But Dale feels he should be paid much more because the revenue generated from the gas pumps he turns on every morning is much higher than the revenue generated by the items that Dana stocks. Assess this argument.

8. A *New York Times* article published in September 2007 observed that the wage of farmworkers in Mexico is $11 an hour but the wage of immigrant Mexican farmworkers in California is $9 an hour.

a. Assume that the output sells for the same price in the two countries. Does this imply that the marginal product of labor of farmworkers is higher in Mexico or in California? Explain your answer, and illustrate with a diagram that shows the demand and supply curves for labor in the respective markets. In your diagram, assume that the quantity supplied of labor for any given wage rate is the same for Mexican farmworkers as it is for immigrant Mexican farmworkers in California.

b. Now suppose that farmwork in Mexico is more arduous and more dangerous than farmwork in California. As a result, the quantity supplied of labor for any given wage rate is not the same for Mexican farmworkers as it is for immigrant Mexican farmworkers in California. How does this change your answer to part a? What concept best accounts for the difference between wage rates between Mexican farmworkers and immigrant Mexican farmworkers in California?

c. Illustrate your answer to part b with a diagram. In this diagram, assume that the quantity of labor demanded for any given wage rate is the same for Mexican employers as it is for Californian employers.

9. Kendra is the owner of Wholesome Farms, a commercial dairy. Kendra employs labor, land, and capital. In her operations, Kendra can substitute between the amount of labor she employs and the amount of capital she employs. That is, to produce the same quantity of output she can use more labor and less land; similarly, to produce the same quantity of output she can use less labor and more land. However, if she uses more land, she must use more of both labor and capital; if she uses less land, she can use less of both labor and capital. Let w^* represent the annual cost of labor in the market, let r_L^* represent the annual cost of a unit of land in the market, and let r_K^* represent the annual cost of a unit of capital in the market.

a. Suppose that Kendra can maximize her profits by employing less labor and more capital than she is currently using but the same amount of land. What three conditions must now hold for Kendra's operations (involving her value of the marginal product of labor, land and capital) for this to be true?

b. Kendra believes that she can increase her profits by renting and using more land. What three conditions must hold (involving her value of the marginal product of labor, land, and capital) for this to be true?

10. Research consistently finds that despite nondiscrimination policies, African-American workers on average receive lower wages than white workers do. What are the possible reasons for this? Are these reasons consistent with marginal productivity theory?

11. Greta is an enthusiastic amateur gardener and spends a lot of her free time working in her yard. She also has demanding and well-paid employment as a freelance advertising consultant. Because the advertising business is going through a difficult time, the hourly consulting fee Greta can charge falls. Greta decides to spend more time gardening and less time consulting. Explain her decision in terms of income and substitution effects.

12. Wendy works at a fast-food restaurant. When her wage rate was $5 per hour, she worked 30 hours per week. When her wage rate rose to $6 per hour, she decided to work 40 hours. But when her wage rate rose further to $7, she decided to work only 35 hours.

a. Draw Wendy's individual labor supply curve.

b. Is Wendy's behavior irrational, or can you find a rational explanation? Explain your answer.

13. You are the governor's economic policy adviser. The governor wants to put in place policies that encourage employed people to work more hours at their jobs and that encourage unemployed people to find and take jobs. Assess each of the following policies in terms of reaching that goal. Explain your reasoning in terms of income and substitution effects, and indicate when the impact of the policy may be ambiguous.

a. The state income tax rate is lowered, which has the effect of increasing workers' after-tax wage rate.

b. The state income tax rate is increased, which has the effect of decreasing workers' after-tax wage rate.

c. The state property tax rate is increased, which reduces workers' after-tax income.

14. A study by economists at the Federal Reserve Bank of Boston found that between 1965 and 2003 the average American's leisure time increased by between 4 and 8 hours a week. The study claims that this increase is primarily driven by a rise in wage rates.

    a. Use the income and substitution effects to describe the labor supply for the average American. Which effect dominates?

b. The study also finds an increase in female labor force participation—more women are choosing to hold jobs rather than exclusively perform household tasks. For the average woman who has newly entered the labor force, which effect dominates?

c. Draw typical individual labor supply curves that illustrate your answers to part a and part b above.

Market Failure and the Role of Government

For many people in the northeastern United States, there is no better way to relax than to fish in one of the region's thousands of lakes. But in the 1960s, avid fishermen noticed something alarming: lakes that had formerly teemed with fish were now almost empty. What had happened?

The answer was acid rain, caused mainly by coal-burning power plants. When coal is burned, it releases sulfur dioxide and nitric oxide into the atmosphere; these gases react with water, producing sulfuric acid and nitric acid. The result in the Northeast, downwind from the nation's industrial heartland, was rain sometimes as acidic as lemon juice. Acid rain didn't just kill fish; it also damaged trees and crops, and in time even began to dissolve limestone buildings.

You'll be glad to hear that the acid rain problem today is much less serious than it was in the 1960s. Power plants have reduced their emissions by switching to low-sulfur coal and installing scrubbers in their smokestacks. But they didn't do this out of the goodness of their hearts; they did it in response to government policy. Without such government intervention, power companies would have had no

For many polluters, acid rain is someone else's problem.

incentive to take the environmental effects of their actions into account.

The Gulf of Mexico oil spill of 2010 is among the reminders that environmental problems persist. Neglected pollution is one of several reasons why markets sometimes fail to deliver efficient quantities of goods and services. We've already seen that inefficiency can arise from market power, which allows monopolists and colluding oligopolists to charge prices above marginal cost, thereby preventing mutually beneficial transactions from occurring. In this section we will consider other reasons for market failure. In Modules 74 and 75, we will see that inefficiency can arise from *externalities,* which create a conflict between the best interests of an individual or a firm and the best interests of society as a whole. In Module 76, we will focus on how the characteristics of goods often determine whether markets can deliver them efficiently. In Modules 77 and 78, we look at the role of government in addressing market failures. The investigation of sources of inefficiency will deepen our understanding of the types of policy that can make society better off.

What you will learn in this **Module:**

- What externalities are and why they can lead to inefficiency in a market economy

- Why externalities often require government intervention

- The difference between negative and positive externalities

- The importance of the Coase theorem, which explains how private individuals can sometimes remedy externalities

Module 74
Introduction to Externalities

The Economics of Pollution

Pollution is a bad thing. Yet most pollution is a side effect of activities that provide us with good things: our air is polluted by power plants generating the electricity that lights our cities, and our rivers are sullied by fertilizer runoff from farms that grow our food. Why shouldn't we accept a certain amount of pollution as the cost of a good life?

Actually, we do. Even highly committed environmentalists don't think that we can or should completely eliminate pollution—even an environmentally conscious society would accept *some* pollution as the cost of producing useful goods and services. What environmentalists argue is that unless there is a strong and effective environmental policy, our society will generate *too much* pollution—too much of a bad thing. And the great majority of economists agree.

To see why, we need a framework that lets us think about how much pollution a society *should* have. We'll then be able to see why a market economy, left to itself, will produce more pollution than it should. We'll start by adopting a framework to study the problem under the simplifying assumption that the amount of pollution emitted by a polluter is directly observable and controllable.

Costs and Benefits of Pollution

How much pollution should society allow? We learned previously that "how much" decisions always involve comparing the marginal benefit from an additional unit of something with the marginal cost of that additional unit. The same is true of pollution.

The **marginal social cost of pollution** is the additional cost imposed on society as a whole by an additional unit of pollution. For example, acid rain harms fisheries, crops, and forests; and each additional ton of sulfur dioxide released into the atmosphere increases the harm.

The **marginal social benefit of pollution** is the additional benefit to society from an additional unit of pollution. This concept may seem counterintuitive—what's good

The **marginal social cost of pollution** is the additional cost imposed on society as a whole by an additional unit of pollution.

The **marginal social benefit of pollution** is the additional gain to society as a whole from an additional unit of pollution.

about pollution? However, pollution avoidance requires the use of money and inputs that could otherwise be used for other purposes. For example, to reduce the quantity of sulfur dioxide they emit, power companies must either buy expensive low-sulfur coal or install special scrubbers to remove sulfur from their emissions. The more sulfur dioxide they are allowed to emit, the lower are these avoidance costs. If we calculated how much money the power industry would save if it were allowed to emit an additional ton of sulfur dioxide, that savings would be the marginal benefit to society of emitting that ton of sulfur dioxide.

The **socially optimal quantity of pollution** is the quantity of pollution that society would choose if all the costs and benefits of pollution were fully accounted for.

Using hypothetical numbers, Figure 74.1 shows how we can determine the **socially optimal quantity of pollution**—the quantity of pollution that makes society as well off as possible, taking all costs and benefits into account. The upward-sloping marginal social cost curve, labeled *MSC,* shows how the marginal cost to society of an additional ton of pollution emissions varies with the quantity of emissions. (An upward slope is likely because nature can often safely handle low levels of pollution but is increasingly harmed as pollution reaches high levels.) The marginal social benefit curve, labeled *MSB,* is downward sloping because it is progressively harder, and therefore more expensive, to achieve a further reduction in pollution as the total amount of pollution falls—increasingly more expensive technology must be used. As a result, as pollution falls, the cost savings to a polluter of being allowed to emit one more ton rises.

figure 74.1

The Socially Optimal Quantity of Pollution

Pollution yields both costs and benefits. Here the curve *MSC* shows how the marginal cost to society as a whole from emitting one more ton of pollution emissions depends on the quantity of emissions. The curve *MSB* shows how the marginal benefit to society as a whole of emitting an additional ton of pollution emissions depends on the quantity of pollution emissions. The socially optimal quantity of pollution is Q_{OPT}; at that quantity, the marginal social benefit of pollution is equal to the marginal social cost, corresponding to $200.

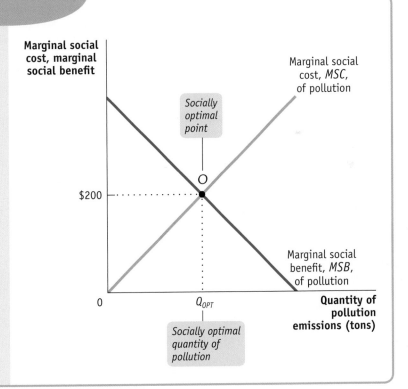

The socially optimal quantity of pollution in this example isn't zero. It's Q_{OPT}, the quantity corresponding to point *O*, where the marginal social benefit curve crosses the marginal social cost curve. At Q_{OPT}, the marginal social benefit from an additional ton of emissions and its marginal social cost are equalized at $200.

But will a market economy, left to itself, arrive at the socially optimal quantity of pollution? No, it won't.

An **external cost** is an uncompensated cost that an individual or firm imposes on others.

Pollution: An External Cost

Pollution yields both benefits and costs to society. But in a market economy without government intervention, those who benefit from pollution—like the owners of power companies—decide how much pollution occurs. They have no incentive to take into account the costs of pollution that they impose on others.

To see why, remember the nature of the benefits and costs from pollution. For polluters, the benefits take the form of monetary savings: by emitting an extra ton of sulfur dioxide, any given polluter saves the cost of buying expensive, low-sulfur coal or installing pollution-control equipment. So the benefits of pollution accrue directly to the polluters.

The costs of pollution, though, fall on people who have no say in the decision about how much pollution takes place: for example, people who fish in northeastern lakes do not control the decisions of power plants.

Figure 74.2 shows the result of this asymmetry between who reaps the benefits and who pays the costs. In a market economy without government intervention to protect the environment, only the benefits of pollution are taken into account in choosing the quantity of pollution. So the quantity of emissions won't be the socially optimal quantity Q_{OPT}; it will be Q_{MKT}, the quantity at which the marginal social benefit of an additional ton of pollution is zero, but the marginal social cost of that additional ton is much larger—$400. The quantity of pollution in a market economy without government intervention will be higher than its socially optimal quantity.

The reason is that in the absence of government intervention, those who derive the benefit from pollution—the owners of polluting firms—don't have to compensate those who bear the cost. So the marginal cost of pollution to any given polluter is zero (the assumption being that the polluter isn't also the pollution victim): polluters have no incentive to limit the amount of emissions. For example, before the Clean Air Act of 1970, midwestern power plants used the cheapest type of coal available, despite the fact that cheap coal generated more pollution, and they did nothing to scrub their emissions.

The environmental cost of pollution is perhaps the best-known and most important example of an **external cost**—an uncompensated cost that an individual or firm

figure 74.2

Why a Market Economy Produces Too Much Pollution

In the absence of government intervention, the quantity of pollution will be Q_{MKT}, the quantity at which the marginal social benefit of pollution equals the price polluters pay for each unit of pollution they emit: $0. This is an inefficiently high quantity of pollution because the marginal social cost, $400, greatly exceeds the marginal social benefit, $0.

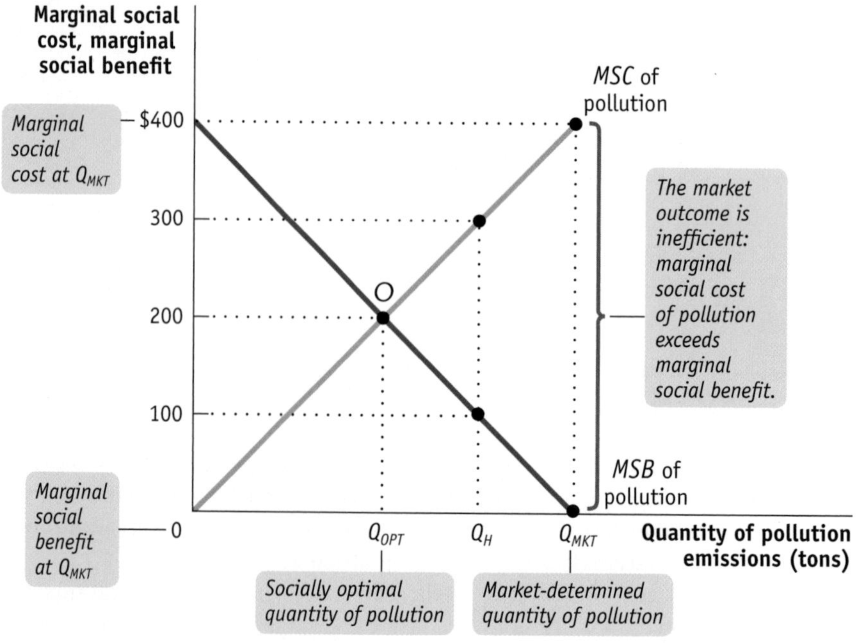

imposes on others. There are many other examples of external costs besides pollution. Another important, and certainly familiar, external cost is traffic congestion—an individual who chooses to drive during rush hour increases congestion and so increases the travel time of other drivers.

We'll see in the next module that there are also important examples of **external benefits**, benefits that individuals or firms confer on others without receiving compensation. External costs and external benefits are jointly known as **externalities.** External costs are called **negative externalities** and external benefits are called **positive externalities.**

As we've already suggested, externalities can lead to individual decisions that are not optimal for society as a whole. Let's take a closer look at why, focusing on the case of pollution.

Traffic congestion is a negative externality.

fyi

Talking and Driving

Why is that woman in the car in front of us driving so erratically? Is she drunk? No, she's talking on her cell phone.

Traffic safety experts take the risks posed by driving while talking very seriously. Using hands-free, voice-activated phones doesn't seem to help much because the main danger is distraction. As one traffic safety consultant put it, "It's not where your eyes are; it's where your head is." And we're not talking about a trivial problem. One estimate suggests that people who talk on their cell phones while driving may be responsible for 600 or more traffic deaths each year.

The National Safety Council urges people not to use phones while driving. But a growing number of people say that voluntary standards aren't enough; they want the use of cell phones while driving made illegal, as it already is in eight states and the District of Columbia, as well as in Japan, Israel, and many other countries.

Why not leave the decision up to the driver? Because the risk posed by driving while talking isn't just a risk to the driver; it's also a safety risk to others—especially people in other cars. Even if you decide that the benefit to you of taking that call is worth the cost, you

aren't taking into account the cost to other people. Driving while talking, in other words, generates a serious—sometimes fatal—negative externality.

The Inefficiency of Excess Pollution

We have just shown that in the absence of government action, the quantity of pollution will be *inefficient:* polluters will pollute up to the point at which the marginal social benefit of pollution is zero, as shown by quantity Q_{MKT} in Figure 74.2. Recall that an outcome is inefficient if some people could be made better off without making others worse off. We have already seen why the equilibrium quantity in a perfectly competitive market with no externalities is the efficient quantity of the good, the quantity that maximizes total surplus. Here, we can use a variation of that analysis to show how the presence of a negative externality upsets that result.

Because the marginal social benefit of pollution is zero at Q_{MKT}, reducing the quantity of pollution by one ton would subtract very little from the total social benefit from pollution. In other words, the benefit to polluters from that last unit of pollution is very low—virtually zero. Meanwhile, the marginal social cost imposed on the rest of society of that last ton of pollution at Q_{MKT} is quite high—$400. In other words, by reducing

An **external benefit** is a benefit that an individual or firm confers on others without receiving compensation.

External costs and benefits are known as **externalities.**

External costs are **negative externalities,** and external benefits are **positive externalities.**

the quantity of pollution at Q_{MKT} by one ton, the total social cost of pollution falls by $400, but total social benefit falls by virtually zero. So total surplus rises by approximately $400 if the quantity of pollution at Q_{MKT} is reduced by one ton.

If the quantity of pollution is reduced further, there will be more gains in total surplus, though they will be smaller. For example, if the quantity of pollution is Q_H in Figure 74.2, the marginal social benefit of a ton of pollution is $100, but the marginal social cost is still much higher at $300. This means that reducing the quantity of pollution by one ton leads to a net gain in total surplus of approximately $300 − $100 = $200. Thus Q_H is still an inefficiently high quantity of pollution. Only if the quantity of pollution is reduced to Q_{OPT}, where the marginal social cost and the marginal social benefit of an additional ton of pollution are both $200, is the outcome efficient.

Private Solutions to Externalities

Can the private sector solve the problem of externalities without government intervention? Bear in mind that when an outcome is inefficient, there is potentially a deal that makes people better off. Why don't individuals find a way to make that deal?

In an influential 1960 article, economist and Nobel laureate Ronald Coase pointed out that in an ideal world the private sector could indeed deal with all externalities. According to the **Coase theorem,** even in the presence of externalities, an economy can reach an efficient solution, provided that the legal rights of the parties are clearly defined and the costs of making a deal are sufficiently low. In some cases it takes a lot of time, or even money, to bring the relevant parties together, negotiate a deal, and carry out the terms of the deal. The costs of making a deal are known as **transaction costs.**

To get a sense of Coase's argument, imagine two neighbors, Mick and Christina, who both like to barbecue in their backyards on summer afternoons. Mick likes to play golden oldies on his boombox while barbecuing, but this annoys Christina, who can't stand that kind of music.

Who prevails? You might think it depends on the legal rights involved in the case: if the law says that Mick has the right to play whatever music he wants, Christina just has to suffer; if the law says that Mick needs Christina's consent to play music in his backyard, Mick has to live without his favorite music while barbecuing.

But as Coase pointed out, the outcome need not be determined by legal rights, because Christina and Mick can make a private deal as long as the legal rights are clearly defined. Even if Mick has the right to play his music, Christina could pay him not to. Even if Mick can't play the music without an OK from Christina, he can offer to pay her to give that OK. These payments allow them to reach an efficient solution, regardless of who has the legal upper hand. If the benefit of the music to Mick exceeds its cost to Christina, the music will go on; if the benefit to Mick is less than the cost to Christina, there will be silence.

The implication of Coase's analysis is that externalities need not lead to inefficiency because individuals have an incentive to make mutually beneficial deals—deals that lead them to take externalities into account when making decisions. When individuals *do* take externalities into account when making decisions, economists say that they **internalize the externalities.** If externalities are fully internalized, as when Mick must forgo a payment from Christina *equal to the external cost he imposes on her* in order to play music, the outcome is efficient even without government intervention.

Why can't individuals always internalize externalities? Our barbecue example implicitly assumes the transaction costs are low enough for Mick and Christina to be able to make a deal. In many situations involving externalities, however, transaction costs prevent individuals from making efficient deals. Examples of transaction costs include the following:

- *The costs of communication among the interested parties.* Such costs may be very high if many people are involved.

- *The costs of making legally binding agreements.* Such costs may be high if expensive legal services are required.

Thank You for Not Smoking

New Yorkers call them the "shiver-and-puff people"—the smokers who stand outside their workplaces, even in the depths of winter, to take a cigarette break. Over the past couple of decades, rules against smoking in spaces shared by others have become ever stricter. This is partly a matter of personal dislike—nonsmokers really don't like to smell other people's cigarette smoke—but it also reflects concerns over the health risks of second-hand smoke. As the Surgeon General's warning on many packs says, "Smoking causes lung cancer, heart disease, emphysema, and may complicate pregnancy." And there's no question that being in the same room as someone who smokes exposes you to at least some health risk.

Second-hand smoke, then, is clearly an example of a negative externality. But how important is it? Putting a dollar-and-cents value on it—that is, measuring the marginal social cost of cigarette smoke—requires researchers to not only estimate the health effects but also put a value on these effects. Despite the difficulty, economists have tried. A paper published in 1993 in the *Journal of Economic Perspectives* surveyed the research on the external costs of both cigarette smoking and alcohol consumption.

According to this paper, conclusions regarding the health costs of cigarettes depend on whether the costs imposed on members of smokers' families, including unborn children, are counted along with the costs borne by

smokers. If not, the external costs of second-hand smoke have been estimated at about $0.19 per pack smoked. (Using this method of calculation, $0.19 corresponds to the *average* social cost of smoking per pack at the current level of smoking in society.) A 2005 study raised this estimate to $0.52 per pack smoked. If the effects on smokers' families are included, the number rises considerably—family members who live with smokers are exposed to a lot more smoke. (They are also exposed to the risk of fire, which alone is estimated at $0.09 per pack.) If you include the effects of smoking by pregnant women on their unborn children's future health, the cost is immense—$4.80 per pack, which is more than twice the wholesale price charged by cigarette manufacturers.

■ *Costly delays involved in bargaining.* Even if there is a potentially beneficial deal, both sides may hold out in an effort to extract more favorable terms, leading to increased effort and forgone utility.

In some cases, transaction costs are low enough to allow individuals to resolve externality problems. For example, while filming *A League of Their Own* on location in a neighborhood ballpark, director Penny Marshall paid a man $100 to stop using his noisy chainsaw nearby. But in many other cases, transaction costs are too high to make it possible to deal with externalities through private action. For example, tens of millions of people are adversely affected by acid rain. It would be prohibitively expensive to try to make a deal among all those people and all those power companies.

When transaction costs prevent the private sector from dealing with externalities, it is time to look for government solutions—the subject of the next module.

Module 74 AP Review

Solutions appear at the back of the book.

Check Your Understanding

1. Wastewater runoff from large poultry farms adversely affects residents in neighboring homes. Explain the following:
   a. why this is considered an externality problem
   b. the efficiency of the outcome with neither government intervention nor a private deal
   c. how the socially optimal outcome is determined and how it compares with the no-intervention, no-deal outcome

2. According to Yasmin, any student who borrows a book from the university library and fails to return it on time imposes a negative externality on other students. She claims that rather than charging a modest fine for late returns, the library should charge a huge fine, so that borrowers will never return a book late. Is Yasmin's economic reasoning correct?

Tackle the Test: Multiple-Choice Questions

1. The socially optimal level of pollution is
   a. less than that created by the market, but not zero.
   b. more than that created by the market.
   c. whatever the market creates.
   d. determined by firms.
   e. zero.

2. Which of the following is a source of negative externalities?
   a. loud conversations in a library
   b. smokestack scrubbers
   c. a beautiful view
   d. national defense
   e. a decision to purchase dressy but uncomfortable shoes.

3. Inefficiencies created by externalities can be dealt with through
   a. government actions only.
   b. private actions only.
   c. market outcomes only.
   d. either private or government actions.
   e. neither private nor government actions.

4. The Coase theorem asserts that, under the right circumstances, inefficiencies created by externalities can be dealt with through
   a. lawsuits.
   b. private bargaining.
   c. vigilante actions.
   d. government policies.
   e. mediation.

5. Which of the following makes it more likely that private solutions to externality problems will succeed?
   a. high transaction costs
   b. high prices for legal services
   c. delays in the bargaining process
   d. a small number of affected parties
   e. loosely defined legal rights

Tackle the Test: Free-Response Questions

1. Draw a correctly labeled graph showing the market-determined quantity of pollution, and explain why that quantity will be chosen in the absence of intervention and private deals. On the same graph, show the socially optimal level of pollution.

Answer (6 points)

1 point: The vertical axis is labeled "Marginal social cost, marginal social benefit" or "Dollars per unit" and the horizontal axis is labeled "Quantity of pollution" or "Q."

1 point: The marginal social cost curve is labeled and upward sloping.

1 point: The marginal social benefit curve is labeled and downward sloping.

1 point: The market-determined level of pollution is shown on the horizontal axis where the marginal social benefit curve reaches the horizontal axis.

1 point: In the absence of intervention and private deals, the marginal cost to a polluter of polluting is zero. Thus, pollution will continue until the marginal social benefit (all of which goes to the polluter) equals the polluter's marginal cost of zero, which occurs at the horizontal intercept of the marginal social cost curve.

1 point: The socially optimal level of pollution is shown on the horizontal axis below the intersection of *MSC* and *MSB*.

2. a. Define the marginal social cost of pollution.
   b. Define the marginal social benefit of pollution, and explain why polluting more can provide benefits to a firm even when it could produce the same quantity of output without polluting as much.
   c. Define the socially optimal level of pollution.

Module 75
Externalities and Public Policy

What you will learn in this Module:

- How external benefits and costs cause inefficiency in the markets for goods

- Why some government policies to deal with externalities, such as emissions taxes, tradable emissions permits, and Pigouvian subsidies, are efficient, although others, including environmental standards, are not

Policies Toward Pollution

Before 1970 there were no rules governing the amount of sulfur dioxide that power plants in the United States could emit—which is why acid rain got to be such a problem. In 1970, the Clean Air Act set rules about sulfur dioxide emissions; thereafter, the acidity of rainfall declined significantly. Economists argued, however, that a more flexible system of rules that exploited the effectiveness of markets could achieve lower pollution levels at a lower cost. In 1990 this theory was put into effect with a modified version of the Clean Air Act. And guess what? The economists were right!

In this section we'll look at the policies governments use to deal with pollution and at how economic analysis has been used to improve those policies.

Environmental Standards

Because the economy, and life itself, depend on a viable environment, external costs that threaten the environment—air pollution, water pollution, habitat destruction, and so on, are worthy of attention. Protection of the environment has become a major focus of government in every advanced nation. In the United States, the Environmental Protection Agency is the principal enforcer of environmental policies at the national level and is supported by the actions of state and local governments.

How does a country protect its environment? At present the main policy tools are **environmental standards,** rules that protect the environment by specifying actions by producers and consumers. A familiar example is the law that requires almost all vehicles to have catalytic converters, which reduce the emission of chemicals that can cause smog and lead to health problems. Other rules require communities to treat their sewage, factories to limit their pollution emissions, and homes to be painted with lead-free paint, among many other examples.

Environmental standards came into widespread use in the 1960s and 1970s with considerable success. Since the United States passed the Clean Air Act in 1970, for example, the emission of air pollutants has fallen by more than a third, even though the

Environmental standards are rules that protect the environment by specifying limits or actions for producers and consumers.

Environmental standards are helping to erase the Los Angeles smog.

population has grown by a third and the size of the economy has more than doubled. Even in Los Angeles, still famous for its smog, the air has improved dramatically: in 1988 ozone levels in the surrounding South Coast Air Basin exceeded federal standards on 178 days; in 2008, on only 28 days.

Despite these successes, economists believe that when regulators can control a polluter's emissions directly, there are more efficient ways than environmental standards to deal with pollution. By using methods grounded in economic analysis, society can achieve a cleaner environment at lower cost. Most current environmental standards are inflexible and don't allow reductions in pollution to be achieved at the lowest possible cost. For example, two power plants—plant A and plant B—might be ordered to reduce pollution by the same percentage, even if their costs of achieving that objective are very different.

How does economic theory suggest that pollution should be controlled? We'll examine two approaches: taxes and tradable permits. As we'll see, either approach can achieve the efficient outcome at the minimum feasible cost.

Emissions Taxes

One way to deal with pollution directly is to charge polluters an **emissions tax.** Emissions taxes are taxes that depend on the amount of pollution a firm produces. For example, power plants might be charged $200 for every ton of sulfur dioxide they emit.

Consider the socially optimal quantity of pollution, Q_{OPT}, shown in Figure 75.1. At that quantity of pollution, the marginal social benefit and the marginal social cost of an additional ton of emissions are equal at $200. But in the absence of government intervention, power companies have no incentive to limit pollution to the socially optimal quantity Q_{OPT}; instead, they will push pollution up to the quantity Q_{MKT}, at which the marginal social benefit is zero.

An **emissions tax** is a tax that depends on the amount of pollution a firm produces.

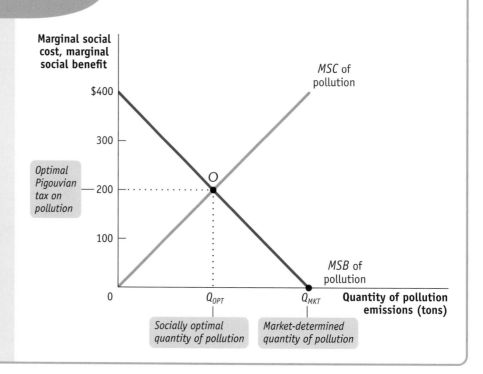

figure 75.1

In Pursuit of the Efficient Quantity of Pollution

The market determined quantity of pollution, Q_{MKT}, is too high because polluters don't pay the marginal social cost, and thus pollute beyond the socially optimal quantity, Q_{OPT}, at which marginal social cost equals marginal social benefit. A Pigouvian tax of $200—the value of the marginal social cost of pollution when it equals the marginal social benefit of pollution—gives polluters the incentive to emit only the socially optimal quantity of pollution. Another solution is to provide permits for only the socially optimal quantity of pollution.

It's now easy to see how an emissions tax can solve the problem. If power companies are required to pay a tax of $200 per ton of emissions, they face a marginal cost of $200 per ton and have an incentive to reduce emissions to Q_{OPT}, the socially optimal quantity. This illustrates a general result: an emissions tax equal to the marginal social cost at the socially optimal quantity of pollution induces polluters to internalize the externality—to take into account the true cost to society of their actions.

Why is an emissions tax an efficient way (that is, a cost-minimizing way) to reduce pollution but environmental standards generally are not? Because an emissions tax ensures that the marginal benefit of pollution is equal for all sources of pollution, but an environmental standard does not. Figure 75.2 shows a hypothetical industry consisting of only two plants, plant A and plant B. We'll assume that plant A uses newer technology than plant B and so has a lower cost of reducing pollution. Reflecting this difference in costs, plant A's marginal benefit of pollution curve, MB_A, lies below plant B's marginal benefit of pollution curve, MB_B. Because it is more costly for plant B to reduce its pollution at any output quantity, an additional ton of pollution is worth more to plant B than to plant A.

In the absence of government action, polluters will pollute until the marginal social benefit of an additional unit of emissions is equal to zero. Recall that the marginal

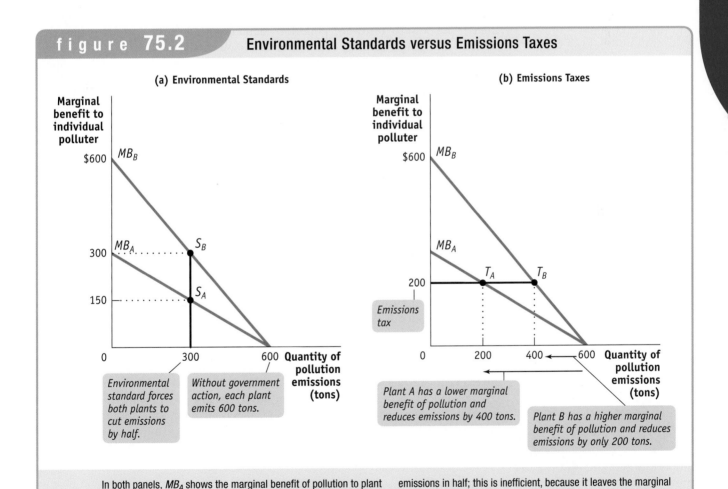

figure 75.2   **Environmental Standards versus Emissions Taxes**

In both panels, MB_A shows the marginal benefit of pollution to plant A and MB_B shows the marginal benefit of pollution to plant B. In the absence of government intervention, each plant would emit 600 tons. However, the cost of reducing emissions is lower for plant A, as shown by the fact that MB_A lies below MB_B. Panel (a) shows the result of an environmental standard that requires both plants to cut emissions in half; this is inefficient, because it leaves the marginal benefit of pollution higher for plant B than for plant A. Panel (b) shows that an emissions tax achieves the same quantity of overall pollution efficiently: faced with an emissions tax of $200 per ton, both plants reduce pollution to the point where its marginal benefit is $200.

social benefit of pollution is the cost savings, at the margin, to polluters of an additional unit of pollution. As a result, without government intervention each plant will pollute until its own marginal benefit of pollution is equal to zero. This corresponds to an emissions quantity of 600 tons each for plants A and B—the quantity of pollution at which MB_A and MB_B are each equal to zero. So although plant A and plant B value a ton of emissions differently, without government action they will each choose to emit the same amount of pollution.

Now suppose that the government decides that overall pollution from this industry should be cut in half, from 1,200 tons to 600 tons. Panel (a) of Figure 75.2 shows how this might be achieved with an environmental standard that requires each plant to cut its emissions in half, from 600 to 300 tons. The standard has the desired effect of reducing overall emissions from 1,200 to 600 tons but accomplishes it in an inefficient way. As you can see from panel (a), the environmental standard leads plant A to produce at point S_A, where its marginal benefit of pollution is \$150, but plant B produces at point S_B, where its marginal benefit of pollution is twice as high, \$300.

This difference in marginal benefits between the two plants tells us that the same quantity of pollution can be achieved at lower total cost by allowing plant B to pollute more than 300 tons but inducing plant A to pollute less. In fact, the efficient way to reduce pollution is to ensure that at the industry-wide outcome, the marginal benefit of pollution is the same for all plants. When each plant values a unit of pollution equally, there is no way to rearrange pollution reduction among the various plants that achieves the optimal quantity of pollution at a lower total cost.

We can see from panel (b) how an emissions tax achieves exactly that result. Suppose both plant A and plant B pay an emissions tax of \$200 per ton so that the marginal cost of an additional ton of emissions to each plant is now \$200 rather than zero. As a result, plant A produces at T_A and plant B produces at T_B. So plant A reduces its pollution more than it would under an inflexible environmental standard, cutting its emissions from 600 to 200 tons; meanwhile, plant B reduces its pollution less, going from 600 to 400 tons. In the end, total pollution—600 tons—is the same as under the environmental standard, but total surplus is higher. That's because the reduction in pollution has been achieved efficiently, allocating most of the reduction to plant A, the plant that can reduce emissions at lower cost.

The term *emissions tax* may convey the misleading impression that taxes are a solution to only one kind of external cost, pollution. In fact, taxes can be used to discourage any activity that generates negative externalities, such as driving during rush hour or operating a noisy bar in a residential area. In general, taxes designed to reduce external costs are known as **Pigouvian taxes,** after the economist A.C. Pigou, who emphasized their usefulness in a classic 1920 book, *The Economics of Welfare.* Look again at Figure 75.1. In our example, the optimal Pigouvian tax is \$200; as you can see from Figure 75.1, this corresponds to the marginal social cost of pollution at the optimal output quantity, Q_{OPT}.

Are there any problems with emissions taxes? The main concern is that in practice government officials usually aren't sure at what level the tax should be set. If they set the tax too low, there will be too little improvement in the environment; if they set it too high, emissions will be reduced by more than is efficient. This uncertainty cannot be eliminated, but the nature of the risks can be changed by using an alternative strategy, issuing tradable emissions permits.

Tradable Emissions Permits

Tradable emissions permits are licenses to emit limited quantities of pollutants that can be bought and sold by polluters. They are usually issued to polluting firms according to some formula reflecting their history. For example, each power plant might be issued permits equal to 50% of its emissions before the system went into

Taxes designed to reduce external costs are known as **Pigouvian taxes.**

Tradable emissions permits are licenses to emit limited quantities of pollutants that can be bought and sold by polluters.

effect. The more important point, however, is that these permits are *tradable*. Firms with differing costs of reducing pollution can now engage in mutually beneficial transactions: those that find it easier to reduce pollution will sell some of their permits to those that find it more difficult. In other words, firms will use transactions in permits to reallocate pollution reduction among themselves, so that in the end those with the lowest cost will reduce their pollution the most and those with the highest cost will reduce their pollution the least. Assume that the government issues 300 permits each to plant A and plant B, where one permit allows the emission of one ton of pollution. Under a system of tradable emissions permits, commonly known as a *cap-and-trade program,* plant A will find it profitable to sell 100 of its 300 government-issued permits to plant B. The effect of a cap-and-trade program is to create a market in rights to pollute.

Just like emissions taxes, tradable permits provide polluters with an incentive to take the marginal social cost of pollution into account. To see why, suppose that the market price of a permit to emit one ton of sulfur dioxide is $200. Then every plant has an incentive to limit its emissions of sulfur dioxide to the point where its marginal benefit of emitting another ton of pollution is $200. This is obvious for plants that buy rights to pollute: if a plant must pay $200 for the right to emit an additional ton of sulfur dioxide, it faces the same incentives as a plant facing an emissions tax of $200 per ton. But it's equally true for plants that have more permits than they plan to use: by *not* emitting a ton of sulfur dioxide, a plant frees up a permit that it can sell for $200, so the opportunity cost of a ton of emissions to the plant's owner is $200.

In short, tradable emissions permits have the same cost-minimizing advantage as emissions taxes over environmental standards: either system ensures that those who can reduce pollution most cheaply are the ones who do so. The socially optimal quantity of pollution shown in Figure 75.1 could be efficiently achieved either way: by imposing an emissions tax of $200 per ton of pollution or by issuing tradable permits to emit Q_{OPT} tons of pollution. If regulators choose to issue Q_{OPT} permits, where one permit allows the release of one ton of emissions, then the equilibrium market price of a permit among polluters will indeed be $200. Why? You can see from Figure 75.1 that at Q_{OPT}, only polluters with a marginal benefit of pollution of $200 or more will buy a permit. And the last polluter who buys—who has a marginal benefit of exactly $200—sets the market price.

It's important to realize that emissions taxes and tradable permits do more than induce polluting industries to reduce their output. Unlike rigid environmental standards, emissions taxes and tradable permits provide incentives to create and use technology that emits less pollution—new technology that lowers the socially optimal level of pollution. The main effect of the permit system for sulfur dioxide has been to change *how* electricity is produced rather than to reduce the nation's electricity output. For example, power companies have shifted to the use of alternative fuels such as low-sulfur coal and natural gas; they have also installed scrubbers that take much of the sulfur dioxide out of a power plant's emissions.

The main problem with tradable emissions permits is the flip-side of the problem with emissions taxes: because it is difficult to determine the optimal quantity of pollution, governments can find themselves either issuing too many permits (that is, they don't reduce pollution enough) or issuing too few (that is, they reduce pollution too much).

After first relying on environmental standards, the U.S. government has turned to a system of tradable permits to control acid rain. Current proposals would extend the system to other major sources of pollution. And in 2005 the European Union created an emissions-trading scheme with the purpose of controlling emissions of carbon dioxide, a greenhouse gas. The European Union scheme is part of a larger global market for the trading of greenhouse gas permits. The FYI that follows describes these two systems in greater detail.

Cap and Trade

The tradable emissions permit systems for both acid rain in the United States and greenhouse gases in the European Union are examples of *cap and trade programs:* the government sets a *cap* (a total amount of pollution that can be emitted), issues tradable emissions permits, and enforces a yearly rule that a polluter must hold a number of permits equal to the amount of pollution emitted. The goal is to set the cap low enough to generate environmental benefits and, at the same time, to give polluters flexibility in meeting environmental standards and motivate them to adopt new technologies that will lower the cost of reducing pollution.

In 1994 the United States began a cap and trade system for the sulfur dioxide emissions that cause acid rain by issuing permits to power plants based on their historical consumption of coal. The cap of 8.95 million tons set for 2010 was about half the level of sulfur dioxide emissions in 1980. Economists who have analyzed the sulfur dioxide cap and trade system point to another reason for its success: it would have been a lot more expensive—80% more to be exact—to reduce emissions by this much using a non-market-based regulatory policy.

The European Union cap and trade scheme is the world's only mandatory trading scheme for greenhouse gases and covers all 27 member nations of the European Union. Available data indicate that within the system, 3,093 metric tons of emissions were transacted in 2008 and 6,326 metric tons in 2009, an astonishing increase of 105%. Although it is still too early to evaluate the system's performance, at the time of this writing the U.S. Senate was impressed enough with the preliminary results to consider proposing an American cap and trade system for greenhouse gases.

Despite all this good news, however, cap and trade systems are not silver bullets for the world's pollution problems. Although they are appropriate for pollution that's geographically dispersed, like sulfur dioxide and greenhouse gases, they don't work for pollution that's localized, like mercury or lead contamination. In addition, the amount of overall reduction in pollution depends on the level of the cap. Under industry pressure, regulators run the risk of issuing too many permits, effectively eliminating the cap. Finally, there must be vigilant monitoring of compliance if the system is to work. Without oversight of how much a polluter is actually emitting, there is no way to know for sure that the rules are being followed.

Production, Consumption, and Externalities

Nobody imposes external costs like pollution out of malice. Pollution, traffic congestion, and other negative externalities are side effects of activities, like electricity generation, manufacturing, or driving, that are otherwise desirable. We've just learned how government regulators can move the market to the socially optimal quantity when the side effects can be directly controlled. But as we cautioned earlier, in some cases it's not possible to directly control the side effects, only the activities that cause them can be influenced. As we'll see shortly, government policies in these situations must instead be geared to changing the levels of production and consumption that create externalities, which in turn changes the levels of the externalities themselves.

This approach, although slightly more complicated, has several advantages. First, for activities that generate external *costs,* it gives us a clear understanding of how the desirable activity is affected by policies designed to manage its side effects. Second, it helps us think about a question that is different but related to the problem of external costs: what should be done when an activity generates external *benefits*. It's important to realize that not all externalities are negative. There are, in fact, many positive externalities that we encounter every day; for example, a neighbor's bird-feeder has the side effect of maintaining the local wild bird population for everyone's enjoyment. And a beautiful flower garden in front of a neighbor's house can be enjoyed by many passersby.

Using the approach of targeting the activity behind the externalities, we'll now turn our attention to the topic of positive externalities.

Private versus Social Benefits

Earlier, we pointed out that getting a flu shot has benefits to people beyond the person getting the shot. Under some conditions, getting a flu vaccination reduces the expected number of *other* people who get the flu by as much as 1.5. This prompted one economist to suggest a new T-shirt slogan, one particularly suited for the winter months: "Kiss Me, I'm Vaccinated!" When you get vaccinated against the flu, it's likely that you're conferring a substantial benefit on those around you—a benefit for others that you are not compensated for. In other words, getting a flu shot generates a positive externality.

The government can directly control the external costs of pollution because it can measure emissions. In contrast, it can't observe the reduction in flu cases caused by you getting a flu shot, so it can't directly control the external benefits—say, by rewarding you based on how many fewer people caught the flu because of your actions. So if the government wants to influence the level of external benefits from flu vaccinations, it must target the original activity—getting a flu shot.

From the point of view of society as a whole, a flu shot carries both costs (the price you pay for the shot, which compensates the vaccine maker and your health care provider for the inputs and factors of production necessary to grow the vaccine and deliver it to your bloodstream) and benefits. Those benefits are the private benefit that accrues to you from not getting the flu yourself, but they also include the external benefits that accrue to others from a lower likelihood of catching the flu. However, you have no incentive to take into account the beneficial side effects that are generated by your actions. As a result, in the absence of government intervention, too few people will choose to be vaccinated.

Panel (a) of Figure 75.3 illustrates this point. The market demand curve for flu shots is represented by the curve D; the market, or industry, supply curve is given by the curve S. In the absence of government intervention, market equilibrium will be at point E_{MKT}, with Q_{MKT} flu shots being bought and sold at the market price of P_{MKT}.

Your flu shot provides positive externalities to those whom you would otherwise make sick.

figure 75.3 — Positive Externalities and Consumption

(a) Positive Externality

(b) Optimal Pigouvian Subsidy

Consumption of flu shots generates external benefits, so the marginal social benefit curve, *MSB*, of flu shots, corresponds to the demand curve, *D*, shifted upward by the marginal external benefit. Panel (a) shows that without government action, the market produces Q_{MKT}. It is lower than the socially optimal quantity of consumption, Q_{OPT}, the quantity at which *MSB* crosses the supply curve, *S*. At Q_{MKT}, the marginal social benefit of another flu shot, P_{MSB}, is greater than the marginal private benefit to consumers of another flu shot, P_{MKT}. Panel (b) shows how an optimal Pigouvian subsidy to consumers, equal to the marginal external benefit, moves consumption to Q_{OPT} by lowering the price paid by consumers.

At that point, the marginal cost to society of another flu shot is equal to the marginal benefit *gained by the individual consumer who purchases that flu shot,* measured by the market price.

So far we have studied goods in the absence of external benefits, so the marginal benefit to the consumer has been no different from the marginal benefit to society. When a good like flu shots creates positive externalities, there is a difference between the marginal benefit to the consumer, which we'll distinguish by calling it the **marginal private benefit,** and the marginal benefit to society, called the **marginal social benefit of a good** (or similarly, of a service or activity). The difference between the marginal private benefit (*MPB*) and the marginal social benefit (*MSB*) is the **marginal external benefit** (*MEB*) that indicates the increase in external benefits to society from an additional unit of the good:

(75-1) $MSB = MPB + MEB$

The demand curve represents the marginal benefit that accrues to *consumers of the good:* the marginal private benefit. It does not incorporate the benefits to society as a whole from consuming the good—in this case, the reduction in the number of flu cases. As you can see from panel (a) of Figure 75.3, the marginal social benefit curve, *MSB,* corresponds to the demand curve, *D, shifted upward* by the amount of the marginal external benefit.

With the marginal social benefit curve and the supply curve, we can find the socially optimal quantity of a good or activity that generates external benefits: it is the quantity Q_{OPT}, the quantity that corresponds to point *O* at which *MSB* and *S* cross. Because the external benefit is not accounted for in market decisions, Q_{OPT} is greater than Q_{MKT}; it's the quantity at which the marginal cost of a good (measured by *S*) is equal to the marginal social benefit (measured by *MSB*).

So left to its own, a market will bring about too little production and consumption of a good or activity that generates external benefits. Correspondingly, without government action, the price to consumers of such a good or activity is too high: at the market output level Q_{MKT}, the unregulated market price is P_{MKT} and the marginal benefit to consumers of an additional flu shot is lower than P_{MSB}, the true marginal benefit to society of an additional flu shot.

How can the economy be induced to produce Q_{OPT}, the socially optimal level of flu shots shown in Figure 75.3? The answer is by a **Pigouvian subsidy:** a payment designed to encourage activities that yield external benefits. The optimal Pigouvian subsidy, shown in panel (b) of Figure 75.3, is equal to the marginal external benefit of consuming another unit of flu shots. In this example, a Pigouvian subsidy works by lowering the price of consuming the good: consumers pay a price for a flu shot that is equal to the market price *minus* the subsidy. In 2001, Japan began a program of subsidizing 71% of the cost of flu shots for the elderly in large cities. A 2005 study found that the subsidy significantly reduced the incidence of pneumonia, and influenza-caused mortality, at a net benefit to Japanese society of $1.08 billion dollars.

The most important single source of external benefits in the modern economy is the creation of knowledge. In high-tech industries such as the semiconductor, software design, and bioengineering industries, innovations by one firm are quickly emulated by rival firms and put to use in the development of further advancements in related industries. This spreading of cutting-edge information among high-tech firms is known as **technology spillover.** Such spillovers often take place through face-to-face contact. For example, bars and restaurants in California's Silicon Valley are famed for their technical chitchat. Workers know that the best way to keep up with the latest technological innovations is to hang around in the right places, have a drink, and gossip. Such informal contact helps to spread useful knowledge, which may also explain why so many high-tech firms are clustered close to one another.

Private versus Social Costs

Now let's turn briefly to consider a case in which production of a good creates external costs—namely, the livestock industry. Whatever it is—cows, pigs, chicken, sheep, or salmon—livestock farming produces prodigious amounts of what is euphemistically known as "muck." But that's not all: scientists estimate that the amount of methane gas produced by livestock currently rivals the amount caused by the burning of fossil fuels in the creation of greenhouse gases. From the point of view of society as a whole, then, the cost of livestock farming includes both direct production costs (payments for factors of production and inputs) and the external environmental costs imposed as a by-product of farming.

When a good like pork involves negative externalities, there is a difference between the marginal cost to the *firm*, which we distinguish as the **marginal private cost,** and the marginal cost to *society,* the **marginal social cost of a good** (or likewise of a service or activity). The difference between the marginal private cost (MPC) and the marginal social cost (MSC) is the **marginal external cost** (MEC)—the increase in external costs to society from an additional unit of the good:

(75-2) $MSC = MPC + MEC$

Panel (a) in Figure 75.4 shows the marginal social cost curve, MSC, of livestock; it corresponds to the industry supply curve, S, *shifted upward* by the amount of the marginal external cost. (Recall that in a competitive industry, the industry supply curve is the horizontal sum of the individual firms' supply curves, which are the same as their

The social cost of livestock production is felt beyond the farm.

The **marginal private cost** of a good is the marginal cost of producing that good, not including any external costs.

The **marginal social cost of a good** is equal to the marginal private cost of production plus its marginal external cost.

The **marginal external cost** of a good is the increase in external costs created by one more unit of the good.

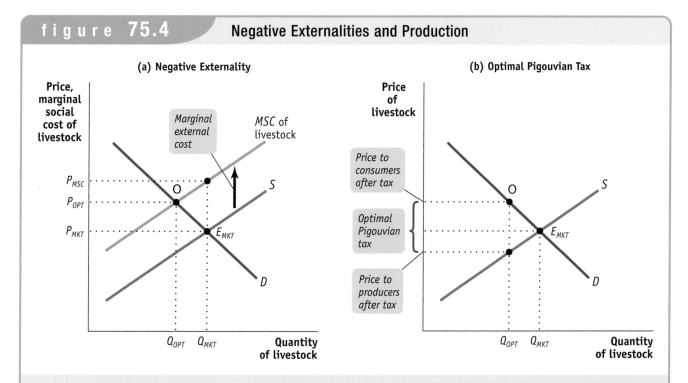

figure 75.4   Negative Externalities and Production

Livestock production generates external costs, so the marginal social cost curve, MSC, of livestock, corresponds to the supply curve, S, shifted upward by the marginal external cost. Panel (a) shows that without government action, the market produces the quantity Q_{MKT}. It is greater than the socially optimal quantity of livestock production, Q_{OPT}, the quantity at which MSC crosses the demand curve, D. At Q_{MKT}, the market price, P_{MKT}, is less than P_{MSC}, the true marginal cost to society of livestock production. Panel (b) shows how an optimal Pigouvian tax on livestock production, equal to its marginal external cost, moves the production to Q_{OPT}, resulting in lower output and a higher price to consumers.

marginal cost curves.) In the absence of government intervention, the market equilibrium will be at point E_{MKT}, yielding an equilibrium quantity of Q_{MKT} and an equilibrium price of P_{MKT}.

The ever-important socially optimal quantity of a good is the quantity at which *marginal social benefit equals marginal social cost.* In the livestock example, this criterion is met at point *O*, where the *MSC* and *D* curves cross. Why can we substitute the demand curve for marginal social benefit in this case? Because although the demand curve represents the marginal benefit to consumers—the marginal private benefit—there are no external benefits to separate the marginal private benefit from the marginal social benefit. That means that when $MSC = D$ and there are no external benefits, it is also true that $MSC = MPB = MSB$.

Unfortunately, the market equilibrium quantity Q_{MKT} is greater than Q_{OPT}, the socially optimal quantity of livestock. So left to its own, the market produces too much of a good that generates an external cost in production, and the price to consumers of such a good is too low: P_{MKT} is less than P_{MSC}, the true marginal cost to society of another unit of livestock. As panel (b) of Figure 75.4 shows, an optimal Pigouvian tax on livestock production, equal to the marginal external cost, moves the market to the socially optimal level of production, Q_{OPT}.

In the flu shot example, we explained that the socially optimal quantity was found where the *MSB* and *S* curves crossed. That point met the $MSB = MSC$ criterion for the socially optimal quantity as well because in the absence of external costs, marginal social cost equals marginal private cost, which is indicated by the supply curve. That is, when $MSB = S$ and there are no external costs, it is also true that $MSB = MPC = MSC$.

At this point, you might ask whether a regulator would choose a method of control that targets pollution directly, such as a cap and trade program, or control the production of the associated good with a Pigouvian tax. Generally, it is a good idea to target the pollution directly whenever feasible. The main reason is that this method creates incentives for the invention and adoption of production methods that create less pollution. For example, the AgCert company has found a way to capture greenhouse gases emitted from animal waste for use as tradable emissions reductions in a cap and trade program.

Network Externalities

There is one type of externality that has no inherently favorable or adverse effect on society at large, but it does affect other users of the associated good or service. Suppose you were the only user of Twitter in the world. What would it be worth to you? The answer, of course, is nothing. Twitter derives its value only from the fact that other people also use Twitter and you can send or receive tweets. In general, the more people who use Twitter, the more valuable it is to you.

A **network externality** exists when the value to an individual of a good or service depends on how many other people use the same good or service. Sometimes referred to as the "fax machine effect," the phenomenon of network externalities is so named because the classic examples involve networks of telephones, computers, and transportation systems. When it comes to sharing digital information, it helps to have more users of the same software, hardware, and online networking services. In other contexts, it's better to have more users of the same stock exchanges, gauges of railroad line, and sizes of electrical plugs, among many examples. Congestion creates a form of negative network externality: it can make things worse for you when more people use the same highway, elevator, or swimming pool.

A good is subject to a **network externality** when the value of the good to an individual is greater when more other people also use the good.

Module 75 AP Review

Solutions appear at the back of the book.

Check Your Understanding

1. Some opponents of tradable emissions permits object to them on the grounds that polluters that sell their permits benefit monetarily from their involvement in polluting the environment. Assess this argument.

2. For each of the following cases, explain whether an external cost or an external benefit is created and identify an appropriate policy response.
   a. Trees planted in urban areas improve air quality and lower summer temperatures.
   b. Water-saving toilets reduce the need to pump water from rivers and aquifers. The cost of a gallon of water to homeowners is virtually zero.
   c. Old computer monitors contain toxic materials that pollute the environment when improperly disposed of.

Tackle the Test: Multiple-Choice Questions

1. Which of the following policy tools is inefficient even when correctly administered?
   a. environmental standards
   b. emissions taxes
   c. tradable emissions permits
   d. Pigouvian taxes
   e. cap and trade programs

2. An efficient Pigouvian subsidy for a good is set equal to the good's
   a. external cost.
   b. marginal social benefit.
   c. marginal external cost.
   d. marginal external benefit.
   e. price at which $MSC = MSB$.

3. Which of the following is true in the case of a positive externality?
   a. $MSC > MSB$
   b. $MPB > MSC$
   c. $MSB > MPB$
   d. $MPB > MSB$
   e. $MSC > MPC$

4. One example of a source of external benefits is
   a. technology spillover.
   b. traffic congestion.
   c. pollution.
   d. subsidies for polluters.
   e. taxes on environmental conservation.

5. Marginal social benefit equals marginal private benefit plus
   a. marginal external benefit.
   b. marginal private cost.
   c. total external benefit.
   d. total external cost.
   e. marginal social cost.

Tackle the Test: Free-Response Questions

1. The purchase of antivirus software by one person provides benefits to other people because they are less likely to receive a virus from the software purchaser. Draw a correctly labeled graph showing how the market will determine the quantity of antivirus software purchased. On the same graph, show the socially optimal quantity of antivirus software. List two different government policies that could be used to achieve the optimal quantity of antivirus software.

2. The use of plastic water bottles creates external costs as the result of plastic production, bottle transportation, litter, and waste disposal. Draw a correctly labeled graph showing how the market will determine the quantity of water bottles purchased. On the same graph, show the marginal external cost, the socially optimal quantity of water bottles, and the size of a Pigouvian tax that could be used to achieve the socially optimal quantity of water bottles.

Answer (8 points)

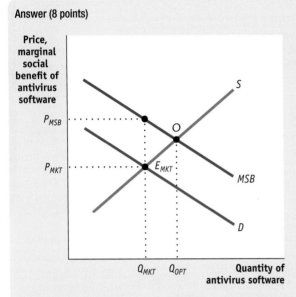

1 point: Vertical axis labeled "Price, marginal social benefit" or "Dollars per unit," horizontal axis labeled "Quantity of antivirus software" or "Q"

1 point: Upward-sloping supply (or equivalently, marginal cost) curve. (Note that with no external costs, marginal private cost equals marginal social cost.)

1 point: Downward-sloping demand (or equivalently, marginal private benefit) curve

1 point: The market quantity of antivirus software is found at the intersection of supply and demand and shown on the horizontal axis.

1 point: Downward-sloping marginal social benefit curve drawn above demand curve

1 point: The optimal quantity of antivirus software is found at the intersection of supply and marginal social benefit and shown on the horizontal axis.

1 point: A Pigouvian subsidy equal to the marginal external benefit at the socially optimal quantity

1 point: A government regulation requiring the optimal quantity of antivirus software

Module 76
Public Goods

In this module, we take a somewhat different approach to the question of why markets sometimes fail. Here we focus on how the characteristics of goods often determine whether markets can deliver them efficiently. When goods have the "wrong" characteristics, the resulting market failures resemble those associated with externalities or market power. This alternative way of looking at sources of inefficiency deepens our understanding of why markets sometimes don't work well and how government can take actions that improve the welfare of society.

Private Goods—And Others

What's the difference between installing a new bathroom in a house and building a municipal sewage system? What's the difference between growing wheat and fishing in the open ocean?

These aren't trick questions. In each case there is a basic difference in the characteristics of the goods involved. Bathroom appliances and wheat have the characteristics necessary to allow markets to work efficiently. Public sewage systems and fish in the sea do not.

Let's look at these crucial characteristics and why they matter.

Characteristics of Goods

Goods like bathroom fixtures and wheat have two characteristics that are essential if a good is to be provided in efficient quantities by a market economy.

- They are **excludable:** suppliers of the good can prevent people who don't pay from consuming it.
- They are **rival in consumption:** the same unit of the good cannot be consumed by more than one person at the same time.

When a good is both excludable and rival in consumption, it is called a **private good.** Wheat is an example of a private good. It is *excludable:* the farmer can sell a bushel to one consumer without having to provide wheat to everyone in the county. And it is *rival in consumption:* if I eat bread baked with a farmer's wheat, that wheat cannot be consumed by someone else.

But not all goods possess these two characteristics. Some goods are **nonexcludable**—the supplier cannot prevent consumption of the good by people who do not pay for it.

A good is **excludable** if the supplier of that good can prevent people who do not pay from consuming it.

A good is **rival in consumption** if the same unit of the good cannot be consumed by more than one person at the same time.

A good that is both excludable and rival in consumption is a **private good.**

When a good is **nonexcludable,** the supplier cannot prevent consumption by people who do not pay for it.

A good is **nonrival in consumption** if more than one person can consume the same unit of the good at the same time.

Fire protection is one example: a fire department that puts out fires before they spread protects the whole city, not just people who have made contributions to the Firemen's Benevolent Association. An improved environment is another: pollution can't be ended for some users of a river while leaving the river foul for others.

Nor are all goods rival in consumption. Goods are **nonrival in consumption** if more than one person can consume the same unit of the good at the same time. TV programs are nonrival in consumption: your decision to watch a show does not prevent other people from watching the same show.

Because goods can be either excludable or nonexcludable, and either rival or nonrival in consumption, there are four types of goods, illustrated by the matrix in Figure 76.1:

- *Private goods,* which are excludable and rival in consumption, like wheat
- *Public goods,* which are nonexcludable and nonrival in consumption, like a public sewer system
- *Common resources,* which are nonexcludable but rival in consumption, like clean water in a river
- *Artificially scarce goods,* which are excludable but nonrival in consumption, like pay-per-view movies on cable TV

figure 76.1

Four Types of Goods

There are four types of goods. The type of a good depends on (1) whether or not it is excludable—whether a producer can prevent someone from consuming it; and (2) whether or not it is rival in consumption—whether it is impossible for the same unit of a good to be consumed by more than one person at the same time.

	Rival in consumption	Nonrival in consumption
Excludable	**Private goods** • Wheat • Bathroom fixtures	**Artificially scarce goods** • Pay-per-view movies • Computer software
Non-excludable	**Common resources** • Clean water • Biodiversity	**Public goods** • Public sanitation • National defense

There are, of course, many other characteristics that distinguish between types of goods—necessities versus luxuries, normal versus inferior, and so on. Why focus on whether goods are excludable and rival in consumption?

Why Markets Can Supply Only Private Goods Efficiently

As we learned in earlier modules, markets are typically the best means for a society to deliver goods and services to its members; that is, markets are efficient except in the case of market power, externalities, or other instances of market failure. One source of market failure is rooted in the nature of the good itself: markets cannot supply goods and services efficiently unless they are private goods—excludable and rival in consumption.

To see why excludability is crucial, suppose that a farmer had only two choices: either produce no wheat or provide a bushel of wheat to every resident of the county who wants it, whether or not that resident pays for it. It seems unlikely that anyone would grow wheat under those conditions.

Yet the operator of a public sewage system consisting of pipes that anyone can dump sewage into faces pretty much the same problem as our hypothetical farmer.

A sewage system makes the whole city cleaner and healthier—but that benefit accrues to all the city's residents, whether or not they pay the system operator. The general point is that if a good is nonexcludable, rational consumers won't be willing to pay for it—they will take a "free ride" on anyone who *does* pay. So there is a **free-rider problem.** Examples of the free-rider problem are familiar from daily life. One example you may have encountered happens when students are required to do a group project. There is often a tendency of some group members to shirk their responsibilities, relying on others in the group to get the work done. The shirkers *free-ride* on someone else's effort.

Because of the free-rider problem, the forces of self-interest alone do not lead to an efficient level of production for a nonexcludable good. Even though consumers would benefit from increased production of the good, no one individual is willing to pay for more, and so no producer is willing to supply it. The result is that nonexcludable goods suffer from *inefficiently low production* in a market economy. In fact, in the face of the free-rider problem, self-interest may not ensure that any amount of the good—let alone the efficient quantity—is produced.

When the benefits from a group project are nonexcludable, there is a temptation to free-ride on the efforts of others.

Goods that are excludable and nonrival in consumption, like pay-per-view movies, suffer from a different kind of inefficiency. As long as a good is excludable, it is possible to earn a profit by making it available only to those who pay. Therefore, producers are willing to supply an excludable good. But the marginal cost of letting an additional viewer watch a pay-per-view movie is zero because it is nonrival in consumption. So the efficient price to the consumer is also zero—or, to put it another way, individuals should watch TV movies up to the point where their marginal benefit is zero. But if the cable company actually charges viewers $4, viewers will consume the good only up to the point where their marginal benefit is $4. When consumers must pay a price greater than zero for a good that is nonrival in consumption, the price they pay is higher than the marginal cost of allowing them to consume that good, which is zero. So in a market economy goods that are nonrival in consumption suffer from *inefficiently low consumption*.

Now we can see why private goods are the only goods that will be produced and consumed in efficient quantities in a competitive market. (That is, a private good will be produced and consumed in efficient quantities in a market free of market power, externalities, and other sources of market failure.) Because private goods are excludable, producers can charge for them and so have an incentive to produce them. And because they are also rival in consumption, it is efficient for consumers to pay a positive price— a price equal to the marginal cost of production. If one or both of these characteristics are lacking, a market economy will lack the incentives to bring about efficient quantities of the good.

Yet there are crucial goods that don't meet these criteria—and in these cases, the government can offer assistance.

Public Goods

A **public good** is the exact opposite of a private good: it is both nonexcludable and nonrival in consumption. A public sewage system is an example of a public good: you can't keep a river clean without making it clean for everyone who lives near its banks, and my protection from sewage contamination does not prevent my neighbor from being protected as well.

Here are some other examples of public goods:

- *Disease prevention.* When a disease is stamped out, no one can be excluded from the benefit, and one person's health doesn't prevent others from being healthy.

Goods that are nonexcludable suffer from the **free-rider problem:** individuals have no incentive to pay for their own consumption and instead will take a "free ride" on anyone who does pay.

A **public good** is both nonexcludable and nonrival in consumption.

- *National defense.* A strong military protects all citizens.
- *Scientific research.* In many cases new findings provide widespread benefits that are not excludable or rival.

Because these goods are nonexcludable, they suffer from the free-rider problem, so private firms would produce inefficiently low quantities of them. And because they are nonrival in consumption, it would be inefficient to charge people for consuming them. As a result, society must find nonmarket methods for providing these goods.

Providing Public Goods

Public goods are provided in a variety of ways. The government doesn't always get involved—in many cases a non-governmental solution has been found for the free-rider problem. But these solutions are usually imperfect in some way.

Some public goods are supplied through voluntary contributions. For example, private donations help support public radio and a considerable amount of scientific research. But private donations are insufficient to finance large programs of great importance, such as the Centers for Disease Control and national defense.

Some public goods are supplied by self-interested individuals or firms because those who produce them are able to make money in an indirect way. The classic example is broadcast television, which in the United States is supported entirely by advertising. The downside of such indirect funding is that it skews the nature and quantity of the public goods that are supplied, while imposing additional costs on consumers. TV stations show the programs that yield the most advertising revenue (that is, programs best suited for selling antacids, hair-loss remedies, antihistamines, and the like to the segment of the population that buys them), which are not necessarily the programs people most want to see. And viewers must endure many commercials.

Some potentially public goods are deliberately made excludable and therefore subject to charge, like pay-per-view movies. In the United Kingdom, where most television programming is paid for by a yearly license fee assessed on every television owner (£145.50, or about $229 in 2010), television viewing is made artificially excludable by the use of "television detection vans": vans that roam neighborhoods in an attempt to detect televisions in non-licensed households and fine them. However, as noted earlier, when suppliers charge a price greater than zero for a nonrival good, consumers will consume an inefficiently low quantity of that good.

In small communities, a high level of social encouragement or pressure can be brought to bear on people to contribute money or time to provide the efficient level of a public good. Volunteer fire departments, which depend both on the volunteered services of the firefighters themselves and on contributions from local residents, are a good example. But as communities grow larger and more anonymous, social pressure is increasingly difficult to apply, compelling larger towns and cities to tax residents and depend on salaried firefighters for fire protection services.

On the prowl: a British TV detection van at work.

As this last example suggests, when other solutions fail, it is up to the government to provide public goods. Indeed, the most important public goods—national defense, the legal system, disease control, fire protection in large cities, and so on—are provided by government and paid for by taxes. Economic theory tells us that the provision of public goods is one of the crucial roles of government.

How Much of a Public Good Should Be Provided?

In some cases, the provision of a public good is an "either-or" decision: a city can either have a sewage system—or not. But in most cases, governments must decide not only whether to provide a public good but also *how much* of that public good to provide. For example, street cleaning is a public good—but how often should the streets be cleaned? Once a month? Twice a month? Every other day?

Imagine a city with only two residents, Ted and Alice. Assume that the public good in question is street cleaning and that Ted and Alice truthfully tell the government how much they value a unit of the public good, one unit being one street cleaning per month. Specifically, each of them tells the government his or her *willingness to pay* for another unit of the public good supplied—an amount that corresponds to that individual's *marginal private benefit* from another unit of the public good.

Using this information along with information on the cost of providing the good, the government can use marginal analysis to find the efficient level of providing the public good: the level at which the *marginal social benefit* of the public good is equal to the marginal social cost of producing it. Recall that the marginal social benefit of a good is the benefit that accrues to society as a whole from the consumption of one additional unit of the good.

But what is the marginal social benefit of another unit of a public good—a unit that generates utility for *all* consumers, not just one consumer, because it is nonexcludable and nonrival in consumption? This question leads us to an important principle: *In the special case of a public good, the marginal social benefit of a unit of the good is equal to the sum of the marginal private benefits enjoyed by all consumers of that unit.* Or to consider it from a slightly different angle, if a consumer could be compelled to pay for a unit before consuming it (the good is made excludable), then the marginal social benefit of a unit is equal to the *sum* of each consumer's willingness to pay for that unit. Using this principle, the marginal social benefit of an additional street cleaning per month is equal to Ted's marginal private benefit from that additional cleaning *plus* Alice's marginal private benefit.

Why? Because a public good is nonrival in consumption—Ted's benefit from a cleaner street does not diminish Alice's benefit from that same clean street, and vice versa. Because Ted and Alice can simultaneously "consume" the same unit of street cleaning, the marginal social benefit is the *sum* of their marginal private benefits. And the efficient quantity of a public good is the quantity at which the marginal social benefit is equal to the marginal social cost of providing it.

Figure 76.2 on the next page illustrates the efficient provision of a public good, showing three marginal benefit curves. Panel (a) shows Ted's marginal private benefit curve from street cleaning, MPB_T: he would be willing to pay $25 for the city to clean its streets once a month, an additional $18 to have it done a second time, and so on. Panel (b) shows Alice's marginal private benefit curve from street cleaning, MPB_A. Panel (c) shows the marginal social benefit curve from street cleaning, MSB: it is the vertical sum of Ted's and Alice's marginal private benefit curves, MPB_T and MPB_A.

To maximize society's welfare, the government should increase the quantity of street cleanings until the marginal social benefit of an additional cleaning would fall below the marginal social cost. Suppose that the marginal social cost is $6 per cleaning. Then the city should clean its streets 5 times per month, because the marginal social benefit of each of the first 5 cleanings is more than $6, but going from 5 to 6 cleanings would yield a marginal social benefit of only $2, which is less than the marginal social cost.

One fundamental rationale for the existence of government is that it provides a way for citizens to tax themselves in order to provide public goods—particularly a vital public good like national defense.

figure 76.2

A Public Good

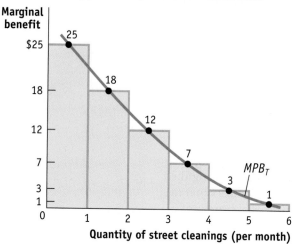

(a) Ted's Marginal Private Benefit Curve

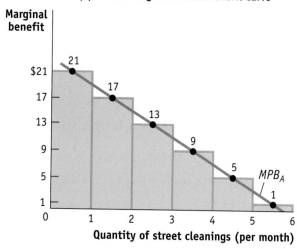

(b) Alice's Marginal Private Benefit Curve

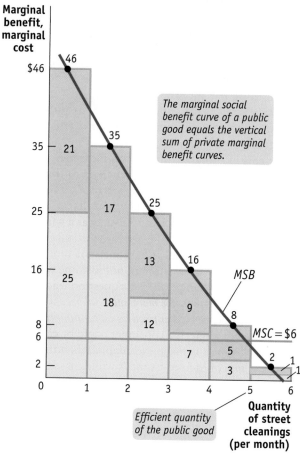

(c) The Marginal Social Benefit Curve

> The marginal social benefit curve of a public good equals the vertical sum of private marginal benefit curves.

Efficient quantity of the public good

Panel (a) shows Ted's marginal private benefit curve, MPB_T, and panel (b) shows Alice's marginal private benefit curve, MPB_A. Panel (c) shows the marginal social benefit of the public good, equal to the *sum* of the marginal private benefits to all consumers (in this case, Ted and Alice). The marginal social benefit curve, *MSB*, is the vertical sum of the marginal private benefit curves MPB_T and MPB_A. At a constant marginal social cost of $6, there should be 5 street cleanings per month, because the marginal social benefit of going from 4 to 5 cleanings is $8 ($3 for Ted plus $5 for Alice), but the marginal social benefit of going from 5 to 6 cleanings is only $2.

Of course, if society really consisted of only two individuals, they would probably manage to strike a deal to provide the good. But imagine a city with a million residents, each of whose marginal private benefit from a good is only a tiny fraction of the marginal social benefit. It would be impossible for people to reach a voluntary agreement to pay for the efficient level of a good like street cleaning—the potential for free-riding would make it too difficult to make and enforce an agreement among so many people. But they could and would vote to tax themselves to pay for a city-wide sanitation department.

Voting as a Public Good

It's a sad fact that many Americans who are eligible to vote don't bother to. As a result, their interests tend to be ignored by politicians. But what's even sadder is that this self-defeating behavior may be completely rational.

As the economist Mancur Olson pointed out in a famous book titled *The Logic of Collective Action*, voting is a public good, one that suffers from severe free-rider problems.

Imagine that you are one of a million people who would stand to gain the equivalent of $100 each if some plan is passed in a statewide referendum—say, a plan to improve public schools. And suppose that the opportunity cost of the time it would take you to vote is $10. Will you be sure to go to the polls and vote for the referendum? If you are rational, the answer is

no! The reason is that it is very unlikely that your vote will decide the issue, either way. If the measure passes, you benefit, even if you didn't bother to vote—the benefits are nonexcludable. If the measure doesn't pass, your vote would not have changed the outcome. Either way, by not voting—by free-riding on those who do vote—you save $10.

Of course, many people do vote out of a sense of civic duty. But because political action is a public good, in general people devote too little effort to defending their own interests.

The result, Olson pointed out, is that when a large group of people share a common political interest, they are likely to exert too little effort promoting their cause and so will be ig-

nored. Conversely, small, well-organized interest groups that act on issues narrowly targeted in their favor tend to have disproportionate power.

Is this a reason to distrust democracy? Winston Churchill said it best: "Democracy is the worst form of government, except for all the other forms that have been tried."

Common Resources

A **common resource** is a good that is nonexcludable but is rival in consumption. An example is the stock of fish in a fishing area, like the fisheries off the coast of New England. Traditionally, anyone who had a boat could go out to sea and catch fish—fish in the sea were a nonexcludable good. Yet the total number of fish is limited: the fish that one person catches are no longer available to be caught by someone else. So fish in the sea are rival in consumption.

Other examples of common resources include clean air, water, and the diversity of animal and plant species on the planet (biodiversity). In each of these cases the fact that the good is rival in consumption, and yet nonexcludable, poses a serious problem.

The Problem of Overuse

Because common resources are nonexcludable, individuals cannot be charged for their use. But the resources are rival in consumption, so an individual who uses a unit depletes the resource by making that unit unavailable to others. As a result, a common resource is subject to **overuse**: an individual will continue to use it until his or her marginal private benefit is equal to his or her marginal private cost, ignoring the cost that this action inflicts on society as a whole.

Fish are a classic example of a common resource. Particularly in heavily fished waters, my fishing imposes a cost on others by reducing the fish population and making it harder for others to catch fish. But I have no personal incentive to take this cost into account, since I cannot be charged for fishing. As a result, from society's point of view, I catch too many fish. Traffic congestion is another example of overuse of a common resource. A major highway during rush hour can accommodate only a certain number of vehicles per hour. If I decide to drive to work alone rather than carpool or work at home, I cause many other people to have a longer commute; but I have no incentive to take these consequences into account.

A **common resource** is nonexcludable and rival in consumption: you can't stop me from consuming the good, and more consumption by me means less of the good available for you.

Overuse is the depletion of a common resource that occurs when individuals ignore the fact that their use depletes the amount of the resource remaining for others.

In the case of a common resource, as in the earlier examples involving marginal external costs, the *marginal social cost* of my use of that resource is higher than my *marginal private cost,* the cost to me of using an additional unit of the good. Figure 76.3 illustrates this point. It shows the demand curve for fish, which measures the marginal private benefit of fish (as well as the marginal social benefit because there are no external benefits from catching and consuming fish). The figure also shows the supply curve for fish, which measures the marginal private cost of production of the fishing industry. We know that the industry supply curve is the horizontal sum of each individual fisherman's supply curve—equivalent to his or her marginal private cost curve. The fishing industry supplies the quantity Q_{MKT} at which its marginal private cost equals the price. But the efficient quantity is Q_{OPT}, the quantity of fish that equates the marginal social benefit (as reflected by the demand curve) to the marginal social cost, not to the fishing industry's marginal private cost of production. Thus, the market outcome results in overuse of the common resource.

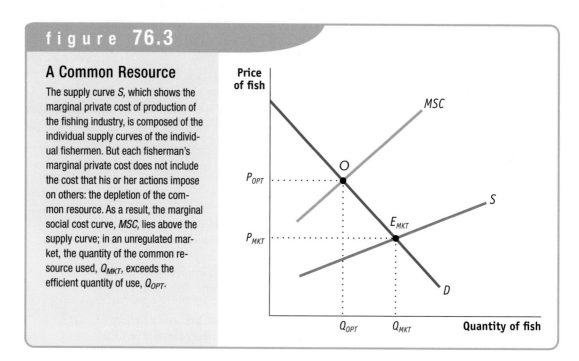

figure 76.3

A Common Resource

The supply curve *S,* which shows the marginal private cost of production of the fishing industry, is composed of the individual supply curves of the individual fishermen. But each fisherman's marginal private cost does not include the cost that his or her actions impose on others: the depletion of the common resource. As a result, the marginal social cost curve, *MSC,* lies above the supply curve; in an unregulated market, the quantity of the common resource used, Q_{MKT}, exceeds the efficient quantity of use, Q_{OPT}.

As we noted, there is a close parallel between the problem of managing a common resource and the problem posed by negative externalities. In the case of an activity that generates a negative externality, the marginal social cost of production is greater than the marginal private cost of production, the difference being the marginal external cost imposed on society. Here, the loss to society arising from a fisher's depletion of the common resource plays the same role as the external cost when there is a negative externality. In fact, many negative externalities (such as pollution) can be thought of as involving common resources (such as clean air).

The Efficient Use and Maintenance of a Common Resource

Because common resources pose problems similar to those created by negative externalities, the solutions are also similar. To ensure efficient use of a common resource, society must find a way to get individual users of the resource to take into account the costs they impose on others. This is the same principle as that of getting individuals to internalize a negative externality that arises from their actions.

There are three principal ways to induce people who use common resources to internalize the costs they impose on others:

- Tax or otherwise regulate the use of the common resource
- Create a system of tradable licenses for the right to use the common resource
- Make the common resource excludable and assign property rights to some individuals

The first two solutions overlap with the approaches to private goods with negative externalities. Just as governments use Pigouvian excise taxes to temper the consumption of alcohol, they use alternative forms of Pigouvian taxes to reduce the use of common resources. For example, in some countries there are "congestion charges" on those who drive during rush hour, in effect charging them for the use of highway space, a common resource. Likewise, visitors to national parks in the United States must pay an entry fee that is essentially a Pigouvian tax.

A second way to correct the problem of overuse is to create a system of tradable licenses for the use of the common resource, much like the systems designed to address negative externalities. The policy maker issues the number of licenses that corresponds to the efficient level of use of the good. Making the licenses tradable ensures that the right to use the good is allocated efficiently—that is, those who end up using the good (those willing to pay the most for a license) are those who gain the most from its use.

If it weren't for fees and restrictions, some common resources would be overrun.

But when it comes to common resources, often the most natural solution is simply to assign property rights. At a fundamental level, common resources are subject to overuse because *nobody owns them*. The essence of ownership of a good—the *property right* over the good—is that you can limit who can and cannot use the good as well as how much of it can be used. When a good is nonexcludable, in a very real sense no one owns it because a property right cannot be enforced—and consequently no one has an incentive to use it efficiently. So one way to correct the problem of overuse is to make the good excludable and assign property rights over it to someone. The good now has an owner who has an incentive to protect the value of the good—to use it efficiently rather than overuse it. This solution is applicable when currently nonexcludable goods can be made excludable, as with the privatization of parks and even roads, but it cannot be applied to resources that are inherently nonexcludable, including the air and flowing water.

Artificially Scarce Goods

An **artificially scarce good** is a good that is excludable but nonrival in consumption. As we've already seen, pay-per-view movies are a familiar example. The marginal cost to society of allowing an individual to watch a movie is zero because one person's viewing doesn't interfere with other people's viewing. Yet cable companies prevent an individual from seeing a movie if he or she hasn't paid. Goods like computer software and audio files, which are valued for the information they embody (and are sometimes called "information goods"), are also artificially scarce.

Markets will supply artificially scarce goods because their excludability allows firms to charge people for them. However, since the efficient price is equal to the marginal cost of zero and the actual price is something higher than that, the good is "artificially scarce" and consumption is inefficiently low. The problem is that, unless the producer can somehow earn revenue from producing and selling the good, none will be produced, which is likely to be worse than a positive but inefficiently low quantity.

Artificially scarce good is a good that is excludable but nonrival in consumption.

We have seen that, in the cases of public goods, common resources, and artificially scarce goods, a market economy will not provide adequate incentives for efficient levels of production and consumption. Fortunately for the sake of market efficiency, most goods are private goods. Food, clothing, shelter, and most other desirable things in life are excludable and rival in consumption, so the types of market failure discussed in this module are important exceptions rather than the norm.

Module 76 AP Review

Solutions appear at the back of the book.

Check Your Understanding

1. For each of the following goods, indicate whether it is excludable, whether it is rival in consumption, and what kind of good it is.
   a. a public space such as a park
   b. a cheese burrito
   c. information from a website that is password-protected
   d. publicly announced information about the path of an incoming hurricane

2. Which of the goods in Question 1 will be provided by a private producer without government intervention? Which will not be? Explain your answer.

Tackle the Test: Multiple-Choice Questions

1. Which of the following types of goods are always nonrival in consumption?
   a. public goods
   b. private goods
   c. common resources
   d. inferior goods
   e. goods provided by the government

2. The free-rider problem occurs in the case of
   a. private goods.
   b. common resources.
   c. artificially scarce goods.
   d. motorcycles.
   e. all of the above.

3. Public goods are sometimes provided through which of the following means?
   I. voluntary contributions
   II. individual self-interest
   III. the government
   a. I only
   b. II only
   c. III only
   d. I and III only
   e. I, II, and III

4. Market provision of a public good will lead to
   a. the efficient quantity.
   b. the efficient price.
   c. inefficiently high production of the good.
   d. inefficiently low production of the good.
   e. none of the good being provided.

5. The overuse of a common resource can be reduced by which of the following?
   a. a Pigouvian tax
   b. government regulations
   c. tradable licenses
   d. the assignment of property rights
   e. all of the above

Tackle the Test: Free-Response Questions

1. Suppose Austin and Ally are the only soccer enthusiasts in a village where any number of public soccer clinics could be put on by visiting experts for $80 each. There are no external costs involved. Austin's marginal private benefit curve for soccer clinics is horizontal at $60. Ally's marginal private benefit curve is a straight line starting at $100 on the vertical axis and ending at 10 clinics on the horizontal axis. Draw a correctly labeled graph for soccer clinics showing the marginal social cost, the marginal social benefit, and each resident's marginal private benefit. Label the quantity of clinics that Austin would purchase if he were the only resident as Q_{Austin}. Label the quantity of clinics that Ally would purchase if she were the only resident as Q_{Ally}. Label the optimal quantity of clinics for society as $Q_{Optimal}$.

2. a. Identify and explain the two characteristics shared by every public good.

   b. Suppose a new resident moves to a community that purchases a public good for the benefit of every member of the community. What is the additional cost of providing the public good to the new community member? Explain.

Answer (6 points):

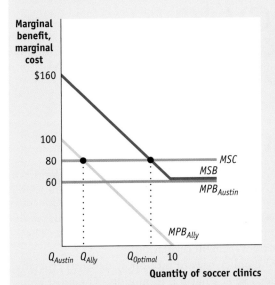

Quantity of soccer clinics

1 point: Correct axis labels ("Marginal benefit, marginal cost" or "Dollars per unit" on the vertical axis, "Quantity of soccer clinics" or "Q" on the horizontal axis)

1 point: *MSC* curve horizontal at a height of $80

1 point: *MSB* curve starts at a height of $160 where the quantity is zero, slopes downward to a height of $60 where the quantity is 10, and then coincides with *MPB*_{Austin}

1 point: Q_{Austin} labeled at a quantity of zero (because *MSC* exceeds *MPB*_{Austin} for every clinic)

1 point: Q_{Ally} found at the intersection of *MSC* and *MPB*_{Ally} and shown on the horizontal axis

1 point: $Q_{Optimal}$ found at the intersection of *MSC* and *MSB* and shown on the horizontal axis

Module 77
Public Policy to Promote Competition

Promoting Competition

We have seen that, in general, equilibrium in a competitive market with no externalities is efficient. On the other hand, imperfectly competitive markets—for example, those with a monopoly or an oligopoly—generally create inefficient outcomes. Concern about the higher prices, lower quantities, and lower quality of goods that can result from imperfect competition has led to public policies to promote competition. These policies include antitrust laws and direct government regulation.

As we discussed in Module 62, public policy toward monopoly depends crucially on whether or not the industry in question is a natural monopoly. The most common approach to a natural monopoly is for the government to allow one firm to exist but to regulate that firm to increase the quantity and lower the price relative to the monopoly outcome.

In this module, we first focus on ways to promote competition in cases that don't involve natural monopolies. If the industry is *not* a natural monopoly, the best policy is to prevent monopoly from arising or break it up if it already exists. These policies are carried out through antitrust laws. Later in this module we will turn to the more difficult problem of dealing with natural monopoly.

Antitrust Policy

As we discussed in Module 66, imperfect competition first became an issue in the United States during the second half of the nineteenth century when industrialists formed trusts to facilitate monopoly pricing. By having shareholders place their shares in the hands of a board of trustees, major companies in effect merged into a single firm. That is, they created monopolies.

Eventually, there was a public backlash, driven partly by concern about the economic effects of the trust movement, partly by fear that the owners of the trusts were simply becoming too powerful. The result was the Sherman Antitrust Act of 1890, which was intended both to prevent the creation of more monopolies and to break up existing ones. Following the Sherman Act, government passed several other acts intended to clarify antitrust policy.

The Sherman Antitrust Act of 1890

When Microsoft Corporation bundled its Internet Explorer web browser software with its Windows operating system, the makers of competing Netscape Navigator cried foul. Netscape advocates claimed the immediate availability of Internet Explorer to Windows users would create unfair competition. The plaintiffs sought protection under the cornerstone of U.S. antitrust policy (known in many other countries as "competition policy"), the Sherman Antitrust Act. This Act was the first of three major federal antitrust laws in the United States, followed by the Clayton Antitrust Act and the Federal Trade Commission Act, both passed in 1914. The Department of Justice, which has an Antitrust Division charged with enforcing antitrust laws, describes the goals of antitrust laws as protecting competition, ensuring lower prices, and promoting the development of new and better products. It emphasizes that firms in competitive markets attract consumers by cutting prices and increasing the quality of products or services. Competition and profit opportunities also stimulate businesses to find new and more efficient production methods.

The Sherman Antitrust Act of 1890 has two important provisions, each of which outlaws a particular type of activity. The first provision makes it illegal to create a contract, combination, or conspiracy that unreasonably restrains interstate trade. The second provision outlaws the monopolization of any part of interstate commerce. In addition, under the law, the Department of Justice is empowered to bring civil claims and criminal prosecutions when the law is violated. Indeed, it was the Department of Justice that filed suit against Microsoft in the web browser case. The initial court ruling, by the way, was that Microsoft should be broken up into one company that sold Windows and another that sold other software components. After that ruling was overturned on appeal, a final settlement kept Microsoft intact, but prohibited various forms of predatory behavior and practices that could create barriers to entry.

As the ambiguities of the Microsoft case suggest, the law provides little detail regarding what constitutes "restraining trade." And the law does not make it illegal to *be* a monopoly but to "monopolize," that is, to take illegal actions to become a monopoly. If you are the only firm in an industry because no other firm chooses to enter the market, you are not in violation of the Sherman Act.

The two provisions of the Sherman Act give very broad, general descriptions of the activities it makes illegal. The act does not provide details regarding specific actions or activities that it prohibits. The vague nature of the Sherman Act led to the subsequent passage of two additional major antitrust laws.

The Clayton Antitrust Act of 1914

The Clayton Antitrust Act of 1914 was intended to clarify the Sherman Act, which did not identify specific firm behaviors that were illegal. The Clayton Act outlaws four specific firm behaviors; price discrimination, anticompetitive practices (exclusive dealing and tying arrangements), anticompetitive mergers and acquisitions, and interlocking directorates (two corporate boards of directors that share at least one director in common).

You are already familiar with the topic of price discrimination from our discussion of market structures. The Clayton Act makes it illegal to charge different prices to different customers for the same product. Obviously, there are exceptions to this rule that allow the price discrimination we see in practice, for example, at movie theaters where children pay a different price from adults.

By prohibiting exclusive dealing, the Clayton Act makes it illegal for a firm to refuse to do business with you just because you also do business with its competitors. If a firm had the dominant product in a given market, exclusive dealing could allow it to gain monopoly power in other markets. For example, a company that sells an extremely popular felt-tip marker—the only one of its kind—could set a condition that customers who want to purchase the marker must purchase all of their office supplies from the company. This would allow the marker company to expand its existing market power into the market for other office supplies.

The Clayton Act outlaws tying arrangements because, otherwise, a firm could expand its monopoly power for a dominant product by "tying" the purchase of one product to the purchase of a dominant product in another market. Tying arrangements occur when a firm stipulates that it will sell you a specific product, say a printer, only if you buy something else, such as printer paper, at the same time. In this case, tying the printer and paper together expands the firm's printer market power into the market for paper. In this way, as with exclusive dealing, tying arrangements can lessen competition by allowing a firm to expand its market power from one market into another.

Mergers and acquisitions happen fairly often in the U.S. economy; most are not illegal despite the Clayton Act stipulations. The Justice Department regularly reviews proposed mergers between companies in the same industry and, under the Clayton Act, bars any that they determine would significantly reduce competition. To evaluate proposed mergers, they often use the measures we discussed in the oligopoly modules: *concentration ratios* and the *Herfindahl-Hirschman Index*. But the Justice Department is not the only agency responsible for enforcing antitrust laws. Another of our major antitrust laws created and empowers the Federal Trade Commission to enforce antitrust laws.

The Federal Trade Commission Act of 1914

Passed in 1914, the Federal Trade Commission Act prohibits unfair methods of competition in interstate commerce and created the Federal Trade Commission (FTC) to enforce the Act. The FTC Act outlaws unfair competition, including "unfair or deceptive acts." The FTC Act also outlaws some of the same practices included in the Sherman and Clayton Acts. In addition, it specifically outlaws price fixing (including the setting of minimum resale prices), output restrictions, and actions that prevent the entry of new firms. The FTC's goal is to promote lower prices, higher output, and free entry—all characteristics of competitive markets (as opposed to monopolies and oligopolies).

The Federal Trade Commission promotes fair practices, free entry by firms, and the virtues of competitive markets.

Dealing with Natural Monopoly

Antitrust laws are designed to promote competition by preventing business behaviors that concentrate market power. But what if a market is a natural monopoly? As you will recall, a natural monopoly occurs when economies of scale make it efficient to have only one firm in a market. Now we turn from promoting competition to establishing a monopoly, but seeking a public policy to prevent the relatively high prices and low quantities that result when there is only one firm.

Breaking up a monopoly that isn't natural is clearly a good idea: the gains to consumers outweigh the loss to the firm. But what about the situation in which a large firm has a lower average total cost than many small firms—the case of natural monopoly we discussed in Section 9? The goal in these circumstances is to retain the advantage of lower average total cost that results from a single producer and still curb the inefficiency associated with a monopoly. In Module 62, we presented two ways to do this—public ownership and price regulation.

While there are a few examples of public ownership in the United States, such as Amtrak, a provider of passenger rail service, the more common answer has been to leave the industry in private hands but subject it to regulation.

Price Regulation Most local utilities are natural monopolies with regulated prices. By having only one firm produce in the market, society benefits from increased efficiency. That is, the average cost of production is lower due to economies of scale. But without price regulation, these firms would be tempted to restrict output and raise price. How, then, do regulators determine an appropriate price?

Since the purpose of regulation is to achieve efficiency in the market, a logical place to set price is at the level at which the marginal cost curve intersects the demand curve. This is called **marginal cost pricing.** (Because we are no longer discussing situations with externalities, we will refer to a single marginal cost that is both marginal social cost and marginal private cost.) We have seen that it is efficient for a competitive firm to set price equal to marginal cost. So should regulators require marginal cost pricing?

Figure 77.1 illustrates this situation. In the case of a natural monopoly, the firm is operating on the downward-sloping portion of its average total cost curve (it is experiencing economies of scale). When average total cost is falling, it must be that marginal cost is below average total cost, pulling it down. If the firm had to set price equal to marginal cost and sell Q_1 units (the quantity demanded when price equals marginal cost), price would be below average total cost and the firm would incur a loss: for each unit sold, the firm would lose the difference between average total cost and price. The firm would not continue to operate at a loss in the long run unless it received a subsidy equal to the amount of the loss. Government could require the efficient price and subsidize the firm, resulting in an overall increase in efficiency for society. But firm subsidies funded from tax revenues are often politically unpopular. What other options do regulators have?

figure 77.1

Price Setting for a Regulated Monopoly

This figure shows the marginal cost curve, MC, and the average total cost curve, ATC. When price is set equal to marginal cost (where the MC curve crosses the demand curve), the firm incurs a loss. When price is set equal to average total cost (where ATC crosses the demand curve) the firm breaks even, but price and quantity are not at the efficient level.

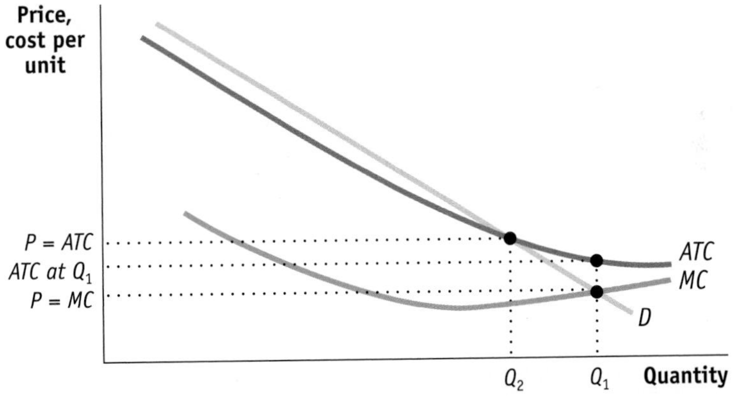

If regulators want to set the price so that the firm does not require a subsidy, they can set the price at which the demand curve intersects the average total cost curve and the firm breaks even. This is called **average cost pricing.** As Figure 77.1 illustrates, average cost pricing results in output level Q_2. The result, a lower quantity at a higher price than with marginal cost pricing, seems to fly in the face of what antitrust regulation is all about. But remember that there are always trade-offs, and it may be best to avoid subsidizing a loss even if it results in less than the efficient quantity.

Allowing a natural monopoly to exist permits the firm to produce at a lower average total cost than if multiple firms produced in the same market. And price regulation seeks to prevent the inefficiency that results when an unregulated monopoly limits output and raises price. This all looks terrific: consumers are better off, monopoly

Marginal cost pricing occurs when regulators set a monopoly's price equal to its marginal cost to achieve efficiency.

Average cost pricing occurs when regulators set a monopoly's price equal to its average cost to prevent the firm from incurring a loss.

profits are avoided, and overall welfare increases. Unfortunately, things are rarely that easy in practice. The main problem is that regulators don't always have the information required to set the price exactly at the level at which the demand curve crosses the average total cost curve. Sometimes they set it too low, creating shortages; at other times they set it too high, increasing inefficiency. Also, regulated monopolies, like publicly owned firms, tend to exaggerate their costs to regulators and to provide inferior quality to consumers.

fyi

The Regulated Price of Power

Power doesn't come cheap, and we're not just talking about the nearly $2 billion spent on congressional races in 2010. By 2017, Georgia Power plans to add two 1,100-megawatt nuclear reactors to its Vogtle Electric Generating Plant in eastern Georgia at an estimated cost of $14 billion. In Kentucky, Louisville Gas and Electric will spend $1.2 billion to add a 750-megawatt coal-fired generating unit. With high start-up costs like these, power plants are natural monopolies. If many plants competed for customers in the same region, none would sell enough energy to warrant the cost of each plant. Here we see the spreading effect from Module 55 in action—having just one plant allows the production level to be relatively high and the average fixed cost to be tolerably low.

On October 6, 2010, U.S. Interior Secretary Ken Salazar and representatives from Cape Wind Associates signed the lease for a wind farm off the coast of Massachusetts. The $2.5 billion project will generate 468 megawatts of electricity. With lower output and higher start-up costs than the coal-fired power plant, the spreading effect is smaller, making the average fixed cost and the average total cost relatively high. If regulators set prices for this natural monopoly in accordance with average total cost, we would expect coal-fired plants to be held to a lower price per kilowatt-hour (kWh) than the relatively expensive wind power plants. Indeed, Cape Wind plans to charge 19 cents per kWh, more than twice the 8 cents per kWh allowed for electricity from coal-fired plants in Kentucky and Massachusetts.

Why the interest in generating energy from wind when energy from coal is cheaper for the consumer? The dynamics of supply and demand provide one reason: as supplies of coal decrease and energy demand increases, the equilibrium price for coal energy will rise, helping investments in wind energy to pay off. Another reason relates to the external costs discussed in Module 75: wind turbines create no emissions. The U.S. Department of Energy reports that if 20 percent of the nation's energy needs were satisfied with wind, carbon dioxide emissions would fall by 825 million metric tons annually. Like coal-fired power plants, wind farms do create some negative externalities. The potential for noise and obstructed views elicit cries of "not in my back yard (or even five miles off my coast)!" As with lunches, there's no such thing as a free kWh, which highlights the importance of cost-benefit analysis.

Module 77 AP Review

Solutions appear at the back of the book.

Check Your Understanding

1. Would each of the following business practices be legal under antitrust law? Explain.
   a. You have a patent for a superior fax machine and therefore are the only person able to sell that type of fax machine. In order to buy your fax machine, you require the purchaser to buy a service contract from you (even though other firms provide excellent service for your machine).
   b. You have invented a new type of correction fluid that does an amazing job covering up mistakes made on paper forms.

   In order to buy your correction fluid, you require purchasers to buy all of their office supplies from you.
   c. You own a car dealership and plan to buy the dealership across the street and merge the two companies. There are several other car dealerships in town.
   d. You and your only other competitor in the state have an agreement that, any time a new firm tries to enter the market, you will drop your prices for long enough to run the new entrant out of business before returning to your previous prices.

2. The FYI in this module discusses the possibility that regulators set prices for wind energy on the basis of average total cost. Explain why policymakers who don't want to pay subsidies would choose average cost pricing over marginal cost pricing in the market for wind energy.

Tackle the Test: Multiple-Choice Questions

1. The Sherman Antitrust Act of 1890 sought to do which of the following?
   a. break up existing monopolies
   b. prevent the creation of new monopolies
   c. stop monopoly behavior engaged in by trusts
   d. respond to the increasing power of trusts in the economy
   e. all of the above

2. A natural monopoly exists when, over the relevant range, increasing the output level results in a lower
   a. total cost.
   b. average total cost.
   c. average variable cost.
   d. average fixed cost.
   e. marginal cost.

3. Which of the following is the most common policy approach to a natural monopoly?
   a. public ownership
   b. price regulation
   c. quantity regulation
   d. quality regulation
   e. a breakup of the monopoly into smaller firms

For questions 4 and 5, refer to the graph provided.

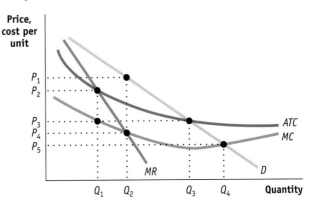

4. Without government intervention, a monopolist will produce _____ and charge _____.
   a. Q_3, P_3
   b. Q_2, P_4
   c. Q_2, P_1
   d. Q_1, P_3
   e. Q_1, P_2

5. The lowest regulated price the government could expect this monopolist to maintain in the long run is
   a. P_1.
   b. P_2.
   c. P_3.
   d. P_4.
   e. P_5.

Tackle the Test: Free-Response Questions

1. a. Draw a correctly labeled graph showing a natural monopoly. On your graph, label the price and quantity the monopoly will choose if unregulated as P_U and Q_U.
   b. On the same graph, shade in and label consumer surplus and the firm's profit in the absence of regulation.
   c. On the same graph, label the lowest price that regulators could expect the monopoly to maintain in the long run as P_R and the resulting quantity as Q_R.
   d. What happens to the size of consumer surplus when the firm is required to charge P_R rather than P_U? What happens to the firm's profit?

Answer (10 points)

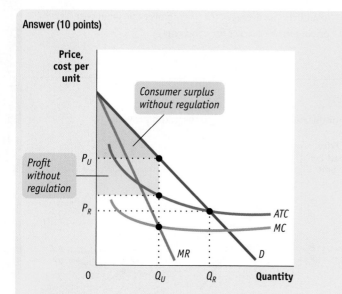

1 point: Correctly labeled axes ("Price, cost per unit" or "Dollars per unit" on the vertical axis, "Quantity" or "Q" on the horizontal axis)

1 point: Downward-sloping *ATC* curve

1 point: Downward-sloping *MC* curve below the *ATC* curve

1 point: Unregulated quantity Q_U shown on the horizontal axis where $MC = MR$

1 point: Unregulated price P_U found on a downward-sloping demand curve above Q_U and shown on the vertical axis

1 point: Correct profit rectangle

1 point: Consumer surplus triangle shown below the demand curve and above the price

1 point: Regulated price and quantity P_R and Q_R shown on the appropriate axes, corresponding to where the demand curve crosses the average total cost curve.

1 point: Consumer surplus will increase

1 point: Profit will decrease to zero

2. List and describe three different public policy approaches to monopoly.

Module 78
Income Inequality and Income Distribution

What you will learn in this Module:

- What defines poverty, what causes poverty, and the consequences of poverty
- How income inequality in America has changed over time
- How programs like Social Security affect poverty and income inequality

For at least the past 70 years, every U.S. president has promised to do his best to reduce poverty. In 1964 President Lyndon Johnson went so far as to declare a "war on poverty," creating a number of new programs to aid the poor. Antipoverty programs account for a significant part of the U.S. *welfare state*—the system whereby the government takes responsibility for the welfare of its citizens—although social insurance programs are an even larger part. In this module, we look at the problem of poverty and the issue of income distribution, and learn how public policy can affect them.

The Problem of Poverty

What, exactly, do we mean by poverty? Any definition is somewhat arbitrary. Since 1965, however, the U.S. government has maintained an official definition of the **poverty threshold,** a minimum annual income that is considered adequate to purchase the necessities of life. Families whose incomes fall below the poverty threshold are considered poor.

The official poverty threshold depends on the size and composition of a family. In 2009 the poverty threshold for an adult living alone was $10,956; for a household consisting of two adults and two children, it was $21,756.

Trends in Poverty

Contrary to popular misconceptions, although the official poverty threshold is adjusted each year to reflect changes in the cost of living, it has *not* been adjusted upward over time to reflect the long-term rise in the standard of living of the average American family. As a result, as the economy grows and becomes more prosperous, and average incomes rise, you might expect the percentage of the population living below the poverty threshold to steadily decline.

Somewhat surprisingly, however, this hasn't happened. Figure 78.1 on the next page shows the U.S. **poverty rate**—the percentage of the population living below the poverty

The **poverty threshold** is the annual income below which a family is officially considered poor.

The **poverty rate** is the percentage of the population with incomes below the poverty threshold.

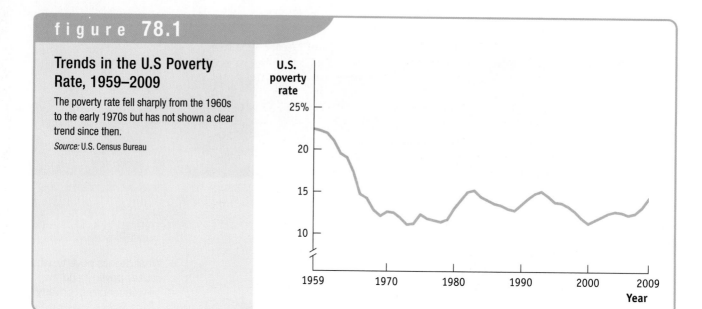

figure 78.1

Trends in the U.S Poverty Rate, 1959–2009

The poverty rate fell sharply from the 1960s to the early 1970s but has not shown a clear trend since then.

Source: U.S. Census Bureau

threshold—from 1959 to 2009. As you can see, the poverty rate fell steeply during the 1960s and early 1970s. Since then, however, it has fluctuated up and down, with no clear trend. In fact, in 2009 the poverty rate was higher than it had been in 1973.

Who Are the Poor?

Many Americans probably hold a stereotyped image of poverty: an African-American or Hispanic family with no husband present and the female head of the household unemployed at least part of the time. This picture isn't completely off-base: poverty is disproportionately high among African-Americans and Hispanics as well as among female-headed households. But a majority of the poor don't fit the stereotype.

In 2009, about 43.5 million Americans were in poverty—14.3% of the population, or about one in seven persons. About one-quarter of the poor were African-American and a roughly equal number, Hispanic. Within these two groups, poverty rates were well above the national average: 25.9% of African-Americans and 25.3% of Hispanics. But there was also widespread poverty among non-Hispanic whites, who had a poverty rate of 9.4%.

There is also a correlation between family makeup and poverty. Female-headed families with no husband present had a very high poverty rate: 32.5%. Married couples were much less likely to be poor, with a poverty rate of only 5.8%; still, about 39% of poor families were married couples.

What really stands out from the data, however, is the association between poverty and lack of adequate employment. Adults who work full time are very unlikely to be poor: only 3.6% of full-time workers were poor in 2008. Adults who worked part time or not at all during the year made up 87.3% of the poor in 2008. Many industries, particularly in the retail and service sectors, now rely primarily on part-time workers. Part-time work typically lacks benefits such as health plans, paid vacation days, and retirement benefits, and it also usually pays a lower hourly wage than comparable full-time work. As a result, many of the poor are members of what analysts call the *working poor:* workers whose income falls at or below the poverty threshold.

What Causes Poverty?

Poverty is often blamed on lack of education, and educational attainment clearly has a strong positive effect on income level—those with more education earn, on average, higher incomes than those with less education. For example, in 1979 the average hourly wage of men with a college degree was 36% higher than that of men with only a high school diploma; by 2009 the "college premium" had increased to 81%. Lack of proficiency in English is also a barrier to higher income. For example, Mexican-born male workers in the United States—two-thirds of whom have not graduated from high school and many of whom have poor English skills—earn less than half of what native-born men earn. And it's important not to overlook the role of racial and gender discrimination; although less pervasive today than 50 years ago, discrimination still erects formidable barriers to advancement for many Americans. Non-whites earn less and are less likely to be employed than whites with comparable levels of education. Studies find that African-American males suffer persistent discrimination by employers in favor of whites, African-American women, and Hispanic immigrants. Women earn lower incomes than men with similar qualifications.

In addition, one important source of poverty that should not be overlooked is bad luck. Many families find themselves impoverished when a wage-earner loses a job or a family member falls seriously ill.

Consequences of Poverty

The consequences of poverty are often severe, particularly for children. Currently, more than 17.4% of children in the United States live in poverty. Poverty is often associated with a lack of access to health care, which can lead to further health problems that erode the ability to attend school and work later in life. Affordable housing is also frequently a problem, leading poor families to move often and disrupting school and work schedules. Recent medical studies have shown that children raised in severe poverty tend to suffer from lifelong learning disabilities. As a result, American children growing up in or near poverty don't have an equal chance at the starting line: they tend to be at a disadvantage throughout their lives. For example, even talented children who come from poor families are unlikely to finish college.

Table 78.1 shows the results of a long-term survey conducted by the U.S. Department of Education, which tracked a group of students who were in eighth grade in 1988. That year, the students took a mathematics test that the study used as an indicator of their innate ability; the study also scored students by the socioeconomic status of their families, a measure that took into account their parents' income and employment. As you can see, the results were disturbing: only 29% of students who were in the highest-scoring 25% on the test but whose parents were of low status finished college. By contrast, the equally talented children of high-status parents had a 74% chance of finishing college—and children of high-status parents had a 30% chance of finishing college even if they had low test scores. What this tells us is that

table 78.1

Percent of Eighth-Graders Finishing College, 1988

	Mathematics test score in bottom quartile	Mathematics test score in top quartile
Parents in bottom quartile	3%	29%
Parents in top quartile	30	74

Source: National Center for Education Statistics, *The Condition of Education 2003*, p. 47.

The Impeccable Economic Logic of Early Childhood Intervention Programs

One of the most vexing problems facing any society is how to break what researchers call the "cycle of poverty": children who grow up with disadvantaged socioeconomic backgrounds are far more likely to remain trapped in poverty as adults, even after we account for differences in ability. They are more likely to be unemployed or underemployed, to engage in crime, and to suffer chronic health problems.

Early childhood intervention has offered some hope of breaking the cycle. A 2006 study by the RAND Corporation found that high-quality early-childhood programs that focus on education and health care lead to significant social, intellectual, and financial advantages for kids who would otherwise be at risk of dropping out of high school and of engaging in criminal behavior. Children in programs like Head Start were less likely to engage in such destructive behaviors and more likely to end up with a job and to earn a high salary later in life. Another study by researchers at the University of Pittsburgh in 2003 looked at early-childhood intervention programs from a dollars-and-cents perspective, finding from $4 to $7 in benefits for every $1 spent on early-childhood intervention programs. The study also pointed to one program whose participants, by age 20, were 26% more likely to have finished high school, 35% less likely to have been charged in juvenile court, and 40% less likely to have repeated a grade compared to individuals of similar socioeconomic background who did not attend preschool. The observed external benefits to society of these programs are so large that the Brookings Institution predicts that providing high-quality preschool education to every American child would result in an increase in GDP, the total value of a country's domestic output, by almost 2%, representing over 3 million more jobs.

poverty is, to an important degree, self-perpetuating: the children of the poor start at such a disadvantage relative to other Americans that it's very hard for them to achieve a better life.

Economic Inequality

The United States is a rich country. In 2008, the average U.S. household had an income of more than $68,000, far exceeding the poverty threshold. How is it possible, then, that so many Americans still live in poverty? The answer is that income is unequally distributed, with many households earning much less than the average and others earning much more.

Table 78.2 shows the distribution of pre-tax income among U.S. families in 2008—income before federal income taxes are paid—as estimated by the Census Bureau. Households are grouped into *quintiles*, each containing 20% or one-fifth of the popula-

table **78.2**

U.S. Income Distribution in 2008

Income group	Income range	Average income	Percent of total income
Bottom quintile	Less than $20,712	$11,656	3.4%
Second quintile	$20,712 to $39,000	29,517	8.6
Third quintile	$39,000 to $62,725	50,132	14.7
Fourth quintile	$62,725 to $100,240	79,760	23.3
Top quintile	More than $100,240	171,057	50.0
Top 5%	More than $180,000	294,709	21.5
Mean Income = $68,424		**Median Income = $50,303**	

Source: U.S. Census Bureau.

tion. The first, or bottom, quintile contains households whose income put them below the 20th percentile in income, the second quintile contains households whose income put them between the 20th and 40th percentiles, and so on. The Census Bureau also provides data on the 5% of families with the highest incomes.

For each group, Table 78.2 shows three numbers. The second column shows the range of incomes that define the group. For example, in 2008, the bottom quintile consisted of households with annual incomes of less than $20,712; the next quintile of households with incomes between $20,712 and $39,000; and so on. The third column shows the average income in each group, ranging from $11,656 for the bottom fifth to $294,709 for the top 5 percent. The fourth column shows the percentage of total U.S. income received by each group.

At the bottom of Table 78.2 are two useful numbers for thinking about the incomes of American households. **Mean household income,** also called average household income, is the total income of all U.S. households divided by the number of households. **Median household income** is the income of a household in the exact middle of the income distribution—the level of income at which half of all households have lower income and half have higher income. It's very important to realize that these two numbers do not measure the same thing. Economists often illustrate the difference by asking people first to imagine a room containing several dozen more or less ordinary wage-earners and then to think about what happens to the mean and median incomes of the people in the room if a billionaire Wall Street tycoon walks in. The mean income soars, because the tycoon's income pulls up the average, but median income hardly rises at all. This example helps explain why economists generally regard median income as a better guide to the economic status of typical American families than mean income: mean income is strongly affected by the incomes of a relatively small number of very-high-income Americans, who are not representative of the population as a whole; median income is not.

What we learn from Table 78.2 is that income in the United States is quite unequally distributed. The average income of the poorest fifth of families is less than a quarter of the average income of families in the middle, and the richest fifth have an average income more than three times that of families in the middle. The incomes of the richest fifth of the population are, on average, about 15 times as high as those of the poorest fifth. In fact, the distribution of income in America has become more unequal since 1980, rising to a level that has made it a significant political issue. The FYI at the end of this section discusses long-term trends in U.S. income inequality, which declined in the 1930s and 1940s, was stable for more than 30 years after World War II, but began rising again in the late 1970s.

It's often convenient to have a single number that summarizes a country's level of income inequality. The **Gini coefficient,** the most widely used measure of inequality, is based on how disparately income is distributed across the quintiles. A country with a perfectly equal distribution of income—that is, one in which the bottom 20% of the population received 20% of the income, the bottom 40% of the population received 40% of the income, and so on—would have a Gini coefficient of 0. At the other extreme, the highest possible value for the Gini coefficient is 1—the level it would attain if all of a country's income went to just one person.

One way to get a sense of what Gini coefficients mean in practice is to look at international comparisons. Figure 78.2 on page 767 shows the most recent estimates of the Gini coefficient for many of the world's countries. Aside from a few countries in Africa, the highest levels of income inequality are found in Latin America; countries with a high degree of inequality, such as Brazil, have Gini coefficients close to 0.6. The most equal distributions of income are in Europe, especially in Scandinavia; countries with very equal income distributions, such as Sweden, have Gini coefficients around 0.25. Compared to other wealthy countries, the United States, with a Gini coefficient of 0.468 in 2009, has unusually high inequality, though it isn't as unequal as in Latin America.

How serious an issue is income inequality? In a direct sense, high income inequality means that some people don't share in a nation's overall prosperity. As we've seen, rising inequality explains how it's possible that the U.S. poverty rate has failed to fall for the

Mean household income is the average income across all households.

Median household income is the income of the household lying in the middle of the income distribution.

The **Gini coefficient** is a number that summarizes a country's level of income inequality based on how unequally income is distributed across the quintiles.

Long-Term Trends in Income Inequality in the United States

Does inequality tend to rise, fall, or stay the same over time? The answer is yes—all three. Over the course of the past century, the United States has gone through periods characterized by all three trends: an era of falling inequality during the 1930s and 1940s, an era of stable inequality for about 35 years after World War II, and an era of rising inequality over the past generation.

Detailed U.S. data on income by quintiles, as shown in Table 78.2, are only available starting in 1947. The figure shows the annual rate of growth of income, adjusted for inflation, for each quintile over two periods: from 1947 to 1980, and from 1980 to 2008. There's a clear difference between the two periods. In the first period, income within each group grew at about the same rate—that is, there wasn't much change in the inequality of income, just growing incomes across the board. After 1980, however, incomes grew much more quickly at the top than in the middle, and more quickly in the middle than at the bottom. So inequality has increased substantially since 1980. Overall, inflation-adjusted income for the top quintile rose 48% between 1980 and 2008, but it rose only 8.7% for the bottom quintile.

Although detailed data on income distribution aren't available before 1947, economists have instead used other information including income tax data to estimate the share of income going to

the top 10% of the population all the way back to 1917. Panel (b) of the figure shows this measure from 1917 to 2008. These data, like the more detailed data available since 1947, show that American inequality was more or less stable between 1947 and the late 1970s but has risen substantially since. The longer-term data also show, however, that the relatively equal distribution of 1947 was something new. In the late nineteenth century, often referred to as the Gilded Age, American income was very unequally distributed; this high level of inequality persisted into the 1930s. But inequality declined sharply between the late 1930s and the end of World War II. In a famous paper, Claudia Goldin and Robert Margo, two economic historians, dubbed this narrowing of income inequality "the Great Compression."

The Great Compression roughly coincided with World War II, a period during which the U.S. government imposed special controls on wages and prices. Evidence indicates that these controls were applied in ways that reduced inequality—for example, it was much easier for employers to get approval to increase the wages of their lowest-paid employees than to increase executive salaries. What remains puzzling is that the equality imposed by wartime controls lasted for decades after those controls were lifted in 1946.

Since the 1970s, as we've already seen, inequality has increased substantially. In fact, pretax income appears to be as unequally distributed

in America today as it was in the 1920s, prompting many commentators to describe the current state of the nation as a new Gilded Age—albeit one in which the effects of inequality are moderated by taxes and the existence of the welfare state. There is intense debate among economists about the causes of this widening inequality. The most popular explanation is rapid technological change, which has increased the demand for highly skilled or talented workers more rapidly than the demand for other workers, leading to a rise in the wage gap between the highly skilled and other workers. Growing international trade may also have contributed by allowing the United States to import labor-intensive products from low-wage countries rather than making them domestically, reducing the demand for less skilled American workers and depressing their wages. Rising immigration may be yet another source. On average, immigrants have lower education levels than native-born workers and increase the supply of low-skilled labor while depressing low-skilled wages.

All of these explanations, however, fail to account for one key feature: much of the rise in inequality doesn't reflect a rising gap between highly educated workers and those with less education, but rather growing differences among highly educated workers themselves. For example, schoolteachers and top business executives have similarly high levels

(a) Rates of Income Growth Since 1947

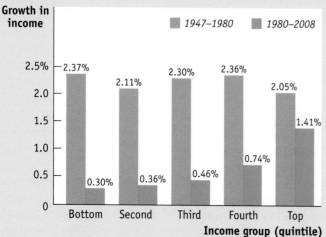

(b) The Richest 10% of Americans, 1917–2008

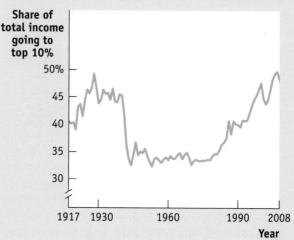

of education, but executive paychecks have risen dramatically and teachers' salaries have not. For some reason, the economy now pays a few "superstars"—a group that includes literal superstars in the entertainment world but also such groups as Wall Street traders and top corporate executives—much higher incomes than it did a generation ago. It's still not entirely clear what caused the change.

past 35 years even though the country as a whole has become considerably richer. Also, extreme inequality, as found in Latin America, is often associated with political instability, because of tension between a wealthy minority and the rest of the population.

It's important to realize, however, that the data shown in Table 78.2 overstate the true degree of inequality in America, for several reasons. One is that the data represent a snapshot for a single year, whereas the incomes of many individual families fluctuate over time. That is, many of those near the bottom in any given year are having an unusually bad year and many of those at the top are having an unusually good one. Over time, their incomes will revert to a more normal level. So a table showing average incomes within quintiles over a longer period, such as a decade, would not show as much inequality. Furthermore, a family's income tends to vary over its life cycle: most people earn considerably less in their early working years than they will later in life, and then experience a considerable drop in income when they retire. Consequently, the numbers in Table 78.2, which combine young workers, mature workers, and retirees, show more inequality than would a table that compares families of similar ages.

Despite these qualifications, there is a considerable amount of genuine inequality in the United States. Moreover, the fact that families' incomes fluctuate from year to year

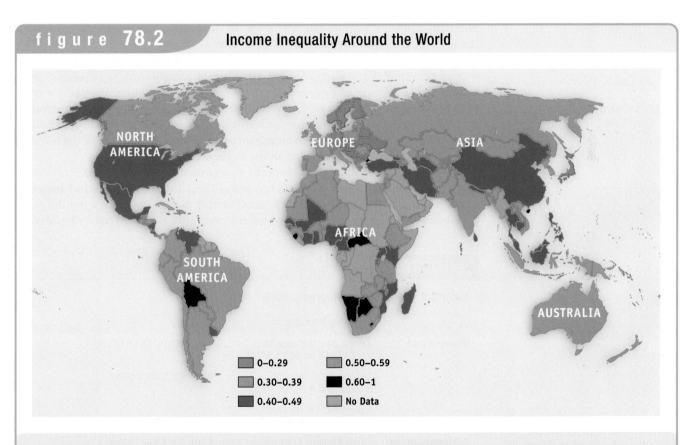

figure 78.2   **Income Inequality Around the World**

Legend:
- 0–0.29
- 0.30–0.39
- 0.40–0.49
- 0.50–0.59
- 0.60–1
- No Data

The highest levels of income inequality are found in Africa and Latin America. The most equal distributions of income are in Europe, especially in Scandinavia. Compared to other wealthy countries, the United States, with a Gini coefficient of 0.468 in 2009, has unusually high inequality.

Source: World Bank, *Human Development Report 2007–2008*

isn't entirely good news. Measures of inequality in a given year *do* overstate true inequality. But those year-to-year fluctuations are part of a problem that worries even affluent families—economic insecurity.

Economic Insecurity

The rationale for the welfare state rests in part on the benefits of reducing economic insecurity, which afflicts even relatively well-off families. One source of economic insecurity is the risk of a sudden loss of income, as occurs when a family member loses a job and either spends an extended period without work or is forced to take a new job that pays considerably less. In a given year, according to recent estimates, about one in six American families will see their income cut in half. Related estimates show that the percentage of people who find themselves below the poverty threshold for at least one year over the course of a decade is several times higher than the percentage of people below the poverty threshold in any given year.

Even if a family doesn't face a loss in income, it can face a surge in expenses. The most common reason for such surges is a medical problem that requires expensive treatment, such as heart disease or cancer. Many Americans have health insurance that covers a large share of their expenses in such cases, but a substantial number either do not have health insurance or rely on insurance provided by the government.

U.S. Antipoverty Programs

U.S. antipoverty programs include three huge programs—Social Security, Medicare, and Medicaid—several other fairly big programs, including Temporary Assistance for Needy Families, food stamps, the Earned Income Tax Credit, and a number of smaller programs. Table 78.3 shows one useful way to categorize these programs, along with the amount spent on each listed program in 2009.

First, the table distinguishes between programs that are **means-tested** and those that are not. In means-tested programs, benefits are available only to families or individuals whose income and/or wealth falls below some minimum. Basically, means-tested programs are poverty programs designed to help only those with low incomes. By contrast, non-means-tested programs provide their benefits to everyone, although, as we'll see, they tend in practice to reduce income inequality by increasing the incomes of the poor by a larger proportion than the incomes of the rich.

Second, the table distinguishes between programs that provide monetary transfers that beneficiaries can spend as they choose and those that provide **in-kind benefits,** which are given in the form of goods or services rather than money. As the numbers suggest, in-kind benefits are dominated by Medicare and Medicaid, which pay for health care.

table 78.3

Major U.S. Welfare State Programs, 2009

	Monetary transfers	In-kind
Means-tested	Temporary Assistance for Needy Families: $20.1 billion	Food stamps: $54.6 billion
	Supplemental Security Income: $42.4 billion	Medicaid: $369.3 billion
	Earned Income Tax Credit: $66.6 billion	
Not means-tested	Social Security: $664 billion	Medicare: $500.3 billion
	Unemployment insurance: $129.4 billion	

A **means-tested** program is available only to individuals or families whose incomes fall below a certain level.

An **in-kind benefit** is a benefit given in the form of goods or services.

Means-Tested Programs

When people use the term *welfare*, they're often referring to monetary aid to poor families. The main source of such monetary aid in the United States is Temporary Assistance for Needy Families, or TANF. This program does not aid everyone who is poor; it is available only to poor families with children and only for a limited period of time.

TANF was introduced in the 1990s to replace a highly controversial program known as Aid to Families with Dependent Children, or AFDC. The older program was widely accused of creating perverse incentives for the poor, including encouraging family breakup. Partly as a result of the change in programs, the benefits of modern "welfare" are considerably less generous than those available a generation ago, once the data are adjusted for inflation. Also, TANF contains time limits, so welfare recipients—even single parents—must eventually seek work. As you can see from Table 78.3, TANF is a relatively small part of the modern U.S. welfare state.

Other means-tested programs, though more expensive, are less controversial. The Supplemental Security Income program aids disabled Americans who are unable to work and have no other source of income. The Supplemental Nutrition Assistance Program (formerly known as the Food Stamp Program) helps low-income families and individuals to buy food staples.

Finally, economists use the term **negative income tax** for a program that supplements the earnings of low-income workers. For example, in the United States, the Earned Income Tax Credit (EITC) provides additional income to millions of workers. It has become more generous as traditional welfare has become less generous. As an incentive to work, only workers who earn income are eligible for the EITC. And as an incentive to work more, over a certain range of incomes, the more a worker earns, the higher the amount of EITC received. That is, the EITC acts as a negative income tax for low-wage workers. In 2009, married couples with two children earning less than $12,570 per year received EITC payments equal to 40% of their earnings. Payments were slightly lower for single-parent families or workers without children. At higher incomes, the EITC is phased out, disappearing at an income of $40,295 in 2009.

A **negative income tax** is a program that supplements the income of low-income workers.

AP Photo/Rich Pedroncelli

The Supplemental Nutrition Assistance Program helps those with low-incomes put food on the table. Purchases are made using an electronic benefits transfer card that works like a debit card but can be used only to purchase food.

Social Security and Unemployment Insurance

Social Security, the largest program in the U.S. welfare state, is a non-means-tested program that guarantees retirement income to qualifying older Americans. It also provides benefits to workers who become disabled and "survivor benefits" to family members of workers who die. Social Security is supported by a dedicated tax on wages: the Social Security portion of the payroll tax pays for Social Security benefits. The benefits workers receive on retirement depend on their taxable earnings during their working years: the more you earn up to the maximum amount subject to Social Security taxes ($106,800 in 2010), the more you receive in retirement. Benefits are not, however, strictly proportional to earnings. Instead, they're determined by a formula that gives high earners more than low earners, but with a sliding scale that makes the program relatively more generous for low earners.

Because most senior citizens don't receive pensions from their former employers, and most don't own enough assets to live off the income from their assets, Social Security benefits are an enormously important source of income for them. Fully 60% of Americans 65 and older rely on Social Security for more than half their income, and 20% have no income at all except for Social Security.

Unemployment insurance, although a much smaller amount of government transfers than Social Security, is another key social insurance program. It provides workers who lose their jobs with about 35% of their previous salary until they find a new job or until 26 weeks have passed. (This period is sometimes extended when the economy is in a slump.) Unemployment insurance is financed by a tax on employers.

The Effects of Programs on Poverty and Inequality

Because the people who receive government transfers tend to be different from those who are taxed to pay for those transfers, the U.S. welfare state has the effect of redistributing income from some people to others. Each year the Census Bureau estimates the effect of this redistribution in a report titled "The Effects of Government Taxes and Transfers on Income and Poverty." The report calculates only the *direct* effects of taxes and transfers, without taking into account changes in behavior that the taxes and transfers might cause. For example, the report doesn't try to estimate how many older Americans who are now retired would still be working if they weren't receiving Social Security checks. As a result, the estimates are only a partial indicator of the true effects of the welfare state. Nonetheless, the results are striking.

Table 78.4 shows how taxes and government transfers affected the poverty threshold for the population as a whole and for different age groups in 2008. It shows two numbers for each group: the percentage of the group that *would have had* incomes below the poverty threshold if the government neither collected taxes nor made transfers, and the percentage that actually fell below the poverty threshold once taxes and transfers were taken into account. (For technical reasons, the second number is somewhat lower than the standard measure of the poverty rate.) Overall, the combined effect of taxes and transfers is to cut the U.S. poverty rate nearly in half. The elderly derived the greatest benefits from redistribution, which reduced their potential poverty rate of 47.4% to an actual poverty rate of 9.7%.

table 78.4

Effects of Taxes and Transfers on the Poverty Rate, 2008

Group (by age)	Poverty rate without taxes and transfers	Poverty rate with taxes and transfers
All	21.4%	12.1%
Under 18	22.0	15.9
18 to 64	15.9	11.1
65 and over	47.4	9.7

Source: Census.gov, ASEC: Table 2. Percent of Persons in Poverty, by Definition of Income and Selected Characteristics: 2008

Table 78.5 shows the effects of taxes and transfers on the share of aggregate income going to each quintile of the income distribution in 2005. Like Table 78.4, it shows both what the distribution of income *would have been* if there were no taxes or government transfers and the actual distribution of income taking into account both

table 78.5

Effects of Taxes and Transfers on the Income Distribution, 2005

Quintiles	Share of aggregate income without taxes and transfers	Share of aggregate income with taxes and transfers
Bottom quintile	1.5%	4.4%
Second quintile	7.3	9.9
Third quintile	14.0	15.3
Fourth quintile	23.4	23.1
Top quintile	53.8	47.3

Source: U.S. Census Bureau.

taxes and transfers. The effect of government programs was to increase the share of income going to the poorest 60% of the population, especially the share going to the poorest 20%, while reducing the share of income going to the richest 20%.

The Debate Over Income Redistribution

The goals of income redistribution seem laudable: to help the poor, protect everyone from financial risk, and ensure that people can afford essential health care. But good intentions don't always make for good policy. There is an intense debate about how large the antipoverty programs should be, a debate that partly reflects differences in philosophy but also reflects concern about the possibly counterproductive effects of antipoverty programs. Disputes about the role of government in income redistribution are also one of the defining issues of modern politics.

Problems with Income Redistribution

There are two different lines of argument against antipoverty programs. One is based on philosophical concerns about the proper role of government. Some political theorists believe that redistributing income is not a legitimate role of government—that government's role should be limited to maintaining the rule of law, providing public goods, and managing externalities.

The more conventional argument against income redistribution involves the trade-off between efficiency and equity. A government with extensive antipoverty programs requires more revenue, and thus higher marginal tax rates, than one that limits itself mainly to the provision of public goods such as national defense. Table 78.6 shows "social expenditure," a measure that roughly corresponds to welfare state spending, as a percentage of GDP in the United States, Britain, and France; it also compares this with an estimate of the marginal tax rate faced by an average wage-earner, including payroll taxes paid by employers and state and local taxes. As you see, France's large welfare state goes along with a high marginal rate of taxation. Some, but not all, economists believe that this high rate of taxation is a major reason the French work substantially fewer hours per year than Americans.

table 78.6

Social Expenditure and Marginal Tax Rates

	Social expenditure in 2005 (% of GDP)	Marginal tax rate in 2008
US	16.3%	34.4%
UK	22.1	38.8
France	29.5	52.0

Sources: OECD Social Expenditure Database; OECD Taxing Wages Database.

The trade-off between antipoverty programs and high marginal tax rates seems to suggest that we should try to hold down the cost of these programs. One way to do this is to means-test benefits: make them available only to those who need them. But means-testing, it turns out, creates a different kind of trade-off between equity and efficiency. Consider the following example: Suppose there is some means-tested benefit, worth $2,000 per year that is available only to families with incomes of less than $20,000 per year. Now suppose that a family currently has an income of $19,500 but that one family member is deciding whether to take a new job that will raise the family's income to $20,500. Well, taking that job will actually make the family worse off because it will gain $1,000 in earnings but lose the $2,000 government benefit.

This situation, in which earning more actually leaves a family worse off through lost benefits, is known as a *notch*. It is a well-known problem with programs that aid the poor and behaves much like a high marginal tax rate on income. Most welfare state programs are designed to avoid creating a notch. This is typically done by setting a sliding scale for benefits such that they fall off gradually as the recipient's income rises. As long as benefits are reduced by less than a dollar for every additional dollar earned, there is an incentive to work more if possible. Current programs are not always successful in providing incentives for work. The combined effects of the major means-tested programs shown in Table 78.3, plus additional means-tested programs such as housing aid that are offered by some state and local governments, can be to create very high effective marginal tax rates. For example, one 2005 study found that a family consisting of two adults and two children that raised its annual income from $20,000—just above the poverty threshold in 2005—to $35,000 would find almost all of its increase in after-tax income offset by the loss of benefits such as food stamps, the Earned Income Tax Credit, and Medicaid.

The Politics of Income Redistribution

In 1791, in the early phase of the French Revolution, France had a sort of congress, the National Assembly, in which representatives were seated according to social class: nobles, who pretty much liked the way things were, sat on the right; commoners, who wanted big changes, sat on the left. Ever since, it has been common in political discourse to talk about politicians as being on the "right" (more conservative) or on the "left" (more liberal).

But what do modern politicians on the left and right disagree about? In the modern United States, they mainly disagree about the appropriate size of antipoverty programs.

You might think that saying that political debate is really about just one thing—how big should government's involvement in income redistribution be—is a huge oversimplification. But political scientists have found that once you carefully rank members of Congress from right to left, a congressperson's position in that ranking does a very good job of predicting his or her votes on proposed legislation. Modern politics isn't completely one-dimensional—but it comes pretty close.

The same studies that show a strong left–right spectrum in U.S. politics also show strong polarization between the major parties on this spectrum. Thirty years ago there was a substantial overlap between the parties: some Democrats were to the right of some Republicans, or, if you prefer, some Republicans were to the left of some Democrats. Today, however, the rightmost Democrats appear to be to the left of the leftmost Republicans. There's nothing necessarily wrong with this. Although it's common to decry "partisanship," it's hard to see why members of different political parties shouldn't have different views about policy.

Can economic analysis help resolve this political conflict? Only up to a point.

Some of the political controversy over the welfare state involves differences in opinion about the trade-offs we have just discussed: if you believe that the disincentive effects of generous benefits and high taxes are very large, you're likely to look less favorably on welfare state programs than if you believe they're fairly small. Economic analysis, by improving our knowledge of the facts, can help resolve some of these differences.

To an important extent, however, differences of opinion on income redistribution reflect differences in values and philosophy. And those are differences economics can't resolve.

Module 78 AP Review

Solutions appear at the back of the book.

Check Your Understanding

1. Recall that the poverty threshold is not adjusted to reflect changes in the standard of living. As a result, is the poverty threshold a relative or an absolute measure of poverty? That is, does it define poverty according to how poor someone is relative to others or according to some fixed measure that doesn't change over time? Explain.

Tackle the Test: Multiple-Choice Questions

1. Which of the following is true of the U.S. poverty rate?
   a. It fell in the 1960s.
   b. There has been a clear upward trend since 1973.
   c. It was lower in 2009 than in 1973.
   d. It has remained unchanged since the mid 1970s.
   e. It has been steadily decreasing since 1959.

2. In 2009, approximately what percentage of the U.S. population lived in poverty?
   a. 2%
   b. 12%
   c. 20%
   d. 26%
   e. 32%

3. Average household income in the United States in 2008 was approximately
   a. $12,000.
   b. $22,000.
   c. $33,000.
   d. $48,201.
   e. $68,000.

4. Programs designed to help only those with low incomes are called
   a. welfare programs.
   b. in-kind programs.
   c. means-tested programs.
   d. income maintenance programs.
   e. social programs.

5. If a country has a perfectly equal distribution of income, its Gini coefficient equals
   a. 0.
   b. 1.
   c. 10.
   d. 50.
   e. 100.

Tackle the Test: Free-Response Questions

1. There are 100 households in the economy of Equalor. Initially, 99 of them have an income of $10,000 each, and one household has an income of $1,010,000.
   a. What is the median income in this economy? What is the mean income?

   Through its poverty programs, the government of Equalor now redistributes income: it takes $990,000 away from the richest household and distributes it equally among the remaining 99 households.
   b. What is the median income in this economy now? What is the mean income? Which indicator (mean or median household income) is a better indicator of the typical Equalorian household's income?

Answer (5 points)
1 point: median income = $10,000
1 point: mean income = $20,000
1 point: median income = $20,000
1 point: mean income = $20,000
1 point: median

2. In your opinion, what is the strongest argument for and against government programs to redistribute income? To what extent can economics be used to resolve the debate?

Section 14 Review

Summary

1. When pollution can be directly observed and controlled, government policies should be geared directly to producing the **socially optimal quantity of pollution,** the quantity at which the **marginal social cost of pollution** is equal to the **marginal social benefit of pollution.** In the absence of government intervention, a market produces too much pollution because polluters take only their benefit from polluting into account, not the costs imposed on others.

2. The cost to society of pollution from a power plant is an example of an **external cost;** the benefit to neighbors of beautiful flowers planted in your yard is an example of an **external benefit.** External costs and benefits are jointly known as **externalities,** with external costs called **negative externalities** and external benefits called **positive externalities.**

3. According to the **Coase theorem,** when externalities exist, bargaining will cause individuals to **internalize the externalities,** making government intervention unnecessary, as long as property rights are clearly defined and **transaction costs**—the costs of making a deal—are sufficiently low. However, in many cases transaction costs are too high to permit such deals.

4. Governments often deal with pollution by imposing **environmental standards,** an approach, economists argue, that is usually inefficient. Two efficient (cost-minimizing) methods for reducing pollution are **emissions taxes,** a form of **Pigouvian tax,** and **tradable emissions permits.** The optimal Pigouvian tax on pollution is equal to its marginal social cost at the socially optimal quantity of pollution. These methods also provide incentives for the creation and adoption of production technologies that cause less pollution.

5. When a good yields external benefits, such as **technology spillovers,** the **marginal social benefit of the good** is equal to the **marginal private benefit** accruing to consumers plus its **marginal external benefit.** Without government intervention, the market produces too little of the good. An optimal **Pigouvian subsidy** to producers, equal to the marginal external benefit, moves the market to the socially optimal quantity of production. This yields higher output and a higher price to producers.

6. When there are external costs from production, the **marginal social cost of a good** exceeds its **marginal private cost** to producers, the difference being the **marginal external cost.** Without government action, the market produces too much of the good. The optimal Pigouvian tax on production of the good is equal to its marginal external cost, yielding lower output and a higher price to consumers. A system of tradable production permits for the right to produce the good can also achieve efficiency at minimum cost.

7. Communications, transportation, and high-technology goods are frequently subject to **network externalities,** which arise when the value of the good to an individual is greater when more people use the good.

8. Goods may be classified according to whether or not they are **excludable,** meaning that people can be prevented from consuming them, and whether or not they are **rival in consumption,** meaning that one person's consumption of them affects another person's consumption of them.

9. Free markets can deliver efficient levels of production and consumption for **private goods,** which are both excludable and rival in consumption. When goods are nonexcludable, nonrival in consumption, or both, free markets cannot achieve efficient outcomes.

10. When goods are **nonexcludable,** there is a **free-rider problem:** consumers will not pay for the good, leading to inefficiently low production. When goods are **nonrival in consumption,** any positive price leads to inefficiently low consumption.

11. A **public good** is nonexcludable and nonrival in consumption. In most cases a public good must be supplied by the government. The marginal social benefit of a public good is equal to the sum of the marginal private benefits to each consumer. The efficient quantity of a public good is the quantity at which marginal social benefit equals the marginal social cost of providing the good. As with a positive externality, the marginal social benefit is greater than any one individual's marginal private benefit, so no individual is willing to provide the efficient quantity.

12. One rationale for the presence of government is that it allows citizens to tax themselves in order to provide public goods. Governments use cost-benefit analysis to determine the efficient provision of a public good. Such analysis is difficult, however, because individuals have an incentive to overstate the good's value to them.

13. A **common resource** is rival in consumption but nonexcludable. It is subject to **overuse,** because an individual does not take into account the fact that his or her use depletes the amount available for others. This is similar to the problem with a negative externality: the marginal social cost of an individual's use of a common resource is always higher than his or her marginal private cost. Pigouvian taxes, the creation of a system of tradable licenses, and the assignment of property rights are possible solutions.

14. **Artificially scarce goods** are excludable but nonrival in consumption. Because no marginal cost arises from allowing another individual to consume the good, the efficient price is zero. A positive price compensates the producer for the cost of production but leads to inefficiently low consumption.

15. Antitrust laws and regulation are used to promote competition. When the industry in question is a natural monopoly, price regulation is used.

16. The Sherman Act, the Clayton Act, and the Federal Trade Commission Act were the first major antitrust laws.

17. **Marginal cost pricing** and **average cost pricing** are examples of price regulation used in the case of natural monopoly to allow efficiencies from large scale production without allowing the deadweight loss that results from unregulated monopoly.

18. Despite the fact that the **poverty threshold** is adjusted according to the cost of living but not according to the standard of living, and that the average income in the United States has risen substantially over the last 30 years, the **poverty rate,** the percentage of the population with an income below the poverty threshold, is no

lower than it was 30 years ago. There are various causes of poverty: lack of education, the legacy of discrimination, and bad luck. The consequences of poverty are particularly harmful for children.

19. **Median household income,** the income of a family at the center of the income distribution, is a better indicator of the income of the typical household than **mean household income** because it is not distorted by the inclusion of a small number of very wealthy households. The **Gini coefficient,** a number that summarizes a country's level of income inequality based on how unequally income is distributed across quintiles, is used to compare income inequality across countries.

20. **Means-tested** programs target aid to people whose income falls below a certain level. The major **in-kind benefits** programs are Medicare and Medicaid, which pay for medical care. Due to concerns about the effects on incentives to work and on family cohesion, aid to poor families has become significantly less generous even as the **negative income tax** has become more generous. Social Security, the largest U.S. welfare program, has significantly reduced poverty among the elderly. Unemployment insurance is another key social insurance program.

Key Terms

Marginal social cost of pollution, p. 724
Marginal social benefit of pollution, p. 724
Socially optimal quantity of pollution, p. 725
External cost, p. 726
External benefit, p. 727
Externalities, p. 727
Negative externalities, p. 727
Positive externalities, p. 727
Coase theorem, p. 728
Transaction costs, p. 728
Internalize the externalities, p. 728
Environmental standards, p. 731
Emissions taxes, p. 732
Pigouvian taxes, p. 734
Tradable emissions permits, p. 734

Marginal private benefit, p. 738
Marginal social benefit of a good, p. 738
Marginal external benefit, p. 738
Pigouvian subsidy, p. 738
Technology spillover, p. 738
Marginal private cost, p. 739
Marginal social cost of a good, p. 739
Marginal external cost, p. 739
Network externality, p. 740
Excludable, p. 743
Rival in consumption, p. 743
Private good, p. 743
Nonexcludable, p. 743
Nonrival in consumption, p. 744
Free-rider problem, p. 745

Public good, p. 745
Common resource, p. 749
Overuse, p. 749
Artificially scarce good, p. 751
Marginal cost pricing, p. 757
Average cost pricing, p. 757
Poverty threshold, p. 761
Poverty rate, p. 761
Mean household income, p. 765
Median household income, p. 765
Gini coefficient, p. 765
Means-tested, p. 768
In-kind benefits, p. 768
Negative income tax, p. 769

Problems

1. What type of externality (positive or negative) is present in each of the following examples? Is the marginal social benefit of the activity greater than or equal to the marginal benefit to the individual? Is the marginal social cost of the activity greater than or equal to the marginal cost to the individual? Without intervention, will there be too little or too much (relative to what would be socially optimal) of this activity?

   a. Mr. Chau plants lots of colorful flowers in his front yard.

   b. Your next-door neighbor likes to build bonfires in his backyard, and sparks often drift onto your house.

   c. Maija, who lives next to an apple orchard, decides to keep bees to produce honey.

   d. Justine buys a large SUV that consumes a lot of gasoline.

2. The loud music coming from the sorority next to your dorm is a negative externality that can be directly quantified. The accompanying table shows the marginal social benefit and the marginal social cost per decibel (dB, a measure of volume) of music.

Volume of music (dB)	Marginal social benefit of dB	Marginal social cost of dB
90		
	$36	$0
91		
	30	2
92		
	24	4
93		
	18	6
94		
	12	8
95		
	6	10
96		
	0	12
97		

a. Draw the marginal social benefit curve and the marginal social cost curve. Use your diagram to determine the socially optimal volume of music.

b. Only the members of the sorority benefit from the music and they bear none of the cost. Which volume of music will they choose?

c. The college imposes a Pigouvian tax of $3 per decibel of music played. From your diagram, determine the volume of music the sorority will now choose.

3. Many dairy farmers in California are adopting a new technology that allows them to produce their own electricity from methane gas captured from animal wastes. (One cow can produce up to 2 kilowatts a day.) This practice reduces the amount of methane gas released into the atmosphere. In addition to reducing their own utility bills, the farmers are allowed to sell any electricity they produce at favorable rates.

a. Explain how the ability to earn money from capturing and transforming methane gas behaves like a Pigouvian tax on methane gas pollution and can lead dairy farmers to emit the efficient amount of methane gas pollution.

b. Suppose some dairy farmers have lower costs of transforming methane into electricity than others. Explain how this system leads to an efficient allocation of emissions reduction among farmers.

4. The accompanying table shows the total revenue and the total cost that accrue to steel producers from producing steel. Producing a ton of steel imposes a marginal external cost of $60 per ton.

Quantity of steel (tons)	Total revenue	Total cost to producers
1	$115	$ 10
2	210	30
3	285	60
4	340	100
5	375	150

a. Calculate the marginal revenue per ton of steel and the marginal cost per ton of steel to steel producers. Then calculate the marginal social cost per ton of steel.

b. What is the market equilibrium quantity of steel production?

c. What is the socially optimal quantity of steel production?

d. What is the optimal Pigouvian tax to remedy the problem created by the negative externality?

5. Voluntary environmental programs were extremely popular in the United States, Europe, and Japan in the 1990s. Part of their popularity stems from the fact that these programs do not require legislative authority, which is often hard to obtain. The 33/50 program started by the Environmental Protection Agency (EPA) is an example of such a program. With this program, the EPA attempted to reduce industrial emissions of 17 toxic chemicals by providing information on relatively inexpensive methods of pollution control. Companies were asked to voluntarily commit to reducing emissions from their 1988 levels by 33% by 1992 and by 50% by 1995. The program actually met its second target by 1994.

a. As in Figure 75.2 draw marginal benefit curves for pollution generated by two plants, A and B, in 1988. Assume that without government intervention, each plant emits the same amount of pollution, but that at all levels of pollution less than this amount, plant A's marginal benefit of polluting is less than that of plant B. Label the vertical axis "Marginal benefit to individual polluter" and the horizontal axis "Quantity of pollution emissions." Mark the quantity of pollution each plant produces without government action.

b. Do you expect the total quantity of pollution before the program was put in place to have been less than or more than the optimal quantity of pollution? Why?

c. Suppose the plants whose marginal benefit curves you depicted in part a were participants in the 33/50 program. In a replica of your graph from part a, mark targeted levels of pollution in 1995 for the two plants. Compare the amounts by which the two plants reduced emissions. Was this solution necessarily efficient?

d. What kind of environmental policy does the 33/50 program most closely resemble? What is the main shortcoming of such a policy? Compare it to two other types of environmental policy discussed.

6. Smoking produces a negative externality because it imposes a health risk on others who inhale second-hand smoke. Cigarette smoking also causes productivity losses to the economy due to the shorter expected life span of a smoker. The U.S. Centers for Disease Control (CDC) has estimated the average social cost of smoking a single pack of cigarettes for different states by taking these negative externalities into account. The accompanying table provides the price of cigarettes and the estimated average social cost of smoking in five states.

State	Cigarette retail price with taxes (per pack)	CDC estimate of smoking cost in 2006 (per pack)
California	$4.40	$15.10
New York	5.82	21.91
Florida	3.80	10.14
Texas	4.76	9.94
Ohio	4.60	9.19

a. At the current level of consumption, what is the optimal retail price of a pack of cigarettes in the different states? Is the current price below or above this optimal price? Does this suggest that the current level of consumption is too high or too low? Explain your answer.

b. In order to deal with negative externalities, state governments currently impose excise taxes on cigarettes. Are current taxes set at the optimal level? Justify your answer.

c. What is the correct size of an additional Pigouvian tax on cigarette sales in the different states if the CDC's estimate for smoking cost does not change with an increase in the retail price of cigarettes?

7. Education is an example of an activity that generates a positive externality: acquiring more education benefits the individual student and having a more highly educated workforce is good for the economy as a whole. The accompanying table illustrates the marginal benefit to Sian per year of education and the marginal cost per year of education. Each year of education has a marginal external benefit to society equal to $8,000. Assume that the marginal social cost is the same as the marginal cost paid by an individual student.

Quantity of education (years)	Sian's marginal benefit per year	Sian's marginal cost per year
9		
	$20,000	$15,000
10		
	19,000	16,000
11		
	18,000	17,000
12		
	17,000	18,000
13		
	16,000	19,000
14		
	15,000	20,000
15		
	14,000	21,000
16		
	13,000	22,000
17		

a. Find Sian's market equilibrium number of years of education.

b. Calculate the marginal social benefit schedule. What is the socially optimal number of years of education?

c. You are in charge of education funding. Would you use a Pigouvian tax or a Pigouvian subsidy to induce Sian to choose the socially optimal amount of education? How high would you set this tax or subsidy per year of education?

8. Planting a tree improves the environment: trees transform greenhouse gases into oxygen, improve water retention in the soil, and improve soil quality. Assume that the value of this environmental improvement to society is $10 for the expected lifetime of the tree. The following table contains a hypothetical demand schedule for trees to be planted.

Price of tree	Quantity of trees demanded (thousands)
$30	0
25	6
20	12
15	18
10	24
5	30
0	36

a. Assume that the marginal cost of producing a tree for planting is constant at $20. Draw a diagram that shows the market equilibrium quantity and price for trees to be planted.

b. What type of externality is generated by planting a tree? Draw a diagram that shows the optimal number of trees planted. How does this differ from the market outcome?

c. On your diagram from part b, indicate the optimal Pigouvian tax/subsidy (as the case may be). Explain how this moves the market to the optimal outcome.

9. The government is involved in providing many goods and services. For each of the goods or services listed, determine whether it is rival or nonrival in consumption and whether it is excludable or nonexcludable. What type of good is it? Without government involvement, would the quantity provided be efficient, inefficiently low, or inefficiently high?

a. street signs

b. Amtrak rail service

c. regulations limiting pollution

d. an interstate highway without tolls

e. a lighthouse on the coast

10. An economist gives the following advice to a museum director: "You should introduce 'peak pricing': at times when the museum has few visitors, you should admit visitors for free. And at times when the museum has many visitors, you should charge a higher admission fee."

a. When the museum is quiet, is it rival or nonrival in consumption? Is it excludable or nonexcludable? What type of good is the museum at those times? What would be the efficient price to charge visitors during that time, and why?

b. When the museum is busy, is it rival or nonrival in consumption? Is it excludable or nonexcludable? What type of good is the museum at those times? What would be the efficient price to charge visitors during that time, and why?

11. In many planned communities, various aspects of community living are subject to regulation by a homeowners' association. These rules can regulate house architecture; require snow removal from sidewalks; exclude outdoor equipment, such as backyard swimming pools; require appropriate conduct in shared spaces such as the community clubhouse; and so on. Suppose there has been some conflict in one such community because some homeowners feel that some of the regulations mentioned above are overly intrusive. You have been called in to mediate. Using what you have learned about public goods and common resources, how would you decide what types of regulations are warranted and what types are not?

12. A residential community has 100 residents who are concerned about security. The accompanying table gives the total cost of hiring a 24-hour security service as well as each individual resident's total benefit.

Quantity of security guards	Total cost	Total individual benefit to each resident
0	$ 0	$ 0
1	150	10
2	300	16
3	450	18
4	600	19

a. Explain why the security service is a public good for the residents of the community.

b. Calculate the marginal cost, the individual marginal benefit for each resident, and the marginal social benefit.

c. If an individual resident were to decide about hiring and paying for security guards on his or her own, how many guards would that resident hire?

d. If the residents act together, how many security guards will they hire?

13. The accompanying table shows Tanisha's and Ari's individual marginal benefit of different numbers of street cleanings per month. Suppose that the marginal cost of street cleanings is constant at $9 each.

Quantity of street cleanings per month	Tanisha's individual marginal benefit	Ari's individual marginal benefit
0		
	$10	$8
1		
	6	4
2		
	2	1
3		

a. If Tanisha had to pay for street cleaning on her own, how many street cleanings would there be?

b. Calculate the marginal social benefit of street cleaning. What is the optimal number of street cleanings?

c. Consider the optimal number of street cleanings. The last street cleaning of that number costs $9. Is Tanisha willing to pay for that last cleaning on her own? Is Ari willing to pay for that last cleaning on his own?

14. Anyone with a radio receiver can listen to public radio, which is funded largely by donations.

a. Is public radio excludable or nonexcludable? Is it rival in consumption or nonrival? What type of good is it?

b. Should the government support public radio? Explain your reasoning.

c. In order to finance itself, public radio decides to transmit only to satellite radios, for which users have to pay a fee. What type of good is public radio then? Will the quantity of radio listening be efficient? Why or why not?

15. Your economics teacher assigns a group project for the course. Describe the free-rider problem that can lead to a suboptimal outcome for your group. To combat this problem, the instructor asks you to evaluate the contribution of your peers in a confidential report. Will this evaluation have the desired effects?

16. The accompanying table shows six consumers' willingness to pay (his or her individual marginal benefit) for one MP3 file copy of a Dr. Dre album. The marginal cost of making the file accessible to one additional consumer is constant, at zero.

Consumer	Individual marginal benefit
Adriana	$ 2
Bhagesh	15
Chizuko	1
Denzel	10
Emma	5
Frank	4

a. What would be the efficient price to charge for a download of the file?

b. All six consumers are able to download the file for free from a file-sharing service, Pantster. Which consumers will download the file? What will be the total consumer surplus to those consumers?

c. Pantster is shut down for copyright law infringement. In order to download the file, consumers now have to pay $4.99 at a commercial music site. Which consumers will download the file? What will be the total consumer surplus to those consumers? How much producer surplus accrues to the commercial music site? What is the total surplus? What is the deadweight loss from the new pricing policy?

17. Software has historically been an artificially scarce good—it is nonrival because the cost of replication is negligible once the investment to write the code is made, but software companies make it excludable by charging for user licenses. Recently, however, open-source software has emerged, most of which is free to download and can be modified and maintained by anyone.

a. Discuss the free-rider problem that might exist in the development of open-source software. What effect might this have on quality? Why does this problem not exist for proprietary software, such as the products of a company like Microsoft or Adobe?

b. Some argue that open-source software serves an unsatisfied market demand that proprietary software ignores. Draw a typical diagram that illustrates how proprietary software may be underproduced. Put the price and marginal cost of software on the vertical axis and the quantity of software on the horizontal axis. Draw a typical demand curve and a marginal cost curve (MC) that is always equal to zero. Assume that the software company charges a positive price, P, for the software. Label the equilibrium point and the efficient point.

18. In developing a vaccine for the H1N1 virus, a pharmaceutical company incurs a very high fixed cost. The marginal cost of delivering the vaccine to patients, however, is negligible (consider it to be equal to zero). The pharmaceutical company holds the exclusive patent to the vaccine. You are a regulator who must decide what price the pharmaceutical company is allowed to charge.

   a. Draw a diagram that shows the price for the vaccine that would arise if the company is unregulated, and label it P_M. What is the efficient price for the vaccine? Show the deadweight loss that arises from the price P_M.

   b. On another diagram, show the lowest price that the regulator can enforce that would still induce the pharmaceutical company to develop the vaccine. Label it P^*. Show the deadweight loss that arises from this price. How does it compare to the deadweight loss that arises from the price P_M?

   c. Suppose you have accurate information about the pharmaceutical company's fixed cost. How could you use price regulation of the pharmaceutical company, combined with a subsidy to the company, to have the efficient quantity of the vaccine provided at the lowest cost to the government?

19. According to a report from the U.S. Census Bureau, "the average [lifetime] earnings of a full-time, year-round worker with a high school education are about $1.2 million compared with $2.1 million for a college graduate." This indicates that there is a considerable benefit to a graduate from investing in his or her own education. Tuition at most state universities covers only about two-thirds to three-quarters of the cost, so the state applies a Pigouvian subsidy to college education. If a Pigouvian subsidy is appropriate, is the externality created by a college education a positive or a negative externality? What does this imply about the differences between the costs and benefits to students compared to social costs and benefits? What are some reasons for the differences?

20. Fishing for sablefish has been so intensive that sablefish were threatened with extinction. After several years of banning such fishing, the government is now proposing to introduce tradable vouchers, each of which entitles its holder to a catch of a certain size. Explain how fishing generates a negative externality and how the voucher scheme may overcome the inefficiency created by this externality.

21. The two dry-cleaning companies in Collegetown, College Cleaners and Big Green Cleaners, are a major source of air pollution. Together they currently produce 350 units of air pollution, which the town wants to reduce to 200 units. The accompanying table shows the current pollution level produced by each company and each company's marginal cost of reducing its pollution. The marginal cost is constant.

Companies	Initial pollution level (units)	Marginal cost of reducing pollution (per unit)
College Cleaners	230	$5
Big Green Cleaners	120	2

   a. Suppose that Collegetown passes an environmental standards law that limits each company to 100 units of pollution. What would be the total cost to the two companies of each reducing its pollution emissions to 100 units?

   Suppose instead that Collegetown issues 100 pollution vouchers to each company, each entitling the company to one unit of pollution, and that these vouchers can be traded.

   b. How much is each pollution voucher worth to College Cleaners? to Big Green Cleaners? (That is, how much would each company, at most, be willing to pay for one more voucher?)

   c. Who will sell vouchers and who will buy them? How many vouchers will be traded?

   d. What is the total cost to the two companies of the pollution controls under this voucher system?

22. Ronald owns a cattle farm at the source of a long river. His cattle's waste flows into the river and down many miles to where Carla lives. Carla gets her drinking water from the river. By allowing his cattle's waste to flow into the river, Ronald imposes a negative externality on Carla. In each of the two following cases, do you think that through negotiation, Ronald and Carla can find an efficient solution? What might this solution look like?

   a. There are no telephones, and for Carla to talk to Ronald, she has to travel for two days on a rocky road.

   b. Carla and Ronald both have e-mail access, making it costless for them to communicate.

23. **a.** EAuction and EMarketplace are two competing Internet auction sites, where buyers and sellers transact goods. Each auction site earns money by charging sellers for listing their goods. EAuction has decided to eliminate fees for the first transaction for sellers that are new to their site. Explain why this is likely to be a good strategy for EAuction in its competition with EMarketplace.

   b. EMarketplace complained to the Justice Department that EAuction's practice of eliminating fees for new sellers was anticompetitive and would lead to monopolization of the Internet auction industry. Is EMarketplace correct? How should the Justice Department respond?

c. EAuction stopped its practice of eliminating fees for new sellers. But since it provided much better technical service than its rival, EMarketplace, buyers and sellers came to prefer EAuction. Eventually, EMarketplace closed down, leaving EAuction as a monopolist. Should the Justice Department intervene to break EAuction into two companies? Explain.

d. EAuction is now a monopolist in the Internet auction industry. It also owns a site that handles payments over the Internet, called PayForIt. It is competing with another Internet payment site, called PayBuddy. EAuction has now stipulated that any transaction on its auction site must use PayForIt, rather than PayBuddy, for the payment. Should the Justice Department intervene? Explain.

Appendix

Modules 79 and 80 present optional material. While these topics are not currently part of the AP exam, the economics of information and indifference curves are an important part of contemporary economic theory and you will be sure to see them in future courses.

- The special problems posed by private information—situations in which some people know things that other people do not (also known as *asymmetric information*)

- How information asymmetries can lead to the problem of adverse selection (otherwise known as the *lemons problem*)

- How firms deal with the need for information, using screening and signaling

- How information asymmetries can lead to the problem of moral hazard

Module 79
The Economics of Information

Private Information: What You Don't Know Can Hurt You

Markets do very well at dealing with situations in which nobody knows what is going to happen. However, markets have much more trouble with situations in which *some people know things that other people don't know*—situations of **private information** (also known as "asymmetric information"). As we will see, private information can distort economic decisions and sometimes prevent mutually beneficial economic transactions from taking place.

Why is some information private? The most important reason is that people generally know more about themselves than other people do. For example, you know whether or not you are a careful driver; but unless you have already been in several accidents, your auto insurance company does not. You are more likely to have a better estimate than your health insurance company of whether or not you will need an expensive medical procedure. And if you are selling me your used car, you are more likely to be aware of any problems with it than I am.

But why should such differences in who knows what be a problem? It turns out that there are two distinct sources of trouble: *adverse selection*, which arises from having private information about the way things are, and *moral hazard*, which arises from having private information about what people do.

Adverse Selection: The Economics of Lemons

Suppose that someone offers to sell you an almost brand-new car—purchased just three months ago, with only 2,000 miles on the odometer and no dents or scratches. Will you be willing to pay almost the same for it as for a car direct from the dealer?

Probably not, for one main reason: you cannot help but wonder why this car is being sold. Is it because the owner has discovered that something is wrong with it—that it is a "lemon"? Having driven the car for a while, the owner knows more about it than you do—and people are more likely to sell cars that give them trouble.

Private information is information that some people have that others do not.

You might think that the fact that sellers of used cars know more about them than buyers do represents an advantage to the sellers. But potential buyers know that potential sellers are likely to offer them lemons—they just don't know exactly which car is a lemon. Because potential buyers of a used car know that potential sellers are more likely to sell lemons than good cars, buyers will offer a lower price than they would if they had a guarantee of the car's quality. Worse yet, this poor opinion of used cars tends to be self-reinforcing, precisely because it depresses the prices that buyers offer. Used cars sell at a discount because buyers expect a disproportionate share of those cars to be lemons. Even a used car that is not a lemon would sell only at a large discount because buyers don't know whether it's a lemon or not. But potential sellers who have good cars are unwilling to sell them at a deep discount, except under exceptional circumstances. So good used cars are rarely offered for sale, and used cars that are offered for sale have a strong tendency to be lemons. (This is why people who have a compelling reason to sell a car, such as moving overseas, make a point of revealing that information to potential buyers—as if to say "This car is not a lemon!")

The end result, then, is not only that used cars sell for low prices but also that there are a large number of used cars with hidden problems. Equally important, many potentially beneficial transactions—sales of good cars by people who would like to get rid of them to people who would like to buy them—end up being frustrated by the inability of potential sellers to convince potential buyers that their cars are actually worth the higher price demanded. So some mutually beneficial trades between those who want to sell used cars and those who want to buy them go unexploited.

Although economists sometimes refer to situations like this as the "lemons problem" (the issue was introduced in a famous 1970 paper by economist and Nobel laureate George Akerlof entitled "The Market for Lemons"), the more formal name of the problem is **adverse selection.** The reason for the name is obvious: because the potential sellers know more about the quality of what they are selling than the potential buyers, they have an incentive to select the worst things to sell.

Adverse selection does not apply only to used cars. It is a problem for many parts of the economy—notably for insurance companies, and most notably for health insurance companies. Suppose that a health insurance company were to offer a standard policy to everyone with the same premium. The premium would reflect the *average* risk of incurring a medical expense. But that would make the policy look very expensive to healthy people, who know that they are less likely than the average person to incur medical expenses. So healthy people would be less likely than less healthy people to buy the policy, leaving the health insurance company with exactly the customers it doesn't want: people with a higher-than-average risk of needing medical care, who would find the premium to be a good deal. In order to cover its expected losses from this sicker customer pool, the health insurance company is compelled to raise premiums, driving away more of the remaining healthier customers, and so on. Because the insurance company can't determine who is healthy and who is not, it must charge everyone the same premium, thereby discouraging healthy people from purchasing policies and encouraging unhealthy people to buy policies.

Adverse selection can lead to a phenomenon called an *adverse selection death spiral* as the market for health insurance collapses: insurance companies refuse to offer policies because there is no premium at which the company can cover its losses. Because of the severe adverse selection problems, governments in many advanced countries assume the role of providing health insurance to their citizens. The U.S. government, through its various health insurance programs including Medicare, Medicaid, and the Children's Health Insurance Program, now disburses more than half the total payments for medical care in the United States.

In general, people or firms faced with the problem of adverse selection follow one of several well-established strategies for dealing with it. One strategy is **screening:** using observable information to make inferences about private information. If you apply to purchase health insurance, you'll find that the insurance company will demand documentation of your health status in an attempt to "screen out" sicker applicants, whom

Adverse selection occurs when one person knows more about the way things are than other people do. Adverse selection exists, for example, when sellers offer items of particularly low (hidden) quality for sale, and when the people with the greatest need for insurance are those most likely to purchase it.

Adverse selection can be reduced through **screening:** using observable information about people to make inferences about their private information.

they will refuse to insure or will insure only at very high premiums. Auto insurance also provides a very good example. An insurance company may not know whether you are a careful driver, but it has statistical data on the accident rates of people who resemble your profile—and it uses those data in setting premiums. A 19-year-old male who drives a sports car and has already had a fender-bender is likely to pay a very high premium. A 40-year-old female who drives a minivan and has never had an accident is likely to pay much less. In some cases, this may be quite unfair: some adolescent males are very careful drivers, and some mature women drive their minivans as if they were F-16s. But nobody can deny that the insurance companies are right on average.

Another strategy is for people who are good prospects to somehow *signal* their private information. **Signaling** involves taking some action that wouldn't be worth taking unless they were indeed good prospects. Reputable used-car dealers often offer warranties—promises to repair any problems with the cars they sell that arise within a given amount of time. This isn't just a way of insuring their customers against possible expenses; it's a way of credibly showing that they are not selling lemons. As a result, more sales occur and dealers can command higher prices for their used cars.

Finally, in the face of adverse selection, it can be very valuable to establish a good **reputation:** a used-car dealership will often advertise how long it has been in business to show that it has continued to satisfy its customers. As a result, new customers will be willing to purchase cars and to pay more for that dealer's cars.

Moral Hazard

In the late 1970s, New York and other major cities experienced an epidemic of suspicious fires—fires that appeared to be deliberately set. Some of the fires were probably started by teenagers on a lark, others by gang members struggling over turf. But investigators eventually became aware of patterns in a number of the fires. Particular landlords who owned several buildings seemed to have an unusually large number of their buildings burn down. Although it was difficult to prove, police had few doubts that most of these fire-prone landlords were hiring professional arsonists to torch their own properties.

Why burn your own buildings? These buildings were typically in declining neighborhoods, where rising crime and middle-class flight had led to a decline in property values. But the insurance policies on the buildings were written to compensate owners based on historical property values, and so would pay the owner of a destroyed building more than the building was worth in the current market. For an unscrupulous landlord who knew the right people, this presented a profitable opportunity.

The arson epidemic became less severe during the 1980s, partly because insurance companies began making it difficult to over-insure properties and partly because a boom in real estate values made many previously arson-threatened buildings worth more unburned.

The arson episodes make it clear that it is a bad idea for insurance companies to let customers insure buildings for more than their value—it gives the customers some destructive incentives. You might think, however, that the incentive problem would go away as long as the insurance is no more than 100% of the value of what is being insured.

But, unfortunately, anything close to 100% insurance still distorts incentives—it induces policyholders to behave differently from how they would in the absence of insurance. The reason is that preventing fires requires effort and cost on the part of a building's owner. Fire alarms and sprinkler systems have to be kept in good repair, fire safety rules have to be strictly enforced, and so on. All of this takes time and money—time and money that the owner may not find worth spending if the insurance policy will provide close to full compensation for any losses.

Of course, the insurance company could specify in the policy that it won't pay if basic safety precautions have not been taken. But it isn't always easy to tell how careful a building's owner has been—the owner knows, but the insurance company does not.

The point is that the building's owner has private information about his or her own actions; the owner knows whether he or she has really taken all appropriate precautions.

As a result, the insurance company is likely to face greater claims than if it were able to determine exactly how much effort a building owner exerts to prevent a loss. The problem of distorted incentives arises when an individual has private information about his or her own actions but someone else bears the costs of a lack of care or effort. This is known as **moral hazard.**

To deal with moral hazard, it is necessary to give individuals with private information some personal stake in what happens, a stake that gives them a reason to exert effort even if others cannot verify that they have done so. Moral hazard is the reason salespeople in many stores receive a commission on sales: it's hard for managers to be sure how hard the salespeople are really working, and if they were paid only straight salary, they would not have an incentive to exert effort to make those sales. Similar logic explains why many stores and restaurants, even if they are part of national chains, are actually franchises, licensed outlets owned by the people who run them.

Insurance companies deal with moral hazard by requiring a **deductible:** they compensate for losses only above a certain amount, so that coverage is always less than 100%. The insurance on your car, for example, may pay for repairs only after the first $500 in loss. This means that a careless driver who gets into a fender-bender will end up paying $500 for repairs even if he is insured, which provides at least some incentive to be careful and reduces moral hazard.

In addition to reducing moral hazard, deductibles provide a partial solution to the problem of adverse selection. Your insurance premium often drops substantially if you are willing to accept a large deductible. This is an attractive option to people who know they are low-risk customers; it is less attractive to people who know they are high-risk—and so are likely to have an accident and end up paying the deductible. By offering a menu of policies with different premiums and deductibles, insurance companies can screen their customers, inducing them to sort themselves out on the basis of their private information.

As the example of deductibles suggests, moral hazard limits the ability of the economy to allocate risks efficiently. You generally can't get full (100%) insurance on your home or car, even though you would like to buy full insurance, and you bear the risk of large deductibles, even though you would prefer not to.

> **Moral hazard** occurs when an individual knows more about his or her own actions than other people do. This leads to a distortion of incentives to take care or to exert effort when someone else bears the costs of the lack of care or effort.
>
> A **deductible** is a sum specified in an insurance policy that the insured individuals must pay before being compensated for a claim; deductibles reduce *moral hazard*.

Module 79 AP Review

Solutions appear at the back of the book.

Check Your Understanding

1. Your car insurance premiums are lower if you have had no moving violations for several years. Explain how this feature tends to decrease the potential inefficiency caused by adverse selection.

2. A common feature of home construction contracts is that when it costs more to construct a building than was originally estimated, the contractor must absorb the additional cost. Explain how this feature reduces the problem of moral hazard but also forces the contractor to bear more risk than she would like.

3. True or false? Explain your answer, stating what concept analyzed in this module accounts for the feature.

   People with higher deductibles on their auto insurance
   a. generally drive more carefully.
   b. pay lower premiums.

Tackle the Test: Multiple-Choice Questions

1. Which of the following is true about private information?
   - I. It has value.
   - II. Everyone has access to it.
   - III. It can distort economic decisions.
   - a. I only
   - b. II only
   - c. III only
   - d. I and III only
   - e. I, II, and III

2. Due to adverse selection,
   - a. mutually beneficial trades go unexploited.
   - b. people buy lemons rather than other fruit.
   - c. sick people buy less insurance.
   - d. private information is available to all.
   - e. public information is available to no one.

3. When colleges use grade point averages to make admissions decisions, they are employing which strategy?
   - a. signaling
   - b. screening
   - c. profit maximization
   - d. marginal analysis
   - e. adverse selection

4. Moral hazard is the result of
   - a. asymmetric information.
   - b. signaling.
   - c. toxic waste.
   - d. adverse selection.
   - e. public information.

5. A deductible is used by insurance companies to
   - a. allow customers to pay for insurance premiums using payroll deduction.
   - b. deal with moral hazard.
   - c. make public information private.
   - d. compensate policyholders fully for their losses.
   - e. avoid all payments to policyholders.

Tackle the Test: Free-Response Questions

1. Identify whether each of the following situations reflects moral hazard or adverse selection. Propose a potential solution to reduce the inefficiency that each situation creates.
   - a. When you buy a second-hand car, you do not know whether it is a lemon (low quality) or a plum (high quality), but the seller knows.
   - b. People with dental insurance might not brush their teeth as often, knowing that if they get cavities, the insurance will pay for the fillings.
   - c. A company does not know whether individual workers on an assembly line are working hard or slacking off.
   - d. When making a decision about hiring you, prospective employers do not know whether you are a productive worker or not.

2. Individuals or corporations (for example home-buyers or banks) believe that the government will "bail them out" in the event that their decisions lead to a financial collapse. This is an example of what problem created by asymmetric information? How does this situation lead to inefficiency? What is a possible remedy for the problem?

> **Answer (8 points)**
>
> **1 point:** Adverse selection
>
> **1 point:** Sellers could offer a warranty with the car that pays for repair costs.
>
> **1 point:** Moral hazard
>
> **1 point:** The insured can be made to pay a co-payment of a certain dollar amount each time they get a filling.
>
> **1 point:** Moral hazard
>
> **1 point:** Pay the workers "piece rates," that is, pay them according to how much they have produced each day.
>
> **1 point:** Adverse selection
>
> **1 point:** Provide potential employers with references from previous employers.

Module 80
Indifference Curves
and Consumer Choice

What you will learn in this Module:

- Why economists use indifference curves to illustrate a person's preferences

- The importance of the marginal rate of substitution, the rate at which a consumer is just willing to substitute one good for another

- An alternative way of finding a consumer's optimal consumption bundle, using indifference curves and the budget line

Mapping the Utility Function

Earlier we introduced the concept of a utility function, which determines a consumer's total utility, given his or her consumption bundle. Here we will extend the analysis by learning how to express total utility as a function of the consumption of two goods. In this way we will deepen our understanding of the trade-off involved when choosing the optimal consumption bundle and of how the optimal consumption bundle itself changes in response to changes in the prices of goods. In order to do that, we now turn to a different way of representing a consumer's utility function, based on the concept of *indifference curves*.

Indifference Curves

Ingrid is a consumer who buys only two goods: housing, measured by the number of rooms in her house or apartment, and restaurant meals. How can we represent her utility function in a way that takes account of her consumption of both goods?

One way is to draw a three-dimensional picture. Figure 80.1 on the next page shows a three-dimensional "utility hill." The distance along the horizontal axis measures the quantity of housing Ingrid consumes in terms of the number of rooms; the distance along the vertical axis measures the number of restaurant meals she consumes. The altitude or height of the hill at each point is indicated by a contour line, along which the height of the hill is constant. For example, point A, which corresponds to a consumption bundle of 3 rooms and 30 restaurant meals, lies on the contour line labeled 450. So the total utility Ingrid receives from consuming 3 rooms and 30 restaurant meals is 450 utils.

A three-dimensional picture like Figure 80.1 helps us think about the relationship between consumption bundles and total utility. But anyone who has ever used a topographical map to plan a hiking trip knows that it is possible to represent a three-dimensional surface in only two dimensions. A topographical map doesn't

figure 80.1

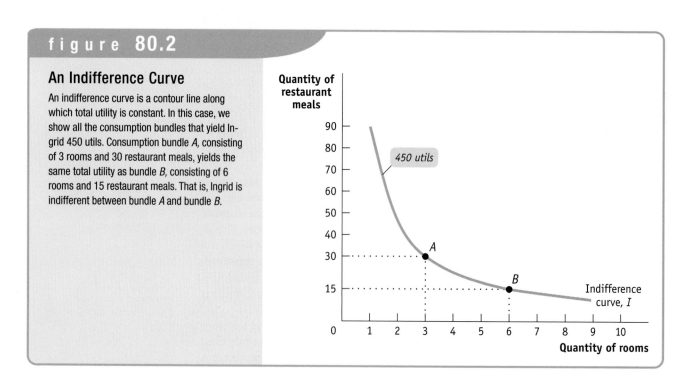

Ingrid's Utility Function

The three-dimensional hill shows how Ingrid's total utility depends on her consumption of housing and restaurant meals. Point *A* corresponds to consumption of 3 rooms and 30 restaurant meals. That consumption bundle yields Ingrid 450 utils, corresponding to the height of the hill at point *A*. The lines running around the hill are contour lines, along which the height is constant. So every point on a given contour line generates the same level of utility.

offer a three-dimensional view of the terrain; instead, it conveys information about altitude solely through the use of contour lines.

The same principle can be applied to the representation of a utility function. In Figure 80.2, Ingrid's consumption of rooms is measured on the horizontal axis and her consumption of restaurant meals on the vertical axis. The curve here corresponds to the contour line in Figure 80.1, drawn at a total utility of 450 utils. This curve shows all the consumption bundles that yield a total utility of 450 utils. One point on that contour line is *A*, a consumption bundle consisting of 3 rooms and 30 restaurant meals. Another point on that contour line is *B*, a consumption bundle consisting of 6 rooms but only 15 restaurant meals. Because *B* lies on the same contour line, it yields Ingrid

figure 80.2

An Indifference Curve

An indifference curve is a contour line along which total utility is constant. In this case, we show all the consumption bundles that yield Ingrid 450 utils. Consumption bundle *A*, consisting of 3 rooms and 30 restaurant meals, yields the same total utility as bundle *B*, consisting of 6 rooms and 15 restaurant meals. That is, Ingrid is indifferent between bundle *A* and bundle *B*.

the same total utility—450 utils—as A. We say that Ingrid is *indifferent* between A and B: because bundles A and B yield the same total utility level, Ingrid is equally well off with either bundle.

A contour line that maps consumption bundles yielding the same amount of total utility is known as an **indifference curve.** An individual is always indifferent between any two bundles that lie on the same indifference curve. For a given consumer, there is an indifference curve corresponding to each possible level of total utility. For example, the indifference curve in Figure 80.2 shows consumption bundles that yield Ingrid 450 utils; different indifference curves would show consumption bundles that yield Ingrid 400 utils, 500 utils, and so on.

A collection of indifference curves that represents a given consumer's entire utility function, with each indifference curve corresponding to a different level of total utility, is known as an **indifference curve map.** Figure 80.3 shows three indifference curves—I_1, I_2, and I_3—from Ingrid's indifference curve map, as well as several consumption bundles, A, B, C, and D. The accompanying table lists each bundle, its composition of rooms and restaurant meals, and the total utility it yields. Because bundles A and B generate the same number of utils, 450, they lie on the same indifference curve, I_2.

Although Ingrid is indifferent between A and B, she is certainly not indifferent between A and C: as you can see from the table, C generates only 391 utils, a lower total utility than A or B. So Ingrid prefers consumption bundles A and B to bundle C. This is represented by the fact that C is on indifference curve I_1, and I_1 lies below I_2. Bundle D, though, generates 519 utils, a higher total utility than A and B. It is on I_3, an indifference curve that lies above I_2. Clearly, Ingrid prefers D to either A or B. And, even more strongly, she prefers D to C.

An **indifference curve** is a line that shows all the consumption bundles that yield the same amount of total utility for an individual.

The entire utility function of an individual can be represented by an **indifference curve map,** a collection of indifference curves in which each curve corresponds to a different total utility level.

figure 80.3   An Indifference Curve Map

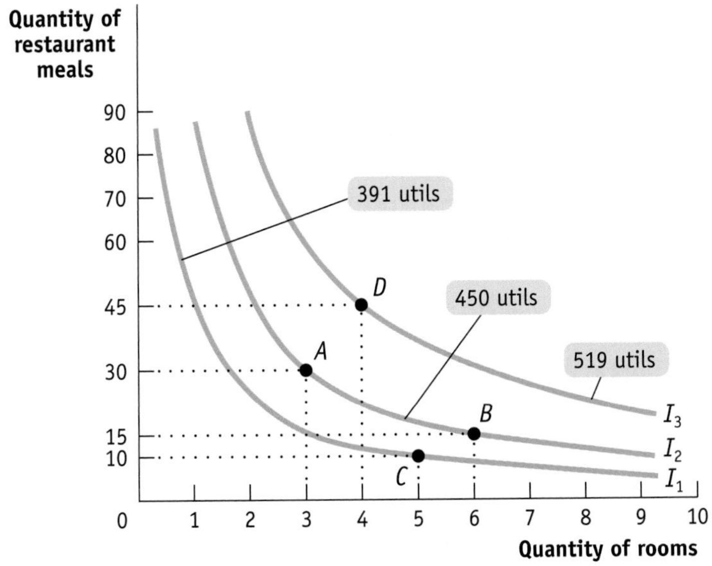

Consumption bundle	Quantity of rooms	Quantity of meals	Total utility (utils)
A	3	30	450
B	6	15	450
C	5	10	391
D	4	45	519

The utility function can be represented in greater detail by increasing the number of indifference curves drawn, each corresponding to a different level of total utility. In this figure bundle C lies on an indifference curve corresponding to a total utility of 391 utils. As in Figure 80.2, bundles A and B lie on an indifference curve corresponding to a total utility of 450 utils. Bundle D lies on an indifference curve corresponding to a total utility of 519 utils. Ingrid prefers any bundle on I_2 to any bundle on I_1, and she prefers any bundle on I_3 to any bundle on I_2.

In the table that accompanies Figure 80.3, we give the number of utils achieved on each of the indifference curves shown in the figure. But is this information actually needed?

The answer is no. As you will see shortly, the indifference curve map tells us all we need to know in order to find a consumer's optimal consumption bundle. That is, it's important that Ingrid has higher total utility along indifference curve I_2 than she does along I_1, but it doesn't matter *how much higher* her total utility is. In other words, we don't have to measure utils in order to understand how consumers make choices.

Economists say that consumer theory requires an *ordinal* measure of utility—one that ranks consumption bundles in terms of desirability—so that we can say that bundle *X* is better than bundle *Y*. The theory does not, however, require *cardinal* utility, which actually assigns a specific number to the total utility yielded by each bundle.

So why introduce the concept of utils at all? The answer is that it is much easier to understand the basis of rational choice by using the concept of measurable utility.

Properties of Indifference Curves

No two individuals have the same indifference curve map because no two individuals have the same preferences. But economists believe that, regardless of the person, every indifference curve map has two general properties. These are illustrated in panel (a) of Figure 80.4.

a. *Indifference curves never cross.* Suppose that we tried to draw an indifference curve map like the one depicted in the left diagram in panel (a), in which two indifference curves cross at *A*. What is the total utility at *A*? Is it 100 utils or 200 utils? Indifference curves cannot cross because each consumption bundle must correspond to one unique total utility level—not, as shown at *A*, two different total utility levels.

b. *The farther out an indifference curve lies—the farther it is from the origin—the higher the level of total utility it indicates.* The reason, illustrated in the right diagram in panel (a), is that we assume that more is better—we consider only the consumption bundles for which the consumer is not satiated. Bundle *B*, on the outer indifference curve, contains more of both goods than bundle *A* on the inner indifference curve. So *B*, because it generates a higher total utility level (200 utils), lies on a higher indifference curve than *A*.

Furthermore, economists believe that, for most goods, consumers' indifference curve maps also have two additional properties. They are illustrated in panel (b) of Figure 80.4:

c. *Indifference curves slope downward.* Here, too, the reason is that more is better. The left diagram in panel (b) shows four consumption bundles on the same indifference curve: *W, X, Y,* and *Z*. By definition, these consumption bundles yield the same level of total utility. But as you move along the curve to the right, from *W* to *Z*, the quantity of rooms consumed increases. The only way a person can consume more rooms without gaining utility is by giving up some restaurant meals. So the indifference curve must slope downward.

d. *Indifference curves have a convex shape.* The right diagram in panel (b) shows that the slope of each indifference curve changes as you move down the curve to the right: the curve gets flatter. If you move up an indifference curve to the left, the curve gets steeper. So the indifference curve is steeper at *A* than it is at *B*. When this occurs, we say that an indifference curve has a *convex* shape—it is bowed-in toward the origin. This feature arises from diminishing marginal utility, a principle we discussed in Module 51. Recall that when a consumer has diminishing marginal utility, consumption of another unit of a good generates a smaller increase in total utility than the previous unit consumed. Next we will examine in detail how diminishing marginal utility gives rise to convex-shaped indifference curves.

figure 80.4 — Properties of Indifference Curves

(a) Properties of All Indifference Curves

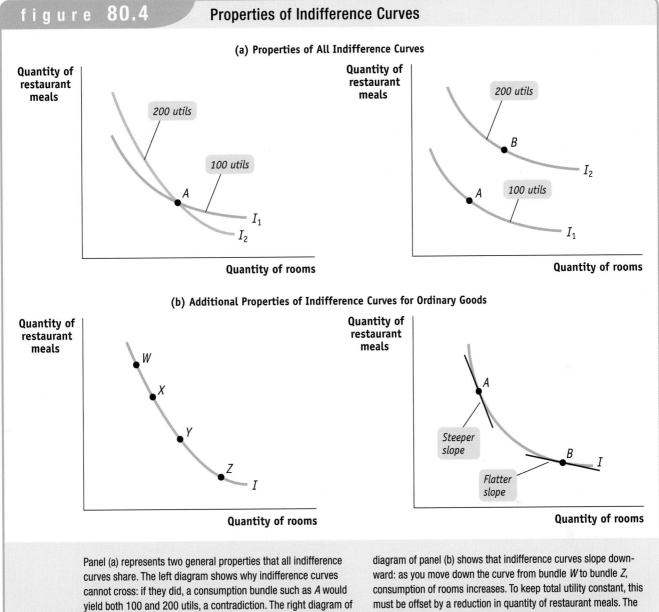

Panel (a) represents two general properties that all indifference curves share. The left diagram shows why indifference curves cannot cross: if they did, a consumption bundle such as *A* would yield both 100 and 200 utils, a contradiction. The right diagram of panel (a) shows that indifference curves that are farther out yield higher total utility: bundle *B*, which contains more of both goods than bundle *A*, yields higher total utility. Panel (b) depicts two additional properties of indifference curves for ordinary goods. The left diagram of panel (b) shows that indifference curves slope downward: as you move down the curve from bundle *W* to bundle *Z*, consumption of rooms increases. To keep total utility constant, this must be offset by a reduction in quantity of restaurant meals. The right diagram of panel (b) shows a convex-shaped indifference curve. The slope of the indifference curve gets flatter as you move down the curve to the right, a feature arising from diminishing marginal utility.

Goods that satisfy all four properties of indifference curve maps are called *ordinary goods*. The vast majority of goods in any consumer's utility function fall into this category. Below we will define ordinary goods more precisely and see the key role that diminishing marginal utility plays for them.

Indifference Curves and Consumer Choice

Above we used indifference curves to represent the preferences of Ingrid, whose consumption bundles consist of rooms and restaurant meals. Our next step is to show how to use Ingrid's indifference curve map to find her utility-maximizing consumption bundle, given her budget constraint, which arises because she must choose a consumption bundle that costs no more than her total income.

It's important to understand how our analysis here relates to what we did in Module 51. We are not offering a new theory of consumer behavior in this module—consumers are assumed to maximize total utility as before. In particular, we know that consumers will follow the *optimal consumption rule*: the optimal consumption bundle lies on the budget line, and the marginal utility per dollar is the same for every good in the bundle.

But as we'll see shortly, we can derive this optimal consumer behavior in a somewhat different way—a way that yields deeper insights into consumer choice.

The Marginal Rate of Substitution

The first element of our approach is a new concept, the *marginal rate of substitution*. The essence of this concept is illustrated in Figure 80.5.

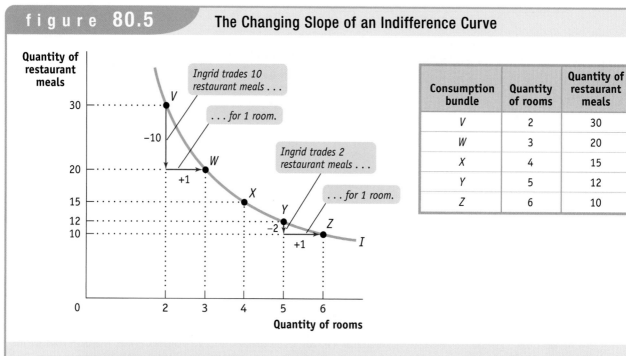

figure 80.5 **The Changing Slope of an Indifference Curve**

Consumption bundle	Quantity of rooms	Quantity of restaurant meals
V	2	30
W	3	20
X	4	15
Y	5	12
Z	6	10

This indifference curve is downward sloping and convex, implying that restaurant meals and rooms are ordinary goods for Ingrid. As Ingrid moves down her indifference curve from V to Z, she trades reduced consumption of restaurant meals for increased consumption of housing. However, the terms of that trade-off change. As she moves from V to W, she is willing to give up 10 restaurant meals in return for 1 more room. As her consumption of rooms rises and her consumption of restaurant meals falls, she is willing to give up fewer restaurant meals in return for each additional room. The flattening of the slope as you move from left to right arises from diminishing marginal utility.

We have just seen that for most goods, consumers' indifference curves are downward sloping and convex. Figure 80.5 shows such an indifference curve. The points labeled *V*, *W*, *X*, *Y*, and *Z* all lie on this indifference curve—that is, they represent consumption bundles that yield Ingrid the same level of total utility. The table accompanying the figure shows the components of each of the bundles. As we move along the indifference curve from *V* to *Z*, Ingrid's consumption of housing steadily increases from 2 rooms to 6 rooms, her consumption of restaurant meals steadily decreases from 30 meals to 10 meals, and her total utility is kept constant. As we move down the indifference curve, then, Ingrid is trading more of one good for less of the other, with the *terms* of that trade-off—the ratio of additional rooms consumed to restaurant meals sacrificed—chosen to keep her total utility constant.

Notice that the quantity of restaurant meals that Ingrid is willing to give up in return for an additional room changes along the indifference curve. As we move from *V* to *W*, housing consumption rises from 2 to 3 rooms and restaurant meal consumption falls from 30 to 20—a trade-off of 10 restaurant meals for 1 additional room. But as we move from *Y* to *Z*, housing consumption rises from 5 to 6 rooms and restaurant meal consumption falls from 12 to 10, a trade-off of only 2 restaurant meals for an additional room.

To put it in terms of slope, the slope of the indifference curve between *V* and *W* is −10: the change in restaurant meal consumption, −10, divided by the change in housing consumption, 1. Similarly, the slope of the indifference curve between *Y* and *Z* is −2. So the indifference curve gets flatter as we move down it to the right—that is, it has a convex shape, one of the four properties of an indifference curve for ordinary goods.

Why does the trade-off change in this way? Let's think about it intuitively and then work through it more carefully. When Ingrid moves down her indifference curve, whether from *V* to *W* or from *Y* to *Z*, she gains utility from her additional consumption of housing but loses an equal amount of utility from her reduced consumption of restaurant meals. But at each step, the initial position from which Ingrid begins is different. At *V*, Ingrid consumes only a small quantity of rooms; because of diminishing marginal utility, her marginal utility per room at that point is high. At *V*, then, an additional room adds a lot to Ingrid's total utility. But at *V* she already consumes a large quantity of restaurant meals, so her marginal utility of restaurant meals is low at that point. This means that it takes a large reduction in her quantity of restaurant meals consumed to offset the increased utility she gets from the extra room of housing.

At *Y*, in contrast, Ingrid consumes a much larger quantity of rooms and a much smaller quantity of restaurant meals than at *V*. This means that an additional room adds fewer utils, and a restaurant meal forgone costs more utils, than at *V*. So Ingrid is willing to give up fewer restaurant meals in return for another room of housing at *Y* (where she gives up 2 meals for 1 room) than she is at *V* (where she gives up 10 meals for 1 room).

Now let's express the same idea—that the trade-off Ingrid is willing to make depends on where she is starting from—by using a little math. We do this by examining how the slope of the indifference curve changes as we move down it. Moving down the indifference curve—reducing restaurant meal consumption and increasing housing consumption—will produce two opposing effects on Ingrid's total utility: lower restaurant meal consumption will reduce her total utility, but higher housing consumption will raise her total utility. And since we are moving down the indifference curve, these two effects must exactly cancel out:

Along the indifference curve:

(80-1) (Change in total utility due to lower restaurant meal consumption) + (Change in total utility due to higher housing consumption) = 0

or, rearranging terms,

Along the indifference curve:

(80-2) −(Change in total utility due to lower restaurant meal consumption) = (Change in total utility due to higher housing consumption)

Let's now focus on what happens as we move only a short distance down the indifference curve, trading off a small increase in housing consumption in place of a small decrease in restaurant meal consumption. Following our notation from before, let's use MU_R and MU_M to represent the marginal utility of rooms and restaurant meals, respectively, and Q_R and Q_M to represent the changes in room and meal consumption, respectively. In general, the change in total utility caused by a small change in consumption of a good is equal to the change in consumption multiplied by the *marginal utility* of that good. This means that we can calculate the change in Ingrid's total utility generated by a change in her consumption bundle using the following equations:

(80-3) Change in total utility due to a change in restaurant meal consumption
$$= MU_M \times Q_M$$

and

(80-4) Change in total utility due to a change in housing consumption
$$= MU_R \times Q_R$$

So we can write Equation 80-2 in symbols as:

Along the indifference curve:

(80-5) $-MU_M \times Q_M = MU_R \times Q_R$

Note that the left-hand side of Equation 80-5 has a negative sign; it represents the loss in total utility from decreased restaurant meal consumption. This must equal the gain in total utility from increased room consumption, represented by the right-hand side of the equation.

What we want to know is how this translates into the slope of the indifference curve. To find the slope, we divide both sides of Equation 80-5 by Q_R, and again by $-MU_M$, in order to get the Q_M, Q_R terms on one side and the MU_R, MU_M terms on the other. This results in:

(80-6) *Along the indifference curve:* $\dfrac{\Delta Q_M}{\Delta Q_R} = -\dfrac{MU_R}{MU_M}$

The left-hand side of Equation 80-6 is the slope of the indifference curve; it is the rate at which Ingrid is willing to trade rooms (the good on the horizontal axis) for restaurant meals (the good on the vertical axis) without changing her total utility level. The right-hand side of Equation 80-6 is the negative of the ratio of the marginal utility of rooms to the marginal utility of restaurant meals—that is, the ratio of what she gains from one more room to what she gains from one more meal, with a negative sign in front.

Putting all this together, Equation 80-6 shows that, along the indifference curve, the quantity of restaurant meals Ingrid is willing to give up in return for a room, $\frac{\Delta Q_M}{\Delta Q_R}$, is exactly equal to the negative of the ratio of the marginal utility of a room to that of a meal, $-\frac{MU_R}{MU_M}$. Only when this condition is met will her total utility level remain constant as she consumes more rooms and fewer restaurant meals.

Economists have a special name for the ratio of the marginal utilities found in the right-hand side of Equation 80-6: it is called the **marginal rate of substitution,** or *MRS,* of rooms (the good on the horizontal axis) in place of restaurant meals (the good on the vertical axis). That's because as we slide down Ingrid's indifference curve, we are substituting more rooms for fewer restaurant meals in her consumption bundle. As we'll see shortly, the marginal rate of substitution plays an important role in finding the optimal consumption bundle.

Recall that indifference curves get flatter as you move down them to the right. The reason, as we've just discussed, is diminishing marginal utility: as Ingrid consumes more housing and fewer restaurant meals, her marginal utility from housing falls and her marginal utility from restaurant meals rises. So her marginal rate of substitution, which is equal to the negative of the slope of her indifference curve, falls as she moves down the indifference curve.

The flattening of indifference curves as you slide down them to the right—which reflects the same logic as the principle of diminishing marginal utility—is known as the principle of **diminishing marginal rate of substitution.** It says that an individual who consumes only a little bit of good A and a lot of good B will be willing to trade off a lot of good B in return for one more unit of good A, and an individual who already consumes a lot of good A and not much of good B will be less willing to make that trade-off.

We can illustrate this point by referring back to Figure 80.5. At point V, a bundle with a high proportion of restaurant meals to rooms, Ingrid is willing to forgo 10 restaurant meals in return for 1 room. But at point Y, a bundle with a low proportion of restaurant meals to rooms, she is willing to forgo only 2 restaurant meals in return for 1 room.

From this example we can see that, in Ingrid's utility function, rooms and restaurant meals possess the two additional properties that characterize ordinary goods. Ingrid requires additional rooms to compensate her for the loss of a meal, and vice versa; so her indifference curves for these two goods slope downward. And her indifference curves are convex: the slope of her indifference curve—*the negative of* the marginal rate of substitution—becomes flatter as we move down it. In fact, an indifference curve is convex only when it has a diminishing marginal rate of substitution—these two conditions are equivalent.

With this information, we can define **ordinary goods,** which account for the great majority of goods in any consumer's utility function. A pair of goods are ordinary goods in a consumer's utility function if they possess two properties: the consumer requires more of one good to compensate for less of the other, and the consumer experiences a diminishing marginal rate of substitution when substituting one good for the other.

Next we will see how to determine Ingrid's optimal consumption bundle using indifference curves.

The principle of **diminishing marginal rate of substitution** states that the more of good R a person consumes in proportion to good M, the less M he or she is willing to substitute for another unit of R.

Two goods, R and M, are **ordinary goods** in a consumer's utility function when (1) the consumer requires additional units of R to compensate for fewer units of M, and vice versa; and (2) the consumer experiences a diminishing marginal rate of substitution when substituting one good for another.

The Tangency Condition

Now let's put some of Ingrid's indifference curves on the same diagram as her budget line to illustrate an alternative way of representing her optimal consumption choice. Figure 80.6 shows Ingrid's budget line, BL, when her income is $2,400 per month,

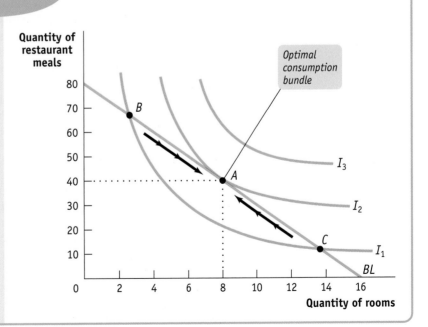

figure 80.6

The Optimal Consumption Bundle

The budget line, BL, shows Ingrid's possible consumption bundles, given an income of $2,400 per month, when rooms cost $150 per month and restaurant meals cost $30 each. I_1, I_2, and I_3 are indifference curves. Consumption bundles such as B and C are not optimal because Ingrid can move to a higher indifference curve. The optimal consumption bundle is A, where the budget line is just tangent to the highest possible indifference curve.

Quantity of restaurant meals

Optimal consumption bundle

Quantity of rooms

housing costs $150 per room each month, and restaurant meals cost $30 each. What is her optimal consumption bundle?

To answer this question, we show several of Ingrid's indifference curves: I_1, I_2, and I_3. Ingrid would like to achieve the total utility level represented by I_3, the highest of the three curves, but she cannot afford to because she is constrained by her income: no consumption bundle on her budget line yields that much total utility. But she shouldn't settle for the level of total utility generated by B, which lies on I_1: there are other bundles on her budget line, such as A, that clearly yield higher total utility than B.

In fact, A—a consumption bundle consisting of 8 rooms and 40 restaurant meals per month—is Ingrid's optimal consumption choice. The reason is that A lies on the highest indifference curve Ingrid can reach given her income.

At the optimal consumption bundle A, Ingrid's budget line *just touches* the relevant indifference curve—the budget line is *tangent* to the indifference curve. This **tangency condition** between the indifference curve and the budget line applies to the optimal consumption bundle when the indifference curves have the typical convex shape.

To see why, let's look more closely at how we know that a consumption bundle that *doesn't* satisfy the tangency condition can't be optimal. Reexamining Figure 80.6, we can see that consumption bundles B and C are both affordable because they lie on the budget line. However, neither is optimal. Both of them lie on the indifference curve I_1, which cuts through the budget line at both points. But because I_1 cuts through the budget line, Ingrid can do better: she can move down the budget line from B or up the budget line from C, as indicated by the arrows. In each case, this allows her to get onto a higher indifference curve, I_2, which increases her total utility.

Ingrid cannot, however, do any better than I_2: any other indifference curve either cuts through her budget line or doesn't touch it at all. And the bundle that allows her to achieve I_2 is, of course, her optimal consumption bundle.

The Slope of the Budget Line

Figure 80.6 shows us how to use a graph of the budget line and the indifference curves to find the optimal consumption bundle, the bundle at which the budget line and the indifference curve are tangent. But rather than rely on drawing graphs, we can determine the optimal consumption bundle by using a bit more math. As you can see from Figure 80.6, at A, the optimal consumption bundle, the budget line and the indifference curve have the same slope. Why? Because two curves can only be tangent to each other if they have the same slope at the point where they meet. Otherwise, they would cross each other at that point. And we know that if we are on an indifference curve that crosses the budget line (like I_1, in Figure 80.6), we can't be on the indifference curve that contains the optimal consumption bundle (like I_2).

So we can use information about the slopes of the budget line and the indifference curve to find the optimal consumption bundle. To do that, we must first analyze the slope of the budget line, a fairly straightforward task. We know that Ingrid will get the highest possible utility by spending all of her income and consuming a bundle on her budget line. So we can represent Ingrid's budget line, the consumption bundles available to her when she spends all of her income, with the equation:

(80-7) $(Q_R \times P_R) + (Q_M \times P_M) = N$

where N stands for Ingrid's income. To find the slope of the budget line, we divide its vertical intercept (where the budget line hits the vertical axis) by its horizontal intercept (where it hits the horizontal axis) and then add a negative sign. The vertical intercept is the point at which Ingrid spends all her income on restaurant meals and none on housing (that is, $Q_R = 0$). In that case the number of restaurant meals she consumes is:

(80-8) $Q_M = \dfrac{N}{P_M} = \$2{,}400/(\$30 \text{ per meal}) = 80 \text{ meals}$

$= \text{Vertical intercept of budget line}$

At the other extreme, Ingrid spends all her income on housing and none on restaurant meals (so that $Q_M = 0$). This means that at the horizontal intercept of the budget line, the number of rooms she consumes is:

The **relative price** of good R in terms of good M is equal to $\frac{P_R}{P_M}$, the rate at which R trades for M in the market.

(80-9) $Q_R = \dfrac{N}{P_R} = \dfrac{\$2{,}400}{(\$150 \text{ per room})} = 16 \text{ rooms}$

$\quad\quad\quad = \text{Horizontal intercept of budget line}$

Now we have the information needed to find the slope of the budget line. It is:

(80-10) $\text{Slope of budget line} = -\dfrac{(\text{Vertical intercept})}{(\text{Horizontal intercept})} = -\dfrac{\dfrac{N}{P_M}}{\dfrac{N}{P_R}} = -\dfrac{P_R}{P_M}$

Notice the negative sign in Equation 80-10; it's there because the budget line slopes downward. The quantity $\frac{P_R}{P_M}$ is known as the **relative price** of rooms in terms of restaurant meals, to distinguish it from an ordinary price in terms of dollars. Because buying one more room requires Ingrid to give up the quantity $\frac{P_R}{P_M}$ of restaurant meals, or 5 meals, we can interpret the relative price $\frac{P_R}{P_M}$ as the rate at which a room trades for restaurant meals in the market; it is the price—in terms of restaurant meals—Ingrid has to "pay" to get one more room.

Looking at this another way, the slope of the budget line—the negative of the relative price—tells us the opportunity cost of each good in terms of the other. The relative price illustrates the opportunity cost to an individual of consuming one more unit of one good in terms of how much of the other good in his or her consumption bundle must be forgone. This opportunity cost arises from the consumer's limited resources—his or her limited budget. It's useful to note that Equations 80-8, 80-9, and 80-10 give us all the information we need about what happens to the budget line when relative price or income changes. From Equations 80-8 and 80-9 we can see that a change in income, N, leads to a parallel shift of the budget line: both the vertical and horizontal intercepts will shift. That is, how far out the budget line is from the origin depends on the consumer's income. If a consumer's income rises, the budget line moves outward. If the consumer's income shrinks, the budget line shifts inward. In each case, the slope of the budget line stays the same because the relative price of one good in terms of the other does not change.

In contrast, a change in the relative price $\frac{P_R}{P_M}$ will lead to a change in the slope of the budget line. We'll analyze these changes in the budget line and how the optimal consumption bundle changes when the relative price changes or when income changes in greater detail later in the module.

Prices and the Marginal Rate of Substitution

Now we're ready to bring together the slope of the budget line and the slope of the indifference curve to find the optimal consumption bundle. From Equation 80-6, we know that the slope of the indifference curve at any point is equal to the negative of the marginal rate of substitution:

(80-11) $\text{Slope of indifference curve} = -\dfrac{MU_R}{MU_M}$

As we've already noted, at the optimal consumption bundle the slope of the budget line and the slope of the indifference curve are equal. We can write this formally by putting

Equations 80-10 and 80-11 together, which gives us the **relative price rule** for finding the optimal consumption bundle:

(80-12) *At the optimal consumption bundle:* $-\dfrac{MU_R}{MU_M} = \dfrac{P_R}{P_M}$

or, *cancelling the negative signs,* $\dfrac{MU_R}{MU_M} = \dfrac{P_R}{P_M}$

That is, at the optimal consumption bundle, the marginal rate of substitution between any two goods is equal to the ratio of their prices. To put it in a more intuitive way, starting with Ingrid's optimal consumption bundle, the rate at which she would trade a room for more restaurant meals along her indifference curve, $\dfrac{MU_R}{MU_M}$, is equal to the rate at which rooms are traded for restaurant meals in the market, $\dfrac{P_R}{P_M}$.

What would happen if this equality did not hold? We can see by examining Figure 80.7. There, at point *B*, the slope of the indifference curve, $-\dfrac{MU_R}{MU_M}$, is greater in absolute value than the slope of the budget line, $-\dfrac{P_R}{P_M}$. This means that, at *B*, Ingrid values an additional room in place of meals *more* than it costs her to buy an additional room and forgo some meals. As a result, Ingrid would be better off moving down her budget line toward *A*, consuming more rooms and fewer restaurant meals—and because of that, *B* could not have been her optimal bundle! Likewise, at *C*, the slope of Ingrid's indifference curve is less in absolute value than the slope of the budget line. The implication is that, at *C*, Ingrid values additional meals in place of a room *more* than it costs her to buy additional meals and forgo a room. Again, Ingrid would be better off moving along her budget line—consuming more restaurant meals and fewer rooms—until she reaches *A*, her optimal consumption bundle.

But suppose we transform the last term of Equation 80-12 in the following way: divide both sides by P_R and multiply both sides by MU_M. Then the relative price rule becomes the optimal consumption rule:

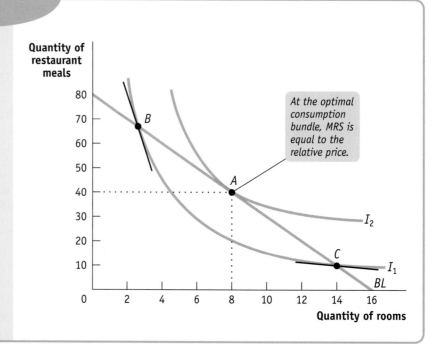

figure 80.7

Understanding the Relative Price Rule

The *relative price* of rooms in terms of restaurant meals is equal to the negative of the slope of the budget line. The *marginal rate of substitution* of rooms for restaurant meals is equal to the negative of the slope of the indifference curve. The *relative price rule* says that at the optimal consumption bundle, the marginal rate of substitution must equal the relative price. This point can be demonstrated by considering what happens when the marginal rate of substitution is not equal to the relative price. At consumption bundle *B*, the marginal rate of substitution is larger than the relative price; Ingrid can increase her total utility by moving down her budget line, *BL*. At *C*, the marginal rate of substitution is smaller than the relative price, and Ingrid can increase her total utility by moving up the budget line. Only at *A*, where the relative price rule holds, is her total utility maximized, given her budget constraint.

(80-13) *Optimal consumption rule:* $\dfrac{MU_R}{P_M} = \dfrac{MU_M}{P_M}$

So using either the optimal consumption rule or the relative price rule, we find the same optimal consumption bundle.

Preferences and Choices

Now that we have seen how to represent the optimal consumption choice in an indifference curve diagram, we can turn briefly to the relationship between consumer preferences and consumer choices.

When we say that two consumers have different preferences, we mean that they have different utility functions. This in turn means that they will have indifference curve maps with different shapes. And those different maps will translate into different consumption choices, even among consumers with the same income and who face the same prices.

To see this, suppose that Ingrid's friend Lars also consumes only housing and restaurant meals. However, Lars has a stronger preference for restaurant meals and a weaker preference for housing. This difference in preferences is shown in Figure 80.8,

figure 80.8

Differences in Preferences

Ingrid and Lars have different preferences, reflected in the different shapes of their indifference curve maps. So they will choose different consumption bundles even when they have the same possible choices. Each has an income of $2,400 per month and faces prices of $30 per meal and $150 per room. Panel (a) shows Ingrid's consumption choice: 8 rooms and 40 restaurant meals. Panel (b) shows Lars's choice: even though he has the same budget line, he consumes fewer rooms and more restaurant meals.

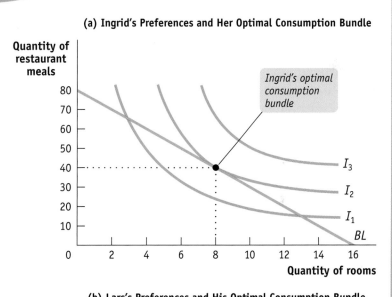

(a) Ingrid's Preferences and Her Optimal Consumption Bundle

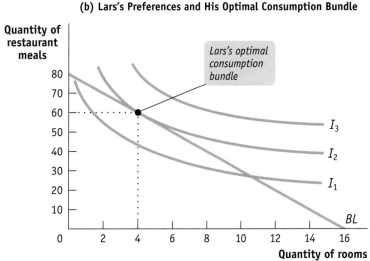

(b) Lars's Preferences and His Optimal Consumption Bundle

which shows *two* sets of indifference curves: panel (a) shows Ingrid's preferences and panel (b) shows Lars's preferences. Note the difference in their shapes.

Suppose, as before, that rooms cost $150 per month and restaurant meals cost $30. Let's also assume that both Ingrid and Lars have incomes of $2,400 per month, giving them identical budget lines. Nonetheless, because they have different preferences, they will make different consumption choices, as shown in Figure 80.8. Ingrid will choose 8 rooms and 40 restaurant meals; Lars will choose 4 rooms and 60 restaurant meals.

Module (80) AP Review

Solutions appear at the back of the book.

Check Your Understanding

1. The accompanying table shows Samantha's preferences for consumption bundles composed of chocolate kisses and licorice drops.

Consumption bundle	Quantity of chocolate kisses	Quantity of licorice drops	Total utility (utils)
A	1	3	6
B	2	3	10
C	3	1	6
D	2	1	4

   a. With chocolate kisses on the horizontal axis and licorice drops on the vertical axis, draw hypothetical indifference curves for Samantha and locate the bundles on the curves. Assume that both items are ordinary goods.

   b. Suppose you don't know the number of utils provided by each bundle. Assuming that more is better, predict Samantha's ranking of each of the four bundles to the extent possible. Explain your answer.

2. On the left diagram in panel (a) of Figure 80.4, draw a point *B* anywhere on the 200-util indifference curve and a point *C* anywhere on the 100-util indifference curve (but *not* at the same location as point *A*). By comparing the utils generated by bundles *A* and *B* and those generated by bundles *A* and *C*, explain why indifference curves cannot cross.

3. Lucinda and Kyle each consume 3 comic books and 6 video games. Lucinda's marginal rate of substitution of books for games is 2 and Kyle's is 5.

   a. For each person, find another consumption bundle that yields the same total utility as the current bundle. Who is less willing to trade games for books? In a diagram with books on the horizontal axis and games on the vertical axis, how would this be reflected in differences in the slopes of their indifference curves at their current consumption bundles?

   b. Find the relative price of books in terms of games at which Lucinda's current bundle is optimal. Is Kyle's bundle optimal given this relative price? If not, how should Kyle rearrange his consumption?

Tackle the Test: Multiple-Choice Questions

1. Which of the following is true along an individual's indifference curve for ordinary goods?
   a. The slope is constant.
   b. Total utility changes.
   c. The individual is indifferent between any two points.
   d The slope is equal to the ratio of the prices of the consumption bundles.
   e. The individual doesn't care if utility is maximized.

2. Which of the following is/are true of indifference curves for ordinary goods?
   I. They cannot intersect.
   II. They have a negative slope.
   III. They are convex.

   a. I only
   b. II only
   c. III only
   d. I and II only
   e. I, II, and III

3. Moving from left to right along an indifference curve, which of the following increases?
   a. The marginal utility of the vertical axis good
   b. The marginal utility of the horizontal axis good
   c. The absolute value of the slope
   d. The marginal rate of substitution
   e. The demand for the vertical axis good

4. If the quantity of good X is measured on the horizontal axis and the quantity of good Y is measured on the vertical axis, the marginal rate of substitution is equal to

   a. $\dfrac{\Delta Q_X}{\Delta Q_Y}$.

   b. $\dfrac{MU_X}{MU_Y}$.

   c. $\dfrac{P_X}{P_Y}$.

   d. the ratio of the slope of the budget line and the slope of the indifference curve.

   e. 1 at the optimal level of consumption.

5. If the quantity of good X is again measured on the horizontal axis and the quantity of good Y is measured on the vertical axis, which of the following is true? The optimal consumption bundle is found where

   a. $\dfrac{MU_X}{MU_Y} = \dfrac{P_X}{P_Y}$.

   b. the slope of the indifference curve equals the slope of the budget line.

   c. the indifference curve is tangent to the budget line.

   d. $\dfrac{MU_X}{P_X} = \dfrac{MU_Y}{P_Y}$.

   e. all of the above are true.

Tackle the Test: Free-Response Questions

1. Each of the combinations of iPod song downloads and DVD rentals shown in the table below give Kathleen an equal level of utility.

Quantity of songs	Quantity of DVDs
0	8
1	6
2	4
3	2
4	0

   a. Graph Kathleen's indifference curve.

   b. Economists believe that the individual indifference curves for ordinary goods exhibit what two properties?

   c. Does Kathleen's indifference curve exhibit the two properties from part b? Explain.

1 point: Axes labeled "Quantity of songs" and "Quantity of DVDs"

1 point: Correctly plotted indifference curve points

1 point: Negative slope

1 point: Convex shape

1 point: Negative slope—yes

1 point: As *more* DVDs are rented, there must be *fewer* song downloads to give Kathleen the same level of utility as before. This trade-off of more of one good for less of another gives the indifference curve a negative slope.

1 point: Convex shape—no

1 point: The indifference curve is a straight line with a constant slope, rather than being a convex line with a slope that decreases in absolute value from left to right.

Answer (8 points)

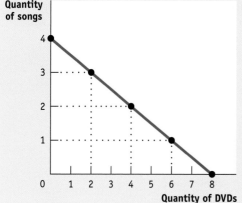

2. Kathleen has $20 to spend on iPod song downloads and DVD rentals each week. The price of an iPod song download is $2 and the price of a DVD rental is $5.

   a. Graph Kathleen's budget line.

   b. Suppose all of Kathleen's indifference curves have the same shape and slope as the one in Question 1. How many song downloads and DVD rentals will Kathleen purchase to maximize her utility? Explain.

Summary

1. **Private information** can cause inefficiency in the allocation of risk. One problem is **adverse selection,** the result of private information about the way things are. It creates the "lemons problem" in the used-car market because buyers will pay only a price that reflects the risk of purchasing a lemon (bad car), which encourages sellers of high-quality cars to drop out of the market. Adverse selection can be limited in several ways—through the **screening** of individuals, through **signaling** that people use to reveal their private information, and through the building of a **reputation.**

2. A related problem is **moral hazard:** individuals have private information about their actions, which distorts their incentives to exert effort or care when someone else bears the costs of that lack of effort or care. It limits the ability of markets to allocate risk efficiently. Insurance companies try to limit moral hazard by imposing **deductibles,** placing more risk on the insured.

3. Preferences can be represented by an **indifference curve map,** a series of **indifference curves.** Each curve shows all of the consumption bundles that yield a given level of total utility. Indifference curves have two general properties: they never cross and greater distance from the origin indicates higher total utility levels. The indifference curves of ordinary goods have two additional properties: they slope downward and are convex in shape.

4. The **marginal rate of substitution,** or **MRS,** of some good R in place of some good M—the rate at which a consumer is willing to substitute more R for less M—is equal to MU_R/MU_M and is also equal to the negative of the slope of the indifference curve when R is on the horizontal axis and M is on the vertical axis. Convex indifference curves get flatter as you move to the right along the horizontal axis and steeper as you move upward along the vertical axis because of *diminishing marginal utility:* a consumer requires more and more units of R to substitute for a forgone unit of M as the amount of R consumed rises relative to the amount of M consumed.

5. Most goods are **ordinary goods,** goods for which a consumer requires additional units of some other good as compensation for giving up some of the good, and for which there is a **diminishing marginal rate of substitution.**

6. A consumer maximizes utility by moving to the highest indifference curve his or her budget constraint allows. Using the **tangency condition,** the consumer chooses the bundle at which the indifference curve just touches the budget line. At this point, the **relative price** of R in terms of M, P_R/P_M (which is equal to the negative of the slope of the budget line when R is on the horizontal axis and M is on the vertical axis) is equal to the marginal rate of substitution of R in place of M, MU_R/MU_M (which is equal to the negative of the slope of the indifference curve). This gives us the **relative price rule:** at the optimal consumption bundle, the relative price is equal to the marginal rate of substitution. Rearranging this equation also gives us the optimal consumption rule. Two consumers faced with the same prices and income, but with different preferences and so different indifference curve maps, will make different consumption choices.

Key Terms

Private information, p. 782
Adverse selection, p. 783
Screening, p. 783
Signaling, p. 784
Reputation, p. 784

Moral hazard, p. 785
Deductible, p. 785
Indifference curve, p. 789
Indifference curve map, p. 789
Marginal rate of substitution (*MRS*), p. 794

Diminishing marginal rate of substitution, p. 795
Ordinary goods, p. 795
Tangency condition, p. 796
Relative price, p. 797
Relative price rule, p. 798

Problems

1. You are considering buying a second-hand Volkswagen. From reading car magazines, you know that half of all Volkswagens have problems of some kind (they are "lemons") and the other half run just fine (they are "plums"). If you knew that you were getting a plum, you would be willing to pay $10,000 for it: this is how much a plum is worth to you. You would also be willing to buy a lemon, but only if its price was no more than $4,000: this is how much a lemon is worth to you. And someone who owns a plum would be willing to sell it at any price above $8,000. Someone who owns a lemon would be willing to sell it for any price above $2,000.

   a. For now, suppose that you can immediately tell whether the car that you are being offered is a lemon or a plum. Suppose someone offers you a plum. Will there be trade?

   Now suppose that the seller has private information about the car she is selling: the seller knows whether she has a lemon or a plum. But when the seller offers you a Volkswagen, you do not know whether it is a lemon or a plum. So this is a situation of adverse selection.

   b. Since you do not know whether you are being offered a plum or a lemon, you base your decision on the expected value to you of a Volkswagen, assuming you are just as likely to buy a lemon as a plum. Calculate this expected value.

   c. Suppose, from driving the car, the seller knows she has a plum. However, you don't know whether this particular car is a lemon or a plum, so the most you are willing to pay is your expected value. Will there be trade?

2. You own a company that produces chairs, and you are thinking about hiring one more employee. Each chair produced gives you revenue of $10. There are two potential employees, Fred Ast and Sylvia Low. Fred is a fast worker who produces ten chairs per day, creating revenue for you of $100. Fred knows that he is fast and so will work for you only if you pay him more than $80 per day. Sylvia is a slow worker who produces only five chairs per day, creating revenue for you of $50. Sylvia knows that she is slow and so will work for you if you pay her more than $40 per day. Although Sylvia knows she is slow and Fred knows he is fast, you do not know who is fast and who is slow. So this is a situation of adverse selection.

   a. Since you do not know which type of worker you will get, you think about what the expected value of your revenue will be if you hire one of the two. What is that expected value?

   b. Suppose you offered to pay a daily wage equal to the expected revenue you calculated in part a. Whom would you be able to hire: Fred, or Sylvia, or both, or neither?

   c. If you knew whether a worker were fast or slow, which one would you prefer to hire and why? Can you devise a compensation scheme to guarantee that you employ only the type of worker you prefer?

3. For each of the following situations, draw a diagram containing three of Isabella's indifference curves.

   a. For Isabella, cars and tires are perfect complements, but in a ratio of 1:4; that is, for each car, Isabella wants exactly four tires. Be sure to label and number the axes of your diagram. Place tires on the horizontal axis and cars on the vertical axis.

   b. Isabella gets utility only from her caffeine intake. She can consume Valley Dew or cola, and Valley Dew contains twice as much caffeine as cola. Be sure to label and number the axes of your diagram. Place cola on the horizontal axis and Valley Dew on the vertical axis.

   c. Isabella gets utility from consuming two goods: leisure time and income. Both have diminishing marginal utility. Be sure to label the axes of your diagram. Place leisure on the horizontal axis and income on the vertical axis.

   d. Isabella can consume two goods: skis and bindings. For each ski she wants exactly one binding. Be sure to label and number the axes of your diagram. Place bindings on the horizontal axis and skis on the vertical axis.

   e. Isabella gets utility from consuming soda. But she gets no utility from consuming water: any more, or any less, water leaves her total utility level unchanged. Be sure to label the axes of your diagram. Place water on the horizontal axis and soda on the vertical axis.

4. Use the four properties of indifference curves for ordinary goods illustrated in Figure 80.4 to answer the following questions.

   a. Can you rank the following two bundles? If so, which property of indifference curves helps you rank them?

   Bundle A: 2 movie tickets and 3 cafeteria meals
   Bundle B: 4 movie tickets and 8 cafeteria meals

   b. Can you rank the following two bundles? If so, which property of indifference curves helps you rank them?

   Bundle A: 2 movie tickets and 3 cafeteria meals
   Bundle B: 4 movie tickets and 3 cafeteria meals

   c. Can you rank the following two bundles? If so, which property of indifference curves helps you rank them?

   Bundle A: 12 videos and 4 bags of chips
   Bundle B: 5 videos and 10 bags of chips

   d. Suppose you are indifferent between the following two bundles:

   Bundle A: 10 breakfasts and 4 dinners
   Bundle B: 4 breakfasts and 10 dinners

   Now compare bundle A and the following bundle:
   Bundle C: 7 breakfasts and 7 dinners

   Can you rank bundle A and bundle C? If so, which property of indifference curves helps you rank them? (*Hint:* It may help if you draw this, placing dinners on the horizontal axis and breakfasts on the vertical axis. And remember that breakfasts and dinners are ordinary goods.)

>> Solutions to AP Review Questions

This section offers suggested answers to the AP Review Questions that appear at the end of each module.

Module 1
Check Your Understanding

1. Land, labor, capital, and entrepreneurship are the four categories of resources. Possible examples include fisheries (land), time spent working on a fishing boat (labor), fishing nets (capital), and the opening of a new seafood market (entrepreneurship).

2. **a.** time spent flipping burgers at a restaurant: labor
   b. a bulldozer: capital
   c. a river: land

3. **a.** Yes. The increased time spent commuting is a cost you will incur if you accept the new job. That additional time spent commuting—or equivalently, the benefit you would get from spending that time doing something else—is an opportunity cost of the new job.
   b. Yes. One of the benefits of the new job is that you will be making $50,000. But if you take the new job, you will have to give up your current job; that is, you have to give up your current salary of $45,000, so $45,000 is one of the opportunity costs of taking the new job.
   c. No. A more spacious office is an additional benefit of your new job and does not involve forgoing something else, so it is not an opportunity cost.

4. **a.** This is a normative statement because it stipulates what should be done. In addition, it may have no "right" answer. That is, should people be prevented from all dangerous personal behavior if they enjoy that behavior—like skydiving? Your answer will depend on your point of view.
   b. This is a positive statement because it is a description of fact.

Tackle the Test:
Multiple-Choice Questions

1. d
2. d
3. b
4. b
5. a

Tackle the Test:
Free-Response Question

2. In positive economics there is a "right" or "wrong" answer. In normative economics there is not necessarily a "right" or "wrong" answer. There is more disagreement in normative economics because there is no "right" or "wrong" answer. Economists disagree because of (1) differences in values and (2) disagreements about models and about which simplifications are appropriate.

Module 2
Check Your Understanding

1. We talk about business cycles for the economy as a whole because recessions and expansions are not confined to a few industries—they reflect downturns and upturns for the economy as a whole. The data clearly show that in the steep downturns, almost every sector of the economy reduces output and the number of people employed. Moreover, business cycles are an international phenomenon, sometimes moving in rough synchrony across countries.

2. Recessions cause a great deal of pain across the entire society. They cause large numbers of workers to lose their jobs and make it difficult for workers to find new jobs. Recessions reduce the standard of living of many families and are usually associated with a rise in the number of people living below the poverty line, an increase in the number of people who may lose their houses because they can't afford their mortgage payments, and a fall in the percentage of Americans with health insurance. Recessions also reduce the profits of firms.

Tackle the Test:
Multiple-Choice Questions

1. a
2. d
3. e
4. c
5. b

Tackle the Test:
Free-Response Question

2. Inflation is an overall increase in the price of goods and services throughout an economy. If inflation occurs, the price of donuts will most likely increase, but an increase in the price of this one good does not indicate inflation. For example, the price of donuts might have increased due to an increase in the price of sugar, while the prices of most other goods in the economy have remained unchanged.

Module 3
Check Your Understanding

1. **a.** False. An increase in the resources available to Tom for use in producing coconuts and fish changes his production possibilities curve by shifting it outward, because he

can now produce more fish and coconuts than before. In the accompanying graph, the line labeled "Tom's original PPC" represents Tom's original production possibilities curve, and the line labeled "Tom's new PPC" represents the new production possibilities curve that results from an increase in resources available to Tom.

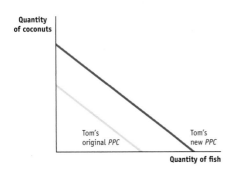

b. True. A technological change that allows Tom to catch more fish for any amount of coconuts gathered results in a change in his production possibilities curve. This is illustrated in the accompanying graph. The new production possibilities curve is represented by the line labeled "Tom's new PPC," and the original production possibilities curve is represented by the line labeled "Tom's original PPC." Since the maximum quantity of coconuts that Tom can gather is the same as before, the new production possibilities curve intersects the vertical axis at the same point as the old curve. But since the maximum possible quantity of fish is now greater than before, the new curve intersects the horizontal axis to the right of the old curve.

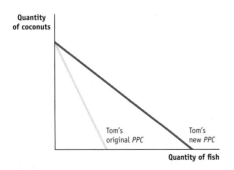

c. False. Production efficiency is achieved at points along a production possibilities curve, but every point inside a PPC is inefficient because more of either good could be produced without producing less of the other. Points outside the PPC are simply unobtainable.

Tackle the Test:
Multiple-Choice Questions

1. c
2. d
3. d
4. e
5. a

Tackle the Test:
Free-Response Question

2.

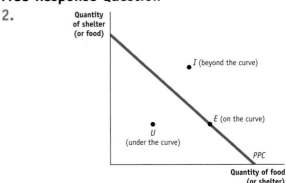

Module 4

Check Your Understanding

1. **a.** The United States has an absolute advantage in automobile production because it takes fewer Americans (6) to produce a car in one day than it takes Italians (8). The United States also has an absolute advantage in washing machine production because it takes fewer Americans (2) to produce a washing machine in one day than it takes Italians (3).

    b. In Italy the opportunity cost of a washing machine in terms of an automobile is $\frac{3}{8}$. In other words, $\frac{3}{8}$ of a car can be produced with the same number of workers and in the same time it takes to produce 1 washing machine. In the United States the opportunity cost of a washing machine in terms of an automobile is $\frac{2}{6} = \frac{1}{3}$. In other words, $\frac{1}{3}$ of a car can be produced with the same number of workers and in the same time it takes to produce 1 washing machine. Since $\frac{1}{3} < \frac{3}{8}$, the United States has a comparative advantage in the production of washing machines: to produce a washing machine, only $\frac{1}{3}$ of a car must be given up in the United States but $\frac{3}{8}$ of a car must be given up in Italy. This means that Italy has a comparative advantage in automobiles. This can be checked as follows. The opportunity cost of an automobile in terms of a washing machine in Italy is $\frac{8}{3}$, equal to $2\frac{2}{3}$. In other words, $2\frac{2}{3}$ washing machines can be produced with the same number of workers and in the time it takes to produce 1 car in Italy. And the opportunity cost of an automobile in terms of a washing machine in the United States is $\frac{6}{2}$, equal to 3. In other words, 3 washing machines can be produced with the same number of workers and in the time it takes to produce 1 car in the United States.

    c. The greatest gains are realized when each country specializes in producing the good for which it has a comparative advantage. Therefore, based on this example, the United States should specialize in washing machines and Italy should specialize in automobiles.

2. At a trade of 1 fish for 1½ coconuts, Hank gives up less for a fish than he would if he were producing fish himself—that is, he gives up less than 2 coconuts for 1 fish. Likewise, Tom gives up less for a coconut than he would

if he were producing coconuts himself—with trade, a coconut costs 1½ = ⅔ of a fish, less than the ⅘ of a fish he must give up if he does not trade.

Tackle the Test:
Multiple-Choice Questions

1. a

2. a

3. a

4. d

5. d

Tackle the Test:
Free-Response Questions

2. a. Country A: opportunity cost of 1 bushel of wheat = 4 units of textiles
Country B: opportunity cost of 1 bushel of wheat = 6 units of textiles

b. Country A has an absolute advantage in the production of wheat (15 versus 10)

c. Country A: opportunity cost of 1 unit of textiles = ¼ bushel of wheat
Country B: opportunity cost of 1 unit of textiles = ⅙ bushel of wheat
Country B has the comparative advantage in textile production because it has a lower opportunity cost of producing textiles. (Alternate answer: Country B has the comparative advantage in the production of textiles because Country A has a comparative advantage in the production of wheat based on opportunity costs shown in part a.)

Appendix
Check Your Understanding

1. a. Panel (a) illustrates this relationship. The higher price of movies causes consumers to see fewer movies. The relationship is negative, and the slope is therefore negative. The price of movies is the independent variable, and the number of movies seen is the dependent variable. However, there is a convention in economics that, if price is a variable, it is measured on the vertical axis. So the quantity of movies is measured on the horizontal axis.

b. Panel (c) illustrates this relationship. Since it is likely that firms would pay more to workers with more experience, then years of experience is the independent variable that would be shown on the horizontal axis, and the resulting income, the dependent variable, would be shown on the vertical axis. The slope is positive.

c. Panel (d) illustrates this relationship. With the temperature on the horizontal axis as the independent variable, and the consumption of hot dogs on the vertical axis as the dependent variable, we see that there is no change in hot dog consumption regardless of the temperature. The slope is zero.

d. Panel (c) illustrates this relationship. When the price of ice cream goes up, this causes consumers to choose a close alternative, frozen yogurt. The price of ice cream is the independent variable and the consumption of frozen yogurt is the dependent variable. However, there is a con-

vention in economics that, if price is a variable, it is measured on the vertical axis. The quantity of frozen yogurt that consumers buy is on the horizontal axis. The slope is positive.

e. Panel (d) illustrates this relationship. Because the intent is for diet books to influence the number of pounds lost, the number of diet books is the independent variable and belongs on the horizontal axis. The number of pounds lost is the dependent variable measured on the vertical axis. The absence of a discernable relationship between the number of diet books purchased and the weight loss of the average dieter results in a horizontal curve. The slope is zero.

f. Panel (b) illustrates this relationship. Although price is the independent variable and salt consumption the dependent variable, by convention the price appears on the vertical axis and the quantity of salt on the horizontal axis. Since salt consumption does not change regardless of the price, the curve is a vertical line, and the slope is infinity.

2. a. The income tax rate is the independent variable and is measured on the horizontal axis. Income tax revenue is the dependent variable and is measured on the vertical axis.

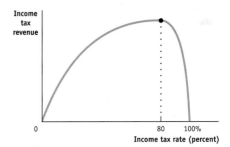

b. If the income tax rate is 0% (there is no tax), tax revenue is zero.

c. If the income tax rate is 100% (all of your income is taxed), you will have no income left after tax. Since people are unwilling to work if they receive no income after tax, no income will be earned. As a result, there is no income tax revenue.

d. For tax rates less than 80%, tax rate and tax revenue are positively related, so the Laffer curve has a positive slope. For tax rates higher than 80%, the relationship between tax rate and tax revenue is negative, so the Laffer curve has a negative slope. Therefore, the Laffer curve looks like the accompanying graph with a maximum point at a tax rate of 80%.

Module 5
Check Your Understanding

1. a. The quantity of umbrellas demanded is higher at any given price on a rainy day than on a dry day. This is a rightward *shift of* the demand curve, since at any given price the quantity demanded rises. This implies that any specific quantity can now be sold at a higher price.

b. The quantity of weekend calls demanded rises in response to a price reduction. This is a *movement along* the demand curve for weekend calls.

c. The demand for roses increases the week of Valentine's Day. This is a rightward *shift of* the demand curve.

d. The quantity of gasoline demanded falls in response to a rise in price. This is a *movement along* the demand curve.

Tackle the Test:
Multiple-Choice Questions

1. e
2. a
3. c
4. d
5. a

Tackle the Test:
Free-Response Question

2.

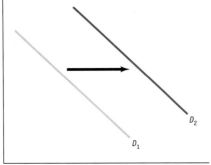

Price of apples

D_2

D_1

Quantity of apples

Module 6

Check Your Understanding

1. **a.** The quantity of houses supplied rises as a result of an increase in prices. This is a *movement along* the supply curve.

    b. The quantity of strawberries supplied is higher at any given price. This is an *increase in* supply, which shifts the supply curve to the right.

    c. The quantity of labor supplied is lower at any given wage. This is a *decrease in* supply, which shifts the supply curve leftward compared to the supply curve during school vacation. So, in order to attract workers, fast-food chains have to offer higher wages.

    d. The quantity of labor supplied rises in response to a rise in wages. This is a *movement along* the supply curve.

    e. The quantity of cabins supplied is higher at any given price. This is an *increase in* supply, which shifts the supply curve to the right.

2. **a.** This is an increase in supply, so the supply curve shifts rightward. At the original equilibrium price of the year before, the quantity of grapes supplied exceeds the quantity demanded, and the result is a surplus. The price of grapes will fall.

    b. This is a decrease in demand, so the demand curve shifts leftward. At the original equilibrium price, the quantity of hotel rooms supplied exceeds the quantity demanded. The result is a surplus. The rates for hotel rooms will fall.

c. Demand increases, so the demand curve for second-hand snowblowers shifts rightward. At the original equilibrium price, the quantity of second-hand snowblowers demanded exceeds the quantity supplied. This is a case of shortage. The equilibrium price of second-hand snowblowers will rise.

Tackle the Test:
Multiple-Choice Questions

1. d
2. d
3. c
4. b
5. d

Tackle the Test:
Free-Response Question

2.

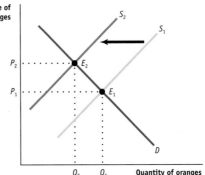

Price of oranges

S_2

S_1

P_2 E_2

P_1 E_1

D

Q_2 Q_1 Quantity of oranges

Module 7

Check Your Understanding

1. **a.** The decrease in the price of gasoline caused a rightward shift in the demand for large cars. As a result of the shift, the equilibrium price of large cars rose and the equilibrium quantity of large cars bought and sold also rose.

    b. The technological innovation has caused a rightward shift in the supply of fresh paper made from recycled stock. As a result of this shift, the equilibrium price of fresh paper made from recycled stock has fallen and the equilibrium quantity bought and sold has risen.

    c. The fall in the price of pay-per-view movies causes a leftward shift in the demand for movies at local movie theaters. As a result of this shift, the equilibrium price of movie tickets falls and the equilibrium number of people who go to the movies also falls.

2. Upon the announcement of the new chip, the demand curve for computers using the earlier chip shifts leftward (demand decreases), and the supply curve for these computers shifts rightward (supply increases).

    a. If demand decreases relatively more than supply increases, then the equilibrium quantity falls, as shown here:

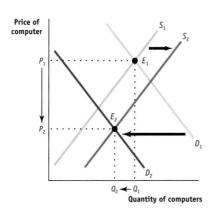

b. If supply increases relatively more than demand decreases, then the equilibrium quantity rises, as shown here:

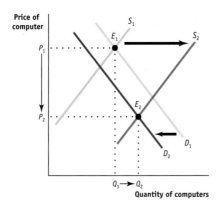

In both cases, the equilibrium price falls.

Tackle the Test:
Multiple-Choice Questions

1. d
2. b
3. a
4. a
5. c

Tackle the Test:
Free-Response Question

2.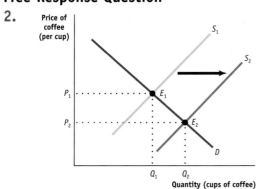

Module 8
Check Your Understanding

1.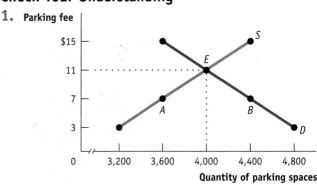

a. Fewer homeowners are willing to rent out their driveways because the price ceiling has reduced the payment they receive. This is an example of a fall in price leading to a fall in the quantity supplied. This is shown in the accompanying diagram by the movement from point E to point A along the supply curve, a reduction in quantity of 400 parking spaces.

b. The quantity demanded increases by 400 spaces as the price decreases. At a lower price, more fans are willing to drive and rent a parking space. It is shown in the diagram by the movement from point E to point B along the demand curve.

c. Under a price ceiling, the quantity demanded exceeds the quantity supplied; as a result, shortages arise. In this case, there will be a shortage of 800 parking spaces. It is shown by the horizontal distance between points A and B.

d. Price ceilings result in wasted resources. The additional time fans spend to guarantee a parking space is wasted time.

e. Price ceilings lead to the inefficient allocation of goods—here, the parking spaces—to consumers. If less serious fans with connections end up with the parking spaces, diehard fans have no place to park.

f. Price ceilings lead to black markets.

2. **a.** False. By lowering the price that producers receive, a price ceiling leads to a decrease in the quantity supplied.

b. True. A price ceiling leads to a lower quantity supplied than in an efficient, unregulated market. As a result, some people who would have been willing to pay the market price, and so would have gotten the good in an unregulated market, are unable to obtain it when a price ceiling is imposed.

c. True. Those producers who still sell the product now receive less for it and are therefore worse off. Other producers will no longer find it worthwhile to sell the product at all and so will also be made worse off.

3.

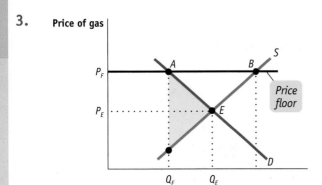

Quantity of gas

a. Some gas station owners will benefit from getting a higher price. Q_F indicates the sales made by these owners. But some will lose; there are those who make sales at the market equilibrium price of P_E but do not make sales at the regulated price of P_F. These missed sales are indicated on the graph by the fall in the quantity demanded along the demand curve, from point E to point A.

b. Those who buy gas at the higher price of P_F will probably receive better service; this is an example of *inefficiently high quality* caused by a price floor as gas station owners compete on quality rather than price. But opponents are correct to claim that consumers are generally worse off—those who buy at P_F would have been happy to buy at P_E, and many who were willing to buy at a price between P_E and P_F are now unwilling to buy. This is indicated on the graph by the fall in the quantity demanded along the demand curve, from point E to point A.

c. Proponents are wrong because consumers and some gas station owners are hurt by the price floor, which creates "missed opportunities"—desirable transactions between consumers and station owners that never take place. The deadweight loss, the net gains forgone because of missed opportunities, is indicated by the shaded area in the accompanying figure. Moreover, the inefficiency of wasted resources arises as consumers spend time and money driving to other states. The price floor also tempts people to engage in black market activity. With the price floor, only Q_F units are sold. But at prices between P_E and P_F, there are drivers who together want to buy more than Q_F and owners who are willing to sell to them, a situation likely to lead to illegal activity.

Tackle the Test:
Multiple-Choice Questions

1. e
2. b
3. e
4. b
5. c

Tackle the Test:
Free-Response Question

2.

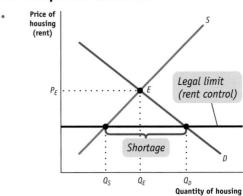

Quantity of housing

Module 9

Check Your Understanding

1. a. The price of a ride is $7 since the quantity demanded at this price is 6 million: $7 is the *demand price* of 6 million rides. This is represented by point A in the accompanying figure.

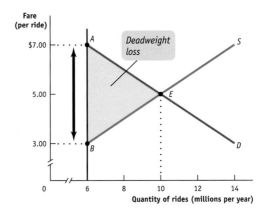

b. At 6 million rides, the supply price is $3 per ride, represented by point B in the figure. The wedge between the demand price of $7 per ride and the supply price of $3 per ride is the quota rent per ride, $4. This is represented in the figure above by the vertical distance between points A and B.

c. The quota discourages 4 million mutually beneficial transactions. The shaded triangle in the figure represents the deadweight loss.

d. At 9 million rides, the demand price is $5.50 per ride, indicated by point C in the accompanying figure, and the supply price is $4.50 per ride, indicated by point D. The quota rent is the difference between the demand price and the supply price: $1. The deadweight loss is represented by the shaded triangle in the figure. As you can see, the deadweight loss is smaller when the quota is set at 9 million rides than when it is set at 6 million rides.

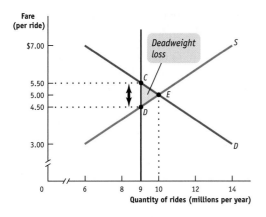

Tackle the Test:
Free-Response Question

2.

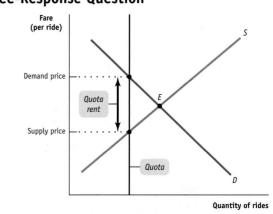

2. The accompanying figure shows a decrease in demand by 4 million rides, represented by a leftward shift of the demand curve from D_1 to D_2: at any given price, the quantity demanded falls by 4 million rides. (For example, at a price of $5, the quantity demanded falls from 10 million to 6 million rides per year.) This eliminates the effect of a quota limit of 8 million rides. At point E_2, the new market equilibrium, the equilibrium quantity is equal to the quota limit; as a result, the quota has no effect on the market.

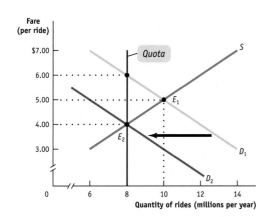

Tackle the Test:
Multiple-Choice Questions

1. d
2. b
3. b
4. d
5. a

Module 10
Check Your Understanding

1. Let's start by considering the relationship between the total value added of all domestically produced final goods and services, and aggregate spending on domestically produced final goods and services. These two quantities are equal because every final good and service produced in the economy is either purchased by someone or added to inventories, and additions to inventories are counted as spending by firms. Next, consider the relationship between aggregate spending on domestically produced final goods and services and total factor income. These two quantities are equal because all spending that is channeled to firms to pay for purchases of domestically produced final goods and services is revenue for firms. Those revenues must be paid out by firms to their factors of production in the form of wages, profit, interest, and rent. Taken together, this means that all three methods of calculating GDP are equivalent.

2. Firms make sales to other firms, households, the government, and the rest of the world. Households are linked to firms through the sale of factors of production to firms, through purchases from firms of final goods and services, and through lending funds to firms in the financial markets. Households are linked to the government through their payment of taxes, their receipt of transfers, and their lending of funds to the government to finance government borrowing via the financial markets. Finally, households are linked to the rest of the world through their purchases of imports and transactions with foreigners in financial markets.

3. You would be counting the value of the steel twice—once as it was sold by American Steel to American Motors and once as part of the car sold by American Motors.

Tackle the Test:
Multiple-Choice Questions

1. c
2. e

3. a

4. b

5. a

Tackle the Test:
Free-Response Question

2. This diagram should resemble Figure 10.1 plus the top half (the Government section) of Figure 10.2. The leakages in this scenario are taxes and private savings that feed into government borrowing and the injections are government purchases of goods and services and government transfers.

Module 11
Check Your Understanding

1. a. In 2009 nominal GDP was $(1,000,000 \times \$0.40) + (800,000 \times \$0.60) = \$400,000 + \$480,000 = \$880,000$. The total value of sales of french fries in 2010 was $900,000 \times \$0.50 = \$450,000$. The total value of sales of onion rings in 2010 was $840,000 \times \$0.51 = \$428,400$. Nominal GDP in 2010 was $\$450,000 + \$428,400 = \$878,400$. To find real GDP in 2010, we must calculate the value of sales in 2010 using 2009 prices: $(900,000 \times \$0.40) + (840,000 \times \$0.60) = \$360,000 + \$504,000 = \$864,000$.

    b. A comparison of nominal GDP in 2009 to nominal GDP in 2010 shows a decline of $((\$880,000 - \$878,400) / \$880,000) \times 100 = 0.18\%$. But a comparison using real GDP shows a decline of $((\$880,000 - \$864,000) / \$880,000) \times 100 = 1.8\%$. That is, a calculation based on real GDP shows a drop 10 times larger (1.8%) than a calculation based on nominal GDP (0.18%): in this case, the calculation based on nominal GDP underestimates the true magnitude of the change because it incorporates both quantity changes and price changes.

2. A price index based on 1990 prices will contain a relatively low price of housing compared to a price index based on 2000 prices. This means that a 2000 price index used to calculate real GDP in 2010 will magnify the value of housing production in the economy and increase the relative size of the housing sector as a component of real GDP.

Tackle the Test:
Multiple-Choice Questions

1. d

2. b

3. c

4. c

5. c

Tackle the Test:
Free-Response Question

2. a. Country A: $(4,000-2,000/2,000) \times 100 = 100\%$
Country B: $(6,000-2,000/2,000) \times 100 = 200\%$

    b. Country A: It stayed the same.
Country B: It doubled.

    c. Country A: $4,000 (There was no price increase so it is the same.)
Country B: $6,000/2 = $3,000 (Prices doubled.)

    d. Country A: $(4,000-2,000/2,000) \times 100 = 100\%$
Country B: $(3,000-2,000/2,000) \times 100 = 50\%$

    e. Country A: $4,000/20 = \$200$ versus Country B: $3,000/15 = \$200$. It is the same.

Module 12
Check Your Understanding

1. The advent of websites that enable job-seekers to find jobs more quickly will reduce the unemployment rate over time. However, websites that induce discouraged workers to begin actively looking for work again will lead to an increase in the unemployment rate over time.

2. a. Not counted as unemployed because not actively looking for work, but counted in broader measures of labor underutilization as a discouraged worker.

    b. Not counted as unemployed—considered employed because the teacher has a job.

    c. Unemployed: not working, actively looking for work.

    d. Not unemployed, but underemployed: working part-time for economic reasons. Counted in broader measures of labor underutilization.

    e. Not unemployed, but considered "marginally attached." Counted in broader measures of labor underutilization.

3. Items (a) and (b) are consistent with the observed relationship between growth in GDP and changes in the unemployment rate. Item (c) is not.

Tackle the Test:
Multiple-Choice Questions

1. e

2. b

3. a

4. d

5. b

Tackle the Test:
Free-Response Questions

2. a. Employed (underemployed); she is not working up to her full potential.

    b. Not in the labor force (discouraged). Once a worker stops actively seeking work, he or she falls out of the labor force.

    c. Employed (part-time); individuals are classified as employed if they work full or part time.

    d. Not in the labor force; he is not actively seeking employment.

Module 13
Check Your Understanding

1. a. Frictional unemployment is unemployment due to the time workers spend searching for jobs. It is inevitable because workers may leave one job in search of another for a variety of reasons. Furthermore, there will always be new entrants into the labor force who are seeking a first job. During the search process, these individuals will be counted as part of the frictionally unemployed.

b. When the unemployment rate is low, frictional unemployment will account for a larger share of total unemployment because other sources of unemployment will be diminished. So the share of total unemployment composed of the frictionally unemployed will rise.

2. A binding minimum wage represents a price floor below which wages cannot fall. As a result, actual wages cannot move toward equilibrium. So a minimum wage causes the quantity of labor supplied to exceed the quantity of labor demanded. Because this surplus of labor reflects unemployed workers, it affects the unemployment rate. Collective bargaining has a similar effect—unions are able to raise the wage above the equilibrium level. This will act like a minimum wage by causing the number of job seekers to be larger than the number of workers firms are willing to hire. Collective bargaining causes the unemployment rate to be higher than it otherwise would be, as shown in the accompanying figure.

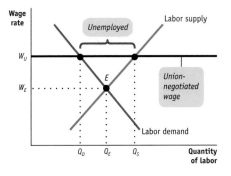

3. An increase in unemployment benefits reduces the cost to individuals of being unemployed, causing them to spend more time searching for a new job. So the natural rate of unemployment would increase.

Tackle the Test:
Multiple-Choice Questions

1. a
2. c
3. b
4. d
5. e

Tackle the Test:
Free-Response Question

2. **a.** Frictional. Melanie is between jobs.
   b. Structural. Melanie is unemployed because wages are not at the market equilibrium.
   c. Cyclical. Melanie is unemployed due to an economic slowdown (recession).

Module 14
Check Your Understanding

1. Shoe-leather costs as a result of inflation will be lower because it is now less costly for individuals to manage their assets in order to economize on their money hold-ings. ATM machines, for example, give customers 24-hour access to cash in thousands of locations. This reduction in the cost of obtaining money translates into lower shoe-leather costs.

2. If inflation came to a complete stop for several years, the inflation rate of zero would be less than the expected inflation rate of 2–3%. Because the real interest rate is the nominal interest rate minus the inflation rate, the real interest rates on loans would be higher than expected, and lenders would gain at the expense of borrowers. Borrowers would have to repay their loans with funds that had a higher real value than had been expected.

Tackle the Test:
Multiple-Choice Questions

1. e
2. c
3. b
4. d
5. c

Tackle the Test:
Free-Response Question

2. **a.** 0%
   b. You borrowed enough money to buy a couch and paid back just enough to buy the same couch (after inflation). Therefore, you gained the benefit of the loan without paying any real interest for it.
   c. Whoever gave you the loan lost. The loan was paid back after prices unexpectedly increased, so the lender received a real interest rate of 0% for letting you use the money for a year.

Module 15
Check Your Understanding

1. Pre–frost, this market basket costs $(100 \times \$0.20) + (50 \times \$0.60) + (200 \times \$0.25) = \$20 + \$30 + \$50 = \$100$. The same market basket, post-frost, costs $(100 \times \$0.40) + (50 \times \$1.00) + (200 \times \$0.45) = \$40 + \$50 + \$90 = \$180$. So the price index is $(\$100/\$100) \times 100 = 100$ before the frost and $(\$180/\$100) \times 100 = 180$ after the frost, implying a rise in the price index of 80%. This increase in the price index is less than the 84.2% increase calculated in the text. The reason for this difference is that the new market basket of 100 oranges, 50 grapefruit, and 200 lemons contains proportionately more of an item that has experienced a relatively small price increase (the lemons, the price of which has increased by 80%) and proportionately fewer of an item that has experienced a relatively large price increase (the oranges, the price of which has increased by 100%). This shows that the price index can be very sensitive to the composition of the market basket. If the market basket contains a large proportion of goods whose prices have risen faster than the prices of other goods, it will lead to a higher estimate of the increase in the price level. If it contains a large proportion of goods whose prices have risen more slowly than the prices of other goods, it will lead to a lower estimate of the increase in the price level.

2. a. A market basket determined 10 years ago will contain fewer cars than at present. Given that the average price of a car has grown faster than the average prices of other goods, this basket will underestimate the true increase in the price level because it contains relatively too few cars.

b. A market basket determined 10 years ago will not contain broadband Internet access, so it cannot track the fall in prices of Internet access over the past few years. As a result, it will overestimate the true increase in the price level.

3. Using Equation 15-2, the inflation rate from 2006 to 2007 is $(207.3 - 201.6)/201.6 \times 100 = 2.8\%$.

Tackle the Test:
Multiple-Choice Questions

1. d
2. c
3. e
4. b
5. b

Tackle the Test:
Free-Response Question

2.

	GDP Deflator	CPI
2004–05:	$(3.2/96.8) \times 100 = 3.3\%$	$(6.4/188.9) \times 100 = 3.4\%$
2005–06:	$(3.3/100.0) \times 100 = 3.3\%$	$(6.3/195.3) \times 100 = 3.2\%$

Module 16
Check Your Understanding

1. A decline in investment spending, like a rise in investment spending, has a multiplier effect on real GDP—the only difference in this case is that real GDP falls instead of rises. The fall in I leads to an initial fall in real GDP, which leads to a fall in disposable income (because less production means a decrease in payments to workers), which leads to lower consumer spending, which leads to another fall in real GDP, and so on. So consumer spending falls as an indirect result of the fall in investment spending.

2. When MPC is 0.5, the multiplier is equal to $1/(1 - 0.5) = 1/0.5 = 2$. When MPC is 0.8, the multiplier is equal to $1/(1 - 0.8) = 1/0.2 = 5$.

3. If you expect your future disposable income to fall, you would like to save some of today's disposable income to tide you over in the future. But you cannot do this if you cannot save. If you expect your future disposable income to rise, you would like to spend some of tomorrow's higher income today. But you cannot do this if you cannot borrow. If you cannot save or borrow, your expected future disposable income will have no effect on your consumer spending today. In fact, your MPC must always equal 1: you must consume all your current disposable income today, and you will be unable to smooth your consumption over time.

4. a. An unexpected increase in consumer spending will result in a reduction in inventories as producers sell items from their inventories to satisfy this short-term increase in demand. This is negative unplanned inventory investment: it reduces the value of producers' inventories.

b. A rise in the cost of borrowing is equivalent to a rise in the interest rate: fewer investment spending projects are now profitable to producers, whether they are financed through borrowing or retained earnings. As a result, producers will reduce the amount of planned investment spending.

c. A sharp increase in the rate of real GDP growth leads to a higher level of planned investment spending by producers as they increase production capacity to meet higher demand.

d. As sales fall, producers sell less, and their inventories grow. This leads to positive unplanned inventory investment.

Tackle the Test:
Multiple-Choice Questions

1. d
2. c
3. b
4. d
5. a

Tackle the Test:
Free-Response Question

2. 1. The interest rate is the price (or opportunity cost) of investing, thus they are negatively related.

2. Expected future real GDP—if a firm expects its sales to grow rapidly in the future, it will invest in expanded production capacity.

3. Production capacity—if a firm finds its existing production capacity insufficient for its future production needs, it will undertake investment spending to meet those needs.

Module 17
Check Your Understanding

1. a. This is a shift of the aggregate demand curve. A decrease in the quantity of money raises the interest rate, since people now want to borrow more and lend less. A higher interest rate reduces investment and consumer spending at any given aggregate price level, so the aggregate demand curve shifts to the left.

b. This is a movement up along the aggregate demand curve. As the aggregate price level rises, the real value of money holdings falls. This is the interest rate effect of a change in the aggregate price level: as the value of money falls, people want to hold more money. They do so by borrowing more and lending less. This leads to a rise in the interest rate and a reduction in consumer and investment spending. So it is a movement along the aggregate demand curve.

c. This is a shift of the aggregate demand curve. Expectations of a poor job market, and so lower average disposable incomes, will reduce people's consumer spending today at any given aggregate price level. So the aggregate demand curve shifts to the left.

d. This is a shift of the aggregate demand curve. A fall in tax rates raises people's disposable income. At any given aggregate price level, consumer spending is now higher. So the aggregate demand curve shifts to the right.

e. This is a movement down along the aggregate demand curve. As the aggregate price level falls, the real value of assets rises. This is the wealth effect of a change in the aggregate price level: as the value of assets rises, people will increase their consumption plans. This leads to higher consumer spending. So it is a movement along the aggregate demand curve.

f. This is a shift of the aggregate demand curve. A rise in the real value of assets in the economy due to a surge in real estate values raises consumer spending at any given aggregate price level. So the aggregate demand curve shifts to the right.

Tackle the Test:
Multiple-Choice Questions

1. d
2. c
3. c
4. a
5. a

Tackle the Test:
Free-Response Question

2. The two effects that cause the aggregate demand curve to have a downward slope are the wealth effect and the interest rate effect of a change in the aggregate price level.

The wealth effect: When the price level increases, the purchasing power of money decreases, causing consumers to scale back on spending. Because consumer spending is a component of aggregate demand, increases in the aggregate price level lead to decreases in the quantity of aggregate output demanded. The opposite is true for decreases in the price level. This negative relationship between the price level and the quantity of aggregate output demanded results in a downward-sloping aggregate demand curve.

The interest rate effect: Increases in the aggregate price level cause people to want to hold more money, which increases the demand for money and drives interest rates up. Higher interest rates reduce investment spending because it costs more to borrow money. Thus, a rise in the price level leads to less investment spending, which is a component of aggregate demand, and causes the quantity of aggregate output demanded to decrease (and vice versa). The result is a downward-sloping aggregate demand curve.

Module 18

Check Your Understanding

1. a. This represents a movement along the SRAS curve because the CPI—like the GDP deflator—is a measure of the aggregate price level, the overall price level of final goods and services in the economy.

b. This represents a shift of the SRAS curve because oil is a commodity. The SRAS curve will shift to the right because production costs are now lower, leading to a higher quantity of aggregate output supplied at any given aggregate price level.

c. This represents a shift of the SRAS curve because it involves a change in nominal wages. An increase in legally mandated benefits to workers is equivalent to an

increase in nominal wages. As a result, the SRAS curve will shift leftward because production costs are now higher, leading to a lower quantity of aggregate output supplied at any given aggregate price level.

2. You would need to know what happened to the aggregate price level. If the increase in the quantity of aggregate output supplied was due to a movement along the SRAS curve, the aggregate price level would have increased at the same time as the quantity of aggregate output supplied increased. If the increase in the quantity of aggregate output supplied was due to a rightward shift of the LRAS curve, the aggregate price level might not rise. Alternatively, you could make the determination by observing what happened to aggregate output in the long run. If it fell back to its initial level in the long run, then the temporary increase in aggregate output was due to a movement along the SRAS curve. If it stayed at the higher level in the long run, the increase in aggregate output was due to a rightward shift of the LRAS curve.

Tackle the Test:
Multiple-Choice Questions

1. e
2. a
3. c
4. d
5. e

Tackle the Test:
Free-Response Questions

2. a. The vertical axis should be labeled "Aggregate price level" (or "Price level"), the horizontal axis should be labeled "Real GDP" and the graph should show an upward sloping curve labeled "SRAS."

b. SRAS shifts to the left.

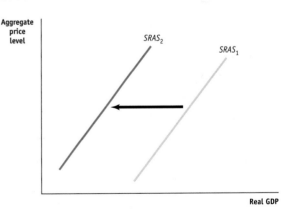

c. an increase in commodity prices, an increase in nominal wages, and a decrease in productivity

Module 19

Check Your Understanding

1. a. An increase in the minimum wage raises the nominal wage and, as a result, shifts the short-run aggregate supply curve to the left. As a result of this negative supply

shock, the aggregate price level rises and aggregate output falls.

b. Increased investment spending shifts the aggregate demand curve to the right. As a result of this positive demand shock, both the aggregate price level and aggregate output rise.

c. An increase in taxes and a reduction in government spending both result in negative demand shocks, shifting the aggregate demand curve to the left. As a result, both the aggregate price level and aggregate output fall.

d. This is a negative supply shock, shifting the short-run aggregate supply curve to the left. As a result, the aggregate price level rises and aggregate output falls.

2. As long-run growth increases potential output, the long-run aggregate supply curve shifts to the right. If, in the short run, there is now a recessionary gap (aggregate output is less than potential output), nominal wages will fall, shifting the short-run aggregate supply curve to the right. This results in a fall in the aggregate price level and a rise in aggregate output. As prices fall, we move along the aggregate demand curve due to the wealth and interest rate effects of a change in the aggregate price level. Eventually, as long-run macroeconomic equilibrium is reestablished, aggregate output will rise to be equal to potential output, and the aggregate price level will fall to the level that equates the quantity of aggregate output demanded with potential output.

Tackle the Test:
Multiple-Choice Questions

1. c
2. a
3. d
4. b
5. b

Tackle the Test:
Free-Response Question

2.

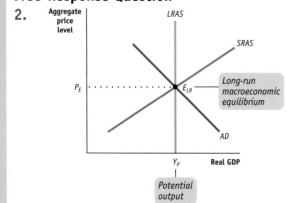

Module 20

Check Your Understanding

1. **a.** This is a contractionary fiscal policy because it is a reduction in government purchases of goods and services.

b. This is an expansionary fiscal policy because it is an increase in government transfers that will increase disposable income.

c. This is a contractionary fiscal policy because it is an increase in taxes, which will reduce disposable income.

2. Federal disaster relief that is quickly disbursed is more effective at stabilizing the economy than legislated aid because there is very little time lag between the time of the disaster and the time when relief is received by victims. In contrast, the process of creating new legislation is relatively slow, so legislated aid is likely to entail a time lag in its disbursement, potentially destabilizing the economy.

3. **a.** An economy is overstimulated when an inflationary gap is present. This will arise if an expansionary monetary or fiscal policy is implemented when the economy is currently in long-run macroeconomic equilibrium. This shifts the aggregate demand curve to the right, in the short run raising the aggregate price level and aggregate output and creating an inflationary gap. Eventually, nominal wages will rise and shift the short-run aggregate supply curve to the left, and aggregate output will fall back to potential output. This is the scenario envisaged by the speaker.

b. No, this is not a valid argument. When the economy is not currently in long-run macroeconomic equilibrium, an expansionary monetary or fiscal policy does not lead to the outcome described above. Suppose a negative demand shock has shifted the aggregate demand curve to the left, resulting in a recessionary gap. An expansionary monetary or fiscal policy can shift the aggregate demand curve back to its original position in long-run macroeconomic equilibrium. In this way, the short-run fall in aggregate output and deflation caused by the original negative demand shock can be avoided. So, if used in response to demand shocks, fiscal or monetary policy is an effective policy tool.

Tackle the Test:
Multiple-Choice Questions

1. e
2. e
3. b
4. b
5. a

Tackle the Test:
Free-Response Questions

2. **a.**

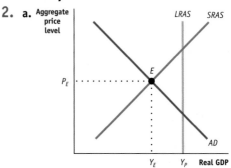

b. Expansionary

c. Decrease taxes, increase government purchases of goods and services, or increase government transfers

Module 21
Check Your Understanding

1. A $500 million increase in government purchases of goods and services directly increases aggregate spending by $500 million, which then starts the multiplier in motion. It will increase real GDP by $500 million × $1/(1 − MPC)$. A $500 million increase in government transfers increases aggregate spending only to the extent that it leads to an increase in consumer spending. Consumer spending rises by $MPC \times \$1$ for every $1 increase in disposable income, where MPC is less than 1. So a $500 million increase in government transfers will cause a rise in real GDP only MPC times as much as a $500 million increase in government purchases of goods and services. It will increase real GDP by $500 million × $MPC/(1 − MPC)$.

2. If government purchases of goods and services fall by $500 million, the initial fall in aggregate spending is $500 million. If there is a $500 million tax increase, the initial fall in aggregate spending is $MPC \times \$500$ million, which is less than $500 million because some of the tax payments are made with money that would otherwise have been saved rather than spent.

3. Boldovia will experience greater variation in its real GDP than Moldovia because Moldovia has automatic stabilizers while Boldovia does not. In Moldovia the effects of slumps will be lessened by unemployment insurance benefits, which will support residents' incomes, while the effects of booms will be diminished because tax revenues will go up. In contrast, incomes will not be supported in Boldovia during slumps because there is no unemployment insurance. In addition, because Boldovia has lump-sum taxes, its booms will not be diminished by increases in tax revenue.

Tackle the Test:
Multiple-Choice Questions

1. c
2. b
3. b
4. c
5. e

Tackle the Test:
Free-Response Questions

2. **a.** $50 million
   multiplier = $1/(1 − MPC) = 1/(1 − 0.75) = 1/0.25 = 4$
   change in G × 4 = $200 million
   change in G = $50 million
   b. 10
   $20 × multiplier = $200 million
   multiplier = 200/20 = 10
   c. 0.1
   $1/(1 − MPC) = 1/MPS = 10$
   MPS = 0.1

Module 22
Check Your Understanding

1. The transaction costs for (a) a bank deposit and (b) a share of a mutual fund are approximately equivalent because each can typically be accomplished by making a phone call, going online, or visiting a branch office. Transaction costs are highest for (c) a share of a family business since finding a buyer for the share consumes time and resources. The level of risk is lowest for (a) a bank deposit, since these deposits are insured by the Federal Deposit Insurance Corporation (FDIC) up to $250,000; somewhat higher for (b) a share of a mutual fund since despite diversification, there is still risk associated with holding stocks; and highest for (c) a share of a family business since this investment is not diversified. The level of liquidity is the lowest for (c) a share of a family business, since it can be sold only with the unanimous agreement of other members and it will take some time to find a buyer; higher for (b) a share of a mutual fund, since it will take only a few days between selling your shares and the payment being processed; and highest for (a) a bank deposit, since withdrawals can usually be made immediately.

2. Economic development and growth are the result of, among other factors, investment spending on physical capital. Since investment spending is equal to savings, the greater the amount saved, the higher investment spending will be, and so the higher growth and economic development will be. So the existence of institutions that facilitate savings will help a country's growth and economic development. As a result, a country with a financial system that provides low transaction costs, opportunities for diversification of risk, and high liquidity to its savers will experience faster growth and economic development than a country that doesn't.

Tackle the Test:
Multiple-Choice Questions

1. d
2. e
3. a
4. d
5. b

Tackle the Test:
Free-Response Questions

2. **Mutual fund**–a financial intermediary that creates a stock portfolio by buying and holding shares in companies and then selling *shares of the stock portfolio* to individual investors.
   Life insurance company–a firm that guarantees a payment to the policyholder's beneficiaries (typically, the family) when the policyholder dies.
   Bank–an institution that helps resolve the conflict between lenders' needs for liquidity and the illiquid financing needs of borrowers who don't want to use the stock or bond markets.
   Pension fund–a nonprofit institution that collects the savings of its members and invests those funds in a variety of assets, providing its members with income when they retire.

Module 23

Check Your Understanding

1. The defining characteristic of money is its liquidity: how easily it can be used to purchase goods and services. Although a gift certificate can easily be used to purchase a very defined set of goods or services (the goods or services available at the store issuing the gift certificate), it cannot be used to purchase any other goods or services. A gift certificate is therefore not money since it cannot easily be used to purchase all goods or services.

2. Again, the important characteristic of money is its liquidity: how easily it can be used to purchase goods and services. M1, the narrowest definition of the money supply, consists only of currency in circulation, traveler's checks, and checkable bank deposits. CDs aren't checkable–and they can't be made checkable without incurring a cost because there's a penalty for early withdrawal. This makes them less liquid than the assets counted in M1.

3. Commodity-backed money uses resources more efficiently than simple commodity money, like gold and silver coins, because commodity-backed money ties up fewer valuable resources. Although a bank must keep some of the commodity—generally gold and silver—on hand, it has to keep only enough to satisfy demand for redemptions. It can then lend out the remaining gold and silver, which allows society to use these resources for other purposes, with no loss in the ability to achieve gains from trade.

Tackle the Test:
Multiple-Choice Questions

1. d
2. c
3. e
4. a
5. b

Tackle the Test:
Free-Response Questions

2. **a.** its official status given by the U.S. government
b. fiat money
c. commodity money–money that has intrinsic value in other uses.
Commodity-backed money–money that has no intrinsic value but can be converted into valuable goods on demand.

Module 24

Check Your Understanding

1. **a.** The net present value of project A is unaffected by the interest rate since it is money received today; its present value is still $100. The net present value of project B is now $-10 + \$115/1.02 = \$102.75$. The net present value of project C is now $119 - \$20/1.02 = \$99.39$. Project B is now preferred.
b. When the interest rate is lower, the cost of waiting for money that arrives in the future is lower. For example, at a 10% interest rate, $1 arriving one year from today is

worth only $\$1/1.10 = \$0.91$. But when the interest rate is 2%, $1 arriving one year from today is worth $\$1/1.02 = \$0.98$, a sizable increase. As a result, project B, which has a benefit one year from today, becomes more attractive. And project C, which has a cost one year from today, becomes less attractive.

Tackle the Test:
Multiple-Choice Questions

1. e
2. b
3. c
4. d
5. b

Tackle the Test:
Free-Response Questions

2. **a.** $\$1,000 \times (1.05)^3 = \$1,000 \times 1.16 = \$1,157.63$
b. $\$1,000/(1.05)^3 = \$863.84$

Module 25

Check Your Understanding

1. Even though you know that the rumor about the bank is not true, you are concerned about other depositors pulling their money out of the bank. And you know that if enough other depositors pull their money out, the bank will fail. In that case, it is rational for you to pull your money out before the bank fails. All depositors will think like this, so even if they all know that the rumor is false, they may still rationally pull their money out, leading to a bank run. Deposit insurance leads depositors to worry less about the possibility of a bank run. Even if a bank fails, the FDIC will currently pay each depositor up to $250,000 per account. This will make you much less likely to pull your money out in response to a rumor. Since other depositors will think the same, there will be no bank run.

2. The aspects of modern bank regulation that would frustrate this scheme are *capital requirements* and *reserve requirements*. Capital requirements mean that a bank has to have a certain amount of capital—the difference between its assets (loans plus reserves) and its liabilities (deposits). So the con artist could not open a bank without putting any of his own wealth in because his bank would need the required amount of capital—that is, it needs to hold more assets (loans plus reserves) than deposits. So the con artist would be at risk of losing his own wealth if his loans turn out badly.

3. Since they have to hold only $100 in reserves, instead of $200, banks now lend out $100 of their reserves. Whoever borrows the $100 will deposit it in a bank (or spend it, and the recipient will deposit it in a bank), which will lend out $100 \times (1 - rr) = \$100 \times 0.9 = \$90$. The borrowed $90 will likewise find its way into a bank, which will lend out $90 \times 0.9 = \$81$, and so on. Overall, deposits will increase by $100/0.1 = \$1,000$.

4. Silas puts $1,000 in the bank, of which the bank lends out $1,000 \times (1 - rr) = \$1,000 \times 0.9 = \$900$. Whoever borrows the $900 will keep $450 in cash and deposit $450 in the bank. The bank will lend out $450 × 0.9 = $405. Whoever borrows the $405 will keep $202.50 in cash and deposit $202.50 in the bank. The bank will lend out $202.50 × 0.9 = $182.25, and so on. Overall this leads to an increase in deposits of $1,000 + $450 + $202.50 + . . . But it decreases the amount of currency in circulation: the amount of cash is reduced by the $1,000 Silas puts into the bank. This is offset, but not fully, by the amount of cash held by each borrower. The amount of currency in circulation therefore changes by –$1,000 + $450 + $202.50 + . . . The money supply therefore increases by the sum of the increase in deposits and the change in currency in circulation, which is $1,000 – $1,000 + $450 + $450 + $202.50 + $202.50 + . . . and so on.

Tackle the Test:
Multiple-Choice Questions

1. d
2. a
3. e
4. c
5. d

Tackle the Test:
Free-Response Questions

2. a. The bank must hold $5,000 as required reserves (5% of $100,000). It is holding $10,000, so $5,000 must be excess reserves.
    b. The bank must hold an additional $50 as reserves because that is the reserve requirement multiplied by the deposit: 5% of $1,000. The bank can lend out $950.
    c. The money multiplier is 1/0.05 = 20. An increase of $2,000 in excess reserves can increase the money supply by $2,000 × 20 = $40,000.

Module 26
Check Your Understanding

1. The Panic of 1907, the S&L crisis, and the crisis of 2008 all involved losses by financial institutions that were less regulated than banks. In the crises of 1907 and 2008, there was a widespread loss of confidence in the financial sector and collapse of credit markets. Like the crisis of 1907 and the S&L crisis, the crisis of 2008 exerted a powerful negative effect on the economy.

2. The creation of the Federal Reserve failed to prevent bank runs because it did not eradicate the fears of depositors that a bank collapse would cause them to lose their money. The bank run eventually stopped after federal deposit insurance was instituted and the public came to understand that their deposits were protected.

3. The balance sheet effect occurs when asset sales cause declines in asset prices, which then reduce the value of other firms' net worth as the value of the assets on their balance sheets declines. In the vicious cycle of deleveraging, the balance sheet effect on firms forces their creditors to call in their loan contracts, forcing the firms to sell assets

to pay back their loans, leading to further asset sales and price declines. Because the vicious cycle of deleveraging occurs across different firms and no single firm can stop it, it is necessary for the government to step in to stop it.

Tackle the Test:
Multiple-Choice Questions

1. a
2. a
3. b
4. d
5. e

Tackle the Test:
Free-Response Questions

2. a. oversee the Federal Reserve System and serve on the Federal Open Market Committee
    b. 7
    c. the president of the United States
    d. 14-year terms
    e. to insulate appointees from political pressure
    f. 4 years; may be reappointed

Module 27
Check Your Understanding

1. An open-market purchase of $100 million by the Fed increases banks' reserves by $100 million as the Fed credits their accounts with additional reserves. In other words, this open-market purchase increases the monetary base (currency in circulation plus bank reserves) by $100 million. Banks lend out the additional $100 million. Whoever borrows the money puts it back into the banking system in the form of deposits. Of these deposits, banks lend out $100 million × (1 – rr) = $100 million × 0.9 = $90 million. Whoever borrows the money deposits it back into the banking system. And banks lend out $90 million × 0.9 = $81 million, and so on. As a result, bank deposits increased by $100 million + $90 million + $81 million + . . . = $100 million/rr = $100 million/0.1 = $1,000 million = $1 billion. Since in this simplified example all money lent out is deposited back into the banking system, there is no increase of currency in circulation, so the increase in bank deposits is equal to the increase in the money supply. In other words, the money supply increases by $1 billion. This is greater than the increase in the monetary base by a factor of 10: in this simplified model in which deposits are the only component of the money supply and in which banks hold no excess reserves, the money multiplier is 1/rr = 10.

Tackle the Test:
Multiple-Choice Questions

1. d
2. e
3. d
4. b
5. c

Tackle the Test:
Free-Response Question

2. 1) provide financial services to depository institutions—regional Federal Reserve banks
    2) supervise and regulate banking institutions—regional Federal Reserve banks and the Board of Governors
    3) maintain the stability of the financial system—the Board of Governors
    4) conduct monetary policy—the Federal Open Market Committee

Module 28

Check Your Understanding

1. **a.** By increasing the opportunity cost of holding money, a high interest rate reduces the quantity of money demanded. This is a movement up and to the left along the money demand curve.
    b. A 10% fall in prices reduces the quantity of money demanded at any given interest rate, shifting the money demand curve leftward.
    c. This technological change reduces the quantity of money demanded at any given interest rate, so it shifts the money demand curve leftward.
    d. Payments in cash require employers to hold more money, increasing the quantity of money demanded at any given interest rate. So it shifts the money demand curve rightward.

2. **a.** A 1% purchase fee on debit/credit card transactions for purchases less than $50 increases the benefit of holding cash because consumers will save money by paying with cash.
    b. An increase in the interest paid on six-month CDs raises the opportunity cost of holding cash because holding cash requires forgoing the higher interest paid.
    c. A fall in real estate prices has no effect on the opportunity cost or benefit of holding cash because real estate is an illiquid asset and therefore isn't relevant in the decision of how much cash to hold. Also, real estate transactions are generally not carried out using cash.
    d. Because many purchases of food are made in cash, a significant increase in the cost of food increases the benefit of holding cash.

Tackle the Test:
Multiple-Choice Questions

1. d
2. d
3. b
4. d
5. e

Tackle the Test:
Free-Response Question

2.

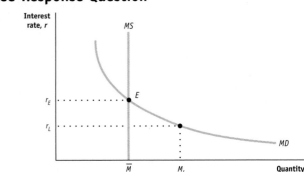

At an interest rate below equilibrium, the quantity of money demanded exceeds the quantity of money supplied. People want to shift more of their wealth out of interest-bearing assets such as CDs and hold it as money instead. Because the quantity of interest-bearing nonmoney assets demanded is less than the quantity supplied, those trying to sell these assets will have to offer a higher interest rate to attract buyers. As the interest rate rises, the quantity of money demanded decreases. This process continues until the market returns to equilibrium.

Module 29

Check Your Understanding

1. **a.** As capital flows into the economy, the supply of loanable funds increases. This is illustrated by the shift of the supply curve from S_1 to S_2 in the accompanying diagram. As the equilibrium moves from E_1 to E_2, the equilibrium interest rate falls from r_1 to r_2, and the equilibrium quantity of loanable funds increases from Q_1 to Q_2.

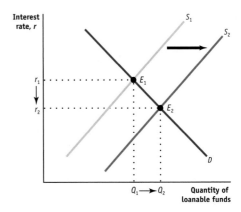

    b. Savings fall due to the higher proportion of retired people, and the supply of loanable funds decreases. This is illustrated by the leftward shift of the supply curve from S_1 to S_2 in the accompanying diagram. The equilibrium moves from E_1 to E_2, the equilibrium interest rate rises from r_1 to r_2, and the equilibrium quantity of loanable funds falls from Q_1 to Q_2.

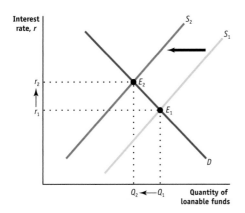

2. We know from the loanable funds market that as the interest rate rises, households want to save more and consume less. But at the same time, an increase in the interest rate lowers the number of investment spending projects with returns at least as high as the interest rate. The statement "households will want to save more money than businesses will want to invest" cannot represent an equilibrium in the loanable funds market because it says that the quantity of loanable funds offered exceeds the quantity of loanable funds demanded. If that were to occur, the interest rate would fall to make the quantity of loanable funds offered equal to the quantity of loanable funds demanded.

3. **a.** The real interest rate will not change. According to the Fisher effect, an increase in expected inflation drives up the nominal interest rate, leaving the real interest rate unchanged.
   b. The nominal interest rate will rise by 3%. Each additional percentage point of expected inflation drives up the nominal interest rate by 1 percentage point.
   c. As long as inflation is expected, it does not affect the equilibrium quantity of loanable funds. Both the supply and demand curves for loanable funds are pushed upward, leaving the equilibrium quantity of loanable funds unchanged.

Tackle the Test:
Multiple-Choice Questions

1. c
2. b
3. b
4. c
5. a

Tackle the Test:
Free-Response Questions

2. **a.** This causes an increase (rightward shift) in the supply of loanable funds.
   b. This causes a decrease (leftward shift) in the demand for loanable funds.
   c. This causes an increase (rightward shift) in the demand for loanable funds.
   d. This causes a decrease (leftward shift) in the supply of loanable funds.

Module 30
Check Your Understanding

1. The actual budget balance takes into account the effects of the business cycle on the budget deficit. During recessionary gaps, it incorporates the effect of lower tax revenues and higher transfers on the budget balance; during inflationary gaps, it incorporates the effect of higher tax revenues and reduced transfers. In contrast the cyclically adjusted budget balance factors out the effects of the business cycle and assumes that real GDP is at potential output. Since, in the long run, real GDP tends to potential output, the cyclically adjusted budget balance is a better measure of the long-run sustainability of government policies.

2. In recessions, real GDP falls. This implies that consumers' incomes, consumer spending, and producers' profits also fall. So in recessions, states' tax revenue (which depends in large part on consumers' income, consumer spending, and producers' profits) falls. In order to balance the state budget, states have to cut spending or raise taxes, but that deepens the recession. States without a balanced-budget requirement don't have to take steps that would make things worse during a recession, and they can use expansionary fiscal policy to lessen the fall in real GDP.

3. **a.** A higher growth rate of real GDP implies that tax revenue will increase. If government spending remains constant and the government runs a budget surplus, the size of the public debt will be less than it would otherwise have been.
   b. If retirees live longer, the average age of the population increases. As a result, the implicit liabilities of the government increase because spending on programs for older Americans, such as Social Security and Medicare, will rise.
   c. A decrease in tax revenue without offsetting reductions in government spending will cause the public debt to increase.
   d. Public debt will increase as a result of government borrowing to pay interest on its current public debt.

4. In order to stimulate the economy in the short run, the government can use fiscal policy to increase real GDP. This entails borrowing, increasing the size of public debt further and leading to undesirable consequences: in extreme cases, governments can be forced to default on their debts. Even in less extreme cases, a large public debt is undesirable because government borrowing "crowds out" borrowing for private investment spending. This reduces the amount of investment spending, reducing the long-run growth of the economy.

Tackle the Test:
Multiple-Choice Questions

1. b
2. d
3. c
4. d
5. e

Tackle the Test:
Free-Response Question

2.

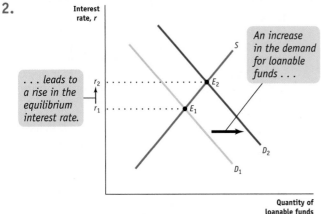

Persistent budget deficits increase the demand for loanable funds, thereby increasing interest rates and decreasing private investment. This is called "crowding out."

Module 31

Check Your Understanding

1. In the accompanying diagram, the increase in the demand for money is shown as a rightward shift of the money demand curve, from MD_1 to MD_2. This raises the equilibrium interest rate from r_1 to r_2.

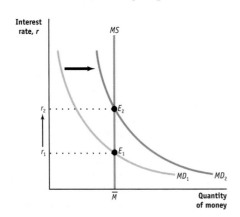

2. In order to prevent the interest rate from rising, the Federal Reserve must make an open-market purchase of Treasury bills, shifting the money supply curve rightward. This is shown in the accompanying diagram as the move from MS_1 to MS_2.

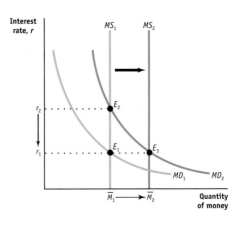

3. a. The money supply curve shifts to the right.
b. The equilibrium interest rate falls.
c. Investment spending rises, due to the fall in the interest rate.
d. Consumer spending rises, due to the multiplier process.
e. Aggregate output rises because of the rightward shift of the aggregate demand curve.

Tackle the Test:
Multiple-Choice Questions

1. a
2. a
3. a
4. c
5. d

Tackle the Test:
Free-Response Questions

2. a. decrease the discount rate, decrease the reserve requirement, open market purchases
b.

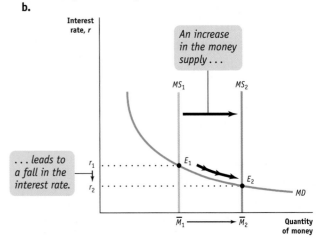

c. No change in aggregate supply; aggregate demand increases. Lower interest rates lead to greater investment spending (and more interest-sensitive consumer spending). Aggregate demand is made up of $C + I + G + (X - IM)$, so an increase in I and C increases AD. Interest rate changes don't affect short-run aggregate supply.

d. As shown in the accompanying figure, aggregate output increases in the short run.

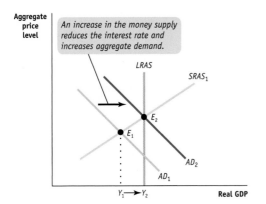

Module 32

Check Your Understanding

1. A 5% increase in the money supply will cause a 5% increase in the aggregate price level in the long run. The process begins in the short run, when the larger money supply decreases the interest rate and promotes investment spending. Investment spending is a component of aggregate demand, so the increase in investment spending leads to an increase in aggregate demand, which causes real GDP to increase beyond potential output. The resulting upward pressure on nominal wages and other input prices shifts aggregate supply to the left until a new long-run equilibrium is reached. Although real GDP returns to its original level, both the increase in aggregate demand and the decrease in aggregate supply cause the aggregate price level to increase. The end result is 5% more money being spent on the same quantity of goods and services, which could only mean a 5% increase in the aggregate price level.

2. A 5% increase in the money supply will have no effect on the interest rate in the long run. As explained in the previous answer, a 5% increase in the money supply is matched by a 5% increase in the aggregate price level in the long run. Changes in the aggregate price level, in turn, cause proportional changes in the demand for money. So a 5% increase in the aggregate price level increases the quantity of money demanded at any given interest rate by 5%. This means that at the initial interest rate, the quantity of money demanded rises exactly as much as the money supply, and the new, long-run interest rate is therefore no different from the initial interest rate.

Tackle the Test:
Multiple-Choice Questions

1. c

2. d

3. c

4. c

5. e

Tackle the Test:
Free-Response Questions

2. a.

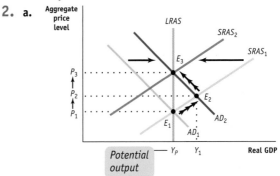

b. The aggregate demand curve shifts to the right, creating a new equilibrium price level and real GDP. The higher money supply leads to a lower interest rate, which increases investment spending and consumer spending, and in turn aggregate demand.

c. Wages rise over time, shifting short-run aggregate supply to the left. This brings equilibrium back to potential output with a higher price level.

Module 33

Check Your Understanding

1. The inflation rate is more likely to quickly reflect changes in the money supply when the economy has had an extended period of high inflation. That's because an extended period of high inflation sensitizes workers and firms to raise nominal wages and prices of intermediate goods when the aggregate price level rises. As a result, there will be little or no increase in real output in the short run after an increase in the money supply, and the increase in the money supply will simply be reflected in a proportional increase in prices. In an economy where people are not sensitized to high inflation because of low inflation in the past, an increase in the money supply will lead to an increase in real output in the short run. This illustrates the fact that the classical model of the price level best applies to economies with *persistently* high inflation, not those with little or no history of high inflation even though they may currently have high inflation.

2. Yes, there can still be an inflation tax because the tax is levied on people who hold money. As long as people hold money, regardless of whether prices are indexed or not, the government is able to use seignorage to capture real resources from the public.

Tackle the Test:
Multiple-Choice Questions
1. d
2. b
3. b
4. c
5. a

Tackle the Test:
Free-Response Question
2.

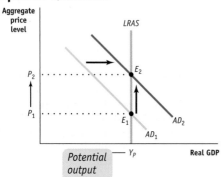

Module 34

Check Your Understanding

1. When real GDP equals potential output, cyclical unemployment is zero and the unemployment rate is equal to the natural rate. This is the case at point E_1 in the figure assuming a natural rate of 6%. Any unemployment in excess of this 6% rate represents cyclical unemployment. An increase in aggregate demand leads to a fall in the unemployment rate below the natural rate (negative cyclical unemployment) and an increase in the inflation rate. This is given by the movement from E_1 to E_2 in the figure and traces a movement upward along the short-run Phillips curve. A reduction in aggregate demand leads to a rise in the unemployment rate above the natural rate (positive cyclical unemployment) and a fall in the inflation rate. This would be represented by a movement down along the short-run Phillips curve from point E_1. So for a given expected inflation rate, the short-run Phillips curve illustrates the relationship between cyclical unemployment and actual inflation rate.

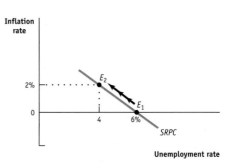

2. There is no long-run trade-off between inflation and unemployment because after expectations of inflation change, wages will adjust to the change, returning employment and the unemployment rate to their equilibrium (natural) levels. This implies that once expectations of inflation fully adjust to any change in actual inflation, the unemployment rate will return to the natural rate of unemployment, or NAIRU. This also implies that the long-run Phillips curve is vertical.

3. Disinflation is costly because to reduce the inflation rate, aggregate output in the short run must typically fall below potential output. This, in turn, results in an increase in the unemployment rate above the natural rate. In general, we would observe a reduction in real GDP. The costs of disinflation can be reduced by not allowing inflation to increase in the first place. The costs of any disinflation will also be lower if the central bank is credible and it announces in advance its policy to reduce inflation. In this situation, the adjustment to the disinflationary policy will be more rapid, resulting in a smaller loss of aggregate output.

4. If the nominal interest rate is negative, an individual is better off simply holding cash, which has a 0% nominal rate of return. If the options facing an individual are to lend and receive a negative nominal interest rate or to hold cash and receive a 0% nominal rate of return, the individual will hold cash. Such a scenario creates the possibility of a liquidity trap, in which monetary policy is ineffective because the nominal interest rate cannot fall below zero. Once the nominal interest rate falls to zero, further increases in the money supply will lead firms and individuals to simply hold the additional cash.

Tackle the Test:
Multiple-Choice Questions
1. b
2. c
3. b
4. e
5. e

Tackle the Test:
Free-Response Questions
2. a. 4%
b. 2%, because 4% − 2% = 2%
c. 0%, because although 4% − 6% = −2%, nominal interest rates can't go below zero
d. Lenders would effectively have to pay people to borrow money, in that what the lenders received back would be

less than what they lent out. No lending would take place. It is better to hold cash than to pay people to borrow money.

    e. Conventional monetary policy (decreasing interest rates) can't happen if the nominal interest rate is already zero. This is called the zero bound OR a liquidity trap.

Module 35

Check Your Understanding

1. A classical economist would have said that the aggressive monetary expansion would have had no short-run effect on aggregate output and would simply have resulted in a proportionate increase in the aggregate price level.

2. Monetarists argue that central banks should implement policy so that the money supply grows at some constant rate. Had the Fed pursued a monetarist policy during this period, we would have observed movements in M1 that would have shown a fixed rate of growth. We would not, therefore, have observed any of the reductions in M1 that are observed in the figure, nor would we have observed the acceleration in the rate of growth of M1 that occurred in 2001.

3. As in Problem 2, a monetarist policy would have resulted in a constant rate of growth in M1. Between 1996 and 2000 the velocity of M1 rose steadily. After 2000 the velocity leveled off a bit and then rose again. Given a constant rate of money growth, these increases in the velocity of M1 would have been expansionary, causing increases in aggregate demand and the aggregate price level, other things equal.

4. The advocacy of fiscal policy (here in the form of tax cuts) to boost economic activity is Keynesian because Keynes promoted fiscal policy as a useful tool to dampen fluctuations in the business cycle. The praise of aggressive monetary policy is not Keynesian because Keynes worried that a liquidity trap would thwart the ability of monetary policy to change interest rates and influence investment spending.

5. a. Rational expectations theorists would argue that only unexpected changes in money supply would have any short-run effect on economic activity. They would also argue that expected changes in the money supply would affect only the aggregate price level, with no short-run effect of aggregate output. So such theorists would give credit to the Fed for limiting the severity of the 2001 recession only if the Fed's monetary policy had been more aggressive than individuals expected during this period.

    b. Real business cycle theorists would argue that the Fed's policy had no effect on ending the 2001 recession because they believe that fluctuations in aggregate output are caused largely by changes in total factor productivity.

Tackle the Test:
Multiple-Choice Questions

1. e

2. d

3. b

4. a

5. d

Tackle the Test:
Free-Response Questions

2. a. The aggregate supply curve is vertical so changes in the money supply affect only the aggregate price level.

    b. Changes in aggregate demand will affect aggregate output.

    c. Business cycles are associated with fluctuations in the money supply.

    d. To avoid inflation, the unemployment rate must be set so that actual inflation equals expected inflation.

    e. Individuals and firms make optimal decisions using all available information.

    f. Fluctuations in total factor productivity growth cause the business cycle by causing the vertical aggregate supply curve to shift.

Module 36

Check Your Understanding

1. The modern consensus has resolved the debate over the effectiveness of both expansionary fiscal and monetary policy. Expansionary fiscal policy is considered effective, although it is limited by the problem of time lags, making monetary policy the stabilization tool of choice except in special circumstances. Expansionary monetary policy is considered effective except in the case of a liquidity trap. The modern consensus has not resolved, however, whether the Fed should adopt an inflation target, whether it should use monetary policy to manage asset price bubbles, and what, if any, kind of unconventional monetary policy it should use in the situation of a liquidity trap.

Tackle the Test:
Multiple-Choice Questions

1. d

2. c

3. e

4. a

5. c

Tackle the Test:
Free-Response Question

2. Your answer can look like the diagram below, or it can have the axes reversed and a curve that resembles a mountain.

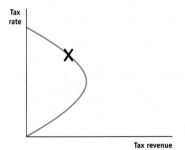

Module 37

Check Your Understanding

1. Economists want a measure of economic progress that rises with increases in the living standard of the average resident of a country. An increase in overall real GDP does not accurately reflect an increase in an average resident's living standard because it does not account for growth in the number of residents. If, for example, real GDP rises by 10% but population grows by 20%, the living standard of the average resident falls: after the change, the average resident has only (110/120) × 100 = 91.6% as much real income as before the change. Similarly, an increase in nominal GDP per capita does not accurately reflect an increase in living standards because it does not account for any change in prices. For example, a 5% increase in nominal GDP per capita generated by a 5% increase in prices results in no change in living standards. Real GDP per capita is the only measure that accounts for both changes in the population and changes in prices.

2. Using the Rule of 70, the amount of time it will take China to double its real GDP per capita is (70/8.8) = 8.0 years; India, (70/4.1) = 17.1 years; Ireland, (70/3.9) = 17.9 years; the United States, (70/1.9) = 36.8 years; France, (70/1.5) = 46.7 years; and Argentina (70/1.2) = 58.3 years. Since the Rule of 70 can be applied to only a positive growth rate, we cannot apply it to the case of Zimbabwe, which experienced negative growth. If India continues to have a higher growth rate of real GDP per capita than the United States, then India's real GDP per capita will eventually surpass that of the United States.

3. The United States began growing rapidly over a century ago, but China and India have begun growing rapidly only recently. As a result, the living standard of the typical Chinese or Indian household has not yet caught up with that of the typical American household.

Tackle the Test: Multiple-Choice Questions

1. d
2. c
3. c
4. b
5. b

Tackle the Test: Free-Response Question

2. Increases in real GDP per capita result mostly from changes in productivity (or labor productivity). Productivity is defined as output per worker or output per hour. Increased labor force participation could also lead to higher real GDP per capita, but the rate of employment growth is rarely very different from the rate of population growth, meaning that the corresponding increase in output does not lead to an increase in output per capita.

Module 38

Check Your Understanding

1. **a.** Significant technological progress will result in a positive growth rate of productivity even though physical capital per worker and human capital per worker are unchanged.
   b. Productivity will grow, but due to diminishing marginal returns, each successive increase in physical capital per worker results in a smaller increase in productivity than the one before it.

2. **a.** If the economy has grown 3% per year and the labor force has grown 1% per year, then productivity—output per worker—has grown at approximately 3% − 1% = 2% per year.
   b. If physical capital has grown 4% per year and the labor force has grown 1% per year, then physical capital per worker has grown at approximately 4% − 1% = 3% per year.
   c. According to estimates, each 1% rise in physical capital, other things equal, increases productivity by 0.3%. So, as physical capital per worker has increased by 3%, productivity growth that can be attributed to an increase in physical capital per worker is 0.3 × 3% = 0.9%. As a percentage of total productivity growth, this is 0.9%/2% × 100% = 45%.
   d. If the rest of productivity growth is due to technological progress, then technological progress has contributed 2% − 0.9% = 1.1% to productivity growth. As a percentage of total productivity growth, this is 1.1%/2% × 100% = 55%.

3. It will take time for workers to learn how to use the new computer system and to adjust their routines. And because there are often setbacks in learning a new system, such as accidentally erasing your computer files, productivity at Multinomics may decrease for a period of time.

Tackle the Test: Multiple-Choice Questions

1. e
2. a
3. d
4. e
5. b

Tackle the Test: Free-Response Questions

2. **a.** Growing physical capital per worker is responsible for 1% productivity growth per year. 2% × 0.5 = 1%
   b. There was no growth in total factor productivity because there was no technological progress. According to the Rule of 70, over 70 years (from 1940 to 2010), a 1% growth rate would cause output to double. Real GDP per capita in this case doubled, as would be expected from a 1% productivity growth rate alone; therefore, there was no change in technological progress.

Module 39

Check Your Understanding

1. A country that has high domestic savings is able to achieve a high rate of investment spending as a percent of GDP. This, in turn, allows the country to achieve a high growth rate.

2. As you can see from panel (b) of the figure on p. 382, although it is important in determining the growth rate for some countries (such as those of Western Europe), the initial level of GDP per capita isn't the only factor. High rates of saving and investment appear to be better predictors of future growth than today's standard of living.

3. The evidence suggests that both sets of factors matter: better infrastructure is important for growth, but so is political and financial stability. Policies should try to address both areas.

4. Growth increases a country's greenhouse gas emissions. The current best estimates are that a large reduction in emissions will result in only a modest reduction in growth. The international burden sharing of greenhouse gas emissions reduction is contentious because rich countries are reluctant to pay the costs of reducing their emissions only to see newly emerging countries like China rapidly increase their emissions. Yet most of the current accumulation of gases is due to the past actions of rich countries. Poorer countries like China are equally reluctant to sacrifice their growth to pay for the past actions of rich countries.

Tackle the Test:
Multiple-Choice Questions

1. d
2. e
3. a
4. c
5. b

Tackle the Test:
Free-Response Question

2. Physical capital, human capital, technology, and natural resources play roles in influencing long-run growth in real GDP per capita. Increases in both physical capital and human capital help a given labor force to produce more over time. Although economic studies have suggested that increases in human capital may explain increases in productivity better than do increases in physical capital per worker, technological progress is probably the most important driver of productivity growth. Historically, natural resources played a prominent role in determining productivity, while today they play a less important role in increasing productivity than do increases in human or physical capital in most countries.

Module 40

Check Your Understanding

1. Long-run economic growth is represented by an outward shift of the production possibilities curve. Short-run fluctuations are represented by a movement from a point below the production possibilities curve toward a point on the production possibilities curve (this shows an economic recovery/expansion) or by a movement to a point farther below the production possibilities curve (this shows a recession/contraction).

2. Long-run economic growth is represented by a rightward shift of the long-run aggregate supply curve. Short-run fluctuations are represented by movements of short-run equilibrium output (the level of real GDP at the intersection of short-run aggregate supply and aggregate demand) above or below potential output.

Tackle the Test:
Multiple-Choice Questions

1. d
2. a
3. a
4. c
5. d

Tackle The Test:
Free-Response Questions

2. a.

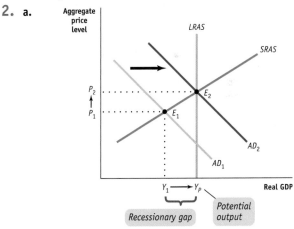

b.

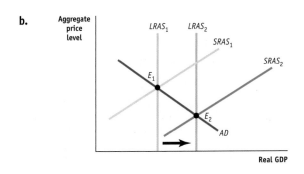

Module 41

Check Your Understanding

1. **a.** The sale of the new airplane to China represents an export of a good to China and so enters the current account.
   b. The sale of Boeing stock to Chinese investors is a sale of a U.S. asset and so enters the financial account.
   c. Even though the plane already exists, when it is shipped to China it is an export of a good from the United States. So the sale of the plane enters the current account.
   d. Because the plane stays in the United States, the Chinese investor is buying a U.S. asset. So this is identical to the answer in part b: the sale of the jet enters the financial account.

Tackle the Test:
Multiple-Choice Questions

1. e
2. a
3. b
4. a
5. a

Tackle the Test:
Free-Response Questions

2.

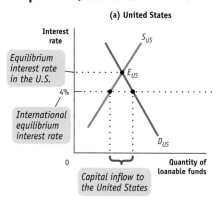

(a) United States

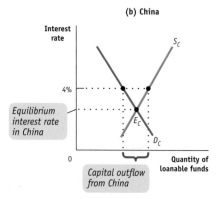

(b) China

Module 42

Check Your Understanding

1. **a.** The increased purchase of Mexican oil would cause U.S. individuals (and firms) to increase their demand for the peso. To purchase pesos, individuals would increase their supply of U.S. dollars to the foreign exchange market, causing a rightward shift in the supply curve of U.S. dollars. This would cause the peso price of the dollar to fall (the amount of pesos per dollar would fall). The peso would appreciate and the U.S. dollar would depreciate as a result.
   b. With the appreciation of the peso it would take more U.S. dollars to obtain the same quantity of Mexican pesos. If we assume that the price level (measured in Mexican pesos) of other Mexican goods and services would not change, other Mexican goods and services would become more expensive to U.S. households and firms. The dollar cost of other Mexican goods and services would rise as the peso appreciated. So Mexican exports of goods and services other than oil would fall.
   c. U.S. goods and services would become cheaper in terms of pesos, so Mexican imports of goods and services would rise.

2. **a.** The real exchange rate equals pesos per U.S. dollar × aggregate price level in the U.S./aggregate price level in Mexico. Today, the aggregate price level in both countries is 100. The real exchange rate today is: $10 \times (100/100) = 10$. The aggregate price level in five years in the U.S. will be $100 \times (120/100) = 120$, and in Mexico it will be $100 \times (1,200/800) = 150$. Thus, the real exchange rate in five years, assuming the nominal exchange rate does not change, will be $10 \times (120/150) = 8$.
   b. Today, a basket of goods and services that costs $100 costs 800 pesos, so the purchasing power parity is 8 pesos per U.S. dollar. In five years, a basket that costs $120 will cost 1,200 pesos, so the purchasing power parity will be 10 pesos per U.S. dollar.

Tackle the Test:
Multiple-Choice Questions

1. d
2. d
3. d
4. b
5. b

Tackle the Test:
Free-Response Questions

2.   In order to purchase more imports from Europe, U.S. consumers must supply more dollars in exchange for euros. As shown in the diagram, the increase in the supply of dollars shifts the dollar supply curve to the right and decreases the exchange rate from XR_1 to XR_2.

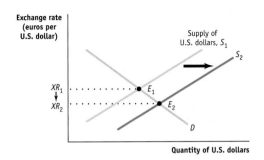

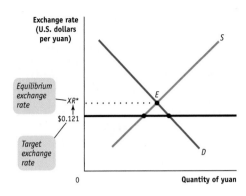

Module 43

Check Your Understanding

1. The accompanying diagram shows the supply of and demand for the yuan, with the U.S. dollar price of the yuan on the vertical axis. In 2005, prior to the revaluation, the exchange rate was pegged at 8.28 yuan per U.S. dollar or, equivalently, 0.121 U.S. dollars per yuan ($0.121). At the target exchange rate of $0.121, the quantity of yuan demanded exceeded the quantity of yuan supplied, creating the shortage depicted in the diagram. Without any intervention by the Chinese government, the U.S. dollar price of the yuan would be bid up, causing an appreciation of the yuan. The Chinese government, however, intervened to prevent this appreciation.

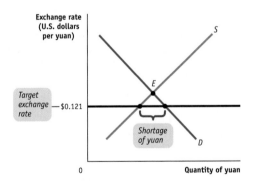

a. If the exchange rate were allowed to float more freely, the U.S. dollar price of the exchange rate would move toward the equilibrium exchange rate (labeled XR^* in the accompanying diagram). This would occur as a result of the shortage, when buyers of the yuan would bid up its U.S. dollar price. As the exchange rate increased, the quantity of yuan demanded would fall and the quantity of yuan supplied would increase. If the exchange rate were allowed to increase to XR^*, the disequilibrium would be entirely eliminated.

b. Placing restrictions on foreigners who want to invest in China would reduce the demand for the yuan, causing the demand curve to shift in the accompanying diagram from D_1 to something like D_2. This would cause a reduction in the shortage of the yuan. If demand fell to D_3, the disequilibrium would be completely eliminated.

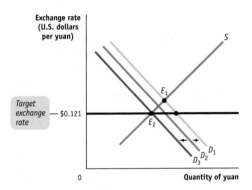

c. Removing restrictions on Chinese who wish to invest abroad would cause an increase in the supply of the yuan and a rightward shift of the supply curve. This increase in supply would reduce the size of the shortage. If, for example, supply increased from S_1 to S_2, the disequilibrium would be eliminated completely, as shown in the accompanying diagram.

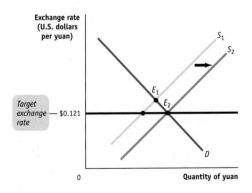

d. Imposing a tax on exports (Chinese goods sold to foreigners) would raise the price of these goods and decrease the amount of Chinese goods purchased. This would also decrease the demand for yuan with which to purchase those goods. The graphical analysis here is virtually identical to that found in the figure accompanying part b.

Tackle the Test:
Multiple-Choice Questions

1.   e
2.   e
3.   b
4.   a
5.   a

Tackle the Test:
Free-Response Questions

2. a. Use foreign exchange reserves. To stabilize an exchange rate through exchange market intervention (e.g., buying its own currency), a country must keep large quantities of foreign currency on hand, which is usually a low-return investment. And large reserves can be quickly exhausted when there are large capital flows out of a country.
  b. Shifting supply and demand curves for currency through monetary policy. If a country chooses to stabilize an exchange rate by adjusting monetary policy rather than through intervention, it must divert monetary policy from other goals, notably stabilizing the economy and managing the inflation rate.
  c. Foreign exchange controls. These regulations distort incentives for importing and exporting goods and services. They can also create substantial costs in terms of red tape and corruption.

Module 44

Check Your Understanding

1.   The devaluations and revaluations most likely occurred in those periods when there was a sudden change in the franc-mark exchange rate: 1974, 1976, the early 1980s, 1986, and 1993–1994.

2.   The high Canadian interest rates caused an increase in capital inflows to Canada. To obtain assets that yielded a relatively high interest rate in Canada, investors first had to obtain Canadian dollars. The increase in the demand for the Canadian dollar caused the Canadian dollar to appreciate. This appreciation of the Canadian currency raised the price of Canadian goods to foreigners (measured in terms of the foreign currency). This made it more difficult for Canadian firms to compete in other markets.

Tackle the Test:
Multiple-Choice Questions

1.   c
2.   b

Tackle the Test:
Free-Response Questions

2.   The decrease in aggregate demand that occurs during a recession includes the demand for goods and services produced abroad as well as at home. When a trading partner experiences a recession, it leads to a fall in their imports. The trading partner's imports are the country's exports.

   A reduction in foreign demand for the country's domestic goods and services leads to a reduction in demand for the domestic currency. With a floating exchange rate, the currency depreciates. This makes domestic goods and services cheaper, so exports don't fall by as much as they would have, and it makes imports more expensive, leading to a fall in imports. Both effects limit the decline in domestic aggregate demand.

Module 45

Check Your Understanding

1. a.

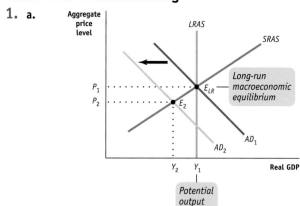

  b. Aggregate demand shifts left, real GDP and the aggregate price level fall.
  c. Nominal wages will decrease as a result of the recessionary gap and the decrease in the aggregate price level, leading to an increase in short-run aggregate supply. The rightward shift in the short-run aggregate supply curve moves the economy back to long-run equilibrium at potential output and a lower aggregate price level.
  d. Lower government spending will decrease the government budget deficit. With less borrowing by the government, the demand for loanable funds will decrease, shifting the demand curve from D_1 to D_2

and decreasing the interest rate from r_1 to r_2 in the accompanying figure.

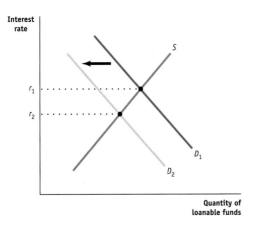

Interest rate

r_1

r_2

S

D_1

D_2

Quantity of loanable funds

Tackle the Test:
Multiple-Choice Questions

1. e
2. b
3. e
4. a
5. e

Tackle the Test:
Free-Response Questions

Graph answers parts a and b.

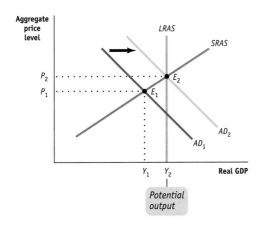

Aggregate price level

LRAS

SRAS

P_2

P_1

E_2

E_1

AD_2

AD_1

Y_1 Y_2 Real GDP

Potential output

2. **a.** The vertical axis is labeled "Aggregate price level" and the horizontal axis is labeled "Aggregate output" or "Real GDP." The AD curve slopes downward, the $SRAS$ curve slopes upward, and the $LRAS$ curve is vertical—all are labeled. The equilibrium aggregate price level and aggregate output are shown on the axes where the AD curve

and the $SRAS$ curve intersect, which is to the left of the $LRAS$ curve.

b. The AD curve shifts to the right. The other curves are unchanged. The new equilibrium price level and aggregate output are shown on the axes at the new equilibrium point. The new equilibrium does not need to be at potential output.

c. Axes are labeled "Interest rate" and "Quantity of loanable funds." The demand curve slopes downward, the supply curve slopes upward, and the curves are labeled. The equilibrium interest rate and quantity are shown on the axes at the point where the curves intersect. The demand for loanable funds shifts to the right and the new equilibrium values are shown on the axes. The interest rate is higher.

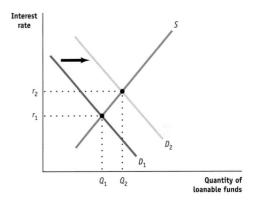

Interest rate

S

r_2

r_1

D_2

D_1

Q_1 Q_2 Quantity of loanable funds

d. Axes are labeled "Exchange rate" and "Quantity of U.S. dollars." The demand curve slopes downward, the supply curve slopes upward, and the curves are labeled. The equilibrium exchange rate and quantity are shown on the axes at the point where the two curves intersect. The supply of U.S dollars decreases, shifting the supply curve to the left, because the higher interest rate in the United States decreases the outflow of capital to countries with a relatively low interest rate.

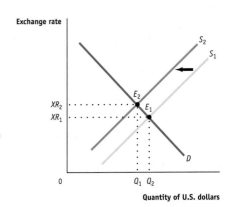

Exchange rate

S_2

S_1

E_2

E_1

XR_2

XR_1

D

0

Q_1 Q_2

Quantity of U.S. dollars

e. The value of the U.S. dollar has increased (it has appreciated). U.S. exports will decline, and aggregate demand will decline.

Module 46

Check Your Understanding

1. a. Since spending on orange juice is a small share of Clare's spending, the income effect from a rise in the price of orange juice is insignificant. Only the substitution effect, represented by the substitution of lemonade for orange juice, is significant.

   b. Since rent is a large share of Delia's expenditures, the increase in rent generates an income effect, making Delia feel poorer. Since housing is a normal good for Delia, the income and substitution effects move in the same direction, leading her to reduce her consumption of housing by moving to a smaller apartment.

   c. Since a meal ticket is a significant share of the students' living costs, an increase in its price will generate an income effect. Students respond to the price increase by eating more often in the cafeteria. So the substitution effect (which would induce them to eat in the cafeteria less often as they substitute restaurant meals in place of meals at the cafeteria) and the income effect (which would induce them to eat in the cafeteria more often because they are poorer) move in opposite directions. This happens because cafeteria meals are an inferior good. In fact, since the income effect outweighs the substitution effect (students eat in the cafeteria more as the price of meal tickets increases), cafeteria meals are a Giffen good.

2. By the midpoint method, the percent change in the price of strawberries is

$$\frac{\$1.00 - \$1.50}{(\$1.50 + \$1.00)/2} \times 100 = \frac{-\$0.50}{\$1.25} \times 100 = -40\%$$

Similarly, the percent change in the quantity of strawberries demanded is

$$\frac{200{,}000 - 100{,}000}{(100{,}000 + 200{,}000)/2} \times 100 = \frac{100{,}000}{150{,}000} \times 100 = 67\%$$

Dropping the minus sign, the price elasticity of demand using the midpoint method is 67%/40% = 1.7.

3. By the midpoint method, the percent change in the quantity of movie tickets demanded in going from 4,000 tickets to 5,000 tickets is

$$\frac{5{,}000 - 4{,}000}{(4{,}000 + 5{,}000)/2} \times 100 = \frac{1{,}000}{4{,}500} \times 100 = 22\%$$

Since the price elasticity of demand is 1 at the current consumption level, it will take a 22% reduction in the price of movie tickets to generate a 22% increase in quantity demanded.

4. Since price rises, we know that quantity demanded must fall. Given the current price of $0.50, a $0.05 increase in price represents a 10% change, using the method in Equation 46-2. So the price elasticity of demand is

$$\frac{\%\ \text{change in quantity demanded}}{10\%} = 1.2$$

so that the percent change in quantity demanded is 12%. A 12% decrease in quantity demanded represents 100,000 × 0.12, or 12,000 sandwiches.

Tackle the Test:
Multiple-Choice Questions

1. d
2. c
3. b
4. e
5. c

Tackle the Test:
Free-Response Questions

2. a. The substitution effect will decrease the quantity demanded. As price increases, consumers will buy other goods instead.

   b. The income effect will increase the quantity demanded. As price increases, real income decreases, so consumers will purchase more of the inferior good.

   c. The substitution effect is larger than the income effect. If the income effect were larger than the substitution effect, more of the good would be purchased as the price increased, and the demand curve would be upward sloping.

Module 47

Check Your Understanding

1. a. Elastic demand. Consumers are highly responsive to changes in price. For a rise in price, the quantity effect (which tends to reduce total revenue) outweighs the price effect (which tends to increase total revenue). Overall, this leads to a fall in total revenue.

   b. Unit-elastic demand. Here the revenue lost to the fall in price is exactly equal to the revenue gained from higher sales. The quantity effect exactly offsets the price effect.

   c. Inelastic demand. Consumers are relatively unresponsive to changes in price. For consumers to purchase a given percent more, the price must fall by an even greater percent. The price effect of a fall in price (which tends to reduce total revenue) outweighs the quantity effect (which tends to increase total revenue). As a result, total revenue decreases.

   d. Inelastic demand. Consumers are relatively unresponsive to price, so a given percent fall in output is accompanied by an even greater percent rise in price. The price effect of a rise in price (which tends to increase total revenue) outweighs the quantity effect (which tends to reduce total revenue). As a result, total revenue increases.

2. a. Once bitten by a venomous snake, the victim's demand for an antidote is very likely to be perfectly inelastic because there is no substitute and it is necessary for survival. The demand curve will be vertical at a quantity equal to the needed dose.

   b. Students' demand for blue pencils is likely to be perfectly elastic because there are readily available substitutes, such as yellow pencils. The demand curve will be horizontal at a price equal to that of non-blue pencils.

Tackle the Test:
Multiple-Choice Questions

1. d
2. d

3. c

4. b

5. c

Tackle the Test:
Free-Response Questions

2. a.

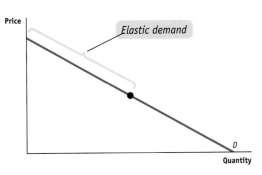

b. An increase in price will decrease total revenue because the negative quantity effect of the price increase is greater than the positive price effect of the price increase.

Module 48

Check Your Understanding

1. By the midpoint method, the percent increase in Chelsea's income is

$$\frac{\$18,000 - \$12,000}{(\$12,000 + \$18,000)/2} \times 100 = \frac{\$6,000}{\$15,000} \times 100 = 40\%$$

Similarly, the percent increase in her consumption of CDs is

$$\frac{40 - 10}{(10 + 40)/2} \times 100 = \frac{30}{25} \times 100 = 120\%$$

Chelsea's income elasticity of demand for CDs is therefore 120%/40% = 3.

2. The cross-price elasticity of demand is 5%/20% = 0.25. Since the cross-price elasticity of demand is positive, the two goods are substitutes.

3. By the midpoint method, the percent change in the number of hours of web-design services contracted is

$$\frac{500,000 - 300,000}{(300,000 + 500,000)/2} \times 100 = \frac{200,000}{400,000} \times 100 = 50\%$$

Similarly, the percent change in the price of web-design services is:

$$\frac{\$150 - \$100}{(\$100 + \$150)/2} \times 100 = \frac{\$50}{\$125} \times 100 = 40\%$$

The price elasticity of supply is 50%/40% = 1.25. Hence supply is elastic.

Tackle the Test:
Multiple-Choice Questions

1. b

2. d

3. d

4. d

5. c

Tackle the Test:
Free-Response Questions

2. a. 40%/20% = 2

b. elastic

c.

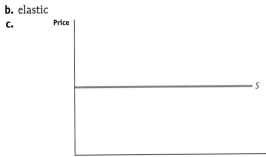

d. Inputs are readily available and can be shifted into/out of production at low cost.

Module 49

Check Your Understanding

1. A consumer buys each pepper if the price is less than (or just equal to) the consumer's willingness to pay for that pepper. The demand schedule is constructed by asking how many peppers will be demanded at any given price. The accompanying table illustrates the demand schedule.

Price of pepper	Quantity of peppers demanded	Quantity of peppers demanded by Casey	Quantity of peppers demanded by Josey
$0.90	1	1	0
0.80	2	1	1
0.70	3	2	1
0.60	4	2	2
0.50	5	3	2
0.40	6	3	3
0.30	8	4	4
0.20	8	4	4
0.10	8	4	4
0.00	8	4	4

When the price is $0.40, Casey's consumer surplus from the first pepper is $0.50, from his second pepper $0.30, from his third pepper $0.10, and he does not buy any more peppers. Casey's individual consumer surplus is therefore $0.90. Josey's consumer surplus from her first pepper is $0.40, from her second pepper $0.20, from her third pepper $0.00 (since the price is exactly equal to her willingness to pay, she buys the third pepper but receives no consumer surplus from it), and she does not buy any more peppers. Josey's individual consumer surplus is therefore $0.60. Total consumer surplus at a price of $0.40 is therefore $0.90 + $0.60 = $1.50.

2. A producer supplies each pepper if the price is greater than (or just equal to) the producer's cost of producing that pepper. The supply schedule is constructed by asking how many peppers will be supplied at any price. The accompanying table illustrates the supply schedule.

Price of pepper	Quantity of peppers supplied	Quantity of peppers supplied by Cara	Quantity of peppers supplied by Jamie
$0.90	8	4	4
0.80	7	4	3
0.70	7	4	3
0.60	6	4	2
0.50	5	3	2
0.40	4	3	1
0.30	3	2	1
0.20	2	2	0
0.10	2	2	0
0.00	0	0	0

When the price is $0.70, Cara's producer surplus from the first pepper is $0.60, from her second pepper $0.60, from her third pepper $0.30, from her fourth pepper $0.10, and she does not supply any more peppers. Cara's individual producer surplus is therefore $1.60. Jamie's producer surplus from his first pepper is $0.40, from his second pepper $0.20, from his third pepper $0.00 (since the price is exactly equal to his cost, he sells the third pepper but receives no producer surplus from it), and he does not supply any more peppers. Jamie's individual producer surplus is therefore $0.60. Total producer surplus at a price of $0.70 is therefore $1.60 + $0.60 = $2.20.

Tackle the Test:
Multiple-Choice Questions

1. c
2. c
3. c
4. b
5. a

Tackle the Test:
Free-Response Questions

2.

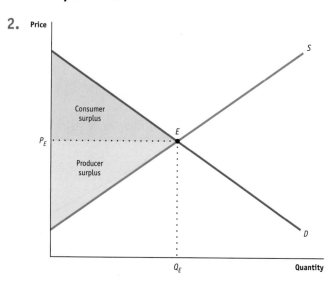

Module 50
Check Your Understanding

1. The quantity demanded equals the quantity supplied at a price of $0.50, the equilibrium price. At that price, a total quantity of five peppers will be bought and sold. Casey will buy three peppers and receive consumer surplus of $0.40 on his first, $0.20 on his second, and $0.00 on his third pepper. Josey will buy two peppers and receive consumer surplus of $0.30 on her first and $0.10 on her second pepper. Total consumer surplus is therefore $1.00. Cara will supply three peppers and receive producer surplus of $0.40 on her first, $0.40 on her second, and $0.10 on her third pepper. Jamie will supply two peppers and receive producer surplus of $0.20 on his first and $0.00 on his second pepper. Total producer surplus is therefore $1.10. Total surplus in this market is therefore $1.00 + $1.10 = $2.10.

2. The following figure shows that, after the introduction of the excise tax, the price paid by consumers rises to $1.20; the price received by producers falls to $0.90. Consumers bear $0.20 of the $0.30 tax per pound of butter; producers bear $0.10 of the tax. The tax drives a wedge of $0.30 between the price paid by consumers and the price received by producers. As a result, the quantity of butter sold is now 9 million pounds.

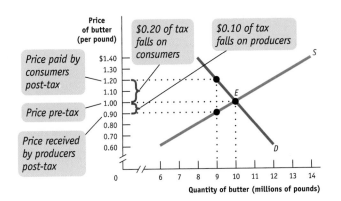

3. a. Without the excise tax, Zhang, Yves, Xavier, and Walter sell, and Ana, Bernice, Chizuko, and Dagmar buy one can of soda each, at $0.40 per can. So the quantity bought and sold is 4.
b. With the excise tax, Zhang and Yves sell, and Ana and Bernice buy one can of soda each. So the quantity sold is 2.
c. Without the excise tax, Ana's individual consumer surplus is $0.70 − $0.40 = $0.30, Bernice's is $0.60 − $0.40 = $0.20, Chizuko's is $0.50 − $0.40 = $0.10, and Dagmar's is $0.40 − $0.40 = $0.00. Total consumer surplus is $0.30 + $0.20 + $0.10 + $0.00 = $0.60. With the tax, Ana's individual consumer surplus is $0.70 − $0.60 = $0.10 and Bernice's is $0.60 − $0.60 = $0.00. Total consumer surplus post-tax is $0.10 + $0.00 = $0.10. So the total consumer surplus lost because of the tax is $0.60 − $0.10 = $0.50.
d. Without the excise tax, Zhang's individual producer surplus is $0.40 − $0.10 = $0.30, Yves's is $0.40 − $0.20 = $0.20, Xavier's is $0.40 − $0.30 = $0.10, and Walter's is $0.40 − $0.40 = $0.00. Total producer surplus is $0.30 + $0.20 + $0.10 + $0.00 = $0.60. With the tax, Zhang's individual producer surplus is $0.20 − $0.10 = $0.10 and Yves's is $0.20 − $0.20 = $0.00. Total producer surplus post-tax is $0.10 + $0.00 = $0.10. So the total producer surplus lost because of the tax is $0.60 − $0.10 = $0.50.
e. With the tax, two cans of soda are sold, so the government tax revenue from this excise tax is 2 × $0.40 = $0.80.
f. Total surplus without the tax is $0.60 + $0.60 = $1.20. With the tax, total surplus is $0.10 + $0.10 = $0.20, and government tax revenue is $0.80. So deadweight loss from this excise tax is $1.20 − ($0.20 + $0.80) = $0.20.

Tackle the Test:
Multiple-Choice Questions

1. c
2. e
3. b
4. d
5. c

Tackle the Test:
Free-Response Questions

2.

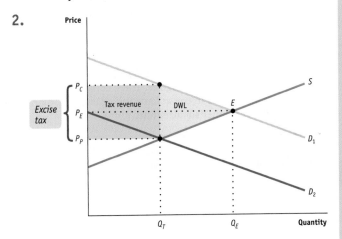

Module 51
Check Your Understanding

1. Consuming a unit that generates negative marginal utility leaves the consumer with lower total utility than not consuming that unit at all. A rational consumer, a consumer who maximizes utility, would not do that. For example, Figure 51.1 shows that Cassie receives 64 utils if she consumes 8 clams, but if she consumes a 9th clam, she loses a util, decreasing her total utility to only 63 utils. Whenever consuming a unit generates negative marginal utility, the consumer is made better off by not consuming that unit, even when that unit is free.

2. a. The accompanying table shows the consumer's consumption possibilities, bundles A through C. These consumption possibilities are plotted in the accompanying diagram, along with the consumer's budget line.

Consumption Bundle	Quantity of popcorn (buckets)	Quantity of movie tickets
A	0	2
B	2	1
C	4	0

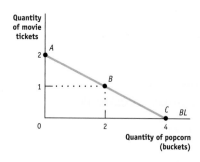

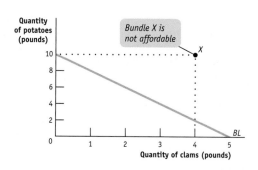

b. The accompanying table shows the consumer's consumption possibilities, *A* through *D*. These consumption possibilities are plotted in the accompanying diagram, along with the consumer's budget line.

Consumption Bundle	Quantity of underwear (pairs)	Quantity of socks (pairs)
A	0	6
B	1	4
C	2	2
D	3	0

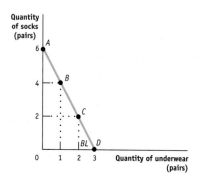

3. From Table 51.3 you can see that Sammy's marginal utility per dollar from increasing his consumption of clams from 3 to 4 pounds and his marginal utility per dollar from increasing his consumption of potatoes from 9 to 10 pounds are the same, 0.75 utils. But a consumption bundle consisting of 4 pounds of clams and 10 pounds of potatoes is not Sammy's optimal consumption bundle because it is not affordable given his income of $20; a bundle of 4 pounds of clams and 10 pounds of potatoes costs $4 × 4 + $2 × 10 = $36, $16 more than Sammy's income. This can be illustrated with Sammy's budget line from Figure 51.3: a bundle of 4 pounds of clams and 10 pounds of potatoes is represented by point *X* in the accompanying diagram, a point that lies outside Sammy's budget line. If you look at the horizontal axis of Figure 51.4, it is quite clear that there is no such thing in Sammy's consumption possibilities as a bundle consisting of 4 pounds of clams and 10 pounds of potatoes.

Tackle the Test: Multiple-Choice Questions

1. d
2. b
3. a
4. b
5. d

Tackle the Test: Free-Response Questions

2. a.

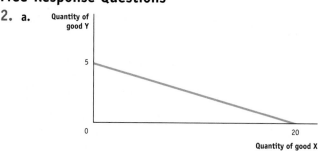

b. Yes, 100/$5 = 400/$20

c. Total utility will increase because marginal utility is positive, while marginal utility will decrease due to the principle of diminishing marginal utility.

Module 52

Check Your Understanding

1. a. Supplies are an explicit cost because they require an outlay of money.

b. If the basement could be used in some other way that generates money, such as renting it to a student, then the implicit cost is that money forgone. Otherwise, the implicit cost is zero.

c. Wages are an explicit cost.

d. By using the van for their business, Karma and Don forgo the money they could have gained by selling it. So use of the van is an implicit cost.

e. Karma's forgone wages from her job are an implicit cost.

2. a. Economic profit is zero, as explained by the following calculations:

Implicit cost = $2,000 + $23,000 = $25,000
Accounting profit = Total revenue − Explicit cost −
Depreciation = $25,000
Economic profit = Total revenue − Explicit cost −
Depreciation − Implicit cost = Accounting profit − Implicit
cost = $25,000 − $25,000 = $0.

b. An economic profit of zero is considered a "normal profit." The resources devoted to this business could not earn
more if used in the next best activity. This is just enough
profit to keep you in this business with no regrets.

Tackle the Test:
Multiple-Choice Questions

1. d
2. e
3. a
4. a
5. c

Tackle the Test:
Free-Response Questions

2. **a.** Total revenue = 2,000 × $2 = $4,000
   b. Accounting profit = $4,000 − $400 − $100 = $3,500
   c. Sunny would need to know the opportunity cost of her
   time.
   d. In general, she would calculate her economic profit and
   operate if she makes at least normal profit (meaning zero
   economic profit). In Sunny's case, she earns $3,500 in
   accounting profit minus the $200 implicit cost of capital
   and the opportunity cost of her time. Because $3,500 −
   $200 = $3,300, she will make at least normal profit if the
   opportunity cost of her time is less than or equal to
   $3,300.

Module 53

Check Your Understanding

1. The profit-maximizing level of output is three units
because marginal cost goes from being below marginal
revenue at a quantity of three to being above marginal
revenue at a quantity of four, thus passing through marginal revenue at the third unit.

2.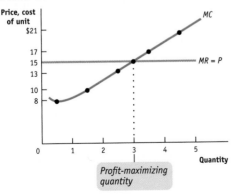

Tackle the Test:
Multiple-Choice Questions

1. c
2. c
3. d
4. e
5. c

Tackle the Test:
Free-Response Questions

2.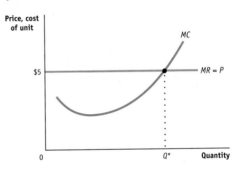

Module 54

Check Your Understanding

1. **a.** The fixed input is the 10-ton machine and the variable
   input is electricity.
   b. As you can see from the declining numbers in the third
   column of the accompanying table, electricity does indeed
   exhibit diminishing returns: the marginal product of each
   additional kilowatt of electricity is less than that of the
   previous kilowatt.

Quantity of electricity (kilowatts)	Quantity of ice (pounds)	Marginal product of electricity (pounds per kilowatt)
0	0	
		1,000
1	1,000	
		800
2	1,800	
		600
3	2,400	
		400
4	2,800	

c. A 50% increase in the size of the fixed input means
that Bernie now has a 15-ton machine, so the fixed
input is now the 15-ton machine. Since it generates
a 100% increase in output for any given amount

of electricity, the quantity of output and the marginal product are now as shown in the accompanying table.

Quantity of electricity (kilowatts)	Quantity of ice (pounds)	Marginal product of electricity (pounds per kilowatt)
0	0	
		2,000
1	2,000	
		1,600
2	3,600	
		1,200
3	4,800	
		800
4	5,600	

Tackle the Test:
Multiple-Choice Questions

1. d
2. e
3. a
4. b
5. a

Tackle the Test:
Free-Response Questions

2.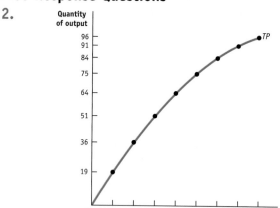

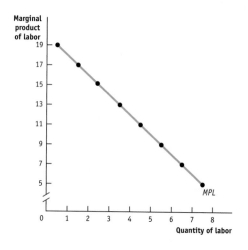

Module 55
Check Your Understanding

1. **a.** As shown in the accompanying table, the marginal cost for each pie is found by multiplying the marginal cost of the previous pie by 1.5. The variable cost for each output level is found by summing the marginal cost for all the pies produced to reach that output level. So, for example, the variable cost of three pies is $1.00 + $1.50 + $2.25 = $4.75. Average fixed cost for Q pies is calculated as $9.00/Q since fixed cost is $9.00. Average variable cost for Q pies is equal to the variable cost for the Q pies divided by Q; for example, the average variable cost of five pies is $13.19/5, or approximately $2.64. Finally, average total cost can be calculated in two equivalent ways: as TC/Q or as $AVC + AFC$.

Quantity of pies	Marginal cost of pie	Variable cost	Average fixed cost of pie	Average variable cost of pie	Average total cost of pie
0		$0.00	—	—	—
	$1.00				
1		1.00	$9.00	$1.00	$10.00
	1.50				
2		2.50	4.50	1.25	5.75
	2.25				
3		4.75	3.00	1.58	4.58
	3.38				
4		8.13	2.25	2.03	4.28
	5.06				
5		13.19	1.80	2.64	4.44
	7.59				
6		20.78	1.50	3.46	4.96

b. The spreading effect dominates the diminishing returns effect when average total cost is falling: the fall in AFC dominates the rise in AVC for pies 1 to 4. The diminishing returns effect dominates when average total cost is rising: the rise in AVC dominates the fall in AFC for pies 5 and 6.

c. Alicia's minimum-cost output is 4 pies; this generates the lowest average total cost, $4.28. When output is less than 4, the marginal cost of a pie is less than the average total cost of the pies already produced. So making an additional pie lowers average total cost. For example, the marginal cost of pie 3 is $2.25, whereas the average total cost of pies 1 and 2 is $5.75. So making pie 3 lowers average total cost to $4.58, equal to (2 × $5.75 + $2.25)/3. When output is more than 4, the marginal cost of a pie is greater than the average total cost of the pies already produced. Consequently, making an additional pie raises average total cost. So, although the marginal cost of pie 6 is $7.59, the average total cost of pies 1 through 5 is $4.44. Making pie 6 raises average total cost to $4.96, equal to (5 × $4.44 + $7.59)/6.

Tackle the Test:
Multiple-Choice Questions

1. c
2. e

3. e

4. e

5. a

Tackle the Test:
Free-Response Questions

2.

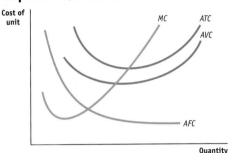

Module 56

Check Your Understanding

1. a. The accompanying table shows the average total cost of producing 12,000, 22,000, and 30,000 units for each of the three choices of fixed cost. For example, if the firm makes choice 1, the total cost of producing 12,000 units of output is $8,000 + 12,000 × $1.00 = $20,000. The average total cost of producing 12,000 units of output is therefore $20,000/12,000 = $1.67. The other average total costs are calculated similarly.

	12,000 units	22,000 units	30,000 units
Average total cost from choice 1	$1.67	$1.36	$1.27
Average total cost from choice 2	1.75	1.30	1.15
Average total cost from choice 3	2.25	1.34	1.05

So if the firm wanted to produce 12,000 units, it would make choice 1 because this gives it the lowest average total cost. If it wanted to produce 22,000 units, it would make choice 2. If it wanted to produce 30,000 units, it would make choice 3.

b. Having historically produced 12,000 units, the firm would have adopted choice 1. When producing 12,000 units, the firm would have had an average total cost of $1.67. When output jumps to 22,000 units, the firm cannot alter its choice of fixed cost in the short run, so its average total cost in the short run will be $1.36. In the long run, however, it will adopt choice 2, making its average total cost fall to $1.30.

c. If the firm believes that the increase in demand is temporary, it should not alter its fixed cost from choice 1 because choice 2 generates higher average total cost as soon as output falls back to its original quantity of 12,000 units: $1.75 versus $1.67.

2. a. This firm is likely to experience diseconomies of scale. As the firm takes on more projects, the costs of communication and coordination required to implement the expertise of the firm's owner are likely to increase.

b. This firm is likely to experience economies of scale. Because diamond mining requires a large initial setup cost for excavation equipment, long-run average total cost will fall as output increases.

Tackle the Test:
Multiple-Choice Questions

1. a

2. e

3. e

4. d

5. e

Tackle the Test:
Free-Response Questions

2.

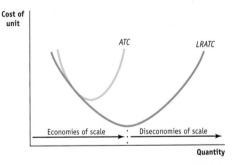

Module 57

Check Your Understanding

1. a. oligopoly

b. perfect competition

c. monopolistic competition

d. monopoly

Tackle the Test:
Multiple-Choice Questions

1. b

2. a

3. d

4. a

5. a

Tackle the Test:
Free-Response Questions

2. a.

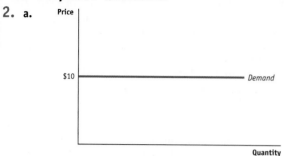

b. $10

Module 58

Check Your Understanding

1. a. The firm maximizes profit at a quantity of 4, because it is at that quantity that $MC = MR$.
  b. At a quantity of 4 the firm just breaks even. This is because at a quantity of 4, $P = ATC$, so the amount the firm takes in for each unit—the price—exactly equals the average total cost per unit.

2. The lowest price that would allow the firm to break even is $10, for the minimum average total cost is $500/50 = $10, and price must at least equal minimum average total cost in order for the firm to break even.

Tackle the Test:
Multiple-Choice Questions

1. d
2. d
3. d
4. c
5. c

Tackle the Test:
Free-Response Questions

2. a.

Q	MC
0	
	16
1	
	6
2	
	8
3	
	12
4	
	16
5	
	20
6	
	24
7	

b. The profit-maximizing quantity is 4.
c. The firm's maximum profit is $TR - TC = (4 \times \$14) - \$56 = \$56 - \$56 = \$0$.

Module 59

Check Your Understanding

1.

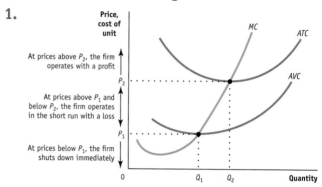

a. The firm should shut down immediately when price is less than minimum average variable cost, the shut-down price. In the accompanying diagram, this is optimal for prices in the range from 0 to P_1.
b. When the price is greater than the minimum average variable cost (the shut-down price) but less than the minimum average total cost (the break-even price), the firm should continue to operate in the short run even though it is making a loss. This is optimal for prices in the range from P_1 to P_2.
c. When the price exceeds the minimum average total cost (the break-even price), the firm makes a profit. This happens for prices in excess of P_2.

2. This is an example of a temporary shut-down by a firm when the market price lies below the shut-down price, the minimum average variable cost. The market price is the price of a lobster meal and the variable cost is the cost of the lobster, employee wages, and other expenses that increase as more meals are served. In this example, however, it is the average variable cost curve rather than the market price that shifts over time, due to seasonal changes in the cost of lobsters. Maine lobster shacks have relatively low average variable cost during the summer, when cheap Maine lobsters are available; during the rest of the year, their average variable cost is relatively high due to the high cost of imported lobsters. So the lobster shacks are open for business during the summer, when their minimum average variable cost lies below price; but they close during the rest of the year, when the price lies below their minimum average variable cost.

Tackle the Test:
Multiple-Choice Questions

1. e
2. d

3. b

4. d

5. c

Tackle the Test:
Free-Response Questions

2. a. 6

   b. $20 \times 6 = \$120$

   c. $29.50 \times 6 = \$177$

   d. $120 - \$177 = -\$57$ (or a loss of 57)

   e. No, because $P < AVC$

Module 60

Check Your Understanding

1. a. A fall in the fixed cost of production generates a fall in the average total cost of production and, in the short run, an increase in each firm's profit at the current output level. So in the long run new firms will enter the industry. The increase in supply drives down price and profits. Once profits are driven back to zero, entry will cease.

b. An increase in wages generates an increase in the average variable and the average total cost of production at every output level. In the short run, firms incur losses at the current output level, and so in the long run some firms will exit the industry. (If the average variable cost rises sufficiently, some firms may even shut down in the short run.) As firms exit, supply decreases, price rises, and losses are reduced. Exit will cease once losses return to zero.

c. Price will rise as a result of the increased demand, leading to a short-run increase in profits at the current output level. In the long run, firms will enter the industry, generating an increase in supply, a fall in price, and a fall in profits. Once profits are driven back to zero, entry will cease.

d. The shortage of a key input causes that input's price to increase, resulting in an increase in average variable and average total cost for producers. Firms incur losses in the short run, and some firms will exit the industry in the long run. The fall in supply generates an increase in price and decreased losses. Exit will cease when the losses for remaining firms have returned to zero.

2. In the accompanying diagram, point X_{MKT} in panel (b), the intersection of S_1 and D_1, represents the long-run industry equilibrium before the change in consumer tastes. When tastes change, demand falls and the industry moves in the short run to point Y_{MKT} in panel (b), at the intersection of the new demand curve D_2 and S_1, the short-run supply curve representing the same number of egg producers as in the original equilibrium at point X_{MKT}. As the market price falls, each individual firm reacts by producing less—as shown in panel (a)—as long as the market price remains above the minimum average variable cost. If market price falls below minimum average variable cost, the firm would shut down immediately. At point Y_{MKT} the price of eggs is below minimum average total cost, creating losses for producers. This leads some firms to exit, which shifts the short-run industry supply curve leftward to S_2. A new long-run equilibrium is established at point Z_{MKT}. As this occurs, the market price rises again, and, as shown in panel (c), each remaining producer reacts by increasing output (here, from point Y to point Z). All remaining producers again make zero profits. The decrease in the quantity of eggs supplied in the industry comes entirely from the exit of some producers from the industry. The long-run industry supply curve is the curve labeled LRS in panel (b).

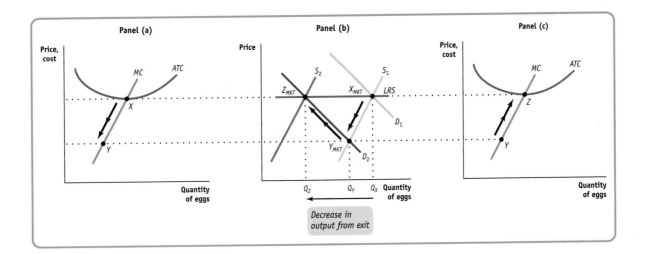

Tackle the Test:
Multiple-Choice Questions

1. d
2. b
3. a
4. e
5. b

Tackle the Test:
Free-Response Questions

2.

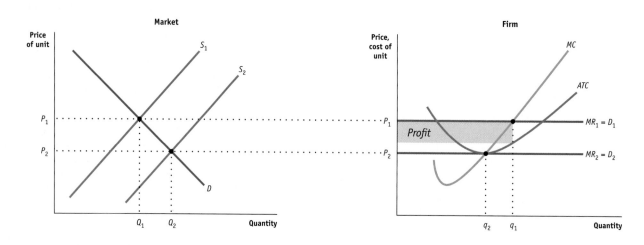

Module 61

Check Your Understanding

1. **a.** The demand schedule is found by determining the price at which each quantity would be demanded. This price is the average revenue, found at each output level by dividing the total revenue by the number of emeralds produced. For example, the price when 3 emeralds are produced is $252/3 = $84. The price at the various output levels is then used to construct the demand schedule in the accompanying table.

   b. The marginal revenue schedule is found by calculating the change in total revenue as output increases by one unit. For example, the marginal revenue generated by increasing output from 2 to 3 emeralds is ($252 − $186) = $66.

   c. The quantity effect component of marginal revenue is the additional revenue generated by selling one more unit of the good at the market price. For example, as shown in the accompanying table, at 3 emeralds, the market price is $84; so, when going from 2 to 3 emeralds the quantity effect is equal to $84.

   d. The price effect component of marginal revenue is the decline in total revenue caused by the fall in price when one more unit is sold. For example, as shown in the table, when only 2 emeralds are sold, each emerald sells at a price of $93. However, when Emerald, Inc. sells an additional emerald, the price must fall by $9 to $84. So the price effect component

in going from 2 to 3 emeralds is (−$9) × 2 = −$18. That's because 2 emeralds can only be sold at a price of $84 when 3 emeralds in total are sold, although they could have been sold at a price of $93 when only 2 in total were sold.

Quantity of emeralds demanded	Price of emerald	Total revenue	Marginal revenue	Quantity effect component	Price effect component
1	$100	$100			
			$86	$93	−$7
2	93	186			
			66	84	−18
3	84	252			
			28	70	−42
4	70	280			
			−30	50	−80
5	50	250			

   e. In order to determine Emerald, Inc.'s profit-maximizing output level, you must know its marginal cost at each output level. Its profit-maximizing output level is the one at which marginal revenue is equal to marginal cost.

2.   As the accompanying diagram shows, the marginal cost curve shifts upward to $400. The profit-maximizing price rises to $700 and quantity falls to 6. Profit falls from $3,200 to $300 × 6 = $1,800. The quantity a perfectly

competitive industry would produce decreases to 12, but profits remain unchanged at zero.

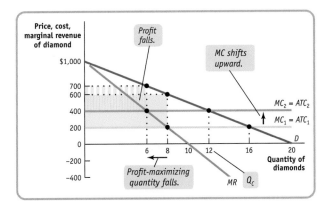

Tackle the Test:
Multiple-Choice Questions

1. b
2. c
3. b
4. d
5. d

Tackle the Test:
Free-Response Questions

2. **a.**

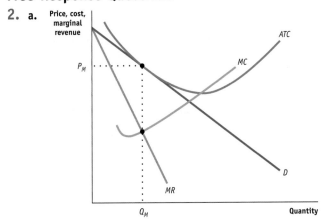

b. Yes, with the help of barriers to entry that keep competitors out.

Module 62

Check Your Understanding

1. **a.** Cable Internet service is a natural monopoly. So the government should intervene if it believes that the current price exceeds average total cost, which includes the cost of laying the cable. In this case it should impose a price ceiling equal to average total cost. If the price does not exceed average total cost, the government should do nothing.

b. The government should approve the merger only if it fosters competition by transferring some of the company's landing slots to another, competing airline.

2. **a.** False. Although some consumer surplus is indeed transformed into monopoly profit, this is not the source of inefficiency. As can be seen from Figure 62.1, panel (b), the inefficiency arises from the fact that some of the consumer surplus is transformed into deadweight loss (the yellow area), which is a complete loss not captured by consumers, producers, or anyone else.

b. True. If a monopolist sold to all customers willing to pay an amount greater than or equal to marginal cost, all mutually beneficial transactions would occur and there would be no deadweight loss.

3. As shown in the accompanying diagram, a "smart" profit–maximizing monopolist produces Q_M, the output level at which $MR = MC$. A monopolist who mistakenly believes that $P = MR$ produces the output level at which $P = MC$ (when, in fact, $P > MR$, and at the true profit-maximizing level of output, $P > MR = MC$). This misguided monopolist will produce the output level Q_C, where the demand curve crosses the marginal cost curve—the same output level that would be produced if the industry were perfectly competitive. It will charge the price P_C, which is equal to marginal cost, and make zero profit. The entire shaded area is equal to the consumer surplus, which is also equal to total surplus in this case (since the monopolist receives zero producer surplus). There is no deadweight loss because every consumer who is willing to pay as much as or more than marginal cost gets the good. A smart monopolist, however, will produce the output level Q_M and charge the price P_M. Profit for the smart monopolist is represented by the green area, consumer surplus corresponds to the blue area, and total surplus is equal to the sum of the green and blue areas. The yellow area is the deadweight loss generated by the monopolist.

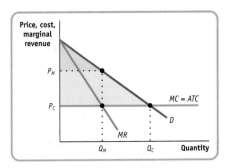

Tackle the Test:
Multiple-Choice Questions

1. a
2. b
3. c
4. a
5. b

Tackle the Test:
Free-Response Questions

2.

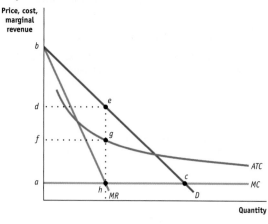

a. triangle *bca*
b. triangle *bed*
c. rectangle *degf*
d. triangle *ech*

Module 63
Check Your Understanding

1. **a.** False. The opposite is true. A price-discriminating monopolist will sell to some customers that would not find the product affordable if purchasing from a single-price monopolist—namely, customers with a high price elasticity of demand who are willing to pay only a relatively low price for the good.
   b. False. Although a price-discriminating monopolist does indeed capture more of the consumer surplus, less inefficiency is created: more mutually beneficial transactions occur because the monopolist makes more sales to customers with a low willingness to pay for the good.
   c. True. Under price discrimination consumers are charged prices that depend on their price elasticity of demand. A consumer with highly elastic demand will pay a lower price than a consumer with inelastic demand.

2. **a.** This is not a case of price discrimination because the product itself is different and all consumers, regardless of their price elasticities of demand, value the damaged merchandise less than undamaged merchandise. So the price must be lowered to sell the merchandise.
   b. This is a case of price discrimination. Senior citizens have a higher price elasticity of demand for restaurant meals (their demand for restaurant meals is more responsive to price changes) than other patrons. Restaurants lower the price to high-elasticity consumers (senior citizens). Consumers with low price elasticity of demand will pay the full price.
   c. This is a case of price discrimination. Consumers with a high price elasticity of demand will pay a lower price by collecting and using discount coupons. Consumers with a low price elasticity of demand will not use coupons.
   d. This is not a case of price discrimination; it is simply a case of supply and demand.

Tackle the Test:
Multiple-Choice Questions

1. d
2. c
3. b
4. e
5. a

Tackle the Test:
Free-Response Questions

2.

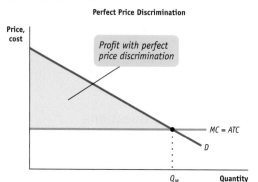

Consumer surplus is zero because each consumer is charged the maximum he or she is willing to pay.

Module 64
Check Your Understanding

1. **a.** This will decrease the likelihood that the firm will collude to restrict output. By increasing output, the firm will generate a negative price effect. But because the firm's current market share is small, the price effect will fall mostly on its rivals' revenues rather than on its own. At the same time, the firm will benefit from a positive quantity effect.
   b. This will decrease the likelihood that the firm will collude to restrict output. By acting noncooperatively and raising output, the firm will cause the price to fall. Because its rivals have higher costs, they will lose money at the lower price while the firm continues to make profits. So the firm may be able to drive its rivals out of business by increasing its output.
   c. This will increase the likelihood that the firm will collude. Because it is costly for consumers to switch products, the firm would have to lower its price substantially (with a commensurate increase in quantity) to induce consumers to switch to its product. So increasing output is likely to be unprofitable, given the large negative price effect.
   d. This will increase the likelihood that the firm will collude. It cannot increase sales because it is currently at maximum production capacity, making attempts to undercut rivals' prices as under the Bertrand model fruitless due to the inability to produce the output needed to steal the rivals' customers. This makes the option to cooperate in restricting output relatively attractive.

Tackle the Test:
Multiple-Choice Questions

1. a
2. e
3. d
4. e
5. b

Tackle the Test:
Free-Response Questions

2. **a.** The first major reason is that cartels are illegal in the United States. The second major reason is that cartels set prices above marginal cost, which creates an incentive for each firm to cheat on the cartel agreement in order to make more profit. This incentive to cheat tends to cause cartels to fall apart.
   b. Under the Cournot model, each firm treats the production of other firms as fixed and chooses the quantity that will maximize profit. This type of quantity competition results in relatively low production levels and positive economic profit. Under the Bertrand model, firms undercut the prices of their rivals until price equals marginal cost. This type of price competition results in normal profit (zero economic profit), as under perfect competition.

Module 65
Check Your Understanding

1. **a.** A Nash equilibrium is a set of actions from which neither side wants to deviate (change actions), given what the other is doing. Both sides building a missile is a Nash equilibrium because neither player wants to deviate from the decision to build a missile. To switch from building to not building a missile, given that the other player is building a missile, would result in a change from −10 to −20 utils. There is no other Nash equilibrium in this game because for any other set of actions, at least one side is not building a missile, and would be better off switching to building a missile.
   b. Their total payoff is greatest when neither side builds a missile, in which case their total payoff is 0 + 0 = 0.
   c. This outcome would require cooperation because each side sees itself as better off by building a missile. If Margaret builds a missile but Nikita does not, Margaret gets a payoff of +8, rather than the 0 she gets if she doesn't build a missile. Similarly, Nikita is better off if he builds a missile but Margaret doesn't: he gets a payoff of +8, rather than the 0 he gets if he doesn't build a missile. Indeed, both players have an incentive to build a missile regardless of what the other side does. So unless Nikita and Margaret are able to communicate in some way to enforce cooperation, they will act in their own individual interests and each will pursue its dominant strategy of building a missile.

2. **a.** Future entry by several new firms will increase competition and drive down industry profits. As a result, there is less future profit to protect by behaving cooperatively today. This makes each oligopolist more likely to behave noncooperatively today.
   b. When it is very difficult for a firm to detect if another firm has raised output, it is very difficult to enforce cooperation by playing "tit for tat." So it is more likely that a firm will behave noncooperatively.
   c. When firms have coexisted while maintaining high prices for a long time, each expects cooperation to continue. So the value of behaving cooperatively today is high, and it is likely that firms will engage in tacit collusion.

Tackle the Test:
Multiple-Choice Questions

1. b
2. b
3. c
4. a
5. c

Tackle the Test:
Free-Response Questions

2.

Module 66
Check Your Understanding

1. **a.** This is evidence of tacit collusion. Firms in the industry are able to tacitly collude by setting their prices according to the published "suggested" price of the largest firm in the industry. This is a form of price leadership.
   b. This is not evidence of tacit collusion. Considerable variation in market shares indicates that firms have been competing to capture each other's business.
   c. This is not evidence of tacit collusion. These features make it less likely that consumers will switch products in response to lower prices. So this is a way for firms to avoid any temptation to gain market share by lowering price. This is a form of product differentiation used to avoid direct competition.
   d. This is evidence of tacit collusion. In the guise of discussing sales targets, firms can create a cartel by designating quantities to be produced by each firm.
   e. This is evidence of tacit collusion. By raising prices to-gether, each firm in the industry is refusing to undercut its rivals by leaving its price unchanged or lowering

it. Because it could gain market share by doing so, refusing to do so supports the conclusion that there is tacit collusion.

Tackle the Test:
Multiple-Choice Questions

1. d
2. d
3. c
4. e
5. a

Tackle the Test:
Free-Response Questions

2. **a.** A large number of firms: having more firms means there is less incentive for any firm to behave cooperatively.
   b. Complex products/pricing schemes: keeping track of adherence to an agreement is more difficult.
   c. Differences in interests: firms often have different views of their own interests and of what a fair agreement would entail.
   d. Bargaining power of buyers: firms are less able to raise prices for buyers with significant bargaining power, which can result from size or access to many options.

Module 67

Check Your Understanding

1. **a.** An increase in fixed cost shifts the average total cost curve upward. In the short run, firms incur losses because price is below average total cost. In the long run, some firms will exit the industry, resulting in a rightward shift of the demand curves for those firms that remain, since each firm now serves a larger share of the market. Long-run equilibrium is reestablished when the demand curve for each remaining firm has shifted rightward to the point where it is tangent to the firm's new, higher average total cost curve. At this point each firm's price just equals its average total cost, and each firm makes zero profit.
   b. A decrease in marginal cost shifts the average total cost curve and the marginal cost curve downward. In the short run, firms earn positive economic profit. In the long run new entrants are attracted into the industry by the profit. This results in a leftward shift of each existing firm's demand curve because each firm now has a smaller share of the market. Long-run equilibrium is reestablished when each firm's demand curve has shifted leftward to the point where it is tangent to the new, lower average total cost curve. At this point each firm's price just equals average total cost, and each firm makes zero profit.

2. If all the existing firms in the industry joined together to create a monopoly, they could achieve positive economic profit in the short run. But this would induce new firms to create new, differentiated products and then enter the industry and capture some of the profit. So, in the long

run, thanks to the lack of barriers to entry, it would be impossible to maintain such a monopoly.

3. **a.** False. As illustrated in panel (b) of Figure 67.4, a monopolistically competitive firm sells its output at a price that exceeds marginal cost—unlike a perfectly competitive firm, which sells at a price equal to marginal cost. Not only does a monopolistically competitive firm maximize profit by charging more than marginal cost, but in long-run equilibrium, a price equal to marginal cost would be below average total cost and cause the firm to incur a loss.
   b. True. Firms in a monopolistically competitive industry could achieve higher profit (*monopoly profit*) if they all joined together as a single firm with a single product. Because each of the smaller firms possesses excess capacity, a single firm producing a larger quantity would have a lower average total cost. The effect on consumers, however, is ambiguous. They would experience less choice. But if consolidation substantially reduced industry-wide average total cost and increases industry-wide output, consumers could experience lower prices with the monopoly.
   c. True. Fads and fashions are promulgated by advertising and a desire for product differentiation, which are common in oligopolies and monopolistically competitive industries, but not in monopolies or perfectly competitive industries.

Tackle the Test:
Multiple-Choice Questions

1. b
2. e
3. b
4. b
5. e

Tackle the Test:
Free-Response Questions

2.

Module 68

Check Your Understanding

1. a. This type of advertising is likely to be useful because it provides new information on an important product.
   b. This type of advertising is likely to be wasteful because it is focused on promoting Bayer aspirin over a rival's aspirin despite the two products being medically indistinguishable.
   c. This is useful because the longevity of a business gives a potential customer information about its quality.

2. A successful brand name indicates a desirable attribute, such as quality, to a potential buyer. So, other things equal—such as price—a firm with a successful brand name will achieve higher sales than a rival with a comparable product but without a successful brand name. This is likely to deter new firms from entering an industry in which an existing firm has a successful brand name.

Tackle the Test:
Multiple-Choice Questions

1. e
2. d
3. a
4. e
5. d

Tackle the Test:
Free-Response Questions

2. Product differentiation is efficient when it conveys useful information to consumers and the marginal benefit of the product differentiation exceeds the marginal cost. It is not efficient from a societal standpoint if it does not convey useful information or other benefits worth more than the resources devoted to it. This is likely to be the case, for example, if it misleads consumers or creates undesirable market power.

Module 69

Check Your Understanding

1. Many college professors will depart for other lines of work if the government imposes a wage that is lower than the market wage. Fewer professors will result in fewer courses taught and therefore fewer college degrees produced. It will adversely affect sectors of the economy that depend directly on colleges, such as the local shopkeepers who sell goods and services to students and faculty, college textbook publishers, and so on. It will also adversely affect firms that use the "output" produced by colleges: new college graduates. Firms that need to hire new employees with college degrees will be hurt as a smaller supply results in a higher market wage for college graduates. Ultimately, the reduced supply of college-educated workers will result in a lower level of human capital in the entire economy relative to what it would have been without the policy. And this will hurt all sectors of the economy that depend on human capital. The sectors of the economy that might benefit are firms that compete with colleges in the hiring of would-be college professors. For example, accounting firms will find it easier to hire people who would otherwise have been professors of accounting, and publishers will find it easier to hire people who would otherwise have been professors of English (easier in the sense that the firms can recruit would-be professors with a lower wage than before). In addition, workers who already have college degrees will benefit; they will command higher wages as the supply of college-educated workers falls.

2. a. The demand curve for labor shifts to the right.
   b. The demand curve for labor shifts to the left.

Tackle the Test:
Multiple-Choice Questions

1. b
2. e
3. d
4. b
5. a

Tackle the Test:
Free-Response Questions

2. a.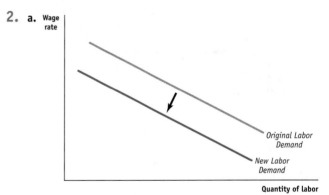

b.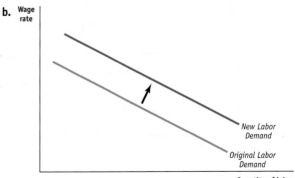

c.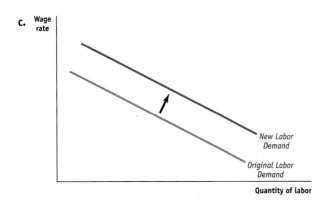

Module 70

Check your Understanding

1. a. This would increase the supply of land, shifting the supply curve to the right and leading to a new equilibrium at a lower rental rate and a higher quantity.

b. This would increase the marginal product of land and thus the value of the marginal product of land. The *VMP* curve for land would shift to the right, leading to a new equilibrium at a higher rental rate and a higher quantity.

2. When firms from different industries compete for the same land, an inter-industry land market develops and, other things being equal, each unit of land used by the various industries will rent for the same equilibrium rental rate, *R*. According to the marginal productivity theory of income distribution, *VMP* for land = *R* for the last unit of land rented. Because each industry rents until *VMP* for land = *R*, the last unit of land rented in each of these different industries will have the same value of the marginal product of land.

Tackle the Test:
Multiple-Choice Questions

1. a
2. c
3. a
4. c
5. e

Tackle the Test:
Free-Response Questions

2.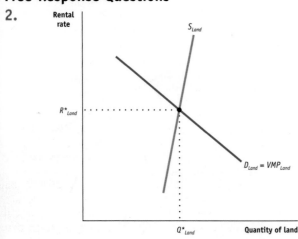

Module 71

Check Your Understanding

1. a. Clive is made worse off if, before the new law, he had preferred to work more than 35 hours per week. As a result of the law, he can no longer choose his preferred time allocation; he now consumes fewer goods and more leisure than he would like.

b. Clive's utility is unaffected by the law if, before the law, he had preferred to work 35 or fewer hours per week. The law has not changed his preferred time allocation.

c. Clive can never be made better off by a law that restricts the number of hours he can work. He can only be made worse off (case a) or equally as well off (case b).

2. The substitution effect would induce Clive to work fewer hours and consume more leisure after his wage rate falls—the fall in the wage rate means the price of an hour of leisure falls, leading Clive to consume more leisure. But a fall in his wage rate also generates a fall in Clive's income. The income effect of this is to induce Clive to consume less leisure and therefore work more hours, since he is now poorer and leisure is a normal good. If the income effect dominates the substitution effect, Clive will in the end work more hours than before.

Tackle the Test:
Multiple-Choice Questions

1. d
2. a
3. e
4. c
5. d

Tackle the Test:
Free-Response Questions

2.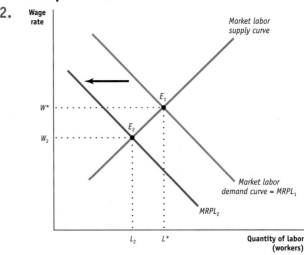

Module 72

Check Your Understanding

1. Yes, the firm is employing the cost-minimizing combination of inputs because the marginal product per dollar is equal for capital and labor: 500/$100 = 1,000/$200 = 5 units of output per dollar.

Tackle the Test:
Multiple-Choice Questions

1. c
2. b
3. c
4. a
5. d

Tackle the Test:
Free-Response Questions

2. **a.** 20
   b. 10/$10 = 1 pencil per dollar
   c. The firm would hire 6 workers.
   d. No. The marginal product per dollar spent on capital is 100/$50 = 2 pencils per dollar. Thus, the firm is not following the cost-minimization rule because the marginal product per dollar spent on labor (1) is less than the marginal product per dollar spent on capital (2).

Module 73
Check Your Understanding

1. **a.** False. Income disparities associated with gender, race, and ethnicity can be explained by the marginal productivity theory of income distribution, provided that differences in marginal productivity across people are correlated with gender, race, or ethnicity. One possible source for such correlation is past discrimination. Such discrimination can lower individuals' marginal productivity by, for example, preventing them from acquiring the human capital that would raise their productivity. Another possible source of the correlation is differences in work experience that are associated with gender, race, or ethnicity. For example, in jobs for which work experience or length of tenure is important, women may earn lower wages because on average more women than men take child-care-related absences from work.

   b. True. Companies that discriminate when their competitors do not are likely to hire less able workers because they discriminate against more able workers who are considered to be of the wrong gender, race, ethnicity, or other characteristic. And with less able workers, such companies are likely to earn less profit than their competitors who don't discriminate.

   c. Ambiguous. In general, workers who are paid less because they have less experience may or may not be the victims of discrimination. The answer depends on the reason for the lack of experience. If workers have less experience because they are young or have chosen to do something else rather than gain experience, then they are not victims of discrimination as long as the lower earnings are commensurate with the lower level of experience (as opposed, for example, to earning a lot less while having just a little less experience). But if workers lack experience because previous job discrimination prevented them from gaining experience, then they are indeed victims of discrimination when they are paid less.

Tackle the Test:
Multiple-Choice Questions

1. a
2. a
3. a
4. b
5. e

Tackle the Test:
Free-Response Questions

2. **a.** Market power—firms with market power can organize to pay lower wages than would result in a perfectly competitive labor market. Monopsonies pay less than the value of the marginal product of labor. And unions can organize to demand higher wages than would result in a perfectly competitive labor market.
   b. Efficiency wages—some firms pay high wages to boost worker performance and encourage loyalty.
   c. Discrimination—some firms pay workers differently solely on the basis of worker characteristics that do not affect marginal productivity.

Module 74
Check Your Understanding

1. **a.** This is an externality problem because the cost of wastewater runoff is imposed on the farms' neighbors with no compensation and no other way for the farms to internalize the cost.
   b. Since the large poultry farmers do not take the external cost of their actions into account when making decisions about how much wastewater to generate, they will create more runoff than is socially optimal. They will produce runoff up to the point at which the marginal social benefit of an additional unit of runoff is zero; however, their neighbors experience a high, positive level of marginal social cost of runoff from this output level. So the quantity of wastewater runoff is inefficient: reducing runoff by one unit would reduce total social benefit by less than it would reduce total social cost.
   c. At the socially optimal quantity of wastewater runoff, the marginal social benefit is equal to the marginal social cost. This quantity is lower than the quantity of wastewater runoff that would be created in the absence of government intervention or a private deal.

2. Yasmin's reasoning is not correct: allowing some late returns of books is likely to be socially optimal. Although you impose a marginal social cost on others every day that you are late in returning a book, there is some positive marginal social benefit to you of returning a book late—you get a longer period during which to use it for education and pleasure. If you need it for a book report, the additional benefit from another day might be large indeed.

   The socially optimal number of days that a book is returned late is the number at which the marginal social benefit equals the marginal social cost. A fine so stiff that it prevents any late returns is likely to result in a situation in which people return books although the marginal social benefit of keeping them another day is greater than the marginal social cost—an inefficient outcome. In that case, allowing an overdue patron another day would increase total social benefit more than it would increase total social cost. So charging a moderate fine that reduces the number of days that books are returned late to the socially optimal number of days is appropriate.

Tackle the Test:
Multiple-Choice Questions

1. a
2. a
3. d
4. b
5. d

Tackle the Test:
Free-Response Questions

2. **a.** The marginal social cost of pollution is the additional cost imposed on society by an additional unit of pollution.
    b. The marginal social benefit of pollution is the additional benefit to society from an additional unit of pollution. Even when a firm could provide the same quantity of output without polluting as much, there is a benefit from polluting more because the firm can devote less money and resources to pollution avoidance.
    c. The socially optimal level of pollution is that level at which the marginal social benefit of pollution equals the marginal social cost.

Module 75

Check Your Understanding

1. This is a misguided argument. Allowing polluters to sell emissions permits makes polluters face a cost of polluting: the opportunity cost of not being able to sell the permits that cover that pollution. If a polluter chooses not to reduce its emissions, it cannot sell its emissions permits. As a result, it forgoes the opportunity of making money from the sale of the permits. So, despite the fact that the polluter receives a monetary benefit from selling the permits, the scheme has the desired effect: to make polluters internalize the externality of their actions and reduce the total amount of pollution.

2. **a.** Planting trees imposes an external benefit: the marginal social benefit of planting trees is higher than the marginal private benefit to individual tree planters because many people (not just those who plant the trees) can enjoy the improved air quality and lower summer temperatures. The difference between the marginal social benefit and the marginal private benefit to individual tree planters is the marginal external benefit. A Pigouvian subsidy equal to the marginal external benefit could be placed on each tree planted in urban areas in order to increase the marginal private benefit to individual tree planters to the same level as the marginal social benefit.
    b. Water-saving toilets create an external benefit: the marginal private benefit to individual homeowners from replacing a traditional toilet with a water-saving toilet is almost zero because water is very inexpensive. But the marginal social benefit is large because fewer critical

rivers and aquifers need to be pumped. The difference between the marginal social benefit and the marginal private benefit to individual homeowners is the marginal external benefit. A Pigouvian subsidy for installing water-saving toilets equal to the marginal external benefit could bring the marginal private benefit to individual homeowners in line with the marginal social benefit.
    c. Disposing of old computer monitors imposes an external cost: the marginal private cost to those disposing of old computer monitors is lower than the marginal social cost, since environmental pollution is borne by people other than the person disposing of the monitor. The difference between the marginal social cost and the marginal private cost to those disposing of old computer monitors is the marginal external cost. A Pigouvian tax on the disposal of computer monitors equal to the marginal external cost, or a system of tradable permits for their disposal, could raise the marginal private cost to those disposing of old computer monitors up to the level of the marginal social cost.

Tackle the Test:
Multiple-Choice Questions

1. a
2. d
3. c
4. a
5. a

Tackle the Test:
Free-Response Questions

2.

Module 76

Check Your Understanding

1. **a.** A public space is generally nonexcludable, but it may or may not be rival in consumption, depending on the level of congestion. For example, if you and I are the only users of a jogging path in the public park, then your use will not prevent my use—the path is nonrival in consumption. In this case the public space is a public good. But the space is rival in consumption if there are many people trying to use the jogging path at the same time or

if my use of the public tennis court prevents your use of the same court. In this case the public space becomes a common resource.

b. A cheese burrito is both excludable and rival in consumption. Hence it is a private good.

c. Information from a password-protected website is excludable but nonrival in consumption. So it is an artificially scarce good.

d. Publicly announced information about the path of an incoming hurricane is nonexcludable and nonrival in consumption, so it is a public good.

2. A private producer will supply only a good that is excludable; otherwise, the producer won't be able to charge a price for it that covers the cost of production. So a private producer would be willing to supply a cheese burrito and information from a password-protected website but unwilling to supply a public park or publicly announced information about an incoming hurricane.

Tackle the Test:
Multiple-Choice Questions

1. a
2. b
3. e
4. d
5. e

Tackle the Test:
Free-Response Questions

2. **a.** Nonrival in consumption: the same unit of the good can be consumed by more than one person at the same time. Nonexcludable: suppliers of the good can't prevent people who don't pay from consuming the good.

b. The additional cost is zero. Public goods are nonrival, so the same unit can be provided to additional community members at no added cost.

Module 77

Check Your Understanding

1. **a.** This practice would be illegal because it constitutes a tying arrangement.

b. This practice would be illegal because it constitutes exclusive dealing.

c. This is legal because the merger does not lead to monopolization.

d. This practice would be illegal because it is a collusive agreement to restrain trade.

2. Wind energy is created by a natural monopoly, which means that marginal cost is below average total cost in the relevant range of production. (If fact, the marginal cost of wind energy is virtually zero, because the wind itself is free.) Thus, a requirement to charge a price equal to marginal cost would result in a price below average total cost and cause the firm to incur a loss. Only with subsidies could the firm survive with marginal cost pricing. If policymakers chose average cost pricing instead, the operator of the wind farm would make a normal profit and no subsidy would be necessary.

Tackle the Test:
Multiple-Choice Questions

1. e
2. b
3. b
4. c
5. c

Tackle the Test:
Free-Response Questions

2. Antitrust policy: prohibit practices that create monopolies and break up existing monopolies.
Public ownership: have government operate the monopoly with the goal of efficiency rather than profit.
Price regulation: restrict price to the lowest price that does not cause losses, which is the price at which the average total cost curve intersects the demand curve.

Module 78

Check Your Understanding

1. The poverty threshold is an absolute measure of poverty. It defines individuals as poor if their incomes fall below a level that is considered adequate to purchase the necessities of life, irrespective of how well other people are doing. And that measure is fixed: in 2009, for instance, it took $10,956 for an individual living alone to purchase the necessities of life, regardless of how well-off other Americans were. In particular, the poverty threshold is not adjusted for an increase in living standards: even if other Americans are becoming increasingly well-off over time, in real terms (that is, in terms of how many goods an individual at the poverty threshold can buy) the poverty threshold remains the same.

Tackle the Test:
Multiple-Choice Questions

1. a
2. b
3. e
4. c
5. a

Tackle the Test:
Free-Response Questions

2. (Answers to the first part of the question will differ.) Economics can add to our knowledge of the facts regarding trade-offs involved in implementing government programs to redistribute income. However, economics can't resolve differences in values and philosophies.

Module 79

Check Your Understanding

1. The inefficiency caused by adverse selection is that an insurance policy with a premium based on the average risk of all drivers will attract only an adverse selection of

bad drivers. Good (that is, safe) drivers will find this insurance premium too expensive and so will remain uninsured. This is inefficient. However, safe drivers are also those drivers who have had fewer moving violations for several years. Lowering premiums for only those drivers allows the insurance company to screen its customers and sell insurance to safe drivers, too. This means that at least some of the good drivers now are also insured, which decreases the inefficiency that arises from adverse selection. In a way, having no moving violations for several years is a way of building a reputation as a safe driver.

2. The moral hazard problem in home construction arises from private information about what the contractor does: whether she takes care to reduce the cost of construction or allows costs to increase. The homeowner cannot, or can only imperfectly, observe the cost-reduction efforts of the contractor. If the contractor were fully reimbursed for all costs incurred during construction, she would have no incentive to reduce costs. Making the contractor responsible for any additional costs above the original estimate means that she now has an incentive to keep costs low. However, this imposes risk on the contractor. For instance, if the weather is bad, home construction will take longer, and will be more costly, than if the weather had been good. Since the contractor pays for any additional costs (such as weather-induced delays) above the original estimate, she now faces risk that she cannot control.

3. **a.** True. Drivers with higher deductibles have more incentive to take care in their driving in order to avoid paying the deductible. This is a moral hazard phenomenon.
   b. True. Suppose you know that you are a safe driver. You have a choice of a policy with a high premium but a low deductible or one with a lower premium but a higher deductible. In this case, you would be more inclined to choose the cheap policy with the high deductible because you know that you will be unlikely to have to pay the deductible. When there is adverse selection, insurance companies use screening devices such as this to infer private information about how skillful people are as drivers.

Tackle the Test:
Multiple-Choice Questions

1. d
2. a
3. b
4. a
5. b

Tackle the Test:
Free-Response Questions

2. This is an example of moral hazard. The government bears the cost of any lack of care in the individual/corporate decisions. Distorted incentives lead the individual/corporation to make riskier decisions because, if a decision is bad, the cost falls on others. The individuals/corporations must be given a personal stake in the result of their decisions. This could be achieved by making the individuals/corporations repay at least some portion of the bailout cost.

Module 80
Check Your Understanding

1. **a.** As you can see from the accompanying diagram the four bundles are associated with three indifference curves: B on the 10-util indifference curve, A and C on the 6-util indifference curve, and D on the 4-util indifference curve.

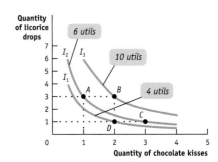

   b. From comparing the quantities of chocolate kisses and licorice drops, you can predict that Samantha will prefer B to A because B gives her one more chocolate kiss and the same number of licorice drops as A. Next, you can predict that she will prefer C to D because C gives her one more chocolate kiss and the same number of licorice drops as D. You can also predict that she prefers B to D because B gives her two more licorice drops and the same number of chocolate kisses as D. But without data about utils, you cannot predict how Samantha would rank A versus C or D because C and D have more chocolate kisses but fewer licorice drops than A. Nor can you rank B versus C, for the same reason.

2. Bundles A and B each generate 200 utils since they both lie on the 200-util indifference curve. Likewise, bundles A and C each generate 100 utils since they both lie on the 100-util indifference curve. But this implies that A generates 100 utils and also that A generates 200 utils. This is a contradiction and so cannot be true. Therefore, indifference curves cannot cross.

3. **a.** The marginal rate of substitution of books for games, MU_B/MU_G, is 2 for Lucinda and 5 for Kyle. This implies that Lucinda is willing to trade 1 more book for 2 fewer games and Kyle is willing to trade 1 more book for 5 fewer games. So starting from a bundle of 3 books and 6 games, Lucinda would be equally content with a bundle of 4 books and 4 games and Kyle would be equally content with a bundle of 4 books and 1 game. Lucinda finds it more difficult to trade games for books: she is willing to give up only 2 games for a book but Kyle is willing to give up 5 games for a book. If books are measured on the horizontal axis and games on the vertical axis, Kyle's indifference curve will be steeper than Lucinda's at the current consumption bundle.
   b. Lucinda's current consumption bundle is optimal if P_B/P_G, the relative price of books in terms of games, is 2. Kyle's current consumption bundle is not optimal at this relative price; his bundle would be optimal only if the relative price of books in terms of games were 5. Since, for

Kyle, $MU_B/MU_G = 5$, if $P_B/P_G = 2$, he should consume fewer games and more books to lower his MU_B/MU_G until it is equal to 2.

Tackle the Test:
Multiple-Choice Questions

1. c
2. e
3. a
4. b
5. e

Tackle the Test:
Free-Response Questions

2. **a.**

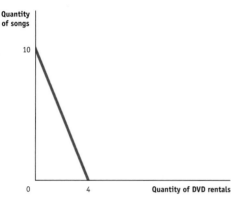

b. Kathleen would purchase 10 song downloads and 0 DVD rentals. We know that Kathleen wants to be on the highest indifference curve possible. We also know that there is no tangency point in this case because the indifference curve and the budget line are both straight lines with different slopes. Thus, the highest indifference curve that touches the budget line will touch it on one of the axes. Since the slope of the budget line is steeper than the slope of the indifference curve (−2.5 versus −0.5), the highest indifference curve that can be afforded, given the budget line, is at the point 10 songs and 0 DVD rentals.

Italicized terms within definitions are key terms that are defined elsewhere in this glossary.

absolute advantage the advantage conferred by the ability to produce more of a good or service with a given amount of time and resources; not the same thing as *comparative advantage*. (p. 27)

accounting profit a business's revenue minus the *explicit cost* and depreciation. (p. 531)

actual investment spending the sum of *planned investment spending* and *unplanned inventory investment*. (p. 169)

AD–AS model the basic model used to understand fluctuations in *aggregate output* and the *aggregate price level*. It uses the *aggregate demand curve* and the *aggregate supply curve* together to analyze the behavior of the *economy* in response to shocks or government policy. (p. 190)

administrative costs (of a tax) the *resources* used (which is a cost) by government to collect the tax, and by taxpayers to pay it, over and above the amount of the tax, as well as to evade it. (p. 508)

adverse selection occurs when an individual knows more about the way things are than other people do. Adverse selection problems can lead to market problems: private information leads buyers to expect hidden problems in items offered for sale, leading to low prices and the best items being kept off the market. (p. 783)

aggregate consumption function the relationship for the *economy* as a whole between aggregate current *disposable income* and aggregate *consumer spending*. (p. 164)

aggregate demand curve shows the relationship between the *aggregate price level* and the quantity of *aggregate output* demanded by *households*, *businesses*, the government, and the rest of the world. (p. 172)

aggregate output the economy's total production of *final goods and services* for a given time period, usually a year. *Real GDP* is the numerical measure of aggregate output typically used by economists. (pp. 12, 113)

aggregate price level a measure of the overall level of prices in the economy. (p. 142)

aggregate production function a hypothetical function that shows how productivity (*real GDP* per worker) depends on the quantities of *physical*

capital per worker and *human capital* per worker as well as the state of technology. (p. 376)

aggregate spending the total spending on domestically produced *final goods and services*; the sum of *consumer spending* (C), *investment spending* (I), *government purchases of goods and services* (G), and *exports* minus *imports* (X – IM). (p. 106)

aggregate supply curve a graphical representation that shows the relationship between the *aggregate price level* and the total quantity of *aggregate output* supplied. (p. 179)

antitrust policy legislative and regulatory efforts undertaken by the government to prevent oligopolistic industries from becoming or behaving like *monopolies*. (p. 653)

appreciation a rise in the value of one currency in terms of other currencies. (p. 422)

artificially scarce good a good that is *excludable* but *nonrival in consumption*. (p. 751)

automatic stabilizers government spending and taxation rules that cause *fiscal policy* to be automatically expansionary when the *economy* contracts and automatically contractionary when the economy expands. Taxes that depend on *disposable income* are the most important example of automatic stabilizers. (p. 212)

autonomous change in aggregate spending an initial rise or fall in *aggregate spending* that is the cause, not the result, of a series of income and spending changes. (p. 160)

autonomous consumer spending the amount of money a *household* would spend if it had no *disposable income*. (p. 162)

average cost pricing occurs when regulators set a monopoly's price equal to its average cost to prevent the firm from incurring a loss. (p. 757)

average fixed cost the *fixed cost* per unit of output. (p. 553)

average total cost *total cost* divided by quantity of output produced. Also referred to as *average cost*. (p. 552)

average variable cost the *variable cost* per unit of output. (p. 553)

balance of payments accounts a summary of a country's transactions with

other countries, including two main elements: the *balance of payments on the current account* and the *balance of payments on the financial account*. (p. 410)

balance of payments on the current account (current account) a country's *balance of payments on goods and services* plus net international transfer payments and factor income. (p. 412)

balance of payments on the financial account (financial account) the difference between a country's sales of assets to foreigners and its purchases of assets from foreigners during a given period. (p. 413)

balance of payments on goods and services the difference between the value of *exports* and the value of *imports* during a given period. (p. 412)

balance sheet effect the reduction in a firm's net worth from falling asset prices. (p. 258)

bank a *financial intermediary* that provides *liquid* assets in the form of *bank deposits* to lenders and uses those funds to finance the *illiquid* investments or *investment spending* needs of borrowers. (p. 229)

bank deposit a claim on a bank that obliges the bank to give the depositor his or her cash when demanded. (p. 229)

bank reserves currency held by *banks* in their vaults plus their deposits at the Federal Reserve. (p. 243)

bank run a phenomenon in which many of a *bank's* depositors try to withdraw their funds due to fears of a bank failure. (p. 246)

barrier to entry something that prevents other firms from entering an industry. Crucial in protecting the profits of a *monopolist*. There are four types of barriers to entry: control over scarce *resources* or *inputs*, increasing returns to scale, technological superiority, and government-created barriers such as *licenses*. (p. 571)

black market a market in which goods or services are bought and sold illegally, either because it is illegal to sell them at all or because the prices charged are legally prohibited by a *price ceiling*. (p. 81)

bond loan in the form of an IOU that pays interest. (p. 104)

brand name a name owned by a particular firm that distinguishes its products from those of other firms. (p. 672)

break-even price the market price at which a firm earns zero profits. (p. 592)

budget balance the difference between tax revenue and government spending. A positive budget balance is referred to as a *budget surplus;* a negative budget balance is referred to as a *budget deficit.* (p. 223)

budget constraint the cost of a consumer's *consumption bundle* cannot exceed the consumer's income. (p. 514)

budget deficit the difference between tax revenue and government spending when government spending exceeds tax revenue. (p. 223)

budget line all the *consumption bundles* available to a consumer who spends all of his or her income. (p. 514)

budget surplus the difference between tax revenue and government spending when tax revenue exceeds government spending. (p. 223)

business cycle the short-run alternation between economic downturns, known as *recessions,* and economic upturns, known as *expansions.* (p. 10)

capital manufactured goods used to make other goods and services. (p. 3)

capital inflow the net inflow of funds into a country; the difference between the total inflow of foreign funds to the home country and the total outflow of domestic funds to other countries. A positive net capital inflow represents funds borrowed from foreigners to finance domestic investment; a negative net capital inflow represents funds lent to foreigners to finance foreign investment. (p. 223)

cartel an agreement among several producers to obey output restrictions in order to increase their joint profits. (p. 639)

central bank an institution that oversees and regulates the banking system and controls the *monetary base.* (p. 253)

chain-linking the method of calculating changes in *real GDP* using the average between the growth rate calculated using an early base year and the growth rate calculated using a late base year. (p. 115)

change in demand a shift of the *demand curve,* which changes the quantity demanded at any given price. (p. 51)

change in supply a shift of the *supply curve,* which changes the quantity supplied at any given price. (p. 60)

checkable bank deposits *bank* accounts on which people can write checks. (p. 231)

classical model of the price level a model of the price level in which the real quantity of money is always at its long-run equilibrium level. This model ignores the distinction between the short run and the long run but is useful for analyzing the case of high inflation. (p. 322)

Coase theorem the proposition that even in the presence of *externalities* an *economy* can always reach an *efficient* solution as long as *transaction costs* are sufficiently low. (p. 728)

collusion cooperation among producers to limit production and raise prices so as to raise one another's profits. (p. 639)

command economy industry is publicly owned and a central authority makes production and consumption decisions. (p. 2)

commercial bank a *bank* that accepts deposits and is covered by *deposit insurance.* (p. 257)

commodity-backed money a *medium of exchange* that has no intrinsic value whose ultimate value is guaranteed by a promise that it can be converted into valuable goods on demand. (p. 233)

commodity money a *medium of exchange* that is a good, normally gold or silver, that has intrinsic value in other uses. (p. 233)

common resource a *resource* that is *nonexcludable* and *rival in consumption.* (p. 749)

comparative advantage the advantage conferred if the *opportunity cost* of producing the good or service is lower for another producer. (p. 26)

compensating differentials wage differences across jobs that reflect the fact that some jobs are less pleasant or more dangerous than others. (p. 711)

competitive market a market in which there are many buyers and sellers of the same good or service, none of whom can influence the price at which the good or service is sold. (p. 48)

complements pairs of goods for which a rise in the price of one good leads to a decrease in the demand for the other good. (p. 53)

concentration ratios measure the percentage of industry sales accounted for by the "X" largest firms. (p. 573)

constant returns to scale long-run *average total cost* is constant as output increases. (p. 563)

consumer price index (CPI) a measure of the cost of a *market basket* intended to represent the consumption of a typical urban American family of four. It is the most commonly used measure of prices in the United States. (p. 144)

consumer spending *household* spending on goods and services from domestic and foreign *firms.* (p. 103)

consumer surplus a term often used to refer both to *individual consumer surplus* and to *total consumer surplus.* (p. 485)

consumption function an equation showing how an individual household's *consumer spending* varies with the household's current *disposable income.* (p. 162)

consumption possibilities the set of all consumption bundles that are affordable, given a consumer's income and prevailing prices. (p. 514)

contractionary fiscal policy *fiscal policy* that reduces aggregate demand by decreasing government purchases, increasing taxes, or decreasing transfers. (p. 205)

contractionary monetary policy *monetary policy* that, through the raising of the *interest rate,* reduces aggregate demand and therefore output. (p. 310)

convergence hypothesis a theory of economic growth that holds that international differences in *real GDP per capita* tend to narrow over time because countries with low *GDP per capita* generally have higher growth rates. (p. 383)

copyright the exclusive legal right of the creator of a literary or artistic work to profit from that work; like a *patent,* it is a temporary monopoly. (p. 572)

cost (of potential seller) the lowest price at which a seller is willing to sell a good. (p. 489)

cost-minimization rule hire factors so that the marginal product per dollar spent on each factor is the same; a firm uses this rule to determine the cost-minimizing combination of inputs. (p. 708)

cost-push inflation inflation that is caused by a significant increase in the price of an input with economy-wide importance. (p. 327)

crowding out the negative effect of *budget deficits* on private investment, which occurs because government borrowing drives up interest rates. (p. 281)

currency in circulation actual cash held by the public. (p. 231)

current account see *balance of payments on the current account.*

cyclical unemployment unemployment resulting from the business cycle; equivalently, the difference between the actual rate of *unemployment* and the *natural rate of unemployment.* (p. 130)

cyclically adjusted budget balance an estimate of what the *budget balance* would be if *real GDP* were exactly equal to *potential output.* (p. 298)

deadweight loss losses associated with quantities of *output* that are greater than or less than the efficient level, as can result from market intervention such as taxes, or from externalities such as pollution. (pp. 92, 506)

debt deflation the reduction in aggregate demand arising from the increase in the real burden of outstanding debt caused by *deflation;* occurs because borrowers, whose real debt rises as a result of deflation, are likely to cut spending sharply, and lenders, whose real assets are now more valuable, are less likely to increase spending. (p. 339)

debt–GDP ratio government debt as a percentage of GDP, frequently used as a measure of a government's ability to pay its debts. (p. 301)

decreasing returns to scale long-run *average total cost* increases as output increases (also known as *diseconomies of scale*). (p. 563)

deductible a sum specified in an insurance policy that the insured individuals must pay before being compensated for a claim; deductibles reduce *moral hazard.* (p. 785)

default when a borrower fails to make payments as specified by the bond contract. (p. 226)

deflation a fall in the overall level of prices. (p. 12)

demand curve a graphical representation of the *demand schedule,* showing the relationship between *quantity demanded* and price. (p. 49)

demand price the price of a given quantity at which consumers will demand that quantity. (p. 89)

demand-pull inflation inflation that is caused by an increase in *aggregate demand.* (p. 327)

demand schedule a list or table showing how much of a good or service consumers will want to buy at different prices. (p. 49)

demand shock any event that shifts the *aggregate demand curve.* A positive demand shock is associated with higher demand for *aggregate output* at any price level and shifts the curve to the right. A negative demand shock is associated with lower demand for aggregate output at any price level and shifts the curve to the left. (p. 191)

deposit insurance a guarantee that a *bank's* depositors will be paid even if the bank can't come up with the funds, up to a maximum amount per account. (p. 246)

depreciation of currency a fall in the value of one currency in terms of other currencies. (pp. 400, 422)

depression a very deep and prolonged downturn. (p. 10)

derived demand for a factor results from (or is derived from) the demand for the output being produced. (p. 681)

devaluation a reduction in the value of a currency that is set under a *fixed exchange rate regime.* (p. 438)

diminishing marginal rate of substitution the principle that the more of one good that is consumed in proportion to another, the less of the second good the consumer is willing to substitute for another unit of the first good. (p. 795)

diminishing returns to an input the effect observed when an increase in the quantity of an *input,* while holding the levels of all other inputs fixed, leads to a decline in the *marginal product* of that input. (p. 545)

diminishing returns to physical capital in an *aggregate production function* when the amount of *human capital* per worker and the state of technology are

held fixed, each successive increase in the amount of *physical capital* per worker leads to a smaller increase in productivity. (p. 376)

discount rate the interest rate the Fed charges on loans to *banks.* (p. 263)

discount window an arrangement in which the Federal Reserve stands ready to lend money to *banks.* (p. 246)

discouraged workers nonworking people who are capable of working but have given up looking for a job due to the state of the job market. (p. 120)

discretionary fiscal policy *fiscal policy* that is the direct result of deliberate actions by policy makers rather than rules. (p. 212)

discretionary monetary policy the use of changes in the *interest rate* or the *money supply* to stabilize the *economy.* (p. 348)

diseconomies of scale long-run average total cost increases as output increases. (p. 562)

disinflation the process of bringing down *inflation* that has become embedded in expectations. (p. 139)

disposable income income plus *government transfers* minus taxes; the total amount of *household* income available to spend on consumption and saving. (p. 105)

diversification investment in several different assets with unrelated, or independent, risks, so that the possible losses are *independent events.* (p. 225)

dominant strategy in *game theory,* an action that is a player's best action regardless of the action taken by the other player. (p. 646)

duopolist one of the two firms in a *duopoly.* (p. 638)

duopoly an *oligopoly* consisting of only two firms. (p. 638)

economic aggregates economic measures that summarize data across different markets for goods, services, workers, and assets. (p. 5)

economic growth an increase in the maximum amount of goods and services an economy can produce. (p. 13)

economic profit a business's revenue minus the *opportunity cost* of resources; usually less than the *accounting profit.* (p. 532)

economics the study of scarcity and choice. (p. 2)

economies of scale long-run average total cost declines as output increases. (p. 562)

economy a system for coordinating a society's productive and consumptive activities. (p. 2)

efficiency wages wages that employers set above the *equilibrium* wage rate as an incentive for workers to deliver better performance. (p. 130)

efficiency-wage model a model in which some employers pay an above-equilibrium wage as an *incentive* for better performance. (p. 714)

efficient describes a market or *economy* that takes all opportunities to make some people better off without making other people worse off. (p. 17)

elastic demand the *price elasticity* of demand is greater than 1. (p. 467)

emissions tax a tax that depends on the amount of pollution a firm produces. (p. 732)

employed people currently holding a job in the economy, either full time or part time. (p. 119)

employment the total number of people currently employed for pay in the *economy*, either full-time or part-time. (p. 12)

entrepreneurship the efforts of entrepreneurs in organizing resources for production, taking risks to create new enterprises, and innovating to develop new products and production processes. (p. 3)

environmental standards rules established by a government to protect the environment by specifying actions by producers and consumers. (p. 731)

equilibrium an economic situation in which no individual would be better off doing something different. (p. 66)

equilibrium exchange rate the *exchange rate* at which the quantity of a currency demanded in the *foreign exchange market* is equal to the quantity supplied. (p. 423)

equilibrium price the price at which the market is in *equilibrium*, that is, the quantity of a good or service demanded equals the quantity of that good or service supplied; also referred to as the *market-clearing price*. (p. 66)

equilibrium quantity the quantity of a good or service bought and sold at the *equilibrium* (or *market-clearing*) *price*. (p. 66)

equilibrium value of the marginal product the additional value produced by the last unit of a factor employed in the *factor market* as a whole. (p. 712)

excess capacity when firms produce less than the output at which *average total cost* is minimized; characteristic of *monopolistically competitive* firms. (p. 665)

excess reserves a *bank's reserves* over and above the reserves required by law or regulation. (p. 249)

exchange market intervention government purchases or sales of currency in the *foreign exchange market*. (p. 432)

exchange rate the price at which currencies trade, determined by the *foreign exchange market*. (p. 421)

exchange rate regime a rule governing policy toward the *exchange rate*. (p. 431)

excise tax a tax on sales of a particular good or service. (p. 499)

excludable referring to a good, describes the case in which the supplier can prevent those who do not pay from consuming the good. (p. 743)

expansion period of economic upturn in which output and employment are rising; most economic numbers are following their normal upward trend; also referred to as a recovery. (p. 10)

expansionary fiscal policy *fiscal policy* that increases aggregate demand by increasing government purchases, decreasing taxes, or increasing transfers. (p. 205)

expansionary monetary policy *monetary policy* that, through the lowering of the *interest rate*, increases aggregate demand and therefore output. (p. 310)

explicit cost a cost that involves actually laying out money. (p. 530)

exports goods and services sold to other countries. (p. 105)

external benefit an uncompensated benefit that an individual or firm confers on others; also known as *positive externalities*. (p. 727)

external cost an uncompensated cost that an individual or firm imposes on others; also known as *negative externalities*. (p. 726)

externalities *external costs* and *external benefits*. (p. 727)

factor distribution of income the division of total income among labor, land, and capital. (p. 681)

factor markets where resources, especially capital and labor, are bought and sold. (p. 103)

federal funds market the financial market that allows *banks* that fall short of *reserve requirements* to borrow funds from banks with *excess reserves*. (p. 263)

federal funds rate the *interest rate* at which funds are borrowed and lent in the *federal funds market*. (p. 263)

fiat money a *medium of exchange* whose value derives entirely from its official status as a means of payment. (p. 234)

final goods and services goods and services sold to the final, or end, user. (p. 106)

financial account see *balance of payments on the financial account*.

financial asset a paper claim that entitles the buyer to future income from the seller. *Loans, stocks, bonds,* and *bank deposits* are types of financial assets. (p. 224)

financial intermediary an institution, such as a *mutual fund, pension fund, life insurance company,* or *bank,* that transforms the funds it gathers from many individuals into *financial assets*. (p. 227)

financial markets the banking, *stock,* and *bond* markets, which channel *private savings* and foreign lending into *investment spending, government borrowing,* and foreign borrowing. (p. 105)

financial risk uncertainty about future outcomes that involve financial losses and gains. (p. 225)

firm an organization that produces goods and services for sale. (p. 103)

fiscal policy the use of taxes, government transfers, or government purchases of goods and services to stabilize the economy. (p. 176)

fiscal year the time period used for much of government accounting, running from October 1 to September 30. Fiscal years are labeled by the calendar year in which they end. (p. 300)

Fisher effect the principle by which an increase in expected future *inflation* drives up the nominal *interest rate*, leaving the expected real interest rate unchanged. (p. 283)

fixed cost cost that does not depend on the quantity of output produced. It is the cost of the fixed input. (p. 548)

fixed exchange rate an *exchange rate regime* in which the government keeps the *exchange rate* against some other currency at or near a particular target. (p. 431)

fixed input an *input* whose quantity is fixed for a period of time and cannot be varied (for example, land). (p. 542)

floating exchange rate an *exchange rate regime* in which the government lets the *exchange rate* go wherever the market takes it. (p. 431)

foreign exchange controls licensing systems that limit the right of individuals to buy foreign currency. (p. 433)

foreign exchange market the market in which currencies are traded. (p. 421)

foreign exchange reserves *stocks* of foreign currency that governments can use to buy their own currency on the *foreign exchange market*. (p. 432)

free entry and exit describes an industry that potential producers can easily enter or current producers can leave. (p. 570)

free-rider problem when individuals have no *incentive* to pay for their own consumption of a good, they will take a "free ride" on anyone who does pay; a problem that with goods that are *nonexcludable*. (p. 745)

frictional unemployment *unemployment* due to time workers spend in *job search*. (p. 127)

gains from trade An economic principle that states that by dividing tasks and trading, people can get more of what they want through *trade* than they could if they tried to be self-sufficient. (p. 23)

game theory the study of behavior in situations of *interdependence*. Used to explain the behavior of an *oligopoly*. (p. 644)

GDP deflator a price measure for a given year that is equal to 100 times the ratio of *nominal GDP* to *real GDP* in that year. (p. 146)

GDP per capita GDP divided by the size of the population; equivalent to the average GDP per person. (p. 115)

Gini coefficient a number summarizes a country's level of income inequality based on how unequally income is distributed across the quintiles. (p. 761)

government borrowing the amount of funds borrowed by the government in financial markets to buy goods and services. (p. 105)

government purchases of goods and services total purchases by federal, state, and local governments on goods and services. (p. 105)

government transfers payments by the government to individuals for which no good or service is provided in return. (p. 105)

gross domestic product (GDP) the total value of all *final goods and services* produced in the *economy* during a given period, usually a year. (p. 106)

growth accounting estimates the contribution of each of the major factors (physical and human capital, labor, and technology) in the *aggregate production function*. (p. 378)

Herfindahl–Hirschman Index, or HHI is the square of each firm's share of market sales summed over the industry. It gives a picture of the industry market structure. (p. 573)

household a person or a group of people who share income. (p. 103)

human capital the improvement in labor created by the education and knowledge embodied in the workforce. (pp. 373, 680)

illiquid describes an asset that cannot be quickly converted into cash without much loss of value. (p. 226)

implicit cost a cost that does not require the outlay of money; it is measured by the value, in dollar terms, of forgone benefits. (p. 530)

implicit cost of capital the *opportunity cost* of the capital used by a business; that is the income that could have been realized had the capital been used in the next best alternative way. (p. 532)

implicit liabilities spending promises made by governments that are effectively a debt despite the fact that they are not included in the usual debt statistics. In the United States, the largest implicit liabilities arise from Social Security and Medicare, which promise transfer payments to current and future retirees (Social Security) and to the elderly (Medicare). (p. 303)

imports goods and services purchased from other countries. (p. 105)

incentive anything that offers rewards to people who change their behavior. (p. 2)

income effect the change in the quantity of a good consumed that results from the change in a consumer's purchasing power due to the change in the price of the good. (p. 459)

income-elastic demand when the *income elasticity of demand* for a good is greater than 1. (p. 476)

income elasticity of demand the percent change in the quantity of a good demanded when a consumer's income changes divided by the percent change in the consumer's income. (p. 476)

income-inelastic demand when the *income elasticity of demand* for a good is positive but less than 1. (p. 476)

increasing returns to scale long-run *average total cost* declines as output increases (also referred to as *economies of scale*). (p. 562)

indifference curve a contour line showing all *consumption bundles* that yield the same amount of total utility for an individual. (p. 789)

indifference curve map a collection of *indifference curves* for a given individual that represents the individual's entire *utility function*; each curve corresponds to a different total *utility* level. (p. 789)

individual choice the decision by an individual of what to do, which necessarily involves a decision of what not to do. (p. 2)

individual consumer surplus the net gain to an individual buyer from the purchase of a good; equal to the difference between the buyer's *willingness to pay* and the price paid. (p. 485)

individual demand curve a graphical representation of the relationship between *quantity demanded* and price for an individual consumer. (p. 55)

individual labor supply curve a graphical representation showing how the quantity of labor supplied by an individual depends on that individual's wage rate. (p. 696)

individual producer surplus the net gain to an individual seller from selling a good; equal to the difference between the price received and the seller's *cost*. (p. 490)

individual supply curve a graphical representation of the relationship between *quantity supplied* and *price* for an individual producer. (p. 63)

industry supply curve a graphical representation that shows the relationship between the price of a good and the total output of the industry for that good. (p. 599)

inefficient allocation of sales among sellers a form of inefficiency in which sellers who would be willing to sell a good at the lowest price are not always those who actually manage to sell it; often the result of a *price floor*. (p. 84)

inefficient allocation to consumers a form of inefficiency in which people who want a good badly and are willing to pay a high price don't get it, and those who care relatively little about the good and are only willing to pay a low price do get it; often a result of a *price ceiling*. (p. 80)

inefficiently high quality a form of inefficiency in which sellers offer high-quality goods at a high price even though buyers would prefer a lower quality at a lower price; often the result of a *price floor*. (p. 85)

inefficiently low quality a form of inefficiency in which sellers offer low-quality goods at a low price even though buyers would prefer a higher quality at a higher price; often a result of a *price ceiling*. (p. 81)

inelastic demand when the *price elasticity of demand* is less than 1. (p. 467)

inferior good a good for which a rise in income decreases the demand for the good. (p. 54)

inflation a rise in the overall price level. (p. 12)

inflation rate the annual percent change in a price index—typically the *consumer price index*. The inflation rate is positive when the *aggregate price level* is rising (*inflation*) and negative when the aggregate price level is falling (*deflation*). (p. 135)

inflation targeting an approach to monetary policy that requires that the central bank try to keep the *inflation rate* near a predetermined target rate. (p. 312)

inflation tax the reduction in the value of money held by the public caused by *inflation*. (p. 325)

inflationary gap exists when *aggregate output* is above *potential output*. (p. 196)

infrastructure *physical capital*, such as roads, power lines, ports, information networks, and other parts of an *economy*, that provides the underpinnings, or foundation, for economic activity. (p. 389)

in-kind benefit a benefit given in the form of goods or services. (p. 768)

input a good or service used to produce another good or service. (p. 62)

interdependent the outcome (profit) of each firm depends on the actions of the other firms in the market. (p. 638)

interest rate the price, calculated as a percentage of the amount borrowed, charged by lenders to borrowers for the use of their savings for one year. (p. 222)

interest rate effect of a change in the aggregate price level the effect on *consumer spending* and *investment spending* caused by a change in the purchasing power of consumers' money holdings when the *aggregate price level* changes. A rise (fall) in the aggregate price level decreases (increases) the purchasing power of consumers' money holdings. In response, consumers try to increase (decrease) their money holdings, which drives up (down) interest rates, thereby decreasing (increasing) consumption and investment. (p. 174)

intermediate goods and services goods and services, bought from one *firm* by another firm, that are inputs for production of *final goods and services*. (p. 106)

internalize the externality when individuals take into account *external costs* and *external benefits*. (p. 728)

inventories stocks of goods and raw materials held to satisfy future sales. (pp. 105, 168)

inventory investment the value of the change in total *inventories* held in the *economy* during a given period. Unlike other types of *investment spending*, inventory investment can be negative, if inventories fall. (p. 168)

investment bank a *bank* that trades in *financial assets* and is not covered by *deposit insurance*. (p. 257)

investment spending spending on productive *physical capital*, such as machinery and construction of structures, and on changes to *inventories*. (p. 106)

job search when workers spend time looking for *employment*. (p. 127)

labor the effort of workers. (p. 3)

labor force the number of people who are either actively employed for pay or unemployed and actively looking for work; the sum of *employment* and *unemployment*. (pp. 12, 119)

labor force participation rate the percentage of the population age 16 or older that is in the *labor force*. (p. 119)

labor productivity (productivity) output per worker. (p. 372)

land all resources that come from nature, such as minerals, timber, and petroleum. (p. 3)

law of demand the principle that a higher price for a good or service, other things equal, leads people to demand a smaller quantity of that good or service. (p. 50)

law of supply other things being equal, the price and quantity supplied of a good are positively related. (p. 60)

leisure the time available for purposes other than earning money to buy marketed goods. (p. 696)

leverage the degree to which a financial institution is financing its investments with borrowed funds. (p. 258)

liability a requirement to pay income in the future. (p. 224)

license gives its owner the right to supply a good or service. (p. 88)

life insurance company a *financial intermediary* that sells policies guaranteeing a payment to a policyholder's beneficiaries when the policyholder dies. (p. 228)

liquid describes an asset that can be quickly converted into cash without much loss of value. (p. 226)

liquidity preference model of the interest rate a model of the market for money in which the interest rate is determined by the supply and demand for money. (p. 273)

liquidity trap a situation in which *monetary policy* is ineffective because *nominal interest rates* are up against the zero bound. (p. 339)

loan a lending agreement between an individual lender and an individual borrower. Loans are usually tailored to the individual borrower's needs and ability to pay but carry relatively high *transaction costs*. (p. 226)

loanable funds market a hypothetical market in which the demand for funds is generated by borrowers and the supply of funds is provided by lenders. The market equilibrium determines the quantity and price, or *interest rate,* of loanable funds. (p. 277)

loan-backed securities assets created by pooling individual *loans* and selling shares in that pool. (p. 227)

long run the time period in which all inputs can be varied. (p. 542)

long-run aggregate supply curve a graphical representation of the relationship between the *aggregate price level* and the quantity of *aggregate output* supplied if all prices, including *nominal wages,* were fully flexible. The long-run aggregate supply curve is vertical because the aggregate price level has no effect on aggregate output in the long run; in the long run, aggregate output is determined by the *economy's potential output.* (p. 184)

long-run average total cost curve a graphical representation showing the relationship between *output* and *average total cost* when *fixed cost* has been chosen to minimize average total cost for each level of output. (p. 561)

long-run industry supply curve a graphical representation that shows how *quantity supplied* responds to price once producers have had time to enter or exit the industry. (p. 603)

long-run macroeconomic equilibrium a situation in which the *short-run macroeconomic equilibrium* is also on the *long-run aggregate supply curve;* so *short-run equilibrium aggregate output* is equal to *potential output.* (p. 194)

long-run market equilibrium an economic balance in which, given sufficient time for producers to enter or exit an industry, the *quantity supplied* equals the *quantity demanded.* (p. 602)

long-run Phillips curve a graphical representation of the relationship between *unemployment* and *inflation* in the long run after expectations of inflation have had time to adjust to experience. (p. 336)

long-term interest rate the *interest rate* on *financial assets* that mature a number of years into the future. (p. 270)

long-term reputation allows an individual to assure others that he or she isn't concealing adverse private information. (p. 784)

lump-sum taxes taxes that don't depend on the taxpayer's income. (pp. 211, 508)

macroeconomic policy activism the use of *monetary policy* and *fiscal policy* to smooth out the business cycle. (p. 346)

macroeconomics the branch of *economics* that is concerned with the overall ups and downs in the *economy.* (p. 5)

marginal analysis the study of *marginal decisions.* (p. 3)

marginal cost curve a graphical representation showing how the cost of producing one more unit depends on the quantity that has already been produced. (p. 538)

marginal cost pricing occurs when regulators set a monopoly's price equal to its marginal cost to achieve efficiency. (p. 757)

marginal external benefit the addition to external benefits created by one more unit of the good. (p. 738)

marginal external cost the increase in external costs created by one more unit of a good. (p. 739)

marginal factor cost of labor (MFCL) the additional cost of hiring an additional worker. The marginal factor cost of land and the marginal factor cost of capital are equivalent concepts. (p. 700)

marginal private benefit the marginal benefit that accrues to consumers of a good, not including any external benefits. (p. 738)

marginal private cost the marginal cost of producing a good, not including any external costs. (p. 739)

marginal product the additional quantity of output produced by using one more unit of that *input.* (p. 543)

marginal productivity theory of income distribution every *factor of production* is paid its *equilibrium value of the marginal product.* (p. 692)

marginal propensity to consume (*MPC*) the increase in *consumer spending* when income rises by $1. Because consumers normally spend part but not all of an additional dollar of disposable income, *MPC* is between 0 and 1. (p. 159)

marginal propensity to save (*MPS*) the increase in household savings when disposable income rises by $1. (p. 159)

marginal rate of substitution (*MRS*) the ratio of the *marginal utility* of one good to the marginal utility of another. (p. 794)

marginal revenue the change in *total revenue* generated by an additional unit of output. (p. 537)

marginal revenue curve a graphical representation showing how *marginal revenue* varies as output varies. (p. 538)

marginal revenue product of labor (MRPL) equals the marginal product of labor times the marginal revenue received from selling the additional output. The marginal revenue product of land and the marginal revenue product of capital are equivalent concepts. (p. 700)

marginal social benefit of a good or activity the *marginal benefit* that accrues to consumers plus the marginal *external benefit.* (p. 738)

marginal social benefit of pollution the additional gain to society as a whole from an additional unit of pollution. (p. 724)

marginal social cost of a good or activity the *marginal cost* of production plus the marginal *external cost.* (p. 739)

marginal social cost of pollution the additional cost imposed on society as a whole by an additional unit of pollution. (p. 724)

marginal utility the change in total *utility* generated by consuming one additional unit of a good or service. (p. 513)

marginal utility curve a graphical representation showing how *marginal utility* depends on the quantity of a good or service consumed. (p. 513)

marginal utility per dollar the additional *utility* from spending one more dollar on a good or service. (p. 518)

marginally attached workers nonworking individuals who say they would like a job and have looked for work in the recent past but are not currently looking for work. (p. 120)

market basket a hypothetical consumption bundle of consumer purchases of goods and services, used to measure changes in overall price level. (p. 142)

market economy an *economy* in which decisions of individual producers and consumers largely determine what, how, and for whom to produce, with little government involvement in the decisions. (p. 2)

market share the fraction of the total industry output accounted for by a firm's output. (p. 569)

mean household income the average income across all households. (p. 765)

means-tested program a program in which benefits are available only to individuals or families whose incomes fall below a certain level. (p. 768)

median household income the income of the household lying in the middle of the *income distribution*. (p. 765)

medium of exchange an asset that individuals acquire for the purpose of trading for goods and services rather than for their own consumption. (p. 232)

menu cost the real cost of changing a listed price. (p. 137)

merchandise trade balance (trade balance) the difference between a country's exports and imports of goods alone—not including services. (p. 412)

microeconomics the branch of *economics* that studies how people make decisions and how those decisions interact. (p. 5)

midpoint method a technique for calculating the percent change in which changes in a variable are compared with the average, or midpoint, of the starting and final values. (p. 462)

minimum-cost output the quantity of output at which *average total cost* is lowest—the bottom of the U-*shaped average total cost curve*. (p. 555)

minimum wage a legal floor on the wage rate. The wage rate is the market price of labor. (p. 82)

model a simplified representation of a real situation that is used to better understand real-life situations. (p. 14)

monetarism a theory of *business cycles,* associated primarily with Milton Friedman, that asserts that GDP will grow steadily if the *money supply* grows steadily. (p. 348)

monetary aggregate an overall measure of the *money supply*. The most common monetary aggregates in the United States are M1, which includes *currency in circulation,* traveler's checks, and *checkable bank deposits,* and M2, which includes M1 as well as *near-moneys.* (p. 234)

monetary base the sum of *currency in circulation* and *bank reserves.* (p. 249)

monetary neutrality the concept that changes in the *money supply* have no real effects on the *economy* in the long run and only result in a proportional change in the price level. (p. 317)

monetary policy the central bank's use of changes in the quantity of money or the interest rate to stabilize the economy (p. 177)

monetary policy rule a formula that determines the *central bank's* actions. (p. 349)

money any asset that can easily be used to purchase goods and services. (p. 231)

money demand curve a graphical representation of the negative relationship between the quantity of money demanded and the interest rate. The money demand curve slopes downward because, other things equal, a higher interest rate increases the *opportunity cost* of holding money. (p. 270)

money multiplier the ratio of the *money supply* to the *monetary base;* indicates the total number of dollars created in the banking system by each $1 addition to the monetary base. (p. 250)

money supply the total value of *financial assets* in the *economy* that are considered *money.* (p. 231)

money supply curve a graphical representation of the relationship between the quantity of money supplied by the Federal Reserve and the *interest rate.* (p. 273)

monopolist a firm that is the only producer of a good that has no close substitutes. (p. 571)

monopolistic competition a market structure in which there are many competing firms in an industry, each firm sells a differentiated product, and there is *free entry into and exit* from the industry in the *long run.* (p. 575)

monopoly an industry controlled by a *monopolist.* (p. 571)

monopsonist a single buyer in a market. (p. 701)

monopsony a market in which there is only one buyer. (p. 701)

moral hazard the situation that can exist when an individual knows more about his or her own actions than other people do. This leads to a distortion of incentives to take care or to exert effort when someone else bears the costs of the lack of care or effort. (p. 785)

movement along the demand curve a change in the *quantity demanded* of a good that results from a change in the price of that good. (p. 51)

movement along the supply curve a change in the *quantity supplied* of a good that results from a change in the price of that good. (p. 60)

multiplier the ratio of total change in *real GDP* caused by an *autonomous change in aggregate spending* to the size of that autonomous change. (p. 160)

mutual fund a *financial intermediary* that creates a stock portfolio by buying and holding shares in companies and then selling shares of this portfolio to individual investors. (p. 228)

Nash equilibrium in *game theory,* the *equilibrium* that results when all players choose the action that maximizes their *payoffs* given the actions of other players, ignoring the effect of that action on the *payoffs* of other players; also known as *noncooperative equilibrium.* (p. 646)

national income and product accounts an accounting of *consumer spending,* sales of producers, business *investment spending,* and other flows of money between different sectors of the *economy;* also referred to as *national accounts.* Calculated by the Bureau of Economic Analysis. (p. 102)

national savings the sum of *private savings* and the government's *budget balance;* the total amount of savings generated within the *economy.* (p. 223)

natural monopoly a *monopoly* that exists when *increasing returns to scale* provide a large cost advantage to having all output produced by a single firm. (p. 571)

natural rate hypothesis the hypothesis that the unemployment rate is stable in the long run at a particular natural rate. According to this hypothesis, attempts to lower the unemployment rate below the natural rate of unemployment will cause an ever-rising inflation rate. (p. 350)

natural rate of unemployment the unemployment rate that arises from the effects of frictional plus structural unemployment. (p. 130)

near-money a *financial asset* that can't be directly used as a *medium of exchange* but can be readily converted into cash or *checkable bank deposits.* (p. 235)

negative income tax a government program that supplements the income of low-income working families. (p. 769)

net exports the difference between the value of *exports* and the value of *imports*. A positive value for net exports indicates that a country is a net exporter of goods and services; a negative value indicates that a country is a net importer of goods and services. (p. 108)

net present value the *present value* of current and future benefits minus the present value of current and future costs. (p. 240)

network externality when the value of a good to an individual is greater when more people also use the good. (p. 739)

new classical macroeconomics an approach to the *business cycle* that returns to the classical view that shifts in the *aggregate demand curve* affect only the *aggregate price level*, not *aggregate output*. (p. 351)

new Keynesian economics theory that argues that market imperfections can lead to price stickiness for the economy as a whole. (p. 352)

nominal GDP the value of all *final goods and services* produced in the *economy* during a given year, calculated using the prices current in the year in which the output is produced. (p. 114)

nominal interest rate the *interest rate* actually paid for a loan, not adjusted for inflation. (p. 138)

nominal wage the dollar amount of any given wage paid. (p. 180)

nonaccelerating inflation rate of unemployment (NAIRU) the *unemployment* rate at which, other things equal, *inflation* does not change over time. (p. 336)

noncooperative behavior actions by firms that ignore the effects of those actions on the profits of other firms. (p. 640)

nonexcludable referring to a good, describes the case in which the supplier cannot prevent those who do not pay from consuming the good. (p. 743)

nonprice competition competition in areas other than price to increase sales, such as new product features and advertising; especially engaged in by firms that have a tacit understanding not to compete on price. (p. 656)

nonrival consumption referring to a good, describes the case in which the same unit can be consumed by more than one person at the same time. (p. 744)

normal good a good for which a rise in income increases the demand for that good—the "normal" case. (p. 53)

normal profit an economic profit equal to zero. It is an economic profit just high enough to keep a firm engaged in its current activity. (p. 534)

normative economics the branch of economic analysis that makes prescriptions about the way the *economy* should work. (p. 6)

oligopolist a firm in an industry with only a small number of producers. (p. 573)

oligopoly an industry with only a small number of producers. (p. 573)

open-market operation a purchase or sale of U.S. Treasury bills by the Federal Reserve, undertaken to change the *monetary base*, which in turn changes the *money supply*. (p. 264)

opportunity cost the real cost of an item: what you must give up in order to get it. (p. 3)

optimal consumption bundle the *consumption bundle* that maximizes the consumer's total *utility* given his or her *budget constraint*. (p. 515)

optimal consumption rule when a consumer maximizes *utility*, the *marginal utility per dollar* spent must be the same for all goods and services in the *consumption bundle*. (p. 520)

optimal output rule profit is maximized by producing the quantity of output at which the *marginal revenue* of the last unit produced is equal to its *marginal cost*. (p. 537)

ordinary goods in a consumer's *utility function*, those for which additional units of one good are required to compensate for fewer units of another, and vice versa; and for which the consumer experiences a *diminishing marginal rate of substitution* when substituting one good in place of another. (p. 795)

other things equal assumption in the development of a model, the assumption that all relevant factors except the one under study remain unchanged. (p. 14)

output the quality of goods and services produced. (p. 12)

output gap the percentage difference between actual *aggregate output* and *potential output*. (p. 196)

overuse the depletion of a *common resource* that occurs when individuals ignore the fact that their use depletes the amount of the resource remaining for others. (p. 749)

patent a temporary monopoly given by the government to an inventor for the use or sale of an invention. (p. 572)

payoff in *game theory*, the reward received by a player in a game (for example, the profit earned by an oligopolist). (p. 644)

payoff matrix in *game theory*, a diagram that shows how the *payoffs* to each of the participants in a two-player game depend on the actions of both; a tool in analyzing *interdependence*. (p. 644)

pension fund a type of *mutual fund* that holds assets in order to provide retirement income to its members. (p. 228)

perfectly competitive industry an industry in which all producers are price-takers. (p. 569)

perfectly competitive market a market in which all market participants are price-takers. (p. 568)

perfectly elastic demand the case in which any price increase will cause the *quantity demanded* to drop to zero; the *demand curve* is a horizontal line. (p. 467)

perfectly elastic supply the case in which even a tiny increase or reduction in the price will lead to very large changes in the *quantity supplied*, so that the *price elasticity of supply* is infinite; the perfectly elastic *supply curve* is a horizontal line. (p. 479)

perfectly inelastic demand the case in which the *quantity demanded* does not respond at all to changes in the price; the *demand curve* is a vertical line. (p. 466)

perfectly inelastic supply the case in which the *price elasticity of supply* is zero, so that changes in the price of the good have no effect on the *quantity supplied*; the perfectly inelastic *supply curve* is a vertical line. (p. 478)

perfect price discrimination a situation in which a monopolist charges each consumer his or her willingness to pay—the maximum that the consumer is willing to pay. (p. 627)

physical asset a claim on a tangible object that gives the owner the right to dispose of the object as he or she wishes. (p. 224)

physical capital human-made goods such as buildings and machines used to produce other goods and services. (pp. 373, 680)

Pigouvian subsidy a payment designed to encourage activities that yield *external benefits*. (p. 738)

Pigouvian taxes taxes designed to reduce *external costs*. (p. 734)

planned investment spending the *investment spending* that *firms* intend to undertake during a given period. Planned investment spending may differ from actual investment spending due to *unplanned inventory investment*. (p. 166)

political business cycle a *business cycle* that results from the use of macroeconomic policy to serve political ends. (p. 351)

positive economics the branch of economic analysis that describes the way the *economy* actually works. (p. 6)

potential output the level of *real GDP* the *economy* would produce if all prices, including *nominal wages*, were fully flexible. (p. 185)

poverty rate the percentage of the population with incomes below the *poverty threshold*. (p. 761)

poverty threshold the annual income below which a family is officially considered poor. (p. 761)

present value the amount of money needed at the present time to produce, at the prevailing *interest rate*, a given amount of money at a specified future time. (p. 239)

price ceiling the maximum price sellers are allowed to charge for a good or service; a form of *price control*. (p. 77)

price controls legal restrictions on how high or low a market price may go. (p. 77)

price discrimination charging different prices to different consumers for the same good. (p. 624)

price floor the minimum price buyers are required to pay for a good or service; a form of *price control*. (p. 77)

price index a measure of the cost of purchasing a given *market basket* in a given year, where that cost is normalized so that it is equal to 100 in the selected base year; a measure of overall price level. (p. 143)

price elasticity of demand the ratio of the percent change in the *quantity demanded* to the percent change in the price as we move along the *demand curve* (dropping the minus sign). (p. 460)

price elasticity of supply a measure of the responsiveness of the quantity of a good supplied to the price of that good; the ratio of the percent change in the *quantity supplied* to the percent change in the price as we move along the *supply curve*. (p. 477)

price leadership a pattern of behavior in which one firm sets its price and other firms in the industry follow. (p. 656)

price regulation a limitation on the price that a *monopolist* is allowed to charge. (p. 619)

price stability when the aggregate price level is changing only slowly. (p. 13)

price-taking consumer a consumer whose actions have no effect on the market price of the good or service he or she buys. (p. 568)

price-taking firm a firm whose actions have no effect on the market price of the good or service it sells. (p. 568)

price-taking firm's optimal output rule the profit of a price-taking firm is maximized by producing the quantity of output at which the market price is equal to the *marginal cost* of the last unit produced. (p. 585)

price war a collapse of prices when *tacit collusion* breaks down. (p. 654)

principle of diminishing marginal utility the proposition that each successive unit of a good or service consumed adds less to total *utility* than does the previous unit. (p. 513)

principle of marginal analysis the proposition that the *optimal quantity* is the quantity at which *marginal benefit* is equal to *marginal cost*. (p. 537)

prisoners' dilemma a game based on two premises: (1) Each player has an incentive to choose an action that benefits itself at the other player's expense; and (2) When both players act in this way, both are worse off than if they had acted cooperatively. (p. 645)

private good a good that is both *excludable* and *rival in consumption*. (p. 743)

private information information that some people have that others do not. (p. 782)

private savings *disposable income* minus *consumer spending*; disposable income that is not spent on consumption but rather goes into *financial markets*. (p. 105)

producer price index (PPI) a measure of the cost of a typical basket of goods and services purchased by producers. Because these commodity prices respond quickly to changes in demand, the PPI is often regarded as a leading indicator of changes in the *inflation rate*. (p. 145)

producer surplus a term often used to refer to either *individual producer surplus* or to *total producer surplus*. (p. 490)

product differentiation the attempt by firms to convince buyers that their products are different from those of other firms in the industry. If firms can so convince buyers, they can charge a higher price. (p. 655)

product markets where goods and services are bought and sold. (p. 103)

production function the relationship between the quantity of *inputs* a firm uses and the quantity of output it produces. (p. 542)

production possibilities curve illustrates the trade-offs facing an economy that produces only two goods; shows the maximum quantity of one good that can be produced for each possible quantity of the other good produced. (p. 16)

progressive tax a tax that takes a larger share of the income of high-income taxpayers than of low-income taxpayers. (p. 499)

property rights the rights of owners of valuable items, whether *resources* or goods, to dispose of those items as they choose. (p. 3)

proportional tax a tax that is the same percentage of the *tax base* regardless of the taxpayer's income or wealth. (p. 499)

public debt government debt held by individuals and institutions outside the government. (p. 300)

public good a good that is both *nonexcludable* and *nonrival in consumption*. (p. 745)

public ownership when goods are supplied by the government or by a firm owned by the government to protect the interests of the consumer in response to *natural monopoly*. (p. 619)

purchasing power parity (between two countries' currencies) the nominal exchange rate at which a given basket of goods and services would cost the same amount in each country. (p. 427)

quantity control (quota) an upper limit, set by the government, on the quantity of some good that can be bought or sold; also referred to as a *quota*. (p. 88)

quantity demanded the actual amount of a good or service consumers are willing to buy at some specific price. (p. 49)

quantity supplied the actual amount of a good or service producers are willing to sell at some specific price. (p. 59)

Quantity Theory of Money a theory that emphasizes the positive relationship between the price level and the money supply. It relies on the equation ($M \times V = P \times Y$). (p. 349)

quota rent the earnings that accrue to the license-holder from ownership of the right to sell the good. (p. 91)

rate of return (of an investment project) the profit earned on an investment project expressed as a percentage of its cost. (p. 278)

rational expectations a theory of expectation formation that holds that individuals and *firms* make decisions optimally, using all available information. (p. 352)

real business cycle theory a theory of *business cycles* that asserts that fluctuations in the growth rate of *total factor productivity* cause the business cycle. (p. 352)

real exchange rate the *exchange rate* adjusted for international differences in *aggregate price levels*. (p. 425)

real GDP the total value of all *final goods and services* produced in the *economy* during a given year, calculated using the prices of a selected base year. (p. 114)

real income income divided by the price level. (p. 135)

real interest rate the *nominal interest rate* minus the *inflation rate*. (p. 138)

real wage the wage rate divided by the price level. (p. 135)

recession a period of economic downturn when output and unemployment are falling; also referred to as a contraction. (p. 10)

recessionary gap exists when *aggregate output* is below *potential output*. (p. 195)

regressive tax a tax that takes a smaller share of the income of high-income taxpayers than of low-income taxpayers. (p. 499)

relative price the ratio of the price of one good to the price of another. (p. 797)

relative price rule at the *optimal consumption bundle*, the *marginal rate of substitution* of one good in place of another equal to their relative price. (p. 798)

rental rate the cost, explicit or implicit, of using a unit of either land or capital for a given period of time. (p. 691)

required reserve ratio the smallest fraction of deposits that the Federal Reserve allows banks to hold. (p. 244)

research and development (R & D) spending to create and implement new technologies. (p. 388)

reserve ratio the fraction of *bank deposits* that a *bank* holds as reserves. In the United States, the minimum required reserve ratio is set by the Federal Reserve. (p. 244)

reserve requirements rules set by the Federal Reserve that set the minimum *reserve ratio* for banks. For *checkable bank deposits* in the United States, the minimum reserve ratio is set at 10%. (p. 246)

resource anything, such as land, labor, and capital, that can be used to produce something else; includes natural resources (from the physical environment) and human resources (labor, skill, intelligence). (p. 3)

revaluation an increase in the value of a currency that is set under a *fixed exchange rate regime*. (p. 438)

rival in consumption referring to a good, describes the case in which one unit cannot be consumed by more than one person at the same time. (p. 743)

Rule of 70 a mathematical formula that states that the time it takes *real GDP* per capita, or any other variable that grows gradually over time, to double is approximately 70 divided by that variable's annual growth rate. (p. 371)

savings and loans (thrifts) deposit-taking *banks*, usually specialized in issuing home loans. (p. 257)

savings–investment spending identity an accounting fact that states that savings and *investment spending* are always equal for the *economy* as a whole. (p. 222)

scarce in short supply; a *resource* is scarce when there is not enough of the resource available to satisfy all the various ways a society wants to use it. (p. 3)

screening using observable information about people to make inferences about their *private information*; a way to reduce *adverse selection*. (p. 783)

securitization the pooling of loans and mortgages made by a financial institution and the sale of shares in such a pool to other investors. (p. 259)

self-correcting refers to the fact that in the long run, shocks to *aggregate demand* affect *aggregate output* in the short run, but not the long run. (p. 196)

shoe-leather costs (of inflation) the increased costs of transactions caused by *inflation*. (p. 137)

shortage the insufficiency of a good or service that occurs when the *quantity demanded* exceeds the *quantity supplied*; shortages occur when the price is below the *equilibrium price*. (p. 68)

short run the time period in which at least one *input* is fixed. (p. 542)

short-run aggregate supply curve a graphical representation of the relationship between the *aggregate price* level and the quantity of *aggregate output* supplied that exists in the short run, the time period when many production costs can be taken as fixed. The short-run aggregate supply curve has a positive slope because a rise in the aggregate price level leads to a rise in profits, and therefore output, when production costs are fixed. (p. 181)

short-run equilibrium aggregate output the quantity of *aggregate output* produced in *short-run macroeconomic equilibrium*. (p. 190)

short-run equilibrium aggregate price level the *aggregate price level* in *short-run macroeconomic equilibrium*. (p. 190)

short-run individual supply curve a graphical representation that shows how an individual producer's profit-maximizing output quantity depends on the market price, taking *fixed cost* as given. (p. 594)

short-run industry supply curve a graphical representation that shows how the *quantity supplied* by an industry depends on the market price, given a fixed number of producers. (p. 600)

short-run macroeconomic equilibrium the point at which the quantity of *aggregate output* supplied is equal to the *quantity demanded*. (p. 190)

short-run market equilibrium an economic balance that results when the *quantity supplied* equals the *quantity demanded*, taking the number of producers as given. (p. 601)

short-run Phillips curve a graphical representation of the negative short-run relationship between the unemployment rate and the *inflation rate*. (p. 331)

short-term interest rate the *interest rate* on *financial assets* that mature within less than a year. (p. 269)

shut-down price the price at which a firm ceases production in the short run because the price has fallen below the minimum average variable *cost*. (p. 593)

signaling taking some action to establish credibility despite possessing *private information*; a way to reduce *adverse selection*. (p. 784)

single-price monopolist a *monopolist* that offers its product to all consumers at the same price. (p. 624)

social insurance government programs—like Social Security, Medicare, unemployment insurance, and food stamps—intended to protect families against economic hardship. (p. 204)

socially optimal quantity of pollution the quantity of pollution that society would choose if all the costs and benefits of pollution were fully accounted for. (p. 725)

specialization a situation in which different people each engage in the different task that he or she is good at performing. (p. 23)

stabilization policy the use of government policy to reduce the severity of *recessions* and to rein in excessively strong *expansions*. There are two main tools of stabilization policy: *monetary policy* and *fiscal policy*. (p. 199)

stagflation the combination of *inflation* and falling *aggregate output*. (p. 193)

standardized product output of different producers regarded by consumers as the same good; also referred to as a *commodity*. (p. 569)

sticky wages *nominal wages* that are slow to fall even in the face of high *unemployment* and slow to rise even in the face of labor shortages. (p. 180)

stock a share in the ownership of a company held by a shareholder. (p. 104)

store of value an asset that is a means of holding purchasing power over time. (p. 232)

strategic behavior actions taken by a firm that attempt to influence the future behavior of other firms. (p. 647)

structural unemployment *unemployment* that results when there are more people seeking jobs in a labor market than there are jobs available at the current wage rate. (p. 128)

subprime lending lending to home buyers who don't meet the usual criteria for borrowing. (p. 259)

substitutes pairs of goods for which a rise in the price of one of the goods leads to an increase in the demand for the other good. (p. 53)

substitution effect the change in the quantity of a good demanded as the consumer substitutes the good that has become relatively cheaper for the good that has become relatively more expensive. (p. 458)

sunk cost a cost that has already been incurred and is nonrecoverable. (p. 563)

supply and demand model a model of how a *competitive market* works. (p. 48)

supply curve a graphical representation of the *supply schedule*, showing the relationship between *quantity supplied* and price. (p. 59)

supply price the price of a given quantity at which producers will supply that quantity. (p. 90)

supply schedule a list or table showing how much of a good or service producers will supply at different prices. (p. 59)

supply shock an event that shifts the *short-run aggregate supply curve*. A negative supply shock raises production costs and reduces the *quantity supplied* at any *aggregate price level*, shifting the curve leftward. A positive supply shock decreases production costs and increases the quantity supplied at any aggregate price level, shifting the curve rightward. (p. 192)

surplus the excess of a good or service that occurs when the *quantity supplied* exceeds the *quantity demanded*; surpluses occur when the price is above the *equilibrium price*. (p. 68)

sustainable describes continued *long-run economic growth* in the face of the limited supply of natural resources and the impact of growth on the environment. (p. 391)

T-account a simple tool that summarizes a business's financial position by showing, in a single table, the business's assets and liabilities, with assets on the left and liabilities on the right. (p. 243)

tacit collusion cooperation among producers, without a formal agreement, to limit production and raise prices so as to raise one anothers' profits. (p. 649)

tangency condition on a graph of a consumer's *budget line* and available *indifference curves* of available *consumption bundles*, the point at which an indifference curve and the budget line just touch. When the indifference curves have the typical convex shape, this point determines the *optimal consumption bundle*. (p. 796)

target federal funds rate the Federal Reserve's desired level for the *federal funds rate*. The Federal Reserve adjusts the *money supply* through the purchase and sale of Treasury bills until the actual rate equals the desired rate. (p. 307)

tax incidence the distribution of the tax burden. (p. 502)

Taylor rule for monetary policy a rule for setting the *federal funds rate* that takes into account both the *inflation rate* and the *output gap*. (p. 311)

technology the technical means for the production of goods and services. (pp. 21, 373)

technology spillover an *external benefit* that results when knowledge spreads among individuals and firms. (p. 738)

time allocation the decision about how many hours to spend on different activities, which leads to a decision about how much labor to supply. (p. 695)

tit for tat in *game theory*, a strategy that involves playing cooperatively at first, then doing whatever the other player did in the previous period. (p. 647)

total consumer surplus the sum of the *individual consumer surpluses* of all the buyers of a good in a market. (p. 485)

total cost the sum of the *fixed cost* and the *variable cost* of producing a quantity of output. (p. 548)

total cost curve a graphical representation of the *total cost,* showing how total cost depends on the quantity of output. (p. 549)

total factor productivity the amount of output that can be produced with a given amount of factor inputs. (p. 379)

total producer surplus the sum of the *individual producer surpluses* of all the sellers of a good in a market. (p. 490)

total product curve a graphical representation of the *production function,* showing how the quantity of output depends on the quantity of the *variable input* for a given quantity of the *fixed input.* (p. 543)

total revenue the total value of sales of a good or service (the price of the good or service multiplied by the quantity sold). (p. 468)

total surplus the total net gain to consumers and producers from trading in a market; the sum of the *consumer surplus* and the *producer surplus.* (p. 495)

tradable emissions permits *licenses* to emit limited quantities of pollutants that can be bought and sold by polluters. (p. 734)

trade when individuals provide goods and services to others and receive goods and services in return. (p. 23)

trade-off when you give up something in order to have something else. (p. 16)

transaction costs the expenses of negotiating and executing a deal. (p. 225)

underemployed people who work part time because they cannot find full-time jobs. (p. 120)

unemployed people who are actively looking for work but are not currently employed. (p. 119)

unemployment the total number of people who are actively looking for work but aren't currently employed. (p. 12)

unemployment rate the percentage of the total number of people in the *labor force* who are unemployed, calculated as *unemployment/(unemployment + employment).* (pp. 12, 119)

unions organizations of workers that try to raise wages and improve working conditions for their members by bargaining collectively. (p. 713)

unit-elastic the price elasticity of demand is exactly 1. (p. 467)

unit of account a measure used to set prices and make economic calculations. (p. 233)

unit-of-account costs (of inflation) costs arising from the way *inflation* makes money a less reliable unit of measurement. (p. 137)

unplanned inventory investment unplanned changes in inventories, which occur when actual sales are more or less than businesses expected; sales in excess of expectations result in negative unplanned inventory investment. (p. 169)

U-shaped average total cost curve a distinctive graphical representation of the relationship between output and *average total cost;* the average total cost curve at first falls when output is low and then rises as output increases. (p. 553)

util a unit of utility. (p. 512)

utility (of a consumer) a measure of the satisfaction derived from consumption of goods and services. (p. 511)

value added (of a producer) the value of a producer's sales minus the value of input purchases. (p. 107)

value of the marginal product the value of the additional output generated by employing one more unit of a given factor, such as labor. (p. 684)

value of the marginal product curve a graphical representation showing how the *value of the marginal product* of a factor depends on the quantity of the factor employed. (p. 684)

variable cost a cost that depends on the quantity of output produced; the cost of the *variable input.* (p. 548)

variable input an *input* whose quantity the firm can vary at any time (for example, labor). (p. 542)

velocity of money the ratio of *nominal GDP* to the *money supply.* (p. 349)

vicious cycle of deleveraging describes the sequence of events that takes place when a *firm's* asset sales to cover losses produce negative *balance sheet effects* on other firms and force creditors to call in their *loans,* forcing sales of more assets and causing further declines in asset prices. (p. 258)

wasted resources a form of inefficiency in which people expend money, effort, and time to cope with the shortages caused by a *price ceiling.* (p. 80)

wealth (of a *household*) the value of accumulated savings. (p. 224)

wealth effect of a change in the aggregate price level the effect on *consumer spending* caused by the change in the purchasing power of consumers' assets when the *aggregate price level* changes. A rise in the aggregate price level decreases the purchasing power of consumers' assets, so they decrease their consumption; a fall in the aggregate price level increases the purchasing power of consumers' assets, so they increase their consumption. (p. 174)

wedge the difference between the *demand price* of the quantity transacted and the *supply price* of the quantity transacted for a good when the supply of the good is legally restricted. Often created by a *quota* or a tax. (p. 91)

willingness to pay the maximum price a consumer is prepared to pay for a good. (p. 483)

zero bound the lower bound of zero on the *nominal interest rate.* (p. 339)

zero-profit equilibrium an economic balance in which each firm makes zero profit at its profit-maximizing quantity. (p. 661)